Mastering
Windows Server® 2012 R2

Mark Minasi
Kevin Greene
Christian Booth
Robert Butler
John McCabe
Robert Panek
Michael Rice
Stefan Roth

SYBEX®
A Wiley Brand

Acquisitions Editor: Mariann Barsolo
Development Editor: Tom Cirtin
Technical Editor: Gavin McShera
Production Editor: Rebecca Anderson
Copy Editor: Linda Recktenwald
Editorial Manager: Pete Gaughan
Production Manager: Tim Tate
Vice President and Executive Group Publisher: Richard Swadley
Associate Publisher: Chris Webb
Book Designers: Maureen Forys, Happenstance Type-O-Rama; Judy Fung
Proofreader: Sarah Kaikini, Word One New York
Indexer: J&J Indexing
Project Coordinator, Cover: Katherine Crocker
Cover Designer: Ryan Sneed
Cover Image: ©Getty Images, Inc./Thomas Northcutt

Dear Reader,

Thank you for choosing *Mastering Windows Server 2012 R2*. This book is part of a family of premium-quality Sybex books, all of which are written by outstanding authors who combine practical experience with a gift for teaching.

Sybex was founded in 1976. More than 30 years later, we're still committed to producing consistently exceptional books. With each of our titles, we're working hard to set a new standard for the industry. From the paper we print on, to the authors we work with, our goal is to bring you the best books available.

I hope you see all that reflected in these pages. I'd be very interested to hear your comments and get your feedback on how we're doing. Feel free to let me know what you think about this or any other Sybex book by sending me an email at contactus@wiley.com. If you think you've found a technical error in this book, please visit http://sybex.custhelp.com. Customer feedback is critical to our efforts at Sybex.

Best regards,

Chris Webb
Associate Publisher, Sybex

Acknowledgments

The author team wishes to thank Gavin McShera for his extensive assistance and constructive criticisms as technical editor (Gavin blogs at mcshera.com), and thanks also go to developmental editor Tom Cirtin, who wrestled our widely varying original drafts into publishable form. We thank the production team at Wiley: editorial manager Pete Gaughan, acquisitions editor Mariann Barsolo, production editor Rebecca Anderson, copy editor Linda Recktenwald, and proofreader Sarah Kaikini.

—*The authors*

Special thanks first to my beautiful wife, Laura, for her patience and support throughout the long hours I've spent writing my chapters for this book! Of course a big thanks has to go to my two sons, Matthew and Dylan, for making sure I woke up early on weekends to continue writing!

Thanks to Mariann Barsolo and Pete Gaughan for asking me to come on board with this book and for giving me the opportunity to work with some fantastic technical minds throughout the process. I found it very inspiring working with the other authors, contributors, and editors on this project—even though we had to rewrite half the book for the R2 release!

Another thank you has to go to my colleagues at Ergo, who've given me the opportunity to work on the type of enterprise-level projects that helped me gain the experience required to write a book like this.

Finally, I would like to dedicate my work in this book to my father-in-law, Cecil Anderson, who has been a father figure to me for many years. His strength and courage are an inspiration to us all.

—*Kevin Greene*

I would like to thank my family for their support. The time invested in this book seemed like an eternity, with lots of weekends involving me stuck at the keyboard writing chapters. I am very thankful for your patience. I love you all! Go Braves!

—*Christian Booth*

I would like to thank my wife Nicole, and our two boys Alex and Miles. Their love and support help me through everything I do.

—*Robert Butler*

I'd like to thank my wife, Sharon, and three kids, Sophie, Adam, and Sam, for their patience throughout the last year. It's not easy trying to balance a hectic workload with family life!

—*John McCabe*

First, I have to thank Kevin Greene for giving me the opportunity to work on this book and guiding me through the first steps. Also special thanks to my wife, Simona, for her patience and accepting the hours I spent with the book instead of with her!

My final thanks go to my family, my friends, and my company, itnetx, for supporting me in many ways so I could keep up with the project.

—*Stefan Roth*

About the Authors

Mark Minasi is a best-selling author, popular technology columnist, commentator, keynote speaker, and IT consultant. He first got the chance to play with a computer at a university class in 1973. At that time, he learned two things:

◆ First, computers are neat. (People still said "neat" back in 1973. Hey, it was back in the 20th Century.)

◆ Second, many technical people are very nice folks, but they can sure put you to sleep in an instant while explaining technical things.

Mark transformed those two insights into a career making computers and networking easier and more fun to understand. He's done that by writing over a thousand computer columns, several dozen best-selling technical books, and explaining operating system and networking planning, installation, maintenance, and repair to crowds from two to two thousand. An independent voice hailed as "Favorite Technical Author" by CertCities four times out of four, Mark has the unusual ability to take even the most technical topics, filter out the hype and explain them in plain English. Perhaps that's why when TechTarget hired him to deliver a webcast on PC tuning, he drew three times as many attendees as any of their previous webcasts, crashing Yahoo's servers, and why he's been hired to deliver keynote addresses at hundreds of techie conferences around the world.

Mark is probably best known for his *Mastering Windows Server* and *Complete PC Upgrade and Maintenance Guide* books, both of which have seen more than 12 editions and sold over 1 million copies.

Mark's humorous, provocative and yet informative style makes him a favorite of audiences around the world. Through his firm, MR&D (`www.minasi.com`), Mark offers technical seminars, classes, and talks, as well as a technical forum. You can also sign up for Mark's newsletter.

Kevin Greene, who led the team of authors on this book, is a Microsoft MVP for System Center Cloud and Datacenter Management and has been working in IT since 1999. He is employed as a subject matter expert for System Center at Ergo in Dublin, Ireland. In this role, he works with clients to deliver enterprise-grade solutions with Windows Server and System Center. In the past, he has held such roles as IT administrator, IT engineer, technical team lead, and senior consultant. He has been on the Microsoft certification track since the days of Windows NT 4.0 and holds qualifications that include MCSE, MCSA, MCITP, MCP, and MCTS. Kevin is an active participant in the Windows Server and System Center (WSSC) community through his blog at `http://kevingreeneitblog.blogspot.com`, and he can also be found hanging around Twitter as @kgreeneit.

He regularly delivers presentations and participates in podcasts on Windows Server and System Center and is a co-author of *Mastering System Center 2012 Operations Manager* (Sybex, 2012).

Kevin lives in Sallins, Co. Kildare, Ireland, with his wife, Laura, and two sons, Matthew and Dylan. When he's not working on his laptop, he spends his free time with his family and supporting Manchester United. He also holds a second-degree black belt in freestyle kickboxing, and although not as involved in the sport as he used to be, he's still an avid follower of the martial arts.

Christian Booth was previously a Microsoft MVP in the System Center: Cloud and Datacenter Management discipline and recently retired his MVP to work fulltime at Microsoft as senior program manager for the System Center team, focusing on the Cloud and Datacenter Management MVP program.

He has worked as a director, lead technical architect, and solutions engineer in the Seattle area for the last 17 years. His experience and focus have always been on the Microsoft platform with specialization in System Center, Windows Server, and virtualization.

Christian has contributed as a subject matter expert, exam item writer, training designer, and technical reviewer on many Microsoft Official Curriculum (MOC) courses. You can find out more about Christian at http://about.me/chbooth.

Robert Butler has been an IT professional for the past 17 years. He works for Affirma Consulting, where he specializes in integrating the various parts of the Microsoft System Center stack into existing environments.

He has been a Microsoft Certified Professional for the last 16 years, and he currently holds many other Microsoft certifications including MCSE PC, MCSA 2012, MCITP EA, and MCTS for SCCM 2012.

Robert lives in Seattle, Washington, with his wife, Nicole, and two children, Alex and Miles. You can find more information on Robert at his System Center blog, http://rbutler.me, or by following him on Twitter at @robert_butler.

John McCabe works for Microsoft as a premier field engineer. Through this role, he gets to work with some of the world's largest companies supporting various technologies ranging from unified communications to private cloud and everything in between. Before joining Microsoft, he was an MVP for Unified Communications.

John lives in Ireland with his wife, Sharon, and three kids, Sophie, Adam, and Samuel. When not working, he enjoys training in martial arts, namely Bujinkan Budo Taijitsu and when time permits you will find him behind some turntables.

Robert Panek is an independent consultant who has enjoyed a successful career in IT and software development. Since 1995 Robert has worked for companies such as AIG, L-3, Radianse, and IPOSyndicate, where in 2000 his work was awarded *Forbes Magazine*'s "Best of the Web" for four consecutive quarters. Due to his vast achievements at IPOSyndicate, he advanced to chief technology officer.

Throughout his 19 years working in IT, Robert has achieved qualifications such as MCP, MCSA, MCSE, MCSD – Web Applications, and MCDBA, and his experience along with his mentoring of junior-level IT professionals has brought him to Sybex publishing to further educate and certify students.

Robert is currently living in New Hampshire with his wife, Jeannie.

Michael Rice continues to thrive as a talented and successful datacenter administrator for a Department of Defense contracting company, Intelligent Software Solutions Inc.

He specializes in leading the way for corporate infrastructure in the areas of virtualization, storage, and systems administration. Over the past eight years as an IT professional, he has earned multiple IT certifications such as MCP, MCTS, MCSA, MCSE, VCP 5, and Net + and has received numerous awards for outstanding performance and dedication to excellence.

Michael lives in the beautiful state of Colorado with his wife, Jessica, and his two wonderful children, Kristen and Anthony. He plans to one day become a certified trainer and further differentiate his career by leading the way in technology for other IT professionals around the globe.

Stefan Roth works as a private cloud architect at itnetx gmbh, a consulting and engineering company located in Switzerland, which was awarded Microsoft's "Partner of the Year – Datacenter" in 2011, 2012, and 2013. He presents at technical events and works closely with his customers and Microsoft to evangelize cloud and datacenter technologies.

Working in IT for the past 13 years, he was previously employed as a systems engineer and consultant for national and international companies, where he gained a great deal of experience in datacenter management. His main focus is Active Directory, System Center Operations Manager, and System Center Orchestrator, and he has achieved certification from Microsoft in the MCITP: Enterprise Administrator and MCSE: Private Cloud disciplines.

You can get more information about Stefan on his System Center Operations Manager blog at `http://blog.scomfaq.ch` or on Twitter at @scomfaq.

Contents at a Glance

Introduction . . . . *xxxi*

Chapter 1 • What's New in Windows Server 2012 R2 1

Chapter 2 • Installing and Upgrading to Windows Server 2012 19

Chapter 3 • Introduction to Server Core 105

Chapter 4 • Windows Server 2012 R2 Networking Enhancements 147

Chapter 5 • IP Address Management and DHCP Failover 175

Chapter 6 • DNS and Name Resolution in Windows Server 2012 R2 . . . . • 211

Chapter 7 • Active Directory in Windows Server 2012 257

Chapter 8 • Creating and Managing User Accounts 377

Chapter 9 • Group Policy: AD's Gauntlet and Active Directory Delegation. 467

Chapter 10 • Active Directory Federation Services. 533

Chapter 11 • Shared Storage and Clustering Introduction 561

Chapter 12 • Windows 2012 R2 Storage: Storage Spaces,
SANish Abilities, and Better Tools 589

Chapter 13 • Files, Folders, and Basic Shares 649

Chapter 14 • Creating and Managing Shared Folders 703

Chapter 15 • Dynamic Access Control: File Shares, Reimagined. 759

Chapter 16 • Sharing Printers on Windows Server 2012 R2 Networks . . . . • 827

Chapter 17 • Remote Server Administration 883

Chapter 18 • Connecting Windows and Mac Clients 929

Chapter 19 • Web Server Management with IIS 979

Chapter 20 • Advanced IP: Routing with Windows 1025

Chapter 21 • Getting from the Office to the Road: VPNs. 1065

Chapter 22 • Adding More Locations: Sites in Active Directory 1123

Chapter 23 • The Third DC: Understanding Read-only Domain Controllers 1153

Chapter 24 • Creating Larger Active Directory Environments:
Beyond One Domain 1185

Chapter 25 • Migrating, Merging, and Modifying Your Active Directory 1243

Chapter 26 • Advanced User Account Management and User Support 1267

Chapter 27 • Server Virtualization with Hyper-V 1339

Chapter 28 • Managing Virtual Machines 1399

Chapter 29 • Installing, Using, and Administering Remote Desktop Services . . . 1435

Chapter 30 • Monitoring Windows Server 2012 R2 1479

Chapter 31 • Patch Management 1531

Chapter 32 • Windows Server 2012 R2 and Active Directory Backup and
Maintenance 1555

Appendix • The Bottom Line 1585

Index 1631

Contents

Introduction . . . . *xxxi*

Chapter 1 • What's New in Windows Server 2012 R2 . . . . **1**
Windows Server 2012 R2 Introduction 1
Windows Server Editions 2
    Standard Edition 2
    Datacenter Edition 2
    Foundation Edition 2
    Essentials Edition 3
Desktop Changes 3
Active Directory Changes 3
    Active Directory Domain Services Changes 4
    Active Directory Rights Management Services 7
    Active Directory Certificate Services 8
Virtualization 8
    Hyper-V 8
    Virtual Desktop Infrastructure 10
Networking Changes 11
    EAP-TTLS 11
    DNS 11
    IP Address Management 11
    NIC Teaming 11
Management Tools 12
    Server Manager 12
    The Remote Tools: WinRM and WinRS 13
    Remote Desktop Services 13
    Group Policy Object Improvements 14
File and Print Sharing 14
    BranchCache 14
    SMB 3.0 15
    File Server Resource Manager 15
Web-based Services 15
    Web Server IIS 15
    FTP Server 17

Chapter 2 • Installing and Upgrading to Windows Server 2012 R2 . . . . . . **19**
What Has Changed? 19
    Installation Requirements 20
    64-Bit Support 22
Installing the Operating System 23
    Performing a Clean Installation 23
    Performing an Upgrade Installation 31

Server Manager Dashboard 42
Using Server Manager to Configure Your Servers 43
Changes to Server Manager 45
Common Configuration Tasks 45
Adding and Removing Roles and Features 56
Troubleshooting Roles and Features 70
Wrapping Up Server Manager 76
Upgrading Active Directory 76
An Overview of Active Directory: New Functionality
in Windows Server 2012 R2 76
Active Directory Upgrade Strategies 80
Unattended Installations 81
Installing Windows Assessment and Deployment Kit 82
Creating an Answer File 87
Using an Answer File 100
Installing a Sample Server Network for
This Book's Examples 102
The Bottom Line 103

Chapter 3 • Introduction to Server Core 105
What's New in Server Core 105
Installing Server Core 106
Server Core Survival Guide 109
Switching between Server Core and the GUI and Vice Versa 109
Accessing Task Manager 109
Closing the Command Prompt 110
Changing the Administrator's Password 110
Accessing File Shares 111
Finding Commands from A to Z 112
Reading Text Files with Notepad 112
Editing the Registry 112
Rebooting and Shutting Down 112
Initial Configurations for Server Core 113
Providing Computer Information 113
Updating the Server 116
Customizing This Server 117
Administering Server Core Remotely 119
Configuring Roles and Features 131
Creating a Domain Controller and Managing DNS 132
Configuring the DHCP Service 133
Setting Up a File Server 135
Setting Up a Print Server 140
Managing Licenses with the Key Management Service 142
Protecting Data with Windows Backup Server 144
The Bottom Line 145

Chapter 4 • Windows Server 2012 R2 Networking Enhancements......147

The Journey to IPv6 147
    The Benefits of IPv6 148
    IPv6 Transition Technologies 148
Better Networking Manageability with PowerShell 150
    Networking Cmdlets and Modules 150
Microsoft NIC Teaming 152
    Understanding the Benefits of a Windows
        Server 2012 R2 NIC Team 152
    NIC Team Configurations 152
Configuring NIC Teaming 155
Enhanced QoS 160
    Minimum Bandwidth 161
    Data Center Bridging 161
    Hyper-V QoS 163
    Policy-Based QoS 164
802.1X Authenticated Access 165
BranchCache Improved 165
Managing Network Performance 167
    Performance Analysis and Tools 168
    Server Performance Advisor Tool 169
The Bottom Line 172

Chapter 5 • IP Address Management and DHCP Failover...........175

IPAM 175
    IPAM Requirements 177
    IPAM Components 178
    Topology Deployment Options 179
IPAM Installation 180
    Installing the IPAM Server Feature 180
    Installing the IPAM Client Feature 182
    Configure IPAM Provisioning 182
    Configure Server Discovery 184
    Run Server Discoveries 185
    Choosing Servers for Management 185
    Retrieving Data 189
Using IPAM 190
    Overview and Server Inventory 190
    IP Address Space 191
    Virtualized IP Address Space 193
    Monitor and Manage 196
    Event Catalog 198
IPAM Delegation 199
IPAM Troubleshooting 203
    Using the Event Viewer 203
    Common Issues 203

DHCP Failover 204
    Clustering vs. Split-scope 205
    What Is DHCP Failover? 205
    DHCP Failover Requirements. 205
Installing DHCP Failover 206
The Bottom Line 209

Chapter 6 • DNS and Name Resolution in Windows Server 2012 R2 211
Understanding the DNS Server Role 211
Installing DNS 214
    Configuring a Stand-Alone DNS Server 214
    Integrating with Other DNS Servers. 217
    Implementing Zones to Manage Namespaces. 221
    Understanding Record Types. 228
    Managing DNS Clients and Name Resolution. 232
Understanding Active Directory's DNS. 239
    Configuring DNS Automatically 239
    Understanding SRV Records and Clients. 241
    Windows Server 2012 R2 Additional Features. 242
Supporting Internet-based DNS Resolution 245
    Supporting External DNS Domains 245
    Resolving External Namespaces 246
Administration and Troubleshooting with DNS Tools 248
    Administering the DNS Server with the DNS
       Management Console and PowerShell. 248
    Leveraging NsLookup and DcDiag. 250
    Helpful DNS Troubleshooting Links. 254
The Bottom Line. 255

Chapter 7 • Active Directory in Windows Server 2012. 257
An Introduction and Active Directory Basics 258
    Creating a Single-domain Forest 260
    Benefits of a Single domain. 261
    Creating a Single-domain Forest 262
    Adding a Second DC 279
    Creating Organizational Units, Accounts, and Groups 285
    Delegating Control Using Organizational Units. 297
    Domain Maintenance Tasks 297
Fine-grained Password Policies. 310
    Creating the Password Settings Object. 310
    Password Settings Object Precedence. 312
SYSVOL: Old and NEW. 313
    The Old: File Replication Service 313
    The New: Distributed File System Replication 317
Upgrading Your Active Directory. 331
    Upgrade the Schema to Windows Server 2012. 331

Upgrade the Domain to 2012 334
Migrating with a Swing Migration 339
Migrating with a Clean and Pristine Migration 343
Using Microsoft's Free Migration Tool: ADMT........................... 347
An Example Migration Setup 348
Establishing the Trust 350
Getting Both Sides ADMT-friendly 351
Starting Up ADMT and Migrating 354
Testing the Migrated Group's Access to Resources........................ 363
Translating Local Profiles 364
Migrating Computer Accounts.. 366
Rollback Considerations 367
The Path to the 2012 Forest Functional Level............................. 367
An Introduction to Windows Azure Active Directory 368
Getting Started with Windows Azure Active Directory 368
How to Interact with Windows Azure Active Directory 370
Synchronizing Windows Azure Active Directory 371
Active Directory Logon Flavors 372
Overview of Workplace Join... 374
What Is Workplace Join? 374
The Bottom Line... 375

Chapter 8 • Creating and Managing User Accounts **377**
Creating and Managing User Accounts..................................... 378
Creating Local User Accounts 378
Creating Domain User Accounts 382
Setting Local User Account Properties 388
Setting Domain-Based User Account Properties........................... 396
Managing Groups 412
Local Groups 413
Active Directory Groups 424
Monday Morning Admin Tasks 433
Forgotten Passwords 434
Locked-Out Users... 435
Using the New Features for User and Group Management 437
Active Directory Administrative Center................................. 437
ADAC Essentials.. 437
Navigating ADAC... 440
PowerShell History Viewer 448
Active Directory Module for Windows PowerShell.......................... 451
Creating Users.. 452
Setting Passwords... 453
Creating Many Users at Once 455
Unlocking a User Account.. 457
Enabling an Account 459
Disabling an Account.. 459

Removing a Group 464
The Bottom Line. 464

Chapter 9 • Group Policy: AD's Gauntlet and Active
Directory Delegation **467**
Group Policy Concepts 467
Policies Are "All or Nothing" 468
Policies Are Inherited and Cumulative. 469
Group Policy Power! Refresh Intervals . . . . ˙. . 469
Group Policy Basics 469
Replication of Group Policy Is Built In 470
GPOs Undo Themselves When Removed. 470
You Needn't Log On to Apply GPO Settings 470
Local Policies and Group Policy Objects 470
Administrators or Non-Administrators LGPO 471
User-specific LGPO. 473
Creating GPOs 474
Modifying Group Policy Default Behavior 479
Group Policy Policies 480
Group Policy Application 481
How Group Policy Is Applied. 481
Filtering Group Policy with Access Control Lists 482
Enforcing and Blocking Inheritance 486
Group Policy Setting Possibilities 486
Decrypting User and Computer Configuration Settings. 487
Using Group Policy to Set Password and Account Lockout Policy 502
Group Policy Preferences. 504
The New and Improved GPMC. 509
Starter GPOs 510
Backing Up and Restoring GPOs 511
Troubleshooting Group Policies. 513
The Resultant Set of Policy Tool 513
Group Policy Results Using the GPMC. 514
Group Policy Modeling Using the GPMC. 516
gpresult. 516
Using Event Viewer 517
Troubleshooting 101: Keep It Simple 517
Active Directory Delegation. 518
Delegating Group Policy Administration. 518
Delegating Control Using Organizational Units 521
Creating a New Organizational Unit 522
Moving User Accounts into an OU 522
Creating a MktPswAdm Group 522
Delegating the Marketing OU's Password
Reset Control to MktPswAdm 523
Advanced Delegation: Manually Setting Permissions. 525

Finding Out Which Delegations Have
Been Set, or Undelegating 530
The Bottom Line 531

Chapter 10 • Active Directory Federation Services . . . . **.533**
Understanding AD FS Key Components
and Terminology 534
AD FS Commonly Used Terms and Components 534
Understanding AD FS Certificates 536
Planning, Installing, and Configuring
an AD FS Infrastructure 537
Planning for AD FS Deployment 537
Installing the AD FS Roles and Features Using Server Manager 539
Creating a Trusted SSL Certificate Using IIS 543
Using the AD FS Server Configuration Wizard 544
Using Windows PowerShell with AD FS 547
Adding a Trusted Relying Party 549
Additional Configuration Options for AD FS 551
Automating Client Configurations Using Group Policy 559
The Bottom Line 560

Chapter 11 • Shared Storage and Clustering Introduction . . . . **.561**
Shared Storage Basics 561
Storage Area Network 562
iSCSI 562
Fiber Channel 563
SAS Enclosures 563
RAID 563
SMB 3.0 563
Windows Server 2012 R2 File and Storage Services 564
Clustering 566
Clustering Requirements 566
Clustering Functionality 567
Cluster Shared Volumes 568
Clusters and Virtualization 569
Understanding Quorums 570
Highly Available Storage 571
Storage Spaces 571
Clustering inside Virtual Machines 573
Setting Up a Cluster 573
Cluster Configuration 574
Storage 575
Adding the First Node in Your Cluster 575
Adding a Second Node to the Cluster 585
Setting Up a Guest-based Cluster 587
The Bottom Line 588

Chapter 12 • Windows 2012 R2 Storage: Storage Spaces, SANish Abilities, and Better Tools 589

What's New in Windows Server 2012 R2 Storage? 589
Tiered Storage Spaces. 590
Write-back Cache 590
Parallelized Repair 591
Low-level Improvement: Native 4K Sector Support 591
UEFI BIOS Support Allows GPT Drives 592
CHKDSK Gets Smarter 592
Online Self-healing. 592
Online Verification 592
Online Identification and Logging 593
Precise and Rapid Correction. 593
In-depth Look at Storage Spaces 594
Reusing Technology from Microsoft's Cloud. 595
Providing SAN-like Capabilities with Microsoft Management Tools 595
Creating a Storage Space 598
Creating a Pool 599
Pool Limitations 602
Viewing Drives in Disk Management. 603
Pooling with PowerShell 604
Allocating Pool Space to a Virtual Disk 606
Storage-tiering Demo and Setup Using PowerShell 619
iSCSI on Storage Spaces. 623
Adding the iSCSI Target Service 623
Connecting to an iSCSI Virtual Disk from the Client Side 628
NFS Shares 631
Where to Use an NFS Share 631
Quick NFS Share Setup 632
Connecting to NFS from the Client Side. 636
Deduplication: Disk and Network. 636
Configuring Data Dedup with Server Manager 638
Configuring Data Dedup with PowerShell. 641
Checking for Corrupt Volumes 646
The Bottom Line. 647

Chapter 13 • Files, Folders, and Basic Shares 649

Understanding the File and Storage Services Role. 650
Additional Role Services and Features 651
How to Add Roles to the File and Storage Services Role 653
Creating Shares 657
Creating Shares with Server Manager 657
Creating Shares on Remote Computers Using Server Manager 660
Publishing Shares in Active Directory 664
Managing Permissions 666

NTFS Permissions. 666
Share Permissions. 667
Share and NTFS Permission Similarities 667
Modifying Share and NTFS Permissions 669
Combining Share and NTFS Permissions 671
Connecting to Shares 672
"A Set of Credentials Conflicts" 674
Using net use on a WAN 674
Common Shares 675
File Server Resource Manager 676
Creating Quota Policies 676
Creating File Screen Policies. 682
Generating Reports. 684
File Server Resource Manager Options. 687
Understanding SMB 3.0. 688
Compatibility with SMB 2.0 and 1.0. 689
SMB Security 691
Implementing BitLocker 692
What's New in BitLocker. 692
Hardware Requirements 693
Enabling BitLocker 695
Using Offline Files/Client-Side Caching 697
How Offline Files Works 698
BranchCache 699
Enabling Offline Files on the Server 699
The Bottom Line. 701

Chapter 14 • Creating and Managing Shared Folders. 703
Creating Shared Folders 703
Creating Shares from Explorer. 705
Remotely Creating Shares with the Computer Management Console. 707
Managing Permissions 711
Creating Share Permissions 711
Understanding File and Directory Permissions 715
Working with Hidden Shares. 732
Exploring the Distributed File System 734
Understanding DFS Terminology 736
Choosing Stand-Alone vs. Domain-Based DFS 737
Creating a DFS Root 738
Adding Links to a DFS Root 743
Configuring DFS Replications 745
Understanding DFS Replication. 747
Managing DFS Replication 747
Exploring the Network File System. 751
The Bottom Line. 756

Chapter 15 • Dynamic Access Control: File Shares, Reimagined. 759

A New Way to Secure File Shares 760

Access Control Using Groups and User AD Attributes 765

Securing Data by Machine Attributes. 766

Centrally Control Permissions Using Templates 767

Using Effective Permissions to Troubleshoot Access Control 769

Automatic File Classification 769

DAC Players: User, Device, Resources, and Claims 769

User 769

Device 770

Resources 770

Claims 770

Enabling DAC 771

Pieces of an Access Policy 774

Side Task 778

Access Denied Assistance 796

Claims—Using Different Attributes 799

Step 1: Create the Claim. 800

Step 2: Create the Resource Property 802

Step 3: Add to the Resource Property List 802

Step 4: Create Central Access Rules. 802

Step 5: Create a Central Access Policy and Deploy It via Group Policy 803

Step 6: Apply the Policy to the Engineering Folder. 803

Step 7: Test with Effective Access 803

Classification. 804

Classifying a Document 804

Classification Properties 806

Classification Rules. 807

Expression Types 813

Understanding Regular Expressions. 818

Securing Data Using DAC and File Classification. 819

The Bottom Line. 824

Chapter 16 • Sharing Printers on Windows Server 2012 R2 Networks . . .827

Print Services Overview 827

The Print Spooler 828

The Printer Driver. 829

Installing the Print and Document Services Role. 832

Adding the Print and Document Services Role. 832

Working in the Print Management Console. 834

Adding the Print Services Role to Server Core 845

PowerShell Cmdlets Reference 847

Deploying Printers to the Masses 847

Adding a Printer to a Client Manually 848

Adding a Printer Using Active Directory Search 849

Deploying Printers via GPO 853

Viewing Deployed Printers. 856
Adjusting Print Server Settings. 857
    Server Properties 857
    Printer Migration 861
Managing Printer Properties 862
    Printer Properties Sharing Tab. 862
    Printer Properties Ports Tab 863
    Printer Properties Security Tab 864
    Printer Properties Advanced Tab. 870
Managing Print Jobs 876
Using Custom Filters 878
Troubleshooting Printer Problems 879
    Basic Troubleshooting: Identifying the Situation 879
    Restarting the Spooler Service 881
    Isolating Printer Drivers 881
The Bottom Line. 882

Chapter 17 • Remote Server Administration. 883
Remote Desktop for Administration. 883
    Configuring the Server for Remote Desktop 884
    Using Remote Desktop Connection. 886
    Remote Desktop Gateway 906
    Configuring a Server for Remote Assistance 917
Windows Remote Management Service. 919
    Enabling WinRM 920
    Using WinRS 921
Remote Server Administration Tools 922
    RSAT Compatibility Issues 923
    RSAT Tools. 923
    Installing RSAT. 924
    Remote Desktop and PowerShell 925
The Bottom Line. 926

Chapter 18 • Connecting Windows and Mac Clients 929
What to Know Before You Begin. 929
    Understanding Client-side Software Requirements. 930
    Domain Accounts and Local Accounts 931
Verifying Your Network Configuration 932
    Verifying Local Area Connection Settings. 933
    Testing Network Connectivity with the *ping* Command 935
    Verifying and Setting Local Area Connection
        Information Using the GUI. 935
Joining the Domain 942
    Joining a Domain from Windows 8 943
    Joining a Domain with PowerShell 950

Changing Domain User Passwords 951
 Changing Domain Passwords from Windows 8 and Windows 7 952
Connecting to Network Resources 955
 Publishing Resources with Group Policy Objects 956
Connecting Mac OS X Clients 969
 Connecting a Mac to the Domain 971
 Connecting to File Shares 973
 Connecting to Printers 974
 Using Remote Desktop from a Mac Client 974
 Troubleshooting 976
The Bottom Line 977

Chapter 19 • Web Server Management with IIS **979**
What's New in IIS 8.0 and 8.5 979
Installing IIS 8 981
 Adding the Web Server Role via Service Manager 981
 Installing IIS 8 via PowerShell 985
 Renovating IIS Construction 986
 Adding Role Services to the Web Server Role for Bigfirm 986
Website Provisioning 991
 Understanding Global Settings 992
 Planning Bigfirm's Apples and Oranges Websites 992
 Creating a Simple Website 994
 Constructing Bigfirm's Websites 995
 Configuring Site Settings 1001
Hosting Multiple Websites 1002
 Deploying Sites 1003
 Site Uniqueness 1005
 Setting Up an Anonymous Account 1005
 Managing Multiple Sites for Bigfirm 1006
 Delegating Administration 1007
Installing and Configuring SMTP 1008
 Getting Started 1008
 Adding the SMTP Server Feature 1009
 Setting Up an SMTP Server 1010
 Adding the SMTP E-mail Feature to an IIS 8 Website 1012
Integrating FTP into IIS 8 Web Pages 1013
 The FTP File Transfer Publishing Service 1014
 Adding FTP to an IIS 8 Website 1014
Advanced Administration 1016
 Using Web Management Services 1017
 Connecting, Securing, Logging 1019
 Backing Up and Restoring Data 1023
The Bottom Line 1024

Chapter 20 • Advanced IP: Routing with Windows **1025**

The Life of an IP Packet. 1025
    First, the Simple Case: No Routing Required. 1027
    Now the Hard Case: With Routing 1030
From Classes to Classless 1034
    In the Beginning Was the Class 1034
    Unusable Host Addresses 1035
    Broadcast Gets Narrower: The First Unroutable Addresses 1035
    Routing the Unroutable, Part I: Private Addresses 1036
Sockets, Ports, and Winsock. 1042
    Winsock: Why We Can All Use the Internet 1045
    Routing the Unroutable, Part II: NAPT and PAT. 1045
    Routing the Unroutable, Part III: Application Layer Gateways. 1047
    Installing a NAT 1047
Testing and Troubleshooting 1057
    Using the Application Itself. 1057
    Pinging a Remote Computer with ping 1058
    Pinging a Remote Computer with traceroute. 1059
    Checking Your Configuration with ipconfig 1060
    Showing Routing and Neighbors. 1060
    Using Network Monitor. 1060
    Which Card Do You Monitor? 1061
The Bottom Line. 1062

Chapter 21 • Getting from the Office to the Road: VPNs **1065**

Introducing VPNs 1065
    Gateway-to-Gateway VPN 1066
Understanding the Tunneling Protocols 1067
    Layer 2 Tunneling Protocol. 1067
    Secure Socket Tunneling Protocol 1067
    Internet Key Exchange Version 2 1068
Using the Network Policy and Access Services Role 1068
    Installing the Network Policy and Access Services Role 1069
Using the Remote Access Role 1070
    Installing the Remote Access Role. 1071
    Configuring Routing and Remote Access. 1072
    Configuring Policies. 1074
    Authenticating VPN Clients 1097
    Configuring Accounting 1100
    Exploring Routing and Remote Access. 1102
Introducing DirectAccess. 1110
    How DirectAccess Works 1110
    DirectAccess Requirements 1112
Installing DirectAccess 1112

Configuring a DirectAccess Client 1118

Managing DirectAccess 1120

The Bottom Line.. 1121

Chapter 22 • Adding More Locations: Sites in Active Directory 1123

Mastering Site Concepts 1123

Sites and Replication 1125

Understanding Site Terminology................................... 1126

Exploring Sites 1128

How Sites Work.. 1128

Renaming Default-First-Site-Name 1130

Defining a Site.. 1130

Deciding on DCs in Remote Locations 1131

Defining a Subnet and Placing It in a Site..................... 1135

Placing a Server in a Site 1137

Adding Site Links.. 1137

Configuring Intersite Replication 1141

Bridgehead Servers.. 1144

Forcing Replication.. 1145

Configuring Clients to Access the Next Closest Site 1146

Configuring Next Closest Site with Group Policy............. 1147

Configuring Next Closest Site through the Registry 1148

Using PowerShell.. 1150

The Bottom Line.. 1152

Chapter 23 • The Third DC: Understanding Read-only
Domain Controllers 1153

Introducing RODCs... 1153

Making Changes on a Read-only Domain Controller 1155

RODC Contents.. 1156

RODC Requirements 1161

RODC and Server Applications 1167

Installing the RODC 1168

Installing RODC on Server Core 1174

Viewing the RODC Properties 1174

Modifying the Allowed List 1176

Staged Installations 1177

DNS on the RODC 1182

Active Directory Integrated DNS................................. 1183

Read-only DNS 1183

The Bottom Line.. 1184

Chapter 24 • Creating Larger Active Directory Environments:
Beyond One Domain 1185

The Foundations of Multiple-Domain Designs...................... 1185

Domains.. 1186

Forests. 1188
Trees 1188
You Must Build Trees and Forests Together. 1190
Planning Your Active Directory Environment 1191
Satisfying Political Needs 1192
Connectivity and Replication Issues 1192
Multiple Domains: When They Make Sense 1193
The Case for an Empty Root 1194
Active Directory Design Pointers. 1196
Creating Multiple Domains 1198
Naming Multidomain Structures 1198
Preparing the DC for the Second Domain 1199
Creating a Second Domain 1200
Functional Levels. 1205
Domain Functional Levels 1205
Forest Functional Levels 1207
FSMOs and GCs 1209
Multimaster vs. Single-Master Replication. 1209
But Not Everything Is Multimaster 1209
Domain Naming: A FSMO Example 1210
Why Administrators Must Know about FSMOs 1210
Global Catalogs 1211
FSMO Roles 1213
Schema Master 1213
Domain Naming Master FSMO 1217
RID Pool FSMO 1217
Infrastructure Operations Master 1218
PDC Emulator FSMO 1219
Transferring FSMO Roles 1219
Time Sync. 1223
Trusts 1226
Defining the Domain: "Trust" 1226
Trust Relationships in More Detail 1227
Trusts Have Direction 1227
Some Trusts Are Transitive. 1228
Trusts Do Not Remove All Security. 1228
Trusts Involve Administrators from Both Sides 1229
Four Kinds of Trusts. 1229
Understanding Transitive Forest Trusts 1230
Manually Creating Trusts 1230
The Bottom Line. 1240

Chapter 25 • Migrating, Merging, and Modifying
Your Active Directory 1243
Upgrade and Migration Strategies 1243
Upgrade Capabilities 1244

Migrating with an In-place Upgrade 1245
Swing Migrations from Windows Server 2003 1255
Active Directory Domain Migration 1258
Using Microsoft's Free Migration Tool: ADMT 1262
Version Incompatibility 1262
Establishing the Trust 1263
Getting Both Sides ADMT-friendly 1264
The Bottom Line 1265

Chapter 26 • Advanced User Account Management and
User Support **1267**
Experiencing the Flexible Desktop 1268
Configuring Home Directories 1269
Setting Up the Lab 1270
Creating the Home Directories 1270
Creating Home Directories 1277
Home Directory vs. Local Storage 1280
Creating Roaming Profiles 1280
Creating a Roaming Profiles Share: The Easy Way 1282
Creating a Roaming Profiles Share: The Hard Way 1290
Configuring Mandatory Profiles 1293
Configuring Super Mandatory Profiles 1299
Configuring a Default Network Profile 1299
Managing Roaming Profiles 1300
Machine Settings 1301
User Settings 1306
Redirecting Folders 1306
Basic Folder Redirection 1308
Advanced Folder Redirection 1314
Managing Folder Redirection 1316
Work Folders 1319
Installing Work Folders 1319
Sync Share Configuration 1319
Client Configuration 1322
Managing the Desktop Using Group Policy 1323
Managing Users with Group Policy
Preferences and Logon Scripts 1328
Managing Drive Mappings 1328
Executing Commands at Logon 1331
Multiple Logon Scripts 1334
Managing Logon Scripts with Group Policy 1335
Managing Shutdown Tasks with Logoff Scripts 1336
The Bottom Line 1337

Chapter 27 • Server Virtualization with Hyper-V **1339**

Understanding Server Virtualization 1339
  What Use Is Server Virtualization? 1341
  Getting Started with Hyper-V 1343
What's New in Hyper-V 2012 R2? 1345
Understanding the Hyper-V Architecture 1352
  The Management OS Partition 1354
  Virtual Machine (Guest) Partitions 1357
Installing and Configuring Hyper-V 1359
  Working with the Console 1363
  Exploring the Actions Pane 1364
Understanding Virtual Disks 1366
  Virtual Disks and Their Controllers 1367
  Creating a New Virtual Disk 1368
  Disk Maintenance 1371
Understanding Virtual Switches 1374
  Choosing a Virtual Switch 1374
  Creating a Virtual Switch 1375
Getting Started with Virtual Machines 1377
  Installing a Virtual Machine 1388
  Working with VLANs 1392
  Time Travel with Checkpoints 1393
The Bottom Line 1396

Chapter 28 • Managing Virtual Machines **1399**

Domain Controllers and Hyper-V 1399
  Virtual DCs That Just Work 1400
  Quick Domain Controller Deployment 1402
Moving VMs: Export and Import 1407
  Quick Migration and Live Migration 1411
  Cluster-free Live Migrations 1414
VM Maintenance 1418
  Backing Up and Restoring Virtual Machines 1418
  Malware Protection and Patching 1421
Disaster Recovery 1422
  Cheap DR with Hyper-V Replica 1423
Online Resources for Hyper-V 1431
The Bottom Line 1432

**Chapter 29 • Installing, Using, and Administering
             Remote Desktop Services** **1435**

Who Needs Remote Desktop Services? 1435
  Centralized Deployment of Applications 1436
  Supporting Remote Users 1436

Supporting PC-Unfriendly Environments 1436
Reducing Hardware Refreshes. 1437
Simplifying the User Interface 1438
Providing Help-Desk Support 1439
Deploying RDS RemoteApp 1439
Understanding the Remote Desktop
  Services Processing Model. 1440
Son of Mainframe? 1440
Anatomy of a Thin-Client Session 1441
Server and Client Requirements 1444
Server Hardware. 1444
Client Hardware 1447
Adding Remote Desktop Services. 1449
Required Role Services 1450
Easy Print. 1452
Single Sign-On. 1452
Network Level Authentication 1453
Licensing Mode. 1453
Remote Desktop Users Group. 1454
Adding the Remote Desktop Services Role 1454
Adding Applications 1458
Connecting to an RDS Session 1459
Adding an RDS RemoteApp Application 1460
Virtual Desktop Infrastructure 1464
Monitoring Remote Desktop Services 1472
Common Tasks and How to Do Them 1473
Remote Desktop Licensing Manager. 1475
The Bottom Line. 1477

Chapter 30 • Monitoring Windows Server 2012 R2 . . . .**1479**
Using Server Manager to Monitor Multiple Servers 1479
Adding Servers to Manage 1480
Creating a Server Group for Monitoring. 1481
Monitoring with Server Groups. 1481
Utilizing the Best Practice Analyzers 1483
Monitoring Your System with Event Viewer. 1485
Viewing an Event 1485
Understanding Event Levels. 1486
Creating and Using Custom Views 1487
Understanding Windows Logs. 1492
Understanding Applications and Services Logs 1493
Configuring Event Log Properties. 1493
Subscribing to Event Logs. 1495
Understanding Subscription Types. 1496
Selecting Events 1498
Setting Advanced Options 1499

Understanding Event Subscription Protocols 1500
Configuring Event Subscriptions. 1501
Troubleshooting Event Forwarding 1505
Checking the Runtime Status. 1505
Using the Windows Event Collector Utility 1505
Monitoring Performance. 1507
Using Monitoring Tools. 1508
Using Data Collector Sets 1510
PAL and PerfView 1519
Introducing PAL 1519
PerfView. 1523
Advanced Monitoring with System Center 2012 R2. 1523
Introduction to Operations Manager. 1524
The Bottom Line. 1528

Chapter 31 • Patch Management **1531**
What's New in Windows Server 2012 R2 Windows
  Server Update Services. 1531
New Features of WSUS v6 in Windows Server 2012 R2. 1532
Software Requirements for WSUS Servers and Clients 1532
Deployment Scenarios 1533
Complex Hierarchies with WSUS 1535
Installation and Configuration of Patch Management. 1536
Installing the WSUS Role on Windows Server 2012 R2 1536
Configuring WSUS for Deployments 1540
Deploying Updates and Migration for Windows Server Update Services. 1544
Configuring Group Policies for Windows Update 1544
Configuring Clients for Windows Updates 1547
Migration from WSUS 3.0 to Windows Server 2012 R2 1550
Backing Up Your WSUS Database 1550
Review Additional Considerations 1551
Operational Management and Tools. 1551
The Bottom Line. 1554

**Chapter 32 • Windows Server 2012 R2 and Active
                Directory Backup and Maintenance** **1555**
Introducing Windows Server Backup. 1555
Installing Windows Server Backup 1556
Backing Up and Restoring a Full Server. 1557
Backing Up and Restoring Files and Folders 1566
Backing Up to the Cloud 1569
Stopping and Restarting Active Directory. 1570
Stopping and Starting AD DS. 1570
Defragmenting Active Directory Offline 1570
Checking the Integrity of an Active Directory Database 1571
Capturing Active Directory Snapshots 1573

Creating an Active Directory Snapshot. 1573
Mounting an Active Directory Snapshot 1574
Working with Mounted Active Directory Snapshots 1574
Backing Up and Restoring Active Directory. 1576
Introducing the Active Directory Recycle Bin. 1577
Creating an Active Directory Backup 1579
Restoring an Active Directory Backup 1580
Performing an Authoritative Restore 1582
The Bottom Line. 1583

Appendix • The Bottom Line . . . . **.1585**
Chapter 2: Installing and Upgrading to Windows Server 2012 1585
Chapter 3: Introduction to Server Core 1586
Chapter 4: Windows Server 2012 R2 Networking Enhancements 1587
Chapter 5: IP Address Management and DHCP Failover 1589
Chapter 6: DNS and Name Resolution in Windows Server 2012 R2 1591
Chapter 7: Active Directory in Windows Server 2012 1592
Chapter 8: Creating and Managing User Accounts 1593
Chapter 9: Group Policy: AD's Gauntlet and Active Directory Delegation 1597
Chapter 10: Active Directory Federation Services 1599
Chapter 11: Shared Storage and Clustering Introduction 1600
Chapter 12: Windows 2012 R2 Storage: Storage Spaces, SANish
Abilities, and Better Tools 1600
Chapter 13: Files, Folders, and Basic Shares. 1602
Chapter 14: Creating and Managing Shared Folders 1603
Chapter 15: Dynamic Access Control: File Shares, Reimagined. 1605
Chapter 16: Sharing Printers on Windows Server 2012 R2 Networks 1606
Chapter 17: Remote Server Administration. 1607
Chapter 18: Connecting Windows and Mac Clients. 1608
Chapter 19: Web Server Management with IIS 1611
Chapter 20: Advanced IP: Routing with Windows. 1612
Chapter 21: Getting from the Office to the Road: VPNs 1614
Chapter 22: Adding More Locations: Sites in Active Directory 1614
Chapter 23: The Third DC: Understanding Read-Only Domain Controllers 1616
Chapter 24: Creating Larger Active Directory Environments: Beyond One Domain 1617
Chapter 25: Migrating, Merging, and Modifying Your Active Directory. 1619
Chapter 26: Advanced User Account Management and User Support. 1620
Chapter 27: Server Virtualization with Hyper-V 1621
Chapter 28: Managing Virtual Machines. 1623
Chapter 29: Installing, Using, and Administering Remote Desktop Services. 1624
Chapter 30: Monitoring Windows Server 2012 R2 1625
Chapter 31: Patch Management 1627
Chapter 32: Windows Server 2012 R2 and Active Directory Backup and
Maintenance 1628

Index. *1631*

Introduction

Welcome to this book on Windows Server 2012 R2. All of the enhancements and new features that this latest release of Microsoft's flagship enterprise operating system offers have definitely raised the bar for future versions of Windows Server. To give you an insight into how much extra you get with 2012 R2, you only have to look at the original Windows Server 2012 release that reached general availability in September 2012. Shortly after that version hit the shelves, Sybex got this group of authors together to write a book on it, but just as we were coming to the final edits of our chapters, Microsoft announced that Windows Server 2012 R2 was to be released in October 2013—that's just over 12 months since the original version of Server 2012. In that short period of time, the amount of new functionality that was packed into Server 2012 R2 meant that we literally had to rewrite nearly half of the original Server 2012 book!

The team of authors who have worked on this book have an abundance of experience designing, deploying, managing, and troubleshooting Windows Server in large-scale enterprise environments, and we're really excited to tell you all about this version of the product.

If you're new to Windows Server, then this book will strive to give you the knowledge you require to go out and start working with it straight away. If you're an experienced administrator or consultant and are already familiar with it, then don't worry; we definitely have loads of new information in here for you to learn to help keep you ahead of the pack.

Who Should Read This Book?

Like every other book in the *Mastering Windows Server* series, we've aimed this book at people who need to know how to install, configure, maintain, and troubleshoot a Windows Server environment. We assume that you already have at least a basic understanding of standard TCP/IP networking and that you have a basic working level of comfort with previous versions of the Windows GUI and Microsoft Management Console (MMC) in particular.

As complex as software products are becoming, no one can be an expert on all of them. If you are like most administrators, you have time to learn only enough about a product so that you can manage it effectively. However, there is probably a lot more that you could be doing with any one product. This book will get you up to speed quickly and then help you through some of the more arcane topics.

Not every administrator will have the same type of infrastructure to work with. What works well in a large corporation does not always work for small companies. What works well for small companies may not scale well for large organizations. Microsoft has attempted to address the differences among companies and deliver a product that can be implemented quickly for a small company yet will still scale well for large organizations. No matter which scenario fits you, you will want to learn how this product will work for you.

What's Inside?

Chapter 1 starts out with an overview of what's new in Windows Server 2012 R2 (let's henceforth abbreviate that to "Server 2012 R2"), and Chapter 2 shows you how to install it on your servers and how to begin to integrate it with your existing network, if you have one.

Veterans of Windows networking will expect Server 2012 R2 to look like other versions of Windows does, with a desktop, a Start menu, and a host of graphically based tools, but as you will quickly learn, there's a whole new GUI to get to grips with. Chapter 3 gets you started on Server Core, and we recommend that you spend time learning it. Chapter 4 looks at the networking enhancements in Server 2012 R2, and Chapter 5 introduces you to some new functionality around IPAM and DHCP Failover. Chapter 6 walks you through DNS, answering the question, "How do I build a DNS infrastructure that is both secure and crafted to serve an Active Directory best?"

Speaking of AD, Chapter 7 is the first chapter to address that essential Windows Server technology, with an explanation of how to build the most common, and simplest, type of Active Directory: one that contains just one domain and just one location. Even if you're going to build huge, globe-spanning ADs, this first look provides a necessary foundation, so don't skip it. Then, once you have your AD up, you'll need to create and manage user accounts, and Chapter 8 shows you how. Once you have a working AD in place, then it's time to get some payback from all your design and setup work, and the tool for that is Group Policy. The good news is that Group Policy is a great way to control 10 or 10,000 machines and user accounts centrally; the bad news is that Group Policy can be a mite complex—but Chapter 9 helps on that score. The fourth AD-related chapter, Chapter 10, covers Active Directory Federation Services, which is a way to provide single sign-on access to your resources across organizational boundaries.

In Chapter 11 and Chapter 12 you get an introduction to shared storage and clustering, which are the pillar components of delivering a highly available IT infrastructure back to the business, along with an introduction to the new "SANish" capabilities of Server 2012 R2 using Storage Spaces.

Chapter 13 through Chapter 15 give you a three-part series on sharing files and folders in Windows Server by initially covering the basics of sharing folders and files and using Windows's security to control who can get to particular files. You will then be walked through Dynamic Access Control, which is a new way of controlling and auditing your file share access. Many servers serve not only files but shared printers as well, and Chapter 16 shows you how to accomplish this with Server 2012 R2.

Following that, Chapter 17 shows you how to maintain and control your servers remotely using a number of built-in technologies, including Remote Desktop. By now, you have some working servers (which is nice) but no clients to use those services (which makes the whole thing sort of pointless), so Chapter 18 shows you how to hook up the various varieties of Windows created in the past decade to a Windows Server 2012 R2 network. What's that, you say? You've got a Mac? No problem, you'll learn how to connect that up too.

Chapter 19 gets you up and running with one of Windows's most complex Server add-ons, Microsoft's Internet Information Services (IIS), better known as the web server. You'll learn how to get IIS running, how to set up a simple website, and how to find your way around the IIS management tools built into Server 2012 R2.

Chapter 20 discusses how a Server 2012 R2 system can facilitate IP routing, which may sound like an odd topic until you consider that you need to understand a bit of IP routing on a Windows Server before you can tackle Chapter 21, which shows you how to use your Server

2012 R2 system to set up a virtual private network. In Chapter 21, you will also learn about the really cool DirectAccess functionality that comes out of the box with Server 2012 R2.

Now it's time to return to Active Directory and take on some more advanced AD topics with four chapters. Chapter 22 shows you how to add multi-location awareness to your AD with a look at sites, site links, and subnets, AD-style. And if you have multiple sites, then you may have some sites that you might be a bit uneasy about installing a domain controller into—which is why we have read-only domain controllers (RODCs); learn about them in Chapter 23. After that, it's time to consider when you'd need to complicate your AD a bit by adding one, two, or a hundred more domains to it, in Chapter 24. Mergers, acquisitions, or just plain-old reorganizations may require you to reshape your AD in a manner that's not all that easy, unless you learn about domain migrations, SID histories, and trust relationships—as you will in Chapter 25. Continuing the Active Directory theme, Chapter 26 dives deep into advanced user account management and support.

You might have already read that Hyper-V is a pretty big thing in Windows Server 2012 R2, so we can't call the book complete without a couple of chapters on that topic—step forward Chapters 27 and 28. Even if you don't do virtualization, give these two chapters a look, because they will help you understand the technology and issues in server virtualization, which is a must-know field.

In Chapter 29, we will walk you through installing, using, and administering Remote Desktop Services, which will help you to design and deliver an optimal remote access and application publishing solution to your organization.

Up to this point, you'll have a lot of time invested in getting your server up and running, so to wrap up the final sections of the book you'll be ready for Chapters 30 through 32—monitoring your system's performance, patching it, and backing it up.

The *Mastering* Series

The *Mastering* series from Sybex provides outstanding instruction for readers with intermediate and advanced skills, in the form of top-notch training and development for those already working in their field and clear, serious education for those aspiring to become pros. Every *Mastering* book includes:

- Real-World Scenarios, ranging from case studies to interviews that show how the tool, technique, or knowledge presented is applied in actual practice.

- Skill-based instruction, with chapters organized around real tasks rather than abstract concepts or subjects.

- Self-review test questions, so you can be certain you're equipped to do the job right.

Final Comments

Make sure you take the time to become familiar with Windows Server 2012 R2. The more comfortable you are with it, the more you will be able to do with it. At the very end of each chapter, you'll find Master It self-tests that help reinforce the topics in the chapters. Instructions have been included that allow you to create a small lab environment. Building a lab environment can come in handy when you are trying to work through a new topic or troubleshoot a problem.

Most of all, have fun as you are going through the topics contained herein. Once you find out how much power this product has in store for you, you will be amazed at some of the things you can do.

How to Contact the Authors

You can contact any of the authors by using the personal blog or Twitter links mentioned in their bios earlier.

Sybex strives to keep you supplied with the latest tools and information you need for your work. Please check our website at www.sybex.com/go/masteringwindowsserver2012r2, where we'll post additional content and updates that supplement this book if the need arises.

Chapter 1

What's New in Windows Server 2012 R2

Windows Server 2012 R2 has over 300 new features, and it's the first Microsoft Server OS that has connectivity with the cloud. Explaining all of those features would take much more than a chapter (which is, of course, why we wrote a book!), but let's use these first few pages to give you the lay of the land. Now, we realize that some reading this book are just getting started with Windows Server, and so for them, *everything* is new, but many others of you reading this already know tons about Windows networking and would just like a summary of what's new in Server—this chapter summarizes that and where *to* find it in the book.

By now, we've sat through about a zillion Microsoft presentations on Windows Server, and they all start the same way, so apparently we're required by law (or at least by custom) to present the following as the first heading when doing an overview.

In this chapter, you'll learn about:

◆ The dramatic changes to the user interface

◆ New Active Directory features enhancing deployment and manageability

◆ Improvements to PowerShell

◆ New technology added to Hyper-V

◆ Enhancements to Windows networking, making it faster and more secure

◆ The new management tools

◆ The important features of IIS 8.0

Windows Server 2012 R2 Introduction

Well, with a slogan like, "Built from the cloud up," it doesn't take a mental heavyweight to figure out what was intended with Windows Server 2012 R2. So what is cloud technology? In a nutshell, it's the practice of using a network of remote servers to store, manage, and process data, rather than a local server. Windows Server 2012 R2 extends these technologies to corporations to be used in the same way for their employees. All corporate data using either virtual machines or individual workstations can be backed up directly to the cloud either on or off site. Cloud technologies are the driving force for the way the world conducts business today and in the near future.

From small business to some of the largest datacenters in the world, Windows Server 2012 R2 is one hot ticket. With virtually hundreds of new features from virtualization, networking, storage, usability, and much more, Windows Server 2012 R2 will not disappoint. The more we use it, the more we like it, and we think you will too!

The following sections offer a brief overview of what's new in this book and where to read more about those features.

Because this is an introductory chapter, all of the topics covered here will be talked about in depth elsewhere in the book.

Windows Server Editions

When Windows Server 2012 was released, you had the choice between Standard and Datacenter editions in both the Server Core and GUI versions. With the release of Windows Server 2012 R2, you have two more editions to choose from: Foundation and Essentials. Not only does each version have different features, but the price for each license reflects each version's features. Let's discuss the differences among all the editions.

Standard Edition

This is the enterprise-class cloud server and is the flagship OS. This chapter will cover in detail the changes affecting the Standard edition, because this is the most popular choice. This server is feature rich and will handle just about all your general networking needs. This server can be used for multipurpose or individual roles. It can be stripped down to its core for an even more secure and better-performing workhorse.

Datacenter Edition

This is Microsoft's "heavy-duty" virtualization server version. This is best used in highly virtualized environments because it sports unlimited virtual instance rights. That's right, I said unlimited! This is really the only difference between Datacenter and Standard, and of course this is reflected in the price; Datacenter costs about four times as much as Standard edition.

Foundation Edition

Foundation contains most core features found in the other editions, but there are some important limitations you should understand before you deploy it. Active Directory certificate service roles are limited to only certificate authorities. Here are some other limitations:

- The maximum number of users is 15.

- The maximum number of Server Message Block (SMB) connections is 30.

- The maximum number of Routing and Remote Access (RRAS) connections is 50.

- The maximum number of Internet Authentication Service (IAS) connections is 10.

- The maximum number of Remote Desktop Services (RDS) Gateway connections is 50.

- Only one CPU socket is allowed.

- It cannot host virtual machines or be used as a guest virtual machine.

Essentials Edition

This server is intended for very small companies with fewer than 25 users and 50 devices. This is a very cost-effective way to provide small business networking. Here are some but not all new features of Windows Server 2012 R2 Essentials:

◆ Improved client deployment

◆ Can be installed as virtual machine or on a server

◆ User group management

◆ Improved file history

◆ Includes BranchCache

◆ Uses the dashboard to manage mobile devices

◆ Includes System Restore

Desktop Changes

In Windows Server 2012, Microsoft removed the Start button from the lower left. In R2 the Start button has been put back so you can access your application menu. You can still hit the Windows key to access your menu if you've already gotten used to using it. If you're not familiar with where the Windows key is, it's to the left of the left Alt key on a standard keyboard. There is also a hotspot in the lower-right corner, which brings up a vertical menu bar. This dynamic menu contains these buttons: the Start menu, the Desktop settings, and Explorer search.

The new look and feel will take a bit of getting used to, but we think you will like the new UI changes. Server Manager has had a major overhaul also and grabs your attention with its colorful display warnings on the dashboard when a problem exists.

One user-requested feature that Server lacked was the ability to switch from the GUI version to Server Core. Often times requirements change that may require you to change over to Server Core. Previously you would have had to do a complete reinstall of Server Core. An administrator now has the ability to convert from the GUI version to Server Core and vice versa.

You can read more about this throughout the book starting in Chapter 2, "Installing and Upgrading to Windows Server 2012 R2."

Active Directory Changes

As you may know, Active Directory (AD) is in many ways the keystone piece of Windows networking, in other words, the central database of user and machine authentication data. Server 2012 R2 ADs include several useful new capabilities for Active Directory Certificate Services, Active Directory Rights Management Services, and Active Directory Domain Services. Collectively, the new features focus on deployment and manageability. The plan is to make it fast and easy to deploy Active Directory services and to have more flexibility accessing files while having better file security. Administration has also improved to make graphical and scripted management more consistent and user friendly.

You can read more about this in Chapter 7, "Active Directory in Windows Server 2012 R2."

Active Directory Domain Services Changes

Microsoft is always striving to make Active Directory Domain Services (AD DS) a more robust directory structure service. In the following sections we will explain what has been improved pertaining to Active Directory Domain Services.

Cloning Domain Controllers

Windows Server 2012 R2 gives you the ability to clone an existing domain controller to speed up deployment. Using the domain controller interface in Server Manager, you can promote a single virtual domain controller. You may then, within the same domain, deploy additional virtual domain controllers.

Cloning will reduce the number of repetitive steps in the deployment process. It will also let you deploy additional domain controllers configured and authorized by Active Directory. This is achieved by creating a copy of a virtual domain controller and then authorizing the source controller and running the appropriate Windows PowerShell cmdlets. Windows PowerShell will create a configuration file with promotion instructions. This file will contain Domain Name Server (DNS) information, name, IP address, and other pertinent information.

You can read more about this in Chapter 7.

Fine-Grained Password Policy Improvements

Active Directory does a lot of things besides just keeping a list of user account names and passwords, but if we had to choose the most important of its tasks, we think it'd be reasonable to say that protecting and maintaining passwords would be that task.

Prior to Windows Server 2008, the issue that we all faced was that everyone in the domain had to follow the same password rules. So, for example, the admin staff had to follow the same password rules as the sales team. Administrators should know how to protect their passwords better than salespeople. If not, you better find new administrators!

In Windows Server 2008, Microsoft introduced fine-grained password policies. This allows you to put separate password policies on separate groups. So now, the administrators can have their own policies and the salespeople can have their own.

In Windows Server 2012 R2, fine-grained password policies have been improved so that you now have the option to create and administer your password-settings objects (PSO) using the Active Directory Administrative Center. This new feature helps simplify your PSO management. Prior to Server 2012 R2, all PSOs had to be created using the Active Directory Schema Interface (ADSI Edit) tool.

You can read more about this in Chapter 7 also.

Active Directory Recycle Bin

We think the best way to explain the Active Directory Recycle Bin is to give you a real-world example and how this technology can save the day.

John is junior administrator for Wiley Books. It took him hours to add 20 new authors to Active Directory. Later when John was finished, he accidently deleted one of the company's Organizational Units (OU).

Wiley backs up all of their data on a nightly basis using Microsoft Windows Backup. Because of this, when restoring Active Directory, it is an all-or-nothing restore. Microsoft Windows

Backup does not give you the ability to restore just the OU. So now that we have to restore Active Directory, John would lose those hours of work because Active Directory's version would be from the previous night's tape backup. This is where the Active Directory Recycle Bin can help.

With Active Directory Recycle Bin, John can simply restore the OU without reverting to another location in time using backups.

Through the use of its new graphical user interface, administrators can now easily un-delete Active Directory objects without going through the tedious process that Windows Server 2008 offered. You can see it in action in Figure 1.1.

FIGURE 1.1
Sample Recycle Bin GUI

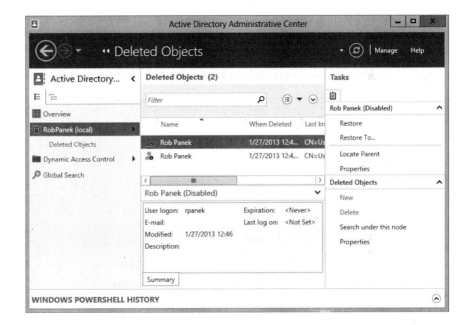

You can read more about Active Directory Recycle Bin in Chapter 7 as well.

PowerShell and AD Administrative Center

Ever since the advent of Windows, Microsoft has shipped operating systems whose administrative tools have, in the main, been graphically based tools; in fact, many Windows administrators can go weeks at a time without having to open a command line. That's good in that it means learning Windows administration is easier for new administrators than it would be for novices trying to learn Unix/Linux administration, because that latter group of operating systems is more heavily dependent on command-line administrative tools than GUI-based administrative tools.

What being command-line-centric does for the Unix/Linux world, however, is to make automating administrative tasks easier in Unix/Linux than it would be to automate many Windows administrative tasks. (You can put a command-line instruction into a batch file, which can then automate whatever task you're trying to accomplish. You can't put mouse clicks in a batch file.) So, Microsoft is trying to give Windows the "automate ability" that it lacks and that Unix and Linux have with a command shell called PowerShell. It's designed to let you take boring, repetitive tasks and automate them easily. Until now the learning curve to use PowerShell was quite steep.

Windows Server 2012 R2 introduces the PowerShell History Viewer, which allows administrators using Active Directory Administrative Center to view the Windows PowerShell commands that are executed. The PowerShell 3.0 improvements are as follows:

- Windows PowerShell workflow
- Windows PowerShell web access
- New Windows PowerShell ISE features
- Support for Microsoft .NET Framework 4.0
- Support for Windows' preinstallation environment
- Disconnected sessions
- Robust session connectivity
- Updatable help system
- Enhanced online help
- CIM integration
- Session configuration files
- Scheduled jobs and Task Scheduler integration
- Windows PowerShell language enhancements
- New core cmdlets
- Improvements to existing core cmdlets and providers
- Remote module import and discovery
- Enhanced tab completion
- Module autoloading
- Module experience improvements
- Simplified command discovery
- Improved logging, diagnostics, and Group Policy support
- Formatting and output improvements
- Enhanced console host experience

◆ New cmdlet and hosting APIs

◆ Performance improvements

◆ RunAs and shared host support

◆ Special character-handling improvements

As you can see by the long list of improvements, Microsoft intends to make PowerShell (see Figure 1.2) as important an administrative platform as the host of GUI tools that exist today.

You will read more about PowerShell throughout the entire book starting in Chapter 2, where you will use it to add roles and features.

FIGURE 1.2
Using PowerShell to install a server role

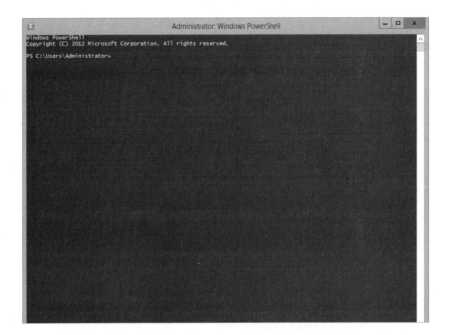

Active Directory Rights Management Services

Passing secure documents and files within your company is vital to the company's information integrity. Your company's CFO, for example, may have a report listing the salaries of all the employees in the company. The CFO wants only other executives in the company to have access to the file. This is where Active Directory Rights Management Services (AD RMS) will be called on to secure the file. With AD RMS the CFO can encrypt or apply authentication to the file.

Prior to Windows Server 2012 R2, AD RMS setup required that only a user with local administrator privileges be allowed to install on the computer that hosted the SQL Server database. This was because AD RMS needed to read the SQL Server settings from the registry during installation. Microsoft implemented the following changes to deal with the AD RMS and how SQL Server is accessed:

- AD RMS now requires that the installer have sysadmin permissions in the SQL Server installation.

- The browser service for SQL Server must be running in order to locate any available SQL Server instances.

- Any ports used by AD RMS setup on the SQL Server computer should have Firewall exceptions enabled. You will need to enable TCP port (default port 1433) for the SQL instance and the UDP port (default port 1434) for the SQL Server Browser Service.

Another piece of AD RMS setup was upgraded. In previous server versions you would have to deploy from the computer where AD RMS was installed. In Windows Server 2012 R2 you are allowed to remotely deploy at targeted server computers.

You can read more about AD RMS starting in Chapter 7.

Active Directory Certificate Services

You can bind the identity of services, devices, and people to a private key using Active Directory Certificate Services (AD CS). This enhanced security feature allows access only to participating applications that support AD CS.

Listed here are some of the changes affecting Windows Server 2012 R2:

- Server Manager integration.

- Deployment and management using Windows PowerShell.

- AD CS role services can be run on Server Core on any version of Windows Server 2012 R2.

- Automatic certificate renewal is now supported for joined computers not in a domain.

- Certificate renewal with same key is enforced.

- International domain name support.

- CA role service has increased security enabled by default.

You can read more about AD CS starting in Chapter 7.

Virtualization

Virtualization allows you to put multiple computer operating systems on one physical machine. In the past, you would have used four servers for your domain controller, Exchange Server, DNS server, and DHCP server. Now you can have one physical box and four virtual servers. This saves money (on hardware) and also saves space (four servers before/one server now). Virtualization in Windows Server 2012 R2 is continuing to improve.

Hyper-V

Server virtualization—breaking one physical server up into a bunch of *virtual machines*—is one of the most significant changes in server management in the past 10 years. We wrote "server management" in lowercase because it's used not just in Windows Server but in various flavors of Linux, Unix, Sun Solaris, and so on. Being able to buy one big, powerful, reliable piece of hardware and fool it into believing that it's actually 10 or 20 smaller separate pieces of computer hardware and then installing separate server OSes on those bits of "virtual server hardware" has greatly simplified server management for operations big and small. Furthermore, it has solved a server management problem that has bedeviled server room planners for years: underutilized hardware. The tool that fools the computer into thinking that it is actually many separate computers is generically called a *virtual machine manager* (VMM).

You see, ever since the start of server computing, most organizations have preferred to put each server function—email, AD domain controller, file server, web server, database server—on its own separate physical server. Thus, if you needed a domain controller, a web server, and an email server for your domain, you would commonly buy three separate server computers, put a copy of Windows Server on each one, and make one a DC, one a web server (by enabling Internet Information Services, R2's built-in web server software, on the server), and one an Exchange Server. The downside of this was that each of those servers would probably run at fairly low load levels: it wouldn't be surprising to learn that the DC ran about 5 percent of the CPU's maximum capacity, the web server a bit more, and the email server a bit more than that. Running a bunch of pieces of physical server hardware below their capacity meant wasting electricity, and that's just not green thinking, y'know? In contrast, buying one big physical server and using a VMM to chop it up into (for example) three virtual servers would probably lead to a physical server that's working near capacity, saving electricity and cooling needs.

First, let's cover the new technology added in this version. Since there are so many improvements to Hyper-V, we're just going briefly touch on each one:

- Client Hyper-V gives desktop Windows Hyper-V technology without the need for installing a server OS.

- A Hyper-V module for Windows PowerShell provides more than 160 cmdlets to manage Hyper-V.

- Hyper-V Replica allows you to replicate virtual machines between storage systems, clusters, and datacenters in two sites. This helps provide business continuity and disaster recovery.

- Resource metering helps track and collect data about network usage and resources on specific virtual machines.

- Simplified authentication groups administrators as a local security group. By doing so, fewer users need to be created to access Hyper-V.

- Single-root I/O virtualization (SR-IOV) is a new feature that allows you to assign a network adapter directly to a virtual machine.

- Storage migration allows you to move the virtual hard disks to a different physical storage while a virtual machine is running.

- SMB 3.0 file share is a new feature that provides virtual machines with shared storage, without the use of a storage area network (SAN).

- The virtual Fibre Channel allows you to virtualize workloads and applications that require direct access to Fibre Channel-based storage. It also makes it possible to configure clustering directly within the guest operating system (sometimes referred to as guest clustering).

- Virtual Non-Uniform Memory Architecture (NUMA) allows certain high-performance applications running in the virtual machine to use NUMA topology to help optimize performance.

Now let's briefly talk about some of the enhancements made to existing Hyper-V technology that many administrators will find useful.

♦ Dynamic memory allows you to configure Smart Paging so your virtual machines can more efficiently restart. If a virtual machine has less startup memory, dynamic memory can be configured to support it.

♦ Importing virtual machines has received a tune-up to better handle configuration problems that would normally prevent an import. Until now the process included copying a virtual machine but never checked for configuration issues.

♦ Live migrations make it possible to complete a live migration in a nonclustered environment. This improvement will make moving a live virtual machine easier.

♦ Larger storage resources, increased scale, and better hardware error-handling are offered in this version. The intention is to help you configure large, high-performance virtual machines with the ability to scale.

♦ Virtual Hard Disk Format (VHDX) increases the maximum storage size of each virtual hard disk. The new format supports up to 64 terabytes of storage. It also comes with built-in hardware protection against power failures. This format will also prevent performance falloff on large-sector physical disks.

♦ You no longer need to shut down the live virtual machine to recover deleted storage space. Virtual machine snapshots will now free up the space the snapshot consumed once it is deleted.

You can read more about this in Chapter 27, "Virtualization with Hyper-V."

REMOVED OR DEPRECATED ITEMS IN WINDOWS SERVER 2012 R2

VM Chimney, also referred to as TCP offload, has been removed and will no longer be available to guest operating systems. The WMI root\virtualization namespace is changed to just root\virtualization\v2 and will eventually be taken out completely in future Server versions. Authorization Manager (AzMan) has also been deprecated in this version and will be phased out in future releases. The new management tools for virtual machines will be the new standard.

Virtual Desktop Infrastructure

In Windows Server 2012 R2, Microsoft has made vast improvements to the virtual desktop infrastructure (VDI), with simpler administration, increased value, and better overall user experience.

Supporting mobile devices is a must in today's market. Virtual desktop infrastructure helps bridge the compatibility gap between devices by virtualizing resources. VDI provides stronger security and higher efficiency that improves productivity with a UI that the user is familiar with. Windows Server 2012 R2 and VDI make it a snap to deploy virtual resources across devices.

Windows Server 2012 R2 VDI, if running in a datacenter, will allow access for mobile devices using Hyper-V and Remote Desktop Services. Microsoft offers three different deployment types in a single solution: pooled desktops, personal desktops, and remote desktop sessions.

You can read more about VDI in Chapter 27.

Networking Changes

Servers are no good without the ability to talk to one another, but—of course—the downside of being able to communicate with other systems means that *infected* systems can try to spread their malware joy. ("Want to secure your server? Easy...disconnect the Ethernet cable!") Server 2012 R2 offers some networking changes to make Windows networking a bit faster and a bit more secure.

EAP-TTLS

With Windows Server 2012 R2 an exclusive protocol is being introduced as an Extensible Authentication Protocol (EAP) type called Tunneled Transport Layer Security (TTLS). This protocol is used with 802.1X Authenticated Wired and Wireless access. This new standards-based protocol provides a secure tunnel for client authentication. 802.1X provides a security shield that prevents unauthorized access to your intranet.

DNS

Although DNS has been around forever, the process by which it translates names seems to get better with each version. Changes in Windows Server 2012 R2 affect both DNS Server and Client. Let's take a look at the changes for Windows Server 2012 R2.

In PowerShell, DNS management has received some improvements. The DNS Server role, for example, has had some improvements to installation and removal using PowerShell. Additional developments in PowerShell include user interface, client query, and server configuration on older operating systems. The LLMNR query time-out has been 300 msec, which was not enough time for computers in power save mode. With the new improvements to DNS Client, this time-out has been increased to 820 msec.

IP Address Management

The IP Address Management (IPAM) framework is a new set of technologies for managing, monitoring, and auditing IP address space. By monitoring DHCP and DNS, IPAM can locate IP address servers within your network and allows you to manage them from a single central UI.

NIC Teaming

NIC Teaming technology in Windows Server 2012 R2 can take multiple network interface cards and team them together to interface as one. Doing so helps with failover should one device become inoperative. Load balancing is also improved when NICs are teamed because the bandwidth is combined into a single larger bandwidth.

You can read more about these topics and new features in Chapter 4, "Windows Server 2012 R2 Networking Enhancements," and Chapter 5, "IP Address Management and DHCP Failover."

Management Tools

Any good networking operating system should offer ways to simplify the job of keeping one server or one thousand servers up and running. The server should also stay up and running with the smallest amount of effort possible on the part of the humans doing the server administration. No one operating system has *the* answer for server administration, but Windows Server has gotten a bit better in 2012 R2 with some useful new tools.

Server Manager

Prior to Windows Server 2008, when an administrator had to configure and maintain a server, the administrator would have to use *many* different tools. Windows Server 2008 changed all that by introducing Server Manager, a one-stop shop for all of your configuration and management tools.

In Windows Server 2012 R2 (Figure 1.3), Microsoft has expanded this functionality even further. Server Manager now lets administrators manage multiple servers (virtual or physical/local or remote) as long as they are no older than Windows Server 2003.

FIGURE 1.3
Server
Manager

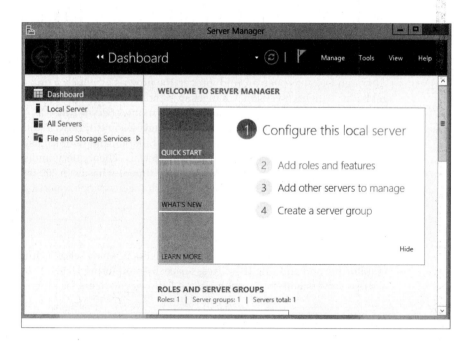

Adding roles and features in Server Manager has gotten even smarter. As you make your selections, the Add Roles and Features Wizard dynamically changes. The wizard assists you in deciding which subset of tools and features are needed for the requested role.

Server Manager has a new dashboard that can show you if problems exist using color-coded boxes. If, for example, an error occurred from within the DNS event log, the DNS box on the dashboard would turn red. This is an excellent tool for troubleshooting your server, and since the dashboard is the first thing you see when you log in, you can't miss it.

Speaking of troubleshooting your server, Server Manager has a host of new troubleshooting tools that we will show you more about in Chapter 2. These tools are all inside the role, inside Server Manager, so you do not have to open multiple applications like Event Viewer or Performance Analyzer to see the results—they're all in one spot!

You can read more about Server Manager in Chapter 2.

The Remote Tools: WinRM and WinRS

It's the case all too often that new operating systems include some really important and useful features that go largely unnoticed. Windows Server 2012 R2 contains one of those neat but largely unknown features in a new network protocol called Windows Remote Management (WinRM). To understand why WinRM is a great feature, let's consider what WinRM is intended to replace: a protocol known as the Remote Procedure Call (RPC).

Even if you've never heard of RPC, chances are that you've been using it for years. RPC's job is to allow one program to talk to another program, even if those programs are running on different computers. For example, if you've ever started up Outlook to read your email on an Exchange Server instance, then you've used RPC: it's how Outlook can tap Exchange on the shoulder and say, "Can I have my email, please?" Or if you've ever used an MMC snap-in like DNS, DHCP, or Computer Management to remotely control those functions on a remote computer from your desktop, you've used RPC.

RPC is a protocol that has provided much service over the years, but it has one big problem: it's hard to secure. Microsoft invented RPC back in the days when there was no Internet, and the vast majority of LANs extended no farther than the distance from the first floor to the top floor in an office building, so security wasn't all that big a concern. Years later, when security became a big concern, Microsoft tried to retrofit security onto RPC with some optional changes wrought first by XP SP2, but by that point the horse was out of the barn, and requiring RPC security would just end up breaking hundreds or perhaps thousands of RPC-dependent applications.

Clearly, the time had come for a change in how Windows programs talk to each other, so Microsoft decided to adopt a protocol that did the same sort of thing that RPC did, with a few changes:

- It's not proprietary but is standards-based and platform-independent—there are similar implementations popping up on Linux and Mac OS.

- It's a modified form of HTTPS.

- Its communications are encrypted.

- It requires authentication to use.

Components of Windows 2012 R2 that use WinRM include event log collection; the ability to use the new Server Manager snap-in on remote servers; and my personal favorite, a secure remote command shell called Windows Remote Shell, or `winrs`. If you need a secure, low-bandwidth remote-control tool, look to `winrs`. Read more about WinRM in Chapter 17, "Remote Server Administration."

Remote Desktop Services

In Windows Server 2012 R2 Microsoft has made large strides in improving the user and management experience. Microsoft intended to improve the user experience regardless of the kind of device being used to connect. They wanted to make sure connecting through a WAN or LAN (to virtual desktops, RemoteApp programs, or session-based desktops) provides a rich experience to the user. Microsoft also wanted to make the remote desktop management experience better. We agree that they did make it better by adding a centralized console so administrators can manage Remote Desktop Services from a single location.

You can read more about Remote Desktop Services in Chapter 17.

Group Policy Object Improvements

What got better? Plenty. Managing Group Policy objects (GPOs) got easier with the built-in Group Policy Management Console. In previous Windows versions, one problem that administrators had was manually forcing a GPO to update. Even though GPOs automatically update every 90 minutes, there are times when you need a GPO to take effect immediately. Administrators had to remote in to the specific computer and run gpupdate.exe from the command line to manually update a GPO.

Now if an administrator wants to manually force a GPO update, the administrator can use the context menu for an OU in the Group Policy Management Console and schedule gpupdate.exe to run on multiple computers at the same time. Administrators can also achieve this by using the PowerShell utility and the new Invoke-GPUpdate cmdlet.

Here are some additional changes to Group Policy in Windows Server 2012 R2:

◆ When dealing with monitoring replication issues at the domain level, you no longer need to download and run separate tools.

◆ For devices running Windows RT, you can now configure local Group Policy. By default it is disabled, and the service must be started and set to automatic.

◆ Group Policy has been upgraded to support Internet Explorer 10.

You can read more about Group Policy in Chapter 9, "Group Policy: AD's Gauntlet and Active Directory Delegation."

File and Print Sharing

Back before we ran web or email services on our Windows servers, we only used Server to share two things: big hard drives and expensive printers. File and print are the oldest services offered by Microsoft networks, but apparently they're not too old to learn a few new tricks.

BranchCache

BranchCache is a technology that optimizes WAN bandwidth by copying content from either your main location or cloud server to your branch office. Once content is copied to the branch, users can access it locally rather than over the WAN. Having the ability to cache files will conserve bandwidth and improve security. BranchCache can support any size office and is not limited to how many it can service. BranchCache can be deployed with just a single Group Policy object (GPO). This technology uses the Windows file server to divide files into small encrypted pieces. The cool thing about dividing the files into smaller pieces is that client computers can download only the pieces that changed. BranchCache will also check for duplicate content and only download one instance of the content, saving disk space.

In Windows Server 2012 R2, BranchCache improvements include automatic client computer configuration and big performance and scalability increases. Client computers can be configured through the use of a Group Policy object. If a GPO has not been configured for BranchCache, then BranchCache will check the hosted cache server and use those settings by default.

One of the new advantages of BranchCache is the ability to preload specific content, like media and DVDs, on a hosted cached server and then have that content sent to the client cache.

Another very nice advantage is the improvements that have been made to allow for better database performance. BranchCache has done this by using the Extensible Storage Engine (ESE). This is the same database technology used by Microsoft Exchange Server. It allows scaling of a single hosted cache server to handle the increased demands of more people without having to increase hardware.

Hosted cache servers no longer need a server certificate issued by a certificate authority (CA). This will greatly reduce costs involved with deploying a public key with multiple CAs.

SMB 3.0

Windows' file server service bears the official name of SMB, which stands unhelpfully for Server Message Block. (Blame IBM, not Microsoft, because an IBM guy first designed it.) SMB has changed little over its roughly 25 years of life, with its biggest changes being support of somewhat bigger block sizes so as to be able to make use of networks faster than 100 Mbps (appeared in 2000), the ability to handle multiple paths, and the addition of digital signatures so as to foil man-in-the-middle attacks (appeared in 2001).

Windows Server 2012 R2 sports a somewhat reworked version of SMB that handles slow networks better, handles encryption more intelligently, cranks up throughput on file transfers, and supports PowerShell.

File Server Resource Manager

You can manage data stored on a file server using the tools in File Server Resource Manager. Some of the tools included help you to automate classification and reporting and manage files and quotas.

With Dynamic Access Control's File Classification Infrastructure you can control and audit access to files on the file server. You can now get more control on how your files are classified on your file servers. With the enhanced features, classifying files can be done manually or automatically.

You can read more about this topic starting in Chapter 13, "Files, Folders, and Basic Shares."

Web-based Services

Finally, there's the subset of the Internet that's become more important than all the rest of the Net put together: the Web and related services. They're important to Windows, and they saw some big changes in 2012 R2.

Web Server IIS

Windows' file services may not have changed much over the years, but that's not the case for Windows' *web* server. One key to hardening any server product is to keep the amount of code exposed to the Internet to a bare minimum; if a web server can support, for example, something called FastCGI but your website doesn't *need* FastCGI, then why run FastCGI on an Internet-facing server and risk the possibility that someone discovers a way to use IIS's FastCGI to hack the server? Clearly you wouldn't, so it'd be nice to just strip your web server software of the things that you aren't going to need. (Security folks call this "minimizing the attack surface." Sometimes we think they play too much *Halo*.)

The perfect web server, then, would be composed of dozens of small modules, each of which could be removed or added as needed to allow the web administrator to build a web server that did exactly what she needed it to do...but no more. That was the guiding light for Windows Server 2008's IIS 7.0, a complete overhaul of IIS including some of the latest security technologies, including WinRM. (When you're doing remote administration of an IIS 7 box, you're using that protocol rather than RPC.)

HACKING IIS 7.0

No one has hacked IIS 7 yet to my knowledge, nor have they taken down IIS 7.5, which is the update shipped with Windows Server 2008 R2. Web admins also liked the cleaner, task-oriented interface of 7.x's IIS administration tools.

Knowing how companies live and breathe on the Internet in today's market, we would expect no less from Microsoft than for it to wave its technology wand across the web server. With the release of Windows Server 2012 R2 comes the newest version of the web server, IIS 8.0 (Figure 1.4). IIS 8.0 has also received a wealth of new rich features to administer and secure your website. Here are a few important changes made in IIS 8.0:

FIGURE 1.4
IIS's new management tool

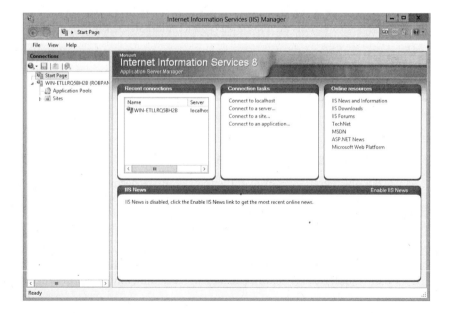

- Application initialization

- Dynamic IP address restrictions

- Centralized SSL Certificate Support

- CPU throttling

- FTP logon attempt restrictions

- Server Name Indication (SNI) support

- Improved SSL and configuration scalability

- Support for multicore scaling on NUMA hardware

Even if you're not a webslinger by trade, it's never a bad idea to understand the current Windows web server—so don't skip Chapter 19, "Web Server Management with IIS."

MICROSOFT MANAGEMENT CONSOLE GETS THE AX!

In Windows Server 2012 R2 the Microsoft Management Console (MMC) snap-in is deprecated for Internet Information Services (IIS) Manager 6.0. In future releases of Windows Server, this will be removed.

FTP Server

Microsoft gets some things right and some things wrong. In a few cases, the company gets things terribly wrong, as was the case with the built-in File Transfer Protocol (FTP) server software that shipped with Windows for the past 15 years or so. It was so clunky, was so difficult to configure, and offered such minimally useful logs and an inability to configure things that *should* have been childishly easy to configure (such as user home directories) that just about everyone who needed a Windows FTP server ended up shelling out a few bucks for a third-party FTP server. Starting with Windows Server 2008 and R2, however, things changed considerably. As far as we can see, Microsoft tossed out all the FTP server code and rebuilt it from scratch. In Windows Server 2012 R2, they also added the ability to restrict the number of failed logon attempts that can be made to an FTP account in a certain period. So if you need a Windows-based FTP server, flip over to the IIS chapter (Chapter 19) to learn about the new changes to the FTP server.

You can read more about web server management in Chapter 19.

Chapter 2

Installing and Upgrading to Windows Server 2012 R2

Experienced Windows Server administrators and consultants might feel the urge to skip this chapter. You might be thinking that you don't need to go through this material again. We urge you to think twice about that. We will be covering the fundamentals, but we will also be going through some details that you will probably not already know and that you will find useful.

Your first experience of Windows Server is probably going to be a manual installation of the operating system on a lab or virtual machine. Depending on the complexity of your environment and your upgrade/migration plans, you may decide to continue with manual installations or even consider automated installations. No matter what you choose, you'll probably want to read this chapter to understand what the typical installation steps are.

In this chapter, we'll cover a clean manual installation and a manual upgrade of Windows Server. From there we'll delve into installation and upgrade strategies for Active Directory. If you are performing many installations of Windows Server, then you will like this next piece. We will discuss how you can save some time and keyboard wear and tear by automating your installations of Windows Server 2012 R2 using an unattended installation answer file that you will create using Windows System Image Manager.

In this chapter, you'll learn to:

◆ Upgrade your old servers

◆ Configure your server

◆ Build a small server farm

What Has Changed?

We think you'll find installing Windows Server 2012 R2 much simpler than installing any previous version of Windows Server. If you have installed Windows 8 or Windows Server 2008, then you have a good idea of what to expect from Windows Server 2012 R2 installations. The installation routine really has been trimmed down to ask for just the basics to give you a secure installation that you can then customize.

Let's look at that last sentence. It's something we've heard before, but you might not have noticed much of a difference. You'll see it straightaway with Windows Server 2012 R2. What does that mean? There is much less functionality installed. Microsoft has not made any assumptions about what you will need this server to do. A clean, default installation of

Windows Server 2012 R2 can't really do very much. It has no functionality installed. It's actually up to you to decide what this server will do on your network and what *functionality* should be installed. The result of this is that the server has a much smaller attack surface. What does that mean? The more functionality you install on a computer, the more targets you present to attackers. The goal should be to install only the functionality you require, in other words, to reduce the number of targets or minimize your attack surface. Furthermore, on the security side, the operating system is locked down by default. The first thing it does when it initially boots up is request a new administrator password. You'll also find that the Windows Firewall is on by default. This operating system pretty much isolates itself from the network until you configure it. Microsoft puts you in total control of how this new server interacts with your network and/or the Internet.

Does this sound like it is going to be a lot of work to get a server up and running? Maybe, but actually Microsoft has made it pretty easy. If you are doing a few manual installations or upgrades, then you can quickly configure your servers using Group Policy and Server Manager. We'll talk about Server Manager later. If you're deploying many servers, then you'll want to look at automated solutions such as Windows Deployment Services or your favorite third-party solution. Again, you can use Group Policy to deploy policies and use the command-line version of Server Manager, called PowerShell, in a scripted manner to customize the roles and features of the server.

HOW ABOUT SERVER CORE?

You can learn a bit more about the Server Core installation of Windows Server in Chapter 3, "Managing a Server without a Desktop: Server Core." The Server Core installation uses some different tools for configuring the functionality installed on a server.

How are you going to deploy Windows Server 2012 R2? There are some complications here. Windows Server 2012 R2 is available with only 64-bit architectures. Microsoft is shifting all of its server products to be 64-bit only. This means you cannot upgrade from 32-bit installations of Windows Server 2008. You'll have to do a clean install on new hardware and move any services or data. If you have 64-bit server deployments, then you can do an in-place upgrade. This can be a time-saver, but it's not usually recommended. Microsoft pretty much urges you to do a clean install every time. However, if your server is running just Microsoft features, roles, and applications (all being 64-bit), then an in-place upgrade is possible. We've done this and had reliable servers afterward.

Installation Requirements

In previous versions of Windows Server, there would be different requirements for each edition of Server you wanted to install, that is, Enterprise versus Standard edition. In Windows Server 2012 R2, Enterprise edition is no longer available and the requirements have been scaled down to just one set for all editions.

As usual, you are given a set of minimum and recommended requirements with the operating system. Be aware that *minimum* means exactly that; the operating system will run, but it will not necessarily run very well. You should also take account of the applications that will be installed and the load that will be placed on your server.

This can vary wildly depending on applications and organizations, so there are no hard-and-fast rules on what your server specifications should be. The best thing to do to get accurate specifications is to develop a pilot environment and generate loads on your "proof-of-concept" servers while monitoring the performance and responsiveness of the servers and applications. However, if your server is going to have moderate loads in a small environment, then you're probably going to be OK with the recommended specifications.

Table 2.1 describes the requirements from Microsoft for Windows Server 2012 R2.

TABLE 2.1:   Windows Server 2012 R2 Requirements

ITEM	MINIMUM	RECOMMENDED	MAXIMUM
CPU	1.4 GHz for x64	2 GHz	64 processor
RAM	512 MB	2 GB or more	32 GB for Standard, 4 TB for Datacenter Edition
Disk	32 GB	40 GB plus additional space for applications or data, 10 GB Server Core Installation	
DVD-ROM	Required to access the installation media; CD-ROM no longer supported		
Display	Super-VGA (800×600) or higher		
Input devices	Keyboard and compatible pointing device, such as a mouse		
Internet Access	Required		

AUDITING YOUR CURRENT INFRASTRUCTURE

It is critical that you accurately audit your existing infrastructure if planning a major change such as a server operating system deployment. Microsoft has provided a free suite of tools in the Microsoft Assessment and Planning Toolkit for Windows Server 2012 R2 (`http://tinyurl.com/ycpuk3l`). This easy-to-use toolkit can audit your servers as well as check hardware and driver compatibility. From this you can create reports to plan any changes.

64-Bit Support

Windows Server 2012 R2 is available only as a 64-bit product. We'll reinforce that: *there are no x86 or 32-bit versions of Windows Server 2012 R2.*

Here are some notes on deploying x64 servers:

◆ Your hardware support for x64 is probably not a huge issue: The major vendors have been selling x64 processors for years for their mainstream products. You can do a quick audit of your server hardware and check for 64-bit support.

◆ A lot of 32-bit applications should be able to run on the x64-only Windows Server 2012 R2: This is thanks to 32-bit emulation provided by the Windows-on-Windows (WOW32) subsystem. Don't count just on this; please check with application vendors, and test in a lab before making firm plans to upgrade servers from Windows Server 2008 to Windows Server 2012 R2.

◆ You cannot do an upgrade from x86 to x64: This precludes upgrading from an x86 installation of Windows Server 2003 or Windows Server 2008 to Windows Server 2012 R2. Getting your servers from x86 to x64 will require a migration plan from one physical server to another.

◆ 64-bit builds of Windows require digitally signed kernel mode drivers: Sure, the operating system will allow you to install those drivers with a warning, but they will never actually load. Make sure your hardware vendor provides suitably signed x64 drivers for Windows Server 2012 R2. Very often we see people complaining about Microsoft for driver issues, but this is really something that your hardware vendor is responsible for. Printer drivers do appear to be something in particular to watch out for!

As with any project, preparation is the key to success. Review the hardware requirements, and check out application and service compatibility before moving forward with any deployment of Windows Server 2012 R2.

 Real World Scenario

SO, WHAT ARE YOU GOING TO DEPLOY?

Many who deployed Windows Server 2008 knew that x86 support from Microsoft in the datacenter was ending. They deployed x64-builds wherever possible. They did the same for their customers. Key products like SQL Server 2008 have native x64 editions. When deploying Windows Server 2008, they were already doing an operating system deployment project, so they decided this was the best time to make that 64-bit jump. Sure, there have been times when they have been forced to go with x86 builds because of third-party application vendor support statements. That'll mean there will be a migration at some later point.

Check the hardware, drivers, application vendor support, and printers. Test everything in a lab. If all is well, then deploy that server as Windows Server 2012 R2 depending on your licensing and your project aims.

For a lab, you might want to look at Microsoft's virtualization solution, Hyper-V. Hyper-V is included as part of Windows Server 2012 R2; you run virtual machines with x64 or x86 operating systems, even Xen-enabled Linux. Hyper-V also requires CPU-assisted virtualization and Data Execution Prevention (DEP) to be turned on in the BIOS. We recommend taking advantage of this technology (or even one of the competitors if you prefer them). You can learn more about Hyper-V later in this book.

Installing the Operating System

Your first installations of Windows Server 2012 R2 in your live or laboratory environment will probably be either a clean installation or an upgrade installation. There are some other, more advanced ways to install Windows:

◆ An unattended installation: We'll talk about that a little later in this chapter.

◆ A cloned installation using ImageX from the Windows Automated Installation Kit.

◆ One of Microsoft's deployment solutions such as Windows Deployment Services (WDS): This is an advanced installation performed over the network using functionality that is included in Windows Server 2012 R2.

◆ Third-party solutions: Ghost is the classic example of a third-party cloning solution that works in conjunction with Microsoft's sysprep tool.

We're going to look at the clean installation and the upgrade installation processes now. We've already mentioned that the installation process is pretty simple.

The clean installation process is very simple in Windows Server 2012 R2. You're pretty much only being asked to do the following:

1. Select a language, time and currency format, and keyboard method.

2. Choose an edition and build of Windows Server.

3. Agree to the license agreement.

4. Choose between a manual and upgrade installation.

5. Configure the disk.

6. Set the default administrator password.

7. Log in.

There are some options during this flow:

◆ Install a driver if needed.

◆ Repair an existing installation of the operating system on the computer.

In the next section, we'll cover completing this flow for a clean installation and an upgrade installation. Then we'll cover some of the options that are presented during the installation and follow that up with showing how to customize the installation of the operating system.

Performing a Clean Installation

A *clean* installation refers to installing the operating system onto a computer that does not have an installation present or one that you want to keep. In our example, we are dealing with a computer that has no previous installation. We are assuming that you have not done any of this before, so we are going to get back to basics. More advanced readers might be tempted to skip ahead to another section, but we recommend that you at least skim this section to see what has changed.

Windows Server 2012 R2 comes on a DVD. It's a pretty large installation. Ensure your server has a DVD-ROM drive, and then insert the DVD media. Alternatively, if you are using a virtual machine, you can redirect the virtual CD/DVD to the Windows Server DVD ISO image that you have downloaded from Microsoft or created from your original media.

WHAT, NO DVD DRIVE?

You may have a server that doesn't have a DVD drive. If so, you could look at one of the advanced network installation methods mentioned earlier. But you can also install Windows Server 2012 R2 from a USB thumb drive. You can find a set of instructions on this blog post by a Microsoft employee: `http://tinyurl.com/ktz5fq`.

Once the media is loaded, you should power up your server and ensure that your server boots from the DVD drive. Normally, a computer with a blank hard disk will boot from the DVD drive by default. If the computer fails to boot from the DVD, then there may be one of a few things going on. There may be a valid operating system on the hard disk that is booting up by default. You might have a boot menu available in your computer that is briefly made available during or after the Power-On Self Test (POST). Alternatively, your server might not get the option to boot from DVD because of a boot configuration. You can alter this by entering the BIOS and making a change there. These two options will vary depending on your hardware, so you should consult your hardware vendor's documentation or contact their support desk. In most cases it will show something like "Boot Order." We have also seen situations where we have burned the DVD from an ISO file but we used a write-speed that was too fast to ensure a good burn.

In the following examples, we'll cover how to install Windows Server 2012 R2.

Figure 2.1 is the first screen you'll see. It allows you to customize the installation language, time and currency format, and the keyboard settings of the server. You'll need to change some settings here if the defaults do not match your language, region, and keyboard. For example, if you are in Ireland using an Irish-based keyboard, then these defaults won't suit you at all! The time zone won't work correctly, currency symbols will be wrong, and the keyboard layout will be totally wrong. For example, you will struggle to find the backslash (\), which is kind of important in the Windows world.

The "Language to install" option will vary depending on the languages supported by your DVD. Most people reading this book will probably deal with English-based media, even those in non–English speaking nations. But you may be choosing Spanish, French, German, Chinese, and so on, depending on where you are and what your company standards are.

The "Time and currency format" setting affects how Windows presents and formats those regional-specific settings. You'll probably always want to ensure that this matches the location where your server is located.

The "Keyboard or input method" setting should match the keyboard that is physically attached to the computer. Keyboards can often vary from country to country, so make sure that this is correct. Don't worry; it won't affect your ability to manage a server using Remote Desktop. An RDP session will use the keyboard settings of the client computer that connects to the server.

The screen shown in Figure 2.2 allows you to do a couple different things:

◆ You can kick off an installation.

◆ You can troubleshoot and repair an existing installation of Windows Server 2012 R2.

In this example, you'll install Windows Server 2012 R2, so click the Install Now button.

FIGURE 2.1
Setup environment to install Windows

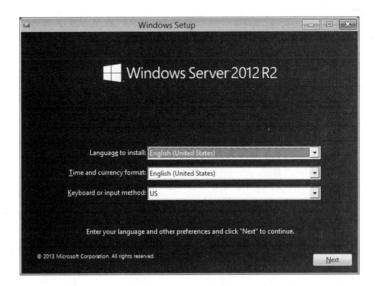

FIGURE 2.2
Install Windows now.

GUI INSTALLATION OR SERVER CORE

You'll also see that you have a choice of installation types. This was introduced with Windows Server 2008. The GUI installation has lots of Windows and graphical user interfaces. The Server Core installation strips that GUI away and assumes you're comfortable with command-line and remote administration techniques

You'll learn a lot more about the Server Core installation in Chapter 3.

In this example, we'll show how to set up a lab, so we want most of the functionality available in Windows Server 2012 R2. Select the Windows Server 2012 R2 Standard Evaluation (Server with a GUI) option (see Figure 2.3).

FIGURE 2.3
Choosing an edition and installation type

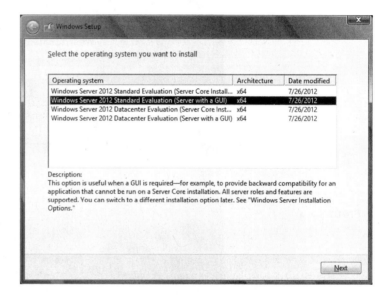

You now get the opportunity to read the legendary Microsoft end user license agreement (EULA), as shown in Figure 2.4. Most techies are going to just click "I accept the license terms" and click Next without ever reading it.

This screen in Figure 2.5 allows you to choose between a new or custom installation of Windows Server 2012 R2 and an in-place upgrade. You can choose to do an upgrade only when you have a previous version of Windows Server 2008 R2 to upgrade. Remember that you cannot upgrade from x86 to x64. You also cannot upgrade from a Server Core installation to a full installation, or vice versa. For this example, you're doing a clean or new installation, so choose Custom. Click Custom to continue.

FIGURE 2.4
Agreeing to the EULA

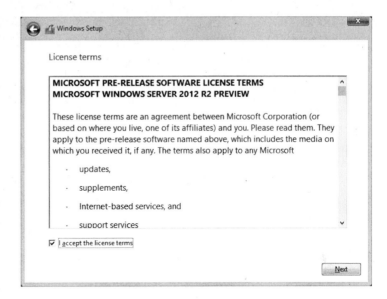

FIGURE 2.5
Upgrade or clean
installation?

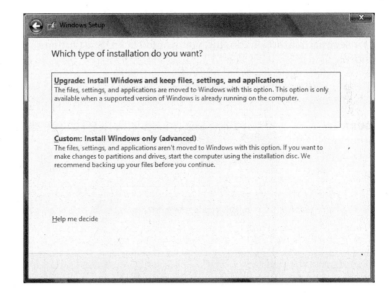

A few different things are going on in Figure 2.6. You'll probably click Next if you're dealing with a simple server where you want all the space in your first disk to be in your C drive. Clicking Next will cause Windows to create a volume called C that will consume the entire first disk in the server.

FIGURE 2.6
Setting up the drive to
install Windows

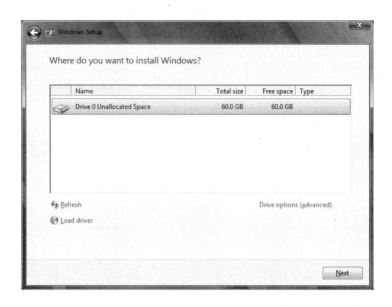

However, what will you do if you want to partition that disk into different volumes? For example, you might want to create a volume to separate web content from the operating system for security reasons. To do this, you would click Drive Options. The screen shown in Figure 2.7 opens.

FIGURE 2.7
Drive options

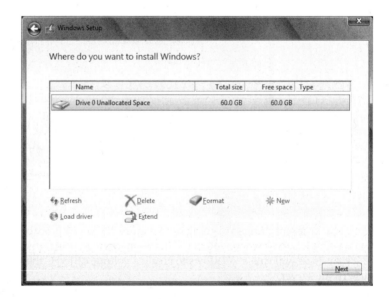

On this screen, you can delete, create, and format volumes as you need them. You'll find yourself coming in here when you don't want to accept the default of using the entirety of your first disk (Disk 0) for the C drive. If you choose to add a new partition, simply click New and then select the size of the partition you need and select Apply.

But what if your installer fails to find any disks at all? You've double-checked your hardware and found nothing wrong. The cables are fine, and your BIOS can see all of your disks. Well, odds are the installer doesn't have the required driver to access your storage controller. As time goes by, this will become more and more common as newer storage controllers are released into the market. You can add a driver by clicking Load Driver. The dialog box shown in Figure 2.8 opens.

FIGURE 2.8

Adding a mass storage controller driver

It used to be that the storage controller had to be present on a floppy drive. That would be a problem considering that servers usually don't come with a floppy drive anymore and Microsoft really wants to kill off the need to use disks. This dialog box allows you to navigate to a floppy disk, CD, DVD, or even a USB flash drive to access the required storage driver. Make sure your driver media is inserted, wait a few moments, and then navigate to find it.

Return to the "Where do you want to install Windows?" screen, and then configure your disk before continuing.

You're getting close to the end now. The dialog box in Figure 2.9 is where the installer actually installs Windows Server 2012 R2 for you. It takes a little while, depending on your install media and destination drive. You can probably get a coffee or answer some of those emails that never seem to stop arriving in your inbox.

Figure 2.10 shows the first screen you'll see when you come back from your break. Before you can log in, Windows Server 2012 R2 wants you to set the password of the local administrator account. A complex password is required, comprised of eight or more characters with a mix of uppercase and lowercase letters and numbers.

FIGURE 2.9
Windows installation
progress

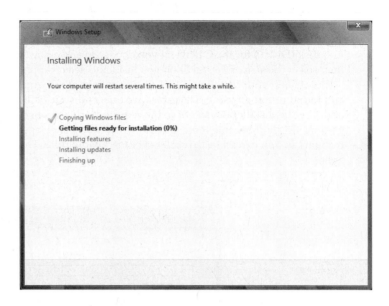

FIGURE 2.10
Setting the
administrator
password

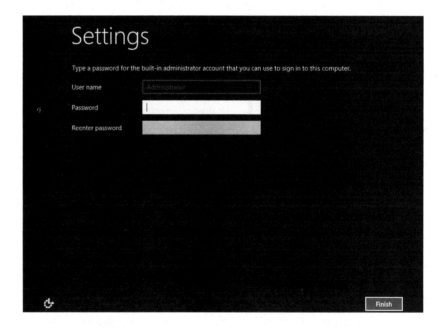

Set your password to something strong. In fact, use a passphrase. We suggest you read, "The Great Debates: Pass Phrases vs. Passwords" at http://tinyurl.com/3hrbg.

Setting the new password will log you on as the local administrator.

You are eventually logged in. Before I continue I want to point out in Figure 2.11, the return of the "START" button in the lower-left corner. I would have to make an assumption and say that this is back by popular demand! The first thing you'll see, other than the start button I just pointed out, is the Server Manager dashboard so that you can customize your server. We will configure the server using both Server Manager and the command-line alternative, PowerShell, a little later in the chapter.

FIGURE 2.11
Logged in as administrator

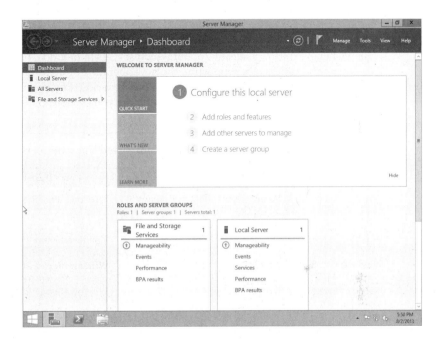

So, that's your first Windows Server 2012 R2 machine up and running. Congratulations! It doesn't do very much, but it is a minor victory. Grab a celebratory drink of something, and then we'll take a look at upgrading an existing installation of Windows Server to Windows Server 2012 R2.

Performing an Upgrade Installation

Most organizations will have existing servers in production, and they will want to know how they can deploy Windows Server 2012 R2 onto those networks without needlessly rebuilding their servers or migrating applications to new hardware.

Although Microsoft says that you should try to avoid in-place upgrades, there just seem to be certain scenarios where it just makes sense:

◆ A small organization that has recently invested in servers will not have the budget to buy a new server to do some sort of rolling upgrade. They will want to reuse existing installations.

◆ Large organizations will not consider a migration of all servers because of the huge costs associated with this process.

◆ Migrations of complex production environments could be costly in terms of effort and downtime.

We think it is realistic to expect that any move toward Windows Server 2012 R2 is likely going to include a mix of clean and upgrade installations. OK…the good news is that upgrade installations are supported, and they do work. It has been done before with production servers, but we believe in being selective about which servers to upgrade, wanting them to be without problems and completely supporting the new operating system. Table 2.2 shows the supported upgrade scenarios. Note that these are outline scenarios. Any upgrade that you are planning should be tested and cleared with vendors before you proceed.

TABLE 2.2:   Windows Server 2012 R2 Supported Upgrade Scenarios

EXISTING OPERATING SYSTEM	SUPPORTED UPGRADE
Windows Server 2008 Standard with SP2 or Windows Server 2008 Enterprise with SP2	Windows 2012 R2 Standard or Datacenter
Windows Server 2008 Datacenter with SP2	Windows Server 2012 R2 Datacenter
Windows Web Server 2008	Windows Server 2012 R2 Standard
Windows Server 2008 R2 Standard with SP1 or Windows Server 2008 R2 Enterprise with SP1	Windows Server 2012 R2 Standard or Datacenter
Windows Server 2008 R2 Datacenter with SP1	Windows Server 2012 R2 Datacenter
Windows Web Server 2008 R2	Windows Server 2012 R2 Standard
Windows Server 2012 Datacenter	Windows Server 2012 R2 Datacenter
Windows Server 2012 Standard	Windows Server 2012 R2 Standard or Windows Server 2012 R2 Datacenter

There are various upgrade scenarios to consider when you think about the combinations of x86, x64, Server Core, and full installations.

Here are some things to note:

◆ You cannot upgrade from x86 to x64, or vice versa.

◆ You cannot upgrade directly from Windows Server 2003. You will first have to upgrade to Windows Server 2008 before moving to Windows Server 2012 R2.

◆ You cannot upgrade from Windows Server 2003 to Windows Server 2012 R2 Server Core editions.

◆ Although you can upgrade from one edition to a higher edition, such as Windows 2008 R2 Standard to Windows 2012 R2 Datacenter, you should ensure that you have a valid Windows license.

◆ You must have licensing for the upgrade operating system, such as Windows Server 2012 R2, before you can upgrade from Windows Server 2008. This will mean either having Software Assurance or purchasing the required Windows Server 2012 R2 license for each upgraded server and the required client access licenses (CALs) for end-user access.

◆ You cannot upgrade from one language to another.

Getting from x86 servers to x64 servers is going to require some sort of migration. The likely process will involve introducing new hardware. This might be done as part of a scheduled recycling of all hardware that is no longer supported by the manufacturer. It could be part of a migration to a virtualized datacenter. Or it might be a rolling process, something we have seen done before because it minimizes hardware spending. Here's an example:

1. Server A, server B, and so on, are running Windows 2008 x86 in the computer room.

2. Server X is purchased for the network upgrade.

3. Server X is built with Windows Server 2012 R2 to closely match server A.

4. Services are migrated from server A to server X.

5. Server A is rebuilt with Windows Server 2012 R2 to closely match server B.

6. Services are migrated from server B to server A.

7. The process continues with all remaining Windows Server 2008 machines.

Plenty of Windows 2000 machines are still knocking around. What are you going to do with them? To upgrade to Windows Server 2012 R2, you will first have to upgrade them to Windows Server 2003 and then 2008 R2. Realistically, that's probably not going to happen in most situations. Windows 2000 had no x64 release for Intel and AMD chipsets. There was an Itanium release, but that's not the same as x64. That means there is no in-place upgrade path from Windows 2000 to Windows Server 2012 R2.

Before you even look at doing an upgrade, you have a few chores to go through first:

◆ You will want to double-check that any software or drivers installed on the server that you are going to upgrade will support Windows Server 2012 R2. The products might work, but there is always the support issue from the vendors. There's a strong likelihood that third-party support will be a bit hit-and-miss in the early days, but that will improve over time.

◆ The most important driver to have is the mass storage controller driver. You've already seen in the clean installation process that you might need to provide this on removable media if Windows Server doesn't have a built-in driver for it.

◆ Check the health of your server hardware. Your vendor usually includes some free software for this. Microsoft recommends that you also use their memory diagnostics tool.

◆ If you are upgrading a production or other important server, then you should back it up before going any further. Test that backup if at all possible. If you're using a virtual machine, then this is a lot easier. You can take a snapshot and revert to that point in time if the upgrade fails. Check with your vendor for snapshot support in production environments first.

◆ You should either disable or uninstall your antivirus software on the server to be upgraded. Odds are you will need to uninstall it because there is a good chance that it will interfere with the upgrade or even break the upgraded server. You should ensure that you have a version of your antivirus software ready to deploy for Windows Server 2012 R2 once the upgrade is completed.

◆ If you are running a monitoring solution such as System Center Operations Manager, you will want to either disable monitoring for a few hours or even remove the agent. Check with your vendor for supported scenarios.

◆ Finally, be prepared for Windows Firewall. It may block application traffic destined to your upgraded servers. Know what ports you will need to configure in advance. This may require checking with the application vendor or using a tool like the free Microsoft Network Monitor.

We cannot recommend enough that you try this upgrade process in a virtual lab first. You can do this pretty cheaply using TechNet or demonstration licenses and with one of a myriad of free virtualization solutions you can try. If you are testing Windows Server 2012 R2, then you can use the following:

◆ Microsoft's free Hyper-V Server 2012

◆ VMware Server, which will run on a Windows Server host

◆ VMware Workstation 9.0

◆ Citrix XenServer, another hypervisor that is a close relative of Microsoft's Hyper-V

Note that you must use a virtualization technology, such as those just listed, that will support 64-bit virtual machines or guests when testing Windows Server 2012 R2.

USING HYPER-V

You're learning about Windows Server 2012 R2, so to us it seems logical to use Hyper-V. We strongly recommend reading Chapter 27, "Virtualization with Hyper-V," and Chapter 28, "Deploying Virtual Machines with Hyper-V," to learn how you can deploy a virtualization environment for your test lab.

All of the formalities are out of the way, so now let's take a look at an upgrade in action. You cannot perform an in-place upgrade if you boot up your server from the DVD or USB device. This method allows only a clean installation. If you want to do an upgrade, then you will have to boot up your Windows Server and insert the DVD or USB or, in the case of a virtual machine, mount your Windows Server 2012 R2 media ISO image. This allows the upgrade program to download updates from Microsoft and to properly scan your server before any changes are made.

This is an existing Windows Server 2008 R2 x64 machine that we are planning to upgrade to Windows Server 2012 R2 (see Figure 2.12). We ran `winver.exe` to check the version and build of the installed operating system. The presence of a `C:\Program Files (x86)` folder means that the installed operating system is a 64-bit one. The process is similar to upgrading from Windows Server 2003 x86 to Windows Server 2008 x86. To get moving, log into the server you want to upgrade, and insert or mount your Windows Server 2012 R2 media.

The dialog box in Figure 2.13 will appear automatically if you have AutoPlay enabled on your DVD drive. If it doesn't appear, then run `setup.exe` from the root of your Windows Server 2012 R2 media.

FIGURE 2.12
Windows 2008 R2 is installed.

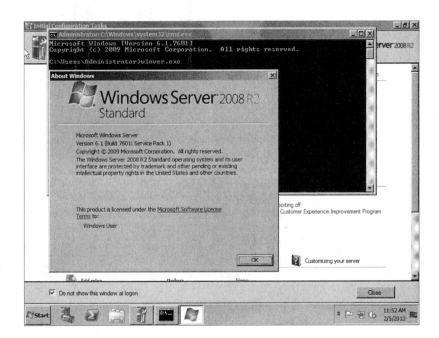

FIGURE 2.13
`setup.exe` startup screen

You'll notice that the upgrade process is almost identical to that of a clean install. It's pretty light on the keyboard and mouse work that you have to do.

Click Install Now when you are ready to proceed with the upgrade as seen in Figure 2.14.

Setup will begin copying temporary files; this may take a few minutes as Windows Server 2012 R2 prepares to install.

The screen in Figure 2.14 allows you to download updates from Microsoft to improve the installation process. The process relies on the server and the currently logged-in user having access to the Internet. Microsoft gives four reasons to go through an installation update:

FIGURE 2.14
Getting updates for the setup

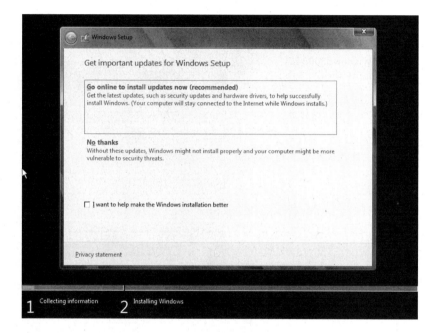

- ◆ Updates for the installation process are downloaded. This can resolve issues that are discovered over time.

- ◆ Driver updates are available to improve the plug-and-play process during installation.

- ◆ Windows updates are included to patch the operating system.

- ◆ Updates for the Microsoft Windows Malicious Software Removal Tool are included to help protect your new server.

Our advice is that you should go through this process if your server is important to you. If you are just doing lab work, then you might not be concerned unless your installation fails, and an update can resolve the issue.

As you can see in Figure 2.15, we've chosen to go through the update, so the installer connects to Microsoft to download any available updates.

We've already discussed the options here; they're the same as in the clean installation process.

You have to choose the required installation, and you must also confirm that you have a license for it. Let's do that now.

FIGURE 2.15
Updates are
downloading.

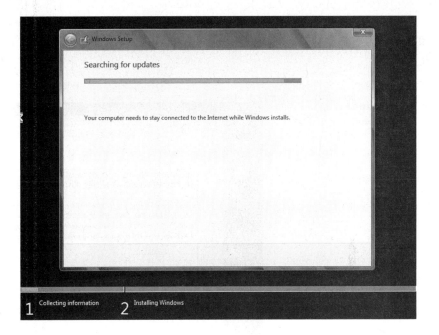

Hold on! Why are you seeing the screen in Figure 2.16? Aren't you doing an upgrade? Well, you haven't actually told the installer that yet. You could be installing a new operating system at this point. Make sure you pick a valid edition choice for your upgrade. Please refer to Table 2.2, which describes valid upgrade paths to Windows Server 2012 R2 if you are actually doing an upgrade.

FIGURE 2.16
Choosing an
edition and
installation
type

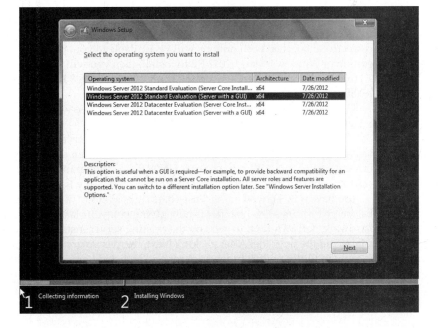

You will have, of course, poured over the EULA and have completely understood it before accepting the licensing terms (see Figure 2.17). Seriously, you will not be able to install Windows Server 2012 R2 if you do not agree to Microsoft's terms.

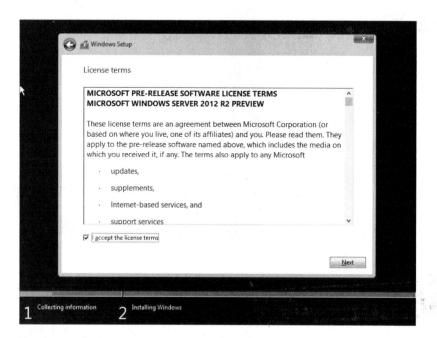

The dialog box shown in Figure 2.18 presents you with the option to do either an upgrade or a custom or clean installation of Windows Server 2012 R2. If you have followed the instructions correctly so far, then both options will be available to you. However, if you selected an invalid edition of Windows Server 2012 R2 to install, then you will not be able to upgrade.

In this example, we are upgrading from Windows 2008 R2 Standard edition to Windows 2012 R2 Standard edition with GUI, so click Upgrade.

The installer now scans the existing installation to see whether there are any known incompatibilities with Windows Server 2012 R2.

The installer will check to see whether the existing server is compatible. If it isn't, then you will get a reason why in a compatibility report, such as an error when trying to upgrade an evaluation version of Windows Server 2008 R2, as shown in Figure 2.19, and you will have to start the upgrade from the beginning after resolving any issues.

You have now arrived at the "last-chance gas station." You had better pull in here and fill up before proceeding. The installer is now giving you your last opportunity to confirm that all the hardware, software, and drivers on the existing server installation will work when you have completed the upgrade. After clicking Next, there is no going back! But seriously, any known incompatibilities with Windows Server will be listed here.

FIGURE 2.18
Choosing to
perform an
upgrade

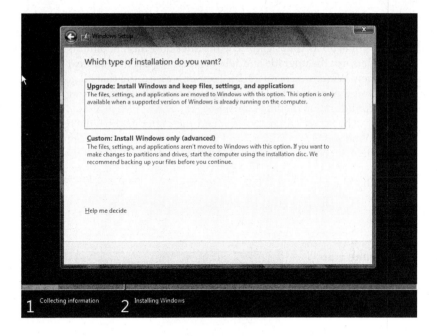

FIGURE 2.19
The compatibility
report

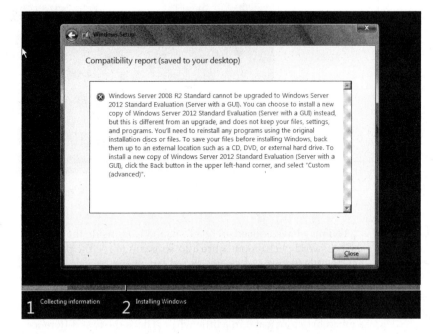

If you get a warning that one of your drivers might not work after the upgrade, you can fix that after the upgrade is completed.

It is break time again! The installer now has enough information from you to proceed. It will perform the upgrade and reboot when required. Your next action will be to log into your shiny new Windows Server 2012 R2 server—assuming that all goes to plan. Don't stray too far because you will need to log in to make sure everything is working correctly and to make any required configuration modifications.

The server will reboot several times; after a while, the server automatically will reboot into Windows Server 2012 R2 and wait for you to log in (see Figure 2.20). How long it takes to get here depends on your hardware. Your server might be quick or slow; for example, a computer with cheap and slow storage will obviously take longer to upgrade. That's why you are warned that the upgrade *may* take several hours.

FIGURE 2.20
The upgrade is complete.

You may have noticed an "eye" shaped icon inside the password field in Figure 2.20. That is the password peekaboo feature allowing you to see the password you typed, this is actually a handy little feature in case you typed the wrong password. Go ahead and log in, and you will eventually see what your upgraded server looks like.

Instead of getting the Initial Configuration Tasks utility, you get to see Server Manager when you log in (see Figure 2.21). For now, don't worry too much about Server Manager; you'll take a much better look at it in a little while. That's the first difference you'll see between a clean installation and an upgrade. As you scroll through the details pane in the middle, you'll see that your Windows Firewall status is inherited from the previous installation.

FIGURE 2.21
Server Manager

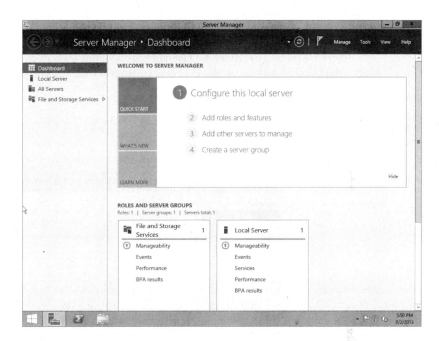

You can also see that some *roles* and *features* are installed. You may remember that we said that a Windows Server 2012 R2 installation has nothing installed by default. That's true. But in this example we just upgraded a server. The server that we just upgraded had no additional components installed. But Windows Server 2012 R2 saw it very differently. It saw important functionality that it believed should be retained in case it is being used. You'll later learn how to use Server Manager or PowerShell to add or remove roles and features.

You will probably want to ensure at this point that you complete the following:

- Check the logs in Event Viewer to see whether there are any problems that need to be resolved.

- Join a domain, if required, and make sure all applicable policies are applied.

- Install all available security updates.

- Install any security software such as antivirus software, and apply any required manual security configurations.

- You may have third-party software to install, configure, or diagnose.

That's an upgrade completed. It wasn't all that painful, was it? This would be an appropriate time for you to customize your server.

Server Manager Dashboard

The Server Manager dashboard is the default screen you will see the first time you log in (see Figure 2.21). When you do a clean installation or upgrade of your server, this tool will allow you to quickly get some essential tasks done.

Before we go into detail let me just summarize what we will cover later in this chapter. Clicking Local Server opens the property settings window shown in Figure 2.22. We will be setting up our computer in the next section and will cover the following items:

FIGURE 2.22
Local Server
Properties
window

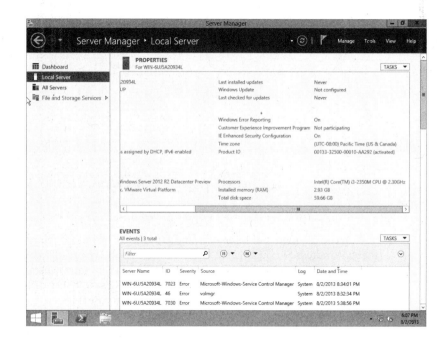

Activate Windows   Every copy of Windows Server 2012 R2 needs to be activated either via the Internet or via a telephone call with Microsoft. Failure to activate will render the server inoperable until you activate it.

Set Time Zone   Just above the Product ID link is a link to set the time zone. Here you can set the time zone and the time.

Configure Networking   The Ethernet link allows you to configure your server's connectivity to the network.

Provide Computer Name and Domain   Using this link you can set the computer name and configure domain membership for the server.

Enable Automatic Updating and Feedback   You really should do this either manually or via Group Policy. Automatic Updates will enable you to download important updates and security updates from Microsoft, usually on a monthly basis.

Download and Install Updates   You can manually force an update to protect your server immediately. We strongly recommend this.

Add Roles   We'll talk more about *roles* and *features* in the next section.

Add Features   Just like with the previous item, this allows you to add functionality to the server.

Enable Remote Desktop   You probably will manage your server via Remote Desktop once it is on the network. This allows you to do that.

Configure Windows Firewall   Your server's Windows Firewall will be on by default. You can configure this automatically using Active Directory Group Policy, or you can do this manually. You need to configure the firewall to allow remote access to network services hosted on this server.

By default, Server Manager will continue to appear whenever you log into the servers that you performed a clean installation on.

You'll now take a look at that tool and how you can manage your server with it.

Using Server Manager to Configure Your Servers

For many years, Microsoft has been trying to get people to use a single tool for managing the configuration of servers. In the past, when we logged into the newest version of Windows Server, we were greeted by some tool that promised to do pretty much that. We looked at it briefly and saw a little check box that said something like "Do not display this again at logon," selected that, and then closed the tool so it would never again see the light of day. The only other time we heard of that tool was while studying for some sort of Microsoft certification exam. We just knew better…why use that tool when we could get exactly what we wanted from Control Panel's Add/Remove Programs in a much shorter time?

You probably noticed early on that Windows Server 2012 R2 is quite different from its predecessors. Before 2012 the default tool was the Initial Configuration Tasks utility. Now you are greeted by the Server Manager dashboard every time you log in. Trust us; you will want to use Server Manager (see Figure 2.21) instead of the old utility.

Now another tool pops up all by itself. Welcome to Server Manager. It's in the *superbar* (or the taskbar) in Windows Server 2012 R2. You will find additional ways to access Server Manager by starting it from Administrative Tools, by running `compmgmtlauncher.exe`, or by using Programs and Features in Control Panel.

WELCOME BACK START BUTTON

In Windows Server 2012 to get to your program listing's shown in the following graphic, you had to hit the Windows key on your keyboard to the left of the left Alt key.   In Windows Server 2012 R2 the Start Button has returned to its original position in the lower left corner of the task bar. This will once again allow you quick access to your main programs that get installed with Windows Server 2012. As you add programs and roles, you will see the new buttons added here.

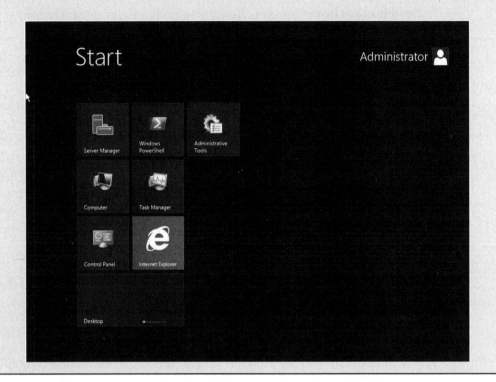

SERVER MANAGER TIP!

Server Manager has a habit of popping up every time you log in. That will get pretty old in a very short time. You can control this by editing the REG_DWORD value of DoNotOpenServerManagerAtLogon in HKEY_LOCAL_MACHINE\SOFTWARE\Microsoft\Server Manager. The default is 0, which causes Server Manager to appear every time you log in. Setting it to 1 will disable this. Another way to disable Server Manager from appearing at login is to select the Manage drop-down menu in the top-right corner of Server Manager. Then select Server Manager Properties. A small pop-up will appear with check box called "Do not show me this console at logon." You will probably want to select this because waiting for Server Manager to open and closing it every time you log in could rapidly become tiresome.

Server Manager is the tool that you will use to manage the configuration of your Windows Server 2012 R2 machines. Using it, you can add and remove native functionality, manage that functionality, and diagnose problems. You can also use a command-line alternative called PowerShell to manage the native functionality that is installed on Windows Server 2012 R2.

Changes to Server Manager

There are some differences between Server Manager in Windows Server 2008 and Windows Server 2012 R2:

◆ As stated earlier in this chapter the Initial Configuration Tasks utility is no longer the default tool upon login; Server Manager is. The Local Server tab will open all the local server properties you can use to manage the server.

◆ You will notice immediately that the GUI is different from any previous version of Server Manager. With new metro like boxes and a cleaner look, it may take a bit to get used to, but in the long run you will appreciate it more.

◆ With Server Manager you now have multiserver remote management support. You can easily add servers to your network from within this tool. An added feature is group management, which allows you to send commands to all servers within the group.

◆ The event logs and services can now be accessed from Server Manager for both local and remote servers.

◆ The Add Roles Wizard has some new screens with a few addition options before getting to roles selection. The first new screen is called Installation Type. The second new screen is called Server Selection. We will discuss these new screens and how they are used a little later in the chapter.

◆ `Servermanagercmd.exe` has been deprecated. PowerShell is now the command-line tool to use.

◆ Adding a feature using the GUI is now part of the Add Roles Wizard and is no longer a separate tool.

This sounds like a lot of differences, but Server Manager is more alike than different on Windows Server 2008 and Windows Server 2012 R2.

Common Configuration Tasks

When you have installed a new server, you need to go through some common tasks to get the server onto the network. We'll now walk you through some samples using Server Manager.

You can see a link on the left of the dashboard called Local Server. If you click it, you will see a large Properties window with all the server properties listed (see Figure 2.22).

As you can see, next to each item listed is a text link. This text link opens up the properties window for that item. Let's get started configuring your new server.

ACTIVATING WINDOWS

If you are using an OEM license, then it will be on a sticker that is affixed to the case of your computer. That license and product key are tied to that computer and can be used only with that computer. If you purchased a retail or individual copy of the license, then the key will likely be in the DVD container. If you have volume licensing from Microsoft, then you will obtain your single reusable license key either from a Microsoft licensing website or from your channel supplier or large account reseller (LAR).

Depending on your license agreement, you can activate each installation directly with Microsoft or via a locally hosted product activation service. Volume licensing and activation are pretty complex subjects, and they are subject to change over time. It's best to go directly to the latest materials that Microsoft has. Currently that's the Volume Activation Overview, which you can find at http://technet.microsoft.com/en-us/library/hh831612.aspx.

Next to Product ID is a linked product key. Click the link to open the Windows Activation screen. To complete the activation process, simply add your key into the text box shown in Figure 2.23, and click the Activate button.

FIGURE 2.23
Windows
Activation
screen

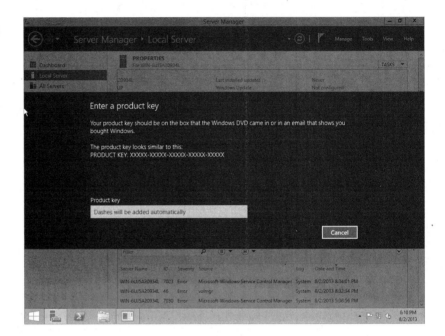

CHANGING NETWORK PROPERTIES

One of the first things you will commonly do with a server is to give it a static IPv4 network configuration. This is required in an IPv4 network so that the server can see other network devices and services.

As stated earlier, next to each listing is a link to change the setting. In this particular case you want to select the link next to Ethernet. Here you can see each of the network interface cards (NICs) on your server. Our server is pretty simple. It only has one network interface for us to configure (see Figure 2.24).

Your server may have two. You might want to look into binding those two NICs into one fault-tolerant and/or load-balancing virtual interface. Your hardware vendor probably supplies software and instructions for doing that.

Here's a handy trick. You can run ncpa.cpl in PowerShell to quickly open the Network Connections properties sheet.

To configure your server's NIC, right-click it, and choose Properties. That opens the dialog box shown in Figure 2.25.

FIGURE 2.24
Network
Connections

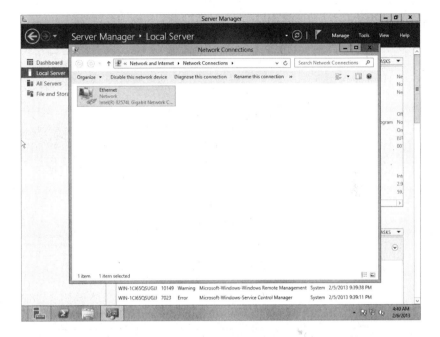

FIGURE 2.25
Local area
connection
properties

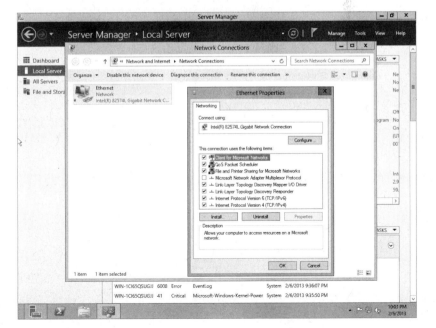

Next select Internet Protocol Version 4 (TCP/IPv4), and click Properties. The dialog box shown in Figure 2.26 will open.

By default, a new Windows Server 2012 R2 server will not have a configured IP address. It will attempt to obtain a TCP/IPv4 configuration from a DHCP server. This is normally not desired for a production server, so you will want to change this to a static configuration (see Figure 2.27).

FIGURE 2.26

IPv4 properties

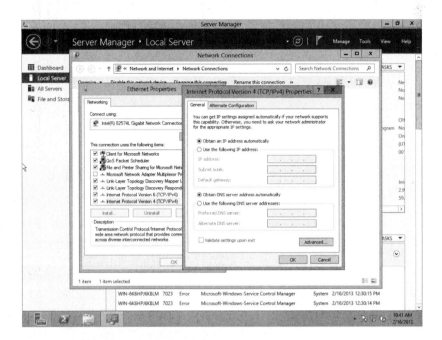

FIGURE 2.27

Configured IPv4 properties

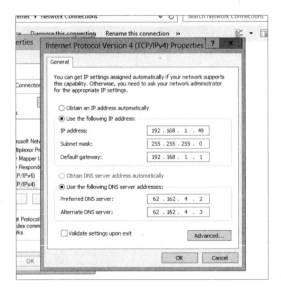

Obtain a configuration for the new server from your network administrators, and then enter the details similar to how we have entered them in Figure 2.27. Click OK to save your settings, and close all the remaining dialog boxes.

There is a command-line way to do this too using the `netsh` command. You'll need to find the name of your network interface, and you can use the `ipconfig` command to get it:

```
C:\>netsh interface ip set address name="Local Area Connection" static
192.168.1.49 255.255.255.0 192.168.1.1
```

The syntax for the `netsh` command is as follows:

```
C:\>netsh interface ip set address name="<Name of the Network Interface" static
<Desired IP Address> <Desire Subnet Mask> <Desired Default Gateway>
```

That saves the address configuration of the server. You'll also want to set the DNS server addresses. This first `netsh` command will set the primary DNS server:

```
C:\>netsh interface ip set dns "Local Area Connection" static 192.168.1.21

C:\>
```

The syntax is as follows:

```
netsh interface ip set dns "<Name of the Network Interface>" static <IP Address
of the Primary DNS Server>
```

If you have a secondary DNS server, then you should also configure it. The command is slightly different:

```
C:\>netsh interface ip add dns "Local Area Connection" 192.168.1.22

C:\>
```

Your new IPv4 configuration should now be applied. You might want to run the `ipconfig` command from command prompt to verify your work:

```
C:\>ipconfig
Windows IP Configuration

Ethernet adapter Local Area Connection:
   Connection-specific DNS Suffix  . :
   Link-local IPv6 Address . . . . . : fe80::5819:d35b:1b24:de7f%10
   IPv4 Address. . . . . . . . . . . : 192.168.1.49
   Subnet Mask . . . . . . . . . . . : 255.255.255.0
   Default Gateway . . . . . . . . . : 192.168.1.1

Tunnel adapter Local Area Connection* 8:
   Media State . . . . . . . . . . . : Media disconnected
   Connection-specific DNS Suffix  . :

Tunnel adapter Local Area Connection* 9:
   Connection-specific DNS Suffix  . :
```

```
IPv6 Address. . . . . . . . . . . : 2001:0:4137:9e50:1817:3f21:3f57:fc97
Link-local IPv6 Address . . . . . : fe80::1817:3f21:3f57:fc97%12
Default Gateway . . . . . . . . . : ::

C:\>
```

You can see that the adapter with the name Local Area Connection now has the new IPv4 configuration. Note that you can get lots more information by running ipconfig /all.

The next step is to test connectivity. You can do this from the command prompt by using the ping command to send a test packet to a network device or a server:

```
C:\>ping 192.168.1.1

Pinging 192.168.1.1 with 32 bytes of data:
Reply from 192.168.1.1: bytes=32 time=13ms TTL=128
Reply from 192.168.1.1: bytes=32 time<1ms TTL=128
Reply from 192.168.1.1: bytes=32 time<1ms TTL=128
Reply from 192.168.1.1: bytes=32 time<1ms TTL=128

Ping statistics for 192.168.1.1:
    Packets: Sent = 4, Received = 4, Lost = 0 (0% loss),
Approximate round trip times in milli-seconds:
    Minimum = 0ms, Maximum = 13ms, Average = 3ms

C:\>
```

In our example, we tested using the default gateway that was defined in our IPv4 network configuration. That's normally a good first step. You can see that we got a response for every test packet that was sent. If you get no responses, then there is a problem with the hardware, drivers, network configuration, cables, or maybe even the network itself.

If you have devices beyond the local gateway, then you should try to ping one of them, assuming that your network administrators allow for such ICMP traffic. This test will confirm that your server can route to remote network nodes.

RENAMING THE SERVER

Every Windows computer should have a unique computer name to uniquely identify it on the network. Every organization has its own practice. Some have tightly structured names that describe the location and function, some use nondescriptive names with incremental numbers, and some use names of characters from their favorite TV show or players from a team that they support.

Click the link next to Computer Name, which you can find in the details pane of Server Manager, as shown in Figure 2.28, to control the name of this server and the domain or workgroup membership of this server. You should name this server according to the naming standards of the organization. You should click Change to do this in the dialog box shown in Figure 2.29.

FIGURE 2.28
Local server
properties

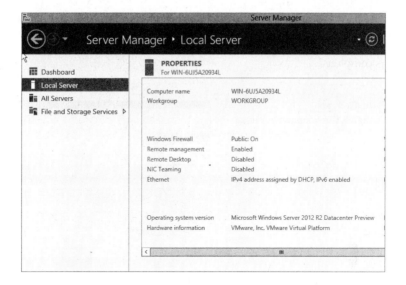

FIGURE 2.29
Computer name

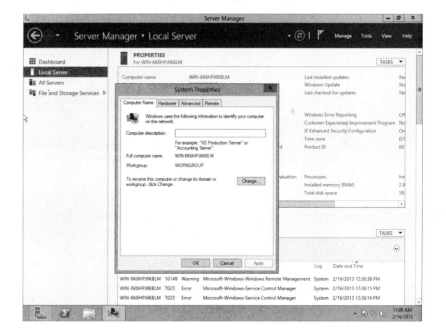

This was a clean installation of Windows. You may remember that the install routine didn't ask you for a computer name. Instead, the server was given a randomly generated name. Some security experts like this, but we like to be able to keep track of our servers, so we try to give them structured names.

To do this, you should change the name under "Computer name," and click OK (see Figure 2.30). Make sure that the name is unique on the network; otherwise, you will encounter problems.

You're now told that you need to reboot in order for this change to be applied (see Figure 2.31). Close down the remaining dialog boxes, and reboot the server when you are prompted to do so. The server will assume the new computer name that you have assigned once the reboot is completed.

FIGURE 2.30
Configure the computer name.

FIGURE 2.31
Restarting after the computer name change

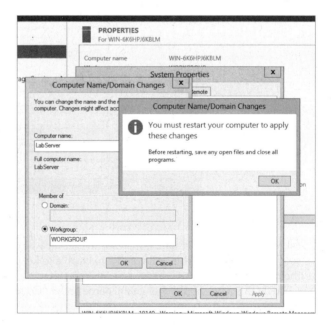

You can alternatively accomplish the previous renaming procedure by running the netdom command from the command prompt:

```
C:\>netdom /renamecomputer WIN-DCL9MRNLVOH /newname:BIGFIRMAPPSVR1
This operation will rename the computer WIN-DCL9MRNLVOH
to BIGFIRMAPPSVR1.

Certain services, such as the Certificate Authority, rely on a fixed machine
name. If any services of this type are running on WIN-DCL9MRNLVOH,
then a computer name change would have an adverse impact.

Do you want to proceed (Y or N)?
y
The computer needs to be restarted in order to complete the operation.

The command completed successfully.
C:\>
```

The syntax for the command is as follows:

```
netdom /renamecomputer <Current Computer Name> /newname:<Desired Computer Name>
```

You will need to manually reboot the server after running this netdom command.

After the reboot, log in again, and fire up Server Manager. You'll see that your new computer name is present in Computer Information.

JOINING A DOMAIN

Odds are you will want to join the server to a domain so that it can use shared resources and be centrally managed. Return to the Computer name properties.

We are joining this server to a domain that has the DNS name of BigFirm.com (see Figure 2.32). Once you've entered that name, click OK. You will then be asked to enter the username and password of a user who has permission to add this server to the domain. That might be bigfirm\administrator, or it might be bigfirm\jbloggs if the user jbloggs has been given those delegated rights in Active Directory. Close all the dialog boxes and reboot, and you'll soon have a server that is a member of the domain and able to take advantage of Group Policy, Active Directory user accounts and security groups, centralized administration, and so on.

Alternatively, you can also do the previous procedure from command line:

```
C:\>netdom join bigfirmappsvr1 /Domain: bigfirm.com /UserD:bigfirm\administrator
/PasswordD:*
Type the password associated with the domain user:
```

The computer needs to be restarted in order to complete the operation:

```
The command completed successfully.
C:\>
```

The syntax for the command is as follows:

```
netdom join <name of computer joining domain> /Domain:<domain to be joined> /
UserD:<name of domain user with permission to join the domain> /PasswordD:*
```

FIGURE 2.32
Domain membership
change

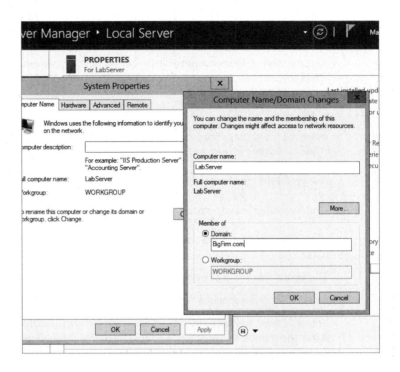

After you run this command, you are prompted for the username of the user account. Once the join command is run, you are told that you need to reboot. You could initiate an automated reboot by adding the /REBoot flag, as shown here. You might prefer to control the timing of reboots as much as possible and instead initiate a manual reboot.

```
netdom join bigfirmappsvr1 /Domain: bigfirm.com /UserD:bigfirm\administrator /
PasswordD:* /REBoot
```

WHY THE COMMAND LINE?

You might be wondering why we are showing you these command-line alternatives. You will need to know these things if you are doing any of the following:

◆ Working with Windows Server 2012 R2 Server Core where there is no alternative. Windows Server 2012 R2 includes a handy tool called sconfig.

◆ Being able to run these commands without reference can be quicker than navigating through a GUI.

◆ If you are building many servers by hand or using some third-party cloning solution, then you might want to script as much as possible.

ENABLING REMOTE ADMINISTRATION

Most Windows administrators want to be able to manage their servers from their desktops. Who really wants to go trotting off to the computer room every time you need to make some change on a server? You can do this by enabling Remote Desktop on your server. You can then use the Remote Desktop tool on your PC or laptop to connect to it over TCP 3389, in other words, the Remote Desktop Protocol (RDP). Your organization's security policies will define when this remote administration can be enabled, if at all.

If you want to enable RDP access, inside the Local Server Properties window click the link next to Remote Desktop, which should currently be labeled Disabled.

You can see in Figure 2.33 that RDP is disabled by default.

FIGURE 2.33
Configuring
Remote Desktop

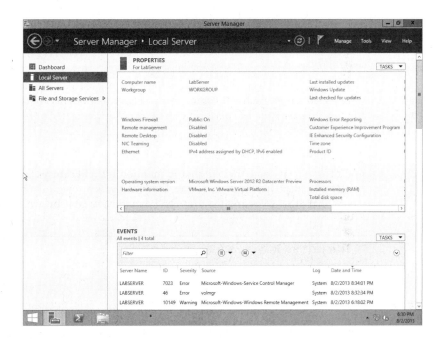

There are two other options:

Allow Connections from Computers Running Any Version of Remote Desktop (Less Secure)   This allows versions of the Remote Desktop tool prior to version 6 to connect to your new server. Version 8 includes new security functionality, so Microsoft would prefer you to use it. Note that Remote Desktop version 8 is included in Windows Server 2012 R2. Older operating systems such as Windows XP and Windows Server 2003 require a free update that you can get from Windows Update or from the Microsoft website.

Allow Connections Only from Computers Running Remote Desktop with Network Level Authentication (More Secure)   This is Microsoft's preference if you do enable RDP access. Note that you must have at least version 6 of Remote Desktop on all possible administrative computers to use this option.

By default, only those people who are members of the local Administrators group on your server will be able to access it via RDP. That suits most scenarios. However, you might want to delegate certain low-level functions to non-administrators. If so, you will need to click Select Users and add the user account names or, preferably, the security group names of those to whom you are granting RDP connectivity rights.

At this point, your server is on the network, you have added it to a domain, and you have enabled Remote Desktop so that you can work on it from your desktop. It's time to add some functionality to your Windows Server 2012 R2 machine.

Adding and Removing Roles and Features

So far, you have installed a new Windows Server 2012 R2 machine, and you have configured it so that it is on the network and can be managed remotely. You're ideally sitting at your desk with a nice drink. You can complete the rest of the configuration in relative comfort. That sounds much better than standing in front of a tiny monitor in a noisy and cold server room.

Before you go forward with Server Manager, we'll define some terminology that you've seen several times in this chapter already:

Roles   A role is a generic function that a server hosts. It could be something like a DNS server or a web server. Each role comes with a set of functionality that can be installed onto a server to allow that computer to perform those tasks. They're called *role services*.

Features   A feature is a specific piece of software that adds a very granular piece of functionality to a server.

One important note that we should mention is that Features is now part of the Add Roles and Features Wizard. In Windows Server 2008 R2 it was a separate tool. This set is extensible. This means that other roles and features can be made available by Microsoft as time goes by.

Inherited Roles and Features

A clean installation of Windows Server 2012 R2 will have no installed features or roles. Microsoft is not going to make any assumptions for you. This allows you to build customized servers with a minimized security risk. However, an upgraded server will include roles and features that Windows Server 2012 R2 can identify on the preexisting Windows 2008 server. For example, if your Windows 2008 server was a DNS server, then your upgraded server with Windows Server 2012 R2 will have a DNS server role installed. You may actually decide that you want to remove some of these inherited roles or features because they are inappropriate for your Windows 2012 R2 server.

Adding a Role

A role can be described as a major function that a server can play in your network. When you install a role, you are installing a set of components to enable that functionality. There is a default set of components for each role that you can customize.

You'll now learn how you can add a role using Server Manager and PowerShell. First, fire up Server Manager. You can see on the left side of the Server Manager dashboard the menu items Dashboard, Local Server, All Servers, and File and Storage Services. What you don't see are any roles or features, not yet anyway. Under Welcome To Server Manager is the link "Add roles and features" (see Figure 2.34). Just click the link to launch the Add Roles and Features Wizard.

FIGURE 2.34
Roles in Server
Manager

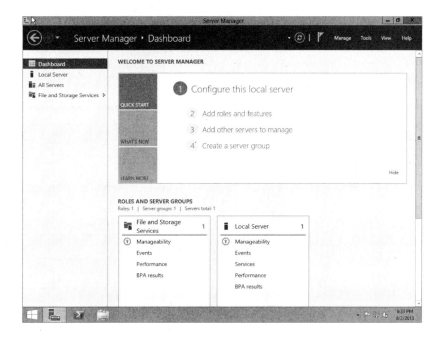

THE ADD ROLES AND FEATURES WIZARD

The new Add Roles and Features Wizard is gigantic in scope and is dynamic to your selections. We could write an entire book on all the options and features in this wizard because they change depending on your choices. We are only going to show you the most common administrator uses.

Lots of these new wizards have a welcome screen that describes the role of the wizard (see Figure 2.35). You can disable the welcome screen from popping up again by selecting the "Skip this page by default" check box.

On the next wizard screen (see Figure 2.36) you can select between "Role-based or feature-based installation" and "Remote Desktop Services installation"; this is all new in Windows Server 2012 R2.

On the "Select installation type" page, you have two choices. You may need a role-based installation if you want to install (all parts) roles or features on a single server. Or you may select "Remote Desktop Services installation" to install either a virtual machine-based desktop or a session-based desktop for Remote Desktop Services. The "Remote Desktop Services installation" option distributes (only logical parts of) the Remote Desktop Services role across different servers. We are going to use role-based for a single server.

FIGURE 2.35
"Before you
begin" screen

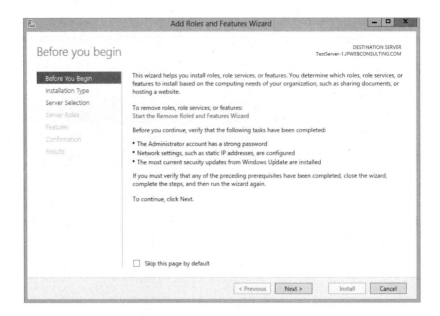

FIGURE 2.36
"Select installation
type" screen

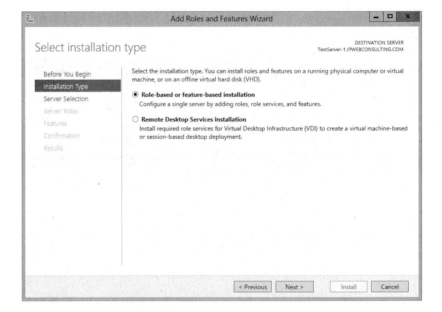

When you select the role-based installation you arrive at the "Select destination server" screen (see Figure 2.37). This too is a new wizard screen in Windows Server 2012 R2.

Server　Select the top option to install on a server from your server pool.

Virtual Hard Disk (VHD)　The second option is a little more complicated and has some requirements that must be met for you to add a VHD file:

FIGURE 2.37
Server
Selection

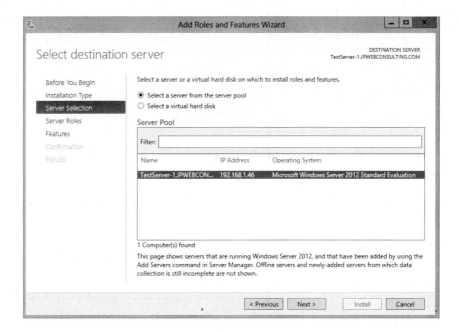

- VHDs must be running Windows Server 2012 R2.

- VHDs cannot have more than one system volume or partition.

- The network shared folder in which the VHD file is stored must grant the following access rights to the computer account of the server that you have selected to mount the VHD file.

- Read/Write access on the File Sharing dialog box.

- Full Control access on the Security tab, File or Folder Properties dialog box.

ACCESS TIP!

User-only account access is not sufficient for installing a role on a VHD. The share can grant Read and Write permissions to the Everyone group to allow access to the VHD, but for security reasons, this is not recommended.

For now, click the top radio button to select a server from your server pool. Then, from the list of servers highlight the server you wish to use and click Next.

You'll now see a listing of all the available roles that you can install (see Figure 2.38). Clicking each one gives you a brief description of that role. The new server we set up is going to be a web server, so select Web Server (IIS).

A pop-up screen appears when you select the Web Server role, informing you that additional management tools will need to be installed with your selection (see Figure 2.39). Click the Add Features button; then click Next on the "Select Server roles" screen.

FIGURE 2.38
Selecting the server
roles to install

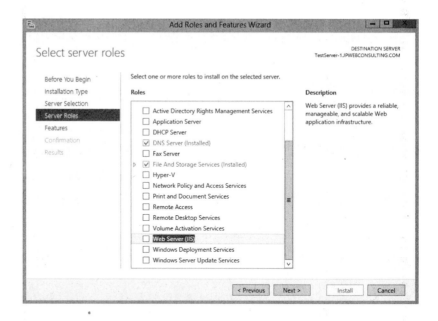

FIGURE 2.39
IIS: Additional tools
required

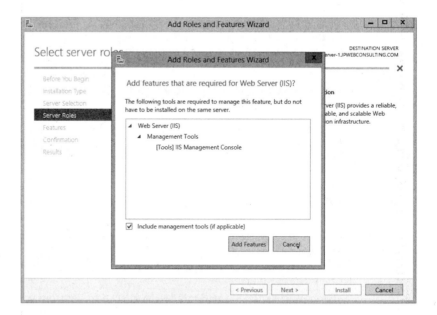

As you can see, the wizard dynamically changes with your selections. This is really handy because the wizard keeps an eye out for additional features that are needed for the server to do its job in that role.

As shown in Figure 2.40, you now have a list of features you can install. Just like the roles, you can click each one to get a brief description of each feature. Click the Next button to continue the wizard.

You now get a summary of the role you've chosen to install, which is IIS in this example (see Figure 2.41).

FIGURE 2.40
Install features
for IIS

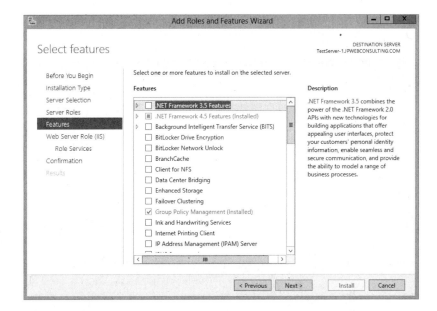

FIGURE 2.41
Web Server Role
summary

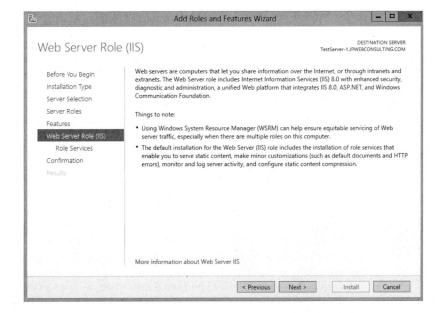

HMM...ROLES AND FEATURES DO MAKE SENSE

Note that you are told that you need to install additional features with IIS. This is the first hint that there is some intelligence behind all of this roles and features functionality in Windows Server 2012 R2. You will continue to see the wizard add more screens of options as we move forward.

A role service is a subcomponent of a role. It is either the core component of the role or an optional component. Each role has one or a set of default role services. You can see in Figure 2.42 that the Web Server role has several additional services checked by default. Also shown are a number of optional role services that you can install if you require them.

FIGURE 2.42
Role Services

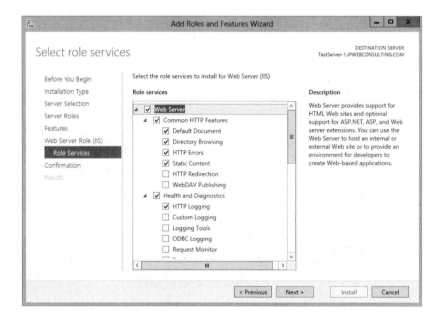

Microsoft has modeled all the available roles, role services, and features. It knows the relationships, the dependencies, and the conflicts. This is applied in Server Manager. For example, if a role requires a certain role service, then clearing that role service will result in clearing the role. It removes the guesswork for administrators, which is a good thing.

You get a confirmation screen where you can verify your new configuration before anything is installed (see Figure 2.43). Click Install to kick that off.

Some roles and role services can take a little time to install. You get a progress screen so you can track the progress.

The installation will eventually finish. You can see that our role installation succeeded. Since you have not configured automatic updating for patching this server yet, you may receive a warning depending on the role you install. You'll probably see this while playing in a lab, so you can safely ignore it. It is a valid warning, though. You should configure your updates either manually or via Group Policy and then deploy them as soon as possible.

You can see that the left menu on Server Manager now lists the IIS Services role that you've just installed (see Figure 2.44).

So, that's how you can add a role and role services by using the GUI. You can also do this using the command prompt in PowerShell. This is where a lot of Windows administrators start skipping pages. Don't do it! Trust us; you will want to know this stuff.

FIGURE 2.43
Confirming the installation

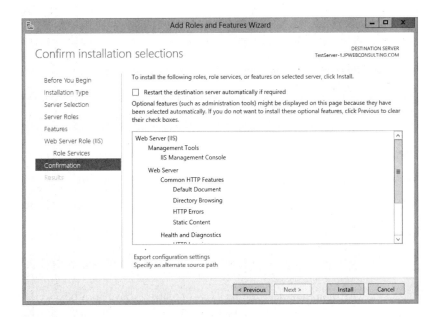

FIGURE 2.44
Viewing the roles in the Server Manager dashboard

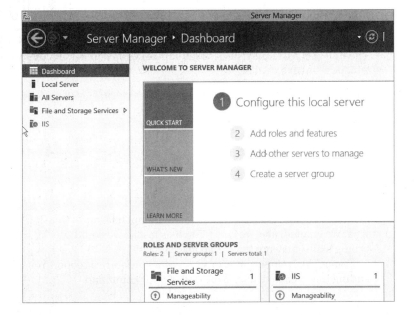

Installing Roles Using PowerShell

You can install roles and features using PowerShell. If you are managing Windows Server 2012 R2, then you'll need to use PowerShell, Microsoft's scripting and command language. The subject of PowerShell is pretty huge. We'll just cover the relevant Server Manager–related cmdlets (pronounced "command-lets") here.

At first, PowerShell might seem a bit clunky to use. But you will find that after a little while it is quicker to use than the GUI. Not only that, but you can also use it in a scripted form for customizing servers. That's very handy if you use a cloning or unattended mechanism for installing Windows or even if you are building loads of servers by hand. You just deploy one image and run the appropriate script or unattended answer file to customize that generic image to be the server you require.

You can launch PowerShell from the superbar, or a really cool way to open it is by pressing the start button and then right-clicking the large PowerShell button-box. You will see a new menu bar appear at the bottom. Make sure you launch it with administrative rights. The PowerShell modules related to Server Manager are not loaded by default. Run this command to load them:

```
PS C:\Users\Administrator> import-module Servermanager
```

You can run the command with the `Get-WindowsFeature` cmdlet to report on what roles, role services, and features are installed:

```
PS C:\Users\Administrator>Get-WindowsFeature
```

The generated report is pretty long, so you'll have to forgive us for not including the entire thing (see Figure 2.45)! We have rain forests to think about, so we've only included snippets of the query results.

None of the roles, role services, or features have an X next to them. That X designates that the role, role feature, or feature is installed as is with our IIS since we already added that one. Hence, we are working with a fairly blank server. You will see in Figure 2.46 that our Web Server IIS is installed.

For this example, you want to install an FTP server, which as you can see at the bottom of Figure 2.45 is still available to be installed. Note in that figure that the role has a Name column. The FTP Service name listed is Web-Ftp-Server. We'll use that designation with the `Install-WindowsFeature` cmdlet.

```
PS C:\Users\Administrator> Install-WindowsFeature -Name Web-Ftp-Server -Restart..


Success     RestartNeeded     Exit Code     Feature Result
-------     -------------     ---------     --------------
True        No                Success       {Web-Ftp-Server, Web-Ftp-Service}


PS C:\Users\Administrator>
```

That was pretty simple, eh? And it was much faster than using the GUI wizard. We knew what we wanted, and we could run it as fast as we could type it, which, depending on your typing skills, may not have been all that fast!

Some roles, role services, or features will require a reboot. You can have this be automatic by adding the `-restart` flag to the end of your command.

FIGURE 2.45
PowerShell
Get-WindowsFeature

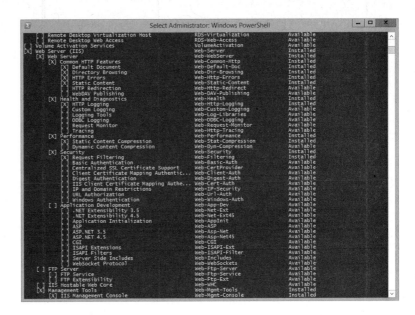

Let's verify the installation. Run PowerShell again with the Get-WindowsFeature cmdlet to check the results, as shown in Figure 2.46:

```
PS C:\Users\Administrator> Get-WindowsFeature
```

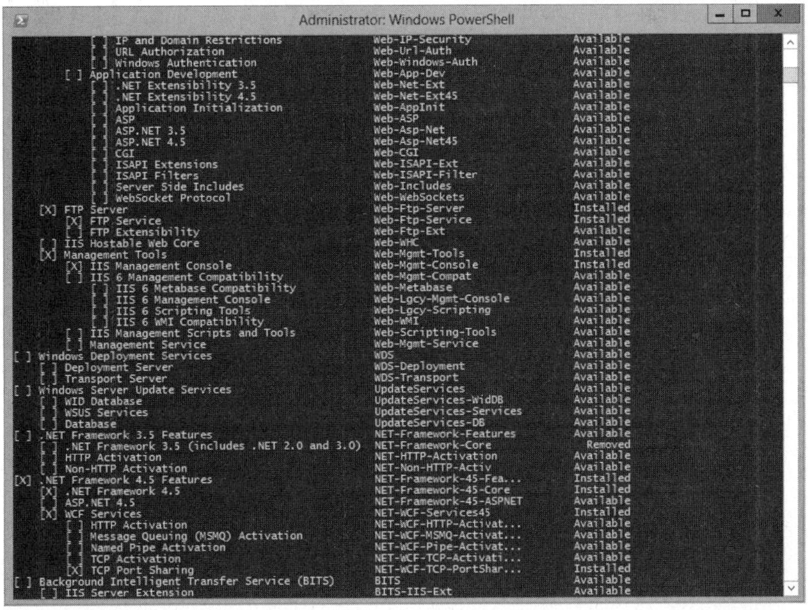

FIGURE 2.46
Checking our
installed role

The roles and role services that you requested are designated with an *X*, which means that they are installed. You can also see that the required features for the FTP Service are also installed. You can ensure that the results are identical to those obtained using the GUI by launching Server Manager.

Anyone who was a little scared of command-line administration might now be getting a little intrigued.

If you want a text report on your server configuration, then you could run this next command. It will export the report to a file called c:\InstalledFeatures.txt:

```
PS C:\Users\Administrator> get-windowsfeature > C:\InstalledFeatures.txt
```

A nice feature is that you can check out what would happen if you ran the command without actually running it. You can do that by adding the -whatif flag:

```
Add-WindowsFeature Name -whatif
```

If you're going to add the File-Services role and the FS-Resource-Manager role service, for example, here's what would happen if you ran that command:

```
PS C:\Users\Administrator> add-windowsfeature File-Services,FS-Resource-Manager
-whatif
What if: Checking if running in 'WhatIf' Mode.
What if: Performing operation "Add-WindowsFeature" on Target "[File Services]
File Server Resource Manager".
What if: Performing operation "Add-WindowsFeature" on Target "[File Services]
File Server".
What if: This server may need to be restarted after the installation completes.

Success Restart Needed Exit Code Feature Result
------- -------------- --------- --------------
True    Maybe          Success   {}
```

Nothing has been changed on the server thanks to the -whatif flag. Notice that you might need to reboot? It is good to know that once this command executes, you'll need to do a reboot. This will allow you to plan for the reboot and warn users of any services hosted by this machine.

Installing Roles on Multiple Servers Using Scripts in PowerShell

Imagine that you were setting up many more roles, role services, and features. You could bundle everything into this one script and run it as required. With that command-line option in PowerShell, you could automatically reconfigure hundreds or thousands of servers using something like Microsoft System Center Configuration Manager. You should now understand the power of PowerShell. You could easily save hours of work on your server deployments or configuration projects.

Before you go too far into setting up a script installation, you need to first check to see if you are allowed to run scripts. Open PowerShell and run the following cmdlet:

```
PS C:\Users\Administrator> get-executionpolicy
Restricted
```

This command shows that scripts are disabled on our server. That's the default in PowerShell. To run the script if scripts are disabled on your server, you'll have to run this command:

```
PS C:\Users\Administrator> set-executionpolicy unrestricted

Execution Policy Change
The execution policy helps protect you from scripts that you do not trust.
Changing the execution policy might expose
you to the security risks described in the about_Execution_Policies help topic.
Do you want to change the execution
policy?
[Y] Yes  [N] No  [S] Suspend  [?] Help (default is "Y"): Y
```

You can verify the change by rerunning the Get-ExecutionPolicy command:

```
PS C:\Users\Administrator> get-executionpolicy
Unrestricted
```

Your server is now set up to allow scripts. For security reasons, I would suggest when you've finished installing your scripts that you change it back to Restricted.

Let's look at using a script with PowerShell. You'll find it handy when you want to add roles, role services, or features to multiple servers. You will need a configuration file to achieve this. Just to show you how to do this, we will use the Add Roles and Features Wizard and export the role installation to an XML file.

Since the previous pages explained how to add a role using the wizard, go ahead and add a Remote Desktop Services role, but stop when you get to the role confirmation page. On the confirmation page (the last screen in the wizard), there is a link at the bottom allowing you to export the configuration to a file (see Figure 2.47).

FIGURE 2.47
Exporting a role to a configuration XML file

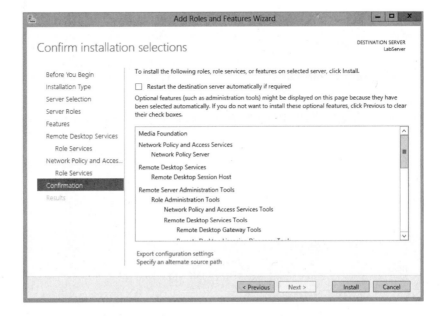

Save the file as **RemoteDesktopConfig.xml** on your C drive root or any convenient location you choose. If you want to open it with Internet Explorer to see what it looks like, feel free. In Figure 2.48 is a partial screenshot of the file. You can go ahead and cancel the wizard now that you've saved the file. Do not hit the Install button!

FIGURE 2.48
XML configuration file

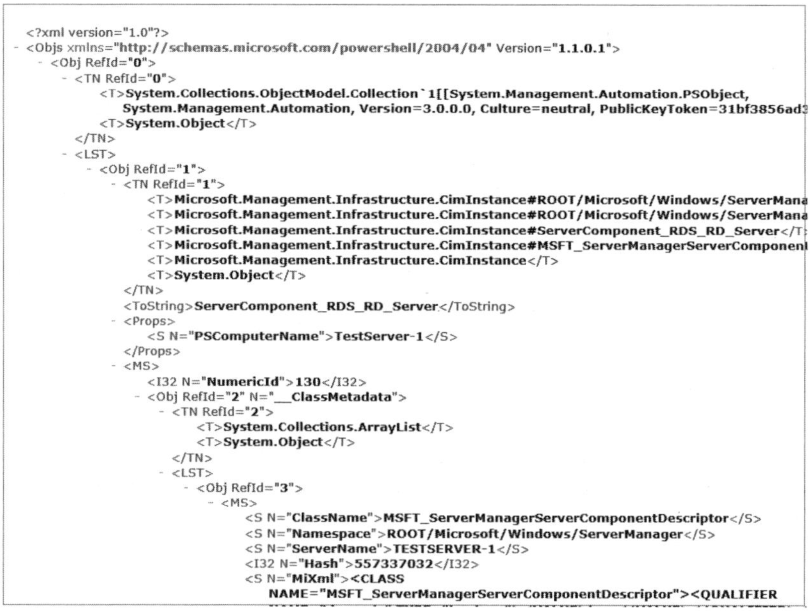

```
<?xml version="1.0"?>
- <Objs xmlns="http://schemas.microsoft.com/powershell/2004/04" Version="1.1.0.1">
  - <Obj RefId="0">
    - <TN RefId="0">
        <T>System.Collections.ObjectModel.Collection`1[[System.Management.Automation.PSObject,
          System.Management.Automation, Version=3.0.0.0, Culture=neutral, PublicKeyToken=31bf3856ad3
        <T>System.Object</T>
      </TN>
    - <LST>
      - <Obj RefId="1">
        - <TN RefId="1">
            <T>Microsoft.Management.Infrastructure.CimInstance#ROOT/Microsoft/Windows/ServerMana
            <T>Microsoft.Management.Infrastructure.CimInstance#ROOT/Microsoft/Windows/ServerMana
            <T>Microsoft.Management.Infrastructure.CimInstance#ServerComponent_RDS_RD_Server</T
            <T>Microsoft.Management.Infrastructure.CimInstance#MSFT_ServerManagerServerComponen
            <T>Microsoft.Management.Infrastructure.CimInstance</T>
            <T>System.Object</T>
          </TN>
          <ToString>ServerComponent_RDS_RD_Server</ToString>
        - <Props>
            <S N="PSComputerName">TestServer-1</S>
          </Props>
        - <MS>
            <I32 N="NumericId">130</I32>
          - <Obj RefId="2" N="__ClassMetadata">
            - <TN RefId="2">
                <T>System.Collections.ArrayList</T>
                <T>System.Object</T>
              </TN>
            - <LST>
              - <Obj RefId="3">
                - <MS>
                    <S N="ClassName">MSFT_ServerManagerServerComponentDescriptor</S>
                    <S N="Namespace">ROOT/Microsoft/Windows/ServerManager</S>
                    <S N="ServerName">TESTSERVER-1</S>
                    <I32 N="Hash">557337032</I32>
                    <S N="MiXml"><CLASS
                      NAME="MSFT_ServerManagerServerComponentDescriptor"><QUALIFIER
```

OK, you are ready to install the Remote Desktop Services role to multiple computers using a script file. Open PowerShell by right-clicking the PowerShell icon in the taskbar, and select Run as Administrator.

Inside PowerShell add the following function:

```
function Invoke-WindowsFeatureBatchDeployment {
    param (
        [parameter(mandatory)]
        [string[]] $ComputerNames,
        [parameter(mandatory)]
        [string] $ConfigurationFilePath
    )

    # Deploy the features on multiple computers simultaneously.
    $jobs = @()
    foreach($ComputerName in $ComputerNames) {
        $jobs += Start-Job -Command {
```

```
        Install-WindowsFeature -ConfigurationFilePath
$using:ConfigurationFilePath -ComputerName $using:ComputerName -Restart
        }
    }

    Receive-Job -Job $jobs -Wait | Select-Object Success, RestartNeeded,
ExitCode, FeatureResult
}
```

As you can see, this function is expecting a few parameters, a list of computer names that will receive the Remote Desktop role, and the file path of your script. So to invoke this function you will use the following code snippet to pass in the parameters you need.

```
# Sample Invocation
$ServerNames = 'TestServer_01', 'LabServer_02'
Invoke-WindowsFeatureBatchDeployment -ComputerNames $ServerNames
-ConfigurationFilePath C:\RemoteDesktopConfig.xml
```

The following line from this snippet is the server names you will change to match yours. As you can see, my servers are TestServer_01 and LabServer_02 and are comma delimited. You can add as many servers as you wish to this line:

```
$ServerNames = 'TestServer_01', ' LabServer_02'
```

The next line from this snippet you will edit is the path of your XML file. Just change it to the path you saved your file to:

```
-ConfigurationFilePath C:\RemoteDesktopConfig.xml
```

Once you make your edits, hit Enter and you will see the install begin. It takes a little while to execute.

You can now verify the installation by running:

```
PS C:\Users\Administrator> Get-WindowsFeature
```

Once again, any role, role service, or feature that is installed will be marked with an *X*. Take note of the Name column. You'll be using that for future commands. If you already know what role or feature you're interested in learning about, try running something like this:

```
PS C:\Users\Administrator> get-windowsfeature RSAT-RDS-Tools
```

Display Name	Name	Install State
[X] Remote Desktop Services Tools	RSAT-RDS-Tools	Installed

REMOVING A ROLE

Removing roles, role services, and features with PowerShell is just as easy as it was to install them. The Remove-WindowsFeature cmdlet is similar to the Install-WindowsFeature cmdlet:

```
Remove-WindowsFeature <Role>,<RoleService>,<Feature> -restart -whatif
```

Here's the syntax:

- Enter the role, role service, or feature that you want to remove. You can use commas to specify many of them.

- Use the -restart flag to initiate an automatic reboot if you need to do so.

- Use the -whatif flag to simulate the command.

This command will simulate removing the FTP server you installed earlier:

```
PS C:\Users\Administrator> remove-windowsfeature Web-Ftp-Server -whatif
What if: Continue with removal?
What if: Performing uninstallation for "[Web Server (IIS)] FTP Server".
What if: Performing uninstallation for "[Web Server (IIS)] FTP Service".
What if: The target server may need to be restarted after the removal completes.


Success Restart Needed Exit Code     Feature Result
------- -------------- ---------     --------------
True    Maybe          Success       {FTP Server, FTP Service}
```

Once you are happy that the command will run OK, you can remove the -whatif flag:

```
PS C:\Users\Administrator> remove-windowsfeature Web-Ftp-Server
Success Restart Needed Exit Code     Feature Result
------- -------------- ---------     --------------
True    Yes            SuccessRest... {FTP Server, FTP Service}
WARNING: You must restart this server to finish the removal process.
Success Restart Needed Exit Code Feature Result
```

You now need to reboot. You can automate the reboot with this line:

```
PS C:\Users\Administrator> remove-windowsfeature Web-Ftp-Server
 -restart
```

That completes the role removal. To install just features, repeat the role-installation process. When you get to the roles screen, click Next to skip adding any roles. You will then arrive at the features screen, where you can select any features you need. Just complete the process as you would with a role.

Troubleshooting Roles and Features

As an IT administrator, one of your jobs is to maintain the health of your servers. This includes monitoring all the roles and features of your network to make sure the servers are performing at their peak levels.

Server Manager can help you do this. For starters, the Server Manager dashboard is now color-coded. If a problem exists, it will appear in red. If you take a look at Figure 2.49, you will see we have three issues with BPA results in DNS. We should, as the awesome administrators that we are, start investigating these issues. We are going to click DNS in the left menu to see all the performance tools available to help us find the problem.

Inside each role you can view the following information:

FIGURE 2.49
New color-coded
warnings in
Server Manager

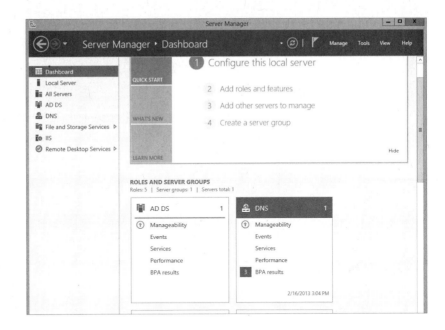

Servers   This section lists the servers the role is installed on (see Figure 2.50). Inside this window there are a few things you can do to get more information. If you right-click the header, as shown in Figure 2.51, you can add more columns of information. We added operating system version so we can quickly see what version each server is running. For one server as we have, it may not be that important, but if you have a server pool or web farm, this can be handy.

FIGURE 2.50
Servers dialog
box

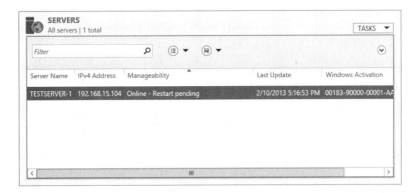

Events   This is a very useful tool to help you diagnose problems. Just like event viewers in previous operating systems, this delivers some great troubleshooting information. We have a warning on our DNS role. You get a short, "at a glance" look at the warning or error. If you click on the error, it will give a detailed description of the problem, as shown in Figure 2.52.

FIGURE 2.51
Adding columns
of information

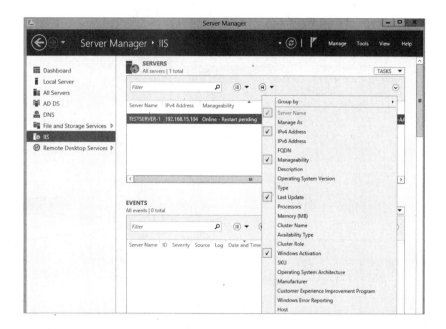

FIGURE 2.52
The Events
window

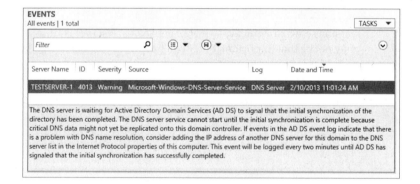

Services This tool is a great feature because it will only show the services associated with this role. If you click Local Server you will see all the services running on the local machine. From within this window you can also start, stop, restart, and pause the service (see Figure 2.53).

Best Practices Analyzer This tool scans your roles and measures best-practice compliance in eight different categories:

- Security
- Performance
- Configuration
- Policy
- Operation
- Pre-Deployment
- Post-Deployment
- Prerequisites

Running a scan is easy. Just click the Tasks button in the Best Practices Analyzer window of the role, as shown in Figure 2.54.

FIGURE 2.53
The Services window

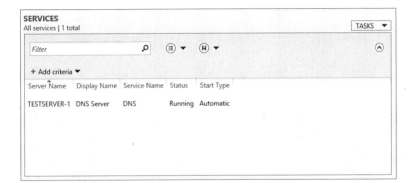

FIGURE 2.54
Running Best Practices Analyzer

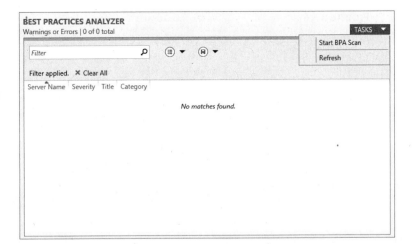

You now need to select a server to run the scan against (see Figure 2.55).

The scan will take a few minutes to run. Just like in the Event Viewer, you will get a list of errors and warnings, as shown in Figure 2.56.

You can click the warning or error and get a detailed description of the error. At the bottom of the description is also a link to more information about the issue.

FIGURE 2.55
Selecting a server to scan

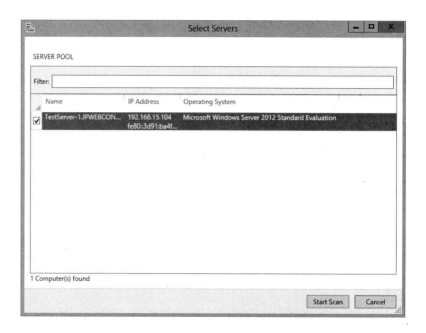

FIGURE 2.56
Best Practices Analyzer results

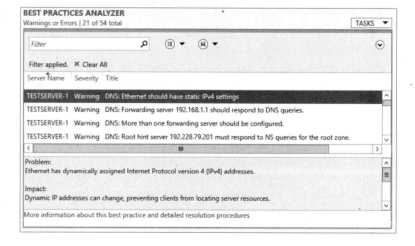

Performance   This window displays performance on a particular role (see Figure 2.57). By default, the performance counter is turned off. Just right-click the server in the list and start the performance counter.

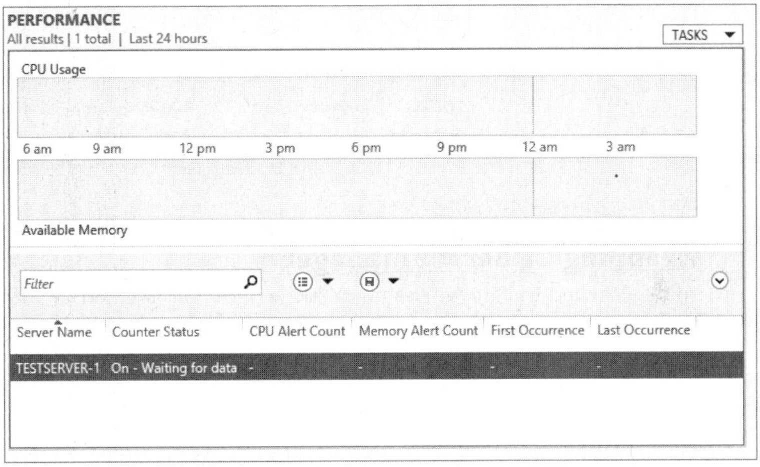

FIGURE 2.57
Performance analyzer

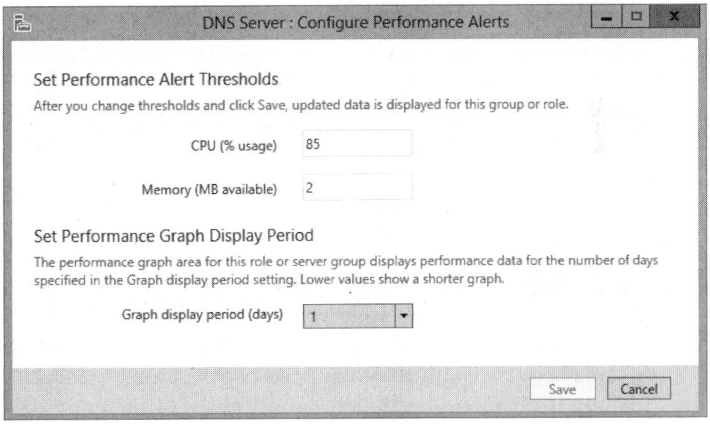

FIGURE 2.58
Performance settings

On the Configure Performance Alerts screen, you can configure the settings for CPU usage, memory usage, and the number of days you want to graph (see Figure 2.58).

Roles And Features   This window displays additional features associated with the role. If you look at Figure 2.59, you will see we're in the IIS role. All the roles and features having to do with IIS are listed.

These tools help you manage and troubleshoot your installed roles and features without having to open up five different programs as you had to do in legacy servers.

FIGURE 2.59
Roles And Features
window

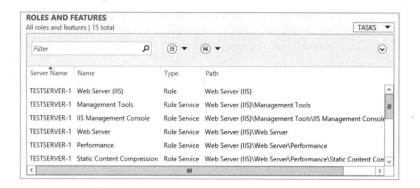

FIGURE 2.59
Roles And Features
window

Wrapping Up Server Manager

You've learned that `servermanagercmd` is being deprecated by Microsoft, and you've learned how to install and remove roles and features using PowerShell and the Server Manager GUI. You have also seen how you can use Server Manager to diagnose roles and features including using the Best Practices Analyzer.

So it's time we mentioned domain controllers and Active Directory—cue the *Jaws*-like dramatic music.

Upgrading Active Directory

OK folks, some good news. We're not going to cover this subject in detail yet. That will be covered in Chapter 7, "Active Directory in Windows Server 2012 R2," but we wanted to mention it here for the readers who have worked with Active Directory (AD) in the past. If you haven't, then don't worry about it—feel free to skip the next couple of pages, and you'll learn about AD in Chapter 7.

An Overview of Active Directory: New Functionality in Windows Server 2012 R2

As usual, a new version of Server comes along, and you get new functionality and design opportunities in Active Directory. A lot of this new functionality will be pretty exciting to people because it appears to be based on customer feedback. Some of these new options will definitely answer some of those questions we frequently see on Internet support forums.

WHAT'S NEW IN ACTIVE DIRECTORY DOMAIN SERVICES

Active Directory Domain Services (AD DS) allows you to deploy domain controllers either locally or on your cloud. There are a host of administration tasks in deploying domain controllers that can be easily completed using AD DS. Let's discuss some of the new features you may find useful.

Active Directory Recycle Bin

Do you hear that? That's the cheering of Active Directory administrators all around the world. Every domain administrator's worst nightmare has been the deletion of objects. When Windows

Server 2008 R2 added this feature, it became possible to recover objects if they were recently deleted without going through nasty backup and recovery processes. The Active Directory Recycle Bin allowed you to quickly recover accidentally deleted objects with a new simpler and supported process. The only problem was that it did not have a user-friendly user interface (UI). Windows Server 2012 R2 addresses this problem with a rich UI that simplifies object recovery. Recovery time is reduced since you have a consistent view of the deleted objects.

Fine-Grained Password Policies

One of the most common questions since the initial release of Active Directory has been, "How can I have more than one password policy?" The official Microsoft answer was that you needed more than one domain to do this. Of course, this contradicts the basic design goal of trying to reduce the number of domains in networks. It also muddied the waters when it comes to no longer thinking of the domain as a security boundary—the domain is a policy boundary, and the forest is a security boundary.

The solution, without using third-party products that Microsoft might not support, was to create a domain for every password policy that you needed (which could create a lot of child domains) or to turn to a third-party solution that would allow you to have more than one password policy in a single domain.

The objective of fine-grained password policies is to associate stronger policies with user accounts of greater significance, in other words, where they have greater access to systems or to valuable data. What ended up happening, however, was that manually defined policy values did not behave as desired and became very time consuming. Windows Server 2012 R2 now allows you to manage policies using the Active Directory Administrative Center, which makes the management of password-settings objects easier.

Rapid Deployment with Cloning

Cloning, by definition, means "making an identical copy of." So how is cloning used with AD DS? The short answer is you can now make an exact replica or clone an existing virtual domain controller in AD DS.

You can promote a single virtual domain controller by using the domain controller promotion interface in Server Manager and then rapidly deploy additional virtual domain controllers within the same domain, through cloning. First, create a copy of an existing virtual domain controller and authorize the original domain controller to be cloned in AD DS. Using PowerShell cmdlets you can create a configuration file with detailed promotion instructions such as name, IP address, and DNS servers. By cloning you can save time by eliminating repetitive tasks of deployment.

Simplified Management

Many of the following areas were addressed with the intent of making the AD DS management experience easier:

- Dynamic Access Control
- Direct Access Offline Domain Join
- Active Directory Federation Services (AD FS)
- Windows PowerShell History Viewer

- Active Directory Recycle Bin user interface
- Active Directory Replication and Topology
- Windows PowerShell cmdlets
- Active Directory Based Activation (AD BA)
- Group Managed Service Accounts (gMSA)

Windows PowerShell History Viewer

If you have been following along in this chapter, then you are practically a PowerShell expert. PowerShell will be getting a lot of developer love in this release and future releases of Windows Server. This is because more and more administrators are learning and using PowerShell.

At some point you're going to realize that performance, security, and deployment speed are the way to manage instead of a fancy graphical UI (and the overhead that goes with it). Remember DOS? Well, think of PowerShell as DOS on steroids! Once you start using it, you will start to see the benefits. Windows PowerShell History Viewer will help with the learning curve associated with PowerShell and will get even more administrators using it.

For example, using the Active Directory Administration Center you add a user. The UI displays the equivalent Windows PowerShell for Active Directory command. The admin can then copy the syntax that can later be used in scripts.

WHAT'S NEW IN AD CS

Let's discuss the new and enhanced features that came out in this version in Active Directory Certificate Services (AD CS). First off, let's just go over briefly what AD CS is. This very important security tool provides services for managing and dispensing public key certificates. This is primarily used on software security systems that use public key technologies. These services are customizable to enhance your security by binding the identity of a device, person, or service to a private key.

Integration with Server Manager

You can now install AD CS and its six associated roles using Server Manager. So just like we did earlier in the "Adding a Role Section," you can easily add AD CS using the Add Roles and Features Wizard. It will then appear in the Server Manager dashboard like any other role. And just like any other role, you can manage it on multiple servers from one location.

Deployment and Management Using Windows PowerShell

AD CS role services can be deployed using PowerShell cmdlets just as we discussed earlier in this chapter about using PowerShell to add a role. Here are the new install and uninstall cmdlets with the AD CS and associated roles:

`Install-AdcsCertificationAuthority`   Certification Authority role service

`Install-AdcsEnrollmentPolicyWebService`   Certificate Enrollment Policy Web role service

`Install-AdcsEnrollmentWebService`   Certificate Enrollment Web role service

`Install-AdcsNetworkDeviceEnrollmentService`   Network Device Enrollment service

Install-AdcsOnlineResponder   Online Responder role service

Install-AdcsWebEnrollment   Certification Authority Web Enrollment role service

Uninstall-AdcsCertificationAuthority   Removes Certification Authority role service

Uninstall-AdcsEnrollmentPolicyWebService   Removes Certificate Enrollment Policy Web role service

Uninstall-AdcsEnrollmentWebService   Removes Certificate Enrollment Web role service

Uninstall-AdcsNetworkDeviceEnrollmentService   Removes Network Device Enrollment role service

Uninstall-AdcsOnlineResponder   Removes Online Responder role service

Uninstall-AdcsWebEnrollment   Removes Certification Authority Web Enrollment role service

What's New in Active Directory Rights Management Services

The role of Active Directory Rights Management Services (AD RMS) is to help you develop and maintain security solutions. Authentication, encryption, and certificates can all be maintained by AD RMS. Let's take a look at what is new in AD RMS.

Changes in AD RMS That Affect SQL Server

In previous releases of Windows Server you would need local administrator permissions to install AD RMS on any SQL Server machine if you planned on storing the AD RMS data. This was because you had to be able to read the SQL Server settings from the registry to do the install. The requirements for configuring SQL Server with AD RMS have changed. The installer account for AD RMS must have sysadmin permissions in the SQL Server installation.

You will also need to have the SQL Server browser running so AD RMS can see there is a SQL Server instance running.

Changes in Deployment of AD RMS for Server Manager and Windows PowerShell

Another fault AD RMS had in previous releases of Windows Server was that it only could be deployed at the same server it was to be installed on. With the vast improvements made to Server Manager and its integration with AD RMS, it now supports remote deployment at targeted server computers.

Using Windows PowerShell to Deploy AD RMS

As described in the previous section on how to use Windows PowerShell commands to install roles, you can now install AD RMS the same way. In the following list we provide you with the new cmdlets to get the job done:

Add-WindowsFeature ADRMS -IncludeAllSubFeature -IncludeManagementTools   This cmdlet adds all AD RMS role services and tools. It downloads all supporting files needed to work with AD RMS.

Add-WindowsFeature ADRMS-Server   This cmdlet adds the AD RMS Server role only. It also downloads all files needed to support an AD RMS server installation.

Add-WindowsFeature ADRMS-Identity   This cmdlet adds identity federation support for AD RMS. It downloads all files needed to support AD RMS working with AD FS.

Active Directory Upgrade Strategies

There are a few different scenarios for upgrading Active Directory. You cannot do a direct upgrade from 32-bit Windows 2008 to Windows Server 2012 R2. You can do an in-place upgrade from Windows 2008 R2 to Windows Server 2012 R2 because both versions are x64.

The following are some Active Directory upgrade scenarios from Windows 2008:

◆ When you want to decommission all old domain controllers:

1. Prepare the forest.

2. Prepare the domain.

3. Install Windows 2012 R2 member servers and promote them to be domain controllers.

4. Decommission old domain controllers.

◆ When all old domain controllers are x64:

1. Prepare the forest.

2. Prepare the domain.

3. Upgrade x64 domain controllers to Windows 2012 R2.

◆ When there is a mix of new and old hardware and a mix of x86 and x64 domain controllers:

1. Prepare the forest.

2. Prepare the domain.

3. Upgrade newer domain controllers to Windows 2012 R2.

4. Install new Windows 2012 R2 member servers and promote them to be domain controllers. These will replace older Windows domain controllers.

5. Decommission old domain controllers.

All of these strategies have a pair of steps in common. A tool called adprep is used to upgrade the forest schema, in other words, prepare the forest. This is done once by a user who is a member of Schema Admins, Enterprise Admins, and Domain Admins in the domain that contains the Schema Master forest-wide FSMO role. The same tool is also used to prepare any domain that will contain Windows 2008 domain controllers. This will be done by a user who is a domain administrator of that domain.

The side-by-side approach, of upgrading from Windows Server 2008 to Windows Server 2012 R2, requires one more step. It is necessary to apply permissions to Group Policy objects so that they can be managed by the Group Policy Management console.

Your final way to get to Windows Server 2012 R2 is a drastic one. You may find that your network is not in a healthy or known state. Sometimes it's better to cut your losses and start again with a new Active Directory that is well planned, documented, controlled, and maintained. You can build a new forest/domain. You can then migrate users, data, and services to the new Active Directory. We've done that in the past when we joined a new company that was going through a spin-off closely followed by a series of mergers. It paid off with a much more stable and manageable working environment.

This all sounds very high level, and it is meant to be. It is just a taste of what you can expect in Chapter 7.

Unattended Installations

We bet you thought you were finally getting to the end of this chapter. Surely, there is no more we could discuss about installing Windows Server 2012 R2, right? Well, think again.

Smaller organizations will be happy with the manual approach for installing or upgrading Windows Server 2012 R2 that we discussed earlier in the chapter. However, you may want to invest some effort in alternative approaches. You could use a cloning solution such as Windows Deployment Services, as found in Windows Server since Service Pack 2 for Windows Server 2003, or the free Microsoft Deployment Toolkit 2012. Maybe you already use a third-party solution. There is another way that might be of interest for you that does not require a server to manage the process.

Unattended installations of Windows extend the installation media by customizing their installation. Part of the process is to answer those questions that you probably get sick of answering all the time. The idea is that you can start an installation and walk away knowing that you will not have to answer any questions. Your new server will install all by itself according to your predefined answers. The new installation routine for Windows 8 and Server 2012 R2 is quite small, but if you are building lots of machines, you will soon get tired of entering product keys, selecting OS editions, and so on. The other, more powerful part is the ability to tweak the installation in ways that are not revealed in the manual installation process. How would you like to install some components of the operating system that are not revealed in the GUI? This could simplify your post-installation customization and streamline your deployments.

All of this is possible by using an answer file that you supply to the installation routine. This approach might be familiar to engineers who have deployed older versions of Windows. In the past you might have used a tool called Setup Manager to create a simple text-based answer file, which you probably then had to customize a fair bit in Notepad.

The release of Windows Vista changed all that. With Vista came the release of the Windows Automated Installation Kit (WAIK), which has seen some updates including support for Windows Server 2008, Windows 7, and Windows Server 2008 R2. With the release of Windows Server 2012 R2, this kit's name has changed to Windows Assessment and Deployment Kit (Windows ADK). ADK is a very powerful set of tools that include the ability to create a boot DVD. This boots up using Windows PE, a trimmed-down version of Windows that you can use for many tasks including OS deployment and troubleshooting. More important for this chapter, it includes Windows System Image Manager (WSIM). WSIM is the replacement for Setup Manager and is used to create answer files for Windows 8 and Windows Server 2012 R2.

The other big change you'll see is the format of the answer files that you are going to use. It used to be pretty simple to edit text files. Heck, Setup Manager actually did little other than set up the skeleton of the answer file. You generally had to do a lot more work on the answer file in Notepad. WSIM creates XML files. Uh-oh! There's that word: XML! Don't let it scare you. It scares many administrators at first because they are far from being programmers. But the WSIM interface does pretty much everything you'll need. You can still go in and edit the file by hand in Notepad or whatever your favorite XML editor is. The only time you might really do that is to jump in and change a product key.

We'll now cover how to deploy Windows Server 2012 R2 in an unattended fashion. You'll see how to install ADK, use WSIM to create an answer file, and then use that answer file to get a silent installation working.

Note that much, if not all, of what is covered in this section can also be used to deploy Windows 8.

Installing Windows Assessment and Deployment Kit

The exercise that you are now going to go through will demonstrate how to deploy an edition of Windows Server 2012 R2 with very little human intervention. You need to deploy several Windows Server 2012 R2 Standard edition servers. It makes sense to automate those builds. You do this by using an answer file to answer the questions that you encountered during the manual installation of Windows Server 2012 R2. We'll show how to create that answer file using Windows System Image Manager, and then we will go through the process of deploying Windows in an unattended fashion.

ADK is a free set of tools that you can download from Microsoft. We are hesitant to include a URL for a download here because Microsoft has updated its deployment kits a few times since the initial release. Your best bet is to visit www.microsoft.com/downloads and search for *Windows ADK*. This will ensure that you get the latest version of ADK.

You'll be asked by the setup program whether you would like to set up on the computer you're using or to download the setup program to be loaded on another machine. If you select to install on the computer you're using to download the ADK, it will download and install it at the same time. For this reason, we suggest you download it to be installed on another computer, which does not do an install and only downloads the software. This way you have a complete copy of the software should you need to reinstall it.

NEW ADK RELEASED FOR WINDOWS 8

The download is very large, about 5.1 GB at the time of writing this chapter. You may have previously downloaded ADK before the release of Windows Server 2012 R2. However, Microsoft released a new version to coincide with the release of Windows 8 to support the new server operating systems, so you will need to download a fresh copy of ADK.

The next thing you are going to need is an administrative workstation. An administrative workstation is a PC that you will use to prepare future builds. This might just be your PC, but that might not be a good location because you're going to be messing around with ADK and WSIM once you start getting to know them; you'll likely be making a mess of the administrative PC, so using your day-to-day machine might not be sensible!

Ensure you have lots of disk space to play with. You'll soon see why. Our preference is to have either a dedicated machine or, even better, a virtual machine. The latter offers the benefit of being economical and having the ability to save and restore states. With virtual machines, you can also mount ISO files, which is of great benefit because you won't waste time messing with utilities and blank disks. Speaking of virtual machines, you're going to need something to test your new answer files with. Virtual machines are great for testing for the same reasons that we like them as administrative workstations.

You will have support if you are running Windows Vista or later. The .NET Framework 4.0 (it will install 4.0 for you) is the only prerequisite.

Using Windows Explorer, navigate to the directory where you downloaded your ADK software and run adksetup.exe.

The first screen will appear, asking for an install location (see Figure 2.60). After you enter a location or use the default, click the Next button to continue.

FIGURE 2.60
ADK setup splash
screen

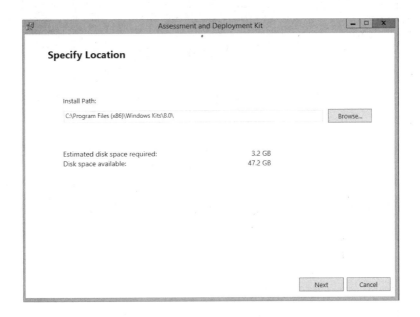

The next screen is the Microsoft Customer Experience Improvement Program (CEIP); see Figure 2.61.

The next screen you see is the License Agreement. Select Accept to agree to the licensing terms that are set out by Microsoft for ADK (see Figure 2.62).

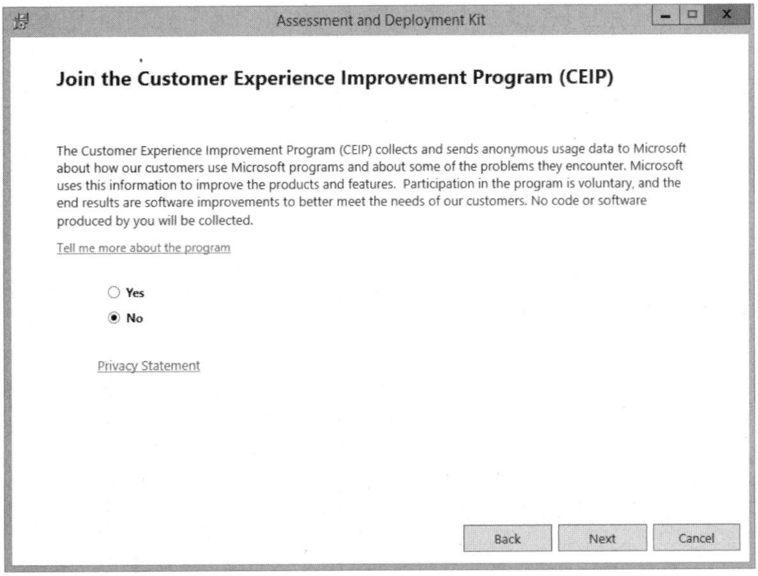

FIGURE 2.61
ADK Customer
Experience
Improvement
Program

FIGURE 2.62
ADK EULA

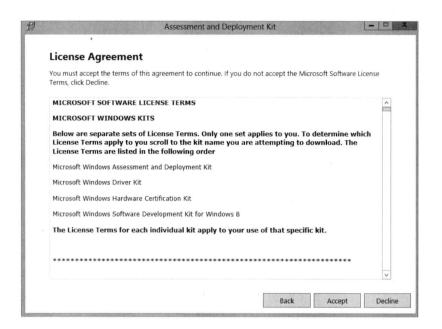

 **Real World Scenario**

A BETTER DESTINATION

Rhonda Layfield, a colleague and a deployment guru, has a great tip for when you are installing ADK. You're asked to choose a location for installing ADK. We usually choose the default of `C:\Program Files(x86)\Windows Kits\8.0\`. Once you start using ADK a lot, however, you'll realize how much command-line stuff you might need to do. Burying your software in a deep path full of lots of long names isn't exactly command-line friendly. Rhonda's tip is to simply install ADK into `C:\ADK`. That will save a lot of keyboard wear and tear.

You have arrived on the ADK select features screen. Let's take a moment to discuss these features. You will notice in the list in Figure 2.67 that SQL Server Express is not shown. This is because I already have SQL Server on my computer. If you do not have SQL Server, then the SQL Server Express option will be in the list and is required for the Application Compatibility Toolkit (ACT).

FIGURE 2.63
ADK features

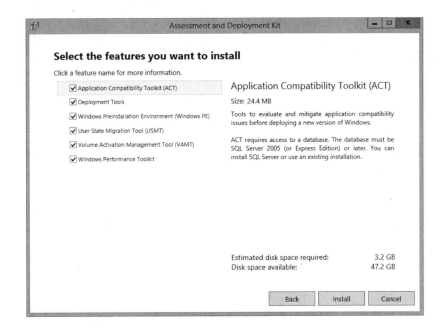

Application Compatibility Toolkit (ACT) This toolkit checks the compatibility of the computers you are going to do the unattended installation on.

Deployment Tools The deployment tools are required to do unattended installations since they are what actually does the automated installation. This is really a subset of tools for ADK. It contains several support programs such as the Deployment Image Servicing and Management (DISM) tool, OEM Activation tool, and Windows System Image Manager, to name a few.

Windows Preinstallation Environment (Windows PE) This is a bare-bones operating system that is placed on the target machine. This is needed to prepare for the install process with the host computer.

User State Migration Tool (USMT) The User State Migration Tool migrates user account data and application settings to the target machine. This saves the administrator time by not having to set the system back up to the original specifications.

Volume Activation Management Tool (VAMT) The Volume Activation Management Tool is self-explanatory. It handles the operating system software activations.

Windows Performance Toolkit This is another subset of tools used to trace the installation process and record events should they occur during the install. This is possible because it is built on the Event Tracing for Windows (ETW) infrastructure.

SQL Server Express SQL Server Express is a portable version of SQL Server and is required by the Application Compatibility Toolkit (ACT) because it stores data that will be used during the installation process.

Click Install if you are ready to commit to the installation of ADK. It can take several minutes for ADK to install (see Figure 2.64). You now have yet another opportunity to respond to some emails.

Eventually ADK is installed (see Figure 2.65). You will notice a check box on this screen to launch the Getting Started Guide. This is an excellent guide to each of the tools in the ADK. We suggest you take a look at it.

FIGURE 2.64
ADK installation
progress

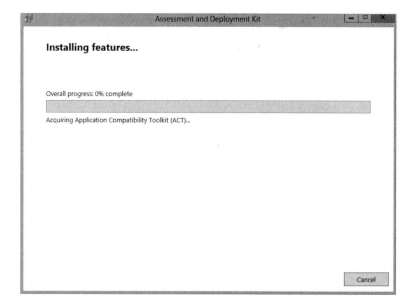

FIGURE 2.65
Completed ADK
installation

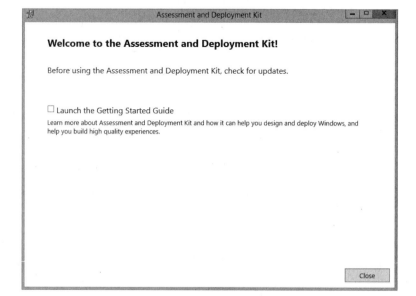

You can find the tools that you're after by hitting the start button on your task bar (see Figure 2.66).

FIGURE 2.66
ADK on the Start menu

Creating an Answer File

Before you actually create an answer file, you should understand a little of what it is and what's going on behind the scenes.

You have been reading about it thus far, but what exactly is an answer file? An answer file is an XML file that answers installation questions for you during the installation process. If you have ever installed an operating system, then you know at some point you will need to set the time zone, for example. Instead of setting your time zone manually, you could specify the time zone in the answer file. Then where the installation would normally prompt you for the time zone, the answer file will answer this question for you. This may not mean that much to you if you're installing just one or two computers, but when you have many computers to do, this process will really shine, and you will be glad you read this section.

When Windows 8 or Windows Server 2012 R2 is installing, the installation routine goes through some or all of seven *configuration passes*, described in Table 2.3. Each of these passes is responsible for carrying out certain tasks. You can think of them as stages. Some tasks can be performed in more than one of the passes. Typically only three of those passes actually need to be executed for Windows to install.

TABLE 2.3: The Configuration Passes

PASS	DESCRIPTION
windowsPE	Boots up the Windows PE installation environment, configures the product key, and configures the installation disk.
offlineServicing	Applies updates to the Windows image, including packages, patches, and languages.
Specialize	Configures settings that might be unique to the system, such as network configuration, regional, and domain.
Generalize	Removes system-specific information. It is executed only when you run sysprep / generalize.
auditSystem	Processes unattended setup steps before a user logs on. This pass runs only if you boot into audit mode.
auditUser	Processes unattended setup steps after a user logs on. It runs only if you boot into audit mode.
oobeSystem	Applies settings before the Windows welcome screen can start, in other words, before you log on.

You will see some of these passes when you create your answer file in WSIM. This will start to get a little clearer once you get into WSIM.

For this section you will need your Windows Server 2012 R2 DVD. Inside the \Sources folder on your installation media you will find a WIM file called install.wim. This file contains everything needed to install the new operating systems. The clever thing about this WIM file is that it contains everything required to install all editions of the operating system on the media. For example, Standard Full, Datacenter Full, Standard Core, and Datacenter Core are all on the Windows Server 2012 R2 DVD. This is because the WIM file uses single-instance storage; instead of having the same identical file six times, it stores it once and creates a reference point for each of the five subsequent copies.

WSIM is going to need a copy of that file on your administrative PC. WSIM uses this *install image* to know what tasks can be performed for the version and edition of Windows that you are working with. These will vary depending on whether you're using Windows 8, Windows Server 2012 R2 Standard, Windows Server 2012 R2 Datacenter, and so on. Why put this on the hard disk and not use the one on your DVD? WSIM needs to create a catalog of the contents of the image file, and it uses the folder containing the image as a working folder. You cannot write to read-only media such as a DVD.

For this example, say you are working with the DVD for Windows Server 2012 R2. You have copied \sources\install.wim into C:\W2012\install.wim on your administrative PC.

Now launch WSIM and get this process rolling by selecting File ➢ Select Windows Image. Navigate to your install image (see Figure 2.67), which is C:\W2012\install.wim, and open it.

You can now see a little of the magic of the WIM file in action. The installation media has a number of different versions of Windows in it. Select the version of Windows that you want to install in an unattended fashion. We have selected the Standard edition of Windows Server 2012 R2 in Figure 2.68.

FIGURE 2.67
Adding a Windows
image to WSIM

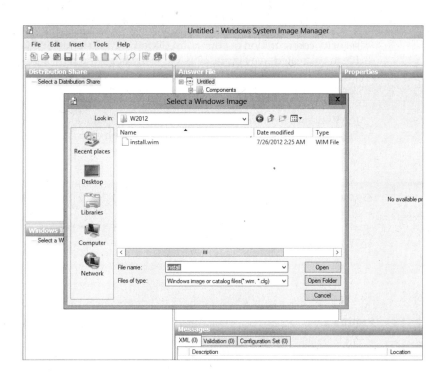

You are now warned that a catalog file of this image cannot be opened because it does not exist. You can either create a catalog file or cancel this process. Click Yes in the dialog box shown in Figure 2.69 to create a catalog file. Note that you must be a local administrator on an administrative PC.

FIGURE 2.68
Selecting the Windows image

FIGURE 2.69
Building a catalog file

User Account Control (UAC) might trigger a request before proceeding depending on the security configuration of your administrative workstation. It takes a little while for a catalog file to be created (see Figure 2.70). We really hope you have a lot of email to respond to or like to drink lots of coffee. Operating system deployment has been sometimes correctly referred to as "progress bar engineering"!

Eventually the catalog is created in C:\W2012 alongside the image file. You can see that the Windows Image pane in WSIM has been populated with Components and Packages (see Figure 2.71). You're not going to be working with distribution shares, so you might as well expand the Windows Image pane to give it more space.

FIGURE 2.70
Generating the catalog file

FIGURE 2.71
Added Windows image

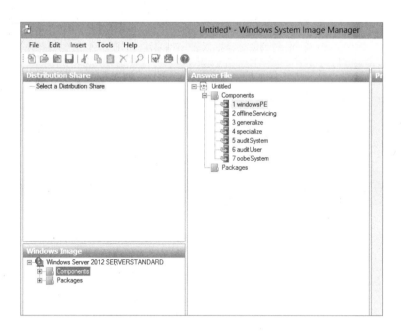

You're interested in working with Components here, so go ahead and expand that (see Figure 2.72). A *component* is a set of related settings that are used as building blocks for constructing an answer file. Each component answers a question or a set of questions during the installation. You can selectively choose components to create your desired unattended installation. The manual installation had only a few questions to answer; strangely, with an unattended installation, more answers are required to get the same results. If you take the time to navigate around the components, you'll also notice that there are more options available. We highly recommend that you read the documentation that is installed as part of ADK. The Unattended Windows Setup Reference goes into great detail on what each of the components is responsible for.

The next step is to create a new answer file within WSIM. Open the File menu, and click New Answer File. It will prompt you to save the answer file. Save it in the same directory, C:\W2012.

FIGURE 2.72

Browsing the Windows image components

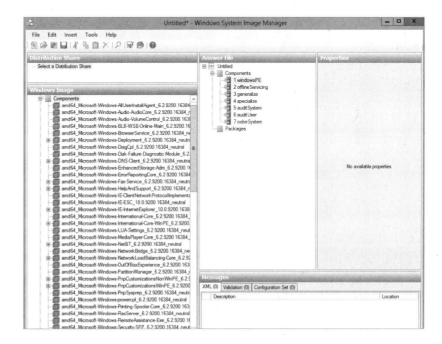

The Answer File pane is now populated (see Figure 2.73). Does what you see look familiar? It should. You can see each of the available configuration passes that are used for installing Windows underneath the Components object. You'll add components to the necessary passes to build up the answer file now.

Under Components in the Windows Image pane, navigate to amd64_Microsoft-Windows-International-Core-WinPE (Figure 2.74).

This component is responsible for configuring the Windows installation environment settings. You'll remember how you had to configure language settings in the manual clean installation at the start of the chapter. This component will automate that step. Right-click the component, and select Add Setting to Pass1 windowsPE.

You can now see that this component has been added to the new answer file in the Answer File pane under pass 1 windowsPE (see Figure 2.75). You can also see that the properties of the component are now available to edit in the top-right details pane. Notice that this component can be expanded to reveal a child object. It also can have properties that can be edited. You select an edit box of a property value and press F1 on your keyboard to access the help on that property. As you progress, you will need to do that to find out what the property does and what its possible values are.

FIGURE 2.73
Starting a new answer file

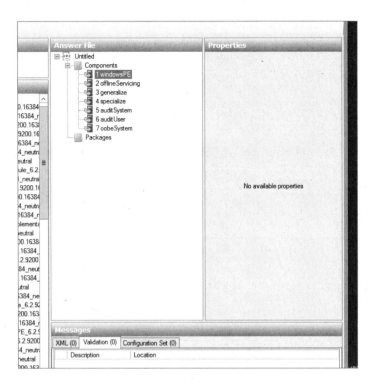

FIGURE 2.74
Select
component
to add to the
answer file

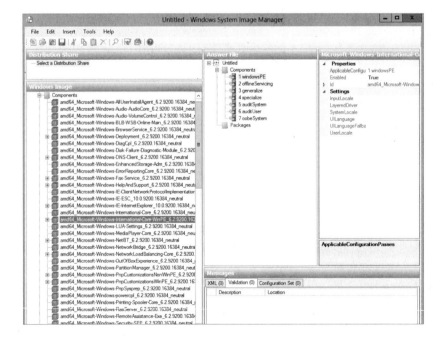

You can now edit the component. Add the following values:

Pass	Component	Property	Value
1	amd64_Microsoft-Windows-International-Core\ SetupUILanguage	InputLocale	en-us
		UserLocale	en-us
		UILanguage	en-us
		SystemLocale	en-us
		UILanguage	en-us

What you have done here is configured each of these settings to be US English (see Figure 2.75). Pressing F1 on any one of those properties will lead you to the help that gives the codes for alternative regional settings. Note that you have also edited the UILanguage property in the child component SetupUILanguage.

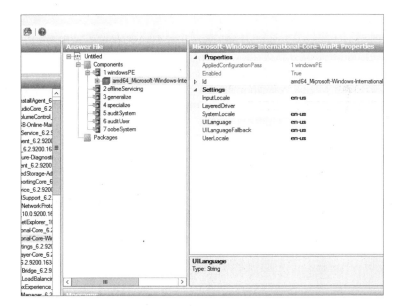

FIGURE 2.75
Configuring
the answer file
component

You'll now add some more components and edit their properties. (We will continue to use the previous table format; make sure you add the components to the pass mentioned in the first column of each table.)

Pass	Component	Property	Value
1	AMD64_Microsoft-Windows-Setup\ DiskConfiguration\Disk	DiskID	0
		WillWipeDisk	True

This Disk subcomponent that you are adding to the answer file in pass 1 tells the installer to manage Disk 0 in the server. Remember that in Microsoft-speak Disk 0 is the first disk in the computer. You have also told the installer to wipe this disk.

In the Answer File pane, you should expand the Disk subcomponent. You'll see two subcomponents called CreatePartitions and ModifyPartitions. Right-click each of those two subcomponents, and select Insert New. This will allow you to create a volume on your newly wiped Disk 0 and then format it using the following subcomponent property settings:

Pass	Component	Property	Value
1	AMD64_Microsoft-Windows-Setup\DiskConfiguration\ Disk\CreatePartitions\CreatePartition	Extend	True
		Order	1
		Type	Primary

Here you are instructing Windows Installer to create a partition and extend it, in other words, fill the entirety of Disk 0 with the new volume. Order instructs the installer to label the volume as 1 because you will refer to this label again in a moment.

You might not want to fill Disk 0 with one partition because it is signified by the setting Extend = True. You can instead set Size to whatever size in megabytes you want partition 1 to be, such as 40960 for a 40 GB volume. You should not set a value for size *and* set Extend = True because that would cause a conflict.

Pass	Component	Property	Value
1	AMD64_Microsoft-Windows-Setup\ DiskConfiguration\Disk\CreatePartitions\ ModifyPartition	Active	True
		Format	NTFS
		Label	Windows
		Letter	C
		Order	1
		PartitionsID	1

Here you can see where we refer to Order again. You're instructing the installer to format the previously created volume for you. It is set up as partition 1 using PartitionsID. In Microsoft-speak, partition 1 is the first partition; there is no partition 0. You set the volume as Active because you want to be able to boot from it. You format it with NTFS, label the volume as Windows, and give it the letter C.

The next part is a bit tricky. We've found that using the help documentation that we have already referred to is useful. But you'll also see how you will need another tool from ADK.

Pass	Component	Property	Value
1	AMD64_Microsoft-Windows-Setup\InstallImage\OSImage\InstallFrom\Metadata	Key	/IMAGE/NAME
		Value	Windows Server 2012 SERVERSTANDARD

When we originally tried to install Windows Server 2012 R2 using an unattended approach, the install would always stop to ask us to choose between the available editions of Windows on the DVD. This was obviously not what we wanted; we wanted an unattended installation. A search through the help file in ADK found that this subcomponent could help us select the correct edition. Unfortunately, it did not tell us what we should put in the property values. What it did tell us was that the values we needed were contained within our install image, install.wim.

So, we opened the Deployment and Imaging Tools Environment (command prompt), which is part of ADK and can be accessed using the start button on our task bar. We then ran the following command:

```
IMAGEX /info C:\W2012\INSTALL.WIM
```

The IMAGEX command is an ADK utility that allows you to manage WIM files. The syntax for the previous command is as follows:

```
IMAGEX.EXE /info <Path to Desired WIM File>
```

This produced a report on the contents of the Windows Server 2012 R2 x64 install image (see Figure 2.76).

Here's the snippet from Figure 2.76 that you need:

```
<NAME>Windows Server 2012 SERVERSTANDARD</NAME>
<DESCRIPTION> Windows Server 2012 SERVERSTANDARD</DESCRIPTION>
```

The Metadata subcomponent allows you to specify a key to search for in these results and then a value to match. In the previous snippet, you can see that there is a NAME key. It is under the path /IMAGE/PATH. The NAME key is used to uniquely identify each of the available editions of Windows contained within the install image. You can see the one you want for this example under IMAGE INDEX="2". That NAME key is set to Windows Server 2012 SERVERSTANDARD. Therefore, you set your Metadata component to search for and match a key called /IMAGE/NAME with a value of Windows Server 2012 SERVERSTANDARD. That image will be the one that the installer should install on the server. Phew! That's the hardest thing you'll do here; we promise.

The following tells the OS installer to install the selected image into the disk you previously selected and into the volume you have just created and formatted, in other words, the first partition on the first disk.

FIGURE 2.76
Server name
image snippet

Pass	Component	Property	Value
1	AMD64_Microsoft-Windows-Setup\ImageInstall\ OSImage\InstallTo	DiskID	0
		PartitionID	1

You use the UserData subcomponent to enter licensing information for this installation of Windows. You accept Microsoft's licensing terms by setting AcceptEula to True. Enter the name of the company for FullName and Organization, which is a common practice to signify ownership of the license. And our product key, which is shown only for illustrative purposes, is entered into Key in the subcomponent:

Pass	Component	Property	Value
1	AMD64_Microsoft-Windows-Setup\ UserData	AcceptEula	True
		FullName	Bigfirm
		Organization	Bigfirm
	AMD64_Microsoft-Windows-Setup\ UserData\ProductKey	Key	HFG76-34GFT-O6ID9-MNBW4-IYUSD

Add the following component into pass 4, "4 specialize." You use ComputerName, well, to set the name of the computer. That's not very mysterious. Set it to *. This tells the OS installer to generate a random name. You could type in something there if you wanted. Use TimeZone to configure the system clock. In this example, we've set it to the USA Eastern Standard Time Zone. A list of available zones is available by pressing F1:

Pass	Component	Property	Value
4	AMD64_Microsoft-Windows-Shell-Setup	ComputerName	*
		TimeZone	Eastern Standard Time

Add the following subcomponent to pass 7, "7 oobeSystem." Configure the Windows Firewall using NetworkLocation. Setting it to Work configures the firewall to be enabled but loosened suitably for a typical corporate network. ProtectYourPC turns on automatic updates and configures it to install updates automatically.

This component shows you how you can add a little extra to your installation that is not otherwise available in a manual installation:

Pass	Component	Property	Value
7	AMD64_Microsoft-Windows-Shell-Setup\OOBE	HideEULAPage	True
		NetworkLocation	Work
		ProtectYourPC	1

The last component you'll set up is a good one to keep in mind for laboratory environments where you might be using MSDN or TechNet licensing. Those subscriptions give you a limited number of activations for every license key. Your typical lab machine has a very short life, so it is pointless to use up your valuable activations.

This component allows you to disable the default process of autoactivation of your installation:

Pass	Component	Property	Value
7	AMD64_Microsoft-Windows-Security-Licensing-SPP-UX	SkipAutoActivation	False

Those are all the components you want to add. What you're now going to do is validate the answer file. On the Tools menu, select Validate Answer File. This will go through the properties and the values that you have entered. Anything that is glaringly wrong will lead to an error in the Messages pane. Everything should be OK if you've entered the components and property values as illustrated so far (see Figure 2.77).

You can save your answer file now. Click the File menu, and select Save Answer File As.

Save it as **autounattend.xml** in a location of your choice, such as `C:\Answer\autounattend.xml` (see Figure 2.78).

FIGURE 2.77
A validated
answer file

FIGURE 2.78
Saving the answer file

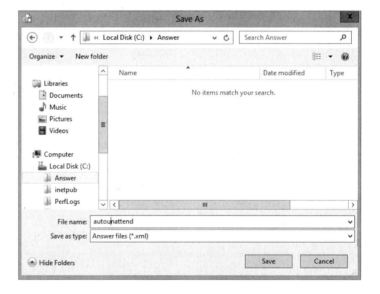

You might as well take a look at the XML file that you've created. Using Notepad, open your new answer file. You should have something like this:

```
<?xml version="1.0" encoding="utf-8"?>
<unattend xmlns="urn:schemas-microsoft-com:unattend">
    <settings pass="windowsPE">
```

```xml
        <component name="Microsoft-Windows-International-Core-
WinPE" processorArchitecture="amd64" publicKeyToken="31bf3856ad364e35"
language="neutral" versionScope="nonSxS" xmlns:wcm="http://schemas.microsoft.com/
WMIConfig/2002/State" xmlns:xsi="http://www.w3.org/2001/XMLSchema-instance">
            <InputLocale>en-us</InputLocale>
            <UserLocale>en-us</UserLocale>
            <UILanguage>en-us</UILanguage>
            <SystemLocale>en-us</SystemLocale>
            <UILanguageFallback>en-us</UILanguageFallback>
        </component>
        <component name="Microsoft-Windows-Setup" processorArchitecture="amd64"
publicKeyToken="31bf3856ad364e35" language="neutral" versionScope="nonSxS"
xmlns:wcm="http://schemas.microsoft.com/WMIConfig/2002/State" xmlns:xsi="http://
www.w3.org/2001/XMLSchema-instance">
            <DiskConfiguration>
                <Disk wcm:action="add">
                    <CreatePartitions>
                        <CreatePartition wcm:action="add">
                            <Extend>true</Extend>
                            <Order>1</Order>
                            <Type>Primary</Type>
                        </CreatePartition>
                    </CreatePartitions>
                    <ModifyPartitions>
                        <ModifyPartition wcm:action="add">
                            <Active>true</Active>
                            <Format>NTFS</Format>
                            <Label>Windows</Label>
                            <Letter>C</Letter>
                            <Order>1</Order>
                            <PartitionID>1</PartitionID>
                        </ModifyPartition>
                    </ModifyPartitions>
                    <DiskID>0</DiskID>
                    <WillWipeDisk>true</WillWipeDisk>
                </Disk>
            </DiskConfiguration>
            <ImageInstall>
                <OSImage>
                    <InstallFrom>
                        <MetaData wcm:action="add">
                            <Key>/IMAGE/NAME</Key>
                            <Value>Windows Server 2012 SERVERSTANDARD</Value>
                        </MetaData>
                    </InstallFrom>
                    <InstallTo>
                        <DiskID>0</DiskID>
```

```
                            <PartitionID>1</PartitionID>
                        </InstallTo>
                    </OSImage>
                </ImageInstall>
                <UserData>
                    <ProductKey>
                        <Key>HFG76-34GFT-06ID9-MNBW4-IYUSD</Key>
                    </ProductKey>
                    <AcceptEula>true</AcceptEula>
                    <FullName>BigFirm</FullName>
                    <Organization>BigFirm</Organization>
                </UserData>
            </component>
        </settings>
        <settings pass="specialize">
            <component name="Microsoft-Windows-Shell-Setup"
processorArchitecture="amd64" publicKeyToken="31bf3856ad364e35"
language="neutral" versionScope="nonSxS" xmlns:wcm="http://schemas.microsoft.com/
WMIConfig/2002/State" xmlns:xsi="http://www.w3.org/2001/XMLSchema-instance">
                <ComputerName>*</ComputerName>
                <TimeZone>Eastern Standard Time</TimeZone>
            </component>
        </settings>
        <settings pass="oobeSystem">
            <component name="Microsoft-Windows-Shell-Setup"
processorArchitecture="amd64" publicKeyToken="31bf3856ad364e35"
language="neutral" versionScope="nonSxS" xmlns:wcm="http://schemas.microsoft.com/
WMIConfig/2002/State" xmlns:xsi="http://www.w3.org/2001/XMLSchema-instance">
                <OOBE>
                    <HideEULAPage>true</HideEULAPage>
                    <NetworkLocation>Work</NetworkLocation>
                    <ProtectYourPC>1</ProtectYourPC>
                </OOBE>
            </component>
        </settings>
        <cpi:offlineImage cpi:source="wim:c:/w2012/install.wim#Windows Server 2012
SERVERSTANDARD" xmlns:cpi="urn:schemas-microsoft-com:cpi" />
</unattend>
```

You now have an answer file that is capable of answering all the questions that will be asked while installing Windows. All you need to do now is supply it to the OS installer.

Using an Answer File

This process is easy enough. You need to store the file autounattend.xml on the root of some form of removable storage. You will then boot up the new server using the correct Windows Server 2012 R2.

A WORD OF CAUTION

Don't go messing with this stuff on a machine that is valuable to you. Test it in a lab first. This is a destructive process; in other words, the hard disk on the computer you use for this will be wiped.

In our example, that will be the Windows Server 2012 R2 DVD. As soon as the server starts to boot from the DVD, you should also insert the removable storage that contains your answer file. The supported forms of removable storage are as follows:

CD/DVD   This requires your server to have two drives: a DVD drive, to boot and install Windows Server 2012 R2 from, and another drive to read the answer file CD or DVD.

Disk   How many servers have disk drives now? This will be OK for lab or older machines.

USB Memory Stick   This is the most likely of all the choices.

Pick your choice of media that is suitable for the server that you are going to build, and copy the answer file onto the root of that storage device.

If you are using a virtual machine, then here's a neat trick. Add a second virtual CD/DVD to the virtual machine where you intend to install Windows Server 2012 R2. Make sure your boot DVD has mounted the correct ISO for installing Windows. Create an ISO file that contains only your autounattend.xml file. You don't have a tool for that? That's OK, because there is one in ADK. Try running the following from your Deployment and Imaging Tools command prompt:

```
oscdimg -n C:\Answer C:\answer.iso
```

This will create an ISO file on C:\ called answer.iso using the contents of the folder C:\ Answer. Please make sure you have not placed your autounattend.xml in C:\ and are trying to make an ISO file from your entire hard disk! It's an easy trap to fall into. The syntax for the previous is as follows:

```
oscdimg -n <Folder to Use as a Source> <Location and Name of the New ISO Image>
```

OK, let's get rocking! Insert your Windows Server 2012 R2 DVD into your boot DVD drive on your server.

You should insert your answer file media as soon as the server has started to boot from the DVD. The first few times you do this you should watch what goes on to make sure the process runs cleanly. What should happen is that Windows Server 2012 R2 silently kicks off an installation, reboots, and waits for you to set the administrator password so you can log in. If the answer file has a mistake, then something else will happen such as the following:

◆   A dialog box with a question will appear and wait for human input.

◆   An error dialog box will appear.

◆   A critical failure will occur and cause a reboot.

You will need to revisit your answer file in WSIM if any of these happen.

If you have gotten everything right, then you now have an answer file that will completely automate your manual installations of Windows Server 2012 R2. You've also gotten a peek into some of the steps required for automated installations.

Installing a Sample Server Network for This Book's Examples

You are going to need a laboratory or test network to practice what you learn in this book.

To follow along with the examples, build two servers using the clean installation or unattended installation method. Our recommendation is that you use both methods for your first attempt to build this lab network. You can then use the unattended installation method for all future builds to speed things along.

Customize each of the two servers using the following settings:

SERVER 1

ITEM	CONFIGURATION
Full Computer Name	bf1.bigfirm.com
IPv4 Configuration	Address: 192.168.1.51
Subnet mask: 255.255.255.0	
Default gateway: 192.168.1.1	
DNS1: <blank>	
DNS2: <blank>	

SERVER 2

ITEM	CONFIGURATION
Full Computer Name	bf2.bigfirm.com
IPv4 Configuration	Address: 192.168.1.52
Subnet mask: 255.255.255.0	
Default gateway: 192.168.1.1	
DNS1: <blank>	
DNS2: <blank>	

At this point, you will be the proud owner of your very first Windows Server 2012 R2 server network.

The Bottom Line

Upgrade your old servers.   Microsoft has provided several upgrade options for Windows Server 2012 R2.

> **Master It**   You have a Windows 2008 x86 file server. What will your upgrade path be to Windows Server 2012 R2?

Configure your server.   Windows Server 2012 R2 allows you to use Server Manager and PowerShell to add or remove roles, role services, and features.

> **Master It**   You have started to deploy Windows Server 2012 R2. You are planning on automating as much of the build process as possible. What tool will you use to add or remove roles, role services, and features?

Build a small server farm.   Installing Windows Server normally requires that you sit in front of the machine and answer a number of questions. This is time-consuming and distracts administrators from other engineering or project tasks that they could be working on. A number of alternative techniques can be employed.

> **Master It**   You have been instructed to build four new servers with Windows Server 2012 R2. This will be the first time your organization will deploy Windows Server 2012 R2. Your department is short-staffed because a number of your colleagues are on vacation. You want to do this job quickly and efficiently. How will you do it?

Chapter 3

Introduction to Server Core

Microsoft designs and develops the next version of its products based on what the market demands. In addition, it fends off the competition by integrating the strengths and features the others have to offer. Thus, with Server Core, introduced in Windows Server 2008 and improved in Windows Server 2012 R2, Microsoft has enhanced its Windows operating systems to combat its competitors' and meet the demands of system administrators who want to work from the command line. Within this chapter, we'll explore what's new in the Windows Server 2012 R2 operating system and how to manage it using PowerShell.

In this chapter, you will learn to:

- ◆ Use the new functionality in Server Core
- ◆ Install and configure Server Core
- ◆ Set up Server Core for a branch-office deployment
- ◆ Remotely manage the operating system

What's New in Server Core

You're installing Windows Server 2012 R2 for the first time, and a couple of screens into the installation you see the installation options. Should you use the GUI or not? You like the benefits Server Core has with regard to security and overhead savings, but you like the point-and-click UI that comes with the GUI version. We have good news for you: In Windows Server 2008 R2, once Server Core was set up you couldn't switch back, but in Windows Server 2012 R2 you can now switch back and forth between Server Core and the GUI. The default installation choice is Server Core, but should you choose to install using the GUI, you will still have PowerShell available. Once you have the server set up and ready to run in production, you can simply switch over to Server Core.

Keep in mind as you read this chapter that even though you can switch to the GUI version to accomplish the same tasks, we will be using Server Core to do those tasks. For example, we will be showing you how to validate your copy of Windows using Server Core. You may find it easier to switch to the GUI version to accomplish this, and that's fine if you choose to do it that way. Most of the samples in this chapter are also in Chapter 2, "Installing and Upgrading to Windows Server 2012 R2," if you want to use the GUI for these tasks. PowerShell 3.0 now offers you more cmdlets to administer your Server Core server. The cmdlets' syntax is now simpler to understand. Many of the existing cmdlets have had parameters added to extend their functionality. See the Survival Guide later in this chapter for a complete list of the new cmdlets added in Windows Server 2012 R2.

WHAT IS SERVER CORE?

Server Core is Windows Server stripped to the minimum requirements to run an operating system. It runs without the GUI, Windows Explorer, Internet Explorer, and other dependent components. Removing the extras means that we have to cope without many of the administration tools that we know and love, namely, snap-ins built on the Microsoft Management Console. This leaves the PowerShell command prompt as our primary interface to the operating system.

So what does this all mean to you, the administrator?

Reduced Maintenance   Less code means fewer updates to perform.

Reduced Attack Surface   Without the fluff, there is less to attack. Roles and features can be installed as needed and the limited number of services will reduce the areas for attack.

Reduced Performance Requirements   Server Core takes fewer CPU cycles and less hard disk space, so the opportunity to repurpose hardware is increased with this option.

Installing Server Core

Before you install Server Core, keep in mind that since you can switch between Server Core and the GUI, it does not matter which version you initially set up. This allows you to set up the server in the GUI, as we showed you in Chapter 2, and then switch it over to Server Core.

The process for installing Windows Server 2012 R2 Server Core is as straightforward as other Windows Server 2012 R2 installations. You pop in the installation DVD and allow the server to boot from it. Then you "follow the bouncing ball." You can use an unattended installation .xml file to configure the OS all the way down to the installed features. You can generate the file with the Windows Automated Installation Kit, which we won't cover in this chapter.

The Setup program lets you select the operating system to install, as shown in Figure 3.1.

FIGURE 3.1
Selecting to install Server Core from the various editions of Windows Server 2012 R2

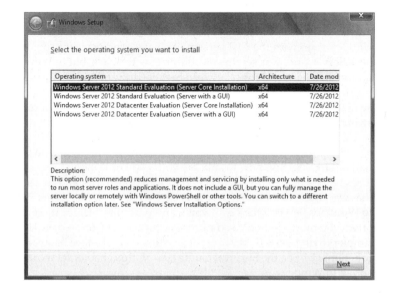

1. For Server Core, select the desired edition, Standard or Datacenter, and click Next.

2. Accept the license terms and click Next.

   The next screen asks which type of installation you want.

3. Since you are doing a clean install, select Custom.

   The next screen asks, "Where do you want to install Windows?" as shown in Figure 3.2.

FIGURE 3.2
Choosing the
installation
partition

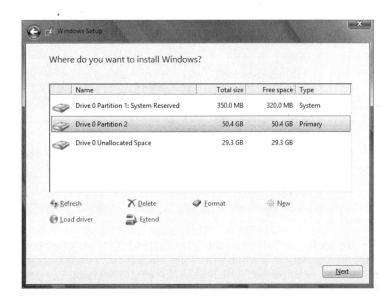

We prefer dividing the drive into two partitions: 50 GB for the operating system and the remainder for data or applications. This provides a smaller backup for the system drive. The tricky part of this is projecting the right size. Additional applications, service packs, security updates, and patches can drive up the overall size to the capacity of the small partition. This can cause system instability and potentially require a rebuild.

4. Using the options on the bottom of the screen, click New to create the 50 GB partition.

   Windows Setup also created the 350 MB system partition. This holds the recovery console operating system. You can't delete this partition. Don't worry about this unavailable space; thumb drives come in bigger sizes now.

5. After a successful installation, use the Administrator account to log on as with a full installation.

6. There is no assigned password, so enter a new one.

Once the installation finishes building the administrator's profile, the desktop appears, as shown in Figure 3.3, which looks very spartan. There's no Server Manager, no taskbar, no system tray—no nuttin'. There's just an open command prompt.

FIGURE 3.3
The barren
Server Core
user interface

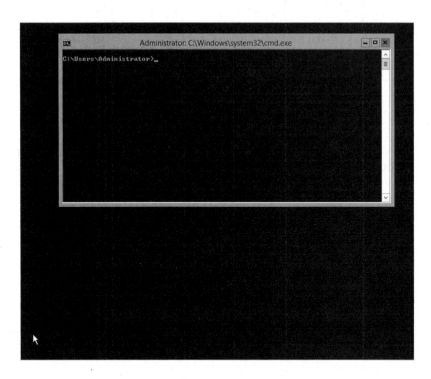

For this book, we've changed the default settings for the PowerShell command prompt for readability. The default is white letters on a black background. You can make similar changes by right-clicking the upper-left corner of the screen and selecting Properties. Then you can modify the color of the fonts and backgrounds on the Colors tab, as shown in Figure 3.4.

FIGURE 3.4
Modifying
the command
prompt
window

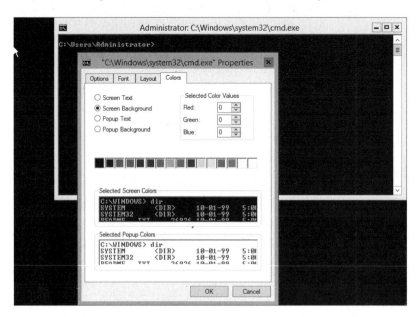

Server Core Survival Guide

Before getting into the details, you need to learn a few survival tips for handling this operating system. We'll discuss accessing Task Manager to control processes, start tasks, and view performance. Then we'll cover basic commands that we typically neglect when a flashy GUI is available. These will help you perform routine administration tasks and allow access to the network.

Switching between Server Core and the GUI and Vice Versa

I'm placing this at the top of the Survival Guide because it may prove to be very handy should you need to switch from Server Core to the GUI and vice versa. Many administrators complete the initial setup using the GUI and switch over to Server Core for production.

You will need to download the script located here: `http://gallery.technet .microsoft.com/scriptcenter/Switch-between-Windows-9680265d/file/70875/1/ SwitchGUIServerCORE.zip`.

This script is used no matter which version you are switching to. Before you run the script, you need to enable scripts on the server; they are disabled by default. To do this, run the following cmdlet:

```
PS C:\>Set-ExecutionPolicy AllSigned
```

Using PowerShell, you can now run the script from the location where you downloaded the file, as shown in Figure 3.5.

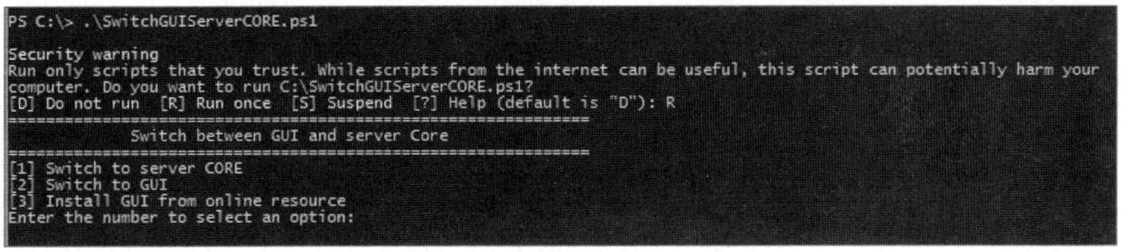

FIGURE 3.5
Running the PowerShell script

Where prompted, add the integer value as follows:

1—To switch to Server Core

2—To switch to the GUI

3—To install the GUI from an online resource

Be patient; this process takes a few minutes to complete. Once it has finished, you will be prompted to reboot the server. When the server reboots, you should be in the version you need.

Accessing Task Manager

Server Core provides a few graphical user interfaces. The most important is Task Manager. It's the same one you have come to know and love with other Windows versions. There are two primary ways to open Task Manager:

Ctrl+Alt+Del   You can open the trustworthy Security dialog box by pressing the Ctrl+Alt+Del key combination. On this page, you can opt to lock the workstation, log out, or start Task Manager.

Ctrl+Shift+Esc   You can use the "MSCE secret handshake" method of Ctrl+Shift+Esc to start Task Manager. Now that you know this, you're part of an elite club. It was once one of those undocumented features.

Closing the Command Prompt

As a good system administrator, you close applications when you've finished using them so as not to consume valuable resources, such as memory and CPU cycles, right? So, you will probably close the command prompt after completing a task while logged onto Server Core.

After realizing that you just closed your only interface to the OS, you can perform the following steps to return to the command prompt:

1. Open Task Manager, as discussed earlier.

2. Click File ➤ New Task (Run). This is just like the Run prompt you find on the Start menu.

3. Enter **cmd** and then click OK, as shown in Figure 3.6.

FIGURE 3.6
"Create new task" window

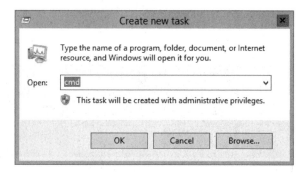

4. Enter **PowerShell** at the command prompt, which will switch you to the PowerShell command prompt.

Changing the Administrator's Password

You'll use PowerShell for most administration tasks, but there are still a few command-line tools that are easier to use, and so we include them in our examples.

After logging onto a Server Core installation for the first time, you might be wondering how you can change the administrator password in the future.

You can do so with the net user command:

```
PS C:\Users\Administrator>net user administrator *
Type a password for the user:
```

```
Retype the password to confirm:
The command completed successfully.
```

The asterisk prompts you for the new password.

The net command is a really old one. It was old when NT was new technology.

One of the newer ways to change a password is using the PowerShell cmdlet Set-ADAccountPassword. The following is the complete cmdlet with properties:

```
Set-ADAccountPassword [-Identity] <ADAccount> [-AuthType {<Negotiate> | <Basic>}]
[-Credential <PSCredential>] [-NewPassword <SecureString>] [-OldPassword
<SecureString>] [-Partition <string>] [-PassThru <switch>] [-Reset <switch>]
[-Server <string>] [-Confirm] [-WhatIf] [<CommonParameters>]
```

Accessing File Shares

Given that Windows Server is a network operating system, you will have to access shares on the network. If you're dependent on Windows Explorer, you may have never attempted to connect to a shared folder with the command prompt. First, to display the shares on a server, use the net view command:

```
PS C:\Users\Administrator>net view \\bf1
Shared resources at \\bf1

Share name  Type    Used as  Comment

-------------------------------------------------------------------------------
isos        Disk
netlogon    Disk
Public      Disk
SYSVOL      Disk
temp        Disk
The command completed successfully.
```

Then, to access a volume, use the net use command, which maps a share to a drive letter:

```
PS C:\Users\Administrator>net use Z: \\bf1\temp
The command completed successfully
```

Within the command prompt, you can switch to that drive by entering the drive letter, like **Z:**. Then use your MS-DOS commands to get around the folders.

To remove the mapped drive, use the following command:

```
PS C:\Users\Administrator>net use Z: /del
Z: was deleted successfully
```

You can also use PowerShell's get-psdrive cmdlet to get drive information and New-PSDrive to map a new drive. Here is the complete New-PSDrive cmdlet for your reference:

```
New-PSDrive [-Name] <String> [-PSProvider] <String> [-Root] <String> [-Credential
<PSCredential> ] [-Description <String> ] [-Persist] [-Scope <String> ]
[-Confirm] [-WhatIf] [-UseTransaction] [ <CommonParameters>]
```

Finding Commands from A to Z

Command-line references are very handy. There is one in Windows Server 2012 R2 for help on the full installation; however, it has Internet hyperlinks to the explanations for all of those commands. The best location for finding a list of available commands is the Command-Line Reference (http://technet.microsoft.com/en-us/library/cc754340.aspx), which offers an A–Z menu. To find a command that will do the job, this is the first place to go.

Most of the PowerShell cmdlets can be located from this parent page (http://technet.microsoft.com/en-us/library/hh801904.aspx).

You will see all the administration categories with links to hundreds of cmdlets.

Reading Text Files with Notepad

In a full installation, you use Notepad to edit text files. It's also available in Server Core as well. This Notepad utility is "old-school"; it was a rerelease of a very early version. It's not as old-school as VI, but it has been resurrected from the days of NT. (If you get that comment, you *are* old.)

Incredibly, the designers of Server Core were actually thinking about dropping this handy tool until the marketing guys got feedback from users. This would have been a huge mistake. Notepad is an essential tool for Server Core.

We have a sample text file called ipconfigCommand.txt. To open the text file, use the following command:

```
C:\Users\Administrator>notepad documents\ipconfigCommand.txt
```

We like using Notepad to construct complex commands. At the bottom of a help text file like this one, you can cut, copy, paste, and edit the examples to get what you need. Then you can copy and paste them into the command prompt. The output can be copied from the command window using the Mark command in the context menu, which you display by right-clicking the window. Then paste it back into Notepad.

Editing the Registry

SCRegedit.wsf is a script developed by the Server Core team to perform common tasks that involve editing the registry. You can use the parameter /cli to list common tasks on Server Core. It may not be all-inclusive for what you need to do, but it does list the MSCE secret handshake for opening Task Manager.

Since scregedit.wsf is a VB script, you have to run it through an interpreter. It's located in the System32 folder, so you have to change the directory to it:

```
C:\Windows\System32>cscript scregedit.wsf /cli
```

Rebooting and Shutting Down

There's also a PowerShell command to reboot and shut down the server. You can even enter the reason for the reboot or shutdown as a remark. Use the following command for rebooting a server:

```
PS C:\> Restart-Computer
```

To restart remote computers you can use this example, which shuts down two remote computers (Server01 and Server02) and the local computer (localhost):

```
PS C:\> Restart-Computer -ComputerName Server01, Server02, localhost
```

Initial Configurations for Server Core

As we stated earlier in this chapter you can activate the GUI and manage your server via Server Manager, as shown in Figure 3.7, and then switch back to the command line when you're satisfied with the configuration. We want to show you how to configure the Server Core server should you choose not to install the GUI, so we will walk you through using the command prompt to get the server running.

FIGURE 3.7
Server Manager local properties window on a standard Windows installation

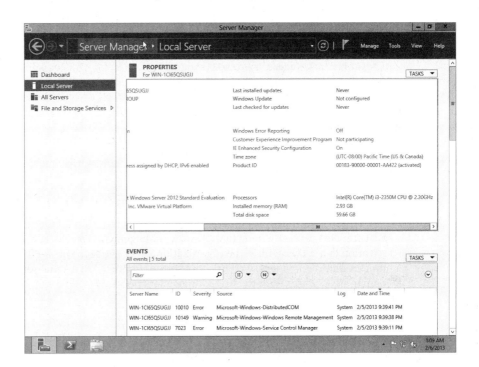

Providing Computer Information

First, we'll examine four of the most basic configuration tasks you would normally perform in Server Manager when doing a fresh GUI installation of Windows Server. All of these can also be performed from the command line:

- Add a product ID key and activate the server.
- Set the time zone.
- Configure networking.
- Provide a computer name and domain.

ENTERING THE PRODUCT KEY AND ACTIVATING THE INSTALLATION

If you haven't noticed, the Windows Server 2012 R2 installation process doesn't require a product key. The operating system will require it eventually; for Windows Server 2012 R2, the time frame is 60 days. On full installations when the grace period is up, you will experience reduced functionality mode (RFM). This will give you a black desktop and persistent notifications, and Windows Update will apply only critical security patches.

The `slmgr.vbs` script provides the product key and activates the server. The traditional process includes entering the key followed by activating the server online. Note in the following command example and later ones that `rem` is a remark that isn't processed by the command prompt or batch files:

```
rem Entering the product ID key
cscript c:\windows\system32\slmgr.vbs
-ipk q7y83-w4fvq-6mc6c-6qqtd-tpm88
Microsoft (R) Windows Script Host Version 5.8
Copyright (C) Microsoft Corporation. All rights reserved.

Installed product key q7y83-w4fvq-6mc6c-6qqtd-tpm88 successfully.
```

The online activation is also performed with the same script:

```
rem online activation
cscript c:\windows\system32\slmgr.vbs -ato
```

In larger environments, volume licensing is the predominant method of obtaining Microsoft software. This process can include the Key Management Service (KMS), which centralizes the activation to a server within the organization. Since the scenario we'll be discussing is for a branch-office deployment, we'll discuss setting up the KMS on this server later in the section, "Managing Licenses with the Key Management Service."

SETTING THE TIME ZONE

Server Core isn't completely devoid of control panel GUIs: the Time and Date control panel remains. The following command opens it:

```
control timedate.cpl
```

After you set the time and date settings you can verify the change, by using this command:

```
PS C:\Users\Administrator>w32tm /tz
Time zone: Current:TIME_ZONE_ID_DAYLIGHT Bias: 300min (UTC=LocalTime+Bias)
  [Standard Name:"Eastern Standard Time" Bias:0min Date:(M:10 D:5 DoW:0)]
  [Daylight Name:"Eastern Daylight Time" Bias:-60min Date:(M:4 D:1 DoW:0)]
```

CONFIGURING THE NETWORK SETTINGS

The primary item that needs to change for the network is the static IP address.

You can use ipconfig or use a PowerShell cmdlet to get some basic network configuration info:

```
PS C:\Users\Administrator> get-netipconfiguration

InterfaceAlias       : Ethernet
InterfaceIndex       : 12
```

```
InterfaceDescription : Intel(R) 82574L Gigabit Network Connection
NetProfile.Name      : Network
IPv4Address          : 192.168.1.20
IPv6DefaultGateway   :
IPv4DefaultGateway   : 192.168.1.1
DNSServer            : 192.168.1.1
```

By default, the configuration uses the Local Area Connection. You can use the PowerShell New-NetIPAddress cmdlet to change it. Here is the cmdlet with properties:

```
New-NetIPAddress [-IPAddress] <String> -InterfaceAlias <String> [-AddressFamily
<AddressFamily> ] [-AsJob] [-CimSession <CimSession[]> ] [-DefaultGateway
<String> ] [-PolicyStore <String> ] [-PreferredLifetime <TimeSpan> ]
[-PrefixLength <Byte> ] [-SkipAsSource <Boolean> ] [-ThrottleLimit <Int32>
] [-Type <Type> ] [-ValidLifetime <TimeSpan> ] [-Confirm] [-WhatIf] [
<CommonParameters>]
```

PROVIDING A COMPUTER NAME AND DOMAIN

To add a computer to a domain, what PowerShell cmdlet should you use? Hmm... add a computer, how about Add-Computer? Too easy!

```
PS c:\Users\Administrator>Add-Computer
```

With PowerShell cmdlets you do not have numerous switches and parameters. Many of the cmdlets prompt you for the parameter, making the learning curve much easier, because you need to remember only the cmdlet, not all the parameters. With that said, you will see a pop-up prompting you for the login credentials (Figure 3.8).

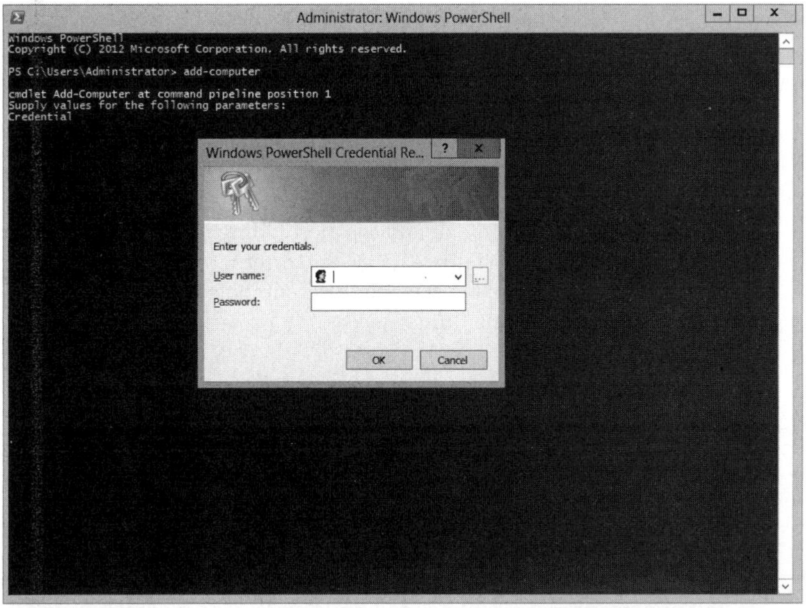

FIGURE 3.8
Enter your
login credentials.

After you log in, you will be asked for the domain name:

```
cmdlet Add-Computer at command pipeline position 1
Supply values for the following parameters:
Credential
DomainName: BigFirm.com
```

By default, the Windows Setup program assigns a really imaginative computer name. You can find that using the hostname command:

```
PS c:\Users\Administrator>hostname
WIN-AG6PVO7DM2A
```

Since that name isn't very user friendly, we'll change it to **Bfsc1.** (It's not a huge improvement, but at least you can type it without your fingers getting in a knot.) The following command tells PowerShell that you want to rename the computer:

```
PS c:\Users\Administrator>Rename-Computer
```

PowerShell will then prompt you for the new computer name:

```
cmdlet Rename-Computer at command pipeline position 1
Supply values for the following parameters:
NewName:bfsc1
```

Updating the Server

Next, you'll perform the typical housekeeping chores to update the server with the latest revisions and security patches. This consists of two steps:

1. Enable automatic updating and feedback.

2. Download and install updates.

ENABLING AUTOMATIC UPDATING

You can modify how automatic updates behave with just a few commands using SCONFIG. At the command prompt type **SCONFIG**. You will see a menu appear in your command window. Select option 5, Windows Update Settings. It will first tell you the current setting, which is Manual by default. To change it to Automatic, simply type the letter **A**. Figure 3.9 shows the Server Configuration menu and the alert telling us that automatic updates have been set.

You can also see in Figure 3.9 all the different tasks you can use SCONFIG for. We have covered some of these tasks using different tools like PowerShell, but this tool is another option to accomplish the same thing.

DOWNLOADING AND INSTALLING UPDATES

For this step on a full installation, we prefer to open the system properties of the computer and navigate to the Automatic Updates tab. Then we click the hyperlink Windows Update Web Site to kick off the download and installation of patches. However, this uses Internet Explorer, which isn't installed on Server Core. If you look back at Figure 3.9, you will see that option 6, Download and Install Updates, can take care of this for you.

After you enter **6** at the command prompt, SCONFIG will ask you if you want to search for all updates or just recommended updates. When you make your selection, it will return your results. You can then choose to install all, none, or just individual updates.

FIGURE 3.9
Automatic
updates using
SCONFIG

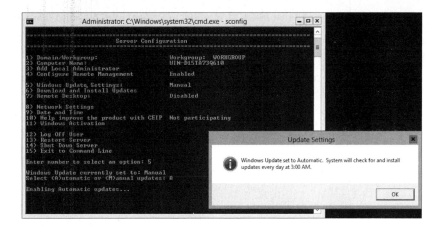

SAMPLE SCRIPT DISCLAIMER

Remember, scripts you find on the Microsoft websites are samples, which means "You are on your own." Microsoft stands behind the object model that it develops, but scripting is different. You have the ability to modify the script; thus, you have the opportunity to destroy your setup. You should understand that your scripts and samples may error-out or have syntax errors. It's up to you to generate an error-free script to do what you want it to do. Since this chapter is devoted to explaining Server Core, a description of VBS scripting and detailed discussions of any samples are outside our focus area.

Customizing This Server

In this stage, you get into applying the infrastructure roles and enabling for remote administration. Here are the steps:

1. Add roles and features.

2. Enable Remote Desktop.

3. Configure Windows Firewall.

ADDING ROLES AND FEATURES

The Server Manager console introduced in the full installation of Windows Server 2012 made the installation of roles and features straightforward. Basically, you select the box, and it's installed. If there are prerequisites that need to be installed in addition to the desired role, the Add Roles and Features Wizard will notify you. Then it will install them as you move through the wizard. In Server Core, the process is similar. The command results will notify you of any prerequisites but won't install them. Then you will have to issue multiple commands to add the prerequisites and roles.

The roles we are going to add are a domain controller (Active Directory Domain Services), DNS, DHCP, and Print and Document Services. Basic file services are already installed and supported with the File Server role service. We'll add a couple of features as well, including Windows Server Backup to provide backup capability.

The following PowerShell cmdlet lists the available roles and features:

```
rem list available (enabled and disabled) roles
PS C:\Users\administrator>Get-WindowsFeature
```

Now that you have the list in front of you, you can see the name of the role to add to the next cmdlet. The following list shows the DHCP Server role. You want to use the entry in the Name column as a parameter for the cmdlet.

```
Display Name                            Name                   Install State
[ ]DHCP Server                          DHCP                   available
[ ]Active Directory Domain Services     AD-Domain-Services     available
[ ]DNS Server                           DNS                    available
[ ]Print and Document Services          Print-Services         available
PS C:\Users\administrator>Add-WindowsFeature DHCP
```

Each role may take a few minutes to install. PowerShell will let you know if there are any problems with the installation. It will also let you know if any prerequisites are required. After you add the role, you can run Get-WindowsFeature again to see if the status shows Installed. Let's install the remaining features:

```
PS C:\Users\administrator>Add-WindowsFeature AD-Domain-Services
PS C:\Users\administrator>Add-WindowsFeature DNS
PS C:\Users\administrator>Add-WindowsFeature Print-Services
```

ENABLING REMOTE DESKTOP

Again, SCONFIG comes to our assistance. If you refer back to Figure 3.9, you will see this as option 7, Remote Desktop. After you enter **7** at the command prompt, it will ask you to enable or disable Remote Desktop. Select Enable by typing the letter **E**. You will be prompted whether to allow clients running any version of Remote Desktop or only clients running Remote Desktop with Network Level Authentication.

Enter your choice; it will send you a confirmation pop-up and you're finished!

CONFIGURING THE FIREWALL

You have some firewall configurations to perform. The firewall needs to allow Remote Administration protocols through it. This includes configuring the ports to allow communication that the Microsoft Management Console snap-ins require. The following command enables protocols associated with the Remote Administration group:

```
netsh advfirewall firewall set rule group="Remote Administration" new enable=yes
```

This group includes all the MMC ports that can be accessed on the server. There are subsets of the protocols so you can have fine-grained firewall policies to remotely manage specific MMC operations, such as Event Viewer, Disk Management, File and Print Services, and Task Scheduler.

Surprisingly, this group doesn't include Remote Desktop. It is part of its own group of the same name. It should be enabled with the following command, which, by the way, is the example in the embedded help of netsh advfirewall firewall set rule. No real wizardry is performed in generating this one. (The new parameter indicates adding a new setting to the rule.)

```
netsh advfirewall firewall set rule group="Remote Desktop" new enable=yes
```

If you want to administer the firewall from the MMC, you will need to also run the following command:

```
netsh advfirewall set currentprofile settings remotemanagement enable
```

Although the firewall should stay enabled, there may be times, such as testing a new application, when you may want to disable it. Here are the commands for turning it on and off:

```
netsh advfirewall set allprofiles state on
netsh advfirewall set allprofiles state off
```

You can also reset the firewall with this command should you make a configuration mistake:

```
netsh advfirewall reset
```

The last firewall command we will show you is probably the most commonly used, which is to enable or disable a port. Here is an example of how to add and delete port 1433 for SQL Server:

```
netsh advfirewall firewall add rule name="Open SQL Server Port 1433" dir=in
action=allow protocol=TCP localport=1433

netsh advfirewall firewall delete rule name="Open SQL Server Port 1433"
protocol=tcp localport=1433
```

We also need to show you the PowerShell cmdlet with properties that you can use to configure the firewall. You can use this cmdlet to set rules, modify rules, and control behavior by changing the properties:

```
Set-NetFirewallProfile -Profile Domain,Public,Private -Enabled True
```

To remove a firewall rule just use this:

```
Remove-NetFirewallRule -Action Block
```

Administering Server Core Remotely

Before you get into configuring the roles you installed on the server, you need to be aware of the options for remote administration. We've touched on them briefly, and you will see them being used in the configurations of the roles in the following sections.

Remote Desktop is a very reliable and secure method of administering remote standard installations, and it is available on Server Core as well. The Microsoft Management Console and its snap-ins are excellent for Server Core administration as long as the network supports it. A new option is Windows Remote Shell, which provides a command-line connection to the remote server.

MANAGING SERVERS WITH REMOTE DESKTOP

Terminal Services (Administration mode) was released with Windows 2000. It was a welcome addition because it provided a virtual desktop environment of the computer you connected to. Windows Server 2003 improved it by making it a default installation. It is an essential method to perform remote work on servers. We have commonly installed and configured applications on Windows servers located on the opposite side of the North American continent using this method. This is a reliable option for Server Core.

With Windows Server 2012 Server Core, you have to realize the desktop is still just the command prompt and a few GUI tools. It's the same as being logged on locally. There are methods for publishing just the command prompt of Server Core to your desktop as a RemoteApp, but we don't recommend doing so. You will still need GUI tools such as Task Manager, Notepad, and the Registry Editor, which are part of your Server Core essentials.

Remember, Remote Desktop and its firewall policy must be enabled to be available. We did this earlier in the "Initial Configurations for Server Core" section.

Managing Remotely with MMC Snap-Ins

Administrators have found the Microsoft Management Console to be a versatile method of managing remote computers. Its strength lies in the use of the RPC protocol and integrated Windows authentication, making it quick and efficient in managing domain-based computers within a LAN.

You can work around the authentication with alternate credentials. On the workstation, you can run the following command to register these credentials:

```
cmdkey /add:bfsc1 /user:Administrator /pass:P@ssw0rd
```

You could opt to leave the /pass parameter off to be prompted for the password. After registering your credentials, you can connect to the server through the snap-in.

In previous versions of Windows Server, you needed to install the adminpak.msi package to have the snap-ins manage all the Windows services. In Windows Server 2012, the adminpak.msi package is replaced by the Remote Server Administration Tools feature. This makes its installation easier and more fine-tuned. In Figure 3.10, you can see that Remote Server Administration Tools has been enabled through the Add Roles and Features Wizard.

FIGURE 3.10
Installing the Remote Server Administration Tools feature

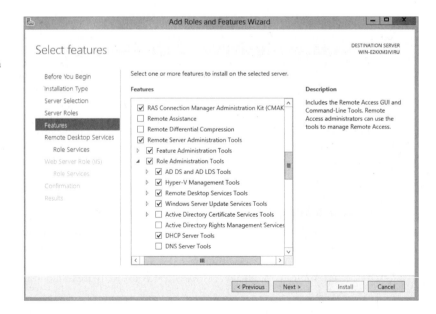

If you like, you can connect to another computer when you add a snap-in to a new MMC. Some snap-ins allow multiple servers to be added into one tree for consolidated administration. The following steps create an MMC for managing the DHCP service on the Windows Server 2012 Server Core installation. Please note that these steps can be performed only after the DHCP service is started and authorized. This is discussed in the "Configuring the DHCP Service" section.

1. After installing the Remote Server Administration Tools on a full installation, at the Run prompt enter **MMC**.

2. From the File drop-down menu, select Add/Remove Snap-in.

3. The Add/Remove Snap-in window is presented and lists the available snap-ins you can add to this MMC instance.

4. Select the DHCP snap-in, and click Add. Then click OK.

5. In the MMC, right-click the DHCP icon, and select Add Server.

6. In the Add Server window, the authorized DHCP servers are listed in the bottom area, as shown in Figure 3.11. Select the Server Core instance.

FIGURE 3.11
Adding a DHCP
server to an MMC

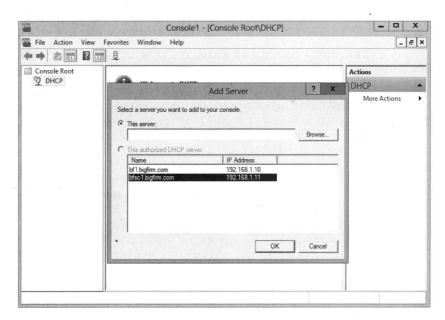

7. Click OK, and the selected DHCP server will be displayed and can be navigated through, as shown in Figure 3.12.

FIGURE 3.12
DHCP console focused on the Server Core instance

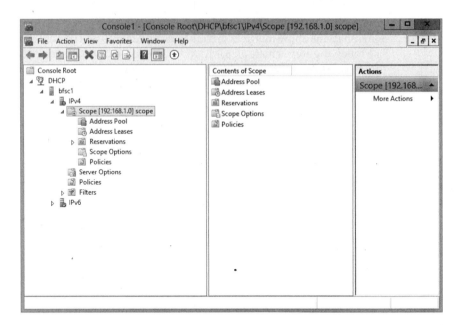

SENDING COMMANDS REMOTELY: WINDOWS REMOTE SHELL

Windows Remote Shell allows commands to be sent to a server. Similar to Telnet, this will allow you to connect to a server and then run a command from a remote command prompt. However, it doesn't allow a continuous connection like the one Telnet provides. It sends the command, receives the results, and then closes the connection.

This is a light client-server application based on Simple Object Access Protocol (SOAP) technology. For this service, all you really need to understand about SOAP is that the client uses XML-formatted text to send the command to the server, and the output sent back to the client is in the same format using HTTP. Text-based communication can be easily read with text editors like Notepad, and HTTP is easy to sniff with a protocol analyzer. So, don't consider it a secure method of managing a server. You have to lock it down.

Microsoft offers an option for test-driving Windows Remote Shell with the `winrm quickconfig` command. However, it sets it up with HTTP and TCP port 5985. This setup, as they recommend, is not meant for production environments. To lock it down, you need to ensure that the communication is encrypted and the server is authenticated. IPsec provides this security, but you may not have that available. You can set Windows Remote Shell for HTTPS (SSL) communication, which uses a server-based certificate to authenticate the server and encrypt the connection.

We will go through the basic steps to get this flying.

GETTING A CERTIFICATE

There are two options in getting a certificate: buy one from a repudiated certificate authority or set up your own certificate authority and request a certificate from it. The latter is much less expensive, especially using Windows Server.

Your own certificate authority is also not hard to set up; however, you should have a fully baked plan on how this will be accomplished for a production Active Directory environment. You need to consider decisions that will have lasting effects throughout the organization. And these effects will require manual administration to remove them. We won't go into detail about this in this section. We're going to be "quick and dirty" on this as in a lab environment.

On the full-installation Windows Server 2012 domain controller, the Active Directory Certificate Services role is installed. A typical installation of this role would include the web enrollment component. This would require Internet Information Services (IIS). We won't go through getting that installed. We will only select the Certificate Authority service. This will allow the creation and administration of certificates. In addition, it will allow the computers of the domain to request certificates using the RPC protocol and Kerberos authentication. We will install a *trusted root enterprise certificate authority*. Root is selected because it is the first and only domain in the organization. Enterprise is selected because it uses Active Directory to verify servers and users are trustworthy. Because it uses Active Directory, it automatically issues verified users and computers. Since Bfsc1 is a domain controller, it automatically requests a certificate. Quick and dirty.

We want to view the certificate using Server Core. (We first tried using the MMC remotely, but for security reasons, this is not an option.) There are two methods of viewing certificates on the Server Core installation—the `certutil` command or PowerShell's `dir` command:

```
rem using certutil
PS C:\Users\Administrator.BIGFIRM\Documents>certutil -viewstore my
my
```

The my refers to the local machine store's own certificates. When you run `certutil`, a window appears listing the installed certificates, as shown in Figure 3.13.

FIGURE 3.13
Certificates displayed by `certutil`

Notice the hyperlink underneath the only installed certificate, "Click here to view certificate properties." This will open the certificate information.

PowerShell offers another route to get to the certificates through its providers. Generally, the provider is a group of objects that PowerShell navigates through. The file system is an example of a provider, so you can do operations on file and folder objects within it. Another provider is the certificate store. You can navigate through the certificate store to view and manage certificates.

The `dir` command is an alias created by the PowerShell developers for the `get-items` command. Thus, you can use your standard MS-DOS command prompt to navigate through the file system. The following command lists the same location as the `certutil` command did earlier:

```
rem starting powershell
C:\Users\Administrator.BIGFIRM >powershell

PS C:\Users\administrator.BIGFIRM> dir cert:\localmachine\my | FL

Subject      : CN=BFSC1.bigfirm.com
Issuer       : CN=bigfirm-BF1-CA, DC=bigfirm, DC=com
Thumbprint   : 03ADB670C63E8D1CDB764CD7AA589C51D854307C
FriendlyName :
NotBefore    : 7/23/2009 6:55:41 PM
NotAfter     : 7/23/2010 6:55:41 PM
Extensions   : {System.Security.Cryptography.Oid, System.Security.Cryptography
               .Oid, System.Security.Cryptography.Oid, System.Security.Cryptogra
               phy.Oid...}
```

The `| FL` parameter is actually another command in shorthand. It formats the output of the `dir` command into a line-delimited list. We like using this format because the values are not truncated as the table format tends to do. In this specific case, the table format (not shown) doesn't truncate the most important value, the thumbprint.

CREATING A LISTENER

The listener tells the Windows Remote Shell service which port and IP address to listen to and respond to client requests. By default, the HTTP port is 5985, and the HTTPS port is 5986. You can view the default settings with the following command. In the output, the attributes `<cfg:HTTP>` and `<cfg:HTTPS>` indicate the port settings. Despite what you may think about XML, the parameter of the command is `format:pretty`. The output appears redundant. However, the top half starting with `<cfg:Client>` is for the client settings that would send requests to other servers. The lower half starting with `<cfg:Service>` is for the service that receives the requests to run on this server.

```
PS C:\Users\administrator.BIGFIRM>winrm get winrm/config -format:pretty
<cfg:Config xml:lang="en-US" xmlns:cfg="http://schemas.microsoft.com/wbem/wsman/
1/config">
    <cfg:MaxEnvelopeSizekb>150</cfg:MaxEnvelopeSizekb>
    <cfg:MaxTimeoutms>60000</cfg:MaxTimeoutms>
    <cfg:MaxBatchItems>32000</cfg:MaxBatchItems>
```

```
<cfg:MaxProviderRequests>4294967295</cfg:MaxProviderRequests>
<cfg:Client>
    <cfg:NetworkDelayms>5000</cfg:NetworkDelayms>
    <cfg:URLPrefix>wsman</cfg:URLPrefix>
    <cfg:AllowUnencrypted>false</cfg:AllowUnencrypted>
    <cfg:Auth>
        <cfg:Basic>true</cfg:Basic>
        <cfg:Digest>true</cfg:Digest>
        <cfg:Kerberos>true</cfg:Kerberos>
        <cfg:Negotiate>true</cfg:Negotiate>
        <cfg:Certificate>true</cfg:Certificate>
        <cfg:CredSSP>false</cfg:CredSSP>
    </cfg:Auth>
    <cfg:DefaultPorts>
        <cfg:HTTP>5985</cfg:HTTP>
        <cfg:HTTPS>5986</cfg:HTTPS>
    </cfg:DefaultPorts>
    <cfg:TrustedHosts></cfg:TrustedHosts>
</cfg:Client>
<cfg:Service>
    <cfg:RootSDDL>O:NSG:BAD:P(A;;GA;;;BA)S:P(AU;FA;GA;;;WD)(AU;SA;GWGX;;;WD)
</cfg:RootSDDL>
    <cfg:MaxConcurrentOperations>4294967295</cfg:MaxConcurrentOperations>
    <cfg:MaxConcurrentOperationsPerUser>15</cfg:MaxConcurrentOperationsPerUs
er>
    <cfg:EnumerationTimeoutms>60000</cfg:EnumerationTimeoutms>
    <cfg:MaxConnections>25</cfg:MaxConnections>
    <cfg:MaxPacketRetrievalTimeSeconds>120</cfg:MaxPacketRetrievalTimeSecond
s>
    <cfg:AllowUnencrypted>false</cfg:AllowUnencrypted>
    <cfg:Auth>
        <cfg:Basic>false</cfg:Basic>
        <cfg:Kerberos>true</cfg:Kerberos>
        <cfg:Negotiate>true</cfg:Negotiate>
        <cfg:Certificate>false</cfg:Certificate>
        <cfg:CredSSP>false</cfg:CredSSP>
        <cfg:CbtHardeningLevel>Relaxed</cfg:CbtHardeningLevel>
    </cfg:Auth>
    <cfg:DefaultPorts>
        <cfg:HTTP>5985</cfg:HTTP>
        <cfg:HTTPS>5986</cfg:HTTPS>
    </cfg:DefaultPorts>
    <cfg:IPv4Filter>*</cfg:IPv4Filter>
    <cfg:IPv6Filter>*</cfg:IPv6Filter>
    <cfg:EnableCompatibilityHttpListener>false</cfg:EnableCompatibilityHttpL
```

```
istener>
        <cfg:EnableCompatibilityHttpsListener>false</cfg:EnableCompatibilityHttp
sListener>
        <cfg:CertificateThumbprint></cfg:CertificateThumbprint>
    </cfg:Service>
    <cfg:Winrs>
        <cfg:AllowRemoteShellAccess>true</cfg:AllowRemoteShellAccess>
        <cfg:IdleTimeout>180000</cfg:IdleTimeout>
        <cfg:MaxConcurrentUsers>5</cfg:MaxConcurrentUsers>
        <cfg:MaxShellRunTime>2147483647</cfg:MaxShellRunTime>
        <cfg:MaxProcessesPerShell>15</cfg:MaxProcessesPerShell>
        <cfg:MaxMemoryPerShellMB>150</cfg:MaxMemoryPerShellMB>
        <cfg:MaxShellsPerUser>5</cfg:MaxShellsPerUser>
    </cfg:Winrs>
</cfg:Config>
```

The listener also allows the mapping of a certificate to the port and IP address. So, using the trusty technique of copying the example from the embedded documentation from the winrm /? command, we crafted the following command to create a listener:

```
winrm create winrm/config/Listener?Address=*+Transport=HTTPS @{Hostname="bfsG1
.bigfirm.com";CertificateThumbprint="03ADB670C63E8D1CDB764CD7AA589C51D854307C"}
```

Here's an explanation of the parameters:

Address=*   The service will listen on all available IP addresses.

Transport=HTTPS   There are only two options: HTTP and HTTPS. They use the default ports 5985 and 5986, respectively.

Hostname=   This has to match the name of the host on the certificate.

CertificateThumbprint=   This is the thumbprint obtained with the certutil command.

CREATING AN INBOUND FIREWALL RULE

The next requirement is to enable an inbound firewall rule to receive the client requests. There is one available for the unsecure HTTP, which would be set up with the /quickconfig option, but you need to build one for the HTTPS port.

If you're a burly, leatherneck system admin type, you might be inclined to torture yourself learning the extensive parameters of the netsh advfirewall firewall command. The MMC snap-in is for those French-vanilla-latte-sipping, pencil-neck-geek system admins. In this book, we appease both the leathernecks and the pencil necks.

We'll start with the latte-sipping style. It helps to see the essential parameters in constructing a rule. Wizards like the New Inbound Rule Wizard are useful because they walk you through configurations without missing important ones. They will assist you in constructing a command line to create the same rule. Just as in the "Server Core Survival Guide" section, we recommend creating the rules through a wizard first on a standard installation and then trying it with the command line. Another option is to take the easy way out and create it on a standard installation and simply convert it to Server Core, as explained in the survival guide section.

Using Windows Firewall with Advanced Security focused on the Server Core installation, we'll walk you through the New Inbound Rule Wizard.

The first page, shown in Figure 3.14, allows you to select a port rule.

FIGURE 3.14
Selecting the type of inbound rule

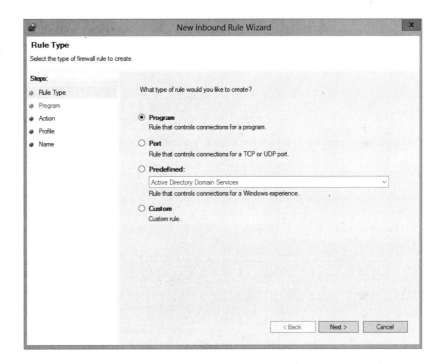

On the Protocol and Ports page, select TCP and enter **5986** for the port, as shown in Figure 3.15.

The Action page provides three options, as shown in Figure 3.16:

◆ "Allow the connection"—This is what you want for this example.

◆ "Allow the connection if it is secure"—As the window explains, this requires IPSec communication to continue the connection. The Network Access Protection feature can be used to set the IPSec policies within a network for this.

◆ "Block the connection"—This blocks the connection.

FIGURE 3.15
Entering the protocol and
port for the inbound rule

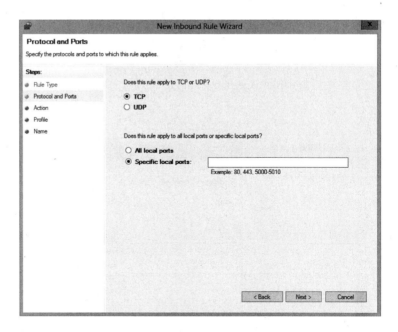

FIGURE 3.16
Selecting the action
for the inbound rule

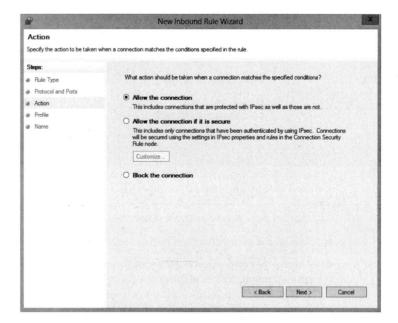

The Profile page applies the rule to any of the three profiles you select, as shown in Figure 3.17. The public and private profiles are meant for computers that are mobile so you can work at home or at a wireless hotspot. Since this server is a domain controller, the concepts of private and public don't apply. We'll stick with the domain profile just to be secure.

FIGURE 3.17
Limiting the
rule to domain
communication

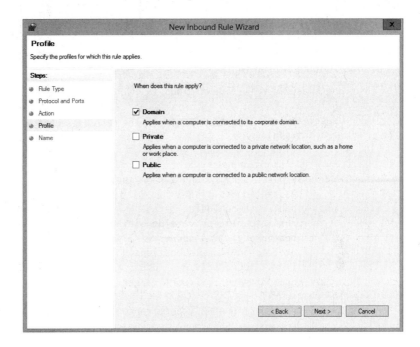

The Name page allows you to enter the name and optional description for the new rule, as displayed in Figure 3.18.

FIGURE 3.18
Providing a
descriptive name
for the rule

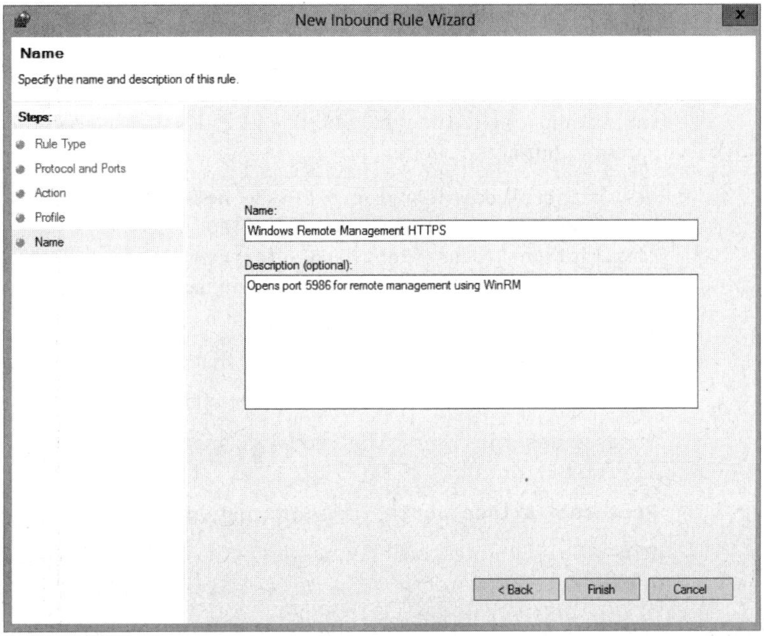

Now that you know the parameters required to create an inbound rule, we'll look at the leatherneck method. The embedded help information provides the following syntax for creating a firewall rule. Note that this was performed in the `netsh` interactive shell. It could be done as one command line as well:

```
netsh advfirewall firewall>add rule ?

Usage: add rule name=<string>
       dir=in|out
       action=allow|block|bypass
       [program=<program path>]
       [service=<service short name>|any]
       [description=<string>]
       [enable=yes|no (default=yes)]
       [profile=public|private|domain|any[,...]]
       [localip=any|<IPv4 address>|<IPv6 address>|<subnet>|<range>|<list>]
       [remoteip=any|localsubnet|dns|dhcp|wins|defaultgateway|
          <IPv4 address>|<IPv6 address>|<subnet>|<range>|<list>]
       [localport=0-65535|<port range>[,...]|RPC|RPC-EPMap|IPHTTPS|any
(default=any)]
       [remoteport=0-65535|<port range>[,...]|any (default=any)]
       [protocol=0-255|icmpv4|icmpv6|icmpv4:type,code|icmpv6:type,code|
          tcp|udp|any (default=any)]
       [interfacetype=wireless|lan|ras|any]
       [rmtcomputergrp=<SDDL string>]
       [rmtusrgrp=<SDDL string>]
       [edge=yes|deferapp|deferuser|no (default=no)]
       [security=authenticate|authenc|authdynenc|authnoencap|notrequired
          (default=notrequired)]
```

The list of parameters is long and intimidating. However, the "Server Core Survival Guide" section told you that you could look for examples at the end of the embedded help. You can edit them in Notepad to create what you need. Notice that the command line doesn't give you much fanfare for your accomplishment:

```
PS C:\Users\administrator.BIGFIRM> netsh advfirewall firewall add rule
name="Windows Remote Management HTTPS"
description="Opens  Port 5986  for remote management using WinRM" protocol=TCP
dir=in localport=5986 profile=domain action=allow
Ok
```

Here's an explanation of the parameters that translate to the earlier wizard pages:

Add rule   In the snap-in, we had to right-click the Inbound Rules object and select New.

Name= & description=   This is the information added in the last page of the wizard, as shown in Figure 3.18.

Protocol= & localport=   This information was added in Figure 3.15.

Dir=   This indicates the inbound part of the rule. The direction was set by selecting the New Inbound Rule Wizard.

Profile= This was set in Figure 3.17. The options in the syntax gave the same values: [profile=public|private|domain|any[,...]].

Action= This was set in Figure 3.16. The options are almost copied in the syntax: action=allow|block|bypass. However, bypass is the equivalent to "Allow if the connection is secure."

Note in Figure 3.15 that the type of rule is implied with the selection of a local port. A rule that is based on a program or a service has its own structure that has examples listed in the embedded help text.

TESTING WITH WINRS

The current client available for Windows Remote Shell is winrs.exe. It is available on Windows 7 and 8 and Windows Server 2012 installations. We hashed out the following command using the winrs.exe help for testing the service:

```
rem test winrs with fire wall enabled.
PS C:\Users\Administrator.BIGFIRM>winrs -r:https://bfsc1.bigfirm.com:5896 ipconfig

Windows IP Configuration


Ethernet adapter Internal:

   Connection-specific DNS Suffix  . :
   Link-local IPv6 Address . . . . . : fe80::b5a1:157f:7220:4f4c%3
   IPv4 Address. . . . . . . . . . . : 192.168.1.11
   Subnet Mask . . . . . . . . . . . : 255.255.255.0
   Default Gateway . . . . . . . . . : 192.168.1.254
```

Configuring Roles and Features

Now you are ready to get this lean, mean infrastructure machine into production. The plan for this Server Core instance is to set up a branch-office infrastructure server. This will provide authentication, file and print services, and other common network support for a small group of computers in a corporate network isolated by WAN links.

The roles that were installed on the computer during the initial tasks are Active Directory Domain Services, DNS, DHCP, and Print and Document Services. Each of these roles needs to be configured. We'll primarily cover the initial tasks for each service using both command-line and GUI tools.

Two additional services already installed are the File Server role service and the Key Management Service. You will configure the File Server role service to provide network access to local folders. The Key Management Service will manage the activation of the volume-licensed operating systems within a network. As a branch-office server, it may prove to be the best platform to obtain the activation information from the Microsoft licensing servers for the branch.

Since the branch-office server is isolated from the corporate datacenter, it needs to perform backup operations of the data residing on the shared folders. The Windows Server Backup feature was installed in the initial configurations as well, and we'll run through the commands to adequately back up the data.

Throughout the book, you will find additional details on configuring Server Core for a given feature.

Creating a Domain Controller and Managing DNS

In previous versions of Windows Server, you would use DCPromo from the command line to create and promote domain controllers. In Windows Server 2012, DCPromo has been deprecated and can only be used with an answer file. Therefore, we are going to teach you the newer way—using PowerShell—to create a domain controller. Since you already installed Active Directory Domain Services (AD DS) earlier in this chapter, much of the work is already done.

You will need to use a prerequisite check that is new in Windows Server 2012. This check will help show you what the server needs to properly install the domain controller.

Test-ADDSDomainControllerInstallation checks the prerequisites for the domain controller installation as if you were performing the actual installation. You will be prompted for domain and login credentials, as shown in Figure 3.19.

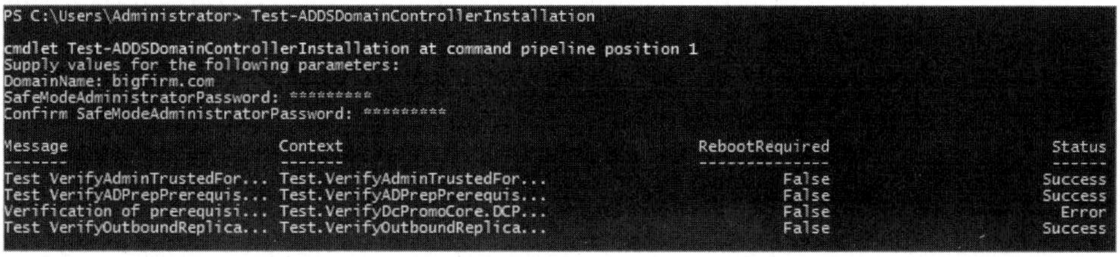

FIGURE 3.19
Running
Test-
ADDSDomain
Controller
Installation

You're ready to install the domain controller. The cmdlet Install-ADDSDomainController will install DNS at the same time. If you do not add any parameters, the following default settings will be used:

Read-only domain controller: No

Global catalog: Yes

DNS server: Yes

Database folder: C:\Windows\NTDS

Log file folder: C:\Windows\NTDS

SYSVOL folder: C:\Windows\SYSVOL

There are plenty of scripts that you can download and use to configure all the different parameters. Here is the complete parameter format in case you need to change the configuration:

```
Install-ADDSDomainController -DomainName <String> [-ADPrepCredential
<PSCredential> ] [-AllowDomainControllerReinstall]
[-ApplicationPartitionsToReplicate <String[]> ] [-CreateDnsDelegation]
[-Credential <PSCredential> ] [-CriticalReplicationOnly] [-DatabasePath
<String> ] [-DnsDelegationCredential <PSCredential> ] [-Force]
```

```
[-InstallationMediaPath <String> ] [-InstallDns] [-LogPath <String> ]
[-MoveInfrastructureOperationMasterRoleIfNecessary] [-NoDnsOnNetwork]
[-NoGlobalCatalog] [-NoRebootOnCompletion] [-ReplicationSourceDC <String>
] [-SafeModeAdministratorPassword <SecureString> ] [-SiteName <String>
] [-SkipAutoConfigureDns] [-SkipPreChecks] [-SystemKey <SecureString> ]
[-SysvolPath <String> ] [-Confirm] [-WhatIf] [ <CommonParameters>]
```

Go ahead and run the cmdlet:

```
PS C:\Users\administrator> Install-ADDSDomainController
```

You will be prompted with the following:

```
The target server will be configured as a domain controller and restarted when
this operation is complete.
Do you want to continue with this operation?
[Y] Yes  [A] Yes to All  [N] No  [L] No to All  [S] Suspend  [?] Help (default is
"Y"):Y
```

When you select Yes, the installation will begin (Figure 3.20). This process may take several minutes to complete.

FIGURE 3.20
Installing the
domain controller

Configuring the DHCP Service

When Windows Server 2003 came out, Microsoft was starting to kick up sand onto the ultra-geek's Linux system. It increased the available suite of commands to provide ultra-geek wannabes with the tools to configure as much as possible. That's when the netsh command came into fashion.

When considering how to manage this service, this command came to mind. We looked up the command on TechNet's Command-Line Reference A–Z list and then printed out the documentation for netsh dhcp. After collating the 40 pages, we logged onto the Server Core instance to get busy. With netsh, you can construct one-line commands or use the interactive shell within the command prompt. In this instance, you'll use the latter.

A branch office requires a basic DHCP implementation, including a single scope with standard scope options of default gateway, DNS servers, and DNS domain name. But before setting that up, you need to authorize it in Active Directory, by using the add server option. In the following code, interactive mode is utilized to enter the commands:

```
netsh> dhcp
netsh dhcp>add server bfsc1.bigfirm.com 192.168.1.11

Adding server bfsc1.bigfirm.com, 192.168.1.11

Command completed successfully.
```

```
netsh dhcp>show server

1 Servers were found in the directory service:

        Server [bfsc1.bigfirm.com] Address [192.168.1.11] Ds location: c
n=bfsc1.bigfirm.com


Command completed successfully.
```

To add a scope, you need to switch to the `netsh dhcp server` prompt and use the add scope command. The required parameters are the subnet and subnet mask that the scope represents, the scope name, and any comments:

```
netsh dhcp>server
netsh dhcp server>add scope 192.168.1.0 255.255.255.0 "Branch Office 1"
 "Sample DHCP scope"


Command completed successfully.
netsh dhcp server>show scope

===============================================================================
 Scope Address  - Subnet Mask   - State   - Scope Name    -  Comment

===============================================================================


  192.168.1.0   - 255.255.255.0  -Active   -Branch Office 1 -Sample DHCP scope

 Total No. of Scopes = 1
Command completed successfully.
```

The scope needs a range of IP addresses to serve to DHCP clients and the standard scope options. The scope options are identified with the option code, a three-digit identifier. You can see the code identifiers in the DHCP Management Console. The options have values in byte, word, dword, string, or IP address format. For our example, we have the following options, identifiers, and values:

- IP range: 192.168.1.50 - 100

- Default gateway: 003, 192.168.1.254

- DNS server: 006, 192.168.1.11

- DNS domain name: 015, bigfirm.com

```
netsh dhcp server>scope 192.168.1.0

Changed the current scope context to 192.168.1.0 scope.
netsh dhcp server scope>add iprange 192.168.1.50 192.168.1.100

Command completed successfully.
```

```
netsh dhcp server scope>set optionvalue 003 IPADDRESS 192.168.1.254

Command completed successfully.
netsh dhcp server scope>set optionvalue 006 IPADDRESS 192.168.1.11

Command completed successfully.
netsh dhcp server scope>set optionvalue 015 STRING bigfirm.com

Command completed successfully.
netsh dhcp server scope>show optionvalue

Options for Scope 192.168.1.0:

        DHCP Standard Options :
        General Option Values:
        OptionId : 51
        Option Value:
                Number of Option Elements = 1
                Option Element Type = DWORD
                Option Element Value = 691200
        OptionId : 3
        Option Value:
                Number of Option Elements = 1
                Option Element Type = IPADDRESS
                Option Element Value = 192.168.1.254
        OptionId : 6
        Option Value:
                Number of Option Elements = 1
                Option Element Type = IPADDRESS
                Option Element Value = 192.168.1.11
        OptionId : 15
        Option Value:
                Number of Option Elements = 1
                Option Element Type = STRING
                Option Element Value = bigfirm.com
Command completed successfully.
```

After running through these commands on Server Core, you can also connect to the service from a remote server and verify the configuration with a GUI.

Setting Up a File Server

The File Server role service provides basic file-sharing capabilities. We didn't have to install any specific role or feature to support this. Like many of the other roles, the procedures to share folders on full installations are typically handled by the MMC or other GUI-based applications, such as Windows Explorer. We'll explore the command-line alternative for this.

CREATING A PRIMARY PARTITION

The first task is to provide a data partition. In the following example, we decided to set the size to 10 GB.

The DiskPart command is perfect for this operation. It manages all the functionality of the Disk Management Console in a command-line format or an interactive shell format. The following is in the interactive shell format. The first set of commands displays the disks and volumes on the computer. Notice that the listed volumes include volumes on other disks. Our data partition has not yet been allocated, so it is not listed in the volumes. To create the data partition, you have to select the disk, which is indicated by the value in the list disk output.

```
PS C:\Windows\system32>diskpart

Microsoft DiskPart version 6.1.7000
Copyright (C) 1999-2008 Microsoft Corporation.
On computer: BFSC1

DISKPART> list disk

  Disk ###  Status          Size     Free     Dyn  Gpt
  --------  -------------   -------  -------   ---  ---
  Disk 0    Online    `     75 GB    55 GB


DISKPART> list volume

  Volume ###  Ltr  Label        Fs     Type       Size     Status     Info
  ----------  ---  -----------  -----  ---------  -------  ---------  --------
  Volume 0    D    GB1SXFRE_EN  UDF    CD-ROM     2850 MB  Healthy
  Volume 1              NTFS    Partition  200 MB   Healthy    System
  Volume 2    C              NTFS    Partition   19 GB   Healthy    Boot
DISKPART> select disk 0

Disk 0 is now the selected disk.
```

Now, you will create the primary partition. The help information is displayed first. Noting that the size is listed in MB, you have some mental calculations to perform: 10 GB = 10,000 MB. After the primary partition is created, you need to select it. This allows you to assign a drive letter to it:

```
DISKPART> help create partition primary
.....
Example:

    CREATE PARTITION PRIMARY SIZE=1000
rem size is in MB so 55 gb is 55000
DISKPART> create partition primary size=10000

DiskPart succeeded in creating the specified partition.
```

```
DISKPART> list partition

    Partition ###   Type              Size      Offset
    -------------   ----------------  -------   -------
    Partition 1     Primary           200 MB    1024 KB
    Partition 2     Primary            19 GB     201 MB
  * Partition 3     Primary            10 GB      20 GB

DISKPART> select partition 3

Partition 3 is now the selected partition.

DISKPART> assign letter=e

DiskPart successfully assigned the drive letter or mount point.
```

With the partition created, you can view it as an available volume. You need to select it and then format it with NTFS:

```
DISKPART> list volume

    Volume ###   Ltr   Label         Fs     Type        Size      Status      Info
    ----------   ---   -----------   -----  ----------  -------   ---------   --------
    Volume 0     D     GB1SXFRE_EN   UDF    CD-ROM      2850 MB   Healthy
    Volume 1                         NTFS   Partition    200 MB   Healthy     System
    Volume 2     C                   NTFS   Partition     19 GB   Healthy     Boot
  * Volume 3     E                   RAW    Partition     10 GB   Healthy

DISKPART> select volume 3

Volume 3 is the selected volume.

DISKPART> format fs=ntfs label="Data volume" quick

    100 percent completed

DiskPart successfully formatted the volume.
```

CREATING THE FOLDERS AND EDITING PERMISSIONS

In this example, you'll create a Sales folder. To make your folder, you'll use the PowerShell cmdlet New-Item: NEW-ITEM E:\Sales -type directory. You then have to trim the security for the folder. You will assign the Administrators group Full Control to the Sales folder.

When a home folder is designated in user properties through Active Directory Users and Computers, the home folder is created automatically with the user having Full Control. Inherited permissions are applicable on this folder, so the default Users group with Read permissions are also assigned. You will need to remove the Users group's permissions from the Sales folder and give the Administrators group Full Control.

SPELLING COUNTS

You should use the %username% system variable to automatically apply usernames to the home folder path. Thus, in the Active Directory Users and Computers console, the home folder path found in the user's properties can look like this: \\bfsc1.bigfirm.com\users\%username%. Remember, spelling counts. If this variable is spelled incorrectly, the literal string is applied as the user's folder name. Invariably we've seen some home folders named similarly to %usrename% or %usernam%.

What could you use to ensure you have the right spelling? The echo command! %username% is like other system variables in that it is effective within the command prompt as well. The echo command will repeat the variable's value as follows:

```
rem spelled correctly
C:\>echo %username%
Administrator


rem not spelled correctly
C:\>echo %uesername%
%uesername%
```

Once you confirm the correct spelling, you can copy and paste it for later use within Active Directory Users and Computers or within a script.

The following are the PowerShell cmdlets to modify the permissions on the Sales folder. The first cmdlet, Get-Acl, will retrieve the folder permissions. If you notice, the Format-List property we used will lay out the results in a clear, readable format for you. You will then use the Set-Acl cmdlet to set the permissions on the folder:

```
rem Display the permissions to the sales folder
Get-Acl E:\sales | Format-List
 Path    : Microsoft.PowerShell.Core\FileSystem::C:\sales
Owner   : BUILTIN\Administrators
Group   : BFSC1\None
Access  : NT AUTHORITY\SYSTEM Allow  FullControl
          BUILTIN\Administrators Allow  FullControl
          BUILTIN\Users Allow  ReadAndExecute, Synchronize
          BUILTIN\Users Allow  AppendData
          BUILTIN\Users Allow  CreateFiles
          CREATOR OWNER Allow  268435456
Audit   :
Sddl    : O:BAG:S-1-5-21-4204471083-1189308523-3240350476-
513D:AI(A;OICIID;FA;;;SY)(A;OICIID;FA;;;BA)(A;OICIID;0x1200a9;
          ;;BU)(A;CIID;LC;;;BU)(A;CIID;DC;;;BU)(A;OICIIOID;GA;;;CO)
```

Here is a handy little script that allows you to modify group permissions on a folder. It will change the permissions on the Sales folder to allow only the Administrators group Full Control.

```
$acl = Get-Acl "E:\Sales"
$Group1 = "Administrators"
$rule1 = New-Object System.Security.AccessControl.FileSystemAccessRule
-ArgumentList @($Group1,"FullControl","ContainerInherit, ObjectInherit",
"None","Allow")
$acl.SetAccessRule($rule1)
$acl |Set-Acl
$acl.SetAccessRuleProtection($true,$false)
$acl |Set-Acl
```

Here are the results of running that script on the Sales folder. As you can see, only the Administrators group now has Full Control:

```
Path    : Microsoft.PowerShell.Core\FileSystem::E:\sales
Owner   : BUILTIN\Administrators
Group   : BFSC1\None
Access  : BUILTIN\ Administrators Allow  FullControl
Audit   :
Sddl    : O:BAG:S-1-5-21-4204471083-1189308523-3240350476-513D:PAI(A;OICI;FA;;;BU)
```

Sharing the Folder

Sharing the folders is a piece of cake with the net share command. Yes, it's that venerable command introduced in the ancient days of LAN Manager. The following command creates the share. The name of the share equals the path, followed by the permissions. The /Unlimited parameter is the number of connections allowed to this share.

```
rem create shares
E:\>net share SALES=e:\sales /grant:bigfirm\sales,FULL /Unlimited
Sales was shared successfully.
```

Of course, we needed to verify the share. So we went to a client and typed the UNC path in the Run prompt, and the results are displayed in Figure 3.21.

FIGURE 3.21
Verifying shares
on Server Core

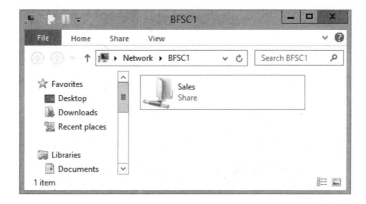

Setting Up a Print Server

e-Print services require components of the Print and Document Services role to be installed. Then, like the other roles, you have to configure the role. In previous versions of Windows, adding a printer was wizard driven, with all components rolled up into one routine. These components included the driver selection and port selection and possibly creating a TCP port and printer configurations. The functionality hasn't changed that much—just the look has, so we won't be going into too much detail on this.

There may be commands to perform each of these procedures within the command prompt, but as in the Miller's tale, it would be "a pain in the arse." With Windows Server 2012, the printer configurations are managed in the Print Management console, another MMC snap-in. We'll eagerly take that route first and then engage in our own Miller's tale.

An administrator responsible for printers will have to install the console by installing either the Print and Document Services role or just the Print and Document Services tool in Remote Server Administration Tools on a compatible workstation.

Once you've installed the Print Management console, you can open it and add the Server Core instance, as shown in Figure 3.22. Each component is separated into its own object category, so now you have a wizard for each of them.

FIGURE 3.22
The Print Management console for configuring the print service

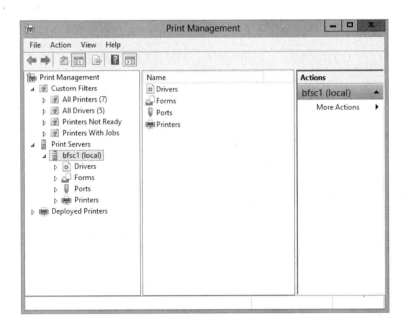

To add a driver, you right-click Drivers and then opt to add the driver. The wizard looks similar to the ones in previous Windows operating systems.

Forms are pretty standard, so there's no need to mess with them; however, ports are very important. Typically, office printers are not locally attached to the server; they're connected to the network. So, you need to create a standard TCP port. Again, it looks eerily familiar, as shown in Figure 3.23.

FIGURE 3.23
Adding a TCP
port

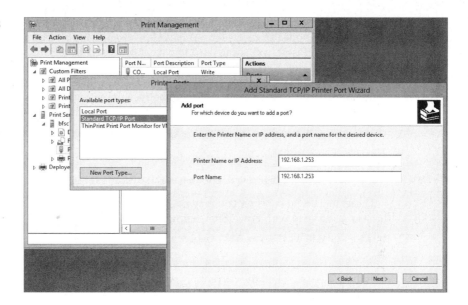

You can then create the printer with the specific driver, port, name, share name, permissions, and other configurations using the Network Printer Installation Wizard, as shown in Figure 3.24.

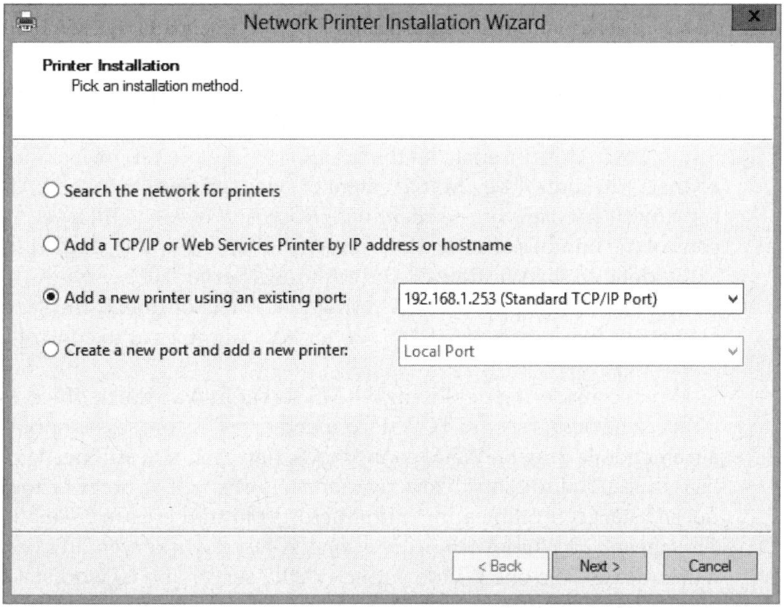

FIGURE 3.24
Network Printer
Installation
Wizard

Now let's look at how to configure a printer using PowerShell cmdlets instead of using the older script methods in Server Core. You can still use the .vbs scripts if you choose, but as we said earlier, Microsoft is pushing hard to have PowerShell as its primary command-prompt administration.

To add a printer, use the Add-Printer cmdlet. This cmdlet can be used for either a local printer or network printer. We'll show you both examples.

First, adding a local HP 5150 printer for the Sales department:

```
PS C:\> Add-Printer -Name "Sales Printer" -DriverName "HP 5150"
```

Now, add a network printer to the print server you set up earlier:

```
PS C:\> Add-Printer -ConnectionName \\bfsc1\192.168.1.253
```

There may be times when you may not have the driver on the server. Adding a print driver to the server is a snap with PowerShell using the following cmdlet:

```
PS C:\> Add-PrinterDriver -Name "HP 5150"
```

You now have a printer installed, but you need to configure the print properties, such as color. First, take a look at the current properties so you can see what needs to be changed:

```
PS C:\> Get-PrintConfiguration -PrinterName " HP 5150"
```

PrinterName	ComputerName	Collate	Color	DuplexingMode
HP 5150		True	True	OneSided

Now that you have the configuration, you can change the Color property to false, as follows:

```
PS C:\> Set-PrintConfiguration -PrinterName "HP 5150" -Color $false
```

Managing Licenses with the Key Management Service

Microsoft has introduced the Volume Activation 3.0 process with Windows 8 and Windows Server 2012. This differs from the familiar online activation. Volume-licensed installations connect to a central Key Management Service server within the LAN, which will register an activation "license" for the client with Microsoft over the Internet. This allows Microsoft to control the number of activations under the same volume product key.

By default, the Windows 8 and Windows Server 2012 servers are configured to connect to the KMS server prior to attempting to connect online. If the server can't find one but does activate online, it acts as a KMS server. You might want to control this process by getting ahead of it.

When considering deploying a KMS server into a branch office, there are two key decision points. The first is secure TCP/IP connectivity. This process is seriously lightweight, so it isn't a tremendous drag on WAN connections; however, you still need connectivity that isn't the big white cloud to centralize activations to one site. The other factor is "25." A KMS server doesn't start communicating with Microsoft until there are 25 qualified licenses to activate. This means 25 Windows 8 installations. A Windows Server 2012 license counts as five Windows 8 installations. So one Windows Server 2012 server and 20 workstations would be enough to trigger communication.

Before the communication is triggered, the computers are running under a grace period and eventually will time out. This turns on "reduced functionality mode."

In a branch office that has more than 25 licenses but not a secure TCP/IP connection to headquarters, setting up a KMS server is a realistic option. If you don't meet the "25" threshold, Microsoft offers the Volume License Multiple Activation Key (MAK), which works similarly to the online activation of product keys.

The following sections detail the steps to set up the KMS server on a branch-office Server Core installation.

DETERMINING THE USE OF SRV PUBLISHING

SRV records are found in DNS and publish the existence of services within a network. This will be discussed in detail in Chapter 5, "IP Address Management and DHCP Failover." By default, the KMS server publishes the service with an SRV record in the primary DNS domain. For our Windows Server 2012 Server Core example, this is BigFirm.com.

In the BigFirm.com DNS domain, you would see an SRV record for `_VLMCS._TCP.Bigfirm .com`. It would have the following properties:

- Name: _vlmcs._TCP

- Type: SRV

- Priority: 0

- Weight: 0

- Port: 1688

- Hostname: Bfsc1.bigfirm.com

If you want this to happen, you would need to add permissions on the DNS zone to allow updates to the KMS servers. We recommend using a domain controller as the KMS server. The service is light, and the domain controller already has permissions to register SRV records in DNS.

However, with SRV records, there is no control over which KMS server the clients will go to if they are located in a branch office. They would query DNS and receive a response for a server located elsewhere. To keep the communication local, the KMS server must be registered on the client. In addition, DNS SRV publishing should be disabled for the branch-office server. This is done by creating a `DisableDNSPublishing` dword value of 1 in the `HKEY_LOCAL_MACHINE\ SOFTWARE\Microsoft\Windows NT\CurrentVersion\SL` key.

ENABLING THE FIREWALL

There is already an inbound rule listed in the Windows Firewall configurations, and it's part of the Key Management Service rule group. You need to enable it. The command for this is as follows:

```
netsh advfirewall firewall set rule group="Key Management Service" new enable=yes
```

ACTIVATING THE INSTALLATION

Just as you activated the Server Core instance, the branch-office KMS server needs to be activated with the `slmgr.vbs` `/ipk` and `/ato` options.

POINTING CLIENTS TO THE KMS

By default, Volume Activation 3.0 clients (Windows 8 and Windows Server 2012) attempt to connect to the KMS automatically using the SRV records. Since the process isn't site aware, it will go to any provided KMS server. You can manually assign the KMS host on each client of the branch location with the following command:

```
cscript c:\windows\system32\slmgr.vbs /skms bfsc1.bigfirm.com:1688
```

You could use a Group Policy object–assigned startup script to distribute this throughout the site.

Protecting Data with Windows Backup Server

This is the one of the features we added in the Server Core installation. It's a good idea to back up data. Your environment may pooh-pooh the use of native backup tools and prefer a third-party enterprise-class backup solution. We don't blame it. However, there's always a point in between installation and full production when the enterprise-class backup solution's client isn't installed or configured. We have found through experience that NTBackup Utility is excellent for CYA data backups.

Microsoft reengineered its native backup utility and named it Windows Server Backup. It takes advantage of the Volume Shadow Copy Service to freeze the state of the data for the backup. Originally, it was designed to provide only off-site backups on a set of portable hard drives. Tape backups were eliminated, so removable hard drives were the only backup option. Fortunately, Microsoft broadened the application to include UNC paths to shared folders and locally attached hard drives by time of the release.

In this discussion, we'll explore the PowerShell cmdlets that manage Windows Server Backup. First, you need to install the Windows Server Backup feature. We provided the proper name for you but you can run `Get-WindowsFeature` to see the list of names. You can also get a list of all cmdlets associated with Windows Server Backup if you run `get-command *wb* -commandtype cmdlet`.

```
PS  c:\Users\Administrator>Install-WindowsFeature Windows-Server-Backup
```

If the feature installed properly, you will see the following output in PowerShell:

```
Success Restart Needed Exit Code      Feature Result
------- -------------- ---------      --------------
True    No             Success        {Windows Server Backup}
```

You will need to create a new backup policy. The backup policy is the set of instructions for automating your backup. When you create a new one, it is empty by default. So you will create it and then fill it with instructions. These instructions include scheduling the backup and setting the backup target location, files, and several others parameters, which you will see as soon as you install the policy. To install it you will use the New-WBPolicy cmdlet:

```
PS  c:\Users\Administrator> New-WBPolicy

Schedule              :
BackupTargets         :
VolumesToBackup       :
```

```
FilesSpecsToBackup    :
FilesSpecsToExclude   :
ComponentsToBackup    :
BMR                   : False
SystemState           : False
OverwriteOldFormatVhd : False
VssBackupOptions      : VssCopyBackup
```

Now that you see the New-WBPolicy properties, you can use the following script to set them. This script will set the policy to back up everything in the Sales folder every morning at 9 a.m.:

```
PS C:\Users\Administrator> $policy = New-WBPolicy

$fileSpec = New-WBFileSpec -FileSpec C:\Sales
Add-WBFileSpec -Policy $policy -FileSpec $filespec

Add-WBBareMetalRecovery $policy

$disks = Get-WBDisk
$backupLocation = New-WBBackupTarget -Disk $disks[2]
Add-WBBackupTarget -Policy $policy -Target $backupLocation

Set-WBSchedule -Policy $policy 09:00

Set-WBPolicy -Policy $policy
```

That will get you started using PowerShell to handle your Windows Server Backup. You can reference the complete cmdlet listing for Windows Server Backup at http://technet.microsoft.com/en-us/library/ee706683.aspx.

The Bottom Line

Use the new functionality in Server Core. The Windows Server 2012 Server Core operating system is a trimmed-down version of its full installation. The removed code reduces the profile for security threats and also reduces performance demands. The primary administration interface is the command prompt. It can perform several but not all of the roles available with the full installation.

Master It The Windows Server 2012 Server Core version differs from the original release in Windows Server 2008. What are those key differences, and how does that impact the roles the server can perform?

Install and configure Server Core. The installation of Server Core is the same as installing a full installation of Windows Server 2012. The full installation provides a list of initial configuration tasks such as joining the domain, initiating automatic updates, and installing features. Each of these operations has a command associated with it.

Master It Server Core has a specific script to perform several common tasks that edit the registry. What is this script's name? What parameter can provide a list of additional commands to perform many of the common configuration tasks?

Set up Server Core for a branch-office deployment. The branch-office deployment is one possible scenario for the Server Core implementation. The infrastructure roles of Active Directory Domain Services, DNS, DHCP, File Services, and Print and Document Services would be installed and configured on a server, which would provide these basic services to the users within a small office environment. The configurations of these services could be performed remotely.

Master It To configure Active Directory Domain Services and DNS, the Active Directory Domain Services Installation Wizard (DCPromo) is run from the command line. What is needed to enter the parameters for the command?

Remotely manage the operating system. Server Core can be remotely managed by three options. Remote Desktop administration is available, but only the command prompt and provided GUIs with Server Core can be used. The MMC snap-ins can connect to the server's services to manage with the standard Windows tools. Finally, a new service, Windows Remote Shell, provides single-command connections to the server.

Master It The Windows Remote Shell offers a quickconfig option. What security concerns should system administrators be aware of when using this option? What can be done to address these concerns?

Chapter 4

Windows Server 2012 R2 Networking Enhancements

When Microsoft first released Windows Server 2012, the new networking capabilities were arguably the most hyped and eagerly awaited features of the operating system. With the release of Windows Server 2012 R2, networking has been further enhanced. In this chapter we will explain how IPv6 and Windows PowerShell enhance the Windows Server 2012 R2 networking experience, and we will discuss functionality such as Network Interface Card (NIC) Teaming and enhanced Quality of Service (QoS). Some familiar networking features, such as BranchCache and 802.1X authenticated access, get a refresh here too. Toward the end of the chapter, we'll delve into networking performance and management to ensure that you get the most out of your networking deployments.

In this chapter, you will learn to:

◆ Understand IPv6

◆ Use PowerShell for better networking manageability

◆ Implement NIC Teaming

◆ Understand the new QoS features

◆ Manage network performance

The Journey to IPv6

Because Windows Server 2012 networking is built on Internet Protocol version 6 (IPv6), it's worth going back in history a bit to explore the development of the Transmission Control Protocol (TCP) and its journey to where we are now. When TCP was combined with the first publicly available version of Internet Protocol (IPv4), we got TCP/IP, which is the basis of all modern computer networking. Microsoft first developed its TCP stack in the 1990s. It evolved as Microsoft developed the various versions of its operating systems, but at its core it remained mostly unchanged right up to Windows Server 2003. At that point, it became apparent that the old TCP/IP (v4) stack couldn't evolve further and was starting to become a bottleneck. Microsoft saw the need for a new stack to be able to take advantage of new technologies and opportunities that its customers and partners were encountering. As a result, they started work on the new version of TCP/IP, which would include a suite of protocols and standards newly developed by the Internet Engineering Task Force (IETF) known as IPv6.

The transition to IPv6 began in 1998 while Microsoft was developing Windows 2000, and our first glimpse of the next-generation TCP/IP (an integrated IPv4/IPv6 stack in a dual–IP layer architecture) was in Windows Vista. Since then, all of Microsoft's new client and server operating systems have the same next-generation TCP stack at the core of their networking, including, of course, Windows Server 2012.

The Benefits of IPv6

The transition to IPv6 networking brings with it a number of benefits when compared to IPv4, such as these:

Large Address Scaling   With the growing usage of consumer Internet-connected mobile devices, IPv4 was becoming saturated with the demand for more IP addresses. The solution was to create a protocol that could handle trillions of IP addresses, and that's where IPv6 comes into its own. IPv6 addresses are 128 bytes in length in comparison to IPv4 addresses, which are only 32-bit. With IPv6, obtaining a public address space is very easy, and on your local area network a private address space that uses Unique Local Address (ULA) prefixes can apply to each site of your organization. The combination of public address space and ULA prefixes allows you to scale your intranet to an enormous size.

Efficient Internet Connectivity   IPv6 in Windows Server 2012 detects potential routing-path issues between the IPv4 and IPv6 Internets and can prevent the initial problematic connection attempt. This feature, along with other benefits such as fixed-length IP packet headers and aggregated address allocation, from the outset delivers a much more efficient Internet connectivity experience.

Enhanced Security   In IPv6, IPSec support is a protocol requirement; this was optional in IPv4. This requirement provides a standards-based solution for your network security needs, promotes interoperability between different IPv6 implementations, and is applicable for devices, applications, and services.

Integrated Quality of Service   QoS enables you to measure and throttle the levels of bandwidth available to your network interface cards (NICs). It's been available in Microsoft's operating systems for a number of years but wasn't too widely used by administrators and IT pros because of more favorable hardware-based solutions on the market. QoS is fully integrated into Windows Server 2012, and it works by using a 20-bit Flow Label field and an 8-bit Traffic Class field in the IPv6 header to determine how traffic is dealt with.

IPv6 Transition Technologies

The journey from IPv4 to IPv6 will definitely not happen in a short time frame, and it became apparent to the original designers of IPv6 that both protocols would have to coexist and work together on the same infrastructure. The caveat, though, is that IPv4 and IPv6 cannot natively talk to each other, and a solution had to be developed to address the communication barriers between these two protocols for the duration of this transitional period. A set of transitional technologies and address types were created so that IPv6 nodes can communicate with each other in a mixed-protocol environment, even if they are separated by an IPv4-only infrastructure.

The original IPv6 designers created Request for Comment (RFC) 2893, "Transition Mechanisms for IPv6 Hosts and Routers." This RFC defined the different IPv4 and IPv6 node types on the Internet, and Table 4.1 explains what they are.

TABLE 4.1:   RFC 2893 Node Type Definitions

NODE TYPE	DESCRIPTION
IPv4-only node	Implements only IPv4 (has only IPv4 addresses) and does not run IPv6. This node type is pretty common today, and Windows Server 2003 and Windows XP are good examples.
IPv6-only node	Implements only IPv6 (and has only IPv6 addresses) and does not support IPv4. This node is able only to communicate with IPv6 nodes and applications. It's an uncommon node type since it's purely IPv6, but this type will become more prevalent as IPv6-enabled devices mature.
IPv6/IPv4 node	Implements both IPv6 and IPv4 and is the most common node type available on the Internet today. Windows Server 2012, Windows Server 2008, Windows 8, and Windows 7 are examples.
IPv4 node	A node that implements IPv4 but can also be an IPv4-only node or an IPv6/IPv4 node.
IPv6 node	A node that implements IPv6 and also can be an IPv6-only node or an IPv6/IPv4 node.

Organizations can migrate to IPv6 while still running side-by-side with their existing IPv4 infrastructure. RFC 2893 outlines these different scenarios that allow you to tunnel traffic between IPv6 and IPv4 infrastructures:

◆   Router-to-router

◆   Host-to-router or router-to-host

◆   Host-to-host

IPv6 for Windows Server 2012 supports the following automatic tunnelling technologies:

ISATAP Tunnelling   The Intra-site Automatic Tunnel Addressing Protocol (ISATAP) provides connectivity for IPv6 hosts across an IPv4 intranet using the host-to-host, host-to-router, and router-to-host scenarios mentioned earlier. The two main components for an ISATAP network are the ISATAP router and ISATAP hosts. A DNS record for the ISATAP router must be configured on the network to enable detection of the router by an ISATAP host. Once detected, the router facilitates IPv6 and IPv4 communication by forwarding packets between the two different protocol type networks.

6to4 Tunnelling   6to4 delivers address assignment and router-to-router, host-to-router, and router-to-host automatic tunneling technology. It doesn't need any explicit tunnels to deliver IPv6 packets over an IPv4 infrastructure. With 6to4, you don't need to request an external IPv6 address from your ISP because you can simply assign external (global) IPv6 addresses inside your network, which will enable you to communicate with locations on the external IPv6 Internet.

Teredo Tunneling   With Teredo, you can perform address assignment and host-to-host automatic tunnelling even from behind network address translation (NAT) devices such as home routers. These devices have no direct native connection to an IPv6 network. Teredo has been designed as a last-resort transition technology for IPv6 connectivity. Teredo will not be used if native IPv6, ISATAP, or 6to4 connectivity is present between communicating nodes. As 6to4 support becomes more prevalent across IPv4 edge devices and IPv6 connectivity becomes the norm, Teredo will be used less and less until finally it is not used at all.

If you want to learn more about IPv6 architecture, then check out the IPv6 Survival Guide here:

```
http://social.technet.microsoft.com/wiki/contents/articles/1728.ipv6-survival-
guide.aspx
```

If you're so inclined, you can also read the original RFC 2893 document from this link:

```
http://www.ietf.org/rfc/rfc2893.txt
```

Better Networking Manageability with PowerShell

Windows PowerShell was first introduced as a built-in operating system feature in Windows Server 2008 and is used by many Microsoft applications, such as Exchange Server, SQL Server, SharePoint, and System Center, to expose their management interfaces and to take administration and automation of tasks to the next level. Windows Server 2012 R2 has PowerShell 4.0 built in, and this comes with an extensive set of Windows PowerShell commands—more commonly referred to as cmdlets (pronounced "command lets")—to perform command-line and script-based configuration of IPv6 and other network-related settings.

Historically, the Netsh.exe (Network Shell) command-line utility was used for managing IPv6, and although using Netsh.exe commands for IPv6 configuration is still supported, it's recommended to now use Windows PowerShell when managing your network configurations in Windows Server 2012 R2. This section will discuss how to leverage PowerShell to get the most out of your networking functionality.

Networking Cmdlets and Modules

Whereas Windows Server 2008 had approximately 200 PowerShell cmdlets, Windows Server 2012 R2 has closer to 2,500! From this enormous pool of new cmdlets, you can use literally hundreds to view, configure, and monitor all of the different networking components and services that feature in Windows Server 2012. You can perform a wide variety of tasks using these cmdlets ranging from simple IP address configuration to more specialized functions like configuring Quality of Service and virtualization networking parameters. Learning PowerShell is the key to managing and automating your servers in your datacenter and to ensuring a simplified Windows Server 2012 networking experience.

PowerShell cmdlets are grouped into sets of related functionalities called modules. Due to the large number of cmdlets available to use for Windows Server 2012 networking and the fact that it would take a lot more than just this chapter to cover them, Table 4.2 shows the relevant networking PowerShell modules and provides links to the cmdlet references contained within them.

TABLE 4.2:   Networking Modules

MODULE NAME	MODULE DESCRIPTION	CMDLETS REFERENCE LINK
BrancheCache	BranchCache	http://tinyurl.com/branchecache
NetAdapter	Network Adapter	http://tinyurl.com/ws2012netadapter
NetConnection	Network Connectivity Status	http://tinyurl.com/ws2012netconnectivity
NetLBFO	NIC Teaming	http://tinyurl.com/ws2012nicteaming
NetQos	QoS	http://tinyurl.com/ws2012qos
NetSecurity	Network Security	http://tinyurl.com/ws2012netsecurity
NetSwitchTeam	Network Switch Team	http://tinyurl.com/ws2012netswitchteam
NetTCPIP	TCP/IP	http://tinyurl.com/ws2012nettcpip
NetworkTransition	Network Transition	http://tinyurl.com/ws2012nettransition
NetWNV	Windows Network Virtualization	http://tinyurl.com/ws2012netwnv

---

THE NEW PING?

Another really cool and definitely useful cmdlet available in Windows Server 2012 R2 is Test-NetConnection. This cmdlet is a serious contender to replace the old but very widely used ping command. If you just run Test-NetConnection without any additional parameters, it will attempt to automatically resolve to an external Microsoft address (internetbeacon.msedge.net) and will return information such as the remote IP address, Internet alias, and PingReplyDetails (RTT in milliseconds). This can be a time-saver when you need to check if a particular server has Internet connectivity, for example.

Running the cmdlet with the –ComputerName parameter gives you the option to specify a specific computer name to run the test against similar to this:

```
Test-NetConnection - ComputerName Host2
```

This will return the following output:

```
PS C:\Windows\system32> test-netconnection –computername Host2
ComputerName           : Host2
RemoteAddress          : 192.168.0.200
InterfaceAlias         : Ethernet
SourceAddress          : 192.168.0.100
PingSucceeded          : True
PingReplyDetails (RTT) : 0 ms
```

Microsoft NIC Teaming

The purpose of NIC Teaming is to combine two or more network interface adapters to create a single logical adapter to provide fault tolerance or bandwidth aggregation for your network connections. Adapters that are members of a NIC team each maintain their own separate physical existence and each connect to separate network cables.

In earlier releases of Windows Server, NIC Teaming was available only through the use of third-party software solutions—such as HP, Intel, and Dell—and required specific network adapter hardware. If you had a network-connectivity problem on a server that had NIC Teaming configured and had to make a support call to Microsoft to troubleshoot the problem, you would be told to contact the third-party vendor for help because NIC Teaming wasn't Microsoft's responsibility. In Windows Server 2012 R2, however, NIC Teaming is built into the operating system, and the cool thing is that it's vendor, hardware, and line-speed agnostic. This section will help you to understand the benefits of Windows Server 2012 R2 NIC Teaming, and we will show you how to easily create and manage a NIC team in your environment.

Understanding the Benefits of a Windows Server 2012 R2 NIC Team

In today's always-connected world, it's essential that the network connections on your servers remain fault tolerant and that they can maintain uptime in the event of a failed adapter. Windows Server 2012 R2 helps to deliver this fault tolerance through the use of NIC Teaming—also known as load balancing and failover (LBFO). It negates the need to purchase any additional (and potentially expensive) hardware or software. With NIC Teaming, multiple network adapters work together as a single logical connection, ensuring that connectivity is maintained even if one network adapter fails. It provides a scenario whereby a server can tolerate network adapter and port failure up to the first switch segment.

You can also use it to aggregate bandwidth from multiple network adapters to deliver better and faster network throughput. For example, if you had three 1-Gbps adapters in a server and decided to create a NIC team with them all, then you would end up with a new logical teamed adapter that provides an aggregate of 3 Gbps of throughput.

Other benefits of NIC Teaming are that it provides a common set of management tools for all network adapter types, eliminates potential problems caused by proprietary solutions, and, of course, is fully supported by Microsoft.

NIC Team Configurations

When you deploy NIC Teaming in Windows Server 2012 R2, you can choose from three basic teaming modes:

Static Teaming　Also known as switch-dependent, this type of configuration requires the switch to be aware of and to participate in the NIC Teaming. Since the NIC team is dependent on the switch, you must ensure that all of the members of the NIC team be connected to the same physical switch and not spread across multiple different switches, as shown in Figure 4.1.

Switch-independent Teaming　Choosing a switch-independent teaming configuration does not require the switch to participate in the teaming. Here, the switch doesn't know that the network adapter is part of a team in the host, and so the adapters can be connected to different switches to provide basic fault tolerance at the switch level too. This teaming configuration will work with any switches, including non-intelligent/team-aware ones, since all of the intelligence required to support NIC Teaming is handled inside Windows Server 2012. Figure 4.2 shows an example of switch-independent teaming.

FIGURE 4.1
Switch-dependent teaming

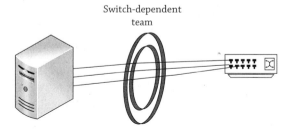

Switch-dependent
team

FIGURE 4.2
Switch-independent teaming

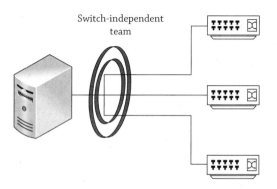

Switch-independent
team

LACP Similar to static teaming, the Link Aggregation Control Protocol (LACP) mode requires that the switches be preconfigured to enable LACP. Once enabled, it can be used to automatically combine multiple NICs into one logical link any time the switch is reconfigured. This removes administrative overhead and makes the network admin's job easier.

When you've chosen the teaming mode, you need to decide on a load-balancing mode to determine how the traffic is handled once it passes through your NIC team. Windows Server 2012 R2 has the following three load-balancing modes to work with:

Address Hash When packets are received on your team using this mode, they first get inspected and then a hashing algorithm is carried out on the destination information—typically the port, IP, and MAC addresses. Using the results of the algorithm, the NIC team then determines which physical NIC will be used to send the packet.

Hyper-V Port This mode can be deployed when you are configuring a NIC team to be used with the Hyper-V role (hence the name). It's not a prerequisite for configuring your virtual networking, but it does have some benefits over address hashing when using Hyper-V. For example, it can be more predictable when sending packets through NICs that are used for Hyper-V, particularly if the team is connected to an external virtual switch.

Dynamic This is a new load-balancing mode that was introduced with Windows Server 2012 R2. This gives you the best of the other two load-balancing modes. Both inbound and outbound traffic can be spread out evenly across the members of your NIC team using a concept called *flowlets*, which essentially breaks up a large flow of traffic into smaller pieces to deliver optimal data transfer.

Depending on whether you are planning to create your NIC team on a physical server or from inside a virtual server, there are a few requirements and limitations to consider:

NIC Teaming on a Physical Server Windows Server 2012 R2 supports up to 32 NICs in a team that has been created on a physical server. You must have at least one NIC to create a team: a one-NIC team could be used for VLAN traffic separation, but a minimum of two NICs are recommended to provide for fault tolerance.

NIC Teaming inside a Virtual Machine If you decide to deploy NIC Teaming from inside a virtual machine, then you will be limited to using only two NIC members to form the team. The reason for this boils down to supportability from Microsoft and doesn't necessarily mean that you can't create larger NIC teams for demo or test purposes.

Supported NIC Types Just about any Ethernet NIC can be used for NIC Teaming, providing it has passed the Windows Hardware Qualification Loop test. The following NIC types, however, *are not* supported:

◆ WLAN

◆ Bluetooth

◆ WWAN

◆ Infiniband

Mixing Different NIC Speeds If you are creating your NIC team for the purpose of load balancing and better throughput (as opposed to for failover reasons), then you must ensure that each NIC in the team has the same speed connection (all 1 Gbps, for example). Mixing NICs with different speeds—such as some 1 Gbps and others 100 Mbps—in a team is not supported, and undesired results will occur if you deploy your team in this way.

NIC TEAMING ONLINE RESOURCES

If you want to learn more about NIC Teaming in Windows Server 2012, then take the time to read over this excellent series of blog posts by Irish Hyper-V MVP Aidan Finn:

```
http://www.aidanfinn.com/?p=13984
```

Another resource worth checking out is the "What's New in Windows Server 2012 R2 Networking" session that was recorded at Microsoft's TechEd North America 2013 conference and is available here:

```
http://channel9.msdn.com/Events/TechEd/NorthAmerica/2013/MDC-B216
```

Configuring NIC Teaming

Creating and managing a NIC team in Windows Server 2012 R2 is really easy. You can either create the team with a few simple mouse clicks directly from the graphical user interface (GUI) or just use PowerShell cmdlets to achieve the same goal. This section will walk you through both scenarios.

To configure your NIC team using the GUI, follow these steps:

1. Log on to your Windows Server 2012 machine with an account that has administrative permissions, and open Server Manager.

2. Click Local Server from the menu options on the left side, and you should see in the properties pane that NIC Teaming is currently disabled, as shown in Figure 4.3.

FIGURE 4.3
Verifying
NIC Teaming
status

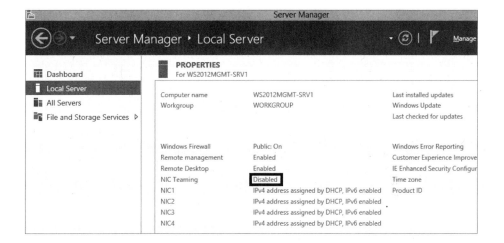

3. Click the Disabled link next to NIC Teaming to open the NIC Teaming dialog box, as shown in Figure 4.4.

4. While in the Adapters and Interfaces section of the NIC Teaming dialog box, hold down the Ctrl key on your keyboard and then, with your mouse, click each of the adapters that you want to create a new team with.

5. Now right-click the selected adapters and choose the Add to New Team option from the context menu, as shown in Figure 4.5.

6. When the New Team dialog box opens, enter a name for your new team in the Team Name field, and ensure that all of the network adapters that you want to add have been selected in the Member Adapters section.

FIGURE 4.4
NIC Teaming
dialog box

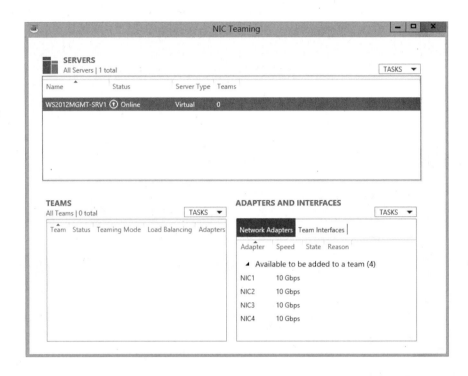

FIGURE 4.5
Adding adapters to a team

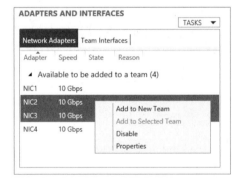

As you can see from Figure 4.6, expanding the Additional Properties option will enable you to configure the Teaming and Load Balancing modes.

7. Choose which adapter will be configured as standby (if applicable) and select the primary team interface with VLAN membership (if applicable).

8. Click OK to create the new NIC team.

After a few seconds, you will see that the team has been created and added to the Teams section of the NIC Teaming dialog box, as shown in Figure 4.7.

FIGURE 4.6
New Team dialog box

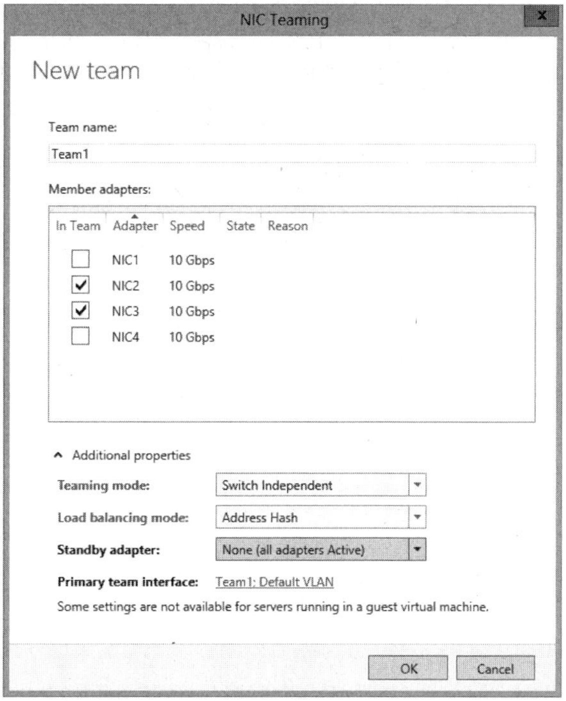

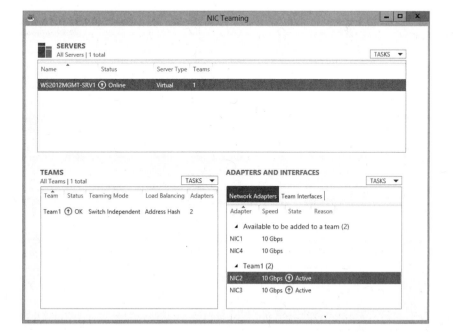

FIGURE 4.7
Newly created NIC team

If you open Network Connections from the control panel, you can see the new NIC team object that has been created, and when you check its status and configured speed, you will see that it has combined the speed of all the NICs in the team. Our example in Figure 4.8 shows a speed of 20 Gbps because we have added two virtual NICs to our team.

FIGURE 4.8

NIC team status

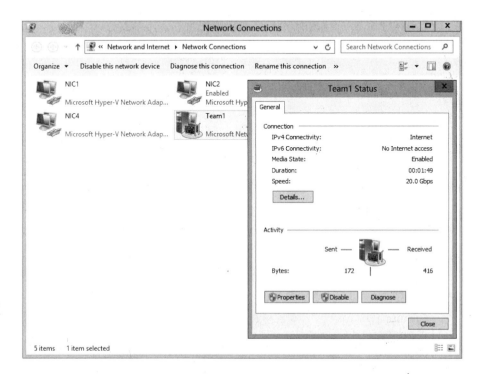

NIC Teaming in Virtual Machines

If you choose to deploy NIC Teaming inside your Hyper-V virtual machines (VMs), first be aware that you can use only synthetic NICs as members of a NIC team and not legacy NICs. Synthetic NICs are the default configuration for a VM in Hyper-V. Second, failover between teamed NICs in a VM might result in traffic being sent with the wrong MAC address reference, and this could drastically affect load balancing. To alleviate this issue, you must ensure that each Hyper-V switch port on the Hyper-V host that is associated with a VM using NIC Teaming is configured to allow teaming. To do this, using an account with administrative permissions, run the following PowerShell command on each host:

```
Set-VMNetworkAdapter -VMName <YourVMnameHere> -AllowTeaming On
```

If you want to be able to create your NIC team using PowerShell, then follow these steps (we've configured our NIC team here the same way as we had it when we used the GUI to create it earlier):

1. Open a PowerShell window with an account that has administrative permissions, and type the following (make sure to substitute the team and NIC names to match your own environment):

```
New-NetLbfoTeam Team1 NIC3,NIC4
```

2. Type Y for yes, and then hit Enter to confirm that you want to perform the action.

In Figure 4.9, you can see that the new NIC team has been created from inside PowerShell.

FIGURE 4.9

Creating a NIC team with PowerShell

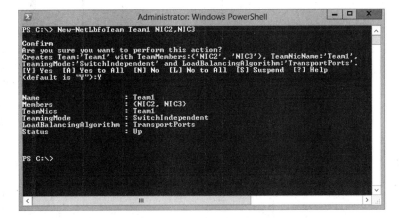

🌐 Real World Scenario

DON'T MIX DIFFERENT TEAMING SOLUTIONS

Dylan was a Windows Server 2012 administrator working on the internal support team in a shared-hosting multi-tenant datacenter. His responsibility was to maintain network connectivity and uptime on the Windows Server 2012 cluster environment being used by customers.

When he was creating the original cluster, Dylan had configured the new NIC Teaming functionality that came built in with Windows Server 2012 and was very happy with the performance and link aggregation that it provided. While Dylan was away on vacation, however, one of his colleagues on the support team decided to do some patching and general maintenance on the cluster after hours. Unfortunately, this colleague wasn't very familiar with the new NIC Teaming feature in Windows Server 2012 and didn't realize it had been configured on the cluster. As a result, he deployed a third-party NIC Teaming solution on top of the existing one and made one of the Microsoft NIC Teaming member NICs a part of the third-party NIC team. This meant that when Dylan returned from vacation, there were now two different NIC Teaming solutions in place on the cluster and both shared the same NICs.

Over the next few days, the cluster continually lost network connectivity and became unstable. When Dylan began to troubleshoot the issue, he quickly realized that there were two different NIC Teaming solutions in place. On investigation, he found an article on Microsoft's Windows Server 2012 TechNet support site that offered the following advice:

"It is strongly recommended that no system administrator ever run two teaming solutions at the same time on the same server. The teaming solutions are unaware of each other's existence resulting in potentially serious problems.

"In the event that an administrator violates these guidelines and gets into the situation described above, the following steps may solve the problem:

1. Reboot the server. Forcibly power-off the server if necessary to get it to reboot.

2. When the server has rebooted run this Windows PowerShell cmdlet:

   ```
   Get-NetLbfoTeam | Remove-NetLbfoTeam
   ```

3. Use the third-party teaming solution's administration tools and remove all instances of the third-party teams.

4. Reboot the server again.

"Microsoft continues its longstanding policy of not supporting third-party teaming solutions. If a user chooses to run a third-party teaming solution and then encounters networking problems, the customer should call their teaming solution provider for support. If the issue is reproducible without the third-party teaming solution in place, please report the problem to Microsoft."

Once Dylan carried out the steps listed in the TechNet article, removing the third-party NIC Teaming solution and re-creating the Windows Server 2012 NIC team, the cluster started to function properly again.

Enhanced QoS

Quality of Service has been a feature of Microsoft operating systems for years, and it allows administrators to configure and deploy policies that predetermine which applications or services should be prioritized when it comes to allocating bandwidth. In other words, traffic for specific network applications will be transmitted before or after other applications. Administrators can determine critical interactive services such as Voice over IP (VoIP) and line-of-business (LOB) applications that must have acceptable levels and bandwidth available to them whenever they seek it.

Even though QoS is delivered through the Windows operating system, the network devices (such as adapters, switches, routers, and gateways) that are responsible for communications between hosts must also be QoS aware. Any non-QoS-aware devices that handle QoS-assigned traffic will deal with the traffic on a best-effort "first come, first served" basis, in the same way that standard network communications work.

QoS INSIDE VIRTUAL MACHINES

Enabling QoS in Windows Server 2012 when it's running as a guest virtual machine within a virtualized environment is not recommended. QoS is designed for traffic management on physical networks rather than virtual networks and should instead be configured in the management operating system on a physical host server with the Hyper-V role deployed.

Minimum Bandwidth

In earlier operating systems, you could use QoS only to enforce maximum bandwidth consumption—also known as rate limiting—and you didn't have the ability to specify minimum bandwidth. Instead of a bandwidth-reservation system, it was more like a bandwidth-throttling solution. This was a big problem when trying to achieve the right QoS bandwidth-management policy in virtual datacenter environments and, as a result, didn't lend itself well to enterprises that were quickly embracing cloud-hosting solutions.

To solve this problem, Minimum Bandwidth was introduced as a new feature to QoS in Windows Server 2012. Minimum Bandwidth provides the bandwidth-reservation solution that was missing with previous iterations and gives you the ability to ensure different types of network traffic get the granular bandwidth configurations that they require.

If you want to learn about Microsoft's best practices for deploying QoS Minimum Bandwidth, then take a look at their guide located here: http://tinyurl.com/ws2012qosmb.

RECOMMENDED ADAPTER SPEEDS FOR MINIMUM BANDWIDTH

Microsoft has determined that Minimum Bandwidth works best on either 1-gigabit Ethernet network adapters or 10-gigabit Ethernet network adapters. Adapters with lower capacity than these are not suitable for QoS.

Data Center Bridging

Data Center Bridging (DCB) is a supported feature in Windows Server 2012 that provides guaranteed bandwidth to different types of network traffic on a converged network infrastructure or converged fabric. Converged traffic has different mixed classes, such as high-speed SAN, VoIP, and traditional LAN—all of which you would typically want to keep isolated from each other. DCB offloads QoS calculations and policy from the main processor and onto the NIC. For this reason, if you want to use DCB in your environment, make sure that your network adapters and switches support DCB functionality.

An example of the benefits here would be from a hosted cloud provider's perspective. When they implement DCB, it could be particularly efficient in helping to reduce complexity by allowing all traffic to flow over the same hardware infrastructure as a converged single subnet with isolated segments, thus removing the requirement for specific isolated hardware that SAN storage typically requires to keep the storage traffic separate from the LAN traffic.

MANAGING DCB

You have to manage DCB through Windows Management Instrumentation (WMI) and PowerShell once the Data Center Bridging feature has been enabled on your Windows Server 2012 servers. The following procedure will enable DCB from the GUI:

1. Log on to your Windows Server 2012 machine with an account that has administrative permissions and open Server Manager.

2. In the Configure This Local Server dialog box, click the Add Roles and Features option, and then click Next in the Before You Begin dialog box of the Add Roles and Features Wizard.

3. Select the Role-Based or Feature-Based installation option and then click Next.

4. In the Select Destination Server dialog box, choose the "Select a Server from the Server Pool" option.

5. Ensure that your server is selected in the Server Pool section; then click Next to proceed.

6. In the Select Server Roles dialog box, just click Next to continue.

7. Select the check box beside Data Center Bridging in the "Select features" dialog box, as shown in Figure 4.10, and then click Next.

FIGURE 4.10
Enabling Data
Center Bridging

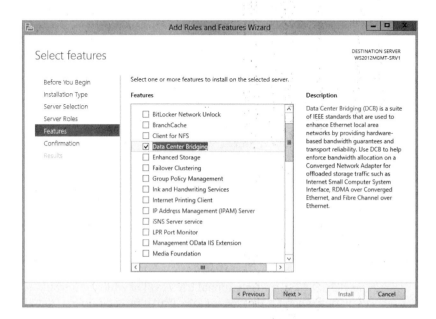

8. In the Confirm Installation Selections dialog box, click Install to enable DCB.

Once you have enabled DCB, you can use the PowerShell cmdlets listed in Table 4.3 to manage it.

TABLE 4.3: DCB PowerShell Cmdlets

CMDLET	DESCRIPTION
Get-NetQosFlowControl	Gets the priority-based flow control (PFC) settings
Set-NetQosFlowControl	Sets the flow control settings
Enable-NetQosFlowControl	Enables link-level flow control based on the IEEE 802.1p priority
Disable-NetQosFlowControl	Disables link-level flow control based on the IEEE 802.1p priority

TABLE 4.3:   DCB PowerShell Cmdlets   *(CONTINUED)*

CMDLET	DESCRIPTION
Get-NetQosDcbxSetting	Gets the data center bridging exchange (DCBX) settings
Set-NetQosDcbxSetting	Sets the DCBX settings
Get-NetQosTrafficClass	Gets the traffic class settings
New-NetQosTrafficClass	Creates a new traffic class
Set-NetQosTrafficClass	Sets the traffic class settings
Remove-NetQosTrafficClass	Removes a traffic class

To learn more about managing DCB through PowerShell, check out the DCB Windows PowerShell User Scripting Guide here: http://tinyurl.com/ws2012dcb.

CAN MINIMUM BANDWIDTH AND DCB WORK TOGETHER?

Although Minimum Bandwidth and DCB have the same functionality, that is, to ensure that a workload receives its fair share of bandwidth when network congestion occurs, they are not designed to work together. It's important to note that you should never enable both Minimum Bandwidth and DCB for workloads that share the same networking stack or NIC because it would cause major bandwidth and performance issues on your network.

Hyper-V QoS

QoS for Hyper-V can be extremely useful to organizations that offer multi-tenant cloud-hosting services where they are held accountable to service-level agreements (SLAs) on network bandwidth. By utilizing Hyper-V QoS, these organizations can ensure that throttling and segmentation of network traffic are delivered seamlessly.

Microsoft defines the following capabilities for Hyper-V QoS:

◆ Enforce minimum bandwidth and maximum bandwidth for traffic flow, which is identified by a Hyper-V virtual switch port number.

◆ Configure minimum bandwidth and maximum bandwidth per Hyper-V virtual switch port by using either PowerShell cmdlets or Windows Management Instrumentation.

◆ Configure multiple virtual network adapters in Hyper-V, and specify QoS on each virtual network adapter individually.

Hyper-V QoS can take advantage of DCB-supported hardware to converge multiple workload types of Hyper-V network traffic (such as live migration, cluster shared volume, and storage traffic) onto a single network adapter with a guaranteed bandwidth SLA assigned to each type. Doing this would then enable far more efficient utilization of expensive high-speed network adapters such as 10-gigabit Ethernet.

Policy-Based QoS

Using Group Policy, you can determine an application's QoS by the following settings:

◆ The sending application and directory path

◆ The destination and source IP addresses and ports

◆ The protocol, either TCP or UDP

◆ Active Directory users or groups

Working together, these settings will determine the Differentiated Services Code Point (DSCP) value. TCP will use this to inject a value from 0 to 63 into the Type of Service (TOS) field in a TCP IPv4 packet. Note that it also injects the value into the Traffic Class field in an IPv6 packet. Routers on the network will then use the DSCP value to determine which packets to prioritize or throttle. The higher the DSCP value assigned by an administrator via Group Policy, the higher the routers will prioritize the associated packets.

Policy-based QoS can be configured either through local Group Policy or Active Directory domain Group Policy configurations, and a QoS policy can be created at the computer level, at the user level, or at both levels if you so wish. It's generally recommended to apply your QoS policy at the computer level, though, because that ensures that no matter which users log onto the device, they will all receive the same QoS configuration. Figure 4.11 shows the Policy-based QoS container inside the Local Computer Policy Computer Configuration view.

FIGURE 4.11
Policy-based QoS in the Group Policy Editor

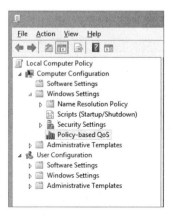

Let's look at an example. An administrator needs to prioritize the LOB application when it is being used by sales staff and directors. You know it operates on TCP 3299 and that you have user groups in Active Directory for sales and for directors. You can build a group policy targeting TCP 3299 and the aforementioned user groups while placing a higher than normal DSCP value of 60 on the application. This value will be injected into all packets on TCP 3299 that are associated with those users in the user groups. The network routers will then interrogate this value in the IPv4 or IPv6 packets and prioritize them as instructed.

The prerequisites for policy-based QoS are as follows:

◆ The managed computers must be running Windows Server 2012, Windows Server 2008 R2/R1, Windows 8, Windows 7, or Windows Vista.

◆ They must be members of an Active Directory domain so that you can deploy your policies using Group Policy.

◆ The routers that reside between the clients and servers must be capable of being configured for DSCP (see RFC 2474 at `http://tinyurl.com/nb852k`).

Be sure to check off each of these prerequisites before you start your QoS deployment. You don't want to think that you have control of everything using QoS only to find that QoS isn't actually doing anything all! The network routers are the prerequisite that could cause the most pain. There could be significant cost and maybe even some difficulty if you've completely outsourced your WAN deployment. Deploying QoS will require a good deal of planning and research on your part. Every organization will have different needs, and you will have to work quite closely with management and the business to design your solution.

802.1X Authenticated Access

The 802.1X authentication protocol is defined by the Institute of Electrical and Electronics Engineers (IEEE) Standards Association and provides an additional layer of security for devices that you want to connect to your local area network (LAN) or wireless local area network (WLAN) environments. It operates at the network adapter port level and can be used to ensure any unwanted computers that cannot perform a successful authentication are denied access to your intranet.

Although 802.1X has been around for a number of years and has had varied levels of support from Microsoft since Windows 2000, there is some new functionality in Windows Server 2012 that wasn't available in the earlier operating system releases. Step forward the Extensible Authentication Protocol (EAP) Tunneled Transport Layer Security (TTLS), otherwise known as EAP-TTLS.

EAP-TTLS is essentially a standards-based EAP tunneling method that supports mutual authentication. It enables client authentication security by providing a secure tunnel using a combination of EAP methods, legacy authentication databases, and legacy password mechanisms.

You can learn more about 802.1X wired and wireless authentication at these locations: `http://tinyurl.com/8021wired` and `http://tinyurl.com/8021wireless`.

BranchCache Improved

BranchCache has been around for some time and is a built-in feature that you can deploy to Windows Server 2012 R2 that enables WAN optimization for organizations with remote branch offices. When remote content is requested by computers in the branch office from the head office or datacenter, BranchCache will store that content on the local (requesting) network, either on a dedicated server or among assigned client workstations. This provides access to files and folders at faster speeds while using less bandwidth. As the remote content gets cached on the local network, any other clients that subsequently request the same content can then access it immediately from the LAN instead of having to download it from the WAN.

BranchCache can be configured as two different modes:

Distributed Cache Mode   When BranchCache is configured in this mode, there's no need to have any server computers located in the branch offices. Instead, when data gets requested and downloaded from the main office by client computers that are located in the branch office, they cache the data locally. The next time other client computers in the same branch office request the same content, they simply access it from the cache on the original client computers.

Hosted Cache Mode   With Hosted Cache mode, server computers must be located at the branch offices. These computers act as local content servers, and when the branch office client computers request and download data from the main office, the content servers then retrieve and cache the data until such time as other client computers in the same branch office need it.

Although BranchCache has been available in previous versions of Windows Server, it has some significant enhancements in Windows Server 2012:

Deep Windows File Server Integration   Utilizing the new data de-duplication functionality of Windows Server 2012 to index content, BranchCache can ensure that bandwidth savings are optimal. Chapter 12 discusses the data de-duplication feature of Windows Server 2012 in greater detail.

Duplicate Content Handling   When duplicate content exists inside a single file or even spread across many different files, BranchCache will store only one instance of that content, ensuring better bandwidth and disk space savings.

No Limit to Office Sizes or Number of Branch Offices   When BranchCache is deployed in Hosted Cache mode, there's no limit to the number of branch offices that you can have as part of your BranchCache solution.

Simplified Deployment with Active Directory   No matter what size organization you deploy BranchCache into, the configuration is managed through a single Active Directory Group Policy object (GPO) ensuring easy management for your infrastructure team.

Automatic Client Computer Configuration   Active Directory Group Policy can also be used to configure client computers as Distributed Cache mode clients by default. If the clients are configured in this way, and they find that a hosted cache server is present, they will then automatically configure themselves as Hosted Cache mode clients instead.

Faster Performance through Offline Content Creation   If BranchCache has been enabled on your servers, then the calculations for content information gathering are performed offline before any of the client computers actually request the data. The result of this is enhanced performance and better bandwidth savings.

Encrypted Cache Data   By default, all of your cached data is now stored with encryption, ensuring data security and integrity are always maintained.

PowerShell and WMI Management   You can now utilize PowerShell and WMI scripting to help manage your BranchCache server and client environments.

If you choose to deploy BranchCache in Hosted Cache mode with Windows Server 2012 R2, then you can take advantage of the following improvements:

More Than One Hosted Cache Server per Location Previously, you could deploy only a single hosted cache server at each office location in the organization. With Windows Server 2012 (or higher) in Hosted Cache mode, you have the capability to deploy multiple hosted cache servers at each location, thus aiding scalability.

Better Database Technology Extensible Storage Engine (ESE) database technology now runs inside the BranchCache databases, delivering far superior performance and storage functionality than previous iterations. This is the same technology that powers Microsoft Exchange Server and is a proven database enhancer in the enterprise.

Managing Network Performance

Understanding how to manage the performance of your networking environment is paramount to ensuring that your business can maintain an optimal level of productivity. This section discusses some of the features and tools that can help you to achieve this goal. In Chapter 30, "Monitoring Windows Server 2012 R2," we talk about performance monitoring in greater detail.

When we talk about network performance being good or bad, there's typically at least one of the performance metrics in Table 4.4 involved in the end result.

TABLE 4.4: Performance Metrics

METRIC	DESCRIPTION
Latency	The time required for an operation to complete. Lower is better.
Scalability	The ability to adapt to increasing demand on system resources. Higher is better.
Throughput	The amount of data transferred or processed in a given time period. Higher is better.
Path Length	The number of CPU cycles divided by the throughput. Lower is better.
Jitter	Fluctuation in throughput and/or latency. Lower is better.

If you want to deliver top performance to your networks by managing these performance metrics, then you need to understand and be able to leverage some of the following Windows Server 2012 R2 features:

Receive Segment Coalescing If your servers are constantly under stress with heavy receive workloads, then you can take advantage of Receive Segment Coalescing (RSC) to remove the overhead from the server and pass it on to RSC-compatible NICs instead. It works by combining smaller packets of data flows into a single larger packet to increase performance.

Registered I/O Registered I/O (RIO) is primarily targeted at application developers who are writing applications that need to send and receive data at microsecond granularity. It enables send and receive operations to be performed with preregistered buffers using queues for requests and completions. Low latency is achieved with RIO by pinning the application memory and therefore reducing the CPU cost.

Receive-Side Scaling   Receive-Side Scaling (RSS) works well with web servers and file servers, and it can be used to distribute the receive network traffic across multiple processors so that packets that belong to the same TCP connection are processed on the same logical processor. As NIC speeds increase (10 Gbps is a lot more prevalent these days), so too will the amount of processing that your CPUs have to do. Without implementing RSS for very heavy workload servers with high network traffic loads, you run the risk of maxing out your CPU utilization and ultimately having to purchase new hardware. To take advantage of RSS, you will, of course, need to have RSS-capable NICs in your servers.

Performance Analysis and Tools

If you want to carry out an analysis of your network performance, then a good place to begin is by using the `Perfmon.exe` tool that comes as part of Windows Server 2012 R2 and examining the data generated by the network-related performance counters listed in Table 4.5.

TABLE 4.5:   Network-Related Performance Counters

OBJECT	ANALYZING	COUNTER
IPv4, IPv6	Resource utilization	Datagrams Received/sec
		Datagrams Sent/sec
TCPv4, TCPv6	Resource utilization	Segments Received/sec
		Segments Sent/sec
		Segments Retransmitted/sec
Network Interface Network Adapter	Resource utilization	Bytes Received/sec
		Bytes Sent/sec
		Packets Received/sec
		Packets Sent/sec
		Output Queue Length
Processor Information	Resource utilization	% Processor Time
		Interrupts/sec
		DPCs Queued/sec
Network Interface Network Adapter	Potential network problems	Packets Received Discarded
		Packets Received Errors
		Packets Outbound Discarded
		Packets Outbound Errors
WFPv4, WFPv6	Potential network problems	Packets Discarded/sec
UDPv4, UDPv6	Potential network problems	Datagrams Received Errors

TABLE 4.5: Network-Related Performance Counters *(CONTINUED)*

OBJECT	ANALYZING	COUNTER
TCPv4, TCPv6	Potential network problems	Connections Failures
		Connections Reset
Network QoS Policy	Potential network problems	Packets Dropped
Per Processor Network Interface Card Activity	Potential network problems	Low Resource Received Indications/sec
		Low Resource Received Packets/sec
Microsoft Winsock BSP	Potential network problems	Dropped Datagrams
		Dropped Datagrams/sec
		Rejected Connections
		Rejected Connections/sec
Network Adapter	RSC performance	TCP Active RSC Connections
		TCP RSC Average Packet Size
		TCP RSC Coalesced Packets/sec
		TCP RSC Exceptions/sec

Server Performance Advisor Tool

If you're looking for something with a bit more depth than `PerfMon.exe`, then you should take a look at the Microsoft Server Performance Advisor (SPA) tool; download version 3.0 from `http://tinyurl.com/ws2012spa` (you'll need a Windows Live ID first). The goal of this tool is to help system administrators assess and troubleshoot their server-performance issues.

SPA provides data reports and recommendations to system administrators about common configuration and performance issues, and it gathers performance-related data from various sources on servers, such as performance counters, registry keys, WMI queries, configuration files, and Event Tracing for Windows (ETW). Based on the server performance data that it collects, SPA can provide an in-depth look at the current server performance situation and issue recommendations about what can be improved.

SPA 3.0 is designed to run on Windows Server 2012 and is primarily targeted at system administrators who manage fewer than 100 servers in various server roles. It can also be used by support engineers to gather performance data and to troubleshoot performance issues for customers.

SPA 3.0 SCALING LIMITATION

The Server Performance Advisor 3.0 tool does not scale well if you are trying to manage performance for more than 100 servers. If you are managing environments larger than this, then you should consider using System Center 2012 R2 Operations Manager as the monitoring and management tool of choice.

INSTALLING SPA 3.0

SPA 3.0 has the following prerequisites that must be in place before you begin installation:

◆ .NET Framework 4

◆ SQL Server 2008 R2 Express

Once you've met the prerequisites, follow these steps to deploy, configure, and run reports from the SPA 3.0 tool on Windows Server 2012:

1. Download the SPAPlus_amd64.cab file and extract its contents to a location on your hard drive.

   A good tip here would be to use something like WinRAR (rarlab.com) or WinZip (winzip.com) to extract the .cab file. In our experience, using the built-in Explorer option to extract the files didn't create the correct folder structure and stopped SPA 3.0 from working properly.

2. From the location where you have extracted the files, locate the SpaConsole.exe application, right-click it, and then choose the "Run as administrator" option to begin, as shown in Figure 4.12.

FIGURE 4.12

Configuring the SPA console

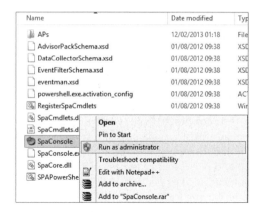

3. Accept the license terms in the Server Performance License Agreement dialog box and then click Next.

4. From the Server Performance Advisor console, click the File option on the menu bar and then choose New Project, as shown Figure 4.13.

5. In the initial New Project Wizard dialog box, click Next.

6. In the Create Project Database dialog box, enter your SQL Server name, and type a SQL database name that you wish to assign to the SPA project. Then click Next.

7. Input the server names that you wish to manage with SPA in the Add Servers dialog box.

FIGURE 4.13

Creating a new project

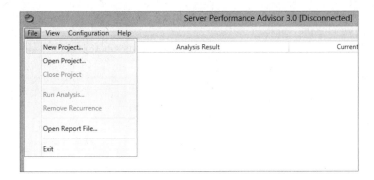

8. Specify the network share that will be used to store the reports, and then click Finish to complete the project setup, as shown in Figure 4.14.

9. Back at the Server Performance Advisor console, select the check box beside your server name, and then click the Run Analysis button to run the report.

10. Choose the advisor packs that are relevant to the system you are running the report against, for example, the Core OS, Hyper-V, or IIS advisor packs; then click OK twice.

FIGURE 4.14

Configuring the server and share

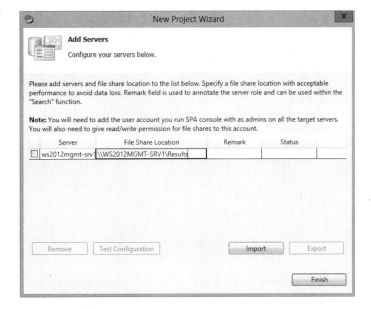

11. Once the analysis has finished, you can then view the report contents through the Report Viewer, as shown in Figure 4.15.

FIGURE 4.15

Viewing the report

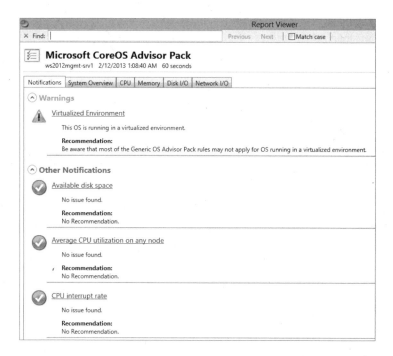

The Bottom Line

Understand IPv6. The journey from IPv4 to IPv6 will definitely not happen in a short time frame, and it became apparent to the designers of IPv6 that both protocols would have to coexist and work together on the same infrastructure. The caveat is that IPv4 and IPv6 cannot natively talk to each other, and for the duration of this transitional period a solution was required to address the communication barriers between these two protocols.

Master It   Which of the following is not an IPv6 transitional technology?

a.   ISATAP

b.   DirectAccess

c.   6to4

d.   Teredo

Use PowerShell for better networking manageability.   Windows Server 2012 R2 has nearly 2,500 PowerShell cmdlets to work with, and from this enormous pool there are literally hundreds that can be used to view, configure, and monitor all of its different networking components and services. You can perform a wide variety of tasks using these cmdlets, ranging from simple IP address configuration to more specialized functions like configuring Quality of Service and virtualization networking parameters.

Master It   Which new cmdlet is built into Windows Server 2012 R2 that is a real contender to replace the traditional `ping` command?

Implement NIC Teaming.   In today's always-connected world, it's essential that the network connections on your servers remain fault tolerant and that they can maintain uptime in the event of a failed adapter. Windows Server 2012 R2 helps to deliver this fault tolerance through the use of NIC Teaming and negates the need to purchase any additional (and potentially expensive) hardware or software.

Master It   If you want to create your NIC team using PowerShell, how would you go about it?

Understand the new QoS features.   Quality of Service (QoS) allows administrators to configure and deploy policies that predetermine which applications or services should be prioritized when it comes to allocating bandwidth. Administrators can determine critical interactive services, such as Voice over IP (VoIP) and line-of-business (LOB) applications, that must have acceptable levels and bandwidth available to them whenever they seek it.

Master It   In earlier operating systems, you could use QoS only to enforce maximum bandwidth consumption, also known as rate limiting. Instead of a bandwidth-reservation system, it was more like a bandwidth-throttling solution. What QoS feature can you use in Windows Server 2012 R2 to solve this problem?

Manage network performance.   Understanding how to manage the performance of your Windows Server 2012 R2 networking environment is paramount to ensuring that your business can maintain an optimal level of productivity.

Master It   Which of the following tools can be used to manage network performance in Windows Server 2012 R2? (Choose two.)

a.   Ipconfig.exe

c.   Perfmon.exe

d.   Dfsrmon.exe

e.   Server Performance Advisor

f.   Networkview.exe

Chapter 5

IP Address Management and DHCP Failover

As network environments get more complex and additional networking protocols such as IPv6 start to become commonplace, the ability to centrally manage and deliver high availability of your IP address configurations is essential. Windows Server 2012 has some additional features to address these requirements delivered through IP Address Management (IPAM) and DHCP Failover. These features work with your existing DNS and DHCP deployments to help you track and reduce outages (and ultimately headaches) related to IP addressing problems.

In this chapter you will learn to:

◆ Implement IPAM

◆ Use IPAM components effectively

◆ Integrate IPAM with System Center 2012

◆ Manage IPAM delegation

◆ Understand DHCP Failover

IPAM

IP Address Management isn't just a new buzz phrase that dictates how you should manage your IP addresses; it's actually a pretty cool (and definitely needed) new feature of Windows Server 2012 that will simplify network complexity through its integration with your existing corporate DNS and DHCP deployments. Microsoft's own words describing IPAM are as follows:

> IPAM is an integrated suite of tools to enable end-to-end planning, deploying, managing and monitoring of your IP address infrastructure, with a rich user experience. IPAM automatically discovers IP address infrastructure servers on your network and enables you to manage them from a central interface.

So, if you're reading that description and thinking, "This sounds like a pretty neat feature, but what kind of problems can I expect it to solve for me?" then here are some typical examples of IP address management issues that you might be able to relate to:

◆ You're trying your best to manually maintain a number of different spreadsheets and custom databases containing (what you hope is) all of the IP addresses for your network environments.

◆ You need to quickly identify a free IP address for a new network computer or device and then ensure it gets registered in DNS.

◆ One of your DHCP scopes has reached its maximum limit, and you need to identify and expand it as quickly as possible.

◆ You have a requirement to track which addresses are in use across multiple different locations and subnets, including virtual address spaces.

◆ You want to make a change to a DHCP option that's spread across all of your different DHCP scopes, such as removing old WINS server references or changing the web proxy.

◆ You're tired of having to open a myriad of different DNS and DHCP consoles each time you want to make a change that is applicable across the entire networking environment.

With IPAM deployed, you can reduce the amount of time spent maintaining existing and new IPv4 and IPv6 address ranges. The more complex your IP address environment is, the more it makes sense to utilize this feature. Furthermore, organizations that have a mixture of physical and virtual networks can now have a unified IP address-management solution across them.

A nice feature of IPAM is that it will automatically search your environment to locate all of your DNS, Domain Controller, and DHCP servers and will give you the option to then bring them under centralized management control or not. If you've deployed the Network Policy Server (NPS) role to any servers in your network, IPAM will not automatically find these, but you can easily add them in manually to bring them under IPAM control. Figure 5.1 shows an example of how IPAM works with your servers to help you centralize your address-management designs.

FIGURE 5.1
IPAM

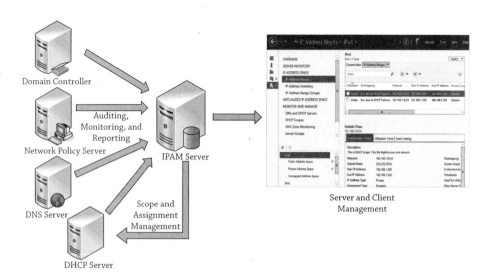

IPAM Requirements

As with any type of configuration or deployment, it's always best practice to ensure that all of the relevant prerequisites have been met. Before you deploy IPAM into your environment, be aware of the following requirements.

WINDOWS SERVER SUPPORT

Because IPAM was introduced with Windows Server 2012, you will need to install it onto a Windows Server 2012 (or higher) computer running either Standard or Datacenter edition. Once installed, IPAM will be able to manage only DHCP, DNS, and Domain Controller servers running Windows Server 2008 or higher. This means that if you still have some legacy Windows Server 2003 or Windows Server 2000 computers on your network, you'll have to manage them the old "decentralized" way.

ACTIVE DIRECTORY SUPPORT

An IPAM server must be a member of an Active Directory domain; non-domain-joined IPAM server deployments are not supported. The IPAM server can operate only within the confines of a single Active Directory forest, but inside that forest you can have a mix of trusted and untrusted domains that can all be managed by the IPAM server. Also, you can manage only domain-joined servers; any servers that are not members of an Active Directory domain will not be supported with IPAM.

CAN I INSTALL IPAM ONTO A DOMAIN CONTROLLER OR DHCP SERVER?

In short, the answer is no. Even though you won't get an error when initially installing the IPAM feature, deploying it onto a server with the Active Directory Services Domain Controller role already in place is not supported. When you later attempt to provision the IPAM server after the initial feature deployment, it will cause you no end of problems and ultimately won't work. Similarly, if you deploy IPAM onto a computer with the DHCP server role installed, then IPAM discovery of DHCP servers on the network will be disabled.

DHCP AND DNS SUPPORT

The following support limits are applicable for DHCP and DNS environments managed by IPAM:

- DHCP and DNS servers must be members of an Active Directory domain.
- A single IPAM server can support up to 150 DHCP servers and up to 6,000 DHCP scopes.
- A single IPAM server can support up to 500 DNS servers and up to 150 DNS zones.

DATABASE SUPPORT

IPAM needs to store all of its configuration and data inside a database. Here's what you need to know about IPAM database support:

◆ What Microsoft calls "forensics data" is stored in the IPAM database for auditing and tracking purposes for up to three years.

This data is made up of a combination of IP address leases, MAC addresses, and login/logoff information for up to 100,000 users. That's a lot of data to store, yet strangely enough Microsoft hasn't provided a database purge policy. You, as the IPAM administrator, must purge the data from the database manually as required.

◆ IPAM in Windows Server 2012 (non-R2) supports only the default Windows Internal Database offering. No other external database is supported.

◆ IPAM in Windows Server 2012 R2, however, gives you the option to use either the Windows Internal Database or a SQL 2008 R2/SQL 2012 database. The SQL database can be co-located on the same server where IPAM is running, or it can be located externally on a remote computer.

NETWORKING SUPPORT

It's a no-brainer to presume that a healthy IPAM deployment is dependent on a fully functional (IPv4/IPv6) networking environment, but here are a few additional things to be aware of on the networking side:

◆ There's no support for non-Microsoft network elements (such as NetBIOS Name Service, DHCP relays, or proxies).

◆ WINS is a legacy Microsoft NetBIOS name-resolution solution and is also not supported by IPAM.

◆ If you want access to IP address utilization trend data from IPAM, then you'll have to make do with just IPv4 reporting because IPv6 address utilization trend data is not yet supported.

◆ IPv6 IP address reclaiming support is not available; only IPv4 support is available.

◆ IPAM does not cross-reference its IP address consistency with routers and switches, so be aware of any DHCP services running on these devices.

IPAM Components

IPAM is made up of three different feature components that integrate to deliver holistic management of your IP address infrastructure. These three components deliver functionality around Multi-Server Management and Monitoring, Address Space Management, and Network Auditing. This section will discuss each of these three features in detail to ensure you have a full understanding of the IPAM suite and knowledge of where each piece can fit into your network-management designs.

MULTI-SERVER MANAGEMENT AND MONITORING

The Multi-Server Management and Monitoring feature of IPAM delivers the automated discovery of manageable DHCP and DNS servers and provides centralization of the resources they serve. If you don't want to use the automatic discovery method, you can still choose to add or remove your DHCP and DNS servers manually. The ability to perform simultaneous updates to all of your DHCP and DNS servers at once stems from this feature.

This feature also provides monitoring functionality that can check the availability of your DHCP scopes and DNS zones.

ADDRESS SPACE MANAGEMENT

The Address Space Management (ASM) feature of IPAM delivers full transparency of your IP address infrastructure from a single centralized console. It includes a neat reporting function that allows you to track IPv4 address utilization trends and produce the data in easy-to-consume reports. Using ASM to ensure better planning, accountability, and control on your network can be the real difference between being proactive (fixing the problem before it happens) or reactive (learning about the problem after it happens) to IP addressing problems.

You can use IPAM ASM to detect overlapping IP address ranges or scopes that have been configured differently across DHCP servers, as well as create DNS and DHCP entries and locate any free IP addresses within a range. Figure 5.2 shows an IP address range utilization trend graph over a one-month period.

FIGURE 5.2
ASM trend graph

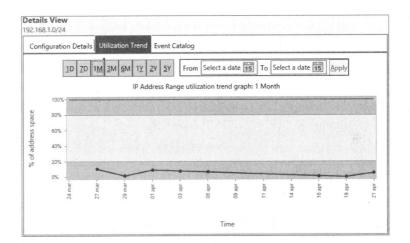

NETWORK AUDITING

The Network Auditing feature of IPAM dives into the Windows event logs on your DHCP servers and gives you a full view of all DHCP configuration changes that have occurred in the environment. It correlates data from the IPAM database, DHCP server lease logs, and your DC and NPS security logs to surface tracking information on users, devices, and IP addresses. With this type of data readily available and fully searchable, you can then run reports on the fly to help identify any configuration issues.

Topology Deployment Options

You have three different topology design options to choose from when deploying IPAM to manage an IP address estate that's spread across multiple physical and logical environments. These types of configurations are categorized and defined in Table 5.1.

TABLE 5.1:   IPAM Topologies

TOPOLOGY	DEFINITION
Centralized	One IPAM server in a central location to manage everything.
Distributed	An IPAM server deployed to each site in the enterprise. The information on each IPAM server will be isolated to each site with no out-of-box replication or syncing of data between the different IPAM servers in the enterprise.
Hybrid	This topology design utilizes a mixture of both the centralized and distributed models and has a central IPAM server deployed along with a number of distributed IPAM servers on different sites.

IPAM Installation

Now that you have an understanding of what IPAM is, we can walk through the installation process. The steps in this section presume that you have either an existing production IP address infrastructure (DC, DNS, DHCP, and the like) to manage or that you have at least followed the steps outlined in this book to build and configure a lab or test network (we're using the Bigfirm.com domain for our sample environment here) that you can deploy IPAM into.

Here are the high-level steps required to get it deployed:

1. Install the IPAM Server feature with the Add Roles and Features Wizard.

2. Configure IPAM provisioning either manually or by using Group Policy.

3. Configure DHCP and DNS server discoveries across your domain(s).

4. Run discovery of your DHCP and DNS servers.

5. Choose discovered servers to be managed.

6. Retrieve data from your managed DHCP and DNS servers.

7. Install the IPAM client on additional computers.

Installing the IPAM Server Feature

In this section, we will walk through the installation of the IPAM feature:

1. To begin, log on to your domain-joined Windows Server 2012 R2 installation with an account that has domain administrative permissions, and from the Server Manager ➢ Local Server ➢ Manage menu, choose the Add Roles and Features option.

2. In the Before You Begin dialog box, click Next.

3. Ensure that Role-based or Feature-based Installation is selected in the Select Installation Type dialog box; then click Next.

4. Under Select Destination Server, leave the default option of "Select a Server from the Server Pool" checked, confirm that your server is highlighted in the Server Pool section, and then click Next to continue.

5. Don't choose any of the options from the Select Server Roles dialog box; just click Next here to move on.

6. When you reach the Select Features dialog box, scroll down until you find the IP Address Management (IPAM) Server option from the Features list and check the box beside it, as shown in Figure 5.3. You'll then be prompted to add some required features here, such as the Group Policy Management console and the Windows Internal Database, so just click the Add Features button in the window that pops up. Click Next again to continue.

FIGURE 5.3
Choosing the
IPAM feature

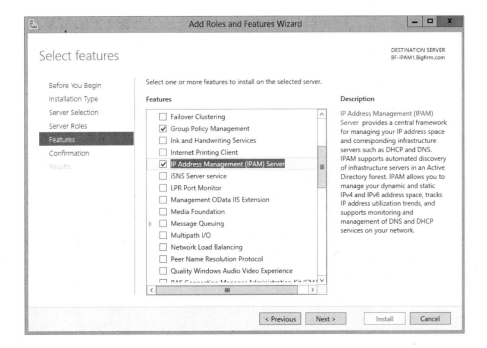

7. When you see the Confirm Installation Selections dialog box, review your selection choice and then click the Install button to start the installation of IPAM.

8. When the install is complete, click the Close button to finish off the wizard.

INSTALLING IPAM WITH POWERSHELL

You can install the IPAM server feature using PowerShell by following these simple steps:

1. Open a Windows PowerShell prompt with elevated permissions by right-clicking the shortcut and choosing the Run As Administrator option. Then enter your admin credentials as required.

2. Type the following command into PowerShell and then press Enter:

```
Install-WindowsFeature IPAM -IncludeManagementTools
```

Installing the IPAM Client Feature

The IPAM client is essentially the same IPAM console that you get when you install the IPAM server feature, but it's installed on a computer that is not your IPAM server. To deploy the IPAM client to a server other than your primary IPAM server, you need to deploy the Remote Server Administration Tools (RSAT). Follow these steps on a Windows Server 2012 or higher computer to deploy the client:

1. To begin, log on to your domain-joined Windows Server 2012 installation with an account that has domain administrative permissions, and from the Server Manager ➢ Local Server ➢ Manage menu, choose the Add Roles and Features option.

2. In the Before You Begin dialog box, click Next.

3. Ensure that Role-based or Feature-based Installation is selected at the Select Installation Type dialog box; then click Next.

4. Under Select Destination Server, leave the default option of "Select a Server from the Server Pool" checked, confirm that your server is highlighted in the Server Pool section, and then click Next to continue.

5. Don't choose any of the options from the Select Server Roles dialog box; just click Next here to move on.

6. When you reach the Select Features dialog box, expand Remote Server Administration Tools and then expand Feature Administration Tools.

7. Check the IP Address Management (IPAM) Client box; then click Next.

8. If you're prompted to add some required features here, such as the Group Policy Management console and the Windows Internal Database, just click the Add Features button from the window that pops up. Click Next again to continue.

9. When you see the Confirm Installation Selections dialog box, review your selection choices, and then click the Install button to start the installation of the IPAM client.

10. After the client installation is complete, click the Close button to exit the wizard.

Configure IPAM Provisioning

Once you have the IPAM feature deployed, you'll need to provision your IP address infrastructure for management. As mentioned earlier, there are two methods of provisioning IPAM: manually or through the use of Active Directory Group Policy. To make things easy (and for the sake of your sanity), we'll focus here on the Group Policy provisioning method. For obvious reasons, if you want to work through this process, you will need to have an Active Directory environment deployed. If you haven't configured your lab with Active Directory yet, then work through the tasks in Chapter 7 and come back to this later.

1. To begin, on the server where you deployed the IPAM server feature, open Server Manager and notice that you now have an option for IPAM in the navigation bar on the left side, as shown in Figure 5.4.

   Clicking the IPAM link from inside Server Manager opens the IPAM Overview console, which will be your main focal point for managing IPAM. Here you can choose from three options: Quick Start, Actions, or Learn More.

2. Click Quick Start to see that the console has already discovered and connected to the local IPAM server that you configured earlier. This is shown in Figure 5.5.

FIGURE 5.4
IPAM in Server Manager

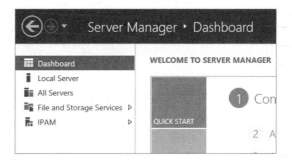

FIGURE 5.5
IPAM
Management

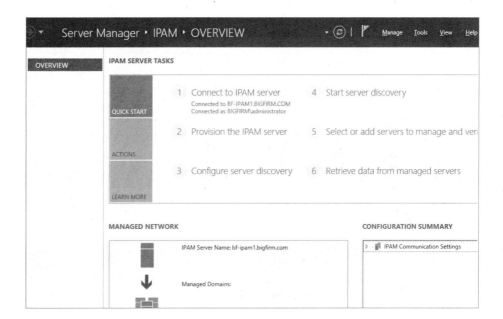

3. Click "Provision the IPAM server" from the Quick Start menu to open the Provision IPAM Wizard.

4. Take a quick read through the text on the Before You Begin dialog box; then click Next.

This should bring you to the Configure Database dialog box, where you can choose from either Windows Internal Database or Microsoft SQL Server as a database option for your IPAM deployment. In this example, we'll leave the default Windows Internal Database option enabled here and click Next.

5. In the "Select provisioning Method" dialog box shown in Figure 5.6, you need to choose from either the Manual or Group Policy Based options. The latter is selected by default and this is the recommended option to go with.

Enter a GPO name prefix into the empty field, and click Next to move on.

FIGURE 5.6
Choosing your provisioning method

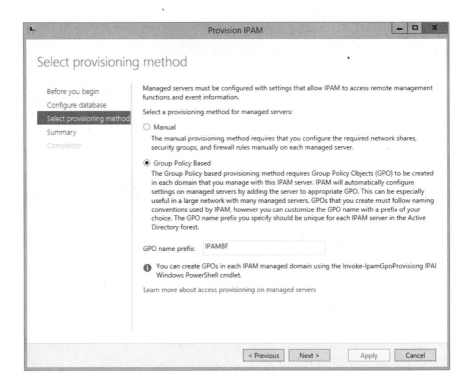

6. The Summary dialog box presents you with the settings that you have chosen, and in our example it lists the GPOs that will be deployed to our managed DHCP, DNS, and NPS servers. Before you click Apply, be warned! Once you click Apply here, you cannot change the provisioning method, and should you wish to revert to a different method, you will need to reinstall IPAM completely.

When you're happy with your choice of provisioning method, click Apply.

7. Once the IPAM provisioning configuration has completed successfully, you can click Close to exit the wizard.

Configure Server Discovery

At this point, you should see that information has started to populate inside the IPAM Overview console, and with the provisioning method now chosen, you can move on to the discovery of your DC, DNS, and DHCP servers:

1. From the IPAM Overview console, click the Quick Start tile and then click Configure Server Discovery.

   In the Configure Server Discovery dialog box, you should see your root domain listed under the Select Domains to Discover drop-down menu.

2. Click the Add button to list this domain as a location to discover your DC, DNS, and DHCP servers, as shown in Figure 5.7.

FIGURE 5.7
Configuring server discovery

3. Click OK to confirm selection and return to the IPAM Overview console.

Run Server Discoveries

Once you have configured the domain where you want to manage servers, it's time to tell IPAM to go out and find them. All you need to do for this task is to click the Start Server Discovery option from the Quick Tasks tile inside the IPAM Overview console. Clicking this will run the IPAM ServerDiscovery task, and you can click the information flag from inside Server Manager to see details of the task progress, as shown in Figure 5.8.

Choosing Servers for Management

After running the discovery task, you can then choose which discovered servers you want to manage through IPAM. To do this you need to first click the "Select or Add Servers to Manage and Verify IPAM Access" option from the Quick Start tile. When you choose this option, you should see your discovered servers listed in the IPv4 section, but you will also notice that they have an IPAM Access Status of Blocked and a Manageability status of Unspecified, as shown in Figure 5.9.

FIGURE 5.8
ServerDiscovery
task details

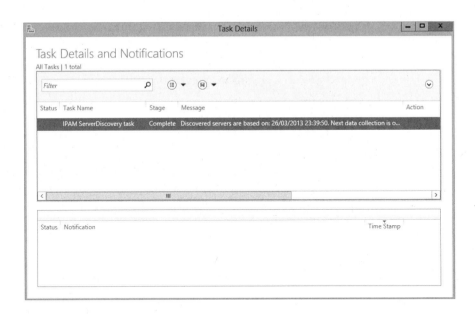

FIGURE 5.9
Blocked
servers

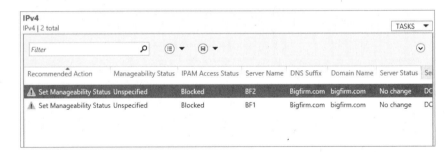

Don't panic; this is expected default behavior, and you just need to initiate those GPOs that you created earlier using the `Invoke-IpamGpoProvisioning` cmdlet in PowerShell. To do this, carry out the following steps:

1. From the IPAM server, ensure you're logged in with an account that has domain administrative permissions.

2. Open Windows PowerShell using the Run as Administrator option to ensure you have elevated rights on the local server.

3. Now type the following command and click Enter (modify as applicable for your own environment):

   ```
   Invoke-IpamGpoProvisioning –Domain Bigfirm.com –GpoPrefixName IPAMBF –
   DelegatedGpouser administrator –IpamServerFqdn BF-IPAM1.bigfirm.com
   ```

4. You should then be prompted to confirm your selection by pressing Y, as shown in Figure 5.10.

FIGURE 5.10
Invoking the
IPAM GPOs

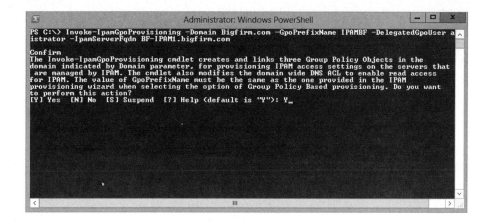

5. The invoke process is relatively quick, and once it's finished, you can confirm that the GPOs have been deployed to your domain by opening the Group Policy Management snap-in from the Server Manager ➤ Tools menu (this was deployed as part of the IPAM server install).

You should see the three IPAM GPOs sitting at the root of your domain, as shown in Figure 5.11.

With the GPOs deployed to the domain, all that's left to do is to choose the servers that you want to be managed by IPAM and let Active Directory do the rest.

FIGURE 5.11
Confirming
the GPOs

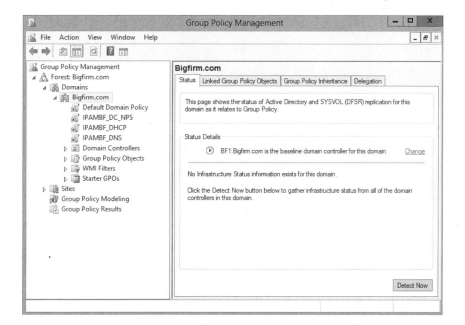

6. To choose the servers, go back to the IPAM Overview console and select Server Inventory from the navigation bar on the left.

   This will bring you back to the view that you saw earlier in Figure 5.9 with the Unspecified servers.

7. Now right-click each server that you want to manage, and select the Edit Server option from the context menu.

8. From the Add or Edit Server dialog box, click the drop-down menu beside Manageability Status and change it to Managed, as shown in Figure 5.12; then click OK.

9. Repeat steps 6–8 for each server that you want to manage.

FIGURE 5.12

Changing manageability status

When each server has been configured as Managed, you can either wait until Active Directory updates Group Policy to the domain (typically every 15 minutes) or run gpupdate /force on each server from either a command prompt or a PowerShell window.

10. Once the GPOs have been pushed out to the domain, go back to the Server Inventory view from within the IPAM console on your IPAM server.

11. Now select and then right-click any servers with a status of Managed, and then choose Refresh Server Access Status from the context menu.

    This will kick off a quick discovery check between the IPAM server and the managed server to ensure that the GPOs have been applied correctly.

12. When the discovery is complete, click the Refresh IPv4 icon at the top of the console, and it should then refresh your managed servers with a status of IPAM Access Unblocked, as shown in Figure 5.13.

FIGURE 5.13
Unblocked
servers

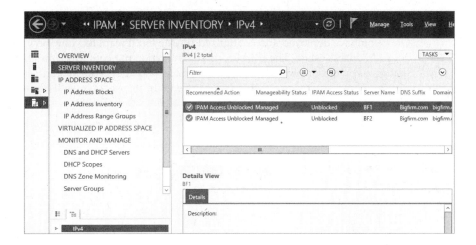

Retrieving Data

With your servers now managed and unblocked, you're just about ready to go. The last thing that you need to do is to right-click these servers and select Retrieve All Server Data from the context menu. This will then populate the IPAM console with your IP scopes and zones.

IPAM DATA REFRESH

If you've followed all of these steps correctly but don't see the DHCP or DNS data populating inside the IPAM console, make sure to click the Refresh icon located to the left of the Notifications flag at the top of the IPAM server console. We've found that data can sometimes take a little longer than expected to come into IPAM the first time a server comes under management, so it doesn't hurt to help it along a little by manually refreshing the console.

When the IPAM server configuration has been completed, you can see a number of new scheduled tasks configured and set to run at different intervals from the Task Scheduler (Local) ➢ Task Scheduler Library ➢ Microsoft ➢ Windows ➢ IPAM view, as shown in Figure 5.14.

FIGURE 5.14
New IPAM
scheduled
tasks

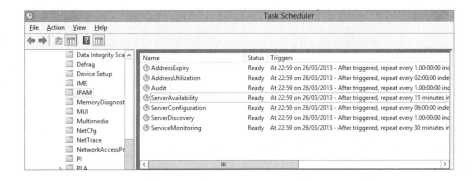

Using IPAM

Once you have deployed and configured IPAM, you'll want to know how to use it to administer your IP address estate. The IPAM console navigation bar contains a number of different links that give you options to view, manage, monitor, and audit your IP address spaces and managed servers. These options are shown in Figure 5.15. In this section we'll discuss some of the different management scenarios and functionalities that IPAM has to offer by working through the various view options in the console.

FIGURE 5.15

IPAM navigation options

Overview and Server Inventory

While installing and configuring IPAM, you've already become pretty familiar with the Overview and Server Inventory views. Here, we'll go into a bit more detail on each.

OVERVIEW

When you click the Overview link, you can choose from three different IPAM server tasks that are presented in the form of tiles called Quick Start, Actions, and Learn More. These tiles are basically quick links to carry out different tasks and actions across your managed network. Here, you will also see a graphical representation of your IPAM servers and managed domains in the Managed Network view along with a Configuration Summary view of all your existing IPAM configuration settings. At the bottom of the Overview window is the Scheduled Tasks view, which is an alternate location to see a list of the scheduled IPAM tasks running on your server.

SERVER INVENTORY

In the IPv4 window here, you get a list of all your managed and unmanaged servers. This list represents only servers that you have either automatically or manually discovered through the IPAM console. From the IPv4 window, you can click the drop-down Tasks menu and add new servers, retrieve server data, or simply export to a Comma-Separated Value (.csv) file. Server

Inventory also has a handy Details view that presents server-specific information (such as hostname, IP descriptions, and IPAM, DHCP, and DNS status) each time you click a server from the IPv4 window.

IP Address Space

Here you really start to see how IPAM can centralize your IP address space management. This view consists of three different sections, as discussed here.

IP ADDRESS BLOCKS

In IPAM, an IP address block is the highest organizational level you can use to group your address spaces. IP address blocks contain IP address ranges that can be sorted into logical chunks (all private addresses in one block, all public addresses in another, for example) to help you easily manage and maintain your IP environment. When you configure an IP address block with IPAM, if the address block comprises both IPv4 and IPv6 address spaces, it will automatically sort the IPv4 ones into public and private address spaces and any IPv6 ones into unicast global addresses.

To create a *private* IPv4 address block, follow this procedure:

1. Open the IPAM console from an administrative account, and from the navigation bar, click through to IP Address Space ➢ IP Address Blocks.

2. From the lower pane in the navigation bar, right-click IPv4 and then choose Add IP Address Block from the context menu, as shown in Figure 5.16.

FIGURE 5.16
Creating an IP address block

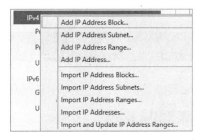

3. In the Add or Edit IPv4 Address Block dialog box, type a private IPv4 address and subnet mask prefix length of your choice into the Network ID and Prefix Length fields, respectively—we've chosen a network ID of 192.168.1.0 and prefix length of 24—then click OK.

    It's worth mentioning that at this point, and depending on the IP and subnet information you have provided, IPAM will automatically add this new IP address block to a public or private address space.

4. To see the newly created IP address block, choose the IP Address Blocks view from the Current View drop-down menu.

5. Now click the IP address block and take a look at the Configuration Details tab to see all of the relevant information pertinent to the criteria you specified.

The Utilization Trend and Event Catalog tabs will start to populate with information once the IP address block starts handling data.

The process of creating a public IPv4 address block is similar to the private process, but there are some additional steps to follow:

1. Open the IPAM console with an administrative account, and from the navigation bar, click through to IP Address Space ➤ IP Address Blocks.

2. From the lower pane in the navigation bar, right-click IPv4 and then choose Add IP Address Block from the context menu, as shown in Figure 5.16.

3. In the Add or Edit IPv4 Address Block dialog box, type a public IPv4 address and subnet mask prefix length of your choice into the Network ID and Prefix Length fields, respectively—we've chosen the public Sybex.com network ID of 208.215.179.132 and a prefix length of 30.

4. Now, since this is a public IP address block, choose the Regional Internet Registry (RIR) that issued the IP addresses (we picked RIPE here) and, if applicable or possible, also complete the Received Date from RIR value, although this isn't required.

5. To see the newly created IP address block, choose the IP Address Blocks view from the Current View drop-down menu, and then in the lower navigation pane, click Public Address Space under IPv4.

6. Verify that your new public address block is available and that you can see information in the Configuration Details tab, as shown in Figure 5.17.

FIGURE 5.17
Public IP
address block

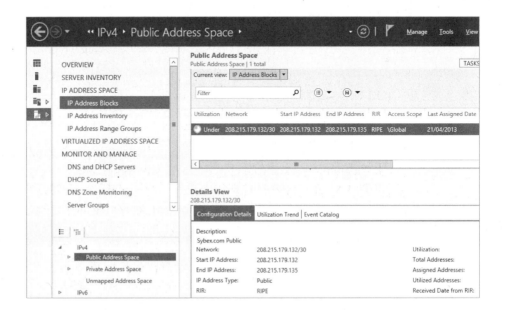

If you want a breakdown of all the IP addresses and IP address ranges that form part of your IP address blocks, then you can easily switch between these options by just clicking the Current View drop-down menu and selecting the type of view that you want.

IPAM ASSIGNMENTS

To better understand IP address blocks, remember that IPAM will automatically assign IP addresses to IP address ranges (similar to DHCP scopes), and then these IP address ranges will be automatically assigned to IP address blocks like this: IP addresses ➢ IP address ranges ➢ IP address blocks.

IP ADDRESS INVENTORY

Here you can see all of the IP addresses available to IPAM as well as the associated device information attached to them (hostnames and device types, for example). There are handy Filter and Add Criteria options here to enable you to scope your IP addresses down to a granular level based on a large number of options, including System Center 2012 Virtual Machine Manager IP address properties. From this view, you can also easily add records and reservations to DNS and DHCP just by right-clicking an IP address that's listed and choosing the relevant option from the context menu.

IP ADDRESS RANGE GROUPS

This final view beneath the IP Address Space section lets you create logical groups to help organize your IP address ranges. You can click the Current View drop-down menu to navigate among IP addresses, IP address ranges, and IP address groups. If you choose the "IP address ranges" option here and then right-click a range and edit it, you can then configure custom fields from the Custom Configurations section that define the IP address range by criteria such as Active Directory site, Country or Region, Business Unit, Device Type, and the like.

You can also specify a value on some of the criteria to gain further granularity and control of your logical address range groups (an example of this would be to specify a value of Reserved for the IP Address State custom field). Once you've edited the IP address ranges here with your custom fields and values, you will be presented with a fully transparent and familiar grouping of your IP address estate. We're sure you'll agree that this beats having to do all this type of grouping and sorting by using a static Excel spreadsheet!

Virtualized IP Address Space

In the original release of IPAM in Windows Server 2012, there was very limited capability to manage virtual IP address spaces that were created using System Center 2012 Virtual Machine Manager (VMM). With all the focus on datacenter and cloud management, it's here that Microsoft has invested the most in enhancing IPAM for Windows Server 2012 R2. The Virtualized IP Address Space section of the IPAM console streamlines the management of your physical and virtual address spaces through a new integration connection with VMM. This integration opens up IP address-management capabilities between your on-premise and cloud-based IP address schemes.

Configuring the integration is relatively simple, but it will work only with Windows Server 2012 R2 and System Center 2012 R2 Virtual Machine Manager. Assuming you have already deployed a VMM 2012 R2 server in the same domain as your IPAM server, here's how you'd integrate them:

1. Using an account with administrative permissions, open the VMM 2012 R2 console and click the Fabric tab in the navigation bar.

2. Click the Add Resources button from the ribbon and choose Network Service, as shown in Figure 5.18.

FIGURE 5.18
Creating a new Network Service in VMM

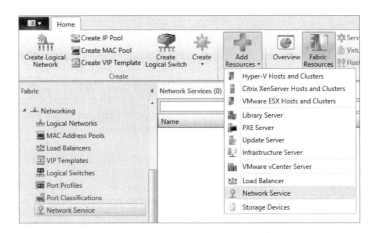

3. In the Name dialog box in the Add Network Service Wizard, type a name (**IPAM**, for example) and a description for the service; then click Next.

4. From the Manufacturer and Model dialog box, leave Microsoft as the manufacturer and choose Microsoft Windows Server IP Address Management from the Model menu, as shown in Figure 5.19; then click Next to move on.

5. Specify a Run As account that will be used to create the integration service; typically this will be an account with administrative permissions on both the VMM and IPAM servers. Click Next.

6. In the Connection String dialog box, input the FQDN of your IPAM server and click Next.

   The Provider dialog box (shown in Figure 5.20) gives you the opportunity to test the connection between the VMM and IPAM servers.

7. It's recommended that you click the Test button here to ensure all is working so far. Click Next to continue.

8. Choose the VMM Host Group that the IPAM service will apply to; then click Next and Finish to complete the process.

FIGURE 5.19
Specifying the IPAM integration model

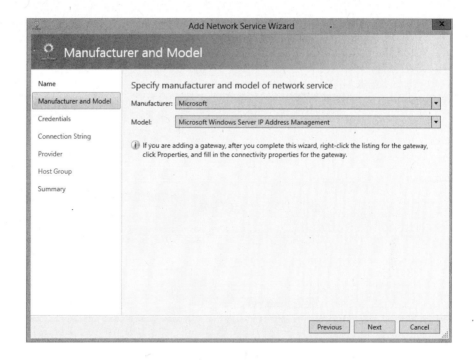

FIGURE 5.20
Testing the connection

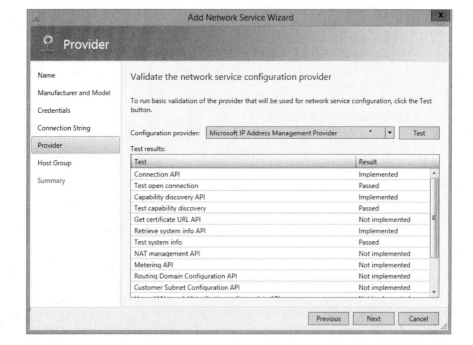

Once you've configured the integration between VMM and IPAM, you can open the IPAM console again and take a look at the Virtualized Address Space section, where you should now see all of your virtual IP address spaces, as shown in Figure 5.21.

FIGURE 5.21
IPAM managing virtual IP address spaces

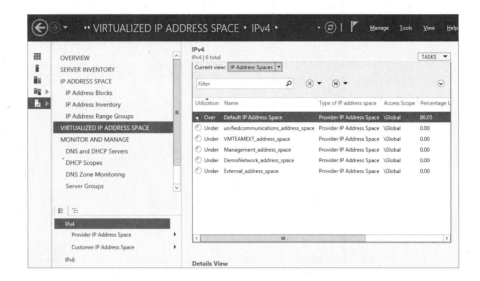

Monitor and Manage

This section of the IPAM console enables you to monitor and manage the DHCP and DNS servers that are under IPAM control. Here you'll find a centralized location that will enable you to carry out a lot of the standard tasks that you previously would have needed to run from each individual server—particularly those related to DHCP management. There are four different views to work with.

DNS AND DHCP SERVERS

This view shows you a list of your DHCP and DNS servers and has a Server Type option to allow you to scope the view to specific DHCP or DNS servers. If you right-click a DHCP server in the list, you will be presented with a number of management tasks for that particular DHCP server that will allow you to edit your DHCP server options, create DHCP scopes, and configure user and vendor classes, to name but a few. Figure 5.22 shows the full menu of choices.

You can also launch the MMC snap-in for both DHCP and DNS by just right-clicking a server and choosing Launch MMC. The Details view provides information on the particular server that you have selected, such as Server Properties, DHCP Options, and DNS Zones.

DHCP SCOPES

This view brings together all of the DHCP scopes that IPAM knows about. You can see key information about each scope's utilization and configured DHCP scope options. There are dedicated sections for IPv4 and IPv6 scopes, and you can filter the views here by public, private, global, and unmapped address space.

FIGURE 5.22
Managing
DHCP with
IPAM

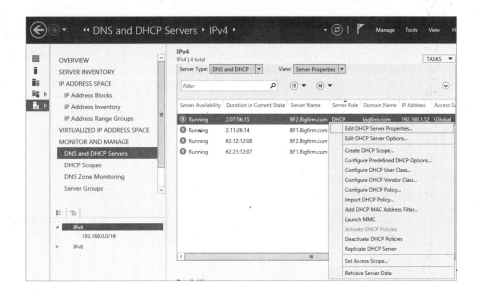

You can perform a number of management actions from this view by highlighting a particular DHCP scope and then right-clicking it. Some of these tasks can be carried out on multiple scopes at the same time, and others must be performed on one scope at a time. Here are some of your options:

◆ Edit DHCP Scope (can run on multiple scopes at once)

◆ Duplicate DHCP Scope (must be run on single scopes one at a time)

◆ Activate DHCP Scope (can run on multiple scopes at once)

◆ Replicate DHCP Scope (must be run on single scopes one at a time)

◆ Deactivate DHCP Scope (can be run on multiple scopes at once)

◆ Delete (can run on multiple scopes at once)

◆ Create DHCP Reservation (must be run on single scopes one at a time)

◆ Configure DHCP Failover

◆ Clear Config Sync Errors

DNS ZONE MONITORING

Here you can see a centralized view of all the DNS forward and reverse lookup zones that IPAM manages. For each zone, you can view the health status (healthy, warning, or error state), the duration it has been in that particular state, information about the server it's running on, and the type of zone it is. If you want to perform any deep management here, however, unlike with DHCP, the only actions you have are Launch MMC, Reset Zone Status, and Retrieve Server Data. Once you launch the MMC, it will scope the connection to the particular zone you had highlighted, and you can then administer the particular zone as you would if you were logged on locally to the DNS server.

MONITORING DNS WITH IPAM OR SYSTEM CENTER OPERATIONS MANAGER?

You might be wondering if this type of DNS monitoring is a substitute or replacement for something like Microsoft System Center Operations Manager. If you already have Operations Manager deployed, then IPAM DNS monitoring is definitely not a substitute for it. Operations Manager is Microsoft's flagship monitoring and management tool that delivers IT service modeling based on their own best practices and recommendations. It takes into account a lot more than just DNS and has a greater array of centralized actions and information than IPAM DNS zone monitoring. Chapter 30, "Monitoring Windows Server 2012 R2," discusses this product in more detail.

If, however, you don't have Operations Manager deployed or the cost implications of deploying System Center 2012 are prohibitive, then IPAM DNS zone monitoring is a good starting point to give you a basic central health overview that may be more than sufficient for your particular environment.

SERVER GROUPS

Similar to the IP address range groups discussed earlier, you can also use custom fields when adding or editing new servers to be managed by IPAM. In these custom fields, you can essentially tag the servers with criteria such as Region, Country, Building, or Floor Number. Once you have these criteria configured on your servers, from the Server Groups view, right-click the IPv4 link and then select the Add Server Group option. When you've added in the custom information, a new server group will be created and can be used to get a more company-specific overview of the IP address server environment.

Event Catalog

We mentioned earlier that IPAM delivers functionality to track IP address and user activity along with configuration changes to your IPAM and DHCP environments. The Event Catalog view provides this information. This view is broken down into the following three subsections.

IPAM CONFIGURATION EVENTS

Here you can track any configuration events that have been made to your IPAM infrastructure. It's a good place to start if you have multiple IPAM admins and need to check back over your change-control processes. You can get information on the account of the specific user who made the configuration change, and you have the option to scope the events into a specific filter to get the information you require quickly. To create one of these filters, simply click the Add Criteria button and then check each of the criteria that you want to filter the list down to.

DHCP CONFIGURATION EVENTS

Very similar to the IPAM Configuration Events view, this view provides information on the configuration events that are specific to your managed DHCP servers. As shown in Figure 5.23, clicking the Tasks menu here will give you the options Purge Event Catalog Data, Retrieve Event Catalog Data, as well as Export, which allows you to export the configuration events to a CSV file for further analysis.

FIGURE 5.23
DHCP
Configuration
Events view

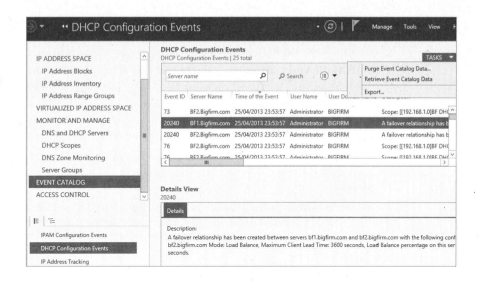

IP ADDRESS TRACKING

This section is where you'll most likely find yourself if you need to track down IP address information based on specific hosts or users. You have four different views here to choose from:

- By IP Address
- By Client ID
- By Hostname
- By User Name

By choosing any of these views, you will be able to decide on the date and time when you want to search, along with whether the search includes or excludes any additional correlated event data that was generated by any managed domain controllers or Network Policy servers. Similar to the DHCP Configuration Events view, clicking the Tasks menu here will allow you to purge, retrieve, or export your data.

IPAM Delegation

When you install the IPAM server role, the installation process automatically creates a number of local security groups that can be used to deliver Role-Based Access Control (RBAC) of your IPAM environment to designated users and administrators. Depending on the type of administrative privileges that you want your users to have, all you need to do is add their accounts to the appropriate security group. Figure 5.24 shows these groups on the IPAM server, and here's a breakdown of what each one offers:

IPAM Administrators   Most likely, you will want to ensure that your own user account is a member of this group. Members of this group have permissions to fully manage and administer IPAM and can run all tasks and views.

IPAM IP Audit Administrators   Members of this group can perform common IPAM management tasks and also have access to the IP address-tracking information so they can carry out IP audits if required.

IPAM ASM Administrators   Any user accounts that are members of this group can carry out tasks related to the IPAM Address Space Management (ASM) functionality.

IPAM MSM Administrators   Any user accounts that are members of this group can carry out tasks across multiple IPAM servers through the IPAM Multi-Server Management (MSM) functionality.

IPAM Users   This is the most basic security group for IPAM, and all users who are members of this group can essentially just view information on server discovery, ASM, and MSM. They can also see information about the operational events that IPAM and DHCP generate, but they cannot view any audit or tracking information.

Layered on top of these security groups and exclusive to IPAM in Windows Server 2012 R2 is the new Access Control feature shown in Figure 5.25.

FIGURE 5.24
IPAM RBAC security groups

FIGURE 5.25
Access Control in IPAM

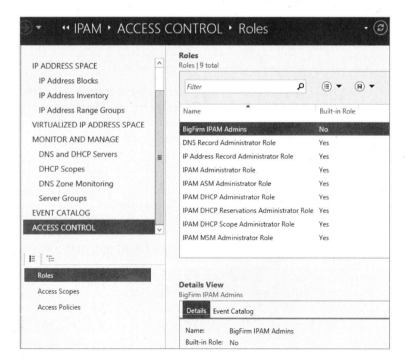

With Access Control, you get eight built-in user roles, but you can also specify custom roles for your IPAM administrators and granularly scope them to different components and policies in IPAM.

Here's a walk-through on configuring a new role, scoping it to specific sections of IPAM, and then delegating that role to a user account in your organization:

1. Click the Access Control view from the IPAM console and ensure that the Roles subview is selected.

2. From the Tasks drop-down menu, choose the Add User Role option to open the Add or Edit Role dialog box shown in Figure 5.26.

3. Type a name for the role and click the OK button.

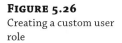

FIGURE 5.26
Creating a custom user role

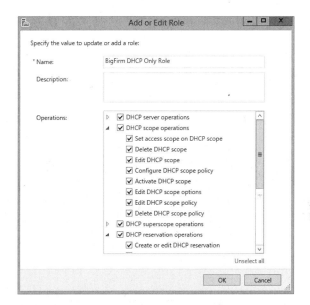

4. Staying in the Access Control view for now, select and then right-click the Access Scopes subview from the navigation pane on the left, and choose the Add Access Scope option.

5. From the Add Access Scope dialog box, click the New button, specify a name and description for the new scope, and then click the Add button to link your new scope to the parent Global access scope, as shown in Figure 5.27.

6. Click OK to continue.

7. Next up, you need to select and then right-click the Access Policies subview from the Access Control view in the console to open the Add Access Policy dialog box.

8. In the User Settings section, browse for the user account that you want to associate with this scoped role; then in the Access Settings section, select the custom role and scope you created previously, as shown in Figure 5.28.

FIGURE 5.27
Configuring an access scope

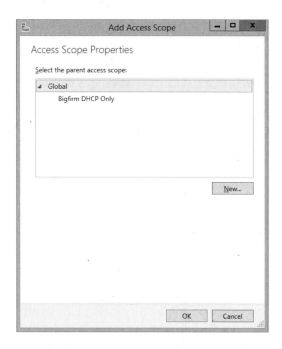

FIGURE 5.28
Adding the access policy

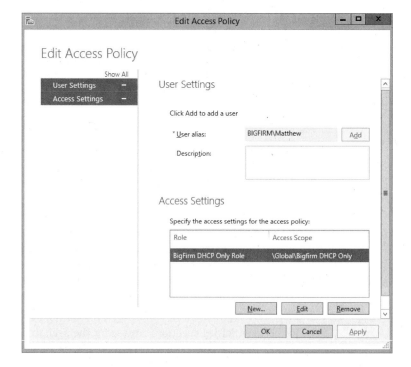

9. Now browse to the particular section in IPAM that you want to scope to this custom access policy—we'll choose the DNS and DHCP Servers view.

10. Right-click a DHCP server (or other managed object), and select the Set Access Scope option from the context menu.

11. Choose the scope that you wish to assign to the managed object, and click OK to complete the process.

IPAM Troubleshooting

Should you run into any problems with your IPAM deployment, then before you log that call with Microsoft support, take a look at some of the information and solutions in this section to see if they help you get to the bottom of the problem.

Using the Event Viewer

As is the case with just about every Microsoft application, role, and feature installation, you will have access to some specific event logs inside the Windows Event Viewer to help you diagnose your troublesome IPAM servers. For IPAM, the event logs are located in Windows Event Viewer ➢ Application and Services Logs ➢ Microsoft ➢ Windows ➢ IPAM. Here's a list and brief description of each:

Admin Channel   Any errors that have been logged unexpectedly as a result of a user action or periodic task can be found here.

Operational Channel   Events being logged to this channel are disabled by default because they are all informational type events based on the operational and health status of IPAM, and there can potentially be a large number of them logged at any given time. You may need to see these alerts only when you're troubleshooting, and that's why this type of logging has been disabled initially.

Configuration Change Channel   Any configuration changes that occur on your IPAM server get logged into this channel. You can use this for auditing IPAM administrators and identifying who made what change (or determining who broke something!).

Analytic Channel   This channel is disabled by default and is used to assist with debugging and trace-logging tasks.

Debug Channel   This channel is also disabled by default and is used to assist with debugging and trace-logging tasks.

Common Issues

In Table 5.2, we detail some common problems with connectivity, provisioning, discovery, and monitoring that you may encounter with IPAM, and we have some suggestions to hopefully help you resolve them.

TABLE 5.2: Common IPAM Issues

ISSUE	SUGGESTED RESOLUTIONS
Can't connect to the IPAM server	◆ Confirm that the account you're using has the relevant permissions to access the IPAM console.
	◆ Ensure that the Windows Internal Database service is running on your IPAM server.
	◆ Ensure that the Windows Process Activation service is running on your IPAM server.
Unable to fetch data from a managed server	◆ Ensure that the access status for your server is set to Unblocked or Not Applicable for DHCP RPC and Audit Share Access Status, DNS RPC Access Status, and Event Log Access Status.
	◆ Confirm that your firewall is not blocking IPAM for any servers listed with a status of Blocked.
	◆ Follow the instructions in the Configure IPAM Provisioning section earlier to ensure you have provisioned the server correctly.
Cannot discover DNS or DHCP servers	◆ If your DNS server is not co-located with a domain controller, make sure that you have registered that DNS server as a name server for the domain zone and that you have also registered your DNS suffix for the domain. Also ensure that the DNS Server service is running on the server.
	◆ If your DHCP server can't be discovered, check to see if that particular DHCP server has been authorized to operate in the domain and ensure that the DHCP Server service is up and running on it.
Not Reachable state shown for a managed server	◆ Confirm that you can communicate with the particular server and that no firewall or other outside variable is blocking access to it.
	◆ Check that the DNS or DHCP Server service is up and running on the server.
	◆ Confirm that the server has been provisioned correctly, and if required, repeat the steps outlined in the Configure IPAM Provisioning section earlier.

DHCP Failover

The Dynamic Host Configuration Protocol (DHCP) is responsible for automatically assigning IP addresses from specified address pools (scopes) to any network-connected devices that need to be identified. It has been an integral part of networking environments for years, and without it, you would need to maintain your own manual lists of IP address allocations. In any kind of reasonably sized environment, this would be an administrative nightmare.

A caveat of traditional Windows Server DHCP implementations, though, was the fact that providing redundancy or high availability (HA) for this critical service wasn't always as straightforward as it should be.

Clustering vs. Split-scope

In Windows Server 2008 R2, your options for HA were to either cluster the DHCP service using the Failover Clustering role or to deploy two or more stand-alone DHCP servers and then split the address scopes so that each server managed only a portion of the overall IP address pool. Both these options had their challenges. With the Failover Clustering role, you needed to have shared storage between each of the cluster nodes, and the cost of purchasing and configuring this option—particularly if it was only for the DHCP service—was quite prohibitive.

If you used the split-scope method, typically with two DHCP stand-alone servers, you had to distribute your IP address scopes in a 70/30 or 50/50 configuration, which meant that should one of your DHCP servers fail over, you then had a deficit in the number of available IP addresses on your network and had to work quickly to get the failed server back online.

What Is DHCP Failover?

In Windows Server 2012, you can still use the Failover Clustering or split-scope option if you want, but Microsoft has given you an even better method of ensuring that your DHCP environment stays up—step forward DHCP Failover!

The new DHCP Failover functionality allows you to configure two DHCP servers in either an active/passive configuration known as *hot standby* or in an active/active configuration known as *load balanced*. The beauty of DHCP Failover is that there is now no need for any expensive shared storage, such as a Storage Area Network (SAN) device, between your DHCP servers. Instead, the IP address lease data is replicated between each server continuously. With both DHCP Failover servers containing a copy of the latest IP address assignment and scope information, you will always be able to sustain a failure of one DHCP server without losing any DHCP functionality.

DHCP FAILOVER AND IPv6

If you've deployed IPv6 across your network, be aware that the DHCP Failover functionality of Windows Server 2012 is supported only with IPv4 addressing. The reason for this is that devices using IPv6 typically determine their own address using stateless IP autoconfiguration. This means that the DHCP server services only the DHCP Option configuration and doesn't manage individual IPv6 addresses. All you have to do here then is to ensure that you have two stand-alone DHCP servers built and configured with the exact same DHCP Option information on each. This will then provide the redundancy that you need in case one of the servers fails.

DHCP Failover Requirements

The following sections outline the prerequisites you need to have in place to deploy DHCP Failover on your network.

WINDOWS SERVER SUPPORT

To deploy DHCP Failover, you need to have two computers running Windows Server 2012 or higher. If you have any DHCP servers running Windows Server 2008 R2, Windows Server 2008, or Windows Server 2003, then you will need to first migrate these to Windows Server 2012.

Microsoft has released the Windows Server Migration Tools to help you with this process, and you can get more information on them here: `http://tinyurl.com/ws2012migtools`.

Also, you cannot create a DHCP Failover configuration with more than two computers because the replication process can occur only between two points.

DOMAIN MEMBERSHIP SUPPORT

As is the case with stand-alone DHCP, you can deploy DHCP Failover onto either domain-joined or workgroup computers. In a domain-joined environment, DHCP Failover can be installed onto DHCP servers that are running on either Domain Controller or Domain Member servers.

Installing DHCP Failover

Once you've met the prerequisites, you're ready to get started with the DHCP Failover installation. In this section, we presume that you've already deployed the DHCP server role to two Windows Server 2012 R2 computers and have configured and activated an address scope on one of the two DHCP servers.

Ensure that you don't have the same scope configured on both servers because if you do, you will get an error during setup stating that the scope on the second failover server needs to be deleted before continuing.

SYNCHRONIZE YOUR SERVER CLOCKS

A gotcha that you might come across when installing DHCP Failover is that the time between the servers must be kept synchronized to within one minute of each other. If it creeps out past one minute during the installation process, you will be greeted with a critical error telling you to go back and get your servers clocks in sync before going any further. You can use something like Active Directory or the Network Time Protocol (NTP) to ensure all is in order here.

---

1. Log on to your first Windows Server 2012 R2 computer (we'll use BF1.Bigfirm.com for our example) with an account that has administrative permissions, and launch the DHCP Manager console MMC snap-in either from the Server Manager ➢ DHCP menu or from within the IPAM console, as discussed earlier.

2. Right-click the scope that you want to create a DHCP Failover relationship for, and then choose Configure Failover, as shown in Figure 5.29.

3. In the Introduction to the DHCP Failover dialog box, ensure that your scope is selected in the Available Scopes section, and click Next.

4. In the Specify The Partner Server To Use For Failover dialog box, click the Add Server button and choose your second server (we've used BF2.Bigfirm.com as an example here) from the list of authorized DHCP servers, click OK, and then click Next.

5. As shown in Figure 5.30, configure your options for the new failover relationship and then click Next. These options are as follows:

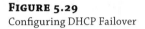

FIGURE 5.29
Configuring DHCP Failover

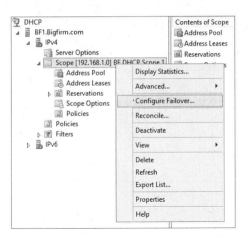

Relationship Name   This is a friendly name for the failover relationship.

Maximum Client Lead Time   This setting defines the maximum amount of time that one server can extend a DHCP lease for a client beyond the time known by the failover server. It has a default value of 1 hour, and this time also determines how long the active server waits with its partner offline before assuming total control of the DHCP scope.

Mode   Choose either Load Balance for an active/active configuration or Hot Standby for an active/passive configuration.

Load-balance Percentage   These values determine the percentage of the IP address range to reserve for each server in the relationship. The default is 50/50.

State Switchover Interval   Turned off by default, it means that an administrator must manually tell DHCP Failover that a server is in a partner-down state. If this setting is enabled, the active DHCP server will automatically place its partner into a partner-down state when it can't communicate with it for the specified amount of time.

Enable Message Authentication   This option enables authentication of the failover replication traffic between partners.

Shared Secret   If you have selected the Enable Message Authentication check box, then you will need to specify a password here for authentication of traffic.

6. Confirm that your settings are correct; then click Finish to complete the Configure Failover Wizard.

7. You should then be presented with a progress dialog box stating that your configuration was successful. When you see this, click the Close button to finish the process.

8. To confirm that the process worked, take a look at the second DHCP server, and you should now see the scope that you selected for failover appear under the IPv4 view, as shown in Figure 5.31.

FIGURE 5.30
Configuring a failover relationship

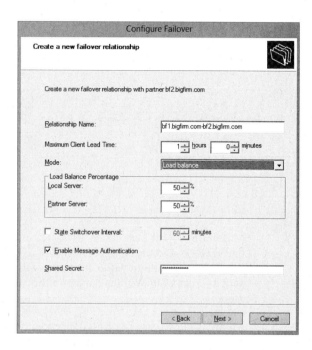

FIGURE 5.31
Synchronized DHCP scope

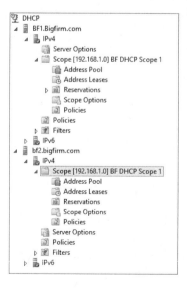

DHCP FAILOVER AND POWERSHELL

With this new feature in Windows Server 2012, you get these seven new PowerShell cmdlets to play around with:

```
Add-DhcpServerv4Failover
Add-DhcpServerv4FailoverScope
Get-DhcpServerv4Failover
Set-DhcpServerv4Failover
Remove-DhcpServerv4Failover
Remove-DhcpServerv4FailoverScope
Invoke-DhcpServerv4FailoverReplication
```

You can use them to quickly deploy, configure, or even remove DHCP Failover. For more information and syntax examples, check out this link from the official Microsoft DHCP product team blog: http://tinyurl.com/ws2012dhcpfailposh.

The Bottom Line

Implement IPAM.   IPAM is an integrated suite of tools to enable end-to-end planning, deploying, managing, and monitoring of your IP address infrastructure, with a rich user experience. IPAM automatically discovers IP address infrastructure servers on your network and enables you to manage them from a central interface.

> **Master It**   IPAM has some specific prerequisites that need to be in place before you can deploy it. What are the requirements for Active Directory that you should be aware of?

Effectively use IPAM components.   IPAM is made up of three different feature components that integrate to deliver holistic management of your IP address infrastructure. These three components deliver functionality for Multi-Server Management, Address Space Management, and Network Auditing.

> **Master It**   Which feature of IPAM enables you to perform simultaneous updates to all of your DHCP and DNS servers? (Choose one.)
>
> **a.** Multi-Server Management
>
> **b.** Address Space Management
>
> **c.** Network Auditing

Integrate IPAM with System Center 2012.   With all the focus on datacenter and cloud management, it's here that Microsoft has invested the most in enhancing IPAM for Windows Server 2012 R2. The Virtualized IP Address Space section of the IPAM console streamlines the management of your physical and virtual address spaces through a new integration connection with VMM. This integration opens up IP address-management capabilities between your on-premise and cloud-based IP address schemes.

Master It What version of Windows Server and VMM do you need to be running to enable IPAM integration?

Manage IPAM delegation. When you install the IPAM server role, the installation process automatically creates a number of local security groups that can be used to deliver Role-Based Access Control of your IPAM environment to designated users and administrators. Depending on the type of administrative privileges that you want your users to have, all you need to do is to add their accounts to the appropriate security group.

Master It There are five local security groups that IPAM creates to deliver RBAC. Which group from the following list *is not* one of them? (Choose one.)

a. IPAM Administrators

b. IPAM IP Audit Administrators

c. IPAM ASM Administrators

d. IPAM Advanced Users

e. IPAM MSM Administrators

f. IPAM Users

Understand DHCP Failover. The beauty of DHCP Failover is that there is now no need for any expensive shared storage, such as a Storage Area Network device, between your DHCP servers. Instead, the IP address lease data is replicated between each server continuously. With both DHCP Failover servers containing a copy of the latest IP address assignment and scope information, you will always be able to sustain a failure of one DHCP server without losing any DHCP functionality.

Master It The new DHCP Failover functionality allows you to configure two different types of failover relationships. What are these relationships called? (Choose two.)

a. Failover clustering (active/active)

b. Hot standby (active/passive)

c. Split-scope (active/passive)

d. Seeded (active/active)

e. Load balanced (active/active)

Chapter 6

DNS and Name Resolution in Windows Server 2012 R2

Computers communicate with each other using IP addresses, whether IPv4 or IPv6. However, it's difficult for most people to remember the IP address for their favorite website or file server. They like using friendly, text-based names. Thus, naming systems are implemented to resolve the friendly names of computers with their assigned IP addresses. The Domain Name System (DNS) is the naming system that Windows Server 2012 R2 servers use. Not only does DNS help users to easily identify devices, but many other services such as Active Directory require DNS so that clients and servers can locate and communicate with domain controllers.

In this chapter, you will learn to:

◆ Explain the fundamental components and processes of DNS

◆ Configure DNS to support an Active Directory environment

◆ Manage and troubleshoot DNS resolution for both internal and external names

Understanding the DNS Server Role

DNS has been around for decades prior to Microsoft developing its first edition of DNS in Windows NT 4.0. There are many different varieties of DNS implementations that support the required features and processes that define DNS. In this section, we'll cover the concepts of Microsoft's Domain Name System and how it's applied in Windows operating systems.

DNS is implemented within Windows Server 2012 R2 to manage IP address name resolution. Once installed on a server, the DNS service will need to communicate with other DNS name servers, which is accomplished using several different methods, such as forwarding, root hints, and delegation. The DNS service will also maintain databases, named *zones*, for the internal Active Directory domain or other namespaces. The domain computers will need to query this DNS service, so you must configure individual computers in order to provide efficient and rapid name resolution.

Windows Server 2012 R2 and previous releases of the Windows Server operating system offer a built-in DNS Server role. Windows Server 2012 R2 DNS is compatible with older versions of DNS going back to Windows Server 2003; however, versions earlier than Windows Server 2008 do not support IPv6 and are functional only with IPv4 addresses.

The following is a short summary of the DNS fundamental concepts referred to in this chapter:

Hostname   This is the (friendly) name of a computer. According to DNS standards, it can be up to 255 characters in length. It is equivalent to a computer's first name, for example, EC01.

Namespace   This is the name of a domain, not specifically an Active Directory domain though. It's a logical set of hosts signified by a name controlled by a set of name servers. This is equivalent to a computer's last name; they're all part of the same family. For example, Bigfirm .com is the namespace for hosts in the Bigfirm.com domain.

Fully Qualified Domain Name   The FQDN is the hostname appended to the domain's namespace, such as EC01.Bigfirm.com.

HOSTS File   This is a text file that statically maps hostnames to IP addresses. This file is located in `c:\windows\system32\drivers\etc` for standard Windows Server 2012 R2 installations and can be used as an entry-level alternative to a DNS server for name resolution in small environments. Don't try to manage a large enterprise environment with static HOSTS file entries though, because it will quickly turn into an administrative nightmare!

Name Server   This is a DNS server that will resolve FQDNs to IP addresses. Name servers also control namespaces for specified domains. They will resolve requests for that namespace from DNS clients throughout the network.

Hierarchical Naming Structure   The namespace is created so that the left part of a name is a subset of the right part of the name as shown in the FQDN. With this, the naming servers can start at the right side of the name, and the responses from the name servers will direct it to the correct naming server for a given namespace. For example, as shown in Figure 6.1, Ec01.Ecoast.Bigfirm.com is the FQDN for a server in the Ecoast.Bigfirm.com domain. This domain is actually a subset, or a *subdomain*, under the control of the Bigfirm.com domain. You can say the same thing about Bigfirm.com for the .com top-level domain name. The strength is that you can ask the .com domain name server where the Bigfirm.com name server is. You can do the same for the Ecoast.Bigfirm.com server, and so on. The FQDN name directs the query to the right name server through a process named *recursion*.

FIGURE 6.1
Hierarchical
DNS naming

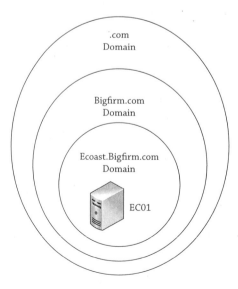

.com
Domain

Bigfirm.com
Domain

Ecoast.Bigfirm.com
Domain

EC01

Recursion This is a server-directed process to resolve an FQDN. If the server cannot resolve the FQDN with its own information, it will send the query to other name servers. The recursion process comprises root servers and domain name servers. Root servers are the top of the hierarchical naming structure. The root servers list the name servers that control the top-level domain names such as .com, .gov, and .edu. The top-level domain servers control the registry of subdomains beneath the top-level domain. For example, name servers for the Sybex.com subdomain are registered on the .com domain servers. When a query occurs, the following occurs (as shown in Figure 6.2):

1. The DNS client requests a name, like www.Sybex.com, from its DNS server.

2. Through the recursive process, the DNS server queries the root servers for the .com domain name servers.

3. The root servers give a list of name servers for the .com domain.

4. Then the DNS server queries the .com name servers for Sybex.com.

5. It receives another list of name servers for the Sybex.com domain.

6. It queries the provided name servers for the www.Sybex.com FQDN.

7. The Sybex.com DNS server coughs up the IP address of the www server to the DNS server.

8. The DNS server passes the IP address to the client.

9. Armed with the IP address, the client connects with the web server www.Sybex.com.

FIGURE 6.2
DNS recursion
process

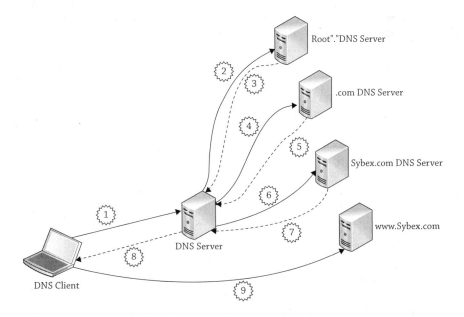

Delegation   This means allowing another name server to control a subdomain of a given namespace. For example, the Bigfirm.com name servers can delegate control of the Ecoast .Bigfirm.com namespace to another server.

Forwarding   This is an alternative to the recursion process. Forwarding is a lateral request to another name server within the network. The forwarding server obtains a response and relays it to the originating name server.

Iteration   This is a client-directed process to resolve an FQDN. If the client receives a negative request from a name server, it will query another name server.

NetBIOS Naming System   This legacy naming system was used primarily within old Microsoft NT 4.0 networks. Its processes are still part of modern-day Windows operating systems, however, particularly when using non-domain (workgroup)–based computers.

Service Records   Service records (SRVs) are records within a DNS namespace to resolve a service to a hostname. This is an essential part of DNS supporting Active Directory.

Dynamic DNS Update   Dynamic DNS (DDNS) update is a process that allows DNS clients to register their hostnames in an assigned namespace such as DHCP. This reduces the need of admins to manually enter records in the name server databases. This is another essential part of DNS supporting Active Directory.

Installing DNS

DNS for Windows Server 2012 R2 can be deployed into several different configurations depending on your scenario. You can choose to install a stand-alone DNS server onto a non-domain-joined computer, or you can deploy it onto either your domain-joined member servers or Active Directory domain controller servers. Whatever the scenario, installing the DNS role is simple. This section will first explain what you need to do to manually deploy DNS onto a non-domain-joined computer in a stand-alone configuration. Later, we will explain how to automatically configure DNS to integrate with Active Directory so as to ensure name resolution runs smoothly inside your domain environment.

Configuring a Stand-Alone DNS Server

First things first: you'll need to have allocated a static IP address to the server that you want to install the DNS role onto, since hitting a moving target is pretty tough for the DNS client! From the desktop, if you hit Ctrl+R and then type **ncpa.cpl** and hit Enter, you will be brought to the Network Connections window. Here, you can right-click your network adapter and then select Properties to open the configuration window. If you double-click Internet Protocol Version 4 (TCP/IPv4), you will be presented with the TCP/IPv4 Properties dialog box. Once there, you can then assign a static IP address, as shown in Figure 6.3.

When you have assigned a static IP address, you should then add the primary DNS suffix, such as Bigfirm.com, into the Advanced TCP/IPv4 Settings dialog box, as shown in Figure 6.4.

We use the word *should* here because it isn't always necessary to add a primary DNS suffix. The primary DNS suffix is modified automatically when the computer joins a domain. If the server is going to operate as part of a workgroup (as is the case in our example here), you will need to add it so other DNS servers can locate it within the DNS structure and the DNS service is properly configured during installation.

FIGURE 6.3
Assigning a static
IP address

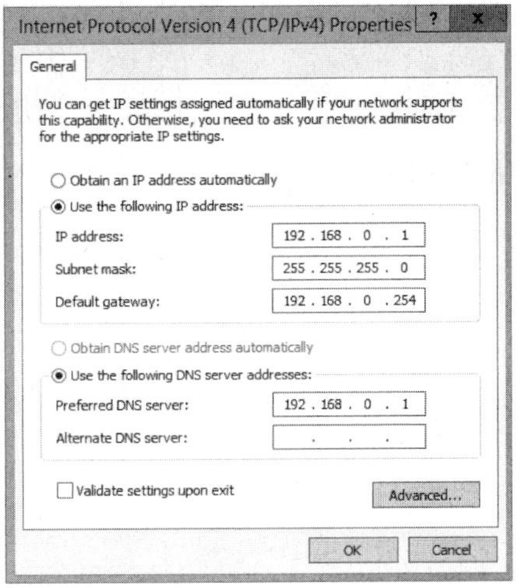

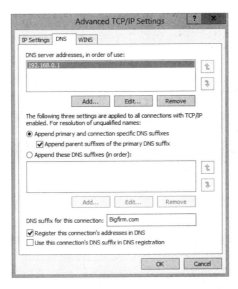

FIGURE 6.4
Adding the DNS
suffix

Once you've configured a static IP address and DNS suffix on your non-domain-joined server, follow these steps to install the DNS role:

1. Open Server Manager, click Dashboard, and then select the "Add roles and features" option, as shown in Figure 6.5.

2. At the "Before you Begin" dialog box inside the Add Roles and Features Wizard, click Next to continue.

3. Choose the "Role-based or Feature-based Installation" option from the Select Installation Type dialog box; then click Next.

FIGURE 6.5
Adding the
DNS role

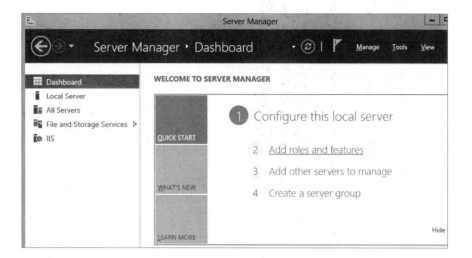

4. Click the "Select a Server from the Server Pool" option and ensure that your server is highlighted in the Select Destination Server dialog box; then click Next to move on.

5. In Select Server Roles dialog box, choose the DNS Server option from the list (if applicable, click the Add Features button from the Add Roles and Features Wizard dialog box that pops up after you select the DNS Server role), as shown in Figure 6.6.

FIGURE 6.6
Selecting the
DNS Server role

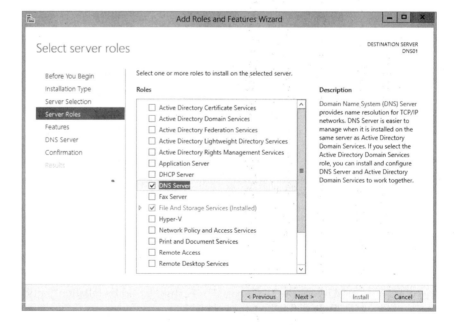

6. Click the Next button in the remaining dialog boxes until you reach the Confirm Installation Selections dialog. Verify that all of your selections are correct, and then click Install to begin the installation.

7. When the DNS Server role installation has completed, click the Close button to finish the process.

Installing the role in this way creates a solitary DNS name server that is talking only with the Internet root servers. It can support a LAN environment for resolving Internet names, but that's about it. The Domain Name System leverages other naming servers to resolve names throughout the DNS structure. For this reason, you'll have to configure the server to talk with other DNS servers that exist in the internal network. Although configuring your DNS server in a stand-alone non-domain configuration can have its merits (such as deploying one in environments where managing multiple static HOSTS files across servers becomes a pain), you will really see the power of Windows Server 2012 R2 DNS when you use it with Active Directory.

Integrating with Other DNS Servers

In "Understanding the DNS Server Role," we mentioned that there are different methods for resolving DNS names, such as forwarding, recursion, delegation, and iteration. These methods are related to the integration with other DNS servers. Before we get started, remember that iteration is basically client driven. If the DNS server doesn't have an answer, the client will go to another DNS server. The server or the client can be configured for iteration only, but it is not the default and is rarely implemented. The other three—forwarding, recursion, and delegation—involve contacting other DNS servers by the queried DNS server.

Recursion is the primary process occurring on the Internet. The queried DNS server starts at the top and works its way down with the referrals it receives from each DNS server it contacts. In Windows DNS servers, the top servers are listed on the Root Hints tab of the DNS server properties, as shown in Figure 6.7. You can display this in the DNS Management snap-in by right-clicking the server icon and selecting Properties. By default, it is populated with "live" Internet DNS servers.

FIGURE 6.7
Root Hints tab

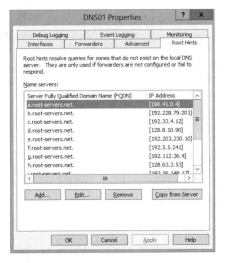

The list is located in a text file named Cache in the c:\windows\system32\dns folder displayed in Figure 6.8.

FIGURE 6.8

The Cache file listing root hints

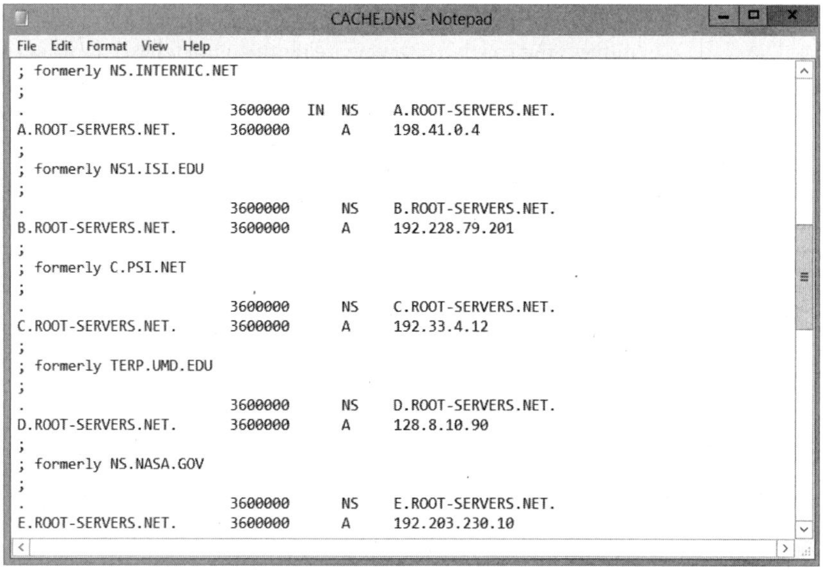

```
; formerly NS.INTERNIC.NET
;
.                         3600000    IN  NS   A.ROOT-SERVERS.NET.
A.ROOT-SERVERS.NET.       3600000        A    198.41.0.4
;
; formerly NS1.ISI.EDU
;
.                         3600000        NS   B.ROOT-SERVERS.NET.
B.ROOT-SERVERS.NET.       3600000        A    192.228.79.201
;
; formerly C.PSI.NET
;
.                         3600000        NS   C.ROOT-SERVERS.NET.
C.ROOT-SERVERS.NET.       3600000        A    192.33.4.12
;
; formerly TERP.UMD.EDU
;
.                         3600000        NS   D.ROOT-SERVERS.NET.
D.ROOT-SERVERS.NET.       3600000        A    128.8.10.90
;
; formerly NS.NASA.GOV
;
.                         3600000        NS   E.ROOT-SERVERS.NET.
E.ROOT-SERVERS.NET.       3600000        A    192.203.230.10
```

In a single Active Directory domain environment, you can leave this alone. DNS servers can use these references to resolve Internet-based namespaces such as Sybex.com when a client requests it. In larger environments, you can remove the root hint entries on other DNS servers and rely on one server to support DNS resolution throughout the external environment. This would essentially be the caching DNS server of the internal structure.

While root hints manage the queries going up the DNS hierarchical structure, delegation manages queries going downward. In our example, the DNS servers that control the .com namespace delegate the control of registered subdomains like Sybex.com. The delegation is simply the listing of these servers. So, the .com name server sends the list of name servers to a DNS server looking for the Sybex.com namespace.

In a Windows environment, you can see delegation in play with multiple Active Directory domains. If you have an Active Directory domain named Bigfirm.com, you have an associated Bigfirm.com DNS namespace. You could create an Active Directory domain named Ecoast.Bigfirm.com. Instead of keeping all the DNS namespaces on the Bigfirm.com DNS server, you can delegate the Ecoast.Bigfirm.com DNS namespace to another DNS server.

Figure 6.9 illustrates this delegation in the DNS management console. The DC01 DNS server supports a forward lookup zone named Bigfirm.com. The Ecoast subdomain, represented by an icon of a gray folder with a text file on top of it, lists only a name server record for EC1.Ecoast.Bigfirm.com with its IP address.

FIGURE 6.9
Delegated domain
for Ecoast.Bigfirm.com

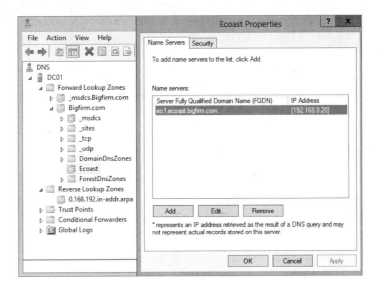

A forwarder is another DNS server to request a lateral query. When a server cannot resolve the DNS name, it can forward the request to another DNS server rather than going through the root hints. In an internal DNS environment, forwarders can be used to resolve other namespaces. For example, the DNS server EC1.Ecoast.Bigfirm.com needs to resolve Bigfirm.com servers and others namespaces, so a forwarder is entered in its properties, as shown in Figure 6.10.

FIGURE 6.10
Forwarders tab

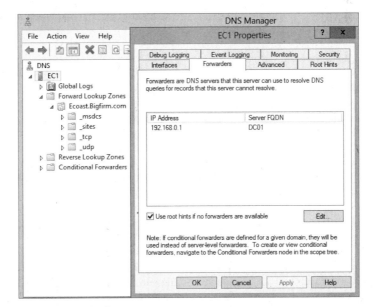

In Figure 6.10, notice the check box "Use root hints if no forwarders are available." You can disable this in a larger environment if you want to centralize the Internet-based DNS queries. Also notice the text concerning conditional forwarders.

Conditional forwarders have their own node in the DNS Manager's scope tree in the left pane. To manage resolution of a specific namespace, the conditional forwarder can direct queries to a specific server. In Figure 6.11, a conditional forwarder was set up for the Otherdomain .local namespace. Thus, any queries for this namespace will go to OS01.Otherdomain.local DNS server.

FIGURE 6.11
Conditional
forwarder

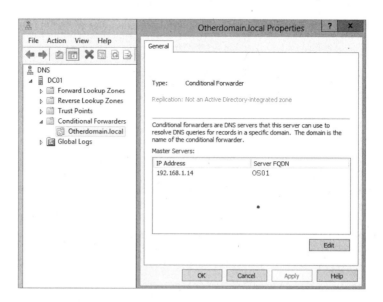

Conditional forwarders are created by right-clicking the Conditional Forwarder folder in the DNS management console and selecting New Conditional Forwarder. The New Conditional Forwarder dialog box provides an option to replicate the setting to other domain controllers in the domain or forest using Active Directory application partitions.

Forwarding also can be used to resolve Internet-based queries instead of using root hints. We prefer to use this in small environments that have an Internet service provider such as cable or DSL. These ISPs will have their own DNS servers that are found on the router configuration. So, these are entered as forwarders on the internal DNS servers. Although root hints can work in this environment, we find this technique more reliable. In addition, it limits the internal DNS server's communication to a specified external source.

The integration with other DNS servers can complete the DNS role configurations. The DNS server could receive requests and then send these requests to other DNS servers. Once it receives the answer, it could cache the information for a period of time, which in Windows Server 2012 R2 is set to one hour by default. This configuration is referred to as a *caching-only server*. If the server is to control a namespace, you have to add zones.

Implementing Zones to Manage Namespaces

A *zone* is the database for a namespace. On the Internet, there is a DNS server that controls the Sybex.com namespace. If you want the IP address for www.sybex.com, this DNS server will look in its zone (database) to find the answer. So, you can create zones on DNS servers to manage namespaces.

In Windows DNS servers, there are four types of zones:

- Standard primary

- Standard secondary

- Active Directory integrated

- Stub

The stub zone doesn't manage a namespace, however, and is more like a conditional forwarder. We'll discuss each of these zone types in the following sections.

UNDERSTANDING THE STANDARD PRIMARY ZONE

Name servers were designed to centralize name resolution for a network. Initially, a DNS server responded to requests based on its text-based HOSTS file. This is essentially what Microsoft named a *standard primary zone*. The standard primary zone is a text file in which the server maintains the records for a given namespace. That's what is *standard* about the Windows DNS implementation. *Primary* refers to replication.

Way back in the old days of Windows NT, there was one master domain controller named the *primary domain controller* (PDC), which controlled any writing to its database. The rest were *backup domain controllers* (BDCs), which had read-only copies. In DNS terms, primary zones mean there is only one master, and this server is it. Other DNS servers can have only read-only copies of this zone; these are secondary.

Creating a zone is easily accomplished with the New Zone Wizard, which you can initiate inside DNS Manager by right-clicking Forward Lookup Zones and selecting New Zone, as shown in Figure 6.12.

FIGURE 6.12

Creating a new zone

The New Zone Wizard prompts for the following information:

- ◆ The namespace or name of the domain such as Primaryzone.local.
- ◆ The name of the text file, which defaults to the `.dns` file extension.
- ◆ The Dynamic DNS Update option. We'll discuss this later in the "Updating DNS Dynamically" section.

After the zone creation, you can view the contents of the text file in the `c:\windows\system32\dns` folder displayed in Figure 6.13. Additional records, CNAME and A, were created for examples that are located at the bottom of the file.

FIGURE 6.13
Standard primary zone file

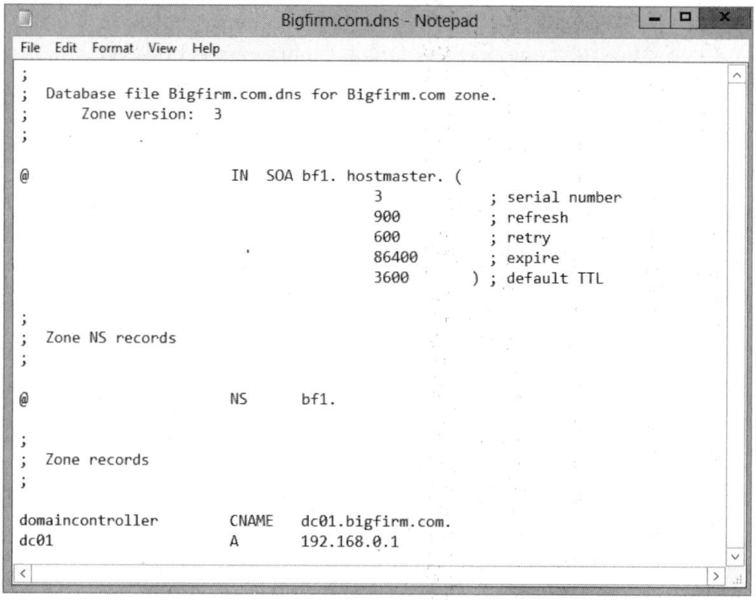

```
Bigfirm.com.dns - Notepad
File  Edit  Format  View  Help

;
;   Database file Bigfirm.com.dns for Bigfirm.com zone.
;       Zone version:  3
;

@                       IN   SOA bf1. hostmaster. (
                                        3               ; serial number
                                        900             ; refresh
                                        600             ; retry
                                        86400           ; expire
                                        3600          ) ; default TTL


;
;   Zone NS records
;

@                       NS        bf1.


;
;   Zone records
;

domaincontroller        CNAME    dc01.bigfirm.com.
dc01                    A        192.168.0.1
```

UNDERSTANDING THE STANDARD SECONDARY ZONE

The *standard secondary zone* is the read-only copy of the standard primary zone or an Active Directory integrated zone. Replication is performed through the zone transfer process, which is configured on the zone's properties. On Windows DNS servers, the default setting for zone transfers is to allow transfers to only the registered name servers of the zone, as shown in Figure 6.14.

You can add a name server, such as EC1.Ecoast.Bigfirm.com to the Name Servers tab, as in Figure 6.15, to permit replication to this server.

Once that is accomplished, you can run through the New Zone Wizard to create a standard secondary zone on EC1. This will require the master server's IP address, which would be the server to request the zone transfer. It doesn't necessarily have to be the DNS server with the standard primary zone. The result is a successful transfer of the zone to EC1, as shown in Figure 6.16.

FIGURE 6.14
Zone Transfers tab
for a primary zone

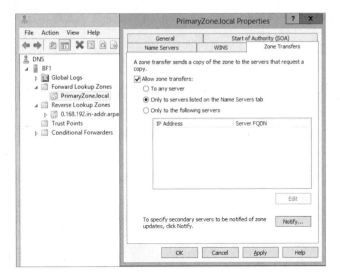

FIGURE 6.15
Name Servers tab
for a primary zone

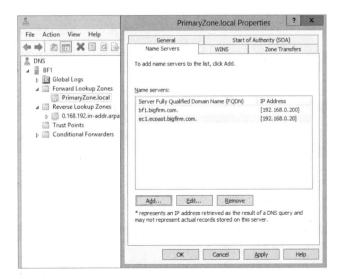

The zone transfer process is not complex. The server for the primary zone keeps track of the changes it has made and has a serial number for the change. When a secondary server contacts the primary server, it checks out the serial number in the Start of Authority record. If the serial number on the secondary server doesn't match, it's time to replicate the changes. This is simply a text-based blast of the database information. Earlier versions of DNS supported AXFR (all zone transfers) replication, which meant the entire zone was replicated to the secondary server. This could be too much traffic to throw onto the line. Windows DNS supports IXFR (which are incremental zone transfers), which replicates just the changes. Windows DNS also supports notification of secondary servers, which reduces the wait time to trigger replication.

FIGURE 6.16
Standard
secondary zone

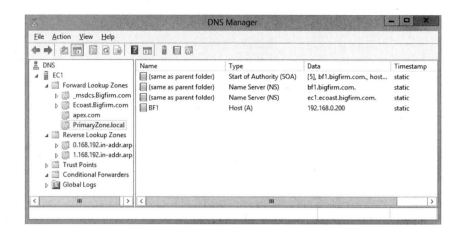

UNDERSTANDING ACTIVE DIRECTORY INTEGRATED ZONES

The third zone, Active Directory Integrated, is the predominant implementation of Windows DNS servers. The name Active Directory says it all:

◆ First, the DNS records are stored in the Active Directory database rather than a text file.

◆ Second, the zones are replicated to all other Active Directory domain controllers in the domain rather than through the zone transfer process.

Since the Active Directory database uses multimaster replication, changes can be made to the DNS zone on any domain controller, and they would be replicated to the other domain controllers. With the integration of DNS in Active Directory, the coupling of DNS and domain controller roles became the norm. For more information concerning the replication process, refer to Chapter 22.

Like the standard zones, an Active Directory integrated zone can be created with the New Zone Wizard. On the first page of the wizard, shown in Figure 6.17, you select the "Store the zone in Active Directory" check box.

FIGURE 6.17
Creating an
Active Directory
integrated zone

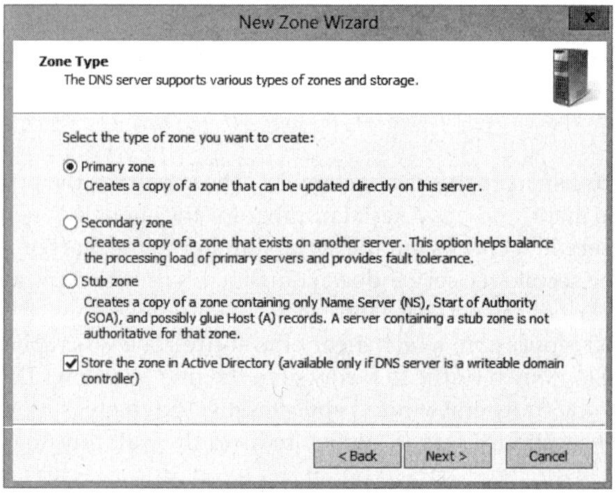

On the next page of the New Zone Wizard, shown in Figure 6.18, you have four options: forest wide, domain wide, domain wide (Windows 2000–compatible), and a specified custom application partition for storing the zone database (this last option is typically grayed out by default, but we will explain in the next paragraph how to enable this). The first two options place the database in automatically created default application partitions: one for the forest and one for the domain that the domain controller is a member of. The Windows 2000–compatible location is the domain partition of the Active Directory database, so the zone database would be replicated to only domain controllers of that domain.

FIGURE 6.18
Active Directory
Zone Replication
Scope screen

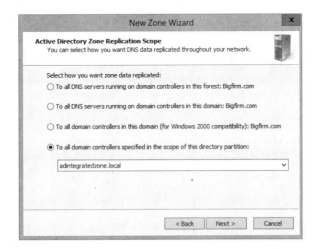

If you want to create custom application partitions, such as the one displayed in the last option in Figure 6.18, then you will need to make use of either the DNSCmd utility or the Add-DNSServerDirectoryPartition cmdlet in PowerShell. Both of these come built into Windows Server 2012 R2, and they provide the ability to manage these types of custom partitions. From a PowerShell session with administrator permissions, type the following command to create a new application partition for the Active Directory integrated zone listed earlier. The name of the partition doesn't have to match the zone name; however, using the same name makes it more understandable when viewing the configurations:

```
C:\Users\administrator.BIGFIRM>Add-DNSServerDirectoryPartition -Name
"adintegratedzone.local"
```

Once the new partition has been created, an Active Directory integrated zone can be assigned to it, as shown in Figure 6.18.

Then the other domain controllers can be configured to support the zone using PowerShell also. On EC1, which is a domain controller for the Ecoast.Bigfirm.com domain, let's say you want to add these two Active Directory zones:

- adintegratedzone.local, which is placed in its own application partition

- The reverse lookup zone for 192.168.0.0 subnet, which is placed in the forest shared partition

First, add the server to the Name Servers tab in the properties of the desired zones, similar to Figure 6.15 shown earlier.

Then, use the following cmdlet to list the available partitions on EC1:

`C:\Users\administrator.BIGFIRM>`**`Get-DNSServerDirectoryPartition`**

From the output, you can see there are four application "directory" partitions. The first one is the custom one created earlier, which the server has enlisted in sharing. The second is the domain application partition that is shared with all of the non-Windows 2000 domain controllers within the Bigfirm.com domain. The third is for the Ecoast.Bigfirm.com domain. The fourth is for all the domain controllers within the forest of domains. EC1 is already enlisted for sharing these two partitions.

USING STUB ZONES TO INTEGRATE WITH OTHER DNS SERVERS

The *stub zone* is another improvement that was first introduced with Windows Server 2003. Its concept and functionality haven't changed in Windows Server 2012 R2, and essentially it's an additional method to integrate with other DNS servers. The stub zone lists only the name server for a given namespace. It holds no control over the zone, so it indicates only what server could support name resolution for the namespace. Like conditional forwarders, it provides a lateral communication to the authoritative DNS server. These zones can also be replicated between domain controllers.

The New Zone Wizard sets up the stub zone with the following parameters:

◆ Type of zone: Stub

◆ Optionally stored in Active Directory with the desired application partition

◆ Namespace of the zone, such as Apex.com

◆ DNS server that supports this namespace

Once the stub zone is created, you can view its contents, as displayed in Figure 6.19. It lists the Start of Authority record for the namespace, the name server record for the namespace, and a host record for the name server.

FIGURE 6.19
Stub zone example

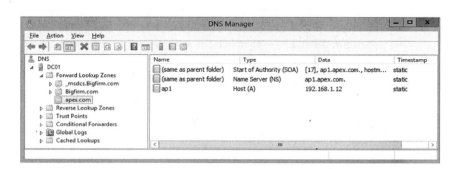

USING REVERSE LOOKUP ZONES TO INCREASE SECURITY

You may have noticed that the zones we created were found in the Forward Lookup Zones folder within the DNS management console. A *forward lookup* means the client provides a fully qualified domain name and the DNS server returns an IP address. A *reverse lookup* does the opposite: the client provides an IP address, and then the DNS server returns an FQDN.

You might be wondering to yourself, "Why would this be necessary?" Well, the primary reasons are security related. Consider a hacker who has set up a malicious service to listen for DNS queries for FQDNs starting with www. on a network. When the rogue service gets a query, it automatically sends a bogus response to the client with the IP address of the hacker's web server. The website loads worms, viruses, Trojans, and other unsafe code before the user knows what's happening. Now, if the web browser could be configured to perform a reverse lookup on the provided IP address, it could compare the result with the queried name. If it didn't match, it wouldn't connect to the web server.

An example of how this type of reverse name resolution lookup works in the real world is with the SMTP service on Windows. This service has an option to perform reverse lookups on connections to the server. The SMTP servers provide their domain names in the communication, and the TCP/IP address is provided in the connection. The reverse lookup can then be performed to verify that things match up as they should do.

The NsLookup command illustrates the use of the reverse lookup. In the following code, the command is started in interactive mode to a server that doesn't have a pointer (PTR) record in a reverse lookup zone. Notice that the default server is listed as UnKnown. DNS queries can be flaky when this is the case.

```
C:\Users\Administrator.BF1>Nslookup
Default Server:   UnKnown
Address:   192.168.0.10
```

If the pointer record is created in the reverse lookup zone, the command output looks better. You can see here that it lists the name of the server:

```
C:\Users\Administrator.BF1>Nslookup
Default Server:   BF1.bigfirm.com
Address:   192.168.0.10
```

To correctly configure reverse lookup zones within your network, you need to understand how reverse resolution works. For IPv4, the IP address is in decimal dot notation with four octets, as in x.y.w.z. IPv6 is similar, but it uses hex numbers and a lot more. Either way, the process is the same. The DNS server that receives the query changes the order of the IP address. So, a query for the FQDN for the IP address of x.y.w.z becomes z.w.y.x, with .in-addr.arpa appended to the end of it. Then the DNS server attempts to resolve the FQDN of z.w.y.x.in-addr.arpa like a normal FQDN. It starts at the top-level domain of .arpa and works its way down to the in-addr. name servers. Each of the decimal values becomes a subdomain of the namespace to the right of it.

In small environments that include only one subnet, the subnet can be represented by a single zone. In our example, the 192.168.0.0 subnet is one zone, as shown in Figure 6.20. When the reverse lookup zone is created, the New Zone Wizard requests the name of the subnet to create the zone.

In larger environments where multiple subnets are in place, the zone for the higher-precedence octet needs to be created, and lower octets should be represented as subdomains or delegated subdomains. For example, if a large organization is using the 10.0.0.0 private IP addressing scheme, it would create a reverse lookup zone for the 10.in-addr.arpa domain name.

With dynamic updates occurring, subdomains would be automatically created for the next octet from 1 to 254, and pointer records would populate the subfolders of the structure. At some point, the subdomains could be delegated to another set of DNS servers, such as domain controllers located in a site that contains these subnets. Then pointer records would be registered in the respective zone that represents the subnet.

FIGURE 6.20
Reverse lookup zone example

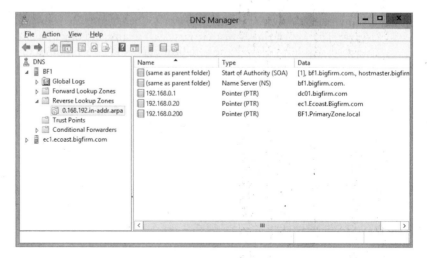

In Figure 6.21, the 10.in-addr.arpa zone was created on BF1. If you wanted the 10.11.0.0 subnets controlled by another server, you would delegate the 11 subdomain. This was delegated to EC1. Within it, the actual subnet of 10.11.12.0 is also represented as a delegated subdomain.

FIGURE 6.21
Reverse lookup zone for the 10.0.0.0 network

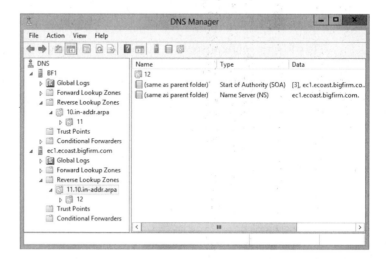

Understanding Record Types

Now that the databases are set up for the clients to retrieve information, you need to add records to the databases. As mentioned previously, Dynamic DNS (DDNS) is a process that allows DNS clients to register their hostnames in an assigned namespace, such as DHCP, and this adds the records for the Windows computers within an environment. However, it will still be necessary to add some records manually and verify that the correct records were created dynamically. More than 25 record types are available for a DNS zone. In this section, we'll review the most common record types found in a Windows DNS implementation.

ROUND-ROBIN AND NETMASK ORDERING

On the Advanced tab in the properties of the DNS server, you will find a number of server options enabled, two of which are:

◆ "Enable round robin"

◆ "Enable netmask ordering"

Round-robin   This is a "poor man's" network load balancing technique. If you register multiple host records of the same name with different IP addresses, the DNS server responds sequentially with a different IP address for each query, starting with the lowest IP address. Although it doesn't spread the client load evenly or smartly to the available hosts, it still provides a balancing capability between servers.

Netmask Ordering   Like round-robin, this uses multiple host records of the same name with a different IP address. Rather than picking randomly, the record that mathematically shows up as being closer is chosen. This is done through a comparison of the subnets. This is good if you have geographically separated hosts and your client needs to contact the one in its own network.

So, when using servers that are geographically separated, you need to decide which method is best. Netmask ordering will keep the response time minimized by nature of a shorter route. Round-robin will distribute the load more evenly if the clients are in a concentrated location.

However, a twist in these processes has come about when using Windows Server 2012 R2 with Windows 7 or Windows 8. The TCP/IP stack for IPv6 and IPv4 "when possible" will perform a similar process to netmask-ordering named, *default address selection*. Thus, it receives the IP addresses from the DNS server and decides on its own which is best.

Like most configurations, this can be overridden with a Group Policy object specifying the following registry change:

```
Hkey_Local_Machine\System\CurrentControlSet
\Services\Tcpip\Parameters\OverrideDefaultAddressSelection
```

A value of 1 will turn off default address selection and allow a random choice of the NLB round-robin servers.

You can see the effect on all this with the use of round robin for geographically split servers. For example, an environment with a disaster recovery site would like to offer two servers located in different sites to perform the same service. In this case, two FTP servers could be available to download data. DNS is rigged to provide two IP addresses for the same name, ftp.Bigfirm.com. Round-robin will resolve the records sequentially. If one server goes down, such as in a disaster, the clients will still have connectivity to ftp.Bigfirm.com. (It will occasionally select the dead server's IP address, but reconnects are still available to keep the data flowing.)

However, if netmask ordering or default address selection is in place, the clients may never get the live FTP server. The DNS server would be making the choice or the client would be. So, this gotcha scenario tells you to apply the time-tried rule: "Test, test, test." Validate which servers are being used in a normal scenario, and validate what happens when a disaster scenario occurs.

HOST AND POINTER RECORDS

Host (A) and pointer (PTR) records are the most common records you will find in the forward lookup zones and the reverse lookup zones, respectively. The A records list the hostname of the computer and return the IP address. The PTR records list the IP address and return an FQDN.

You may have to create these for computers that do not have the DDNS update protocol available.

ALIAS RECORDS

Alias (CNAME) records are created to list a secondary name for a computer. This record will list the name and return the assigned computer's FQDN. These are useful in the event of replacing the server of a published name that the clients use to access applications or services. Without their reconfiguration, clients will still be able to access the alias after replacement.

MAIL EXCHANGER RECORDS

Mail exchanger (MX) records are for SMTP communication. Mail servers request MX records to contact the receiving SMTP server for that namespace. Typically, you will be setting these up in an external DNS zone. However, they may be required internally for specific applications. The MX record requires an FQDN of the SMTP server and a priority value.

The priority helps determine which MX record to contact first, and next when more than one are available. The lower value wins out. Remember "number-one priority."

Say you have a primary SMTP server and a smart host SMTP server to support catching email when the primary server is unavailable. You would want to create MX records for both of them. The primary SMTP server needs a lower-priority value compared to the smart host, such as 10 and 20, respectively. When the primary SMTP server is unavailable, the smart host is contacted.

SERVICE RECORDS

Service records (SRV) are the "big kahunas" for Windows DNS implementations. Without the SRV records, workstations and servers would not be able to find domain controllers. The SRV records by themselves involve only five values:

Service Name This is a standard value typically preceded by an underscore, such as _gc. or _ladp. This is equivalent to a hostname and it would be tacked onto the FQDN of a service.

Server FQDN This is the server that provides the service.

Port This is the TCP or UDP port on which the service is available. The protocol is signified in the registered name, such as _TCP.

Priority This works just like MX records—it has a "number-one priority."

Weight This is the tiebreaker for priority. Leave it at 0 if you're not concerned with ties.

You will see a plethora of SRV records in a Windows DNS zone that supports Active Directory. They are found in subdomain folders because the service name is assigned different FQDNs. The required service is described by the FQDN like _gc._tcp.bigfirm.com. Figure 6.22 illustrates the SRV records.

FIGURE 6.22
SRV record
example

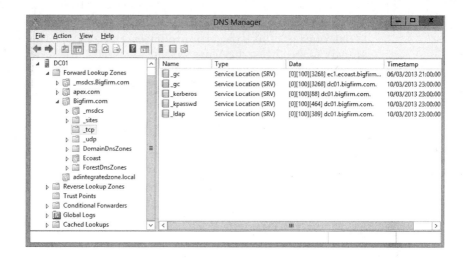

START OF AUTHORITY RECORDS

A Start of Authority (SOA) record is a single record within each zone. It has information about what DNS server controls this zone and parameters on how to treat the resolved records. It contains several values that shouldn't be modified by editing the record. You should edit them on the Start of Authority (SOA) tab in the properties of the zone, as shown in Figure 6.23.

FIGURE 6.23
Start of Authority
(SOA) tab

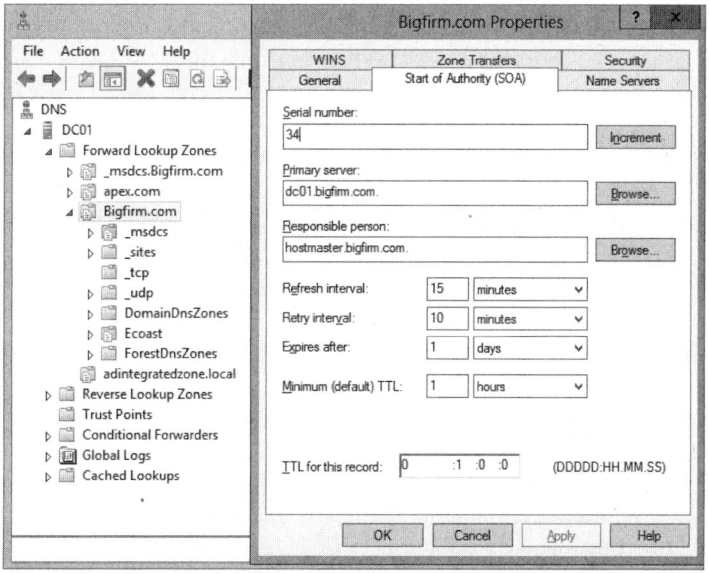

The following are the fields on the tab:

Serial Number   This is the revision number of the zone file. This really counts with standard primary zones because the Active Directory replication has its own serial number, so to speak. Secondary zones can compare their number with it to see whether their information is up to date. If it isn't, it's time for a zone transfer.

Primary Server   This is the server in which the zone was initially set up. You can switch a primary server to a secondary server and vice versa if you want to modify how replication updates in your environment.

Responsible Person   This is supposed to be an email address of the person who administers the zone. Notice that the @ is replaced by a dot (.). If you want to make someone really mad, you put their email address here!

Refresh Interval   This is how long the secondary server can wait before attempting to check changes on the primary server. At this point of time, it compares the serial number of the SOA record with its own. By default it is 15 minutes. The value is listed in seconds within the actual record.

Retry Interval   How long should the secondary server wait before trying again after a failed zone transfer? This is in seconds too and defaults to 10 minutes.

Expires After   How long can the secondary server continue to answer requests on this zone after a zone transfer is performed? The default is one day. This is also in listed in seconds within the record, and the value is 86,400.

Minimum (Default) TTL   How long should these records be cached or, in other words, what's the Time To Live (TTL)? The default is an hour, or 3,600 seconds.

NAME SERVER RECORDS

Name server (NS) records list the servers that can respond to queries for this zone. There will be at least one of these records in the zone. Like the SOA record, this is modified in the properties of the zone on the Name Servers tab, as shown earlier in Figure 6.15. The only value required in the NS record is the FQDN of the server. You'll notice a little note at the bottom of the Name Servers tab stating that the IP address is a retrieved value.

Managing DNS Clients and Name Resolution

You can deduce that every computer is a DNS client. The DNS service is a vital component of the network even if Active Directory is not part of it. In addition, it is the only method for getting to your favorite Internet websites like: www.Sybex.com.

On the Windows operating system, there are two areas concerning the clients of DNS: resolving hostnames and registering hostnames and IP addresses through Dynamic DNS updates.

HOSTNAME RESOLUTION

The Windows computer has two parts in the name-resolution process. This process is so important that we'll call it the "circle of life." One part, which is nearly dead, is NetBIOS, and the other is DNS. (You could call it the hostname process, but most admins call it DNS.) This circle consists of the steps a computer would take in resolving a given name, as illustrated in Figure 6.24.

FIGURE 6.24
The circle of life

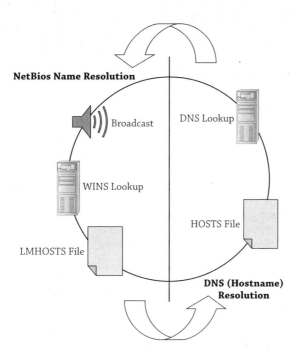

The NetBIOS process involves the following steps:

1. Broadcast the name into the network and see whether someone answers.

2. Look the name up in WINS.

3. Look the name up in the LMHOSTS file. This is another text file similar to the HOSTS file located in the same place: c:\windows\system32\drivers\etc. It lists NetBIOS names instead of hostnames.

The order of the first two steps is configurable, particularly through the DHCP server. The broadcast step can be skipped, or the WINS lookup can be skipped. The default on Windows Server 2012 R2 is to resolve through WINS first and then resolve with a broadcast second. However, the LMHOSTS lookup is always last.

The DNS process involves a shorter list of steps:

1. Look the name up in HOSTS.

2. Look the name up in DNS.

The order of the DNS process steps is not configurable, but you can modify the behavior of the DNS lookup. There are some good and bad points about the HOSTS file being first. If you are unable to access a DNS server or you need to redirect resolution of a name to another place, editing the HOSTS file works great. If the HOSTS file has stale or malicious entries, troubleshooting DNS can be difficult.

The name-resolution process circles through both parts until it comes up with an IP address. It also has a choice of where to start in the circle, either NetBIOS or DNS. This is basically application dependent. Older legacy Windows applications looked at a name and considered it NetBIOS. TCP/IP-based applications thought it was a hostname. This affects how the name is resolved, and it still is part of the Windows operating systems.

Examples of this include the net view command and the ping command.

The net view command is a command from the ancient days of LAN Manager, which relied entirely on NetBIOS. If you attempt to connect to a server using this command, you will see the NetBIOS name cache populated with the server name. This is displayed with the nbtstat -c command. The cache can be cleared with nbtstat -R.

```
rem view the NetBios cache
C:\Users\Administrator.BF1>nbtstat -c

Local Area Connection:
Node IpAddress: [192.168.0.10] Scope Id: []

    No names in cache

rem access the shares on bfsc1
C:\Users\Administrator.BF1>net view \\bfsc1
Shared resources at \\bfsc1


Share name   Type   Used as   Comment

-------------------------------------------------------------------------------
NETLOGON     Disk             Logon server share
SALES        Disk
SYSVOL       Disk             Logon server share
Users        Disk
The command completed successfully.

rem view cache again
C:\Users\Administrator.BF1>nbtstat -c

Local Area Connection:
Node IpAddress: [192.168.0.10] Scope Id: []

                NetBIOS Remote Cache Name Table

        Name              Type      Host Address    Life [sec]
        ------------------------------------------------------------
        BFSC1    <00>  UNIQUE        192.168.0.11      600
```

When you ping a server, the DNS process is used because it was written as a TCP/IP utility. You can see that it resolved the server via DNS by displaying the DNS cache with the ipconfig /displaydns command. The cache is cleared with ipconfig /flushdns.

```
rem clear the DNS cache
C:\Users\Administrator.BF1>ipconfig /flushdns

Windows IP Configuration

Successfully flushed the DNS Resolver Cache.

C:\Users\Administrator.BF1>ping BFSC1

Pinging BFSC1.bigfirm.com [192.168.0.11] with 32 bytes of data:
Reply from 192.168.0.11: bytes=32 time<1ms TTL=128
Reply from 192.168.0.11: bytes=32 time<1ms TTL=128
Reply from 192.168.0.11: bytes=32 time<1ms TTL=128
Reply from 192.168.0.11: bytes=32 time<1ms TTL=128

Ping statistics for 192.168. 0.11:
    Packets: Sent = 4, Received = 4, Lost = 0 (0% loss),
Approximate round trip times in milli-seconds:
    Minimum = 0ms, Maximum = 0ms, Average = 0ms

C:\Users\Administrator.BF1>ipconfig /displaydns

Windows IP Configuration

    BFSC1
    ----------------------------------------
    Record Name . . . . . : BFSC1.bigfirm.com
    Record Type . . . . . : 1
    Time To Live  . . . . : 1185
    Data Length . . . . . : 4
    Section . . . . . . . : Answer
    A (Host) Record . . . : 192.168. 0.11
```

Knowing this helps you decide how to support the DNS client-resolution process and affectively kill or support (as needed) NetBIOS names. The NetBIOS name process is chatty and takes up unnecessary CPU cycles. If the DNS server and client implementation are configured correctly, NetBIOS name-resolution support can be eliminated or at least minimized.

CONFIGURING CLIENTS

You can find the DNS and NetBIOS configurations in the IP properties of the network connection. Both are in the advanced settings. You can find the NetBIOS configurations on the WINS tab. Figure 6.25 displays the WINS tab with the default configurations.

The settings enable LMHOSTS and default the NetBIOS configurations to the DHCP server settings. First, by default the LMHOSTS file is empty. It would be good to disable this because malicious viruses have entered data into this file in the past.

Next, the NetBIOS settings default to what's on the DHCP server. The DHCP server scopes have an option named NBT Node Type (046). This setting orders the first two steps in the NetBIOS process in the circle of life. Four options are indicated by a decimal value:

◆ Broadcast only: "b-node," 1

◆ Contact WINS only: "p-node," 2

◆ Broadcast first and then contact WINS: "m-node," 4

◆ Contact WINS and then broadcast: "h-node," 8

FIGURE 6.25
The WINS tab

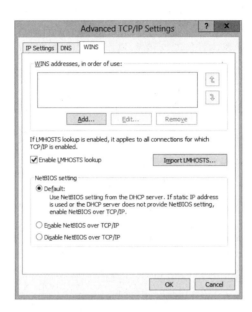

H-node is best for a network relying on NetBIOS because it reduces the chatter in a WINS-supported environment. If no WINS server is available, the computer can at least get some answer in a subnet, such as at home or in a workgroup. If DHCP is not configured with this value, the operating system's default configuration takes place. Windows Server 2012 R2 defaults to h-node, or hybrid mode.

It would be best for Active Directory environments to disable NetBIOS because it reduces the extra chatter and processes. It also helps reduce security threats such as bots that search networks for computers to attack using this naming system. Before doing this, however, you'd need to ensure that DNS name resolution is airtight.

You can find DNS client configurations on the DNS tab of the network properties, which is displayed in Figure 6.26. The obvious need is the DNS server's IP address. It should be connecting to the nearest server, typically a domain controller in its local site. A secondary DNS server is recommended.

The middle portion of the tab deals with unqualified names. This is a hostname without its "last name," the DNS suffix (such as BFSC1 listed earlier in the ping example). The DNS server needs an FQDN, so the DNS client appends DNS suffixes, the "last name," before sending the request. The primary DNS suffix is listed in the System control panel (My Computer properties) under the Computer Name tab. This is managed automatically by the operating system when the computer joins the domain, so you shouldn't need to mess with it. Additional suffixes may be necessary in larger environments, but in single-domain environments, the default settings work. Only in rare occasions would you consider adding a connection DNS suffix.

FIGURE 6.26
DNS tab

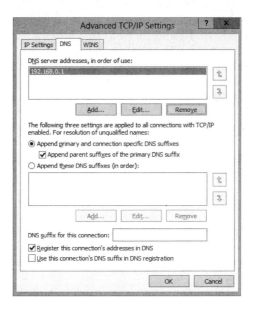

All of this is moot if FQDNs are used regularly. When applications are configured, use FQDNs of servers. When configuring home folders or folder redirection, use FQDNs. When writing scripts that map network drives, use FQDNs. Get the point? On top of this, using FQDNs bypasses the NetBIOS process. Applications can tell the difference between NetBIOS names and FQDNs and will resort to DNS when they recognize an FQDN.

UPDATING DNS DYNAMICALLY

To make the DNS name-resolution process airtight, you need to have all of the computers listed in DNS zones. In the past, DNS became a full-time job for system admins because they had to manually enter the ever-growing number of records for their network. To reduce the work for system admins, Microsoft sought a dynamic solution through WINS when developing NT and then switched to DNS when the Dynamic DNS (DDNS) update protocol was available. The process is pretty simple:

1. The client queries the SOA record for its primary DNS suffix namespace. This will tell it what server can accept DDNS. It also does this for the reverse lookup zone that its IP address is associated with.

2. The client makes the DDNS request to that server.

On standard zones' Start of Authority records, the primary server is listed. On Active Directory integrated zones, the domain controller receiving the request modifies the SOA response with its name. Since it can change the Active Directory database, there's no need to hunt down a domain controller located elsewhere. If the update process fails, it can attempt to find other name servers to perform the update.

The only configuration on the DNS tab concerning DDNS you can make is to the two check boxes on the bottom, as shown in Figure 6.26. You can register the name with the primary DNS suffix or with the connection suffix. The latter check box is deselected by default.

The silly part of this is that the DNS client service doesn't perform the DDNS process. The DHCP client service does. This reminds us of an eventful day when one of us disabled the DHCP client service on a domain controller. "This doesn't need the service running; it has a static IP address," he naively thought. As already mentioned, the DDNS process is used by the domain controllers to list the SRV records for Active Directory. Eventually, the clients couldn't find the domain controller because there were no SRV records for it. Oh, joy! Fortunately, this was in a lab environment.

There are two other locations that manage the DDNS process: the zone for a namespace and the DHCP server.

The DNS zone can be enabled for DDNS updates in the New Zone Wizard or can be modified in the properties of the zone. Figure 6.27 depicts the options for DDNS. The options are secure only, both secure and nonsecure, and disabled. Secure dynamic updates means the DNS client has authenticated with the domain controller prior to the update. Nonsecure means the update is accepted without authentication. Given the name, you can safely assume that hackers can exploit this option. Disabled prevents any DDNS updates from occurring.

FIGURE 6.27
Dynamic DNS
update options

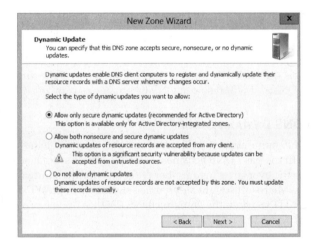

The DHCP server can also participate in the DDNS process. In much earlier versions of Windows Server, there were plenty of Windows clients that didn't have DDNS capabilities. To resolve this, the DHCP server would identify these OSs and perform the updates for them. In addition, the DHCP server would perform the update upon request. Figure 6.28 shows the DNS tab of the IPv4 properties within the DHCP server.

The default settings are displayed, and these settings will be rarely modified. Essentially, DHCP is not performing any updates because clients are doing it themselves. It does perform a cleanup when leases expire. Name protection, which is just a check box reached by clicking the Configure button, basically prevents DHCP server from updating an existing DNS record.

FIGURE 6.28
DDNS options
on DHCP

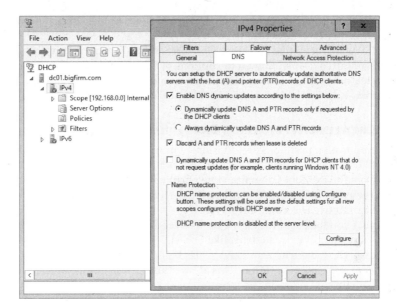

Understanding Active Directory's DNS

Microsoft has integrated DNS and Active Directory so tightly together that it's difficult to discuss the two separately. When an Active Directory environment is created with Windows Server 2012 R2, the Active Directory installation process automatically configures DNS while adding the role. This provides a hands-off capability for the IT generalist in setting up DNS.

In the following sections, we'll cover the way Active Directory configures DNS and uses it to support clients. For a more detailed discussion of the Active Directory terms and concepts, refer to Chapter 7.

Configuring DNS Automatically

Windows Server 2012 R2 offers two ways of installing the DNS service: adding the DNS role on its own (as you've seen earlier in the stand-alone non-domain configuration) or adding the Active Directory Domain Services role. When you opt for the latter, you must run the Active Directory Domain Services Installation Wizard, which performs a number of configurations for the Active Directory Domain Services role, including automatically configuring and integrating the DNS role. In Chapter 7, we will walk you through the Active Directory installation process in detail, but here we take a look at just what happens regarding the DNS role.

First, you must understand the prerequisite for the Active Directory installation process. The prospective domain controller needs to have connectivity to the existing Active Directory DNS structure. Otherwise, it won't be able to connect to the domain controllers and obtain the necessary information. So, the IP configurations must list a DNS server within the Active Directory environment, preferably the forest root's DNS server or a DNS server in the same domain you are about to join. The only exception to this is when you create the very first domain controller in the Active Directory environment. At that point, there is no Active Directory DNS structure to point to.

When the Active Directory Domain Services wizard is run, a new domain controller is configured. Depending on the options selected within the wizard, a new domain may be created. In either case, the DNS service and settings are configured automatically. The following changes are made.

CREATING APPLICATION PARTITIONS

Application partitions are divisions within the Active Directory database that are created for sharing DNS zones between different domains when a new domain or forest is created. The DomainDNSZones.domain.name partition is created for domain controllers within a domain. The ForestDNSZones.domain.name partition is created for sharing between domain controllers of an Active Directory forest.

If you look again at Figure 6.9 from earlier, you will notice the _msdcs.bigfirm.com subdomain is delegated just like Ecoast. It is delegated to the same domain controller, in this case, DC01.Bigfirm.com. The _msdcs.Bigfirm.com zone is created in the ForestDNSZone.Bigfirm.com application partition. This allows this portion of the namespace to be replicated to all domain controllers in the forest.

When additional domain controllers are created, they are automatically enlisted to these application partitions.

ADDING A FORWARDER

Within the DNS server's properties, a forwarder is added and can be viewed and configured from the Forwarders tab. This will typically be the IP address of the original DNS server that the server was using.

MODIFYING IP PROPERTIES

The new domain controller created by the Active Directory Domain Services Wizard is also a new DNS server. The primary DNS server's address in the IP properties is reconfigured to the loopback IP addresses, ::1 (for IPv6) and 127.0.0.1 (for IPv4).

DELEGATING THE SUBDOMAIN

A child domain has a name that is a subdomain within an existing domain namespace. For example, Ecoast.Bigfirm.com is a subdomain within the Bigfirm.com namespace. When the Active Directory Domain Services Wizard does its thing, the new domain's namespace will be supported on the new domain controller as a delegated subdomain.

On the parent domain, a subdomain like Ecoast.Bigfirm.com is delegated to the new domain controller. The delegation will link the parent to the child domain for name resolution. This was illustrated earlier in Figure 6.9.

ADDITIONAL RECOMMENDED CONFIGURATIONS

After a domain controller is created, we recommend that you make the following changes to the DNS settings:

1. In the network adapter TCP/IPv4 properties, change the primary DNS server to the IP address of the primary network connection. For example, if the primary IP address for your server is 192.168.0.1, then this is what you need to change your primary DNS server property to.

   When troubleshooting DNS with the NsLookup utility, the loopback address (127.0.0.1) causes tests to be "unauthoritative." Although this may be merely cosmetic, we have found results to be a little fickle using the loopback address, so it's best to stick with the primary IP address instead.

2. Create the reverse lookup zones in the ForestDNSZones.domain.name application partition.

   The reverse lookup zone for subnets may need to be shared between domain controllers of different domains.

3. Create a stub zone for new domain trees on the root DNS server.

   A domain tree has a different name than the root DNS server. Since the original DNS server entry is listed as a forwarder like the other domain controller promotions, the DNS server can communicate with the rest of the Active Directory DNS structure. However, there are no automatic configurations on the rest of the Active Directory DNS structure to resolve names in the new namespace. For example, we need to set up a conditional forwarder or a stub zone to point the DNS servers to the new domain controller for Apex.com. In Figure 6.19, you can see a stub zone used to assist resolving Apex.com domain FQDNs.

Understanding SRV Records and Clients

Looking at a brand-spanking-new domain's DNS zone, you will notice that it has a lot of new folders or subdomains. Drilling through these folders, you will find service location records by the boatload, as shown earlier in Figure 6.22. As we mentioned, Microsoft needed SRV records and Dynamic DNS updates to make Active Directory work. This is the result of the two technologies working together.

The netlogon service performs DDNS requests to create the SRV records within the Active Directory DNS namespace. The sole reason is to ensure computers can find domain controllers in the domain.

Within the Windows operating system processes, the specific services are sought out with the use of the DNS. In Figure 6.22, you will notice a few different services:

◆ _gc, or global catalog: The LDAP service to look up data within the global catalog

◆ _kerberos: The authentication process

◆ _kpassword: Another part of the authentication process

◆ _ldap: The LDAP service to look up data within the domain

Each of these services is performed by domain controllers within the domain or forest. In Figure 6.22, you see DC01.Bigfirm.com perform all of these roles and what TCP port it is listening on.

So, when a Windows computer needs a specific domain controller service, such as LDAP, it will request an SRV answer for _ldap._tcp.Bigfirm.com. It will then have all it needs to get busy with an IP address and port.

If a Windows computer needs to find a domain controller in its own site, it can look for it within the _sites.Bigfirm.com subdomain. This subdomain will list all the created sites within the Active Directory Sites and Services console.

The idea that admins could possibly support this load of DNS entries manually is incredible. For one domain controller, you can expect at least 16 to 20 different SRV records to be registered. Learning all of them is a daunting task for sure. That's when tools like DcDiag come into play. See the section, "Leveraging NsLookup and DcDiag," later in this chapter for instructions for using these utilities.

Windows Server 2012 R2 Additional Features

Up to this point, the essential features we have discussed and skills you have learned would go a long way toward ensuring you are proficient enough to manage a Windows Server 2012 R2 DNS environment. This section will discuss some of the additional DNS features in Windows Server 2012 R2 that tend not to be implemented as frequently as the other essential features that we have covered already, but nonetheless, they're definitely worth explaining here.

GLOBAL QUERY BLOCK LIST

There are a few common host records that can be registered in DNS by other services. Web Proxy Automatic Discovery Protocol (WPAD) is a very common one. This helps web browsers automatically download the proxy configurations from a server. Since the record doesn't belong to a specific computer, any computer—including potentially compromised hacker computers—could attempt to register the name. Another common host record is Intra-site Automatic Tunneling Addressing Protocol (ISATAP). As you learned from Chapter 4, the purpose of ISATAP is to perform routing for IPv4 to IPv6 networks.

The global query block list specifies the names blocked from DDNS registration. Thus, a hacker computer's attempt to register names, such as WPAD or ISATAP, is rejected.

The following commands illustrate how you can administer this list. You can see this list with Get-DNSServerGlobalQueryBlocklist. Notice that it is populated with wpad and isatap by default:

```
C:\Users\Administrator.BF1>Get-DNSServerGlobalQueryBlocklist

Enable:  True
List:  {wpad, isatap}
```

If you want to add a name to the list, such as www, you can use the Set-DNSServerGlobalQueryBlocklist option. By default, the feature is enabled. You can disable or reenable it using the -Enable option with either a $True or $False Boolean value.

GLOBAL NAMES AND SINGLE NAME RESOLUTION

Even with the decline in the use of WINS, there seem to be some requirements in the marketplace to support some applications' use of the NetBIOS naming process. The GlobalNames feature is a special zone created to resolve a NetBIOS name (15 characters with no dots in it). The DNS client is supposed to perform the query to the GlobalName zone when the primary and alternate DNS suffix searches have failed.

The steps to configure this are not difficult given the earlier discussions:

1. Create a new zone with the name GlobalNames.

   An Active Directory integrated zone is recommended to provide replication to other domain controllers.

2. Enable GlobalNames support with the Set-DNSServerGlobalNameZone command:

   C:\Users\Administrator.BF1>Set-DNSServerGlobalNameZone -Enable $True

3. Replicate the zone to other domain controllers.

   Remember to add these domain controllers to the name servers list of the zone.

4. Add CNAME records in the zone to redirect to specific hosts.

   In our example, www is redirected to hostrecord.PrimaryZone.local, as shown in Figure 6.29.

FIGURE 6.29
The GlobalNames zone

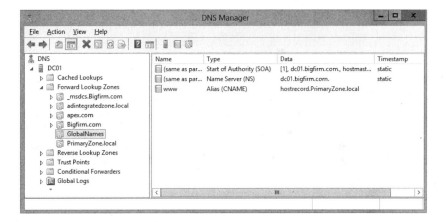

5. Add a service location record if you need other Active Directory forests to query this zone.

You can use the NsLookup utility to test the resolution of the global name:

```
C:\Users\Administrator.DC1>Nslookup
Default Server:  DC01.bigfirm.com
Address:  192.168.0.1

> www
Server:  DC01.bigfirm.com
Address:  192.168.0.1

Name:     hostrecord.primaryzone.local
Address:  192.168.0.21
Aliases:  www.bigfirm.com
```

In most environments that rely on Windows servers, the need for single names (NetBIOS) has been worked around, as we discussed earlier. It has also been minimized through the proper deployment of applications by using FQDNs and leveraging DNS.

BACKGROUND ZONE LOADING

Some older environments have DNS zones so large that it takes the domain controllers more than an hour to restart the DNS service. If you have that problem, you're in luck with background zone loading! We expect a DNS zone must have a massive number of records to cause this issue.

While the DNS service is starting, it will start responding to zones it has loaded. Requests to zones that haven't loaded could be referred to other DNS servers.

DNSSEC

Like HTTP, DNS is an unencrypted and unauthenticated protocol. As we mentioned about reverse zones, hackers can spoof DNS responses. To counter this, the DNS Security Extensions (DNSSEC) were developed, which allow a DNS server to digitally sign the resource records. Windows Server 2012 R2 provides the support to act as secondary zones for a DNSSEC zone. It only responds to queries for the record from a digitally signed zone. It will also provide the necessary resource records to authenticate the signature.

These records are the KEY, SIG, and NXT records. KEY is the public key of the signing DNS server. SIG is the digital signature of the resource record. NXT basically lists all the valid records in the namespace.

With Windows Server 2012 R2, DNSSEC has the following enhancements on its predecessor:

◆ Active Directory integration and support for DNS dynamic updates

◆ Updated DNSSEC standards support (NSEC3 and RSA/SHA-2)

◆ Record validation through the use of the updated DNSSEC standards

◆ Additional PowerShell support for DNSSEC

If you want to test drive DNSSEC in your lab, then check out this step-by-step guide from Microsoft:

```
http://tinyurl.com/dnsseclab
```

TRUST ANCHORS

Trust anchors are the public certificates of DNSSEC servers that the DNS server will trust for communications. The trust anchor certificates will be used to validate the digital signatures of the responses. These are added to the properties of the DNS server in the form of public keys.

Windows Server 2012 R2 contains the following new enhancements for trust anchors:

◆ Use of Active Directory for trust anchor distribution

◆ Automated rollover support

◆ Simplified extraction of the root trust anchor

Trust anchors are displayed in Windows Server 2012 R2 from the DNS Manager console, inside the Trust Points folder that you can see in the tree view on the left side.

Supporting Internet-based DNS Resolution

Within an organization, there is the need to manage Internet namespaces as well. The users within a LAN will need to access websites and other Internet-based services. External users will need to access the organization's websites and mail servers at a minimum. So, you will have to be mindful of these requirements also.

To allow external users access to your websites, an external DNS domain needs to be in place. Thus, you need to consider whether deploying an external DNS server is necessary. The internal computers will resolve external names through the internal DNS servers. Therefore, integration with the Internet DNS structure is required.

Supporting External DNS Domains

Most companies register a DNS namespace to support a website and email. Small- and some medium-size companies will allow an ISP to manage the namespace on their external DNS servers. The benefits are the availability of the servers and the reduced headache of maintaining additional servers on a public Internet-facing subnet. These servers are managed through a web interface and allow only a few types of records such as host, cname, and MX.

Using a Windows Server 2012 R2 server for external DNS operations is possible. The DNS role can be installed on a server that isn't a domain member (as we discussed earlier in "Configuring a Stand-Alone DNS Server"), and then the registered DNS namespace's name server record can be modified to the public IP address of the server. Oh, sure, exposing a stand-alone DNS server to the Internet in this way can be done, but realistically there are some cons to the idea:

- Windows Server 2012 R2 isn't free, and utilizing it simply as an external DNS solution is not the most economical way to do things.

- The Windows Server 2012 R2 server needs to be locked down and secure if exposed externally. Now you are looking at deploying Server Core and hardening that.

- It needs to be highly available, so you'll have to cluster the server or set up multiple DNS servers.

- If it hasn't already been taken care of, you'll need to have a highly available network connection to the Internet, too.

The cost of going in this direction is high, and many companies would rather spend the money elsewhere. This may be where a simple Linux implementation of DNS has an advantage. However, we recommend the approach most have taken—letting an ISP manage the namespace.

SPLIT BRAIN

Many companies have also implemented a "split-brain" scenario when it comes to DNS, although not intentionally. What this means is they have an internal namespace that is the same as the external namespace. For example, we have the registered external namespace Bigfirm .com. The company has decided to build an Active Directory environment with the same name.

CAVEATS TO USING SPLIT-BRAIN DNS

Depending on whom you speak to or what technical document on DNS you read, you might see recommendations telling you not to use the same domain name for your company's internal and external DNS namespace. They will recommend that you use something different that may not be found on the Internet or a registered name you don't ever use.

When companies don't follow this recommendation, they soon realize that they have a conflict with resolving external resources that they own such as www.Bigfirm.com. The internal DNS server can't find the name, so it kicks back a big goose egg for a response. The admins try to fix this by adding the name manually with the external IP address, but adding the external IP address causes routing issues. In addition, the developers are whining that they can't upload new content with the external IP address. They need the internal IP address. This kind of additional administration hassle becomes the norm for dealing with split-brain issues.

Managing this scenario with just one server would be ideal. A split-brain DNS implementation is a cool idea that is supposed to remedy this issue. You could have a single DNS server support an internal and external zone of the same namespace. The IP addresses for the external zone would be provided to external requests and internal IP addresses for the internal requests.

It's a nice idea that Windows Server 2012 R2 doesn't support. Primarily, Microsoft doesn't support your organization exposing the domain controller that hosts the internal DNS namespace to even the edge of the Internet. This is not a secure measure. The Active Directory database is too valuable to hang in a DMZ like a ripe peach. So, you have to come up with an alternative.

Your objective is to provide resolution of external requests with external IP addresses and internal requests with internal IP addresses. Using Microsoft DNS, you will have to administer (a minimum of) two DNS servers to support this scenario. Here are the basic steps:

1. Implement an external DNS server to support Bigfirm.com. Typically, this is already in place with the registration of a domain name with the help of the ISP.

2. Implement the internal DNS structure. Using the Active Directory Domain Services Installation Wizard, this is handled quite readily.

3. Add any external records to the internal zone for Bigfirm.com.

   Remember, the DNS servers within the network will be authoritative for the Bigfirm.com domain. If it can't find www.Bigfirm.com, it doesn't exist. External records must be duplicated in the internal zone so a positive result can be returned. You will have to test routing to ensure that the IP address is accessible. If routing causes problems, you may have to use an internal address.

4. Configure resolving external namespaces using root hints or forwarders. This topic is covered in the following section.

Resolving External Namespaces

We discussed how to integrate a DNS server with others. The primary methods of resolving DNS names in the Internet are the root hints or the forwarders. The root hints were a list of DNS servers that were at the top of the Internet's DNS structure. The DNS server could communicate with these servers to perform recursive queries for external namespaces. Forwarders were lateral requests to another DNS server to see whether that server could come up with the name. We mentioned that in small environments we prefer to use forwarders to an external DNS server that is supported by the ISP, but using root hints still work in this scenario too.

It is important to not mix the two. Don't list root hints servers as forwarders. A query to a root hint is a referral request that always returns the name server for a domain. It doesn't respond with host records, and it doesn't perform the recursive operation that a forwarder would. Forwarders also take precedence over root hints. In Figure 6.10 shown earlier in the chapter, the Forwarders tab includes the check box "Use root hints if no forwarders are available." You can infer that if a forwarder is listed and it comes up with an invalid response, the query is over, and root hints won't be touched.

In extensive internal DNS environments, judicious use of the forwarders and root hints is necessary. The internal subdomain name servers need to resolve queries from the root DNS server. They also have to resolve Internet-based queries. Taking advantage of the caching capability of DNS, they can rely on a server to resolve and store common queries to reduce externally bound traffic. Microsoft recommends that the caching server should not be the root server so the root server will not be overburdened with the additional workload. In addition, they warn internal DNS servers that host zones should not communicate directly with the Internet to reduce their exposure to Internet. Figure 6.30 depicts one solution that could work for our fictitious DNS structure.

FIGURE 6.30
Internal DNS structure

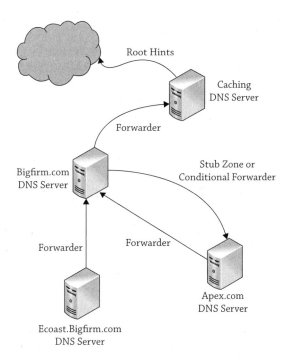

In this example, forwarders are used to send requests to the root DNS server in Bigfirm .com. Root hints could be used by removing the Internet root hints and listing BF1.Bigfirm.com as the root hint server. The caching server is in place to prevent the DNS servers hosting the

Active Directory integrated zones from making queries into the Internet. It performs resolutions via the root hints. To handle queries in the Apex.com domain, a stub zone or a conditional forwarder is used.

Other solutions are possible and may have merit for different reasons. We prefer the simplicity of using the forwarders to manage the integration between the servers.

Administration and Troubleshooting with DNS Tools

In this section, we'll discuss the available tools and troubleshooting techniques for DNS name resolution. Given the importance of DNS, you need to be familiar with the tools that give valuable information to discern where problems lie with name resolution. The standard admin tools, the DNS management console, and PowerShell provide additional information over and above configurations. The NsLookup, DcDiag, and DNSLint utilities provide excellent initial indications of problems concerning DNS resolution.

Administering the DNS Server with the DNS Management Console and PowerShell

To administer the DNS server, we have touched on two tools: the DNS management console, which is an MMC snap-in, and PowerShell, which, of course, is a shell-based command-line tool. PowerShell offers the capability of administering the entire server like the MMC and offers a little more functionality. For example, as you learned earlier, the DNS management console doesn't offer a method of modifying the global query block list or creating directory partitions.

Throughout the chapter, you have seen the DNS management console used to create zones and edit the properties of servers and zones, which are the run-of-the-mill types of tasks you do with it. You can also take advantage of some diagnostic configurations within the console. These are configured in the properties of the DNS server.

Event Logging   A separate Event Viewer log is created for the DNS service. It is attached to the DNS management console. In addition, the server collects all events by default, which is set on the Event Logging tab.

Debug Logging   More detailed logging of the actual communication occurring on the DNS server can be gathered for inspection. Debug logging is disabled by default but can be enabled from the properties of the DNS server; Figure 6.31 displays the Debug Logging tab. This feature is valuable if the DNS server is not acting reliably. Although most DNS issues are resolved with proper IP connectivity, you will find this tool useful when IP connectivity is determined not to be the cause. On rare occasions, we have had to verify whether specific requests were hitting the server, and this tool provided the information.

Monitoring   This tab can also be accessed from inside the DNS server properties and is displayed in Figure 6.32. It's the equivalent to the million-dollar machine that goes "ping!" It's like a blinking light. It can test DNS queries from this server or to another server—not a specific server, mind you, just any indiscriminant server out there. Then you can perform the test at intervals.

The output is just pass or fail. Basically, if the DNS server is having problems, it's a fail. We haven't found any comfort or valuable data in resolving DNS issues on this tab, and most likely it won't tell you anything new. We'd recommend using something like Microsoft's System Center 2012 R2 Operations Manager for monitoring your DNS servers, and this topic is discussed later in Chapter 30.

FIGURE 6.31
Debug Logging
tab

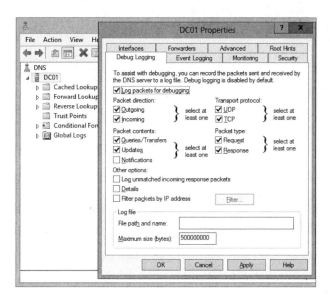

FIGURE 6.32
Monitoring tab

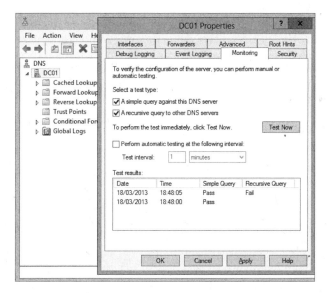

PowerShell offers a number of diagnostic cmdlets as well. These may be useful in collecting and examining data:

◆ `Get-DNSServer` provides configurations of the DNS server.

◆ `Get- Get-DnsServer | Export-Clixml –Path "c:\config\DnsServerConfig.xml"` generates a text file of the configurations and zone properties.

◆ `Get-DNSServerDiagnostics` provides event-logging details of specific DNS operations on the server.

◆ `Clear-DNSServerCache` empties the cache. Occasionally, stale resolved records need to be removed after a problem has been resolved. This is also available in the DNS management console.

Each of these tools provides administration and monitoring features. We find they are useful for the deeper investigation where the frontline tools such as `NsLookup`, `DcDiag`, and `DNSLint` do not immediately indicate the problem.

Leveraging NsLookup and DcDiag

`NsLookup`, `DcDiag`, and `DNSLint` are the tools that you will most likely use the most when troubleshooting DNS issues. `NsLookup` provides immediate indications of something that could be wrong or misconfigured with name resolution. `DcDiag` and `DNSLint` provide initial indications concerning Active Directory–related issues, such as DDNS registration and SRV records. If these tools do not reveal the problem, you can rely on the features of the DNS management console and PowerShell to help you out.

NsLookup

`NsLookup` is the first tool we go to when troubleshooting name-resolution problems. It connects to the listed primary DNS server in the IP configurations and makes requests for DNS queries.

Notice that the utility doesn't perform the name-resolution process, in other words, the circle of life. It narrows down to one portion of the circle. In our discussion on clients, the examples of the `ping` and `net view` commands were provided to show the different parts of the process. The `ping` example showed the DNS process that included the first step of looking the name up in the HOSTS file. So, you will see a disconnect between `ping` and `NsLookup` if the HOSTS file has records for the same hostname in it.

CONFICKER VIRUS

One example of malicious software that uses DNS to cause disruption is the Conficker virus. This "lovely" bit of code originated in 2008 and can (believe it or not) still be found today lingering on computers that haven't been patched with the latest virus definitions and system updates. It prevents browsers on infected systems from hitting important sites within specific DNS namespaces like Microsoft.com, Symantec.com, and Norton.com.

This has a crippling effect. The computer can't go to the Windows update site; it can't even look up possible solutions for the problem. Even if you installed Norton AntiVirus onto the machine, it couldn't access the Symantec update site for the latest definition updates. The machine couldn't fix itself!

When we came across Conficker, `NsLookup` was our first tool of choice to troubleshoot it. The queries to Microsoft.com and Symantec.com were positive, but it wouldn't fly in Internet Explorer or Firefox instances on that computer. This difference helped narrow down where the issue lied. Therefore, the browsers were infected.

Of course, NsLookup provides the IP addresses for the sites we need to hit. But—"Oh, no!"—the Microsoft websites don't play using just the IP address in the URL. So, trying that workaround doesn't work either.

We found the solution using the Microsoft Windows Malicious Software Removal Tool (MSRT). It had to be downloaded on a separate computer, and then using Sneakernet, we transferred the MSRT package to the infected computer. It identified and removed the virus. These days, thankfully, the Conficker virus is restricted to older operating systems with out-of-date or missing antivirus and Windows Update definitions. It's a good example, though, of how name-resolution modifications can be used to create havoc and then how tools, such as NsLookup, can be used to troubleshoot and identify its presence.

When an application cannot access a server, after checking TCP/IP connectivity, we start to poke around with the NsLookup command. Here are some things we look for:

◆ Is the DNS server responding? The command will tell you right at the start if it can connect to the DNS server. If there is a delay or time-out, there's no need to continue. You have a connectivity issue.

◆ Is the default server unknown? This indicates that the reverse lookup performed by NsLookup failed. When it is in this state, we find that the rest of NsLookup tests get squirrely.

◆ Can you resolve a local FQDN? This bypasses a portion of the client's processing. The client will append primary DNS suffixes to search for hostnames.

◆ Can you resolve a hostname without the DNS suffix? This is what the client does so you can walk through the step.

◆ Can you resolve external FQDNs? This will validate that the default DNS server can get out to the Internet.

NsLookup has two methods: single-command queries and interactive mode. The interactive mode is much more powerful, so we opt to use that at the start. This mode offers the ability to perform queries on different types of resource records and allows you to switch to another server. The following are examples of queries we commonly perform (with remarks added for clarity):

```
C:\Users\Administrator.BF1>Nslookup
Default Server:  BF1.bigfirm.com
Address:  192.168.0.10

rem a host record query
> BF1.bigfirm.com
Server:  BF1.bigfirm.com
Address:  192.168.0.10

Name:    BF1.bigfirm.com
```

```
Address:  192.168.0.10

rem a reverse "ptr" record query
> set q=ptr
> 192.168.0.10
Server:  BF1.bigfirm.com
Address:  192.168.0.10

10.1.168.192.in-addr.arpa     name = BF1.bigfirm.com

rem a start of authority query
> set q=soa
> bigfirm.com
Server:  BF1.bigfirm.com
Address:  192.168.0.10

bigfirm.com
        primary name server = BF1.bigfirm.com
        responsible mail addr = hostmaster.bigfirm.com
        serial  = 124
        refresh = 900 (15 mins)
        retry   = 600 (10 mins)
        expire  = 86400 (1 day)
        default TTL = 3600 (1 hour)
BF1.bigfirm.com     internet address = 192.168.0.10

rem a name server query
> set q=ns
> bigfirm.com
Server:  BF1.bigfirm.com
Address:  192.168.0.10

bigfirm.com     nameserver = BF1.bigfirm.com
BF1.bigfirm.com     internet address = 192.168.0.10

rem a resource record query
> set q=srv
> _ldap._tcp.bigfirm.com
Server:  BF1.bigfirm.com
Address:  192.168.0.10

_ldap._tcp.bigfirm.com  SRV service location:
        priority    = 0
        weight      = 100
        port        = 389
        svr hostname = BF1.bigfirm.com
BF1.bigfirm.com     internet address = 192.168.0.10
```

DcDiag

DcDiag was originally part of the administrator support tools (which needed to be installed separately) from earlier versions of Windows Server but is now included by default as part of the Windows Server 2012 R2 installation. It's our first-choice tool to perform a quick health check on the DNS structure. Since it runs through a score of domain controller diagnostics, it must validate that DNS is working as needed. After running the standard battery of tests, you may see errors in attempting to connect to domain controllers. Then you could run additional DcDiag tests specifically for DNS. The following example tests whether a domain controller can perform DDNS to register the SRV records:

```
dcdiag /test:RegisterInDNS /DnsDomain:bigfirm.com /f:documents\
dcdiagRegisterInDNS.txt
```

This produced the following text output:

```
Starting test: RegisterInDNS

      DNS configuration is sufficient to allow this domain controller to

      dynamically register the domain controller Locator records in DNS.

      The DNS configuration is sufficient to allow this computer to dynamically

      register the A record corresponding to its DNS name.

      ...................... BF1 passed test RegisterInDNS
```

DcDiag performs a boatload of domain controller–related tests, including several DNS tests. We mentioned one, the RegisterInDNS test. These tests primarily focus on the integration between the DNS servers within an Active Directory environment. Tests can be performed on delegation, forwarders, dynamic update, and external DNS name resolution.

The following is a portion of the help information for the DcDiag utility. It lists the tests available for DNS. We normally rely on NsLookup to test external name resolution, so we never use the /DnsForwarders and /DnsResolveExtName tests but have listed them here for transparency:

```
DNS
This test checks the health of DNS settings for the whole enterprise. Sub tests
can be run individually using the switches below. By default, all tests except
external name resolution are run

   /DnsBasic             (basic tests, can't be skipped)
   /DnsForwarders        (forwarders and root hints tests)
   /DnsDelegation        (delegations tests)
   /DnsDynamicUpdate     (dynamic update tests)
   /DnsRecordRegistration  (records registration tests)
   /DnsResolveExtName     (external name resolution test)
   /DnsAll               (includes all tests above)
   /DnsInternetName:      <internet name> (for test /DnsResolveExtName)
(default is www.microsoft.com)
```

As discussed earlier with SRV records, the number of SRV records registered by a domain controller is so great that it is difficult to eyeball whether it's working correctly. In addition to the /registerinDNS test, /DnsDynamicUpdate and /DnsRecordRegistration run through checks concerning SRV registration by the domain controllers. Unlike /registerinDNS, these do not have to be run locally on the domain controller. The following command will verify the SRV records for a domain controller. The /v option is for "verbose." The output is lengthy because it lists all of the SRV records for the domain controller:

```
C:\Users\Administrator.BF1>dcdiag /s:BF1.bigfirm.com /test:dns /
dnsrecordregistration /v
```

The following will validate that DDNS update is operational on a zone. It will register a host and delete it from the DNS zone of the server. In this case, that is Ecoast.Bigfirm.com:

```
C:\Users\Administrator.BF1>dcdiag /s:ec1.Ecoast.Bigfirm.com /test:dns /
dnsdynamicupdate /v
```

DIG Deeper than NsLookup

There's a DNS troubleshooting tool that's been around in the Unix world for quite some time called the Domain Information Groper, or DIG for short. If you ask users of DIG for their opinion on how the NsLookup utility stacks up against DIG as a DNS troubleshooting tool, don't be surprised if they start laughing before politely telling you it doesn't stack up at all!

The good news, though, is that you can download DIG for free (http://www.isc.org/software/bind) and install it into your Windows Server 2012 R2 environment to help turbocharge your DNS troubleshooting skills. DIG can be run in typical command-line format but also has a batch mode option that supports the reading of lookup requests from a file.

If you want to learn how to install DIG onto a Windows Server, have a look at the walk-through here: http://tinyurl.com/DIGinstall. You can also review an online usage guide for DIG from this link http://tinyurl.com/DIGusage.

Helpful DNS Troubleshooting Links

The tools we have discussed up to now have all been based on what's available out of the box with Windows Server 2012 R2. Those tools are where you should start your troubleshooting from inside the network. In this section, we want to share some DNS-related websites that you can use to assist with external DNS problems.

www.IntoDNS.com This is such a simple but effective website to add to your DNS troubleshooting armory. When you reach the home page, all you need to do is to enter the DNS name of the domain that you want to get information on and then click the Report button. This will then return all of the available information for the A (parent), NS, SOA, MX, and WWW records for that domain. With this information, you can quickly identify whether any of those records have been configured incorrectly, or you can just use it as a cross-check for the information that you have been given.

www.MXToolbox.com   This site does pretty much what it says on the tin. It's designed to assist with MX record troubleshooting and can prove instrumental in trying to ascertain why mail flow for a particular email domain isn't working. You can run a number of different tests against any given domain, such as MX lookup, Blacklist check, Whois lookup, and SMTP verification. If you haven't used this site before, now's the time to add it to your favorites!

www.DNSStuff.com   This is another popular site that you can use to run DNS reports, Whois, and IP information tests. You can also get access to a large number of additional DNS troubleshooting tools here if you're prepared to sign up for an account with them, but investigate the benefits for yourself with a trial run before purchasing.

The Bottom Line

Explain the fundamental components and processes of DNS.   DNS relies on integrated servers that manage a hierarchical naming structure. On the Internet, this structure starts with root servers and then top-level domain servers, which delegate subdomains to other DNS servers. Within a DNS server, the database of records is known as a *zone*, and it can be replicated between other DNS servers to provide distributed query resolution for a given namespace.

> **Master It**   Several common DNS records were discussed in this chapter. The SRV and MX records both have a parameter named priority. If there were two SRV records for the same service with a priority parameter of 10 and 20, which SRV record would be selected first?

Configure DNS to support an Active Directory environment.   Active Directory requires a DNS namespace to be available to support the assigned name of the domain. Windows Server 2012 R2 provides an automatic capability to create the required DNS structure through the domain controller promotion process. The DNS zones can be stored in the Active Directory database, which provides multimaster replication of the DNS records. With the use of SRV records and DDNS update, the domain controllers can register their services in DNS for clients to access them.

> **Master It**   The DNS service on DCs can create Active Directory integrated zones. In which locations within the Active Directory database can the zones be placed? What scope do these locations provide?

Manage and troubleshoot DNS resolution for both internal and external names.   Internal and external name resolution relies on the connectivity between DNS servers. Forwarding and root hints are the primary methods to allow DNS servers to send queries between them. Several tools are available to assist troubleshooting and monitoring DNS configurations and performance, including NsLookup, PowerShell, and DcDiag.

> **Master It**   The SRV record registration for domain controllers is performed by the netlogon service. It is a very complex and demanding task to attempt to perform this manually. What tests can be performed to verify whether SRV records are correctly registered within a domain?

Chapter 7

Active Directory in Windows Server 2012

Active Directory, what a great concept. The word *Active* implies a kind of dynamic behavior, and the word *Directory* implies some sort of storing and searching tasks of a component. The phrase also describes what Active Directory is all about: a central place where you store and manage all your users and computers and the behavior of your Windows infrastructure. Active Directory has been around since Windows Server 2000 and has been extended through Windows Server 2003, Windows Server 2003 R2, Windows Server 2008, and Windows Server 2008 R2. In today's businesses, Active Directory plays a major role as a centralized identity and access solution.

Although Active Directory has been a very robust solution for some time, Microsoft has tuned and added some more features to make Windows Server 2012 Active Directory a more reliable, scalable, secure, and easier-to-manage solution.

However, just because Active Directory is very easy to set up and install, it does not mean you just can run DCPROMO and click Next, Next, and Finish. This will not work anymore, and there are considerations you need to make before, while, and after installing Active Directory. Otherwise, sooner or later you will end up with a misconfigured and malfunctioning system. In this chapter I would like to shed some light not only on the different aspects of installing and configuring Active Directory but also on managing and maintaining your Active Directory systems.

What probably interests most of you is what's new in Active Directory 2012; in the following chapters you will learn how to install, configure, and maintain Active Directory 2012.

In this chapter, you will learn to:

- ◆ Create a single-domain forest
- ◆ Add a second DC to the domain
- ◆ Decide whether to add a global catalog
- ◆ Create accounts
- ◆ Create fine-grained password policies
- ◆ Understand the Windows Server 2012 forest functional level
- ◆ Upgrade your domain to Windows Server 2012

In this chapter we are going to refer to Windows Server 2012 and Windows Server 2012 R2 just as Windows Server 2012. If there are any features available only in Windows Server 2012 R2, we will point them out specifically.

An Introduction and Active Directory Basics

A good way to get started is to define the terms and definitions. Because Active Directory uses many specific words, we are going to explain the vocabulary that administrators need to know.

Workgroup   A *workgroup* is basically one or more computers on a Windows network (LAN) that are *not* joined to a domain. Every computer resides on itself, so there is no dependency among them. For example, computer 1 has a local user named Joe and computer 2 also has a user named Joe. These users have the same name and are the same person but are completely different users. Therefore, if you want to manage these users' passwords, for example, you'll need to connect to or log onto each computer console and change the password. There is no way to centrally manage these users.

Domain   A *domain* is a collection of objects that share the same database. That means that in our workgroup example you would create one Joe in the central Active Directory database and connect workgroup computers 1 and 2 to this database domain. Why you use a domain? If all objects are managed centrally, you don't need to connect to or walk to each computer to change the user's password. There is much more to a domain, but to get the basic understanding, this example illustrates it pretty well.

Active Directory Domain Services   *Active Directory Domain Services (AD DS)* is a service that is integrated into the Windows Server operating system but is not automatically installed by default. If you are going to promote a Windows server to a domain controller, either to an existing domain or to a completely new domain, you must create the AD DS, the Active Directory database on the server, and many other components that are needed for Active Directory to function properly. Because Active Directory is running as a Windows service in the background, you can stop and start Active Directory. This is a huge improvement because you don't need to boot into recovery mode for Active Directory authoritative restores or database maintenance tasks; instead, you just stop the AD DS service and perform your operation.

Every domain controller has its own copy of the Active Directory database that is dynamically updated by other domain controllers. Because all of the Active Directory joined or integrated systems depend on Active Directory, it is essential to have at least two domain controllers for redundancy purposes. Otherwise, if one domain controller fails and it was the only one, your whole environment grinds to a halt.

Site   Sites represent the physical structure or topology of your network. By definition, a *site* is a collection of well-connected subnets.

In many cases branch offices are created as a site. We assume that the systems are well connected within the branch office network but have a small network connection to their headquarters. In this case you would probably create a site for the branch office. There is much more to say about sites, but for now we will leave it this way.

Replication   *Replication* is probably the most complicated topic pertaining to Active Directory. Active Directory is designed as a multimaster replication system. This means you can perform a change, for example, creating user Joe on domain controller A or domain controller

B, and this change is replicated to the domain controller where you didn't create the user. Of course, you can create, modify, and delete objects, and every change will replicate to each domain controller in the same site within 15 seconds (intersite) and to domain controllers in different sites in as little as 15 minutes (180 minutes by default). Active Directory calculates its best replication path according to an advanced algorithm so that every domain controller receives the latest updates.

Objects In short, everything within Active Directory is an *object*. As an example, user Joe is an object. If you change his first name, you will change a property of Joe that is saved in an attribute called First Name. Also, if you create a computer account, then the groups, organizational units, sites, IP subnets, and so on are objects with properties.

Schema The *schema* holds the classes for the objects you create. You can imagine the schema as a bunch of templates that you will use if you create user Joe. Active Directory needs to know what the user will look like, for example which properties it has, such as first name and last name. This is provided by the schema. If you plan to install other software like Lync or Exchange, the schema will need to be extended. Why? If you look at the user object before and after a schema extension, you will see that there are more options (properties) available on the user object, such as SIP address, after the extension. SIP stands for Session Initiation Protocol, and a SIP address is an address that is used for video and voice communication calls over Internet Protocol (IP).

Group Policy As previously explained, *group policies* are needed to configure settings for users and computers. They are very handy because you can configure one or more settings in one group policy and apply these settings to one or more users or computers by linking the GPO to the respective OU.

As an example, let's say you would like to enable the remote desktop on each server so you can connect using your RDP client. It would be a lot of work to set this on every computer by hand. You would enable the remote desktop setting in the group policy and link it to the OU where your server resides, and all the computers within this OU will be enabled for remote desktop.

You can link GPOs to sites, domains, and OUs. When you promote your server to a domain controller, two policies are in place by default. Every domain has a Default Domain Policy and a Default Domain Controllers Policy.

Organizational Units *Organizational units*, as the name implies, are used to organize objects in Active Directory, mainly users and computer objects. An OU is just a kind of a container that contains similar objects. There are two main reasons for organizing things in Active Directory. The first reason is to link Group Policy objects (GPO) and the second is that you need an OU for delegation of control.

Let's say you create an organizational unit name USERS and put Joe into this OU. Now you want Joe to always receive its network drives mapped. Therefore you need to create a GPO and link this policy to the USERS OU. Now Joe will receive the settings from the GPO and all his network drives.

The icon for an OU looks like a folder from Windows Explorer, and because of a similar usage, administrators often get confused and use the OUs like Windows folders to group things together to find them more easily. This is not the main purpose of OUs. Sure, you can use them to group and organize objects to find the objects more easily in Active Directory, but your main intention as an Active Directory administrator should be to use as many OU as necessary to apply delegation of control and to control the object in the OU through GPOs.

Default Domain Policy The *Default Domain Policy* is created as soon you create your first domain. This policy contains settings for users and computers that will apply to the entire domain. It is important to understand that this policy is essential for you environment and should not be deleted. You can modify this policy, but we don't recommend it. If you need to apply custom settings to the domain, you should create a new policy on the domain level and store your custom settings in your newly created policy.

Default Domain Controllers Policy The *Default Domain Controllers Policy* is also a very important policy that is linked to the Domain Controllers container in your Active Directory. The settings configured in the Default Domain Controllers Policy are specific configurations that apply only to the domain controllers. If you promote a member server to a domain controller, this server is automatically placed into the Domain Controllers container. There are very few cases where you need to touch this policy.

Forest A *forest* is a single instance of Active Directory. Within a forest you can have one or multiple domains that share the same schema. If you set up a single domain controller, you are basically creating the smallest forest possible. It is also called a single-domain forest. A forest is also referred as a security boundary in which users, computers, and other objects are accessible.

Global Catalog A *global catalog* contains information about each object in every domain in a multidomain Active Directory forest. The global catalog is stored on domain controllers that have been enabled as global catalog servers, and its data is distributed through Active Directory replication. There is only one global catalog within a forest but multiple copies of it. Applications like Exchange or clients query the global catalog to get information about objects within the forest. A global catalog in the domain contains full information about the objects in the domain, but it contains only partial information about objects within the forest. A global catalog provides other services as well, such as providing references to other objects in different domains, resolving user principal names (UPN), and universal group membership caching.

Trust A *trust* is a connection between domains to access their resources, such as servers or applications. For example, this could be used if some users need to access file shares or intranet information in the opposite domain. If you install a domain and child domains, Active Directory automatically creates a transitive trust. This way you can access objects from the root domain in the child domains, and vice versa. If you need access to resources in another forest, you could create some form of trust to connect both forests.

Tree If you build one or more domains within the same forest that have contiguous namespace and/or share the same schema, you create a *tree*. A contiguous namespace is a domain that shares the same root domain name. For example, the root domain is bigfirm.com and a possible contiguous namespace is marketing.bigfirm.com. An Active Directory tree is a collection of domains that are built in a transitive trust hierarchy.

Creating a Single-domain Forest

As you learned, a single-domain forest is the simplest Active Directory topology you can build. The general recommendation is to create an Active Directory domain if you have 10 or more users. You could also create a domain if you have fewer users because there is no limit in place; it's just a matter of complexity and cost. The advantages are obvious:

◆ Manage users and permissions in a central place

◆ Centrally secure and manage each system using GPOs

◆ Provide additional Active Directory dependent services

You might wonder if you should stick with one domain or why you might want to add more than one domain to your infrastructure. Whenever possible, you should create just a single-domain forest because it is easier to set up and manage. There are a few situations where you might consider more than one domain. Since Windows Server 2012 Active Directory did not change in terms of design and is as it was in Windows Server 2008 R2, the following rules are still valid. You should use multiple domains in the following situations:

◆ You have very slow WAN links and trouble with replication performance. This is more important if you have also very high number of attribute or object changes in your Active Directory.

◆ You have a legacy domain in place and it needs to persist.

◆ Your domain is very dynamic and the objects change frequently. In this case the replication traffic could be excessive at a threshold of 100,000 objects. To separate replication traffic in general, one option is to divide the domain.

It is important to understand that the reasons for creating multiple domains are not that one domain is reaching its technical limits; the problem lies in the replication, which could lead to several problems in your infrastructure. We previously discussed that a single domain is the smallest forest you can create. Just as you can install multiple domains in one forest, you can also create multiple forests. Here are some reasons for creating multiple forests:

◆ You need to separate the so-called administrative autonomy. Perhaps some departments in your company do not trust each other. Or perhaps there are security reasons, like completely isolating your HR department's IT infrastructure. Or perhaps there is no agreement on schema changes.

◆ You need to separate applications and services from the other infrastructure. You might want to install Hyper-V clusters in a separate forest (fabric) and install your managing tools, such as System Center products, in another forest.

Keep in mind that the more Active Directory forests you build, the degree of complexity and the management effort increase rapidly to a level you might not expect.

Benefits of a Single domain

The benefits of a single domain are obvious:

Cost   If you build one domain, it is recommended that you install at least two domain controllers for redundancy. Of course, if you install additional domain controllers for new domains or forests, the costs for licenses, hardware, software, and managing and maintaining additional servers always increase. Although you can virtualize any domain controller, you still have costs for storage and managing these servers.

Management   Every domain you add will have additional objects you need to control and take care of. In addition, there are many challenges in setting cross-domain or even cross-forest permissions and using group nesting to share resources or keep all domains and forests up and running.

Disaster Recovery   Active Directory is a very complex beast in terms of domain or even forest recovery. It is always easier to recover one domain rather than two or more domains.

Windows Server 2008 introduced fine-grained password policies. This solved a long-term problem that forced you also to create a separate domain. Fine-grained password policies allow you create multiple password policies. In earlier versions of Active Directory there could be only one password policy. In Windows Server 2012 fine-grained password policies are the same they were as in Windows Server 2008, but it offers a user-friendly interface to easily manage and control them.

Creating a Single-domain Forest

You might have realized that there were no changes in the Active Directory basics. Since we have now covered most of the terms and definitions, we are now going to build a single-domain forest. But before we start to build a new domain, there are several points to be aware of and clarify:

- Windows Server 2012 version
- Server configuration
- Deployment configuration
- Operating system compatibility
- Domain name
- Forest functional level
- Domain functional level
- DNS
- File locations
- DSRM administrator password

In the next few pages we will discuss each of these considerations.

WHICH WINDOWS SERVER 2012 VERSION

Microsoft simplified the version jungle and offers two Windows Server 2012 versions you can consider for setting up domain controllers: Windows Server 2012 Standard or Datacenter edition. There is no difference in functionality, availability, or features. The difference is in terms of licensing and the number of virtual machines you can run on top of each edition. At the beginning of this book, we explained the differences between the two versions. If you need to install a domain controller, you can always choose Windows Server 2012 Standard edition, and if your license agreement allows, you can install Windows Server 2012 Datacenter edition. Another thing you need to be aware of is that Windows Server 2012 is available only in 64-bit versions; there is no 32-bit version. This comes into play when you are thinking about upgrading your domain controllers. You cannot perform an in-place upgrade from a 32-bit system to a 64-bit system.

SERVER CONFIGURATION

Once you've installed Windows Server 2012 Standard edition, you need to configure the server name and IP address. Just to clarify, we are using Windows Server 2012 Standard edition because the functionality is identical to the Windows Server 2012 Datacenter edition. The only difference is the licensing.

Server Name

Before promoting a domain controller you need to assign the final computer name. What are good server names? I could write almost a separate book about naming servers, but there are few main things you should consider:

◆ Don't use any company, department, country, or other names that could change over time in your server names.

◆ Keep the names short; your administrator will thank you.

◆ Use acronyms to identify your server roles.

A common naming scheme for domain controllers is DC01, DC02, and so on. You can rename a domain controller using the GUI or `Netdom` tool.

IP Addressing

Because clients and servers locate the domain controller using DNS and your domain controller has mainly the DNS role installed, you must always assign a static IP address. Otherwise, your domain controller becomes a moving target for other systems if they are trying to locate it. If you are configuring an IPv4 address only, it is best practice to leave IPv6 enabled.

Now you might think you're ready to run `DCPromo`. Good idea, but what you will experience is a friendly message box letting you know that this does not work anymore.

Installing a Domain Controller Server Role

If you need to install the domain controller server role, you need to start Server Manager, choose Manage, and then select Add Roles and Features (see Figure 7.1).

FIGURE 7.1
Adding the Active Directory role to your server

A wizard will start and let you choose which role or feature to install. In Windows Server 2008 R2, there were two separate wizards to install a role or a feature. The Add Roles and Features Wizard will install all binaries needed to run the Active Directory Domain Services Configuration Wizard (ADDSCW) afterward.

When the wizard has finished, you will need go back to Server Manager and click the yellow exclamation mark (see Figure 7.2).

FIGURE 7.2
Starting the
installation
wizard

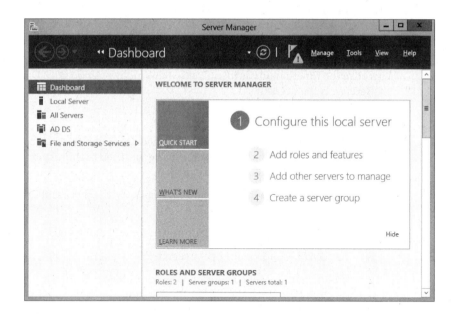

This will give you the opportunity to promote the server to a domain controller (see Figure 7.3). The next steps are very similar to the DCPromo utility you were used to in Windows Server 2008 R2.

FIGURE 7.3
Promoting the server

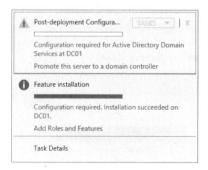

The wizard will give you several options; you need to either select or type in the appropriate information. Depending on the options you select, the wizard changes the dialog accordingly.

DEPLOYMENT CONFIGURATION

The deployment configuration option allows you to identify whether you're creating a new domain in a new forest or adding it to an existing forest. If you're adding it to an existing forest, you can add another domain controller to an existing domain (which is covered later in this chapter) or create a new domain.

For the first DC, your choice is simple. You'll be creating a new domain in a new forest.

AUTHENTICATION PITFALL

Domain controllers running Windows 2008 and later including Windows Server 2012 have the "Allow cryptography algorithms compatible with Windows NT 4" setting disabled by default. The legacy cryptographic algorithms used in Windows NT 4.0 can be cracked with today's technologies.

Therefore, Microsoft made their domain controller more secure by using a Group Policy setting to prevent logons from hardware and clients that use weak Windows NT 4.0 cryptographic algorithms. This could be a SAMBA Server Message Block (SMB) client that cannot establish a secure channel to a Windows Server 2008 or higher-based domain controller or an SMB storage device that cannot create a secure channel to the domain controller. The work-around is to enable this setting in the Default Domain Controller Policy. You can find more details on this page:

    http://support.microsoft.com/kb/942564/

OPERATING SYSTEM COMPATIBILITY

In Windows Server 2012 Microsoft introduces the Resilient File System (ReFS). This file system is, as its name says, more resilient than NTFS. It provides higher integrity and scalability, and it also has proactive error identification built in. You may be tempted to choose this file system for all your upcoming server projects because of its qualities, but sadly there are limitations you need to be aware of:

- ReFS is only available in Windows Server 2012.

- ReFS is only used for data volumes. There is no way to use ReFS as an operating system volume or boot volume.

As an Active Directory administrator, you need to know these best practices:

- Use only NTFS to store your SYSVOL, Active Directory database, and the Active Directory log files.

- Do not install SYSVOL on an ReFS-formatted volume or disk.

- Do not install the Active Directory database on an ReFS-formatted volume or disk.

If you try to select an ReFS formatted disk for the SYSVOL, the Active Directory database, or a log file, you will receive an error saying that you need to select an NTFS-formatted drive.

DOMAIN NAME

Because this is the first domain controller, you will choose to add a new forest. Thus, you will also need to install DNS and the global catalog. Both DNS and GC are required for the first domain controller in your new forest. It is not possible to install a read-only domain controller (RODC) as the first domain controller; you cannot select this option.

NAMING YOUR ROOT DOMAIN

Giving a name to a new root domain is probably the most difficult part. If you're setting up a lab domain controller, you needn't care about the name. But the situation is different if you have to build a domain or forest in a productive environment. Because the NetBIOS name of the domain will appear somewhere on the client side, management may not like seeing that name on their desktop when they log in. We highly recommend discussing and getting a commitment from the responsible manager when choosing the domain name.

What should a domain name look like? As you know, a valid Active Directory root domain name looks like a fully qualified domain name (FQDN). There are two parts: the actual name and a suffix, such as bigfirm.com, mydomain.local, or forest.com. These are all valid domain names. In Windows Server 2003 you could choose a single-label domain name like bigfirm, mydomain, or forest, and it would be supported by Microsoft. But as applications, such as Exchange evolved and depended on Active Directory and DNS, you were no longer allowed to create single-label domains. If you try to create a single-label domain in Windows Server 2012, you will get an error.

For the second part of a top-level domain you could use a suffix such as .com, .gov, .ch, or .net, or perhaps you might prefer some other suffix, such as .local or .domain.

The advantages of having the same name for Active Directory and the public DNS name, such as bigfirm.com, are these:

◆ The company web applications URL is the same whether it is internal or external.

◆ You can use public certificates internally

◆ The Lync SIP address is the same as the email and login address.

◆ The logon could be used as the email address.

One big disadvantage is that it isn't easy to distinguish from a firewall perspective between internal and external zones. Many administrators specifically try to avoid using Internet top-level domain names to avoid confusion with their internal networks.

As you can see, there are advantages and disadvantages to each of these options. We cannot recommend one naming convention in general. In the end the name has to fit your technical requirements and also meet your company's security policy.

Active Directory and DNS

It is essential to know that Active Directory heavily depends on DNS. No DNS, no Active Directory. Why? Active Directory registers all kinds of service (SRV) records in DNS to locate specific services that are needed for Active Directory to function correctly. I guess that 80 percent of problems of a nonfunctioning Active Directory are related to DNS.

When you installed your domain controller, a warning appeared that a delegation for the DNS could not be created. This is because the Active Directory wizard configures DNS for you; it also tries to create a delegation for the DNS server, but there is no DNS installed. Confirm the dialog and continue.

Domain Functional Levels

During the Active Directory setup wizard you are prompted to select the domain functional level. The domain functional level depends on the operating system you are using for your domain controller. You cannot select a higher domain functional level than the one your oldest version of the operating system has.

The following domain functional levels are available in Windows Server 2012.

◆ Windows Server 2003

◆ Windows Server 2008

◆ Windows Server 2008 R2

◆ Windows Server 2012

The minimum level required to join a Windows Server 2012 domain controller to another domain is forest functional level 2003. That means no operating system older than Windows Server 2003 is valid. There is no way to install a domain controller into a forest with forest functional level 2000.

If you install a domain controller, you can choose any domain functional level including up to Windows Server 2012. Be aware that if you choose domain functional level Windows Server 2012, you will not be able to add domain controllers other than Windows Server 2012 domain controllers. Therefore, if you are joining a Windows Server 2012 domain controller to a Windows Server 2008 R2 domain functional level, you cannot raise the functional level to Windows Server 2012 if you have a Windows Server 2008 R2 domain controller.

Here are two important things to remember:

◆ If you meet the requirements, you can always raise a functional level.

◆ You can almost never lower a functional level.

There is one exception. You can lower the forest and domain functional level from the Windows Server 2012 forest level to a Windows Server 2008 R2 domain and forest functional level. See the sidebar, "Functional Levels Can(not) Be Lowered," later in this chapter for more details.

This is like adding salt to soup. You can always add more salt, but if you put too much in, you can't take it back out. If you are unsure, it is better to first choose a lower functional level like Windows Server 2008.

FUNCTIONAL LEVEL APPLIES TO DCs, NOT MEMBER SERVERS

If the domain functional level is Windows Server 2012, the domain will support only those DCs running Windows Server 2012. Older member servers are fine, but not older DCs.

There is always confusion about these levels. Customers often ask questions like these:

◆ Can a domain running Windows Server 2012 domain functional level add a member server running Windows Server 2008? Yes!

◆ Can a domain running Windows Server 2012 domain functional level support a Windows Server 2008 R2 domain controller? No!

◆ Can I add Windows Server 2012 to a domain running Windows Server 2008 R2 domain functional level? Yes. You are adding just a member server, not a domain controller.

When you run the Active Directory Domain Services Configuration Wizard, you can select the domain functional level (see Figure 7.4).

FIGURE 7.4
Active Directory
Domain Services
Configuration
Wizard

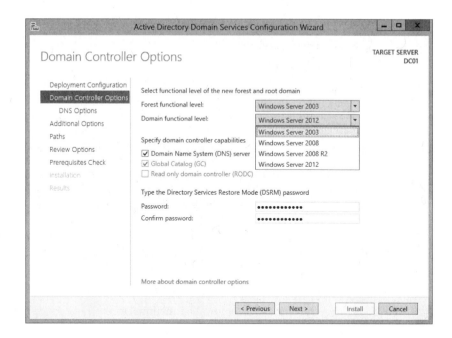

In earlier versions of Windows Server, the features available in your domain forest depended on your Active Directory functional levels.

Windows Server 2003 domain functional level

◆ You could rename domain controllers using Netdom.exe.

◆ The lastLogonTimestamp attribute was added.

◆ You had the ability to redirect Users and Computers containers.

◆ There was selective authentication to specify who has access to which resource in a trusted forest.

◆ You had constraint delegation to secure delegate user credentials using Kerberos.

Windows Server 2008 domain functional level

◆ It offers DFS-R support for the SYSVOL directory.

◆ You have AES 128 and AES 256 support for Kerberos.

◆ It provides detailed last interactive logon information.

◆ It uses fine-grained password policies.

Windows Server 2008 R2 domain functional level

◆ Authentication mechanism assurance determines the logon method used by a user. This is stored in the Kerberos token.

◆ Automatic SPN management is available for Managed Service Accounts.

In Windows Server 2012 domain functional level

◆ KDC support is available for claims, compound authentication, and Kerberos armoring via two settings: "Always provide claims" and "Fail unarmored authentication requests."

For a detailed list of the features available in each functional level, see this URL:

```
http://technet.microsoft.com/en-us/library/understanding-active-directory-
functional-levels(WS.10).aspx
```

FOREST FUNCTIONAL LEVELS

The forest functional level identifies the capabilities within the forest. The domain functional level depends on the operating system of the domain controllers. The forest functional level depends on the domain functional level of the domain. You cannot raise a forest functional level higher than the lowest domain functional level in the forest.

You can also select the forest functional level during the Active Directory installation. The following forest functional levels are supported:

◆ Windows Server 2003

◆ Windows Server 2008

◆ Windows Server 2008 R2

◆ Windows Server 2012

As with the domain functional level, you can raise the forest functional level after the DC has been promoted. You first raise the domain functional level of each domain in the forest to the same functional level, and then you raise the forest functional level to the same level. Remember that all domain functional levels must be on the same level before you can raise the forest functional level (see Figure 7.5).

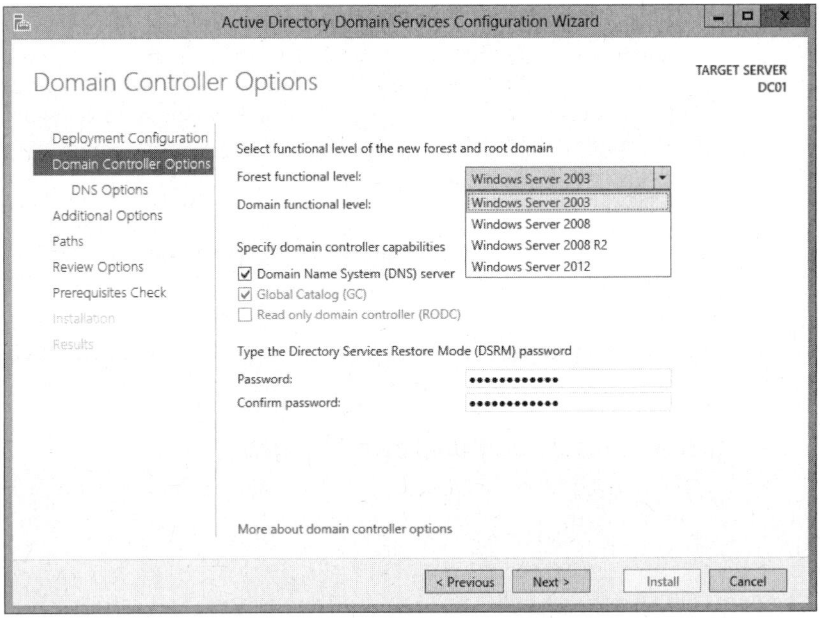

FIGURE 7.5
Selecting the forest functional level in the Active Directory wizard

Just as the different domain functional levels add features to your domain, the different forest functional levels also provide various features.

Windows Server 2003   Windows Server 2003 provides the following features:

- ◆ Ability to create forest trusts

- ◆ Ability to rename a domain

- ◆ Ability to deploy a read-only domain controller (RODC)

- ◆ Improved Knowledge Consistency Checker (KCC)

- ◆ Improved linked-value replication so that only the differences of group memberships are replicated

- ◆ Access-based enumeration in the DFS namespace

Windows Server 2008   The Windows Server 2008 forest functional level does not provide any additional features.

Windows Server 2008 R2   The Active Directory Recycle Bin lets you restore deleted objects without starting the domain controller in Active Directory Restore Mode. You need to enable the Active Directory Recycle Bin using PowerShell commands. Active Directory Recycle Bin is a great feature that was improved in Windows Server 2012. It is now much easier to set up and manage, as you will see later in this book.

Windows Server 2012   The Windows Server 2012 forest functional level offers no new features.

WHAT'S DIFFERENT IN WINDOWS SERVER 2012 R2 FUNCTIONAL LEVELS

As we are writing this book, we are testing with a preview version of Windows Server 2012 R2. Although little in Active Directory has changed, there are some changes in functional levels from its predecessor.

You can add a Windows Server 2012 R2 domain controller into an existing 2003 functional level environment. But be aware that the Windows Server 2003 domain and forest functional level is deprecated. When you deploy a Windows Server 2012 R2 into an existing Windows Server 2003 environment, you will be prompted to move to a higher functional level.

The lowest functional level that you can select in Windows Server 2012 R2 is the Windows Server 2008 domain and forest functional level.

You can find a full-featured overview of the new functional level on TechNet. Hopefully, Microsoft will have it updated by the time this book is published. Go to:

```
http://technet.microsoft.com/en-us/library/understanding-active-directory-
functional-levels.aspx
```

LOCATIONS FOR FILES AND SYSVOL

The Active Directory Domain Services Configuration Wizard prompts you for the location of various Active Directory files and the location of the SYSVOL shared folder.

The SYSVOL shared folder is used to share information, such as scripts and elements of Group Policy objects between domain controllers. SYSVOL and the Active Directory database and log files must be placed on an NTFS formatted drive. The database and log files can be located on different drives, but those also must be formatted as NTFS (see Figure 7.6).

FIGURE 7.6
File paths

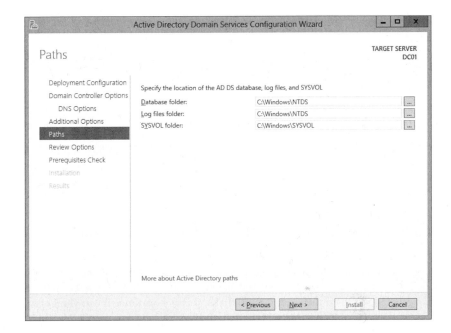

Windows Server 2012 introduces the new Resilient File System. ReFS offers higher integrity and scalability, and it has proactive error identification built in. You might think that it would be a perfect place for an Active Directory component, but as discussed earlier, this is not supported. Nor can you place the Active Directory database, Active Directory log file, or SYSVOL directory on ReFS.

At its core, Active Directory is a large database, and databases have a primary data file and a transaction log file. Changes to the database are first written to the transaction log file, and then periodically the transaction log file is check-pointed—that's just a fancy way of saying that changes in the transaction log are committed to the database.

The transaction log provides significant fault tolerance and recovery capabilities to the Active Directory database. If the server loses power in the middle of any change, Active Directory can use the log to ensure that the database is in a consistent state when the server is rebooted. Any changes recorded in the log are committed to the database, and any unfinished changes recorded in the log are ignored.

From a performance perspective, it is possible to increase the performance of your DC by moving the database and transaction log files to different drives. For optimal disk performance of Active Directory, you may use a configuration similar to this:

◆ C:\ drive: Operating system

◆ D:\ drive: Active Directory database file and SYSVOL

◆ E:\ drive: Transaction log file

In this configuration, each of the drives needs to be a separate spindle (a separate physical disk). A single drive with three partitions wouldn't provide any performance gain. Additionally, if your disk drives have different speeds, you should put the operating system on the fastest disk, the transaction log on the next fastest, and the Active Directory database file and SYSVOL on the slowest disk. The operating system and the transaction log file will receive the heaviest usage.

To optimize your domain controller just a bit more, you can distinguish between heavy read and heavy write operations. If you have heavy read operations, you should add sufficient memory to the domain controller so that it can cache the database in memory. For heavy write operations, you can improve performance by adding the following:

◆ Hardware RAID controllers

◆ High RPM disks

◆ Battery backend write-caching (BBWC) on the RAID controller

This sounds good and makes sense, but what will happen if you virtualize your domain controller? In this case it's a good idea to add sufficient memory for your domain controller so that it can cache the database. If you are going to place the transaction log, database, and SYSVOL on different virtual disks, the performance improvement will probably be minimal. The problem is that all the virtual disks are on the same LUN, and this LUN is spread over an array of disks. That means that all virtual disks share the same physical disks in the storage. From a theoretical standpoint, it would be best to place each file on a separate array or LUN. In any case, you should use the fastest storage you have.

For a good starting point to figure out if you have a disk performance problem, you can use these performance counters. Each of these counters should have a low value:

◆ Avg. Disk Queue Length

◆ Avg. Disk Read Queue Length

◆ Avg. Disk Write Queue Length

Let's look at an example. If your domain includes 100 users, you can store the database and log files on the C drive with the operating system and not notice any performance problems. On the other hand, if you are supporting 50,000 users, you may want to squeeze every ounce of performance out of the server, so you will locate the database and log files on different drives. If you are building a test system, there is nothing wrong with leaving everything on C.

MOVING THE DATABASE AND LOG FILES

Windows Server 2012 introduces restartable Active Directory Domain Services (AD DS), which you can use to perform database management tasks without restarting the domain controller in Directory Services Restore Mode (DSRM). If you need to relocate the log or database onto a different drive, you can use the command-line utility NTDSUtil. Because of the AD DS, you don't have to restart the domain controller in DSRM; you just need to stop the Windows AD DS service and perform your task.

DIRECTORY SERVICES RESTORE MODE PASSWORD

If you ever need to perform maintenance or restoration of Active Directory, you would use Directory Services Restore Mode. You can access DSRM by pressing F8 to access the Advanced Options menu. You can also access the different Safe Mode options from this menu.

After selecting Directory Services Restore Mode, you will be prompted to log on. However, Active Directory will not be running, so you can't use an Active Directory account. Instead, you will use a special administrator account with a different password. The Active Directory Domain Services Configuration Wizard prompts you to set the password for the DSRM account, as shown in Figure 7.7.

FIGURE 7.7
Setting the Directory Services Restore Mode password

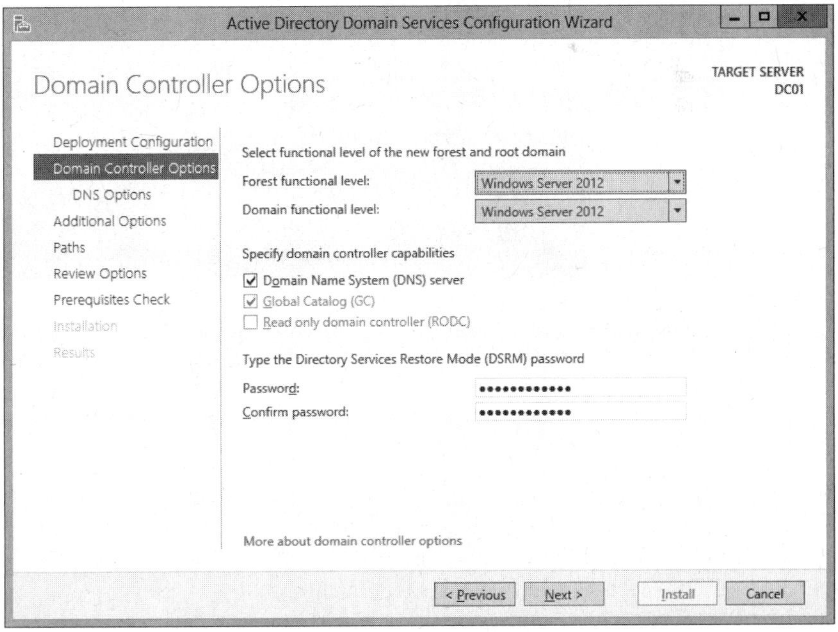

Make sure you document the password you set here. Many organizations document critical passwords by writing them down and storing them in a safe. You won't be able to access DSRM without this password. The DSRM administrator account password is sometimes confused with the regular administrator password you set for the Domain Admins account, but it is different. From a security standpoint, this DSRM password is critical in that you can locally log onto a domain controller and use it to gain access to the Active Directory database. If you realize that all passwords are stored in this database, you will think twice about where you store the DSRM password.

CHANGING THE DSRM PASSWORD

If you have 100 domain controllers, it is somewhat difficult to control each DSRM password, or you might need to change a DSRM password. You can do it the old way and change the password by running the DSMGMT or NTDSUtil command on a running domain controller. You don't need to enter DSRM mode to change the DSRM password. You can find more about this on TechNet:

http://technet.microsoft.com/en-us/library/cc753343.aspx.

One geeky way to keep your DSRM password known to you or to change it is to synchronize the password with a domain user account. How does this work? First, you need to create a domain user account, let's say DSRMAccount. This can be a regular domain user account. Next, start an elevated command prompt and type the following command:

```
NTDSUtil
Set dsrm password
SYNC FROM DOMAIN ACCOUNT DSRMAccount
Q
Q
```

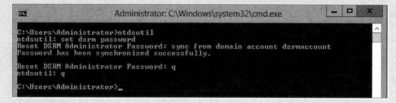

Now your DSRM account is synchronized with the DSRM Account in Active Directory. But this does not permanently synchronize the password; it just synchronizes it for the moment. Therefore, if you change the DSRM Account password, you'll need to execute the command again. What you could do is either apply a GPO to all domain controllers with a scheduled task to execute this command on a regular basis or write a PowerShell script to execute this command on all domain controllers. You would just need to call C:\Windows\System32\NTDSUtil.exe and submit the parameters as shown here:

"SET DSRM PASSWORD" "SYNC FROM DOMAIN ACCOUNT DSRMAccount" Q Q

There is a great post about this on TechNet:

http://blogs.technet.com/b/askds/archive/2009/03/11/ds-restore-mode-password-maintenance.aspx

RUNNING THE ACTIVE DIRECTORY DOMAIN SERVICES CONFIGURATION WIZARD

Now that you know what you will encounter, the next step is to add the Active Directory role and then run the Active Directory Domain Services Configuration Wizard. In Windows Server 2012 adding the Active Directory role basically adds all the necessary binaries and then you can configure Active Directory.

The following steps assume you have a clean installation of Windows Server 2012 without any additional roles installed. If you have installed additional roles, you may have some minor differences.

1. Log onto a Windows Server 2012 server using an account with local administrator privileges.

2. Start Server Manager and choose Manage ➢ Add Roles and Features.

3. Review the information on the "Before you begin" page.

4. Select "Role-based or feature-based installation."

5. Select your destination server for the server pool (see Figure 7.8).

FIGURE 7.8
Selecting the server

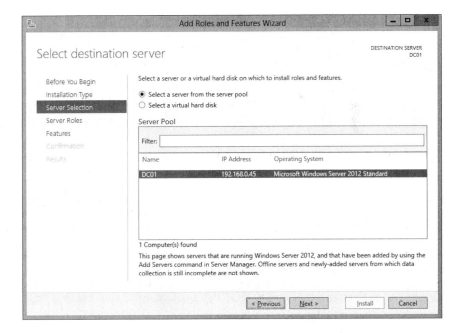

6. Select the Active Directory Domain Services role and add the recommended features, such as Remote Server Administration Tools.

7. On the Features dialog you don't need to select anything.

8. Review the Active Directory Domain Services dialog.

9. If you want to restart the server automatically, select the option "Restart the destination server automatically if required."

    After the binaries are installed, a yellow exclamation mark appears in Server Manager.

10. Click the yellow exclamation mark and click the "Promote this server to a domain controller" link.

    This will start the Active Directory Domain Services Configuration Wizard.

11. On the Active Directory Deployment Configuration dialog, select "Add a new forest" and enter a name for the root domain (see Figure 7.9). Choose any two-part domain name you like. Click Next.

FIGURE 7.9
Add a new forest

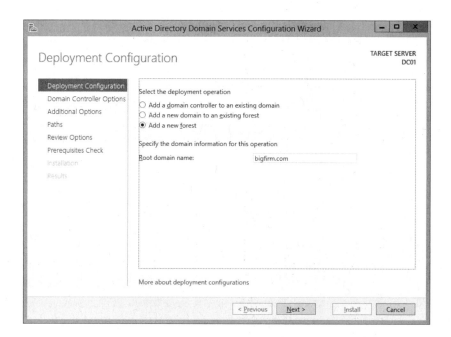

12. Leave the forest and domain functional level at its default Windows Server 2012. Make sure the Domain Name System (DNS) Server option is selected to install the DNS role. The Global Catalog (GC) option is selected and cannot be changed, because this is the first domain controller in the domain. Enter the Directory Services Restore Mode (DSRM) password twice. Click Next.

    Active Directory will attempt to locate a DNS server. If you haven't pre-staged a DNS server, you will now receive a warning, letting you know the zone for your domain can't be created. This is normal.

13. Click Next to continue.

14. There is no reason to change the NetBIOS name for the domain. Leave it as its default and click Next.

15. The path for database, log file, and SYSVOL will appear. You could change the path of the files but accept the defaults and click Next.

16. Review the options on the summary page and click Next to continue. Notice in the lower-right corner there is a button called "View script" (see Figure 7.10).

FIGURE 7.10
"View script"
option

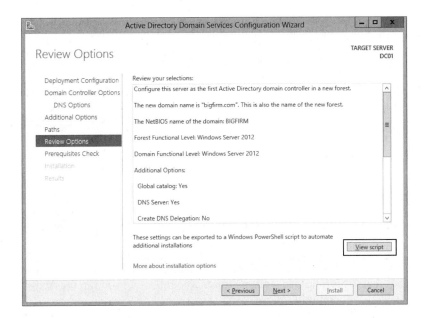

If you click this button a Notepad window will open and present the PowerShell command to set up an exact same forest with all the options you selected before.

17. Review all the commands and all the options (see Figure 7.11).

You could open a PowerShell command window on any Windows Server 2012 server where you have the Active Directory Domain Services role installed and copy and paste these commands. At the PowerShell command prompt you will be prompted for the DSRM password. Because of security reasons the wizard scrubs out the password, and the DSRM password will not be visible in the PowerShell script.

But if you want to provide the password without being prompted every time you execute the script, you could use the line I added in the previous example that will provide the password to the script:

```
-SafeModeAdministratorPassword (ConvertTo-SecureString "P@ssw0rd" -AsPlainText
-Force)`
```

18. When you finish the wizard you will be on the On Prerequisite Check page and two warnings will appear, but the wizard will show a green check mark indicating that all prerequisites passed successfully. As previously discussed, these warnings are normal. Click Install.

FIGURE 7.11
PowerShell commands generated by the wizard

Now it is time to take a break and let the server install the forest. Once the wizard finishes running and reboots, you will be prompted to log on.

19. Press Ctr+Alt+Del to log on.

The password for the domain administrator account is the same as the password was for the local administrator account before you ran the Active Directory Domain Services Configuration Wizard.

That's it. You have created a single-domain forest. Your next logical step is to create a second DC.

Figure 7.12 shows the screen when you promote a Windows Server 2012 domain controller using PowerShell, as described in step 17.

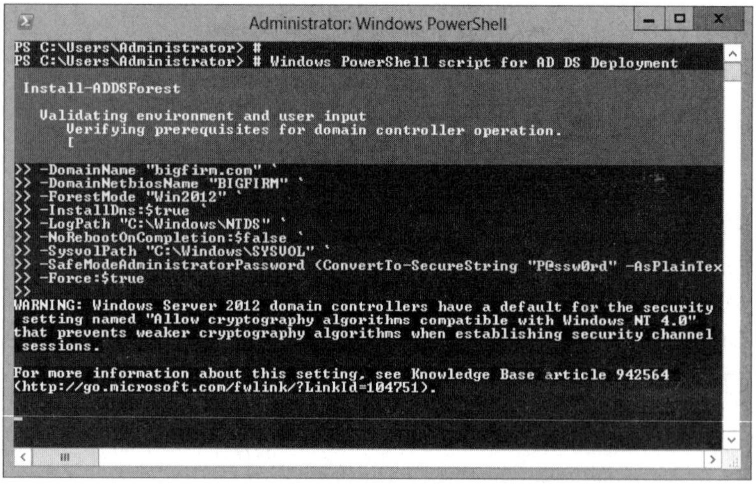

FIGURE 7.12
Installing a domain controller using PowerShell

ADMINISTERING WINDOWS SERVER 2012 REMOTELY

The recommended way of administering a Windows server is not logging onto the server itself; instead, you can install Remote Server Administration Tools (RSAT) on your client. Microsoft offers RSAT as a separate download; first you run Setup on your client and then you turn on the features.

RSAT for Windows 8 can manage Windows Server 2012 and has limited functionality for Windows Server 2008 and Windows Server 2003. For an overview of what can be managed in which version of Windows Server, see the following web page:

    http://support.microsoft.com/kb/2693643/en-us

To download RSAT for Windows 8 go to:

    http://www.microsoft.com/en-us/download/details.aspx?id=28972

RSAT for Windows 8.1 is needed to manage Windows Server 2012 R2 and Windows Server 2012. There is also limited functionality for Windows Server 2008 R2 and Windows Server 2008. To download the RSAT for Windows 8.1 (Preview) go to:

    http://www.microsoft.com/en-us/download/details.aspx?id=39296

Adding a Second DC

Whenever possible, you should have a second DC in place. A second DC will make routine and disaster recovery much simpler. A single domain controller is at significant risk of being a single point of failure. If it goes down, your entire network can go down, and you will find yourself in crisis mode. In Windows Server 2012 nothing has changed in this respect.

If you have a second DC and either the first or second DC fails, the network will continue to hum along. User will still be able to log onto the domain, and they won't experience any interruption in their work, group policies will still be applied, and normal administration of the domain can still be done. You will still have work to do, but it won't be a crisis. Additionally, restoring a failed DC is much simpler if another DC is still running in the domain. You can even create a new DC from scratch without a backup if it comes to that. If your last DC in the domain fails, you will need a recent backup of Active Directory, and you will have a significant amount of work to do to restore the domain. Besides that, you will have several nervous managers hovering over your shoulder frequently asking things like, "How much longer?" or, "Do you need any help?"

Just as you ran the Active Directory Domain Services Configuration Wizard to create the first DC, you will run this wizard to create the second. An account with Domain Admins permission is required to add a domain controller. You will also need to consider the following choices:

◆ Deployment configuration

◆ DNS

◆ Global Catalog

Before Running the Configuration Wizard

Install the Active Directory Domain Services role onto a fresh Windows Server 2012 by running the Add Roles and Features Wizard. Next, you need to have a static IP address assigned to your second DC. The DNS IP address points to the first DC so the server can locate the domain.

You will need to access the TCP/IP properties for the NIC. The easiest way to access the network adapters is to follow these steps:

1. Press WIN+R on your Windows 2012 server keyboard.

2. Type **ncpa.cpl** and click OK.

3. Click the Local Area Connection. Click the Properties button.

4. Select Internet Protocol Version 4 (TCP/IPv4) and select Properties.

   Ensure that you have a statically assigned IP address compatible with your network.

5. Enter the address of the DNS server, as shown in Figure 7.13.

   In this example network, the DNS server has an address of 192.168.0.45, so we have entered it as the IP address for the DNS server (see Figure 7.13).

FIGURE 7.13
Configuring network settings

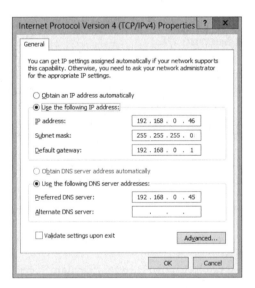

6. Close all the windows and dialog boxes.

You don't need to join the server to the domain prior to promoting it to a domain controller. The configuration wizard will automatically take the necessary steps and move the computer object into the Domain Controller container in Active Directory.

Deployment Configuration for the Second DC

Since you already have a domain, you will have different choices to make with the deployment configuration. If you want to add a second DC, you will select "Add a domain controller to an existing domain," as shown in Figure 7.14.

This would be the same selection for every new domain controller you wanted to add to the domain. If you needed to create a child domain, you would select "Add a new domain to an existing forest."

FIGURE 7.14
Adding a second
domain controller

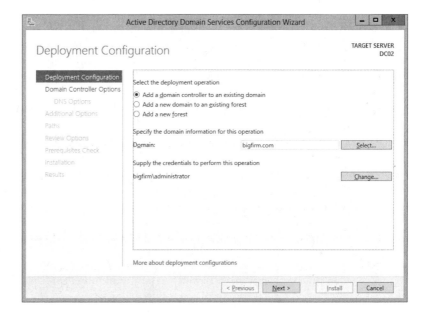

DNS for the Second DC

Should you add DNS to the second DC? Yes!

If your first DC is running DNS (as recommended), then your second DC should also be running DNS. If you followed the steps for promoting the first DC, then it is running an Active Directory integrated (ADI) zone. By adding DNS to the second DC, you will add redundancy with very little overhead. You can also use the second DNS server for load balancing.

Remember, Active Directory depends on DNS. If there is no DNS available for your DC to locate SRV records to find domain controllers and necessary services, Active Directory will not function. It is essential for Active Directory to have a working DNS in place.

With two DNS servers you can configure servers and clients to use both DNS servers. It is recommended to add one preferred and one alternate server for the computers in your network. These computers will only query the alternate DNS server if the preferred DNS server does not respond to queries.

One-half of your computers should use DNS server 1 as the preferred DNS server, and the other half of the computers should be configured to use DNS server 2 as preferred DNS server.

If you have dynamically assigned IP addresses and options, you can configure half of the DHCP client scopes to deploy DNS server 1 as the preferred DNS server and the other half of the DHCP client scopes to deploy DNS server 2 as preferred DNS server.

One very important step to remember is that after you promote your domain controller, you need to reconfigure the DNS network settings. Make sure you set the domain controller's primary DNS to its own IP address. It is best practice that domain controllers always point to themselves first if DNS is installed on the server.

GLOBAL CATALOG FOR THE SECOND DC

Should the second DC be a global catalog server? Yes!

In this chapter, you are creating only a single-domain forest. In a single-domain forest, you should always make all of your domain controllers global catalog servers. There is no additional cost involved and doing so ensures that the DC provides full functionality if the other DC fails.

GLOBAL CATALOG PLACEMENT DIFFERENCES

There are always questions about the GC placement. Microsoft states the following very clearly in KB223346 found at `http://support.microsoft.com/kb/223346/en-us`.

SINGLE-DOMAIN FOREST

In a forest that contains a single Active Directory domain, there are no phantoms. A *phantom* is a reference to an object in a different naming context. For example, if you add user B from domain B into a group A in domain A, you may have noticed that a different kind of icon is shown in the Member tab of the group. This is a phantom. Because no such phantoms are created, the infrastructure master has no work to do. The infrastructure master may be placed on any domain controller in the domain, regardless of whether that domain controller hosts the global catalog or not. If you don't know yet what the infrastructure master and other FSMO roles are, read the section, "FSMO Roles and How to Move Them," on the upcoming pages.

MULTIDOMAIN FOREST

If every domain controller in a domain that is part of a multidomain forest also hosts the global catalog, there are no phantoms or work for the infrastructure master to do. The infrastructure master may be put on any domain controller in that domain. In practical terms, most administrators host the global catalog on every domain controller in the forest.

If no domain controller in a given domain that is located in a multidomain forest hosts the global catalog, the infrastructure master must be placed on a domain controller that does not host the global catalog.

RUNNING THE AD DS CONFIGURATION WIZARD FOR THE SECOND DC

You can follow these steps to promote a second server to a domain controller. In these steps, the server is not a member of the domain. If you have joined your server to the domain, you might see minor differences.

1. Log onto the server using an account with local administrator privileges.

2. If you have not already done so, install the Active Directory Domain Services role. Open Server Manager and choose Manage/Add Roles and Features. Then follow the wizard as you did for the first domain controller.

   Alternatively, you could open a PowerShell command prompt and run the following cmdlet; this will install the same features as running the wizard:

   ```
   Add-WindowsFeature AD-Domain-Services,RSAT-AD-AdminCenter,RSAT-ADDS-Tools,GPMC
   ```

3. In Server Manager click the yellow exclamation mark and click "Promote this server to a domain controller."

   If the yellow exclamation mark did not appear after you ran the PowerShell command, click the refresh icon in Server Manager.

4. On the first Deployment Configuration page, select "Add a domain controller to an existing domain." Specify the domain name and provide domain administrator credentials for bigfirm.com domain. If the account you used to log onto the server isn't a member of the Domain Administrators group in the target domain, you will also need to enter alternate credentials. Click Next.

AD PROBLEMS? CHECK DNS!

If you receive an error indicating that a domain controller for the domain can't be contacted, double-check the spelling of the domain name and then check that DNS is running on the DNS server. Ensure your system is configured to use this DNS server. A simple check is to ping the domain name. For example, if your domain name is bigfirm.com, you would type in ping bigfirm.com and you should receive four replies. If you don't receive any replies, it is a clear indication that either you are not reaching DNS (check your TCP/IP and firewall settings) or DNS is not functioning correctly.

---

5. On the Domain Controller Options page, select both "Domain Name System (DNS) server" and Global Catalog (GC), as shown in Figure 7.15. Make sure Default-First-Site-Name is selected. You also need to enter a DSRM password. A good practice would be to choose the same DSRM password for your second DC as you did for your first DC. Click Next.

6. If a DNS delegation warning appears, click Next.

7. On the Additional Options page, you could specify to install Active Directory from media.

   You could use NTDSUtil to create installation media from a current Active Directory database. NTDSUtil will create a kind of a point-in-time snapshot that you then provide as input for this wizard. The advantage is that you only need to replicate the differences for the time after the snapshot. This feature is very useful if you have a slow WAN link and you don't want to replicate the entire Active Directory database over this slow network link.

FIGURE 7.15
Adding DNS
and GC to the
second DC

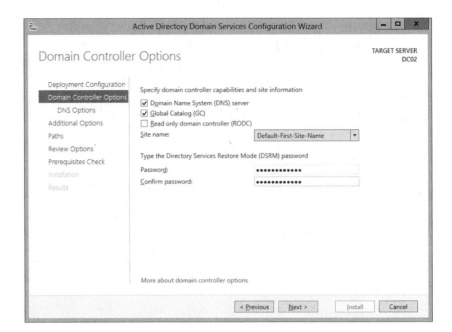

8. In this case, choose to replicate from "Any domain controller." Click Next.

9. On the Paths page, leave the database, log file, and SYSVOL, and click Next.

10. Review the Review Options page, and if desired click the View Script option to save your selected options so that you can run the same setup at a later time. Click Next.

11. Verify on the Prerequisites Check page that the check is successful. You will notice the same warnings as we discussed for the first domain controller. Click Install.

12. After the installation is finished click Close, and the domain controller will reboot automatically.

13. Log onto the domain controller, and the Active Directory Domain Services Configuration Wizard will finish the task.

INSTALLING ACTIVE DIRECTORY FROM MEDIA

In a previous step we mentioned that you could use NTDSUtil to create a kind of a snapshot from your current Active Directory and then use this point-in-time copy to promote a new domain controller. The next step is to copy this snapshot to your portable disk or drive and then install a domain controller using this media. If you want to know how to create media like this, there is a detailed guide on TechNet:

http://technet.microsoft.com/en-us/library/cc770654.aspx

Creating Organizational Units, Accounts, and Groups

Once you have created your domain, you will want to create your OUs, user accounts, computer accounts, groups, and so on. There are two tools to choose from: either you stay with the legacy Active Directory Users and Computers (ADUC) tool or you choose to work with the Active Directory Administrative Center (ADAC). Microsoft will push upcoming new features and management tasks to the ADAC, so it makes sense to start using this new console.

Both tools allow you to create everything with point-and-click ease. However, you can also run the tasks from the command line, preferably with PowerShell. This is very handy in a couple of situations:

◆ You need to create or modify many objects and you want to script the process.

◆ You are running Server Core and you don't want to use the ADUC or ADAC GUI tools.

CREATING ORGANIZATIONAL UNITS

Organizational units are used to organize objects within Active Directory. Any object (such as users, computers, groups, and so on) can be placed within an OU to make them easier to administer. The two primary technical reasons why you will create an OU are these:

◆ Management through Group Policy

◆ Administrative delegation

MANAGEMENT THROUGH GROUP POLICY

Group Policy objects (GPOs) can be created and linked to sites, domains, and OUs. If you want some users to have a specific group policy assigned to them, you can create an OU, place the accounts within the OU, and link the GPO to the OUs.

However, if you haven't created any OUs, one way GPOs can be assigned to regular accounts is through the Default Domain Policy that is applied to all users and computers equally. Imagine that you wanted to deploy an application to all users in the sales department using Group Policy. If you link your GPO to the domain, all users in the entire company would get the application, not just the users in the sales department.

Instead, you would create an OU (let's call it Sales), move the sales department user and computer accounts into this OU, and then link the GPO to the Sales OU. If you had other groups or users that you wanted to apply specific Group Policy objects to, you would create an OU for them and place their user and computer objects within that OU.

Another way of applying GPOs to some users or computer objects is to create an Active Directory security group and add into the group all your users who need to get the policy settings applied. After you have your group created and provisioned, you could add this group to the GPO's Security Filtering section and remove the default Authenticated Users group from the Security Filtering settings. For detailed steps read Chapter 9, "Group Policy: AD's Gauntlet and Active Directory Delegation." It will show you how to accomplish this and more.

ACTIVE DIRECTORY ADMINISTRATIVE CENTER

Windows Server 2008 R2 already had an Active Directory Administrative Center built-in, but it was a challenge to create objects if you were used to the Active Directory Users and

Computers console. In Windows Server 2012, Microsoft brings a more evolved Active Directory Administrative Center. It is redesigned and fully based on PowerShell. Because of that you can always copy the latest commands from the Windows PowerShell History windows, modify the commands, and build your own script to accomplish the task faster.

However, the Active Directory Users and Computers MMC is still available and works with Windows Server 2012, and it has the same functionality as Windows Server 2008 R2.

CREATING OUs WITH ADAC

To create an OU using Active Directory Administrative Center, follow these steps:

1. Launch Windows Server 2012. On the Start page click Active Directory Administrative Center. Alternatively you can press WIN+R to get the Run window, type **dsac.exe**, and click OK.

2. Right-click the domain, and select New ➢ Organizational Unit.

3. Enter **Sales** in the Name text box and ensure that the check box "Protect from accidental deletion" is selected. Your display will look similar to Figure 7.16.

FIGURE 7.16
Creating an OU named Sales

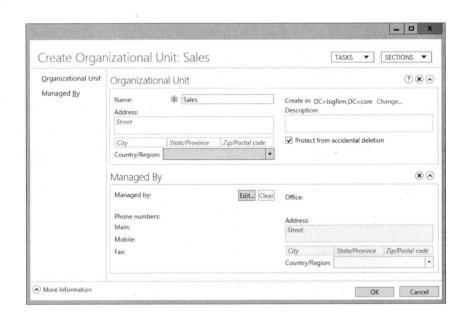

4. Click OK and your OU is created.

5. It is also possible to create child OUs. Right-click the Sales OU you just created, and select New ➢ Organizational Unit.

6. Type in **Users** for the name and click OK. Your display should look similar to Figure 7.17 with the Users OU as a child of the Sales OU.

FIGURE 7.17
OUs in Active
Directory
Administrative
Center

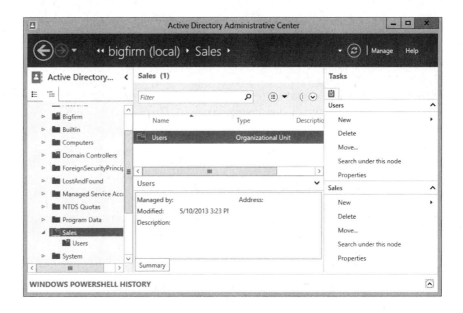

PROTECT FROM DELETION

"Protect from accidental deletion" is a neat feature that prevents anyone (even administrators) from accidentally deleting an object. Even though ADAC prompts you with the "Are you sure?" question, many of us click right through these confirmation dialog boxes. However, when this option is set, the object cannot be deleted until the option is cleared.

If you really want to delete an object, you still can. Modify this setting by right-clicking the object in ADAC, choose Properties, and deselect the option.

You may notice that you have two Users objects within Active Directory, but they are very different. The Users OU within the Sales OU is an OU and can have GPOs linked to it. The Users container under the domain is only a container (not an OU) and cannot have GPOs linked to it. OUs have slightly different icons to identify them—it is not just a folder but instead a folder with an icon embedded on the front of the folder reminding you that it is something more.

LDAP DISTINGUISHED NAMES

Active Directory uses the Lightweight Directory Access Protocol (LDAP) for communication. LDAP uses a distinguished name (DN) to uniquely identify each object within the directory. Before looking at how to create objects from the command line or scripts, you should understand the components of a DN.

The format of a DN uses objectType=objectName with several object types separated by commas. For example, a domain named bigfirm.com has two domain components (bigfirm and com) that are identified this way:

```
dc=bigfirm, dc=com.
```

Organizational units have an object type of OU, and the Users and Computers containers are identified with cn (for "common name"). The Sales OU would have this DN:

```
ou=Sales,dc=bigfirm,dc=com
```

The Users container would have this DN:

```
cn=Users,dc=bigfirm,dc=com
```

A *container* is an Active Directory object that is created within Active Directory when you promote a server to a domain controller. This object contains default users and groups for Active Directory and also entirely different attributes than an OU. One other big difference is that you cannot apply group policies to this container.

An account with a name of Sally.Smith located in the Sales OU would have this DN:

```
cn=Sally.Smith,ou=Sales,dc=bigfirm,dc=com
```

An account with a name of Joe.Johnson located in the Users container would have this DN:

```
cn=Joe.Johnson,cn=Users,dc=bigfirm,dc=com
```

If OUs are nested, or have OUs within them, the lowest level OU comes first in the DN name. For example, if the Sales OU had a child OU named Users and then had a user named Maria within it, the DN would be as follows:

```
cn=Maria,ou=Users,ou=Sales,dc=bigfirm,dc=com
```

If the DN includes any spaces, it needs to be enclosed with quotes to ensure it is interpreted correctly. For example, this doesn't require quotes because there are no spaces:

```
cn=Maria,ou=Users,ou=Sales,dc=bigfirm,dc=com
```

However, the same DN with spaces must include quotes:

```
"cn=Maria,ou=Users,ou=Sales,dc=bigfirm,dc=com"
```

LDAP DNs are not case sensitive. The following two DNs will be interpreted as the same object:

```
cn=Maria,ou=Users,ou=Sales,dc=bigfirm,dc=com
CN=Maria,OU=Users,OU=Sales,DC=bigfirm,DC=com
```

CREATING OUs WITH POWERSHELL

PowerShell has been around for a few years, and it is becoming more important to know what PowerShell is all about. In Windows Server 2008 R2, PowerShell 2.0 was built in and already had good support for several features and roles. Because PowerShell is object oriented it has a solid, well-designed architecture. Microsoft pushes PowerShell extensively so you can use it to control almost anything in Windows Server 2012.

In Windows Server 2012, PowerShell 3.0—or in Windows Server 2012 R2, PowerShell 4.0—is built in with tons of new commands for more easily controlling your server. Exploring all these new features would require several books on the subject. Here we'll just continue with our example to give you a feel for what it's all about. If you don't know which command-line tool to use, such as DSAdd, Windows Script Host (WSH), or PowerShell, then learn PowerShell—it is the present and future technology.

If you installed your second domain controller according to our step-by-step guide, you should have already the Active Directory PowerShell commands available. Verify that you have the AD DS Snap-Ins and Command-Line Tools installed. You can find out if you start the Add Roles and Features Wizard and click Next until you reach the page where you select the features. It should look similar to the one shown in Figure 7.18.

FIGURE 7.18

Adding a PowerShell cmdlet

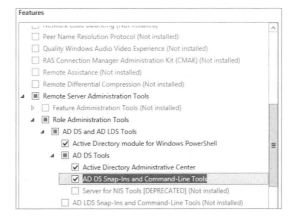

In Windows Server 2012 click the PowerShell icon on the taskbar; this will launch the PowerShell command window showing the prompt PS C:\Users\administrator>. In the next section you will learn how to use PowerShell to create an OU named PS_OU.

POWERSHELL AND ACTIVE DIRECTORY

PowerShell has a large set of commands available that basically need only some additional parameters to do their work. These commands are referred to as cmdlets and are the work horses in PowerShell. If you have certain roles installed in Active Directory, new cmdlets are available, but in order to get them to work you need first to import these cmdlets into your PowerShell session. Most of the time new cmdlets come in a type of module, and you need to load these modules to have the new functionalities available.

You do this by typing:

```
Import-Module ActiveDirectory
```

This will take a moment and you will be prompted again. Next, type the command to create an OU named PS_OU.

```
New-ADOrganizationalUnit –Name PS_OU –Server DC02.bigfirm.com –Path
"DC=bigfirm,DC=com"
```

You may need to modify the server name DC02.bigfirm.com and the domain component "DC=bigfirm,DC=com" to match your domain controller and your domain name. If it doesn't work and you get an error, check first to see if you have any typos. PowerShell is in general case insensitive. This means it doesn't matter whether you write the command in uppercase or lowercase; it will work either way.

In PowerShell 3.0 it's no longer necessary to import the module first by typing Import-Module ActiveDirectory as we did in the example. PowerShell 3.0 will recognize the New-ADOrganizationalUnit cmdlet and import the appropriate module. If the module has already been imported, PowerShell will skip this step and not import the module again.

The first New-ADOrganizationalUnit cmdlet consists of a verb and a noun separated by a dash (-). This is a basic design principal in PowerShell to make cmdlets easy to remember. For example, if you want to get an OU, you could type **Get-ADOrganizationalUnit**, or to remove an OU you could type **Remove-ADOrganizationalUnit**.

We provided several parameters for the New-ADOrganizationalUnit cmdlet, so let's have a brief look at these. The -Name parameter specifies the name of the OU; notice that there is a space between Name and the PS_OU name. -Server specifies the domain controller where you want to create the OU, and -Path specifies the placement of the new OU. There are many more parameters you could provide. To see all the options type Get-Help New-ADOrganizationalUnit or just help New-ADOrganzationalUnit.

You might be wondering if there is a way to create a script to speed things up. It might not make much sense in our example to create a script, because it's just one line of code. But we've not even touched on the tip of the iceberg; what if you wanted to create 10 OUs at a time, for example, PS_OU1, PS_OU2, and so on, and delete those OUs and re-create them? I think it's worth creating a script for that.

In Windows Server 2012 you get an integrated scripting environment for developing and running PowerShell scripts right out of the box. This tool is called Windows PowerShell ISE. ISE stands for Integrated Scripting Environment. It is a script editor that helps you build scripts faster and also allows you to run the scripts right from your console. Windows PowerShell ISE has some great features like Intellisense, which helps you find the right cmdlet and provides a command section with detailed information about the cmdlets. There is much more to explore; here we will just briefly touch on the experience of writing a script in the Windows PowerShell ISE. You can create and execute a PowerShell script by following these steps:

1. Launch Windows PowerShell ISE by right-clicking the PowerShell icon on your taskbar. In the context menu you will see a task called Windows PowerShell ISE.

    The PowerShell icon should be pinned on the taskbar; if it is not, launch Windows PowerShell ISE from the Start screen.

2. Choose the View menu and make sure Show Script Pane is selected.

3. Type the following lines into the Script pane (upper-white section) in Windows PowerShell ISE (see Figure 7.19):

```
Import-Module ActiveDirectory
ForEach ($i in 1..10) {
New-ADOrganizationalUnit -Name "PS_OU$i" -Server DC01.bigfirm.com `
-Path "DC=bigfirm,DC=com"
}
```

FIGURE 7.19

Running
PowerShell
in PowerShell
ISE

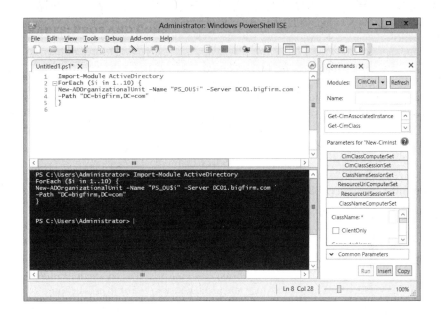

Notice that the second line uses a `ForEach` loop to iterate 10 times. `$i` contains the current number from each loop. For example, the first time the loop is executed, `$i` contains the number 1; the second time the loop is executed, `$i` contains the number 2; and so on. And every time the loop starts, the `New-ADOrganizationalUnit` cmdlet gets executed. Because the cmdlet needs to split over two lines, there is a back-tick (`` ` ``) at the end of the third line; this allows the command to wrap to the next line.

4. Choose File ➢ Save As, and save this script in your Documents library as **Create100Us .ps1**.

   At this point, you have a PowerShell script you can run, but you probably won't be able to run it without modifying the environment.

5. Return to Windows PowerShell ISE. Type **Get-Ex**, and press the Tab key. Notice that you get a menu that shows you all the commands that start with `Get-Ex*`. This functionality is called Intellisense. In this case, there is only one cmdlet, `Get-ExecutionPolicy`.

6. The command will become `Get-ExecutionPolicy`. Press Enter. Go to the menu bar and click the green triangle that looks like a Play button from a tape recorder, or press F5.

   If you have a default installation, the result will show Restricted in the blue window underneath the Script pane, and you can't run the script.

7. Clear the Script pane, type the following command to change Execution Policy, and press the F5 key:

   ```
   Set-ExecutionPolicy RemoteSigned
   ```

8. When prompted to allow the change, click Yes. This will allow you to execute local scripts.

9. Choose File ➢ Open, and select your previously saved script, `Create100Us.ps1`.

10. You can now execute your script by pressing F5.

If all goes well, you can launch Active Directory Administrative Center and view your new OUs. If there are errors, review the script. It is common for errors to occur the first time you type the script, especially if they are several lines long.

POWERSHELL 4.0 IN WINDOWS SERVER 2012 R2

Windows Server 2012 R2 ships with the latest and greatest PowerShell, version 4.0. It is important to understand that PowerShell 4.0 is backward-compatible with earlier versions. This means that our examples work under Windows Server 2012 PowerShell 3.0 and Windows Server 2012 R2 PowerShell 4.0.

CREATING ACCOUNTS

Once you have created some OUs, you will want to create some accounts. Both users and computers need accounts in order to access the domain. Just as with OUs, you can use either Active Directory Users and Computers, Active Directory Administrative Center, DSAdd, or PowerShell to create the accounts.

The creation of computer accounts is often automated. When a computer joins the domain, a computer account is automatically created. By default, the account is created in the Computers container, but you can modify this using the `redircmp` command-line tool. The syntax is as follows:

```
Redircmp DN
```

For example, if a user joined a computer to a domain and you wanted the computer account to be created in the Sales OU, you would enter the following command:

```
Redircmp "OU=Sales,DC=bigfirm,DC=com"
```

If you need to set it back to the default setting, type:

```
Redircmp "CN=Computers,DC=bigfirm,DC=com"
```

Don't forget to adjust the domain controller ($DC=xxx$) settings according to your environment.

CREATING ACCOUNTS WITH ACTIVE DIRECTORY ADMINISTRATIVE CENTER

To create a user account using Active Directory Administrative Center, follow these steps:

1. Launch Active Directory Administrative Center by pressing WIN+R to start the Run dialog, enter **dsac.exe** into the text field, and click OK.

2. Right-click the Sales OU you created earlier, and select New ➢ User.

3. Enter the first name, last name, and user logon name for the user.

4. Enter a password on the same page, confirm it, and ensure the check box is selected for "User must change password at next log on."

This will ensure that the user changes the password and no one else knows it, not even you. Your display will look similar to Figure 7.20.

FIGURE 7.20
Creating a user
in ADAC

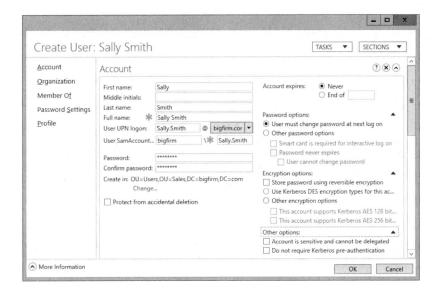

If the account is shared by multiple users (such as a temporary job filled by different workers), you may want to select "User cannot change password." If you are creating service accounts (user accounts used to start services), you may select "Password never expires" to ensure an expired password doesn't lock out the account. Finally, if the account isn't going to be used for a while, consider disabling it.

5. Click Next.

6. Review the information on the page, and click OK.

CREATING USERS WITH POWERSHELL

Before PowerShell was born, we used a tool called DSAdd to create users and other Active Directory objects. It was a great tool back then, but today it's considered it a legacy tool that's still around and works great. It might be a step into batch scripting and offers a first touch into the automated command-line world. But the only way to get serious about automating and making life easier is to use PowerShell.

Just as you used PowerShell to create OUs, you can also create user accounts. You will be surprised to learn that the basic cmdlet doesn't differ much from the DSAdd command. The cmdlet you need is the following:

```
New-ADUser -Path "OU=Sales,DC=bigfirm,DC=com" -AccountPassword (ConvertTo-
SecureString P@ssword -AsPlainText -force) -Name "Maria Smith" -Givenname Maria
-Surname Smith `
-DisplayName "Maria Smith" -SamAccountName "Maria.Smith" `
-UserPrincipalName "Maria.Smith@bigfirm.com" -ChangePasswordAtLogon 1 -Enabled 1
```

This PowerShell example and DSAdd both create a user named Maria Smith with the exact same parameters. You might think that, the PowerShell command has more code than the DSAdd command in the previous example. Now you are probably wondering what the advantage is if you have to type more to achieve the same thing. The strength of PowerShell lies in its fully object-oriented approach with all its bells and whistles.

Notice in the example that we could not just specify a password in string format; we needed to convert this string into a SecureString first and then submit this to the –AccountPassword parameter. The –ChangePasswordAtLogon and –Enabled parameters need an input value of type Boolean. Boolean means either 0 (= false) or 1 (= true). Review the rest of the command and you will see that it is self-explanatory.

CREATING GROUPS

You may also want to create some groups. The most common reason to create groups is to organize users. More specifically, global security groups are created to organize users and then assign permissions to the groups. Whenever possible, you should assign permissions to groups rather than users. You may have heard the old saying "Users come and go, but groups stay forever." Well, maybe you haven't heard it before since we just made it up, but it makes sense, and it is a good way to remember that you always assign permissions to groups instead of users.

As an example, you could have several users in the sales department. Instead of assigning permissions to each individual in the sales department, you could create a single global security group name G_Sales. Place all the users in the sales department into this group and assign permissions to the G_Sales group. If a user leaves, take him out of the G_Sales group and he will no longer have the permissions of the group. If a user joins the sales team, put her into the G_Sales group, and she will have the same permissions as everyone else in the group.

That sounds pretty easy, but there is not just one type of group; there are several types and each of them has its own purpose. The two types of groups are distribution and security. Distribution groups are used for email, and security groups are used to assign permissions. Security groups can also be used for email.

There are three group scopes:

Global Global groups are used to organize users. This is the most commonly used group and the one you will create later in this chapter. Users will be placed in the global groups, and permissions can be assigned to the global groups.

Domain Local In some domain implementations, domain local groups are used in an AGDLP group strategy where *A* indicates accounts, *G* indicates global groups, *DL* indicates domain local groups, and *P* indicates permissions. User accounts are placed in global groups. Global groups are placed into domain local groups, and permissions are assigned to the domain local groups. When used this way, the domain local groups are an added layer used to identify resources. The recommended approach is to design your group strategy using the AGDLP principle.

Universal   Universal groups are used only in multiple-domain environments. For example, in a network with two domains, Europe and UnitedStates, and global group G_Sales in each domain, you can create a universal group UG_Sales that has as its members the two G_Sales groups, UnitedStates\G_Sales and Europe\G_Sales. The UG_Sales group can then be used anywhere in the enterprise. Any changes in the membership of the individual G_Sales groups will not cause replication of the UG_Sales group. Now you can add the universal group into a domain local group and thus give resource permission to the sales team all over the world. This strategy is referred to as AGUDLP, where *U* stands for universal group.

The most common way to create these groups is with Active Directory Users and Computers or with Active Directory Administrative Center. You can use the following steps to create a global security group:

1. Launch Active Directory Administrative Center by pressing WIN+R to start the Run dialog, type **dsac.exe** into the text box, and click OK.

2. Right-click the Sales OU, and select New ➤ Group.

3. Enter **G_Sales** in the "Group name" box. Your display will look similar to Figure 7.21. Click OK.

FIGURE 7.21
Creating a group using Active Directory Administrative Center

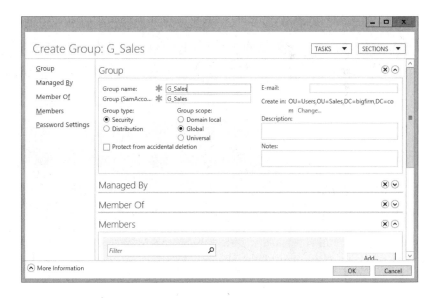

4. Right-click the Sales OU, and select New ➤ Group. Then enter **G_SalesAdmins** in the "Group name" box. Click OK.

Your G_SalesAdmins group is created, and now you could use this group to assign permissions, for example, delegating control to an OU as described in the upcoming section.

CREATING GROUPS WITH POWERSHELL (ADAC WINDOWS POWERSHELL HISTORY)

In the previous examples you created OUs and users using PowerShell. We showed you the command you needed to create the object. But what if you don't know the command or you could use some help? If you followed the steps for creating the groups using the Active Directory Administrative Center, then you already have everything in front of you:

1. After you create the G_SalesAdmins group, click the down arrow within a circle on the right side of where it says Windows PowerShell History in your console, as shown in Figure 7.22.

   Now you will see all the tasks previously executed in the ADAC. You should also see the last two New-ADGroup commands, as shown in Figure 7.22.

2. Click the + sign on the left side of the cmdlet to expand it and see all its parameters.

FIGURE 7.22
Viewing
PowerShell
History

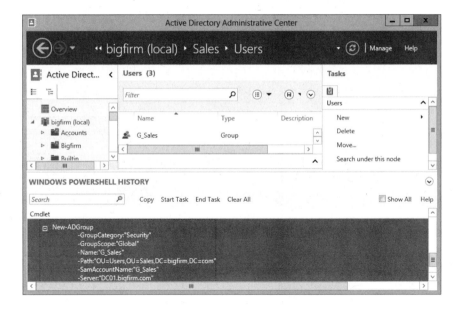

3. Right-click the first New-ADGroup cmdlet, and copy and paste it into a PowerShell window. Then change the Name and SamAccountName fields of the group to something else, for example:

```
New-ADGroup -GroupCategory:"Security" -GroupScope:"Global" -Name:"G_
SalesPowerUsers" `
 -Path:"OU=Sales,DC=bigfirm,DC=com" -SamAccountName:"G_SalesPowerUsers" `
-Server:"DC02.bigfirm.com"
```

4. Execute the command by pressing Enter.

If you don't receive any errors, you will have just created another global group.

PowerShell History Viewer

You just saw in Figure 7.22 how tasks previously executed in Active Directory Administrative Center are translated into PowerShell and displayed in Windows PowerShell History. Because ADAC is on top of PowerShell, everything will be shown in the PowerShell History as commands. Windows Server 2012 Active Directory has now more than 140 PowerShell cmdlets, and it would take a lot of time to learn the commands and the specific syntax. Therefore we recommend that you keep an eye on this window because it will help you in learning these commands.

At the top of the PowerShell History window are several fields:

Copy You can use Copy to copy one or multiple commands. For copying multiple commands you can hold Ctrl and click each of the commands you would like to copy.

Search With the Search field you can search any cmdlet within PowerShell History. Just type the first few letters, and the pane will narrow down your search results.

Start Task and End Task If you want to group your commands, you can click Start Task before executing any action in ADAC and give it a name, and click End Task as soon you have finished executing the action. For the next group of commands, you would repeat these steps.

Clear All This will clear your history commands.

Show All If you select Show All, every task you perform in the ADAC will be shown in the History window. If you deselect this option, only tasks that manipulate Active Directory will show up. The default is for the check box to be deselected.

Delegating Control Using Organizational Units

Earlier in this chapter, I mentioned that one of the reasons for creating an OU was to delegate control, and certainly one of AD's strengths is that it can let you grant partial or complete administrative powers to a group of users. This means that it would be possible for a one-domain network to be subdivided into, say, Uptown and Downtown, or Marketing, Engineering, and Management, or whatever. Probably the most common requirement or reason to delegate control to an OU is to give helpdesk people permission to reset user passwords. Another quite often requested permission is to be able to modify only certain attributes of users or group objects. Of course there are many other requirements you will be facing during your Active Directory administration career. Even if you're not terribly interested in delegation, Chapter 9 gives you a very good head start on delegating control in Active Directory.

Domain Maintenance Tasks

After you have established your domain, you will need to do some domain maintenance. Although this section doesn't cover everything you will need to do, it does cover some basic tasks:

- Joining a domain
- Decommissioning a DC
- Troubleshooting ADI DNS
- Raising the domain and forest functional levels

- Using `Netdom`
- Managing the domain time
- Moving FSMO roles

JOINING A DOMAIN

Follow these steps to join a Windows Server 2012 to a domain. Once the server is joined to a domain, it is referred to as a member server.

1. Log on to the local server.
2. Start Server Manager and click Local Server.
3. In the upper-left click the link right next to Domain.
4. The System Properties dialog will appear. Select the Computer Name tab and click the Change button.
5. Select the Domain radio button, and enter the name of the domain you are joining. Your display will first look similar to Figure 7.23, which shows the WORKGROUP, and then in Figure 7.24 we added the domain that we want to join. Click OK.

   You will be prompted to provide the credentials of an account that has permission on the domain.
6. Enter the credentials, and click OK.
7. After a moment, you will see a Welcome dialog box. Click OK. You will then be prompted to restart the computer. Click OK.
8. Click Close to close the System Properties dialog box.
9. You will receive another reminder saying the server must be restarted. Click Restart Now.

After the server has rebooted, it will be a member of the domain—a member server.

FIGURE 7.23
System currently in a workgroup

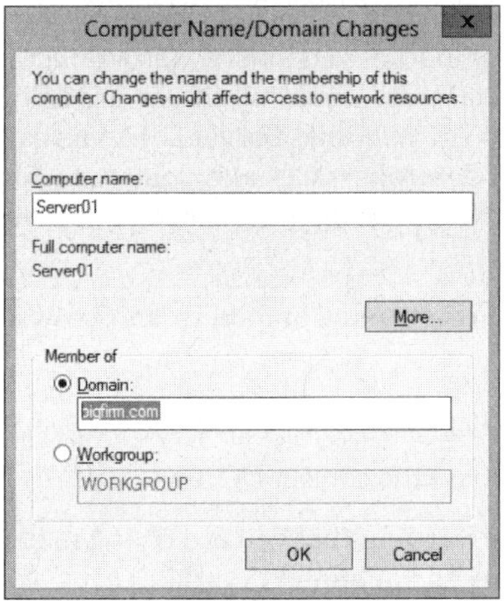

FIGURE 7.24
System joining
a domain

OFFLINE DOMAIN JOIN

Windows Server 2008 R2 introduced a new feature that allows you to join a Windows 7/8 or Windows Server 2008 R2/2012 system to a domain without contacting a domain controller. This can be useful if the computer doesn't have reliable connectivity to the corporate network. Windows Server 2012 does also offer this feature but there is still no GUI available to configure. For more details about an offline domain join, check out the article on TechNet at `http://technet.micro` `soft.com/en-us/library/dd392267.aspx`, which has been updated for Windows Server 2012.

DECOMMISSIONING A DC

If it's ever necessary to take one of the domain controllers out of service, it is imperative that you properly decommission it. When you decommission it, you remove all Active Directory components and return the domain controller to a member server role.

Properly decommissioning the DC is especially important if you need to take the first DC out of service. The first DC in the domain includes several Operations Master roles, sometimes called FSMO roles, that are integral to the proper operation of the domain. If this server simply fails and you are never able to bring it back up, you are going to have some problems until you properly decommission it.

The easiest method of decommissioning a DC is to simply run the PowerShell cmdlet `Uninstall-ADDSDomainController`. In Windows Server 2008 R2, you were able to run `DCPromo` to demote a domain controller, but at this Windows Server 2012 version `DCPromo` is gone. The tasks this cmdlet will perform are very similar to the `DCPromo` in the past Windows versions. If the domain controller you are running this cmdlet on is still operational and holds all the FMSO roles, it will transfer the roles to a new domain controller, demote the domain controller, move the computer object from the Domain Controllers OU into the Computers container, and take care of several other details. The DNS server role will be still installed and running, but if your DNS zones were Active Directory integrated (ADI), they are no longer available.

If this server just fails and you are not able to run `Uninstall-ADDSDomainController`, you will need to remove all the dependencies from the domain, like DNS SRV records that pointed to this domain controller and other deeply hidden traces in Active Directory from this domain controller. In previous Windows versions, it was a rather lengthy and tedious process using NTDSUtil and some manual work. However, if you are using the Active Directory Users and Computers snap-in available in Windows Server 2012, you can simply delete the domain controller object in the Domain Controllers OU, and you are finished.

For anyone who has gone through the lengthy metadata process using NTDSUtil and other tools, this is a great addition:

1. Launch Active Directory Users and Computers, and browse to the Domain Controllers OU.

2. Locate the DC you want to decommission. Right-click it, and select Delete.

3. Verify that you have selected the correct DC, and click Yes in the confirmation dialog box.

   A dialog box will appear warning that you are trying to delete a DC from AD without using the Active Directory Installation Wizard.

4. Select the check mark where it says "This Domain Controller is permanently offline and can no longer be demoted…" and click Delete (see Figure 7.25).

FIGURE 7.25
Deleting a domain controller

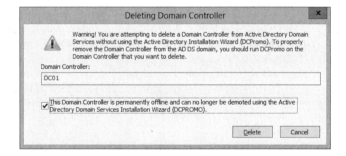

If the DC is a global catalog server, you will receive a warning asking if you want to continue.

5. Click Yes.

   If the server was holding any Operations Master roles, you will be prompted to have the role(s) transferred to another domain controller.

6. Click OK, and the role(s) will be seized by this DC.

If the failed DC is later recovered, you won't be able to remove Active Directory using Uninstall-ADDSDomainController. However, there is a work-around. Instead of just entering Uninstall-ADDSDomainController alone, enter **Uninstall-ADDSDomainController -ForceRemoval**. The –ForceRemoval switch will allow Active Directory to be removed without accessing another DC in the domain. There are other options available with this cmdlet that you can explore by typing **Get-Help Uninstall-ADDSDomainController**. For example, the –Force switch will suppress any upcoming warnings, which can be useful if you want to use it in a script, or –DemoteOperationMasterRole, which will force a demotion of the Active Directory even an Operations Master role is discovered. Of course, you can combine all these parameters to remove Active Directory from your orphaned domain controller.

ASK BEFORE YOU SHOOT

Wouldn't it be nice to have some sort of view into the future to see what would happen if you did certain things? Let's say you have a domain controller that you would like to demote, but you are not sure if all prerequisites have been met. PowerShell 3.0 is your friend and gives you cmdlets that you can try before you actually shoot. In our example you could run **Test-ADDSDomainControl lerUninstallation**. This will run an actual check to find out if all prerequisites for a demotion have been met. After running this cmdlet, you will be prompted with a status success or failure and other useful information. As with all other cmdlets, you can run **Get-Help** or just run **Test-ADD SDomainControllerUninstallation** to get more optional parameters for this cmdlet.

If you are digging a bit more in PowerShell 3.0, there are several other "Test" cmdlets, for example, Test-ADDSDomainControllerInstallation, Test-ADDSDomainInstallation, Test-ADDSReadOnlyDomainControllerAccountCreation, and so on. Check the TechNet article at http://technet.microsoft.com/en-us/library/hh974719.aspx for more information on this topic.

TROUBLESHOOTING AD DNS

A common problem that occurs with DNS is that SRV records aren't created when the server is rebooted. The netlogon service is responsible for creating these records, and sometimes it just seems to hiccup after rebooting the server.

As a reminder, the SRV records are used to locate domain controllers in a domain running specific services or holding specific roles within a domain. As a few examples, services within the domain often need to locate a global catalog server, a PDC emulator, a domain controller within a specific site, or simply a domain controller in the domain. Services query DNS for the appropriate SRV records, and as long as they exist, the server can be located. However, occasionally these records aren't created after a reboot. Figure 7.26 shows the DNS Manager console open to show that the records have been correctly created. Notice that there are several folders starting with an underscore (_msdcs, _sites, _tcp, and _udp). Each of these folders includes SRV records.

FIGURE 7.26
DNS service records (SRV)

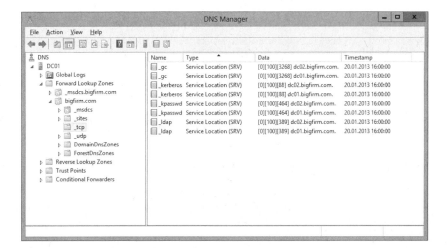

If you are experiencing connectivity problems and you notice that DNS is missing these records, there is a simple fix. Go to command prompt and issue the following two commands:

```
Net stop netlogon
Net start netlogon
```

The `netlogon` service will re-create the records, and you will be back in business.

RAISING DOMAIN AND FOREST FUNCTIONAL LEVELS

You may want to raise your domain and/or forest functional levels after you have initially created your forest or after upgrading from a Windows Server 2008 environment. The primary reason why you would want to do so is to take advantage of additional features available at the higher levels. Although Window Server 2012 forest functional levels don't offer any new features, you might still want to raise the domain functional level to Windows Server 2012. Anyhow, the big-picture steps you would take are as follows:

1. Ensure that all your domain controllers are running Windows Server 2012.

2. Raise the domain functional level to Windows Server 2012.

3. Raise the forest functional level to Windows Server 2012.

It is important to remember that once you raise the level, there is no turning back. If your current domain functional level is Windows Server 2008 R2 and you raise it to Windows Server 2012, you will no longer be able to promote anything less than a Windows Server 2012 server to a domain controller. If that fits in your plans, raise the levels.

FUNCTIONAL LEVELS CAN(NOT) BE LOWERED

Well, that's not exactly true. If you have a forest functional level of 2012, you could lower the forest and domain functional level to Windows Server 2008 R2. It does not work in the GUI but you could run two PowerShell commands to accomplish the task.

First, you lower the forest mode to Windows Server 2008 R2:

```
Set-ADForestMode -Identity "bigfirm.com" -ForestMode Windows2008R2Forest
```

And as a second step you lower the domain mode to Windows Server 2008 R2:

```
Set-ADDomainMode -Identity "bigfirm.com" -DomainMode Windows2008R2Domain
```

Keep in mind that lowering the forest functional level will also break the depending features, for example, Dynamic Access Control.

There are four tools you could use to raise the domain forest levels:

◆ Active Directory Users and Computers (to raise the domain functional level)

◆ Active Directory Domains and Trusts (to raise the forest functional level)

◆ Active Directory Administrative Center (to raise the domain and forest functional levels)

◆ PowerShell 3.0 (to raise the domain and forest functional levels)

Depending on your version, choose whichever method is appropriate for you. Because the Active Directory Administrative Center is new, we will now have a look at this console and how to raise the domain forest level there.

You can raise the domain functional level by following these steps:

1. Launch the Active Directory Administrative Center by pressing WIN+R to start the Run dialog and typing **dsac.exe** into the text box. Click OK.

2. Also start the console for the Start screen.

3. Right-click the domain name, and select "Raise the domain functional level," as shown in Figure 7.27.

FIGURE 7.27
Raising functional levels in Active Directory Administrative Center

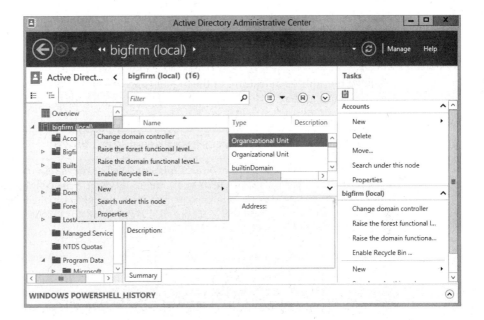

4. Review the information on the Raise Domain Functional Level page.

Notice that this page informs you what the current functional level is and gives you the option to raise it. Select Windows Server 2012 from the drop-down box.

5. Click OK.

You will receive another warning reminding you that this action isn't reversible.

6. Click OK.

After a moment, a dialog box will indicate that the level was raised successfully.

7. Click OK.

You can raise the forest functional level the same way you raised the domain functional level:

1. Launch the Active Directory Administrative Center by pressing WIN+R to start the Run dialog and typing **dsac.exe** into the text box. Click OK.

2. Also start the console for the Start screen.

3. Right-click the domain name and select "Raise the forest functional level."

4. Review the information on the Raise Forest Functional Level page.

   Notice that this page informs you what the current functional level is and gives you the option to raise it. Select Windows Server 2012 from the drop-down box.

5. Click OK.

   You will receive a warning reminding you that this action isn't reversible.

6. Click OK.

   After a moment, a dialog will indicate the level was raised successfully.

7. Click OK.

Many of the additional features of the higher functional levels will be available automatically. Only a few (such as the Active Directory Recycle Bin) require additional steps to enable them.

RAISE DOMAIN FORESTS LEVELS THE POWERSHELL WAY

Raising domain functional levels or forest functional levels is not an administrator's daily task. If ever, you will do it probably few times in your career, and you will probably not use a script to raise these levels. Therefore, this might not be a perfect case for using PowerShell. But to point out what is possible with the new PowerShell 3.0, we will show you how this is done.

To raise the domain functional level, start a PowerShell command window and type:

```
Set-ADDomainMode -Identity "bigfirm.com" -DomainMode Windows2012Domain
```

You will need to confirm this action by typing **Y**, which stands for Yes. After that your bigfirm.com domain will be raised to Windows Server 2012 domain functional level.

To raise the forest functional level, start a PowerShell command window and type:

```
Set-ADForestMode -Identity "bigfirm.com" -ForestMode Windows2012Forest
```

You will need to confirm this action by typing **Y**, which stands for Yes. After that your bigfirm.com forest will be raised to Windows Server 2012 forest functional level.

USING NETDOM

A valuable command-line tool is Netdom (short for "domain manager"). It is available at the command prompt on any server that has been promoted to a domain controller. Although Netdom is primarily used to manage trusts in environments with more than one domain, it also has several other uses.

Rename Computers (Including Domain Controllers)

You can use the `netdom computername` command to safely rename domain controllers and member servers. In early versions of Windows, renaming a domain controller wasn't possible unless you first demoted it. Be aware that even if you use `Netdom` to rename a domain controller, it may take a couple of reboots before everything settles—especially in DNS. More important, you should not rename servers that are certificate servers (those running Active Directory Certificate Services). A certificate server needs to keep the same name. The name embedded in a certificate identifies the server it is issued to and the server that issued the certificate. Certificates are validated by querying the original server, but if the name is changed, none of the certificates can be validated.

Renaming a DC involves giving it an alternate name and changing the alternate name to the DC's primary name. For example, if you have a domain controller named DC01 in the domain bigfirm.com but you want to rename it to DC03, you first give it an alternate name of DC03 with the following command:

```
Netdom computername DC01 /add:DC03.bigfirm.com
```

At this point, the server has two names: its primary name and an alternate name. Next, rename the computer to the alternate name with this command:

```
Netdom computername DC01 /makeprimary:DC03.bigfirm.com
```

`Netdom` will indicate success and prompt you to reboot the server. With the reboot, your domain controller will change the alternate name to its primary name.

As a last step you need to remove the old name DC01 from the domain controller computer object with this command:

```
Netdom computername DC03 /remove:DC01.bigfirm.com
```

Now your domain controller has a new name.

Join a Computer to a Domain

If you want to join a computer to a domain from the command prompt or via a script, you can use `Netdom`. The simplest implementation is as follows:

```
Netdom join server01 /d:bigfirm.com /reboot
```

This command will join the computer named server01 to the domain bigfirm.com and force a reboot. Normally, the computer account for a computer that just joined the domain is placed into the Computers container. As mentioned previously, you can use the `redircmp` command to have computer accounts created somewhere else.

It is also possible to get fancier with `Netdom`, but it tends to be more difficult than using the directory service command-line tools (such as `DSMove`). For example, if you want to move the computer account from the Computers container to the Sales OU, you could follow the `NetDom Join` command with the `DSMove` command.

```
Dsmove "CN=Server01,CN=Computers,DC=bigfirm,DC=com" -newparent
"OU=Sales,DC=bigfirm,DC=com"
```

Join the PowerShell Way

Netdom is a very good tool to use to manage your domain, and there are certain tasks that only Netdom can fulfill. In terms of joining computers to the domain, PowerShell can help you if you need to add multiple computers to a domain or even if you need to remotely add workgroup computers to the domain. The basic command to add a Windows 2012 server named Server01 to the bigfirm.com domain is:

```
Add-Computer -ComputerName Server01 -LocalCredential Server01\Administrator
-DomainName "bigfirm.com" -OUPath "OU=Sales,DC=bigfirm,DC=com"-Credential
bigfirm\administrator -Restart -Force
```

You can run this command from a Windows Server 2012 domain controller and remotely join Server01 to the domain. If you run this command, you will be prompted twice for a password; the first prompt is to set the local administrator password (-LocalCredential parameter) and the second prompt is the account that needs permission in the domain to create the computer account (-Credential parameter).

Other Netdom Commands

Netdom includes many other commands that can be used to manage your domain. Check out the full online reference for Netdom at http://technet.microsoft.com/en-us/library/cc772217.aspx.

These are some other commands that may be of interest to you:

NetDom Reset   Resets a machine's account. Sometimes you will sit down at a system and be unable to log onto the domain because the machine has lost its domain account, or so it says. Sometimes just resetting it does the job.

NetDom Reset Pwd   Resets a machine's domain password. You must be sitting at the machine for this to run. If a machine has not connected to the domain for an extended period, it's possible that this account's password has expired, and this command can resolve the problem.

NetDom Remove   Removes a system from a domain.

NetDom query fsmo   Sometimes you need a quick way to find your Operations Master roles within your domain. Instead of clicking through different GUIs, just run this command and all your Operations Master roles will be displayed.

MANAGING THE DOMAIN TIME

The Kerberos authentication protocol used by Active Directory requires that all computers in the domain be synced with each other. If any computer becomes more than five minutes off from a domain controller, you will be able to connect to the network but all services might not work properly until the time is corrected.

Because of this, time synchronization is very important in a domain. Time synchronization is achieved through a hierarchy. It starts with the server holding the role of the PDC Operations Master (normally the first domain controller created in the domain) and extends to each system in a domain. You can check which server holds this role by following these steps:

1. Launch Active Directory Users and Computers.

2. Right-click the domain and select Operations Masters.

3. Select the PDC tab, as shown in Figure 7.28.

FIGURE 7.28

Operations Masters PDC tab

Ideally, the domain controller hosting the PDC role is configured to synchronize with a valid Network Time Protocol (NTP) source. The rest of the computers in the domain will get their time from this server.

- All domain controllers will synchronize their time with the time on the PDC.

- All computers and member servers will synchronize their time with the time on their authenticating domain controller.

- If a computer is specially configured so that it doesn't get its time from the authenticating DC, it should be synchronized with an NTP server just like the PDC Operations Master DC.

As long as the PDC has the correct time and users don't change the time on their systems, everything works well.

RESTRICT TIME CHANGES WITH GROUP POLICY

It is not uncommon for administrators to configure Group Policy to prevent users from changing the time and accidentally removing their systems from the domain. The System Time Group Policy setting is located in Computer/Policies/Windows Settings/Security Settings/Local Policies/User Right Assignment.

You will use the Windows Time Service (w32tm) to check and synchronize the time. W32tm is executed from the command-line.

You can use the following command to check five samples of current time against Microsoft's time server (at time.windows.com) and verify how accurate they are. The output will indicate whether the time on your server is ahead (indicated with a +) or behind (indicated with a -):

```
W32tm /stripchart /computer:time.windows.com /samples:5 /dataonly
```

You can synchronize the time on the PDC Operations Master using an internal time source if you have one or an external time source if not. If you synchronize with an external NTP server using the w32tm service, you will need to ensure that UDP port 123 is open.

Use the following command to have your system synchronize its time with an external time server. Several time servers are available, but this example is using Microsoft's time server (time.windows.com) and the NIST time server (time.nist.gov):

```
W32tm /config "/manualpeerlist:time.nist.gov,time.windows.com"/
syncfromflags:manual /reliable:yes /update
```

The `syncfromflags` parameter specifies that the server will synchronize with one of the servers in the `manualpeerlist` group. You can add just a single time server (and omit the quotes) or add multiple time servers separated by a comma, as shown.

It is also a good idea to restart the time service using the following commands:

```
Net start w32time
Net stop w32time
```

After you restart the service, you can use the earlier w32tm command to verify that the time is now accurate. If you change the time, it may take as long as five minutes before w32tm synchronizes again and resets the time to the proper time.

This section covered several maintenance tasks and techniques you will likely find useful to keep your network running. It is certainly not an all-encompassing list, but it should help you master some of the basics. A neat newer feature that can help you reduce the amount of maintenance you will need to do is *fine-grained password policies*. This feature allows you to set multiple password account lockout policies without creating a new domain.

FSMO ROLES AND HOW TO MOVE THEM

Active Directory holds the Flexible Single Master Operations roles (FSMO), which are used for different tasks within the forest and domain. There are two forest-wide roles and three domain-wide roles. Table 7.1 lists the role name, the scope, and its purpose.

TABLE 7.1:   FSMO roles

FSMO ROLE	SCOPE	PURPOSE
Schema Master	Forest	Hold the forest's schema
Domain Naming Master	Forest	Manage the domain names
Infrastructure Master	Domain	Ensure cross-domain object references
PDC Emulator	Domain	Responsible for the time in the forest
		Handle password changes
		Connection point for managing GPOs
		Account lockouts
RID Master	Domain	Manage and replenish the RID pools

In certain situations, for example, decommissioning a domain controller, upgrading the domain, or even for performance issues, you will need to move these roles to a new domain controller. Active Directory must have each of these roles available all the time. One way to migrate or move these roles to a new domain controller is using the NTDSUtil command.

To move the domain FSMO roles, follow these steps:

1. Open a command prompt (cmd.exe) and type **NTDSUtil**. Press Enter.

2. Type **roles** and press Enter.

3. Type **connections** and press Enter again.

4. Now you need to connect to the server that will hold the FSMO roles in the future. Type **connect to server [Servername]** and press Enter.

5. Type **quit** and press Enter.

6. First you will transfer the PDC Emulator role. Type **transfer pdc** and press Enter. You need to confirm your request by clicking Yes.

7. If needed, you can type **transfer rid master** and press Enter to move the RID Master role. You need to confirm your request by clicking Yes.

8. If needed, you can type **transfer infrastructure master** and press Enter to move the Infrastructure Master role. You need to confirm your request by clicking Yes.

9. Now that you have finished moving all domain FSMO roles, type **quit** and press Enter; then type **quit** again to exit to the command prompt.

Of course, you would need to repeat these steps for each domain.

If you decide to move the forest-wide FSMO roles, follow these steps:

1. Open a command prompt (cmd.exe) and type **NTDSUtil**. Press Enter.

2. Type **roles** and press Enter.

3. Type **connections** and press Enter again.

4. Now you need to connect to the server that will hold the FSMO roles in the future. Type **connect to server [Servername]** and press Enter.

5. Type **quit** and press Enter.

6. First you will transfer the Schema Master role. Type **transfer schema master** and press Enter. You need to confirm your request by clicking Yes.

7. If needed, you can type **transfer naming master** and press Enter to move the Domain Naming Master role. You need to confirm your request by clicking Yes.

8. Now that you've finished moving all forest FSMO roles, type quit and press Enter; then type **quit** again to exit to the command prompt.

After you have moved all your FSMO roles to the new domain controller(s), you might want to check to see if everything is the way you expect. We suggest that you run the **netdom query fsmo role** command in the command prompt, which will show you which domain controller holds which FSMO role.

Fine-grained Password Policies

Before you can implement fine-grained password policies, you need to ensure that your environment meets the minimum requirements.

◆   You have deployed a Windows Server 2012 domain controller to your domain.

◆   The domain functional level must be set to Windows Server 2008.

Only members of the Domain Admins group can create password-settings objects (PSOs).

Creating the Password Settings Object

In Windows Server 2012 you have a perfect GUI for creating the Password Settings objects. Under the hood nothing changed from Windows Server 2008 R2; the features are the same. However, it will be a great advantage to be able to manage the PSOs using the GUI, especially when it comes to typing time values as duration entries, because this was a big pain before.

You will create a PSO for the G_ITAdmins groups with the following steps:

1.   Start Active Directory Administrative Center by pressing WIN+R, open the Run dialog, and enter **dsac.exe** into the text box. Click OK. You can also start the Active Directory Administrative Center from the Start screen.

2.   Change to the tree view and scroll down to System/Password Settings Container.

3.   Right-click Password Settings Container and click New/Password Settings, as shown in Figure 7.29.

FIGURE 7.29
ADAC Password Settings Container

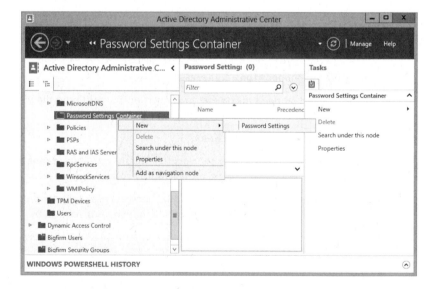

4.   Type **PSO_G_ITAdmins** and choose the value 10 for Precedence.

5.   Enforce a minimum password length of 15 characters.

6. Enforce a minimum password age of 30 days.

7. Enforce an account lockout policy with the number of failed attempts allowed set to 5.

8. Under Directly Applies To, click Add. Select the G_ITAdmins group and click OK.

9. Leave the rest of the settings at their default. You should see a dialog similar to the one in Figure 7.30.

FIGURE 7.30
Password
Settings

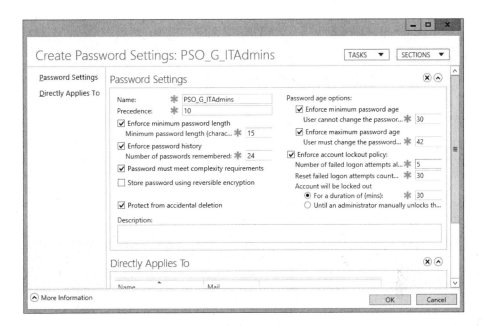

10. Click OK to close the dialog.

You should see now in your Password Settings container in Active Directory Administrative Center a PSO called PSO_G_ITAdmins.

Now you need some kind of proof that this PSO works and what settings you have. In our previous examples we created a user named Sally Smith. Let's assume that this user is an IT administrator, and therefore we are going to add Sally Smith into the G_ITAdmins group. Sally should now receive the new password settings; you can easily prove it by logging onto a server using the sally.smith account. Another way to see what kind of PSO rules are applied to a user is as follows:

1. Open Active Directory Administrative Center.

2. Navigate into the Sales OU where the user Sally Smith has been created.

3. Right-click Sally Smith, and click "View resultant password settings," as shown in Figure 7.31.

FIGURE 7.31
View resultant
password settings

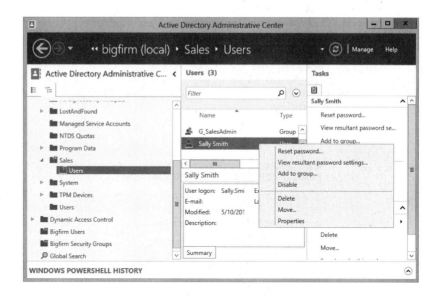

4. The PSO_G_ITAdmins dialog opens and you can see the PSO object that applies to Sally Smith.

5. Click OK to close the dialog.

It is important to know that you can link PSOs to other groups in addition to global security groups. However, when the Resultant Set of Policy (RSOP) for the user object is determined, only those PSOs are considered that are directly linked to the user object or the global security group that the user is member of. PSOs linked to distribution groups or other security groups are ignored.

Password Settings Object Precedence

In the previous example you configured several password settings that are set up similarly to those in the Default Domain Policy in your domain. There is one more setting to look at. In the PSO configuration dialog shown in Figure 7.30, you can configure the Precedence parameter. This identifies which PSO will take precedence, if multiple PSOs apply to a user.

Let's take the G_ITAdmins group and apply two PSOs, one with precedence of 10 and one with precedence of 5. The PSO with precedence of 5 will win, because a lower precedence value is a higher precedence.

This makes sense if you are just using groups and apply the PSO to the group level. But what happens if you apply a PSO to the group G_ITAdmins (Sally Smith is still a member) and you apply a PSO directly to Sally Smith?

Let's take the G_ITAdmins group again, where Sally Smith is a member, and apply a PSO with a precedence of 10. Create another PSO with a precedence of 15 and apply this PSO directly to the user Sally Smith. The PSO directly applied to Sally will win, although the precedence value is higher.

The way that the PSO applied is determined is as follows:

A PSO that is linked directly to the user object is the resultant PSO. If no PSO is linked to the user object, the global security group memberships of the user—and all PSOs that are applicable to the user based on those global group memberships—are compared. The PSO with the lowest precedence value is the resultant PSO.

SYSVOL: Old and NEW

The really cool thing about Active Directory back in the year 2000, and still cool today, is that Active Directory is a distributed database. It can have more than one domain controller that houses a writable copy of the directory database, thus eliminating the need for primary (writable) and secondary (nonwritable) servers. Inside each Active Directory domain controller were a couple of folders, which were public-facing shares, used to provide access and replication capabilities for the various domain controllers throughout the domain. The directory that stored and made these shares available was titled SYSVOL. It contains netlogon shares (logon scripts and Group Policy objects for client computers in the domain), user logon scripts, Windows Group Policy, File Replication Service staging, folders and files for synchronization, and file system junctions.

This section addresses the following topics:

♦ Introduction to the File Replication Service

♦ Migration to Distributed File System Replication

♦ Discovering the current migration state of a domain controller using the `dfsrmig` command

The Old: File Replication Service

Often when we consider something in the world of technology as old, there is a negative connotation associated with it. In this case, the old stuff simply makes reference to the way that something has been done in the past. In this particular case, the changes made to SYSVOL, in Windows Server 2008 R2 and also in Windows Server 2012, are encompassed in a new methodology for conducting replication of SYSVOL materials between replication partners throughout the domain.

DID FRS CHANGE IN WINDOWS SERVER 2012?

No. FRS works the same way as in Windows Server 2008 R2, but its successor is called DFS-R.

The new way of using Distributed File System Replication (DFS-R) has some significant improvements over the old File Replication Service (FRS) method, but that doesn't necessarily mean the old way is bad. In fact, all versions of Active Directory with the exception of Windows Server 2008 R2 and Windows Server 2012 use the "old" method. It is worth exploring and gaining an understanding of FRS because it is so prevalent on the networks to which you will add Windows Server 2012.

Before you start using the cool new features of DFS Replication, it is important that you understand FRS and its functionality so that you can easily migrate from FRS to DFS-R. But when do you need to upgrade? If you're upgrading from Windows 2003 to a Windows Server 2012 domain or if you are upgrading a Windows 2008 (R2) domain that has not yet implemented DFS-R and you are going to upgrade to Windows Server 2012 domain. FRS replication uses something called file system junctions to maintain the integrity of the SYSVOL folder. You will want to understand the operation of FRS and some of the operations associated with FRS replication. Each domain controller that runs FRS contains the following shares and components of SYSVOL:

- Netlogon shares
- User logon scripts
- Windows Group Policy
- FRS staging folders and files
- File system junctions

File system junctions are used extensively throughout the SYSVOL structure. They are a feature of the NTFS version 3.0 file system. That's the same file system that was released with Windows Server 2000. Junction points work to eliminate data loss or corruption that can occur when you modify the SYSVOL structure.

SYSVOL uses junction points to manage a single-instance store. A single-instance store is place where a single copy of the content is used by multiple consumers for example computers. Junction points are also referred to as reparse points. A junction point is a physical location on a hard disk that points to a piece of data that is located somewhere else on your hard drive or on some other physical storage device. In a single-instance store, the physical files exist only one time on the file system; however, in SYSVOL, the file exists in SYSVOL\staging\domain or in SYSVOL\enterprise and SYSVOL\staging\enterprise. These additional directory structures are the reparse points that redirect file input and or output to the original locations.

This configuration of junction points/reparse points maintains the data consistency by making sure that a single instance of the data exists. This configuration also permits more than one access point for a given piece of data. The idea is that you get data redundancy without data duplication. Junction points graft the namespace of the destination file system to the local NTFS volume. An underlying reparse point permits NTFS to transparently remap an operation to the destination object. The result is that if you modify the data in the SYSVOL structure, the changes will occur directly on these physical files. If you were to perform a cut-and-paste operation, for example, in the SYSVOL structure that contains the junction points, then the operation would occur in the junction point.

UNDERSTANDING FILE REPLICATION SERVICE

FRS was released with Windows 2000 Server to replicate Distributed File System (DFS) folders and the SYSVOL folder. It replicates files and folders stored in SYSVOL on domain controllers and DFS shared folders. When FRS sees that a change has been made to a file or folder within a replicated share, then FRS will automatically replicate the updated folder to the other servers. FRS is a multimaster replication service, meaning any of the servers that participate in the replication can trigger updates and subsequent replications and can also resolve conflicts among both files and folders to maintain data consistency among the servers participating as replication partners. FRS keeps data synchronized across multiple servers and enables networks to increase the availability of data to their clients. If a single server becomes unavailable, the files and folders are still available because they exist on another server. FRS is good at replication in geographically dispersed wide area network environments because data can be synchronized to each physical location, which can eliminate the need for clients to use the WAN for access to information from SYSVOL or DFS. FRS is probably most commonly known for its role in replicating SYSVOL data between domain controllers in a domain. Each domain controller has a SYSVOL folder structure containing files and folders that must be available and synchronized between domain controllers in a domain. The netlogon share, system policies, and Group Policy settings all are part of the SYSVOL structure and need to be replicated to each of the domain controllers for the domain.

BENEFITS OF REPLICATION WITH FRS

When you make additions, modifications, or deletions to SYSVOL, the FRS will take over and replicate those changes to the other domain controllers in the domain. FRS has some benefits that it implements when replicating data between servers, including the following:

Encrypted RPC   FRS uses Kerberos authentication for authenticating remote procedure calls (RPCs) to encrypt the data that is sent between members of a replication partnership.

Compression   FRS compresses files in the staging folder using NTFS compression. Files that are being sent across the network between replication members are sent in their compressed form to save network bandwidth.

Conflict Resolution   FRS resolves conflicts with files and folders to make the data consistent among replica members. If two identically named files are created or modified, the FRS uses a simple rule to resolve the conflict. The rule is called "last writer wins." FRS will simply take the most recent update and use that as the authoritative file and will then replicate this version of the file to the other members of the replication partnership. Now if two identically named folders are created on separate servers, FRS will identify the conflict and use a different methodology to resolve the conflict. In this case, FRS will rename the folder that was most recently created and replicate both folders to the replication members. Using this strategy, an administrator is then able to manually resolve the conflict without potential data loss.

Continuous Replication   FRS provides continuous replication between members of replication groups. FRS changes are replicated within three seconds of the change being made.

Fault-Tolerant Replication Path   FRS does not use broadcasts to replicate. It can provide multiple paths for connection between servers. If a replica member is unavailable, then FRS will send the data on a different path. FRS prevents identical files from being sent more than once to any replica member.

Replication Scheduling   One of the cool things about FRS is that you can schedule replication to occur at specified times and intervals. This really comes in handy when it is necessary to replicate data across WAN links. You can schedule the replication to occur during off-peak hours on your WAN line.

Replication Integrity   FRS maintains replication integrity using update sequence numbers to log changes to files on a replica member. FRS is able to manage replication even if one of the replica members is shut down without notice. When the member comes back online, FRS will replicate changes that happened in the member's absence as well as updates made to local files on the member before the shutdown. In pre-Windows 2008 environments, FRS is used primarily in two network situations, DFS and SYSVOL replication. FRS can be used to keep data in DFS hierarchies synchronized among replica members in the replication topology. FRS and DFS are independent technologies, and DFS does not require FRS. You could use other replication methods to ensure the DFS members were kept up to date.

In pre-Windows 2008 environments, FRS is used primarily in two network situations, DFS and SYSVOL replication. FRS can be used to keep data in DFS hierarchies synchronized among replica members in the replication topology. FRS and DFS are independent technologies and DFS does not require FRS. You could use other replication methods to ensure the DFS members were kept up to date.

SOURCE MATERIAL

Much of the information in this section and the next is taken from Microsoft's TechNet website:

```
http://technet.microsoft.com/en-us/library/cc781582(v=WS.10).aspx
```

Please see that site for additional information.

FRS REQUIREMENTS AND DEPENDENCIES

SYSVOL replication is handled by FRS. FRS replicates SYSVOL using the topology generated by the Knowledge Consistency Checker (KCC) and also has its own Active Directory objects that are replicated using Active Directory replication. The KCC is responsible for building the Active Directory replication topology. It uses a highly sophisticated algorithm to calculate the most efficient way to build the connection objects between the domain controllers.

WHAT ABOUT AD?

It is important to remember that although FRS is used to replicate SYSVOL, it is not used as the mechanism for replicating Active Directory. There are two parts that need to be replicated. One part is the content of Active Directory, such as users, computers, and groups, and the other part is the content of the SYSVOL directory, such as group policies. FRS is used only for replicating the SYSVOL part and not the Active Directory part.

FRS does have some requirements and dependencies in order to operate:

Active Directory Replication   FRS requires Active Directory replication to be functioning properly so that the FRS objects in Active Directory reside on all domain controllers in the domain.

DFS   If you are going to use FRS to keep data synchronized in folders on separate physical servers, you must first build a DFS namespace. (This does not apply to replicating SYSVOL.)

DNS   FRS requires an operational DNS infrastructure. FRS uses DNS for name resolution services for the replica members.

Kerberos Authentication   FRS requires a functioning Kerberos environment.

NTFS   FRS uses the USN journal in NTFS volumes to identify changes or updates to files.

Remote Procedure Calls   FRS requires both traditional IP connections and RPC to communicate with replication members and domain controllers in the domain.

WHAT IS THE FUTURE OF FRS?

FRS is going to die in the near future. Windows Server 2012 still supports SYSVOL replication with FRS, but it is an old technology and its future is DFS-R, which has many advantages over FRS. If you install a brand-new Active Directory on Windows Server 2012, you'll get DFS-R right after promoting your server.

FRS IN WINDOWS SERVER 2012 R2

The File Replication Service is deprecated in Windows Server 2012 R2 but is still available. Now that this feature has been declared as deprecated by Microsoft, it is time start planning to use DFS-R.

The New: Distributed File System Replication

As you learned earlier in this chapter, FRS has been used since the inception of Active Directory on Windows Server 2000 for SYSVOL replication to domain controllers throughout the Active Directory domain. Windows Server 2008 R2 introduced a new option for replicating SYSVOL throughout the domain called Distributed File System Replication. This option is continued in Windows Server 2012. DFS-R is a state-based, multimaster replication engine that supports replication scheduling and bandwidth throttling. DFS-R uses a compression algorithm known as Remote Differential Compression (RDC). RDC is a "difference over the wire" protocol used to update clients and servers over the network. RDC detects insertions, removals, and modifications of data files and replicates only the changes to its replication partners, instead of the entire files. RDC can provide significant improvements to the replication of SYSVOL between domain controllers in your domain.

UNDERSTANDING DFS-R

Many of you are familiar with the Distributed File System. DFS is used to provide a single transparent namespace in which users can access shared resources located in diverse target locations throughout the network. This DFS namespace can be hosted in multiple locations. As its name suggests, it is truly a distributed file system. DFS is not new to Windows Server 2012; it has been around for years. In fact, the DFS namespace is one of the two scenarios (along with SYSVOL replication) under which you will find FRS.

When Windows Server 2008 R2 was released, Microsoft updated the way in which DFS replicated files and folders. Instead of using FRS, it included a new feature with DFS called DFS-R. DFS-R replaces FRS in DFS, as well as in SYSVOL replication in Active Directory domains where the domain functional level is at least Windows Server 2008. RDC, described in the previous section, is great because as it detects changes in files and folders, instead of replicating the entire file or folder (which is what FRS did), it replicates only the changes made to the file or folder. RDC can save a tremendous amount of network bandwidth during replication. DFS-R uses replication groups to replicate files and folders. A *replication group* is really just a set of servers where each of the servers is called a *member* of the group. Each member participates in the replication of one or more replicated folders. A *replicated folder* is a folder that stays synchronized on each member of the replication group.

The topology, schedule, and bandwidth throttling for the replication group are applied to each replicated folder. Each replicated folder has unique settings, such as the file and folder filters, so that you can filter out files and subfolders for each replicated folder. DFS-R can be managed by using the DFS management tool or from the command line using DFSRADMIN, DFSRDIAG, DFSUTIL, DFSCMD, and DFSDIAG.

The gotcha with DFS-R is that your domain controllers need to be at least Windows Server 2008, Windows Server 2008 R2, or Windows Server 2012. If you are still running Window Server 2003, or heaven forbid Windows 2000, you will be stuck with FRS until you can arrange to migrate to the newer-version domain controllers and migrate to DFS-R.

WHAT'S NEW IN DFS-R WINDOWS SERVER 2012

The DFS-R in Windows Server 2012 doesn't contain many new features. The improvements are mostly limited to bug fixes and improvements in troubleshooting; it has also been made more resilient. To find detailed information on what's new see TechNet for impovement in Windows Server 2012, see http://technet.microsoft.com/en-us/library/dn270370.aspx and for Windows Server 2012 R2 http://technet.microsoft.com/en-us/library/dn281957.aspx

---

MIGRATING TO DFS-R

The requirement for using DFS-R is that your domain functional level be at least Windows Server 2008. This means a little more than getting all your domain controllers to Windows Server 2008 or higher. You would think you could just upgrade your Windows Server 2003 DCs to Windows Server 2008 or higher and you would be good to go. It just doesn't quite work that way. The migration process from FRS to DFS-R actually works through a number of states, during which SYSVOL replication transitions from FRS replication to DFS-R. The steps and states are clearly defined in the following section.

I really urge you to migrate your FRS replication to DFS-R. FRS is supported in Windows Server 2012, but there are rumors that FRS might not be supported in upcoming versions of Windows Server. Therefore, plan ahead and take these steps.

MIGRATION STEPS

The following migration steps for Windows Server 2012 are the same as they were in Windows Server 2008 R2. The migration process involves setting migration rules on the domain controller that is the primary domain controller emulator (PDC emulator) and waiting for other domain controllers to act on those rules. Migration states can be defined as local to the DC or global to the DCs in the domain. The global migration state is set with the `dfsrmig` command-line utility, which is used for setting one of the phases of the migration process. This setting is made in Active Directory and is then replicated to all domain controllers. Each domain controller has its own local migration state. DFS-R on each DC polls Active Directory to determine the global migration state to which the DC should migrate. If the global migration state is different from the local migration state, then DFS-R will attempt to move the local state to match the global state. The local migration state can be any one of the stable states or the transition states. The SYSVOL migration proceeds through four primary states (usually called stable states) and six temporary states (usually called transition states). The transition states lead a DC to the stable states.

There are four stable states, or phases, to SYSVOL migration from FRS to DFS-R. The states are called start, prepared, redirected, and eliminated. They are also referenced by ordinal numbers from 0 to 3, respectively:

Start (state 0) Before the SYSVOL migration begins, FRS replicates the shared SYSVOL folder.

Prepared (state 1) FRS still replicates the shared SYSVOL folder that the domain uses, while DFS-R replicates a copy of the shared SYSVOL folder. This copy of SYSVOL is not used to service requests from other DCs.

Redirected (state 2) The DFS-R copy of SYSVOL becomes responsible for servicing requests from other DCs. FRS continues to replicate the original SYSVOL folder, but DFS-R now replicates the production SYSVOL folder that the DCs in the redirected state use.

Eliminated (state 3) DFS-R continues to handle all the SYSVOL replication. Windows deletes the original SYSVOL folder, and FRS no longer replicates SYSVOL data.

SOURCE MATERIAL

Much of the information of this section is taken from Microsoft's TechNet website:

> http://technet.microsoft.com/en-us/library/dd641052.aspx

Please see that site for additional information.

You use the `dfsrmig` command during the migration to step through the four stable states. Some visible changes occur during the process:

1. The migration process creates a copy of the SYSVOL folder. FRS replicates the original SYSVOL folder located at `c:\windows\SYSVOL`. DFS-R replicates the copy of the SYSVOL folder located at `c:\windows\SYSVOL_dfsr`.

2. The mapping of the SYSVOL shared folder changes from FRS to DFS-R. Originally the SYSVOL shared folder mapping, `c:\windows\SYSVOL`, is used for the information that is actively replicated by FRS. Later in the migration process, the SYSVOL shared folder location will be mapped to `c:\windows\SYSVOL_dfsr`, and the information actively used by Active Directory will be replicated by DFS-R.

3. The migration process will delete the original copy of the SYSVOL folder.

TRANSITION STATES

Each domain controller will also cycle through a series of transition states as they move from one stable state to another. There are five transition states, and the states are numbered from 4 through 9. The states each have names that explain exactly what is occurring during the transition:

◆ Preparing (state 4)

◆ Waiting for initial synchronization (state 5)

◆ Redirecting (state 6)

◆ Eliminating (state 7)

◆ Undo redirecting (state 8)

◆ Undo preparing (state 9)

Figure 7.32 shows the process of migration through the four stable states and the transition states involved between each stable state.

FIGURE 7.32
DFS-R migration states

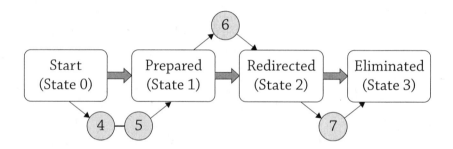

You are probably wondering exactly how DFS-R migrates between states. Remember that the DFS-R service on each DC polls Active Directory for the current global migration state. If the global state is different from the local state on the DC, then DFS-R takes steps (transitional states) to match the state of the global state.

When you are ready to migrate the domain controllers in your domain to DFS-R, all the domain controllers will begin at the start state. You will open a command prompt and use the dfsrmig tool to move your domain controllers from the start state to the eliminated state. The cool thing about this migration process is that not only can you move forward through the migration process, but you can also go backward if need be, as long as you have not completed step 3, the elimination. For example, maybe you are working along and your DC is at the prepared state and you decide you need to move back to the start state, for whatever reason. You can use the dfsrmig tool and change the state back to start. It is important to know that once you have moved to state 3, there is no going back. The migration will be complete at that point. The original SYSVOL will be deleted. There is no going back from eliminated. You will want to methodically move from state to state as you migrate from FRS to DFS-R.

Migrating to the Prepared State

Before you actually get to the process of migrating anything, you will need to meet some requirements. Remember that in order to use DFS-R, your domain will need to be raised to the functional level of Windows Server 2008. This means that each of your domain controllers will need to be Windows Server 2008, Windows Server 2008 R2, or Windows Server 2012. If you are still using domain controllers from the 2000 or 2003 families, you are not quite ready for DFS-R. Once again, Windows Server 2012 is still supporting FRS, but it is not certain that FRS will be deprecated in upcoming Windows Server versions.

Verifying Active Directory

Before you raise the domain functional level to Windows 2008, you should check the health of Active Directory and verify that the existing SYSVOL is replicating correctly. If Active Directory replication is not working the way it should, then you need to take care of that problem before you try to migrate. A failure on a single domain controller could be perpetuated to the rest of the domain. This is your chance to address any existing issues with AD. Do the following:

1. Microsoft recommends that you use the `net share` command to verify that the SYSVOL folder is shared by each domain controller and that this share folder still maps to the SYSVOL folder that FRS is replicating. When you type the `net share` command, the output will display the share names for the netlogon share and the SYSVOL share along with their respective current directory locations.

2. You will want to make certain that you have sufficient disk space to make a copy of your SYSVOL folder structure.

3. Use the Ultrasound tool to monitor FRS and verify its functionality. It can be downloaded free of charge at `http://www.microsoft.com/en-us/download/details.aspx?id=3660`.

4. On one of the domain controllers of the domain, open a command prompt, and type `repadmin /replsum`. This command will verify that Active Directory replication is working properly. The output should not indicate any errors. If it does, take the opportunity to correct them before you continue.

5. Open a command prompt, and type **DCDIAG**. This will perform several checks on your system. The output should not indicate any errors. If it does, take the opportunity to correct them before you continue. If you want to run DCDIAG for a remote server, type **DCDIAG /s:DC02.bigfirm.com**. This will run the utility for DC02.bigfirm.com.

6. Using the Registry editor on each domain controller in the domain, navigate to HKEY_LOCAL_MACHINE\System\CurrentControlSet\Services\Netlogon\Parameters, and verify that the value of the SYSVOL Registry entry is *drive*:\windows_folder\SYSVOL\SYSVOL and that the value of the SYSVOLReady Registry entry is set to 1.

7. On each domain controller, go to the Services tool, and verify that the DFS Replication service is started and that the start-up type is set to Automatic.

Raising the Domain Functional Level

Now that you have taken the steps to ensure the functionality of Active Directory, FRS, and SYSVOL, and you have checked the Registry for the correct entries and settings, you are ready to raise the domain functional level to Windows Server 2008. To raise the domain functional level to Windows Server 2008, perform the following steps:

1. Open Active Directory Administrative Center.

2. Right-click the domain, and click Raise Domain Functional Level.

3. In the Domain Functional Level box, select Windows Server 2008.

4. Click OK.

5. In the warning message box, click OK.

6. In the confirmation box, click OK.

Each time you move from one state to the next, you will do a series of verification activities. Once these activities are complete, you move to the next state. In this case, you have verified Active Directory and SYSVOL for functionality. You have checked the Registry Editor and raised the domain functional level. There is one detail left before you make the migration to the prepared state, and that's making a backup. At this point, it is time to make certain that you have a good current backup of your system state data. If things go really, really wrong, you want to be able to get back to this point. So, take a few minutes to make, and verify, a system state backup. Then you will be ready to migrate to the prepared state.

PERFORMING THE MIGRATION

The process of migrating from the starting state to the prepared state is a short one. You will need to open a command prompt and type the following command (see Figure 7.33):

```
dfsrmig /setglobalstate 1
```

At this point, you will need to verify that the global migration state has been updated. To do this, you will again use the command prompt and type the following command:

```
dfsrmig /getglobalstate
```

FIGURE 7.33
DFS-R set global state 1

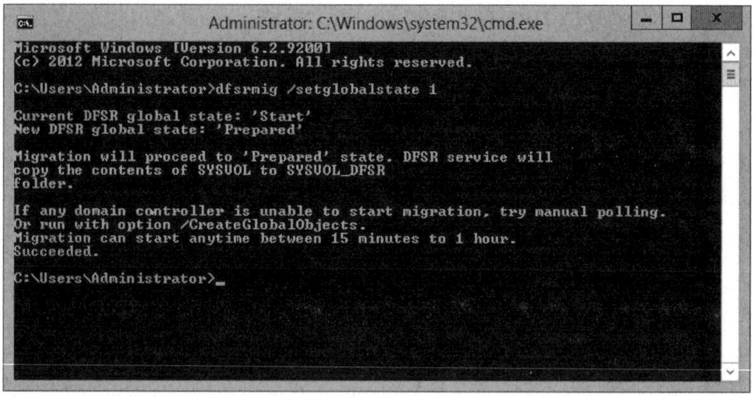

This command will return the current global state with a message indicating success (see Figure 7.34).

There is one last command to verify that all the domain controllers in the domain have moved to the prepared state:

```
dfsrmig /getmigrationstate
```

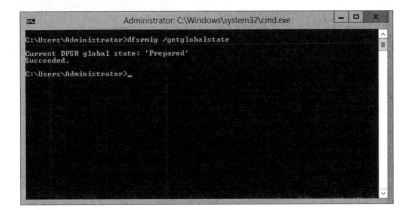

FIGURE 7.34
DFS-R get global state

Remember that this command can take some time before it comes back with the message that all domain controllers in the domain have migrated to the prepared state. Active Directory takes a while to replicate, so be patient. Now that you have set the process in motion for moving to the prepared state, you will want to verify that the domain has properly migrated to this state before you move to the next phase of the migration process. There are very simple steps you can perform to make certain you have successfully made the move to the prepared state:

1. On each domain controller in the domain, you can open a command prompt and type **net share** to verify that SYSVOL is shared by each domain controller in the domain and that the shared folder still maps to the SYSVOL folder that FRS is replicating.

2. Use the Ultrasound tool to verify that FRS on the original shared folder remains operational.

3. Check the file system, and verify the creation of the new SYSVOL_DFSR folder in the c:\ windows\SYSVOL_dfsr directory and that the contents of the original SYSVOL folder have been copied there (see Figure 7.35 and Figure 7.36).

4. Use the DFS management tool to generate a diagnostic report.

   If you do not already have the DFS management tool installed, you can add it as a feature in Server Manager under Manage ➢ Add Roles and Features ➢ Remote Server Administration Tools and File Services Tools ➢ DFS Management Tools.

FIGURE 7.35
Output from the getmigrationstate command

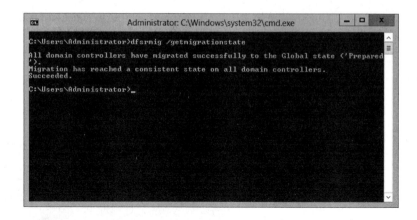

FIGURE 7.36
The new SYSVOL_DFSR folder

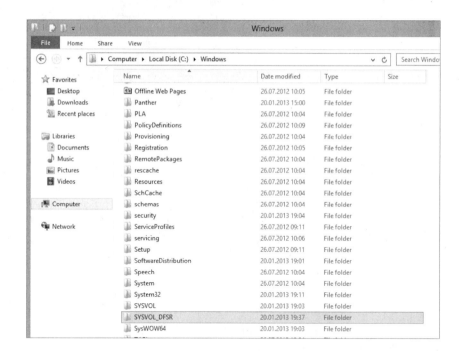

When you use the DFS Manager snap-in, it is possible to run two types of diagnostic reports called the Health report and the Propagation report. You should really run both of the reports and review them to check for problems (Figure 7.37). To generate these reports, use the following steps:

1. Open DFS Manager.

2. In the console tree under the Replication node, click Domain System Volume.

3. Click the Membership tab.

4. Click Membership Status.

5. Verify that the Enabled box is selected for a local path of `c:\windows\SYSVOL_dfsr\your domain`.

6. Right-click Domain System Volume.

7. Click Create Diagnostic Report.

8. When the Diagnostic Report Wizard opens, select the types of reports to run, and follow the steps of the wizard.

FIGURE 7.37
Creating a DFS Manager report

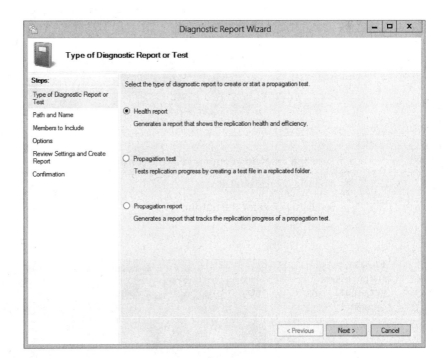

When you have verified the successful move of your DCs to the prepared state, you are ready to move on to the redirected state.

After verifying that your DCs are successfully working in the prepared state, you are ready to move them to the redirected state. In the redirected state, DFS-R will take on the responsibility of replicating the SYSVOL folder for the domain. There are two parts to this piece of the migration process. First you will migrate to the redirected state, and then you will verify that the domain has successfully migrated to the redirected state.

MIGRATING TO THE REDIRECTED STATE

To migrate the domain to the redirected state, you will perform the following tasks:

1. Type the following command at the command line:

   dfsrmig /setglobalstate 2

   See Figure 7.38 for the output.

FIGURE 7.38
Output of the
setglobalstate
2 command

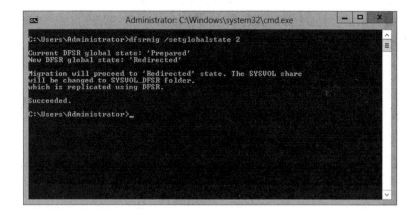

2. Type the following command at the command line:

   dfsrmig /getglobalstate

   See Figure 7.39 for the output.

FIGURE 7.39
Output of the
getglobalstate
command

3. Type **dfsrmig /getmigrationstate** to confirm that all DCs in the domain have reached the redirected state (see Figure 7.40).

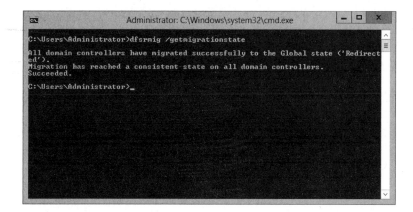

At this point, you have successfully completed the steps necessary to migrate the domain to the redirected state; however, before you move ahead to the eliminated state, you will want to verify that the domain has successfully moved to the redirected state. To verify successful migration into this state, you should do the following:

1. Open a command prompt, and type **net share**.

   The output of this command will show you the new SYSVOL_DFSR share in its authoritative state, as shown in Figure 7.41.

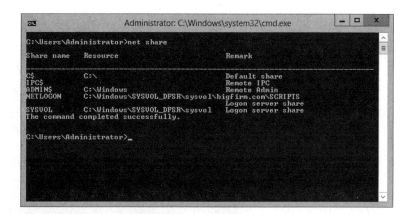

2. Use DFS Manager to create another set of diagnostic reports just like you did in the verification of the prepared state.

3. Use the Ultrasound tool to verify that the FRS replication of the original SYSVOL folder is healthy.

   You will recall that DFS-R is actually responsible for the domain replication of the new SYSVOL folder share; however, it is important to verify the functionality of the FRS replication process should you want to go back to the prepared state.

When you have verified that the domain controllers in your domain have successfully made the migration to the redirected state, you can make the final move to the eliminated state.

MIGRATING TO THE ELIMINATED STATE

You've come a long way, baby! It's time to make the last migration step in the move from FRS to DFS-R. At this point, all your domain controllers should be running happily in the redirected state. DFS-R is successfully replicating the SYSVOL shared folders, and FRS is faithfully keeping up its old SYSVOL shares. It's time to decommission, or in this case eliminate, FRS. There are a few things you will want to do before you actually move to the eliminated state. Remember, once you make this migration step, there is no going back. So, verify the redirected state once more to make sure everything is working:

1. Type the command **dfsrmig /getmigrationstate**, and make certain all your domain controllers are running in redirected state.

2. Type the command **repadmin /replsum** to verify that Active Directory replication is working properly. Make sure there are no errors.

3. Save the state of the Active Directory just in case you should need to recover from backup.

If you are satisfied that your domain is functioning as desired in the redirected state, then it is time to migrate to the eliminated state. Perform the following steps on the domain controller:

1. Type the command **dfsrmig /setglobalstate 3** (Figure 7.42).

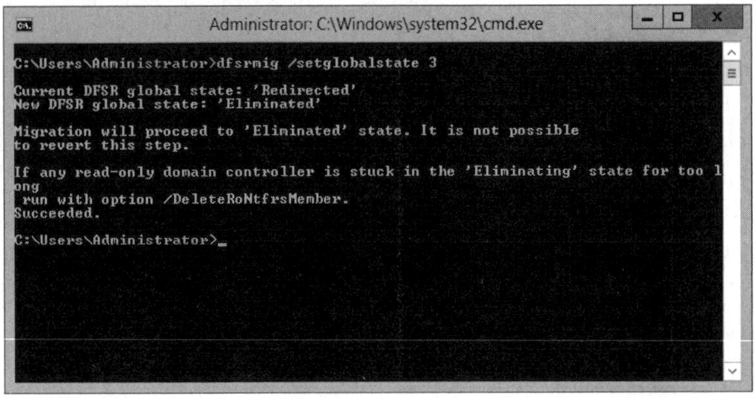

FIGURE 7.42
Output of
setglobalstate 3
command

2. Type **dfsrmig /getglobalstate** to verify that the global state is eliminated (Figure 7.43).

3. Type **dfsrmig /getmigrationstate** to confirm that all domain controllers in the domain have successfully migrated (Figure 7.44).

FIGURE 7.43
Output of
getglobalstate
command

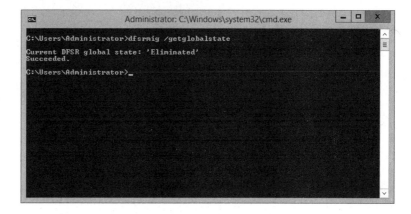

FIGURE 7.44
Output of
getmigrationstate
command

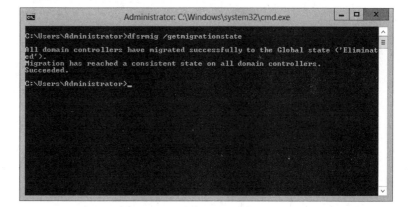

4. On each domain controller, open a command prompt and type **net share** to verify the SYSVOL shared folder location (Figure 7.45).

5. Use DFS Manager to generate the same general diagnostic and propagation reports you created in the prepared and redirected state verifications.

6. On each domain controller, open Windows Explorer and verify that the c:\windows\ SYSVOL shared folder has been removed.

FIGURE 7.45
Final output of the net
share command

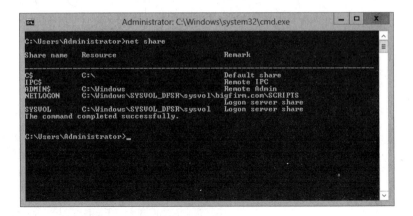

It is OK if some of the folders stay resident; however, you will want to ensure that they
are empty of any contents. The idea is to have only the new SYSVOL_DFSR structure, as
shown in Figure 7.46.

FIGURE 7.46
Eliminated state
file system with
no old SYSVOL
directory

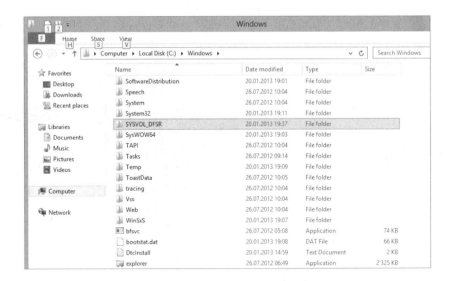

If you look at the Windows Services console, you will see that the File Replication Service has
been set to Disabled (Figure 7.47).

With that stroke, you have successfully migrated your SYSVOL replication infrastructure
from FRS to DFS-R and garnered all the benefits of remote differential compression. You have
taken something that is truly old in the SYSVOL folder and FRS replication and migrated it to
something new in SYSVOL_DFSR and DFS replication.

FIGURE 7.47
FRS is disabled
after migration.

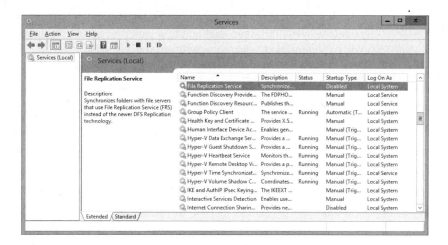

Upgrading Your Active Directory

Active Directory Server 2012 has arrived and you are anxious to get your current infrastructure up to the latest release because you want to stay current with your infrastructure.

Before, we assumed there was no existing network and we were going to build a new network from scratch. This is not the case in most situations. Active Directory has been around for over a decade and most companies have some version of Active Directory. As this section title says, we are going to focus on upgrading your domain to Windows Server Active Directory 2012. But before we can dive into this adventure, you need to understand the path we are going to take and what the prerequisites might be.

ARE YOUR SERVERS READY? NT SERVERS ARE NOT INVITED TO THIS PARTY!

There is no way for a Windows NT 4.0 domain controller to live near a Windows Server 2012 domain controller. Since Windows Server 2008 R2, there is no longer any support for NT 4.0 domain trusts, and you can't install a Windows NT 4.0 Server into a Windows Server 2012 domain. Besides that, Microsoft's support for Windows Server NT 4.0 ended years ago. Therefore, Windows Server NT 4.0 is probably the most unsecure system on this planet.

Upgrade the Schema to Windows Server 2012

In earlier versions of Windows Server, if you planned to upgrade your domain, you had to run a tool called adprep.exe. This tool would prepare and extend your forest schema to support new features, and it would also prepare your domain to create new groups and containers as needed. Additional options like /gpprep would prepare the domain to set the permission Group Policy objects for replicating to the Windows Server domain controller and /rodcprep would add support for the Read-only Domain Controller accounts.

We have good news and even better news. In Windows Server 2012 adprep.exe still exists in the \support\adprep directory on your Windows Server 2012 sources. But there is no 32-bit version of adprep.exe, only the 64-bit version, which you can run on a 64-bit Windows Server

2008 and higher. You don't have to run `adprep.exe` on a domain controller; you can run it remotely on a Windows server that is a member server of a domain or even a workgroup server. If you execute `adprep.exe /?`, you get all the available options.

If you need to extend your schema from a 64-bit Windows 2008 server, you need to type the following command:

```
Adprep /forestprep /forest w2k3domain.com /user administrator /userdomain
w2k3domain.com /password P@ssw0rd
```

After successfully extending the schema, you can run the following command to extend the domain:

```
Adprep /domainprep /gpprep /domain w2k3domain.com /user administrator /userdomain
w2k3domain.com /password P@ssw0rd
```

In order to extend the support for Read-only Domain Controllers you need to execute the following command:

```
Adprep /rodcprep /domain w2k3domain.com /user administrator /userdomain
w2k3domain.com /password P@ssw0rd
```

The better news is that you don't have to execute `adprep.exe` at all. In Windows Server 2012 there is a new Active Directory Domain Services Configuration Wizard, which you used earlier in this chapter to promote your first domain controller. This wizard is available after you have the Active Directory Domain Services role installed. The wizard takes care of all necessary steps you need to take to successfully promote your Windows Server 2012 member server to a domain controller. Microsoft has integrated `adprep.exe` into this wizard to make the promotion as comfortable as possible.

If you are going to promote your server and you have provided all the necessary information, once you click Install, the wizard checks the environment and prepares the forest, schema, and domain, as shown in Figure 7.48.

FIGURE 7.48
ADDSCW preparing the target domain

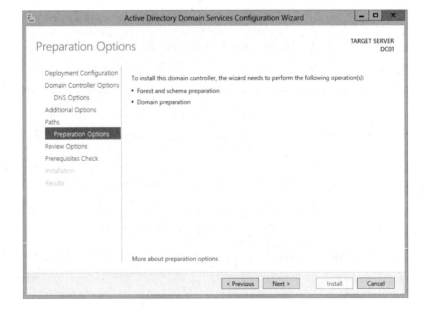

Figure 7.49 shows the wizard upgrading the forest, via `adprep /forestprep`.
Next, the wizard upgrades the domain, as shown in Figure 7.50, using `adprep.exe /domainprep`.

FIGURE 7.49
ADDSCW
preparing the
forest

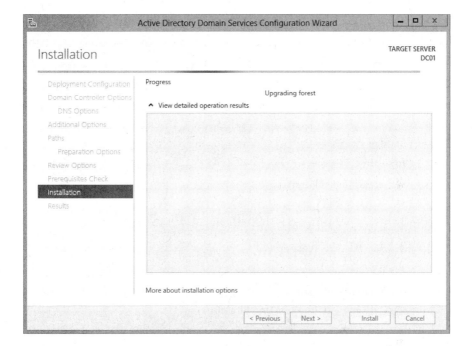

FIGURE 7.50
ADDSCW
preparing the
domain

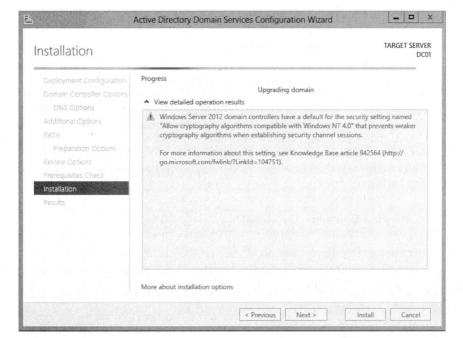

But why does Microsoft provide the adprep.exe tool and also implement it in the Active Directory Domain Services Configuration Wizard? It is because there are companies that need to document each step they perform on their infrastructure in a service-management or change-management system because it is required by their change-management process. In such a case, running adprep.exe from the command line gives you the opportunity to follow exactly what has changed.

If you don't have a change-management process in place, you can use the comfortable way of extending your forest or domain by doing all the work from the wizard.

NEW GROUPS IN WINDOWS SERVER 2012

In Windows Server 2012 Active Directory new groups are available that are created during the upgrade process.

In the BUILTIN container in ADAC or ADUC:

◆ Access Control Assistance Operators

◆ Hyper-V Administrators

◆ RDS Endpoint Servers

◆ RDS Management Servers

◆ RDS Remote Access Servers

◆ Remote Management Users

In the Users container in ADAC or ADUC:

◆ Cloneable Domain Controllers

Upgrade the Domain to 2012

Before we start talking about migration, we'll offer a bit of advice that quite frankly you would be crazy not to take. If you're migrating, then that means you probably already have a domain that currently works. You intend to convert this domain to a Server 2012–based AD domain that works. The scary part is in getting from the "before" to the "after." You'll really make people unhappy if you mess up along the way, because a working domain is better than no domain at all, and messing up along the way leaves you with a broken one. So, here's the advice: don't even think about starting your migration until you've tried the process on a test network. The availability of virtual technology makes the testing process quick and painless—almost a no-brainer.

There are three basic philosophies of migrating to a Windows 2012 domain:

In-place Upgrade This would be conducted through the setup process of installing the Windows Server 2012 operating system on top of an existing 64-bit Windows domain controller.

Swing Migration A Windows Server 2012 member server is promoted and becomes a domain controller in the existing domain. This is referred to as an Active Directory upgrade or domain migration.

Clean and Pristine Migration A "pure as the driven snow" Windows Server 2012 Active Directory is created. User accounts, groups, and computers are migrated into this new domain with the use of tools, such as the Active Directory Migration Tool (ADMT). The latest released version is 3.2.

These approaches are explained in detail in the following sections.

MIGRATING WITH AN IN-PLACE UPGRADE

An in-place upgrade means installing a Windows Server 2012 installation over an existing domain controller. The upgrade process is more or less a Next, Next, Finish job. But as easy it may sound, there are some consequences you have to be aware of. Everything in the domain will stay more or less the same. That means users, computers, and groups are not touched, and all are happy that not much has changed. But the downside might be that all the good things and the bad things are carried forward and stay the same. Or some applications that are installed on the system are not compatible. If something goes wrong, it could hit you really hard because the upgrade is more or less an all-or-nothing step. Therefore, make sure you have a tested backup available. Even though Microsoft assures you that nothing should go wrong, Murphy might be sitting in the corner waiting for you.

It is important to know that all the roles that are installed on the domain controller will also be upgraded. This means that if you have, for example, DNS and DHCP roles installed on your system, these roles will be also upgraded to the Windows Server 2012 versions.

If you decide to do an in-place upgrade of your domain controller, you need to know which version of Windows Server you can actually upgrade.

Domain controllers that run 64-bit versions of Windows Server 2008 or Windows Server 2008 R2 can be upgraded to Windows Server 2012 (as shown in Table 7.2). There is no way to upgrade domain controllers that run Windows Server 2003 or 32-bit versions of Windows Server 2008. To replace them, you must install domain controllers that run Windows Server 2012 in the domain, and then remove the domain controllers that run Windows Server 2003.

TABLE 7.2:   Upgrade Path

IF YOU ARE RUNNING THESE EDITIONS...	YOU CAN UPGRADE TO THESE EDITIONS...
Windows Server 2008 Standard with SP2	Windows Server 2012 Standard
or	or
Windows Server 2008 Enterprise with SP2	Windows Server 2012 Datacenter
Windows Server 2008 Datacenter with SP2	Windows Server 2012 Datacenter
Windows Web Server 2008	Windows Server 2012 Standard
Windows Server 2008 R2 Standard with SP1	Windows Server 2012 Standard
or	or
Windows Server 2008 R2 Enterprise with SP1	Windows Server 2012 Datacenter
Windows Server 2008 R2 Datacenter with SP1	Windows Server 2012 Datacenter
Windows Web Server 2008	Windows Server 2012 Standard

Before considering doing an in-place upgrade, you need to check several requirements of Windows Server 2012:

◆ Make sure your server hardware supports 64-bit operating systems.

   Because Windows Server 2012 is available only in 64-bit, there is no way to use 32-bit hardware.

◆ The minimum hardware requirement for Windows Server 2012 is a 1.4 GHz 64-bit processor, 512 MB RAM, 32 GB free disk space, and a screen resolution of 800 × 600. These requirements are probably easy to meet nowadays.

◆ It only makes sense to do an in-place upgrade of a server that has an estimated additional life cycle of three to four years. Make sure you get also hardware vendor support for the lifespan of the server.

◆ Verify that each piece of software installed on the server is supported by Windows Server 2012, especially antivirus software, hardware drivers, and applications. If you try to fix incompatibility issues during the upgrade, you could get in big trouble. If you are not sure, we recommend removing the antivirus software before the upgrade and reinstall it after a successful upgrade.

◆ Make a backup of the domain controller and system state.

UPGRADE PATH FOR WINDOWS SERVER 2012 R2

It is important to note that Windows Server 2012 R2 does not allow you to upgrade from Windows Server 2008 SP2 anymore. You need at least Windows Server 2008 R2 SP1 to upgrade from.

If you need to upgrade from Windows Server 2012 Datacenter, you can upgrade to Windows Server 2012 R2 Datacenter. If you have Windows Server 2012 Standard installed, you can upgrade to Windows Server 2012 R2 Standard or Windows Server R2 Datacenter.

The minimum requirements for Windows Server 2012 R2 are the same as for Windows Server 2012.

As a best practice I recommend backing up the entire C:\ partition and system state. To create the backup, I highly recommend making backups using two different backup tools. First, back up the C:\ partition and system state using your company backup tool that you have in place. For the second backup, use the Windows internal backup tool to back up the boot partition and system state. The reason is that in case of problems Microsoft used to support only backups done by their own utility.

At this stage you have verified that your system is ready for upgrading and that you have valid backups. The next steps are to make sure that your domain controller does not have any errors or replication problems.

To verify the domain controller's health state use `repadmin` to check the replication by running the following command:

```
repadmin /replsum /bysrc /bydest /sort:delta
```

This command will show replication errors in your domain sorted by replication source and replication destination and largest delta of replication. If the output shows any errors, try to fix the problems in advance.

AD REPLICATION STATUS TOOL

In 2012 Microsoft released the AD Replication Status Tool. This is a small GUI-based tool that can be installed on a Windows client or Windows server operating system. This tool allows you to analyze the replication status for the domain controller in your domain or forest. It easily shows you any errors and allows you to export the results to a CSV or XPS file for further analysis. You can download it here: http://www.microsoft.com/en-us/download/details.aspx?id=30005.

On your domain controller run the command DCDIAG and make sure all tests are passed. DCDIAG needs to be installed separately on Windows Server 2003. The source suptools.msi can be found on the source media in: \support\tools.

If all tests pass, open Windows Event Viewer on your domain controller, look into the event logs for any errors or warnings, and try to fix the problems.

Here's how to do an in-place upgrade from a 2008-based AD:

1. Prep the forest's schema to be compatible with Windows Server 2012.

2. Prep the domain for Windows Server 2012.

3. Run the setup program to upgrade the domain controller.

PREPPING THE FOREST/SCHEMA AND DOMAIN

During an in-place upgrade, not all domain controllers must be Windows Server 2008. However, some FSMO roles must be located on this system. The domain naming master of the forest, which is by default the first domain controller in the forest, must be Windows Server 2008. The PDC emulator of each domain within the forest is required to be Windows Server 2008 as well. These by default are the first domain controllers in each domain. It is recommended to start the upgrade process on a domain controller that doesn't hold any FSMO role. If the domain controller that you want to upgrade currently holds an FSMO role, you can move the FSMO role and then, after a successful upgrade, move the role back to the new Windows Server 2012 domain controller.

In addition, all domain controllers need to be running Windows Server 2003 or higher. Also, the domain functional level is Windows 2003 native or better.

Before you upgrade even one domain of your Windows Server 2003/2008 forest to Windows Server 2012, you have to change your entire forest schema to Windows Server 2012. You will do that on the forest's schema operations master FSMO role. Pop the Windows Server 2012 Setup CD into the computer's CD drive, open a command prompt, and navigate to the support\ adprep directory on whatever drive holds the CD. So, for example, if your CD drive is drive D, you would open a command prompt, type **D:**, and press Enter; then you would type cd \ support\adprep and press Enter again. Adprep.exe is compiled in only 64-bit. There is no longer a 32-bit version.

1. Run adprep on the schema master role by typing **adprep /forestprep**, and press Enter.

   A warning will appear verifying that all servers are running Windows Server 2003 or higher.

2. Confirm by typing **C** and then pressing Enter.

3. Next, on the infrastructure master role in your domain that you want to prepare, run adprep /domainprep /gpprep and press Enter.

4. Finally, run adprep /rodcprep on the infrastructure master role.

In step 1, when you extended the forest schema, you might have noticed while running the command that a lot of text appears and runs in a matrix style through your command prompt. This step imports all the necessary schema changes. If you have Exchange or Lync or any other application that needed a schema extension installed in the past, step 1 did not change or interfere with those schema changes.

Step 4 prepared the domain for Windows Server 2012 and changed the permission for Group Policy objects for replication with Windows Server 2012. As a last step, you added the opportunity to add a Read-only Domain Controller. It is a good idea to run adprep /rodcprep now because at a later time when you are back in production, it might require more effort to do this.

To summarize, before you can upgrade a Windows 2008–based AD domain to a Server 2012–based AD domain, you must do the following:

1. Apply Service Pack 2 to all Windows Server 2008 domain controllers and apply Service Pack 1 to all Windows Server 2008 R2 domain controllers to cover the upgrade requirements.

2. Upgrade the forest by running adprep /forestprep on the schema FSMO computer for your forest, even if that machine is not in the domain that you are going to upgrade.

3. Upgrade the domain structure by running adprep /domainprep /gpprep on the infrastructure FSMO for the domain that you are going to upgrade.

4. Optionally, run /rodcprep to prepare for read-only domain controllers.

RUNNING SETUP

Now you're ready to run Setup. Put in the DVD, double-click it in My Computer if it doesn't autostart, and select the Upgrade option. When you are asked about getting the latest updates, select this option so that you will have the latest updates available. The wizard will warn you about anything that will change in this upgrade. It will also check that you've forest-prepped and domain-prepped properly. Before you click Start, you will get a dialog showing any application or driver compatibility issues. If you accept the results, Setup runs hands-off, and there's nothing for you to do until it's done and you log onto your newly upgraded Server 2012 DC for the first time. At this point, you're upgraded!

IN-PLACE UPGRADES: PROS AND CONS

To summarize, the things in favor of in-place upgrades are the following:

◆ They don't require new machines.

◆ Your users keep their old SIDs, and the domain keeps its old trust relationships, so any servers in other domains—resource domains containing perhaps file and print servers or email servers, for example—will still recognize those users without trouble.

◆ The users keep their old passwords.

◆ It's a simple, quick upgrade.

◆ If you're going from 2008-based ADs to 2012-based ADs, then the upgrade seems pretty trouble free.

Although in-place upgrades have a lot going for them, we recommend that many people *not* do them. Here's why:

◆ The upgrade path is very limited. Windows Server 2012 is 64-bit only. Many organizations still have 32-bit domain controllers, so it may not be an option.

◆ It's all or nothing. You upgrade *all* the accounts, and it's a one-way trip—there's no AD rollback wizard. (However, you can, as we've suggested, restore the system state data.) We prefer more gradual approaches.

◆ Any leftover junk remains in your Active Directory database.

Migrating with a Swing Migration

A gradual and smooth step forward to your Windows Server 2012 domain is referred to as a swing migration. It is also widely known as an Active Directory migration. What you do is add a Windows Server 2012 member server to your domain and then promote this server to a domain controller. The Active Directory data is replicated, and you have your first Windows Server 2012 domain controller added. In this scenario everything stays the same except you add more servers. The downside of this procedure is that you will need more hardware if you install the server physically, or if you are going to virtualize, you will need more storage, memory, and CPU resources. This does not mean you will have more domain controllers because you can demote the old domain controllers. If you are not willing to spend money and resources, you also can install a spare server as a Windows Server 2012 domain controller and demote the old domain controller, and then after a successful demotion you can redeploy the server with Windows Server 2012.

This entire migration is a very safe way to upgrade your domain; you don't have an all-or-nothing situation. Although you need to extend the schema of the forest, I would not consider it a critical step.

Redeploying a domain controller can be a project on its own. Depending on which domain controller you are going to replace, you need to carefully plan each step. There might be dependent services, such as DNS, DHCP, FSMO roles, applications that query this domain controller, or file shares that depend on this domain controller. Therefore, you need to take time and get to know your environment very well.

PREPARING TO PROMOTE THE MEMBER SERVER

Before you promote your Windows Server 2012 member server to a domain controller, make sure the domain has a forest functional level of at least Windows Server 2003. If you are going to promote a Windows Server 2012 into a forest with a forest functional level of 2000, you will get an error.

PERFORM A SWING MIGRATION

A swing migration involves these basic steps:

1. Check your domain for errors.

2. Add the Active Directory role to the member server.

3. Run the Active Directory Domain Services Configuration Wizard with Schema Admin, Enterprise Admin, and Domain Admin permissions.

   The ADDSCW will automatically run adprep /forestprep and adprep /domainprep on the schema-respective infrastructure master.

4. Perform post-migration steps, such as placing FSMO roles, changing the IP address, and other changes.

5. Redeploy the source domain controller as necessary.

PREPPING THE FOREST/SCHEMA AND DOMAIN

As with the in-place upgrade, the existing forest and target domain need to be prepped for Windows Server 2012's Active Directory changes. ForestPrep, DomainPrep, and GPprep are required to be run as listed in the "Migrating with an In-place Upgrade" procedures.

The other way of extending the schema and domain is to start the Active Directory Domain Services Configuration Wizard right away. As we mentioned before, adprep.exe is integrated into the wizard, and it will take care of all the necessary steps. Whichever way you choose, the rollback procedures at this point of the game are the same as for the in-place upgrade. Restore the system state data on the schema master domain controller.

BUILDING A WINDOWS SERVER 2012 MEMBER SERVER

The target domain controller will start as a Windows Server 2012 member server in the original domain. In preparation, the Active Directory Domain Services role and DNS role must be installed prior to running the Active Directory Domain Configuration Wizard.

VERIFYING DNS

Since the new domain controller will support DNS, it should be added as a name server to the applicable forward and reverse zones. Once the member server is promoted as a domain controller, the DNS zones will be replicated.

To ensure proper name resolution of the domain controllers, the DNS resolution should be tested. Perform checks of the service resource records using NsLookup and DcDiag, which we covered earlier in this chapter.

PREPPING THE SOURCE DOMAIN CONTROLLER

You need to decide what will be done with the source domain controller prior to performing the operation. If the server is to remain in the domain as a domain controller, little needs to be done. If it will be redeployed, you must consider how to replace the network's reliance on this server.

The following data for the source server should be collected in order to apply similar settings to the target member server after the domain controller promotion:

◆   Server name.

◆   IP addresses (IPv4 and IPv6).

◆   Assigned Active Directory site.

◆   Assigned OU.

◆   Applied GPOs and RSOP output. You can type,

    gpresult /scope computer > GPOResult.txt

    to push the results to a text file.

◆   Assigned FSMO roles. These will be transferred if the server will be decommissioned.

◆   Global catalog role.

◆   Additional services, such as DHCP, file and printer sharing, and Internet Authentication Services for VPN connections.

Finally, perform system state data backups for all domain controllers and file system backups for essential services to be migrated outside Active Directory Domain Services.

PROMOTING THE MEMBER SERVER

The Active Directory Domain Services Configuration Wizard does the meat of the work. You should select the option "Add a domain controller to an existing domain" for the deployment configuration. Also, you should enable the options for the DNS and Global Catalog roles as required.

After the wizard has finished, a restart is performed and the DNS service should be configured on the target domain controller. Although the Active Directory integrated DNS zones have been replicated to the domain controller, the DNS service may not be showing them.

1.   On the source server, enumerate the DNS zones and application partitions:

     dnscmd /enumzones
     dnscmd /enumdirectorypartitions

2.   On the target server, enumerate the DNS application partitions and zones using the previous command.

3.   Compare the results between the two servers.

     If they are not listed, you can use the dnscmd /enlistdirectorypartitions command to force the new DNS server to start sharing the partitions. The zones should be listed since the domain controller is listed as a name server for the zones.

```
dnscmd /EnlistDirectoryPartition <FQDN of partition>
```

4. As a last step, examine the DNS server settings and configure them to your company standard.

POST-MIGRATION PROCEDURES

You should verify the domain services. You can perform tool-based tests with the Event Viewer, DcDiag, and NetDiag to see if there are any initial problems. You should perform user acceptance tests as well, such as attempting to log on and accessing network resources with the new domain controller as the available authentication service.

Given the plans for the migration process, you should perform the following:

◆ FSMO role transfers and GC assignment.

◆ IP address reassignment.

◆ Network name reassignment. The domain controller can be renamed using the System applet (sysdm.cpl) in Control Panel or the netdom renamecomputer command.

◆ For DNS, reassignment of the standard primary zones may be required.

GOOD TO KNOW...

After adding a Windows Server 2012 domain controller to an existing domain, you should transfer the FSMO roles to the newest domain controller.

REPURPOSING HARDWARE

The swing migration provides the opportunity to redeploy an existing domain controller as a Windows Server 2012 domain controller, although it may not have the correct upgrade path available. For example, you may have a domain controller capable of running both 64- and 32-bit versions of Windows Server. Remember, Windows Server 2012 comes in 64-bit only, so upgrading the original server wouldn't be possible.

This procedure requires an available virtual machine or hardware that can support Windows Server 2012. This spare machine provides an intermediate phase between the two Active Directory states. Follow these general steps:

1. Prep the forest/schema and domain.

2. Build a Windows Server 2012 member server on the spare machine.

3. Verify that DNS is supporting Active Directory adequately.

4. Prep the source server.

5. Promote the spare member server.

Similar to the post-migration procedures, you will want to ensure everything is stable within the network and that users can access resources.

6. Run `DCPromo` to uninstall Active Directory from the original domain controller. After that, it will be listed as a member server in the domain.

7. Build a Windows Server 2012 member server on the original hardware.

   You can use the same name and IP address of the original server as long as you delete the computer account in Active Directory.

8. Promote the member server to a domain controller.

9. Perform post-migration procedures including reviewing the FSMO placement.

   The spare domain controller may have FSMO roles assigned to it through the decommissioning of the source domain controller.

10. Once the domain and the domain controller services are validated, the spare can be decommissioned by removing the Active Directory Domain Services role or running the PowerShell command `Uninstall-ADDSDomainController`.

SWING MIGRATION: PROS AND CONS

To summarize, these are the benefits of swing migrations:

◆ They are gradual in implementation. Once the first Windows Server 2012 domain controller is introduced, the rest of the domain controllers can be upgraded or replaced as necessary.

◆ Your users keep their old SIDs and the domain keeps its old trust relationships, so any servers in other domains—resource domains containing perhaps file and print servers or email servers, for example—will still recognize those users without trouble.

◆ The users keep their old passwords.

◆ The swing migration offers the opportunity to redeploy Windows Server 2012 on the original server.

There are few disadvantages of this method. These are the most common pain points:

◆ More preparation and planning are required to ensure a smooth delivery.

◆ Any leftover junk remains in your Active Directory database.

Migrating with a Clean and Pristine Migration

The third approach is characterized as clean and pristine (C&P). In this approach, you leave your existing domains alone and create a new, empty AD domain. Then you use a migration tool to copy user and machine accounts from the old domain (or domains) into the new AD domain.

The advantage of this method is that it is gradual. The migration can span a period of time when testing can be conducted and issues can be resolved. During this time, users will still need access to their data. Access can be maintained by reassigning permissions or relying on the capability of SID history.

C&P Is Gradual

In specific cases, you need the C&P approach. For one thing, it's gradual if you need to restructure your forest. With an in-place upgrade, you walk your domain through a one-way door. If you find later that Server 2012–based ADs just aren't the thing for you, then too bad; you're stuck. But if you have a new domain and you copy some subset of your users over to that domain, then you just tell those users to log into this new domain. If they start using the new domain and you find after a week or two that the AD is just not the tool for you, then you can always just tell the users to go back to their old domain accounts.

Although the swing migration approach is gradual as well, the process still leaves the junk that may have contributed to the poor performance and issues that instigated the migration in the first place. Over time, unknowledgeable administrators can configure Active Directory in some manner that confounds the wise chaps who've read this book. These changes will still be there to work through after the domain is migrated to a later version.

The C&P approach also provides an intermediate phase that is not available with the other two. During this phase, you have the opportunity to test the process, proving users will be able to access their resources and uncovering some common issues that may arise with later production runs of the migration. This reduces the headaches and heart attacks that could arise upon crossing the threshold of the one-way door.

INTRA-FOREST MIGRATIONS

Keep in mind that these same processes are applicable to intra-forest migrations too. "Intra-what?" you might ask. This merely means within a forest. You learned in this book that the forest is a group of domains built in relation to each other.

Users, computers, and groups may need to be transferred to another domain within the forest. You migrate these objects from one domain to another domain "in the forest" using these procedures. The primary difference is that objects, like users and groups, must be moved rather than copied. The source user account is deleted after the target account is created. The ADMT is used to migrate the accounts back to the source domain in a rollback. New computer accounts are created in the new domain, but the old computer accounts are disabled for rollback purposes.

There are two combinations of objects that need to be migrated together. This is referred to as, closed sets.

Users and Global Groups   Global groups allow only users and other global groups from the same domain as members. When the user changes domains, it can't be a member of its original group. When a global group is moved, the members from the original domain are dropped as well. These need to be migrated together to maintain access within the limits of global group membership rules.

Resource Computers and Domain Local Groups   Resources cannot assign permissions to domain local groups from other domains. If the computer is migrated without the assigned domain local groups, the computer will not be able to "see" the group's SID on the user's security token to provide it access. As an alternative, you can opt to change the scope of the domain local group to universal, but this will impact the global catalog size.

HANDLING PERMISSIONS WITH THE NEW DOMAIN

Suppose you decide to go the C&P route. Since there will be an intermediate phase, you can expect that the users of the organization will be members of old domains or the new one. This will require users in the new domain to be able to access files and other resources in an old one. Straddling the two domains, the organization will be heavily dependent on the trusts between the domain controllers until all servers that hold the resources are on the same side as the users.

How will the users in the new domain maintain the same access to resources as they did in the old domain? Business continuity is a big-ticket item for management; they need to ensure their people will be able to get to their data. A seamless migration will minimize any access outages.

There are two approaches to maintain access to the resources: re-ACLing and SID histories. ACL stands for access control list, a techie term for the security tab of a resource like a shared folder. The SID is the security identifier, which is the unique number assigned to accounts to identify it within the permission structure. If you don't blink after opening the security tab of a file, you may see the SID listed on the ACL before the computer resolves the SID to a friendly display name.

 Real World Scenario

THE RANDOM HORDE AND THEIR JUNK

A group of venture capitalists acquired two IT private firms. The management of the newly formed corporation wanted to merge the two firms' Active Directory forests into one to provide a unified message system based on Exchange and reduce the administrative overhead.

The network environment of one firm seemed to be held together with duct tape and Super Glue. Unexplained system downtime was common, and performance slowed down after a few days of operations between reboots.

You might think that an IT firm would have been able to apply its expertise to its own environment. They had the know-how to deliver a top-of-the-line example of their services. However, did they have the time and money to do so? No.

As one employee explained, the environment was the result of a random horde. To address issues in an aging and piecemeal environment, part-time administrators and IT professionals provided stop-gap measurements. These in turn became the long-term solutions. Similar solutions existed in Active Directory. The number of user accounts tripled the number of actual employees. The number of computer accounts surpassed the number of actual computers as well. The undocumented VPN solution that relied on the original domain controller could not be reconfigured. (They lost the admin password.) Thus, an upgrade or swing migration would potentially collapse the remote users' tunnel into the network. A C&P approach was a must.

Re-ACLing the Server

One approach is the obvious (and somewhat laborious) way: just walk over to all those old servers and add Joe's new account to the permissions lists on those servers. This is called re-ACLing because the other name for a list of permissions on a network service is the access control list. It can be a real pain, but some migration tools will do that for you automatically.

Outside of the total excitement this process offers, especially when you may have to do this for 100+ shares for 100+ groups or users, the potential of error is high. The possibility of unintentionally removing access for one group, adding access to the wrong group, or forgetting to add another required group will ensure this to be a fun-filled adventure for all involved!

Using SID Histories

You know that every user has an SID. That's been true since NT 3.1. But under Windows 2000 native and Windows Server 2003 domain functional levels, Active Directory lets users keep more than one SID. As migration tools create the new AD user accounts, those accounts of course get new SIDs. But the migration tools can tack the user's old SIDs onto the new user account as well, exploiting a feature called SID history. Then, when a user tries to access some resource that he had access to under his old account, his workstation tries to log him in to that resource using his new Active Directory account.

As with all domain logons, AD builds a token for the user that contains both his user SID and the SIDs of any global and universal groups to which he belongs. Here's the trick to SID histories: AD says, "He's a member of a group with this SID," and sends along his old SID from the old domain! Even though it's a user account's SID, the AD domain controller passes the SID along as if it were a global group SID, and apparently this is acceptable. The resource, reviewing the token, says, "Hmmm…do I know any of these guys? Well, there's this user SID…nope, I don't know that guy…but wait, look, he's a member of the 'Joe from the old domain' group. I have an ACL for that 'group,' so I guess he's in." Thus, even though Joe is logged in as a person from the new group with a new SID, he's dragging the old SID around, and it gets him access to his old stuff.

Using this method is preferred over the re-ACLing method because the resources' permissions can remain unchanged. The key is ensuring that the SID history is recorded during the migration and the trusts do not filter them when the user is "crossing the trust" to access the resource.

WHAT YOU NEED TO CREATE SID HISTORIES

Several notes about SID histories are important:

◆ You need a migration tool that knows how to create SID histories. Microsoft's free Active Directory Migration Tool, which we'll cover a bit later in this chapter, can do that. Other migration tools are available, but you have to pay for them. Quest Software, for example, offers a suite of industry-approved migration tools.

◆ Migration tools create SID histories as they copy user accounts from older domains to your new 2003/2008/2012 functional level domain. (Remember, Windows Server 2012 can exist in these functional levels.) Before a migration tool can work, you must create a trust relationship between the old and new domains. But no matter which migration tool you have, your migration tool cannot create SID histories unless you have created that trust relationship with netdom or with ADDT's New Trust Wizard.

◆ When you create that new clean-and-pristine AD domain, make sure that it's already shifted into Windows Server 2012 functional level—after all, you're building a fresh new domain; you may as well get the most out of it—before creating the trust relationship and running the migration tool.

You can keep SID histories for quite a while, but SID histories are really just temporary measures, because you only need your old SIDs as long as your old domains are around. That probably won't be for long. Once you've moved all your servers and workstations out of the old domain, the old SIDs are of no value. So, it'd be convenient to be able to trim those old SID histories off your user accounts. You can do that with a short VBScript that Microsoft describes in Knowledge Base article 295758:

```
http://support.microsoft.com/kb/295758
```

Using Microsoft's Free Migration Tool: ADMT

If you're thinking about a clean and pristine migration, then you need a migration tool, and if you've priced migration tools, then you might be reconsidering a C&P. But you needn't, because Microsoft offers a migration tool called the Active Directory Migration Tool (ADMT). Originally written for Microsoft by NetIQ, ADMT v3.2 maintains the ease of use of the first version and adds some nice features as well.

CLEAN AND PRISTINE MIGRATION: PROS AND CONS

Here are C&P's advantages:

◆ C&P lets you do gradual upgrades.

◆ C&P *copies* user accounts; it doesn't *move* them. The old accounts are still there if something goes wrong.

◆ C&P lets you create your DCs from clean installs, avoiding the extra complexity and potential bugs of an in-place upgrade.

◆ C&P lets you consolidate domains, collapsing a morass of many domains into just one or just a few.

Although we've said that C&P has the advantage of reversibility, thus helping you manage your risk, it's not without costs:

◆ You need more machines than you would if you were just upgrading. You'll need machines to act as domain controllers in the new domain.

◆ Most migration tools cannot copy passwords. ADMT provides a separate service to install on the source domain for this. Otherwise, the users will have to create new passwords the first time they log into the new AD domain. This isn't a showstopper, but for a large remote workforce, this would cause heartache.

◆ You have to buy a migration tool. There *is* ADMT, but it's really intended for small-scale migrations of 1,000 users at best. These tools aren't cheap, starting somewhere in the neighborhood of $10 per user. That's *per user*, not per administrator.

◆ You cannot create an Active Directory domain with the same NetBIOS name or FQDN as the original domain, because that would require you to be able to create two domains with the same name (since you don't decommission the old domains when you do a clean and pristine migration).

◆ It's more work. You have to worry about when to move any given set of users and groups, you may have to re-ACL or translate local profiles, and so on.

VERSION INCOMPATIBILITY

At the time of this writing, ADMT 3.2 is the latest version for this tool. However, it is only compatible with Windows Server 2008 R2. When you try to install the Active Directory Migration Tool (ADMT) 3.2 on a Windows Server 2012 server, you receive the following error: "The Active Directory Migration Tool v3.1 must be installed on Windows Server 2008." ADMT 3.2 and PES 3.1 are not supported for installation on Windows Server 2012. The installers intentionally block unsupported operating systems. There is a Knowledge Base article about this problem:

```
http://support.microsoft.com/kb/2753560/en-us
```

What would be the recommended solution? Install ADMT 3.2 onto a Windows Server 2008 R2 in the target domain. To have a supported scenario you also need to install a Windows Server 2008 R2 as target domain controller in the new domain.

But what happens if you already specified a Windows Server 2012 forest functional level? Well, luckily you can lower the forest and domain functional levels to Windows Server 2008 R2 using two PowerShell commands.

First, you need to lower the forest functional level by executing:

```
Set-AdForestMode -identity bigfirm.com -forestmode Windows2008R2Forest
```

You need to confirm your input and wait a few seconds for the command to successfully finish. Next, you need to lower the domain functional level by executing this command:

```
Set-AdDomainMode -identity bigfirm.com -domainmode Windows2008R2Domain
```

Again, you need to confirm your command and after successfully lowering the domain functional level you can install a Windows Server 2008 R2 domain controller.

If you're already using Dynamic Access Control, then you will not be able to use this feature because Windows Server forest functional level 2012 is required.

An Example Migration Setup

To provide a basic run-through of this utility, we'll use this example: Bigfirm has purchased the OtherDomain company. OtherDomain is a Windows Server 2003 Active Directory domain. Bigfirm has built a clean-and-pristine Windows Server 2012 domain named Bigfirm.com for consolidating its domains into one. Microsoft has not published any new ADMT for Windows Server 2012; therefore, for compatibility Bigfirm also has a Windows 2008 R2 domain controller installed just for targeting with ADMT. After the migration, OtherDomain will decommission this domain controller. The forest functional level is set to Windows 2008 R2. The ADMT will be also installed onto a Windows 2008 R2 member server named ADMT01.

The administration department needs to be migrated from OtherDomain's Windows Server 2003 domain. The administration department shares a workstation (they don't get a lot of work done), and their user folders are located on the domain controller named DC2003. During the migration, the department members will need to access their home folders and log onto their workstation to perform their work until these are migrated to the new domain too. In this example, we'll cover the following:

◆ How to migrate user accounts and groups across two forests.

◆ How SID histories allow the migrated user to access resources on the old domain whose ACLs have not been changed.

◆ How ADMT can re-ACL the workstation in the old resource domain. This will also reassign the local profiles of the users to their new accounts.

◆ How ADMT can migrate member servers from the old domain to the new AD domain.

To make this work, we'll set up five systems—two in OtherDomain.local and three in Bigfirm.com. The two in OtherDomain.local are as follows.

We'll set up a DC for OtherDomain.local named DC2003. On DC2003, we'll create the following:

◆ A shared folder named Users with Everyone assigned Full Control permissions. The Active Directory Users and Computers snap-in will configure the NTFS permissions for the specific user accounts.

◆ An organizational unit named Administration.

◆ Domain user accounts for those dependable Administration people.

◆ A home folder mapped to the Z: drive with the UNC path of \\DC2003\ users\%username%.

◆ A global group named Administration Group and its members.

◆ A shared folder named Administration with the Administration Group assigned Full Control permissions.

◆ A Windows 7 client Win7 that needs to be migrated to the bigfirm.com domain.

The Bigfirm.com domain will contain three systems:

◆ A clean Windows Server 2012 domain controller DC01.

◆ A temporary Windows Server 2008 R2 domain controller, which is being used for ADMT as a target. Its name is W2K8DC.

◆ A Windows Server 2008 R2 member server of the domain where ADMT is installed. This server is called ADMT01.

To visualize the entire scenario see Figure 7.51:

FIGURE 7.51
Migration scenario

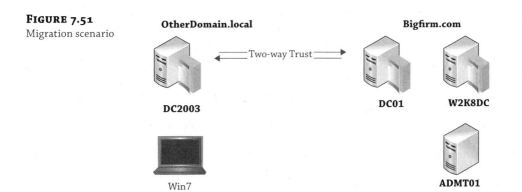

Establishing the Trust

Next, we'll establish the trust between the two domains. The quickest method for this example is using the Active Directory Domains and Trusts console (domain.msc). Use the New Trust Wizard for the following:

1. Specify the type of trust. An external trust is simple and effective for this procedure.

2. Specify a two-way trust. Accounts from each domain will need to access the other's resources.

3. Create the trusts on the other domain. This will require domain admin credentials on that domain.

4. Validate the trust to make certain things are working fine.

We like to stop and test things at this point—is the trust working, and are the permissions correct on DC2003? Since users and global groups from any domain can be members of domain local groups and member server local groups, we attempt to add a user from the opposite domain to a built-in group on the domain controller. This is a required step down the road. So, we search and add the Bigfirm\Administrator to the built-in Administrators group of OtherDomain in Active Directory Users and Computers.

But adding users to groups is not what we *really* want. We want the migrated accounts to be able to access resources in the opposite domain. This is where SID history comes into play. As stated earlier, the SID history is treated as another group on the security token that will be passed to the resource domain for access to the migrated accounts' resources. If you weren't paying attention to the New Trust Wizard and clicked every Next and OK button like a mind-numbing automaton, then you may have missed the window shown in Figure 7.52.

FIGURE 7.52
SID filtering warning

What was that? SID filtering is enabled. SID history can be exploited by an evil hacker in an elevated privilege attack. He could construct a security token with an SID of a domain administrator within the trusting resource domain. Since the SID is recognized as a domain administrator, his account would have the same level of access. SID filtering strips any SIDs that don't originate from the trusted user domain. Basically, our users' security token wouldn't buy a gumball in the source domain with SID filtering enabled because the SID history value would be stripped off. So, following the useful hyperlink "Securing external trusts" in the window, we learn we can use the netdom command to disable and enable SID filtering for migrations such as these.

The `netdom` command comes installed with Windows Server 2012, but earlier versions had it available in the Support Tools. Microsoft released a later version of Support Tools after Windows Server 2003 Service Pack 2, so be sure to search its site for the latest version.

The following commands are run to disable SID filtering. The `/quarantine:no` parameter does the trick. You should be able to deduce how SID filtering would be enabled:

```
Rem performed on dc01.bigfirm.com
Netdom trust otherdomain /domain:bigfirm /quarantine:No
/usero:administrator /passwordo:P@ssw0rd

Rem performed on the DC2003.OtherDomain.local:
Netdom trust bigfirm /domain:otherdomain /quarantine:No
/usero:administrator /passwordo:P@ssw0rd
```

Getting Both Sides ADMT-friendly

ADMT can be an absolutely frustrating nightmare of a program because of its needs. It's a program that takes information that is fairly private and internal to a domain—user accounts and passwords—and reveals it to a completely different domain. Before ADMT can do that, you'll have to open a number of locked doors. The following is what you have to do.

PUTTING A DOMAIN ADMIN IN EACH OTHER'S ADMINISTRATORS GROUPS

The ADMT utility needs an account that is both a member of the Domain Admins group in the target domain, Bigfirm.com, and a member of local Administrator groups of servers and workstations in the source domain, OtherDomain.local. This will allow the ADMT utility to perform changes to permissions, user rights, and other nifty stuff that all powerful administrators have the privileges to do. In this example, we created an account with the imaginative name of ADMT in the Bigfirm.com domain and assigned it to the Domain Admins group. Using the trust relation between the two domains, it was also assigned to the built-in Administrators group in OtherDomain.local and the local Administrators group on Win7 .bigfirm.com.

On the source domain, OtherDomain.local, a similar requirement is needed for the Password Encryption Service (PES). This is an additional service that will read the password of the migrating account, encrypt it, and then store it with the new account's properties. It needs to be a member of the Domain Admins group in the source domain, OtherDomain.local, and a member of the built-in Administrators group in the target domain, Bigfirm.com. We created an account with an equally imaginative name, PES, in OtherDomain.local. Over at Bigfirm.com, we opened up Active Directory Users and Computers and drilled down to the Built-in folder to find the Administrators group. Then we made the PES account a member of that group.

TURNING ON AUDITING

ADMT has some specific auditing needs, presumably so that it can monitor how it's doing. The source domain—the one the users are being copied from, OtherDomain.local—needs both success and failure audits enabled for user and group management.

On the target and source machines (W2K8DC.Bigfirm.com and DC2003.OtherDomain.local), we enable auditing by modifying a group policy called Default Domain Controller Policies. In a standard Windows Server 2003 installation, you can use Active Directory Users and Computers to do this. Right-click the Domain Controllers OU, and choose Properties and then the Group Policy tab; double-click Default Domain Controllers Policy, and the Group Policy editor appears. With Windows Server 2008 R2, the Group Policy Management Console is installed automatically. After opening this console, you drill down to the Group Policy Objects container. Then right-click the Default Domain Controllers Policy, and select Edit.

To get to the policy you're looking for, open Computer Configuration, then Windows Settings, then Security Settings, and then Local Policies; finally inside Local Policies you see Audit Policy. Inside Audit Policy, double-click Audit Account Management, and make sure that Define These Policy Settings is selected, as is Success and Failure. Then click Close, but don't close the GP editor; your work is not nearly done yet.

ENABLING CRYPTOGRAPHIC SETTINGS ON THE TARGET DOMAIN

To migrate computers with previous versions of Windows to a target domain with domain controllers running Windows Server 2008 and higher, another GPO setting is required on the target domain. Within the Security options of the Domain Controller GPO, enable "Allow cryptography algorithms compatible with Windows NT 4.0."

Farther south in Computer Configuration, choose Administrative Templates ➤ System ➤ Netlogon. Right-click "Allow cryptography algorithms compatible with Windows NT 4.0," click Edit, click Enabled, and then click OK.

BEFORE STARTING ADMT

As previously mentioned, C&P stands for clean and pristine. That means you leave all the old stuff behind and move into a new forest or domain. From our experience, although you leave all your unwanted objects behind, you can reduce your stress factor if you start to clean up your old environment before migration. Clean up your old house even though you're moving into a new home? Yes, right! In terms of your domain migration, we recommend doing a few cleanup steps in your source domain.

First, check to see if you have some old SID history on your objects. If you are going to migrate your accounts, groups, and computers, you don't want to have old SID history on your accounts.

Next, make sure all groups, users, and computers you are going to migrate are objects you really need. Don't migrate old, orphaned groups, users, and computers; it doesn't make sense. Therefore, you need to delete your old unused objects before you migrate.

After you've cleaned up your environment, check the group nesting. Make sure that all your group nesting matches the AG(U)DLP principle. AG(U)DLP means an account is nested into a global group, the global group is member of a universal group (if required), and the universal or global group is a member of a domain local group. This domain local group has been assigned permission on the resources.

These are probably the most important premigration steps you need to take, and they will help you to succeed and migrate only those objects you really want.

INSTALLING ADMT AND PES

ADMT is available as a download from Microsoft. Installing the utility is straightforward for a C&P installation since you will not be importing databases from previous versions. It does ask whether the database will be on SQL Express or a standard installation of SQL. In most cases, SQL Express will be the preferred option.

ADMT INSTALLATION ISSUES

Because there are many ways an ADMT installation can fail, we recommend reading the following blog for troubleshooting:

```
http://blogs.technet.com/b/askds/archive/2010/07/09/admt-3-2-common-
installation-issues.aspx
```

Creating a Password Key on the Target

Now, you want your users' passwords to move over with their accounts and ADMT can do that with the help of the Password Encryption Service (PES). Before it will migrate passwords, ADMT requires that you create a password encryption file on ADMT01 and then copy that over to DC2003, and DC2003 will use that to be able to send passwords over the wire—but encrypted.

To do this, you have to run ADMT from the command line. The following is an example of the command syntax:

```
admt key /option:create /sourcedomain:otherdomain
/keyfile:c:\temp\password.pes /keypassword:P@ssw0rd
```

This says to prepare a key that OtherDomain.local can use to transfer passwords to Bigfirm .com. (Bigfirm is not explicitly mentioned because you're working on a Bigfirm.com DC.) The C:\temp\password.pes file just says where to put the file. If your server has a floppy drive, then A:\ works fine too. It doesn't matter where you put it—just understand that you'll have to somehow transport that file to the OtherDomain.local DC, DC2003. When it runs properly, ADMT will return a message looking something like this:

```
The password export server encryption key for domain 'otherdomain' was
successfully created and
saved to 'c:\temp\password.pes'
```

You're finished on ADMT01.Bigfirm.com for the moment. It's time to move to the DC2003.

Moving Over the PES File

Once you're logged in at DC2003, you need to get that PES file from ADMT01.bigfirm.com to a local drive; we usually just create a share and copy it across the network. You can alternatively put it on a floppy, a CD-ROM, or whatever you want—but it has to get over to DC2003 one way or another.

Installing the Password Migration DLL on the Source DC

The Password Encryption Service was once included with earlier versions of ADMT. The 3.1 release is available as a separate download.

The PES is installed with an MSI file called `PWMIG.MSI`; double-click it to start the ADMT Password Migration DLL Installation Wizard, perhaps the world-record holder for wizard name length. The key ingredients required in the installation are the password file and the service account that was created earlier. After the installation, you should be prompted to reboot. Remember the service's autostart configuration is set to Manual. This restart of the source domain controller will have you scratching your head as to why the ADMT utility isn't working if you don't verify that the service is running.

A LITTLE HOUSEWORK ON THE WORKSTATION

If computers are to be migrated, we need to cover some additional steps. The ADMT installs an agent service on a computer to perform security modifications and to trigger a domain membership change. The utility will perform a few checks prior to the install to ensure things are flying correctly. One is a test of the file and printer sharing. With XP, Vista, and Windows 7, the firewall can cause these tests to bomb.

◆ In `firewall.cpl`, on the Advanced tab, configure the ICMP settings to Allow Incoming Echo Requests. This is for your own benefit.

◆ On the Exception tab, select File and Printer Sharing to make it an allowed service.

In addition, we recommend the following:

◆ Add the ADMT account as a member of the local Administrators group, as mentioned earlier.

◆ Reset the local Administrator account to a known password. If the domain membership change fails, this account may be the only way into the workstation to fix it.

Starting Up ADMT and Migrating

When migrating users and computers from one domain to another, the basic sequence of events is as follows:

1. Set up the trusts, registry entries, and so on.

2. Migrate services accounts.

   For brevity, we're not going to detail this here. A service account is migrated to the new domain, and servers are modified on the source domain's servers to use this new account.

3. Migrate the global groups from the old domain to the new domain.

   The new global groups get SID histories from the old ones, so anyone in the new BIGFIRM\Administration group will have access to anything that people in the OtherDomain.local\Administration group has access to. This means that as you migrate users from OtherDomain.local to Bigfirm.com, the users can be automatically placed in the Administration group in Bigfirm.com and they will have immediate access to all their old stuff.

4. Migrate the users.

   Once you have the global groups migrated, you can migrate the users at whatever pace works for you. Users migrated to the new domain will be able to access file shares, shared printers, and other resources from the old domain, because the migrated user accounts have SID histories from the old domain.

5. Migrate the workstations and servers to Bigfirm.com. Change the domain membership from OtherDomain.local to Bigfirm.com.

6. Translate security objects.

   User rights, file and share permissions, and local group membership are a few objects that can be re-ACLed by the ADMT. To ensure access to the resource, new account and group SIDs need to be applied to servers and workstations. Depending on how the migration is conducted, this type of operation can happen before server migration. In our example, the workstation's local profiles need to be mapped to the new accounts. During a long migration, the user and their workstation may not be migrated simultaneously. So, profiles should be translated prior to a computer's domain membership change.

7. Repeat migration processes to fill in gaps.

   Membership of groups may change, user accounts may need to be enabled or disabled, and additional security objects may need translation. All of these require planned runs of the ADMT utility.

8. Migrate domain local groups.

9. Once all the member servers are moved over to Bigfirm.com and you've checked that all the permissions have been correctly changed from OtherDomain.local references to Bigfirm.com references, you can decommission OtherDomain.local—break the trust relationship, shut off the OtherDomain.local DCs, and trim the SID histories from the migrated user accounts.

It's time to migrate the global groups and users, so let's do it. Move over to ADMT.Bigfirm .com, and start up ADMT (Start ➤ Administrative Tools ➤ Active Directory Migration Tool). It's a kind of sparse-looking UI, as shown in Figure 7.53, but here is a list of a few of its available functions:

- Migrate groups

- Migrate service accounts

- Migrate users

- Translate local user profiles

- Migrate workstations and member servers

ADMT does a *lot* of things, more than we can cover in a short time. We'll just cover the basics here. We *strongly* recommend that you read the Help file that comes with it, because ADMT is a powerful and useful tool that can migrate users, groups, machines, and even Exchange setups! In addition, the Migration Guide is available for download from Microsoft.

FIGURE 7.53
The spartan
ADMT console

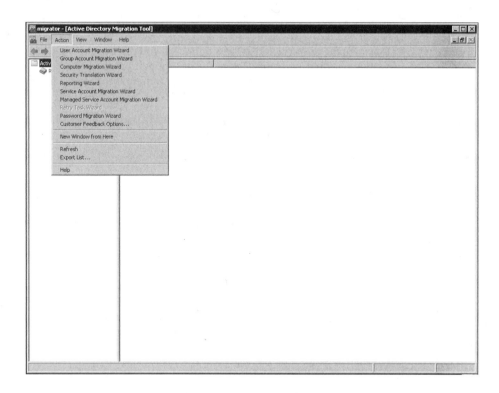

FIGURE 7.53
The spartan
ADMT console

GUI, Command Line, or VBScript

The ADMT utility provides three interfaces for performing the migrations. Each has advantages:

GUI Based on the Microsoft Management Console technology, the ADMT snap-in offers wizards to walk you through each function. This is useful if you are not familiar with the options and required parameters to migrate a specific object. However, it is tedious to click through the wizard for a large quantity of objects.

Command Line Batch files can be created using the command-line ADMT tool. This is useful for migrating larger numbers of accounts. Each command is limited to delivering the accounts to one organizational unit, so it cannot be all-encompassing. The following is the listing of functions available with it. We'll cover some examples in the following sections:

```
admt
The syntax of this command is:

ADMT [ USER | GROUP | COMPUTER | SECURITY | SERVICE |
         REPORT | KEY | PASSWORD | CONFIG | TASK ]
```

VBScript Scripting offers logic to control the ADMT operations. It also provides the functionality of reading input text files and performing individual operations on each entry. So, large numbers of operations with different requirements could be bundled into a batch job more readily. It does require expertise on writing scripts.

We highly recommend performing these operations in a test environment to get a feel for the utility and to develop a game plan on a specific migration. A mix of different methods may be more effective than sticking with just one.

The information required with each method and each function is similar, so it would seem repetitive going through each one. Here we will show some examples of the operations in GUI and command-line format.

USER AND GROUP MIGRATION WITH THE ADMT SNAP-IN

Group migration and user migration are very similar. In this example, we will walk through the User Migration Wizard.

1. On the ADMT menu, choose User Account Migration Wizard, and click Next to see the first panel, the all-familiar Welcome page.

   Earlier versions of ADMT offered a test run of the operations. Version 3.1 isn't as timid. So, be certain to run this in a test environment first for familiarization and then on pilot accounts in the production environment.

2. Click Next on the Welcome page, and you'll see the dialog shown in Figure 7.54.

FIGURE 7.54

Choosing source and destination domains

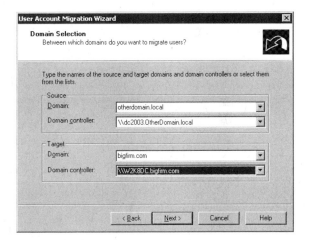

This page is straightforward; you pick the domain that you're moving from and the one that you're moving to. But it's actually quite useful as well, because it serves as a test of connectivity. If DC2003 wasn't up, your only options on both "from" and "to" would be Bigfirm.com, which wouldn't be a very interesting migration.

3. Once you choose the domains, click Next, as shown in Figure 7.55, and you'll notice a pause as the DCs connect.

   The option "Read objects from an include file" requires a file that lists users or groups that would be imported into the wizard.

4. In this case, "Select users from domain" is selected.

FIGURE 7.55
User Selection Option page

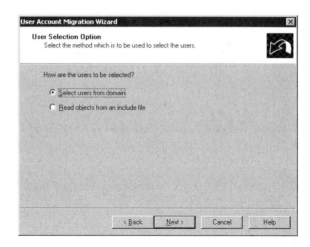

This option displays the User Selection page, as shown in Figure 7.56, which allows you to select which object, or in this case, which users, to migrate. The Add button provides the typical search dialog box you'd see in Active Directory Users and Computers.

FIGURE 7.56
User Selection page

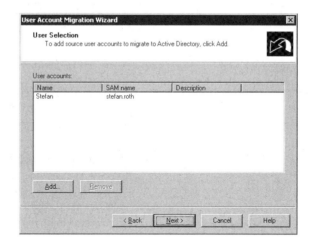

5. For this example, click Add and choose stefan.roth, although you could choose any number of users or groups given in the wizard.

6. Click Next, and you're led to the dialog shown in Figure 7.57, which allows you to choose an OU in the target domain.

   Like all good AD-aware tools, ADMT lets you choose what OU to place the migrated group into. But don't worry that you have to master that cumbersome LDAP-ese.

7. Click the Browse button, and ADMT then lets you navigate though the AD structure.

8. Click Next to see the screen shown in Figure 7.58, which displays the password migration options.

FIGURE 7.57
Organizational Unit Selection page

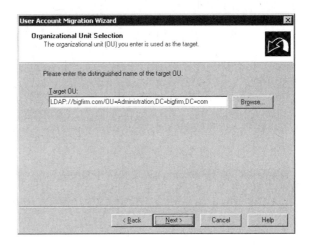

FIGURE 7.58
Password Options page

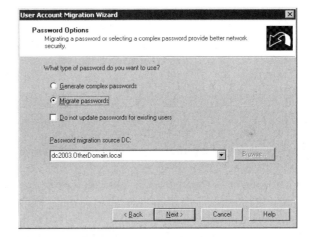

Since passwords are unique to user accounts, password options will be seen only in the User Account Migration Wizard. Basically, you can migrate the passwords or have ADMT come up with new ones for your users. The former needs the PES server. The latter needs a location to store the text file containing all these new passwords. As you can imagine, distributing this file to your users should not be done as an email attachment to the All Users distribution group. So, you will have an additional challenge to get the passwords to the users after the migration.

9. Click Next.

The next page is titled Account Transition Options, as displayed in Figure 7.59. This determines how to handle the target and source accounts after migration. Given the scenario, the accounts may need to be disabled for a period of time. The ADMT can handle both sides. Keep an eye out for the "Migrate user SIDs to target domain" check box. In Mexico, they would say, "Está muy importante." This creates the SID history on the user or group. This is ADMT's way of saying, "Create a SID history item in Bigfirm.com for the stefan.roth user account."

FIGURE 7.59

Account Transition Options page

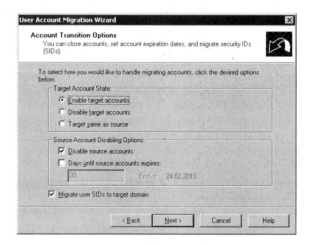

10. Click Next on this page to generate something of a useful diagnostic—if something isn't in place to allow the SID history mechanism to work, ADMT emits an error message. Or it issues a warning, such as creating the OtherDomain$$$ helper group and enabling auditing if you forgot to do so.

    Whenever you use an SID history, the ADMT checks with the old domain, OtherDomain .local in this case, to see whether creating the helper group is acceptable. This group has something to do with how ADMT ensures that the SID histories will work right, but the wizard checks anyway to ensure that it's OK to create the group.

11. Click Yes, and you'll see a login screen, shown in Figure 7.60, as if you haven't already presented your credentials frequently enough.

12. Click Next to go to the User Options page, shown in Figure 7.61.

    Typically, the preferred option for the first migration is "Fix users' group memberships." This will update the SIDs in the groups of which the users were members. The other options can be used later in re-migrating the account to assist in stripping off the old SID history. "Update user rights" will replace the SIDs with the new one. "Translate roaming profiles" will reassign permissions to the new SID.

    Specific properties can be excluded from the migration (see Figure 7.62). Say Bigfirm doesn't want the department or company fields of a user account migrated; these can be singled out and excluded with this page.

FIGURE 7.60
SID history credentials

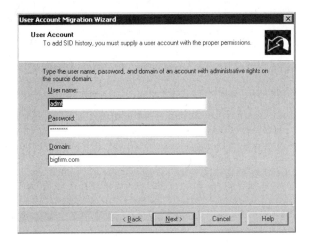

FIGURE 7.61
User Options page

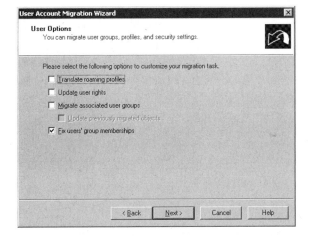

FIGURE 7.62
Object Property Exclusion page

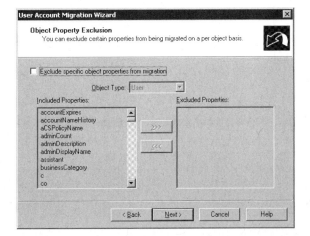

You're migrating a group named Administration, but what if there already *is* a group named Administration? The page shown in Figure 7.63 answers the question.

13. You can skip the migration, zap the existing Administration group, or add a prefix to the name.

14. Walk through the rest of the wizard to the Finish button, and the migration kicks off.

It will display the statistics of the migration process, as shown in Figure 7.64. If errors pop up, view the log with the available button. You can also visit the logs in the c:\windows\ admt folder. The log files are named with a date/timestamp.

FIGURE 7.63

Conflict Management page

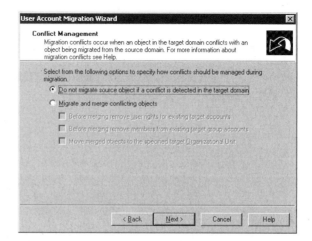

FIGURE 7.64

Migration Progress dialog box

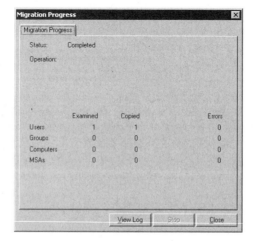

MIGRATING WITH THE COMMAND LINE

As mentioned earlier, the command-line utility `ADMT.exe` offers batch operations, which avoids the tedious button-clicking required with the console's wizards. The first example migrates the Administration global group:

```
rem global group migration
admt group /N "administration group" /sd:"otherdomain.local"
 /td:"bigfirm.com" /to:"administration" /mss:yes /fgm:yes
 /ugr:yes /mms:no /co:Merge+REMOVEUSERRIGHTS+REMOVEMEMBERS
```

Although this example doesn't exhaust all the options for this command, each option is represented with the wizards:

`/N`: The SAM Account name of the group. Additional group names could be listed as well.

`/sd`: Source domain.

`/td`: Target domain.

`/to`: Target organizational unit.

`/mss`: Migrate SIDs. This is equivalent to the check box named "Migrate user SIDs to target domain."

`/fgm`: Fix group membership.

`/ugr`: Update group rights.

`/mms`: Migrate members. If yes, all user accounts as members would also be migrated.

`/co`: Conflict options. In this case, the group will be merged with one of the same name, user rights will be removed from that group, and any existing members will be removed.

The following command migrates the rest of the user accounts in the Administration organizational unit:

```
rem user account migration
admt user /N "stefan.roth" "marcel.zehner" "philipp.witschi" "chris.greuter" /
sd:otherdomain.local /td:bigfirm.local /to:"administration" /mss:yes /co:ignore /
po:copy /ps:dc2003.otherdomain.local /dot:disablesource+enabletarget /uur:yes /
fgm:yes
```

The additional parameters are user-specific:

`/po`: Password option

`/ps`: PES server

`/dot`: Transition options, which manage the state of the accounts after migration

`/uur`: Update user rights

Testing the Migrated Group's Access to Resources

Because the migrated Administration group in Bigfirm.com has an SID matching the one of the Administration group in OtherDomain.local and *that* group has access to \\DC2003\

`Administration`, then anyone in the new Administration group should be able to get to `\\DC2003\Administration`. Let's try it:

1. In the Bigfirm.com domain, log on as the Administrator, and attempt to access the `\\Dc2003\Administration` share.

   This should produce an "access denied" message because the account doesn't have permissions to the share.

2. Assign the Administrator account to the newly migrated Administration group in Bigfirm.com.

3. Log off and log back on as the administrator.

   Note that you will need to do this to rebuild the security token.

4. Attempt to connect to the `\\DC2003\Administration` share again.

Cool, the Administration share opens! The SID history works.

Translating Local Profiles

Assuming the user accounts were successfully migrated, the users will be able to access resources within the OtherDomain.local domain. However, they still have to work on the workstation located in that domain. If they log onto the Win7 workstation now, they will have a new profile created for each of them. They will whine and gripe that they can't find their photographs of loved ones, or, worse yet, their Internet favorites are gone!

To prevent this headache, the Security Transition Wizard provides reassignment of the SIDs on existing profiles on all Windows platforms.

The Security Translation Wizard is used for several types of procedures. The translation of local profiles is just one. It can also reassign permissions for user rights, files and shares, printers, local groups, and Registry Editor settings. The following section will familiarize you with this function.

TRANSLATING PROFILES WITH THE ADMT SNAP-IN

You can start the Security Translation Wizard from the Action drop-down menu (shown earlier in Figure 7.63). It asks for many of the same things that the User and Group Migration wizards require:

- Source domain and domain controller.

- Target domain and domain controller.

- Object selection, in this case computers. These are chosen through the typical search dialog box. In our example, Win7 is the desired computer that the local profiles will be reassigned to for the migrated user.

Then it gets into security specifics (see Figure 7.65). This lists the type of security objects to translate. The ADMT's Help details when to translate each of these. In this example, just the "User profiles" check box is selected.

On the next page, shown Figure 7.66, the three options Replace, Add, and Remove treat the old SID as described in the window. The ADMT's help file specifies which option is required for each type of security object. In this case, the local profiles need to have the security replaced. The Add option with local profiles has a tendency to break software application packages deployed with Group Policy objects.

FIGURE 7.65
Translate Objects page

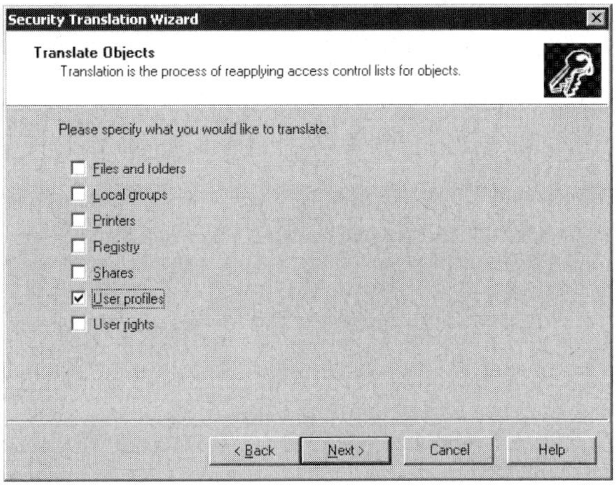

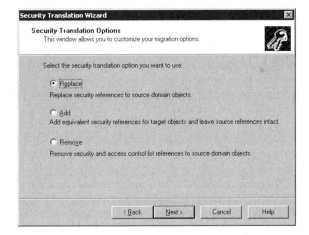

FIGURE 7.66
Security Translation
Options page

The old SID will be replaced with the user account's new SID, so when Bigfirm\Stefan.Roth logs on the workstation, it identifies the original profile with the new account.

After the wizard is complete, a different window displays, as shown in Figure 7.67. The Active Directory Migration Tool Agent Dialog window (say *that* ten times quickly) runs the actual operation on the workstation. You must launch the operation with the desired radio button: "Run pre-check" or "Run pre-check and agent operation." (If you use the ADMT command-line utility, the operation starts automatically.) The pre-check, as mentioned, will test the File and Print Services, but more specifically it checks whether the ADMT account can access the administrative shares like, \\Win7\admin$. The agent operation will install the agent on Win7 and then perform the translation.

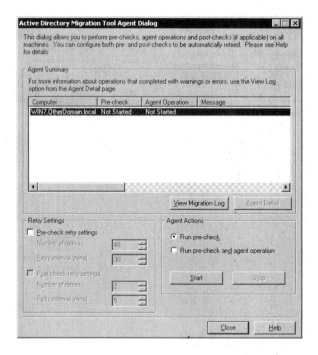

FIGURE 7.67
Active Directory
Migration Tool
Agent Dialog
window

The Agent Summary field displays the progress. For further information, you can view the migration log and agent detail. The agent detail provides another window detailing the agent's installation and run events.

The users need to be logged off the workstation while this operation occurs. A locked workstation will also lock access to the profile. This causes the agent to perform an add operation, but it still could produce an error or unexpected reactions. From our experience, some users may not understand the difference between logged off and locked. We recommend asking users to restart their workstations when knocking off from work. Then run the operation in off-hours.

After the agent operation is completed, the user can log on with the new user account. Their old desktop should be presented, and all the other profile-specific settings are available. In this case, their mapped drives to their home folder should be available. Their access to the home folder will verify whether the SID history is working as well.

In additional runs of the Security Translation Wizard, permissions on the home folder can be re-ACLed.

Migrating Computer Accounts

The process of migrating computer accounts looks similar to the Security Translation Wizard and the Active Directory Migration Tool Agent (see Figure 7.68).

The Agent Summary field includes a Post-check column. The operation performs the domain membership change, which will require a reboot. The verification of change is performed in the post-check. The reboot makes the post-check retry settings important. This sets the number of retries and the interval between each attempt. With a little patience on your part, the operation completes.

FIGURE 7.68
Active Directory Migration Tool Agent
Dialog window for computer migrations

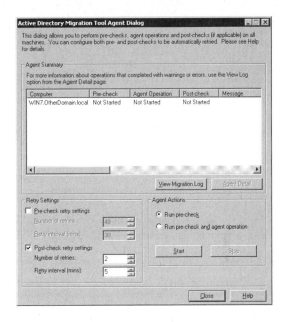

Rollback Considerations

The greatest advantage to the C&P migration is its gradual nature. This also lends itself to gradual rollback plans. Phases of the migration will uncover wrinkles and hiccups. You want these to emerge early in the pilots. If issues or obstacles arise, you can avoid performing a show-stopping "no-go" rollback. Issues can be addressed individually and with proper planning, workarounds and intermediate states can be expected.

The migration process involves copies of accounts and groups. Thus, source accounts and groups are still in place and can be reenabled and used as necessary. Only a few security objects require rollback procedures, such as local user profiles.

So, for each migration phase, plan and test the rollback to the state prior to the specific change within the phase.

The Path to the 2012 Forest Functional Level

Once you decide on which of these migration methods to use, you will start upgrading or migrating as described in the respective section.

In a single-domain forest, you will upgrade each of the domain controllers to Windows Server 2012. After all domain controllers have Windows Server 2012 installed, you can raise the domain functional level to Windows Server 2012. Then you can raise the forest functional level to Windows Server 2012 as well.

In a multidomain environment, you can independently upgrade each domain within a forest that has multiple domains. For example, you can begin upgrading domain controllers in a child domain before you upgrade domain controllers in the root domain of the same forest. As soon you have upgraded all domain controllers in a domain to Windows Server 2012, you can raise the domain functional level in that domain. Continue upgrading each domain to Windows Server 2012 until all domains in the same forest have a domain functional level of Windows Server 2012. Now you can raise the forest functional level to Windows Server 2012.

For a detailed procedure on raising domain and forest functional levels, see the section, "Raising Domain and Forest Functional Levels."

An Introduction to Windows Azure Active Directory

Previously we discussed Active Directory which is on-premises. This means that Active Directory within your company is protected from the outside world. Let's recap why you use Active Directory. You need this directory service to centrally store and manage all your users and computers to control the behavior of your Windows infrastructure.

A few years before Active Directory was developed, IT had a big problem. Without Active Directory, every application needed to store its access credentials locally in a store, such as in a database or locally on the server itself. Windows NT had a modest way of managing users and computers, but that solution was far from meeting the needs of an enterprise. One major reason why Active Directory was developed was to centrally manage the infrastructure. Today, the same problem occurs in Windows Azure. Now the application landscape has gotten fragmented again. Some of your company's cloud applications have a configuration store holding the usernames and passwords so that the application can authenticate and authorize the user to use this application in Windows Azure. But now Windows Azure Active Directory comes into play. In this section we refer to your on-premises Active Directory as "Active Directory" and Azure-hosted Active Directory as "Windows Azure Active Directory" (WAAD, Windows Azure AD, or Azure Active Directory).

Windows Azure Active Directory is a service that provides identity management and access-control capabilities for your cloud applications. Many online cloud applications from Microsoft already use Windows Azure AD. The most common of these is Office 365; others include Dynamics CRM Online and Windows Intune.

WAAD is a multitenant service that can handle millions of companies, far more than 100 million users, and thousands of tenants on the same platform. It is optimized for availability and consistent performance and maximized for scalability. Does that mean you no longer need your on-premises Active Directory? Yes and no. Windows Azure Active Directory can be used on its own, but the most common scenario is that companies integrate Windows Azure AD with their on-premises Active Directory. In an architectural sense, it can be considered as Active Directory in the cloud extended from your current on-premises Active Directory (see Figure 7.69).

Providing this expansion from your on-premise Active Directory into the cloud allows you to manage your users and groups locally and replicate them to WAAD using DirSync, which we will discuss shortly. Because of that mechanism, you will be able to create a single sign-on (SSO) experience for your cloud-hosted application. Be aware that if you are using only DirSync, you won't get an SSO experience. For SSO you also need to deploy Active Directory Federation Services (AD FS) in your on-premises Active Directory. For more details, see the section, "Active Directory Logon Flavors."

Getting Started with Windows Azure Active Directory

How do you get an account for an AD tenant in Azure Active Directory? The easiest way is to sign up for an Office 365 account, and you will immediately have Windows Azure Active Directory along with it. This is because Office 365 uses Windows Azure Active Directory. Another way of getting WAAD is to sign up for it online on Windows Azure (http://www .windowsazure.com/). Whichever method you choose, you will be able to manage your account from both portals.

After you have signed up for Windows Azure, you can start managing your directory, as shown in Figure 7.70.

FIGURE 7.69
Windows Azure Active
Directory integration

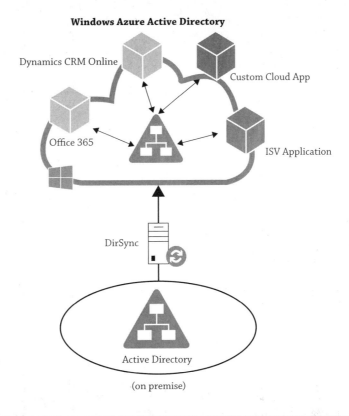

FIGURE 7.70
WAAD portal

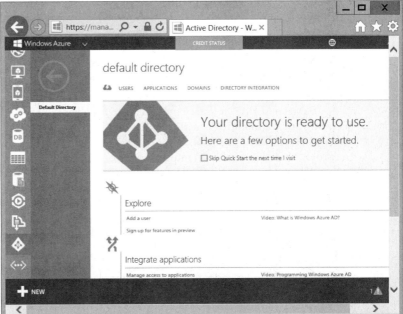

The Windows Azure Management portal, the Windows Azure AD portal, the Office 365 Account portal, the Windows Intune Account portal, and the Windows Azure PowerShell cmdlets all read from and write to a single shared instance of Windows Azure AD that is associated with your organization's tenant, as shown in the Figure 7.71.

FIGURE 7.71
Managing Windows Azure Active Directory

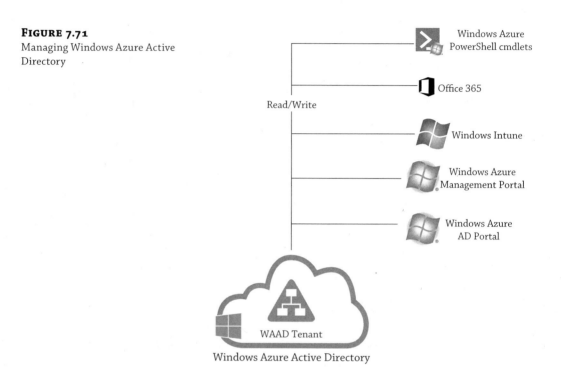

Windows Azure Active Directory

How to Interact with Windows Azure Active Directory

If you're already familiar with Active Directory, you've probably used Lightweight Directory Access Protocol (LDAP) to query the directory for objects. LDAP is an application protocol for accessing and maintaining directory information. However, you can't use LDAP for accessing WAAD because LDAP was not designed for a multitenancy scenario. One other problem is that the protocol must be usable on multiple platforms across many different technologies. Because of this, Microsoft built a RESTful interface for accessing WAAD. Representational State Transfer (REST) is an architecture that uses HTTP to perform create, read, update, and delete (CRUD) actions using the GET, POST, PATCH, and DELETE methods. Microsoft refers to this RESTful interface as Windows Azure Active Directory Graph.

There are several advantages of using this kind of interface:

◆ Platform independent—Any device is capable of using HTTP and calling HTTP methods.

◆ Language independent—Any programming language can use REST architectures to talk to other programming languages; for example, C# can talk to Java.

◆ Standards based—Because it runs on HTTP and is based on the HTTP standard, Windows Azure AD Graph can be used on any platform.

◆ Easily manageable—Firewalls can be easily configured to allow HTTP traffic.

TESTING WINDOWS AZURE ACTIVE DIRECTORY GRAPH

In order to get an idea of how the Graph API works, you can try it out. Microsoft provides a test application in Windows Azure called Graph Explorer that lets you run queries against your tenant.

Go to `http://graphexplorer.cloudapp.net/` and sign in with your Microsoft account; then choose Use Demo Company in the top-right corner. This will send you to a test tenant (GraphDir1) at `https://graph.windows.net/GraphDir1.OnMicrosoft.com` where you can get a look and feel for this technology.

For example, if you want to run a query to return all users from this tenant, you simply add the expression **users** at the end of the URL, like this: `https://graph.windows.net/GraphDir1.OnMicrosoft.com/users`. Or if you just want to return the attributes from a single user called `Daniel@GraphDir1.onmicrosoft.com`, you would run `https://graph.windows.net/GraphDir1.OnMicrosoft.com/users/Daniel@GraphDir1.onmicrosoft.com`.

You will also find a link to additional documentation on Windows Azure Active Directory Graph.

There are additional protocols in Windows Azure Active Directory. REST/HTTP is just one of four protocols needed to access and use WAAD. Table 7.3 provides a brief overview of the entire stack of protocols and the purpose of each. This chapter is not intended to give you a deep dive into these technologies so we won't go any deeper than a brief description.

TABLE 7.3: Windows Azure Active Directory Protocols

PROTOCOL	PURPOSE
REST/HTTP directory access	Create, read, update, and delete directory objects and relationships
OAuth 2.0	Service-to-service authentication Delegated access
SAML 2.0	Web application authentication Single sign-on experience
WS-Federation 1.3	Web application authentication Single sign-on experience

Synchronizing Windows Azure Active Directory

At this point, you have some idea of what WAAD is, where you can manage your WAAD users, and how you can interact with your Windows Azure Active Directory. The real benefit of WAAD starts when you integrate your WAAD with your on-premises Active Directory. Figure 7.69, shown previously, provides a high-level view of the integration concept.

The main goal is to have your on-premises directory act as a source of authority and the Azure directory receive all users, groups, and contact objects. "Source of authority" means that you manage only your on-premises directory, and all changes you make override the settings in Windows Azure AD. The mechanism that updates the Windows Azure AD is a tool called DirSync. This tool allows you to synchronize your objects to WAAD and keep it up to date with your on-premises directory. Once DirSync is installed, it runs in the background synchronizing WAAD every few hours. The latest version of the DirSync tool is also capable of synchronizing the users' passwords in the cloud. Not exactly the plain password, which would be a security issue, but rather the tool synchronizes hash values of the password hashes. Imagine what benefits that brings to your company.

Your users can access the cloud applications using the same credentials as they use for the corporate on-premises network.

THE DIRSYNC TOOL

DirSync is relatively easy to set up. It is a 64-bit tool that requires SQL Server 2008 R2 Express Edition or a full version of SQL Server. Once the tool is installed, it is basically "set and forget," meaning you will not need to touch the installation again.

It's important to understand that if you are going to enable Active Directory synchronization, your on-premises Active Directory will be the authoritative data source and will overwrite changes made to synchronized users in the cloud. There is one exception: if you are going to deploy Exchange Server in a hybrid deployment scenario, some attributes need to be written back to your on-premises Active Directory. Please check the Knowledge Base article at `http://support.microsoft.com/kb/2256198/en-us` for the relevant attributes.

If you need more details on configuring directory synchronization, a good starting point for DirSync is TechNet; see `http://technet.microsoft.com/en-us/library/hh967629.aspx`.

Active Directory Logon Flavors

We have discussed the two directories and explained that you can synchronize objects (users, groups, and contacts) from your on-premises directory into the cloud, including synchronizing user passwords using DirSync. Although you have synchronized the two directories and have applications deployed on both, you might assume that you have single sign-on in place, but that's not correct. At this point, the users can log in to your corporate network and use the applications. If they attempt to access a cloud application, they will be prompted again for the credentials. Yes, the credentials are the same, but they are not transferred to the cloud application. This behavior is called same sign-on.

In order to get a single sign-on experience you need to deploy Active Directory Federation Services (AD FS). Deploying an AD FS infrastructure into your corporate network allows you to establish a relying party trust relationship between your AD FS farm and Windows Azure Active Directory. That relying trust relationship makes it possible to securely pass authentication tokens between your corporate network and Windows Azure AD. In Figure 7.72 you can see how this works from a high-level view.

If you deploy AD FS in your Active Directory, you not only get real single sign-on for your cloud applications, but you also can deploy a two-factor authentication mechanism. A two-factor authentication method forces the users, in addition to providing their credentials, to add another security code in order to authenticate against Windows Azure applications. This additional code adds an additional security layer to your infrastructure.

FIGURE 7.72
Windows Azure Active Directory single sign-on

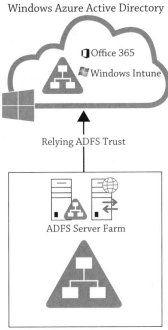

To give you a better overview of the pros (+) and cons (-) you face in every level of deployment, we provide a summary in Table 7.4.

TABLE 7.4:   Windows Azure Active Directory Integration

WINDOWS AZURE ACTIVE DIRECTORY ACCOUNT	WINDOWS AZURE ACTIVE DIRECTORY ACCOUNT + DIRSYNC	WINDOWS AZURE ACTIVE DIRECTORY ACCOUNT + DIRSYNC + ADFS
+ No additional configuration required.	+ On-premises Active Directory is the master source.	+ On-premises Active Directory is the master source.
	+ User has one pair of credentials.	+ Single sign-on experience.
		+ Two-factor authentication.
- User has two pairs of credentials.	- No single sign-on to cloud applications.	- DirSync tool must be installed on a dedicated on-premises server.
- No single sign-on for cloud applications.	- Two-factor authentication cannot be implemented.	- An AD FS farm must be deployed on-premises.
- Two-factor authentication cannot be implemented.	- DirSync tool must be installed on a dedicated on-premises server.	

In this section we introduced you to Windows Azure Active Directory and showed how to manage and integrate it into your environment. Now you should have a basic understanding of the most important terms and technologies that you need to get started with WAAD.

Overview of Workplace Join

Today's companies face huge problems with all kind of devices in their network. Imagine a consultant needing to do work for an IT project. The CEO of this company uses an iPad to do his work. The marketing people need to present their products on a different device, such as a slate. All of these people use their devices at home and in the office, and there is no standard device for all of them. One thing they have in common is that they need access to certain resources on the network.

Since all of these devices require access to the corporate network and applications, it has been a challenge to provide a secure and compliant way of providing access to these resources and managing the devices and data. Until now you only had two choices: either you joined a device to Active Directory (if possible) or you didn't. Both ways had advantages or disadvantages for the user accessing the data and applications as well as for the business managing the devices. Workplace Join was born out of the bring-your-own-device (BYOD) policy, which permits employees to bring their personal devices into their workplace and use them.

What Is Workplace Join?

Workplace Join comes with Windows Server 2012 R2 and is integrated into Windows 8.1; it allows your users to access applications and data from wherever they are without being joined to the domain from any device. In addition, Workplace Join gives the user single sign-on for the corporate applications, and the administrator of the company can still control who has access to the company resources. Of course, this tighter integration of devices brings some risks with it, but for that reason Microsoft has provided multifactor authentication and also added some functionality to Active Directory Federation Services in Windows Server R2 to manage these risks.

Registration is quite simple. Depending on your device, either you register via a URL or you configure the computer settings. In both scenarios, to register the device you provide the user principal name (UPN), which in many companies corresponds to the user's email address. The client device will then connect either from within your company network or from outside (via the Internet) the company's Web Application Proxy and authenticate the user. The Web Application Proxy, which is new in Windows Server 2012, is part of the Remote Access role service that allows you to provide users outside an organization with access to applications that are running on servers inside an organization. Web Application Proxy's strength lies in publishing applications, and this published source can be accessed on any device. If the credentials match, a new service in Windows Server 2012 R2 AD FS called Device Registration Service (DRS) will register the user's device in Active Directory. For that purpose, a new object class has been created in Active Directory. This new device object can be used to give conditional and fine-grained access to the data and resources in your corporate environment. You can think of Workplace Join as domain join lite (see Figure 7.73).

FIGURE 7.73
Workplace Join

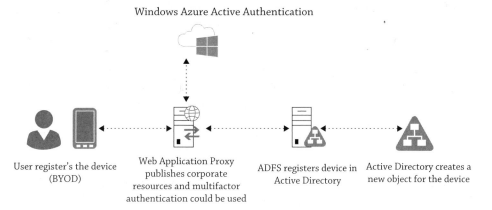

Windows Azure Active Authentication

User register's the device (BYOD)

Web Application Proxy publishes corporate resources and multifactor authentication could be used

ADFS registers device in Active Directory

Active Directory creates a new object for the device

Users who subscribe to this new feature don't give full control over the device to the administrator, but the Windows Server 2012 R2 domain controller administrator can apply a set of security policies and also perform a limited wipe of classified corporate data. This gives the administrator good control over what is happening with the corporate data and how to access it. On the flip side, the users can still use their device the way they want and also get easy and comfortable access to network resources.

GETTING STARTED WITH WORKPLACE JOIN

Workplace Join is a part of Windows Server 2012 R2 and Windows 8.1 and because of that we wanted to give you a short introduction and an idea what Workplace Join is. There is much we could talk about this new technology but this would exceed the volume of this book.

If you would like to play with Workplace Join in your lab, there is a good Step-by-Step guide on TechNet about joining an iOS device and a Windows device using Workplace Join. See the following link for more information: `http://technet.microsoft.com/en-us/library/dn452410.aspx`.

The Bottom Line

Create a single-domain forest.   Any Windows Server 2012 server can be promoted to a domain controller to create a single-domain forest. A DC hosts an instance of Active Directory Domain Services.

> **Master It**   You want to promote a server to a DC and create a single-domain forest. What should you do?

Add a second DC to the domain.   A single DC represents a potential single point of failure. If it goes down, the domain goes down. Often, administrators will add a second DC to the domain.

Master It   You want to add a second DC to your domain. What should you do?

Decide whether to add a global catalog.   A global catalog server hosts a copy of the global catalog. Any domain controller can become a GC, but only the first domain controller is a GC by default.

Master It   You are promoting a second server to a domain controller in your single-domain forest. Should you make it a GC?

Create accounts.   Any domain needs to host user and computer accounts representing users and computers that will access the domain. There are several ways to create user and computer accounts.

Master It   What are four methods that can be used to create a user account? Two have a GUI and the other two are command-line tools.

Create fine-grained password policies.   Windows Server 2012 introduced the ability to create multiple password policies within a domain by using fine-grained password policies. You can use a fine-grained password policy to assign a different password policy to a user or group within the domain.

Master It   You want to create a fine-grained password policy for a group of administrators in your network. What should you create and what tool should you use?

Understand the Windows Server 2012 forest functional level.   Each forest functional level has traditionally offered new functionality to Active Directory. For example, the Windows Server 2008 R2 forest functional level brought support for the Recycle Bin feature.

Master It   What new feature is offered in the Windows Server 2012 forest functional level?

Upgrade your domain to Windows Server 2012.   You currently have a Windows Server 2008 single-forest domain, and you are figuring out how to upgrade this forest. You want to have a Windows Server 2012 forest.

Master It   What methods for upgrading or migrating your forest make the most sense?

Chapter 8

Creating and Managing User Accounts

Probably one of the most common tasks an administrator will do, not only during deployment but also during the life of a Windows Server environment, is to create and manage user accounts. This sounds like a pretty simple task, but it is a very important one because of the time management and security implications. It's important for server administrators or consultants to understand the process. They might think they can ignore it because they don't create user accounts in normal operations. That may be true, but they are usually the people responsible for creating the first users in a new network, defining the processes, and handing over the operation to another team, department, or their customers. The same senior staff members also need to be able to create and manage user accounts for services and applications on their servers by following best practices.

We'll cover the basics of creating and managing user accounts so that everyone has something to gain from this chapter. In every situation where you just have PowerShell available, this chapter will serve you with the necessary skills to master your situation. We'll cover how you can create and manage your user accounts from the command prompt and PowerShell. Don't let that scare you; you've already seen in previous chapters how the keyboard alternative can sometimes be a real time- and effort-saver; you'll see that this trend continues here.

We'll discuss some of the common properties and settings that you can configure for user accounts. We'll also discuss groups, why you would use them, how to add/remove users to/from groups, and best practices for group membership assignment. We'll cover all of these subjects in three environments: a stand-alone Windows Server machine, a Server Core installation, and Active Directory.

We will show you the Windows Server 2012 options, most of which are identical to Windows Server 2008 R2. Windows Server 2012 has some new wrinkles, in the form of a new task and PowerShell-driven management tool called the Active Directory Administrative Center, which is totally built on top of PowerShell. Microsoft has added many more Active Directory modules for management via PowerShell, its shell and scripting language. So, we'll wrap up the chapter with a section covering those subjects. We believe that you'll finish this chapter thinking that those tools will be a major time-saver.

In this chapter, you'll learn to:

◆ Manage users and groups

◆ Use the Active Directory Administrative Center in Windows Server 2012

◆ Manage users and groups with PowerShell

> **WINDOWS SERVER 2012 (R2) COMPATIBILITY**
>
> We would like to point out if we are writing about Windows Server 2012 we are also meaning Windows Server 2012 R2 and all features apply to both versions.

Creating and Managing User Accounts

In this section, we'll cover how to create, manage, and delete local user accounts and domain-based user accounts. You'll learn how to do this using the GUI-based, command line–based, and PowerShell-based administrative tools, although you have to realize that the command-line tools are going to become extinct. Microsoft is going to push PowerShell in a big way.

The working environment for this chapter contains a domain controller called DC01.bigfirm .com and a member server called Server01.bigfirm.com. This will allow us to demonstrate how to create and manage local and domain user accounts.

Creating Local User Accounts

We'll cover how to create local user accounts first. There is one major tool to manage local user accounts, Computer Management. You can find it in Server Manager by choosing Tools ➢ Computer Management. This tool will give you the same options when managing users and groups as in Windows Server 2008 R2.

To follow along with this example, log into Server01.bigfirm.com as Administrator, open Computer Management, and navigate into \Local Users and Groups\Users (see Figure 8.1). You can see two existing user accounts:

FIGURE 8.1
Local users in Computer Management

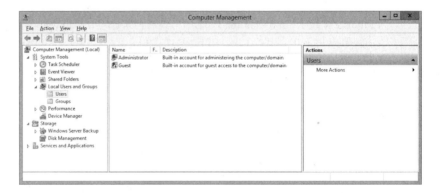

Administrator   This is the default administrative user account. We will talk a little more about this account in a few moments.

Guest   The purpose of this account is to allow people who do not have an actual user account to log into the local computer. This might be something an administrator might want if they have lots of guest users coming and going.

You'll notice that the Guest account has a little down arrow on its icon. This is because best practices dictate that this account should be disabled. Microsoft has done this by default for you. Having a Guest account is not a common requirement on a server, so you might never need to enable it.

Real World Scenario

THE ADMINISTRATOR ACCOUNT

It is critical that you protect the Administrator account in a manner that is suitable for your organization. The local Administrator account has complete control over your server, and the domain Administrator account has complete control over your network! So, it makes sense to have a very strong password for this account.

Administrator is an anonymous account in larger organizations. Take a look at your security logs in Event Viewer and ask yourself, "How do I know who did what using the Administrator account?" It is because of this that you should create a user account with suitable administrative or delegated rights for any administrator who needs them. Using the default Administrator account is often banned unless there is an emergency. To allow every member of IT to be accurately audited by the Security log, you'll need to create Administrator user accounts for each administrator. You then need to ensure that each administrator has only the rights and permissions they need to do their job.

Some organizations choose to disable the Administrator account altogether. That's one solution that you might not be big on because this account is a great backdoor in the case of password lockouts. Administrator is the one user who cannot be locked out. Those organizations could take an alternative approach. You can think of it as the "nuclear" option. You've all seen those movies where two generals have to turn two different keys in order to start a nuclear missile launch. You can do the same thing with the Administrator password. It can be set by two different individuals or even departments, one typing the first half of the password and the other typing the second half. Organizations in need of this sort of option probably have an IT security or internal audit department that is the holder of one half of the password while the server administration team retains the other half.

One final option is to rename the Administrator account. There's some debate about this option because the security identifier (SID, a code that Windows uses internally to uniquely identify an object) of the account can be predicted once you have access to the server or the domain. Some argue that renaming the account is pointless. However, most Internet-based attacks are actually rather robotic and unintelligent. They target typical names such as SA, root, or Administrator and try brute-force attacks to guess the password. It is still worthwhile to rename the Administrator account to defend against these forms of attack.

In the end, the same old security rules apply. Set a very strong password on your Administrator accounts, restrict knowledge of the passwords, restrict remote access where you can, and control physical access to your servers.

In this example, we'll show how to create a user account for a new member of staff called Steve Red. Steve sure does get around, doesn't he? In \Local Users and Groups\Users, right-click in the middle pane and then select New User. The New User dialog box opens.

Now fill in some details about the user with the following fields (see Figure 8.2):

FIGURE 8.2

Creating a new local user

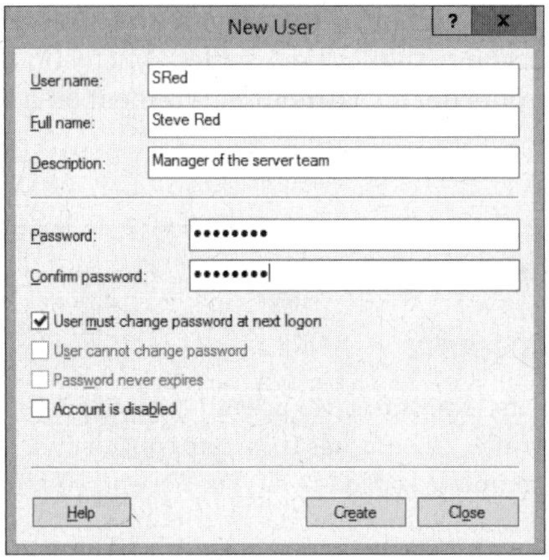

User Name   This is the name that the user will enter whenever they log in. We strongly recommend implementing some sort of naming standard. A smaller organization might get away with SRed for Steve. You might want to add a numeric scheme, such as SRed1SRed, SRedSRed01, or SRed10SRed. Some organizations take things further. Some use the company employee ID as a username. Others use the person's initials (including the middle name) with a number, such as SMRed10. These more anonymous systems might be appropriate where personal data is deemed sensitive.

Full Name   The "Full name" field is just the name of the person who will use the account. You probably don't want to store those names on servers that will be facing the Internet.

Password   Next, you need to set the password. One of the better ways to set a password is to use a *passphrase*. Read the case study to learn more about passphrases.

User Must Change Password at Next Logon   We've left the "User must change password at next logon" option enabled for this example. That does exactly what it says on the tin. You can set an easy-to-communicate password such as "your new passphrase" and leave this box selected (it's on by default). The new user will be able to log on but *must* change their password to complete the logon process. This guarantees that no member of IT will know the user's password. You'll notice that the next two check boxes are grayed out and unavailable to use. To change this, you should clear the "User must change password at next logon" check box. Logically, these boxes conflict with each other.

User Cannot Change Password   You can decide to prevent the account user from being able to change their password. A scenario where you might use this is when you are creating a user account that will be used by an application or a service. Setting this option prevents the program or an attacker of the program from being able to change the password.

Password Never Expires   "Password never expires" overrides any password expiration policies that may be set elsewhere, such as on the local system or in a group policy. You'll likely use this option for service user accounts only. You don't want something like SQL Server shutting down because the service user account's password wasn't changed. Organizations with ultra-tight security might just have a 100 percent ban on this option.

Account Is Disabled   "Account is disabled" is pretty self-explanatory. The account will be created, but it cannot be used until this check box has been deselected. This is what was done with the Guest user account. You might do this if you are creating a large number of users for the future and will enable them only when the users actually start.

Remember that you may have set an easily communicated password for the user account only, and it's probably something that IT regularly or always uses. Using this option will protect the user account against unauthorized use until the employee starts and is forced to change their password using the aforementioned "User must change password at next logon" option.

Clicking Create will create the SRed user for you and clear the fields in the New User dialog box. This allows you to quickly add more new users without having to open more menus and click menu options. You can click Close to exit the dialog box once the user is created.

You can see that the user is now created (see Figure 8.3), and you can either work on the account some more or allow it to be used.

FIGURE 8.3

The new user in Computer Management

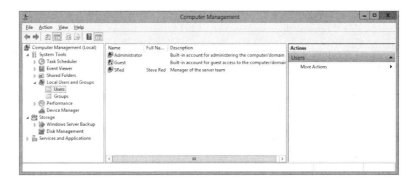

THE CASE FOR PASSPHRASES

Microsoft has been talking about passphrases for a few years now. There has always been some debate about what the best approach is with passwords. People typically have used seven or eight characters for their passwords. They've used complexity such as capital letters, numbers, or symbols to strengthen the password. However, that very same complexity makes that password harder to remember and harder to type. The result is that the help desk has a fun time every Monday morning dealing with locked-out users and password reset requests. This is made worse when you force people to change their password every 30 days, which is done because you need the password to change before it could possibly be cracked by an attacker.

The alternative is to use longer passwords, such as 12 characters, with no enforced complexity. This lengthening makes the password mathematically stronger. You're already thinking that will never fly with management or with the users. Hold on a moment.

The key to the solution is to advertise the concept of a passphrase. Up to now some people enter things like "November1982-1" and increment it every month when their password expires. How about telling people to enter something that means something to them or is easy to remember? For example, a person with a yellow Italian sports car might have "my prancing pony is yellow." That's a long password, but it is easy for that person to remember, and it's easy to type. Here's the winner: the password is so strong that you could allow it to be used for six months. That would be popular! You could advertise the concept of passphrases using posters, emails, briefings, and so on if you decided to introduce the policy. Thanks to fine-grained password policies, you could bring it in gradually with sympathetic pilot users who could spread the good word on your behalf.

You can also create users via the command line. This is helpful when using the Server Core installation of Windows Server 2012, but you may also find it's useful to learn for scripting as well. You can run the following command to create the local user SRed on your server:

```
C:\Users\administrator>net user SRed1 Skyisblue2013 /ADD
The command completed successfully.
```

The syntax of this command is as follows:

```
net user <user name to create> <password to set> /ADD
```

That command creates a user on the local computer. It does pretty much nothing else. None of the other options that we've just talked about are turned on or used. If the password is longer than 14 characters, you will be informed that the password is longer than 14 characters, which could have been a problem on legacy Windows systems. You are asked to confirm that you want such a long password. If you want to add spaces into your password, you can do that by surrounding the password with quotation marks. Here's an example:

```
net user SRED "My d0g is yellow" /ADD
```

You can add a few options to this command to completely re-create what you did in the Computer Management tool:

```
net user SRed Skyisblue2013 /fullname: "Steve Red" /comment: "Manager of the
server team" /logonpasswordchg:yes /add
```

That's a long command. Here's what the options do:

/fullname   This gives the user account a name for future reference.

/comment   This completes the Description field in the properties of the user account.

/logonpasswordchg:yes   This forces the user to change their password when they first log into the server.

Here are some of the other options that we covered for Computer Management:

/passwordchg   This is set to either yes or no to control whether a user can change their own password.

/expires   This is set either to a date (in the format *mm/dd/yy[yy]*) or NEVER.

/active   This either enables or disables the account.

You can get more information on other options by typing **net help user** at the command prompt. Don't fall into the trap of typing net user /?. There isn't much information there.

Creating Domain User Accounts

Let's quickly return to why you might prefer to use domain-based user accounts instead of local accounts. It turns out that your user, Steve Red, will need to be able to log into many servers on the network, not just that stand-alone server. He's going to be using many services, and it has been determined that he needs a single sign-on experience. Administrators also want to set up only one user account and be able to grant rights to just one user account. Steve wants to have only one user account and one password. The solution is simple—use a domain and a domain user account.

To do this, log into your domain controller (in this example, it's DC01.bigfirm.com) to use a tool called Active Directory Users and Computers, which you can find in Administrative Tools on any domain controller. Using the free-to-download Remote Server Administration Tools, you can install this and other server management tools on your Windows 8 computer for remote management. You'll probably prefer to do this when managing a production environment on a day-to-day basis.

🌐 Real World Scenario

SEPARATION OF ADMINISTRATION

One of the things that Windows administrators have been slow to adopt is the concept of separating our roles as office employees and network administrators. Unix administrators have been doing it for decades by simply using the su command. In other words, they log into the network using an ordinary account with normal user rights and elevate their privileges to a higher account whenever they need to do any administrative work. Why would you want to do this? It's pretty simple. Imagine you are surfing the Internet or reading your email. A piece of malware manages to slip through your defense mechanisms and execute. What is it going to run as? That's right; it will run under your account. What is going to stop it from rampaging across your corporate network if you have logged in as a domain administrator or some other privileged account? Absolutely nothing! Windows does offer some protection with User Account Control (UAC), but it's not a perfect defense. Just like physical security, sometimes the simplest solutions are the best ones.

The solution is quite simple and not quite as horrific as many Windows administrators try to make out when they hear it. Staff members with administrative rights should have two accounts. One account will be for their daily office work such as using Microsoft Word, surfing the Internet, or reading email. The second account will be for administrative work. This is where people throw their hands up in the air and start protesting. Let us finish—you'll soon see how easy this can be to use.

Let's say that you have set this scenario up for Steve Red. Steve's normal daily account is SRed. That's what Steve logs into his computer with to do his non-administrative work. You've also set up another account that has rights to manage parts of Active Directory, some servers, and desktops in his office. This account is called SRed-Admin. You could have used a fine-grained password policy to enforce stricter requirements on the administrative account, but you've gone with passphrases for everyone. That's pretty secure.

How does Steve switch between different roles during the day? This is the normal argument against separation of administration: "I don't want to be constantly logging out and in again." There are a few ways to get around this.

You've been able to use the RunAs feature to run programs under alternative user accounts. In Microsoft Windows Server and in Windows client operating systems, you can run programs as a different user than the currently logged-on user. This is known as Run As. If you want to do so, you need to follow these basic steps:

1. Locate the program you want to start.

2. Press and hold down the Shift key while you right-click the program icon, and then click "Run as different user."

3. Enter the credentials for the user you would like to run the program.

Some organizations have used this and even changed the shortcuts for the administrative MMC snap-ins in Administrative Tools to do this by default. Windows 8 and Windows Server 2012 allow you to quickly switch users without having to log out.

There are other approaches to this solution. Some have used Citrix presentation virtualization products to provide an administrative environment in the past. Windows Server 2008 R2/2012 Remote Desktop Services can easily duplicate this now by publishing either desktops or applications to people's computers. Or you could offer a variation on the virtual administrative PC solution by running that virtual PC on your Windows 8 Client; it already has a full-blown Windows Server Hyper-V 3.0 on board. One final solution we implement is management servers. Those servers are dedicated Windows servers just for managing the IT infrastructure. All necessary tools are installed and shared by any administrator who needs to manage the servers. The big advantage is that you can block the Internet connections for those management servers and also control that only those management servers are allowed to manage servers by defining the appropriate firewall access rules. The administrator just needs to connect to those management servers using the Remote Desktop Protocol (RDP).

You should now understand the need to separate the two working lives of an administrator and see that the solutions aren't all that hard to live with; in fact, they can be quite beneficial in saving time and effort.

Figure 8.4 shows Active Directory Users and Computers with the Users container. Users contains a number of built-in users and groups that are important to the functions of Active Directory. Some of them are used now, and some of them will be used when you deploy other functionality on your network. Some people use this container for user accounts that they create. This means that it becomes difficult to separate your ordinary user accounts from built-in ones and to apply policies and delegate administrative rights. We wish Microsoft had used a different name for this container.

FIGURE 8.4
Active Directory
Users and Computers

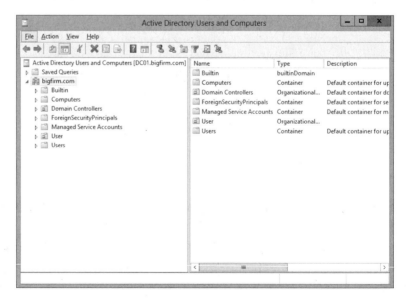

The solution is pretty simple:

1. Create another OU, typically named after the domain or the organization, at the root of the domain. In this case, you'll create one called BigFirm under bigfirm.com.

2. Then create an OU architecture to suit the policy and administrative hierarchy of the organization within this domain. You have a single site organization, so do the following:

    a. Create an OU for the users (Users).

    b. Create another for the computers (Computers).

    c. Create one more for the security groups (Security Groups).

    You can see the solution in Figure 8.5. This allows you to give rights to each of these types of objects with granular control and to treat them differently. You'll be creating the users in the OU\BigFirm\Users within the domain bigfirm.com.

FIGURE 8.5

The Users OU

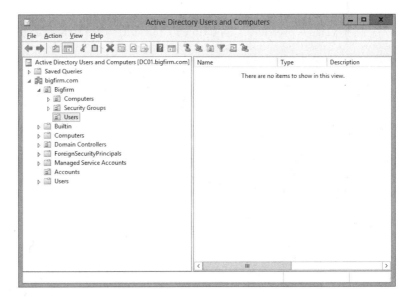

3. Navigate into the OU where you want to create your new user.

4. Right-click in the OU, and select New ➢ User to create the user. This launches the New Object-User Wizard.

    You can see that things are pretty simple here.

5. Enter the first name and last name of the user.

    This automatically completes the full name, which you can alter if you want.

6. Enter the logon name, such as **SRed**, as shown in Figure 8.6.

FIGURE 8.6
Creating a new
Active Directory
user

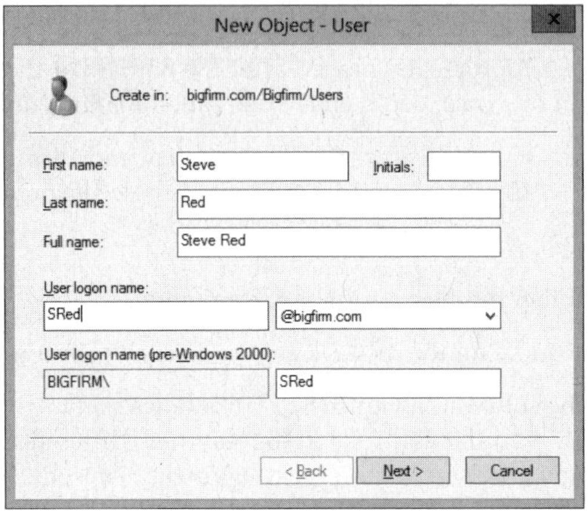

This is probably a good time to introduce some terminology for people new to Active Directory and user account management. Every user has two types of names with which they can access resources on the network:

User Logon Name   This is the name that you are probably most familiar with, such as SRed.

User Principal Name   This is a username that looks like an email address. You can see in Figure 8.6 that the UPN for Steve Red is SRed@bigfirm.com. The UPN suffix (@bigfirm.com) is inherited from the name of the domain by default. This is bigfirm.com in our scenario. Note that you can add UPN suffixes to your Active Directory forest by following the instructions at http://tinyurl.com/3y4zdw.

The user logon name, which was retained by Microsoft for backward compatibility, is visible as SRed. You can also see that the pre–Windows 2000 username is Bigfirm\ SRed. Funnily enough, this pre–Windows 2000 username is exactly what users will be prompted to enter when they log onto the domain!

7. Click Next to go to the New Object - User page, shown in Figure 8.7.

FIGURE 8.7
Setting the
new AD user
password

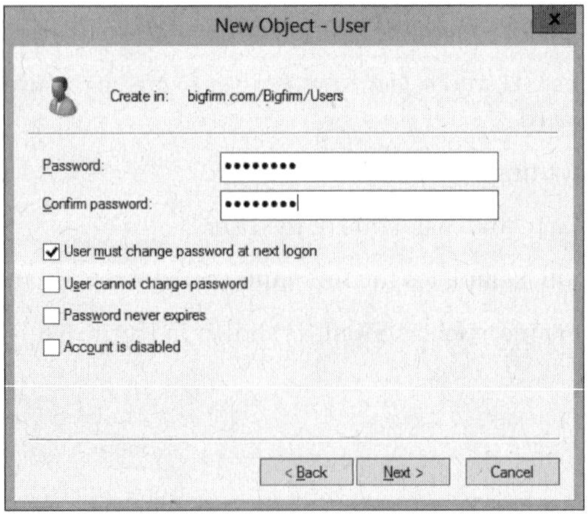

The options here are pretty self-explanatory and work just like those in the local user account. We described them earlier while showing how to create a local user account. A common mistake here is to not enter a password that meets your defined complexity requirements. The default settings are defined in the Default Domain Policy. You may have customized these with another policy object. You won't be able to complete this wizard without meeting the requirements.

8. Finish the wizard to create the user.

You can see in Figure 8.8 that the user is created and that it is located in the \BigFirm\Users OU. That's it. That's pretty simple, right? Let's take a look at how you can do the same thing from command line.

FIGURE 8.8

The new user in
Active Directory

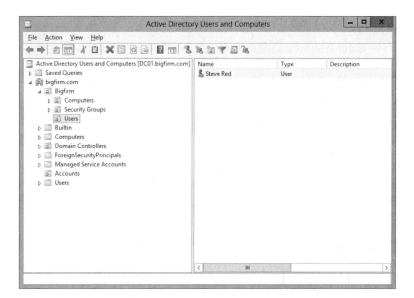

The first command you'll look at is dsadd. The following command will re-create what you've just done in the GUI:

```
dsadd user "CN=Steve Red,OU=Users,OU=BigFirm,DC=bigfirm,DC=com" -samid SRed
-upn SRed@bigfirm.com -fn Steve -ln Red -display "Steve Red" -pwd Mydogisblu3
-mustchpwd yes
```

Wow! That's quite a command. Here's the syntax:

```
dsadd user <Distinguished Name of the user> -samid <user logon name> -upn
<user principal name> -fn <firstname> -ln <surname> -display <full name> -pwd
<password> -mustchpwd <the user must change their password on first logon: yes or
no>
```

What's with this whole distinguished name (DN) thing? The DN describes where in Active Directory the user account object is created and how it is named. The DN in our case is: CN=Steve Red,OU=Users,OU=BigFirm,DC=bigfirm,DC=com. That breaks down as follows:

Component Name (CN)   This is the name of an object. In this case, it is the name of the user account object.

Organization Unit (OU)   You have a number of these to define your path of \BigFirm\ Users. Have you noticed yet how the DN is working its way backward up through the path, as in CN=Steve Red,OU=Users,OU=BigFirm?

Domain Component (DC)   This describes the name of the domain, such as bigfirm.com. Notice that this is *not* backward like the rest of the DN.

You can get more help on creating users using the dsadd command by typing **dsadd user /?**. There's a chance that you've seen that the net user command has a domain option. You are now thinking that it was a simpler command to use and wondering why we haven't chosen to use it here. The reason is that net user does not allow you to specify where in the domain you should create the user account object. You want to create the user in \BigFirm\Users, and dsadd allows you to do this.

Let's now take a look at what you have created and how you can manage those user accounts.

Setting Local User Account Properties

Let's open the user account for Steve Red that is created on the member server, Server01. You should right-click that user and choose Properties. This opens the screen shown in Figure 8.9.

FIGURE 8.9
Local user general properties

This dialog box will look pretty familar. These are the settings you defined for the user account when you created it. The grayed-out check box, "Account is locked out" will be enabled and selected if the user is locked out. An account will be locked out if the password policy defines that it should be locked out after *x* number of failed password entry attempts within a specified time frame. By default, this is defined in the Default Domain Policy. Notice that you cannot select this box; that's because you cannot use this dialog box to lock out a user. The option becomes enabled only when the user is actually locked out.

We will go through the properties of the user object now and discuss the various attributes of a local user account.

MEMBER OF TAB

The Member Of tab is used to control group membership of the user account (see Figure 8.10). We'll return to this tab when we cover groups later in this chapter.

FIGURE 8.10
Local user group membership

PROFILE TAB

The Profile tab, which you can see in Figure 8.11, is used to control a number of settings:

FIGURE 8.11
Local user profile settings

Profile Path   This setting is the location where the user profile is located. A *profile* is a folder structure that contains the settings that are unique to that user. It also contains things such as their My Documents and Favorites folders.

Logon Script   This setting allows you to define a script that will be stored on domain controllers and that will be run every time this user logs on. You might store this logon script locally for a local user account.

Home Folder   This setting allows you to define a network drive that will be dedicated to this user and mapped as a particular drive letter when they log in.

OBTAINING THE DN THE EASY WAY

Administrators can sometimes be pretty lazy, so you might hate typing this stuff. Our tip for obtaining the DN of the OU you are creating is to follow these steps:

1. Open Active Directory Users and Computers.

2. Select View ➢ Advanced Features.

   This makes a lot of things visible to you in the Advanced Users and Computers MMC.

3. Navigate to the OU that you want the DN of, and open its properties.

4. Click the Attribute Editor tab, and scroll down to distinguishedName, as shown here.

5. Double-click this and copy the DN for later reuse.

We mentioned profiles a moment ago. Quite simply, an administrator will create a folder for the user to automatically store their personal data and settings and share the folder on a file server. It will have security permissions placed on it so that only the user in question (as well as local system and local administrators) can access the folder. This will allow the user's profile to be stored in this location when they log out and downloaded when they log in. An example of such a folder might be `\\DC01\profiles\SRed`. This is created as follows:

◆ DC01 is the file server.

◆ Profiles is a shared folder.

 All authenticated users can read and write to the share. The folder in the file system allows only authenticated users to read the contents. Local administrators will probably have full control permissions on the share and the folder. You might consider creating this share as a hidden share that is not visible when you browse the network by naming the share **Profiles$**.

◆ SRed is a folder that is created to store the profile of the user Steve Red.

 Security on this folder allows only the user Steve Red to read and write to this folder via the Modify permission. Administrators of the file server and system will have full control rights.

ENVIRONMENT TAB

The Environment tab shown in Figure 8.12 controls how the working environment is configured when the user logs into the server using Windows Server 2008 Terminal Services or Windows Server 2012 Remote Desktop Services, such as by using the Remote Desktop Connection client.

FIGURE 8.12
Local user
environment settings

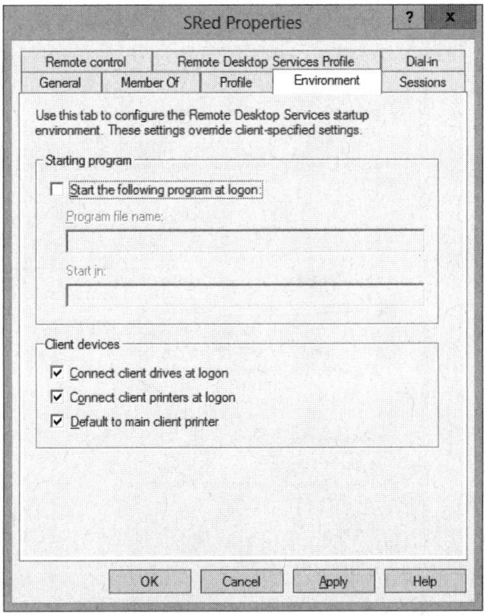

You can configure a particular program to run every time a user logs in by selecting the "Start the following program at logon" option. You should enter the command to run that program and also enter a folder that will be the startup folder for that program.

The Remote Desktop Connection client allows a user to choose to map their local drives and local printers and choose to configure print jobs while using the server to always go to the client computer's default printer. Administrators can forcefully control these options using this tab.

REMOTE DESKTOP SERVICES OR TERMINAL SERVICES

Windows Server 2012 expanded the functionality in Terminal Services to include virtual desktop infrastructure. Microsoft rebranded Terminal Services in Windows Server 2008 R2 as Remote Desktop Services, and in Windows Server 2012 it is still Remote Desktop Services (RDS). That can be a little confusing if you're reading this chapter and still working with Windows Server 2008. Just know that when we refer to Remote Desktop Services, we are usually also talking about Terminal Services on Windows Server 2008/2012.

SESSIONS TAB

You can see the Sessions tab in Figure 8.13. It also controls how Remote Desktop Services will work for this user. A user's session on a server will remain in a disconnected state on a server if they do not choose to log out. This means that they continue to use resources and that their programs continue to execute. More important, this means that one of the two freely available concurrent sessions that are used by administrators on servers will be consumed. Forgetful administrators can quickly consume both of those sessions, which will prevent other administrators from logging in normally by using the Remote Desktop Connection client. Note that administrators can terminate those sessions by using Remote Desktop Services Manager either locally or from a remote computer.

FIGURE 8.13
Local user Sessions tab

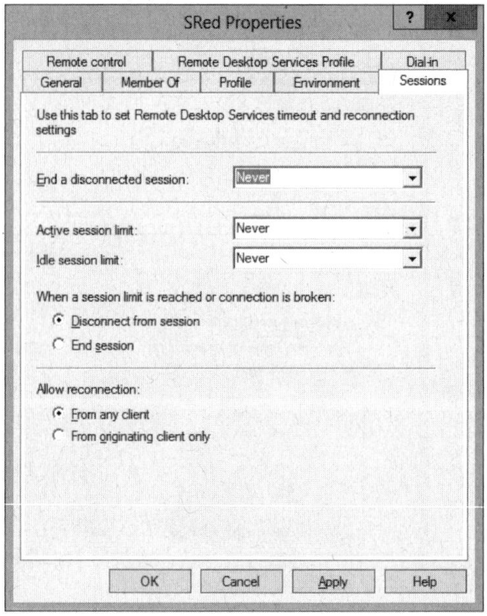

You can force disconnected sessions to terminate automatically after a defined time. Although it's more efficient to configure this centrally using the Windows Server 2012 Remote Desktop Services Configuration, you can do this on a per-user basis by using the "End a disconnected session" drop-down box on the Sessions tab.

Those valuable sessions can be made available by limiting how long an administrator's session can last. You can configure this maximum time by configuring the "Active session limit" drop-down box.

Idle sessions can be terminated automatically by choosing a time limit in the "Idle session limit" drop-down box.

The termination action for "Idle session limit" and "Active session limit" can be configured to be either disconnect the session (that is, the session still runs but is not interactive) or end the session completely.

A user can reconnect to a disconnected session to continue what they were previously doing. This is pretty useful in the following situations:

◆   A session will be disconnected if there is a network outage between the client and server.

◆   A user or administrator may deliberately disconnect a session to leave some task running without any interaction.

It appears from the bottom of this tab that you can control how a user can reconnect to a disconnected session. You may choose to allow the user to reconnect from any client or only from the original client. This latter option might be used for security reasons, but it is a pretty restrictive idea.

REMOTE CONTROL TAB

The Remote Control tab, shown in Figure 8.14, allows administrators to control how an administrator can interact with a user's Remote Desktop Services session. The concept is that an administrator can join the user's session to assist them with some task.

FIGURE 8.14
Local user Remote
Control tab

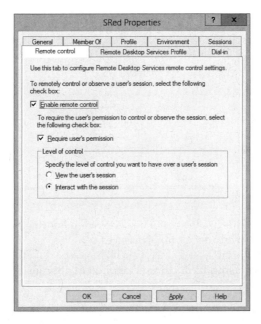

The default is that remote control is enabled. Maybe some user should never have remote control. You can disable remote control of that user's sessions by deselecting the "Enable remote control" check box.

This remote control thing might sound like it could be a little sneaky. The default is that a user will be prompted to either allow or disallow the remote control attempt by an administrator. You could deselect the "Require user's permission" check box to never involve the user in the process.

If you have allowed remote control, then you can configure the level of interaction that the administrator can have with the user's session. You can set it so that the administrator can only view the user's session; in other words, it is read-only with no control. The default is to allow an interactive session where an administrator can use the mouse and keyboard in the user's session.

REMOTE DESKTOP SERVICES PROFILE TAB

The Remote Desktop Services Profile tab, Figure 8.15, allows you to specify a custom profile for when this user logs into the server using Remote Desktop Services. This can allow administrators to provide a dedicated Remote Desktop Services profile or even a restricted profile for this user's session called a *mandatory profile*. The path for your custom profile will logically be placed in the Profile Path field.

FIGURE 8.15

Local user Remote Desktop Services Profile tab

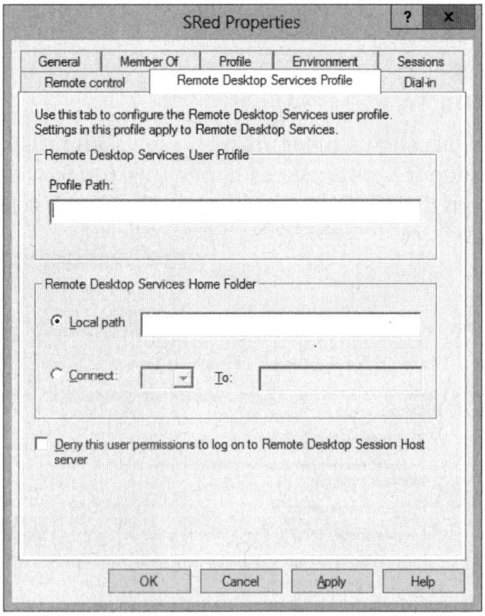

You can also offer this user a special home folder for storing personal information if they connect to the server by using Terminal Services.

At the bottom of the tab, you can see a check box to prevent the user from even being able to log into this server using Terminal Services. You might consider doing this with accounts such as those used for services. This means that even if the account's password should become compromised, you can still prevent it from being used by an attacker via Remote Desktop.

DIAL-IN TAB

The Dial-in tab, as shown in Figure 8.16, allows an administrator to control if and how a user can remotely connect to this server, such as by initiating a VPN tunnel or using a modem to dial in.

FIGURE 8.16
Local user Dial-in tab

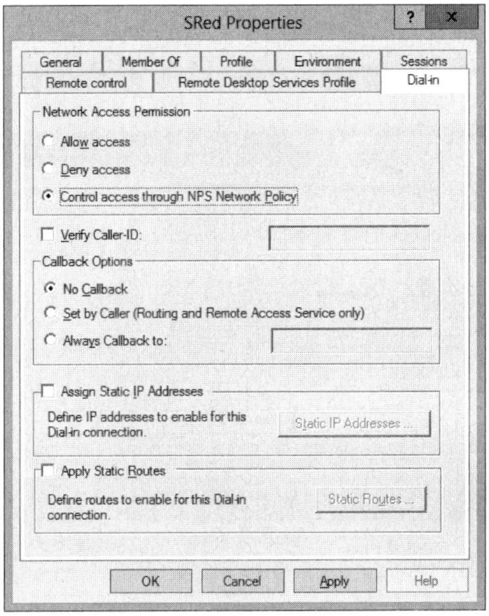

Changing any of the properties in this dialog box is pretty easy using Active Directory Users and Computers, as you've probably realized by now. You can control only *some* of these settings by using the `net user` command. Let's take a look at one or two. This command will change the full name of the local user account:

```
net user SRed /fullname:"Steve Red"
```

This will set the home folder path to that of your choosing:

```
net user SRed /homedir:"D:\Home\SRed"
```

You should make sure that the path is valid before you run the command because the command does not check it. You should also verify that the permissions are OK for this user.

This configures the profile path setting for the user:

```
net user SRed /profilepath:"D:\Profiles\SRed"
```

Again, there is no error-checking built into the command, so you should first make sure that the path and permissions are valid.

Setting Domain-Based User Account Properties

Let's compare what you've just looked at in a local user account with that of a domain-based user account:

1. Log back into the domain controller, DC01.bigfirm.com.

2. Navigate to a user.

3. Select the user object, right-click, and select Properties.

   Note that you should have Advanced Features enabled in the View menu of Active Directory Users and Computers (ADUC). You can see the user's properties in Figure 8.17.

FIGURE 8.17

Active Directory
user account properties

4. Disable the Advanced Features view in ADUC and see how it compares to the following sections.

You'll notice that the advanced view gives you much more power. You can see two things here:

◆ There are a lot more tabs with many more settings available to you in a domain-based user account than there are in a local user account.

   This gives administrators much more control over their users. It also allows you to store more information with each user account. This information can be used by users or by applications.

◆ Both local user accounts and domain-based user accounts share a lot of common settings.

We won't repeat ourselves when it comes to those settings in this section. We are assuming you've read the descriptions in the previous section on local user accounts.

Let's start by looking at the General tab.

GENERAL TAB

You can see, again in Figure 8.17, some descriptive information for your user. You'll see the usual first name and last name. You also have the ability to store some other information about the user in the user account object in Active Directory such as their office, telephone number, email address, and web page. You'll find that you can make use of any defined email address or web page settings for this user by right-clicking the account object in Active Directory Users and Computers. This allows you to open the user's defined web page or send mail to their defined email address.

ADDRESS TAB

The Address tab is shown in Figure 8.18. This allows you to define a postal address for the user in question. Why would you want to do this? Active Directory can be used as a directory for users; in other words, it can be used by users to find out information about other users on the network, or it can be used by applications to store, retrieve, and share information about the users.

FIGURE 8.18

Active Directory
user Address tab

ACCOUNT TAB

You can see the user logon name, the UPN, and the pre–Windows 2000 user logon name that you defined while creating the user in Figure 8.19. You can use these controls to modify those usernames.

FIGURE 8.19
Active Directory
user Account tab

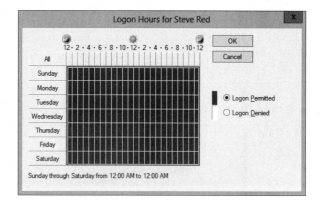

Clicking the Logon Hours button will open the dialog box in Figure 8.20. This allows you to control when a user can log on to the network to access resources. It does not forcibly log the user off. You might consider using this control where security is extremely strict. It's not a common requirement to configure this setting.

FIGURE 8.20
Active Directory
user Logon Hours
dialog

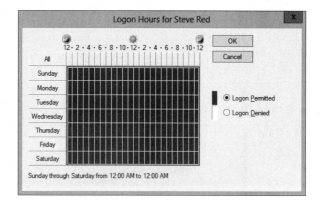

Back on the Account tab is a button called Log On To. The dialog box in Figure 8.21 will open if you click it.

FIGURE 8.21
Active Directory
user Logon
Workstations
dialog box

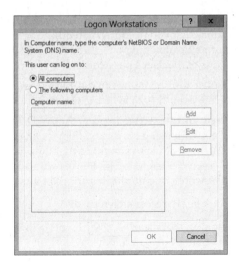

This dialog box allows you to control which computers this user can use to log into Active Directory. You might consider doing this in a few scenarios:

◆ You need to control where some or all of your users log in. This isn't exactly a common configuration request, but we can imagine that some places that have CIA/NSA-like security might want to use this.

◆ You have a consultant or visiting engineer on-site, and you want to restrict the person to the computers they should be working on.

◆ You are creating a user account for an application or a service, and you need to ensure that it is used only on the designated servers. This will restrict any damage (temporarily!) that can be done if that user account is compromised.

The Log On To and the Logon Hours settings on the Account tab can be used together to accomplish your domain-based user account logon restrictions.

Returning to Figure 8.19, have you noticed that you have many more options for controlling the account? It's not necessarily immediately obvious until you scroll down that control in the middle of the dialog box:

User Must Change Password at Next Logon   This is used by an administrator to force a user to change their password after an administrator has set or reset it. This means that the administrator should have no knowledge of what the user will use for their password.

User Cannot Change Password   This would be used by an administrator for a service account to ensure that it cannot be changed.

Password Never Expires   This control overrides any password expiration policies that may be configured in Active Directory. Ideally it won't be used for ordinary user accounts, but it is typically used for service user accounts.

Store Password Using Reversible Encryption   Never enable this setting unless you know with 100 percent certainty that you need it. It is required when applications need to know a user's password for authentication purposes. Microsoft says that it is essentially the same as storing cleartext versions of the user's password.

Account Is Disabled   An administrator can disable a user account to prevent anyone from being able to authenticate or authorize by using the account.

Smart Card Is Required for Interactive Logon   Active Directory can be configured to allow users to sign onto the network using a *smart card* device. It's referred to as *two-factor authentication*. In other words, the user uses something that they have (a unique token) and something that they know (a secret PIN) to log in. It is considered to be a much better solution for authentication than passwords or passphrases, for the following reasons:

- The token cannot be shared or stolen easily.

  The device is unique, so it means that the owner will know if it is stolen, or they cannot log in themselves if they give it to someone else.

- It uses a simple-to-remember PIN. It also uses very strong encryption mechanisms.

  This means that the user doesn't have any passwords that change on a frequent basis—a common cause of headaches for IT on a Monday morning when users forget their long or complex passwords!

The added security might prompt administrators to deploy smart cards to either some or all users depending on security requirements. This check box will force users to log in using their assigned smart card and will not allow them to log in using the traditional username and password.

Account Is Sensitive and Cannot Be Delegated   This configures whether the user can be impersonated by a service. This is done to allow the service to impersonate the user. You might possibly encounter this behavior in the middle tier of an *n*-tier architecture, such as a web front end, a middle-layer application server, and the backend database architecture. The default is that this check box is clear and allows impersonation of this user account.

Use Kerberos DES Encryption Types for This Account   Some applications may require a service account that uses the DES encryption algorithm. You would enable this setting for those service user accounts. You may need to reset the password after changing this setting.

This Account Supports AES 128-Bit Encryption   Some applications may require a service user account with AES 128-bit encryption. You would enable this setting for those accounts.

This Account Supports AES 256-Bit Encryption   See the previous item about AES 128-bit encryption.

Do Not Require Kerberos Preauthentication   This setting can be used to enable users to be able to log in when the network contains mixed variety Kerberos realms, such as an Active Directory and Unix key distribution centers (KDCs).

Notice that there isn't a grayed-out check box to indicate that the user is locked out? This makes it very clear to you that you cannot just go to this dialog box to lock out a user. Instead, you only have a control to unlock a user account near the top middle of the tab.

The last control on this tab is for controlling the automated expiration of this account. You can define a date when the user account will no longer be able to be used. You might use this when creating a user account for visiting engineers/consultants or for temporary/contract staff. Since you would know how long they would be in the office, you could preconfigure when the account would expire so that they could no longer log in. This protects the network nicely against user account misuse.

PROFILE TAB

We discussed in the local user account properties the reasons for having the Profile tab shown in Figure 8.22.

FIGURE 8.22

Active Directory user Profile tab

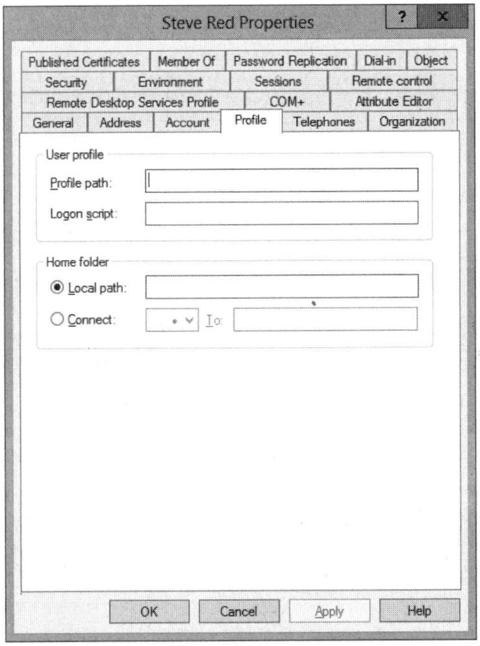

TELEPHONES TAB

The Telephones tab is pretty self-explanatory (see Figure 8.23). You can store telecommunications contact information for the user in their user account object.

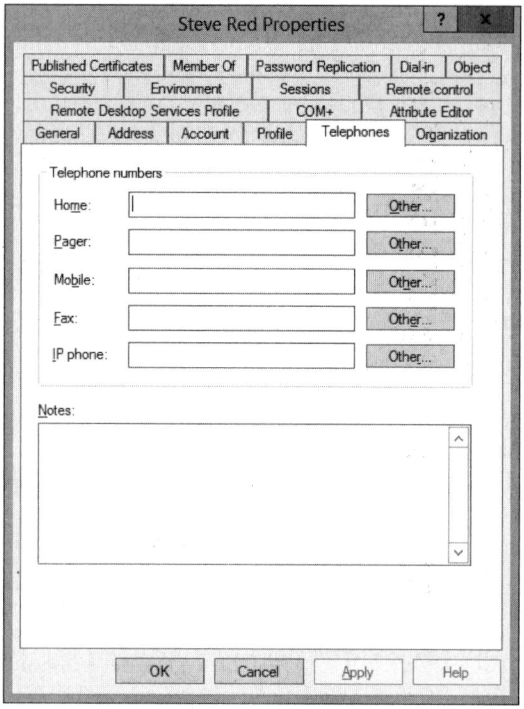

FIGURE 8.23

Active Directory
user Telephones tab

ORGANIZATION TAB

The Organization tab is another one of the information tabs (see Figure 8.24). We've
mentioned several times that applications can use this sort of information. For example,
the settings here could be used by a Windows SharePoint Services (WSS) implementation.
This information is presented in a web interface when users look to find more about an owner
of some documentation or a site within the WSS implementation. WSS loads this information
from the user's Active Directory user account object. For example, if you browsed to view
Steve Red on a WSS server, then the properties of SRed would be read by WSS from Active
Directory.

This tab allows you to describe the role of the user within the organization—it's more of a
human resources thing and doesn't have anything to do with Active Directory delegation or
administration. You can also select their line manager by browsing to another domain-based
user account in Active Directory.

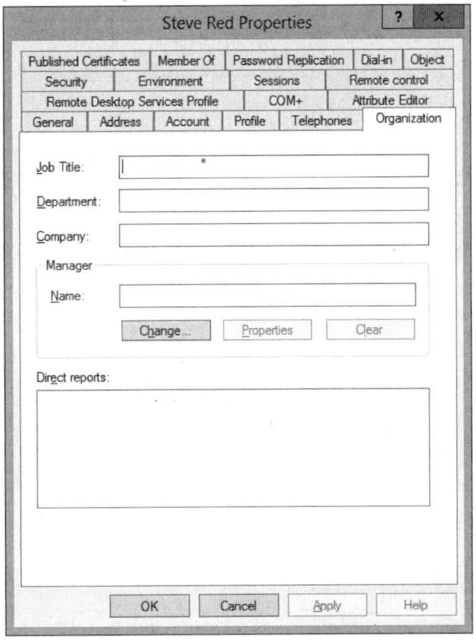

FIGURE 8.24
Active Directory
user Organization
tab

COM+ TAB

You're delving into application programming country with the COM+ tab in Figure 8.25. A
partition is an application configuration. An application can have many configurations. This
means you can have many of these COM+ partitions within Active Directory. You can read more
about application partitions on MSDN.

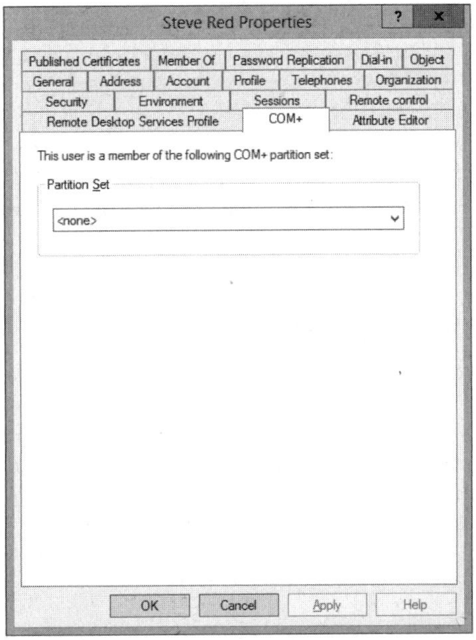

FIGURE 8.25
Active Directory
user COM+ tab

A partition set can contain many partitions. You can link users to partition sets and in turn to the contained partitions. Not only can you link a single user, but you can link all users in an OU by linking the OU to a partition set. You can read more about creating partition sets within Active Directory on MSDN at http://tinyurl.com/2naoft.

ATTRIBUTE EDITOR TAB

You've seen this tab before when you looked at the properties of an OU (see Figure 8.26). You can view or directly edit the properties of a user object here if you want.

FIGURE 8.26
Active Directory
user Attribute
Editor tab

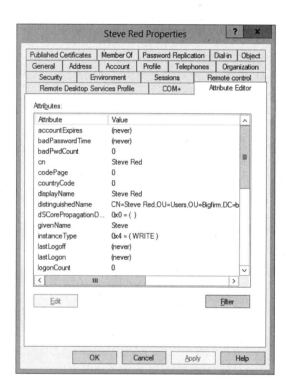

PUBLISHED CERTIFICATES TAB

Certificates give you an encryption-based security mechanism that is used to prove identity (see Figure 8.27).

Here you can view certificates that have been automatically assigned to the user through Active Directory using Certificate Services. You can actually manually assign certificates to a user from your own local certificate stores or from certificates that are stored on the file system.

FIGURE 8.27
Active Directory
user Published
Certificates tab

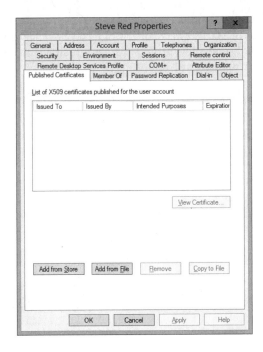

MEMBER OF TAB

The Member Of tab allows you to control group membership of this user account (see Figure 8.28). We'll return to this later when we cover groups and group membership later in this chapter.

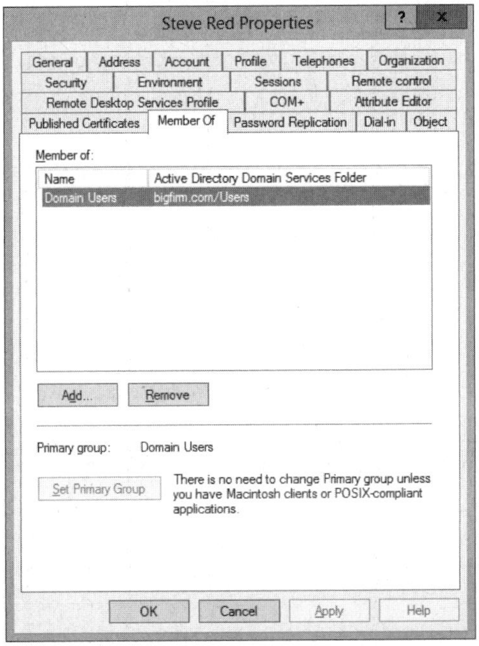

FIGURE 8.28
Active Directory
user group
memberships

You can see that you can also control the primary group of the user. This is required only in POSIX applications or Macintosh client computers. When one of these clients creates a file or folder on a Windows server, this primary group is assigned to the new object. The group must be in the user's own domain, and it must be either a global or universal security group.

PASSWORD REPLICATION TAB

The Password Replication tab is used to view which read-only domain controllers (RODCs) this user's password has been replicated to (see Figure 8.29). An RODC is an Active Directory architecture option that was added with Windows Server 2008. You can place an RODC in branch offices where the physical security of a normal domain controller cannot be guaranteed. In the event of the theft or compromise of an RODC, you can isolate user accounts that have their details stored on that RODC.

FIGURE 8.29
Active Directory
user Password
Replication tab

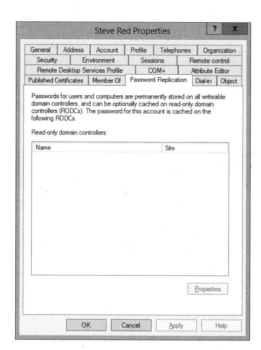

OBJECT TAB

You'll find the Object tab, shown in Figure 8.30, to be quite useful when doing some troubleshooting. You can view some useful information such as the following:

◆ When the object was created

◆ When it was last modified

◆ USN information that is used to control Active Directory replication

FIGURE 8.30

Active Directory
user object
properties

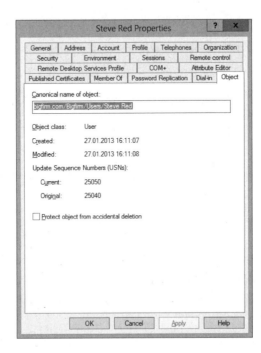

A nice new option on this tab is the ability to protect the user account against accidental deletion using the check box at the bottom. This would be pretty useful to ensure that no one unintentionally deletes the user account for a critical service account, such as the CEO or a senior government official.

SECURITY TAB

The Security tab, as shown in Figure 8.31 allows you to control who can do what to this user account object. This is known as *delegation*. We'll discuss this subject in great depth later in this book.

Take a look at the permissions assigned to SELF by clicking it. SELF is the user in question. That is, what can Steve Red do to the SRed user account? If you scroll down in the "Permissions for SELF" control, you will see that Steve can actually change a lot of settings in his own user account. This means that Steve can alter settings such as who his manager is, what his contact details are, and so on. In theory, you could present users with some web-like application that allows them to easily edit these settings. This approach would be much easier for them to understand than asking them to fire up Active Directory User and Computers and edit their accounts there!

FIGURE 8.31
Active Directory
user object security

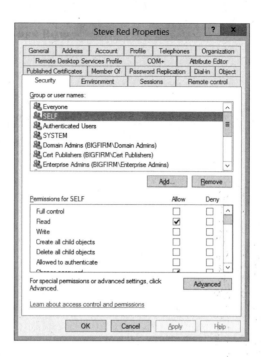

EDITING MANY USER ACCOUNTS AT ONCE

It's pretty easy to change all of those settings for an individual account, as you've just seen. What if you want to modify more than one account at once? That's easy too. For this example, create a couple of new users in the Users OU, as shown in Figure 8.32.

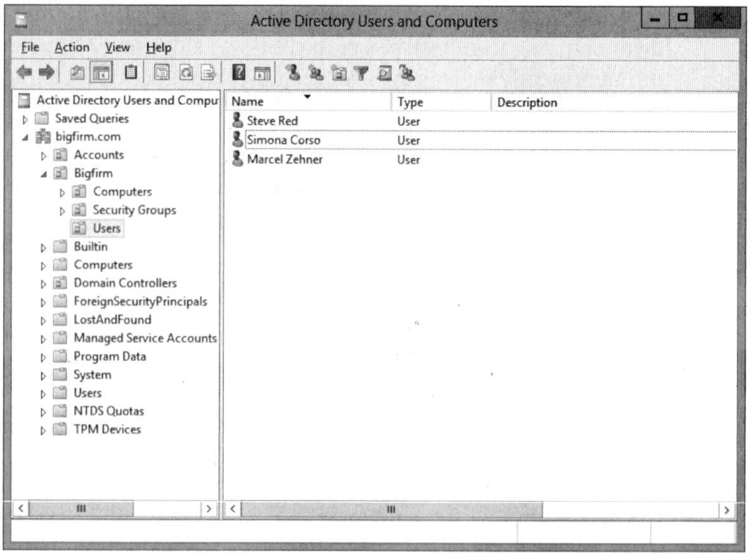

FIGURE 8.32
Additional Active
Directory users

Say you want to modify settings for all the users in this OU. Select all the user accounts, right-click, and select Properties.

This opens up a properties dialog box, shown in Figure 8.33. It actually doesn't make sense to offer all the settings for more than one user, so you see only a subset of the options.

FIGURE 8.33
Properties of multiple Active Directory user objects

To modify a setting, select the check box associated with it. This makes the edit box available to you. You can now edit the setting for all the users you previously selected, as shown in Figure 8.34.

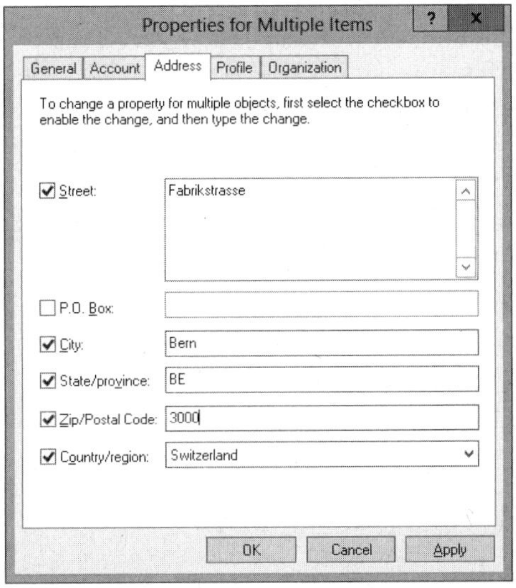

FIGURE 8.34
Changing attributes of multiple Active Directory objects

Managing domain-based user account objects is pretty easy when using Active Directory Users and Computers. You'll now take a look at how to do it when the command prompt is your only option.

MANAGING DOMAIN-BASED USER PROPERTIES AT THE COMMAND LINE

Let's look at how you can do the same thing using the command prompt. You'll be using a command called dsmod with the user option. You can view the help for this by running the following:

```
dsmod user /?
```

Notice that you have to use the DN of the user that you want to modify. Check out the previous tip to get this from the distinguishedName property of the user account object on the Attribute Editor tab (see the "Obtaining the DN the Easy Way" sidebar). That's all well and good if you have a GUI available to you. What happens if you don't? If you know the UPN of the user, then you can run dsquery to get the DN:

```
dsquery user -upn SRed@bigfirm.com
"CN=Steve Red,OU=Users,OU=BigFirm,DC=bigfirm,DC=com"
```

Alternatively, you can run the dsquery command using the SAM account name, which is the friendly name that you know as SRed:

```
C:\Users\Administrator>dsquery user -samid SRed
"CN=Steve Red,OU=Users,OU=BigFirm,DC=bigfirm,DC=com"
```

dsquery is a really powerful command, so it's well worth getting to know it with dsquery /?.

Now you can proceed with dsmod. Let's see how you can configure a home drive and a drive letter to map it for Steve Red:

```
dsmod user "CN=Steve Red,OU=Users,OU=BigFirm,DC=bigfirm,DC=com" -hmdir \\DC01\
home$\SRed -hmdrv P
```

This will configure a home drive (a special network-based shared folder specific to this user) with the drive letter P mapped to \\DC01\home$\SRed whenever Steve Red logs in.

You now want to configure the manager for Steve Red. You've just learned that Marcel Zehner has been promoted to be the department head. You can do this by running the following:

```
dsmod user "CN=Steve Red,OU=Users,OU=BigFirm,DC=bigfirm,DC=com" -mgr "CN= Marcel
Zehner,OU=Users,OU=BigFirm,DC=bigfirm,DC=com"
```

Notice that you didn't enter something like bigfirm\mzehner or mzehner as the manager. You actually used the DN for the account that is the manager.

At first, dsmod looks like a difficult command to use. Play with it for a few minutes, and you'll see that it's not actually that bad.

RENAMING AND DELETING OBJECTS

As you can imagine, the decision to rename or delete something should be considered very carefully. There's a very serious implication to this.

RENAMING OBJECTS

Every object in Windows has a name. You use that name for logins, scripts, application configuration, and so on. For example, if you create a user called SCorso, then Simona Corso will use that label to log in. Windows does not use that name to keep track of the subject. That's because names change. Simona might get married and change her surname to Simona Red. That will require changing her username to SiRed. Windows needs to treat her exactly as it always did. Windows won't want to find every resource on the network where SCorso was used to change the reference to SiRed, such as group memberships, file share permissions, mailbox associations, and so on.

Understanding How a SID Comes into Play

We humans need something we can remember and type easily, so a friendly label is used. Windows has a special code for each object called a *security identifier (SID)*. The SID is a globally unique identifier for every object in Active Directory. Every user object has a SID. Every computer object has a SID. Every group has a SID.

What happens when you rename a user or group, such as a *security principal*? Sure enough, the name you know changes. In the case of Simona, she will need to remember her username. However, Windows tracks her user object only by the SID. Any resource permissions assigned to her user object or any group memberships associated with her user object won't change. Her user object name has changed, but her SID has not. Note that any third-party applications that use object names instead of SIDs will still require some administration to change the referenced object name. But anything that integrates tightly with Active Directory, such as SQL, SharePoint, or Exchange, will be OK.

The thing to remember here is that when you change the name of an Active Directory object, such as a user or group, Windows still sees that as being the same object even if you don't. Permissions given to that object, attributes of that object, group memberships, and so on will not have changed.

DELETING AN OBJECT

The other scenario you need to discuss is when you delete an object. If you assign permissions to SiRed, then Windows maintains a list of permissions that are associated with her SID. The same happens if you assign permissions to a group of users. Windows will maintain the permissions associated with the SID of that group object, not with its name.

Restoring a Deleted Object

You have to be very careful about deleting that user or group object. If you accidentally delete them or you're told to restore them to their prior state, then you cannot just create a new object with an identical name. Remember that the SID is globally unique and is not tied to the name. A replacement SiRed user object will have a different SID. The file share or mailbox that Simona used to have access to won't recognize the new user object because it has a different SID than the old user object. The only way to restore access to a deleted group or user object is to restore the deleted object from a backup.

There's a few ways to do this, which Microsoft discusses at `http://tinyurl.com/2wgo4g`. Microsoft added a new Active Directory Recycle Bin in Windows Server 2012, which will simplify the process of restoring recently deleted objects.

The point to remember is that the name of an object is not how Windows identifies the object. It uses a SID. You might re-create a copy of an object with the same name, but it will be a different object.

A BEST PRACTICE

For this reason, we strongly recommend that you disable users when you are asked to remove a user by your manager or the human resources department. That turns the user off and blocks them out from the network. Additionally we recommend creating a dedicated OU for accounts that have been disabled and that you move every account that you disable to this OU. Doing it this way gives you an immediate overview of all accounts that are not in use anymore. There's always a chance that there has been a miscommunication or the person returns to work. Reenabling their access is easy: enable their account. After an agreed cooling-off period of 30 or 60 days, you can go ahead and delete that object.

For your Active Directory domain, you can use this command to find inactive and disabled accounts:

```
dsquery user -inactive <number of weeks> -disabled
```

For example, this command will find users that are disabled and have been inactive for eight weeks:

```
dsquery user -inactive 8 -disabled
```

To delete a user or a number of users, you simply select them, right-click, and select Delete. Deleting a user isn't much of a challenge from the command prompt. You can run the following to delete a local user account:

```
net user <username> /delete
```

This command will delete the SRed local user account:

```
net user SRed /delete
```

You'll use the dsrm command and the user object's DN to delete an Active Directory user account:

```
dsrm "CN=Steve Red,OU=Users,OU=BigFirm,DC=bigfirm,DC=com"
```

You will be prompted to confirm the deletion. That's not necessarily a bad thing, but you won't want that to happen in a script. You can prevent a confirmation prompt by running this:

```
dsrm "CN=Steve Red,OU=Users,OU=BigFirm,DC=bigfirm,DC=com" -noprompt
```

Managing Groups

Treating a collection of users as a single entity for one or a number of purposes eases a lot of administration tasks. For example, instead of performing 100 operations to assign permissions to each of the 10 users to 10 resources, you can assign the users to a group (1 operation) and assign the group permissions to the resources (11 operations). The math makes it clear why you should use groups. Instead of dealing with individuals, you deal with the collective or the group.

In fact, best practice is that you always use groups for assigning permissions. Therefore, you need to know how to create groups, modify memberships, and remove groups.

You'll now learn about creating, controlling, and deleting local groups and domain-based groups. You'll see how to do this work using Active Directory Users and Computers and the command prompt.

Local Groups

Just like a local user, a local group exists within a member or stand-alone computer, be it a server, laptop, or desktop. It can contain local user accounts that exist on the server. It can also contain users or groups from the Active Directory that the server is a member of. You can manage groups using the same GUI tools that you use to manage local users.

Figure 8.35 shows where you manage local groups on a server. You can see that there are a number of them here by default. Windows will also add more groups if you add certain roles.

FIGURE 8.35
The default local groups

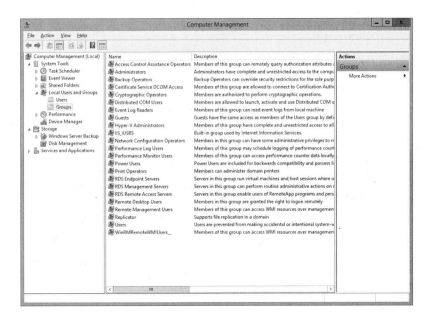

CREATING A GROUP

In this section, you'll create a new group called Fileshare. You can use it to assign permissions to a file share on this server to members of this group:

1. Either click the Action menu or right-click in the center pane, and then select New Group.

   The New Group dialog box will open.

2. Enter the name of the group as Fileshare, as shown in Figure 8.36.

   We recommend that you enter a description for any group you create. You might remember what this group is intended for now, but will you remember what it does in six months when you've been working on countless other projects and come back to fix an issue on this machine? Will your colleagues know what it does when you are out sick or away on vacation?

FIGURE 8.36
Creating a new local group

If you wanted, you could create this group now with no members. For this example, the local user for Steve Red should be made a member of this group, so you'll do that now.

3. Click the Add button.

You can see in Figure 8.37 that the dialog box that opens allows you to search for and add members.

FIGURE 8.37
Selecting group members

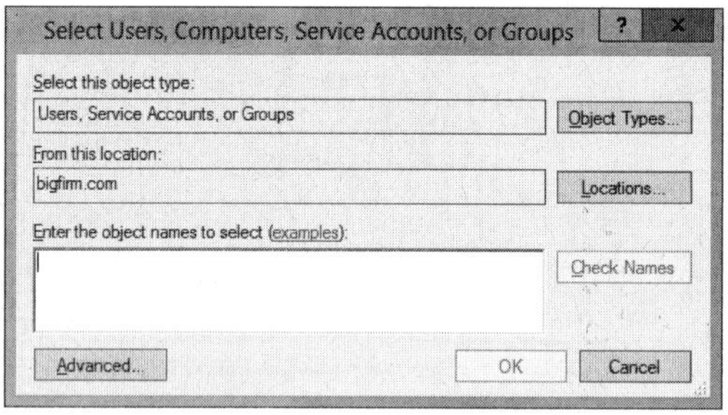

4. Add the following to the group:

◆ Active Directory or local users

◆ Computer accounts from Active Directory

◆ Active Directory groups

The Active Directory–based options are available only if this server is a member of a domain. The server that you are working with, SERVER01, is a member of bigfirm.com.

You can see that at the moment, the "Select this object type" setting allows you to add either users, groups, or service accounts to your group. You can modify this by clicking Object Types.

As shown in Figure 8.38, you can select or deselect Computers, Groups, Users, or Service Accounts. Now you are asking yourself, service accounts? In Windows Server 2012 you now also have the option to select Managed Service Accounts (MSA). Depending on what you select, this will modify what you can add to or remove from your group during this membership edit.

FIGURE 8.38
Potential group
member types

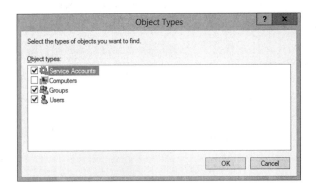

Back in the Select Users, Computers, Service Accounts, or Groups dialog box, you can see that "From this location" is set to the domain that the server is a member of. This is the default for a domain member computer. The location defines from where you can choose the objects that you have selected. A stand-alone server can have only itself as the location. In this example, you can choose either users or computers from the bigfirm.com domain.

5. You want to change this, so select a local user account. Click Locations to do this.

   Note that you could also select another trusted domain by clicking this button. Or you could even browse within the domain to a precise OU to reduce the size of the search for a domain-based user or computer.

   In Figure 8.39, we've expanded the domain to illustrate how you could browse through the OUs. However, you want to choose a local user account.

6. Select the name of the local server, Server01.

   You could alternatively select the domain so you could add a group or user from the Active Directory domain to add into your local group.

FIGURE 8.39
Selecting the object
source location

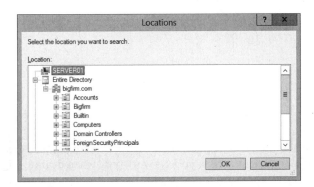

If you believe that you know the username of the local user account to add, then you could simply type it in.

7. Type in **SRed** (for example) and then click Check Names.

The dialog box searches the local account database and is able to confirm that SRed is actually SERVER01\SRed, as shown in Figure 8.40. Alternatively, if you are sure that the name is right, you could just type it and click OK.

FIGURE 8.40
Adding a user to the local group

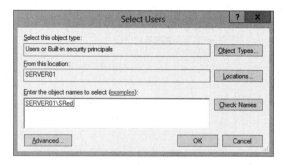

8. If you don't know the precise name, then click Advanced to open the dialog box shown in Figure 8.41.

FIGURE 8.41
Group membership advanced view

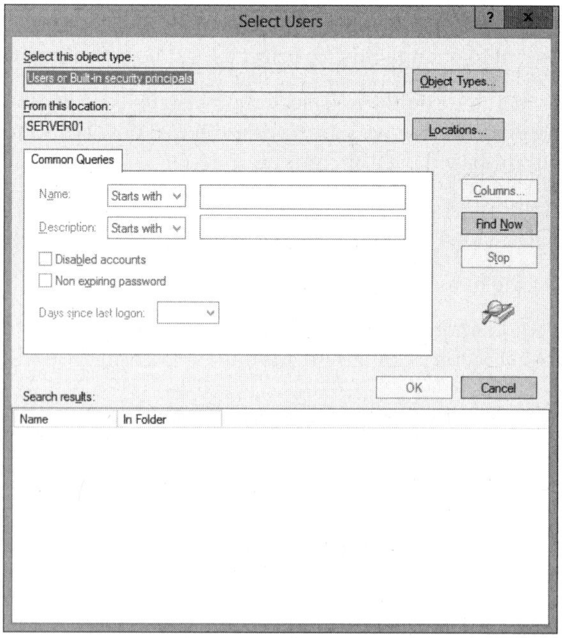

Lots of the search options here are grayed out because you have set the location to the local computer. These options work only when dealing with a domain location.

9. Click Find Now to list all the available accounts that you can add to the group based on the search criteria defined earlier.

Figure 8.42 shows the results of this search. Here you can select the object or objects that you want to add to the group.

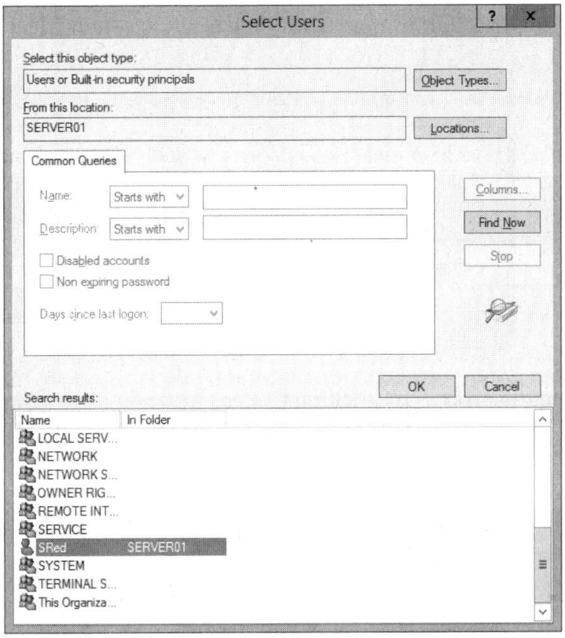

FIGURE 8.42
Selecting a user to add from the advanced view

10. Select SRed, and click OK.

The selected objects are displayed in the Select Users dialog box, as shown in Figure 8.43.

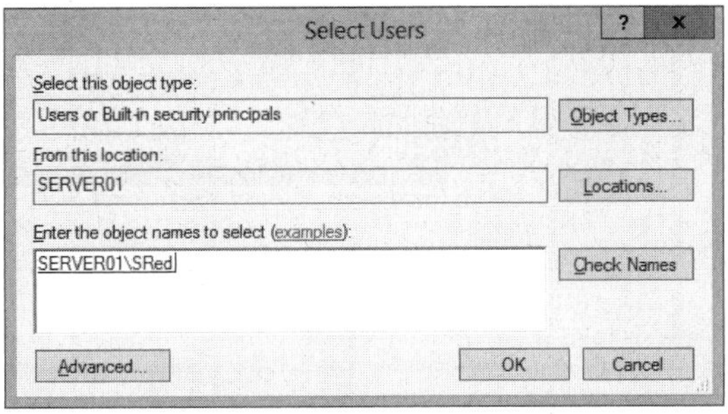

FIGURE 8.43
Checked potential group member

11. Click OK to save this membership.

You can see in Figure 8.44 that the group is ready to be created with its initial membership.

FIGURE 8.44
The potential
new members are
displayed.

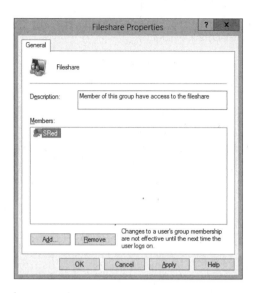

12. Complete the process by clicking Create.

You can see in Figure 8.45 that the new group is created and the user Steve Red has been added to it.

FIGURE 8.45
The new group is
created.

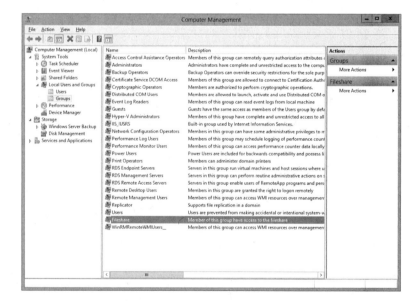

LOGGING IN WITH A NEW GROUP MEMBERSHIP

Here's something important to note. It doesn't matter if you are working with Active Directory or local groups. A user can use their group membership only when they log in *after* the group membership has been modified. Steve Red would not be able to use his new group membership if he was currently logged in. You would have to advise him to log out and log back in again.

CREATING A GROUP AT THE COMMAND LINE

You can do the same thing with the command prompt by using the `net localgroup` command. You can get help by running the following:

```
net help localgroup
```

You can create the group by running this:

```
net localgroup Fileshare /add /comment:"Members assigned permission to the
fileshare on this server"
```

The syntax for this command is as follows:

```
net localgroup <name of the new group> /add /comment:"<a description for the
group>"
```

Note that you cannot add a user to the group while creating it from the command prompt.

ADDING A USER TO GROUP

Let's add a new member to our group. You can do this via the MMC snap-in.

1. Open the properties of the group, which opens the window shown in Figure 8.46.

FIGURE 8.46
Group properties

Here you can see the existing membership of the group.

2. Click Add to add a new member to the group.

Just like before, you can set the criteria for what will be added to the group and from where. You are going to add a domain-based group to the local group. You want everyone who is in the domain to be in the local group. You happen to know that a built-in domain-based group called Domain Users will do this for you.

3. Type in the name of the group, and click Check Name.

You can see in Figure 8.47 that Domain Users will be added to the group.

FIGURE 8.47
Adding a domain
group to a local
group

4. You can also see that BIGFIRM\Domain Users will join SRed as a member of the group. Click OK (see Figure 8.48).

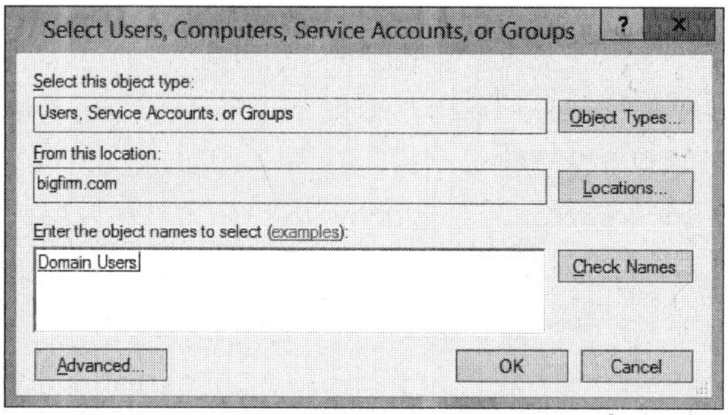

A HANDY TECHNIQUE: ADDING A DOMAIN GROUP TO A LOCAL GROUP

The scenario of adding a domain group to a local group is a powerful one. It allows an administrator to reuse a collection of Active Directory objects in the form of an Active Directory group and give them rights to a resource that is shared on this server. You might consider doing this where an application owner has been granted local administrative access to a single server and nothing else. They can create local groups and populate them with domain groups and users. The application administrator can share their application with domain members without needing any domain administrative rights.

FIGURE 8.48
The potential new
membership of the
group

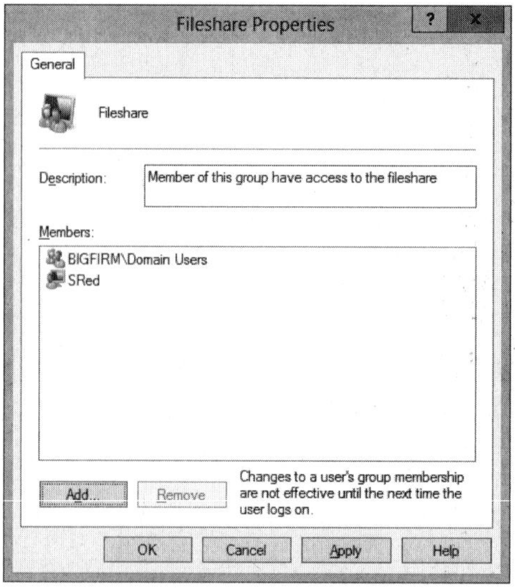

It's time for you to see how you can add members to a group using the command prompt. You'll be using net localgroup again:

```
net localgroup Fileshare SRed /add
```

That's a pretty simple command to add a user to a group. The syntax is pretty simple as well:

```
net localgroup Fileshare <name of object to add to the group> /add
```

The following quickly adds the Domain Users group from the BigFirm domain to your new local group:

```
net localgroup Fileshare "bigfirm\domain users" /add
```

Remember that Member Of tab in the local user account properties dialog box? Let's take a look at the user account object of SRed in Figure 8.49.

FIGURE 8.49

The user's group memberships

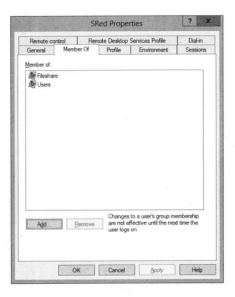

You can see that his group membership has been updated. You can just as easily add Steve to a group here. You have been asked to add Steve's local user account to the local Administrators group. This will make him an administrator of this server and only this server.

1. Click Add, and the dialog box in Figure 8.50 opens.

FIGURE 8.50

Adding a user to a group via the user properties

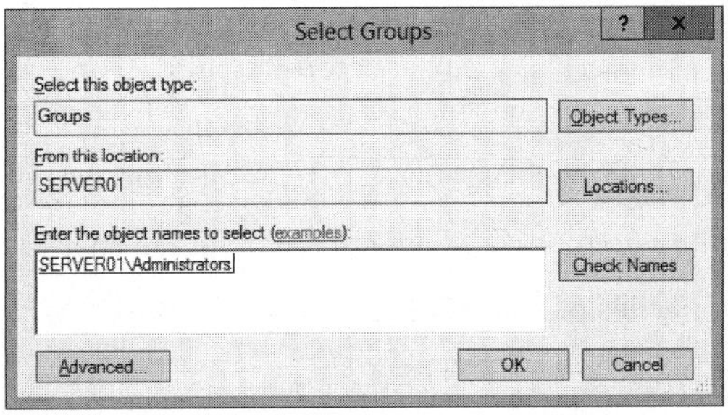

2. Type in the name of the group that you want to add this user to, and then click Check Names to be sure that you have the group name correct.

Note that you can only add local user accounts into local groups. You cannot add local users to domain groups.

The listing of group memberships for the local user account has now been updated, as you can see in Figure 8.51.

FIGURE 8.51

The user's group memberships

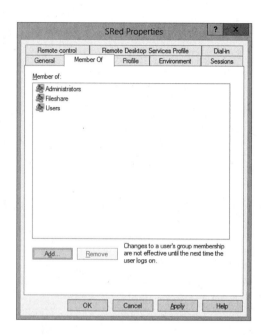

3. Click OK to save these changes.

The only way to replicate this using the command prompt is to manipulate the group itself instead of the user:

```
net localgroup administrators SRed /add
```

REMOVING A USER

Removing a user from a local group is easy too. You can do this in either of these ways:

◆ *Using the user account*: Use the user account if this is a one-off operation or if you're removing multiple rights from a user.

◆ *Using the group*: Use the group if you're removing identical rights from many users.

We'll now show how to modify the membership of Fileshare by removing Steve Red:

1. Open the properties of Fileshare, as shown in Figure 8.52.

FIGURE 8.52
Removing a user
from a local group

2. Select SRed.

   You can select more than one member to remove by using the Shift or Ctrl key.

3. Click Remove once you have highlighted the members to remove.

That's it; there's nothing more to removing a member from a group.

The following command will remove Steve Red from the Fileshare group:

```
net localgroup fileshare SRed /delete
```

To delete a group using the MMC snap-in, follow these steps:

1. Browse to it and select it.

2. Right-click the group and select Delete.

Take note of the dialog box in Figure 8.53 that appears when you say you're going to delete a group. You are about to affect many users or computers who are members of this group.

FIGURE 8.53
Are you really sure
you want to delete
the group?

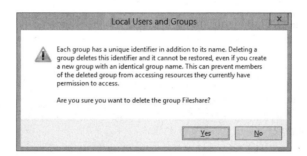

IT'S TIME TO PAY CLOSE ATTENTION AGAIN

This is important enough for us to repeat it: although you see users, computers, and groups as relatively friendly names such as SRed, SERVER01, or Fileshare, Windows does not. It uniquely identifies these *security principals* using a SID. A unique SID is created every time a new security principal is created. This means that if you create SRed, delete it, and re-create it, Windows will see the old and new objects as two different security principals. You see them as one, but they are not. The result is that permissions assigned to the old account are not retained by the new account.

The pop-up in Figure 8.53 warns you of this. You must be certain that the organization is 100 percent sure that it no longer needs a security principal before it deletes it. Here, you need to know that once you delete a group, its assigned permissions, as well as the group membership, are lost. Any user who was granted access to a resource such as a file share via membership of this group, will lose access to that resource.

The following `net localgroup` command will delete the Fileshare group without any warnings or requests for confirmation:

```
net localgroup fileshare /delete
```

Active Directory Groups

The basic concept of Active Directory or domain-based groups does not differ from that of local groups. You use them to collectively treat a number of objects in an identical manner. However, you can do a lot more with Active Directory groups. This is made possible because this type of group is stored in Active Directory on domain controllers and a subset of domain controllers that are configured to be global catalogs. This enables a single group to contain many domain-based security principals, such as users and computers, and to be used across all computers within the domain in which the group resides. In fact, you can use groups outside of their native domain, and there is even a category that can contain members from any domain in a forest.

For the purpose of this section, you should assume that when we say *group*, we mean Active Directory group. These are the two basic group types:

Distribution Group   A distribution group is used to group a number of objects together that will be addressed collectively. A mail server, such as Microsoft Exchange, can present the distribution group to users as a destination address. The user can choose to send mail to the distribution group, and the mail server will attempt to send the mail to all members of the group, assuming that they have email addresses configured.

Security Group   A security group can also perform the mail distribution function. But the primary purpose of this type is given away by the name: security. You can use a security group to assign permissions or rights to an object or a set of objects, such as an organizational unit, a folder, or a component of an application. This allows Active Directory to become not only your single authentication mechanism for your network but also your authorization mechanism. An end user can use a single user account to gain authorization to secured resources across the entire Active Directory forest, not just a domain or a single computer.

There are three group scopes to deal with as well:

Domain Local Group   A domain local group is intended to be used only within the domain that it was created in. It can contain user/computer accounts, global groups, and universal groups from any domain in the forest and domain local groups from the same domain.

Global Group   This is the default scope when you create a group in Active Directory. A global group can be used by computers within the domain that it is a member of and by members of other domains in the Active Directory forest. It can contain user/computer accounts from the domain that the global group is created in.

Universal Group   One thing makes a universal group very different from both of the other group types. Both of the others are stored and replicated to all domain controllers within the domain that they were created in. A universal group is stored on domain controllers that are configured as global catalogs. This implies that the universal group is replicated to domains across the entire forest. That allows a universal group not only to be able to be used by all computers in the forest but also to contain members from any domain within the forest.

A WORD OF CAUTION ABOUT UNIVERSAL GROUPS

Great care must be taken when designing a universal group in larger environments because you are adding to replication loads when you create or modify them. Active Directory will only replicate the changes to universal groups, but just be careful of large-scale changes. You also need to be sure that global catalog–enabled domain controllers are close to services that rely heavily on them.

Single-domain networks do not need to worry too much about universal groups because there isn't much use for them. Universal groups can contain user/computer accounts, global groups, and other universal groups from any domain in the forest.

You probably just noticed something there. Groups can contain other groups. This is commonly referred to as *group nesting*. Why would you consider doing this? Here are two things to consider:

Managing Several Groups at Once   Say you have groups called Accounts Management and Sales Management. You want to be able to deal with both of them at once, maybe having one email address for them all that you will treat as a contact list. You can create a group called Management and add each of the three accounts as members. You can then configure an email address for the Management group.

Managing Organizational Units in Different Departments   Another scenario, shown in Figure 8.54, is where you have created organizational units for different departments; for example, say you have \BigFirm, which contains \BigFirm\Accounts and \BigFirm\Sales. There are two levels of IT. BigFirm has an IT department that runs Active Directory and corporate IT functions. You work in this department. Both Accounts and Sales have small IT teams that can only manage objects in their OUs. This is called *delegation*. You want to be able to have a group called Management that will contain managers for all departments. You do not want to manage these members, and you want departmental IT staff to manage the process instead. You can create the group Accounts Management in \BigFirm\Accounts and create Sales Management in \BigFirm\Sales. This allows departmental IT to manage those two groups. Create the group Management in \BigFirm. Now you can add the departmental groups as members of Management.

FIGURE 8.54
Nested groups

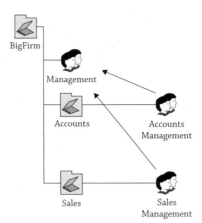

As you can see, there's a little more to Active Directory groups than there is to local groups. It is important to understand why you are creating a group and how that group will be used before you create the group. You can change group scopes and group types, but you must understand what the impact will be, such as that changing from a global group to a universal group will alter Active Directory replication from being between domain controllers within a domain to being between global catalog servers across an entire forest. The extra bit of planning is well worth the effort, as you will find as you progress through the rest of this book. As time goes by, you will find yourself using groups for all sorts of things:

◆ Assigning permissions to file shares

◆ Creating email distribution groups containing members across an entire corporate forest

◆ Assigning rights for deploying operating systems

◆ Controlling what computers will receive an automated deployment of Microsoft Visio

◆ Controlling who will be targeted by a Group Policy object

◆ Delegating administrative rights to parts of Active Directory

You may be thinking that the concept of group nesting sounds pretty complex and nasty. When you combine this with a descriptive naming standard for your groups, you can create a group mechanism that is very easy to deploy and manage and that allows for granular delegated administration.

CREATING ACTIVE DIRECTORY GROUPS

It's time for you to create some Active Directory groups. Say you want to create a group that will be used only within your domain. It will be used to assign rights to anyone who is a manager in the organization. This description tells you that you need a domain local group scope and that you need a security group type.

Earlier you created an OU called \BigFirm\Security Groups within the bigfirm.com domain.

1. Navigate there using Active Directory Users and Groups.

2. Right-click, and select New ➤ Group.

    This opens the New Object-Group dialog box.

3. Enter **Management** as the group name.

   This automatically fills in the pre–Windows 2000 group name, as shown in Figure 8.55, which is maintained to maintain backward compatibility with legacy operating systems.

FIGURE 8.55
Creating a new Active Directory group

4. Selected the desired group scope of "Domain local" and keep the default group type of Security.

5. Click the OK button to create the group.

You've probably noticed that you didn't have the option to edit the properties of the group while you created it. You'll probably want to add a description and add members to the group. You can do this by right-clicking the group and selecting Properties to open the Management Properties dialog box shown in Figure 8.56.

FIGURE 8.56
Adding a group description

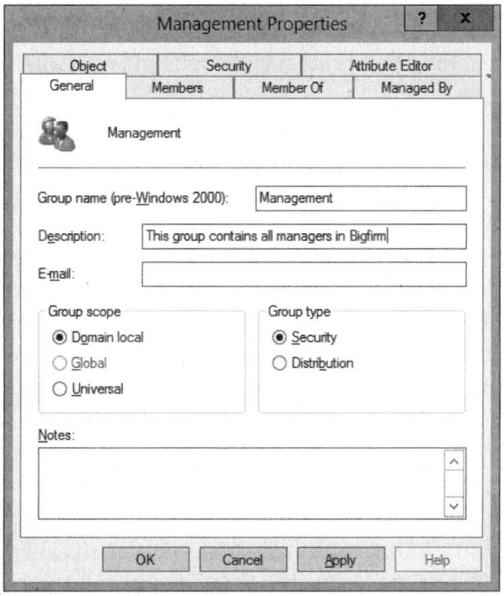

We've already typed in the description for the group. This form of documentation makes it immediately clear to administrators what the purpose of the group is. We discussed the need to do this when we covered local groups. It's infinitely more important to document in this way when dealing with medium- to large-size Active Directory setups where there may be teams of administrators working with the servers.

GROUP NAMING STANDARDS

It is important to adopt a naming standard for groups if your domain will grow to be large or it will be part of a forest. Remember that groups can be used anywhere within a domain or even an Active Directory forest. Even with just two domain controllers, you can support a large user base and a complex organization. How meaningful do you think the name Management would be in an organization containing hundreds or thousands of users? What about a corporate or government forest with many domains and tens of thousands of employees? Management is possibly suitable for a small/medium organization with a single site and a small IT team.

If you have an organization with many departments or many sites, you might consider having Milan-Accounts Management and Milan-IT Management, for example. It's immediately visible that each of these group names is associated with an office in the city of Milan and that the members of the groups are members of management for a department. If you have many domains in a forest, you could consider something like BigFirm-Milan-Senior Management. Any administrator in any domain in the forest knows that the group is from the BigFirm domain, the members are from the Milan office, and all members are from the senior management team in that office.

We also recommend adding some sort of prefix to the group to show what kind of group it is, for example, the prefix DL for domain local, DG for domain global, or UG for universal groups. This would end up in a group name like DG-ITManagement-Milan or DL-ITManagement-Milan. If you do this you can easily distinguish between the group types, which could be helpful while searching or scripting groups.

The bottom of the General tab shows you the type and scope of the group. You may notice that you can change these. However, there are some things to consider before making changes here.

Changing a group from being a security group to a distribution group means that it cannot be used for assigning permissions anymore. You are warned that any permission assigned using this group may fail to function. This is especially important if you are denying access to critical resources using this group.

We've tested this with file shares to see how it worked. We shared a folder using a security group and added some members. We also applied permissions to the folder on the file system. We verified that the members had access to the share and everything looked good. We changed the group type to a distribution group. We checked the share and folder permissions, and the distribution group still had rights. Testing user access showed that the user still had rights to the folder. So far, so good. We then logged the user out and back in again. Uh-oh; the user lost rights. The group that became a distribution group still had rights but was no longer effective. We then reversed the group back to being a security group. A logout and login were required to give the test user access to the share again.

This behavior doesn't have to be something bad—not at all. Let's think about a scenario where you have many global security groups that have been assigned somewhere-permissions on some shares. You can't even remember where this group has been assigned. You take all the steps to figure out where this group is and which share it belongs to. Later you want to delete the group because you think it is not in use anymore. In this scenario you could just change the group scope to distribution and all permissions will be inactive. That means the group is somehow disabled. If you wait for a certain time and users complain that they don't have any access to share XYZ, then you know that the group still is in use. We know it is not a very smooth approach to get the user involved, but many times there is no other way.

Anything that will affect members typically requires the user to log out and back in again. That's the third time we've stated this in this chapter; it has definitely been the solution to almost every group membership and rights assignment question we have dealt with at work. Remember this when you grant a user rights to a resource by adding them to a group.

You cannot directly change a group from being a domain local group to a global group, or vice versa. However, you can change either scope to being a universal group. From there, you can change it back to either a domain local or a global group. Make sure that the member list does not conflict with your preferred group scope. You need to be sure that your group is not used in another domain if you're changing a global group to a domain local group. This would cause loss of access to secured resources for members of the group. Administrators in larger forest implementations need to be aware that they are potentially adding new traffic to global catalog replication when converting an existing group into a universal group.

The member functionality for domain-based groups works just like that of local groups. Open the properties of a group, as shown in Figure 8.57. You can add and remove members using the Add and Remove buttons.

FIGURE 8.57
Adding new members to the Active Directory group

As you can see in Figure 8.58, domain-based groups are capable of containing more types of objects than local groups can, such as the following:

Other Objects   This flexible solution allows you to add members that are created by applications, that is, not the usual users, computers, or groups.

Contacts   These objects are created in Active Directory to store contact information about people or organizations. This could be used for distribution groups.

Service Accounts   This is a new feature of Windows Server 2012 where you can set up dedicated service accounts instead of creating user accounts and assigning them to services.

FIGURE 8.58

Selecting potential member object types

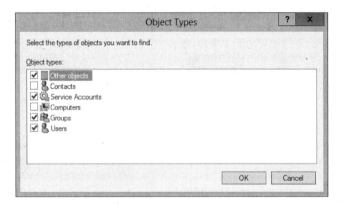

Because you're dealing with the member list of a domain-based group, you cannot add security principals that are local machine based, that is, local users or local groups. These security principals exist only on their computer, so it makes no sense to add them to a domain-wide or forest-wide group. For this reason, the Locations dialog box shown in Figure 8.59 presents only domains that exist in your forest.

FIGURE 8.59

Choosing a new member object location

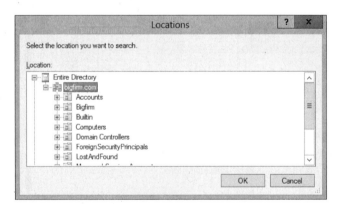

Domain-based groups can be nested; that is, a group can be a member of another group. The Member Of tab in the group's properties, shown in Figure 8.60, allows you to manage what groups this group is a member of.

FIGURE 8.60

What group is this group a member of?

The Managed By tab shown in Figure 8.61 is a nice little feature. As an administrator, you probably have no idea who has a business reason to access secured data. You have enough to do to run the network, let alone know the complete operations of the business. The owner of the data, usually a department head or team lead, is the best person to decide this. What is often (but not always) the best solution? You can put the power of access control into the hands of the data owner. Cut out the middle man, in other words, IT. If the owner can manage access to the resource, then the business can adapt to requirements as needs arise.

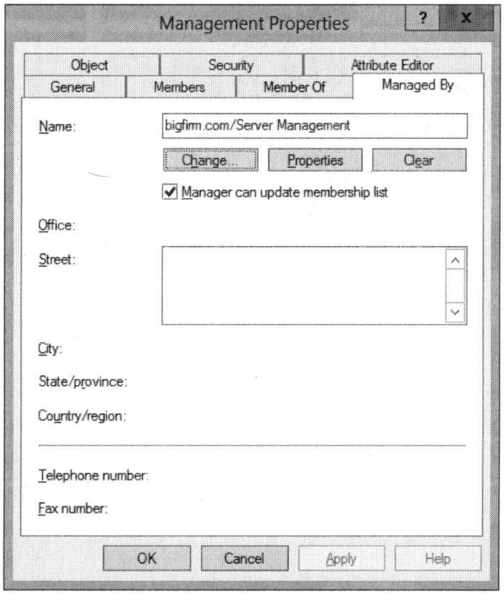

FIGURE 8.61

Active Directory group Managed By tab

The Managed By tab allows you to elect a user or a group that can be the owner of this group. This group can be assigned rights to resources. We've saved the best bit for last. The selected owner can be given rights to manage the membership of the group by selecting the "Manager can update membership list" box. Superb! You don't have to give the manager rights to manage the security rights of a shared folder. Can you imagine the disasters that could arise from that? The simple solution is to let them manage the membership of groups that have the right to use the shared folder. All you have to do is give them a mechanism for editing the group membership, such as the Active Directory Users and Computers snap-in, a script, or maybe a web applet.

CREATING A GROUP AT THE COMMAND LINE

It's important to learn how to manage groups from the command line. You'll first look at how to create a group using dsadd group. You can get more help by typing the following:

```
dsadd group /?
```

The following is a simple command that re-creates what you can do in the GUI. It creates a domain local group called Management in the \BigFirm\Security Groups OU in the bigfirm .com domain.

```
dsadd group "CN=Management, OU=Security Groups,OU=BigFirm,DC=bigfirm,
DC=com" -scope l
```

Here's the syntax:

```
dsadd group <distinguished name of the new group> -scope <Domain Local
= l | Global = g | Universal = u>
```

By default, this creates a security group. You can actually leave out the -scope option if a global group is what you want. You can make a global distribution group instead by running this:

```
dsadd group "CN=Management, OU=Security Groups,OU=BigFirm,DC=bigfirm,
DC=com" -secgrp no -scope g
```

The change in the syntax is as follows:

```
-secgrp <security group = yes | distribution group = no>
```

The default is to create a security group. You don't need to use this option in your command if a security group is what you need to create.

Do you remember that the GUI for creating domain-based groups didn't offer you anything other than the ability to create the group? You had to go back into the properties of the group to set the properties or add members. Well, you can use this command:

```
dsadd group "CN=Senior Management, OU=Security Groups,OU=BigFirm,
DC=bigfirm,DC=com" -scope g -desc "This group contains senior managers"
 -memberof "CN=Management,OU=Security Groups,OU=BigFirm,DC=bigfirm,DC=com"
 -members "CN=Steve Red,OU=Users,OU=BigFirm,DC=bigfirm,DC=com"
 "CN=Simona Corso,OU=Users,OU=BigFirm,DC=bigfirm,DC=com"
```

This command has done quite a bit. You've created a global security group called Senior Management in the Security Groups OU. You've set the group description to "This group contains senior managers." The Senior Management group was added as a member of the Managers group. And finally, you have added two users to the new Senior Managers group.

You can use the `dsmod group` command to modify an existing group. Here's the command to get some help:

```
dsmod group /?
```

This command will add Steve Red and Simona Corso to the Management group:

```
dsmod group "CN=Management, OU=Security Groups,OU=BigFirm,DC=bigfirm,DC=com"
 -addmbr "CN=Steve Red,OU=Users,OU=BigFirm,DC=bigfirm,DC=com" "CN=Simona Corso,OU
=Users,OU=BigFirm,DC=bigfirm,DC=com"
```

The syntax is as follows:

```
dsmod group <DN of the group to manage> -addmbr
<DNs of the users to add to the group>
```

Next you want to remove Steve Red from the group:

```
dsmod group "CN=Management, OU=Security Groups,OU=BigFirm,DC=bigfirm,DC=com"
-rmmbr "CN=Steve Red,OU=Users,OU=BigFirm,DC=bigfirm,DC=com"
```

You can erase the existing member list of a group and add a replacement member list by running this:

```
dsmod group "CN=Management, OU=Security Groups,OU=BigFirm,DC=bigfirm,DC=com"
 -chmbr "CN=Steve Red,OU=Users,OU=BigFirm,DC=bigfirm,DC=com"
```

You can change the group scope to universal by running this:

```
dsmod group "CN=Management, OU=Security Groups,OU=BigFirm,DC=bigfirm,DC=com"
 -scope u
```

The syntax for the `-scope` option is as follows:

```
-scope <Domain Local = l | Global = g | Universal = u>
```

One disappointment here is that you cannot set the manager properties for a group using `dsmod group`.

How about deleting a group? That's pretty easy:

```
dsrm "CN=Management, OU=Security Groups,OU=BigFirm,DC=big firm,DC=com"
```

This command will delete the Management group. You'll get prompted to confirm the deletion. You can skip that by running this:

```
dsrm "CN=Management, OU=Security Groups,OU=BigFirm,DC=big firm,DC=com" -noprompt
```

Monday Morning Admin Tasks

We'll now cover some common operational tasks that you may find yourself doing regularly. Our experience is that anyone in a help-desk role will find their Monday mornings consumed by these tasks if they don't carefully consider how to design their authentication mechanisms.

Check out the discussions on passphrases and smart cards earlier in this chapter to see what we mean. We'll cover domain-based security principals because this is what you will find yourself working with the vast majority of the time.

Forgotten Passwords

The first challenge is dealing with a person who can't remember their password. This is usually the number-one call to the help desk after the weekend. Let's see how you can reset that password for your user. After all, the user is your customer, and you need to provide quality and timely service.

1. If you are using the GUI, navigate to the user account in question in Active Directory Users and Computers.

2. Right-click the user and select Reset Password to open the Reset Password dialog box.

3. Enter a new password for the user, as shown in Figure 8.62

FIGURE 8.62

Resetting the user password

This new password must comply with the password policies that apply to the user. Odds are that you are going to be communicating this password to the user over the phone. Our experience is that you should use a password that is easy to communicate. Be wary that you may be dealing with people whose first language is not the same as yours. Something like Password123456789 is easy to communicate over the phone and complies with the default password requirements. Do you see that the check box to force the user to change their password after logon is selected? This is the default. This is very convenient because, as you can see, the password that you gave to this user is probably the same one that you will use for every user. Forcing the user to change their password will secure their user account, and this means that no one in IT will know their password.

At the bottom is the check box to unlock the account. You can select this just in case the user has been locked out of their account. Users who aren't IT savvy might not be able to understand or communicate the messages on their desktop that explain why they can't log in. Changing the user's password without unlocking the account won't help them log in. It won't do any harm to select this check box if you're dealing with an unsure-sounding user or a repeat offender.

Here's how you can change a user's password using the dsmod user command:

```
C:\Users\Administrator>dsmod user "CN=Steve Red,OU=Users,OU=BigFirm,
DC=bigfirm, DC=com" -pwd *
Enter User Password:

Confirm user password:

dsmod succeeded:CN=Steve Red,OU=Users,OU=BigFirm,DC=bigfirm,DC=com
```

The -pwd * option instructs the command that you will enter the new password and confirm it. Alternatively, you can reset the password in the command:

```
dsmod user "CN=Steve Red,OU=Users,OU=BigFirm,DC=bigfirm,DC=com"
 -pwd Password12345678
```

You can use an additional option with either of these commands to force the user to change their password when they log on:

```
dsmod user "CN=Steve Red,OU=Users,OU=BigFirm,DC=bigfirm,DC=com"
 -pwd Password12345678 -mustchpwd yes
```

Locked-Out Users

Account lockout policies . . . oh, boy! Pretty much most of the "security experts" you will encounter on the Internet or in person love their "three failed logons in 30 minutes should cause a lockout" policy. You know what? That's a great recipe for facilitating a denial-of-service attack. Get access to a desktop computer in your forest with an ordinary user account for a couple of minutes, and you can run a script that will fail five logons for every user on your Active Directory in no time at all. Every single user except for the default domain administrator accounts will be locked out. That'll shut down your business. It's for this reason that real security experts have been telling us to really think hard about using the lockout option for passwords. (Check out the earlier "The Case for Passphrases" sidebar to see an alternative.) It's for this reason that lockouts are disabled by default in the Default Domain Policy. Our opinion is that this is a very good thing. Nevertheless, some organizations will enable this policy. They may have a valid reason for it. For this reason, it's important to know how to unlock a user account.

Note that this is defined in Active Directory in the Default Domain Group Policy object (GPO). The default setting in Windows Server 2012 is 0, that is, to not lock out user accounts after failed login attempts.

Two Simple Lock-Out Scenarios

The first scenario is when the user has reported that their computer is informing them that they are locked out. They know their password, so you don't need to reset it. You can navigate to the user account in Active Directory Users and Computers and open the properties of the account. You can see in the Account tab, shown in Figure 8.63, that there is a message to inform you that the account is locked out. The solution is simple. You unlock the account. Of course, the user may have forgotten their password, so you may need to reset that as well.

FIGURE 8.63
Active Directory
user locked out

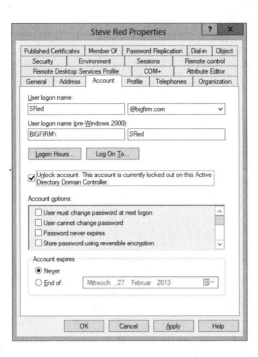

The second scenario is the user whose only knowledge of their problem is that they cannot log in. There could be two problems here (to start with). The user could have forgotten their password, or they could have a locked account. You should just kill two birds with one stone and deal with both possibilities. You can open the dialog box to reset the user's password, shown in Figure 8.64.

FIGURE 8.64
Unlocking user
account and
resetting password

Unfortunately, it appears that there is no command-line option for unlocking user accounts—except for PowerShell, of course.

With that, we've covered all the options for basic user and group management that are common to Windows Server 2012. We'll now move on to cover what's new in Windows Server 2012.

Using the New Features for User and Group Management

Everything we have discussed in this chapter applies to both Windows Server 2008 R2, Windows Server 2012 and Windows Server 2012 R2. Windows Server 2012 has two major changes that are relevant to basic user and group management:

♦ Microsoft has renewed the Active Directory Administrative Center (ADAC) and built it on top of PowerShell. In addition, new features have been integrated into the console, like a GUI for Active Directory Recycle Bin and Fine-grained Password Policies.

♦ Microsoft has added PowerShell History into the ADAC for more easily managing and creating users and groups as well as other objects.

Windows Server 2008 R2 has already natively integrated PowerShell 2.0, and in terms of managing users and groups, there are not any new cmdlets in Windows Server 2012. Although Windows Server 2012 has integrated the brand-new PowerShell 3.0 and Windows Server 2012 R2 PowerShell 4.0, most new cmdlets in the Active Directory field are for managing the Active Directory components and not users and groups.

However, you can download Quest's Free PowerShell Commands for Active Directory from `http://tinyurl.com/5otmff`. These cmdlets have syntax similar to the built-in Windows Server 2012 cmdlets, but in certain ways they offer a bit more support and flexibility, for example, in terms of accessing user attributes. In this section we'll be covering the native Windows Server 2012 PowerShell cmdlets.

Active Directory Administrative Center

Microsoft extended and also graphically adjusted the new Active Directory Administrative Center to give you a more task-oriented command interface. Rumor has it that Active Directory Users and Computers (ADUC) will be discontinued and Microsoft's focus will be on Active Directory Administrative Center. However, in Windows Server 2012 both tools are available, and one cannot work without the other. We consider ADUC as legacy and ADAC the future.

Microsoft's strategy is clear: PowerShell. Since ADAC is just a GUI for PowerShell functionality, it is worth investigating the power of this tool. Microsoft wanted to provide something to make it quick and easy to do frequent, repetitive tasks, such as dealing with those user lockouts on Monday mornings. You'll find ADAC on the Tools menu in Server Manager on a Windows Server 2012 domain controller. You can also use it on Windows 8 if you install the Remote Server Administration Tools for Windows 8; see `http://www.microsoft.com/en-us/download/details.aspx?id=28972`. If you are already running Windows 8.1 and you would like to manage Windows Server 2012 R2, go to `http://www.microsoft.com/en-us/download/details.aspx?id=39296`. It takes a little longer than Active Directory Users and Computers to load, so you might fire this up in the morning and leave it running.

ADAC Essentials

You can see what we mean by *task oriented* when ADAC opens, as shown in Figure 8.65. In the center pane is an interface dedicated to resetting passwords and unlocking user accounts. Those are the most common Active Directory tasks for IT, so it makes sense that the tool is right there.

What happens without ADAC when a user calls the corporate help desk asking to have their password reset or their account unlocked? The help-desk technician needs to search the organizational units in Active Directory for the user. Then they have to right-click the user and perform the task. This assumes the help-desk engineer knows how to search Active Directory. It's also time consuming. As you can see in Figure 8.65, with ADAC the help-desk engineer simply enters the username and new password. The "Unlock account" option is grayed out because the account isn't locked out.

ADAC also makes finding objects easier for the help desk. You can see in Figure 8.66 that they can enter the name of the object to search for.

FIGURE 8.65
Resetting a user password in ADAC

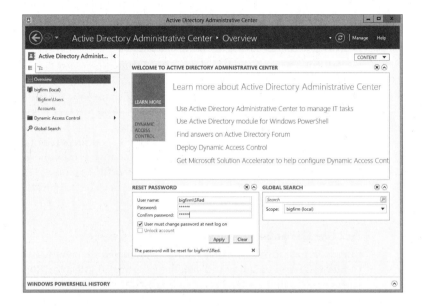

FIGURE 8.66
Searching for an Active Directory object

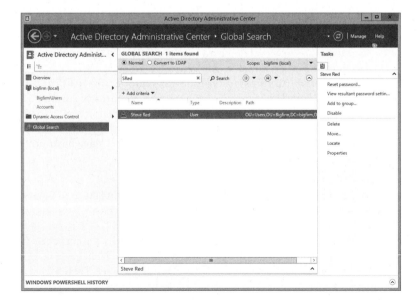

Figure 8.66 shows the results of that search. You can see how easy it was to search for SRed. The engineer can easily right-click this user object to perform administrative tasks on it. The search tool is pretty clever because it searches attributes of the object, that is, the object properties. The engineer could have searched for *S*, *Steve*, or *Steve Red* and still found the SRed user object. This isn't limited to user objects either! You can search for any type of object in the domain, such as groups and computers.

You can reach the Global Search tool by clicking Global Search in the navigation pane on the left. This allows you to jump right in and access some more powerful search options.

Clicking "Add criteria" gives you some really powerful options to qualify the search, as shown in Figure 8.67. Look at those built-in criteria and imagine how useful they could be. Every morning you could kick off the day by searching for locked-out accounts and dealing with them before employees arrive. In the local user accounts section of this chapter, we recommended that you disable accounts instead of immediately deleting them. To use one of these criteria, select the associated box, and then click the Add button.

FIGURE 8.67
Potential search criteria

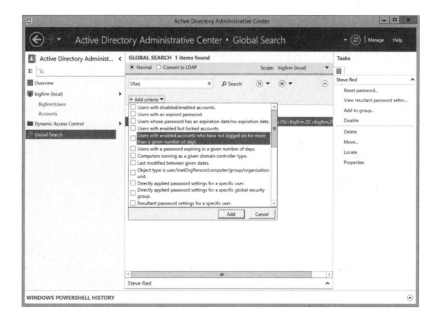

In the figure, we've selected the option "Users with enabled accounts who have not logged on for more than a given number of days." You can see in the center of the dialog in Figure 8.68 where you can select a number of days from a predefined range of options. This is very useful. Ideally, the human resources department should communicate with IT whenever an employee leaves the company. However, we are human, and we make mistakes. Using this query, you can identify "stale" user accounts and disable them. You can remove a search criterion by clicking the grey *X* on the right.

FIGURE 8.68
Finding all users
who have not logged
in for 15 days

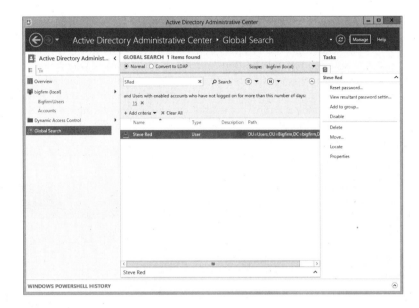

You can even build a more complex query by clicking the "Add criteria" drop-down. For example, the object type could be Computer, and the object name could start with *B*. This means you wouldn't get search results that are polluted with other object types such as groups, users, and OUs.

You can use that little disk icon on the right to save your query for later reuse. You give the query a name (use something descriptive), and you can access the query again by clicking the icon on the left side of the little disk icon. It is also a drop-down box which shows all saved queries after clicking on it. If you select a saved query it will load and execute the result for you.

Once you have found an object, you will want to do something with it. When you select an object, the Tasks pane on the right will display context-sensitive actions. You can click one of those tasks to manage the selected object.

Navigating ADAC

Now that we've covered the basics, let's start navigating ADAC. The navigation pane has a list view (the default) and a tree view. The list view contains a preselected set of locations. This includes the following:

◆ The ADAC Overview where you started out and where you can quickly deal with basic user requests and simple searches

◆ The domain from which you can jump into any OU or container

◆ The Users and Computers containers where you're ideally not adding anything

◆ The Global Search tool, which we've already covered

You can add other locations by right-clicking in the navigation pane and selecting Add Navigation Nodes. That opens a window where you can navigate your Active Directory structure, as shown in Figure 8.69.

FIGURE 8.69

Adding a navigation node

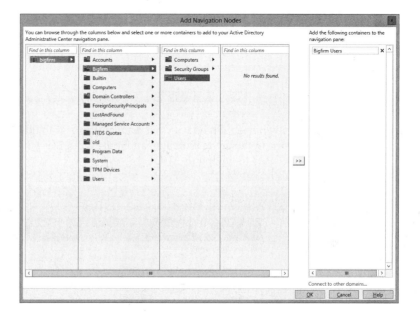

We've browsed to \BigFirm\Users and added that OU to the control in the right side of the window. Did you notice that you can use the "Connect to other domains" control at the bottom right to navigate to OUs or containers in other domains in the forest? You can use this to manage many domains in many forests at once with ADAC.

In Figure 8.70, you can see that we have clicked OK to add the \BigFirm\Users OU to the list view in ADAC. Now you can quickly get to the OU where you are managing user accounts, another time-saver for day-to-day administration. The Tasks pane now contains new actions, allowing you to perform administration within the OU.

FIGURE 8.70
Using a navigation
node

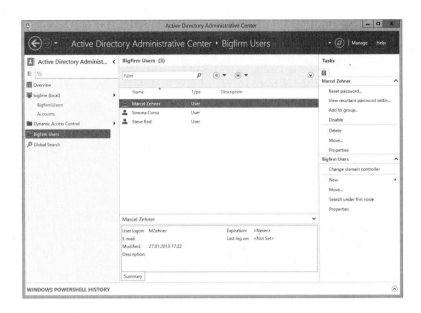

Note that any navigation nodes you create will appear in both the tree and list views.

The tree view in the navigation pane in Figure 8.71 gives you the more traditional navigation method you're used to having in ADUC.

FIGURE 8.71
The tree view in
ADAC

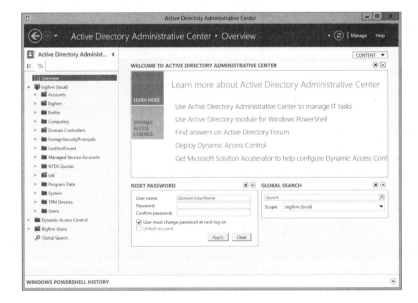

Let's do some work. In this example, you'll create a user. Navigate to \BigFirm\Users using the new navigation node that you just created in the list view, and click New ➤ User in the Tasks pane. That opens up the dialog box shown in Figure 8.72.

FIGURE 8.72

Creating a new user in ADAC

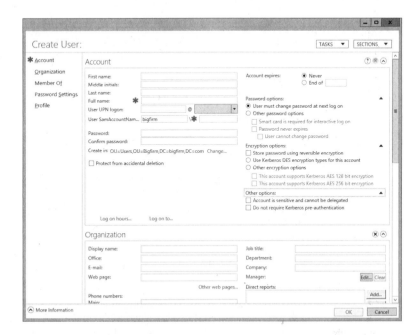

Wow! That's a hefty dialog box, and it might be a bit daunting at first. Let's take a look around before you do anything. First, let's simplify things. You only need to complete the fields with a red * beside them to be allowed to create a user. The left navigation pane tips you off that this window is broken up into sections. You can use the Sections button on the top right to hide or reveal those sections. This allows you to hide any sections that you never use. ADAC will remember what sections are hidden or revealed.

You can see that we've removed the Organization in the center of the dialog and Encryption options sections on the upper-right side of the dialog in Figure 8.73. We have also filled out the dialog box to create a new user called Kevin Greene. Instead of navigating through a wizard and then opening the user properties to complete the operation, you can do everything here. Every commonly used option for setting up the user is available in this dialog box. This initially daunting window will reduce the amount of time it takes to create and configure a user account.

FIGURE 8.73
Removed dialog box
sections in ADAC

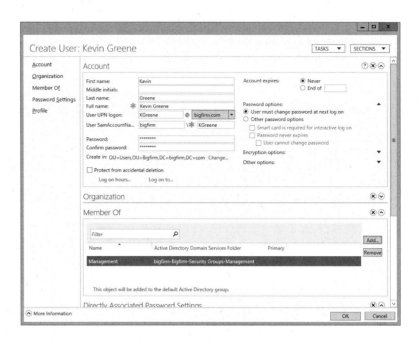

We could have just entered the full name and the SAM account name to create this user. What happens if you don't enter the non-mandatory password? The account will be created, but it will be disabled. You will not be able to enable it because the lack of a password contravenes the default domain password policy. You can reset the password and then enable the account.

Here's what you should do:

1. Enter the username details.

2. Specify the password.

3. Add the user to a group.

4. Click OK.

The user is created and added to the OU that you are in.

You probably noticed that not every single attribute or property for user objects was available. The common ones were, but lots of others weren't. In Active Directory, you will probably configure those properties via policies instead. However, you can still access them.

Figure 8.74 shows the properties of the user account in ADAC. A new section appears in the window called Extensions. This allows you to view and configure those advanced features of the object.

FIGURE 8.74
Viewing the user
properties in ADAC

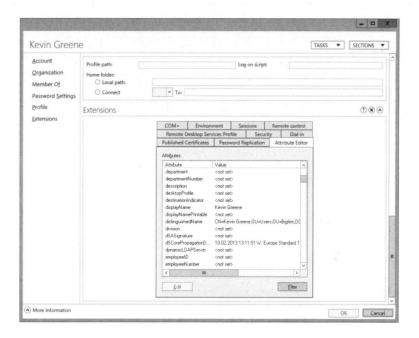

As shown in Figure 8.75, we have returned to the list view and created an additional navigation node for the \BigFirm\Security Groups OU. It's time to manage groups in ADAC. Click New and then Group in the Tasks pane.

FIGURE 8.75
An additional
navigation node for
security groups

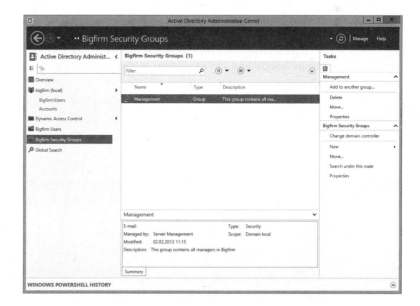

As you can see in Figure 8.76, like with the dialog box for creating a user, you can mask or hide some of the sections. You are going to do that now.

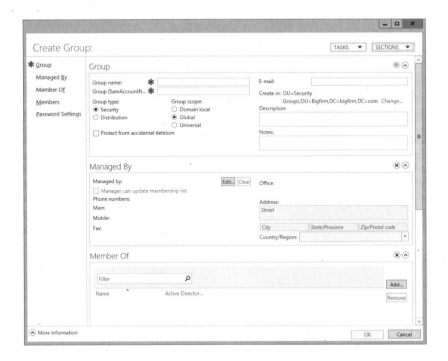

You can simplify the view by clicking the Sections button to remove the Member Of section, for example.

Let's create a group called Helpdesk. Figure 8.77 shows the completed dialog box to create the new Helpdesk group. Again, you can enter a lot of information into a single dialog box, saving you from going through a wizard and then editing the group object properties afterward. Do the following:

1. Enter the group name, and fill in SamAccountName.

2. Specify the group type and scope.

3. Select the "Protect from accidental deletion" check box so you can't delete the group accidentally.

4. Specify an email address for mail distribution (this requires a compatible mail service).

5. Edit the description and the notes.

6. Specify a group manager who can manage the group membership.

   Members of senior management can alter the group membership of the Helpdesk group now.

7. Add two users to the Helpdesk group membership.

8. Click OK to create the group.

FIGURE 8.77
Creating the new
group in ADAC

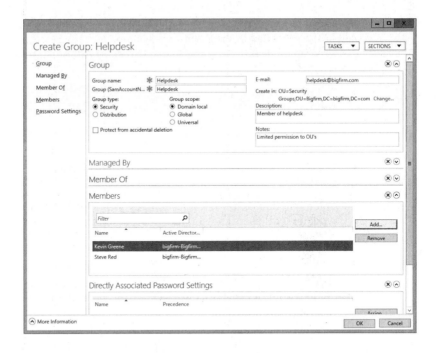

You can return to the group object properties to edit the configuration or the membership of the group, as shown in Figure 8.78.

FIGURE 8.78
Viewing the
group properties
in ADAC

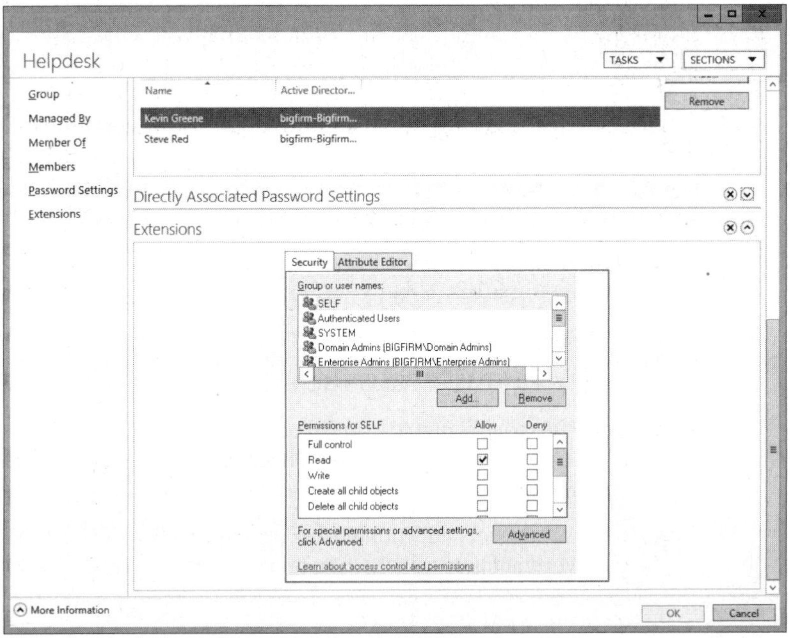

As with the user object properties, those attributes you couldn't see in the object creation dialog box are revealed in the Extensions section.

As we wrap up dealing with the Active Directory Administrative Center, here are a few remaining tips:

- ADAC can be installed only on Windows Server 2012 machines and Windows 8 computers running the Remote Server Administrative Tools (RSAT).

- You can manage domains in your forest or in other forests where a trust exists and you have the appropriate permissions.

- In the navigation pane, you can right-click the domain name to connect to different domain controllers.

  You might do this to work on a domain controller in another site, such as to do some work for local users and get immediate results without waiting for intersite replication.

- Active Directory Web Services (ADWS) must be installed on at least one domain controller in the domain to use ADAC to manage that domain.

  If you install a Windows Server 2012 domain controller, ADWS is installed and started automatically. It provides a web service interface for managing Active Directory using tools such as ADAC and PowerShell.

In the ADAC's Getting Started content in the Administrative Center Overview section you will find hyperlinks to online content for ADAC and the new PowerShell modules for Active Directory management using PowerShell.

PowerShell History Viewer

You may have noticed that there is one new section in ADAC called PowerShell History Viewer. It's mostly hidden, and if you are not aware of it you will easily work with ADAC without ever knowing about it. For PowerShell History to show up you need to click the down-arrow button, as shown in Figure 8.79.

In Figure 8.79 there is a new user called Chris Greuter. Immediately after you click OK in your user-creation dialog, the PowerShell History gets filled with PowerShell commands. For example, for creating a simple enabled user with the minimal input, five different cmdlets are fired off. If you look closer at these commands, you will see that they take these steps:

1. New-ADUser sets up the basic skeleton for the user object without a password. Therefore the account is disabled.

2. Set-ADAccountPassword sets the user password.

3. Enable-ADAccount enables the user account since the password has been set.

4. Set-ADAccountControl sets all the AD account options found on the Account tab of the user object's properties pages. These options are for such things as whether the user can change the password or whether the user's password expires.

5. Set-ADUser sets additional user options such as whether the user needs to change the password at logon or whether smart card login is required.

FIGURE 8.79

Displaying the PowerShell History window

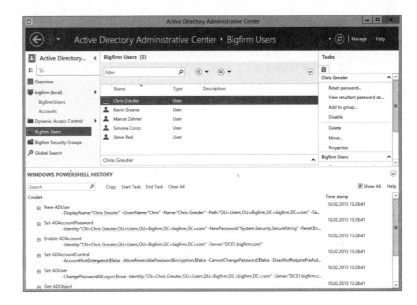

This is how the ADAC works under the hood. Of course, if you are going to create a user object, you will not fire off five cmdlets; instead, you will pack all the necessary information into a one-liner.

It doesn't make a difference whether you create a user or a group or even an OU; ADAC will log every PowerShell step in this window. In order to see the full details on each command you can click the + sign on the left side of the cmdlet. This will expand all the parameters, as you can see in Figure 8.80.

FIGURE 8.80

PowerShell cmdlet expanded

If you think about it, you can click each of them and ADAC will teach you the commands. Is that not a nice feature? It even gets better. On the top of the Windows PowerShell History screen are different tasks. In the Search box you can search for a specific command. As soon you start typing, the result pane will adjust according to your search entry. Next to the Search box are five more tasks plus a Help option:

◆ Copy

◆ Start Task

- ◆ End Task

- ◆ Clear All

- ◆ Show All

The Copy command lets you copy the entire command string from your PowerShell History window, and if you want, you can paste it into the editor of your choice, such as Notepad. You even can select multiple command lines by holding the Ctrl key and selecting all the commands you want and then copy them.

You may have realized that this small window gets filled up quickly, and if you want to track a certain action, you may have trouble determining which cmdlet belongs to which step. Because of that you can use the Start Task, End Task, and Clear All tasks. Before we start, make sure the Show All check box, shown previously in Figure 8.79, is deselected. We will explain later what this option does, but for now leave it unchecked and follow these steps:

1. Click the Clear All task.

   This will empty all the commands from your PowerShell History pane, and you will have a clean command pane.

2. Click Start Task, which will give you a rectangular description box in which you can type a meaningful description of the task you are going to perform, for example, **New User**.

3. Create a new user in Active Directory using the ADAC, click the OK button on the user-creation dialog, and then click End Task.

4. Click Start Task again, and type into the rectangular description box **Delete User**.

5. Go to your previously created user in ADAC and delete it.

6. Click End Task once more. You should have now a grouped view of your commands, as shown in Figure 8.81.

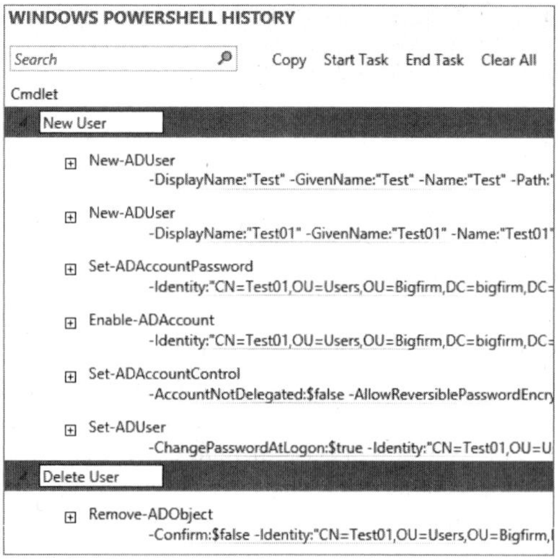

FIGURE 8.81
Grouping PowerShell commands

Not only do you get a structured overview in your window, but if you copy the commands into your editor, you will see that the descriptions "New User" and "Delete User" are added as a comment in your script, which is really helpful.

The last option you can select is Show All. If you select this check box, Active Directory Administrative Center will show even more commands in the PowerShell History.

7. Select the BigFirm Users OU, which we created, and hit F5 to refresh the OU content.

Notice that you get new commands that you didn't see before. Why is that? Think about it: ADAC is on top of PowerShell, and therefore if you refresh your OU, you actually force ADAC to requery the OU. In PowerShell this is done by the `Get-ADObject` cmdlet. You probably don't like to get flooded with PowerShell commands, so you are better off deselecting this option.

Now you've had an introduction to creating objects in PowerShell. In the next section you will get a more detailed dive into basic PowerShell.

Active Directory Module for Windows PowerShell

The Active Directory module for Windows PowerShell allows you to perform command-line and scripted operations using Microsoft's new shell language. Like ADAC, it is available only for Windows Server 2012 and Windows 8 (using the Remote Server Administration Tools). Also like ADAC, it requires the Directory Web Services role to be installed on at least one domain controller in the domain that you wish to manage. You can also install the Directory Web Services Gateway (`http://tinyurl.com/yblxwey`) on Windows Server 2003 or Windows Server 2008 domain controllers in your site for optimum performance. We'll now cover how to manage users and groups using this PowerShell module. We'll cover the more common scenarios, but we strongly recommend that you check out the Microsoft site at `http://technet.microsoft.com/en-us/library/hh852274.aspx` to read more about this subject.

You won't be using the normal PowerShell window. Instead, launch the Active Directory module for Windows PowerShell from Administrative Tools either on your Windows Server 2012 domain controller or on a Windows 8 machine with RSAT installed.

In Windows Server 2008 R2 when you opened a PowerShell windows for the first time, you needed to load the Active Directory module by typing:

```
PS C:\Users\Administrator> Import-Module ActiveDirectory
```

In Windows Server 2012 you are in a comfortable situation in that the module will be loaded automatically. As soon you enter a command that the shell recognizes as an Active Directory cmdlet, the module will be loaded automatically.

The basic PowerShell commands for creating Active Directory objects like users, groups, computers, OUs, and so on didn't change in Windows Server 2012. So if you have created scripts with the PowerShell 2.0 Active Directory module, they will also work in Windows Server 2012 and Windows Server 2012 R2.

UPDATE HELP FILES

We highly recommend before diving into PowerShell 3.0 / 4.0 that you update the local stored help files. You can easily do that by running the command Update-Help. This command will connect to the Internet and download the latest help files for the current modules loaded in your shell and those installed in the PSModulePath environment variable. The help files themselves are CAB files that contain XML files, which will be extracted and copied to the appropriate path automatically.

OK, so what if you don't have an Internet connection? Then you can use the Save-Help command, where you can specify a path to store the files. Then transfer the files to your offline computer, and use, for example, Update-Help -SourcePath C:\Temp to import the help files to your outdated computer.

There is a lot more information available; if you are interested in this topic, go to http://technet .microsoft.com/en-us/library/hh849720.aspx.

Creating Users

Let's start with some user administration operations. It makes sense to create a user first. The PowerShell cmdlet for that is New-ADUser:

```
PS C:\Users\Administrator> New-ADUser "Philipp Witschi"
```

PowerShell contains help and examples. If you want help with New-ADUser, then you can run this command:

```
PS C:\Users\Administrator> Get-Help New-ADUser
```

You can get examples of cmdlet usage like this:

```
PS C:\Users\Administrator> Get-Help New-ADUser -examples
```

Finally, you can get in-depth information about the cmdlet by running the following:

```
PS C:\Users\Administrator> Get-Help New-ADUser -detailed
```

These help commands are consistent with all the cmdlets supplied by Microsoft's modules in PowerShell. There are a few other useful things to note. You can add a -whatif flag to a cmdlet to see what will happen if you run it:

```
PS C:\Users\Administrator> New-ADUser PWitschi -whatif
What if: Performing operation "New" on Target "CN=PWitschi,CN=Users,
DC=bigfirm,DC=com".
```

Nothing is actually done; this just simulates the command and tells you what the result would be if you removed the -whatif flag. You can also tell PowerShell to seek a confirmation before executing the command. That's useful so you can double-check what you have typed before running the command:

```
PS C:\Users\Administrator> New-ADUser PWitschi -confirm

Confirm
Are you sure you want to perform this action?
```

```
Performing operation "New" on Target "CN=PWitschi,CN=Users,DC=bigfirm,DC=com".
[Y] Yes  [A] Yes to All  [N] No  [L] No to All  [S] Suspend  [?] Help
(default is "Y"):
```

You can use -whatif and -confirm on all the following cmdlet examples so you can be sure that what you are doing is correct.

The previous New-ADUser command creates the new user, PWitschi, in the default location for new users, usually the Users container. As we stated earlier, that's not the best place for storing user accounts. It contains a number of special users and groups, so you should treat it as special. You have a location in \BigFirm\Users for your user accounts. Say you want to specify a number of configurations for the user. This is what you can run:

```
PS C:\Users\Administrator> New-ADUser "Philipp Witschi" -SamAccountName
  "PWitschi" -GivenName "Philipp" -Surname "Witschi" -DisplayName "Philipp
Witschi"
  -Path 'OU=Users,OU=BigFirm,DC=bigfirm,DC=com' -UserPrincipalName
  "PWitschi@bigfirm.com"
```

Let's look at the flags in this:

-SamAccountName   This is the user logon name (pre–Windows 2000) property in the user object properties. For example, you entered PWitschi, so the user will be able to log in using the domain name BigFirm\PWitschi.

-GivenName   This refers to the first name of the user.

-Surname   This is the last name of the user.

-DisplayName   This is the display property of the user object.

-Path   This refers to the distinguished name of the OU where you want to create the new user object. In this case, it will be in the \BigFirm\Users OU in the bigfirm.com domain.

-UserPrincipalName   The UPN is the user logon name property in the user object, that is, the one that takes an email-like form.

If you run this command, you'll find your new user is created in the OU that you have specified. You'll also find that the user is disabled. Why? PowerShell wants you to specify that the user should be enabled.

Why would you want to create a user this way? You may want to run a bulk job to create a lot of user accounts. You won't enable the user accounts until the associated people are ready to use them. At that point, you can set a password unique to the user and then enable the account. PowerShell is being flexible.

Setting Passwords

Speaking of passwords, you didn't set one, did you? You're not forced to do so. However, if you want to, you can specify a password using the -AccountPassword flag. There's a catch here: -AccountPassword requires a secure string to be entered, so you can't just add My Passw0rd. You have to create a secure string before creating the user. There are a number of ways to do this; PowerShell is very open in how you can deal with things.

Let's assume you're creating 10 user objects and you want to set them all with the same password and enable the users. You also want to force the users to change their password when they log in for the first time. You can do something like this:

```
PS C:\Users\Administrator> $pw = Read-Host "Please Enter The Password"
 -AsSecureString

Please Enter The Password: ******************

PS C:\Users\Administrator> New-ADUser "Philipp Witschi" -SamAccountName
 "PWitschi" -GivenName "Philipp" -Surname "Witschi" -DisplayName "Philipp
Witschi"
 -Path 'OU=Users,OU=BigFirm,DC=bigfirm,DC=com' -UserPrincipalName
 "PWitschi@bigfirm.com" -AccountPassword $pw -Enabled 1 -ChangePasswordAtLogon 1
```

The first line prompts the administrator to enter a password. When the text is entered, it will be converted into a secure string. It will then be stored in the $pw variable. The $ indicates to PowerShell that pw is a variable or a container where you want to store a value. The Read-Host cmdlet will prompt you for a value. ASSECURESTRING will convert the value you enter in response to the prompt into a secure string. $pw will be stored in memory by this PowerShell session until you either overwrite the value or close the PowerShell window.

When you run the command, you're prompted to enter the password. Respond with an easy-to-communicate string that meets the password complexity and length requirements.

The second command will create your user. You can add a few flags to meet your requirements:

AccountPassword Use the $pw password from the previous command. This passes your desired password for the new user object in a secure string format.

Enable This takes either a 1 (user object to be enabled) or a 0 (user object to be disabled) value.

ChangePasswordAtLogon This takes either a 1 (force a password change) or a 0 (do not force a password change) value.

The result of this combination is that the user object is created with your desired password and is enabled, and the user will be forced to change their password when they log in for the first time.

It seems wasteful to run two commands, doesn't it? It would be for just one user. But with this approach, you can repeat that second command for the other nine users you want to create. Each one would have the same password.

If you wanted to create just one user, then you could do everything in one command. This approach will take advantage of PowerShell's power. You'll be nesting the Read-Host cmdlet:

```
PS C:\Users\Administrator> New-ADUser "Philipp Witschi" -SamAccountName
 "PWitschi" -GivenName "Philipp" -Surname "Witschi" -DisplayName "Philipp
Witschi"
 -Path 'OU=Users,OU=BigFirm,DC=bigfirm,DC=com' -UserPrincipalName
 "PWitschi@bigfirm.com" -AccountPassword (read-host "Please Enter The Password"
 -AsSecureString) -Enabled 1 -ChangePasswordAtLogon 1

Please Enter The Password: **********
```

What you've done here is substitute the `Read-Host` cmdlet for the `$pw` variable, as shown in the previous approach. This will cause the `Read-Host` cmdlet to run before the `New-ADUser` cmdlet can complete and then enter the required secure string as a value for the `-AccountPassword` flag. When you run the command, you are prompted for a password, and then the user object is created.

Creating Many Users at Once

Imagine that you work in a university as an Active Directory administrator. You probably have a forest for student accounts. Every summer you delete all the old student user accounts. You then create new user accounts for each student attending the first semester of the year. You're looking at a task where you might be creating tens of thousands of user objects. Are you really going to use ADUC, ADAC, or one of the previous PowerShell examples to do that? We hope you aren't planning on using one of those approaches.

You can use a powerful one-line PowerShell command to do this work for you with very little effort. What you are going to do is create a comma-separated value (CSV) file in Excel or some other spreadsheet-editing tool. A more advanced network may have a personnel management system that can create this via some export process. The CSV file is a text file that contains a header row dictating value descriptions and is followed by one row for each user. Each row will contain the values that describe the user. Here are the contents of a file called `users.csv` that you can use to create three users:

Name	SamAccountName	GivenName	Surname
Rachel Kelly	RKelly	Rachel	Kelly
Ulrika Gerhardt	UGerhardt	Ulrika	Gerhardt
Tomasz Kozlowski	TKozlowski	Tomasz	Kozlowski
DisplayName	**Path**	**UserPrincipalName**	**AccountPassword**
Rachel Kelly	OU=Users,OU=BigFirm, DC=bigfirm,DC=com	RKelly@bigfirm.com	NewPassw0rd
Ulrika Gerhardt	OU=Users,OU=BigFirm, DC=bigfirm,DC=com	UGerhardt@bigfirm .com	NewPassw0rd
Tomasz Kozlowski	OU=Users,OU=BigFirm, DC=bigfirm,DC=com	TKozlowski@bigfirm .com	NewPassw0rd

If you open that CSV file, `users.csv`, in Notepad, it will look like this:

```
Name,SamAccountName,GivenName,Surname,DisplayName,Path,UserPrincipalName,
AccountPassword
Rachel Kelly,RKelly,Rachel,Kelly,Rachel Kelly,"OU=Users,OU=BigFirm,DC=bigfirm,DC=
com",RKelly@bigfirm.com,NewPassw0rd
Ulrika Gerhardt,UGerhardt,Ulrika,Gerhardt,Ulrika Gerhardt,"OU=Users,OU=BigFirm,
DC=bigfirm,DC=com",UGerhardt@bigfirm.com,NewPassw0rd
Tomasz Kozlowski, TKozlowski,Tomasz,Kozlowski,Tomaz Kozlowski,"OU=Users,OU=BigFirm,
DC=bigfirm,DC=com",TKozlowski@bigfirm
.com,NewPassw0rd
```

NOTICE THE HEADER ROW

The header row is the same as the variables you used earlier with the New-ADUser cmdlet. The rows below the header row in the CSV file contain the values for creating each user.

Now you want to run a command that will read each row from the CSV file that you've saved as C:\users.csv. The command will then execute the New-ADUser cmdlet using the values from the file. Here's the command:

```
PS C:\Users\Administrator> Import-CSV c:\users.csv | foreach
  {New-ADUser -Name $_.Name -SamAccountName $_.SamAccountName -GivenName
  $_.GivenName -Surname $_.Surname -DisplayName $_.DisplayName -Path $_.Path
  -UserPrincipalName $_.UserPrincipalName -AccountPassword (ConvertTo-SecureString
  -AsPlainText $_.AccountPassword -Force) -Enabled $true -ChangePasswordAtLogon 1}
```

Don't let the size of this command scare or confuse you. We promise it is simple to understand once you break it down into its components:

IMPORT-CSV   This PowerShell cmdlet will read the CSV file you created and saved as C:\ users.csv.

| This is a pipe. It's the vertical bar on your keyboard. Part of the power that PowerShell gives you is the ability to feed the results of one cmdlet in as a parameter to another cmdlet. Here you're reading the CSV file and feeding it into the next part of the command.

FOREACH   This cmdlet takes the CSV file, which is read as three items, that is, three rows of data (excluding the header row). The FOREACH cmdlet will now run a task using each of the rows as a parameter.

NEW-ADUSER   You know that this command will create a user. But how does it get its values?

$_   Each flag in the New-User cmdlet requires a value. You know that you have assigned a header to the CSV values. Each of the $_ entries in the command refers to one of those headers. You need to know that $_ represents an object in PowerShell and $_.Name represents the property Name of the object. For example, the $_.Name refers to the Name header in the CSV. So, New-ADUser will take the value Rachel Kelly from the first row and substitute it for $_.Name.

AccountPasword   You're again converting the password value to a secure string to meet the requirements of the flag.

This command will read each of the three data rows from the CSV file. It will load in the values and create three user objects based on these values, such as in the OU you specified in the CSV file. The users will have their password set, be enabled, and then be forced to change their password when they log in.

Nothing is stopping you from adding columns to this CSV and matching additional flags in the command to further populate the attributes of the user object, such as roaming profile, home directory, and so on.

Using this approach, you could manually or automatically (using some developed export tool from a personnel system) create this CSV file and then run this *one* command to create many user accounts. That's exactly what PowerShell is all about: making work easier by automation.

Unlocking a User Account

You can also use PowerShell to do the more mundane work. If you want to unlock a user account, you can run the following:

```
PS C:\Users\Administrator> Unlock-ADAccount -identity SRed
```

The -identity flag takes the name of the user object to unlock. In this example we've used the friendly user logon name. You might want to use the DN to identify the user object:

```
PS C:\Users\Administrator> Unlock-ADAccount -identity "CN=Steve Red,OU=Users,
OU=BigFirm,DC=bigfirm,DC=com"
```

You can reset a user's password using this command:

```
PS C:\Users\Administrator> Set-ADAccountPassword -identity SRed -reset
 -newpassword (read-host "Please Enter The New Password" -AsSecureString)

Please Enter The New Password: **********
```

The Set-ADAccountPassword cmdlet also uses the -identity flag to specify a user object to manage. The -reset flag lets PowerShell know that you aren't doing a normal password change that requires knowing the old password. Instead, you want to change a password for a user object because the user has forgotten their password. You're again using the Read-Host cmdlet to read in a password and convert it to a secure string for the -newpassword flag.

The Get-ADUser cmdlet will retrieve a user object's properties:

```
PS C:\Users\Administrator> Get-ADUser SRed


DistinguishedName: CN=Steve Red,OU=Users,OU=BigFirm,DC=bigfirm,DC=com
Enabled           : True
GivenName         : Steve
Name              : Steve Red
ObjectClass       : user
ObjectGUID        : 5fa7f3ac-93ec-4cf8-bf80-21368f8b3a8d
SamAccountName    : SRed
SID               : S-1-5-21-3625881918-2577536232-3089104624-1108
Surname           : Red
UserPrincipalName: SRed@bigfirm.com
```

By default it retrieves only a small set of the available attributes. If you want to see everything that's available in a user object, then run the Get-ADUser command and ask for all properties using a * wildcard:

```
PS C:\Users\Administrator> Get-ADUser SRed -properties * | more
```

Here you're piping the results into a More cmdlet so that the results pause and require you to press a key to continue. Otherwise, the results just scroll past faster than you can read them. There are probably too many results included, so you can modify the previous results by specifying the properties you do want to see. You'll need to know what properties to ask for, so the wildcard approach is useful after all.

```
PS C:\Users\Administrator> Get-ADUser SRed -properties HomeDirectory


DistinguishedName: CN=Steve Red,OU=Users,OU=BigFirm,DC=bigfirm,DC=com
Enabled           : True
GivenName         : Steve
HomeDirectory     : \\DC01\home$\SRed
Name              : Steve Red
ObjectClass       : user
ObjectGUID        : 5fa7f3ac-93ec-4cf8-bf80-21368f8b3a8d
SamAccountName    : SRed
SID               : S-1-5-21-3625881918-2577536232-3089104624-1108
Surname           : Red
UserPrincipalName: SRed@bigfirm.com
```

This example has requested that the default response to `Get-ADUser` be modified to also include the `HomeDirectory` attribute.

You can return the properties of a number of users at once by specifying some search criteria:

```
PS C:\Users\Administrator> Get-ADUser -Filter 'Name -like "*"' -SearchBase
"OU=Users,OU=BigFirm,DC=bigfirm,DC=com"
```

There are two flags here:

-Filter   Here you are specifying any object with a name similar to the wildcard `*`, in other words, all user objects.

-SearchBase   You've further qualified the search by specifying the \BigFirm\Users OU in the domain.

That command will return the default properties of all user objects in the \BigFirm\Users OU.

If you want to modify the property of a user object, then you will need to run the Set-ADUser cmdlet:

```
PS C:\Users\Administrator> Set-ADUser SCorso -Description "IT Manager"
```

That command specifies the user, SCorso, and that you want to modify the -Description attribute. This example will change this user object's description to IT Manager, giving Simona a promotion. You can get a list of the attributes to modify by running this:

```
PS C:\Users\Administrator> Get-Help Set-ADUser
```

It's possible to change a property of a large number of objects at once. In this example, you'll modify every object in \BigFirm\Users. You'll use the `Get-ADUser` cmdlet that we just discussed to find the users in that OU and then feed the results into Set-ADUser using a pipe:

```
PS C:\Users\Administrator> Get-ADUser -Filter 'Name -like "*"' -SearchBase "OU=Us
ers,OU=BigFirm,DC=bigfirm,DC=com" | Set-ADUser -Description "Member of IT"
```

This uses the same example for finding users as we covered just a moment ago. Once you have the objects, you can feed them in as parameters via the pipe into `Set-ADUser`. You're changing the property of all the found users to Member of IT.

Enabling an Account

Earlier we said that you might want to create a user object and enable it only when the human user was ready to use it. Here's how to enable a user object for Philipp Witschi:

```
PS C:\Users\Administrator> Enable-ADAccount -Identity PWitschi
```

Disabling an Account

We discussed why you might want to disable accounts for a certain amount of time before deleting them. Here's how to disable an account:

```
PS C:\Users\Administrator> Disable-ADAccount -Identity PWitschi
```

Finally, you get to the point where you want to delete a user account:

```
PS C:\Users\Administrator> Remove-ADUser -Identity PWitschi -confirm

Confirm
Are you sure you want to perform this action?
Performing operation "Remove" on Target "CN=PWitschi,CN=Users,DC=bigfirm,DC=com".
[Y] Yes  [A] Yes to All  [N] No  [L] No to All  [S] Suspend  [?] Help
(default is "Y"):
```

We've been very careful by throwing on the -confirm flag at the end of the Remove-ADUser cmdlet. That will force you to read what the result will be and gives you a chance to decide whether you want to continue with this action. Doing things from the command line is very quick, so a deletion is something you need to be careful about. If this will be a script, then you will probably not want to use the -confirm flag because you might not want the script to pause halfway through the execution to ask you to interact with it.

That wraps up our coverage of user management using PowerShell. We'll now move on to group management. To get going, create a group by using the New-ADGroup cmdlet. Have you noticed how similar all these cmdlets are? That's a feature of PowerShell. There's a verb like Get, Set, or New and then something descriptive to indicate what the cmdlet does.

```
PS C:\Users\Administrator> New-ADGroup -Name "IT Administrators" -SamAccountName
"IT Administrators" -GroupCategory Security -GroupScope DomainLocal -DisplayName
"IT Administrators" -Path "OU=Security Groups,OU=BigFirm,DC=bigfirm,DC=com"
-Description "Members of this group are in IT"
```

That command will create a domain local security group called IT Administrators in the \BigFirm\Security Groups OU using these flags:

-Name   This is the name of the group!

-SamAccountName   This is the name associated with the pre–Windows 2000 group object attribute.

-GroupCategory   This will be either Security (or 1) or Distribution (or 0).

-GroupScope   This will be either DomainLocal (or 0), Global (or 1), or Universal (or 2).

-DisplayName This is the name shown for the group.

-Path This is the distinguished name of the OU where the group will be located.

-Description This will fill the description field of the object for future reference.

Once you have a group, you'll want to start adding members to it. You'll be using the Add-ADGroupMember cmdlet to add members. You have lots of ways to do this. You'll start with the simplest one:

```
PS C:\Users\Administrator> Add-ADGroupMember "IT Administrators" -Member SRed
```

You can use the -Identify flag to tell PowerShell which group you want to edit. You then can specify a user to add using the -Member flag. The previous example adds the SRed user object to the IT Administrators security group. Odds are you'll want to add more than one user at once. If you're doing this from the PowerShell command prompt, then you could use this approach:

```
PS C:\Users\Administrator> Add-ADGroupMember "IT Administrators"

cmdlet Add-ADGroupMember at command pipeline position 1
Supply values for the following parameters:
Members[0]:SCorso
Members[1]:MZehner
Members[2]:
```

Using this method, you specify the group to be managed, but you do not list the new members in the command. PowerShell knows that something is missing, so it prompts for a member. You've entered SCorso as member 0, entered MZehner as member 1, and pressed Return on the prompt for another member to end the command. The users you entered will then be added to the group. Alternatively, you can use this approach:

```
PS C:\Users\Administrator> Add-ADGroupMember "IT Administrators" -Member
    SCorso,MZehner
```

You've used a comma delimiter to separate the name of each user account object that you want to add to the IT Administrators group.

You might want to add a very large number of users into a group. You can use a search result generated by using the Get-ADUser cmdlet to do this:

```
PS C:\Users\Administrator> Add-ADGroupMember "IT Administrators" -Member (Get-ADUser
    -Filter 'Name -like "*"' -SearchBase "OU=Users,OU=BigFirm,DC=bigfirm,DC=com")
```

This command nests the Get-ADUser query that you used earlier when you were dealing with user management via PowerShell. You've nested the Get-ADUser cmdlet as a value for the -Member flag of the Add-ADGroupMember cmdlet. Get-ADUser is searching for all users in the \BigFirm\Users OU. The resulting users are added as members to IT Administrators.

Remember that you're not limited to adding just users to a group in Active Directory. You can also add groups to create nested groups:

```
PS C:\Users\Administrator> Add-ADGroupMember "IT Administrators" "Helpdesk"
```

The previous command will add the Helpdesk group to the IT Administrators group.

When you have a group, you'll want to see who are members. This is a simple command using the Get-ADGroupMember cmdlet to list all the members of the IT Administrators group:

```
PS C:\Users\Administrator> Get-ADGroupMember "IT Administrators"

distinguishedName: CN=Helpdesk,OU=Security Groups,OU=BigFirm,DC=bigfirm,DC=com
name             : Helpdesk
objectClass      : group
objectGUID       : 93e9b21b-023a-4e46-88b5-3c4cbf71f218
SamAccountName   : Helpdesk
SID              : S-1-5-21-3625881918-2577536232-3089104624-1115

distinguishedName: CN=Steve Red,OU=Users,OU=BigFirm,DC=bigfirm,DC=com
name             : Steve Red
objectClass      : user
objectGUID       : 5fa7f3ac-93ec-4cf8-bf80-21368f8b3a8d
SamAccountName   : SRed
SID              : S-1-5-21-3625881918-2577536232-3089104624-1108
```

That will return all direct members of the group, not the nested members. The returned list might not be very useful for something like a report. PowerShell allows you to specify which attributes of the returned objects should be presented:

```
PS C:\Users\Administrator> Get-ADGroupMember "IT Administrators" |
  FT ObjectClass,Name

ObjectClass                       Name
-----------                       ----
group                             Helpdesk
user                              Steve Red
```

Here you've piped the results from Get-ADGroupMember into the FT cmdlet. FT is an alias and stands for Format-Table cmdlet. That allows you to specify properties or attributes that you would like listed. In the previous example, you've asked for ObjectClass and Name. That gives you useful reports on what objects are direct members of the IT Administrators group.

However, if a group contains other groups as members, then you might need a complete recursive list of members:

```
PS C:\Users\Administrator> Get-ADGroupMember "IT Administrators" -recursive | FT
  DistinguishedName

DistinguishedName
-----------------
CN=Steve Red,OU=Users,OU=BigFirm,DC=bigfirm,DC=com
CN=Kevin Greene,OU=Users,OU=BigFirm,DC=bigfirm,DC=com
CN=Marcel Zehner,OU=Users,OU=BigFirm,DC=bigfirm,DC=com
```

Here you've added the -Recursive flag to the cmdlet and piped the results into FT or Format-Table to get the distinguished names of all objects that can claim membership in the IT Administrators group.

AUTOMATICALLY ADJUSTING COLUMNS

It's possible that if you run the command with multiple properties, it will not correctly show up in the command prompt. It will look like the columns are not sized correctly. What you then can do is add the switch -auto at the end of the command. As you might know in PowerShell, you don't always have to write the complete switch name. For example, in this case -auto stands for -AutoSize. This will instruct the FT cmdlet to adjust the columns' width automatically. The command will look like this:

```
PS C:\Users\Administrator> Get-ADGroupMember "IT Administrators" -recursive | FT
-auto
```

The next operation you'll want to be able to do with groups is remove members. You'll use the Remove-ADGroupMember cmdlet for that:

```
PS C:\Users\Administrator> Remove-ADGroupMember "IT Administrators" -Member
SRed

Confirm
Are you sure you want to perform this action?
Performing operation "Set" on Target "CN=IT Administrators,OU=Security
Groups,OU=BigFirm,DC=bigfirm,DC=com".
[Y] Yes  [A] Yes to All  [N] No  [L] No to All  [S] Suspend  [?] Help
(default is "Y"):
```

Here you've requested to remove the user SRed from the IT Administrators group. The Remove-ADGroupMember cmdlet always asks for confirmation. You can enter one of a number of options in response to the confirmation request:

Yes   Go ahead and remove the indicated user from the group.

Yes to All   Use this option if you have requested to remove multiple members from the group and you're sure you want to remove them all.

No   Do not remove the indicated user group the group.

L   Abandon all removal operations requested in the command.

S   Suspend the operation. This will return you to the command prompt. You can resume the command to this point by typing **Exit**.

You can run this command for multiple users by using a comma delimiter:

```
PS C:\Users\Administrator> Remove-ADGroupMember -Identity "IT Administrators"
-Member SCorso,SRed

Confirm
Are you sure you want to perform this action?
Performing operation "Set" on Target "CN=IT Administrators,OU=Security
Groups,OU=BigFirm,DC=bigfirm,DC=com".
[Y] Yes  [A] Yes to All  [N] No  [L] No to All  [S] Suspend  [?] Help
(default is "Y"):
```

Here you have separated SCorso and SRed with a comma. You can add many users or even groups to the command this way.

You might want to remove many users or groups using some sort of search. In the following example, you're using the Get-ADUser cmdlet to search for all users in the \BigFirm\Users OU and then remove them from the IT Administrators group:

```
PS C:\Users\Administrator> Remove-ADGroupMember "IT Administrators" -Member
  (Get-ADUser -Filter 'Name -like "*"' -SearchBase "OU=Users,OU=BigFirm,DC=bigfirm,
DC=com")

Confirm
Are you sure you want to perform this action?
Performing operation "Set" on Target "CN=IT Administrators,OU=Security
Groups,OU=BigFirm,DC=bigfirm,DC=com".
[Y] Yes  [A] Yes to All  [N] No  [L] No to All  [S] Suspend  [?] Help
(default is "Y"):
```

You can see that you haven't specified a value for the -Member flag. Instead, you have nested the Get-ADUser cmdlet. That will find all the users you want to remove, and the result is passed to the Remove-ADGroupMember cmdlet. If you confirm this, every user object in the \BigFirm\ Users OU will be removed from the IT Administrators group.

This has a similar catch to when you used the same query approach to add users to the group. The entire Remove-ADGroupMember operation will fail if any of the resulting objects from the Get-ADUser nested query are not members of the indicated group. So, if you query for all users in \BigFirm\OU and one of them is *not* already in the IT Administrators group, then the removal operation will fail.

Maybe you want to remove all members from a group. You can do that by querying for the members of the group and nesting that command in a command to remove members from the group:

```
PS C:\Users\Administrator> Remove-ADGroupMember "IT Administrators" -Member (Get-
ADGroupMember "IT Administrators")

Confirm
Are you sure you want to perform this action?
Performing operation "Set" on Target "CN=IT Administrators,OU=Security
Groups,OU=BigFirm,DC=bigfirm,DC=com".
[Y] Yes  [A] Yes to All  [N] No  [L] No to All  [S] Suspend  [?] Help
(default is "Y"):
```

Here you are retrieving all the members of IT Administrators by running the Get-ADGroupMember cmdlet. That's nested in the Remove-ADGroupMember command and will return the answer as a value for the -Member flag of the command.

That gives you many ways to create a group using PowerShell, add members, query the membership, and remove members. All that remains is to delete that group.

Removing a Group

Removing a group is a pretty simple task. Just use the—you guessed it—Remove-ADGroup cmdlet and specify the name of the group:

```
PS C:\Users\Administrator> Remove-ADGroup "IT Administrators"

Confirm
Are you sure you want to perform this action?
Performing operation "Remove" on Target "CN=IT Administrators,OU=Security
Groups,OU=BigFirm,DC=bigfirm,DC=com".
[Y] Yes  [A] Yes to All  [N] No  [L] No to All  [S] Suspend  [?] Help
(default is "Y"):
```

Here you are deleting the IT Administrators group. It doesn't matter if the group has members or not; it will be removed. Be sure that you don't need the group anymore. Remember that you cannot just re-create the group to restore all the assigned permissions because the SID assigned to the group is globally unique.

Finally, you've reached the end of the section that deals with the Active Directory module for Windows PowerShell. At first it looks like it will be very difficult to use. Sure, in a smaller environment there might not be any advantage to using PowerShell, but it's something you should learn. In medium-size environments, you'll find it can be used to rapidly get results. In large environments, you'll find it's something you'll be able to use to get complex operations done very quickly and with minimum effort.

The Bottom Line

Manage local users and groups.   Local users and groups are stored on a computer and cannot be used to log into or access resources on other computers.

> **Master It**   You have 25 PCs with 25 users on a workgroup network, in other words, a network with no Active Directory or Windows domain. You are installing two file servers. You want to provide authorized-only access to shared resources on the file servers. How will you do this?

Manage users and groups in Active Directory.   Users and groups can be stored in Active Directory. That means administrators can create a single copy of each user and group that is stored in a replicated database and can be used by member computers across the entire Active Directory forest. You can use Active Directory Users and Computers, the command prompt, PowerShell, and Active Directory Administrative Center to manage users and groups on Windows Server 2012.

> **Master It**   List the different types of Active Directory group types and scopes. Why would you use each of them?

Manage users and computers in Windows Server 2012.   You can manage users and computers using either PowerShell or the new Active Directory Administrative Center. ADAC makes it quicker and easier for administrators to perform day-to-day operations such as resetting passwords, unlocking user accounts, and finding objects in the forest that they want to manage. The Active Directory module for Windows PowerShell offers a command-line interface and way to script Active Directory management tasks. You can use this to automate repetitive tasks using scripts or to perform complex and large operations that would consume too much time using an administrative console.

Master It   You are managing the Windows Server 2012 Active Directory forest for an international corporation. The directors have announced that a new call center with 5,000 employees is to be opened soon. The human resources department will be able to produce a file from its database with the names of the new employees thanks to some in-house developers. You want to create the user objects as quickly as possible with minimum human effort. How will you do this?

Delegate group management.   Part of the power of Active Directory is the ability to delegate administrative rights. You can grant permissions to users or groups to manage any organizational unit or object in the domain. You can limit those rights so people only have permissions to do what they need to do for their role in the organization.

Master It   You are a domain administrator in a large organization. Your network contains several file servers. File shares are secured using domain-based security groups. You have delegated rights to help-desk staff to manage these groups. The organization is relying on the help desk to know who should have read, read/write, and no access to the file shares. Mistakes are being made and changes are taking too long, causing employees to be unable to access critical information. You've considered a paper-based procedure where the business owners of the file shares document who should have access. This has proven to be unpopular because it slows down the business. You have been asked to implement a solution that ensures the business is not delayed and where only authorized people have access to sensitive information.

Deal with users leaving the organization.   It is important to understand that Windows tracks users, groups, and computers by their security identifier and not by their visible friendly name. When you delete and re-create an object, the new object is actually a different object and does not keep the old object's rights and permissions.

Master It   The personnel department has informed you that an employee, BKavanagh, is leaving the organization immediately under bad circumstances. The security officer informs you that there is a security risk. You have been asked to deal with this risk without any delay. What do you do? Two hours later you are told that the personnel department gave you the wrong name. The correct name is BCavanagh. BKavanagh has called the help desk to say that she cannot do any work. What do you do to rectify the situation?

Group Policy: AD's Gauntlet and Active Directory Delegation

When you talk about Active Directory, you must also talk about Group Policy. Group Policy is not a new technology for Active Directory, but it has grown and improved with every iteration of the operating system and service pack since it was first introduced in Windows 2000. The Group Policy technology and features that are delivered with Windows Server 2012 R2 are such drastic improvements from the original version that they can almost seem like new technology. Changes and enhancements have come for managing Group Policy (the Group Policy Management Console and the Group Policy Management Editor), managing available settings (with now more than 5,000 settings), controlling targeting objects, and troubleshooting your Group Policy infrastructure. If you are a veteran of Group Policy, you will certainly want to focus on the Group Policy preferences, GPMC, and troubleshooting sections in this chapter.

In this chapter, you will learn to:

◆ Understand local policies and Group Policy objects

◆ Create GPOs

◆ Troubleshoot group policies

◆ Delegate control using organizational units

◆ Use advanced delegation to manually set individual permissions

◆ Find out which delegations have been set

Group Policy Concepts

Let's start with some important concepts, terms, and rules you need to know to master Group Policy. In the process of explaining the functionality of Group Policy, we will mention several settings without actually showing you how to turn them on in the Group Policy snap-in. Just focus on the concepts for now. Later in this section, we'll take you on a full tour of the Group Policy Management console (GPMC); we will cover the Group Policy application (including settings such as Enforce and Block Inheritance) and the expanded settings.

Administrators configure and deploy Group Policy by building *Group Policy objects* (GPOs). GPOs are containers for groups of settings (*policy settings*) that can be applied to user and computer accounts throughout Active Directory. Policy objects are created using the Group Policy Management Editor (GPME), which is invoked by editing a GPO from within the GPMC. The same GPO could specify a set of applications to be installed on all users' desktops, implement a very strict policy of disk quotas and restrictions on the Explorer shell, and define domain-wide password and account lockout policies. It is possible to create one all-encompassing GPO or several different GPOs, one for each type of function.

A GPO is made up of two parts:

Computer Configuration   The computer configuration policies manage machine-specific settings such as disk quotas, security auditing, and Event Log management.

User Configuration   User configuration policies apply user-specific settings such as application configuration, Start menu management, and folder redirection.

However, there is a good bit of overlap between the two, especially now that Group Policy preferences have been introduced (more on Group Policy preferences later in this chapter). It's not unusual to find the same policy available in both the User Configuration and Computer Configuration nodes. Be prepared for a certain amount of head scratching as you search for the policy you want to activate and decide whether to employ the user-based policy or the computer policy. Keep in mind that you can create a policy that uses both types of settings, or you can create separate GPOs to control the User Configuration and Computer Configuration settings.

Contrary to the name, Group Policy objects aren't group oriented at all. Maybe they are called GPOs because a bunch of different configuration management settings are *grouped* together in one location. Regardless, you cannot apply them directly to groups. You can apply them locally, to sites, domains and to OUs (Microsoft abbreviates these collectively with LSDOU in the correct order, which stands for (1) Local, (2) Site, (3) Domain, (4) OU) within a given forest. This act of assigning GPOs to a site, domain, or OU is called *linking*. The GPO-to-LSDOU relationship can be many-to-one (many GPOs linked to one OU, for example) or one-to-many (one GPO linked to several different OUs). Once linked to an LSDOU, user policies affect user accounts within the OU (and sub-OUs), and computer policies affect computer accounts within the OU (and sub-OUs). Both types of policy settings apply at a periodic refresh rate, which is approximately every 90 minutes, for the most part.

When we said GPOs were stored in the AD, that wasn't exactly accurate. GPOs are stored in two parts—a Group Policy container (GPC) and a Group Policy template (GPT), which is a folder structure. The container part is stored in the Active Directory database and contains property information, version information, status, and a list of components. The folder structure path is `Windows\SYSVOL\sysvol\<Domainname>\Policies\GUID\`, where *GUID* is the globally unique identifier for the GPO. This folder contains administrative settings, security settings, information on available applications, registry settings, scripts, and much more.

Policies Are "All or Nothing"

Each GPO contains many possible settings for many functions; usually you'll configure only a handful of them in each GPO. The others will be left "inactive," sort of like putting REM (for a remark) in front of a command in a script or using a semicolon at the beginning of a line in an INF file. Once you've configured policy settings and told AD that "this GPO is linked to the Bigfirm.com domain," for example, the individual settings or types of settings cannot be selectively applied. All User Configuration settings will be applied to all user accounts logged onto Windows 7, 8, and Server 2012 R2 systems in the linked domain. All Computer Configuration settings will be applied to all Windows 7, 8, and Server 2012 R2 machines in the domain. Now, let's say you've created a GPO that deploys a set of standard desktop applications such as Word, Excel, and Outlook, and you threw in a bunch of shell restrictions to prevent users from changing their configurations. If you don't want your IT support group users to be subject to those ridiculously stringent shell restrictions (although those users may need them most of all!), you can do a couple of things:

- ◆ You can create a separate GPO for those policy settings and link the GPO to an OU that contains all the regular users. But that OU will be the only one that gets the Office applications.

- ◆ You can alternately set permissions on the GPO that prevent the policy from being applied to the IT support group (this is called *filtering*). However, if you use filtering to solve this problem, none of the settings in the GPO will apply to the IT support group at all.

Policies Are Inherited and Cumulative

Group Policy settings are cumulative and inherited from parent Active Directory containers. For example, the Bigfirm.com domain has several different GPOs. There is a GPO linked to the domain that sets password restrictions, account lockout, and standard security settings. Each OU in the domain also has a GPO linked to it that deploys and maintains standard applications, as well as folder redirection settings and desktop restrictions. User accounts and computer accounts that are located in the OUs receive settings from both the GPO linked to the domain and the GPO linked to the specific OU. So, some blanket policy settings can be applied to the entire domain, while others can target accounts according to OUs upon which they are linked.

Group Policy Power! Refresh Intervals

Policies apply in the background every 90 minutes, with up to a 30-minute "randomization" to keep the domain controller from getting hit by hundreds or even thousands of computers at once. DCs are different from normal computers and refresh group policies every five minutes. There is, however, a policy to configure all of this, as you'll see later in this chapter. Exceptions to the refresh interval include folder redirection, software installation, script application, Group Policy preference printers, and Group Policy preference drive maps. These are applied only at logon (for user accounts) or system startup (for computer accounts); otherwise, you might end up uninstalling an application while someone is trying to use it. Or a user might be working in a folder as it is being redirected to a new network location. In essence, for data integrity these policy settings apply only in the "foreground" refresh of Group Policy.

Group Policy Basics

To better understand how Group Policy technology works in your Active Directory environment, it is best to understand how some of the Group Policy technology works "under the hood." If you are just becoming familiar with Group Policy, you will quickly see that many of the features that Group Policy possesses are benefits over older technologies, such as system policies.

Replication of Group Policy Is Built In

GPOs replicate themselves automatically, with no work required on your part. Active Directory is replicated using AD Replication (controlled by the Knowledge Consistency Checker and the Intersite Topology Generator) and is controlled by the File Replication Service or Distributed File Replication Service.

GPOs Undo Themselves When Removed

All the administrative template GPO settings write their information to certain parts of the registry and clean up after themselves when the policy setting is removed or the GPO is deleted.

This fixes the dreaded "tattooing" issue that has plagued "policy management" since it was first introduced. For example, suppose you had created a system policy on a legacy system that set everyone's background color to some nauseating hue and also set up a policy that kept them from changing the color. Those changes were written into the system's registry. If you then deleted the policy, the entries in the registry would not be removed, and therefore the ugly background would remain intact on the system. This is called "tattooing". You'd actually have to write a *second* policy to undo the registry effects. With GPOs, that's not necessary. Just removing the policy will undo its effects.

You Needn't Log On to Apply GPO Settings

The true glory of Group Policy is related to the "background refresh." Since all domain-based computers check in to see whether there are any changes every 90 minutes or so, policy settings are constantly being applied. This means that a setting that you make at 6 A.M. on a Monday morning to control some security setting on each desktop won't require that the computers be up and running. Rather, the background refresh will apply to the computer before the user arrives at 8 A.M.

On Windows 2000 and later with Active Directory, machines get their policy settings from the domain they have membership in when they power up (recall that machines log on also), and users get policies from *their* domain when they log on.

Local Policies and Group Policy Objects

When you open the Group Policy tool (gpedit.msc), it automatically focuses on the local machine GPO, as shown in Figure 9.1. Administrators can use the tool to configure account settings (such as the minimum password length and number of bad logon attempts before locking the account), to set up auditing, and to specify other miscellaneous settings. However, the domain-based policy editor, the Group Policy Management Editor, includes a number of settings (including software installation and folder redirection) that are not available for local policies.

GP FOLDER STRUCTURE

The local Group Policy folder structure is similar to that of other domain-based GPOs and is found in \Windows\system32\GroupPolicy.

FIGURE 9.1
The Local Group Policy
Editor—local machine

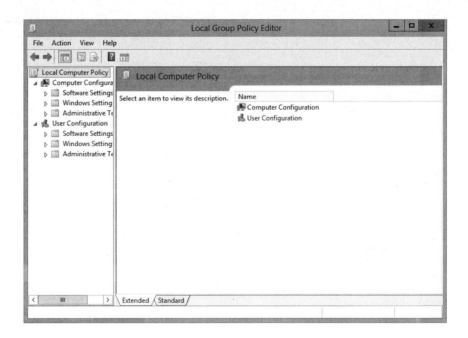

If you happen to be working on a Windows Server 2012 R2 or Windows 8 computer, you have more than the local GPO (LGPO) that you can configure. On these computers, you also have GPOs that can target groups of local users (Administrators or Non-Administrators LGPO) and individual users (User Specific LGPO).

Administrators or Non-Administrators LGPO

As their names represent, the settings in the Administrators and Non-Administrators LGPOs will target either the users in the Administrators group or the users in all other groups. The idea is that when a user has membership in the local Administrators group, that user should have more privileges than a user who is not in this group.

Note that the LGPOs that control these settings modify user-based settings only. There are no settings under these LGPOs that control computer-based settings, which are located under the Computer Configuration node.

Since there are two "types" of groups, there are two LGPOs that control them. For you to control both of these types of users, you will need to configure both LGPOs. To access these LGPOs, you must use the MMC. The steps are similar to those discussed previously, with a slight alteration in the scoping of the Group Policy object that is loaded in the MMC. Instead of choosing Local Computer from the Group Policy Objects list, use the Browse button to look for the Administrators or Non-Administrators group listed on the Users tab, as shown in Figure 9.2.

FIGURE 9.2
You can view the Administrators and Non-Administrators LGPOs using the MMC.

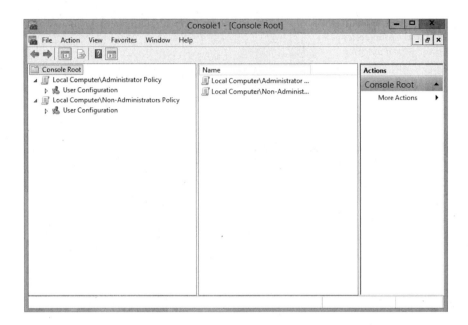

To access both of these local GPOs for editing, follow these steps:

1. Select Start ➤ Run.

2. Type **MMC** in the Open text field.

> **PERMISSIONS REQUIRED**
>
> This is an administrative task; therefore, if you have UAC enabled, you will have to agree to the permissions that opening the Group Policy Management Editor MMC snap-in requires.

3. From within the MMC, select the File menu from the toolbar.

4. Select Add/Remove Snap-in from the drop-down menu.

5. Select Group Policy Object Editor from the list of snap-ins.

6. Leave Local Computer as the entry under Group Policy Object.

7. Click the Browse button.

8. Select the Users tab in the Browse window for a Group Policy Object dialog box.

9. Select Administrators from the list, and then click the OK button.

10. Select Finish in the Select Group Policy Object dialog box.

11. Click OK in the Add or Remove Snap-ins dialog box.

12. Expand the Local Computer\Administrators Policy node in the console window.

Repeat steps 4–12 for the Non-Administrators LGPO, replacing Non-Administrators for Administrators in the appropriate steps.

User-specific LGPO

Finally, you can configure a very granular LGPO on every Windows Server 2012 R2 and Windows 8 computer. This policy is geared to target individual user accounts. There are only user-based policy settings in the LGPO, and the settings target only a single user.

The caveat to using this LGPO is that the user must have an account in the local SAM of the computer that you are configuring.

To view and configure this LGPO, you will also use the MMC and follow the same steps as you did for the Administrators and Non-Administrators LGPOs; however, you will select the user account on the Users tab for which you want to create the LGPO when adding the Group Policy Object Editor snap-in to the MMC. If you have selected the Administrator account, it will show up in the MMC similar to Figure 9.3.

FIGURE 9.3
Once a user is selected for management of the LGPO, it will show up in the MMC with all the User Configuration settings exposed.

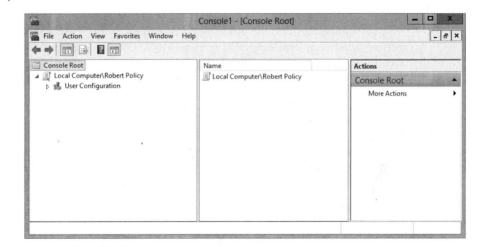

Here are the steps to follow to access the local user-specific GPOs:

1. Select Start ➤ Run.

2. Type **MMC** in the Open text field.

PERMISSIONS REQUIRED

This is an administrative task; therefore, if you have UAC enabled, you will have to agree to the permissions that opening the Group Policy Management Editor MMC snap-in requires.

3. From within the MMC console, select the File menu from the toolbar.

4. Select Add/Remove Snap-in from the drop-down menu.

5. Select Group Policy Object Editor from the list of snap-ins.

6. Leave Local Computer as the entry under Group Policy Object.

7. Click the Browse button.

8. Select the Users tab in the Browse for a Group Policy Object dialog box.

9. Select the desired user account from the list, and then click the OK button.

10. Click Finish in the Select Group Policy Object dialog box.

11. Click OK in the Add or Remove Snap-ins dialog box.

12. Expand the Local Computer\<username> Policy node in the console window.

Creating GPOs

Now that you understand the major concepts involved with Group Policy and know the difference between local GPOs and domain-based GPOs, let's go through the steps of creating and editing a domain-based GPO. In this section, we'll show you all the settings we discussed in the preceding "theory" section.

DOMAIN-BASED GPOS

From this point forward, we will be focusing on only domain-based GPOs, because they are the preferred, logical, and secure way to deploy the settings that exist in a GPO.

You will be using the GPMC to manage all domain-based GPOs. With Windows Server 2012 R2, you will need to install the GPMC using Server Manager, as you saw in Chapter 2, "Installing and Upgrading to Windows Server 2012 R2."

After the GPMC is installed, it shows up under the Start ➤ Administrative Tools menu. Once you select it from this list, the GPMC tool opens and displays the domain in which your management computer has membership, as shown in Figure 9.4.

To create a new GPO in the domain, you will need to expand the GPMC structure such that you can see all the nodes that exist under the domain, as shown in Figure 9.5.

To create a GPO in the domain, follow these steps:

1. Right-click the Group Policy Objects node, and select New.

2. In the New GPO dialog box, type the name for the GPO (in this case **Desktop Security**), and then click the OK button.

This will create a blank GPO called Desktop Security, which is not linked to any container in the domain yet. At this point, you will want to configure the GPO settings and then link it to the site, the domain, or an OU. To link a GPO to a node in Active Directory, follow these steps:

FIGURE 9.4
GPMC is the preferred
GPO management
tool.

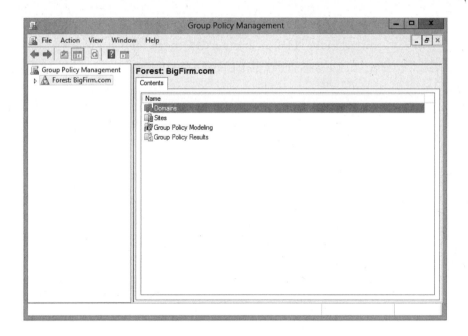

FIGURE 9.5
GPMC expands to
display all the nodes
under the domain.

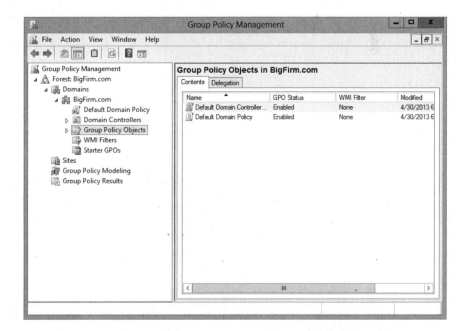

1. Right-click the desired node, in this case Desktops OU.

2. Select the "Link an Existing GPO menu" option.

3. In the Select GPO dialog box, select the Desktop Security GPO, and then click the OK button.

   Notice that the Desktops OU now has a linked GPO associated with it. If you want to create and link a GPO to an OU, you can do this in just a single step. By right-clicking the OU (or domain or site, for that matter), you can select the option called "Create a GPO in this domain, and link it here." This will perform both steps in just a single action.

4. Now, click your GPO, in this case Desktop Security.

   Notice that the GPO has some tabs and properties associated with it in the right pane of the GPMC. Four tabs are associated with each GPO: Scope, Details, Settings, and Delegation (see Figure 9.6).

FIGURE 9.6
GPO tabs and
properties in
the right pane
of the GPMC

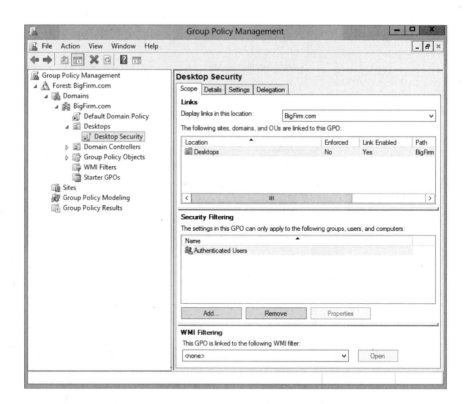

The Scope tab helps keep track of many aspects of the GPO. The most important of these details includes where in Active Directory it is linked to the uppermost area of the tab named Links and the middle area named Security Filtering. The Links area is rather obvious, listing the sites, domains, and OUs the GPO is currently linked to. The Security Filtering area clearly indicates which groups and users have the permission to apply the settings in the GPO. This filtering was referenced earlier, when it was used to control which users in the domain would have the settings from the GPO applied, just by adding or removing them from this tab. The final area of the tab, WMI Filtering, lists the WMI filter that the GPO has a link to, if any. WMI filters allow the targeting of GPOs to computer accounts dependent on the state of the computer at the time the WMI query is run.

The Details tab, as shown in Figure 9.7, helps keep track of the GPO information that is associated with the creation and state of the GPO. Here you will be able to track down the GUID, creation date, version, and so on related to the GPO. You can also configure whether all or part (computer and/or user) of the GPO is enabled or disabled.

FIGURE 9.7
The Details tab of the GPMC provides key information about the GPO.

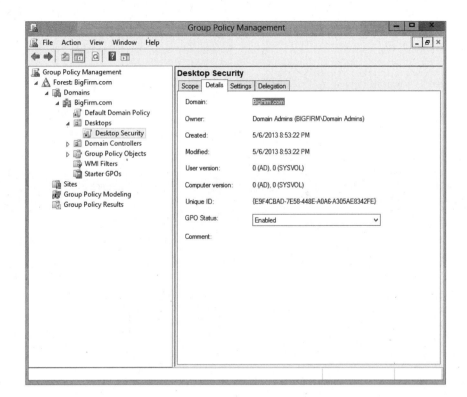

The Settings tab contains dynamic data related to the settings that are configured in the GPO. The tab displays an HTML version of the settings report, as shown in Figure 9.8.

Finally, the Delegation tab shows the current security controlling the administration of the GPO. There are three different levels of administration of the GPO on this tab, as shown in Figure 9.9. Two include editing the GPO, where one is just reading the settings of the GPO.

FIGURE 9.8
The Settings tab of the GPMC displays the current settings in the GPO.

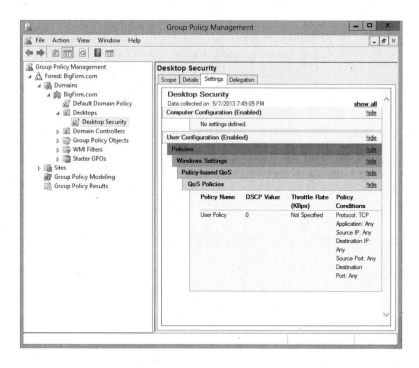

FIGURE 9.9
The Delegation tab of the GPMC displays the level of administration permissions per group and user.

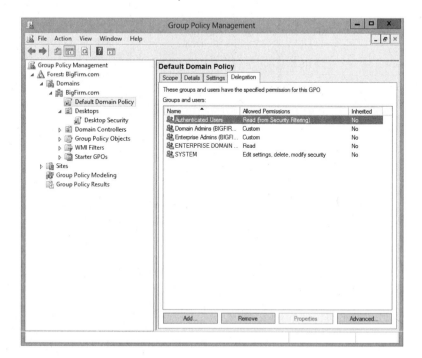

Now let's view and modify the new GPO. Back under the Group Policy Objects node in the GPMC, right-click the GPO, and click Edit. This will open the GPME in a separate window, and you'll see the policy object name at the root of the namespace, in this case Desktop Security [HOST1.BIGFIRM.COM] Policy. This indicates what policy is being viewed and edited. Figure 9.10 shows the policy expanded in the console tree to show the major nodes of the GPO. Remember that HOST1 is the domain controller for the Bigfirm.com domain.

FIGURE 9.10
Group Policy being edited in the GPME

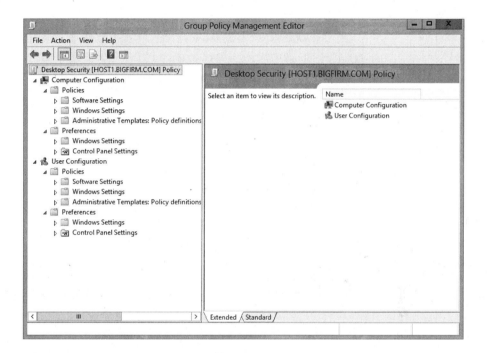

There are two major types of settings, as we mentioned earlier. Computer Configuration settings are applied to computer accounts at startup and during the background refresh interval. User Configuration settings are applied to the user accounts at logon and during the background refresh interval.

Once you've configured your Group Policy settings, simply close the GPME window. There is no Save or Save Changes option. Changes are written to the GPO when you click OK or Apply on a particular setting, although the user or computer will not actually see the change until the policy is refreshed.

Modifying Group Policy Default Behavior

Group Policy is fantastic all by itself, but there are some behaviors that you might want to tweak or control. It might seem cyclical, but there are GPO settings to control the behavior of Group Policy and some of its settings. You will find that many of these settings don't need to be configured, but in the instances where you need to make some minor adjustments, they will come in handy.

Group Policy Policies

You can find the GPO settings to control Group Policy under Administrative Templates of both the User Configuration and Computer Configuration nodes (`Policies\Administrative Templates\System\Group Policy`). The Computer Configuration node contains most of the policies we'll be discussing. Figure 9.11 and Figure 9.12 show the User Configuration and Computer Configuration options for Group Policy. The following paragraphs summarize the most important configuration options.

FIGURE 9.11
User Configuration settings for Group Policy

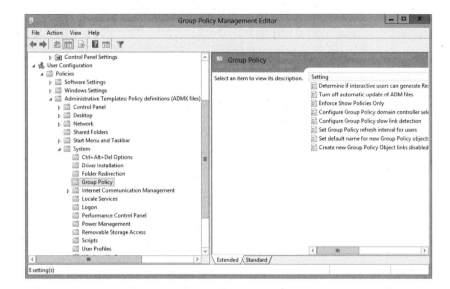

FIGURE 9.11
User Configuration settings for Group Policy

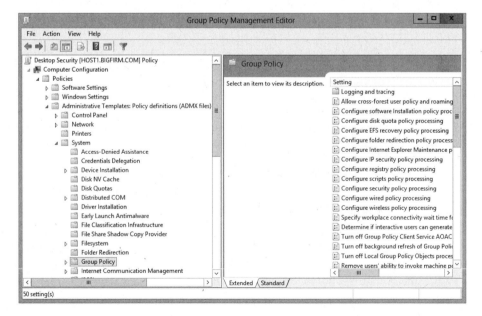

FIGURE 9.12
Computer Configuration settings for Group Policy

Group Policy Refresh Intervals for Users/Computers/Domain Controllers   These separate policies determine how often GPOs are refreshed in the background while users and computers are working. These parameters permit changes to the default background refresh intervals and tweaking of the offset time.

Turn Off Background Refresh of Group Policy   If you enable this setting, policies will be refreshed only at system startup and user logon. This might be useful for performance reasons in your branch offices, since having 1,500 computers refreshing policies every 90 minutes could cause congestion over the WAN.

Group Policy Application

Like most technologies, Group Policy has logic associated with it to ensure that it applies in a reliable manner. For the most part, the application of Group Policy will be straightforward. It is only when you start to have conflicting settings in multiple GPOs and you start to modify the default behavior that the logic becomes more complex. Regardless, when you sit down to design and implement your policy settings, you will need to fully grasp what the end result will be for all of your computers and users.

In this section, we will cover the default Group Policy application, which will resolve all your questions regarding GPO setting conflicts. You know, questions like, "What if I have a GPO at the domain that removes the Run command from the Start menu but a different GPO linked to the Desktops OU that adds the Run command to the Start menu?"

We will also delve into areas that will help you "target" your GPO settings for when too many users and computers (or not enough users and computers) are receiving the policy settings. With WMI filters, enforcement, blocking inheritance, and more, you will certainly not be without options.

How Group Policy Is Applied

Now that you have a GPO or two running, you'll soon find the troublesome part of Group Policy: figuring out what the end result is for each computer and user. Imagine, for example, that a user calls up and asks, "Why is my background purple?" You then realize that there are a *lot* of places that your system gets policies from, and they might disagree on things such as background color. So, which one *wins*?

POLICIES EXECUTE FROM THE BOTTOM UP IN THE GUI

Let's start by considering a simple situation: just policies in a domain. Suppose you look at the domain node using the GPMC and see that it has many GPOs linked to it, as shown in Figure 9.13.

In this (admittedly fanciful) situation, the domain has five group policies, four of which attempt to set a workstation's background color to gray, green, red, or blue. (The other is the Default Domain Policy, which has nothing to say on the issue.) To see the order in which the GPOs have preference, you can click the domain node and view the Linked Group Policy Objects tab in the right pane. So, based on Figure 9.13, which one wins? Gray, red, green, or blue?

FIGURE 9.13
Domain node and
linked GPOs

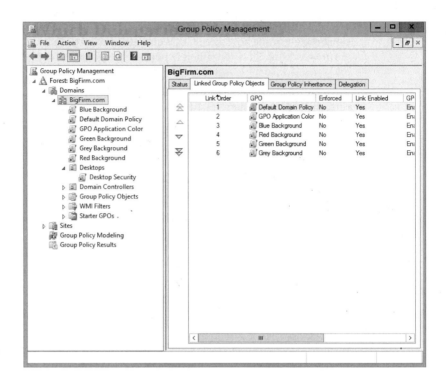

The answer lies in two basic conflict-resolution rules for GPOs:

Rule 1   Listen to the last policy that you heard from.

Rule 2   Execute policies from the bottom up, as they appear in the GUI.

Reading from the bottom of the dialog box up, you see that the system will first see the policy that sets the background gray, then the one that sets it green, then the one that sets it red, and finally the one that sets it blue. Because blue is the last one heard from, it wins, and the effects of the previous three are obviated.

You can also click the Group Policy Inheritance tab, which will display the order in which the GPOs apply from all locations within Active Directory. As you can see in Figure 9.14, the blue background policy wins out over the others.

But what if you *want* the red background policy to win? Notice the up and down arrows to the left of the Linked Group Policy Objects tab? You can shuffle them around to your heart's content.

Filtering Group Policy with Access Control Lists

But we're not *nearly* finished here. It *could* be that although it looks as if many policies apply to your system, in fact, only a small number do. The reason: GPOs have ACLs.

Click any GPO in the GPMC (in our example, the Desktop Security GPO), and view the Scope tab in the right pane. Here, in the Security Filtering section, you see the ACL for the GPO, as shown in Figure 9.15.

FIGURE 9.14
GPO inheritance
for the domain
node

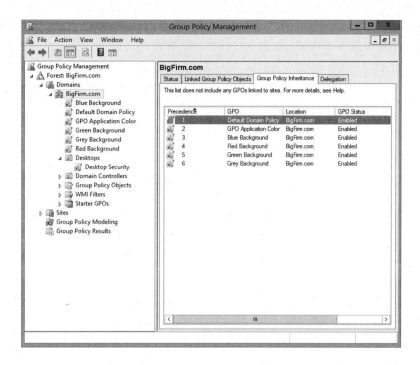

FIGURE 9.15
ACL for a GPO in
the GPMC

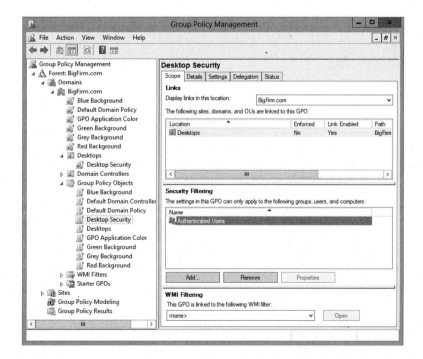

As we pointed out before, Domain Admins and Enterprise Admins have Read and Modify permissions, and Authenticated Users have Read and Apply Group Policy. However, notice that you only see Authenticated Users listed in the list. Why is that? Well, this is a list of only the users, computers, and groups that have the permission to apply the GPO settings. To view the full ACL, you must first select the Delegation tab and then click the Advanced button. The good ol' Security Settings dialog box will display, as shown in Figure 9.16.

FIGURE 9.16
Security Settings dialog box for a GPO

It may happen that you create a GPO to restrict desktops and you don't want to apply it to a certain group of people. The group Authenticated Users includes everyone (user and computer accounts) but guests, so by default the GPO will apply to everyone but guests; that means even Domain Admins and Enterprise Admins will receive the policy settings. To prevent Domain Admins and Enterprise Admins from receiving this policy, you must select the Deny box next to Apply Group Policy (Figure 9.17). A member of both groups will only need the Deny setting for one of the two groups, but you'll need to select the Deny box for both groups if the members of Domain Admins and Enterprise Admins are not the same people. To "excuse" others from receiving the policy, put them all in a security group and add that group to the list. It is not enough to deselect the Allow box for Read and Apply Group Policy; the users in your special security group are also members of Authenticated Users, so you actually need to choose the Deny option for them as well. Deny takes precedence over Allow.

As an alternative to all that ACLing, you can also remove the Authenticated Users group from the Security Filtering part of the Scope tab, add all the users who need to have the settings to a security group, and then add the security group to the Security Filtering part of the Scope tab. This is shown in Figure 9.18.

FIGURE 9.17
Denying the Apply Group Policy permission

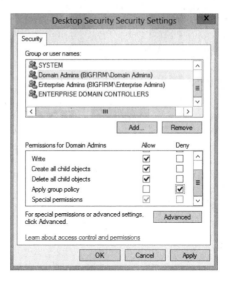

FIGURE 9.18
Group Policy security filtering without Authenticated Users

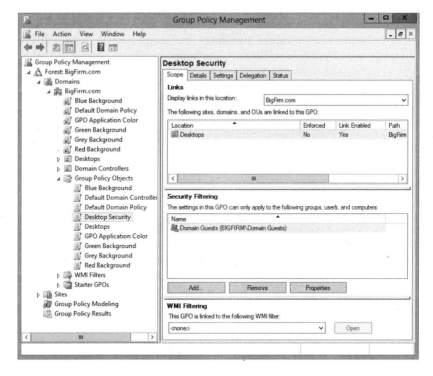

By the way, there is nothing to prevent you from adding individual users to the permissions list for a GPO. However, it is a horrible security and management practice to do so, because it is impossible to track individual users who are placed on ACLs throughout the enterprise! We'll stress, then, that policy filtering is incredibly powerful—you might say that it's the tool that lets you oppress individuals or groups. In the real world, however, adding ACLs to a policy can be a nightmare for the poor fool trying to figure out two years later why a policy is attached to a domain but *isn't bloody applying to most of the people in the domain!*

Enforcing and Blocking Inheritance

Just as security filtering can be used to counter the blanket application of policy application, the Block Inheritance setting is a special setting on an AD node (domain or OU) to prevent higher-level GPOs from trickling down. When the Block Inheritance setting is enabled, the settings of higher policies will not be applied to lower containers at all. For example, if you create a GPO for a specific OU, say Brunswick, and set up all the necessary settings for the Brunswick OU, and then you want to prevent the Bigfirm domain GPOs from affecting the Brunswick OU, you'd enable the Block Inheritance setting on the Brunswick OU. The only GPOs applied will be those linked to the Brunswick OU.

There is also a counter to the block inheritance configuration. When Enforce is turned on for a GPO, the Block Inheritance setting is neutralized for the enforced GPO. Also, the settings in subsequent GPOs are prevented from reversing the ones in the Enforce-enabled GPO. For example, if domain admins have a set of highly disputed settings turned on at the domain level and those renegade Brunswick admins set up their own OU with its own policy settings and select the Block Inheritance setting, the Brunswick OU effectively escapes the disputed settings, but only until the domain admins get wise and select the Enforce setting. Then the domain admins win, and the Brunswick OU people have to live with the same restrictions as everyone else. Enforce beats Block Inheritance (just like paper covers rock).

Like all secret weapons, the Enforce and Block Inheritance settings are best used sparingly. Otherwise, in a troubleshooting situation it becomes rather complicated to determine what GPOs are applied where. This could be detrimental to the mental health (and potentially the job security) of a network administrator.

Whew! Here's a summary of the factors that can decide which Group Policy object wins:

◆ Examine policies in this order: local GPOs, then site GPOs, then domain GPOs, then OU GPOs, then child OU GPOs, and so on.

◆ Within any AD node—site, domain, or OU—examine the policies as they appear in the GUI, from the bottom up.

◆ If policy settings conflict, pay attention only to the setting in the last GPO that you examined, *unless* you already saw a policy that said Enforce. This means that no matter what conflicting policy setting comes afterward, you should ignore these because of the Enforce-enabled GPO.

◆ Before you actually apply a GPO, check its ACL. If the target user or computer does not have the Read and Apply Group Policy permissions (usually through group membership), then the GPO doesn't apply.

Group Policy Setting Possibilities

You can do basically anything with Group Policy settings that you can do to the local system registry and most configurations. Here are a few examples:

Deploy Software You can gather all the files necessary to install a piece of software into a *package*, put that package on a server somewhere, and then use group policies to point a user's desktop at that package. The user sees that the application is available, and again, you accomplish all that from a central location rather than having to visit every desktop. The first time the user tries to start the application, it installs without any intervention from the user.

Restrict the Applications That Users Can Run You can control a user's desktop to the point where that user can run only a few applications—perhaps Outlook, Word, and Internet Explorer, for example.

Control System Settings The easiest way to control disk space quotas is with GPOs. Many Windows systems are most easily controlled with policy settings; with some systems, policies are the *only* method to enable and control those systems.

Set Logon, Logoff, Startup, and Shutdown Scripts GPOs allow any or all of these four events to trigger a script, and you use GPOs to control which scripts run.

Simplify and Restrict Programs You can use GPOs to remove many of the features from Internet Explorer, Windows Explorer, and other programs.

General Desktop Restriction You can remove most or all of the items on a user's Start button, keep her from adding printers, or disallow her from logging out or modifying her desktop configuration at all. With all the policy settings turned on, you can really lock down a user's desktop. (Too much locking down may lead to creating one unproductive employee, however, so be careful.)

There's lots more to work with in policies, but that was a basic introduction to get you started.

Decrypting User and Computer Configuration Settings

Windows Server 2012 R2 and Windows 8 come with a completely new look and feel for the User and Computer Configuration settings in the GPME. The reason for this is that Microsoft has done us all a huge favor! The favor is that it has introduced nearly 3,000 more GPO settings. To give you a better grip on the volume of settings, Microsoft has also adjusted how the settings are presented in the GPME.

As you see in Figure 9.19, there are two main nodes to the GPME interface: User Configuration and Computer Configuration. Both nodes have the following subnodes: Policies and Preferences. The Policies subnode is further broken down into the following subnodes: Software Settings, Windows Settings, and Administrative Templates. The Preferences subnode is broken down into these subnodes: Control Panel and Windows Settings.

The difference between the two levels of nodes is this: settings for User Configuration apply to user accounts, and settings for Computer Configuration apply to computer accounts. For example, if registry settings are involved, as is the case with administrative templates, the changes will be written to HKEY_CURRENT_USER (HKCU) for User Configuration and to HKEY_LOCAL_MACHINE (HKLM) for Computer Configuration settings. You may want to create separate GPOs for machines and users to keep things straight. If a value set in the computer settings is also specified in the user policy settings, the Computer Configuration settings usually take precedence by default. To ensure the behavior, check out the Explain tab within the GPO setting, but the best solution would be to test!

FIGURE 9.19
Group Policy nodes
and subnodes

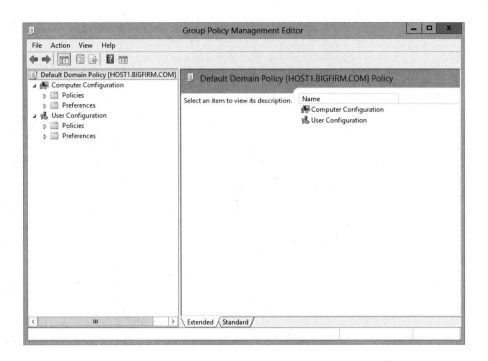

With more than 5,000 settings in a Windows Server 2012 R2 GPO, it's impossible to go over every setting. However, to help you through the settings, you should check out the Excel spreadsheet that Microsoft has provided at:

```
http://www.microsoft.com/downloads/details.aspx?displaylang=en&FamilyID=1
8c90c80-8b0a-4906-a4f5-ff24cc2030fb
```

We will go over some of the more useful policy settings and policy categories in the following sections.

SPECIFY SCRIPTS WITH GROUP POLICY

You can specify logon and logoff scripts, as well as scripts to run at system startup and shutdown, using Windows Settings in either the User Configuration node or the Computer Configuration node. Expand Policies\Windows Settings to reveal Scripts, and then select the script type (Startup, Shutdown, Logon, or Logoff) in the details pane on the right; Figure 9.20 shows the scripts available in User Configuration. From here, double-click the script type (such as Logon), or highlight it and choose Action ➢ Properties. Add Scripts to the list using the Add button, supply a script name and parameters when prompted (see Figure 9.21), and click OK. To edit the script name and parameters (not the script itself), choose Edit. If more than one script is specified, use the up and down buttons to indicate the order in which the scripts should run.

FIGURE 9.20
Group Policy logon
scripts

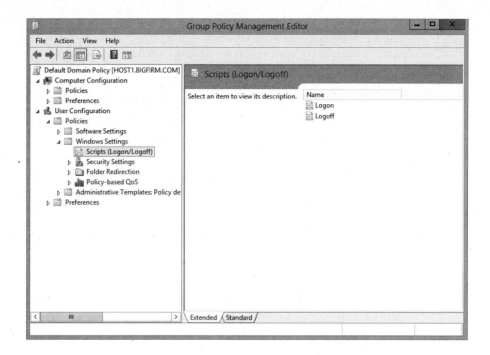

FIGURE 9.21
Adding a script to Group Policy

The scripts you create and assign should be copied to the following path in the directory: \
`Windows\SYSVOL\SysVol\domainname\Policies\{GUID}\Machine\Scripts\Startup`
(or `Shutdown`). (Or they can be copied to `User\Scripts\Logon` or `User\Scripts\Logoff`,
depending on whether you are assigning scripts to the Computer Configuration node or to the
User Configuration node.) The GUID for the Group Policy object is a long string that looks like
{FA08AF41-38AB-11D3-BD1FC9B6902FA00B}. If you want to see the scripts stored in the GPO and
possibly open them for editing, use the Show Files button at the bottom of the properties sheet.
This will open the folder in Explorer.

As you may know, you can also specify a logon script in the properties sheet of the user
account in `dsa.msc`. Microsoft calls these *legacy logon scripts* and encourages you to assign
scripts with Group Policy for Windows AD–aware clients. The advantage to using the Group

Policy scripts is that they run asynchronously in a hidden window. So, if several scripts are assigned or if the scripts are complex, the user doesn't have to wait for them to end. Legacy logon scripts run in a window on the desktop. On the other hand, you might not want the scripts to run hidden (some scripts stop and supply information or wait for user input). In that case, several policy settings are available to help you define the behavior of Group Policy scripts. These settings are located in the System\Scripts\Administrative Templates node. There you'll find settings to specify whether to run a script synchronously or asynchronously and whether it should be visible or invisible.

FOLDER REDIRECTION

One of the more useful things you can do with User Configuration settings in Group Policy is to arrange for a user's AppData, Desktop, Start Menu, Documents, Favorites, and Links folders to follow the user around from computer to computer. These folders are important elements in a user's working environment. AppData stores application-specific user information (Internet Explorer uses it, for example), and Desktop may contain important folders and shortcuts that need to be just one click away for the user. The Start Menu folder contains program groups and shortcuts to programs, and My Documents is the default place to save and retrieve files, sort of like a local home directory.

There are several good reasons to use folder redirection. For one thing, it's convenient for users who log in from several different machines. Also, if you specify a network location for some or all of these folders, they can be backed up regularly and protected by the IT department. If roaming profiles are still in use, setting up folder redirection speeds up the synchronization of the server profile with the local profile at logon and logoff, since the redirected folders need not be updated. Redirecting the Desktop and Start Menu folders to a centralized, shared location facilitates standardization of users' working environments and helps with remote support issues, because help-desk personnel will know that all machines are configured in the same way. Best of all, you can mix and match. It's possible to specify a shared location for the Desktop and Start Menu folders while allowing each user to have their own Documents and AppData folders. Let's take a look.

To set a network location for the Documents folder in Group Policy:

1. Go to User Configuration\Policies\Windows Settings\Folder Redirection\Documents.

2. Right-click the highlighted Documents folder, and choose Properties from the context menu.

   The properties sheet reveals that this setting is not configured by default.

3. Choose Basic from the drop-down list to specify a single location for the Documents folder, to be shared by all the users, or choose Advanced to set locations based on security group membership.

   If you want a single location for a shared Documents folder, just fill in the target location with a network path or browse for it.

4. To designate different locations, first choose a security group and then specify a network path.

Figure 9.22 demonstrates redirecting the My Documents folder for all members of Domain Engineering to the CentralEng share on the server Zooropa. Whether you choose the Basic or Advanced redirection option, the policy permits you to choose from four options:

◆ Redirect the folder to the user's home directory

◆ Create a folder for each user under the root path

◆ Redirect to the following location (which you specify)

◆ Redirect to the local user profile location

FIGURE 9.22
Policy to redirect the user's Documents folder

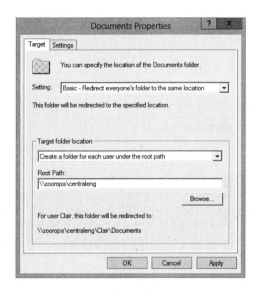

5. For this example, choose the second option; everyone in Engineering will use the same root path, but they will have individual Documents folders.

When you use this option, the system creates a subfolder named after the user in the path you specify.

6. Now click the Settings tab to configure the redirection settings.

For the sake of completeness, the redirection settings for Documents are shown in Figure 9.23.

The options you see in Figure 9.23 show default selections for the Documents folder. Notice that the user will have exclusive access to the folder by default. The contents of the corresponding folder will be moved to the new location by default. Even after the policy is removed, the folder will remain redirected unless you say to "unredirect" it.

FIGURE 9.23
Additional settings in Group Policy to redirect the user's Documents folder

SECURITY SETTINGS

Security settings, along with administrative templates, make up a significant part of Group Policy. The default security settings are purposely open to minimize administrative headaches and to ensure that users and applications work as intended. As security increases, users and applications have more restrictions, and support time goes up. In other words, security is inversely proportionate to convenience. As you start locking down systems, something is bound to stop working. Hey, regular users can't even install applications on a Windows Vista system by default. When you start enforcing passwords that are eight characters or more, contain both letters and numbers, can't use any part of a user's name, and cannot be reused until 15 other passwords have been used, things get complicated for the everyday Joe. For organizations that want to increase security, there are tools and guidelines.

For example, if you have ever "hardened" a Windows server according to established military or other high-security guidelines, you know that you have to set particular permissions on particular folders, change the default permissions on certain registry keys, and change or create other registry entries as well. All in all, it takes a few hours of work on a single server, even for an efficient admin. What if you have 50 servers and 500 workstations? Some things can be scripted, but others can't. There is no Microsoft or third-party tool that does everything automatically for all machines.

Here's where Group Policy comes to the rescue. Assuming you are going to standardize throughout a grouping of servers or workstations, or even a portion of the organization, you have to change those sticky registry permissions and settings only once using Group Policy. You only have to set the NTFS permissions once. The permissions can even be set up in one policy and copied to another. Whether you need a lot of security or just a little more than the default, chances are you'll want to make at least some standardized changes, and the Security Settings node will certainly make your life easier. The bulk of security settings are found under `Computer Configuration\Policies\Windows Settings\Security Settings`, although public key policies and software restriction policies are also found in the User Configuration node in the same path. The following are the major categories of settings under Security Settings:

Account Policies   Specifies password restrictions, lockout policies, and Kerberos policy.

Local Policies   Configures auditing and assigns user rights and miscellaneous security settings.

Event Log   Centralizes configuration options for the event log.

Restricted Groups   Enforces and controls group memberships for certain groups, such as the Administrators group.

System Services   Standardizes services, configurations, and protects against changes.

Registry   Creates security templates for registry key permissions to control who can change what keys and to control read access to parts of the registry.

File System   Creates security templates for permissions on files and folders to ensure that files and directories have and keep the permissions you want them to have.

Public Key Policies   Manages settings for organizations using a public key infrastructure.

Software Restrictions Policies   Places restrictions on what software runs on a system. This new feature is designed to prevent viruses and untrusted software from running on a system.

Leveraging Security Templates

To accomplish your "mass" security rollout from the previous example, you will need some way to get the settings "entered" and then "deployed." The deployment is rather easy, since you have AD and Group Policy. The question then becomes how do you "enter" the security information so it can be tracked, reused, and quickly modified? The answer is security templates. We suggest that if you've been overlooking them, then you *have* to start using them. In this section, you'll see why.

Let's say that you've decided you want to ensure that the Power Users groups on your workstations should be empty—you don't want anyone in those groups. You also are awfully tired of stomping out the latest web server worm on all of those computers that installed IIS, so you're going around and disabling Web Publishing Service on all servers that don't need it.

But, man, that's a lot of work. So, you adopt Plan B: the security requirements document. In this document, you outline exactly what must be done for any workstations or servers approved at Acme Corporation. You distribute the document. And no one has time to read it. Nor is there any easy way to check up on systems to see whether they meet the requirements. Or so it seems.

Wouldn't it be great to just click a button and make those changes on every system? You can, with a few tools: `secedit.exe`, which is an MMC snap-in named Security Configuration and Analysis, and security templates.

What Templates Can Do

Basically, a *security template* is an ASCII file that you feed into a program named `secedit.exe`. That template is a set of instructions—basically a script—that tells `secedit` to make various kinds of changes in your system.

Templates don't let you modify anything that you couldn't modify otherwise; they just provide a nice, scripted, reproducible way to make modifications and then easily audit systems to ensure that they meet the template's requirements. You could make any of these changes by hand with the GUI, but it'd be time-consuming. With templates, you can change the following:

NTFS Permissions   If you want the directory `C:\STUFF` to have NTFS permissions of System/Full Control and Administrators/Full Control and to deny access to everyone else, then a template can make that happen. And because you can apply templates not only to one machine but also to many (provided you're using group policies), you could enforce that set of NTFS permissions on the whole domain.

Local Group Membership Perhaps you have a policy that workstations are set up so that the only accounts in the local Administrators group should be the local Administrator account and the Domain Admins group from the domain. But now and then, some support person "temporarily" elevates a user account to the Administrators group, with the innocent intention of undoing the action "as soon as the need is over." And, because that support person is as busy as all support folks are, that undoing never gets done. By applying a security template that says that "only Administrator and Domain Admins can be in the local Administrators," reapplying the template kicks everybody out who's not supposed to be there.

ENFORCING SECURITY SETTINGS

Templates automate the process of setting some security information, just as if you had sat down and done it from the GUI. There's no magic guardian angel that constantly monitors a system to ensure that your desired template settings are always enforced. The only way to ensure that your settings remain in force is to either reapply the template on some regular basis or create a GPO to apply the template, because security settings in a GPO are updated, regardless of any changes, every 16 hours.

Local Security Policy Settings Every machine has dozens of local security settings, things like, "Should I show the name of the last person who logged in?" and "How often should passwords on locally stored accounts be changed?" and "Who should be allowed to change the time on this system?" to name a few.

Working with Templates

It's easiest to show you how to work with templates with an example, so let's build a template to do three things:

- We'll ensure that no one is in the local Power Users group.

- We'll set NTFS permissions so that the directory C:\SECRET will be accessible only to the local Administrators group.

- Finally, we'll shut down Internet Information Services, that pesky web server that seems to install itself on every operating system that Microsoft makes.

First, you'll need some tools. Let's build an all-in-one tool using the MMC. Also, you'll need two snap-ins: Security Templates and Security Configuration and Analysis. Set it up like so:

1. Click Start, type **mmc /a** in the Start Search field, and then press Enter to bring up the empty MMC.

2. In the empty MMC, choose Add/Remove Snap-in from the File menu.

3. In the Add or Remove Snap-in dialog box, click Security Configuration and Analysis and then the Add button. Then click Security Templates and Add again.

4. Click OK.

5. Save your new custom tool for future use.

Your tool should look like the one in Figure 9.24.

Expand the Security Templates node, and add a new template search path. The path you want to add will be C:\Windows\Security\Templates. Expand that, and you'll see a DC security.inf prebuilt template.

FIGURE 9.24
MMC with Security
Templates and
Security
Configuration and
Analysis snap-ins

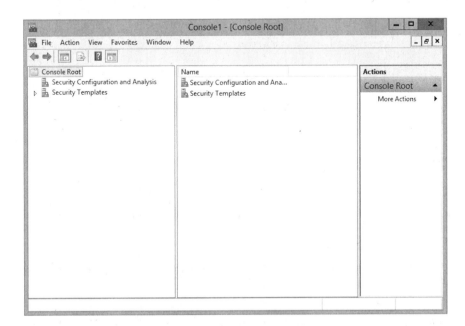

EXPANDING THE SECURITY TEMPLATES

Expand the DC security.inf security template, and you'll see, in the right pane, folders corresponding to everything that you can control:

Account Policies   Sets password, account lockout, and Kerberos policies

Local Policies   Controls audit settings, user rights, and security options

Event Log Settings   Controls parameters of how events are stored

Restricted Groups   Controls what goes into and stays out of various local groups

System Services   Turns services on and off and controls who has the rights to change any of that

Registry Security   Sets permissions to change or view any given registry key (and which keys will have changes audited)

File System   Controls NTFS permissions on folders and files

But you're interested in building a new template from scratch. To do that, right-click the template path, and choose New Template from the context menu. Type in a name for the template and a description if you want. The new template will appear as a folder in the left pane, along with the prebuilt template. We've named ours Simple. First, let's clean out the Power Users group:

1. Open Simple.

2. Inside Simple, you'll see a folder named Restricted Groups. Click it so that it appears in the left pane.

3. Right-click Restricted Groups, and choose Add Group.

4. Type in **Power Users** in the Add Group dialog box, or use the Browse function to select the Power Users group.

    Note that if you are working from a domain controller, then you won't, of course, have a Power Users group.

By default, including a group in a security template tells the template to remove everyone from the group, so you're finished. If you wanted to use the security template to put someone in the group, then just right-click the group and choose Properties, which lets you specify members of the group.

Next, let's set up the security template so that any system with a folder named C:\SECRET will be accessible only to the local administrators.

1. Back in the left pane, right-click File System, and choose Add File.

2. In the dialog box that appears, you can either browse to a particular directory or simply type in the directory name.

    Yes, the menu item was Add File, but you can choose directories as well.

3. Type **C:\SECRET**, and click OK.

    Now you'll see the standard Windows NTFS permissions dialog box.

4. Delete permissions for all users and groups except for Administrators. Grant Full Control Permission to Administrators.

    The program will ask whether you want these permissions to apply only to this folder or to all child folders.

5. Set it as you like, and click OK.

Finally, let's shut down IIS:

1. Click System Services.

2. In the right pane, right-click World Wide Web Publishing Services, and choose Properties.

3. Select the Define This Policy Setting in the Template check box, and click the Disabled radio button.

4. Click OK.

Now save the template—right-click Simple or whatever you called the template, and click Save. Unless you set up a separate folder for your templates as we described earlier, you now have a file named simple.inf in your \Windows\Security\Templates folder.

Creating a Security Database

To see how this template will modify a system or to apply the template setting using the MMC snap-in, you must create a security database. To do this, you have to essentially compile it from its simple ASCII form to a binary form called a *database*. You do that from the other snap-in, Security Configuration and Analysis.

1. Right-click Security Configuration and Analysis and choose Open Database to open the Open Database dialog box, which asks what database you want to load.

    Within the Open Database dialog box, you want to create a new database, but there's no option for that; instead, just type the name of the new database.

2. Using this example, type **Simple,** and press Enter.

    Typing in a name of a new database causes the snap-in to realize that you want to *create* a new database, so it then asks which template to build it out of. (Yup, it's nonintuitive.) By default, a dialog box shows you the files with `.inf` extensions in the `Windows\Security\Templates` folder.

3. If you're following this example, choose `simple.inf`.

    Before you click enter, though, notice the Clear This Database Before Importing check box.

4. Select that option.

    Otherwise, when you're experimenting with a template, the snap-in makes your changes cumulative (which might well be your intention, but it's not usually ours) rather than wiping the slate clean and starting from scratch.

5. Choose the template, and click Open.

    Nothing obvious has happened, but the snap-in has now "compiled" (which is our word, not Microsoft's, but it seems a good shorthand for the process of converting your ASCII template into a binary security database) the template into a security template named `simple.sdb` in `My Documents\Security\Database`. In the details pane, you'll see the Configure and Analyze options.

6. Right-click Security Configuration and Analysis, and you'll see two options: Analyze Computer Now and Configure Computer Now.

    Analyze doesn't change the computer. Instead, it compares the computer's state to the one that you want to create with the template. It then shows you—and saves a log file that explains—how your system varies from what the template instructs. The log file is written to `\Documents\Security\Logs`.

7. To see how your computer measures up to the settings in the database, select the Analyze Computer Now option, and you can see what the current settings are compared to what you want them to be.

8. If you want to jump in headfirst and apply the settings, instead of choosing Analyze Computer Now, select Configure Computer Now to modify the system's settings to fall in line with the template.

That's all very nice, you may be thinking, but how do I apply it to dozens of computers? Do I have to visit each one? Well, you do if you want to use this tool! If you want to use other options, one would be to use a command-line tool. A command-line program called `secedit.exe` will both convert templates into databases and apply databases. To read a template, apply, and then create a database in the process, use the following syntax:

```
Secedit /configure /cfg templatefilename /db databasefilename/overwrite /
log logfilename
```

To apply an existing database without first reading the template, just leave off the `/cfg` switch and argument. To apply the template to your workstations, you could include the `secedit` command in a logon script (be sure to specify full path names for the template, database, and log files) that will reapply it with every logon. You could also use the Task Scheduler service to run a batch file and reapply the template at specific intervals. Or you could enable the Telnet server on your Windows server machines and just apply the template whenever you like.

Automation and scripting are nice, but what if you want to take advantage of the "automatic" background refreshes that Group Policy provides, as well as the 16-hour forced security settings update? That's right, you use Group Policy! You'll learn about this in the next section.

Using Domain-based Group Policies to Apply Templates

`secedit` is nice, but it has to be invoked manually or from a batch file, which means a lot of messy editing of logon batch files or fiddling with the scheduled tasks on all your systems. If you use a login script, the security template gets applied at logon time only. How do you enforce security settings more often? With a GPO.

Domain-based GPOs have a few benefits:

◆ It's easy to control whom they apply to, which is much easier than having to figure out which batch files go where.

◆ They reapply themselves not only at logon time but also throughout the day—the workstation seeks them out every 60 to 120 minutes.

◆ Security settings are "reapplied" every 16 hours, just in case a security setting was modified by the user, an application, and so on.

Importing Security Templates

You already have your security template, `simple.inf`, which you created in the previous section. Now, you want to leverage the deployment of the security settings in the template by using a GPO.

The steps to import the template are very simple. Follow these steps to import the `simple.inf` template into a GPO:

1. Launch the GPMC.

2. Go to an OU that contains the computers that you want to apply the security settings to.

   For example, the `simple.inf` template could apply to all the desktops in your organization.

3. Right-click the OU, and select the "Create a GPO in this domain, and Link it here" menu option.

4. Type in a name for your new GPO; ours is named Desktop Enforcement Policy.

5. Right-click Desktop Enforcement Policy, and select the Edit menu option.

6. From within the GPME, drill down and select the Security Settings node, which is found under `Computer Configuration\Policies\Windows Settings`.

7. Right-click the Security Settings node, and click the Import Policy menu option.

8. Click the `simple.inf` security template (you can browse for this template if you have it on a network share or a USB thumb drive), and select Open.

9. Verify that the settings were imported by going down one level below the Security Settings node to the Restricted Groups node.

10. Click the Restricted Groups node, and ensure your Power Users policy is there.

The big question is, what do you do now? Well, if you can just wait 90 minutes, you don't have to do anything! Just allow the standard background policy refresh to take over and—bam!—all your settings will apply to all computers in the Desktops OU.

New Administrative Templates (ADMX/ADML)

The old-style administrative templates were OK, but they had issues. In fact, these ADM templates were plagued with size issues, scripting complexity, and language barriers. To solve all these issues, Microsoft developed a new type of file that replaces the ADM template, which originated with Windows Server 2008. The new templates are XML based and come in pairs. The new file extensions are ADMX and ADML.

The ADMX and ADML files are now stored in `C:\Windows\PolicyDefinitions`. When you crack open this folder location, you will see more than 100 ADMX files, along with a default folder for English, which is named en-US. The en-US folder contains all the language-specific information for displaying the settings in the GPME.

The new ADMX/ADML files have a few benefits:

♦ These files are not stored in the folder structure of the GPO.

♦ The files can be ported to nearly any language, as long as a new ADML file and folder structure is established for the new language.

♦ There is a central store option that allows for centralized administration of the ADMX/ADML files.

Creating a central store for the storage and administration of these files is as easy as making a copy of the folder structure! That's right—all that needs to be done to centralize the management of these files is to copy the folder structure to the domain controllers. In short, follow these steps to create the central store:

1. Open your Windows 8 or Server 2012 R2 computer to view the `C:\Windows\PolicyDefinitions` folder.

2. Right-click the PolicyDefinitions folder, and select Copy.

3. Open the `C:\Windows\Sysvol\sysvol\<domainname>\Policies` folder on any of the domain controllers for your domain.

4. Right-click the Policies folder, and select Paste.

The end result will be that you have now duplicated the ADMX/ADML folder structure and files on the domain controller, as shown in Figure 9.25. Since the folder exists in the domain controller, it will automatically be replicated to all the other domain controllers in the domain.

FIGURE 9.25
Central store for ADMX/ADML files

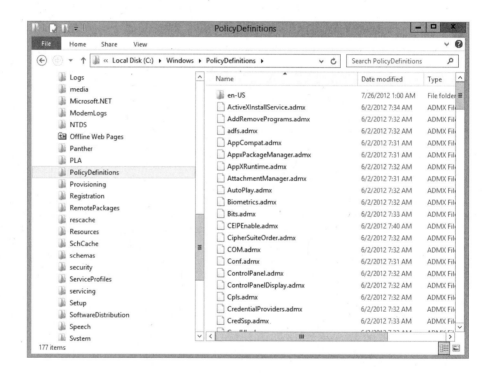

To verify that you are now consuming the ADMX files from the central store, just edit a GPO and view the text after the Administrative Templates node from within the GPME.

If you have a custom ADMX/ADML file combo after creating the central store, all you need to do is copy the ADMX file to the PolicyDefinitions folder and the ADML file to the en-US folder. The new settings will show up in the GPME!

Restricting Internet Explorer

For every setting in Internet Explorer, there seems to be policy to disable it. Considering that a good deal of time at work is spent surfing the Web, it's a particularly cruel and clever thing to impose such control over IE settings (unfortunately, many companies use Firefox instead of Internet Explorer). Here are a few settings that we find useful:

◆ If you want to prevent users from messing with the security zones you set up or if you want Internet Explorer to use the same security zones and proxy settings for all users on the computer, then enable the Security Zones and Proxy settings under Computer Configuration/Policies/Administrative Templates/Windows Components/Internet Explorer.

◆ To prevent users from downloading offline content to their workstations, enable the policy named Disable Adding Schedules for Offline Pages under User Configuration/Policies/ Administrative Templates/Windows Components/Internet Explorer/Offline Pages.

◆ To prevent users from making any changes to IE's Security, Connections, or Advanced Properties pages, disable access to these and other IE Control Panel pages in the User Configuration node under Internet Explorer/Internet Control Panel.

◆ If you want to keep users from downloading any software from the Web, however, that's a little more difficult. There is a policy under the User Configuration/.../Internet Explorer/ Browser Menus that disables the Save This Program to Disk option. However, this won't prevent users from installing the software without saving it, and there are probably a couple of other ways around the restriction for a determined power user.

Prevent Users from Installing or Running Unauthorized Software

While we're on the subject of preventing users from installing software, enable the policy named Prevent Removable Media Source for Any Install found under User Configuration/.../ Windows Components/Windows Installer to keep users from running installations from a CD-ROM or a floppy drive (remember those?). And if you are going to do that, you should also enable the policy to hide the "Add a program from CD-ROM or floppy disk" option in User Configuration/.../Control Panel/Add or Remove Programs. The Control Panel node includes several options to disable or remove all or part of the Add/Remove Programs applet.

Disabling Add/Remove Programs will not prevent users from running setup routines in other ways, however. Anyone who can use a command line can circumvent these restrictions, so you'd need to open the System node of the User Configuration policies and enable the policy called "Prevent access to the command prompt." If you are looking for that infamous policy called "Run only specified Windows applications," it's found in the System node of the User Configuration templates (shown in Figure 9.26). Be careful with this one, though; you have to make a list of all applications that can be launched from Windows Explorer. There is also a setting in the same location called "Don't run specified Windows applications." For this one, you'd need to make a list of disallowed programs.

PREVENTING REGISTRY EDITING

You can create a policy to prevent access to the registry editing tools. Enabling this policy prevents users from running `regedt32.exe` and `regedt.exe`, although regular users only have Read access to the vast majority of the registry anyway.

FIGURE 9.26
Policy to run
only specified
applications

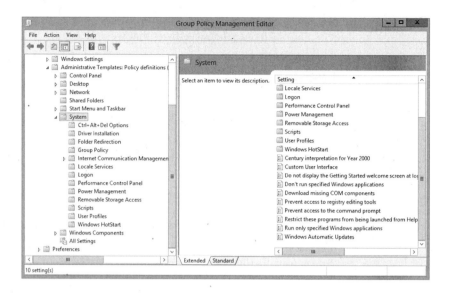

The same principle applies to the Start menu and taskbar option called "Run from the Start menu." Experienced users will not be prevented from running nonapproved programs just because Run is removed from the Start menu, so you have to seek out all the other ways of launching programs and disable them as well (users can also launch programs from Task Manager unless you disable it in the Ctrl+Alt+Del options).

CREATING A CONSISTENT DESKTOP AND START MENU

If you want to achieve a simplified and consistent desktop and Start menu for your organization or department, you'll probably need to combine folder redirection with the restrictions that are available in the administrative templates.

Using Group Policy to Set Password and Account Lockout Policy

One of the most misunderstood and complex aspects of Windows AD is how and where password policies are configured and managed. In this section you will get the skinny on how it works to remove all doubt moving forward. Here is a list of truths and myths about Account Policy settings that should answer all of your FAQs:

Truths

◆ The only way to modify the Account Policy settings for domain user accounts is in a GPO linked to the domain.

◆ Fine-grained password policies can be set up to have users in the same domain have different Account Policy settings. In other words, IT users can have a 20-character password, and executives can have a three-character password.

◆ A GPO linked to an OU will modify the local SAM Account Policy settings for the local users in the SAM of all computer accounts in that OU.

Myths

◆ A GPO can be linked to the Domain Controllers OU to modify the Account Policy settings for domain user accounts.

◆ A GPO can be linked to an OU to modify the Account Policy settings for the user accounts contained within the OU.

◆ The ACL for the Default Domain Policy can be modified to include only certain security groups, thus allowing different password policies in the same domain.

By default in a Windows Server 2012 R2 domain, the Default Domain Policy is used to establish the Account Policy settings for all user accounts in the domain. (This includes both domain user accounts and all local SAM user accounts for computers joined to the domain.) Password and account lockout policy settings are located under Computer Configuration/ Policies/Windows Settings/Security Settings. The password policy includes the following options:

Enforce Password History   Enable this option to specify the required number of consecutive unique passwords before a given password can be used again.

Maximum Password Age   This option sets the amount of time for which a password can be used before the system requires the user to pick a new one. Organizations usually set this interval somewhere between 30 and 90 days.

Minimum Password Age   The value set here is the amount of time for which a password must be used before the user is allowed to change it again.

Minimum Password Length   This option defines the smallest number of characters that a user's password can contain. Seven or eight characters are a good minimum length for passwords. Setting this policy also disallows blank passwords.

Passwords Must Meet Complexity Requirements   In case you are wondering "What requirements?" this setting used to be called Passwords Must Meet Complexity Requirements of Installed Password Filter. A password filter DLL is built into Windows 2000 and later. Password filters define requirements such as the number of characters allowed, whether letters and numbers must be used, whether any part of the username is permitted, and so forth.

If you enable this policy, all new passwords and changed passwords must meet the following requirements:

◆ They must be at least six characters long.

◆ They cannot contain the username or part of the username.

◆ They must use three of the four following types of characters: uppercase letters (A–Z), lowercase letters (a–z), numbers (0–9), and special characters (for example, @, %, &, #).

Store Passwords Using Reversible Encryption   Yes, this policy is definitely a security downgrade, telling the domain controller that it's OK to store passwords in a reversible encryption. This is one step away from cleartext; passwords are normally stored in a one-way hash encryption. If you need this for only individual user accounts (like Mac users), enable the option in the user account properties instead. Reversible encryption is required, however, if you are using CHAP authentication with remote access or Internet Authentication Services.

Account Lockout Policy, once enabled, prevents anyone from logging in to the account after a certain number of failed attempts. The options are as follows:

Account Lockout Duration This setting determines the interval for which the account will be locked out. After this time period expires, the user account will no longer be locked out and the user can try to log in again. If you enable the option but leave the Minutes field blank, the account will stay locked out until an administrator unlocks it.

Account Lockout Threshold This value defines how many times the user can unsuccessfully attempt to log in before the account will be locked out. If you define this setting, be sure to specify the number of permitted attempts, or the account will never lock out.

Reset Account Lockout Counter After This setting defines the time interval after which the count of bad logon attempts will start over. For example, suppose you have a reset count of two minutes and three logon attempts. If you mistype twice, you can wait two minutes after the second attempt, and you'll have three tries again.

Group Policy Preferences

One of the most impressive aspects of Windows Server 2012 R2 (not just Group Policy related, but of the entire new OS) is Group Policy preferences (GPP). Group Policy preferences are extensions to Group Policy, which in normal speak is "new settings in a GPO." These new settings add more than 3,000 policy settings to a GPO, and some of them are just amazing! For example, now you can modify the local Administrator password on every desktop in your environment, within about 90 minutes. You can also control the membership of the local Administrators group on all desktops and servers, without removing the key service accounts and other domain groups that are unique to each computer.

GPP Settings

The GPP settings are a bit different from the other Group Policy settings, primarily because they exist in duplication under both the computer and user areas of a GPO. This gives you great flexibility and power over which setting you want to unleash on the desktops and users in the environment.

For the GPP settings, you will see the list of options displayed in Table 9.1.

TABLE 9.1: Group Policy Preferences Settings

GROUP POLICY PREFERENCES SETTING	AVAILABLE UNDER COMPUTER CONFIGURATION?	AVAILABLE UNDER USER CONFIGURATION?
Applications	No	Yes
Drive Maps	No	Yes
Environment	Yes	Yes
Files	Yes	Yes

TABLE 9.1:   Group Policy Preferences Settings   *(CONTINUED)*

GROUP POLICY PREFERENCES SETTING	AVAILABLE UNDER COMPUTER CONFIGURATION?	AVAILABLE UNDER USER CONFIGURATION?
Folders	Yes	Yes
Ini Files	Yes	Yes
Network Shares	Yes	No
Registry	Yes	Yes
Shortcuts	Yes	Yes
Data Sources	Yes	Yes
Devices	Yes	Yes
Folder Options	Yes	Yes
Internet Settings	No	Yes
Local Users and Groups	Yes	Yes
Network Options	Yes	Yes
Power Options	Yes	Yes
Printers	Yes	Yes
Regional Options	No	Yes
Scheduled Tasks	Yes	Yes
Services	Yes	No
Start Menu	No	Yes

Most of the settings in Table 9.1 are self-explanatory. However, we'll give you a jump-start on how some of these settings might be used. For example, security is always on the top of the IT staff members' minds when it comes to securing desktops, but there is never enough time, right? Take the issue of resetting the local Administrator password on every desktop in your company. We know, we know…that is just crazy talk! However, when was the last time that this task was accomplished for your desktops? At installation? Two years ago? We have heard all of the possible answers, but now with GPP, you can change it as often as you like. To make this setting occur, follow these steps:

1. Modify a GPO that is targeting all of your desktops (the best bet here is to link a GPO to the OU that contains the desktop computers).

2. When you have launched the GPME for the GPO, head to the Computer Configuration\Preferences\Control Panel\Local Users and Groups node.

3. Right-click the node, and select New ➢ Local User, which will open the New Local User Properties dialog box, as shown in Figure 9.27.

FIGURE 9.27
Group Policy Preferences
New Local User Properties
dialog box

UNDERSTANDING NEW USER POLICY

You are not actually creating a new user when you select the New ➤ User option for GPP. Instead, think about it as creating a new user policy! You can create a new user, but there are many more options than just creating a new user. Use this "New XYZ policy" mentality when you create any new GPP setting, and it will help you figure out what you want to do with the setting.

---

4. From here, just type in the name of the user you want to control, which is **Administrator**.

5. Then, type in the password that you want to use, retyping it as the dialog box clearly indicates.

Voilá! This will reset the password for the local Administrator account on every desktop that falls under the Scope of Management to receive the GPO. After about two hours, all of the desktops that are connected to the domain and network will have the setting updated.

Now, wasn't that easy? The rest of the settings are just as easy, and the power that you now have at your fingertips is quite impressive. To give you an idea of what we have seen and what others have already done with GPP, here is a list of ideas per policy setting to get you started:

- Applications
  - Enable the spell-checker for Microsoft Word.
  - Configure the Outlook autoarchive capability.
  - Configure a "company-approved and consistent" signature for Outlook email.
- Drive maps
  - Replace all drive mappings in the logon script with a Group Policy preferences setting.

- Map drives for Terminal Services sessions only.

- Environment

  - Create a laptop environment variable that is used with other Group Policy preferences settings.

  - Establish environment variables for first name, last name, address, and so on, which can then be used in the Outlook signature.

- Files

  - Transfer virus definitions from server to desktop.

  - Deploy application configuration files to desktops.

- Folders

  - Clean up the Temporary Internet Files folder.

  - Create an application folder for desktops that runs secured applications.

- Network shares

  - Control network shares on a server only during business operating hours.

  - Enable access-based enumeration for the server.

- Registry: Uh, you name it—it can and might have been done!

- Data sources

  - Create a centralized data source configuration for salespeople.

  - Create a custom data source configuration for help-desk employees.

- Folder options

  - Allow all IT staff users to see hidden and super-hidden files at every desktop they administer.

  - Configure all IT staff users to see file extensions in Windows Explorer on all desktops they touch.

- Internet settings

  - Configure the Internet Explorer proxy setting for all users in branch office 1.

  - Configure custom Internet Explorer settings that standard Group Policy settings can't handle, such as all the settings on the Advanced tab of the Internet Explorer settings configuration dialog box.

- Local users and groups

  - Reset the local Administrator password on every desktop.

  - Manage local Administrators group members on every desktop and server (by the way, without first deleting the members!).

- Power options: Create a 24-hour power options scheme where users never see a power options scheme during working hours, but after employees leave, their computer is put into Standby mode after five minutes of no activity. (This has been proven to save about $50 per PC per year.)

◆ Printers

  ◆ Eliminate printers from logon scripts.

  ◆ Configure printers for laptop users who go from remote office to remote office, giving them only the printers they need based on their location.

◆ Scheduled tasks: Waking the computer up during the middle of the night to allow maintenance to occur (an excellent combo with power options!).

◆ Services

  ◆ Configure a different service account to increase overall security.

  ◆ Configure the service account password.

  ◆ Configure service behavior if it fails to start gracefully.

ITEM-LEVEL TARGETING

One of the most impressive aspects of GPP is the item-level targeting capabilities. You can now target and apply any GPP setting by first querying different aspects of the computer environment, only applying the setting if the environment is what you want it to be. For example, let's say you have the HR department running an application that exists in a Terminal Services environment. When they launch this application, they need to have a mapped drive for the application. The solution that most companies must use today is to map the drive for the user account, so they have a "bogus" drive mapping even when they are working on their desktop. GPP item-level targeting allows you to provide the drive mapping *only* when they are in the Terminal Services environment.

You can obtain this type of control by leveraging one of many different item-level targeting options. The full list of item-level targeting options is as follows:

Battery Present	IP Address Range	RAM
Computer Name	Language	Registry Match
CPU Speed	LDAP Query	Security Group
Date Match	MAC Address Range	Site
Dial-up Connection	MSI Query	Terminal Session
Disk Space	Operating System	Time Range
Domain	Organizational Unit	User
Environment Variable	PCMCIA Present	WMI Query
File Match	Portable Computer	
	Processing Mode	

> ### 🌐 Real World Scenario
>
> #### ELIMINATING LOGON SCRIPTS USING GROUP POLICY PREFERENCES
>
> Many companies are still using legacy logon scripts to apply settings to desktops such as drive mappings and printer mappings. Using logon scripts is archaic in comparison to the new and improved capabilities of GPP.
>
> Many other companies have switched to using GPP when possible to eliminate some, if not all, of the settings in their logon scripts. You can use the following preferences in lieu of logon scripts:
>
> **Drive Mappings**   Drive mappings can now be targeted to create "just-in-time" mappings that make more sense for users. Item-level targets can be used in conjunction with drive mappings to only provide access to data based on the user having the correct application installed, with the right patch installed, and only when in a Terminal Services session.
>
> **Printers**   Printers are often hard to manage for medium and large organizations that have mobile users. When a user goes to a company branch office, it can be difficult for the user to find and configure the correct printer. The GPP for printers can be used to map all printers in the company. When used with an item-level target (such as an IP address range or AD site), users will get the printer they need in the branch office, just because they are in the branch office.
>
> **Registry**   With the new registry preference, any registry entry can now be placed in a GPO without any custom ADM template or ADMX file. This includes binary and multistring values, which were not possible in ADM templates.

The New and Improved GPMC

The GPMC has been around for quite a while now. The first generation of the GPMC was revolutionary and made administration of GPOs much easier. This generation of the GPMC continues to make the administration of GPOs easy, efficient, and stable. No more are the days when you needed to launch the Active Directory Users and Computers to see, create, link, and manage GPOs. That was archaic to say the least. Now, the new GPMC can run on Windows Server 2012 R2 and Windows 8.

You will need to install the GPMC, because it is not installed by default. For your Windows Server 2012 R2 computers, you can install the GPMC from Server Manager.

1. Launch Server Manager, and select the Features menu option.

2. From here, you just need to click the Add Features option, which will give you a full list of tools you can install, as shown in Figure 9.28.

3. Select the Group Policy Management option, which will take you through some gyrations to get the tool installed.

4. After a restart, you will now have the GPMC installed.

FIGURE 9.28
The GPMC is
installed via Server
Manager.

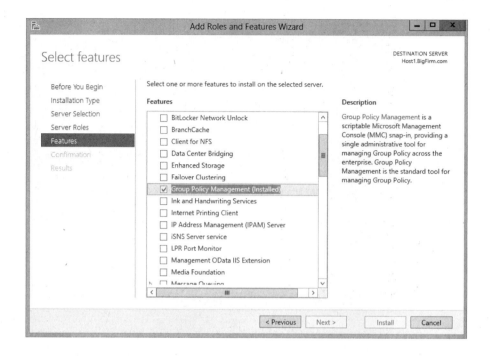

For your Windows 7 or 8 desktops, installing the Remote Server Administration Tools is needed for GPMC. You will need to follow these steps to get the GPMC installed:

1. Install any current service packs (some downloads may include a service pack).

2. Install the Remote Server Administrative Tools.

3. Open the Control Panel from the Start menu.

4. Click the Programs and Features applet.

5. Select the "Turn Windows features on or off" menu option.

Starter GPOs

Microsoft is making strides to make GPO management easier and more efficient. The first attempt at this is Starter GPOs. You can use a Starter GPO to re-create a suite of GPO settings, only to use the Starter GPO again and again and again. Say, for example, that you are in charge of ensuring that Internet Explorer is configured properly for your organization. You could create a Starter GPO that includes all of the required Internet Explorer settings and save the Starter GPO. Then, when any new GPO is created, it uses the IE Starter GPO you created to ensure the Internet Explorer settings are included.

To create a new Starter GPO, select the Starter GPO node in the GPMC. Then, follow these steps:

1. Right-click the Starter GPO node, and select the New menu option.

2. Type in the name of your Starter GPO; we're using **IE Starter GPO**.

3. To configure your IE settings, you now only need to edit the GPO, just like you would any other GPO, by right-clicking it in the GPMC and selecting Edit.

Now that your Starter GPO is created, everyone who has the ability to create a GPO in the domain can use it as a "starter suite of settings." When any new GPO is created in the GPMC, there is a drop-down list for Source Starter GPO in the New GPO dialog box, as shown in Figure 9.29. Keep in mind, however, that one significant limitation of Starter GPOs is that they only include the administrative template settings of the GPO.

FIGURE 9.29
New GPOs can use a Source Starter GPO during creation.

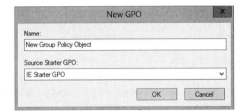

Backing Up and Restoring GPOs

The GPMC is a one-stop shop for all GPO management. One of the most important aspects of protecting your GPO assets is to back them up. (It is like anything in a computer world; you are only as protected as the last time you backed up your data!)

The GPMC provides both backup and restore capabilities, which allows you to archive every version of the GPO that you create and implement. It is very convenient that the GPMC provides these capabilities directly in the interface, because there is no need to launch another application or tool to do this job.

Backing up a GPO is simple:

1. Right-click the GPO that you want to back up.

2. Select the "Back up" menu option.

   The Back Up Group Policy Object dialog box appears.

3. Input the location to store your backups.

   This can be a predetermined location, or you can create a folder during this process.

4. Type in the location or click the Browse button, whichever option suits you best.

5. Now that you have a GPO archive folder selected, simply click the "Back up" button.

   You will see the progress of the backup process in the Backup dialog box.

6. When the GPO has successfully been backed up, click out of that box.

BEFORE-AND-AFTER BACKUPS

Like data and other operating system changes, backups should be performed directly before a change is made, as well as after the change is made to ensure that both states of the GPO are captured.

There will be a time when you want to view the list of GPOs that you have backed up. To see this list, right-click the Group Policy Objects node within the GPMC and select the Manage Backups menu option. This will launch the Manage Backups interface, shown in Figure 9.30. From here, you can restore, delete, and view the settings of a backed-up GPO.

FIGURE 9.30
GPMC allows you to manage the GPOs that you have backed up.

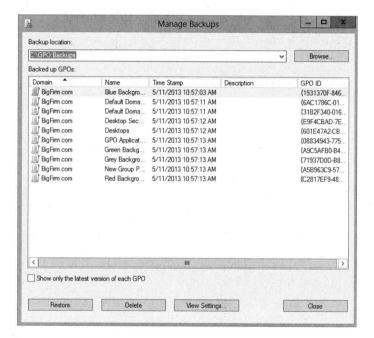

Restore   The Restore feature will allow you to restore the "archived GPO" over the "production GPO." You can imagine how important this might be!

Delete   The Delete option allows you to clean-house the archived GPOs, especially those that are of no use anymore or those that are *really* old. There's no reason to clog up your servers with information you will not need in the future.

View Settings   The View Settings option allows you to view the contents of the GPO, as well as all the other key information such as delegation, security, links, and so on. Figure 9.31 illustrates the HTML page that is displayed from selecting the View Settings option.

FIGURE 9.31
The View Settings option in the backup tool allows you to see all the GPO information.

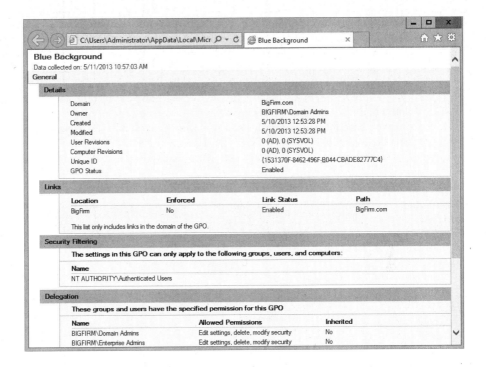

Troubleshooting Group Policies

In case it's not clear by now, group policies are powerful…and also complex. And they can be kind of opaque—sometimes you create a bunch of policy settings for a domain controller that you intend to control some desktop and then restart the desktop, log in, and wait to see the effects of the new policies…but nothing happens.

A few troubleshooting tools are included to assist you in troubleshooting Group Policy issues. The Resultant Set of Policy (RSOP) snap-in and console tool provides a graphical interface, and `gpresult.exe` performs equivalent functions from the command line. `gpotool.exe` is a Windows Resource Kit tool, and it looks for inconsistencies between GPOs that are stored on domain controllers. This little utility can help you identify replication issues that are causing a problem with Group Policy application.

The Resultant Set of Policy Tool

Troubleshooting group policies has been, for administrators, a major obstacle to complete control and domination of the network environment. The problem was the inability to view the cumulative policy settings that were in effect for a user or computer. This little capability to display actual policy settings, the Resultant Set of Policy tool, is built into Windows Server. Using RSOP you can run "What-if" scenarios to diagnose problems. Without RSOP, you have to look at the properties of each site, domain, and OU to see which policies and containers are linked. Then you must view the ACLs and WMI information to see whether there's any filtering and also check out the Disabled, Block Inheritance, and Enforce options. Don't forget the item-level targeting, which can get very granular, thus confusing to try to evaluate by hand. Finally, you need to view the settings of the policies in question before you can get to the bottom of things. You'll need to take notes. Personally, we prefer the RSOP tool.

The RSOP tool is easily launched by typing **rsop.msc** at the command prompt. When it is launched, you will see it working away, determining the resultant set of policy that has been applied based on the computer you are running it on and the user account that is logged in at the time the tool is run.

The result is a window that's similar to that shown in the GPME, as shown in Figure 9.32.

FIGURE 9.32
rsop.msc generates a real-time view of the policy settings that have been applied.

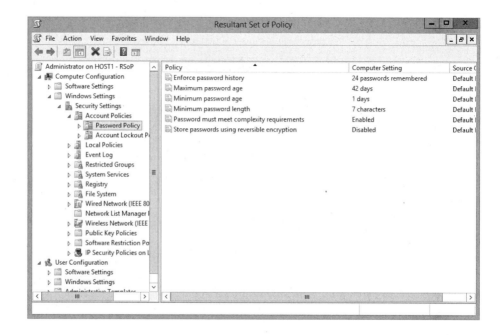

Here are a few things to note about using the rsop.msc tool:

◆ The tool provides only the applied GPOs and the settings from those GPOs.

◆ The tool provides a view of which GPO each setting came from.

Group Policy Results Using the GPMC

Inside the GPMC is a tool that is similar to that of the localized version of the RSOP, but it allows you to query any computer and user on the network to get the RSOP. Imagine that a user calls to indicate that they can't access a website that is required for their job. You could visit their desk, but that would only take time, when you are sure that they are getting their Internet Explorer proxy settings from a GPO. So, instead, follow these steps:

1. Launch the Group Policy Results Wizard in the GPMC.

You can find the Group Policy Results Wizard toward the bottom of the GPMC. When you launch the wizard, you just need to provide the computer and user you want to find results for, and the wizard takes care of the rest, as shown in Figure 9.33.

FIGURE 9.33

Group Policy Results Wizard in the GPMC

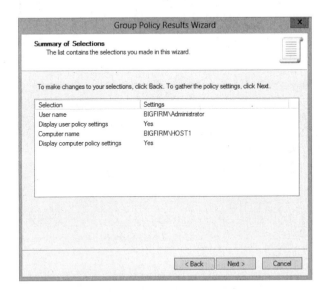

2. Select the user and the desktop they are logged into, and browse to the IE proxy setting.

You notice that the wrong GPO is applied to the computer, since someone set up an enforcement of the GPO linked to the OU above, which is negating your proxy setting. Problem found.

3. Fix the Enforce issue on the GPO, and you are set!

The results from the wizard will display in three different tabs on the right pane—Details, Summary, and Policy Events:

Details The Details tab, shown in Figure 9.34, summarizes all the settings, including the GPOs that were applied, those that failed, the security groups that were considered, WMI filters, and more.

Summary The Summary tab displays any errors that occurred during the creation of the GPOs.

Policy Events The Policy Events tab is unique, in that it displays the settings from the Event Viewer that relate to Group Policy–related events and categories.

If you can see that there is an issue with an applied setting, you can use the contents of all three tabs to track down the issue.

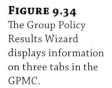

FIGURE 9.34

The Group Policy
Results Wizard
displays information
on three tabs in the
GPMC.

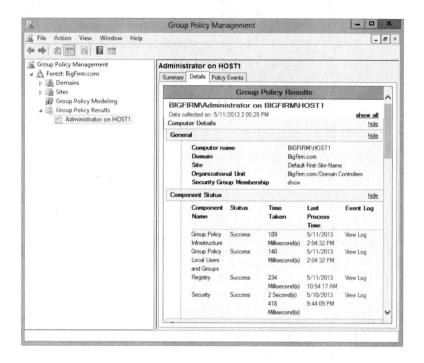

Group Policy Modeling Using the GPMC

The Group Policy Results Wizard in the GPMC is powerful, allowing you to view the existing
state of the GPOs and their settings on any computer and user on the network. However, what
if you have a scenario where you want to move a computer to a different OU or move a user to
a different OU because they are being promoted? You would not want to just move the account
and hope that the settings are correct based on the new location in AD.

gpresult

gpresult.exe is a Group Policy troubleshooting and reporting tool that complements the
RSOP snap-in by adding command-line and batch file capabilities to the RSOP arsenal. When
run without arguments or options, gpresult will generate the following RSOP information for
the current user at the local machine:

- ◆ The DC that the workstation got the policies from

- ◆ When the policies applied

- ◆ Which policies applied

- ◆ Which policies were not applied because of filtering

- ◆ Group memberships

- ◆ User rights information (if used in verbose mode)

To generate RSOP information for a remote user on a remote machine, use the `/S systemname` and `/USER username` arguments. For instance, to get RSOP information on the remote workstation WINDOWS8CLIENT1 for the user dmelber, type **gpresult /S WINDOWS8CLIENT1 /USER dmelber**.

You can get more detailed information with options:

◆ `/V` says to give more verbose information: `gpresult /V`.

◆ `/Z` says to give even *more* information; it is the "Zuper-verbose" option: `gpresult /Z`.

◆ If you know that you're zeroing in on just a machine policy, add `/SCOPE MACHINE`; if you're interested only in user policies, add `/SCOPE USER`.

So, for example, to get the maximum information about the user policies applied to this system, add `gpresult /Z /SCOPE USER`. It's also a simple matter to generate a report by redirecting the output of the command to a text file:

```
gpresult /S WINDOWS8CLIENT1 /USER dmelber /Z > c:\gpinfo.txt
```

Using Event Viewer

You can stop chuckling now! We're serious! There are times that you need to really pat Microsoft on the back, and this is one of those times. Event Viewer has been completely overhauled, and now, to the shock of many, there is an entire node dedicated to Group Policy!

The Group Policy Operational log is a replacement for the `Userenv.log` file that was generated by Group Policy in the past. Now, you don't need to set up any verbose or auditing settings; it just happens. To view the Group Policy log files in the new Event Viewer, just launch Event Viewer. Once Event Viewer is open, expand the Applications and Services Logs\Microsoft\Windows\GroupPolicy node. Here, you will find the Operational log for Group Policy. After clicking the Operational log, you will see the list of events on the right pane.

Here are a few tips and features of the new environment:

◆ The Operational log replaces the `Userenv.log` file from previous versions of Windows Group Policy.

◆ The General and Details tabs provide excellent information for troubleshooting issues.

◆ Double-clicking the event will launch the event in its own window, allowing a single view of the information.

◆ Clicking the System + sign on the Details tab will expose more information about the event.

Troubleshooting 101: Keep It Simple

We predict that, even with the RSOP tool, working with group policies will not be a walk in the park for most. Here are a few suggestions to help minimize troubleshooting time:

◆ Keep your policy strategy simple. Locate users and computers together in OUs if possible, and apply policies at the highest level possible.

◆ Avoid having multiple GPOs with conflicting policies that apply to the same recipients.

◆ Minimize the use of the Enforce and Block Inheritance settings.

◆ Document your Group Policy strategy. You may want to visually depict your policy structure and put it on the wall, like your network topology diagrams. That way, when a problem arises, you can consult the diagram to see what's going on before you go fishing.

◆ Test those GPO settings before deployment! This is absolutely essential to conserve your help-desk resources and ensure that applications and system services continue to run properly.

Active Directory Delegation

Active Directory delegation is a powerful solution to the old-world style of legacy Windows domains, where you had to create multiple domains to create separate control over users, groups, and computers. By implementing delegation within a single Active Directory domain, you don't need multiple domains, you can save money by reducing the number of domain controllers, managing the enterprise is easier with a single domain, and so on.

This feature of Active Directory is so compelling that many companies and enterprises have moved to Active Directory to take full advantage of the benefits that Active Directory delegation provides. One of the most compelling benefits of using delegation is the ability to grant one or more groups the privilege to reset passwords for user accounts. This means you can allow a group of users to reset passwords for just a subset of the users in a domain. For example, you can allow the HR manager to reset passwords for all the employees in the HR department—no more privilege, no less privilege.

Delegating Group Policy Administration

The ability to delegate creation and configuration of GPOs and their settings to administrative personnel (or to others, for that matter) is extremely useful, especially in a large organization. In this section, we'll explain how to allow persons who are not members of Domain Admins or Enterprise Admins to create and manage GPOs for designated sites, domains, or organizational units.

The GPMC provides a simple yet distributed array of options to ensure that you are providing the correct delegation to the correct set of administrators. There are five primary delegations that you will want to configure:

◆ Creating GPOs

◆ Linking GPOs

◆ Managing GPOs

◆ Editing GPOs

◆ Reading GPOs

All of these are configured in the GPMC. The major confusion about establishing delegation in the GPMC for GPO management is scoping. This means that you need to know where to set up the delegation; then once you are there, you need to know how far the delegation will extend. For example, suppose that you are the HR OU administrator. This means that you control everything for HR, including user accounts, group accounts, and even which GPOs are linked to your OU. How do you ensure that you are the only administrator who can link a GPO to your

HR OU? Well, this is one of the delegated tasks that the GPMC can control. Let's take a look at each delegation and the scope.

GPOs, by default, can be created by a member of the Administrators group for the domain or by members of the global group called Group Policy Creator Owners. However, although members of Administrators have full control of all GPOs, members of Group Policy Creator Owners can only modify policies they themselves have created, unless they have been specifically granted permission to modify a policy. So, if you put a designated Group Policy administrator into the security group Group Policy Creator Owners (that's almost as awkward as Active Directory Users and Computers), that person can create new policy objects and modify them.

To delegate who can create a GPO in your domain, you will head down to the Group Policy Objects node in the GPMC. Once you click this node, you will select the Delegation tab in the right pane to view the list of users and groups that have been granted the ability to create GPOs in the domain, as shown in Figure 9.35.

FIGURE 9.35
Delegation of the creation of GPOs using GPMC

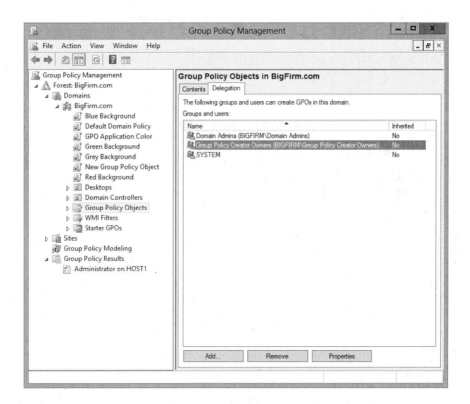

It's one thing to create a GPO; linking that GPO to a site, domain, or OU is another matter. Administrators have this power by default, but a special delegation can be configured, per AD node, to grant other administrators this capability. Here, the scoping is very important to follow.

Unlike the ability to create a GPO, which is per the entire domain, the ability to link a GPO to an AD node is per AD node, which makes logical sense. How about the configuration of this delegation?

To configure who can link a GPO to an AD node, you need to select the target AD node in the GPMC. Then, in the right pane, select the Delegation tab. Each AD node has one. Notice that the default list of users and groups can link a GPO to this node, as shown in Figure 9.36. One key issue to keep in mind is that the delegation of linking to an AD node does not inherit down through the AD structure. Therefore, if you delegate the ability to link a GPO to the domain node, this does not grant the ability to all OUs in the domain.

FIGURE 9.36

Delegation to link a GPO to the domain

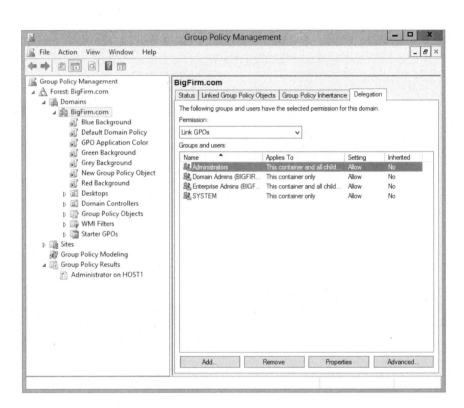

The final three delegations have the same scope, which is per GPO. Again, this makes logical sense, but sometimes logic does not always make it to the keyboard for some people. If this is logical, you should be able to select a GPO in the GPMC; then, in the right pane, you can select the Delegation tab to see the delegations per GPO. This is exactly the case, and you can see the three levels of delegation per GPO in Figure 9.37. Here, you need to right-click the GPO to see the full list of delegations.

The interface does not say "Manage GPO." Instead, it says "Edit settings, delete, modify security" for the GPO.

FIGURE 9.37
Delegations to manage, edit, and read a GPO

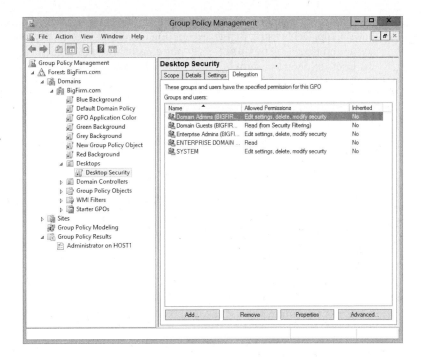

Delegating Control Using Organizational Units

Certainly one of AD's strengths is that it can let you grant partial or complete administrative powers to a group of users, meaning that it would be possible for a one-domain network to subdivide itself into, say, Uptown and Downtown, Marketing and Engineering and Management, or whatever. Let's look at a simple example of how to do that.

Let's suppose that there are five people in marketing: Adam, Betty, Chip, Debbie, and Elaine. They want to designate one of their own, Elaine, to be able to reset passwords. They need this because "I forgot my password—can you reset it for me?" is probably the number-one thing that marketing calls the central IS support folks for. The central IS folks are happy to have someone local to marketing take the problem off their hands, freeing them up to fight other fires.

Here's the process:

1. Create an OU called Marketing.

   You can call it anything that you like, of course, but Marketing is easier to remember later.

2. Move Adam's, Betty's, Chip's, Debbie's, and Elaine's already-existing user accounts into the Marketing OU.

3. Create a group called MktPswAdm, which will be the people who can reset passwords for people in the Marketing OU.

   Again, you can actually give it any name you want.

4. Make Elaine a member of the MktPswAdm group.

5. Delegate password reset control for the Marketing OU to the MktPswAdm group.

If you want to follow this along as an exercise, get ready by creating accounts for Adam, Betty, Chip, Debbie, and Elaine, except don't make them administrators. Or do it from the command line; type **net user** *username* **/add**, and you'll get a basic user account built in the Users folder. For example, create Adam like so:

```
net user Adam Pa$$word /add
```

You've got to be sitting at the domain controller to do this. You can create domain users from any other system at the command line, but you must then add the option /domain, as follows:

```
net user adam /add /domain
```

Creating a New Organizational Unit

Creating a new OU is simple. Just open Active Directory Users and Computers (ADUC), right-click the domain's icon in the left pane, and choose New ➤ Organizational Unit. A dialog box will prompt you for a name of the new organizational unit. Enter **Marketing**, and click OK. You're done.

Moving User Accounts into an OU

Next, to move Adam, Betty, Chip, Debbie, and Elaine to the Marketing OU, open ADUC, open your domain (ours is Bigfirm.com; yours might have another name), and then open the Users folder. (If you created the five accounts somewhere other than Users, then look there.)

You can move all five users by clicking Adam and Ctrl+clicking the other four accounts. Then right-click one of the five accounts, and you'll get a context menu that includes a Move option; select Move, and you'll get a dialog box asking you where to move the "object." It'll originally show you your domain name with a plus sign next to it; just click the plus sign, and the domain will open to show the OUs in your domain. Choose Marketing, and click OK; all five accounts will move to the Marketing OU. In ADUC, you can open the Marketing OU, and you will see that all five accounts are now in that OU.

Or...you can use the drag-and-drop capability. In ADUC, click the Users folder in the left pane. You will be able to see the contents of Users in the right pane. In the left pane, you'll not only be able to see Users, but you should be able to see the Marketing OU as well. Select the users, and then drag them from the right pane to the Marketing OU. Instant OU movement! (What's that you say? You're not impressed? Well, believe us, when you do a lot of user management, you'll find this to be a lifesaver. Trust us on this.)

Creating a MktPswAdm Group

Next, you'll create a group for the folks who can reset Marketing passwords. Again, work in ADUC. First click the Marketing OU to highlight it, and then select Action ➤ New ➤ Group. (You can also right-click the Marketing OU and select New ➤ Group.) You'll see a dialog box like Figure 9.38.

You see that the dialog box gives you the option of creating any one of the three types of groups in Active Directory. A global group will serve our purposes well, although in this particular case—the case of a group in a given domain getting control of an OU in that same domain—either a domain local, global, or universal group would suffice. We've called the group MktPswAdm. Click OK, and it's done.

FIGURE 9.38

Creating a new group

FIGURE 9.38

Creating a new group

Next, put Elaine in the MktPswAdm group. Right-click the icon for MktPswAdm, and choose Properties. Click the Members tab, then the Add button, then Elaine's account, then Add, and then OK. You'll see that Elaine is now a member of MktPswAdm. Click OK to clear the dialog box.

Delegating the Marketing OU's Password Reset Control to MktPswAdm

Now let's put them together. In ADUC again, right-click the Marketing OU. Choose Delegate Control, and the first screen of the Delegation of Control Wizard will appear.

The wizard is a simplified way to delegate, and it'll work fine for this first example. Click Next, and you'll see Figure 9.39.

FIGURE 9.39

Before selecting a group

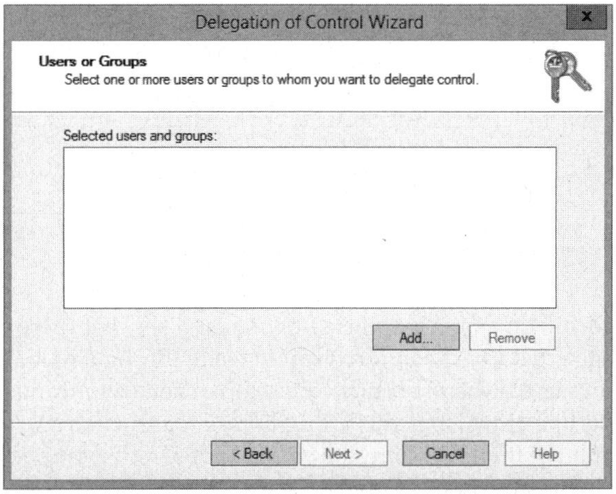

Next, you have to tell it that you're about to delegate some power to a particular group, so you have to identify the group. Click Add, and choose the MkPswAdm group. After choosing MkPswAdm and clicking OK to dismiss the Add dialog box, the screen looks like Figure 9.40. Now click Next, and you'll get a menu of possible tasks to delegate, as you see in Figure 9.41.

FIGURE 9.40
MkPswAdm selected

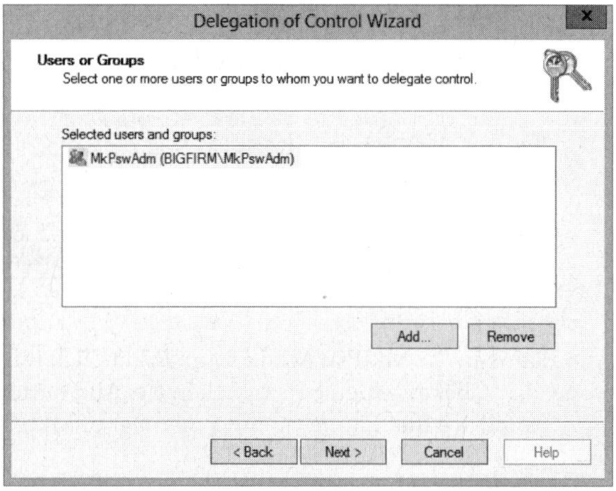

FIGURE 9.41
Options for delegation

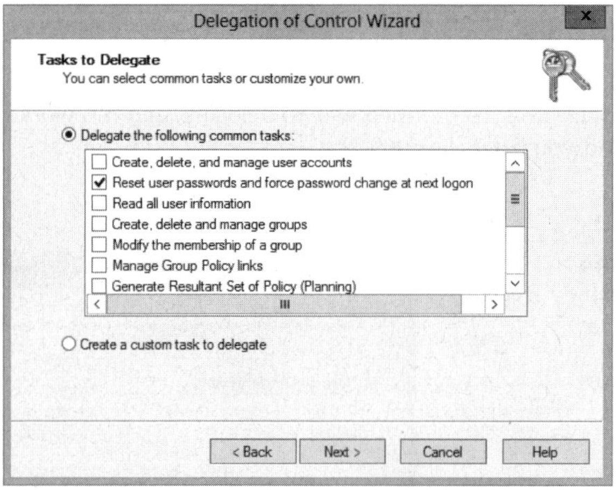

Once you do a bit of exploring here, you'll see that there are many, many functions that can be delegated. Rather than force you to wade through a long list of things that you'll never care about, however, Microsoft picked the top dozen or so things that you'd be most likely to want to delegate, one of which is the ability to reset passwords. We've selected that in the figure; click Next, and the final screen in the wizard appears, as you see in Figure 9.42.

Click Finish, and it's done.

FIGURE 9.42

Confirming your choices

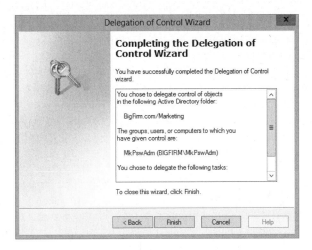

Remember, delegation lets you designate a set of users who have some kind of control over a set of users and/or computers. You accomplish that by putting the controlling users into a group, putting the things that you want them to control into an OU, and then delegating control of the OU to the group.

Advanced Delegation: Manually Setting Permissions

Although the previous scenario is a nice—and useful—example, it only hints at the power of delegation. You actually needn't use the wizard to delegate; it just makes things simpler for a range of common tasks.

BEST PRACTICES FOR DELEGATION

Delegation is a powerful tool for administering your network. If it is used carefully, it will prove quite helpful. So far in this section we have mentioned a few good practices to use when delegating; now we'll expand on these and explore more examples:

◆ *Create groups and OUs that will have delegation applied to them*: This facilitates security as well as administration.

◆ *Avoid assigning permissions directly to a user*: Create a group (see the earlier discussion), and place the user in that group. Creating a group to house one user is not as burdensome as it might seem initially; in fact, it will make your administrative life much easier than trying to track down why this one individual can still perform actions that she or he shouldn't.

◆ *Assign the least amount of permissions to users and groups*. This will help make your network *most* secure. Users might think they are entitled to full control for everything, but they rarely, if ever, require it.

◆ *Use full control sparingly*: Full control can backfire on you when users or groups start taking advantage of your largesse. Full control gives the user an opportunity to work with an object's permissions. That means the users could give themselves greater permissions than the administrator intended. In addition, if someone gains control of this account, then that person could cause more mayhem than they would otherwise.

◆ *To further enforce security and enhance good administration techniques, delegate object creation and object management to different groups*: This is known as *two-person integrity* (TPI). If you split the responsibility between two individuals or groups, there is less likelihood of mismanagement by either. Think of this as splitting the create-backup and restore permissions between two groups. For example, you could give one group of administrators the ability to create groups in an OU, where you give a different group of administrators the ability to control the group's members.

◆ *Create Taskpad views*: Taskpad views are great when you want to delegate tasks to help-desk personnel or other groups that require some permissions but don't want them to have access to the full console. This technique can help train new administrators before you give them the keys to the domain.

◆ *You can delegate at levels higher than an OU, but avoid doing this as a rule*: If you delegate permissions at the domain level, that user or group could have a potentially far greater impact on your network than you anticipated.

STICK AROUND

Even if you're not terribly interested in delegation, stay with this example. It shows how to navigate the three levels of progressive complexity in Windows Server 2012 R2 security dialog boxes.

Here's how you can directly manipulate delegation:

1. First, open ADUC, and select View ➢ Advanced Features. New items will appear on the screen, as in Figure 9.43.

2. Right-click the Marketing OU, and choose Properties.

    You'll get a properties sheet with a Security tab. (By the way, without Advanced Features enabled, you will not have the Security tab available.)

3. Click it, and you'll see something like Figure 9.44.

    Here, I've scrolled down a bit to show what the dialog box tells you about the MkPswAdm group. It appears that the group has powers that can only be described as "special," which isn't all that helpful. This is the top level of a Windows 2012 R2 security dialog box. Think of it as the overview level of security information. We quite frankly find this top-level view pretty limited. About all it really tells us is that there are many entries in this dialog box—you can't see that because they don't all fit in here—and you may recall that each of these entries are called *access control entries* (ACEs). The list in total is called the *access control list* (ACL), pronounced "ackull," rhyming with "shackle."

FIGURE 9.43
ADUC with
View Advanced
Features
enabled

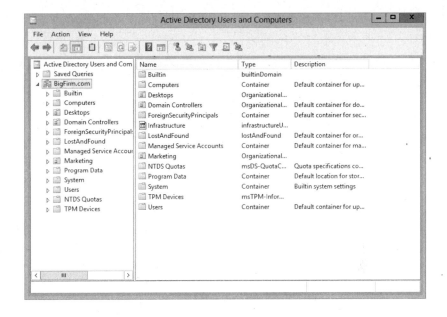

FIGURE 9.44
Security tab on Marketing OU

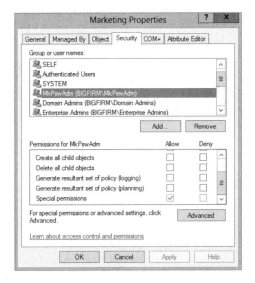

In theory, you should be able to click any of the ACEs in the top part of the dialog box, and in the bottom part you see what powers that ACE gives the thing named in the ACE. For example, you see in Figure 9.44 that MkPswAdm has "special" powers. That's one reason we don't like this dialog box all that much, because "special" doesn't say much. The other reason is that this dialog box only shows a really simplified list of possible powers, so what you see will be sometimes misleading. That's why it's nice that you can zoom in one level by clicking the Advanced button.

4. Do that in ADUC, and you'll see a screen like Figure 9.45.

FIGURE 9.45
Advanced security
settings for
Marketing OU

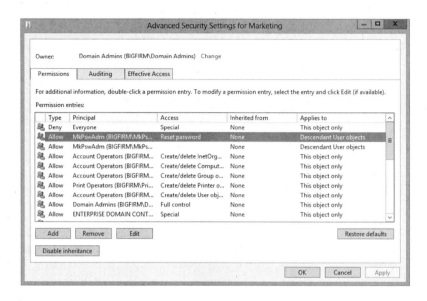

5. Scroll down to highlight MkPswAdm, and you see two entries for it: One lists the "special" permission, while the other does not list anything for the permissions, which is not very helpful at all.

6. Click it and choose Edit when you have one of the entries highlighted, and you'll see something like Figure 9.46.

   Here you see that we've given MkPswAdm the ability to read and write "Descendant User objects" properties, but *only* the pwdLastSet property—AD lingo for being able to select the check box that indicates "User must change password at next logon," which is available in the Reset Password dialog box.

7. Now, go back and look at the other record for MkPswAdm and edit it, and you'll see Figure 9.47.

As you can see from the figure, there are a *lot* of powers that you can grant to a particular group in controlling a particular OU! Believe it or not, you can set more than 10,000 individual permissions for just one OU. And that's counting only the Allow permissions—it's double that for both Allow and Deny.

Where might you make use of this? Well, you gave MkPswAdm the ability to change passwords, but you didn't take it away from the groups that originally had it—the Domain Admins members, the Enterprise Admins members, and the like can still reset passwords. That's not a bad idea, but if you really ever *do* come across a "feuding departments" scenario, wherein marketing wants to be sure that they're the *only* people who can administer accounts, then you'd first delegate the Marketing OU to some group and then go in with the Security tab and rip out all of the other administrators.

FIGURE 9.46
Specific
MktPswAdm
abilities

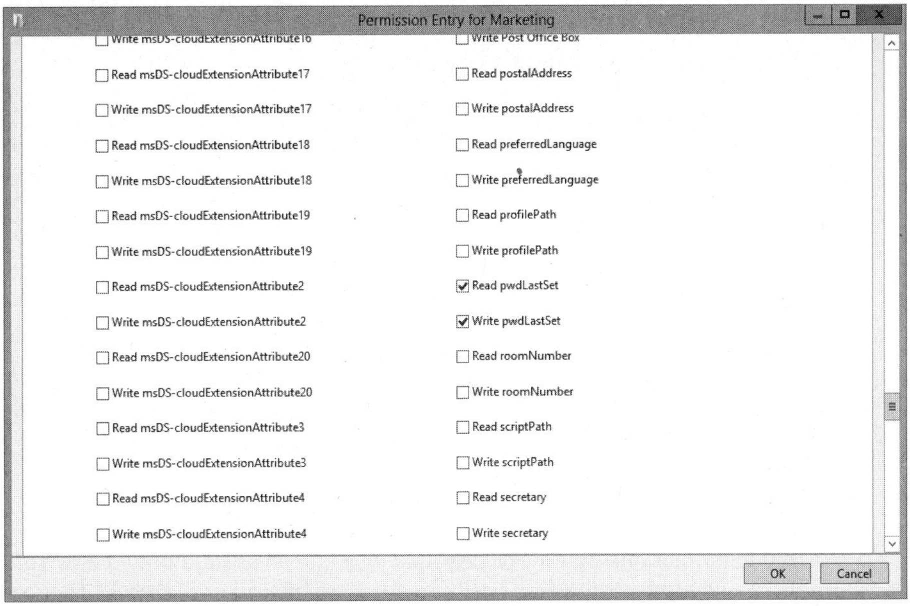

FIGURE 9.47
Giving the
power to reset
passwords

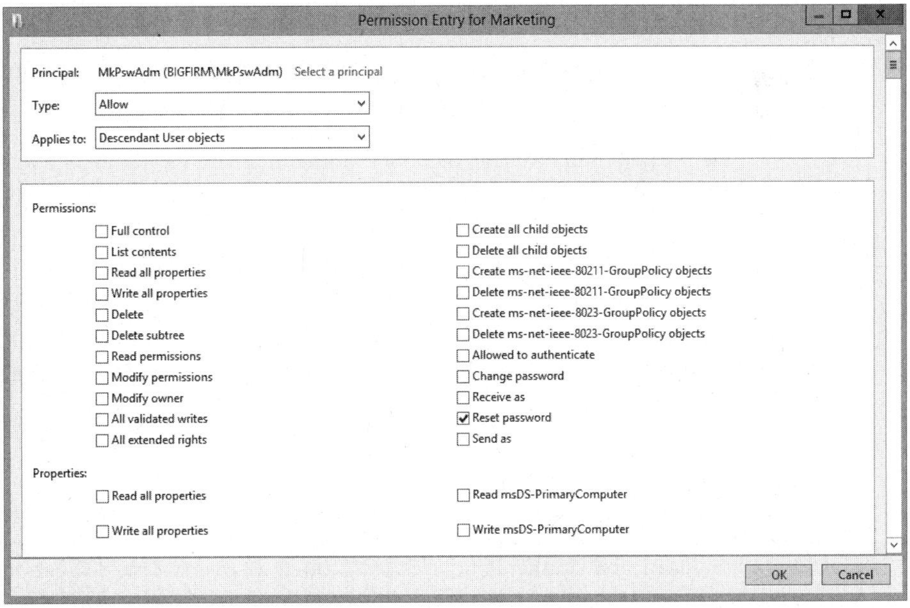

Finding Out Which Delegations Have Been Set, or Undelegating

It's time for some not-so-good news and some bad news.

Suppose you're not the administrator who set up Active Directory. Suppose, instead, you're the *second* administrator—the person hired to clean up the mess that the *first* administrator made. You know these kinds of administrators; they're the "mad scientist" variety—the guys who just click things in the administrative tools until they solve the problem…they think. And *document*? Heck, real administrators don't document; there is never time to document. After all, this network was hard to design; it should be hard to understand!

So, you're wondering what this guy did. How did he change the company's AD from the default AD that you get when you run DCPromo? That's a hard question to answer. First, of course, the OUs that he created are obvious—just look in Active Directory Users and Computers, and you'll see the new folders. But what delegations did he do?

Here's the not-so-good news. Sad to say, but there is no program you can run that will compare the standard AD structure and delegations to the current AD structure and delegations and spit out a "this is what has changed" report. Considering this limitation, we'll offer a really heartfelt piece of advice: always document delegations. *Always*. Try to control who can do delegations, and make clear that delegations are authorized only sparingly. So, why is this news about comparisons *not-so-good* news, instead of *bad* news? The reason is a small tool called dsacls.exe. This tool, part of the core Windows Server 2012 R2 command-line utilities, provides you with detailed listings of the directory service (the ds portion of the tool name) ACLs (the acls portion of the tool name).

To use the tool, you must get to a command prompt:

1. Select Start ➢ Run.

2. From there, type **cmd**, and a command prompt window will open up.

3. From here, type **dsacls** to get the full list of help that accompanies the tool.

   As the help will indicate, the tool requires that you input the path to the OU that you want to view in the official LDAP syntax. This will be something like ou=marketing,dc=bigfirm,dc=com for our example.

   You can just type **dsacls ou=marketing,dc=bigfirm,dc=com**. This will pump the output to the command prompt window, which is not all that friendly or useful to analyze.

4. So, instead of this option, pipe the output to a file, using the following syntax: **dsacls ou=marketing,dc=bigfirm,dc=com > c:\marketing_OU_delegation.txt**.

When you open the marketing_OU_delegation.txt file, you will see a result similar to that in Figure 9.48.

Now, here's the really bad news. The Delegation of Control Wizard is a nice little tool, but it's only a *delegation* wizard, not an *un*delegation wizard. If you want to remove MkPswAdm's ability to change marketing passwords, you have to go into the Security tab, find the references to MkPswAdm, and rip them out. We warn you, if there are some delegations you want to keep and others you want to remove, you will have to manually determine which ones correspond to the delegated task you configured.

FIGURE 9.48
Giving the
power to reset
passwords

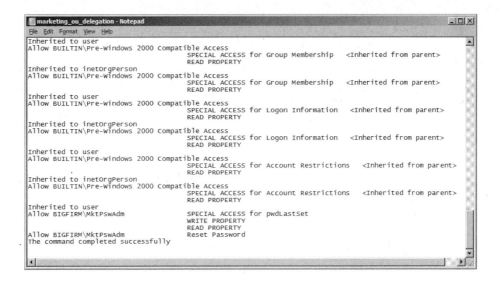

The Bottom Line

Understand local policies and Group Policy objects.   Every Windows computer from Windows 2000 Professional and up has a local group policy. Windows 8 has many local group policies, which can accommodate for various situations where the computer might be located. There are Group Policy objects stored in Active Directory too, which allow for central administration of computers and users who are associated with the domain.

Master It   Which of the following is not a local group policy?

◆ Local Computer Policy

◆ Administrator

◆ Non-Administrator

◆ All Users

Create GPOs.   Group Policy objects can and should be created within your Active Directory domain. These additional GPOs will allow you to control settings, software, and security on the different users and computers that you have within the domain. GPOs are typically linked to OUs but can be linked to the domain node and to AD sites as well. GPOs are created within AD by using the Group Policy Management console.

Master It   Create a new GPO and link it to the HRUsers OU.

Troubleshoot group policies.   At times a GPO setting or group policy fails to apply. There can be many reasons for this, and you can use many tools to investigate the issue. Some tools, such as the rsop.msc tool, are presented in a resulting window, and other tools, such as gpresult, are used on the command line. Regardless of the tool you use, troubleshooting Group Policy is sometimes required.

Master It Which tool would you use to ensure that all settings in all GPOs linked to Active Directory have applied, even if there have not been any changes to a GPO or a setting in a GPO?

Delegate control using organizational units. Delegation is a powerful feature in Active Directory that allows domain administrators to delegate tasks to junior administrators. The idea is that the delegation granted is narrow in scope, providing only limited capabilities within Active Directory and the objects contained within.

Master It Establish delegation on the HRUsers organizational unit such that the HRHelpDesk security group can reset the passwords for all users in the HRUsers OU.

Use advanced delegation to manually set individual permissions. There are thousands of individual permissions for any given AD object. Advanced delegation provides the ability to set any of these permissions to give a user or security group access to the object for the specified permission. The Delegation of Control Wizard is a useful tool to grant common tasks, but when the wizard does not provide the level of detail required, you must grant delegation manually.

Master It *Delegation* is another term for which of the following?

- ◆ Replicating AD database
- ◆ Read-only domain controller
- ◆ Setting permissions on AD objects
- ◆ Using Group Policy to set security

Find out which delegations have been set. It is unfortunate, but the Delegation of Control Wizard is a tool that can only grant permissions, not report on what has been set. To find out what delegations have been set, you have to resort to using other tools.

Master It Name a tool that you can use to view what delegations have been set.

Chapter 10

Active Directory Federation Services

Active Directory has made managing domains so much easier for administrators over the years. We can share with and connect to multiple applications and organizations rather easily in a secure manner. One of the great services offered to us by the Windows Server family ever since Server 2003 R2 is Active Directory Federation Services (AD FS). AD FS is a software component developed by Microsoft that can be installed on Windows Server operating systems to provide users with single sign-on (SSO) capabilities to applications and services across boundaries that were previously unreachable with a single logon account. Using a claims-based access control authorization model, AD FS issues a secure token to an entity, allowing it to cross organizational boundaries while maintaining application security. This technology gives our users the freedom to cross multiple forests and even authenticate into cloud-based applications and websites while using a single trusted account to log into everything.

Windows Server 2012 R2 has taken the previous AD FS abilities to link or federate between multiple AD forests and expanded that functionality to now include the ability to federate between two or more Active Directory Domain Services (AD DS) systems. The newest version, AD FS 2.1, is automatically included with this server edition, allowing us to manage logon identities across multiple platforms, including non-Microsoft environments. This added benefit allows organizations with multiple subsidiaries that house their own individual Active Directories to share and exchange directory information securely among themselves. We can extend this ability even further by provisioning access into cloud services, allowing an SSO user to use one login to reach multiple services and applications well outside the corporate network. As you can imagine, trying to manage all those identities and passwords while synchronizing across a larger realm of directories could prove to be difficult. Luckily for us, Microsoft continues to provide excellent directory synchronization tools like Forefront Identity Manager (FIM). FIM allows organizations to synchronize identity information across a multitude of various heterogeneous directory stores. AD FS and FIM work hand in hand to provide both users and administrators with the proper functionality and ease-of-use to securely provide SSO access to resources across multiple environments around the world.

In this chapter we will take a deep dive into working with AD FS. You will learn to:

◆ Install the AD FS role on a server

◆ Configure the first federation server in a server farm

◆ Configure AD FS performance monitoring

Understanding AD FS Key Components and Terminology

Before we jump in and start building out an AD FS implementation, it's a good idea to go over the key components and terminology that will be used throughout this chapter. AD FS uses terminology from multiple technologies, including Internet Information Services (IIS), Active Directory Domain Services (AD DS), Active Directory Certificate Services (AD CS), Active Directory Lightweight Directory Services (AD LDS), and Web Services. Following is a list of terms and definitions used in this chapter that will help you gain a better understanding of AD FS.

AD FS Commonly Used Terms and Components

The following are the key components and terminology of AD FS:

Account Partner   The account partner is the organization that issues the security tokens used by user accounts to access resources located in the resource partner's environment. It's the account partner's responsibility to store and authenticate user accounts, create the user's claim, and package claims into security tokens used by the resource partner for authentication into their applications and services. Account partners and resource partners work together in a federation trust relationship to provide SSO capability to resources among themselves.

AD FS Configuration Database   The AD FS configuration database is used to store all configuration data that represents a single AD FS instance or federation service. There is an AD FS configuration database for each individual federation server farm. AD FS gives you the option to store the data on a Windows Internal Database (WID), or you can utilize Microsoft SQL Server. Please keep in mind that you can only run either WID or SQL in a single ADFS instance. You cannot run both. You need to consider what database topology will work best for your deployment. SQL is scalable, whereas WID is capped at a limit of five WID servers per federation server farm.

Attribute Store   The attribute store is best defined as a database or directory service that contains attributes about clients. You can use these attributes to issue claims about the clients. AD FS supports a few different possibilities for an attribute store. For the most part, Active Directory and SQL Server are used primarily as the attribute store. Custom attribute stores can be built and used but with additional configuration requirements like building a custom connection string.

Claim   A claim is a statement that one subject makes about itself or another object. For example, the statement can be about a name, email, group, privilege, or capability. Claims are issued and consumed between account partners and resource partners to provide single sign-on access for user accounts to travel freely between organizations or services. These claims are used for logon authentication and authorization purposes in an application shared between the provider and the consumer. Claims identify a group of attributes for a user account such as the user's name or role. The account partner packages claims into security tokens and then sends those tokens to the resource partner requesting user authentication into applications and services hosted by the resource partner.

Federation Metadata   Federation metadata can be described as the data format that is used to communicate configuration data between the relying party and the claims provider. Federation metadata can used to create a trust between the claims provider and the relying party. Federation trusts are required for user accounts to travel securely between organizations, applications, and services. We will create a trust together later in the chapter.

Federation Server   A federation server is a server that has been built and configured for the AD FS role service. A federation server serves as part of a federation service that is used to route authentication requests and host a security token service for user accounts between trusted organizations and services. It is the federation server's job to create and issue security tokens used by user accounts to authenticate into federation services.

Federation Server Farm   When you cluster multiple federation servers together to act as one single federation service on the same load-balanced network, that cluster of servers is referred to as a federation server farm. The farm can consist of many devices such as federation servers, proxies, and AD FS web agents.

Federation Server Proxy   A federation server proxy is a federation server that is placed outside the corporate network to provide an intermediary proxy service between your publically inaccessible firewalled corporate network and clients out on the Internet. In order to allow remote access to the cloud service, such as from a smartphone, home computer, or Internet kiosk, you need to deploy a federation server proxy to act as a middleman between the Internet and the corporate network.

Network Load Balancer   When you have multiple federation servers running together in federation server farm, it is an AD FS requirement to balance the load between servers using some sort of network load balancer (NLB). The NLB can be a piece of hardware such as a multilayer switch or a piece of software such as the built-in NLB functionality with Windows Server. Adding this very important piece offers excellent advantages. In addition to load balancing the AD FS environment, having multiple federation servers with an NLB between them will provide fault tolerance and high availability as added bonuses to the AD FS infrastructure.

Relying Party   A relying party is any organization, application, or service that consumes the claims that are issued from an account provider. A partner organization or cloud service like Office 365 is an excellent example of a relying party.

Relying Party Trust   A relying party trust is a trust that is created between two federation services. Very similar to an Active Directory forest trust, a relying party trust creates the secure tunnel that provides user accounts the ability to securely authenticate into applications and services between entities. Please note: Active Directory forest trusts and federation trusts work independently from one another.

Resource Partner   The resource partner is the other organization part of the federation trust relationship with the account partner. The job of the resource partner is to host the applications and services that the account partner's users wish to access using SSO. The resource partner inspects the security tokens sent by the account partner and decides whether to allow that user account access to its applications and services.

Although there are many additional pieces that make up the entire spectrum of AD FS terminology, these terms and definitions help provide a general understanding of the underlying framework.

Let's also take a minute to examine the four different types of certificates that are used in an AD FS infrastructure. These trusted certificates are required by AD FS and are listed in the next section.

Understanding AD FS Certificates

Certificates are fundamental building blocks for allowing AD FS to work and function properly. Every client that wants to have SSO capabilities needs to have and be able to accept these secure certificates. Certificates are created and issued by both IIS (Internet Information Services) and AD FS to maintain trusted relationships. You use these certificates to securely communicate with all the different objects within an AD FS environment. You cannot implement AD FS as an SSO solution without using these trusted certs. We will create and add certificates together using both IIS and AD FS later in this chapter, but first let's see how they are used. The following are federation server requirements:

Token-Signing Certificate   A token-signing certificate is a secure X509 certificate that is used by a federation server to digitally sign the security tokens that are created and dispersed throughout an AD FS infrastructure. You are required to use a token-signing certificate on a federation server for AD FS to function properly. Out of the four certificates discussed here, this is the one that AD FS actually uses to sign tokens. You can have multiple token-signing certificates. In fact, it is a best practice to keep a few available in a revolving cycle so that just in case the active certificate expires or becomes compromised, you have a backup certificate to roll over to.

Token-Decryption Certificate   The token-decryption certificate is used hand in hand with the token-signing certificate. When an account partner issues a security token for a user account to access an application or service on the resource partner's side of the house, the federation server in the resource partner's environment has to be able to decrypt the security token and verify that it has not changed or been tampered with.

Secure Sockets Layer Certificate   The SSL certificate is designed to be used with traffic between federation server proxies and clients out on the Internet. In order for a web service or client to securely communicate with the federation server proxy, the client must be able to accept the SSL certificate issued by the proxy. Noticing a trend here? All AD FS traffic is secured by encryption and trusted certificates. But think about it: Now that you are granting more access to a single account, more checks and balances are needed to maintain that account's security.

Service Communication Certificate   The service communication certificate provides the same functionality that an SSL certificate does but with one added benefit. In addition to securing traffic between web clients and federation server proxies, this certificate secures communication between Windows Communication Foundation (WCF) clients and applications. Since many web services and web service client applications are built on the WCF framework, by default this is the certificate used by a federation server for the SSL certificate in Internet Information Systems.

Now that you have general understanding of which certificates are required by AD FS and how they are used, let's discuss some best practices for using them. Even though it is entirely possible to use self-signed certs in a lab or test environment, you will want to make sure that you use a trusted certificate authority (CA) for signing all of your production certificates. You can use a trusted CA created by Active Directory Certificate Services (AD CS), or you could use a trusted third-party CA distributor like GoDaddy.com. This helps ensure an added layer of security. AD FS certificates are installed at the root level of federation servers, so the more secure, the better. You wouldn't want an evil hacker to get in and have unauthorized access to all of your federation resources. Have all of your certificates installed and ready to go on all of your federation servers as part of the planning and installation phases of implementing your AD FS deployment.

Planning, Installing, and Configuring an AD FS Infrastructure

AD FS is an extensive and encompassing deployment addition to any corporate infrastructure. It will completely change the way your users access and log into websites, services, and applications across the world. AD FS gives you the fantastic ability to securely traverse corporate, partner, and cloud resources using SSO capabilities. Using just a single user account, you can cross multiple organizational boundaries. This can be a huge relief to administrators and users alike by eliminating the sometimes seemingly endless list of different user accounts and passwords that we use on a daily basis. Together we will plan for, install, and configure an AD FS infrastructure.

Planning for AD FS Deployment

Much time is spent planning for an AD FS implementation. If you have the resources available, it would be a good idea to build a test lab environment for a mock deployment. Since AD FS is supported by virtualization platforms like Hyper-V and VMware, you could completely virtualize a test implementation of AD FS. The same concept holds true in a production environment as well. Currently there is no provided functionality to roll back an AD FS SSO deployment once it has been configured and your users have been fully federated. Therefore, we highly recommend that you run a pilot to test SSO capabilities before turning them on. Use a set of production users, and have that group comprehensively test their SSO capabilities from different sources like from a domain-joined machine, from a home computer, from a partner organization, and from a smartphone. Once you feel comfortable with the users' SSO capabilities, you can safely complete the federation of your production environment.

One of the first things to consider when planning AD FS is how your organization will best benefit from the technology. Will users need to access cloud-based services like Office 365 for email on a daily basis? Does your organization span multiple forests with shared resources that require users to log in multiple times? AD FS makes using these types of scenarios flow so much smoother by federating a user's identity. Normally you would have to stop at every authentication tollbooth and try to remember one of the multitudes of passwords stuck in your head. Using AD FS you can log in at your desk, upload data to a partner organization's repository, and visit multiple cloud-based applications without ever logging in more than once.

One of the most important steps to building a solid AD FS infrastructure is planning the deployment. You have to consider many different aspects like how many servers you will need and where they should be placed, whether you should build a server farm or use a single stand-alone server, whether you should use Windows Internal Database (WID) or SQL for the configuration database, and what other services you will need like network load balancing or federation server proxies. Draw out different deployment topologies on a big whiteboard to see what deployment requirements best fit your organization. Implement and test different deployments in your lab environment. Consider what boundaries users will need to cross. Will partner organizations or cloud services be included with your deployment? Most deployment types like the idea of providing SSO access into cloud services like Microsoft Office 365 or into partner organizations such as a subsidiary's directory services or data repositories. Many of today's corporations host their email and Exchange functionalities through a web-hosted cloud service. Let's take a look at some of the recommended topology considerations for deploying AD FS for SSO capabilities with a cloud service like Office 365. It is recommended to deploy an AD FS server farm with WID as the configuration database when planning to provide SSO user access to a cloud-based application within an environment of 60,000 or fewer users.

How Many AD FS Servers Should You Deploy?

The following information will help you estimate how many AD FS federation servers and federation server proxies you will need in your server farm deployment based on how many users will use SSO access to cloud services and partner organizations:

Up to 1,000 Users   You can get away with using domain controllers to host the AD FS role in a small environment if needed. If you have the resources available, it is still a good idea to segregate infrastructure roles and services as best you can by building dedicated servers for AD FS even though it is not a requirement. For under 1,000 users, it is not necessary to build dedicated federation servers or federation server proxies. However, you still have to utilize an NLB between the two domain controllers that are acting as the two federation servers in the federation server farm.

1,000 to 15,000 Users   If your environment consist of a user base ranging anywhere from 1,000 to 15,000 users, you will want to build out at least two dedicated federation servers on the internal side of the corporate firewall, two federation server proxies on the external side of the corporate firewall (DMZ or extranet), and an NLB configured for each pair to balance the load.

15,000 to 60,000 Users   For larger organizations you could easily find yourself deploying anywhere from three to five dedicated federation servers and at least two federation server proxies. Federation servers scale at one additional dedicated server per 15,000 users. Currently the maximum number of federation servers in a single federation server farm is five, or 60,000 users. For really large enterprises it is completely possible for multiple maxed-out federation server farms to provide SSO capabilities for users all over the globe.

Should You Use WID or SQL for Your Deployment?

Traditionally you would want use a Windows Internal Database for the AD FS configuration database with a web SSO design. At a certain point you can no longer use WID if the environment grows too large. WID caps out and is limited to five federation servers per farm. At that point configuration of a SQL Server database is required. If you have more than 60,000 users who will require SSO access, you will want to plan and deploy SQL Server for the configuration database right from the start. A SQL Server configuration for AD FS provides three added benefits to a WID deployment:

◆ Geographic load-balancing is supported to help provide increases for high traffic based on location.

◆ Administrators can use and take advantage of the high-availability features provided by SQL Server.

◆ SQL Server is not limited to five federation servers per farm.

What Type of Networking Requirements Will Be Expected?

Proper networking is essential to the success of your AD FS deployment. For AD FS to function and work as intended, TCP/IP connections must exist between the client, domain controllers, federation servers, the AD FS web agent, and federation server proxies. DNS plays another very important role in rolling out AD FS. As part of your implementation, you will most likely need to add additional Host A records for additional servers and clusters that are deployed during implementation. For more in-depth instruction on using and configuring DNS, please refer to Chapter 6, "DNS and Name Resolution in Server 2012 R2."

When you use network load balancers or NLB clusters both internally on the corporate network and externally on a DMZ, for example, DNS servers resolve the cluster DNS name to the cluster IP address for the NLB cluster you have configured. For example, bf1.test.com resolves to 172.100.1.3. Keep in mind that a network load balancer is required for proper production deployment as well. An NLB can be a piece of hardware or software that provides load-balancing, high availability, and fault tolerance across multiple devices and machines on a network.

Are Multiple Browsers Supported for AD FS SSO Access to a Microsoft Cloud Service?

You may not be able to sign into the cloud service using integrated Windows authentication from within the corporate network with any other browser than certain versions of Internet Explorer if your computers have Extended Protection for Authentication patches installed. By default, Windows client OSes are preconfigured with Extended Protection for Authentication. If you want to use other browsers like Chrome, Safari, and Firefox to sign into the cloud service, you may have to remove all of the Extended Protection for Authentication patches from the local machine. This is not supported or recommended by Microsoft for security reasons, but it can be done to get you online with your favorite browser. Please visit http://technet.microsoft.com/en-us/library/ff678034.aspx for more information on AD FS browser requirements.

Cookies

One key requirement for client computers to use SSO capabilities is that cookies must be enabled on that machine. AD FS creates session-based and persistent cookies that must be stored locally to each client for proper login access. Please keep in mind that if the client computer is not configured to accept HTTPS authentication cookies, then AD FS will not function properly.

Installing the AD FS Roles and Features Using Server Manager

AD FS 2.1 in Windows Server 2012 R2 uses the same great features that were provided in version 2.0, while bringing to light some new and changed functionality that make this protocol stronger and easier to use than in previous versions. Before Server 2012, you had to download and install AD FS software before you could deploy your server infrastructure. Now you can easily use Server Manager to add the AD FS roles and features right from the server instead of having to download and install the software as required in previous server editions.

Another nice addition in Windows Server 2012 R2 is that AD FS can now also be used with Active Directory Domain Services to provide extended functionality. AD FS can consume AD DS user and device claims that are included in Kerberos tickets because of domain authentication. This greatly expands the capabilities of AD FS. To top it all off, Microsoft didn't forget about AD FS with their new and improved PowerShell cmdlets to automate and administer AD FS through a command-line interface. We will take a look at AD FS PowerShell cmdlets later in the chapter.

Let's install the AD FS role on your first federation server using Server Manager:

1. Launch Server Manager by selecting the Server Manager icon pinned to the taskbar on your desktop or by selecting the Server Manager tile from the Start screen, as shown in Figure 10.1.

FIGURE 10.1
Selecting Server Manager from the taskbar or Start screen

2. From your Dashboard tab, select the link "Add roles and features," as shown in Figure 10.2.

FIGURE 10.2
Launching the
Add Roles and
Features Wizard

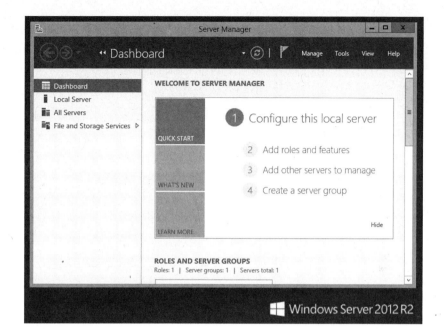

3. When the wizard begins, do the following:

   a. Review the information on the "Before you begin" page.

   b. Keep the default for role-based installation.

   c. Select the server you wish to install the new roles and features on.

   d. Continue into the Server Roles page.

4. On the Server Roles page, select the check box for Active Directory Federation Services, as shown in Figure 10.3.

   If you do not already have IIS, Windows Internal Database, and Active Directory Certificate Services available, make sure to add those roles and features during this wizard as well. Might as well get it all done in one go.

5. Click Next to go to the Features page.

   This will give you the opportunity to add any additional features that you might need.

6. Make your selections, and click Next to continue.

   The AD FS page provides a description of the technology and a few important things to keep in mind about the install. Please note: the Federation Service and the Federation Service Proxy roles cannot live on the same server, and you must be on a domain-joined machine to successfully install the role.

FIGURE 10.3
Selecting the AD
FS server role

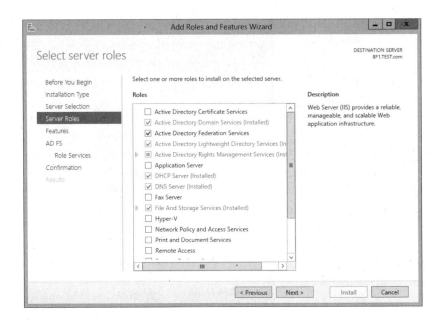

7. Click Next.

   The Role Services page allows you to install the additional role services you will need to launch a fully functional AD FS infrastructure.

8. Read over and select all additional role services except the Federation Service Proxy, keeping in mind the rule from the previous step.

9. Review the information on the Confirmation page to make sure you haven't missed anything.

   The wizard nicely displays all selected roles, features, and tools that support them. There are a few additional options available on this page that can be useful:

   a. Restart the destination server automatically if required.

   b. Export configuration settings.

   c. Specify an alternate source path.

10. Click Install.

    The final page of this wizard is the Results page. An installation progress bar will be displayed, as shown in Figure 10.4. The task will run in the background if you wish to close the page and exit. You can always view task details by clicking Notifications in the command bar.

11. Upon successful installation, reboot the server manually, or if you selected the Restart Automatically option from the Confirmation page, the server will reboot when the install has finished if needed.

FIGURE 10.4
Reviewing the
Results page and
installing the
AD FS roles and
features

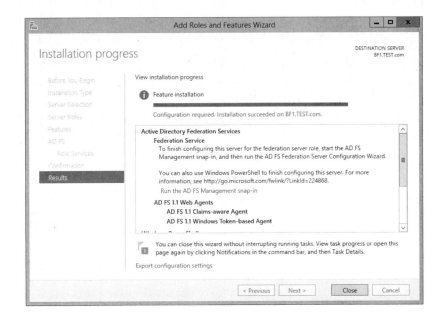

You can now use the Notifications flag in Server Manager to finish the Post-deployment Configuration of AD FS on the server. Before we continue with the Post-deployment Configuration, let's take a minute to create our trusted SSL certificate. You will always want to have your trusted certificate created before you start the Post-deployment Configuration task since the Post-deployment configuration wizard will require the already created SSL certificate in order to complete the AD FS configuration.

Creating a Trusted SSL Certificate Using IIS

We talked about the certificate requirements earlier in the chapter. Now you get to see how those certificates are built and used with IIS. Before you can fully deploy and configure a federation server using the AD FS Server Configuration Wizard, you must first set up a new domain SSL certificate representing your federation service name. Here are the steps for creating the certificate required for the deployment of AD FS:

1. Launch Server Manager, select Tools, and then select Internet Information Services (IIS).

   The IIS Manager will start, allowing you to select your server from the left pane.

2. Highlight the server node, and in the features pane select Server Certificates.

   For this lab exercise you will create and use a self-signed certificate. You would not want to use a self-signed certificate for a production environment because of potential security vulnerabilities.

3. Click Create Self-Signed Certificate to launch the wizard.

4. Specify a friendly name for the certificate: **AD FS**.

This page also gives you the opportunity to select a certificate store for the new certificate.

5. Choose either the Personal or Web Hosting store from the drop-down menu and click OK.

When completed successfully, your screen should look similar to Figure 10.5.

FIGURE 10.5
Viewing a newly created certificate using the IIS Manager tool in Server Manager

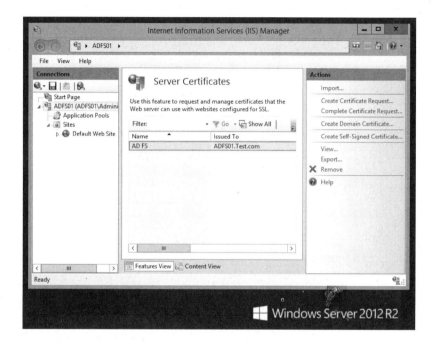

Using the AD FS Server Configuration Wizard

Now that you have your trusted SSL certificate created, you can continue with the Post-deployment Configuration task of configuring AD FS on your server. Depending on the topology layout you go with for your production installation, more certificates may be required, such as token-signing and verification certificates for clients. You can always come back and create other certificates as needed, but for now the wizard will install the remaining needed certificates as part of the configuration process. Let's continue with configuring AD FS on your server:

1. In Server Manager, click the Notification flag and select Configure the federation service on this server.

2. The wizard will start and display a Welcome page, allowing you to choose from two installation options. You can either create a new federation service or add a federation server to an existing federation service. The nice thing about the Welcome page is that there is a hyperlink to all of the AD FS pre-requisites just in case you might have missed a step along the way.

3. Since this is first AD FS server you are installing, keep the default selection of Create the first federation server in a federation server farm.

4. Click Next to display the Connect to AD DS page. As part of the configuration process, AD FS will register itself with your AD DS. You will be required to enter the credentials of an Active Directory domain administrator to continue past this point in the configuration process.

5. After entering the appropriate credentials, click Next to move into the Specify Service Properties page. This is where you are required to attach your trusted SSL Certificate to the Federation Service. If you created your SSL Certificate locally to the server then you can easily select that certificate from the drop-down provided, or you can click the import button to bring in the certificate from a network location. You will notice that as soon as you have selected the certificate you wish to use, the Federation Service Name field will auto-populate with the same name as the certificate, as shown in Figure 10.6. Don't worry too much about the syntax of the Federation Service Name or the name of your SSL Certificate because the very last option given to us on this page of wizard is to create a user friendly Federation Service Display Name that will be displayed when a user signs in. In most cases the name of the Company is used as a Federation Service Display Name.

FIGURE 10.6
Specify Service
Properties page

6. Click Next to go to the Specify Service Account page. On this page of the configuration wizard you will be required to either create a new service account to be used with the Federation Service, or select an existing service account from your Active Directory. It is a best practice to keep service accounts separate between services. You wouldn't want to have multiple services running off of the same account because if that account becomes

locked or compromised then it would affect multiple services and applications instead of just one. Since this is our first time through the configuration wizard, go ahead a create a new dedicated service account for AD FS.

7. Click Next to continue on to the Specify Database page. As we mentioned earlier in the chapter, AD FS can use either Windows Internal Database or a SQL Server Database to store configuration data. For this exercise we will use the WID. If by chance you are ever running through this configuration wizard on server that was previously configured for AD FS, you may have to overwrite that existing database. The nice part is that the wizard automatically detects the previous installation and all you have to do is check the box to Overwrite existing AD FS configuration database data on the Confirm Overwrite sub page and continue as normal through the rest of the wizard.

8. Click Next to go to the Review Options page as shown in Figure 10.7.

FIGURE 10.7
Review
Options page

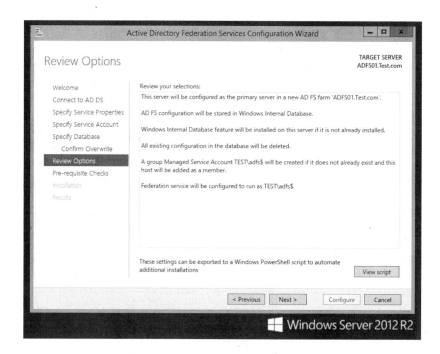

9. Review the information listed carefully and make sure that all of your choices so far are exactly like you want them. Now would be the time to make any changes to your configuration options.

The configuration wizard will automatically create the additional signing and token-encryption certificates that you will need for this deployment during the installation. It also configures the Windows Internal Database with the network service account, provided from the server, with access to the database. In addition to these settings, a browser sign-in will be deployed to the virtual directory under the default website in IIS.

10. ·Click Next to move on into the Pre-requisite Checks page. This is a great addition to the wizard because if you missed anything along the way or mis-configured one of the fields then the configuration wizard will check for any errors or potential conflicts that may occur during the installation. If an error is found, you will need to fix the problem before you can complete the installation. If done properly up until this point, your screen will look similar to Figure 10.8.

FIGURE 10.8
Pre-requisite
Checks page

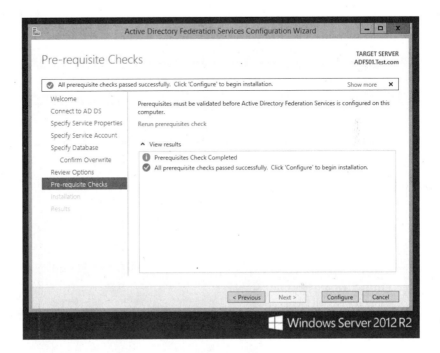

11. Click Configure to begin the installation. It should only take a few minutes to complete. A successful completion message will appear once the installation has finished.

In our example the "Deploy browser sign-in Web site" component was skipped because the website was already built previous to this exercise. Figure 10.8 shows you an example warning upon successful completion.

12. Click Close to complete the installation.

Using Windows PowerShell with AD FS

Let's take a moment to recap what you have completed so far:

- ◆ You have installed the AD FS roles and features on your server.
- ◆ You have created and assigned any needed deployment certificates.
- ◆ You have configured your server for AD FS federation services.

A few things to note at this point are that the AD FS Management snap-in should be installed and registered alongside the Windows PowerShell cmdlets for administering AD FS from the command line. If you go back into the AD FS Management snap-in, you will see that more configuration nodes have been added. You will also notice that the AD FS Overview page has a new wizard called "Add a trusted relying party." This additional configuration step is required to manage single sign-on access for applications and services. We will add a trusted relying party in the next section.

Before we continue into the next portion of your install, let's take a look at the Windows PowerShell cmdlets that are available to you in Windows Server 2012 R2. With the AD FS snap-in registered; your execution policy set to remote signed, and running Windows PowerShell as administrator; run the following command: Get-Command *-ADFS*. This will display the usable PowerShell cmdlets available for AD FS. If you wish to see all the cmdlets that are supported for a particular resource, use this command:

```
Get-Command *-ADFS<object_name>
```

The Help command uses the same principles. To learn more about AD FS in PowerShell, you can always type Get-Help *-ADFS* or Get-Help *-ADFS<object_name> for information on a specific cmdlet. Figure 10.9 shows an example of requesting help for adding a claims provider trust in AD FS:

```
Get-Help Add-ADFSClaimsProviderTrust
```

It is worth taking the time to learn about and use Windows PowerShell on a regular basis for almost all administrative duties extending well beyond AD FS. The automation of tasks can greatly increase productivity.

FIGURE 10.9
Using PowerShell for help with a specific AD FS cmdlet

Adding a Trusted Relying Party

Let's jump back into your AD FS configuration. You need to now add a trusted relying party. This trust can exist between local applications, partner organizations, or cloud services. This wizard helps you establish a trust relationship between the federation service and relying parties like another federation service, application, or service that consumes claims from your organization's federation service. The federation service issues security tokens used by relying parties to make authentication decisions.

For this exercise you will create a trust using federation metadata. Since you don't necessarily have a partner organization handy to share federation metadata with, you will create an AD FS trust to itself. There would be no reason to deploy this topology in a production environment, but for a demonstration or test of the technology's capability and functionality, it will do just fine. In production you would follow the same steps using the federation metadata from the partner, for example, Office 365. Following are the steps for creating the trust:

1. In Server Manager, click Tools, and select AD FS Management.

2. On the AD FS Overview page, select the link "Add a trusted relying party," or select the option from the Actions drop-down menu. Either way will launch the wizard.

3. Review the information on the Welcome page.

   A brief description of how relying party-trusts work is provided in the wizard.

4. Click Start to go to the Select Data Source page.

   There are three ways you can select a data source:

   ◆ You can type in the network path to access federation data published online or on a local network.

   ◆ You can browse for the federation metadata file.

   ◆ You can manually enter the data about the relying partner.

5. Since your federation metadata is local, enter the direct path to your federation metadata by providing a URL, as shown in Figure 10.10, and append `/FederationMetadata/2007-06/FederationMetadata.xml` to the FQDN of your server hosting the data, as shown in the example.

6. Click Next to continue into the Specify Display Name page.

   You can choose to change the default display name and make any notes about this relying party on this page.

7. Click Next to navigate to the Choose Issuance Authorization Rules page.

   These rules determine whether a user is permitted to receive claims from the relying party. You can either permit or deny all users to access this relying party.

8. For testing purposes go ahead and allow all users access.

   If needed in a production environment, the application or service could still deny the user access.

9. Click Next to go to the Ready to Add Trust page. Review the tabs carefully.

   A lot of information goes into adding a trust, as shown in Figure 10.11.

FIGURE 10.10
Select a data source
using the Add Relying
Party Trust Wizard.

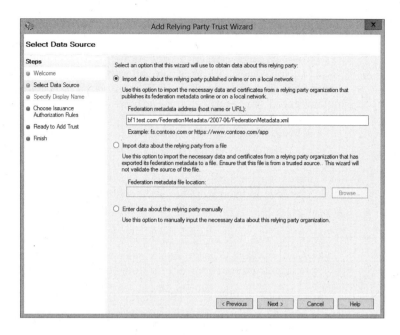

FIGURE 10.11
Ready to Add
Trust page

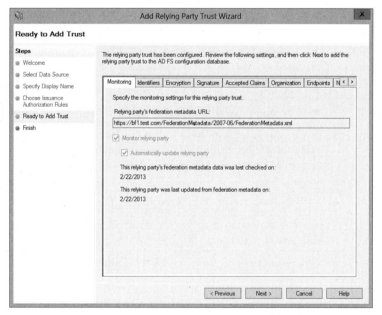

10. Click Next to install the configuration and display the final page of the wizard, the Finish page.

Upon successful completion, this page will display an already selected check box to open the Edit Claim Rules dialog box for this relying party trust when the wizard closes.

11. If you wish to change or add any additional claim rules, keep the default and close the wizard; otherwise deselect the option and click Close.

If you go back into the AD FS Management tool, you'll see that the relying party trust has been added to your trust relationships. You have now successfully deployed AD FS on your new federated server! You can verify that AD FS is working on your server by checking the Event Viewer, as shown in Figure 10.12.

FIGURE 10.12
Verifying that the AD FS service is installed and working using Event Viewer

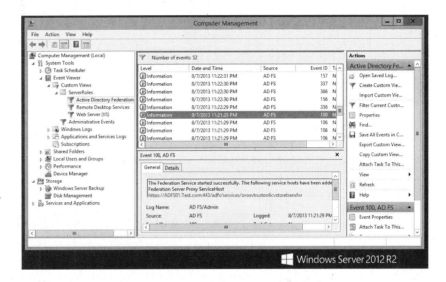

Additional Configuration Options for AD FS

Now that your server is a fully functional federation server, you can take a look at some of the additional management tasks available to you with AD FS. Using the AD FS Management snap-in, you can create additional token certificates, add additional federation servers and federation server proxies (in a federation server farm deployment), configure performance monitoring, and perform a multitude of additional tasks. Let's take a closer look at some of these options.

ADD A TOKEN-SIGNING OR TOKEN-DECRYPTING CERTIFICATE

Certificates are a very important piece of the AD FS puzzle. AD FS requires you to use both token-signing and token-decrypting certificates to securely transfer information between federation servers. These certificates are digitally signed by use of a private key. When an account partner issues a security token for a user identity, the resource partner validates the token for authenticity. As long as the information sent matches the information received, the user is granted access to the desired resources. This type of encryption and decryption security checking prevents hackers from gaining access to your AD FS environment.

As we mentioned earlier in the chapter, it is a best practice to have additional token-signing and token-decrypting certificates available within the environment in case the certificates currently being used are expiring or if suspicion arises that the certificates' security has been compromised. If either event takes place, you will need to roll over to a new certificate. The following steps show how to add an additional token certificate using the AD FS snap-in:

1. Open Server Manager, select Tools, and then select AD FS Management.

2. In the console tree, double-click Service, and then click Certificates.

3. Select either the Add Token-Signing Certificate or the Add Token-Decrypting Certificate link, shown in Figure 10.13.

FIGURE 10.13
Adding a token certificate using the AD FS snap-in

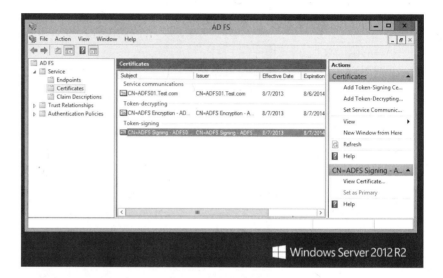

4. Navigate to the certificate file you wish to add using the Browse for Certificate File dialog box, select the appropriate certificate file, and click Open.

CONFIGURE AD FS PERFORMANCE MONITORING

Another great feature automatically included with AD FS is the ability to configure Performance Monitor. This tool allows you to actively monitor the performance of an AD FS infrastructure. You can create and schedule reports as needed to manage the environment properly. This is very useful for keeping a close eye on how well AD FS is running within the enterprise. AD FS comes with its own set of performance counters that monitor all authentication and token transactions used by AD FS. Using the following steps, you will configure performance monitoring for AD FS:

1. Launch Performance Monitor by either selecting the option from Tools in Server Manager or typing **Performance Monitor** on the Start screen.

2. In the console tree, expand Data Collector Sets, right-click User Defined, point to New, and then click Data Collector Set.

   The New Data Collector Set Wizard will appear, as shown in Figure 10.14.

3. Give your new data collector set a name like **AD FS Performance**, select the radio button "Create manually (Advanced)," and then click Next. This page allows you to select what type of data logs to use with AD FS. Keep the default radio button "Create data logs" selected, and put a check mark next to each available option. Alternatively, this page allows you to select and create a performance counter alert instead of creating data logs.

FIGURE 10.14
New Data Collector Set Wizard

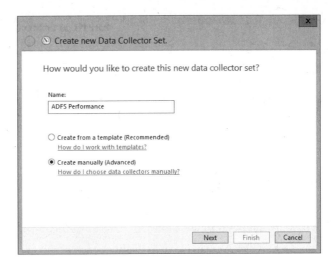

4. Click Next to take you to the Performance Counters page.

5. Click Add to display all the available counters that you have the option to select.

6. Select the AD FS counters and add them to the "Added counters" list, as shown in Figure 10.15.

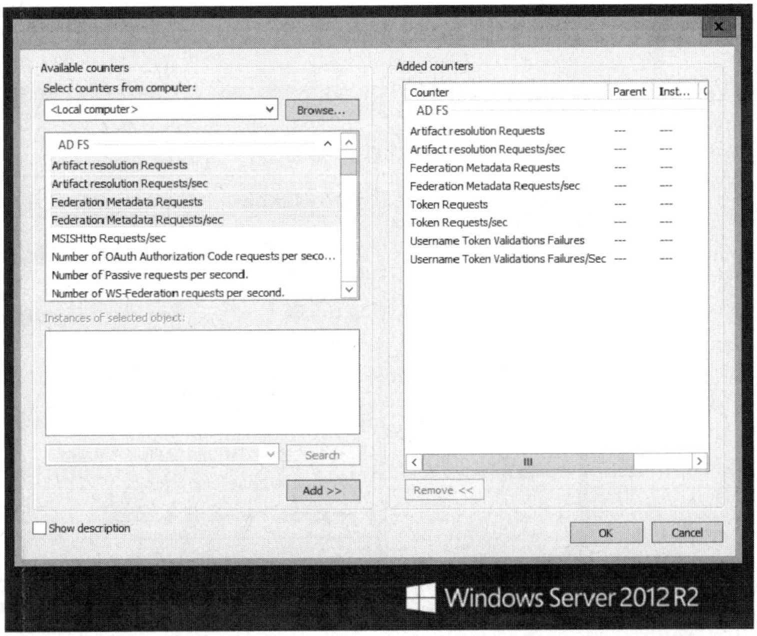

FIGURE 10.15
Adding AD FS performance counters

7. Click OK after all the proper counters have been added.

8. Click Next to go to the Event Trace Providers page.

9. Click Add to browse through event providers, and select AD FS and AD FS Tracing to be added. Click OK.

10. Click Next to add any registry keys for monitoring.

    This task is optional; you do not have to monitor any registry keys unless you want to do so.

11. Click Next to continue.

    You are now prompted for where you want the data to be saved.

12. Accept the default location unless you wish to browse for and select a different location to store the data.

13. Click Next to move to the final page of this wizard.

    You are asked to confirm the creation of your new data collector set.

14. Keep the defaults and click Finish to complete this wizard.

If you go back into Performance Monitor, you will see that the new data collector set has been successfully created. The new data collector set appears in the console tree under the User Defined node. Right-click the AD FS Performance data collector set, and click Start to begin collecting data. You will notice that a new AD FS report is being generated under the Reports node in the console tree, as shown in Figure 10.16. You can now use this report to watch the performance of your AD FS infrastructure.

FIGURE 10.16
Generating an AD FS report using Performance Monitor

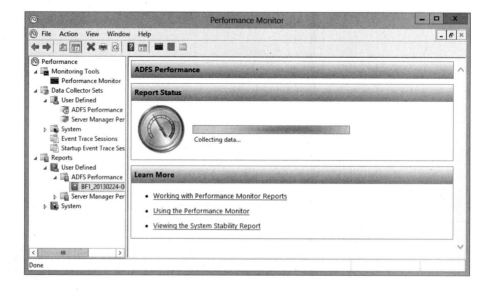

Table 10.1 provides a closer look at the available AD FS performance counters. The table explains what each counter's function is and which servers support these counters. This information is also available on online at `http://technet.microsoft.com/en-us/library/ff627833(v=WS.10).aspx`.

TABLE 10.1:   AD FS Performance Counters

COUNTER	DESCRIPTION	CAN BE USED ON
Artifact Resolution Requests	Monitors the number of incoming federation metadata requests per second that are sent to the federation server	Federation servers
Artifact Resolution Requests/sec	Monitors the number of requests to the artifact resolution endpoint per second that are sent to the federation server	Federation servers
Federation Metadata Requests	Monitors the number of incoming federation metadata requests sent to the federation server	Federation servers
Federation Metadata Requests/sec	Monitors the number of incoming federation metadata requests per second that are sent to the federation server	Federation servers
Token Requests	Monitors the number of token requests sent to the federation server including SSOAuth token requests	Federation servers
Token Requests/sec	Monitors the number of token requests sent to the federation server including SSOAuth token requests per second	Federation servers
Proxy MEX Requests	Monitors the number of incoming WS-Metadata Exchange (MEX) requests that are sent to the federation server proxy	Federation server proxies
Proxy MEX Requests/sec	Monitors the number of incoming MEX requests per second that are sent to the federation server proxy	Federation server proxies
Proxy Requests	Monitors the number of incoming requests sent to the federation server proxy	Federation server proxies
Proxy Requests/sec	Monitors the number of incoming requests per second that are sent to the federation server proxy	Federation server proxies

ADD AN ADDITIONAL SERVER TO A FEDERATION SERVER FARM

Depending on your organizational goals and topology selections, you will probably need to add additional servers to your federation server farm. The placement of these servers depends on how you plan to use SSO access within your organization. If you plan to keep SSO in-house within the corporate network, you could logically place the new server in the same location as the others. If you plan to use SSO capabilities to and from a partner organization for a federated web SSO design, you would need to place a federation server in the resource partner organization as well.

The following exercise shows how to add an additional server to the farm. The server has to meet a few requirements before it can be added. The server must be domain joined to your Active Directory forest, it must have the AD FS roles and features installed, and it must have the required AD FS certificates installed locally to the machine.

1. On the server you wish add, launch the Post-deployment Configuration task from the Notification flag in Server Manager just after installing the AD FS Role like we did when we created our first Federation Server in the farm earlier in the chapter. You will notice that the configuration wizard to add an additional server to the farm is very similar to the creation of the first federated server, but with a few differences.

2. This time when the Welcome page populates, select the second option to Add a federation server to a federation server farm. Notice how the other pages left in the configuration wizard have changed as shown in Figure 10.17.

FIGURE 10.17
Add a federation server to an existing federation service.

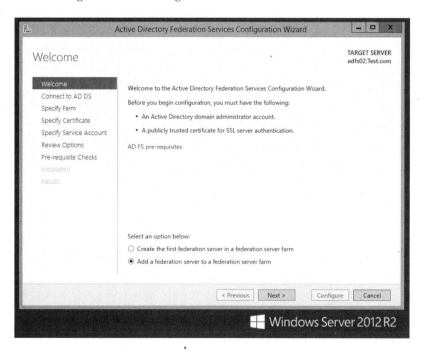

3. Click Next to continue on into the Connect to AD DS page. Just like the first federation server we created, administrator credentials are required for the federation service configuration on this second server in the farm.

4. Click Next. You will notice that this page of the wizard, the Specify Farm page, is different from the configuration of the first federated server in the farm. Since we have already created a farm, an SSL certificate, and a dedicated service account the first time through, all we have to do now is specify the configuration for the second federated server. Since we used WID on the first federated server in the farm, leave the default selection and enter the name of the first federated server that houses the WID.

5. Click Next taking us into the Specify Certificate page. Make sure to attach the same SSL certificate that was used on the first federation server in the farm.

6. Click Next. Now on the Specify Service Account page, click Select to browse your Active Directory and specify the dedicated service account that you created during the first federated server's configuration.

7. The rest of the configuration wizard is the same as we are used to from the first federated server that was created earlier in the chapter. Review all of your choices for accuracy, run the Pre-requisite Checks, and install the service. Make sure to watch for any warnings or errors along the way.

8. The last thing you need to do after the installation completes successfully is verify that the server is operational. Refer back to Figure 10.12. Check the Event Viewer on the new federation server to verify that the service is working properly. Specifically look for AD FS Event ID 100.

VERIFYING FEDERATION SERVER FUNCTIONALITY

Checking the AD FS Event Viewer logs is not the only way you can test and verify that AD FS is working properly on the federation server. Alternatively, you can open up a browser window on a client machine within the same forest and enter the DNS hostname of a federation server appended with `/adfs/fs/federationserverservice.asmx`. For example, you could type `https://bf1 .test.com/adfs/fs/federationserverservice.asmx`. The client may be prompted with the message stating that there is a problem with this website's security certificate. Click "Continue to this website," and you should see a display of XML with the service description document. If access is forbidden or the web page cannot be displayed, then you know IIS is not functioning properly and is not serving up pages as it should. AD FS errors would also be displayed in Event Viewer, pointing you in the right direction for troubleshooting.

ADD THE FEDERATION SERVER PROXY ROLE TO A SERVER

AD FS proxies are federation servers that are placed on the external side of your corporate network. The main purpose of a proxy server is to allow remote internal users access to the server farm from an external source like the Internet, without having to expose your AD FS infrastructure to the outside world. When a remote user requests access to your corporate network, the AD FS proxy server uses forms-based authentication to prompt the user for a username and password.

There are a few server requirements to keep in mind when deploying a federation server proxy:

◆ There must be a federation server on the internal corporate network to communicate with.

◆ The proxy server must have a trusted SSL certificate with a subject name that matches the federation service name.

◆ Proper DNS entries will need to be configured.

The steps for adding the Federation Server Proxy role are similar to configuring a new federation server discussed previously in this chapter:

1. Launch Server Manager, and from the Dashboard tab, select the link Add Roles and Features, or select the same function from the Manage drop-down.

2. Navigate through the wizard as you normally would by selecting the appropriate installation type and server options.

3. When you get to the Server Roles page, select the Federation Service Proxy role, as shown in Figure 10.18.

FIGURE 10.18
Installing the Federation Service Proxy role on a server

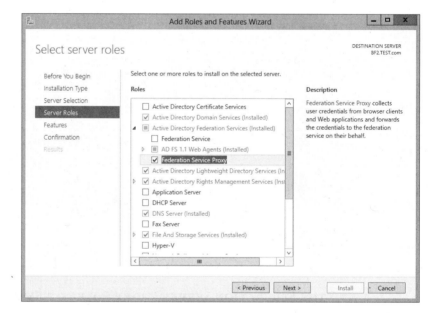

Please note the Federation Service Proxy role and the Federation Service role cannot be installed on the same server.

4. If you need or want any additional features on this server, make sure to add them on the Features page of the wizard.

5. Continue through the Confirmation and Results pages to complete the steps for installing the Federation Server Proxy role.

Automating Client Configurations Using Group Policy

There are some additional configuration changes that need to be made to allow client computers to freely interact with federation applications. Any client computer that wishes to have SSO access to applications and services needs to have the trusted SSL certificate locally installed, and the browser settings for each user profile will need to be configured to trust the account federation server.

As you can imagine, manually configuring each individual machine and user profile would be a tedious and time-consuming task in a larger environment. Thankfully, you can use Group Policy to push the settings and certificates to client computers. Following are the steps to configure the Group Policy settings for distributing certificates. Please note that domain or enterprise administrator credentials are required to perform the following task:

1. On a domain controller, launch Server Manager, navigate to Tools, and then click Group Policy Management.

2. Find an existing Group Policy object or create a new one to contain the certificate settings.

3. Ensure that the GPO is associated with the domain, site, or organizational unit where the appropriate user and computer accounts reside.

4. Right-click the GPO, and then click Edit.

5. In the console tree, open Computer Configuration\Policies\Windows Settings\Security Settings\Public Key Policies, right-click Trusted Root Certification Authorities, and then click Import.

6. On the Welcome to the Certificate Import Wizard page, click Next, as shown in Figure 10.19.

FIGURE 10.19
Certificate Import Wizard

7. On the File to Import page, type the path to the appropriate certificate files (for example, `\\bf1\c$\bf1.cer`), and then click Next.

8. On the Certificate Store page, click "Place all certificates in the following store," and then click Next.

9. On the Completing the Certificate Import Wizard page, verify that the information you provided is accurate, and then click Finish.

10. You can repeat the same steps to add additional certificates for each of the federation servers that live in the federation server farm.

The Bottom Line

Install the AD FS role on a server.   Installing the AD FS role on a server is one of the first steps in implementing an AD FS infrastructure. Windows Server 2012 R2 has made it easier than ever to install and use AD FS. AD FS provides you with single sign-on access within your corporate network, to a partner organization, and to websites and applications hosted on the Internet.

Master It   How do you install AD FS on a server?

Configure the first federation server in a server farm.   A federation server serves as part of a federation service that can issue, manage, and validate requests for security tokens and identity management. Multiple federation servers provide much-needed functionality like high availability and network load balancing in a large AD FS infrastructure. For proper SSO user access between your organization and a partner organization, federation servers must be deployed in the partner's organization as well as your own.

Master It   How do you create the first federation server in a federation services server farm?

Configure AD FS performance monitoring.   AD FS includes its own dedicated performance counters to help you monitor the performance of both federation servers and federation server proxy machines. This is a nice little addition that helps you manage AD FS more easily. Generated reports provide AD FS–specific details that show you how well it is running in the environment. Monitoring performance is an essential part of planning for growth and scalability. High utilization could mean that you need to deploy another federation server to balance the load more proficiently.

Master It   How would you monitor the performance of your AD FS infrastructure?

Chapter 11

Shared Storage and Clustering Introduction

Shared storage and clustering in Windows Server 2012 R2 deliver arguably the most significant functionality that any large enterprise or datacenter infrastructure design requires. Ensuring that resources such as applications, services, files, and folders are delivered in a highly available, centralized, and scalable offering should be paramount to every IT administrator and consultant. Utilizing shared storage and clustering gives organizations the ability to scale out storage on demand, create centralized locations for resources, and make them highly available (HA) to the business.

The concepts of shared storage and clustering aren't new or exclusive to Windows Server 2012 R2, but gaining a clear understanding of each will allow you to confidently deploy the enhanced HA offerings that come out of the box with the operating system. In this chapter you will learn to:

- ◆ Use the available storage options for clustering
- ◆ Use quorums to help in clustering
- ◆ Build out host and guest clusters

Shared Storage Basics

In its most basic form, shared storage offers a central location inside an organization's IT infrastructure to host a specific set of files or applications so that multiple users can have simultaneous access to them. Many different storage devices can be utilized for this technology, examples of which are storage area networks (SANs), Network Attached Storage (NAS), and Serial Attached SCSI (SAS). Depending on your requirements (and budget), which of these options you deploy is up to you. Ultimately, when combined with clustering, they all achieve the same goal of enabling people to keep working with their applications and files in the event of a server outage. A simple example of this is a person named Sarah in Human Resources. Sarah needs to make sure that she has a location to securely store critical documents related to employees, which could include their Social Security numbers. With a properly designed and implemented shared storage solution, Sarah can place these files on a shared location that is encrypted and backed up and could potentially have rights management or other security measures enabled. Other employees with the associated rights to this location have access to these files, and Sarah doesn't have to worry about trying to share the files from her own workstation or even risk losing them if it was to crash.

Storage, and the ability to provide controlled access to it, is one of the most common requirements of any organization. Many different storage options are available. Before we get into the options available in Windows Server 2012 R2, let's review the basic components:

◆ iSCSI SAN

◆ Fiber Channel SAN

◆ SAS enclosures .

◆ SMB 3.0 Server 2012

With the feature advancements in Windows Server 2012 R2 specific to storage, you can start utilizing these components on the infrastructure you already own. Let's dig into these technologies for a brief overview.

Storage Area Network

A storage area network is a network-connected entity that is dedicated to storage. SAN technology is just a basic framework, and each type of SAN solution presents storage in its own unique way. What we are really talking about is block-level storage that is available to resources over the network. The SAN is typically a large device with numerous hard disk drives, and you divide and format them to present to servers and computers on the network.

In addition, a SAN doesn't have to be a traditional network; it could be over Fiber Channel, for example. With Fiber Channel, the same basic principal applies: it's a device filled with disks but the network is fiber optic. In most organizations the storage network has a network switch dedicated and optimized for a SAN. The data transfer network that a SAN communicates on is typically known as the *storage fabric*. The main purpose of a SAN is to allow different types of servers, applications, and users from multiple places to access a storage pool, which can be accessed from any devices that interconnect with that storage fabric. Part of the storage fabric is the host bus adapter (HBA); HBAs are the network interface cards (NICs) that connect the storage fabric to the resources on your network that need to access the storage.

Many organizations and IT pros believe that a SAN provides them the flexibility to deploy and redeploy servers and storage in a much more dynamic fashion. Servers can boot directly from a SAN, giving them the operating system and its configurations in a larger, more highly available location. If the physical server goes down, a new one can be put in its place, and the operating system and the associated disks can be pointed to the new server much faster than rebuilding and restoring from tape.

We recommend that you spend some time investigating these topics at a much deeper level, and if your organization has an existing SAN, you should start by reading through the deployment and administration guides that accompany it.

iSCSI

Internet Small Computer System Interface (iSCSI) has been around for many years and has been used as a way to allow computers or servers to communicate with disk drives or other storage devices such as tape libraries. As SCSI has advanced, so has the network infrastructure connecting your servers and computers. Gigabit-based networks are much more commonplace and allow you to run storage connections natively through these higher-bandwidth connections. iSCSI is used to facilitate the transfer of data over a TCP/IP (Ethernet) network. The iSCSI protocol lets you present the disk drives located in your SAN over an existing network to your servers.

Microsoft's iSCSI Initiator is a software component built into all Windows Server operating systems since 2008 and is also included in Windows 7 and Windows 8. The iSCSI Initiator enables the connections on your Windows devices to utilize this technology.

As with the other storage technologies we are going to talk about here, we won't get into great detail about all of the scaling and performance options available. The purpose of this chapter is to introduce the topics.

Fiber Channel

Fiber Channel (FC) is a high-speed connectivity network link running over twisted-pair copper wire or fiber-optic cable. The connection to your servers and storage is handled through the host bus adapter (HBA) using a protocol similar to TCP, called Fiber Channel Protocol (FCP).

The HBAs communicate in a grouping of zones with specific worldwide names, which essentially act like IP addresses. The Fiber Channel connection to your drives and storage is through a fiber switch and is managed in zones that are allocated to specific network interfaces. This has long been the fastest type of network storage connectivity option available to organizations, but it doesn't come cheap!

SAS Enclosures

Serial Attached SCSI is a way to access devices that employ a serial connection over locally connected cables. Unlike iSCSI and FC, there is no network connectivity in SAS enclosure solutions. The SAS technology supports earlier SCSI technologies, including printers, scanners, and other peripherals. SAS enclosures are large devices similar to a SAN that have multiple disks configured using different RAID levels to provide redundancy in the event of disk failure.

RAID

Redundant Array of Independent Disks consists of multiple disks grouped together. The array allows you to build out fault-tolerant disks and scale disks together to get high levels of performance. Multiple types of RAID exist that offer many different methods of performance and failover. The RAID technologies are the backbone of the internal workings of iSCSI, SAS, and Fiber Channel SAN enclosures. The following link provides information evaluating the types of RAID and when to use them, plus a breakdown of the different types in more detail: http://technet.microsoft.com/en-us/library/cc786889(v=WS.10).aspx.

SMB 3.0

Server Message Block (SMB) is a protocol specifically designed for file sharing and scaling out file shares or servers. It sits on top of TCP/IP but can utilize other network protocols. SMB is used for accessing user data and applications on resources that exist on a remote server. SMB has some specific requirements for setup:

- Windows Server 2012/2012 R2 failover cluster with a minimum of two nodes is required.
- File shares must be able to be created with the Continuous Availability property, which is the default.
- Files shares need to be on CSV volumes.
- Client computers accessing these resources must be Windows 8 or higher.
- Servers utilizing or accessing them must be Windows Server 2012 or higher.

The failover cluster servers running Windows Server 2012/2012 R2 have no extra requirements or roles that need to be installed. SMB 3.0 is enabled by default.

SMB features that are new to Windows Server 2012/2012 R2 include the following:

◆ SMB Transparent Failover—This capability allows you to transparently connect clients to another node seamlessly so that applications and storage are uninterrupted.

◆ SMB Scale Out—Using Cluster Shared Volumes (CSVs) you create a shared disk that all nodes in a cluster use via direct I/O to better serve network bandwidth and load on the file servers. This optimizes performance while giving consumers better access.

◆ SMB Direct—This uses NICs that have RDMA (Remote Direct Memory Access) capabilities and allows you to offload some of the CPU power usage and run higher speeds of data transfer with minimal latency.

These are just a few of the newer features available to SMB. There are many other components, such as SMB-specific PowerShell cmdlets, encryption, and performance counters.

An in-depth look at SMB and the new feature set can be found on TechNet at `http://technet.microsoft.com/en-us/library/hh831795.aspx`.

Windows Server 2012 R2 File and Storage Services

The File and Storage Services role in Windows Server, shown in Figure 11.1, provides all the services and functions you need to manage and create file servers and storage options with Windows Server.

FIGURE 11.1
File and Storage
Services

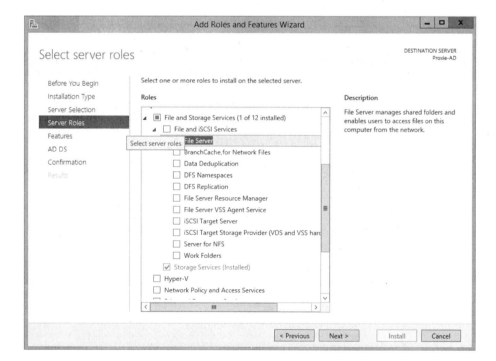

As you can see, the Storage Services component of this role is installed by default and cannot be uninstalled. The other components can be installed and removed as needed.

The File and iSCSI Services component of this role provides multiple other components that will help you manage your file shares, disk size, replication, and branch offices. The following list provides an overview of each of these components and what they offer to your file and storage capabilities with Windows Server 2012 R2:

File Server   This component allows you to manage shares and enable users to access files on this specific server in your organization's network.

BranchCache for Network Files   This component allows your BranchCache servers to have network file services.

Data Deduplication   This service helps you manage and save disk space by looking through your volume and making sure that only a single version of a file exists. Continuing with the earlier example of Sarah and her HR files, let's say that Matthew, an HR coworker of Sarah, saved a copy of a file somewhere else, thinking it wasn't available. Data Deduplication makes sure that only a single version of the specific file exists but that pointers are available so that Matthew can find his file.

DFS Namespaces   Distributed File System (DFS) allows you to set up a group of shared folders that could be hosted on other servers in your organization but appear under one name. Here's an example:

- Server 1—Has a share location named \\Server1\Files.

- Server 2—Has a share location named \\Server2\Stuff.

Using DFS Namespaces, you could locate both of these on \\Bigfirm\Shared.

DFS Replication   This feature enables you to synchronize shared folders across a WAN. It does not require DFS Namespaces but can be used with it.

File Server Resource Manager   File Server Resource Manager (FSRM) is a performance and monitoring tool that will give you more detailed reports on what's happening with your storage. You can build file policies, quotas, and classifications through FSRM as well.

File Server VSS Agent Service   You can use this service to copy applications and data that are stored on the specific server the role is on that is using Volume Shadow Copy Service (VSS). For more information on VSS you can review http://tinyurl.com/c11whatisvss.

iSCSI Target Server   This provides the tools and related services to manage your iSCSI servers.

iSCSI Target Storage Provider (VDS and VSS Hardware Providers)   Works similarly to the File Server VSS Agent Service, but it is specific to servers that are using iSCSI targets with VSS and the Virtual Disk Service (VDS).

Server for NFS   You can enable Network File System (NFS), which is used by Unix/Linux–based computers, so that shares on this installation of Windows Server 2012 R2 are visible to those clients.

Work Folders   This new feature of Windows Server 2012 R2 provides a simple way to manage files that exist on a bunch of different workstations and personal devices. The work folder will act as a host and synchronize the users' files to this location so they can access their files from inside or outside the network. This differs from File Server or DFS Namespaces in that these are client-hosted files. Going back to our example about Sarah and Matthew in the Human Resources department, Matthew and Sarah could be using Work Folders so that files saved in specific locations on their workstations would be synchronized with a file server and updated. If they are working on a project together but from different locations, those files are always available and synchronized.

You can install all of these components through the Server Manager dashboard, which provides details of each component and any required prerequisites. In the next section we will be defining clustering and helping you build out highly available services with failover clustering.

Clustering

In its most basic form, a *cluster* is two or more servers (physical or virtual) that are configured as a logical object and a single entity that manages shared resources and presents them to end users. Servers that are members of a cluster are known as *nodes*. The three most common types of clusters in Windows Server 2012 R2 are file server clusters, SQL clusters, and Hyper-V clusters.

A two-node cluster, for example, would be configured with nodes (physical or virtual), multiple network interface cards, and a shared storage solution such as iSCSI, SAN, or direct attached disks. The purpose of clustering is to allow a specific group of nodes to work together in a shared capacity with highly available resources. This gives your end users high availability for the workloads they need. Clustering provides the following benefits:

◆ The ability to survive a node crashing or going offline

◆ The ability to restart a virtual machine or survive a VM crash

◆ Zero downtime for any patching or maintenance to cluster nodes

◆ The ability to move and disperse the load of servers (such as guest VMs)

The scalability options go well beyond two host servers and can expand up to sixty-four nodes per cluster, with support for even cross-geographic locations. The complexities of geographically distributed clusters for availability and recovery are not the focus of this section, but they will become more important as you start to understand the capabilities of clustering.

Clusters are commonly used in high-capacity, high-visibility, and fault-tolerance scenarios. You design the cluster size and cluster type based on the specific needs of the service or business and on the resources to be hosted. In any scenario, always think of clustering as a solution for making your services, applications, and components more available to the end user.

Windows Server has grown as an operating system over the years, and the requirements for creating a cluster have always been the key to a successful cluster implementation. In the next section we'll take a look at these requirements.

Clustering Requirements

We'll spend some time examining the requirements for setting up a cluster and some of the best practices involved. But before we get into the hardware specifics, make sure to review the TechNet post "Validate Hardware for a Windows Server 2012 Failover Cluster," located at http://technet.microsoft.com/en-us/library/jj134244.aspx.

> ### Validation Information for Windows Server 2012 R2
>
> As of this writing, the Windows Server 2012 R2 validation information has not been published. The requirements stated in the article, "Validate Hardware for a Windows Server 2012 Failover Cluster," apply and will continue to be supported.

Here are at the requirements:

Servers Our team of experts, MVPs, and Microsoft all recommend that you use a set of hardware that contains the same or similar hardware items and configuration.

Network Multiple network interface cards should always be used. In addition, if your clusters are using iSCSI, you should separate network and normal communications traffic either by using physically different network hardware or by logically segmenting the traffic using VLANs on the switches.

Storage If you're utilizing Serial Attached SCSI or Fiber Channel in a cluster, all items should be identical, including HBA drivers and firmware. You should not use multiple versions of firmware or drivers even if the manufacture supports it.

Shared Storage Shared storage is required. With Windows Server 2012 (and R2) you can use shared storage that is local via SAS to the server, along with SMB 3.0 file shares for all of your cluster needs.

Storage Spaces If you plan to use Serial Attached SCSI, Windows Server 2012 and Server 2012 R2 support Storage Spaces. We will be discussing Storage Spaces in Chapter 12, but here are some of the basics in regard to Storage Spaces and clusters:

- You need a minimum of three physical SAS disk drives.

- The drives require a minimum of 4 GB of capacity.

- These drives cannot be startup disks; they need to be dedicated to the storage pool.

- When you configure storage spaces, clusters support only simple or mirror types.

Clustering Functionality

Clustering is a mix of software and hardware, and it can be hosted on physical servers or virtual machines. Windows Server 2012 R2 has the components and tools built in for deploying your clusters, including a handy prerequisites wizard to validate that you have all the components and configurations in place to successfully set up a cluster.

Many improvements have been made to clustering since the Windows Server 2008 R2 version. Clustering is affected by these operating system improvements, but its features are located in the same places and have the same capabilities from prior versions, but with much improvement, such as cluster scalability. Windows Server 2012 and Server 2012 R2 have an increased scalability offering in the Hyper-V Failover Clustering feature, now supporting up to 64 nodes and 8,000 VMs per cluster.

Microsoft has also introduced a concept called *continuous availability*. This includes network interface card teaming, support for Cluster-Aware Updating, and Scale-Out File Servers (SOFS). Continuous availability is end-to-end monitoring, with options to monitor up and down the entire cluster stack.

Cluster-Aware Updating Cluster-Aware Updating is a service supported by the newly revamped Windows Server Update Services (see Chapter 31, "Patch Management," for more information). This feature will move your workloads or virtual machines to another node in the cluster, process the update (rebooting if needed), and then move the workloads right back and proceed to the next node in the cluster.

Using Hyper-V Virtual Disks as Shared Storage Considered to be possibly one of the best features of Windows Server 2012 and 2012 R2 is the ability to utilize your Hyper-V virtual disks (in VHDX format only) as shared storage for guest-based clustering, greatly expanding scale-out and availability inside the virtual infrastructure, and for building out scale-out file servers. Most important is the ability to use your VHDX files for clustering without a SAN.

A well-implemented failover-clustering solution will maximize business productivity and hone in on service levels. A resilient datacenter is one that has resource pools of computing power, storage, and network resources. In building a failover-clustering environment with Windows Server 2012 R2, you begin at the physical layer, starting with the network. Figure 11.2 shows an individual server with two physical NICs and multiple virtual adapters.

FIGURE 11.2
Physical and virtual NICs

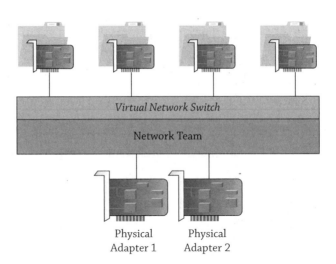

With continuous availability you get not only improved reliability but also improved performance. With this design you team multiple connects to increase the throughput available to the operating system and fault tolerance if an NIC port fails, a cable is pulled, or a physical card goes offline.

Cluster Shared Volumes

Cluster Shared Volumes (CSV) is a component of Failover Clustering and was first introduced in Windows Server 2008 R2. CSVs were designed specifically for virtualization. Their basic use was to simplify storage for virtual machines. If you do not use a CSV with your Hyper-V servers, then your disk can be accessed by only one node at a time. Configuring a CSV allows a common shared disk to be used, simplifies the storage-management needs for Hyper-V, and allows multiple VHDs to exist. You can also minimize downtime and disconnections with fault detection and recovery over the additional connection paths between each node in your cluster (via SAN).

The design of the CSV simplifies storage so that multiple VMs can access the same disk at the same time, which obviously doesn't require as many disk drives to be created. You will gain other abilities through this model; when you are doing a live migration of your virtual machine, the shared volumes create multiple connections between the cluster nodes and the shared disk. So if a connection is lost, the migration can continue via another connection. To utilize CSVs you need only use NTFS partitions; no special settings or configurations are required beyond that.

In Windows Server 2012, CSVs allow multiple nodes to have read/write access to the same disk. The advantage that you gain from this is the ability to quickly move any of the volumes you have from any node in a cluster to another node in the cluster. Dismounting and remounting a volume are greatly improved, which helps simplify managing large numbers of disks in your clusters. Windows Server 2012 also made some significant changes in its advanced capabilities, such as BitLocker volumes, removal of the external authentication dependencies support for storage spaces, and major improvements in validation of Hyper-V to CSV functionally for performance increases. In Windows Server 2012, there is no automatic rebalancing of node assignment for your disks, but in Windows Server 2012 R2, CSV ownership is balanced across all nodes. Previously, all disks could be owned by one or two nodes in, say, a 12-node cluster, but with Windows Server 2012 R2, the disks are evenly disturbed across the 12 nodes. If a node goes down, the cluster automatically starts the process of rebalancing the disk placement. By moving away from a single coordinator node to a distributed node, support for Scale-Out File Servers is much more effective and the risk of failure dramatically drops.

In Windows Server 2012 R2, CSVs have better diagnostics and interoperability than in previous versions. You can view the CSVs on a node-by-node basis to see if I/O is set up to be redirected and the reason for it. Windows Server 2012 R2 has a new PowerShell cmdlet, `Get-ClusterSharedVolumeState`. For interoperability, Windows Server 2012 R2 adds support for the following features:

- Resilient File System (ReFS)
- Disk Deduplication
- Parity storage spaces and tiered storage spaces

The growth and acceptance of virtualization in organizations of all sizes shows that the way clustering is being used today versus even five years ago has dramatically changed. Many datacenters today are building out large-scale clusters. Microsoft has been working diligently on increasing the resiliency of CSVs as well as expanding their utilization beyond just for VMs and extending it to Scale-Out File Servers (SOFS) specifically to shared VHDX. Scale-Out File Servers are discussed in Chapter 13, "Files, Folders, and Basic Shares." The major changes since Windows 2008 R2 in CSVs expand the possibilities for what you can use them for, as well as the scenarios and storage options for your clusters.

Clusters and Virtualization

This section focuses on the improvements in Windows 2012 R2. Since there has been just one year between the releases of Windows Server 2012 and Windows Server 2012 R2, we'll treat them as one release. The features that are specific to Windows Server 2012 R2 will be noted as such. First, let's talk about the new features and how guest (virtual machine) clusters have been given some great options:

Shared VHD   One of the new features is shared VHD (virtual hard disk) for guest clusters, giving you the ability in your Hyper-V environment to use .vhdx as your shared storage solution.

Virtual Machine Drain on Shutdown   The VM drain on shutdown enables the Hyper-V host to start draining a specific node and migrate all of the VMs to a new host. This will also happen if the VM shuts down during an outage.

VM Network Health Monitoring   VM network health monitoring allows you to live migrate VMs if even if a disconnect occurs on your virtual network. Additional new features pertain to things like the Cluster dashboard and node health detection that gets fed into that dashboard.

Live Migrations   Previous to Windows Server 2012, to do a live migration you needed to have a shared storage solution in place that you were leveraging for live migration with no downtime. Windows Server 2012 allows you to move the VMs from host to host with or without a cluster, and with the addition of SMB 3.0 file shares, the files you have set up for this don't need to sit on a SAN. You can do live migrations from VMs that are on local disks attached to the server.

One of the most important factors to understand in clustering is the *quorum*—what it does, why you need one, and what improvements have been made to Windows Server 2012 R2 that improve the quorum's resiliency. In the next subsection we'll explain what a quorum is so that you can gain a deeper understanding of its use in clustering.

Understanding Quorums

According to *Webster's New World College Dictionary, Third Edition*, a quorum is "the minimum number of members required to be present at an assembly or meeting before it can validly proceed to transact business." This definition holds true for the use of the term *quorum* as it pertains to a cluster. The best way to start gathering the technical needs for your cluster is to understand what a quorum is and what it's used for.

The quorum has been around since the inception of clustering and has been a major component and an unsung hero of sorts. In each revision of Windows Server, improvements to the quorum have been made to bring us to where we are now with extremely advanced quorum capabilities in Windows Server 2012. *The quorum is the setting in the failover that determines the number of failures a cluster can have or sustain and keep the cluster (services) online.* Once you have exceeded the quorum's threshold, that cluster goes offline.

The cluster does not count the nodes and resource numbers, so it doesn't look at the current capacity and decided to shut the services down. Think of it like this: There are 100 nodes in a cluster; that does not mean that if 50 of them go down, the cluster shuts off when it reaches 51 nodes down. The cluster is completely unaware of the server count or what resources are being over- or underutilized. Instead, the responsibility of the quorum is to help prevent an anomaly called *split-brain*, where two servers in a cluster are attempting to write the same file or take ownership of the same resources, potentially corrupting them.

The job of the quorum in this capacity is to prevent the problem from happening and essentially decide whether the cluster can or should continue to function, stopping a problematic node's service until it can communicate properly with the rest of the clusters. When the issue is resolved, the quorum will allow the problematic node to rejoin the cluster group and restart all the needed services. The quorum decision is done through votes; each node in a cluster has a single vote, and the cluster itself can be configured as a witness vote. The witness can be a file share or a disk (as a best practice from the Cluster team at Microsoft, you should always configure a cluster with an odd number of members). The odd number of nodes gives you the ability to have an even number of quorum votes, and the odd resource can be the witness for outages. Adding this additional node ensures that if half the cluster goes down, the witness node will keep it alive.

Highly Available Storage

Having a highly available virtual infrastructure is a major factor in the success of your HA plan. Considerations for storage options and how to connect the storage to your virtual machines so that they run uninterrupted when hardware fails are imperative. Design considerations include how to store your VMs and what kinds of components are required to provide the benefits for fault tolerance. The following is a list of highly available storage options:

Hardware Most important is hardware for the storage, whether SAN or iSCSI or JBOD (just a bunch of disks).

Power You need stable power and redundant power supplies. If you can provide secondary power, that is a plus.

Disks HA storage should be able to tolerate a disk failure and continue to meet your needs.

Storage Network Hardware Creating a highly available hardware solution usually involves removing all the single points of failure, including the storage network components such as HBAs or network adapters.

Storage Spaces This new storage virtualization feature introduced in Windows Server 2012 allows you to use USB, Fiber Channel, iSCSI, SAS, and SATA attached disks to create a virtual disk that can span all of them. In Windows Server 2012 R2, when you create these virtual disks they use mirroring or parity for protection, which allows for a disk failure without losing your data. The important part to understand is that this is best utilized by spanning your creation of storage pools across heterogeneous disk types.

Multipath Input/Output Multipath Input/Output (MPIO) is a Windows feature that allows your Fiber Channel and iSCSI storage to be accessible via multiple pathways in order for a client like Hyper-V to have HA as it accesses your storage solution. By having multiple paths, MPIO sees both storage locations as a single device, and it natively supports failover. MPIO does all of the work for you; if something goes offline, it will handle the immediate rerouting over the other connection.

Network Teaming and Fault Tolerance If you are looking to connect Hyper-V hosts to storage, it is highly recommended that you set up the host servers with multiple network cards and pathways. You always want to leverage redundancy with network teaming on any of your clustered resources, and when you use SMB/SMB Multichannel it will give you the best available bandwidth.

Storage Spaces

Storage Spaces is considered one of the great new features of Windows Server 2012 and Server 2012 R2. The main advantage is the ability to manage a bunch of disks as a single virtual disk drive. The virtual disk type dictates how data is written across the physical disks.

Currently there are three choices:

Simple   As the name implies, this is a simple stripe set without parity. Consider this closer to a RAID 0. A simple layout provides no redundancy, so any disk failure can cause problems with data access. It is used primarily to increase throughput and maximize capacity.

Mirror   This is a RAID 1 configuration that increases reliability by using two disks (for example), which allows one disk to fail without causing interruption. The major drawback is the loss of disk space because one of the disks is used as a copy (mirror) of the other.

Parity   This is similar to a RAID 5 configuration; it is a striped set of data across disks with distributed parity. By striping data and information across multiple disks, it increases the reliability. As with RAID 5, you need a minimum of three disks.

If you are unfamiliar with disk RAID, I recommend you look at the following site for full information on the background of RAID and RAID levels: `http://en.wikipedia.org/wiki/RAID`. Storage Spaces has three basic components:

Physical Disks   If you are leveraging physical disks for your storage pools, here are the requirements:

- ◆ Minimum of one physical disk.

- ◆ Two physical disks to create a resilient mirror virtual disk.

- ◆ Three physical disks for resilient mirroring with parity.

- ◆ Five physical disks for three-way mirroring.

- ◆ All hard disks must be blank (unformatted).

- ◆ iSCSI, SATA, SAS, SCSI, and USB are supported disk types.

Storage Pool   A storage pool consists of one or more physical disks that you are using to create a virtual disk. An unformatted blank disk can be added into a storage pool at any time.

Virtual Disks   These are considered the same as physical disks from an application or user perspective. The benefit is that virtual disks are far more flexible, and they have the resiliency of physical disks with built-in mirroring.

Storage Spaces offers different types of provisioning options that determine how much space is being used and how to allocate to the virtual disks. You can define the performance type and what you are willing to utilize to achieve it. Many design factors are involved in an increase or decrease in performance, such as disk speed, size, and type. Having a great plan and design will increase the performance of your system.

The provisioning type is determined by how space is allocated to the disk and your performance choices:

Thin   Thin provisioning allows you to overallocate space while using only the amount of space your files need. It provides flexibility but does reduce performance since the storage has to move and pull disk space from the pool as the size increases.

Fixed   Fixed is reserved targeted space. For example, if you define 40 GB, that is the maximum that the virtual disk gets. It cannot be larger than the disk space of the pool. You can extend the fixed size by adding more disks to your storage pool, and the only performance impact you will see is if you add disks and extend an already defined disk. It takes a little resource time to spin all that up.

Clustering Inside Virtual Machines

When you develop your clustering strategy for printers, file shares, or Hyper-V, you are giving the infrastructure a highly available solution, one that can grow and you can move your critical systems into. To the support of Windows Server 2012 R2 and guest-based clustering, you are adding the next level of HA and increasing the speed of recovery from a system failure. It's not always the hardware that requires high availability; in many cases the software is causing a problem, resulting from memory leaks, software updates, or configuration changes. When you run your cluster-aware applications as virtual workloads, the failover time and the integration with many of the new continuous availability workloads become more enticing because consumers experience no interruption.

To understand the workloads that are capable of this type of clustering, you need to remember the golden rule: If a workload is made for clustering or recommended to cluster for HA or disaster recovery (DR) purposes, it can work in a guest cluster. Microsoft has made the Windows Server 2012 and Server 2012 R2 workloads aware of this virtual guest cluster, in such areas as these:

- Continuously available file shares
- DHCP server
- SQL Server 2012—always on
- Exchange Server
- SharePoint
- Files shares (standard file sharing)
- Print services

To use this technology you utilize a model enabled in Windows Server 2012 R2: a shared VHDX. Windows Server 2012 introduced the VHDX format, which addressed the storage, data protection, and performance needs on large disks. When you create virtual guest clusters, you are attaching a VHDX to a SCSI controller for your VM, enabling sharing to create a connection, and presenting the VHDX as an SAS drive. So you are given the option of building out an infrastructure that doesn't necessarily require iSCSI, Fibre Channel SAN, or block-level storage, but you are getting to use SMB 3.0.

Now that you understand some of the basic building blocks, you can take your knowledge of the shared storage and clustering capabilities of Windows Server 2012 R2 into the next section and dive into setup.

Setting Up a Cluster

In this section we will walk through the basic steps of setting up a host-based cluster. For the purpose of this example we will be creating a two-node cluster and configuring it for file shares. Clustering file shares is a great starting place to introduce you to managing a cluster. The requirements are very simple. We'll take a basic need in any enterprise and provide immediate high availability.

To successfully set this up, you need to work through each of the following sections.

Cluster Configuration

The lab we are going to use for this example is very simple. We have two servers running Windows Server 2012 R2. The servers are named as follows:

Server 1 = Cluster1

◆ Local storage = C:\ drive 30 GB

◆ NIC #1 (primary) IP address: 192.168.1.17

◆ NIC #2 (secondary) IP address: 192.1681.18

Server 2 = Cluster2

◆ Local storage = C:\ drive 30 GB

◆ NIC #1 (primary) IP address: 192.168.1.19

◆ NIC #2 (secondary) IP address: 192.1681.20

The cluster for this example is named DemoCluster, and its IP address is 192.168.1.21.

To examine the basic options of clustering we're going to focus on clustering file services, but we'll spend more time going over how to set up the cluster service on two nodes, step by step.

When prepping to build out a similar example cluster, the steps should be fairly straightforward, and hopefully you will see the value in getting your organization set up and using cluster services. In regard to the quorum that we discussed previously, I have created a share on a separate server; you can utilize a file share as the quorum, as we discussed. The share will be located on the Active Directory domain controller for this example, BF1. The share \\ BF1\#Cluster will be utilized for the witness.

The two servers have two physical NICs. Ideally you would have a minimum of three NICs in a production environment or six if possible. You want to separate the three types of network needs. If you have five or more NICs available, then you can team two NICs for the primary services. Remember, for every NIC you use, you should always use a static IP address. DHCP is supported with clustering, but it's not ideal or advised in most scenarios. The following list is a typical role configuration for NICs:

NIC role 1: cluster management and storage—Do not set the default gateway.

NIC role 2: client traffic (for accessing VMs or apps)

◆ Needs the default gateway

◆ Needs DNS

Once you have set up the NICs and are ready to move on, the next step is taking the host names (rename the servers to something descriptive of your clusters) and joining them to Active Directory. As shown previously, the servers we are using in this example are named Cluster1 and Cluster2.

After you have joined these devices to an Active Directory domain, you need to make sure each cluster node has Remote Desktop and Remote Management installed, and since you are going to be creating a file server cluster, setting up the File Server role is required.

Storage

Before we set up the cluster itself, let's do a quick review of the storage options of clusters. You have several choices, and since it's a requirement, you need to figure out what type of storage solution you want to use. Typical options for shared storage are these:

◆ iSCSI SAN

◆ Fibre Channel SAN

◆ SAS enclosures

◆ SMB 3.0 shared folders on Windows Server 2012

We discussed each of these storage components previously in this chapter. One of the great benefits of the storage options with Windows Server 2012 R2 is that all of the storage solutions used today are supported, so you can leverage the hardware you already have. There's no need to run off and change your storage infrastructure just yet. Windows Server 2012 R2 provides the option, if you haven't invested in a specific storage solution, to build it out with SMB 3.0. As discussed earlier in the chapter, SMB 3.0 was first introduced in Windows Server 2012 with Scale-Out File Servers and Hyper-V in mind, and it was the start of what is now considered continuous availability. You can read up on SMB 3.0 and see ways to leverage it in your organization at the following link: `http://tinyurl.com/c11SMB30`.

Adding the First Node in Your Cluster

One of the first things you need to do is install the Failover Clustering feature, and you have a couple options for doing this. As noted many times in this book, you can use PowerShell to install it. You can find information on installing any Windows feature with PowerShell at the following link: `http://tinyurl.com/c11ClusterInstall`. For this feature, enter the following command from an administrative PowerShell console:

```
Install-WindowsFeature -Name Failover-Clustering
```

You can include the `-IncludeManagmentTools` switch at the end of the command if you have not installed the administrative tools already.

For this example we will be going through Server Manager and adding the File Server role and the Failover Clustering feature. Follow the basic prompts; since the wizard is pretty basic and doesn't ask you any questions when you add the feature, we will jump right to configuring your cluster. If you need assistance in adding roles and features, please see Chapter 7, "Active Directory in Windows Server 2012 R2."

Once the Failover Clustering feature is installed, it will appear on the Apps section of your Start screen, as shown in Figure 11.3.

FIGURE 11.3
Apps section of
the Start screen

Double-click Failover Cluster Manager to open it. As you can see in Figure 11.4, all of the major components you need to create, validate, and manage your cluster are listed in a single window.

FIGURE 11.4
Failover Cluster
Manager

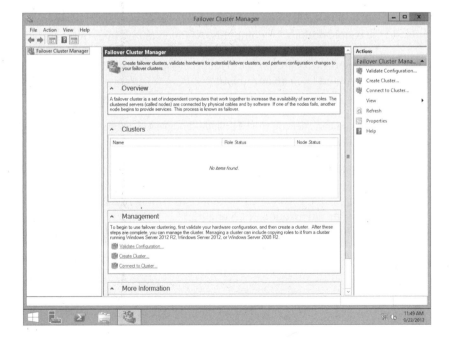

Take some time to examine the console; expand the More Information section and find some of the basic topics on the web that are updated in the console. Since the web links in the console are updated frequently, you can find links to any major changes or updates there. Exploring the cluster console is very important if you have never done this before.

The next step is to create a new cluster; you do this by following these steps:

1. Select Create Cluster by either right-clicking Failover Cluster Manager from the column on the left or selecting Create Cluster from the Actions menu, as shown in Figure 11.5.

FIGURE 11.5
Choose Create Cluster.

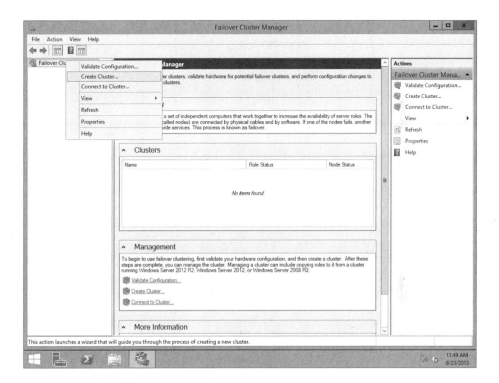

You will see the Before You Begin screen, and it will give you the basics you need to complete this process.

2. Click Next.

You now need to enter the name of the server you want to be a part of this cluster.

3. Enter **Cluster1** as the name of the server (as shown in Figure 11.6), or you can browse and select the server you are using for your setup.

4. Click Next.

When you select the server, you will be prompted with a validation screen; this is to check that the server meets all the requirements.

FIGURE 11.6

Adding a server
to the cluster

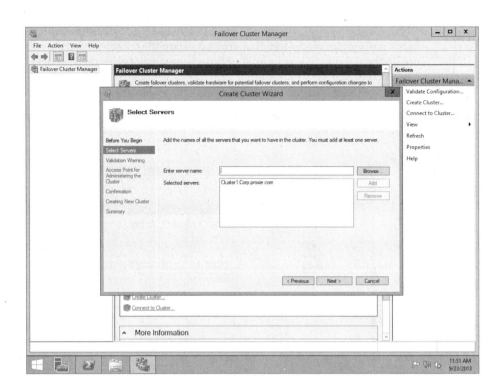

5. You can select No, but it is always recommended to select Yes and let the validation run.

   The cluster-validation process will walk you through a few steps starting with the Before You Begin screen.

   Next is the testing option you want to run against this server cluster. Running all tests is the default and is recommended at minimum for your first node in the cluster.

6. Click Next to accept the default.

7. Confirm your information about which server to test, and click Next to run the validation.

   Figure 11.7 shows the Validate a Configuration Wizard running on a large list of components required to have a successful cluster.

8. Once the validation has completed, quickly review the Summary screen of the wizard, as shown in Figure 11.8.

9. Optionally, you can click the View Report button to open a web form that lets you further examine the items.

FIGURE 11.7
Validate a
Configuration
Wizard

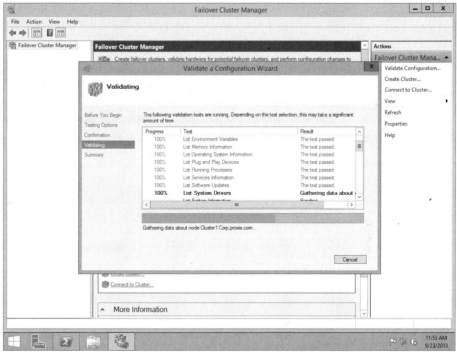

FIGURE 11.8
Validation
Report

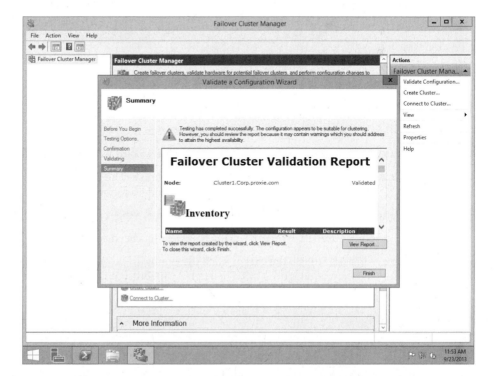

Figure 11.9 shows the Inventory screen of this report. As you can see, the items under Name are hyperlinks that will take you to detailed information about items in the report.

FIGURE 11.9
Validation Report Inventory screen

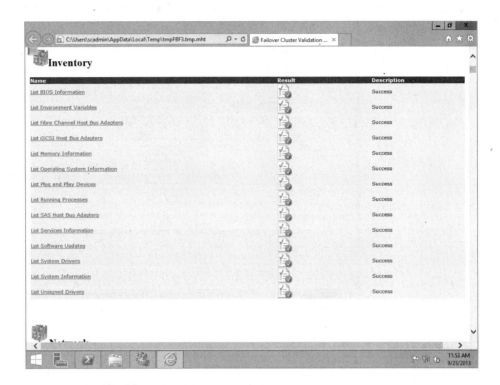

10. Now that you have added the server for nomination into the cluster and gone through the validation process, you need to give your cluster a name and IP address. We are using the name **DemoCluster**, as shown in Figure 11.10. You will use the cluster name to connect to and administer the cluster and nodes referenced by this central IP address.

11. When prompted, confirm the cluster; the wizard will add the brand-new cluster.

12. Once you see the Summary page, click Finish. The Failover Cluster Manager screen will list the newly created cluster with one node, as shown in Figure 11.11.

13. Now expand DemoCluster on the left side of the screen and select Nodes.

    In Figure 11.12 you can see that Cluster1 has been added as a node and is available.

14. To add a role to the cluster, click the Configure Role link on the Summary of Cluster page, as shown in Figure 11.13. The High Availability Wizard will appear.

FIGURE 11.10
Entering a cluster
name

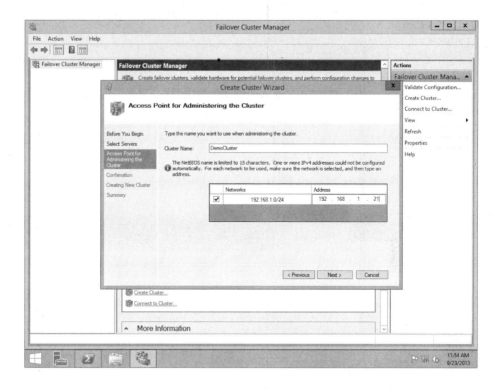

FIGURE 11.11
Creating a cluster
name

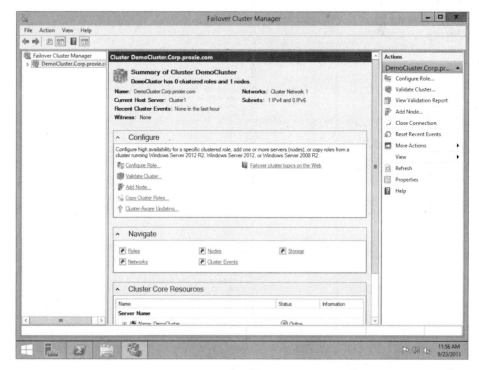

FIGURE 11.12
Viewing newly
added nodes

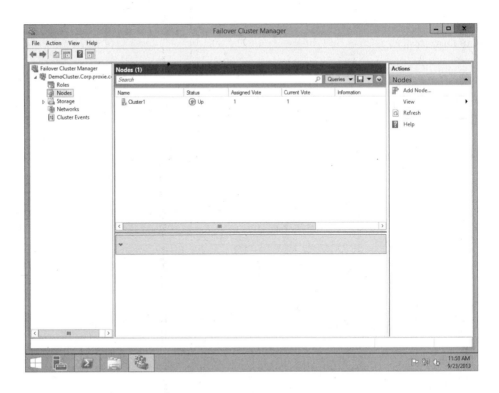

FIGURE 11.13
Starting the High
Availability Wizard

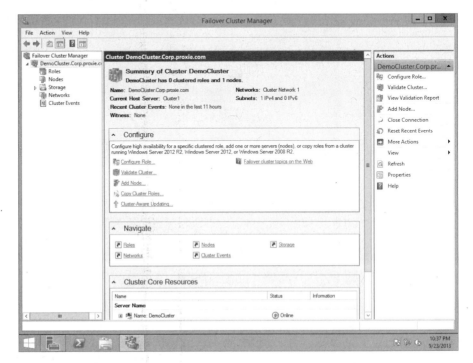

OPTIONS FOR ROLES

Each of the roles that you select will require different options and have its own set of precondi-
tions. I recommend that if you are going to start looking at these different workloads, you review
all the information at `http://blogs.msdn.com/b/clustering/`. This is the primary site for
the Microsoft Cluster team, and it has a ton of resources on each type of cluster workload you
could want to set up.

15. Click Next to bypass the Before You Begin screen, so you can select the specific role to
make highly available.

16. In the High Availability Wizard, select File Server, as shown in Figure 11.14, and click Next.

FIGURE 11.14

Selecting a role

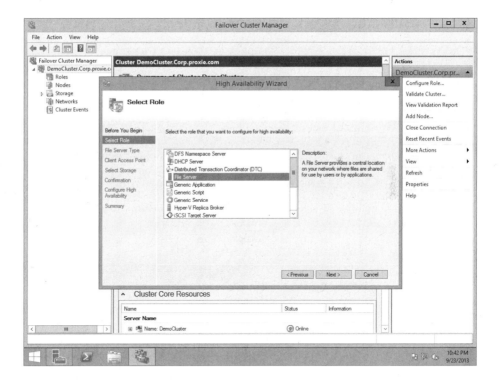

17. Choose the type of file server you want to build out. As shown in Figure 11.15, the options are these:

◆ "File Server for general use"—for basic SMB and NFS file shares

◆ "Scale-Out File Server for application data"—for DFS and file servers that will span multiple nodes

The next few steps are similar to setting up your cluster. You will start by creating a name that the clients will use to access this file cluster. For our example, we will use **DemoFile**.

FIGURE 11.15
File Server Type
screen

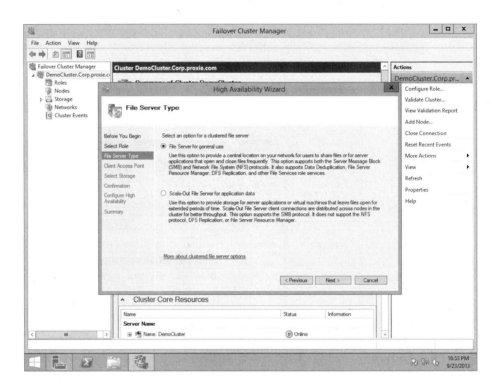

18. Enter the IP address you want the file cluster to be associated with. In our example we will use 192.1681.22.

19. Select the storage you are using for your cluster, click Next, and confirm your configuration.

Once you have gone through the remaining steps and reviewed the summary, the highly available file server will appear under Roles in your Failover Cluster Manager screen, as shown in Figure 11.16.

FIGURE 11.16
File Server
clustered role

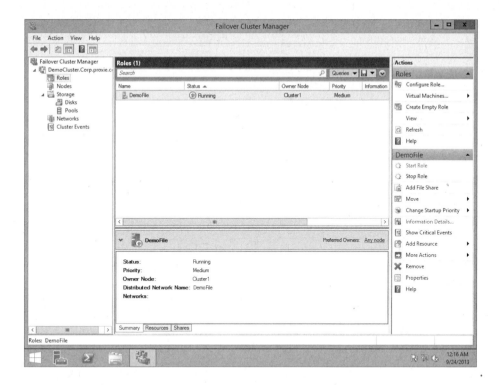

Adding a Second Node to the Cluster

One thing that many people skip before adding the second node in the cluster is validating that the primary node is active and working. So make sure you check through the following before moving onto this next step.

1. Look at the Cluster1 server and make sure it isn't showing any errors or doesn't have a red check mark through it.

2. Validate your storage and that you can confirm connections to the servers.

3. Validate your networking and that all connections are there and showing as connected.

4. Rerun the validation tests and get a report to review all options.

   Some warnings may appear, and you should take the time to evaluate each one and make sure it isn't going to affect you as you add secondary (or more) nodes to this cluster. Each error or warning the report provides will give you links and more detailed information so that you can successfully take care of any issue that is there.

Now onto adding the additional node to your cluster: the important part that may seem obvious is that now you are providing your host services failover. It is exciting to have your first cluster up and running, but without additional nodes it's just a lonely service running on your server. The best place to start is the Failover Cluster Management console; in the Configure section you will see the option Add Node. This is shown in Figure 11.17.

FIGURE 11.17
Add Node option

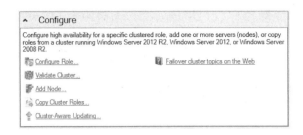

1. Select Add Node and the wizard will start.

2. Enter the server name; for our example it is CLUSTER2.

   You will be prompted again for validation, which will start the validation wizard.

3. For at least the first two nodes in a cluster you should choose "Run all tests."

   Once the validation is completed, you will get another Validation Report, similar to the one shown in Figure 11.9.

4. Verify that everything is in an acceptable state and finalize the additional node.

5. Finally, look under the Failover Cluster Manager\DemoCluster\Nodes to see the two cluster nodes you have added.

   As you can see in Figure 11.18, both of our nodes are showing a status of Up.

FIGURE 11.18
Cluster nodes
status

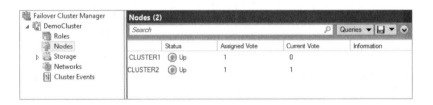

Now that you have both nodes set up, your cluster can provide failover to any of the workloads you wish to support.

You may have noticed in Figure 11.18 two other columns next to Status:

◆ Assigned Vote

◆ Current Vote

Windows Server 2012 R2 provides an advanced quorum configuration option where you can add or evict quorum votes node by node. Out of the box all nodes are assigned a vote. You may decide to remove votes from specific nodes to help with disaster recovery solutions. The most common situation is when you have a geocluster and you want to remove the votes from your recovery site; if you consider doing this, refer to Microsoft's guide on quorum considerations for DR found here: http://tinyurl.com/c11ClusterDR.

Setting up a cluster infrastructure is usually not complex, although it can be depending on your needs and the services you wish to provide with your cluster. The more services, nodes, and sites you add, the more complex the setup becomes, but they are all worth it. The cluster hosts and guest capabilities will make all of your organization's resources highly available, scalable, and recoverable in case of a site failure.

In the next section we will spend some time on guest clustering, why you might want to add it, and how Windows Server 2012 R2 makes things even better!

Setting Up a Guest-based Cluster

As we have mentioned a few times in this section, guest-based clustering means extending the cluster services to inside the virtual machine layer. The idea is to allow your VMs to have high-availability options inside the VM, so you can have an HA application or service sitting on top of a clustered set of hosts. You are now moving into an extremely highly available datacenter, giving all the applications physical or virtual continuous availability.

What can you cluster in your virtual guests? Anything that is supported by Windows clustering will work. You can include all of your major services and common Windows Server workloads such as these:

◆ File shares and services including DFS

◆ DHCP Server

◆ SQL Server

◆ Exchange Server

◆ SharePoint

◆ Internet Information Server

In Windows Server 2008 R2, guest clusters supported the standard OS health detection, application health, and application mobility options. At that point there was no support for VM mobility, so in case of a failover you would have to migrate the VM to another host and spin it up. Windows Server 2012 made great moves in recovery so that guest-level HA recovery is now possible. The clustered service will reboot the VMs if needed, and at the host level if recovery is necessary, the VM will fail over to another node.

Basically, the Role Health Service will detect a failure and automatically recover by moving the VM role to a different VM to allow the OS or applications to update. Now you can connect your VMs to all different types of storage, so you can connect to a SAN for shared storage via Fiber Channel with virtual fiber adapters.

As the health services moves into the monitoring stages, it will accept a first failure, and the applications will move to other nodes. A second or third failure will cause the cluster host to shut down and restart the VM. Configuring this is very simple and requires only that you look at the clustered service properties, set the second and third failures, and set up your application health monitors through the clustered service.

Setting up your guest-based cluster is similar to setting up a host-based cluster in that the components have the same requirements except that these can be virtual. Here are the considerations:

1. Build out a minimum of two virtual machines.

2. Create two virtual network switches based on your requirements.

   If you need to access additional resources, you will need to create additional networks that are specifically external virtual switches.

3. Connect the associated storage solution to your VMs, such as your virtual Fiber Channel, iSCSI, or SMB storage.

4. Install Windows Server 2012 R2 on your virtual machine.

5. Install the Failover Clustering feature on each of the VMs in that cluster.

6. Connect your network and storage to the VMs.

7. Run the Validate Cluster Configuration Wizard and make sure you get a positive report.

Configuring your guest-based clusters is essentially the same as configuring your host cluster; you want to connect and configure all the same settings with the exception of the Hyper-V role, because these are all Hyper-V guests. If you are feeling more knowledgeable now that you have gone through this introduction on shared storage and clustering, we highly recommend looking at the Clustering and High-Availability blog on TechNet at `http://blogs .msdn.com/b/clustering/`.

The Bottom Line

Use the available storage options for clustering.   With the release of Windows Server 2012 R2, many more storage options are available for your clustering and high-availability solutions.

    Master It   You want to build out a JBOD solution and need the most effective type of disk capacity. The failover doesn't matter as much as space and speed. What technology should you consider?

Use quorums to help in clustering.   A quorum is "the minimum number of members required to be present at an assembly or meeting before it can validly proceed to transact business." This definition holds true for the use of a quorum in clustering.

    Master it   You have chosen to deploy an odd-numbered cluster with five nodes, and you will use one node as a file share witness for quorum. Once the cluster is up and running, you host an application. But after the install the application has a major memory leak and starts seizing up the servers and shutting them down. How many nodes will go down before the cluster is completely offline?

Build out host and guest clusters.   Clustering is a mix of software and hardware and can be hosted on physical servers or virtual machines. Windows Server 2012 R2 has the components and tools built in to help you deploy your clusters, including a handy prerequisites wizard to validate that you have all the components and configurations in place to successfully set up a cluster.

    Master it   When planning your host- and guest-based clusters, excluding the Hyper-V role, what is the difference between the two in setting up a cluster?

Chapter 12

Windows 2012 R2 Storage: Storage Spaces, SANish Abilities, and Better Tools

For those who have had some time to play with Storage Spaces in Windows Server 2012, I bet you are excited about the new changes in R2. But before we discuss them, let's do a quick recap of Storage Spaces for those who are new to this feature.

Storage Spaces was introduced in Windows Server 2012 as a native feature. Remember, this is not RAID but is something new that was designed for full-blown enterprise use. The basic function of Storage Spaces is to allow you to take just a bunch of disks (JBOD) and configure them in a pool. From here you can create virtual disks (the actual storage space) and volumes with fault tolerances of various degrees. This type of configuration gives you great flexibility.

Imagine not having to invest in a large, expensive storage area network (SAN) or in the specialized training that your administrators would need to configure and maintain it. A core goal of Storage Spaces is to provide a cost-effective solution for mission-critical storage. Storage spaces and pools are designed to grow on demand. Here is a list of just some of the features in Storage Spaces that are included in Windows Server 2012:

- ◆ Just-in-time provisioning
- ◆ Fault resiliency (mirroring and parity)
- ◆ Intelligent error correction
- ◆ Multi-tenancy support
- ◆ Integration with CSV to allow scale-out scenarios

In this chapter, you will learn to:

- ◆ Create a storage pool on a virtual disk
- ◆ Create additional storage on a virtual disk
- ◆ Use deduplication techniques to reduce file size

What's New in Windows Server 2012 R2 Storage?

Since this book is about Windows Server 2012 R2, we'll now tell you what's new in storage. Microsoft has included technology in Storage Spaces that you previously saw only in expensive storage arrays. The following sections detail the new technology.

Tiered Storage Spaces

There are several classifications of disks in today's storage world, including Serial Advance Technology Attachment (SATA), Serial Attached SCSI (SAS), Solid State Drive (SSD), and Fibre Channel. Choosing the correct storage for the job is essential. For example, if you need a file server, SSD is not a good choice. SSD was designed for speed, not capacity, and because file servers generally need capacity and not speed, SATA, which was designed for capacity rather than speed, in this case may be a better match.

In Windows Server 2012 R2 you can have a maximum of two storage tiers, essentially a fast tier and a slow tier. These tiers use SSD in the fast tier and SATA in the slow tier automatically. The really clever thing here is that an administrator doesn't have to decide up front where to place the data. The Storage Tiers Management Service will automatically analyze the data on your disks in slices of 1 MB. It has two categories for assignment: *hot spots* and *cold spots*. Hot spots are areas of the data that are accessed frequently; the assumption here is that since this is active data, it is a "hot topic." Cold spots are the opposite: data that has not been accessed regularly. After the analysis, hot spots will be promoted to the SSD tier, and any identified cold spots will be assigned to the SATA tier. The analysis happens daily at 1:00 a.m. by default, but you can configure it if you like; see Figure 12.1. But if a file needs to be on the fast tier all the time, the administrator can "pin" the file to the fast tier.

FIGURE 12.1
Storage Tiers Management service in the Task Scheduler

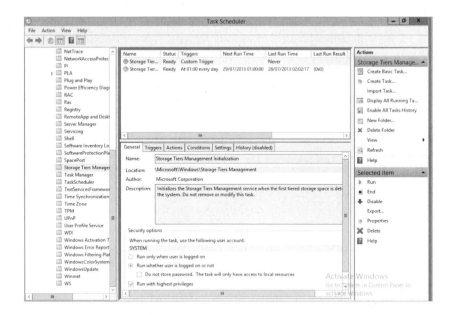

Write-back Cache

Write-back cache refers to how data is written to disk. Data is written to the cache first and will be stored there until it is about to be overwritten; at this point it will be flushed to disk and committed. In general, writing and storing data in cache gives better performance and is considered another type of memory. If an app is writing to the cache, it can hand off its I/O handle quickly and get back to other tasks. Certain workloads traditionally don't like write-back caching because when the app writes data, it must be written to disk to avoid corruption. Hyper-V, for example, requires write-through. Tiered storage can be used in conjunction with a virtual disk (not VHD/VHDX in relation to Hyper-V and virtual machines in this case, but a virtual disk from a Storage Spaces perspective) to absorb any spikes in writes. The fast tier can then be used to overcome the spike and allow Hyper-V to use write-back caching.

Parallelized Repair

When a disk fails in a traditional RAID set, if you have a *hot spare* (a disk that can instantly take over the job of a failed disk in a RAID set), this hot spare will kick in and the RAID array will start rebuilding the data on this disk. A performance impact on the disk subsystem is inevitable during the rebuild because all the data is being written to a single disk. The paralyzed repair process in Storage Spaces is a little different. If a disk fails, the remaining healthy disks that have suitable capacity take ownership of the data that was stored on the failed disk and will serve users' requests across all available spindles. Since all disks are now helping out, there should be no performance impact. The repair process can bring in the hot spare or the administrator can replace the failed disk, and in the background the disk can be brought back into the storage space.

Low-level Improvement: Native 4K Sector Support

Originally, hard disks used a 512-byte-per-sector format, and with this came limitations in storage size and performance. With ever-increasing demand on capacity and speed, a change was needed, and over the course of a few years 4K sector disks became standard. However, software (such as file system utilities, operating systems, and database engines) was not necessarily quick to catch up. Most drive manufacturers shipped 4K sector drives but emulated 512-byte sectors for compatibility. Obviously, this requires a bit of overhead because the entire 4K sector is read into memory, modified, and then written back. Since there is a degree of manipulation happening, there is also a performance impact, which is acceptable in this case.

With native 4K support, the data storage industry no longer emulates 512-byte sectors, which means the performance impact is gone.

The following list shows some of the apps and scenarios for 4K sector support:

- Ability to install Windows to and boot from a 4K sector disk without emulation (4K native disk)

- New VHDX file format

- Full Hyper-V support

- Windows backup

- Full support with the New Technology File System (NTFS)

- Full support with the new Resilient File System (ReFS)

- Full support with Storage Spaces

- Full support with Windows Defender

- Inbox application support

UEFI BIOS Support Allows GPT Drives

Master boot records are special areas located at the beginning of the partitioned space on a disk. They contain information on the underlying partition structure and some chained boot code to allow the operating system to start. Master boot records stored their block address as 32 bits. Originally, a 512-byte sector drive with a block address of 32 bits was limited to 2 TB. This obviously is no longer acceptable. So the industry went to 4K sectors, and now drives have a maximum capacity of 16 TB. It seems like we are getting there, but considering that in today's infrastructure we could be looking at petabytes of data, terabytes just doesn't seem to cut it.

The GUID Partition Table (GPT) provides a 64-bit addressing structure. With a 512-byte sector drive you could have 9.4 zettabytes (9,444,732,965,739,290,426,880) of data. Currently, the GPT supports a maximum disk and partition size of 8 ZB.

I can envision you now rushing to convert your drives to GPT, and you would be right! But be careful; not all operating systems support booting from GPT partitions using standard BIOS. See the following link:

```
http://en.wikipedia.org/wiki/GUID_Partition_Table
```

The *Unified Extensible Firmware Interface* (UEFI) is designed as a direct replacement for the legacy BIOS system. It essentially does the same job but adds functionality like diagnostics and repair of computers with operating systems deployed. UEFI is designed to support booting from GPT, and Windows 2012 R2 fully supports the UEFI BIOS.

CHKDSK Gets Smarter

In all the years I have been computing, this has been one of my staples. CHKDSK has been with us for many generations of DOS and Windows, and it is (for me, anyway) great to see this tool upgraded.

One of the biggest problems that faced CHKDSK before its upgrade was its direct relationship to the number of files on a volume. The larger the number of files, the longer it took to run. Another problem that constantly plagued CHKDSK was that if it detected a problem, it usually had to dismount the volume, rescan everything, detect the problems all over again and then fix the problem. As you can imagine, with large volumes this took a long time, and in our current always-on culture, downtime is simply not acceptable.

The CHKDSK code has been upgraded, and the NTFS health model has also been redesigned. We'll discuss these upgrades in the next few pages, but they essentially lead to the simple conclusion that CHKDSK is no longer needed in its former capacity.

Online Self-healing

Although this feature of NTFS has been around since Windows Vista, the number of issues that it can detect and fix online has greatly increased. This in turn has decreased the actual need for CHKDSK because most issues will be self-healed. And if they self-heal, the volume doesn't have to go offline.

Online Verification

In Windows Server 2012 you can verify an actual corruption. Sometimes errors occur because of memory issues, but this doesn't necessarily mean the disk is corrupt. Now, because of online verification, you can invoke a check. A new service called Spot Verifier is triggered by a file system driver to perform this check, as shown in Figure 12.2. It operates in the background and does not affect system performance.

FIGURE 12.2
Spot Verifier
service

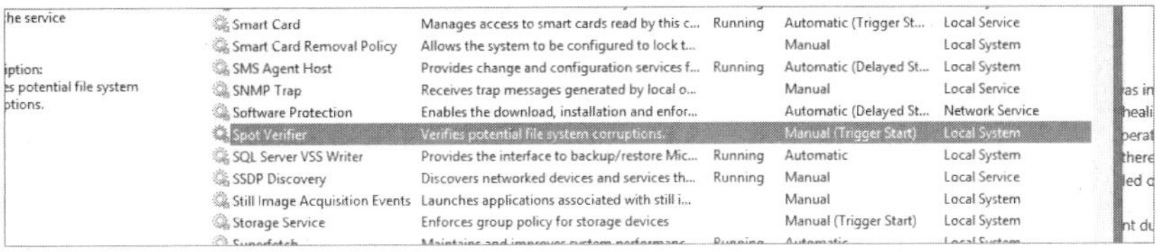

Online Identification and Logging

Once you find a real issue, an online scan of the file system is triggered. This scan is designed to run in conjunction with the operating system and will run only when the system is idle or when utilization is low. Once it finds the problem, it logs it for offline correction.

Precise and Rapid Correction

Because you have logged where the issues are, you don't have to scan the entire file system again when you begin the offline process. This essentially means that when you do take a volume offline to repair the issues, it takes seconds to repair rather than potentially hours. This quick fix is called Spotfix. If you are using Cluster Shared Volumes, there is no downtime, giving you always-on volumes.

With these new improvements, the CHKDSK runtime is no longer based on the number of files but rather on the number of corruptions. Because you can repair so many issues online (with CSV always online), CHKDSK is becoming less required. Figure 12.3 shows the new options that are available in CHKDSK.

FIGURE 12.3
New CHKDSK
options

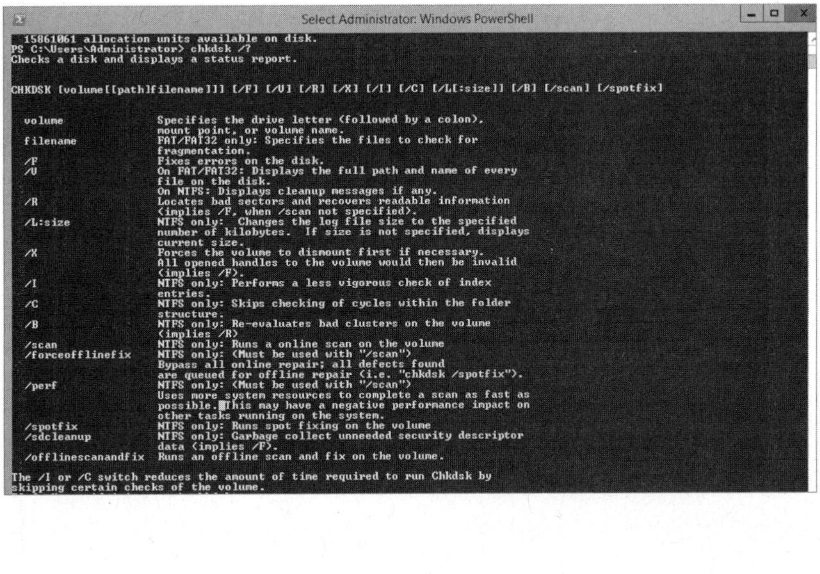

The new options are /scan, /forceofflinefix, /perf, /spotfix, /sdcleanup, and /offlinescanandfix. As you can see, they relate directly to the new health model described previously.

We must stress at this point that another key goal of upgrading CHKDSK was to ensure that users are kept informed of any corruption. Part of the reason was to allow users and administrators to stop actively running CHKDSK to verify the file system; now there is simply no need. The system uses the Action Center included in Windows to notify a user or administrator of file system corruption and recommends an action. See Figure 12.4 for the results of a sample online scan.

FIGURE 12.4
Message in Action Center for online scan

In Figure 12.5 you can see that if the issue cannot be repaired online, the Action Center will ask you to restart the computer to allow an offline repair.

FIGURE 12.5
Message in Action Center for offline scan

In-depth Look at Storage Spaces

In Windows Server 2012 R2, the concept of Storage Spaces is essentially the same as what was released in Windows Server 2012, which we discussed at the start of this chapter. The exceptions are the new features we introduced earlier and now we will go into further detail about.

Reusing Technology from Microsoft's Cloud

Microsoft runs multiple cloud services. I'm sure you've heard of Windows Azure or Office 365. Imagine all the lessons Microsoft learned during the deployment, setup, and day-to-day operations of these environments. Also imagine that if Microsoft had to buy multimillion-dollar storage networks to cope with the ever-growing need for storage in cloud-based environments, how crippling this would be to a cloud-based environment.

Microsoft applies all this knowledge to the new technologies they release, including Storage Spaces. Microsoft needed a cost-effective way to increase storage and maintain essential features found in storage area networks, hence the birth of Storage Spaces. As cloud services develop, you will see improvements in Storage Spaces such as those you have seen between the releases of Windows Server 2012 and Windows Server 2012 R2.

Providing SAN-like Capabilities with Microsoft Management Tools

One of the really interesting things about Microsoft technologies is the familiar interface that they provide for managing their products. You are usually given two options: the GUI and PowerShell.

USING THE GUI

Although the Microsoft Management Console (MMC)—the traditional console for most of the management plug-ins—still exists, most features within Windows Server 2012 R2 are managed via Server Manager, as shown in Figure 12.6. Storage Pools is enabled by default on all systems and can be found as a subfeature under File and Storage Services.

FIGURE 12.6
Server Manager, File and Storage Services

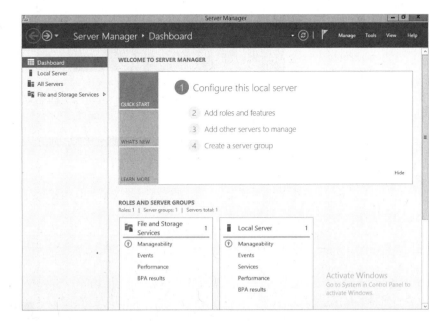

Once you choose File and Storage Services, you will see all the related options to this menu, including Storage Pools, as shown in Figure 12.7.

Clicking Storage Pools will bring you into the main configuration. Take a look at Figure 12.8.

FIGURE 12.7
Suboptions for
File and Storage
Services

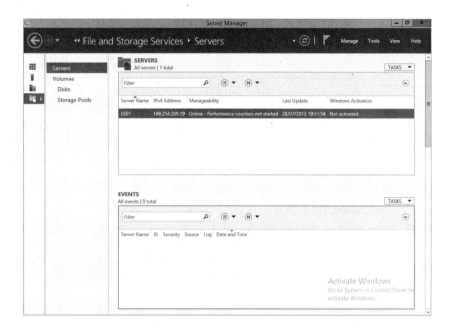

FIGURE 12.8
Storage Pools
configuration

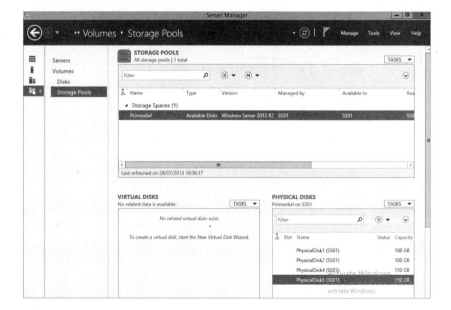

This is the main configuration window, it is split into three main areas:

Storage Pools   This area contains a section called Storage Spaces, and under it is listed Primordial. By default, all disks not assigned to a different pool are assigned to the Primordial pool. As you work with Storage Spaces you will notice that the Primordial pool will disappear when all the disks have been assigned.

As you can see, there are no other pools assigned or configured yet. In the top-right corner of this area, under Tasks, is the option to create a new storage pool. We will play with this later on, so don't worry about it for now.

You can right-click the Primordial pool and examine its properties.

Virtual Disks   Virtual Disks represent the volumes you will create inside a storage pool. Remember, this is not a VHD or VHDX file. You cannot create a virtual disk inside the Primordial pool; you must create a storage pool first.

Physical Disks   Physical disks are the disks that are available to Storage Spaces to assign to storage pools. A disk can be assigned to only one pool at a time. If you right-click a disk in this list, you get the option to toggle (turn off/on) a drive light (toggling drive lights helped you find which disk you are working on in a physical storage array); this will work only if the storage you are using is SCSI Enclosure Services (SES) compliant. SES also works if a drive is failing and will communicate with Storage Spaces to let the administrator know what is happening.

USING POWERSHELL

As mentioned, you can use PowerShell cmdlets to quickly provision Storage Spaces. Some administrators prefer to work with a command-line environment when administering servers. Personally, I like to mix them.

Windows Server 2012 R2 has a new PowerShell module called Storage, which contains all the PowerShell cmdlets you need to work with Storage Spaces.

In Windows Server 2012 and above, a PowerShell module is automatically imported when you attempt to call a cmdlet that is part of that module. To review the cmdlets available to you under the Storage module, open an elevated PowerShell window and type **get-command –module Storage**. In Windows Server 2012 R2, there are 102 cmdlets available to you. Not all are storage pool related.

Hopefully you are familiar with PowerShell and understand its verb/noun structure. If you base what cmdlets you are looking for on Figure 12.8, this would mean you are looking for cmdlets related to physical disks, virtual disks, and storage pools. To help you identify the cmdlets for each of these, try typing **get-command *StoragePool* |where {$_.modulename -eq "Storage"}** and examine the result. Figure 12.9 shows the expected output; each cmdlet has its own set of options, which you can see by using **get-help cmdletname**.

We are not going to go through this here, but we are going to show you some sample output from a couple of the cmdlets. For example, type **get-storagepool** and observe the output. Now type **get-storagepool |fl *** and see the difference. FL is an alias in PowerShell which standards for Format-List, the * option determines which properties you want to display, in this * stands for All properties. The output is shown in Figure 12.10. Repeat for the cmdlets get-physicaldisk and get-virtualdisk and observe the output.

FIGURE 12.9
Storage cmdlets

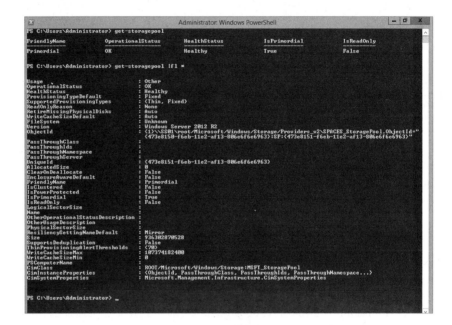

FIGURE 12.10
Sample
output for get-
storagepool

Creating a Storage Space

Storages Spaces is an extremely powerful feature, and as we have mentioned, storage spaces bring many benefits to an organization. They are also simple to configure. No specialized training is required.

In the next few pages we'll walk you through the process of creating a storage space and show you how simple it really is. The general process is as follows:

1. Obtain free physical disks.

2. Create storage pools

3. Create virtual disks

We will show you how to create a storage pool via the GUI and PowerShell. First, however, we will give you a quick introduction to our lab. We have a single server with multiple physical disks, two 100 GB SAS drives, two 150 GB SAS drives, and one 300 GB SATA drive.

Creating a Pool

When you create a storage pool you must decide on the physical disks you want allocated to the pool. It is important to think in terms of what the pool will be used for and, now with the storage-tiering feature, what type of disks should be part of the pool.

To create a pool, follow these steps:

1. Open Server Manager and click File and Storage Services.

2. Choose Storage Pools.

3. Right-click the primordial pool and select New Storage Pool, as shown in Figure 12.11.

FIGURE 12.11
Creating a new storage pool

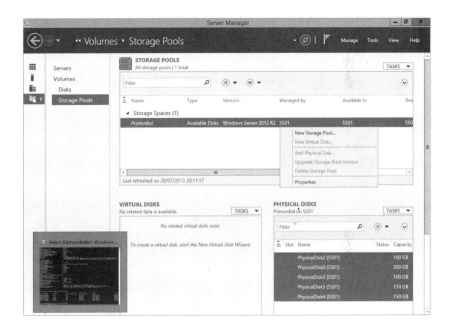

This will open the New Storage Pool Wizard.

4. Click Next to bypass the welcome screen.

5. In the Storage Pool Name screen, shown in Figure 12.12, you must name your storage pool in this case just name it **Test**. You can optionally add a description.

In the bottom half of the window you will see it is using the primordial pool for its available disk pool.

Next, you need to select the physical disks in your pool.

6. In this example, select all the disks, as shown in Figure 12.13.

Notice that you can select both ATA and SAS disks. Figure 12.14 shows the Allocation options: Automatic, Hot Spare, or Manual.

7. In our example we are using Automatic allocation. Click Next to continue.

FIGURE 12.12
Naming your
storage pool

FIGURE 12.13
Selecting disks
for the storage
pool

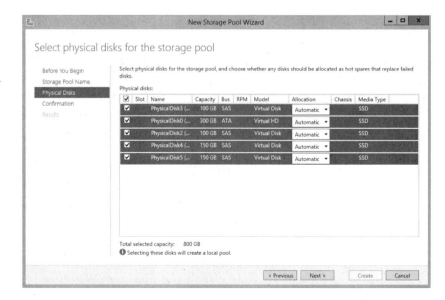

FIGURE 12.14
Disk allocation
options

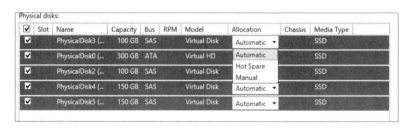

MIXING MANUAL AND AUTOMATIC DISKS

When allocating disks, you can have multiple hot spares in your pool, but you should not mix manual and automatic disks. Choosing Automatic on this screen will balance the pool automatically between hot spares and usable capacity.

You cannot change the disk allocation from manual to automatic after making an assignment in the GUI, but you can do so from PowerShell. See Figure 12.15 for an example of how to identify and change the allocation of a drive.

8. Finally, as with all wizards, you get a chance to review the options you selected before committing the change; see Figure 12.16. Click Create when you are satisfied with your choices.

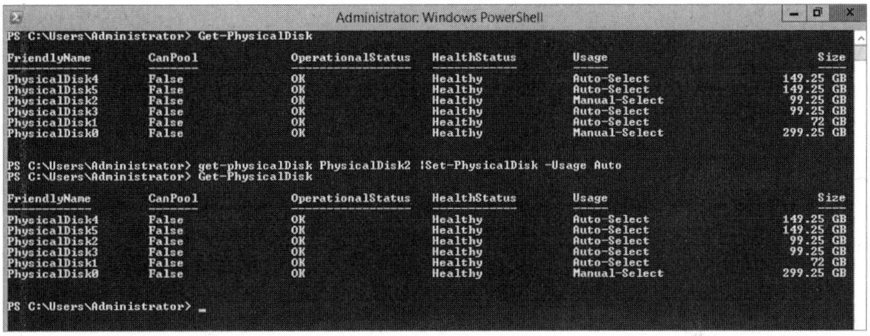

FIGURE 12.15
Changing the drive allocation type in PowerShell

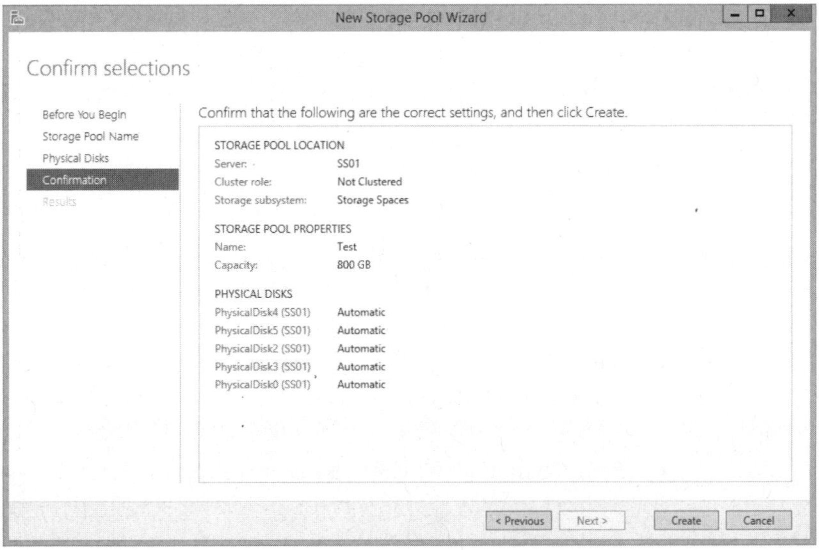

FIGURE 12.16
Reviewing the configuration options before creating a pool

A progress screen will appear and show a status of Completed when the pool is created; see Figure 12.17.

FIGURE 12.17
Storage pool
created
successfully

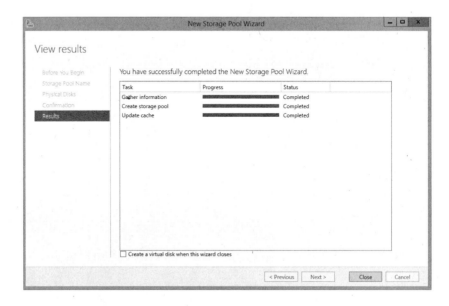

Congratulations on creating your first storage pool.

Pool Limitations

As with all technologies, there are some limitations to storage pools, and although the technology is powerful, it most certainly is not optimal for every situation. With that in mind, let's look at the limitations:

◆ A hard drive must be 10 GB or larger.

◆ You cannot deploy a boot system to a storage space.

◆ Any drives to be added into a storage pool must not be partitioned or formatted. All data on any drive used will be lost.

◆ Three drives are required when parity is used, two drives for two-way mirroring, and three or more for three-way mirroring.

◆ All drives in a pool must be of the same sector size (4K/512e or 512). 512e or 512 Emulation allowed manufacturers to make 4K sector disks and maintain compatibility with software which had not been updated to understand 4K sectors.

◆ Fibre Channel and iSCSI disks are not supported in a storage pool.

◆ All storage must be compatible with `storport.sys`. To check this use the Microsoft Hardware Compatibility List (if your hardware appears on the compatibility list it will work with storport) located at the following URL: `http://www.microsoft.com/en-us/windows/compatibility/CompatCenter/Home?Language=en-US`.

◆ If a virtual disk is to be used in a failover cluster, NTFS must be the file system deployed to the virtual disk.

Viewing Drives in Disk Management

Essentially, a storage pool is a logical container for the disks. For example, in our demo environment we have several disks ready to be assigned to a storage pool. In the Disk Management screen shown in Figure 12.18, you can see all the physical disks listed before we pooled them.

FIGURE 12.18
Unallocated disks in Disk Manager

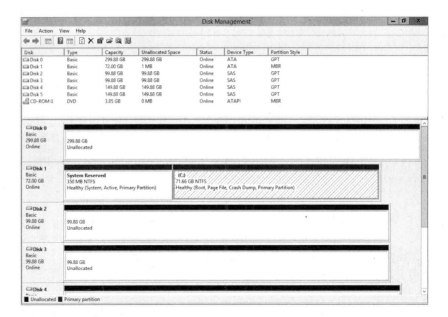

After we added the disks to a storage pool, we refreshed Disk Manager. As you can see in Figure 12.19, they all disappeared. Disk 1 still remains as this is the OS disk and it always will be and you will never be able to include it in a storage space. Where did they go? Remember that a storage pool is a container. You need to create virtual disks in order to see the volumes in Disk Manager again.

FIGURE 12.19
Drives no longer
appearing in
Disk Manager
after being added
to a storage pool

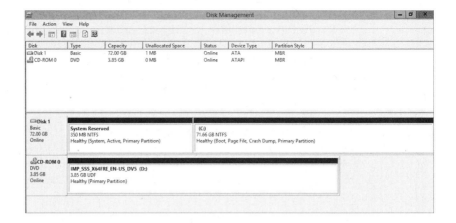

Pooling with PowerShell

We mentioned earlier that everything you can do in the GUI you can do via PowerShell. We will
now show you how to create a storage pool using PowerShell:

1. First, you need to find which disks are available. Use the `Get-PhysicalDisk` cmdlet to
   retrieve a list of all disks in the system. Figure 12.20 shows the results for our example.

2. Look at the `CanPool` property. When its value is `True`, this disk can be used in a storage
   pool.

3. Filter on physical drives that can be pooled, and store the results in a variable for later use
   using the following syntax:

   ```
   $drivestopool = (Get-physicaldisk |where {$_.CanPool -eq $True})
   ```

4. Next, identify the storage subsystem you are running, and again store it in a variable, but
   in this case you are interested only in the `FriendlyName` of the property, as shown in
   Figure 12.21.

FIGURE 12.20
Displaying
available physical
disks

FIGURE 12.21
`storagesubsys-
tem` cmdlet

Use the following syntax to capture the storage system's `FriendlyName`:

`$storagesystem = (get-storagesubsystem).friendlyname`

Now you can create the storage pool.

5. Use following syntax for creating a pool:

```
New-storagepool –friendlyname TestPool –StorageSubSystemFriendlyName
$storagesystem –physicaldisks $drivestopool
```

The `FriendlyName` for the pool can be any string you wish. This syntax will create a pool named TestPool with the disks that can be added into it. See Figure 12.22.

6. Now use the `Get-StoragePool` cmdlet to find out more detailed information about your pool using the following syntax:

`Get-StoragePool TestPool |fl *`

See Figure 12.23 for our example output, and notice the amount of detail that PowerShell provides versus the GUI.

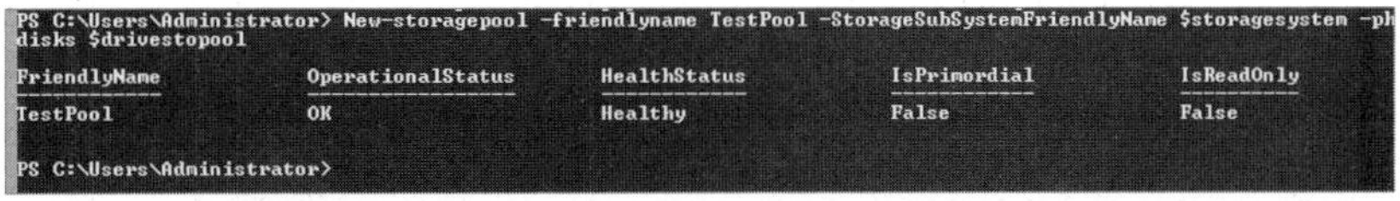

FIGURE 12.22
Output of PowerShell when creating a new storage pool

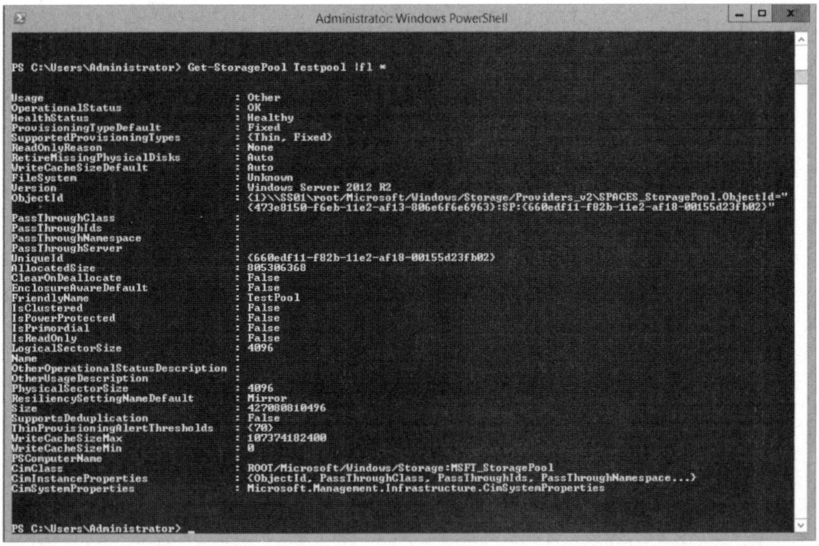

FIGURE 12.23
Output for Get-StoragePool cmdlet

Allocating Pool Space to a Virtual Disk

From the outset of this chapter we have made it clear that when we reference a virtual disk in relation to storage space, we are not talking about VHDX for a virtual machine. In fact, unless you place a virtual machine in the storage space or use it as an iSCSI target store, you will not see a VHD anywhere.

Virtual disks are essentially disks that you carve out of your storage pool. You previously created a pool for your physical disks, and we showed you that from a Disk Manager perspective all the disks disappeared because they now belong to the storage pool. In order to use some of the space contained within your storage pool, you have to create a virtual disk. It is not directly related to a physical disk in the storage pool, but it is representative of a chunk of space you are allocating out of the storage pool. How that chunk comes into existence depends on the options we will discuss next.

One of the great things about virtualization in general is that you maximize the use of the hardware. For example, previously many organizations had one server role, which was a waste, but now you can have multiple roles that are completely isolated assigned to one server. Hopefully you are familiar with virtualization in general at this stage. A similar concept exists in storage pools and virtual disks.

As we have already said, storage pools are essentially logical containers for a set of physical disks that you want to aggregate. The virtual disks will be presented to a server for use as a volume. If you have three physical disks of 500 GB each combined in a storage pool, you have the potential for 1.5 TB of space. See Figure 12.24.

FIGURE 12.24
Storage pool allocation

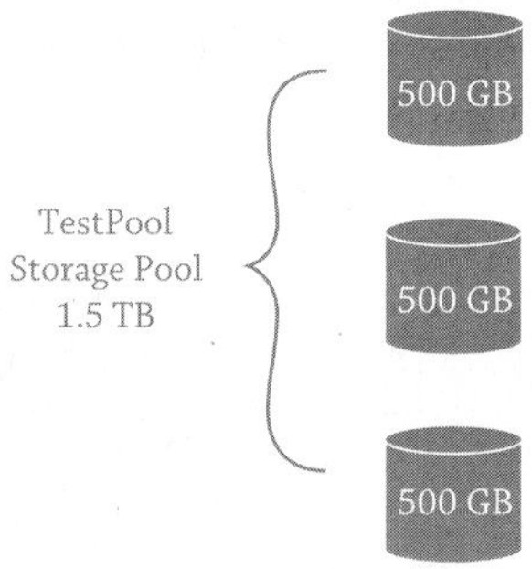

TestPool
Storage Pool
1.5 TB

500 GB

500 GB

500 GB

Pretty cool. (We're not taking into account redundancy just yet, because we will explain this shortly.) Now a system administrator gets a request from a new application team, and they require 2 TB of space for their application. However, when the system administrator reviews the projected growth, they realize that the 2 TB won't be needed upfront, which is good because there is no budget for more disks. Sound familiar? The dilemma is what to do about it.

One of the first choices you have with virtual disks is whether they are fixed or thin provisioned:

Fixed   With fixed, if you ask for 2 TB, you need 2 TB of capacity available for provisioning.

Thin   Thin-provisioned disks use only what is needed at the moment. This is brilliant! In the previous example, the application team thinks they have the 2 TB capacity they asked for, but in fact they are using only a fraction of the 2 TB. See Figure 12.25.

FIGURE 12.25

Fixed and thin-provisioned disks

Fixed Provisioned
Capacity 1 TB
Required 1 TB
Used 1 TB

Thin Provisioned
Capacity 1 TB
Required 1 TB
Used 200 GB

MANAGING THIN-PROVISIONED DISKS

Thin-provisioned disks can lead to overcommitment of resources and need to be managed. You need to create alerts to ensure that you monitor the free space left in the pool and in the virtual disk. The last thing you want is to have an outage because you overcommitted the resources. If used correctly, thin-provisioned disks can help system administrators mitigate storage costs and still meet the needs of the consumers.

DETERMINING DISK LAYOUT

Next, you need to decide on the layout of the virtual disk. There are three resiliency options, as follows:

Simple   In this design, data is striped across all disks in the pool. There is no reliability in this layout. If a disk fails, you potentially lose all your data.

Mirror   Mirroring the data duplicates it across different disks; this gives you maximum reliability but greatly impacts the amount of space you can potentially use. To protect from a single disk failure, you need at least two physical disks in your storage pool; to support two disk failures, you need at least five physical disks.

Parity   Parity essentially writes data in stripes across all the disks but also writes parity information, so if a disk fails it can recover. This gives you excellent reliability and performance. To support a single disk failure you need at least three disks.

Figure 12.26 gives you a visual representation of the different layouts you can potentially use. As you will see in green the data is written across all disks. In yellow you will see if we write the data to one drive in a 4-drive mirror it will get written to a second disk. Finally in blue we show you data is written across all disks but parity information is written with it to allow for recovery.

FIGURE 12.26
Virtual disks
layout

CREATING A VIRTUAL DISK IN THE GUI

The next step is to create a virtual disk. The easiest place to create the virtual disk is within the Storage Pools console of Server Manager, as shown in Figure 12.27.

FIGURE 12.27
Storage Pools
console

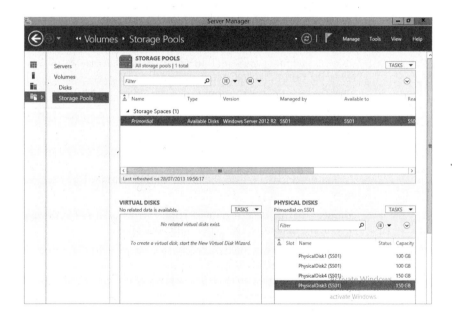

1. In the lower left under Virtual Disks, click Tasks ➢ New Virtual disk, as shown in Figure 12.28.

2. Click Next on the welcome screen of the New Virtual Disk Wizard.

   As shown in Figure 12.29, you need to select the storage pool that you want to create the virtual disk from. In our example we are going to use TestPool.

3. Select your storage pool and click Next.

FIGURE 12.28
Creating a new
virtual disk

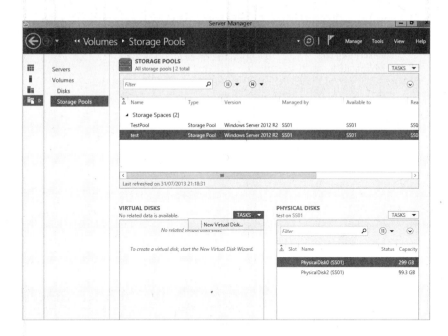

FIGURE 12.29
Select a storage
pool to use for
creating a virtual
disk

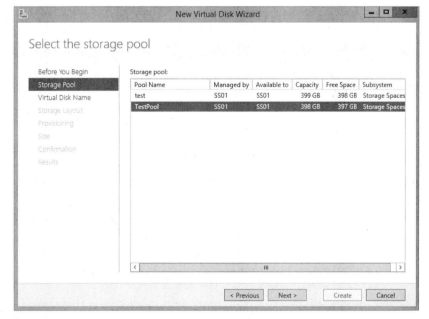

You need to assign a name to the virtual disk. You can also enter a description of what
the virtual disk will be used for.

4. In our example, we're naming it File_Vdisk, as shown in Figure 12.30, and indicating that
it is to be used for file storage.

FIGURE 12.30
Naming and
describing the
virtual disk

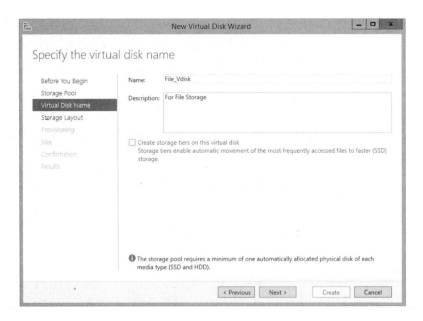

The next step is to choose your storage layout, as shown in Figure 12.31. You have three options: Simple, Mirror, and Parity.

FIGURE 12.31
Storage layout
for virtual disks

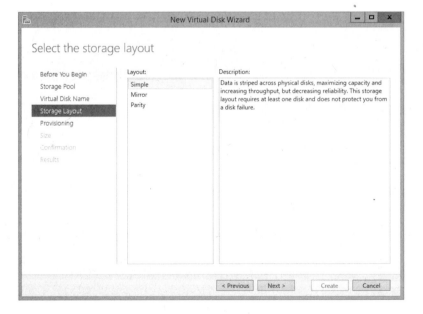

5. For this example, choose Simple and click Next.

Now you need to choose the provisioning type. You have two options, Thin or Fixed, as shown in Figure 12.32.

6. In this example, choose Thin, because you want to maximize your space in the storage pool.

   You now need to decide on the size of the virtual disk. Since it is thinly provisioned, you could in theory enter any value here.

7. Our storage pool is about 400 GB, so we'll assign 500 GB to the virtual disk, as shown in Figure 12.33. Click Next to continue.

FIGURE 12.32
Provisioning type for the virtual disk

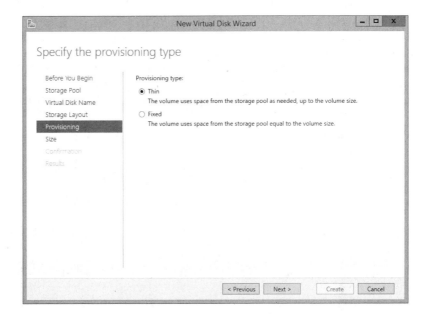

FIGURE 12.33
Setting the size of the virtual disk

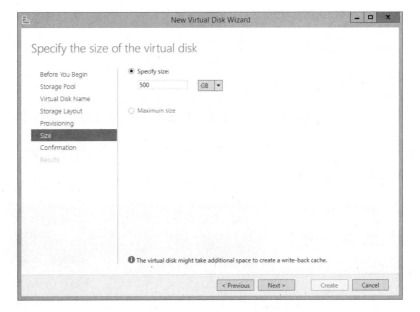

8. Finally, review your choices and confirm the settings by clicking Create.

9. Review the Results screen and ensure that everything is complete, as shown in Figure 12.34. Click Close to end the wizard.

FIGURE 12.34
Results screen for the new virtual disk

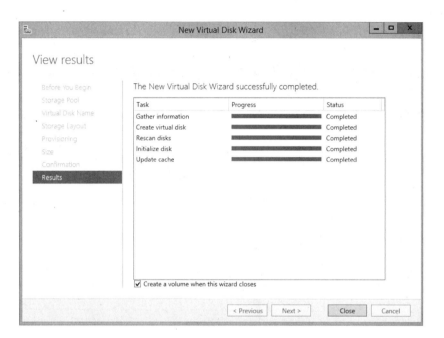

SIDE EXERCISE

Check out Disk Manager now and see what suddenly appeared!

CREATING A VIRTUAL DISK IN POWERSHELL

First, let's use PowerShell to look at the virtual disk we created in the previous example using the GUI. In Figure 12.35 we use the `Get-VirtualDisk` cmdlet to retrieve all information on virtual disks that we've created. As you can see, we have created only one, the 500 GB virtual disk.

FIGURE 12.35
Output of `Get-VirtualDisk`

To create a new virtual disk you need to use the cmdlet `New-VirtualDisk`. But you need to know the storage pool friendly name before you start. Do you remember the command for getting the storage pool friendly name?

Once you have the friendly name, follow these steps:

1. Use the following syntax to store the friendly name of the storage pool in a variable:

```
$sp = (get-storagepool).friendlyname
```

The next step is to create the virtual disk, but we'll show you the full syntax first:

```
New-VirtualDisk -StoragePoolFriendlyName $sp[1] -ResiliencySettingName
Simple -Size 500GB -FriendlyName TestVdisk -ProvisioningType Thin -
NumberofDataCopies 1 -NumberofColumns 2
```

As you can see, there are a few more options to select. Let's look at a few of them:

ResiliencySettingName   Equivalent to the storage layout options of Simple, Mirror, Parity.

NumberofDataCopies   The number of copies of the data you want to keep; this option is directly related to `ResiliencySettingName`. If you choose `Simple`, for example, `NumberofDatacopies` can only be 1. If you choose `Mirror`, the `NumberofDataCopies` will be at least 2, depending on the amount of disk space you have in the system.

NumberofColumns   Directly associated with the number of disks you want to use. A storage pool may have hundreds of disks, but you may want to stripe or mirror or use parity across only five disks. This option gives you the choice. This option also is related to both `ResiliencySettingName` and `NumberofDataCopies`.

The values we selected for `NumberofDataCopies` and `NumberofColumns` are related to the options we selected. For example if we want to mirror our data we increase the `NumberofDataCopies` and if we add to span our Vdisk across multiple disks we increase the `NumberofColumns`. In our case we only want 1 copy of the data and we want to write the data across 2 disks.

2. The `$sp[1]` option we chose selects one element out of all the storage pools we captured using the `get-storagepool` command. For example if we have 5 storage pools the `get-storagepool` command will return all 5, this is no good so using [1] allows us to select the storage pool which is number 2 out of the 5 we captured. The count starts from 0 so the first storage pool can be retrieved using `$sp[0]`.

In our lab environment we have multiple storage pools. If we just referenced `$sp`, the command would fail because it would try to insert (in our case) two storage pool friendly names.

See Figure 12.36, which shows you a sample run of the command we just outlined.

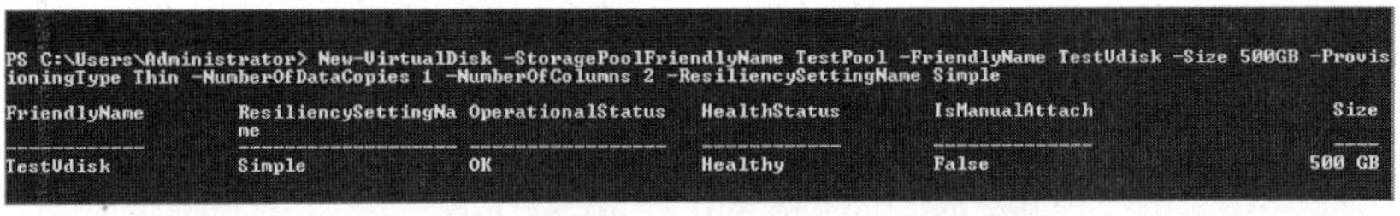

FIGURE 12.36
Sample output from creating Vdisk in PowerShell

3. Run get-virtualdisk now to review the output, and the disk you created should be listed.

Again, as an exercise, view the disk in Disk Manager.

VOLUMES FROM VIRTUAL DISKS

If you have ever provisioned a standard physical disk and created a volume and formatted it, then this should be very familiar territory.

There are several ways you can create volumes. Disk Manager and Diskpart are the two you are most familiar with, and there is absolutely nothing wrong with creating the volume from one of these if you so wish. However, for this example and to show you that you can do everything you need in relation to storage spaces directly from the Storage Pool UI, we will show you how to create a volume from there.

In Figure 12.37 you can see the Storage Spaces UI, and under Virtual Disks you can see File_Vdisk, which we created earlier.

FIGURE 12.37
Storage Spaces UI with our newly created virtual disk

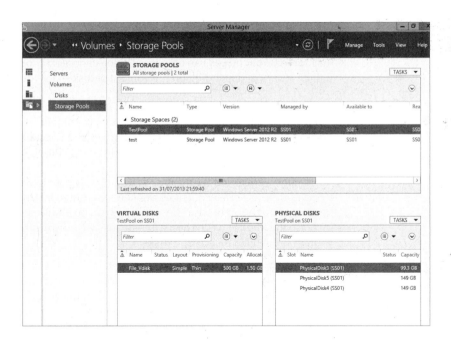

1. Right-click the new virtual disk and select New Volume, as shown in Figure 12.38.

2. Click Next on the welcome screen of the New Volume Wizard.

3. Select the server and disk—SS01 for the server and Disk 6, File_Vdisk, as shown in Figure 12.39—and click Next.

   As with normal disks, just because the full disk may be 500 GB, the volumes you create don't have to be 500 GB. You can create multiple volumes of different sizes if you want. They just have to add up to 500 GB.

FIGURE 12.38
Creating a new volume from a virtual disk

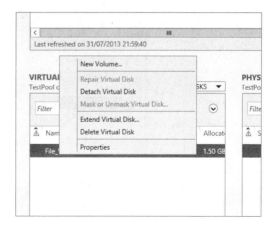

FIGURE 12.39
Selecting the
server and virtual
disk

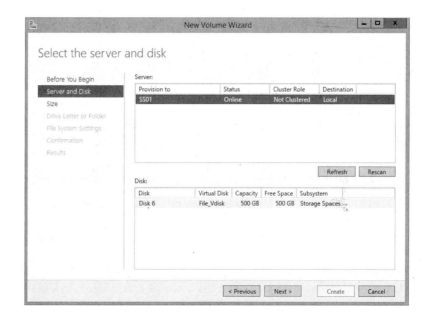

4. In our example, as shown in Figure 12.40, we'll stay with the default size of 500 GB, which will be thinly provisioned.

   Next, as you would for a normal disk, select a drive letter or a folder where you want to mount the volume.

5. In our example, we'll accept the default of E, as shown in Figure 12.41.

FIGURE 12.40
Setting capacity
for the volume

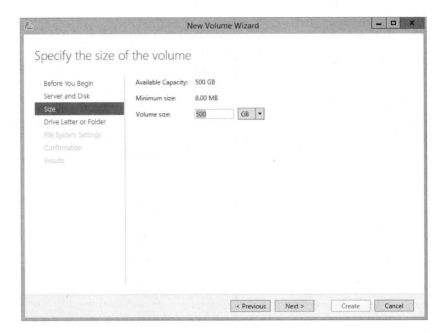

FIGURE 12.41
Selecting a drive
letter for the
volume

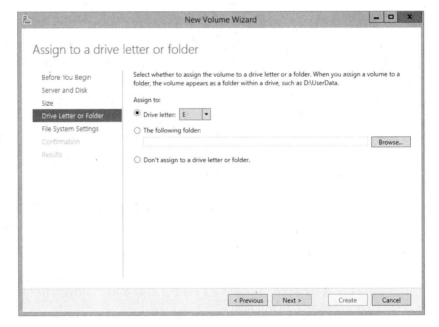

Now you can choose the file system. Notice you can choose only NTFS or ReFS, as shown in Figure 12.42.

FIGURE 12.42
File system
settings

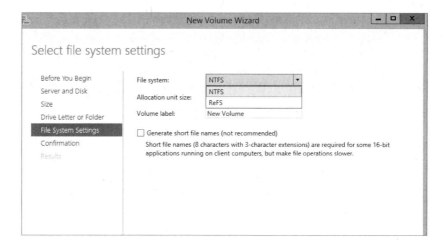

6. Select NTFS.

7. Rename the Volume Label to **Test_Volume** and click Next.

8. Confirm all the values and click Create.

9. Ensure in the Results screen, shown in Figure 12.43, that everything registers Completed, and click Close.

10. Open Windows Explorer and notice that your new volume E: has appeared.

FIGURE 12.43
Results screen
for creating the
volume

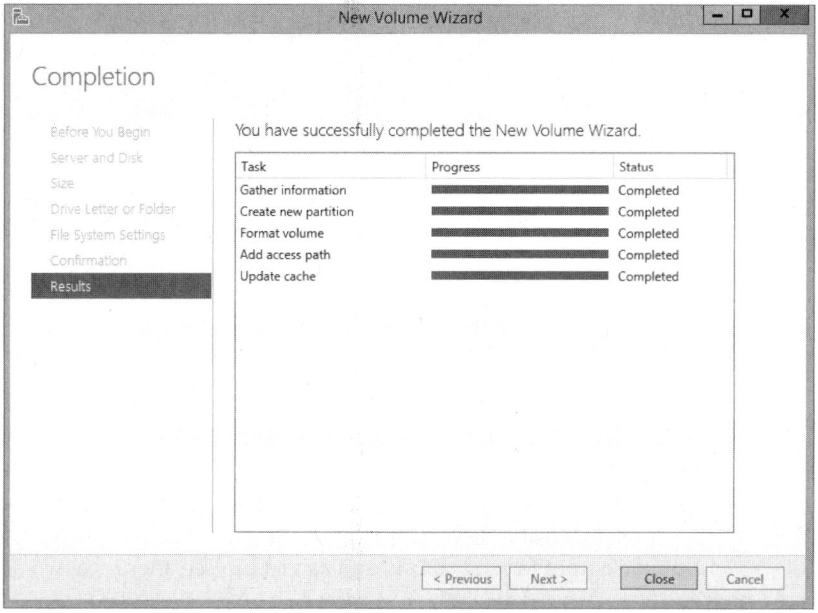

NEW DISKS ARE OFFLINE BY DEFAULT

By default, when you add a physical disk or a VHD or even a new virtual disk, it will always be in an offline state. Normally this is OK, but in a cloud environment always having to bring the disk online is an extra step you could do without. In the command-line utility Diskpart you have the ability to configure an option so that if you create a virtual disk, it will automatically come online.

To set the policy status for SAN disks to Online, in an elevated command line type the following:

```
Diskpart "san policy=OnlineAll"
```

See Figure 12.44 for sample outputs of running Diskpart and setting the SAN policy to Online.

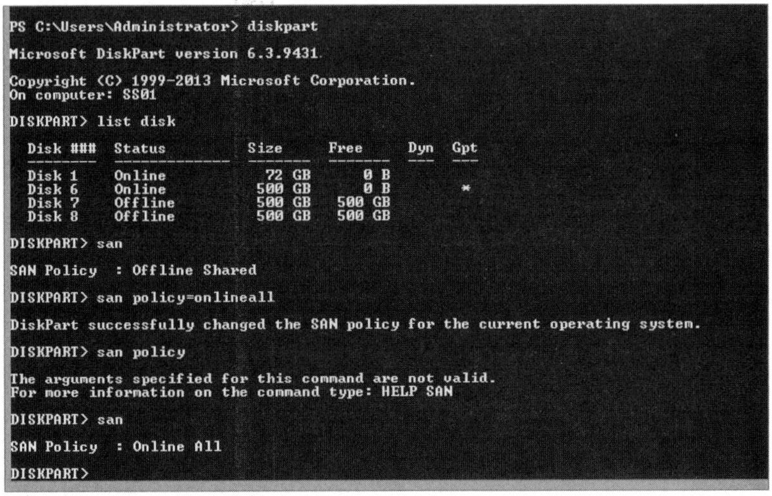

FIGURE 12.44
Sample output
for setting
Diskpart SAN
policy

```
PS C:\Users\Administrator> diskpart

Microsoft DiskPart version 6.3.9431

Copyright (C) 1999-2013 Microsoft Corporation.
On computer: SS01

DISKPART> list disk

  Disk ###  Status         Size     Free     Dyn  Gpt
  --------  -------------  -------  -------  ---  ---
  Disk 1    Online          72 GB      0 B
  Disk 6    Online         500 GB      0 B         *
  Disk 7    Offline        500 GB    500 GB
  Disk 8    Offline        500 GB    500 GB

DISKPART> san

SAN Policy  : Offline Shared

DISKPART> san policy=onlineall

DiskPart successfully changed the SAN policy for the current operating system.

DISKPART> san policy

The arguments specified for this command are not valid.
For more information on the command type: HELP SAN

DISKPART> san

SAN Policy  : Online All

DISKPART>
```

SIDE EXERCISE

Using the steps we previously outlined, create a new virtual disk in TestPool. Does it come online?

MAKING DISKS ONLINE WITH POWERSHELL

As with everything, the old command-line tools are being replaced with PowerShell. Can you guess the cmdlets used to find out what disks are offline and set them online?

First, let's use get-disk to figure out what state our disks are in. Figure 12.45 shows a sample output for get-disk, and as you can see, there are two disks offline.

1. Simply type get-disk and press Enter.

2. You could also filter on just offline disks by typing the following:

   Get-disk |where {$_.operationalstatus -eq "Offline"}

3. To bring them online, you would use the set-disk cmdlet.

4. To bring all the disks online at once using the previous syntax, which we filtered for offline disks, you would pipe its output into the set-disk cmdlet to make it easier.

   The syntax is shown here, and Figure 12.46 shows the sample output:

   Get-disk |where {$_.operationalstatus -eq "Offline"} |set-disk - isoffline $false

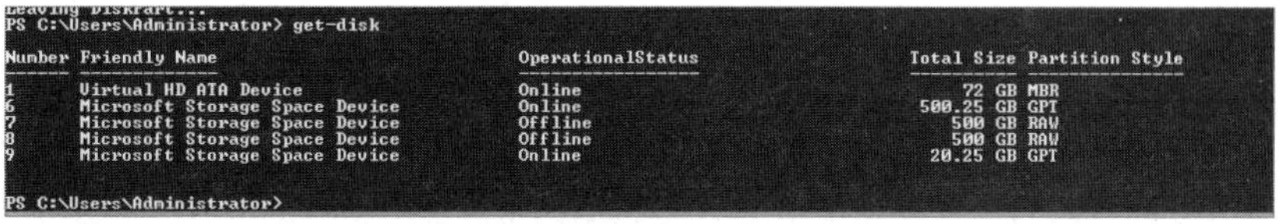

FIGURE 12.45
Output for
get-disk

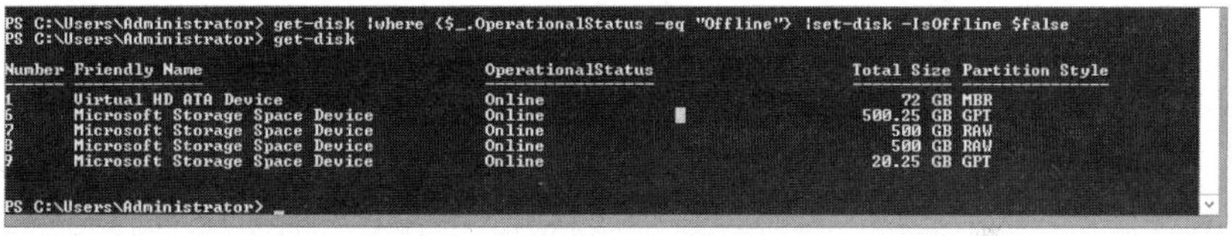

FIGURE 12.46
Bringing all disks
online using
PowerShell

Storage-tiering Demo and Setup Using PowerShell

We have brought you through creating a storage pool, a virtual disk, and volumes for your environment. One of the things we mentioned at the beginning of this chapter was storage tiers. They can be of huge benefit to an environment because they allow you to split up your storage and charge-back based on the resources that the end users require. Essentially, if the end users require high-speed storage, you can allocate and bill accordingly; if they don't, you can allocate low-end storage to serve their needs. If your company does charge-back, this will be of benefit to all end users because storage spaces will automatically move the more frequently accessed data to the fast storage tier and the less accessed data to the slow tier.

Since you are now familiar with the Storage Spaces console, you will notice that there is no place to configure storage pools within the UI. This feature can be configured only via PowerShell.

We've already created our storage pool named TestPool, so let's use this as the friendly name.

As we've already said, you can create only two tiers in Windows Server 2012 R2. Solid State Drive (SSD) and Hard Disk Drive (HDD) are the two media types the system recognizes.

In our lab if we run the PowerShell cmdlet get-physicaldisk, we get the output shown in Figure 12.47.

FIGURE 12.47

Sample output of get-hysical disk for creating storage tiers

CREATING SSD AND HDD POOLS

As you can see, we have SSD and HDD drives in our environment. Now we'll create our storage tiers. We are going to create two tiers in our example (which is also the maximum supported), and then we'll create a virtual disk that will be allocated across the tiers. We will then partition and format the disk for use.

Using the cmdlet New-StorageTier, here is the syntax to use for creating the SSD pool. We have to store it in a variable for later use:

```
$ssdtier = new-storagetier -StoragePoolFriendlyName "TestPool" -
FriendlyName SSD_Tier -Mediatype SSD
```

For the HHD tier we use the following syntax:

```
$hddtier = new-storagetier -StoragePoolFriendlyName "TestPool" -
FriendlyName HDD_Tier -Mediatype HDD
```

The next step is to add a virtual disk and tie it to the storage tiers. Before you ask whether you can remap an existing virtual disk to a storage tier, the answer is no.

With that in mind, we'll create a new virtual disk, which we will tie to our storage tiers. Here is the syntax to use:

```
New-VirtualDisk -StoragePoolFriendlyName TestPool -FriendlyName Tiered_
VDisk -StorageTiers @($ssdtier, $hddtier) -StorageTierSizes @(10GB,
50GB) -ResiliencySettingName Simple
```

Figure 12.48 shows the output of successfully creating a disk.

FIGURE 12.48

Output of creating a virtual disk in storage tiers

Most of the options should be familiar from creating a virtual disk earlier. However, we have two options related to creating a virtual disk in a storage tier:

StorageTiers @($ssdtier, $hddtier)   This specifies the tiers you can use. This is *not* a hash table, so be careful not to use curly brackets. We have stored our tiers in separate variables for ease of reference.

StorageTierSizes @(10GB, 50GB)   This specifies the size of each tier and is referenced in the order you set in the -StorageTier option. As you saw in Figure 12.48, the total size is 60 GB, which is 10 GB + 50 GB.

From here you would need to create a volume as before for storing data. We'll show you a quick PowerShell trick you can use to create a 20 GB volume on the disk and format it all in one line! Here is the syntax:

```
Get-VirtualDisk | Get-Disk | New-Partition -Size 20GB -AssignDriveLetter
| Format-Volume -Force -confirm:$false
```

See Figure 12.49 for the output of the command. Now you can navigate to the drive letter and copy a file.

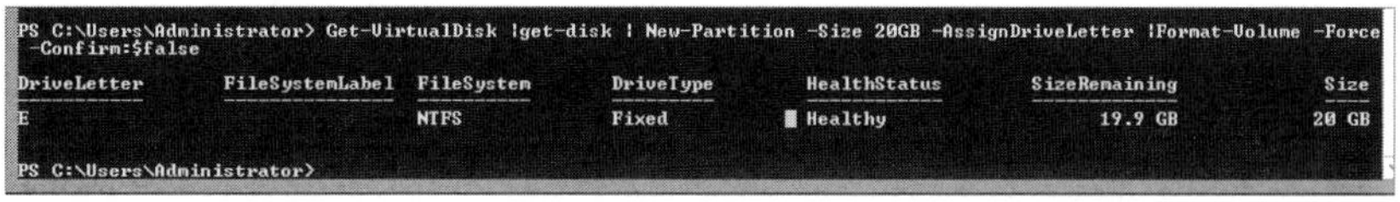

FIGURE 12.49

Creating a new partition and formatting it in PowerShell

Take a moment to review the properties of the virtual disk we previously created. In Figure 12.50 notice how the capacity is split because we set it between the different tiers.

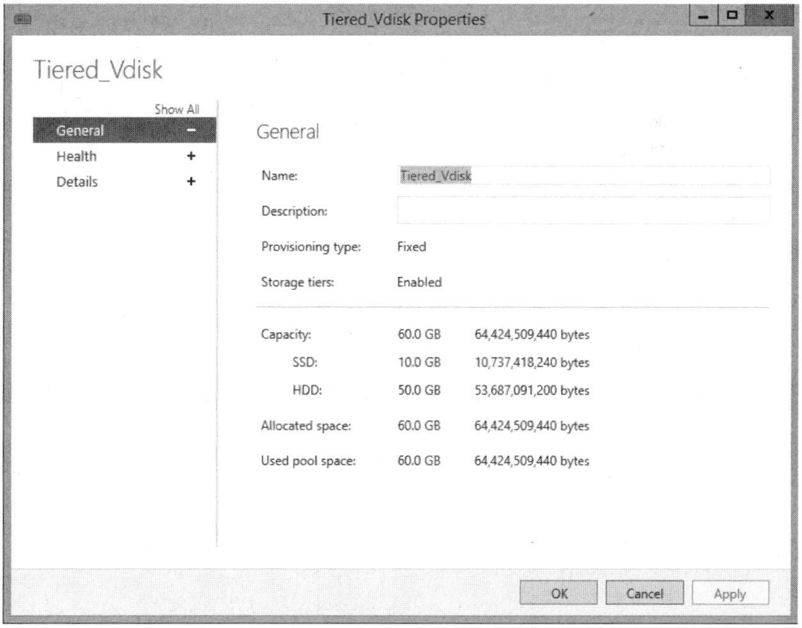

FIGURE 12.50

Properties of a tiered virtual disk

Using the Write-back Cache

Now we'll show you how to use one of the last major features of Storage Spaces in Windows Server 2012 R2, the write-back cache. As with storage tiers, you cannot enable this via the GUI; it must be done via PowerShell. Remember, the write-back cache can help speed up applications because writing to cache is quick and doesn't have to wait for storage to catch up to commit the write.

Take the PowerShell command we used to build our previous storage tier and modify the name and the `StorageTierSizes` options. Then add the `–WriteCacheSize` option with a size setting; in this case you want a write-back cache size of 2 GB:

```
New-VirtualDisk -StoragePoolFriendlyName TestPool1 -FriendlyName Tiered_
VDisk -StorageTiers @($ssdtier, $hddtier) -StorageTierSizes @(20GB,
70GB) -ResiliencySettingName Simple -WriteCacheSize 2GB
```

Voilà You have now created a virtual disk that will use storage tiers, with write-back cache enabled.

Storage Tiers Optimization

The final thing we discussed about storage tiers at the start of this chapter is that every night at 1:00 A.M. it will run a job to reprioritize the storage and move around what needs to be in the fast tier versus the slow tier.

In Task Scheduler, choose Task Scheduler Library ➢ Microsoft ➢ Windows ➢ Storage Tiers Management. Task Scheduler lists a job called Storage Tiers Optimization, as shown in Figure 12.51.

FIGURE 12.51
Storage Tiers Optimization task

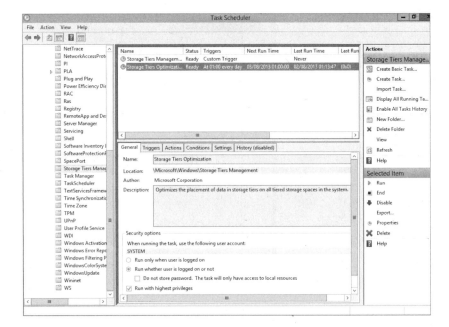

You can modify the task or manually trigger it if necessary.

iSCSI on Storage Spaces

Storage spaces are incredibly useful for providing scalable and reliable back-end storage. Think of the amount of money a company would have to invest to get the abilities we have already outlined. What would be really useful now is to combine all this powerful storage technology with iSCSI so you can allow remote systems (such as file servers, mail systems, virtualization clusters, and the like) to also benefit from these features.

iSCSI requires a few elements to be configured in order for it to present logical unit numbers (LUNs) to remote machines. First, we'll explain a few items that make up iSCSI from a host server and remote server perspective that you'll need to know in order to understand the example we'll use:

iSCSI Target Server   This allows iSCSI initiators to make a connection to the target service, which in turns presents a VHD that's located on a target server's volume. To the target server's operating system, this appears as a VHD file. You can configure access control to secure the disk appropriately.

iSCSI Virtual Disk   The iSCSI virtual disk in this case is an actual VHD when viewed on the target server, but when viewed from a client server or initiator point of view, it appears as a disk that can be brought online or offline and have volumes created on it.

iSCSI Initiator   The initiator is the client software used to connect to a target server and access whichever iSCSI virtual disks have been presented and it is authorized to access.

This technology is commonplace in most businesses today, and it allows them to create clusters for all sorts of business reasons. In my previous place of employment we used a Windows server with the iSCSI target server to create a Hyper-V cluster to run our production network. In the next section we'll walk you through an example of setting up the iSCSI target service, creating a virtual disk, and presenting it to a remote system.

Adding the iSCSI Target Service

By default, the iSCSI target service is not enabled. You must add it, and you'll do this via PowerShell. The syntax for adding the Windows feature iSCSI Target server is:

```
Add-windowsfeature FS-iSCSITarget-Server -IncludeManagementTools
```

A server reboot may be required after adding the feature, so make sure you are in a position to be able to complete the installation.

The iSCSI Target server is a File and Storage Services subfeature, and that means that you can administer it via the Server Manager console under File and Storage Services, as shown in Figure 12.52.

FIGURE 12.52
iSCSI Target server
management

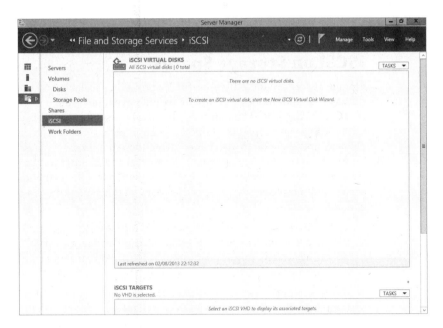

CREATING AN ISCSI VIRTUAL DISK

As you can see from Figure 12.52, there are two main screens: iSCSI Virtual Disks and iSCSI Targets. As we have already said, a target will present the iSCSI virtual disks that have been created. (Don't confuse them with virtual disks in Storage Spaces. They are different; iSCSI virtual disks appear as VHD files on the Target server.)

To demonstrate this, let's create an iSCSI virtual disk. In our example we will be using the E drive we created earlier from our tiered storage pool. Don't worry if you haven't set it up; all you need is a drive and a folder to store the VHD you are going to create.

1. In the center of the iSCSI Virtual Disks window shown in Figure 12.52, click "To create an iSCSI virtual disk, start the new iSCSI Virtual Disk Wizard."

2. Select the Target server that's listed and a volume where you wish to store the iSCSI virtual disk.

   In our example this will be E:, as shown in Figure 12.53.

3. Give the iSCSI virtual disk a descriptive name; for example, if it's for a Hyper-V cluster, type **VMCluster_Vdisk**. Notice the path in Figure 12.54.

4. Next, enter the size of the virtual disk; for our example type **50 GB**.

   Notice the options; you can choose whether you want to provision all the space at once using the fixed option, provision a dynamically expanding disk, or use a differencing disk. These options will seem familiar if you are used to Hyper-V.

5. Choose Dynamically Expanding in this case.

FIGURE 12.53
Selecting a server
and a volume for
an iSCSI virtual
disk

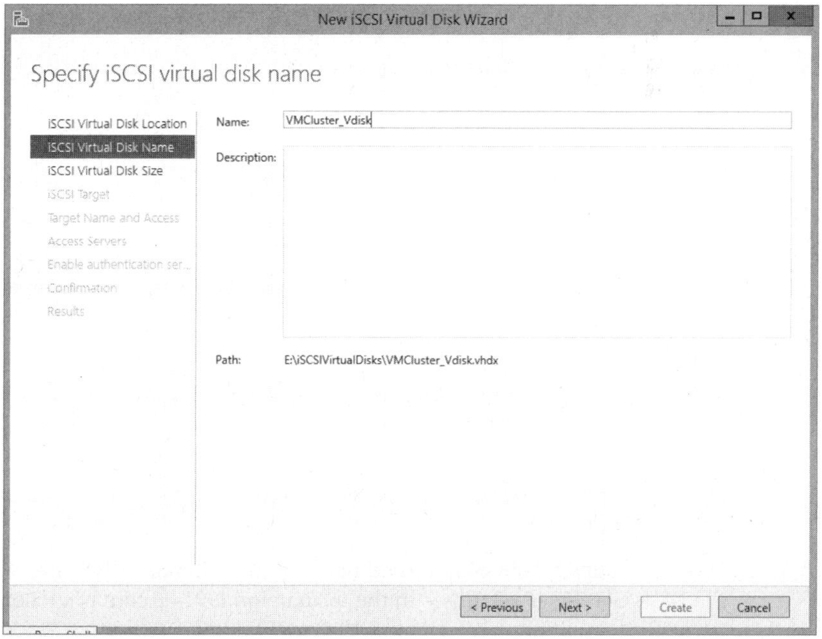

FIGURE 12.54
iSCSI Virtual
Disk Name
screen

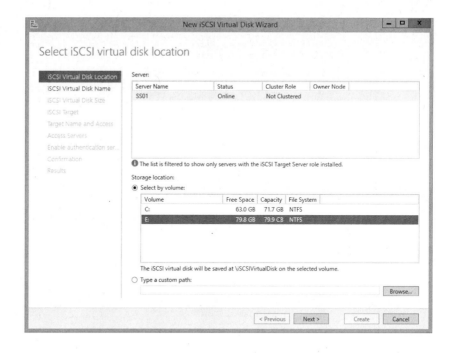

CHOOSING THE FIXED OR DYNAMICALLY EXPANDING OPTION

It is worth noting that you need to be careful when choosing among Fixed, Dynamically Expanding, or Differencing. Choosing the wrong type can dramatically affect performance. As a rule of thumb, if you are unsure and do not know the type of workload that will eventually use that disk, choose Fixed.

---

6. Since this is a new server and you don't have any iSCSI Target servers yet, you need to select the "New iSCSI target" option, as shown in Figure 12.55.

FIGURE 12.55
New iSCSI target

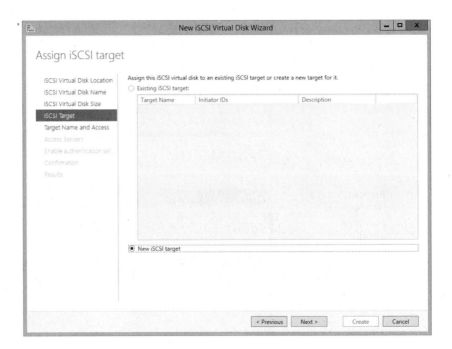

7. Give the iSCSI target a name; for this example type **VMCluster_Target**, as shown in Figure 12.56.

Next, you need to configure access to the iSCSI virtual disk you are creating. You can authorize specific initiators based on their IQN or DNS name, IP address, or MAC address.

The IQN (iSCSI qualified name) is an automatically generated name. For Microsoft Servers it usually is in the format: iqn.1991-06.com.microsoft:*servername*.

FIGURE 12.56
New iSCSI target
name

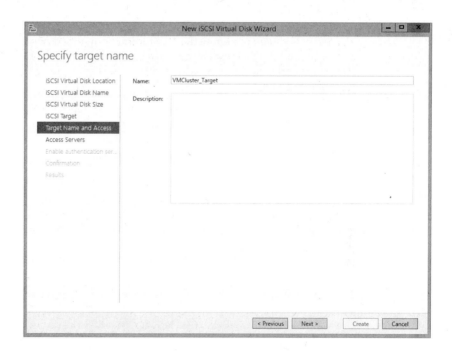

8. On the Specify Access Servers screen of the wizard, click Add.

   This will bring up the "Add initiator ID" window, as shown in Figure 12.57.

FIGURE 12.57
Add initiator ID

If you are familiar with iSCSI, you will notice a new option for Windows Server 2012 and above. If you do not know the iSCSI initiator qualified name, you can query a remote server for it. (IQN is simply a naming convention for iSCSI that is consistent with the format of the machine; usually it follows the format: iqn.1991-05.com.microsoft:server01 .contoso.com.)

When deploying iSCSI in the past, I had a preference for IQNs because they do not change unless you change the machine name. Other options, as described earlier, have the ability to change easily in an environment, and if you are presenting these LUNs to remote machines, you don't want that to happen.

9. As shown in Figure 12.57, select the ID from the initiator cache on the target server.

Next, you can challenge for authentication to a LUN using CHAP (Challenge-Handshake Authentication Protocol is an authentication protocol to control access to resources). In our example we will ignore this.

10. Finally, review all the settings and click Create.

SIDE EXERCISE

Use the iSCSI cmdlets to review the iSCSI Target server and virtual disk deployed.

The cmdlets you require are `get-iscsitargetserver` and `get-iscsivirtualdisk`.

Do you fancy creating a new virtual disk for iSCSI in PowerShell and presenting it to a target? Here are some sample cmdlets you can use:

1. Create the virtual disk using the `New-ISCSIVirtualDisk` cmdlet.

Here is an example:

```
New-IscsiVirtualDisk -path e:\newdisk.vhdx -SizeBytes 20GB -Computer
name SS01
```

2. Add that disk to your target using the `Add-IscsiVirtualDiskTargetMapping` cmdlet.

Here is an example:

```
Add-IscsiVirtualDiskTargetMapping -TargetName VMcluster-Target -path
e:\newdisk.vhdx
```

Done!

Connecting to an iSCSI Virtual Disk from the Client Side

You have provisioned an iSCSI Target server and a new virtual disk, but they are of no use until a client connects to the LUN. Remember that if you set up access lists, you will be able to connect to the LUN only from that specified machine.

1. Select the iSCSI initiator located in the Tools menu under Server Manager, as shown in Figure 12.58.

The iSCSI Initiator Properties window should appear.

FIGURE 12.58
Locating iSCSI
initiator

2. To follow along with our example, simply type **192.168.0.1** in the Quick Connect box and click Quick Connect, as shown in Figure 12.59.

FIGURE 12.59
iSCSI Initiator Properties – Quick Connect

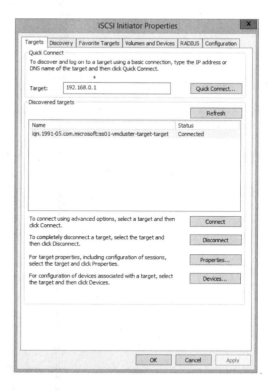

A dialog box will appear verifying the status as Connected. This will ensure the LUN can be seen and you have set up the access rules correctly. See Figure 12.60. Click Done to continue.

FIGURE 12.60
Successful connection to iSCSI target

3. Next, select the Volumes and Devices tab and click Auto Configure, as shown in Figure 12.61.

   This will autopopulate the volumes that are being presented to the client.

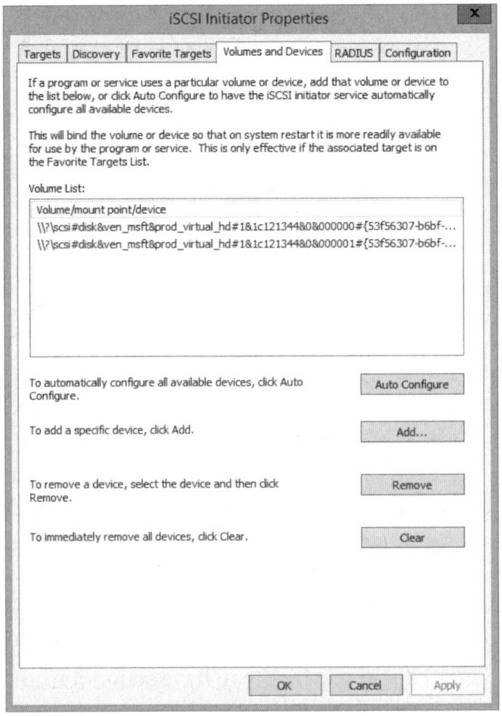

FIGURE 12.61
Volumes and Devices – Auto Configure

4. Finally, from Server Manager, under File and Storage Services, click Volumes ➢ Disks.

As shown in Figure 12.62, we have two new disks with Bus Type listed as iSCSI. They are now available to format and create standard volumes out of.

FIGURE 12.62
Displaying newly
added iSCSI disks

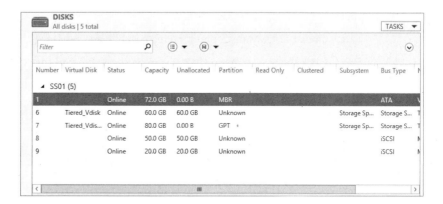

NFS Shares

Network File System (NFS) allows you to share files between a Windows server and a Unix/Linux platform using the NFS Protocol. In Windows Server 2012 the following improvements were introduced:

NFS Version 4.1 Support   This includes easier accessibility through firewalls, RPCSEC_GSS protocol for enhanced security, client and server security negotiation, Windows and Unix file semantics, better support for clustered file servers, and WAN-friendly compound procedures.

Improved Performance   No more tuning is necessary because by using the new native RPC-XDR protocol, you should achieve optimal performance out of the box.

Easier Manageability   You can manage via PowerShell and a unified GUI in Server Manager. RPC port 2049 makes it easier to configure firewalls. Another improvement is better identity mapping, and there is a new WMIv2 provider.

NFSv3 HA Improvements   There are now improved failover times with the new per-physical disk resource and tuned failover paths. This makes failover time fast for NFS clients.

Where to Use an NFS Share

NFS is used in environments where you have a requirement for file shares in a mixed operating system environment (such as Windows and Unix/Linux). With the improvements in Windows Server 2012, you can now present a share with NFS and SMB at the same time.

A common use for this has been found in some third-party hypervisors using Windows Server 2012 NFS shares as data stores for templates and ISOs.

Quick NFS Share Setup

We'll now show you how to provision an NFS share. Since we are in a hurry, let's use PowerShell. Add the NFS service to Windows using the following syntax:

```
Add-WindowsFeature FS-NFS-Service
```

We have a directory we want to share in our lab under the path E:\shares. We will guide you through this process using the GUI:

1. Open Server Manager and navigate to File and Storage Services.

2. Click the Shares menu since we are going to be working with shares.

   This will bring you to the Shares management area, as shown in Figure 12.63.

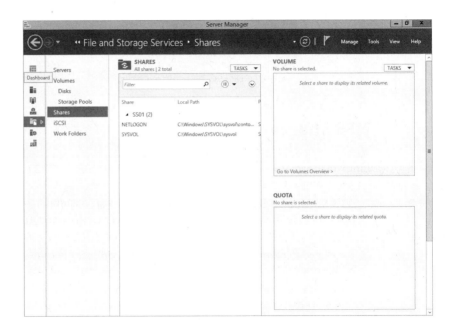

FIGURE 12.63
Share management in Server Manager

3. In the Shares area of the window, click Tasks ➤ New Share.

   This will invoke the New Share Wizard, as shown in Figure 12.64.

4. Click NFS Share - Quick.

5. Select your server. In our lab it will be SS01.

6. In the Share Location screen click "Type a custom path," and enter the path to the share.

   In our lab it is e:\shares, as shown in Figure 12.65.

FIGURE 12.64
New Share Wizard

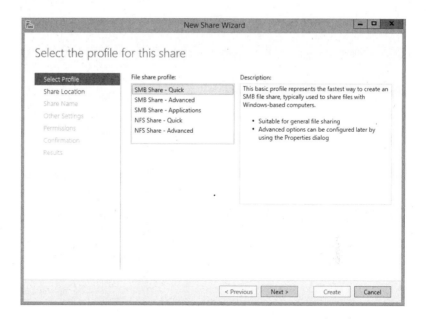

FIGURE 12.65
Server and path
for share

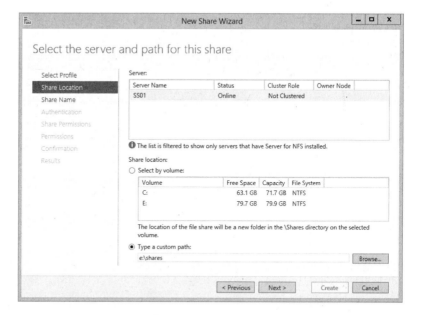

7. Enter a share name. In our lab it is shares, as shown in Figure 12.66.

Selecting the right authentication mechanism is highly dependent on the environment you are integrating into it. In our case we have not enabled our Linux client for Kerberos authentication because it is a stand-alone client. We have chosen No Server Authentication (AUTH_SYS) and "Enable unmapped user access," as shown in Figure 12.67.

FIGURE 12.66
Enter a share
name.

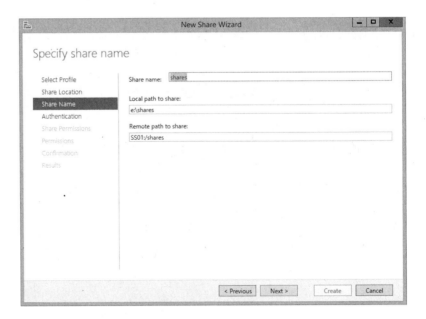

FIGURE 12.67
Authentication
methods

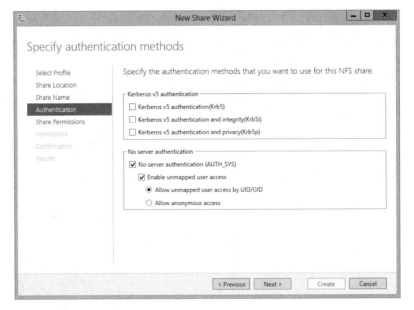

MORE ON STORAGE

The Microsoft Storage team has in-depth articles that you should reference for more detailed configuration and identity mapping if required:

```
http://blogs.technet.com/b/filecab/archive/2012/10/09/nfs-identity-
mapping-in-windows-server-2012.aspx
```

8. Next, under Share Permissions click Add. Then in the Add Permissions dialog, select All Machines, and for "Language encoding" select ANSI. Choose Read / Write for "Share permissions," as shown in Figure 12.68.

9. On the "Specify permissions to control access" screen, verify that the Everyone account exists and has been assigned Full Control, as shown in Figure 12.69.

10. Confirm the details and click Create to create the new NFS share.

11. Verify that it was successful and click Close.

FIGURE 12.68

Adding share permissions

FIGURE 12.69

Permissions to
control access

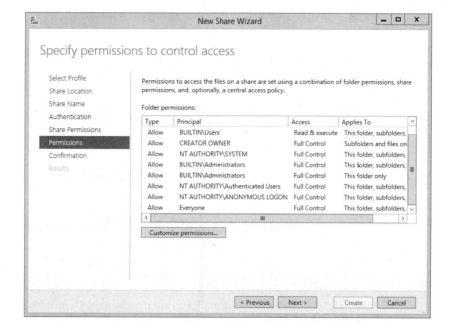

Connecting to NFS from the Client Side

In our lab we have Linux Mint deployed. By default, we are able to connect to the share, but we get various errors when we try to browse the share or create a directory. Linux Mint, along with many other distributions, requires you to install the nfs-common package before you can read from an NFS share. Follow these steps to install the package:

1. From a terminal window type:

   ```
   sudo apt-get install nfs-common
   ```

   This will install the necessary items to allow you to browse the share.

   Now you can mount the share that you previously created on your test Windows server.

2. Again from a terminal window type:

   ```
   sudo mount -t nfs 192.168.0.1:/Shares /mnt/share
   ```

   There is no output; rather, you have to browse to the directory or mount point (/mnt/share) you specified. Here's an explanation of this syntax:

   Sudo   Super user do (Privileged execution for performing certain tasks)

   Mount   Used to mount various types of file systems

   -t nfs   The NFS file system to mount

   192.168.0.1:/Shares   The remote share you are mounting

   /mnt/share   The local mount point

3. Next, browse to the share by typing the following:

   ```
   cd /mnt/share
   ```

4. Now type the following command to list the directory contents:

   ```
   ls
   ```

On Windows Server you have created a file called Readme.txt. You should be able to see this file after you issue the ls command. The Readme.txt file is just an example, try placing some of your own files in the share on the windows server and retry the ls command on the Linux client.

Deduplication: Disk and Network

Windows Server 2012 introduced *Data Deduplication* as a native storage feature. Data Deduplication is a more efficient way of storing data. With the ever-increasing need for storage in cloud technologies, you can imagine the amount of duplicate files that are stored. Even at home I have several copies of ISO files or virtual hard disks for my USB storage and servers. These files are 3–7 GB each. I'm wasting a lot of storage space by keeping multiple copies and not coming up with a proper library system.

This is a simple example but it brings up another point: the files all have similar parts and they all take up space. Wouldn't it be cool if you could identify those common pieces, create a single master reference on disk, and then point to it for every other file that has that common piece? You have this ability in Data Deduplication.

Data Deduplication in Windows uses a concept called the *chunk store*. A file gets split into variable-size chunks usually between 32 KB and 128 KB; on average a chunk is around 64 KB. These chunks are compressed and stored in the chunk store. Each chunk is stored in a chunk container, which grows to about 1 GB in size before a new container is created. You can view the chunk store and its containers on the root of the volume in a folder called System Volume Information. The folder by default is locked down to just the System account, so you must take ownership of it and ensure that the System account remains in full control. A reparse point replaces the normal file. If the file is accessed, the reparse point shows where the data is stored and restores the file. See Figure 12.70.

FIGURE 12.70
Data dedup in action

Although not installed by default, Data Deduplication is designed to be easy to deploy. It also has been designed to have *zero* impact on the users; in fact, the users won't even notice anything. You can turn on Data Deduplication on any of your primary data volumes with minimal impact on performance. It was designed to not interfere with files that are new or that are currently being written to. Rather it will wait, and every hour it will check for files that are eligible for deduplication. You can reschedule the process according to the needs of your company.

Eligibility for deduplication starts with files that are over three days old (again this is configurable based on needs), and it always excludes files that are smaller than 32 KB, have extended attributes, or are encrypted. If you have other files that you don't want part to be of the dedup process, this is also configurable.

Deduplication happens on network traffic as well. As traffic is sent or received, it is assessed to see if it can be deduplicated, effectively reducing the potential amount of traffic that has to be sent or received. Unlike storage deduplication, you cannot modify a schedule or data type for the network dedup.

However, there are a few things to be aware of before continuing. Dedup is supported only on NTFS volumes, and you cannot dedup a boot or system drive. In Windows Server 2012 it can't be used with CSV, live VMs, or SQL databases.

So what's new in Windows Server 2012 R2 for Data Deduplication? The key focus was on allowing deduplication for live VMs. That's right; you can dedup the VHDs and VHDXs that your live VMs are using. Primarily you can use it in VDI scenarios, with a further focus on remote storage. With these enhancements you can dedup your VDI environment. It is also worth noting that although it is not supported for other virtualized workloads, there are no specific blockers to stop you from enabling it. As always, the results cannot be guaranteed.

This is an amazing technology to have natively within Windows Server, and it will provide substantial savings in terms of storage for a business. Next we'll show you how to configure it.

First, you need to add Data Deduplication. You can add this feature using PowerShell. The syntax is as follows:

```
Add-WindowsFeature FS-Data-Deduplication
```

Then you can configure it via Server Manager or PowerShell.

Configuring Data Dedup with Server Manager

We'll explore the Server Manager method first.

1. Open Server Manager, click File and Storage Services, and choose Volumes.

2. Right-click the volume you want to configure Data Deduplication on, and select Configure Data Deduplication, as shown in Figure 12.71.

FIGURE 12.71
Configuring Data Deduplication

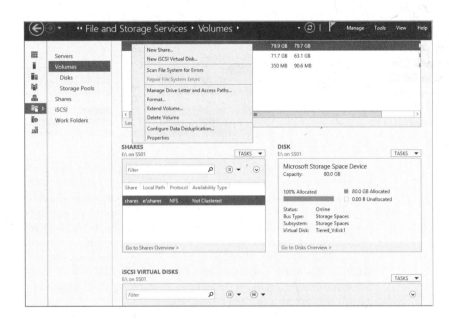

3. Click the drop-down box beside "Data deduplication" and select "General purpose file server."

   Notice the other option, "Virtual Desktop Infrastructure (VDI) server," as shown in Figure 12.72. Click OK.

   Next, you need to decide how old the files must be before they are processed by the dedup engine. This means there will be no impact on newly created files for the specified time.

4. In our example, we'll keep it at 3 days.

   You can modify this value later if you change your mind. See Figure 12.73.

   Also on this screen, you can choose any extensions you wish to exclude from the dedup process. For example, you may not want to dedup a SQL database or an Access database. If you want multiple entries in the field, include a comma between each entry. For example, if you wanted to exclude SQL database files and the Active Directory database file (`ntds.dit`), you would type in the field **mdf,dit**.

FIGURE 12.72
Enabling Data
Deduplication

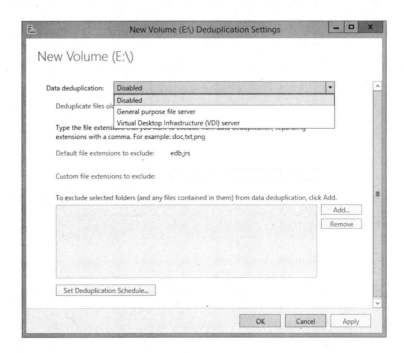

5. Exclude these extensions, as shown in Figure 12.73.

   Excluding a file is great, but you may have some folders in the organization that are highly sensitive, and for that reason you can't dedup them. They may have common chunks, but you can't risk the possibility of a disk corruption on the chunk store, which could potentially affect the information. Of course, this is a highly unlikely scenario, but it does show you that you can exclude a folder of sensitive information.

6. In this case, we'll exclude E:\shares because this is our previously created NFS share.

   We are not 100 percent sure about what is being stored there, and we don't want to take a risk without further investigation.

   At the start of this chapter we said that the dedup engine has a background process that will run every hour by default. In Figure 12.73 you also have the option to change that schedule.

7. Click the Set Deduplication Schedule button, and you will see three check boxes, as shown in Figure 12.74.

   By default background optimization is turned on, but you can also enable throughput optimization, which will force the optimization job through when dealing with large amounts of data. Microsoft says a throughput job can process roughly 2 TB of data per volume in a 24-hour period on a single volume. If you have multiple volumes, you can run this in parallel.

8. For this example, leave the schedule as is.

FIGURE 12.73
Configuring New
Volume Deduplication
Settings

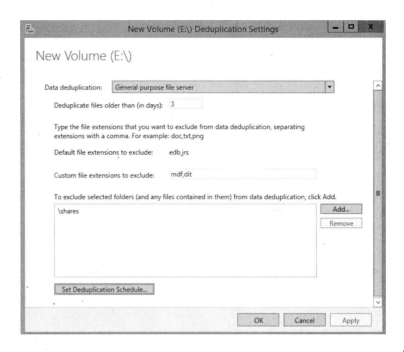

FIGURE 12.74
Changing the dedup
schedule

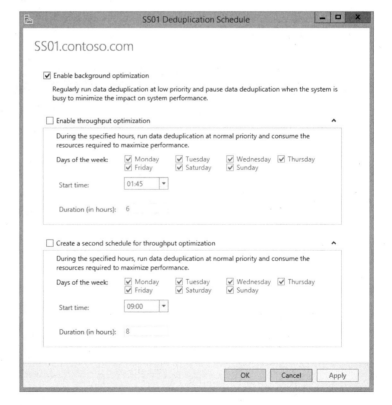

When you review the volume in Server Manager, you will see the Deduplication Rate (measured in %) and Deduplication Savings (measured in bytes) columns, as shown in Figure 12.75.

FIGURE 12.75
Viewing
deduplication
information in
Server Manager

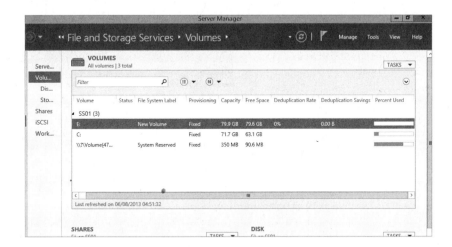

Configuring Data Dedup with PowerShell

We'll now show how to work with deduplication in PowerShell. Figure 12.76 shows the available PowerShell cmdlets.

FIGURE 12.76
PowerShell cmdlets
for deduplication

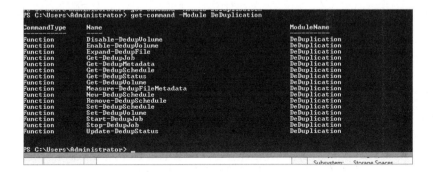

1. To enable dedup for a volume, use the following syntax:

   ```
   Enable-DedupVolume E:\
   ```

   The output is shown in Figure 12.77.

   You know that dedup is enabled, but you'd like to find out how much it has saved you and other such data.

2. Use the `Get-DedupStatus` cmdlet, as shown in Figure 12.78.

FIGURE 12.77
Enabling dedup output with PowerShell

FIGURE 12.78
Get-DeDupStatus output

On the volumes in our lab we haven't had a lot of information to dedup, hence the values in the screenshots are at 0%, but this has been for a reason. In our configuration we excluded E:\shares because we're not 100 percent sure what is stored there, and since it is an NFS share for Linux, we just don't want to take the chance. (In practical terms it doesn't matter what the client is; it is transparent.) Inside E:\shares we copied a Win2012R2_Preview ISO, which is about 4 GB in size. We created an additional folder at E:\TestData and have copied two Win2012R2_Preview ISOs under different names and also a Technical folder, which contains documents on technical information. See Figure 12.79 for our sample data.

FIGURE 12.79
Contents of E:\TestData

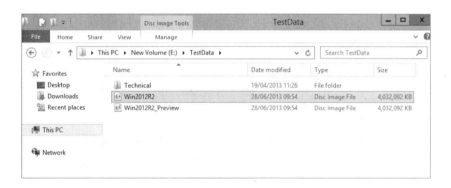

Remember I said that although we have copied this data, we now have to wait three days for it to be included for deduplication? If you can't wait that long, you can use the cmdlet Start-DedupJob to accelerate this.

3. The syntax is as follows:

```
Start-DedupJob -Type Optimization -Volume E:
```

As you can see in Figure 12.80, dedup has started a manual schedule and is in its current state of Queued. You can accelerate it from here if you want.

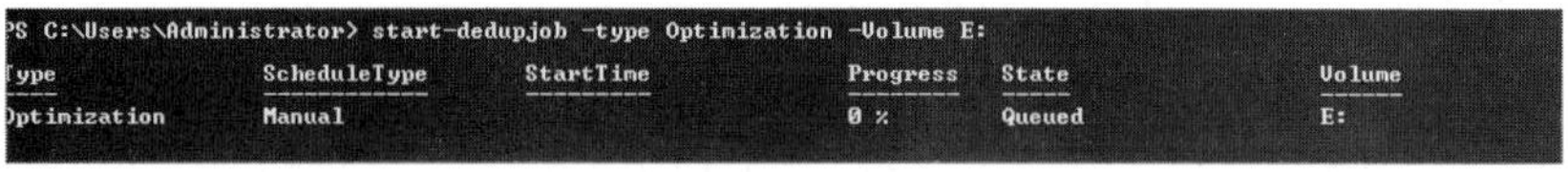

FIGURE 12.80
Output of Start-DedupJob

4. In Task Scheduler, choose Task Scheduler Library ➤ Microsoft ➤ Windows ➤ Deduplication.

As shown in Figure 12.81, you will see three jobs listed (we will explain the last two jobs later in this chapter):

♦ BackgroundOptimization

♦ WeeklyGarbargeCollection

♦ WeeklyScrubbing

FIGURE 12.81

Manually invoking
BackgroundOptimization

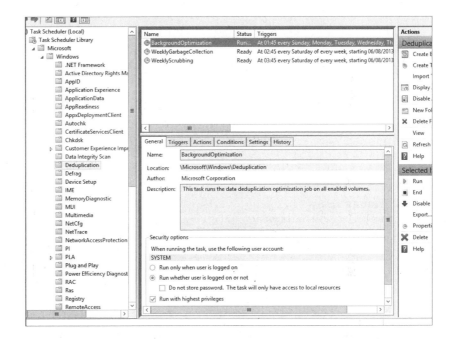

5. Right-click BackgroundOptimization, return to PowerShell, and use the cmdlet `Get-DedupJob`.

See Figure 12.82 for sample output.

FIGURE 12.82

Sample output
of the `Get-
DedupJob`
cmdlet

Figure 12.83 shows just how much it has saved already, and it is not even finished.

6. Now compare the output in Figure 12.84 when the `Get-DedupJob` cmdlet has completed.

In our test lab we have already saved 4.64 GB, which is great because storage is tight!

FIGURE 12.83

Output of Get-Dedup Status while Get-DedupJob is running

FIGURE 12.84

Output of Get-Dedup Status when optimization is complete

7. Try using the Get-DeDupVolume cmdlet for a different output view.

8. As an additional exercise, remove E:\Shares from the excluded folder selection and rerun the optimization job.

   How much space is freed up now?

9. Finally, right-click the E:\TestData folder and view its properties.

   Figure 12.85 shows the properties of the TestData folder in our lab. Notice the difference in the Size and Size on disk values?

FIGURE 12.85

Folder properties after running dedup

So now you have seen dedup in action. But where has the data actually gone?

10. Use the cmdlet Get-DedupMetadata to view information on the chunk store we talked about at the introduction to this section.

See Figure 12.86 for the output of the cmdlet.

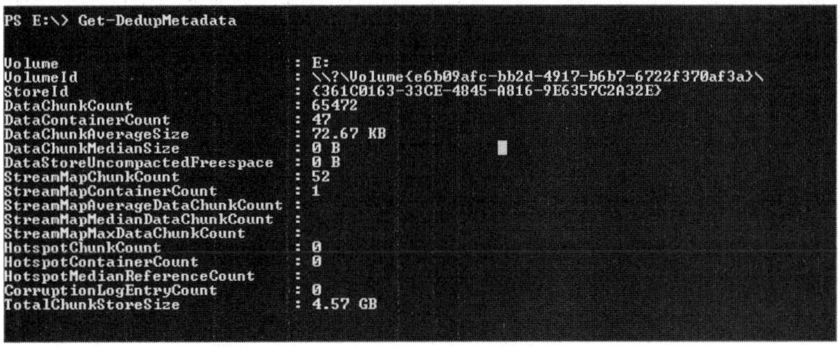

FIGURE 12.86

Get-DedupMeta-
data output

```
PS E:\> Get-DedupMetadata

Volume                         : E:
VolumeId                       : \\?\Volume{e6b09afc-bb2d-4917-b6b7-6722f370af3a}\
StoreId                        : {361C0163-33CE-4845-A816-9E6357C2A32E}
DataChunkCount                 : 65472
DataContainerCount             : 47
DataChunkAverageSize           : 72.67 KB
DataChunkMedianSize            : 0 B
DataStoreUncompactedFreespace  : 0 B
StreamMapChunkCount            : 52
StreamMapContainerCount        : 1
StreamMapAverageDataChunkCount :
StreamMapMedianDataChunkCount  :
StreamMapMaxDataChunkCount     :
HotspotChunkCount              : 0
HotspotContainerCount          : 0
HotspotMedianReferenceCount    :
CorruptionLogEntryCount        : 0
TotalChunkStoreSize            : 4.57 GB
```

As you saw in Figure 12.81, Task Scheduler has two other jobs available that run on a weekly basis. We'll discuss both of them now. First, we'll talk about GarbageCollection.

GarbageCollection is configured to run on a weekly basis by default, but you can invoke it as needed. The GarbageCollection job cleans up the chunk store by removing unused chunks, which releases disk space. You can see that it is an important job.

To manually invoke a garbage collection, use the `Start-DedupJob` cmdlet as follows:

```
Start-DeDupjob -Type GarbageCollection -volume E:
```

This will queue the job until the system is idle, or you can run the job from within Task Scheduler to accelerate it.

SIDE EXERCISE

Delete all the ISO files you used throughout this lab and empty the Recycle Bin. Run an optimization job and then run a garbage-collection job. View the chunk store size after the jobs are complete using the cmdlet `Get-DedupMetadata`. The following illustration shows the reduction in our chunk store when we performed this exercise in the lab.

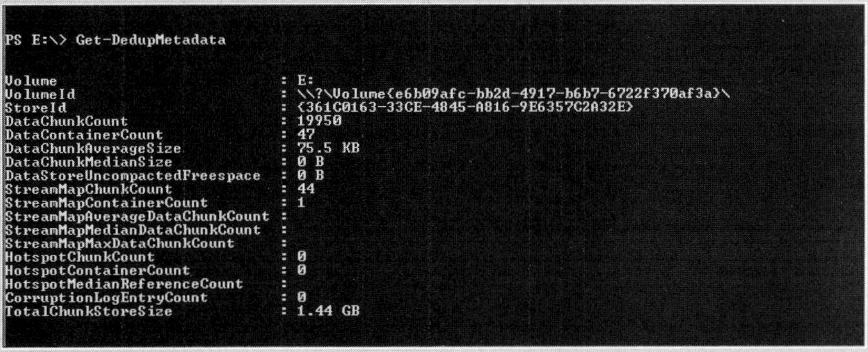

```
PS E:\> Get-DedupMetadata

Volume                         : E:
VolumeId                       : \\?\Volume{e6b09afc-bb2d-4917-b6b7-6722f370af3a}\
StoreId                        : {361C0163-33CE-4845-A816-9E6357C2A32E}
DataChunkCount                 : 19950
DataContainerCount             : 47
DataChunkAverageSize           : 75.5 KB
DataChunkMedianSize            : 0 B
DataStoreUncompactedFreespace  : 0 B
StreamMapChunkCount            : 44
StreamMapContainerCount        : 1
StreamMapAverageDataChunkCount :
StreamMapMedianDataChunkCount  :
StreamMapMaxDataChunkCount     :
HotspotChunkCount              : 0
HotspotContainerCount          : 0
HotspotMedianReferenceCount    :
CorruptionLogEntryCount        : 0
TotalChunkStoreSize            : 1.44 GB
```

Checking for Corrupt Volumes

The last thing in relation to dedup that we will talk about in this chapter is volume corruption checks. As you can imagine, the more commonality found in files, the more the chunk store will grow, and the more reparse points that will exist on disk.

Imagine if the disk sector where part of a chunk exists became corrupted. You'd risk losing potentially hundreds or thousands of files. Although this is a rare occurrence, especially if you combine it with resiliency techniques, there is a potential for it to happen. Dedup has some special built-in checks that will prevent this from happening.

For example, dedup has redundancy for critical metadata; it also provides redundancy for the most accessed chunks (if a chunk is accessed more than 100 times, it becomes a hot spot). It provides a log file to record the details of any corruption, and later through the use of scrubbing jobs it will analyze the log and make repairs.

Repairs can be made from the backup of the working copy when referring to the critical metadata or the hot spots. If you have dedupped a mirrored storage space, dedup can use the mirrored data to repair the chunk.

As with optimization jobs and garbage-collection jobs, scrubbing jobs happen on a scheduled basis and can be configured to happen more often than the default of one week.

You can trigger a job with PowerShell using the following syntax:

```
Start-DeDupJob -Type Scrubbing -Volume E:
```

This will invoke a verification job against the E: drive volume but will check only the entries in the corruption log file.

To check the integrity of the entire deduplicated volume, use the following command:

```
Start-DeDupJon -Type Scrubbing -Volume E: -full
```

To review the output of the scrubbing, check Event Viewer. All output for a scrubbing job is stored in Event Viewer ➤ Applications and Services Logs ➤ Microsoft ➤ Windows ➤ Deduplication ➤ Scrubbing. See Figure 12.87.

FIGURE 12.87
Event Viewer
Scrubbing log

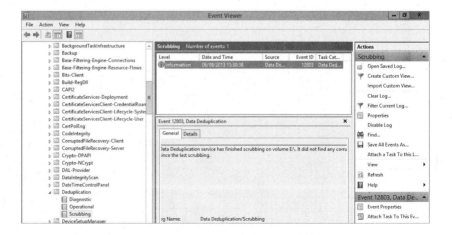

The Bottom Line

Create a storage pool on a virtual disk.   Storage is an ever-growing business requirement. If you were constantly buying SAN solutions to meet this need, it would prove very costly. Also, it is very hard to predict what you may need in a year's time. How would you manage your storage to get the most out of it and to meet your future storage needs?

Master It   In your lab create a storage pool using the GUI with three disks. Create a virtual disk three times the size of the total usable capacity of the disk. Format it and get it ready to use.

Create additional storage on a virtual disk.   A common occurrence in enterprises today is last-minute requests for provisioning of applications that require large amounts of storage. Often the storage available locally in the server is not large enough to meet the need. How can you get additional storage onto the server without adding local storage?

Master It   In your lab deploy an iSCSI target, create a virtual disk, and then connect your server to use the newly created storage.

Use deduplication techniques to reduce file size.   Part of the reason behind data growth in today's environments is the availability of storage, but storage will become a problem sooner rather than later. A high percentage of these files contain a large degree of identical data patterns, but using deduplication techniques can dramatically reduce the disk space required and make better overall use of the storage in place.

Master It   In your lab copy an ISO multiple times into different shares, and repeat for office documents that are not located on your System volume. Enable Deduplication on the data drive, and exclude a share of importance in your environment.

Chapter 13

Files, Folders, and Basic Shares

One of the core functions of any server is to serve resources such as files and folders. In Windows Server 2012 R2, the File Services and Storage Services roles have been combined into one role called File and Storage Services. This role is installed by default; however, any additional roles that serve File and Storage Services will need to be added via the wizard in Server Manager. The File Services role includes role services such as the File Server Resource Manager (FSRM), services for Network File System (to support Unix clients), the Windows Search service, and BranchCache for remote offices. Now that Storage Services is available in conjunction with File Services, Windows Server 2012 R2 has unleashed some new and improved roles and features like Deduplication, Storage Spaces, and Storage Pools that have made this version of Windows Server the best yet.

When you plan on sharing files and folders, it's important that you understand not only how to share the data but also how to protect it with permissions including both New Technology File System (NTFS) and share permissions. Although both sets of permissions are applied independently, they also work with each other cumulatively to provide multiple levels of enhanced security options to us. You should be able to quickly determine what the ultimate permissions are for a user who accesses a share over the network. And, if you want to protect entire hard drives, you can still use BitLocker Drive Encryption to encrypt them just as you could in Windows Server 2008 R2. One of the most notable new features in Windows Server 2012 R2 drive encryption is the new BitLocker Drive Encryption options. You can now use the "Encrypt used disk space only" option! No more waiting for hours for the entire volume to finish encrypting when you are only using a small portion of the total disk space. We will take a deeper dive into BitLocker's new features toward the end of the chapter.

The underlying protocol that handles file transfers is Server Message Block (SMB), which has been upgraded to version 3.0 in Server 2012. SMB 3.0 comes with many new features that have redefined file shares as a foundation for enterprise storage solutions for small and medium-size companies. This protocol stack provides some significant benefits for file transfers over the network—as long as you're connecting to the right kinds of clients. Both SMB 1.0 and SMB 2.0, with all of their inherent challenges, will still be used when connecting to legacy machines. Currently only Windows 8 and the Windows Server 2012 family can take full advantage of the new SMB 3.0 features that will be discussed in this chapter.

In this chapter, you will learn to:

◆ Install additional File and Storage Services roles on a server

◆ Combine share and NTFS permissions

◆ Implement BitLocker Drive Encryption

Understanding the File and Storage Services Role

The File and Storage Services role combines multiple file and storage technologies that assist administrators with setting up file servers for their organization. The default installation would allow basic administration of storage functionality by using Server Manager or PowerShell, but to build a proper file server you would want to install the File Server role alongside other important roles like File Server Resource Manager and DFS Replication. Not that DFS is needed all the time—it can definitely be a great addition when you need replication for availability or geographically dispersed locations. The important thing is to have a plan and an end goal in place for your server roles. Try to get the most out of the wizard the first time around by planning accordingly. We will add roles in the next section.

The core component of any server is its ability to share files. In fact, the Server service in the entire Windows Server family (including Server 2012 R2) handles the server's basic file- and print-sharing capabilities. But what exactly does that mean, and why is it so important? By default, just because you have a server running doesn't mean it has anything available for your users. Before they can actually get to resources on the server, you must share your resources. Let's say you have a folder on your local F drive named Apps with three subfolders, as shown in Figure 13.1.

FIGURE 13.1
Subfolders in the F:\Apps folder

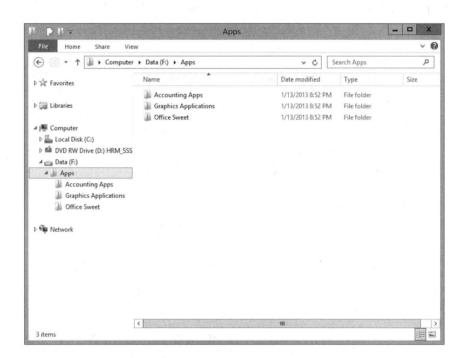

When you share this folder on the network under the name Apps, you allow your clients to map a new drive letter on their machines to your F:\Apps folder. By mapping a drive, you are placing a virtual pointer directly on the remote drive. If you map your client's M drive to the Apps share of the server, the M drive will look identical to the server's F:\Apps folder, as shown in Figure 13.2.

FIGURE 13.2
The BF1\Apps
share mapped
to the M drive

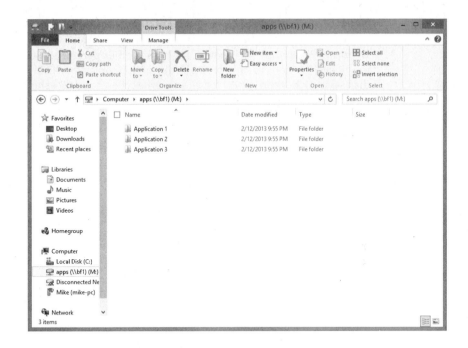

FIGURE 13.2
The BF1\Apps
share mapped
to the M drive

Don't worry; we'll slow down and explain how to create this share and how to connect to it later in this chapter. That's really all there is to it. Sharing resources means that you allow your users to access those resources from the network. No real processing goes into it as far as the server is concerned; it just hands out files and folders as they are.

Additional Role Services and Features

Server Manager is a single console that includes several sections that can be used to manage the different server roles including the File and Storage Services role. File and Storage Services in Windows Server 2012 R2 helps you do much more than just share folders. The File and Storage Services role includes several additional role services:

File Server   This is the primary role service required to support the File and Storage Services role. This role provides you the ability to create and manage shares alongside allowing users to share and access files that are available on the network. One nice feature of File Server is that it is automatically added when a folder is shared. This role uses the new SMB 3.0 protocol, which is discussed in more depth toward the end of this chapter.

Distributed File System   Distributed File System (DFS) includes both DFS Replication and DFS Namespaces and is covered in more depth in Chapter 14, "Creating and Managing Shared Folders."

Data Deduplication   Data Deduplication (Dedup) allows you to save more disk space by locating and removing duplication within data files. Instead of storing multiple copies of the same identical files, only a single copy takes up space and all duplicates reference the original.

The main idea of Data Deduplication is to store more data in less space by segmenting files into small blocks, identify the duplicates, and then maintain a single copy of those duplicates. Dedup on Server 2012 R2 is now block-based at the operating system level; many storage providers' solutions use file-based Dedup at the storage level. Many people wonder how much disk savings they can expect for different file types. Table 13.1 shows some very impressive numbers provided by tests in a lab environment. These tests may be somewhat optimized for better performance.

TABLE 13.1: Storage Savings Dedup Provided in a Test Environment

FILE TYPE	SAVINGS
General files	50–60% storage savings with Deduplication enabled
Documents	30–50% storage savings with Deduplication enabled
Application library	70–80% storage savings with Deduplication enabled
VHD library	80–95% storage savings with Deduplication enabled

File Server Resource Manager   File Server Resource Manager (FSRM) provides a rich set of additional tools that can be used to manage the storage of data on the server, including configuring quotas, defining file-screening policies, and generating storage reports. A full section on FSRM is included later in this chapter in the "File Server Resource Manager" section, including what's new with FSRM in Windows Server 2012 R2.

Network File System   This service enables you to grant access to files from Unix client computers and any other machines that can talk using the Network File System (NFS). Windows Server 2012 R2 has really come a long way since Windows Server 2008 by delivering an impressive clustered implementation solution with this server edition. Server 2012 provides seamless failover for mixed-mode clients in a clustered environment. Recognizing the need for and growth of the virtualization world, Microsoft has designed NFS Server specifically for clustered virtual environments, where I/O continuity exists regardless of the operation being performed at the time of failover. NFS version 4.1 is now used, making the implementation of NFS the most reliable and easiest to deploy within the Windows Server family so far.

Windows Server 2012 R2 also introduces a number of new PowerShell cmdlets for NFS. For a full list of all the cmdlets that are available use the `Get-Command -Module NFS` cmdlet. As you can see, there is a cmdlet for just about everything you would want to do with NFS. For syntax information or to learn more about a particular command, you can use any of the following cmdlets:

◆   `Get-Help <cmdlet name> -Detailed`

◆   `Get-Help <cmdlet name> -Examples`

◆   `Get-Help <cmdlet name> -Full`

Storage Services   Windows Server 2012 R2 has added some great features with Storage Services. It now includes both storage spaces and storage pools. By combining Storage Services with Data Deduplication, Windows Server 2012 R2 can now not only provide but contend with services that would normally require a separate storage area network.

File Server VSS Agent Service   Once enabled, this role will allow you to perform shadow copies of applications that store data on your file server. New to Server 2012, the VSS for SMB File Shares feature allows backups to run while live data is written to SMB file shares. Previous versions of VSS would only allow shadow copies to work on local volumes.

iSCSI Target Server   This role is the server component that provides block storage to other servers and applications on the network. It contains all the management tools needed for iSCSI targets. Target Server runs the iSCSI target over an Ethernet network without having to use any additional hardware. This role service supports heterogeneous storage, which allows a Windows Server to share storage in a mixed software environment by utilizing various types of iSCSI initiators. This role can be managed using the new integrated Server Manager GUI or by using the new Windows PowerShell cmdlets included with Windows Server 2012 R2.

BranchCache for Network Files   BranchCache can be used in a multiple-site environment to allow computers in branch offices to cache commonly downloaded files. BranchCache needs to be enabled on the shared folder. You'll see how to do this in the "Using Offline Files/Client-Side Caching" section later in this chapter.

FILE SERVER ROLE ADDED WHEN A FOLDER IS SHARED

If you just use Windows Explorer to share a folder, the File Server role is added automatically. You don't have to add the role using Server Manager. However, when you plan to utilize any additional roles, you will need to add those roles from the Add Roles and Features Wizard found in Server Manager.

How to Add Roles to the File and Storage Services Role

You can add File and Storage Services roles by following these steps:

1. Launch Server Manager by selecting the Server Manager icon pinned to the taskbar on your desktop or by selecting the Server Manager tile from the Start screen, as shown in Figure 13.3.

2. From your Dashboard tab, select the link "Add roles and features," shown in Figure 13.4.

3. The Add Roles and Features Wizard will walk you through the rest of the process. Review the information on the Before You Begin page, and click Next.

4. The Installation Type page defaults to a role-based or feature-based installation. The second option has role services for VDI deployment. Keep the default, and click Next.

5. On the Server Selection page, choose the server you wish to add role services to, and click Next.

FIGURE 13.3
Selecting Server
Manager from
the taskbar or
Start screen

FIGURE 13.4
Launching the
Add Roles and
Features Wizard

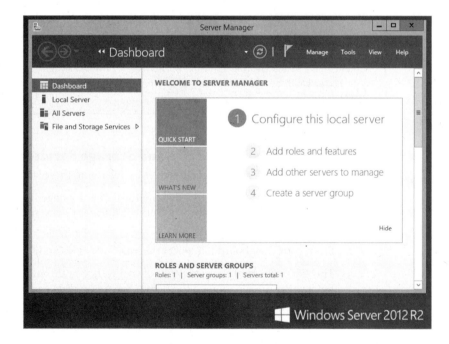

6. On the Server Roles page, select the following role services, as shown in Figure 13.5: File Server, File Server Resource Manager, and BranchCache for Network Files. Click Next.

FIGURE 13.5
Selecting File
and Storage
Services Role
Services

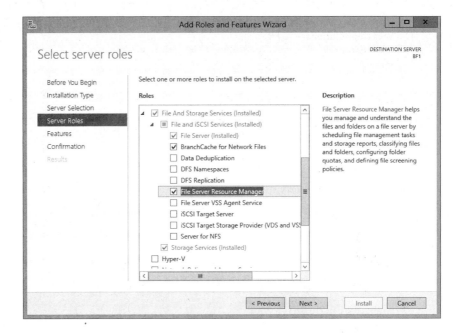

Now that you have selected your roles, it is time to install any additional features that help support your role services. There are many useful features to choose from.

ROLES VS. FEATURES

A role is considered a major function of the server, whereas a feature is a smaller add-on package that usually provides additional support to a major role. Major roles would include Active Directory, DNS, and DHCP. Features like PowerShell, Windows Server Backup, and Remote Assistance provide additional functionality to help you better manage your server roles.

---

7. For the moment let's install BitLocker Drive Encryption, BranchCache, and Enhanced Storage. You will notice that selecting BitLocker Drive Encryption automatically calls out the Enhanced Storage features to be installed as well, shown in Figure 13.6. Click Next.

8. Review the information on the Confirmation page to make sure you haven't missed anything.

   The wizard nicely displays all selected roles, features, and tools that support them. There are a few additional options available on this page that can be useful: "Restart the destination server automatically if required," "Export configuration settings," and "Specify an alternate source path."

FIGURE 13.6
Selecting additional
features for role
services

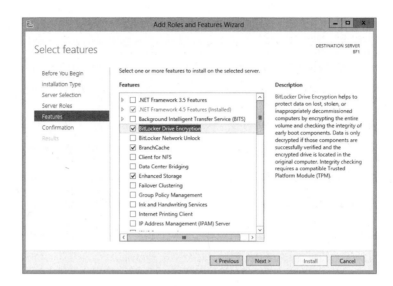

9. Click Install.

The final page of this wizard is the Results page. An installation progress bar will be
displayed. The task will run in the background if you wish to close the page and exit. You
can always view task details in the command bar by clicking Notifications.

10. Upon successful installation, reboot the server manually, or if you selected the Restart
Automatically option from the Confirmation page, the server will reboot when the install
has finished.

At this point, Server Manager now includes all of the roles and features you installed from
the exercise. If you open Server Manager and go to your dashboard, you'll see that you can
now view and use the installed roles and features by clicking tools and selecting the desired
resource. The File Server Resource Manager features are shown in Figure 13.7.

FIGURE 13.7
File Server Resource
Manager tools

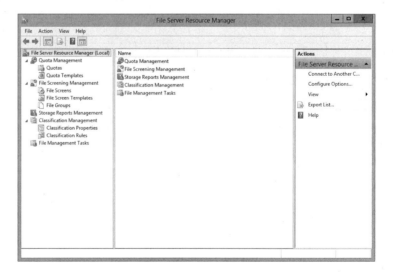

Creating Shares

The process of creating shares has undergone some nice changes in this server edition. It feels as though everything has a wizard to guide us through our tasks and actions. There are many different ways to create shares that are discussed throughout this Mastering book. In this section we will focus on creating shares using Server Manager. No matter which method you use, you'll need either Administrator or Power User rights on the computer where you're creating the shares.

Once a share is created, it can be published to Active Directory to make it easy for users to locate the share. You'll learn how to create shares using Server Manager and publish the shares to Active Directory in this section.

Creating Shares with Server Manager

It's relatively easy to add shares using Server Manager. The Shares tab, found in File and Storage Services, has a New Share Wizard to help you with this task:

1. If it's not already started, launch Server Manager by selecting the Server Manager icon pinned to the taskbar on your desktop, or by selecting the Server Manager tile from the Start screen.

2. Select File and Storage Services, and then select Shares.

3. Right-click the Shared Folder Location page, and click New Share. You can also select New Share from the Tasks drop-down menu. Either action will launch the New Share Wizard, as shown in Figure 13.8.

FIGURE 13.8
Create a new share using Server Manager.

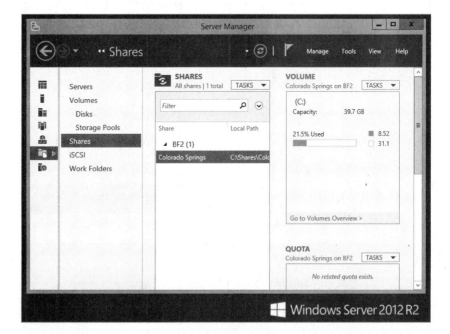

The first screen, Select Profile, gives you the choice of which profile protocols to use when creating your share. There are two main choices and a few subchoices. You can either create an SMB share or an NFS share. In general:

◆ SMB shares are used for Windows operating systems.

◆ NFS shares are used to talk to Unix-based machines.

SMB and NFS have both Quick and Advanced share profile options. The Advanced profile has a few additional configuration options that include enabling quotas. You can always add the extra features later using Server Manager. If you decide to enable quotas, you will be required to build a new quota template first or edit an existing template. SMB has one extra share profile called SMB Share - Applications. This profile creates an SMB file share with additional settings used in a virtual environment.

4. For this exercise let's use the SMB Share - Quick profile shown in Figure 13.9. Select the Quick profile and click Next.

FIGURE 13.9
Selecting a share profile

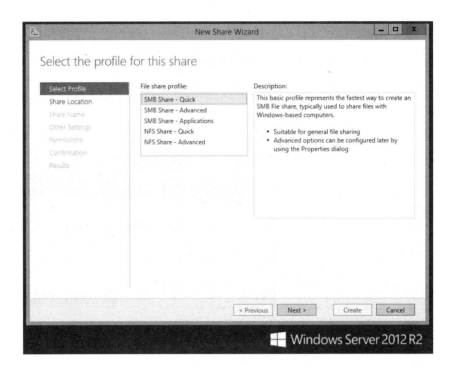

5. On the Share Location page, choose which server will host the share, and also select which volume on the server will serve as the share location.

Please note that you can only create a share on a server that has the File Services Resource Manager role installed.

6. Click Next.

The Share Name page allows you to define the name of the share and provide a share description, and it shows you both the local and remote network paths needed to reach the resource.

7. Take note of this information, because you will need to provide these network paths to your users for access. Figure 13.10 provides an example of naming your share. Click Next.

FIGURE 13.10
Naming a new share

The Other Settings page gives you four additional features to help make your share more robust:

◆ The "Enable access-based enumeration" feature will automatically hide a folder from a user who does not have permission to read the folder.

◆ The "Allow caching" option gives offline users access to the shared data when working offline.

◆ Since you installed the BranchCache role in the previous exercise, you can now select the "Enable BranchCache on the file share" option on this page of the wizard.

◆ The last option on this page, "Encrypt data access," secures remote file access to and from the share.

If you have not yet turned on encryption for server, go ahead and select this option now. If it's greyed out and already checked, then you already have encryption turned on for this server.

8. Make your selections and click Next.

9. The Permissions page gives you an opportunity to change the NTFS permissions if desired. We'll cover NTFS permissions later in the chapter, but for now click Next to accept the default NTFS permissions.

10. The Confirmation page gives you a summary of all the choices you have made for creating your new share. Review them for accuracy, make any desired changes, and then click Create. Figure 13.11 shows the Confirmation page.

FIGURE 13.11
The Confirmation page

The final page of this wizard is the Results page. Two progress bars will be displayed: one bar for the Create SMB Share task and one bar for the Set SMB Permissions task. Once the Status shows Completed, the share is built and ready for use.

11. Click Close to finish the wizard.

Creating Shares on Remote Computers Using Server Manager

It's also possible to perform the previous procedure to create shares on remote computers using Server Manager. Just like in previous server editions, Server Manager can perform management tasks on remote computers. Remote Management is installed and enabled by default with servers running Server 2012. In Figure 13.12 you can see the different options that Server Manager provides when another server has been added.

FIGURE 13.12
Management tasks on a remote server

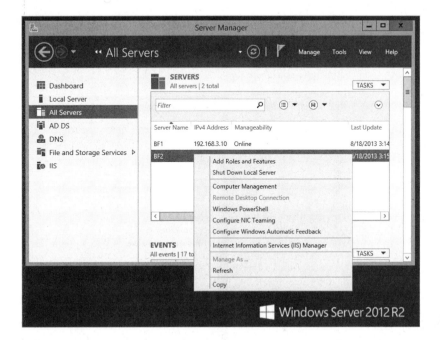

Managing Windows Server 2008 from Server 2012 R2

In order to fully manage servers running Windows Server 2008 or Windows Server 2008 R2, a few updates are required. First install .NET Framework 4.0 and then install Windows Management Framework 3.0. You will then need to ensure the remote computer is configured correctly, which can be done by entering three commands:

1. Enter the following command at the command prompt on the computer that you want to administer remotely. This command will enable the WinRM listener:
   ```
   winrm qc
   ```

2. When prompted, type **Y** and press Enter.

3. Ensure the Virtual Disk Service is running on the remote computer. You can do this from the command line with the following command:
   ```
   sc config vds start= auto
   net start vds
   ```

Real World Scenario

SETTING USER LIMITS

You can configure how many users can connect to a share simultaneously by configuring the "User limit" option on the properties page of the share. To set the user limit; open Administrative Tools, double-click Computer Management, expand Shared Folders, select Shares, right-click the share you wish to set a user limit on, and then select Properties. Here is a screenshot of setting the user limit on a share.

As an example, if an application under your share is licensed for 100 concurrent users, you can configure your server share to maintain that limit, even though you may have 200 users on your network. Just select the "Allow this number of users" radio button, and fill in the appropriate number (it defaults to 1). As users connect to the share, they build up to the user limit. As users log off or disconnect from the share, the number drops. This type of licensing enforcement can be handy in reducing your licensing costs.

Be careful with your licensing, though. Not all applications have a concurrent license mode, although they might have a client license mode. With client license mode, the manufacturer doesn't care how many users are accessing the application at any given time; they just care about how many people have installed the application altogether. This user limit option will not protect you in these cases.

Another thing to keep in mind is that this user connection concurrency limit is based on the entire share. It cannot be defined for each folder within a share. For example, you could have two applications in a single share. Application 1 has a concurrency limit of 100, and application 2 has no limits. You might inadvertently limit access to application 2 when the share limits the connections to 100. The easy solution is to use different shares if different limits are needed.

Finally, you need to consider how your users connect to the share to use these applications before you limit them based on concurrency. If your users all connect to the share upon logging in (such as with a mapped drive) but don't disconnect until logging off, your concurrency limit may be used up based on who shows up for work first, and you'll have 100 people using up your concurrency limit even if only a small percentage of them are actually using the application. If connections are made only when actually using the application, the user limit will work quite nicely.

WATCH THE SPACES WITH SC

The sc config command is used to change the configuration of a service. By default the Virtual Disk Service (VDS) is not started, so you will use this command to automatically start the VDS on the server. You will need this service running to use remote management capabilities. For more information about the sc command's options and features, open up a command-line interface and type **sc config?**. The server config (sc) command is very particular about spaces. The following command has a space after the = symbol and will work:

```
sc config vds start= auto
```

On the other hand, this next command will fail since the space is missing:

```
sc config vds start=auto
```

---

4. Create a firewall exception for the Remote Volume Management group with the following command. Even though this spans two lines in the book, the entire command should be entered on a single line.

```
netsh advfirewall firewall set rule~CA
group="Remote Volume Management" new enable=yes
```

When the command is entered correctly, the output indicates that that it has "Updated 3 rules."

Once the remote computer is configured, you can launch Server Manager on your local computer, select Manage, and then select Add Servers. There are three ways to find and add new machines to your local Server Manager. You can add a server by searching through your Active Directory and selecting a domain-joined computer, you can also add a server using the DNS tab by typing in the computer name or IP address, and lastly the Import tab will let you directly call out the network path to the desired machine or browse network locations to find the needed resource. Using one of these methods, find the machine you wish to manage and click OK. After a moment, Server Manager will be connected to the remote computer. You can now view and manage the remote computer on the All Servers tab in Server Manager. Simply right-click the newly connected remote computer, and a list of management functions will be displayed for you to use, as shown in Figure 13.13.

FIGURE 13.13
Managing a remote
computer

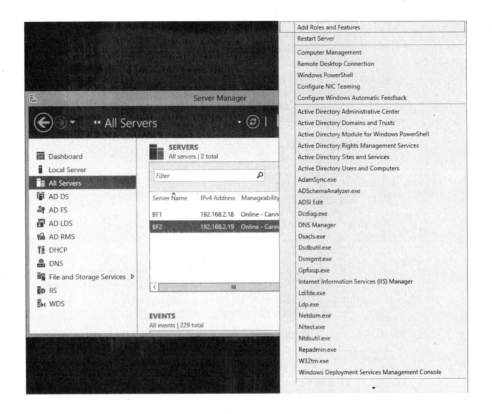

Publishing Shares in Active Directory

One of the great things about Active Directory is that it can unify all resources in an enterprise into a single directory, whether it's printers, groups, users, organizational units, or just about anything you can dream up—or more appropriately, serve up. This counts for shares too. The primary reason to publish a share to Active Directory is to allow users to easily find it.

To publish a share, you need to be in the Active Directory Users and Computers Management Console. Right-click the organizational unit of choice, and select New ➢ Shared Folder. From there, you'll be asked to provide a name for this publication of the share and, of course, the share name. That's all there is to it—your share is now published in Active Directory.

Once the share is published, you can also add keywords to help users easily find the published share:

1. Right-click the shared folder object in Active Directory Users and Computers.

2. Select Properties, and click the Keywords button.

3. Add any keywords you like that users might use to help them find this share.

Figure 13.14 shows keywords being added to the Colorado Springs published share.

FIGURE 13.14
Adding keywords
to a published
share

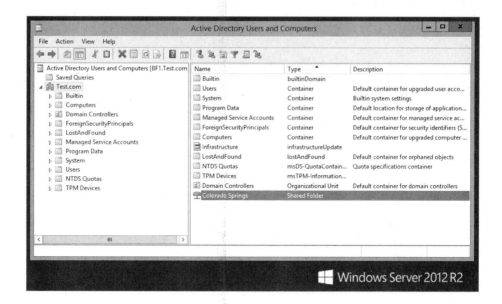

Users can then use the Active Directory Search tool to search based on the keyword.
Figure 13.15 shows the Active Directory Search tool with Shared Folders selected in the Find
drop-down box. We added the keyword *Colorado* and clicked Find Now, and the share was
located. At this point, we could just double-click the share to access it.

FIGURE 13.15
Using Active
Directory Search
to locate a
published share

Managing Permissions

One of the great strengths of both NTFS-formatted drives and shares is the ability to assign permissions and control who can access different files and folders. While Chapter 14 will cover the inner workings of these permissions in much greater detail, this chapter gives a basic introduction to both NTFS and share permissions. You'll notice that not much has changed in regard to permissions with this server edition. Mostly there's just a new way to navigate and use the same features and tools you are familiar with from Windows Server 2008 R2.

There are many similarities between NTFS and share permissions, which you'll learn about in this section. These include how each permission can be assigned Allow or Deny, how permissions are cumulative, how Deny takes precedence, and how the principle of implicit deny is used.

When a user accesses a share that has both NTFS and share permissions applied, the resulting permission is commonly called the least restrictive permission. Since you may be asked to resolve the problem of why a user can't access a file or folder, you should know how to calculate the resulting permission, which you'll learn in this section.

NTFS Permissions

NTFS permissions apply to any file or folder on a disk that has been formatted with NTFS.

Read   When a user is assigned Read permission, the user is allowed to view the contents, permissions, and attributes associated with a file or folder.

Read & Execute   The Read & Execute permission is used to grant permission for a user to execute files. Any executable files (such as .exe, .bat, and .com) are files that can be executed or launched. If a user has only Read permission, and not Read & Execute, the files can't be executed.

List Folder Contents   The List Folder Contents permission allows a user to view the contents of a folder. It will allow a user to see that files exist in a folder but will not apply Read permissions to those files.

Write   If a user is assigned Write permission to a file or folder, the user can modify the file or folder. This includes adding new files or folders to a folder or making changes to existing files or folders. However, it does not include deleting files from a folder.

Modify   Modify includes all of the permissions from Read, Read & Execute, and Change and adds the ability to delete files and folders.

Full Control   Full Control is a combination of all the available permissions. It adds the ability to change permissions and take ownership of files or folders.

Share Permissions

Share permissions apply to shares only when they are accessed over the network. There are only three share permissions:

Read   Users granted Read permission can read files and folders within the share.

Change   Users granted Change permission can read, execute, modify, and delete files and folders within the share.

Full Control   Users granted Full Control permission have all the permissions from Change and can also modify permissions on the share.

Share and NTFS Permission Similarities

Now that you have a basic understanding of the overall NTFS and share permissions, it's easier to explore the similarities, and there are many. These include:

- Both can be assigned either Allow or Deny.

- Both are cumulative.

- Deny takes precedence with both.

- Both support implicit deny.

ASSIGNING ALLOW OR DENY

As you start working with permissions, you'll notice that they have both Allow and Deny check boxes for each of the listed permissions. Here's an overview of how they work:

- If the permission is set to Allow for a user or group, the user or group has this permission.

- If the permission is set to Deny for a user or group, the user or group does not have the permission.

- Permissions are cumulative. If a user has multiple Allow permissions assigned (such as Allow Read and Allow Change), the user has a combination of the assigned permissions.

- If both Allow and Deny permissions are assigned for a user, Deny takes precedence.

If there aren't any permissions assigned to a user, then the user does not have access to the object. This is referred to as an *implicit deny*. Both share permissions and NTFS permissions use the discretionary access control (DAC) model to control access. Each object has a discretionary access control list (DACL, pronounced "dackel"). The DACL is a list of access control entries (ACEs).

Each ACE identifies a user or a group with their associated security identifier (SID) and Allow or Deny permission. Any object can have multiple ACEs in the DACL; said another way, any object can have multiple permissions assigned.

SECURITY IDENTIFIERS

Every user and every group is uniquely identified with a SID. When the user logs on, a token is created that includes the user's SID and the SIDs of any groups where the user is a member. This token is used by the operating system to determine whether a user should have access. The SIDs in the token are compared to the SIDs in the access control entries of the DACL to determine access.

When a user accesses a file, folder, or share, the operating system compares the DACL with the user's account and group memberships. If there's a match, the user is granted the appropriate permission.

CUMULATIVE PERMISSIONS

Objects can have multiple permissions assigned. As an example, imagine a share named ProjectData. Administrators could be granted Full Control, another group could be granted Change, and another group could be granted Read permission. When multiple permissions are assigned, permissions are cumulative. In other words, if multiple permissions apply to a user, the user has the combination of all the permissions.

Imagine that Sally is a member of both the G_Sales group and the G_SalesAdmins group, and these groups are granted the following permissions to the Sales share:

G_Sales   Allow Change permission

G_SalesAdmins   Allow Full Control permission

Since Sally is a member of both groups, she is granted both Change and Full Control; said another way, she is granted the combination of both the Change and Full Control permissions.

DENY TAKES PRECEDENCE

If both Allow and Deny for any permission are assigned to a user, Deny takes precedence. As an example, imagine you have granted the G_Sales group Full Control to a share that includes proprietary information. For some reason, Billy-Joe-Bob (who is a member of the G_Sales group) has fallen out of grace with the company. You're asked to leave him in the G_Sales group so he can access other shares but prevent him from accessing the proprietary share.

Figure 13.16 shows what you can do. The share permissions started with personnel in the G_Sales group having Full Control permissions on the share. To prevent Billy-Joe-Bob from accessing the data at all, his account was added and assigned Deny Full Control. Said another way, his account is explicitly denied.

FIGURE 13.16
Selecting custom
share permissions

Notice the conflict. The user is granted access as a member of the G_Sales group and denied access for his specific account. The conflict is resolved in favor of the Deny permission. This makes sense if you think about it. When you take the extra steps needed to deny access, you don't want anything overriding it. Deny takes precedence.

Implicit Deny

There's also something known as *implicit deny*. If permissions aren't explicitly granted, they are implicitly denied.

Imagine a share named ProjectData where the only group granted access to the share is the G_Sales group. Maria is in the G_HR group and is not a member of the G_Sales group, so she does not have any access to the share. She hasn't been explicitly granted access, so she is implicitly denied access.

This is similar to your home. If you never give the keys to anyone for your house, they shouldn't be able to get in. Of course, you still need to worry about bandits and hackers, but from the basic perspective, giving no permissions results in no access.

Modifying Share and NTFS Permissions

You can modify both the share and NTFS permissions using Server Manager, Computer Management, or Windows Explorer. The steps are a little different for each method, but ultimately you'll get to the same permissions pages. For this discussion, we're limiting the procedure to using Server Manager.

Imagine that you've created a share and granted the Everyone group Read permission. However, now you want to change the permissions so that users in the G_Sales group have Change permissions and no other users besides administrators can view or use this set of folders and files. You can follow these steps to make the changes:

1. Launch Server Manager, and browse to File and Storage Services ➤ Shares.

2. Right-click the Apps share, and select Properties.

3. Click the Permissions button, and then click Customize Permissions. Your display will look similar to Figure 13.17.

FIGURE 13.17
Viewing the share permissions

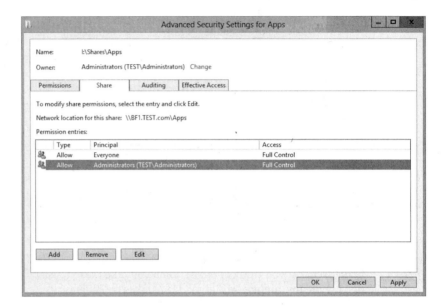

4. On the Share tab, click Add. Then click "Select a principal," and enter the name of the group you want to grant access to the share (for example, **G_Sales**) and click OK.

5. Since you don't want everyone to have access, select the Everyone group, and click Remove. Click OK.

6. Click Apply, and then navigate off the Share tab to the Permissions tab.

   Notice that the Permissions tab delegates NTFS permissions and the Share tab delegates Share permissions. We will go over mixing these permissions in the next section.

7. Now on the Permissions tab, click Add, and enter the name of a group you want to add (such as **G_Sales**). Click OK after you've added the group.

   By default any user or group you add is automatically granted Read, Read & Execute, and List Folder Contents permissions.

8. Select the Allow Write permission for the group you've added to ensure they can also make changes to the files, and then click OK.

9. Remember to remove the Everyone group from this set of permissions as well: Select the Everyone group and click Remove.

   Share permissions and NTFS permissions are managed separately but work together to provide proper permissions. Your display will look similar to Figure 13.18.

FIGURE 13.18
Viewing the NTFS permissions

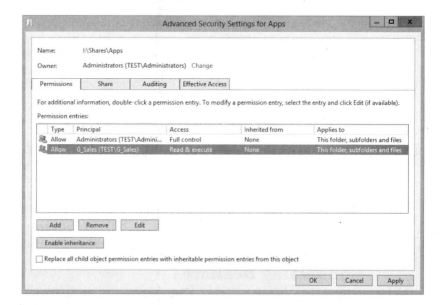

10. Click Apply and OK on the Advanced Security page to finalize permissions.

11. Click Apply and OK on the Apps Properties Permissions page to finish the exercise.

Combining Share and NTFS Permissions

People sometimes find it challenging to identify the permissions a user will have when they access a file or folder via a share. We like to keep it simple with these three steps:

1. Determine the cumulative NTFS permissions.

2. Determine the cumulative share permissions.

3. Determine which of the two provides the least access (commonly called the *most restrictive permission*).

Imagine that Sally is a member of the G_Sales and G_ITAdmins groups. The assigned permissions for the SalesData folder (shared as the SalesData share) are shown in Table 13.2.

TABLE 13.2: Combining NTFS and Share Permissions

GROUP	NTFS PERMISSIONS	SHARE PERMISSIONS
G_Sales	Read, Read & Execute, List Folder Contents	Read
G_ITSalesAdmins	Full Control	Change

In step 1, you need to determine the cumulative NTFS permissions. Sally has the Read, Read & Execute, and List Folder Contents permissions as a member of the G_Sales group. Additionally, she has Full Control permission as a member of the G_IT SalesAdmins group. Since Full Control includes all the other permissions, her cumulative NTFS permissions are Full Control.

In step 2, you need to determine the cumulative share permissions. Sally has the Read permission as a member of the G_Sales group. Additionally, she has the Change permission as a member of the G_IT SalesAdmins group. Since Change includes both Read and Write, her cumulative share permissions are Change.

The last step involves a simple question. Which permission provides the least access or is the most restrictive: Full Control or Change? The answer is Change. Change is the permission that Sally will have if accessing the share over the network.

How about a trick question? What is Sally's permission when she accesses the SalesData folder locally?

The answer is Full Control. Remember that share permissions apply only when a user accesses the share over a network. If the folder is accessed locally, only NTFS permissions apply.

Connecting to Shares

Now that you have these shares, how do people use them? Assuming that you have a share called Apps on a server called BF1, how would someone attached to the network access that share?

Primarily, you connect to a share using the universal naming convention (UNC) of \\ ServerName\ShareName. Alternatively as a simple example, you can press the Windows key + R from the desktop to open the Run dialog box and enter **ServerName** (using the server name of any server connected to your network) followed by a backslash, as shown in Figure 13.19. Another way to open the Run dialog box in Server 2012 is to go to the Start screen, type **Run**, and press Enter. In the figure, we've used **BF2** to connect to the server named BF2.

FIGURE 13.19
Searching for shares

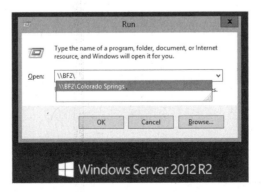

Once the operating system connects, it retrieves a list of shares that are available. On this server there are currently four shares, well, four shares that aren't hidden. Chapter 14 will show you how additional hidden shares are available. You could type in **Apps** to the end of \\BF1\ and complete the entry as **BF1\Apps**, or simply click the Apps share from the menu shown in Figure 13.19 and click OK to connect the Apps share.

Besides using the Search menu, you can connect to the share in the following ways:

Mapping a Drive   You can map a drive letter to a share on your network. For example, users may need access to a share each time they boot. You can right-click either Computer or Network from the Windows Explorer menu and select Map Network Drive. Take a moment to enjoy the new feel of the Server 2012 R2 user interface. With the Windows Explorer page open, select Computer, and then select the Computer option from the top action bar. A new ribbon will be displayed similar to the ones that you are familiar with seeing in programs like Microsoft Word. Many new options are available from the ribbon, including Map a Network Drive. Figure 13.20 shows the Map Network Drive dialog box. With "Reconnect at sign-in" selected, the user will always have the Z drive mapped to the share when they boot.

FIGURE 13.20
Mapping a share to a drive letter

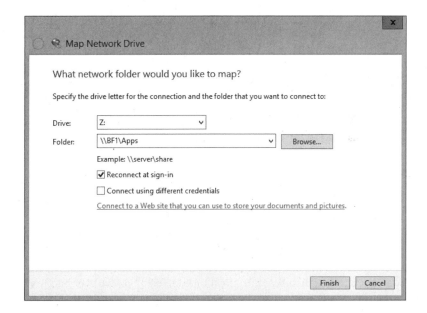

Searching Active Directory   If a client is a member of a domain, the Search Active Directory command appears on the Network console. You can launch Network by selecting Start ➢ Network on Windows Server 2012 R2.

Using net use   You can use the net use command at the command line. The basic syntax is as follows:

```
net use driveletter \\servername\sharename
```

For example, to attach to the share Apps on the server named BF1 and then to be able to refer to that share as drive Z, you could use this command:

```
net use Z: \\BF1\apps
```

If you later want to remove the mapping, you can use this command:

```
net use Z: /delete
```

"A Set of Credentials Conflicts"

Sometimes when you're trying to attach to a share, you'll get an error message that says something like "A set of credentials conflicts with an existing set of credentials on that share."

Here's what's happening. You've already tried to access this share and failed for some reason—perhaps you mistyped a password. The server that the share is on has constructed some security information about you that says you're a deadbeat, and it doesn't want to hear anything else about you. You need to get the server to forget about you so that you can start all over. You can do that with the /d option.

Suppose you've already tried to access the \\BF1\Apps share and apparently failed. It might be that you *are* actually connected to the share but with no permissions. (We know it doesn't make sense, but it happens.) You can find out what shares you're connected to by typing just **net use** all by itself. Chances are, you'll see that \\BF1\Apps is on the list. You have to disconnect from that BF1 server so that you can start over. To do that, type this:

```
net use \\BF1\apps /d
```

Then do another net use to make sure that you have all of those connections cleaned up; you may find that you have *multiple* attachments to a particular server. Or…in a few cases, you may have to disconnect *all* of your file shares with this command:

```
net use * /d
```

With all the connections closed, you can try net use again, and it will work.

Using net use on a WAN

Now you are into one of the most difficult networking areas: connecting to your resources across long distances and great unknowns. If you've ever had to rely on long-distance remote computing, you know not to rely on it. But you have a new little function set in your net use arsenal that takes a lot of the "unknown" out of the picture.

Instead of relying on getting to the appropriate name resolution server, getting through to that server, and getting accurate reliable resolution over an inaccurate and unreliable network link, you can now just map a drive straight to your server via its IP address. Granted, you now need to know that IP address, but it is a good fail-safe. In our case, we work from several different locations connected with frame-relay WAN links. The network isn't always so good about being able to convert server names into IP addresses, so net use \\BF1 usually tells us that our machine couldn't *find* \\BF1. Even if it *does* work, *name resolution*—converting a name such as BF1 to a network address—takes time.

If you know the IP address of the server you're trying to contact, then you can use the IP address in lieu of the server's name. If you know that BF1's IP address is 134.81.12.4, you can simply type this:

```
net use \\134.81.12.4\apps
```

And, because you're probably connecting from a different network, you might have to add the /user: information. And it's never a bad idea to add /persistent:no so that your system doesn't spend five minutes trying to reconnect to it the next time that you start up. So, for example, if BF1 is a member of a domain named BigFirm.com and you have an account on BigFirm
.com named boss, you could ensure that BF1 will know who you are and log you on like so:

```
net use \\134.81.12.4\apps /user:bigfirm.com\boss /persistent:no
```

Although there are many conventional methods of connecting to shares using different GUIs, don't overlook the net use command. You'll find it useful.

Common Shares

In Windows Server, several common shares have already been created for you. Most of these shares are hidden. If you know of these shares, you can connect to any of them using the UNC path.

C$, D$, and So On   All drives, including CD-ROM drives, are given a hidden share to the root of the drive. This share is what is called an *administrative share*. You cannot change the permissions or properties of these shares, other than to configure them for Offline Files (we'll talk about Offline Files at the end of this chapter). Only the Administrators and Backup Operators groups can connect to administrative shares, and you can't stop sharing these administrative shares without modifying the registry or by stopping the Server service (which stops all sharing). These shares come in handy for server administrators who do a lot of remote management. Mapping a drive to the C$ share is the equivalent of being at C:\ on the server.

**ADMIN$**   The ADMIN$ share is another administrative share and it maps to the location of the operating system. If you installed the operating system at D:\Windows, the ADMIN$ share would map to D:\Windows.

PRINT$ Whenever you create a shared printer, the system places the drivers in this share. This allows the drivers to be easily downloaded when clients connect to the shared printer.

**IPC$**   The IPC$ share is probably one of the most widely used shares in interserver communications, though you will rarely interact with it directly. When you try to access shared resources on other computers (to read event logs, for example), the system uses *named pipes*. A named pipe is a piece of memory that handles a communication channel between two processes, whether local or remote, and the IPC$ is used by the named pipes.

NETLOGON   The NETLOGON share is used in conjunction with processing logon requests from users. Once users successfully log in, they are given any profile and script information that they are required to run. This script is often a batch file. For example, we have a common batch file that we want all of our users to run every time they log in. This allows us to have all clients run a standard set of commands, like copying updated network information, mapping standard network drives, and so on. These batch files, scripts, and profiles go in the NET-LOGON share. The NETLOGON share is required on all domain controllers.

SYSVOL The SYSVOL share is used to house Group Policy information and scripts that are accessed by clients on the network. You will always see SYSVOL shares on domain controllers, but they can be replicated to member servers.

File Server Resource Manager

File Server Resource Manager (FSRM) is an important addition that's configurable with the File and Storage Services role. It includes several additional capabilities that make it easier to manage a file server:

◆ Creating and managing quota policies

◆ Creating and managing file screen policies

◆ Viewing reports

These techniques are covered in the following sections.

Creating Quota Policies

NTFS has long included quota management capabilities, but they have been significantly improved with FSRM. In short, quotas allow you to monitor and limit the space users can consume on a volume or folder.

STORAGE USAGE MONITORING VS. QUOTA POLICIES

Although storage usage monitoring uses the same technology as quota policies available with NTFS, it has a subtle difference from the quota policies. Storage monitoring monitors the entire volume and is configured by default to let you know when the drive reaches 85 percent of capacity. Quota policies can be configured on individual folders, which allows you to fine-tune what you monitor.

When creating quotas, you have the ability to set warning limits, set enforcement limits, provide notification of reached limits via email or event log entries, and even execute commands in response to any limit. Quotas can be set for any share on a server or any specific path.

Quotas can be very useful for monitoring storage on file servers. For example, you may have a file server with 2 TB of storage. You may think this is more than enough space, but if some users are creating and editing audio and video files, 2 TB of free space could disappear quickly. A quota policy can help you limit users to a specific amount. However, these audio and video files may be integral to your business, and you may not want to limit the storage space but instead just ensure you're informed when the storage space reaches a certain threshold. Instead of actually limiting the storage, you can use the quota policy to just monitor the usage.

On the surface, quota policies can be very simple to understand and implement. However, you can get pretty sophisticated with them if you need to do so.

QUOTA TEMPLATES

Microsoft has included several quota templates in FSRM that can easily be applied as is, or you can modify them to fit your needs. You can even create your own templates. Figure 13.21 shows the Configure Quota screen with the default templates.

FIGURE 13.21
Viewing the available quota templates

Once you have an idea of how the quotas work, the information on this page gives you the basic information you need to understand what the quota will do. A significant piece of information is the quota type: hard or soft. A *hard* quota limit will enforce the limit and prevent users from exceeding the limit. A *soft* quota limit is just used for monitoring; it will provide notification but does not enforce the limit.

The 200 MB Limit with 50 MB Extension template provides an excellent example of responding to a quota limit being reached. You can view or edit the template properties of any template by right-clicking the template and selecting Edit Template Properties.

The figures in 13.22 show the template being edited. On the left you can see the basic template. Notice on the bottom that there are three notification thresholds that have been configured: 85 percent, 95 percent, and 100 percent. The 85 percent warning only sends an email, the 95 percent warning sends an email and logs an event, and the 100 percent warning also executes a command.

 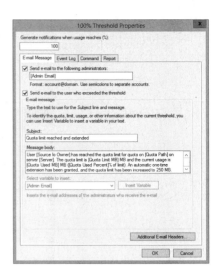

The page on the right of the figure was reached by selecting the Warning (100%) notification threshold and clicking Add. It is using the `dirquota.exe` command-line tool to modify the quota. Specifically, it is changing the quota from a limit of 200 MB to 250 MB. The commands you put here are limited only by your imagination. If necessary, you also set the security context of the command depending on what permissions the command needs to execute.

In addition to executing a command, the other threshold responses are sending an email, logging an event, and creating a report.

E-mail Message Tab

The E-mail Message tab allows you to configure an email response if the threshold is reached. If you want an email sent to an administrator, simply add the administrator's email address (or an administrator's distribution group) on this page in the format of account@domain, such as ITAdmins@bigfirm.com. You can also configure it to send an email to the user who exceeded the threshold simply by selecting a box. FSRM uses Active Directory to look up the user's email address.

The templates include a preconfigured subject line and message body, and both can include variables. In Figure 13.23 the message body includes several variables: Source I/O Owner, Quota Path, Server, and more. If you click within either the subject line or the message body, the variable drop-down box will be enabled. You can select any of these variables to see a short explanation of what it is. We know when we first saw [Source lo Owner], we couldn't figure out what "lo" was, but after selecting it from the drop-down box, we saw it meant I/O, or input/output.

FIGURE 13.23

Viewing the E-mail
Message tab

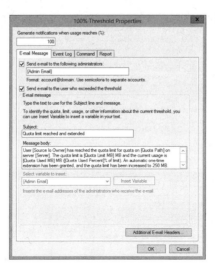

You can add to your email messages by clicking the Additional E-mail Headers button. On the right side of Figure 13.23, you can see the additional headers. It also includes variables that you can add by selecting the variable in the drop-down box and clicking Insert Variable.

SMTP SERVER MUST BE CONFIGURED

For FSRM to send email messages, it must be configured with the server name or IP address of an SMTP server that will accept the email messages. This is done on the File Server Resource Manager Options page, covered later in this chapter.

Event Log Tab

You can configure the events to be logged in the Application log if desired. It's as simple as selecting the Event Log tab and selecting the box to send the warning to the event log, as shown in Figure 13.24. Any events sent from here are logged into the Application log.

FIGURE 13.24
Viewing the Event
Log tab

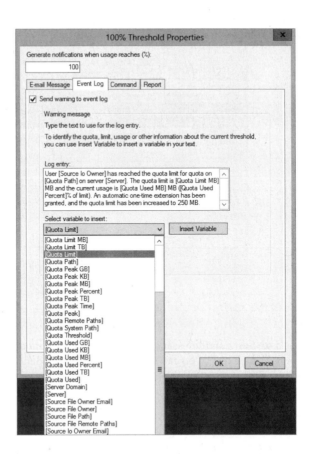

Just as you can add variables to email messages, you can also add variables to log entries. In Figure 13.24, we've selected the variable drop-down box to show some of the variables that can be added. A lot of variables can be selected, but not all of them are showing in the figure.

Report Tab

The fourth tab that can be manipulated for notification thresholds is the Report tab. You can configure reports to be generated in response to a threshold and automatically be sent via email to administrators and/or the user. Reports can also be created on demand, as you'll see later in this chapter.

CREATING A QUOTA

Once you understand the basics, it's pretty simple to create and apply a quota. There are a few different ways in Windows Server 2012 R2 to configure quotas at different share and folder levels. If you already have both share and quota templates created, you can easily configure a quota by right-clicking the share on the Shares tab of the File and Storage Services role in Server Manager and selecting Configure Quota. Adjusting the properties and creating quota templates is done directly through FSRM found in the Tools directory on Server Manager.

Imagine you want to monitor the amount of data that is being stored in a folder named Graphics on your system. Specifically, you want to know whether the amount of storage used is getting close to 500 MB. If the limit is reached, you want to send a report to the user letting her know which files are duplicates, which files are the largest, and which files haven't been used recently.

You can use the following steps to create this quota:

1. Launch Server Manager, and browse to Tools ➢ File Server Resource Manager.

2. Expand Quota Management, right-click Quotas, and select Create Quota.

3. Enter the path to the folder you want to monitor in the Quota Path text box.

    For example, you could enter `I:\ Finance`. Alternately, you could click Browse and browse to the path. You are given the choice here to apply this new quota to only the selected folder, or you can propagate this quota template to all existing and new subfolders within the Graphics directory.

    The next choice on this page allows you to define the quota properties.

4. For this exercise select the 200 MB Limit Reports to User option. We will edit this property later on.

5. Review the summary of quota properties and click Create.

    The new quota will now be displayed, allowing you to further modify your desired settings.

6. Right-click the new quota and select Edit Quota Properties.

    On the Quota Properties page provide a description of your new quota.

7. Then manually adjust the Space limit to 500 MB and keep the default setting of "Hard quota." Now you can edit your Notification thresholds, as shown on the left side of Figure 13.25.

8. Select the Warning (100%) notification threshold, and click Edit.

9. Review the information on the E-mail Message, Event Log, and Command tabs.

    If a warning appears indicating that an SMTP server is not configured, review the information, and click Yes to continue; you can configure the SMTP server later. Notice that you can modify the data on any of these tabs.

10. Click the Report tab. Your display will look similar to the right side of Figure 13.25.

FIGURE 13.25
Viewing the Report
tab of a new quota

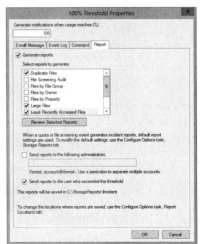

Notice that the reports are already configured. The Generate Reports check box is checked, and three reports are configured to be generated: Duplicate Files, Large Files, and Least Recently Accessed Files. Additionally, the quota is configured to send the report to the user exceeding the threshold.

11. Click OK to close the 100% Threshold Properties page.

12. Click OK to close the Quota Properties page.

Creating File Screen Policies

File screens are used to filter or screen files to ensure certain types of files aren't stored on a server. Imagine that after implementing a quota policy and reviewing some of the reports, you realize that your F drive is almost full because one of the users has stored several gigabytes of backup MP3 files on the server.

Although it's admirable that the user is backing up his files, you may not want him using your server to back up his MP3 files. Additionally, you may not want anyone storing MP3 files or any other type of audio or video files on your server.

You can create a file screen that will block users from saving specific types of files and generate notifications when anyone attempts to save these blocked files on the server. File screens can be created on entire volumes or specific folders, and just as quotas have templates,

FIGURE 13.26
Viewing the file
screen templates

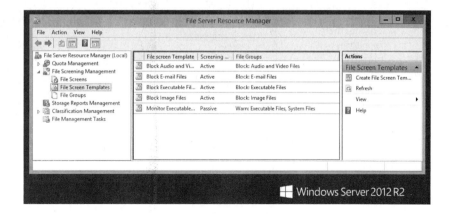

file screens also have templates. Figure 13.26 shows Server Manager open to the file screen templates.

Notice that several well-known file group types are identified in the templates such as audio and video files and image files. The specific extensions of these file types are identified in the File Groups node. For example, audio and video files include .mp1, .mp2, .mp3, .mp4, and .mpeg—and that's not even all of the ms.

When you create a file screen, you can simply select one of the file groups. This will meet your needs most of the time, but if you want to add file types or exclude specific file types from the screen, you can modify the contents to meet your needs.

Imagine that your company has recently learned that many users are storing Outlook .pst files on a server that are more than 1 GB in size and eating up the storage space. The company states that users cannot store email files on a file server. You can use the following steps to enforce the rule:

1. Launch Server Manager, and browse to the File Screen Templates node.

2. Right-click the Block E-mail Files template, and select the Create File Screen from Template option.

3. Enter the volume name that you want to screen (such as **F:**) in the File Screen Path text box.

   Since we chose the Block E-mail Files Template, our screen properties are already preselected. We could also change to a different template's screen properties or define our own custom properties if we wish. Keep the default option and review the summary at the bottom of the page.

4. Click Create.

5. Select the File Screens node (right above File Screen Templates) in the FSRM directory structure.

6. Right-click the new file screen you just created, and select Edit File Screen Properties. Your display will look similar to Figure 13.27.

FIGURE 13.27
Viewing the
properties of a
file screen

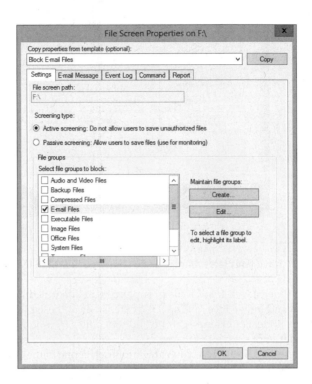

Notice that you can select either Active or Passive screening. Since you want to specifically block users from storing the files on the server, leave it as Active screening. Passive screening is used for monitoring.

7. Click through the E-mail Message, Event Log, Command, and Report tabs.

If a warning appears indicating that an SMTP server is not configured, review the information, and click Yes to continue. You'll see that these are very similar to the tabs used with quotas. Only the notification content is changed.

8. Click OK once you've reviewed the tabs.

Generating Reports

Several different reports are available. You can generate reports as part of any quota policy or file screen policy. You can also configure reports to be generated on a schedule or generate them on demand.

Thankfully, the reports are well-named, and it's easy to determine the primary content just by the name. The different reports available are Duplicate Files, File Screening Audit, Files by File Group, Files by Owner, Files by Property, Large Files, Least Recently Accessed Files, Most Recently Accessed Files, and Quota Usage.

Additionally, you can save the reports in several different formats such as DHTML, HTML, XML, CSV, and text. You can access the reports with the following steps:

1. Launch Server Manager. Right-click the Storage Reports Management node within the File Server Resource Manager, and select Generate Reports Now.

   On the Settings tab, you can select as many reports as you'd like to view, but if you select them all, be patient; they take some time to generate on large volumes. Some of the reports have additional parameters that you can modify. For example, if you select the Quota Usage report, you can click the Edit Parameters button and modify the minimum quota usage that will be included in the report.

2. Select the reports you want to generate and then check the boxes next to the report formats that you'd like to view. Your display will look similar to Figure 13.28.

FIGURE 13.28
Selecting report types and formats

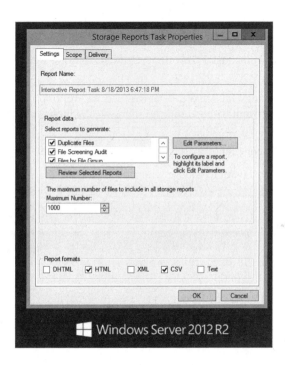

3. Click the Scope tab.

   On this page you get to select what type of data will be accumulated in your reports.

4. After making your file type selections, click Add.

   This allows you to browse to and add the folders you want to run reports against.

5. Make your folder selection and click OK.

   The last tab in Storage Reports Task Properties is the Delivery tab. You can have the reports emailed to an administrator.

6. Simply check the box and fill in the person's email address that you wish to send the reports to.

This comes in handy with Scheduled reports. Have all your reports run on Sunday, and have them waiting in your email Monday morning for you to review.

7. In the Generate Storage Reports dialog box, select Generate Reports in the Background, and click OK.

This will create a report task that will be deleted after it completes. The dialog box defaults to "Wait for the reports to generate and then display them." You can watch the task run, and once it has finished, the reports will be displayed to you. The default location that the reports are saved to locally on the server is \\c$\StorageReports\ Interactive. Depending on the amount of data in the reports, this could take several minutes to complete.

8. While the report task is running, right-click Storage Reports Management, and select Schedule a New Report Task.

9. On the Settings Tab, give your new scheduled report task a proper name, select which reports you want to generate, and then select which report formats to generate the reports in.

10. Select the Scope tab.

Here you will want to choose which type of data to report on and which folders to report against.

FIGURE 13.29
Scheduling reports

11. On the Delivery Tab, check the box, and input an email address to have the reports sent to every week.

A properly configured SMTP server will be required for any email notifications provided by the FSRM.

12. The schedule defaults to Weekly: Select Sunday at 5 a.m. Your display will look similar to Figure 13.29.

13. Click OK to accept the schedule.

The new schedule is now displayed in the FSRM Storage Reports Management window. If you have SMPT configured, right-click the task and run it once now to test your work.

MONITOR DISK CONSUMPTION OF REPORTS

If you create a report schedule that will create report files on your system, you'll want to monitor the amount of space taken up by the reports. The worst-case scenario is that a report schedule is created and reports are regularly created, steadily consuming the disk space. One way to avoid this impacting the operation of the server is to change the default location of the reports by modifying the Report Locations tab of the File Server Resource Manager options.

The report task you created earlier should be done at this point.

14. Navigate to the reports located in the %systemdrive%\StorageReports\Interactive folder. Use Windows Explorer to browse to this folder.

15. Double-click some of the HTML files to view the available information. Double-click any of the text files to see how the information is displayed.

As you can see, FSRM provides rich reporting capabilities.

File Server Resource Manager Options

You can modify several FSRM options. One of them, Email Notifications, must be configured before you can use any of the email capabilities of the server. You can access the options page by right-clicking File Server Resource Manager within Server Manager and selecting Configure Options. A properties sheet appears with seven tabs:

Email Notifications If you want to use email notifications, you must enter the name or IP address of an SMTP server that will accept email from your server. You can also enter the default email address for administrator recipients and a default From address on this page. You can send a test email to make sure your settings are configured properly.

Notification Limits Once a threshold is reached (such as 85 percent usage on a disk), the threshold remains until action is taken. Instead of having the notifications harass the user every 30 seconds, you can set time limits in minutes for these notifications. The default is 60 minutes for each of the threshold responses: email notification, event log entry, command execution, and report generation.

Storage Reports   Many of the reports have parameters that can be modified. Each parameter that can be modified starts with a default. You can use this page to modify the default parameters.

Report Locations   Reports have default locations on the system drive (which is normally c:\). Three folders are created within the %systemdrive%\StorageReports folder. They are Incident (created from notifications), Scheduled (created from scheduled report tasks), and Interactive (created from on-demand reports). You can change the default locations for any of the reports from this page.

File Screen Audit   This page has only one option: "Record file screening activity in an auditing database." If selected, the screening activity will be recorded in a database, which can be reviewed by running a file screen auditing report.

Automatic Classification   It's possible to manage files based on classification properties and rules you create, instead of where files are located within a directory tree. If you use classification management (not many people do), you can use this tab to schedule the execution of classification rules and generate reports. If you'd like to learn more about file classification, check out this TechNet article: http://technet.microsoft.com/library/dd758765.aspx.

Access-Denied Assistance   New with Windows Server 2012, the Access-Denied Assistance tab allows you to customize your own access-denied error message that is displayed to a user who does not have the proper permissions to access a certain folder or file. On top of that, you can enable users to request assistance directly from the error message by clicking the hyperlink. This is a very useful feature.

Although NTFS is a great file system and has included extras such as NTFS quotas, you can get a lot more capabilities by using File Server Resource Manager. If you're managing a file server, these extras are worth digging into.

Understanding SMB 3.0

Server Message Block (SMB) is an application-layer network protocol that is used primarily to provide shared access to files, printers, ports, and communication between machines on a network. SMB is commonly referred to as Common Internet File System (CIFS). This protocol is used primarily for Windows operating systems and serves as the basis for Microsoft's Distributed File System implementation.

SMB 3.0 has changed quite a bit in this server edition. Many new features have made this protocol a robust, high-performance alternative to Fibre Channel and iSCSI appliances. Let's take a look at some of the new features:

SMB Transport Failover   This feature allows administrators to perform maintenance on clustered computers without having to incur any downtime. In the event of a cluster failover, the SMB 3.0 clients will automatically reconnect to another clustered machine without losing any access to the file shares they were using. Clustered file server machines eliminate the single point of failure of having only one file server or a nonclustered environment.

SMB Scale Out   SMB clients are no longer limited to the bandwidth of a single cluster node. When clustered, the machines load balance between themselves using their aggregate resources. Now every server in a file server cluster is an active node serving content to clients. SMB scale-out file shares are always configured with the Continuously Available property set.

SMB Multichannel   This feature allows file servers to use multiple network connections simultaneously, which greatly increases throughput since you can transmit more data across multiple high-speed network adapters at the same time. This also means you have a new level of fault tolerance on the network. While using multiple connections at the same time, the clients will continue to work uninterrupted in the event of a single connection loss. Another nice benefit of SMB Multichannel is automatic discovery. It will discover the existence of available network paths and dynamically add connections as required.

SMB Direct   SMB Direct is a new transport protocol for SMB 3.0 that allows direct data transfers between servers with minimal CPU utilization and low latency when RDMA-capable network adapters are present. This makes a network file server capable of housing local storage for applications like Microsoft SQL Server 2012 and Microsoft Hyper-V.

SMB Windows PowerShell Cmdlets and WMI Objects   Another big win in Server 2012 is all the PowerShell management cmdlets that are now included with the operating system. The new SMB cmdlets allow administrators to manage and monitor file servers and file shares. You can also write scripts to automate common file server administrative tasks. With the new WMI objects, developers benefit from the ability to create automated solutions for file server configuration and monitoring.

SMB Encryption   This new feature allows you to encrypt data in motion on a per-file or per-share server basis. It will protect the data being transferred against eavesdropping and tampering attacks without IPsec or any additional dedicated hardware in place. SMB Encryption is also very useful when remote users are trying to access data from unsecured networks. It will secure the data transmission from the corporate network resources to the user's unsecure remote network. If you recall from earlier in the chapter, we enabled SMB encryption by selecting the check box on the Other Settings page of the New Share Wizard during the creating new shares exercise. This feature can also be directly enabled in Server Manager without the wizard.

SMB Directory Leasing   This feature uses BranchCache to provide faster access to documents over high-latency WAN networks. Directory leasing reduces the communication round-trips from client to server over a WAN. The client caches directory and file metadata in a consistent manner for longer periods of time. The server notifies the client when information changes and initiates a sync that updates the client's cache. This feature is designed to work with user home folders and published shares.

SMB 3.0 PROTOCOL SPECIFICATION

Although we've highlighted some of the important features of SMB 3.0, we certainly haven't covered everything in depth. If you'd like to look at the full protocol specification, you can check it out at http://support.microsoft.com/kb/2709568.

Compatibility with SMB 2.0 and 1.0

To maintain backward compatibility, newer operating systems support both SMB 2.0 and SMB 1.0. To take full advantage of the features available in SMB 3.0, both the server and client must have and be able to use SMB 3.0. Table 13.3 shows which SMB version is used with which operating system. If you match the server operating system across the top row with the client operating system down the left-hand column, the table will show you which version of SMB will be used during communication. For example, if you were to choose Server 2008 R2 from the top row as the server operating system and match a Windows 7 client from the left-hand column, the table would show you that the highest supported version of SMB you could use is SMB 2.1.

TABLE 13.3: SMB Version in Relation to Operating System Version

CLIENT/SERVER OS	WINDOWS 8 WINDOWS SERVER 2012 R2	WINDOWS 7 WINDOWS SERVER 2008 R2	WINDOWS VISTA WINDOWS SERVER 2008	PREVIOUS VERSIONS OF WINDOWS
WINDOWS 8 WINDOWS SERVER 2012 R2	SMB 3.0	SMB 2.1	SMB 2.0	SMB 1.0
WINDOWS 7 WINDOWS SERVER 2008 R2	SMB 2.1	SMB 2.1	SMB 2.0	SMB 1.0
WINDOWS VISTA WINDOWS SERVER 2008	SMB 2.0	SMB 2.0	SMB 2.0	SMB 1.0
PREVIOUS VERSIONS OF WINDOWS	SMB 1.0	SMB 1.0	SMB 1.0	SMB 1.0

SMB 3.0 is used whenever possible by the clients that support it. Since SMB 3.0 is not supported by other operating systems (such as Windows 7 or Windows Server 2008), newer clients can use older versions of the protocol to talk to legacy machines. The good news is that all of this is automatic. You don't need to do any special configuration to take advantage of SMB 3.0 or to switch back to SMB 2.0 or SMB 1.0 for legacy clients. Here's what automatically occurs with SMB:

◆ If both clients support SMB 3.0, SMB 3.0 will automatically be used.

◆ If one of the clients does not support SMB 3.0 (Windows 7, for example), then the OS that it does support (SMB 2.1 in this example) will be used for the session.

You've probably heard some of Microsoft's "Better Together" marketing campaigns. That's not just marketing for marketing's sake. SMB is one example where you'll truly enjoy better performance when you match up new technologies with each other. A network running Windows Server 2012 R2 servers but still running Windows 7 desktops won't be using SMB 3.0. If it's a busy network, the difference will be noticeable.

SMB Security

This server edition has introduced a number of security improvements in SMB 3.0. SMB 3.0 introduces a new algorithm for SMB signing, AES-CMAC. CMAC is based on a symmetric key block cipher (Advanced Encryption Standard (AES)), whereas HMAC used in SMB 2.0 is based on a hash function (Secure Hash Algorithm (SHA)). Advanced Encryption Standard (AES) was the specification adopted by the U.S. government in 2002 and was approved by the National Security Agency for encryption of top secret information.

AES-CMAC provides stronger assurance of data integrity than a checksum or an error-detecting code. CMAC is designed to detect intentional, unauthorized modifications of the data, as well as accidental modifications. The verification of an error-detecting code or of a checksum detects only accidental modifications of the data.

HMAC SHA-256 used in SMB 2.0 provides data integrity—assurances that the data hasn't been modified. Although SMB 1.0 also provides data integrity, the security is better with HMAC SHA-256 and best with AES-CMAC.

A *hash* is simply a number created by performing a hashing algorithm on a packet, message, or file. As long as the packet is the same (not modified), the hashing algorithm will always provide the same hash (the same number). Generically, a hash provides data integrity to packets, messages, or files by following these steps:

1. Create the packet.
2. Calculate the hash on the packet.
3. Send the packet and hash to their destination.
4. The destination calculates the hash on the received packet and compares it to the received hash:
   - If both hashes are the same, data integrity is maintained.
   - If the hashes are different, data integrity has been lost. This could be because an attacker modified the data or simply because bits were lost in transit.

However, if an attacker could modify the data in transit, why not modify the hash in transit too? To prevent this, the hash is encrypted with a session key known only to the client and the server. This is called *digitally signing* the packet in SMB 1.0 and 2.0. The process is as follows:

1. Create the packet.
2. Calculate the hash on the packet.
3. Encrypt the hash with a session key (or shared key).
4. Send the packet with the encrypted hash.
5. The receiver decrypts the encrypted hash.
6. The receiver calculates the hash on the received packet.
7. The receiver compares the two hashes to determine whether integrity is lost.

Enabling digital signing for SMB 1.0 packets could decrease performance by as much as 10 to 15 percent. Although you'll still see a performance hit with SMB 2.0, it won't be as great. One of the primary reasons is that SMB 2.0 is streamlined, resulting in fewer packets being sent and fewer packets needing to be signed.

Implementing BitLocker

BitLocker Drive Encryption is a technology designed to provide protection for entire disk drives. BitLocker To Go is a newer technology that came out with Windows 7 and is designed to allow you to encrypt USB flash drives. Our focus here will simply be using BitLocker Drive Encryption to secure drives on Server 2012.

The primary vision of BitLocker is to encrypt data on hard drives so that if the hard drive is stolen or lost, the data can't be accessed. This has significant application with laptops and servers located where physical security is weak. Laptops are easy to pilfer—people leave them in a conference room for lunch or forget them on a chair, and quickly they're gone.

Similarly, servers located in remote office locations often have weak physical security, or at least weaker physical security than the main business location. You probably have very strong physical security in your primary server room, but your server in a remote office may be hidden behind a closet door that can be jimmied with a crowbar or even a credit card.

BITLOCKER ENHANCES PHYSICAL SECURITY

BitLocker enhances physical security but can't protect against all possible attacks. Malware such as rootkits can introduce weaknesses that might allow access to data if the computer is later stolen.

Additionally, if disk drives on a decommissioned server are not cleaned, they may include data you wouldn't want shared. BitLocker will protect this data from being used inappropriately.

On the surface, it may look like the data on these drives is protected through permissions. However, an attacker could set up a domain and place his account in Enterprise Admins. If he had physical access to your server, he could then remove the drive from your server, place it into his server, and easily take ownership of all the files. At that point, he would own all your data. However, if the files are encrypted, it will be much more difficult to access the data—we hesitate to say impossible, but it will be difficult enough to deter the vast majority of attackers.

What's New in BitLocker

Microsoft has added some new and exciting features to BitLocker with the release of Windows 8 and Windows Server 2012. BitLocker can now be provisioned before the installation, and then only used disk space will need to be encrypted. This saves you a lot of time on both sides of the install. One of the downfalls of the original BitLocker release was how long it took to encrypt a drive. I'm very glad to see the vast performance increases in this Server Edition of BitLocker. Following are some new features and functionality of the latest release:

BitLocker Provisioning   Using the Windows Preinstallation Environment (WinPE), administrators can now enable BitLocker prior to operating system deployment.

Used Disk Space Only Encryption   This feature allows for a much faster encryption experience by only encrypting the used disk space. There are two encryption methods: Full Volume Encryption and Used Disk Space Only.

Standard User PIN and Password Change   Administrative privileges are still required to configure BitLocker, but now standard users are given the ability to change the PIN or password for the operating system volume or a fixed-data volume by default.

Network Unlock   Network Unlock is a new BitLocker protector option for operating system volumes in Windows Server 2012 R2. Domain machines joined to a trusted wired network can have the system volume unlocked upon a system reboot. This is very useful when a PIN is lost.

Support for Encrypted Hard Drives for Windows   Windows 8 and Windows Server 2012 now include BitLocker Support for Encrypted Hard Drives. BitLocker will support pre-encrypted Windows hard drives from the manufacturer.

Encryption for Clustered Shared Volumes   BitLocker volume encryption is supported for failover clusters that are running Windows Server 2012 R2. In an Active Directory environment running at a Windows Server 2012 domain functional level, both traditional clustered disks and clustered shared volumes can use volume-level encryption provided by BitLocker. Each node performs decryption by using the computer account, called the cluster name object (CNO). Doing this enables physical security for deployments outside a secure data center and helps meet compliance requirements for volume-level encryption.

Hardware Requirements

To provide the best protection, your hardware should include Trusted Platform Module (TPM) version 1.2. TPM 1.2 is a hardware component built into the computer, typically on the motherboard.

If the system has TPM 1.2 and BitLocker has been enabled, the system will do an integrity check when it boots up. If it senses changes in the hardware that indicate the hard drive is in a different computer, the drive will lock. It will stay locked until it is manually unlocked using a recovery key.

However, many computers don't have TPM 1.2. There are alternatives that can be used to encrypt drives with BitLocker:

Password   BitLocker can encrypt the drive, and a password can be used to unlock it.

Smart Card   BitLocker can encrypt the drive, and a smart card with a PIN can be used to unlock the drive.

You select TPM, a password, or a smart card when enabling BitLocker on a specific drive. In Figure 13.30, the system does not have a TPM, so only the password and smart card options are shown.

FIGURE 13.30
Unlocking a
BitLocker-protected
drive

It's also possible to select the option to have the drive automatically unlock when accessed on the same computer. This requires that the drive hosting Windows be also protected by BitLocker. When used this way, the encryption will be apparent only when the drive is moved to another computer (or enough hardware is changed in the current computer to make BitLocker think the drive has been moved).

BitLocker can be implemented on partitions without encrypting the entire drive. For example, if your system has a single physical hard drive divided into two partitions (C and D), you can lock the D drive with BitLocker without locking the C drive.

RECOVERY KEY

The BitLocker recovery key can be used if TPM detects that the drive has been moved onto a different computer. Once TPM detects that it has been moved (or the hardware has been changed), it will lock the drive until the recovery key is used to unlock it.

BitLocker includes a recovery mechanism in case the password is forgotten or the smart card is lost. Microsoft recommends that you save the recovery key to Active Directory Domain Services, save it to a file, print it, or store it in a safe place. The BitLocker wizard gives you three options:

◆ Save the recovery key to a USB flash drive.

◆ Save the recovery key to a file.

◆ Print the recovery key.

This key should be protected at a level comparable to the data stored on the drive. In other words, if you have secret proprietary data on the drive, protect the key like its secret proprietary data.

Enabling BitLocker

BitLocker is not enabled by default. Before you can enable BitLocker, you must first add the BitLocker Drive Encryption feature. If you recall from our adding roles exercise in the beginning of the chapter, we have already enabled the BitLocker role. Please refer to that exercise if you need to refresh yourself on the process of adding the role to the server. The following steps assume that TPM 1.2 is not available on your system and the BitLocker role is already installed on the server.

1. Launch Control Panel, and click System and Security.

   At this point, you'll see the BitLocker Drive Encryption feature in the System and Security Center. If you looked here before adding the feature, it didn't appear.

SEARCHING CONTROL PANEL

Control Panel has a neat feature that is quite valuable but easily overlooked. In the upper-right corner is a search box. You can type in any search term (such as BitLocker or User), and it'll list only the relevant applets. This is also available in Windows Vista, Windows 7, Windows 8, and Windows Server 2008. Now if they could only make this feature available for Group Policy.

---

2. Click BitLocker Driver Encryption. You'll see a display similar to Figure 13.31.

FIGURE 13.31
Turning on BitLocker
Drive Encryption

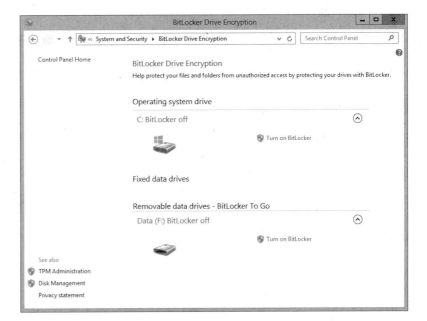

3. Click Turn on BitLocker.

   The BitLocker Drive Encryption page will be displayed, allowing you to select how to unlock this drive. Without TPM installed, the two options present are Use a Password and Use a Smart Card.

4. Select Use a Password to Unlock the Drive, and enter your password twice.

   Alternatively, if you have a smart card and the system supports smart card usage, you could choose to protect it with a smart card.

5. Click Next.

6. Select Save the Recovery Key to a File. Browse to a location on your computer, and click Save.

   Ideally, you'd save this file on a separate drive (such as a USB flash drive). If you attempt to save the file on the same physical drive, you'll be prompted to save it somewhere else, but you can click Yes to override the prompt.

7. Click Next.

   The next page allows you to select how much of your drive to encrypt. Here you can use the new Encrypt Disk Space Only feature. If you choose Encrypt Entire Drive, it can take quite a while depending on the size of the drive. We've seen 1 GB take about 30 seconds, so if you have a 500 GB drive, this might be a good time for a break if you were to select that option.

8. Keep the default and click Next.

   The next page has you verify that you wish to encrypt this drive.

9. When you are ready, click Start Encrypting. A progress bar is displayed.

10. Click Close once the process is completed.

    If you reboot your system, the drive will be listed as encrypted and won't be accessible.

11. You can unlock it by right-clicking the drive and selecting Unlock Drive, as shown in Figure 13.32. Enter your password and unlock the drive.

    Once the drive is unlocked, you can access the data normally.

12. Right-click the drive, and select Manage BitLocker.

    This menu gives you the ability to change the password and manipulate other options for the drive.

FIGURE 13.32
Unlocking an
encrypted drive

BITLOCKER TO GO

BitLocker To Go is a great capability that's easy to use once you've added the feature to the server.

1. Access BitLocker Drive Encryption via Control Panel.

2. Insert your USB flash drive, and click Turn On BitLocker.

3. Enter a password, save your recovery key, and click Start Encrypting.

If the drive is placed into another computer, it won't be readable.

However, you can insert the drive into another computer and enter the password when prompted, and you'll have access to all your data. Although it works best on Windows 8 or Windows Server 2012 R2 you can also access your data on other systems such as Windows 7 by launching the BitLockerToGo.exe file to decrypt and copy the data.

Many organizations are taking extra steps to protect "data at rest," and BitLocker To Go looks like it will meet those needs. We fully expect it to be widely used in the near future.

Using Offline Files/Client-Side Caching

If you have laptop users in your network environment, you'll love the Offline Files or Client-Side Caching (Microsoft uses both names interchangeably) feature. In fact, it will appeal to almost anyone who uses a network. Offline Files provides three main advantages: it makes the network appear faster to its users, smoothes out network "hiccups," and simplifies the task of keeping laptop files and server files in sync.

How Offline Files Works

Offline Files is enabled on shares hosted on a server. When enabled, it automatically caches accessed files, storing the cached copies in a folder on a local hard drive (a folder not surprisingly called Offline Files). It then uses those cached copies to speed up network access (or apparent network access), because subsequent accessing of a file can be handled out of the local hard disk's cached copy rather than over the network.

This is great for users on the road. Offline Files can use the cached copies of the files to act as a stand-in for the network if it isn't present (as it isn't for mobile users) or even if the network has failed.

Offline Files uses a write-through caching mechanism; when you write a file out, it goes to the network location to save it, and it is also cached to your local hard disk. And when you want to access a file that Offline Files has cached, Offline Files would *prefer* to give you the cached (and faster) copy, but first Offline Files checks that the file hasn't changed at the server by examining the file date, time, and size both on the server and in the cache. If they're the same, then Offline Files can give you the file out of the cache without any worries; otherwise, Offline Files fetches the network copy so you have the most up-to-date copy.

Offline Files increases the chances that it has the most up-to-date copies of your cached files by doing background synchronizations in several user-definable ways. This synchronization is largely invisible to the user, who simply utilizes the share over the network.

You'll like Offline Files for several reasons:

Always Offline Mode   This new configurable feature in Windows 8 and Windows Server 2012 provides an improved user experience with faster access to files and lower bandwidth usage by always working offline. Unlike previous editions that switched from online to offline depending on network connectivity, Always Offline Mode stays offline even when connected through a high-speed network connection. Windows will automatically update files by synchronizing with the Offline Files cache. This new feature helps drive better performance. Always Offline Mode requires the machine to be domain joined and have Group Policy Management installed to be configured for use.

Faster Access   Because these oft-used cached files will reside on the local hard disk in the Offline Files folder, you'll immediately see what seems to be an increase in network response speed. Opening a file that appears to be on the network but that is really in a local disk folder will yield apparently stunning improvements in response time, because little or no actual network activity is required.

Reduced Network Traffic   Since cached files don't need to be retransmitted over the LAN, network traffic is reduced. Having frequently used files in a local cache folder also solves the problem of "What do I do when the network's down and I need a file from a server?" If you try to access a file on a server that's not responding (or if you're not physically connected to the network), Offline Files shifts to "offline" mode. When in offline mode, Offline Files looks in your local Offline Files network cache and, if it finds a copy of that file in the cache, it delivers the file to you just as if the server were up, running, and attached to the user's workstation.

Automatic Synchronization   Anyone who's ever had to get ready for a business trip knows two of the worst things about traveling with a laptop: the agony of getting on the plane only to realize that you've forgotten one or two essential files and the irritation of having to remember when you return to make sure that whatever files you changed while traveling get copied back to the network servers. Offline Files greatly reduces the chance of the first of those problems because, again, often-used files can be configured to automatically end up in the local network cache folder. It greatly reduces the work of the second task by automating the laptop-to-server file synchronization process.

BranchCache

BranchCache is designed to optimize the availability of data in branch offices that are connected with slower WAN links. When enabled, BranchCache allows data to be cached on computers in the remote office for use by other computers in the remote office.

Imagine your company headquarters is located in Colorado Springs and a branch office is located in Tampa via a slower link. If users in Tampa needed to access data shared from a server in Colorado Springs, they'd have to connect over the WAN link, even if they just accessed and closed the file a moment previously.

With BranchCache, files can be cached on a computer in the remote office after they are accessed the first time. Users who need to access the file later can access the locally cached copy. BranchCache still checks to ensure the file is the most recent version, but a quick round-trip check of the timestamp is much quicker than downloading the entire file again.

BranchCache supports two modes:

Hosted Cache   Data is hosted on one or more servers in the remote office running either Windows Server 2008 R2 or a later Windows Server operating system like Windows Server 2012 R2.

Distributed Cache   Data is hosted on PCs in the branch office. A server is not needed, but data can only be cached on Windows 7 and Windows 8 computers. Older client OS versions are not supported for hosting.

BranchCache is supported on Windows Server 2008 R2, Windows Server 2012, and Windows Server 2012 R2 servers, as well as Windows Vista, Windows 7, and Windows 8 clients. You can't enable BranchCache on server versions before Windows Server 2008 R2 or client versions older than Windows Vista. When using Distributed Cache mode, data will be cached only on Windows 7 and Windows 8 computers, but a computer running Windows Vista can still access data cached using BranchCache even though the Windows Vista machine cannot be a host. Before BranchCache can be enabled, it must be added as a role service under the File and Storage Services role.

Group Policy includes several settings that you can use to enable and manage BranchCache. These settings are located in the Computer Configuration\Policies\Administrative Templates\ Network\BranchCache node of Group Policy.

Enabling Offline Files on the Server

Offline Files is relatively easy to enable on the server. There are two ways to enable caching of the share. You can enable this setting on the Other Settings page of the New Share Wizard when creating a new share, or if the share is already created you can modify the share properties.

1. Launch Server Manager and browse to the Shares tab of File and Storage Services, where you'll see all the shares that are currently shared on the network.

2. Right-click any of the available shares and then select Properties.

3. Click the Settings button, and then select the Caching tab.

Your display will look similar to Figure 13.33. On this page you can enable both caching of the share and BranchCache if it is not already enabled.

FIGURE 13.33
Viewing Offline Files settings

While this section explained Offline Files and showed you how to configure it on the server, it needs to be configured on the client side as well. Different client operating systems (Windows XP, Windows Vista, Windows 7, and Windows 8) approach this differently. You can check out these web links for different clients:

◆ Windows XP:

   http://support.microsoft.com/kb/307853

◆ Windows Vista:

   http://windows.microsoft.com/en-US/windows-vista/Working-with-network-files-when-you-are-offline

◆ Windows 7:

`http://www.windows7update.com/Windows7-Offline-Files.html`

◆ Window 8:

`http://technet.microsoft.com/en-us/library/hh848267`

The Bottom Line

Install additional File and Storage Services roles on a server.   The File and Storage Services role includes services designed to optimize serving files from the server. A significant addition is the File Server Resource Manager role, which can be used to manage quotas, to add file screens, and to produce comprehensive reports.

Master It   How do you add FSRM to the server?

Combine share and NTFS permissions.   When a folder is shared from an NTFS drive, it includes both share permissions and NTFS permissions. It's important to understand how these permissions interact so that users can be granted appropriate permission.

Master It   Maria is in the G_HR and G_HRManagers groups. A folder named Policies is shared as Policies on a server with the following permissions:

NTFS: G_HR Read, G_HR_Managers Full Control
Share: G_HR Read, G_HR Change

What is Maria's permission when accessing the share? What is her permission when accessing the folder directly on the server?

Implement BitLocker Drive Encryption.   BitLocker Drive Encryption allows you to encrypt an entire drive. If someone obtains the drive that shouldn't have access to the data, the encryption will prevent them from accessing the data.

Master It   What are the hardware requirements for BitLocker Drive Encryption, and what needs to be done to the operating system to use BitLocker?

Chapter 14

Creating and Managing Shared Folders

Maybe you can still remember putting data on floppy disks that you wanted to share with peers. Sharing files and folders is one of the very reasons why server technologies were developed. Microsoft Windows Server 2012 R2 has developed new and advanced ways to share files with services like Network File System (NFS), which provides a file-sharing solution for enterprises that may be running a mix of operating systems. With NFS, you can share files with not only other Windows servers but also Unix, Linux, and Mac OS clients if they exist in your organization. We will look at NFS in depth in this chapter and go over what is new and what has changed with this server edition.

Windows Server 2012 R2 also has revamped its Distributed File System (DFS) technologies by continuing to offer WAN-friendly replication to simplify access to geographically dispersed files and folders. You can share files and folders across the network based on your groupings of them. This function streamlines a complex process that was both tedious and time-consuming in earlier Windows Server releases.

In this chapter, we'll help you dig into DFS and then NFS with step-by-step guides on how to use these exciting functions. You'll find out what they are, how they work, and how to make them work for you.

In this chapter, you will learn to:

◆ Add a File and Storage Services role to your server

◆ Add a shared folder using NFS

◆ Add a DFS root

Creating Shared Folders

Before you can create a shared folder, you must have the appropriate rights to do so. This requires that you be either an administrator or a power user. You can create shares in a couple of ways: you can use the Windows Explorer interface when sitting at the server, or you can use the Share window in Server Manager to create shares either at the server or remotely.

SOME BASICS OF FILE SHARING

One of the core components of any server is its ability to share files. In fact, the Server service in each member of the Windows NT family, including Server 2012 R2, handles the server's ability to share file and print resources. But what exactly does that mean, and why is it so important? By default, just because you have a server running doesn't mean it has anything available for your users. Before they can actually get to resources on the server, you must share your resources. Let's say you have a folder on your local I drive named APPS with three application subfolders, as shown here:

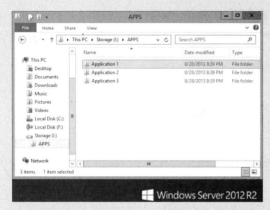

When you share this folder to the network under the name of APPS, you allow your clients to map a new drive letter on their machines to your I:\APPS folder. By mapping a drive, you are placing a virtual pointer directly to where you connected. If you map your client's M drive to the APPS share of the server, their M drive will look identical to the server's I:\APPS, as shown here:

Creating Shares from Explorer

Let's take a step back and look at sharing the APPS folder. If you're sitting at the server, the Explorer interface provides a simple and direct means for creating and managing all properties of a share. Let's go back to the `I:\APPS` folder that you want to make available to the network under the name of APPS.

In Explorer, right-click the APPS folder, and select the Sharing and Security menu option. This will bring up the properties sheet for the folder APPS. Click the Sharing tab. To share the folder, you can use Share or Advanced Sharing, as shown in Figure 14.1.

FIGURE 14.1

Properties for the APPS share

1. There are two options for sharing that you can select from: Share and Advanced Sharing. Use the Advanced Sharing option so that you can use some of the additional features that the wizard provides. The first thing you have to do is turn sharing on by checking the box for "Share this folder."

2. Once you have sharing enabled, you must then decide on your share's name. This is a very important step because this name is how users will connect to the share. Name the share **APPS**.

3. After the share is named, the Comments field will become available, allowing you to provide a share description. You can also set a user limit on this page that will help control share access. Provide a share description, set a realistic number of maximum connections, and then click the Permissions button to go to the next page.

4. The Everyone group is automatically granted Read permissions to a new share. Click the Add button, and a search dialog box will pop up where you can give other users or groups access. Always add an administrator-level user or group first, and then give that object Full Control permissions. This ensures that an administrator can always control and support the share. It is a best practice to give the Full Control permissions only to administrators. You don't want everyone to be able to assign and revoke permissions as they wish. You can imagine how fast things go haywire when a user removes the administrator group and takes control of your share! Since this is an APPS share that you would want everyone to be able to read, leave the Everyone group on the share with Read permissions. Click Apply and OK to continue.

5. The last option on the Advanced Sharing page is Caching. This feature allows you to select additional offline settings like enabling BranchCache, an excellent feature discussed in the previous chapter. Review the available options, make appropriate selections, and click OK. For more information about caching, you can always click the Configure Offline Availability for a Shared Folder hyperlink at the bottom of the page.

6. Review all of the selections made for sharing the folder, and then click Apply and OK to finish up sharing the folder. APPS is now shared across the network.

Now that your APPS folder is shared with users, you can browse to that share using Windows Explorer. There are multiple ways to view shared drives and folders. In the next section we will look at viewing shares using the Computer Management console.

SETTING USER LIMITS

You can configure how many users can connect to a share simultaneously in the User Limit area of the Sharing properties sheet. If the applications under your share are each licensed for 100 concurrent users, you can configure your server share to maintain that limit, even though you may have 200 users on your network. As users connect to the share, they build up to the user limit. As users log off or disconnect from the share, the number drops. This means that you can set a share limit that does not exceed your existing licensing limits, which will help ensure you stay in compliance with your licensing agreements.

Be careful with your licensing, however. Not all applications have a concurrent license mode, although they might have a client license mode. With client license mode, the manufacturer doesn't care how many users are accessing the application at any given time; they just care about how many people have installed the application altogether. This user-limit option will not protect you in these cases.

Finally, you need to consider how your users connect to the share to use these applications before you limit them based on concurrency. If your users all connect to the share upon logging in but don't disconnect until logging off, your concurrency limit may be used up based on who shows up for work first, and you'll have 100 people using up your concurrency limit even if only a small percentage of them are actually using the application. If connections are made only when actually using the application, the user limit will work quite nicely.

Remotely Creating Shares with the Computer Management Console

Windows Server 2012 R2 has added some great improvements in the way you can use Server Manager. From just a single management server, you can create and manage shares across multiple servers with little effort. As long as the remote server is online and available on the network, there is no reason to have to log into it directly. Let's take a look at using the new Server Manager UI to connect to and create a new share on a remote server.

1. Open Server Manager, click All Servers, and right-click the server you wish to remotely manage.

   A new set of options will be displayed, one of which is Computer Management, as shown in Figure 14.2.

FIGURE 14.2
Using Server Manager to connect to another server

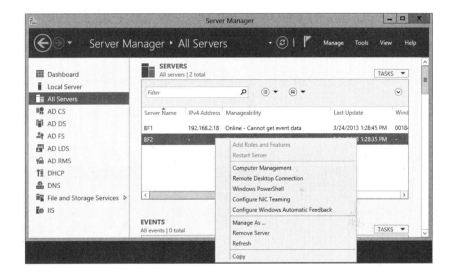

THE COMPUTER MANAGEMENT TOOL

Within your Administrative Tools program group is the Computer Management console. With this tool, you can, among other things, create and manage shares locally or remotely. In contrast, within the Explorer interface, if you right-click a folder that is not local to your machine, you won't see the Sharing menu option. If you are going to create a share using the Computer Management console from your local machine, you're set. If you want to manage a share on a remote server, you have to first connect to that server.

---

2. Select Computer Management, and Server Manager will automatically connect to the remote server.

3. To begin managing the share, select Computer Management ➢ System Tools ➢ Shared Folders ➢ Shares, as shown in Figure 14.3.

FIGURE 14.3
Computer Management
shared folders

4. You can now either select New Share from the Actions menu or right-click in the Shares window and select New Share.

5. Click Next in the initial screen of the Create A Shared Folder Wizard, and you will see the screen shown in Figure 14.4.

FIGURE 14.4
Specifying a folder
location in the Create
A Shared Folder
Wizard

Make sure that the "Computer name" field is correct so that you are creating the share on the right computer. To create the share, you can browse through the given drives and folders, or you can create a new folder on the fly by simply typing the full drive and folder name in the "Folder path" box.

6. For this example, create a new folder called **Graphics** and share the folder as `I:\Graphics`.

7. Once you have completed the path, click Next.

8. You'll then see the screen shown in Figure 14.5. On this page, enter the name you want this share to be given, along with a brief description.

FIGURE 14.5
Assigning a share name and description

9. Click Next to continue through the wizard.

From there, we jump straight into defining the share permissions. On the next screen (Figure 14.6) you are given four options for defining permissions:

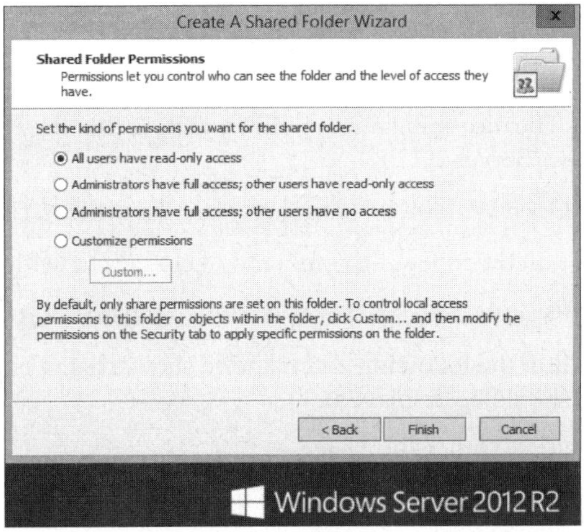

FIGURE 14.6
Controlling computer access in the Create A Shared Folder Wizard

All Users Have Read-Only Access This option allows the Everyone group to have read-only access to the contents of the folder. This is the default setting in Server 2012 and is a great feature that illustrates the extra focus Microsoft has given to security in the past few years. In previous server editions, the default, Everyone having Full Control, included anonymous users coming in across the network! Since Windows Server 2008, when creating a share, you don't have to start with a wide-open door. You start with a closed door and open it per your specifications, at your leisure.

Administrators Have Full Access; Other Users Have Read-Only Access This option ensures that your users can view data and run programs but can't modify or delete anything within the share. This still gives administrators the appropriate rights to manage the data.

Administrators Have Full Access; Other Users Have No Access This option allows the users to do anything they want except delete files or folders, change permissions, or take ownership of the files.

Customize Permissions This option lets you define permissions based on specific users or groups.

KEEPING SHARES SECURE

There are a few very important security aspects to consider when determining proper share permissions. Full Control should only be granted to administrators, and users should only be granted rights appropriate to their job duties. This does two great things for an organization: it ensures no user outside of corporate IT can take control of, change, or delete share permissions and objects, and it also limits the number of high-privilege accounts on the network available to a security breach. If your users can only read and write to a network share and one of those accounts becomes compromised, at least that account will not be able to cause too much damage, like deleting the entire share.

---

10. Once you set up the permissions on your share, click Next to see the final screen of the Create A Shared Folder Wizard, which lists the results and gives you the option to run the wizard again, as shown in Figure 14.7.

For a more advanced approach, you can utilize Windows PowerShell to create SMB file shares. The nice thing about SMB cmdlets is that they are already available by default in Windows Server 2012 R2.

1. Open Windows PowerShell from the taskbar, running the program as an administrator.

2. Run the following command to create a new file share:

```
PS C:\> New-SmbShare -Name ShareName -Path C:\LocalFolder
```

3. Run the following command to show a list of existing file shares; the one you just created should be displayed:

```
PS C:\> Get-SmbShare
```

4. Finally, use this command to remove the share you just created:

```
PS C:\> Remove-SmbShare -Name ShareName
```

FIGURE 14.7
The final screen shows a summary of the share you created.

Managing Permissions

Share permissions are applied when a user accesses a file or folder across the network, but they are not taken into consideration when a user accesses those resources locally, as they would be when sitting directly at the computer or when using resources on a terminal server. NTFS permissions, in contrast, are applied no matter how a user accesses those same resources, whether they are connecting remotely or logging in at the console. So, when accessing files locally, only NTFS permissions are applied. When accessing those same files remotely, the sum of both share and NTFS permissions is applied by calculating the most restrictive permissions of the two types. For more information about NTFS, see Chapter 13, "Files, Folders, and Basic Shares."

Creating Share Permissions

Share permissions are possibly the easiest form of access control you will deal with in Windows Server. Remember that share permissions take effect only whenever you try to access a computer over the network. Consider share permissions to be a kind of access pass to a secure building. When you walk up to the front door and show your identification, the guard looks up your name and gives you a pass that shows your access level for everything on the inside. If your pass says "level 1 access," then your pass will get you into every door on level 1—and nowhere else. Once inside, if you try to get into a room with level 2 access requirements, it won't work. By defining share permissions, you can safely control the access level for each person at the front door.

Keep in mind, though, that this front door—or share-level permission—isn't the entire picture. The share-level permission represents only the *maximum* level of access you will get on the inside. If you get Read permissions at the share, the best you can do once you've connected remotely to the share is read. Likewise, Change permissions will grant change at best. If you want full control to *anything* inside the share, you need Full Control permissions *at* the share. But understand that when we say the share permission is the *maximum* level of access you will get inside the share, it is entirely possible to restrict access more once you're inside by using file-level (or NTFS) permissions. You can have full control at the share, but an object inside can still have NTFS permissions that say only you can read it.

DEFINING SHARE PERMISSIONS

To define share permissions, we will walk you through the Computer Management console:

1. Select the share you want to secure by right-clicking the share name, selecting Properties, and then selecting the Share Permissions tab.

    You can get to the same place from Explorer by right-clicking the locally shared folder, selecting Sharing and Security, and then clicking the Permissions button. Both methods will bring you to the dialog box shown in Figure 14.8.

FIGURE 14.8
The Share Permissions tab

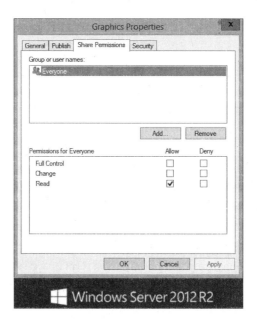

NO MORE EVERYONE

Note that the Everyone group, by default, has Read access permissions, which is a great step forward in the Windows world in terms of security. Until Server 2003, the Everyone group was given Full Control access by default. Another nice feature in Server 2012 is that the Everyone group is no longer added to a folder when it is shared.

In this dialog box, you are shown a "Group or user names" box that lists users and groups assigned to the share; when a user or group is selected, the permissions for that user or group to access the share are revealed. You can assign different levels of permission for different users and groups. At the share level, you have three types of permissions, shown in Table 14.1.

TABLE 14.1:   Types of Permissions

PERMISSION	LEVEL OF ACCESS
Full Control	The assigned group can perform any and all functions on all files and folders through the share.
Change	The assigned group can read and execute, as well as change and delete, files and folders through the share.
Read	The assigned group can read and execute files and folders but has no ability to modify or delete anything through the share.

The example in Figure 14.8 shows Read access for Everyone. Although you won't see the Administrator account listed with any specific rights, note that local administrators always have Full Control access of the shares on the computer. If you want to change share permissions to give all your network administrators Full Control, you will need to add the group and assign them rights.

2. Click the Add button to see the dialog box shown in Figure 14.9.

FIGURE 14.9
Select Users, Computers, Service Accounts, or Groups dialog box

3. Either type in the name of the user or group that you want to add or click the Advanced button, which will bring you to the second Select Users, Computers, Service Accounts, or Groups dialog box, shown in Figure 14.10. This dialog box enables you to search the directory.

FIGURE 14.10

Enumerate users and groups by clicking the Find Now button in this dialog box.

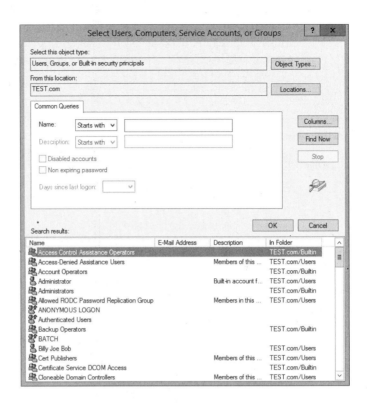

You can either use the Active Directory search functions on the Common Queries tab to narrow down your choices or click the Find Now button, which will enumerate all the users in the directory.

4. From here you locate the group that you want to add—the Domain Administrators group in the example—and click OK and then OK again.

   This brings you back to the Share Permissions tab with the Domain Administrators group added to the display and highlighted.

5. Select the Full Control check box.

Again, keep in mind that share-level permissions are just your first filter for users accessing files over the network. Whatever level of permissions you get at the share level will be the highest level of permissions you can get for files and directories (the most restrictive apply, remember?). If you get Read rights to the share but Full Control rights to the file, the share will not let you do anything other than read.

Understanding Allow and Deny

You probably noticed when you selected the Allow check box on the Full Control permission for the Domain Administrators group in the previous example that there also exists a Deny check box for each permission listed. Share permissions are just about the simplest set of permissions that you'll deal with, so they're a great place to explain this Allow and Deny notion. Here's how they work:

◆ An administrator of a share, file, user account, or whatever can change permissions on that object. (That's almost a complete definition of an administrator, actually.)

There are several kinds of permissions—Full Control, Change, or Read in the case of shares. Anyone can be allowed or denied by the administrator, or the administrator can choose to clear *both* Allow and Deny, leaving a user with neither Allow nor Deny on that permission.

◆ If the user has no permissions—in other words, no Allow or Deny—then the user does not have access to the object.

◆ If the Allow permission is selected, the user can exercise the permission; if Deny is selected, the user can't. We know that's obvious, but let's see how it affects more complex situations.

Understanding File and Directory Permissions

Now that you have a good understanding of share-level permission options, let's take a more granular look at file and directory permission sets. These sets of permissions, commonly referred to as NTFS permissions, allow you to assign specific permissions to folders and files within a share. These additional permissions make it possible to restrict access all the way down to the folder and file levels of a shared directory.

It is a best practice to keep up-to-date documentation of permissions that you manage within a share. Anytime you make permission changes to folders or files, you should record the changes for future reference and to use as a troubleshooting guide to permission issues that arise in the environment. Special circumstances will come up that require you to lock down folders and files and restrict their use to only certain security groups or users. Trying to remember all the special permissions on folders and files in a large environment would be a nightmare. Good, clean documentation is a necessity, especially if you lose the permission sets applied to customized, noninherited folders and files that need to be restored from being corrupted or deleted. Document everything.

Permission Types

Before you assign permissions to your files and folders, you need to have a good understanding of what those permissions mean and how they work. There are two different levels of permissions.

To see the higher level, go to any NTFS folder, right-click it, choose Properties, and then select the Security tab. You'll see a permissions dialog box like the one in Figure 14.11.

FIGURE 14.11

Top-level NTFS permissions dialog box

The permissions you see in Figure 14.11 are actually built up from the lower-level permissions. For example, the high-level permission List Folder Contents comprises five lower-level permissions: Traverse Folder/Execute File, List Folder/Read Data, Read Attributes, Read Extended Attributes, and Read Permissions. You may want to think of them as "molecular" and "atomic" permissions. There are 13 atomic permissions for NTFS. (Other sorts of Active Directory objects, such as organizational units, *can* have child objects because you can create users and other OUs inside OUs.) All AD object types share the same set of atomic permissions, even the ones that are irrelevant—go ahead and grant someone the ability to create child objects for a Group Policy object; it'll be about as useful as granting someone at a brick factory the ability to set the sex of the bricks.

Look at Table 14.2 to see how groups of atomic permissions in the left column make up molecular permissions.

TABLE 14.2:   Atomic and Molecular Permissions

ATOMIC	WRITE	READ	LIST FOLDER CONTENTS	READ & EXECUTE	MODIFY	FULL CONTROL
Traverse Folder/ Execute File			X	X	X	X
List Folder/Read Data	X	X	X	X	X	X
Read Attributes	X	X	X	X	X	X

TABLE 14.2:   Atomic and Molecular Permissions   *(CONTINUED)*

ATOMIC	WRITE	READ	LIST FOLDER CONTENTS	READ & EXECUTE	MODIFY	FULL CONTROL
Read Extended Attributes		X	X	X	X	X
Create Files/Write Data	X				X	X
Create Folders/ Append Data	X				X	X
Write Attributes	X				X	X
Write Extended Attributes	X				X	X
Delete Subfolders and Files						X
Delete					X	X
Read Permissions	X	X	X	X	X	X
Change Permissions						X
Take Ownership						X

ATOMIC PERMISSIONS

We'll start at the atomic level. These permissions are the building blocks of the permissions that we normally speak of, such as Read, Modify, and Full Control. You will probably never see these permissions, much less refer to them on their own.

Traverse Folder/Execute File   The Traverse Folder permission lets you bypass all the locks on the upper levels and essentially "beam yourself" right into level 4. Like Execute File, it's a useful permission, but it has nothing to do with files. What's happening is this: when NTFS is examining a permission, it pulls up the 13 bits. When looking at the first one, it asks itself the question, "Is this a file or a folder?" If it's a file, then it interprets that first bit as the Execute File permission. If it's a folder, then it's the Traverse Folder permission. You'll see this in a somewhat less-extreme manner on some of the other permissions as well.

List Folder/Read Data   List Folder permissions allow you to view file and folder names within a folder. Read Data permissions allow you to view the contents of a file. This atomic right is the core component of Read.

Think of the separation between these two atomic permissions. Is there really much of a difference? Yes, but probably not for long. Remember the days when we called everything files and directories? Now the file and *folder* terminology has become mainstream. Just when we start really getting used to it, another term is coming into play: *objects.* Everything on your machine is an object—both files and folders. This atomic permission could almost be rephrased to *read object*. Regardless of whether this permission applies to a file or folder, this right lets you examine the contents of an object.

Read Attributes   Basic attributes are file properties such as Read-Only, Hidden, System, and Archive. This atomic-level permission allows you to see these attributes.

Read Extended Attributes   Certain programs include other attributes for their file types. For example, if you have Microsoft Word installed on your system and you view the file attributes of a DOC file, all sorts of attributes will show up, such as Author, Subject, Title, and so on. These are called *extended attributes*, and they vary from program to program. This atomic permission lets you view these attributes.

Create Files/Write Data   The Create Files atomic permission allows you to put new files into a folder. Write Data allows you to overwrite existing data within a file. This atomic permission will not allow you to add data to an existing file.

Create Folders/Append Data   Create Folders allows you to create folders within folders. Append Data allows you to add data to the end of an existing file but not change data within the file.

Write Attributes   This permission allows you to change the basic attributes of a file.

Write Extended Attributes   This permission allows you to change the extended attributes of a file.

Delete Subfolders and Files   This atomic permission is strange. Listen to this: with this permission, you can delete subfolders and files, even if *you don't have Delete permissions on that subfolder or file*. Now how could this possibly be? If you were to read ahead to the next atomic permission—Delete—you would see that permission lets you delete a file or folder. What's the difference? Think of it this way: if you are sitting at a file or folder, Delete lets you delete it. But let's say you're sitting at a folder and want to delete its *contents*. This atomic permission gives you that right. There is a very vague difference between the two. One lets you delete a specific object; the other lets you delete the *contents* of an object. If you are given the right to delete the contents of a folder, you don't want to lose that right just because one object within that folder does not want to give you permission. Hey, it's your folder—you can do with it what you want.

Delete   Plain and simple this time, Delete lets you delete an object. Or is it plain and simple? If you have only the atomic permission to delete a folder but not its big-brother atomic permission to delete subfolders and files, and if one file within that folder has no access, can you delete the folder? No. You can't delete the folder until it is empty, which means that you need to delete that file. You can't delete that file without having either Delete rights to that file or Delete Subfolders and Files rights to the file's parent folder.

Read Permissions   The Read Permissions atomic permission lets you view all NTFS permissions associated with a file or folder, but you can't change anything.

Change Permissions   This atomic permission lets you change the permissions assigned to a file or folder.

Take Ownership   We'll talk about what ownership is and what it does in more detail later in the chapter, but this atomic permission allows you to take ownership of a file. Once you are the owner, you have an inherent right to change permissions. By default, administrators can always take ownership of a file or folder.

MOLECULAR PERMISSIONS

A full understanding of what atomic permissions do, as well as an understanding of the atomic makeup of molecular permissions (shown in Table 14.2), provides exceptional insight into what these molecular permissions are and how they work. This section will try to put the atomic makeup of permissions in better perspective, but you should flip back and forth to Table 14.2 while you read about these permissions. This information will form a solid foundation to help you manage permissions later.

Read   Read permissions are your most basic rights. They allow you to view the contents, permissions, and attributes associated with an object. If that object is a file, you can view the file, which happens to include the ability to launch the file, should it be an executable program file. If the object in question is a folder, Read permissions let you view the contents of the folder.

Now, here is a tricky part of folder read. Let's say that you have a folder to which you have been assigned Read permissions. That folder contains a subfolder, to which you have been denied all access, including read access. Logic would say that you could not even see that subfolder at all. Well, the subfolder, before you even get into its own attributes, is *part of* the original folder. Because you can read the contents of the first folder, you can see that the subfolder exists. If you try to change to that subfolder, then—and only then—will you get an Access Denied message.

Write   Write permissions, as simple as they sound, have a catch. For starters, Write permissions on a folder let you create a new file or subfolder within that folder. What about Write permissions on a file? Does this mean you can change a file? Think about what happens when you *change* a file. To change a file, you must usually be able to open the file or read the file. To change a file, Read permissions must normally accompany your Write permissions. There is a loophole, though: if you can simply append data to a file, without needing to open the file, Write permissions will work.

However, if a programmer were to write an application that opens a file in a write-only mode, the file could then truncate it without reading it and then write to the file, all without reading the file; thus, the file would be changed without the reading process taking place.

Read & Execute   Read & Execute permissions are identical to Read but give you the added atomic privilege of traversing a folder.

Modify   Simply put, Modify permissions are the combination of Read & Execute and Write, but they give you the added luxury of Delete. Even when you could change a file, you never really could delete the file. You'll notice that when you select permissions for files and folders, if you select Modify only, then Read, Read & Execute, and Write are automatically selected for you.

Full Control   Full Control is a combination of all the previously mentioned permissions, with the abilities to change permissions and take ownership of objects thrown in. Full Control also allows you to delete subfolders and files, even when the subfolders and files don't specifically allow you to delete them.

List Folder Contents   List Folder Contents permissions apply similar permissions to Read & Execute, but they apply only to folders. List Folder Contents allows you to view the contents of folders. More important, List Folder Contents is only *inherited* by folders, and it is shown only when looking into the security properties of a folder. The permission allows you to see that files exist in a folder—similar to Read—but will not apply Read & Execute permissions to those files. In comparison, if you applied Read & Execute permissions to a folder, you would be given the same capabilities to view folders and their contents but would also propagate Read & Execute rights to files within those folders.

Special Permissions   Special Permissions is simply a customized grouping of atomic rights you can create when one of the standard molecular permissions just covered isn't suited to your specific situation. Although it might appear that the Special Permissions feature was new in Server 2003, it did, in fact, exist in Windows 2000. It just wasn't visible as a molecular permission. In Windows 2000, there wasn't any way to tell whether a folder had customized atomic permissions unless you looked in the Advanced tab of the Securities properties sheet. In Server 2012, you can tell just by looking at the Allow/Deny check boxes used for Special Permissions whether the access control entries (ACEs) have been modified. If the check boxes appear shaded, then, by clicking the Advanced tab, you can view and edit those modifications.

INHERITED PERMISSIONS

A tool that has been around since early Windows Server editions is the *inherited permissions* feature. By now, you are probably accustomed to using this great feature. If a file or folder is set to inherit permissions, it really has no permissions of its own; it just uses its parent folder's permissions. If the parent is also inheriting permissions, you simply keep moving up the chain of directories until you get one that actually has some cold, hard permissions assigned. That being said, the root directory cannot inherit permissions.

For example, say you have a folder named APPS, with three subfolders and files. All the subfolders and files allow inheritable permissions. If you set permissions on APPS to allow Read & Execute permissions for users, all subfolders and files automatically mirror those new permissions. What if you want to customize the permissions on application 1 so that users can also write? You right-click application 1, select Properties, and then click the Security tab to view the permissions on the folder. If the check boxes for anything other than Special Permissions are grayed out, you can tell that the folder is inheriting permissions from its parent. From here, you need to select the Advanced tab in order to see the "Allow inheritable permissions from parent to propagate to this object and all child objects" option (now there's a mouthful). This option shows whether the object is inheriting permissions and lets you choose whether to allow inheritance.

ASSIGNING FILE AND DIRECTORY PERMISSIONS

Once you understand what the different permissions mean, assigning them to files and folders is a piece of cake. Start off in Explorer, and then follow these steps:

1. Find the file or folder you want to assign rights to, right-click it, select Properties, and then select the Security tab. Take a look at Figure 14.12.

FIGURE 14.12

The Security properties tab

The top window shows the different groups or users to whom permissions are assigned, and the bottom window shows the permissions assigned to the selected user or group. You're starting off in an APPS folder for this example. Ideally, because this is for applications, you want all users to have Read & Execute permissions and not have the ability to change, add, or delete anything. You also want to keep administrators in full control so they can still maintain the data, and there is a group of database managers that you want to give Modify rights. Since the Users and Administrators groups already have an entry by default, you'll start by adding the Database Managers group and giving that group Modify rights.

2. Click Edit and then the Add button, and the Select Users, Computers, Service Accounts, or Groups dialog box will appear, as shown earlier in Figure 14.9.

You can type in the name of the user or group, click the Advanced button, and click the Find Now button, or you can set up your query manually to enumerate a list of domain accounts.

3. Since you know the name of the group you want to add in this example (Database Managers), just type it in the Select Users, Computers, Service Accounts, or Groups dialog box and then click the Check Names button.

This will cross-check the manually typed entry with the list of names to find a match.

4. Once the name appears with an underscore, click OK to return to the Security tab of the properties page of APPS.

Now that you have added the Database Managers group, the dialog box should look like the one shown in Figure 14.13.

FIGURE 14.13
The Database Managers group is added.

FASTER ADDITIONS OF USERS AND GROUPS

You can add multiple users and groups at one time using either interface in the previous example. When you type the names in manually, just type the first name, click the Check Names button, and start typing the next name. If you don't type a complete name before clicking Check Names, it will give you the closest match to your typed entry. If you choose to use the Active Directory search interface, you can select multiple accounts by clicking the first entry and then holding the Ctrl key down while you click additional entries.

Now all you have to do is assign the correct permissions, which are Modify rights.

5. Highlight the Database Managers group, and select the Modify box in the Allow column.

The Security tab should now look like Figure 14.14.

FIGURE 14.14

Applying Modify permissions

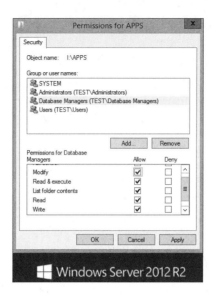

Since the Users and Administrators groups were added by default when you created the share, let's look at the default permissions that were applied and see whether you need to make any adjustments.

6. Click the Users group, and you will see the dialog box shown in Figure 14.15.

FIGURE 14.15

Default User's group permissions

PERMISSION-LEVEL CAUTION

You need to be careful when selecting some permission levels. Selecting Read & Execute includes all of the rights of Read, so Read is automatically selected. If, on the other hand, you want to clear Read & Execute, deselecting the Read & Execute box won't automatically deselect Read.

You can see in Figure 14.15 that the Users group already has some default permissions, including Read & Execute, List Folder Contents, and Read. You can also tell that these are inherited because of the gray shading in the Allow column. However, as you may remember, the shading in the Special Permissions entry doesn't mean that these permissions are inherited (although they might be). The shading here just represents that there are more permission entries than you can see in this particular dialog box.

7. Click the Advanced button to find out more.

If you take a look at Figure 14.16, you will see a much more complex version of the permission entries you saw in Figure 14.15. We're not quite sure why the good folks at Microsoft provide a sort of table of contents for the permissions story, when they could simply provide the whole story all at once.

FIGURE 14.16
Advanced Security Settings for APPS dialog box

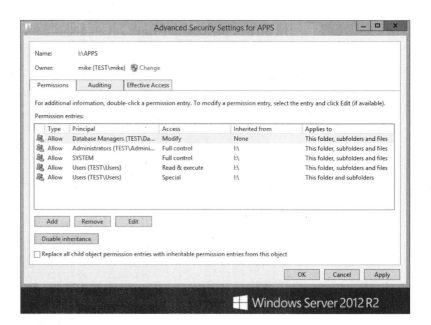

The "Permission entries" box shows your selected groups and users, with a description of their rights. You can disable inheritance, and you can still add and remove entries from this box. So, what is different here? In this window, you get to see a few more details. First, you can see that what might have been one entry in the previous screen can become two or more detailed entries, allowing you to see exactly which rights are inherited and from where or whether the entries were specifically created for this resource by hand. For example, notice that the Users group has two entries, both of which are inherited by the volume. You can also see exactly where the permissions flow downward by looking at the "Applies to" column. Of course, having all these details is great for troubleshooting because you finally have all the information in one place (well, almost).

You have the ability to tailor your extended permissions to the atomic level by choosing an entry and clicking the Edit button. Be careful, though. With so many permissions coming from so many different places (and we aren't even considering share permissions here!), this process can easily become messy to troubleshoot. Try to simplify your resources and users as much as possible, by volume, by group, or by machine, and your life will be a lot simpler when dealing with permissions.

To see what rights the Users group has so you can make sure it has the correct access to the APPS folder, follow these steps:

1. Select the Users entry with Read & Execute permissions.

2. Then click the View button on the Advanced Security Settings page.

3. Next, click "Show advanced permissions," and notice how the options are grayed out here.

If you repeat the same steps on the Database Managers group, why is the View button now an Edit button? Why are the permissions not grayed out for Database Managers? The reason is inheritance is applied to the Users group and not the Database Managers group. If you wanted to edit the Users group here, you would have to break inheritance and re-add the group. Figure 14.17 shows the Users group's atomic permissions.

FIGURE 14.17
Viewing and editing the atomic permissions gives you the most information.

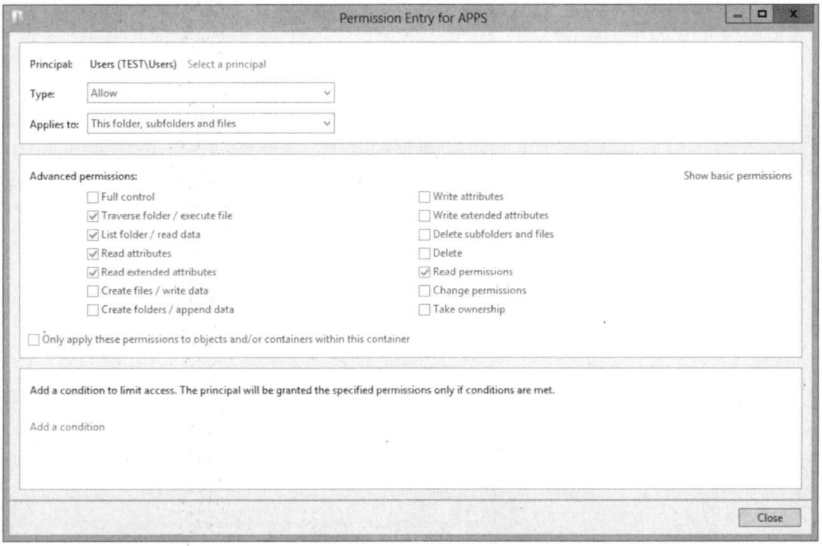

These permissions are Read & Execute by the book. No more, no less; these five atomic permissions make up Read & Execute. Consider it law.

PERMISSION INHERITANCE

You might have noticed that the "Applies to" drop-down list is also unavailable for the Users group entry. Remember, you couldn't remove it because of inheritance, and this is yet another result of inheritance. You can consider inheritance as an order from on high. These permissions *will* be applied to this folder, subfolders, and files unless and until you disable inheritance and create your own custom permissions. Or you could go straight to the source, since, as the administrator, you are the ruler when it comes to inheritance. If you open up the properties for the volume and edit the entries for the Users group, you can remove or modify the permissions; you can then specify exactly where you want them applied throughout the volume by using the Apply Onto button from there.

Notice there were two entries for the Users group. Server 2012's default permissions are more secure than those given to you in previous server editions. Remember, in Windows 2000, Everyone had Full Control on *everything*! Let's examine the atomic permissions for the other Users group entry:

1. If you are still looking at the dialog box in Figure 14.17, click Close—you don't need to modify the Read & Execute entry because that is exactly what you want for the APPS directory.

2. Back in the Advanced Security Settings for APPS window, click the other entry for the Users group and then click Edit. You'll see the dialog box shown in Figure 14.18.

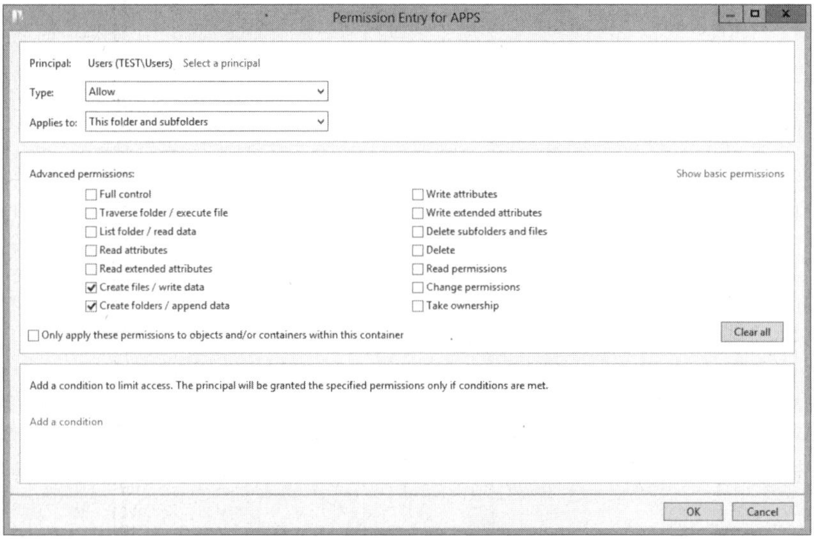

FIGURE 14.18
Editing the special permissions for the Users group

The default permissions for the Users group include the ability to create files and folders on the volume as well as the ability to write data and append data to the files contained within that volume—unless, of course, you specifically deny that ability to any particular resources on the volume. So, what you have here is a set of permissions that is in between two of the molecular groups discussed previously. The first set of atomic permissions you saw for the Users group made up the Read & Execute molecular permission. If you add these two atomic permissions, the molecular set falls somewhere between Read & Execute and Modify. In full, the Modify permission also includes the Write Attributes, Write Extended Attributes, and Delete Files and Folders rights.

For a couple of reasons, the easier of the two solutions is to use the Deny function:

◆ First, you don't have to worry about the rest of your inherited permissions from the volume, some of which you will need to keep. When you remove inheritance, you are given the right to copy the existing inherited permissions and can edit them as you like.

◆ Second, by removing inheritance, you take away your ability to push out permissions from the volume on a global scale, which is a pretty handy feature. As we said before, if you can simplify the permissions by doing things on a global scale, you can save yourself a lot of time and energy.

To disable the ability for the Users group to create files or folders or to write or append data with the APPS folder, simply select the Deny check box (see Figure 14.19) for both of the atomic permission entries, and click OK.

FIGURE 14.19
There isn't enough information to determine the *whole* permissions story from the initial permissions sheet.

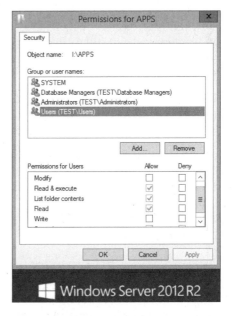

Removing a Group or User

To remove a group or user entry, just click the Remove button from either of the two properties sheets you just saw. If a user or group is there because of inheritance, the Remove option will be unavailable, and you will have to disable inheritance by selecting the "Disable inheritance" option.

Using the Detailed Interface to Get the Whole Story

Look at Figure 14.19. Remember this dialog box? We'll remind you of something we said before about the interfaces used for managing NTFS permissions: this window just doesn't give enough information, and it's kludgey. If you decided to disable inheritance to get rid of the Users group's Write permissions and clicked the Remove button in this dialog box to accomplish that, you'd remove *both* of the Users entries that you saw in Figure 14.16. Also, if you used this window to add a user or group account, you'd only be able to select the molecular permissions boxes you see here—you wouldn't be able to specify exactly where you wanted those permissions applied using inheritance. You'd have to drill down to the dialog box shown in Figure 14.16 to do that. It's best to just bypass this unnecessary dialog box and go straight to the detailed view. That way, you have the full story to start with.

CONFLICTING PERMISSIONS

You can assign permissions to files, and you can assign permissions to directories. Just as share permissions can conflict with file and directory permissions, file permissions can conflict with directory permissions. In share-level conflicts, the share wins; in file and directory permission conflicts, the file wins. The share-level permissions set the maximum allowable access, so if the share-level permission is Read and the NTFS level permission is Write, then the result is Read only. If you assign read-only rights to a directory but you assign change rights to a file within that directory, you will still be able to change the file.

MULTIPLE PERMISSIONS

Now for another problem. You have given your Administrators group full control over the APPS folder, and everyone else has Read & Execute permissions only. Here is where permissions once again come into conflict. Everyone is a user, right? Even administrators are users. Hmmm. How does this work? Well, in the case of multiple permissions, the *least restrictive* permissions will prevail, as long as share permissions aren't involved. Let's say you have an administrator named Bob. Bob is part of the Users group, which has read-only rights on a file. Bob is also part of the Administrators group, which has full control. In this case, Bob will get full control because it is least restrictive.

DENY PERMISSIONS

We talked about Deny permissions with respect to shares earlier and then briefly talked about the effects of inheriting permissions as it relates to Allow and Deny. The same thing applies in file and directory permissions, but in a way that's just a tad bit more complex because of the increased number of security options. Think of a corporate bonus-award spreadsheet file that you are trying to protect. You want everyone to see the file, but you want only the managers to be able to actually change the file. It makes sense: grant the Employees group the right to read and the Managers group full control. Imagine that, somewhere along the line, some low-level supervisor falls into both groups. That person needs to be part of the Managers group for some things but is more like the Employees group in others. If you leave the permissions just described, this supervisor is going to get the best of both worlds with this spreadsheet—full control. For this reason, you decide that you explicitly don't want anyone in Employees to have full control. Now what?

Easy enough: simply deny those excess permissions. What you need to do is determine which permissions you specifically do *not* want employees to have and select them in the Deny column; this way you can make sure that employees are given Read rights only. To do this, follow these steps:

1. Right-click the file.

2. Go to the Security tab, and then click Advanced. (Remember this interface from Figure 14.15?)

3. From here, highlight the entry for the Employees group and click Edit, which will allow you to modify the atomic permissions for the spreadsheet.

4. From the Type drop-down box, select Deny, and then click the "Show advanced permissions" button.

5. Check the attribute boxes for the entries that you see in Figure 14.20.

FIGURE 14.20
Deny permissions

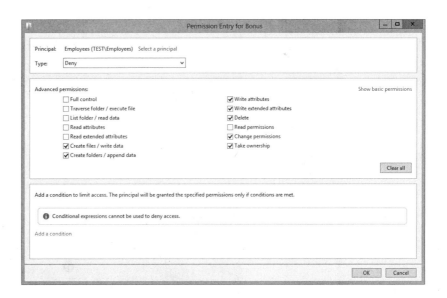

You'll need to individually select the boxes for each attribute. If you check the box for Full Control, however, everything else below that will automatically be selected in the Deny column because Full Control *includes* all permissions. For this example, you want to allow Read and deny Write permissions.

6. Click OK to have these new permissions take effect.

You'll get a warning that tells you that Deny permissions override Allow permissions. Now, in the case of the multiple-permissions scenario, the Deny takes precedence, and even if the supervisor in question has both Managers and Employees memberships, he'll get cut off with the Deny. Notice how now on the Advanced Security Settings page there are two entries for the Employees group: one for the Deny permissions and one for the Allow. The two are no longer combined in a single entity like you are used to seeing in Windows Server releases prior to Windows Server 2008.

EFFECTIVE PERMISSIONS

What is the end result of all of these permissions if some are inherited, some are not, some apply to users, and some apply to groups? Who will get to do what and with which files? How can you tell what the result of all these permissions will be for any group, user, or object? Well, Microsoft has included a tool in Server 2012 that allows you to calculate the effective access for any particular user or group on a particular object. Take a look at the dialog box in Figure 14.21. Once again, it's the advanced properties sheet for your APPS folder that, by now, you should know well. Remember that administrators have Full Control, database managers have Modify, and users have Read & Execute permissions.

FIGURE 14.21
Advanced permissions
for the APPS folder

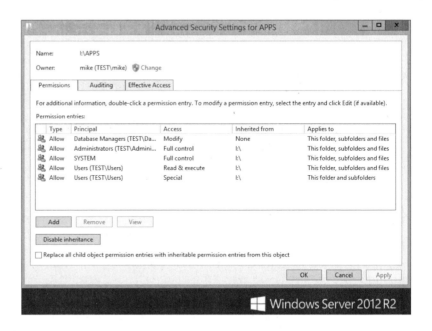

To see how exactly all these permissions work, click the Effective Access tab, and you will see the dialog box shown in Figure 14.22. Windows Server 2012 R2 has changed this page quite a bit with this release. The new Effective Access tab allows you to now easily view a user or group's access to any local or domain-joined machines or groups. You can select a local or network user, include that user's group membership in the query, and view effective access against another group or server. In the following example you can see the effective permissions for the Database Managers group on our test server BF1. The effective access is Modify, just as we set it in previous exercises.

FIGURE 14.22
Effective Access tab

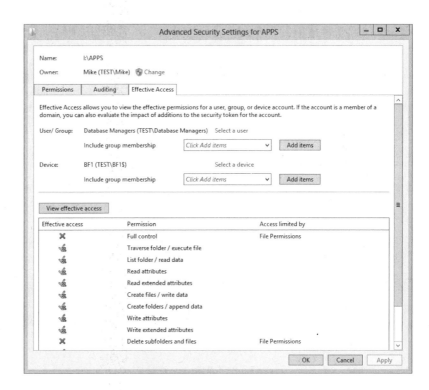

Of course, you need to have the appropriate rights to view the permissions on whatever resource you are checking, and there *are* some limitations in terms of the factors that are used to determine the effective access. For instance, you may not be able to view permissions for every user or group. Consider the local Users group on the server called Storage, where your APPS share is located. Because this server is a member of an Active Directory domain, the global group called Domain Users is automatically nested within the local Users group. You can view the effective permissions on the local Users group by making the following selections on the Effective Access tab of the Advanced Security Settings Page:

1. Click the "Select a user or device" button, and then select the Location button.

2. Select the local location called Storage (instead of the directory).

Because the Domain Users group is nested in the local Users group, domain users have the same rights to the folder, barring the existence of any other set of permissions that would conflict with these. But when you try to get the effective permissions for the Domain Users group using this tool, it comes up with no access because this tool cannot calculate the effective permissions for domain groups that are nested in local groups.

This certainly limits the effectiveness of the tool, but you can still use it to calculate multiple ACEs for a user or group, as you saw in the previous example.

OWNERSHIP

Through the course of assigning and revoking permissions, you are bound to run into the problem where no one, including the administrators, can access a file. And you can't change the file's permissions because you need certain permissions in order to assign permissions. This could be a really sticky situation. Fortunately, ownership can help you.

There is an attribute of every object called an *owner*. The owner is completely separate from permissions. There will always be *some* owner for *every* object. But how does that help you? Well, the owner of an object has a special privilege—the ability to assign permissions.

Taking ownership of a file or folder is a relative easy task as long as the account being used to change ownership has full control over the desired resource. If you refer back to Figure 14.16, you will notice the Owner field underneath the Name field. You will also notice there is a Change option available (if this option is grayed out, then you are not logged in with an account that has privileges to change ownership). If you select Change, a Select User dialog box will appear, allowing you to assign ownership to another user or group.

On a corporate share in a production environment it could be a good idea to make sure that an IT-managed elevated account or more specifically a storage-level service account is the owner of all the files and folders in the share. This configuration is used most heavily for backup and restore purposes. Certain file systems cannot restore files for which they do not have permissions to do so. Imagine trying to restore a share on which users have made themselves owners of folders and files and removed all other access. Those folders or files would be un-restorable by anyone except the owner. This reinforces the good policy of keeping tight and manageable permissions throughout the environment from one controlled, centralized location.

Working with Hidden Shares

Once you share a folder to the network, it becomes visible to the user community. But what if you don't necessarily want everyone to see the share? For example, we have created an installation source share on a server so that whenever we go to a user's workstation, we can install whatever applications we need to without having to bring CDs. It's really just a convenience, but at the same time, we don't want the users clicking through the shares, installing every program they can get their hands on. Sure, we could limit the share to allow permissions only to us, but that is kind of a pain, too. We don't want to log off the user and log in as ourselves every time we do an install, especially if user profiles are being used. This is where creating hidden shares can help. We want the share to be there and available but just not easily visible. Although not a completely secure solution, it is a deterrent to browse-happy users.

To create a hidden share, proceed as normal in sharing a folder, but place a dollar sign at the end of the name. That's it. Now, whenever the server registers its information to the browse list with its available resources, it simply will not register that hidden share.

We'll now show how to create a share called INSTALL$, which will be shared from
`I:\Install`.

1. Create the share as normal, making sure to call it **INSTALL$** instead of INSTALL (see Figure 14.23).

FIGURE 14.23

Creating a hidden share

2. Select the permissions to allow access to *only* administrators (see Figure 14.24).

FIGURE 14.24

Setting administrators permissions on a hidden share

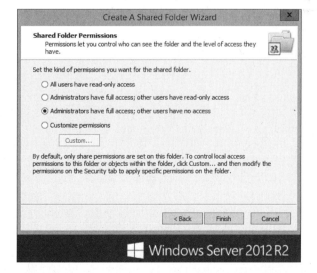

Now, from your client workstations, you will not see the INSTALL$ share listed in the browse list, but you can still map a drive to the INSTALL$ drive connection manually.

3. Select the share name from the Computer Management console, as shown in Figure 14.25.

FIGURE 14.25
Mapping to a
hidden share

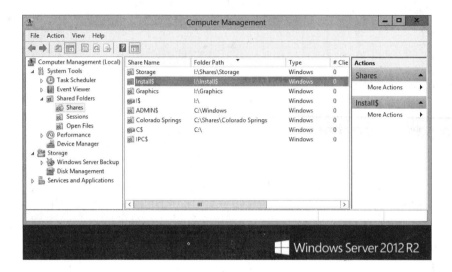

Although the hidden share will not show from your Explorer browser list, the share is visible through the Computer Management console. This helps keep you from forgetting which hidden shares you have created.

Exploring the Distributed File System

What is DFS? Well, with DFS, you can create a single share that encompasses every file share–based resource on your network. Think of it as a home for all the file shares on your network with a "links" page that points the clients to the particular server or servers that actually house those shares. You could have shares that span the entire world. Group them all together under one namespace, and share that namespace to the user base to allow an easy, user-friendly, centralized way of sharing resources. To take it a step further, DFS can replicate changes to the shares on any servers that are members of the replication group, keeping all those servers up to date.

Server 2012 uses two technologies:

DFS Namespaces DFS namespaces gives you the ability to group shared folders that live on different sites and servers into one or more logically structured namespaces. The namespace is then presented to a user as a single shared folder consisting of many subfolders as though all of the shared folders live in a local directory. This is a great functionality that gives you a centralized way of managing and using shares across multiple physically separated servers or site locations. This structure increases availability and automatically connects users to shared folders in the same Active Directory Domain Services site, when available, instead of routing them over WAN connections.

DFS Replication   DFS Replication is an efficient, multiple-master replication engine that you can use to keep folders synchronized between servers across limited-bandwidth network connections. DFS replication can occur across multiple sites and servers that live within the same forest. DFS Replication uses remote differential compression (RDC) to locate and replicate only the changed data blocks of a file. This works hand in hand with the new Data Deduplication features provided by Windows Server 2012 R2. Integrated with the same block-level storage technology, DFS Replication supports replicating folders and files that are housed on volumes that have Dedup enabled on them. Using Dedup to reduce storage requirements on an NTFS file system has no ill effect on DFS Replication.

Before you can use these features, you must first add these new roles to your server. The roles you will need to add are the DFS Namespaces and DFS Replication roles. Use the Add Roles and Features Wizard in Server Manager to add them, as shown in Figure 14.26.

There are a few additional requirements to take note of before running DFS. Your servers will need to be configured using the following steps before you can properly deploy DFS Replication in your environment:

- All the servers that you wish to be members of the replication group must have the DFS Replication role installed.

- You must make sure that your antivirus software is compatible with DFS Replication.

- All member servers must reside within the same forest. DFS Replication works great between domains, but it is not currently possible to replicate between forests.

- Verify that your AD DS schema is up to date with all relevant server edition schema additions. Windows Server 2012 R2 comes already up to date.

- Understand that DFS Replication does not support the FAT or Resilient File System (ReFS), nor does DFS support replicated data that is stored on cluster shared volumes. The data must be present on an NTFS file system to support replication between servers.

FIGURE 14.26
Adding the DFS
Namespaces and
DFS Replication
roles

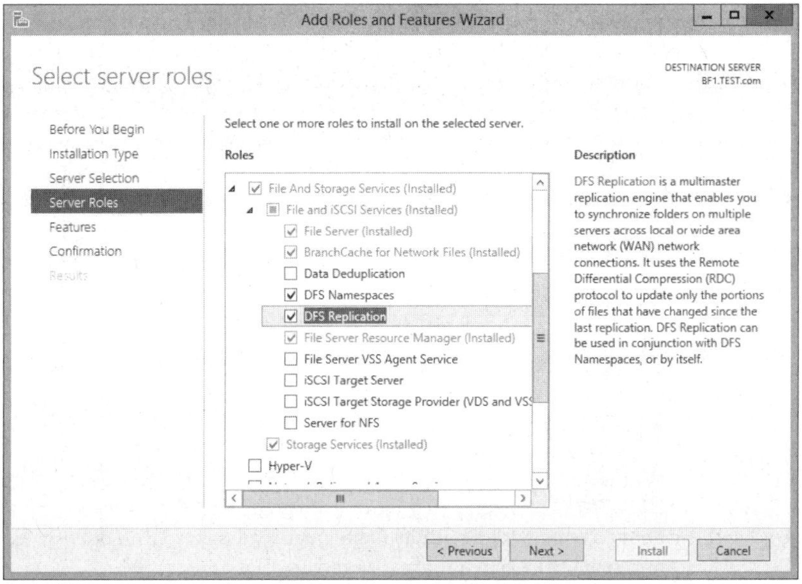

As an alternative to using the Add Roles and Features Wizard, you can always add the roles and features to your server by utilizing Windows PowerShell. Following are a few examples of using PowerShell to add these roles to a server and how to create a DFS namespace:

1. Open Windows PowerShell from the taskbar, running the program as an administrator.

2. Run the following commands to install the DFS role on a server:

```
PS C:\> Import-Module ServerManager
PS C:\> Add-WindowsFeature FS-DFS
PS C:\> Import-Module DFS
```

3. Run the following command to create a stand-alone DFS namespace:

```
PS C:\> New-DfsnRoot -TargetPath "\\Test-FS\Software" -Type Standalone
-EnableSiteCosting -Path "\\Test\Software"
```

4. To see all the new DFS PowerShell cmdlets available in Windows Server 2012 R2, run the following command:

```
PS C:\> Get-Command -Module DFS
```

Understanding DFS Terminology

Before we go much further, you need to understand the terminology of DFS. Just like learning to understand Active Directory, a whole new set of concepts and terms comes into play.

You start with a *root*. This translates roughly into the share that will be visible to the network. In the example, APPS is the root. You can have many roots in your site, and with Server 2012 one server can hold more than one root just like Server 2008. A root is shared to the network and actually operates like any other share. You can have additional files and folders within the shared folder.

Under a root, you add *DFS links*. The link is another share somewhere on the network that is placed under the root. The term *link* is part of our never-ending terminology shift. In this case, it seems to be shifting to more of an Internet nomenclature. Picture the DFS root as a web home page with nothing on it but the name of the page and a bunch of links to other web pages. The links within the DFS hierarchy are like hyperlinks on a web page that automatically direct you to a new location. You, the user, don't need to know where that link will take you, as long as you get the web page you are looking for. Once you find your home page (the DFS root), you will be directed by those hyperlinks (your DFS links) to any other website you want (your shares).

A *target or replica* can refer to either a root or a link. If you have two identical shares on the network, usually on separate servers, you can group them together within the same link, as *DFS targets*. You can also replicate an entire root—you know, the table of contents—as a *root replica member*. Once the targets are configured for replication, the File Replication Service keeps the contents of roots in sync.

Real World Scenario

DFS AND YOU

We started this chapter with a suggestion that you should look into or start playing around with DFS. Well, let us tell you a short story about the day a server died. Now we know you are thinking about a song with a similar name; just read on and find out why using DFS can save critical files and reduce the time required to restore files and or folders.

One day a few years ago one of the authors of this book was looking at his servers and examining the event logs before he left for the day. Everything seemed OK, so he went home, some 45 miles away. Home for about 15 minutes, he got a page from the afternoon support person that the main server at one location was down and he could not log in or see it using the ping command. He drove back fearing the worst, only to arrive and see that production was ongoing and nothing needed to be done. Those critical files needed for that night's production were in use from another server.

The server was restored the next day (a problem with the motherboard) and the company never missed a beat. The time that would have been required to restore from backup would have doubled the mean time to restore (MTTR) and cost millions of dollars in lost production. Those costs included the people who could not work in the plants because of the missing data. If you want to keep the data in play, get comfortable using the DFS function.

Choosing Stand-Alone vs. Domain-Based DFS

Before you begin making a DFS system, you need to decide which kind of DFS you want. This decision will be primarily based on whether you have an Active Directory. The big difference is going to be on the root of the DFS. In an Active Directory–based DFS or domain-based DFS, the root itself can have replicas. In other words, that one single point of failure—the root—has been spread out into the Active Directory. Using root replicas, if you have 27 servers housing the Active Directory, you have 27 places where the DFS information lives. Well, it's not all DFS information; it's just enough information to point clients to one of the DFS root replicas. With that, as long as the Active Directory is alive and available, the DFS is too. Also, when integrated into the Active Directory, link replicas can be configured to use automatic replication. With automatic replication, the File Replication Service takes over the synchronization of the contents of replicated folders to ensure that all replicas contain the same information. It might be safe to say that if you have an Active Directory–based domain, you should choose domain-based DFS.

But here's the really cool part of an Active Directory–based DFS. If you host your DFS in the Active Directory of the test.com domain, not only do your users not need to know which server a particular share is on, but now they don't even need to know which server the DFS itself is on. Instead of having to map a drive to \\servername\DFSname, your users could map a drive to \\test.com\DFSname. Now, using the same logic a client uses to find an available domain controller for Active Directory, the client can search for a host of the DFS. If one fails, the client just calls on another.

A domain-based DFS automatically publishes its topology in Active Directory. What this means is that the actual DFS hierarchy—the roots, links, and targets—is published into Active Directory so that all domain controllers will know where the DFS lives, what it looks like, and how to get to it. It *doesn't* mean that every domain controller is a DFS root replica server.

If you've gotten this far, you probably don't have an Active Directory to publish to. What about the non-AD-based networks? Most companies have migrated to Active Directory. Most have at least put up a few member servers here and there. For those who have not gone through the process of migration, the DFS provides an enhancement to the basic file server that lets an enterprise step out of its physically bound shackles into a more user-friendly and manageable state. A stand-alone DFS is a solid step forward into the world of file sharing from previous Windows Server versions, without requiring a major Active Directory initiative. With a stand-alone DFS, you don't get the nice fault tolerance of the root itself, you don't get the automatic replication, and you don't get the DFS published in the Active Directory. But you still get all the other goodies, such as combining all your network shares into a single namespace and finally killing the dependency on physical server names and locations when it comes to getting your users to their resources. In just a little bit, we'll talk about how these benefits brought to you by the DFS can be put to use in a practical environment—with or without an Active Directory—but first, let's jump into learning how to actually build these things.

Let's say you have the following set of shared resources across the network:

UNC Path	Users' Mapping	Resource Description
\\DC1\APPS	G:	All generic applications
\\RESOURCE1\APPS	G:	The same applications as \\DC1\APPS
\\STORAGE\SALES	S:	The corporate sales data
\\STORAGE2\USERS	H:	All user directories
\\STORAGE\FINANCE	Q:	The corporate financing data
\\RESOURCE2\APP2	P:	Miscellaneous applications

This could become a real pain for users (not to mention administrators!), who have to remember where to go to connect to their various resources. Here, there are five different servers housing resources. This also means that if a client needed to access APPS, SALES, USERS, and FINANCE all at the same time, they would be required to make four different connections. Well, four doesn't sound too bad, but we have been in large networks where there were no more available drive letters left on clients to map another share; every single letter from A to Z was mapped to something. You also have to remember which clients connect to \\DC1\APPS and which connect to \\RESOURCE1\APPS, which are identical shares housed on two different servers. Again, it's not a big deal in this particular example, but if you had 50 servers containing the same set of APPS, this could become a nightmare to keep track of.

BENEFITS OF DFS

As you can probably see, DFS is most beneficial in large enterprises and probably not worth the effort in small-office networks.

Now, let's put this same scenario into DFS instead. You would have one DFS root—we'll call it Corp—with all your corporate shares listed within.

Creating a DFS Root

Your choices for the DFS root type are domain root and stand-alone root. A domain root will publish itself in Active Directory, while a stand-alone root will not. This fundamental difference is the deciding factor on how much functionality you will receive. Keep in mind that a domain

DFS root must be hosted on a domain controller so that there is an Active Directory to post to. One of the most important benefits of being published in Active Directory is that domain roots can have replica roots. Again, a root replica lets you have any domain controller host the root, which greatly improves fault tolerance. Because the roots require Active Directory to be replicas at this level, stand-alone roots cannot be and cannot have replicas. For this exercise we will use our test server BF1 as a stand-alone server, and you will choose that option when we get to that step.

Start by firing up the DFS Management screen shown in Figure 14.27 to begin using the DFS features, which we will describe in a bit.

FIGURE 14.27
DFS Management screen

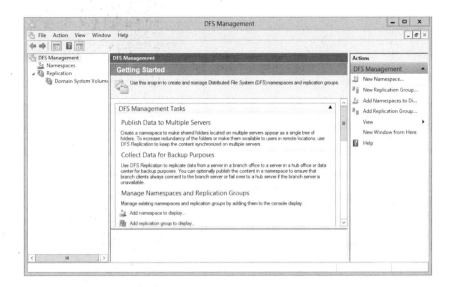

There are two ways to create a new namespace on the DFS Management page. You can click Action and then New Namespace, or you can just right-click the Namespace object and make the same selection. Either action will launch the New Namespace Wizard, which will guide you through this process.

1. If you want, browse to find the correct server name to use, or type in the name directly. See Figure 14.28 with the server name displayed.

USING THE WIZARDS

We recommend using wizards until you are comfortable with the process; this recommendation is true for all of Server 2012.

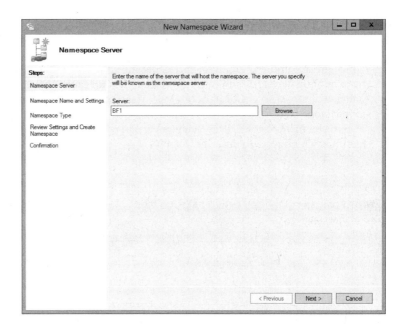

FIGURE 14.28
New namespace
server

2. Next, assign a name for the namespace, as shown in Figure 14.29.

FIGURE 14.29
Namespace name

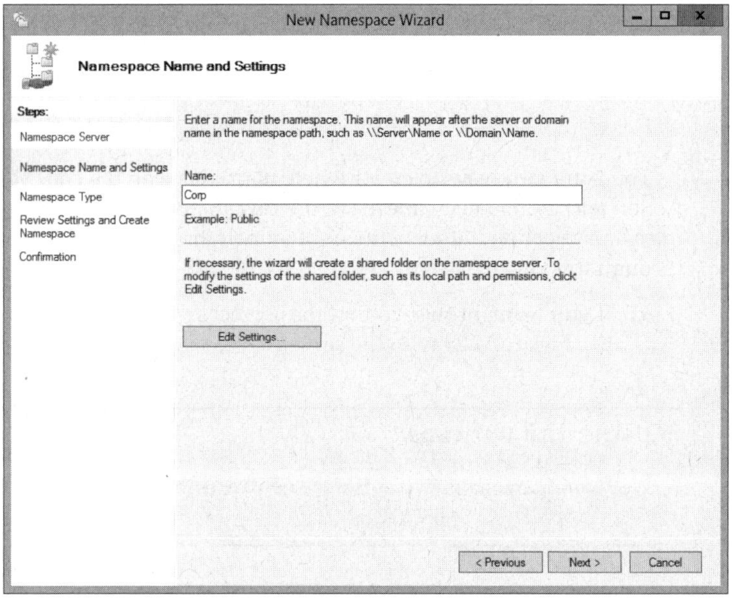

This name will appear after the server name and is used as the name for the collection of files and folders added to the namespace.

Now you will need to assign the type of namespace you wish to create. Your choice is either a domain-based namespace or a stand-alone namespace. The domain-based namespace allows you to store the namespace on one or more namespace servers. The stand-alone namespace allows you to place the namespace on a single namespace server.

3. Use the stand-alone namespace for this example, as shown in Figure 14.30. This will allow you to add files and folders to the namespace later.

FIGURE 14.30
Namespace Type screen

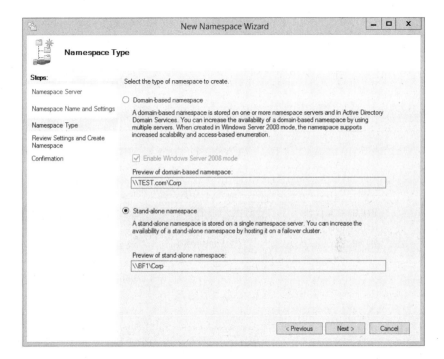

The final screen shows all the settings before the namespace is confirmed and created, as shown in Figure 14.31.

4. If you are OK with these settings, click the Create button to create the namespace. The Confirmation screen is shown in Figure 14.32.

FIGURE 14.31
Review Settings and
Create Namespace
screen

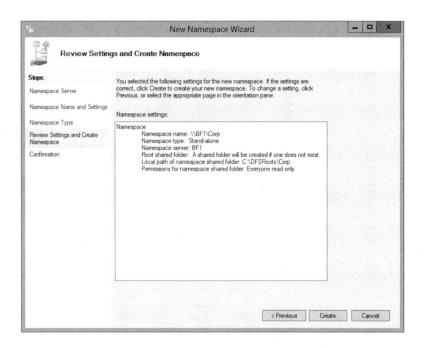

FIGURE 14.32
Confirmation
screen

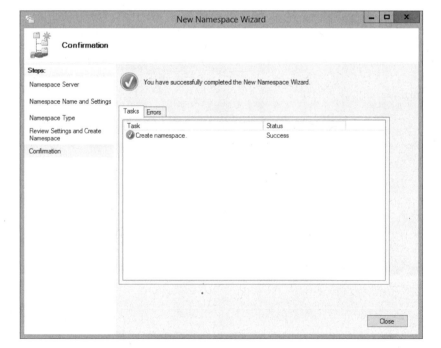

This process may take some time; however, when completed, you will be well on your way to having files and folders shared in one logical location from across the server environment with one name for easy access. In the Shares window in Server Manager, you can then see the Corp folder created with a local path of `c:\DFSRoots\Corp`, as shown in Figure 14.33.

FIGURE 14.33
DFS root path

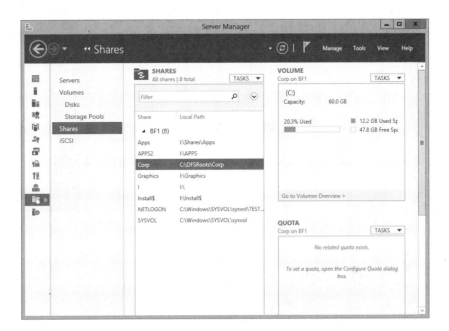

Adding Links to a DFS Root

Under this one root share, you can now add links or files and folders. To do this, all you need to do now is to click the Add Folder target and add any and all files and folders you want. So, let's create a new folder and add those target files and folders.

You will then need to create a new folder within the Corp namespace.

1. To do this, click New Folder in the DFS Management window under Actions on the right, click to add a name to it, and then browse for the folders.

2. Then just browse to add folder targets, as shown in Figure 14.34, and click OK.

   If you are using different servers, their names will change after the \\; however, in this example, we are using only one server because we are in stand-alone mode. If we were using a domain-based mode, we would use only one target folder.

3. Click OK, and if you have not created a replication for the new folder (and who would if you did not know what you were going to name it?), you can then create that now.

FIGURE 14.34
The Browse for Shared Folders dialog box

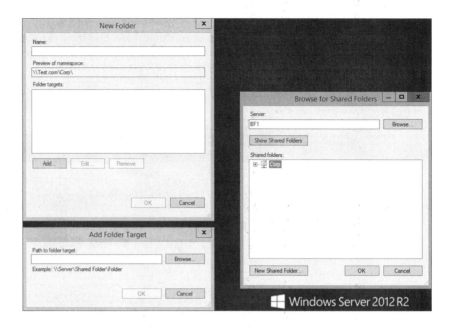

Understand, though, that DFS isn't a new kind of file server. In a sense, it's not a file server at all—it is, instead, a way of putting a kind of "table of contents" on a bunch of existing file shares and pointing the clients to that source of information when they need to connect to a share that is referenced in that table. DFS does *not* create file shares; you must create all the file shares on the various servers first and *then* use DFS to impose some order. To emphasize that point, here's another fact about DFS: the file shares needn't be NT, Server 2003, or Server 2008 file shares. If you had Unix NFS, Banyan VINES, and Novell NetWare client software on your computer, then you could actually create a DFS "share" that points only to NFS, VINES, and NetWare volumes! We will cover NFS next, but first let's finish with DFS.

But does that mean that this new DFS root—this "table of contents"—constitutes a new single point of failure? If that one server that houses the root—the place where all your users go to find their resources—goes dead in the water, so do your users, right? Not necessarily. Combined with Active Directory, DFS roots can be made to be fault tolerant. Instead of the actual, physical root being housed on one server, it can be stored in Active Directory, which is maintained across all domain controllers. Now, if one of those servers housing the root—in Active Directory—goes down, your users are automatically directed to another location to retrieve root information without even a hiccup.

Again, we'll stress the function of DFS. *Fault-tolerant DFS* doesn't mean that you're backing up the data in the file shares. It only means that the "table of contents" that is a DFS root gets backed up so that if the computer hosting the DFS root goes down—and sorry to be stressing this point, but again there's a good chance that the machine hosting the DFS root *does not contain one single byte of shared files*, just the pointers to the servers that contain those files—then there's another computer standing by to assume the role of "table of contents server," or, in Server 2012 language, the DFS root.

Configuring DFS Replications

Can you somehow protect those file shares and their data with some kind of fault tolerance? Yes, you can, by using replication.

1. To do this, go to the DFS Management window, and click the Replication link under the Namespaces link, as shown in Figure 14.35.

FIGURE 14.35
DFS Replication screen

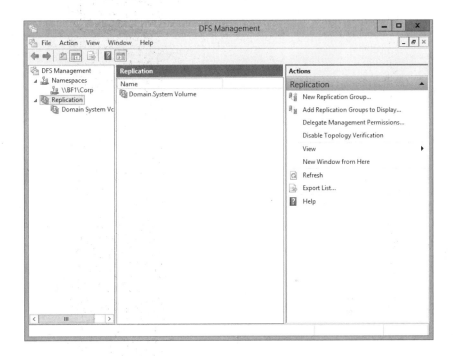

2. Under the Actions section, click New Replication Group.

One of the great features of Server 2012 that we have not pointed out is the use of wizards and how they look different. Notice once you open a wizard that all the steps are clearly listed on the left column. This helps you plan things because you know what to expect next—no more clicking OK or Next and finding something you were not expecting. Also, notice that these steps are explained better than in previous server technologies.

Anyway, let's get back to work—on the first replication screen in the wizard, you have two choices. One is for a multipurpose replication group, and the other is for a replication group for data collection. If you are using the domain-based namespace or stand-alone namespace, then you would choose the default, which is Multipurpose. If you wanted to replicate data to back it up and "collect" data on, say, a hub server, then choose the second option.

3. You will use the default.

4. Next, you will need to give the replication group a name. We'll name it CorpRep, as shown in Figure 14.36.

FIGURE 14.36
New Replication Group Wizard's Name and Domain screen

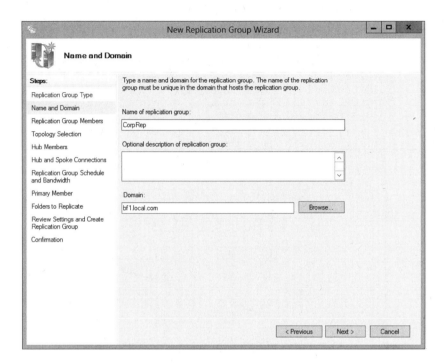

5. Next, you will need to add the servers that will be part of the replication group.

   You should choose these with some thought, because you will add to the amount of data that will flow into and out of the servers selected.

WAITING FOR REPLICATION

Configuration changes are not applied immediately to all members. The new configuration must be replicated to all domain controllers, and each member in the replication group must poll its closest domain controller to obtain the changes. The amount of time this takes depends on AD DS replication latency and the long polling interval (60 minutes) on each member. To poll immediately for configuration changes, open a command-prompt window, and then type the following command once for each member of the replication group: `dfsrdiag.exe pollad`.

---

6. Continue through the wizard, and make your selections for the topology, hub members (if any), hub and spoke connections (if any), replication group schedule and bandwidth, primary member, and folders to replicate.

7. Then review and complete the wizard.

Using the DFS Replication Service (DFSR), DFS can keep all copies of replicated targets in sync with each other. If you have dynamic data within a link at all—and by *dynamic* we mean anything that changes as the users access it, such as Word documents, spreadsheets, databases, or anything else that requires users to change data on the server—you probably shouldn't replicate it. Let's say Jane and Bob are both editing the same document, but both are editing different replicated copies on two different shares. Jane makes her changes and closes the document, and then Bob makes different changes and saves his version. Who wins? Bob will win because he saved it last. Once saved, the document is replicated to the other share, overwriting Jane's changes. So, remember, if a user is editing a document and accessing it on a link that is a replica, their changes will get overwritten the next time the replication occurs. Use caution when using link replicas and replication.

Understanding DFS Replication

Replication itself is simple. In a stand-alone DFS, the replication is manual, and one link replica is the master. In other words, changes from that particular master server propagate to all other replica servers. If the physical share you want to keep synchronized resides on an NTFS volume on a Windows 2012 Server machine, replication is automatic based on the Active Directory replication schedule and uses multimaster replication. With multimaster replication, you can modify files on any one of the link replicas, and the changes will be automatically copied to the other members. Really, with automatic replication, there is no such thing as a master after the initial replication. The first replication will need a master to ensure that all shares have the same starting point. It is advised, though, that you do not mix automatic and manual replication within a single replica set.

The Missing Link

Now that we have covered the replication process, we should note that both Active Directory and DFS replicate at the same time. They are not the same but replicate that way. Once we had problems replicating and found that if we corrected the Active Directory replication process, the FRS, or in this case DFS, would reestablish and replicate as well. If this does not correct replication on your DFS, then you will need to do a more detailed troubleshooting and correction process.

Managing DFS Replication

After you have configured your DFS, there are a few steps you must go through to properly manage the roots, links, and clients that are connected to them. Once you have set up your replication groups, there will come a time when you will need to make changes.

EDITING REPLICATION SCHEDULES AND BANDWIDTH

Perform the following tasks to make changes to the replication or bandwidth for your replication groups.

To edit the schedule and bandwidth for a replication group, follow these steps:

1. In the console tree under the Replication node, right-click the replication group with the schedule that you want to edit, click Properties, and then click Edit Schedule.

2. Use the Edit Schedule dialog box to control when replication occurs, as well as the maximum amount of bandwidth that replication can consume.

To edit the schedule and bandwidth for a specific connection, follow these steps:

1. In the console tree under the Replication node, select the appropriate replication group.

2. Click the Connections tab, right-click the connection that you want to edit, and then click Properties.

3. Click the Schedule tab, select "Custom connection schedule," and then click Edit Schedule.

4. Use the Edit Schedule dialog box to control when replication occurs, as well as the maximum amount of bandwidth that replication can consume.

Enabling or Disabling Replication

From time to time you will also need to enable or disable your replication groups.

To Replicate or Not to Replicate

If you are updating your network and need to control your bandwidth, you may want to disable replication. We always disable replication and change the time to replicate Active Directory whenever we upgrade servers or networking devices. You would not want to cause problems for yourself if you were adding equipment and the servers want to replicate and then fail. This will not only fill up error logs but also start causing problems fast. The best thing here is to disable replication whenever you are making changes to the network's architecture.

To enable or disable replication for a specific connection, perform the following steps:

1. Open Server Manager and choose Tools ➢ DFS Management.

2. In the console tree, under the Replication node, click the replication group that contains the connection you want to edit.

3. In the details pane, click the Connections tab.

4. Do one of the following:

   ◆ To disable a connection, right-click the connection, and then click Disable.

   ◆ To enable a connection, right-click the connection, and then click Enable.

CONNECTION SUPPORT

Microsoft does not support one-way connections for DFS replication. Creating a one-way replication connection can cause numerous issues including health-check topology errors, staging issues, and issues with the DFS replication database. To create a one-way connection, instead make the replicated folder on the appropriate member read-only.

ENABLING OR DISABLING REPLICATION ON A SPECIFIC MEMBER

Sometimes you may also need to enable or disable replication with specific members of a replication group. Caution should be the order of the day. After a disabled member is enabled, the member must complete an initial replication of the replicated folder. Initial replication will cause about 1 KB of data to be transferred for each file or folder in the replicated folder, and any updated or new files present on the member will be moved to the `DfsrPrivate\PreExisting` folder on the member and will be replaced with authoritative files from another member. If all members are disabled, then the first member enabled becomes the primary member, which may not be what you want to do.

TO SHARE OR TO PUBLISH

Membership changes are not applied immediately. The membership changes must be replicated to all domain controllers, and the member must poll its closest domain controller to obtain the changes. The amount of time this takes depends on AD DS replication latency and the short polling interval (five minutes) on the member.

SHARING OR PUBLISHING A REPLICATED FOLDER

Once you have completed the replication wizard, you may want to share or publish the replicated folder. To do this, you must add the folder to an existing or new namespace.

To share a replicated folder without publishing the folder to a DFS namespace, perform the following steps:

1. Open Server Manager and choose Tools ➢ DFS Management.

2. In the console tree, under the Replication node, click the replication group that contains the replicated folder you want to share.

3. In the details pane, on the Replicated Folders tab, right-click the replicated folder that you want to share, and then click Share and Publish in Namespace.

4. In the Share and Publish Replicated Folder Wizard, click "Share the replicated folder," and then follow the steps in the wizard.

To share a replicated folder and publish it to a DFS namespace, perform the following steps:

1. Open Server Manager and choose Tools ➤ DFS Management.

2. In the console tree, under the Replication node, click the replication group that contains the replicated folder you want to share.

3. In the details pane, on the Replicated Folders tab, right-click the replicated folder that you want to share, and then click Share and Publish in Namespace.

4. In the Share and Publish Replicated Folder Wizard, click "Share and publish the replicated folder in a namespace" and then follow the steps in the wizard.

CHECK THE SECURITY REQUIREMENTS

To perform this procedure, you must meet the security requirements for managing DFS replication and namespaces. If folders will be shared as part of the Share and Publish Replicated Folder Wizard, you must also be a member of the local Administrators group on the servers where each folder is shared.

PRACTICAL USES

Before you start setting up your root, throwing in some links, and reorganizing the way your users access their resources, let's take a quick look at some good ways that DFS can actually add value to your network. Remember, it's not about playing with cool new features; it's about making life easier. When you reduce your time on the boxes, you become more efficient and thus more productive.

Consolidated Enterprise Resources

The example DFS we've worked through in this chapter would be a good way to consolidate enterprise resources. You can take all your shared resources across the network and put them under one logical share. Then, instead of having to know which logical drive a resource resides on, you only need to know the subdirectory. The neat thing is that actually configuring the DFS has absolutely no impact on the configuration of your network. You can build and experiment with DFS configurations all day long in a production environment without anyone even knowing that it exists. All of the old shares on your network remain in place, data is untouched, and users don't see anything different. Once you're ready with your new DFS, the hard part comes in—changing your users' drive mappings from one drive per \\server\share to one drive for all shares. Don't underestimate this task. It's more than just mapping a new drive letter to the DFS root. All applications need to know that they will no longer be on drive X, for example, but rather on drive Y.

Life-Cycle Management

The good news is that with DFS, this is the last time you'll ever deal with changing drive mappings. If you need to move data from one server to another for purposes of cycling a new server in and an old one out, you don't need to play the game of backing up data, wiping the server, rebuilding it new with the same name, and restoring data to make it look like it is the same physical machine. With DFS, you can set up a new server and configure it as an offline link replica for the share you want "moved." After you verify that all data has been ported over successfully, bring it online and take the old one off. The users don't know that they are hitting a new server. The DFS handles it all in stride.

Exploring the Network File System

We have covered DFS, so you now know how great it can be to point to one logical location to find files and folders. Now you get to talk to the animals—or share files with all those other knockoff operating systems. Just kidding—you want to be able to share files across the whole organization, and if you are using another OS, Server 2012 offers you a tool to do just that. We will be getting a bit technical in this section, and we want you to know that you may not need to do this; however, if you do, you will want to follow these steps. You must select NFS when adding the File Services role to your server. You had to do this for the DFS section just completed. If you did not select NFS, simply go back into your File and Storage Services and add NFS by selecting the appropriate box. So, we'll begin by discussing what NFS is and what Server 2012 can provide you.

Network File System provides a file-sharing solution for organizations that have a mixed Windows and Unix/Linux environment. NFS gives you the ability to share files across these different platforms when you are running Server 2012. NFS Services include the following features and improvements in Server 2012:

Active Directory Lookup   You have the ability to use Windows Active Directory to access files. The Identity Management for Unix Active Directory schema extension includes Unix user identifier (UID) and group identifier (GID) fields. This enables Server for NFS and Client for NFS to look up Windows-to-Unix user account mappings directly from Active Directory Domain Services. Identity Management for Unix simplifies Windows-to-Unix user account mapping management in Active Directory Domain Services.

Enhanced Server Performance   Services for NFS include a file filter driver, which significantly reduces common server file access latencies.

Unix Special Device Support   Services for NFS support Unix special devices (mknod).

Enhanced Unix Support   Services for NFS support the following versions of Unix: Sun Microsystems Solaris version 9, Red Hat Linux version 9, IBM AIX version 5L 5.2, and Hewlett Packard HP-UX version 11i. However, newer versions will undoubtedly be supported in the future.

You can use command-line tools, but in Server 2012 you can use also the Services for Network File System console, as shown in Figure 14.37. The command-line tools and their use are listed later in the chapter.

FIGURE 14.37
Services for the
Network File
System console

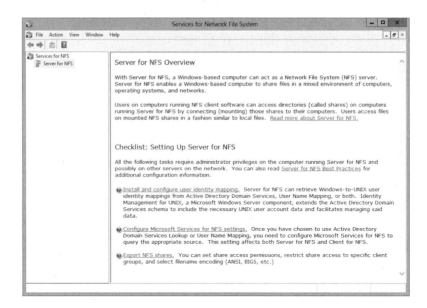

One of the more common scenarios that would create the need to use NFS is for users in a Windows environment using an enterprise resource planning system (ERP) that is Unix based. While in the ERP system, users can create reports and or export accounting data into Microsoft Excel for further analysis. NFS allows you to access these files while still in Windows, which cuts down on both the technical skills and the time required to export the files using a Unix script and then import them into a Windows-based application. Another scenario may be that you have a Unix system used to store files in some storage area network (SAN). Having NFS running on Server 2012 allows users in the organization to access the files stored there without all the overhead of scripting on the Unix side.

NFS Service Components

There are two service components that help run NFS:

Server for NFS   Normally, a Unix-based computer cannot access files on a Windows-based computer. A computer running Windows Server 2012 R2 and Server for NFS, however, can act as a file server for both Windows-based and Unix-based computers.

Client for NFS   Normally, a Windows-based computer cannot access files on a Unix-based computer. A computer running Windows Server 2012 R2 and Client for NFS, however, can access files stored on a Unix-based NFS server.

NFS in Server 2012 R2 also has administrator tools that you can use to manage NFS; you can find these administration functions in the Microsoft Management Console (MMC) snap-in discussed throughout this book.

Before using NFS, there are some prerequisites and assumptions that must be made. You will need to have a basic understanding of both Windows and Unix environments, have some file security knowledge, and know how to administrate Server 2012 R2. A good understanding of what the users need is also a requirement.

NFS PRECAUTIONS

Before installing Services for NFS, you must remove any previously installed NFS components, such as NFS components that were included with Services for Unix. We recommend that you back up or make a record of your configuration before removing NFS components so that you can restore the configuration on Services for NFS.

By default, Server for NFS supports Unix client computers using NFS version 2 or version 3. You can override this, however, and configure Server for NFS to allow access only to clients running NFS version 2. For instructions, see "Configuring Server for NFS" in the Services for NFS help. Client for NFS supports both versions, and this is not configurable.

You will need to gather the list of users, groups, and computers that will be used. Begin with a test ID on both the Windows and Unix servers before you deploy and announce your genius. Start by creating user accounts on the both servers, and then install the Server for NFS role by following these steps:

1. Open Server Manager, click Manage, and then select Add Roles and Features.

2. The Add Roles and Features Wizard will start. Keep the default selected, "Role-based or feature based installation," and click Next.

3. On the Server Selection screen, pick which server to install the role on and click Next.

4. Drill down to the Server for NFS role. To get there, expand File and Storage Services, expand File and iSCSI Services, and select the check box for Server for NFS. Click Next to continue.

5. Select any additional features you may wish to add to the server at this time. Please note that this page is where you could add the Client for NFS feature. For this exercise we will only install Server for NFS. Click Next to move into the Confirmation page.

6. Review the roles and features that will be installed and click Install.

7. When the installation completes, the installation results will appear. Click Close.

You now need to configure NFS authentication and create an NFS shared folder. Make sure you use Server 2012 for this and keep those security updates current. Now that Server for NFS is installed, you get a new tab called NFS Sharing on the properties screen of a folder. Follow these steps to create an NFS shared folder:

1. On the computer running Server for NFS, create a folder to use as the NFS shared folder.

2. Right-click the folder you created, and click Properties.

3. Select the NFS Sharing tab, and click Manage NFS Sharing.

4. On the NFS Advanced Sharing page, check the box to share this folder. The share name defaults to the folder name. If you want to allow anonymous access, select "Allow anonymous access."

5. Click Permissions, click Add, and then do either of the following:

    ◆ In the Names list, click the clients and groups you want to add, and click Add.

    ◆ In the Add Names box, type the names of clients or groups you want to add, separating names in the list with a semicolon (;).

6. In the Type of Access list, click the type of access you want to give the selected clients and groups.

7. Select Allow Root Access if you want a user identified as root to have access other than as an anonymous user. By default, the user identifier (UID) root user is coerced to the anonymous UID.

8. In the Encoding list, click the type of directory name and filename encoding to be used for the selected clients and groups. Stay consistent here!

9. Click OK twice, and then click Apply and OK.

The nice thing about Windows Server 2012 R2 is that you can use PowerShell to accomplish the same tasks we just walked through using the Server UI. Let's take a look at using PowerShell to install the NFS role on a server and to create an NFS file share.

1. Open Windows PowerShell from the taskbar, running the program as an administrator.

2. Run the following commands to install the NFS role on a server:

```
PS C:\> Import-Module ServerManager
PS C:\> Add-WindowsFeature FS-NFS-Services
PS C:\> Import-Module NFS
```

3. Run the following command to create a new NFS file share:

```
PS C:\> New-NfsShare -Name "NFSshare01" -Path "C:\shares\NFSshare01"
```

4. To see all the New NFS PowerShell cmdlets available in Windows Server 2012 R2, run the following command:

```
PS C:\> Get-Command -Module NFS
```

SETTING DEFAULT PERMISSIONS

You will now apply some default permissions for the files and folders you will be creating and then make some minor changes to your firewall on the server you are using for NFS. Remember that the server you use should be behind the organization's main firewalls and be protected. You will need to open all the ports shown here to run NFS:

SERVICES FOR NFS COMPONENT	PORT TO OPEN	PROTOCOL	PORT
User Name Mapping and Server for NFS	Portmapper	TCP, UDP	111
Server for NFS	Network Status Manager	TCP, UDP	1039
Server for NFS	Network Lock Manager	TCP, UDP	1047
Server for NFS	NFS Mount	TCP, UDP	1048
Server for NFS	Network File System	TCP, UDP	2049

To open the firewall ports, follow these steps as necessary:

1. On a computer running the User Name Mapping service or Server for NFS, press the Windows key + R. In the Run field, type **firewall.cpl**, and then click OK.

2. Click the Exceptions tab, and then click Add Port.

3. In the Name field, type the name of a port to open, as listed in the "Setting Default Permissions" sidebar.

4. In the "Port number" field, type the corresponding port number.

5. Select TCP or UDP, and click OK.

6. Repeat steps 2 through 5 for each port to open, and then click OK when finished.

You will then need to add Mapsvc.exe to the exception list in the firewall.

1. On the computer running the User Name Mapping service, press the Windows key + R. In the Run field, type **firewall.cpl**, and then click OK.

2. Click the Exceptions tab, and then click Add Program.

3. Click Browse, click mapsvc.exe, and then click Open. By default, this file is located in %windir%\System32.

4. For testing purposes, click "Change scope," select "Any computer," and then click OK.

5. Click OK two times more.

You are almost finished with this process. Now you will need to enable file and print sharing on the computer running the NFS service. You probably know how to do this if you have been reading along to this point, but we want to be complete, so here are the steps:

1. On a computer running Services for NFS, press the Windows key + R. In the Run field, type **firewall.cpl**, and then click OK.

2. Click the Exceptions tab, select the File and Printer Sharing check box, and then click OK.

3. Repeat these steps on each computer running Services for NFS.

You will want to test this to verify that all the functionality is there before you release it to the masses. The following Microsoft TechNet article will give you four tests you can run: http://technet.microsoft.com/en-us/library/cc753302.aspx.

You can use the netsh command-line tool to configure the firewall as well. See Figure 14.38 for an explanation and listing of available commands.

FIGURE 14.38
netsh command-line utility

The Bottom Line

Add a File and Storage Services role to your server. Before you can create and use DFS or NFS, share files and folders, or perform any other file-related function across the domain in Server 2012, you will need to install the additional File and Storage Services roles.

Master It Go into Server Manager, and add the server roles DFS and NFS.

Add a shared folder using NFS. Once the proper File and Storage Services roles have been added, you can then share folders, such as a folder called APPS.

Master It Create a shared folder called APPS on your Windows Server 2012 R2 server; when you have finished, the wizard should show a successful share.

Add a DFS root. If your organization ends up with a lot of file servers created over time, you may have users who do not know where all the files are located. You can streamline the process of finding and using multiple file servers by creating a DFS root and consolidate the existing file servers into common namespaces.

Master It Create a new namespace called **MYFIRSTNS** on your Windows Server 2012 R2 server; when you have finished, the wizard should show a new namespace called MYFIRSTNS.

Chapter 15

Dynamic Access Control: File Shares, Reimagined

I am sure that as you make your way through this book, you have begun to realize the vast number of features that have been included in Windows Server 2012. Now we come to probably the single most important new feature, Dynamic Access Control. This is a groundbreaking new feature that will shake up file server administrators forever!

Let's start with a short example. When you join a company and you get a user account for the computer, you can be almost sure you are part of a default group called Domain Users. Now as you require access to different resources, you submit the relevant forms to the resource owners and are granted access, which usually means you are placed in the security group that has already been granted access to these resources. (For example, if you want access to financial data, the Finance share gives anyone who is part of the Finance group read-write access to the financial data.) As you want access to more and more resources, you get added to more and more groups. As new resources come online, new groups are created to manage access to them.

Think about how many file servers are deployed around the world today and how many groups are created to control access to these shares, and then add the amount of administrative effort to not only create them but maintain everything afterward. This is the reality of file server administrators today.

Now let us introduce Dynamic Access Control (DAC). This truly is the next generation in securing information that needs to be secure and controlling access to resources to which only authorized people should have access.

Imagine that a not-so-tech-savvy financial director of a large corporation decides to record all the directors' salaries in an Excel spreadsheet and doesn't password-protect it or put it in a secured folder. A disgruntled employee gets hold of this document and publishes it to the world. How embarrassing would that be not only to the company but also to the financial director!

Now imagine a world where the financial director does the same silly thing but the data is automatically secured because it contains keywords that trigger a process to classify the data as sensitive and allow access only to certain groups. Wouldn't that be simply amazing! This is one of the groundbreaking features within DAC. Hopefully, now you get a picture of what we are about to dive into and master!

The key thing to remember is that DAC is not a single piece of technology. It is a file-server solution. It brings together conditional expressions (for example, is this user part of a group, or does the computer a file is accessed from need to be domain joined?), file classification (such as high business importance, classified, and the like), and Central Access Policies (centrally manage all the authorization policies), and with the use of Kerberos it validates "claims" from users. In turn, these technologies come together to form DAC and allow you to create a centrally controlled governance policy across your file servers.

In this chapter, you will learn to:

◆ Secure your data using conditions

◆ Create a new claim type and resource property

◆ Secure hundreds of servers

◆ Classify and secure data without knowing what the data is

A New Way to Secure File Shares

We assume if you are reading this chapter that you know the basics of file shares: how to create them and manage them. If you don't, stop! And turn back to Chapter 13 where you will learn all this. If you are familiar and are ready to proceed, let's go!

Let's dive straight in and look at the share permissions on a file share, as shown in Figure 15.1.

FIGURE 15.1
File share permissions in Windows Server 2012

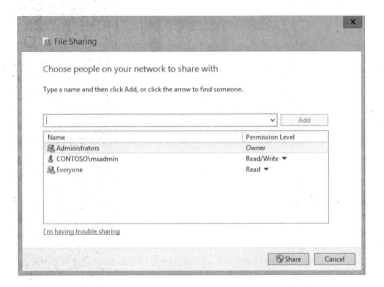

As you can see, no major changes have happened there. The real power in securing file shares is through the security properties, as displayed in Figure 15.2.

FIGURE 15.2
Security tab for a
file share

This Security tab dictates the NTFS permissions to not only the folder but the files as well. But as you can see from this tab, it doesn't look much different than in previous versions of Windows.

Since this is most definitely an advanced feature, it is rightly placed under the Advanced button located at the bottom of the Security tab; see Figure 15.2.

Figure 15.3 shows the Advanced Security settings for a file share, and it is where we can begin to configure the basics of DAC.

FIGURE 15.3
Advanced Security
settings for a file
share

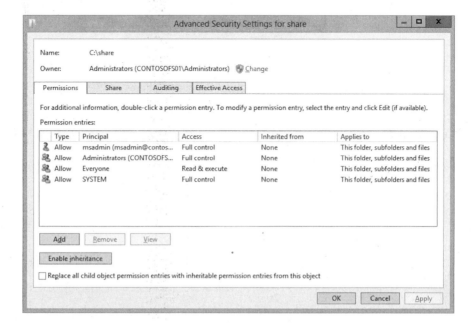

In this example we have a single folder called share. It is shared to everyone for read-only access via its share permissions and read-only via its NTFS permissions, and we also allow our administrators Full Control. As you can see from Figure 15.3, however, the Everyone principal has Read & execute access. Now you can start to see the granular control the Advanced Security settings offer, but this is still not DAC.

Click Add from the Advanced Security Settings screen, and you will be brought to the "Permission Entry for share" screen, as shown in Figure 15.4.

FIGURE 15.4
Permission Entry for share

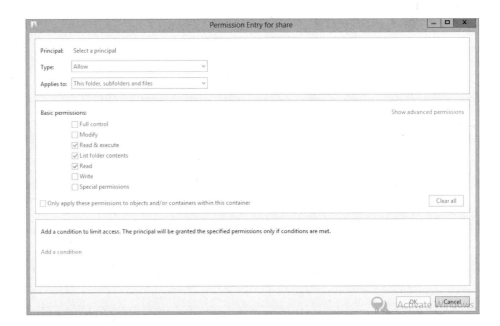

In order to progress, you must select a principal. A principal would be, for example, a user account or a group to which you want to assign privileges. If you don't select a principal at this stage, all the elements will stay grayed out.

As you can see, quite a few options look familiar from previous versions of Windows. However, now there is a new section where you can add a condition. This is where the power of DAC begins: with conditional expressions.

When you click "Add a condition," you will get the chance to create a condition, as shown in Figure 15.5.

FIGURE 15.5
Adding a condition

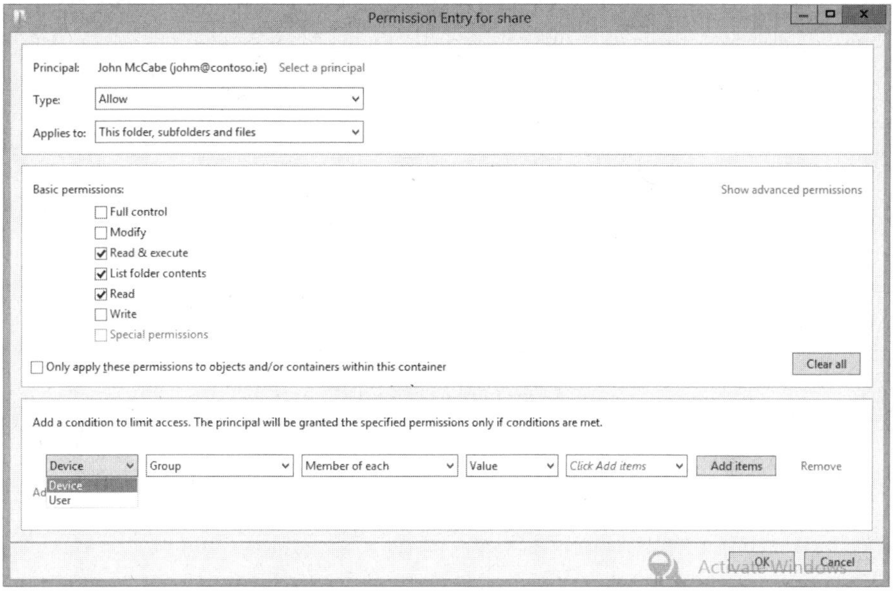

The first condition to choose from is a device or a user. Now you can secure data not only down to the user account but also from the device from which they access the resource. You can ensure that they have to access the resources from a corporate device but not their home laptop. That way, you can ensure the security of the data because you control the corporate laptop/desktop.

In the example in Figure 15.6, we have allowed John McCabe (johm@contoso.ie) Read & Execute, List Folder Contents, and Read permissions, but we have now added a condition that in order to access the share he needs to be on a computer that is part of the Domain Computers group.

FIGURE 15.6
"Permission Entry for share" dialog adding a condition

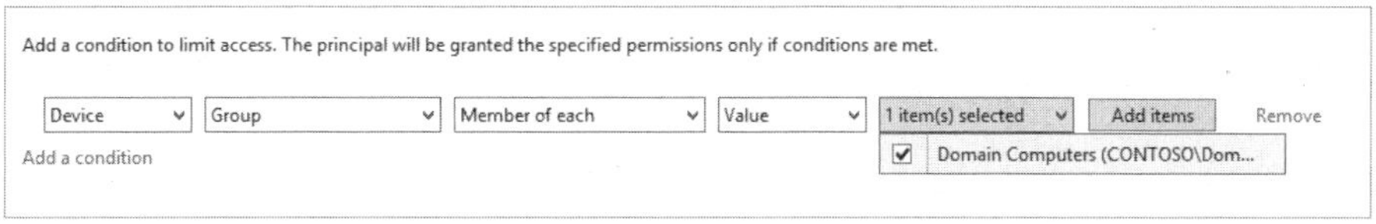

Now, returning to the "Advanced Security Settings for share" screen, you can see the new principal added but the Condition column for John McCabe is now populated, as shown in Figure 15.7.

FIGURE 15.7
Advanced Security
Settings with
Condition listed

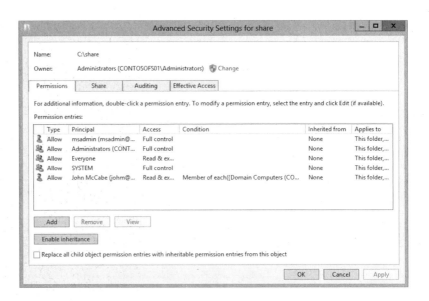

If we re-edit the principal John McCabe (johm@contoso.ie), we can add additional conditions and apply Boolean logic to the conditions using "And" or "Or." "And" ensures that all conditions are true. For example, we could set a device condition to be part of the Domain Computers group and a user condition to be part of the IT group. If both conditions are not met, access is not granted. In the "Or" case, if either condition is true, then access will be granted. See Figure 15.8 for a sample "And" condition.

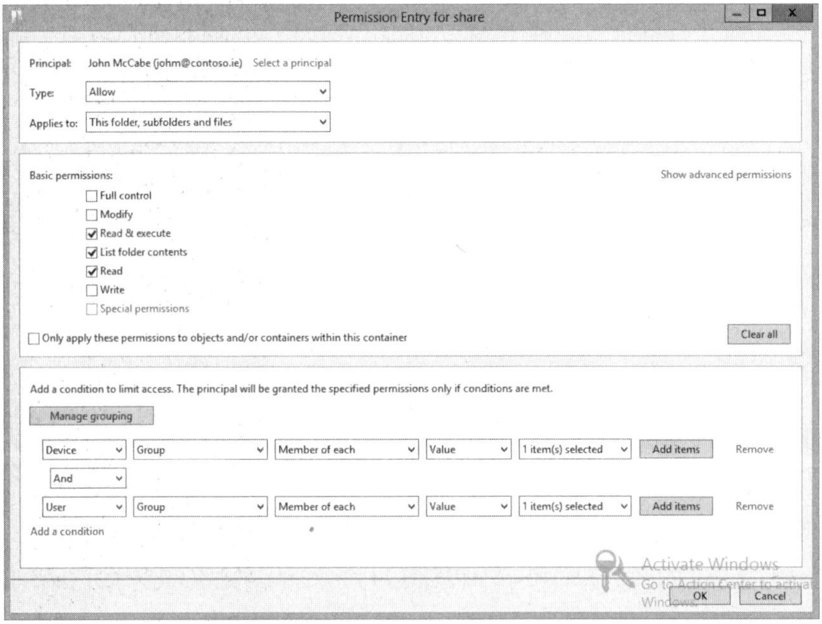

FIGURE 15.8
Sample "And"
condition

Access Control Using Groups and User AD Attributes

As you saw in the previous section we could select a principal (and remember, a principal could be a user or a group) and assign a condition, and then based on the condition, access will be granted or denied. This leads back to an age-old problem of administration of groups.

Think about it. In an enterprise or even a small business, how often do groups in Active Directory get cleared out, and how often are privileges for the existing user base assessed to ensure they are still valid? Should someone really be part of the IT Admins group now that they are a truck driver? What if now you could, for example, change the Department field in the user account in Active Directory, and it would then change the access permissions?

Active Directory stores lots of information with different tags to identify the data, called attributes. For example, when you create a user account, the most basic information you enter would be the first name and last name of the person. This information is stored in an attribute in Active Directory. These attributes can be reviewed and edited (but do be careful because it is not pretty if you mess up). Figure 15.9 shows a sample of some attributes; in this case we are viewing the given name (first name) for the user David McCormick.

A very useful attribute you can use to help secure information is the Department attribute. As you see in Figure 15.9, our user David is part of the IT group. We know IT contains lots of sensitive information, and we certainly don't want usernames and passwords or sensitive network information falling into the wrong hands.

FIGURE 15.9
Department Active Directory attributes

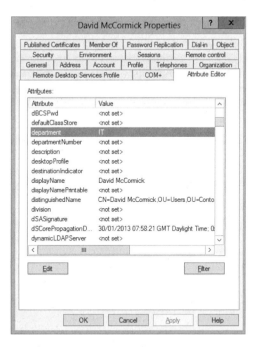

If you review all the attributes available for a user, you will see it's a very long list. In reality only a few fields may prove useful in controlling access to the data. Some examples of this would be EmployeeType (you may not want part-time staff to access certain types of data), Company (you don't want a child company accessing data from Contoso), and PhysicalDeliveryOfficeName (you might not want employees in London accessing data in the New York office).

Don't be limited by the options I mentioned; you can come up with your own options. If the attribute you want doesn't exist, you can create it and use it. This is obviously not for the faint hearted, but it illustrates just how flexible DAC can be.

In Figure 15.5 we had only the User and Device options. Now we have a new option called Resource; see Figure 15.10.

FIGURE 15.10
Resource option
in the "Permission
Entry for share"
screen

The Resource option gives you the claim types (essentially the attributes you publish to present as authorization claims to access resources) you have published. In our example, once we select Resource, the Department option is displayed. Don't worry for now how it got there; we will show you how later in the chapter.

The same logic conditions of Equals or Not Equals exist, but now the last options field automatically provisions a list of common departments to select from. See Figure 15.11.

This list is not pulled from a summary list of all users in your Active Directory. It is a default list provided by DAC when you publish an attribute as a claim type; you can modify it if needed.

FIGURE 15.11
Department
selected and
potential values

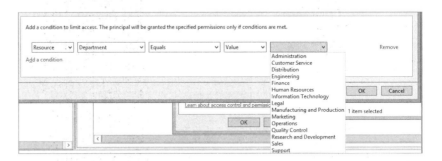

Don't jump ahead! In order for DAC to work, you need to build up the solution, and it is important that you understand the concepts before configuring the solution.

Securing Data by Machine Attributes

In recent years many companies have had to address the bring-your-own-device (BYOD) craze. It has become common for staff to use their own money to purchase the latest devices that suit their personal needs but will also allow them to access data on the corporate network.

These include tablets and laptops and on rare occasions home desktop computers. From an IT administrator's perspective, this can be frustrating when you are asked to tightly control access to information. You can see the problem: because the enterprise doesn't own the asset, there is only so much they can do to control the security of the device. The big issue is how these devices can operate in an environment but be restricted to information that is not sensitive.

Take a few seconds to review Figure 15.5 again; you will see that we have a Device option. This option allows us by default to decide whether a computer is part of a group and whether to allow access to a resource. Imagine you create four groups: one group for desktop machines, the second group for laptops, the third group for Finance, and the fourth group for Engineering. Now you could create rules requiring that only the desktop computers and laptop computers that are also part of the Finance group can access all information contained within the Finance share. That way you can encrypt the Finance machines (desktop or laptop) so that if a user does copy data off the central share, the information is protected. It's a simple example, but straight away you can see how much more control you can implement to protect your company's information.

Centrally Control Permissions Using Templates

You now have a powerful tool to control access to resources, but if you had to manually implement this, it would obviously take a huge amount of time. Like most things in IT now, centralized is best! Could you imagine taking the power of DAC but having to implement it for every file server in your environment?

Windows Server 2012 has a management utility called Active Directory Administrative Center (ADAC). This utility can be found in Server Manager under Tools.

Once the ADAC is launched in the navigation section on the left side, you will see Dynamic Access Control listed. When you click Dynamic Access Control, it brings you to the core area, where you will centrally configure the DAC rules for your environment. Take a look at Figure 15.12, which shows the Active Directory Administrative Center.

FIGURE 15.12
Dynamic Access Control in the ADAC

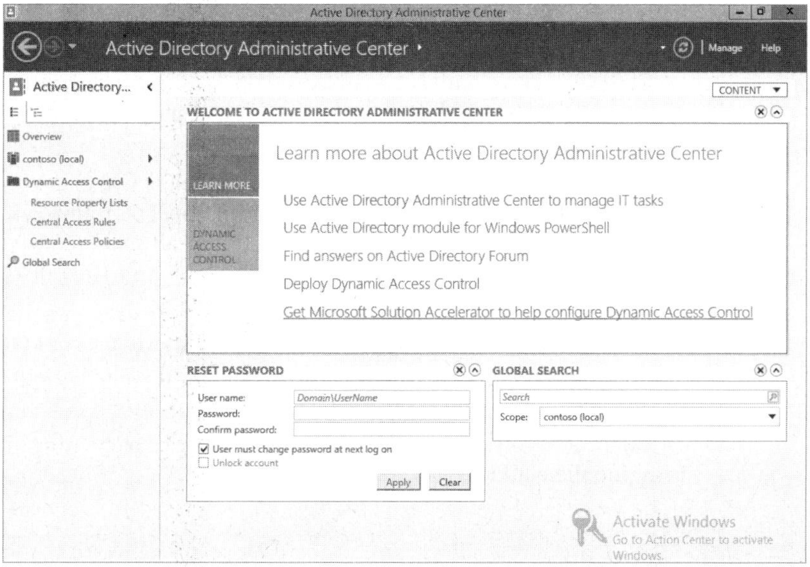

We'll take a minute to explain each of the items you see listed under the main Dynamic Access Control window. These will become important as we progress:

Central Access Policies A Central Access Policy is exactly what its name says. It is the central location for storing the access policies you want to configure. It will give you peace of mind that when you configure it, that configuration will be deployed to all the file servers in the environment.

Central Access Rules Central Access Rules are the rules about how you want to secure the information. A common example would be giving access to resources based on department. Central Access Policies utilize these rules to help you apply the standard across your organization. Figure 15.13 shows the DAC screen for Central Access Rules.

FIGURE 15.13

Central Access Rules

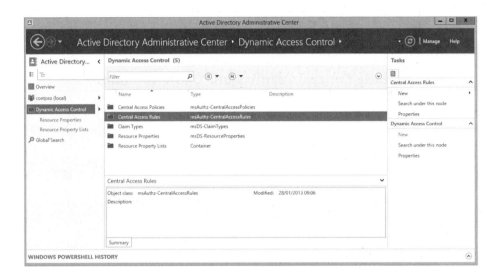

Claim Types Claim types are based on Active Directory attributes. Both user and device-based attributes can be used to configure claims. Claim types end up being used in the authorization process by Kerberos.

Resource Properties Resource properties allow you to use properties that may be defined on a file or a folder to help classify the information. For example, if the Department field on a file is set to HR, this information could be automatically classified as Confidential. This information can also be used by the Central Access Rules to target the correct resource and permissions.

Resource Lists Resource lists give you the ability to categorize resource properties into more useful containers. For example, a resource property list could limit the number of classifications displayed for selection, which may make it easier to keep track of when you don't need all the potential classifications that have been configured.

Later in this chapter we will show you examples of creating all these particular elements and bringing them all together.

Using Effective Permissions to Troubleshoot Access Control

Let's say your company has applied a Central Access Policy to a test share on your file server. This share has several subfolders containing simple folder names based on three departments: Sales, Accounts, and Engineering. The administrator has already configured the policies to authorize access to the each individual folder only by the department.

The administrator wants to ensure that policies are working correctly. With the use of effective permissions you can achieve this, and you can also test individual user accounts without having to obtain their credentials and test their access.

Don't worry if you don't fully understand this right now. Later in this chapter we'll show you how to use effective permissions, and we'll include the appropriate screenshots.

Automatic File Classification

By now you're aware of the considerable power Dynamic Access Control can bring. Think about all the information contained within the files that are hosted on the network shares within your company and then try to imagine how you are going to protect every one of them.

Traditionally, protecting data was a manual process, and what was worse, you had to ensure that the IT administrators and users understood how to manage their documents correctly.

Imagine if someone put the payroll Excel spreadsheet in the wrong place, which didn't have the traditional permissions to protect it! Imagine if your company had intellectual property and it was not secured correctly! Finally imagine the stress of managing and trying to guarantee the security of the data.

In modern IT infrastructures, centralized management—where as many tasks as possible are automated—should be the minimum base for an organization. Applying this simple principle to the classification of data is extremely important.

Using the resource properties mentioned early in this chapter, you can do this! These resource properties allow you to manually set classifications, but when you combine these with the File Server Resource Manager (FSRM) in Windows Server 2012, you can automatically classify the documents. If an end user does misplace a document in a file share, you are confident that no sensitive information can be accessed by unauthorized parties. Later in this chapter we will give you a demonstration on how to complete this.

DAC Players: User, Device, Resources, and Claims

As we progressed through this chapter so far, we touched on the key players in DAC and what makes it work. Before we start enabling DAC and walking you through scenarios, we'll recap on these players and provide some more information about them.

User

Let's start with the user. A user, as we all know, is generally how we identify ourselves and is the primary method of authorization. You can grant access to resources on just the user object. However, user accounts contain an enormous amount of information, which when properly populated will let you use these fields (attributes) to provide additional authorization to resources.

Device

Like users, devices also have a huge amount of information that you can use. You just need to select the attributes you need. A good example would be for sensitive information; to prevent leakage of this data, it would be great to be able to limit access to this information to devices that you know will always be physically located in and connected to the corporate network. You can restrict access to such information based on location. For desktop computers, you can simply enter **Onsite** in its Location field, and for laptops you can enter **Mobile**.

Normally for desktops, corporations restrict access to removable media and physically secure the asset. Because a laptop by its very nature is mobile, it is very difficult to physically secure the asset, and there may be a valid business reason to enable access to removable media. A user can now access the sensitive information, copy it to their laptop, and then copy it onto a USB device. However, with a Device claim you can restrict access to this sensitive information by the type of device the user is on, even if they have full access assigned. If the user is not on a physically secure asset, they can't access the sensitive information, thus preventing data leakage.

Resources

Resources are key. If they haven't been defined, they should be defined. They help classify the data on your file servers, and they will work with the File Server Resource Manager to ensure this happens automatically. This solves the big issue of how to apply this retroactively to your current environment. Microsoft has already done a lot of work out of the box on defining resources within DAC, and it is my opinion that it is best to see what is there. Remember, *you* must spend time planning your resources; if you don't, it will become a big problem later on.

Claims

A *claim* is information from a trusted source about an entity. It is a method of authorization that is based on an attribute (either a device or a user normally) to provide additional security to resources. It could be your office location or your department or any other attribute that is defined to provide you access to information. For example, if your office location is New York, then you can access the America user share.

Claims are of three different types (we've already discussed user and device claims, so we're providing just a brief overview here):

User A user claim is associated with the Active Directory user attributes, for example, your department or your location. Any attribute technically can become part of the user claim model.

Device Like a user claim, a device claim's information comes from the attributes associated with Active Directory computer accounts. For example, location or operating system could be used to create a claim.

Transformation Transformation claims are for cross-forest scenarios. In many enterprises today it is rare to have a single forest where everything is stored and managed. This claim type helps secure data in such a scenario. A transformation claim will help you limit the types of information also being exposed through the inter-forest environment. For example, in the forest contoso.com you are using location and department for claims, but in litware.com you don't want to expose the department; a transformation policy will allow you to hide the department and present only the location. It will also allow you to stop unwanted claim information from entering the environment. So even though a user might include the staff number, department, and manager, you may be interested only in the staff number and can block the rest of the information.

Again, you need to plan this correctly. You must determine what claim types are to be used within an organization and whether inter-forest trusts are place, and if DAC is to be used what transformation policies should be put in place.

Central Access Rules   These rules bring together the resources and claims just described to allow you to control access to information dynamically. These will feed into the Central Access Policy you will define later, which is, in turn, applied to the server base you want to control access to.

You now know the key players, and as you progress enabling DAC and configuring it for your environment, you will begin to put this information into context.

Let's begin.

Enabling DAC

In this section of the chapter I assume you have Windows 2012 installed and ready to play. In our lab environment we have three servers running Windows 2012 and a client running Windows 8. The servers are configured as one domain controller and two file servers. There are several user accounts with certain attributes (for example, Manager, Location, and Department) configured to allow you to create claim types later on.

First, you need to enable support for claims, compound authentication, and Kerberos armoring in the Kerberos Distribution Center (KDC), which is where your Kerberos authentication tickets are generated via Group Policy.

1. On your domain controller, open the Group Policy Management console located in Administrative Tools, or if you love the Search feature within Windows 2012, from the Start menu just start typing **Group Policy** and you will see the tool.

2. Click Group Policy to open it.

3. Under the Group Policy Management tree on the left side, expand Forest ➤ Domains ➤ *yourdomain.com* ➤ Domain Controllers and locate the Default Domain Controllers Policy, as shown in Figure 15.14.

4. Right-click it and select Edit. This will open a new screen called the Group Policy Management Editor; see Figure 15.15.

FIGURE 15.14
Group Policy
Management
Tool showing the
Default Domain
Controllers Policy

FIGURE 15.15
Group Policy
Management
Editor

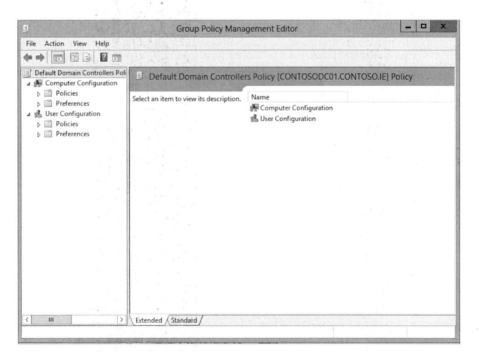

5. In the tree structure on the left, navigate to Computer Configuration ➤ Policies ➤ Administrative Templates ➤ System, as shown in Figure 15.16.

FIGURE 15.16
Location of policy to edit to enable KDC support

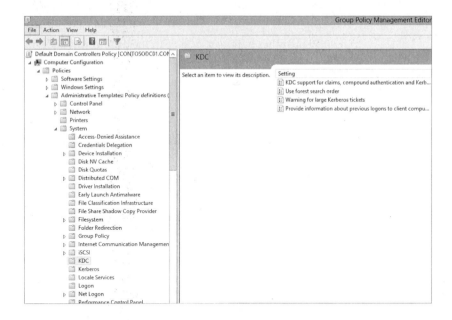

You want to edit the policy in the right side of the screen called "KDC support for claims, compound authentication and Kerberos armoring." Double-click the policy, and the policy editor will pop up and give you options to configure. See Figure 15.17.

FIGURE 15.17
Configuring "KDC support for claims, compound authentication and Kerberos armoring"

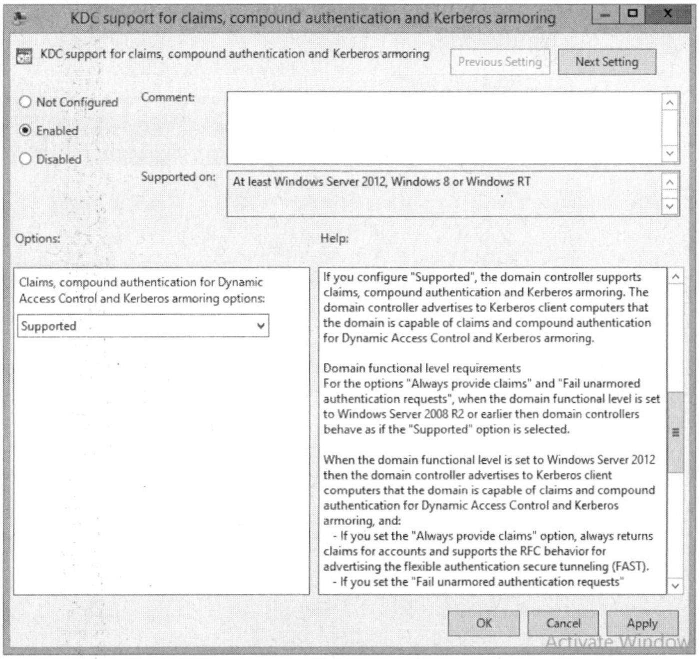

6. Select Enable (notice how the drop-down box gets populated with Supported) and click OK.

   There are other options available in the drop-down box, and the Help window just to the right will give you further information about the options available.

7. Take some time to read through the Help screen, but to simply enable Supported just leave it in the drop-down box and click OK.

8. Close the Group Policy Management tool.

9. Open an elevated command prompt and type **gpupdate/force** to propagate the group policy you just configured, or you could just wait for standard replication and Group Policy refresh.

Earlier in this chapter we showed you the Active Directory Administrative Center. This is where you will configure Dynamic Access Control.

Pieces of an Access Policy

You have learned that in order for DAC to work you have several prerequisites to configure: the claim types, the resources, and the central access rules. We also mentioned that we want to minimize the management overhead. This is where Central Access Policies come into play. They bring all of our configuration work together to easily administer and control access to the information within our environments. In the following pages we will show you how to secure your file servers using DAC centrally and how this can be applied across your organization. The best way to really get to grips with this new technology is to dive right in. Let's build a simple access policy.

CREATING A DYNAMIC ACCESS POLICY

Open the Active Directory Administrative Center and click Dynamic Access Control, as shown in Figure 15.18.

FIGURE 15.18
Active Directory
Administrative
Center

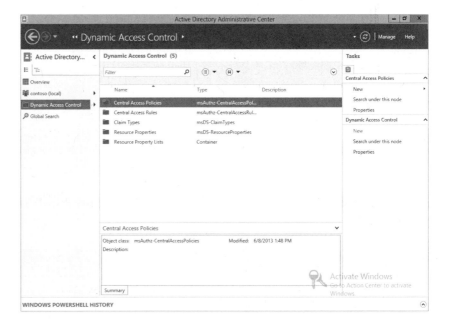

At this point, if you try to create a Central Access Policy, you will not be able to. As we mentioned, you have to create resources, claim types, and central access rules to create a policy.

One thing to notice is the various options in the center window. When you click through them, the Tasks menu on the right changes to suit the option you have selected. First, you will create a new claim type:

1. In the center window click Claim Types, and notice how the Tasks menu changes to suit.

2. On the Tasks menu, under Claim Types select New ➣ Claim Type, as shown in Figure 15.19.

FIGURE 15.19
Creating a new claim type

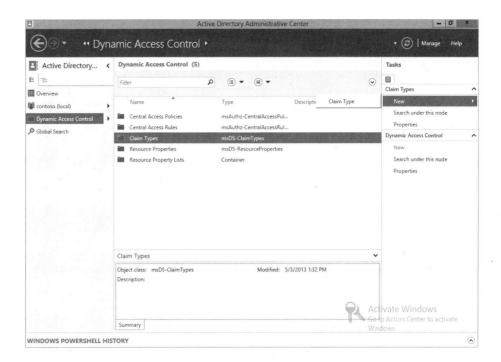

A new window will open for creating the new claim type.

3. Take some time to look at the options; you will see all the attributes that you can potentially select from to create a claim type. The different attributes are for both user and device claims.

For example, browse to the attribute dNSHostName, and you will notice that it belongs to Computer, as shown in Figure 15.20.

FIGURE 15.20
Displaying the
dNSHostName
property

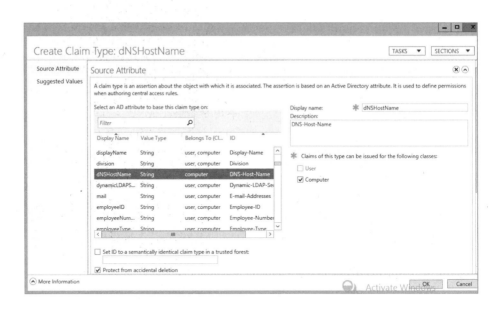

4. In the Source Attribute list, select Department.

5. Modify the "Display name" field on the right to **department_Contoso**; see Figure 15.21.

FIGURE 15.21
Modifying the
department
attribute to
create a claim
type

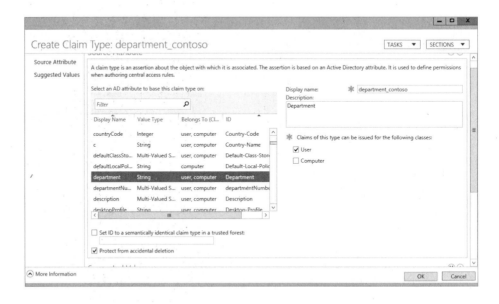

6. Scroll down to Suggested Values; this is where you will put in the information relevant to Contoso; for example, Microsoft has already configured the Department claim type but has not listed any departments.

We are creating a Department claim for Contoso, which has four departments: Sales, IT, Accounts, and HR. You will use these later on to control access to the demo shares. For example, Sales will be allowed access only to Sales data, HR will be allowed access only to HR data, and so on.

7. Under "When a user assigns a value to this claim type," select "The following values are suggested," as shown in Figure 15.22.

FIGURE 15.22
Assigning values to claim types

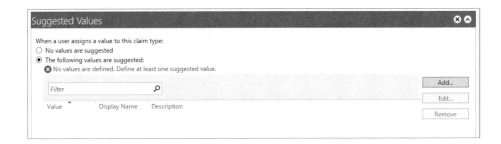

8. Click the Add button; this will bring up the "Add a suggested value" window.

9. Enter **Sales** in both the Value and "Display name" fields, as shown in Figure 15.23, and click OK.

FIGURE 15.23
Adding a suggested value

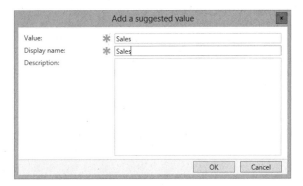

10. Repeat these steps for IT, Accounts, and HR, and click OK when finished.

Your first claim type is finished. Well done.
Now you need to create a resource property:

1. Choose Resource Property, and as before select New from the Tasks menu.

You will see two options listed: the resource property and the reference resource property.

2. Since we've already created a claim type, we're going to use a reference resource property. Select Resource Property if you do not have a claim type already created.

In Figure 15.24 you can see the claim type we created earlier. The "Display name" field is also populated, and you will have a choice under "Value type" between Single-valued Choice and Multi-valued Choice.

FIGURE 15.24
Create Reference
Resource Property
screen

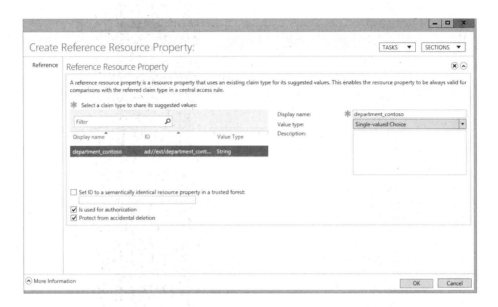

3. Choose Single-valued Choice in this case because in most companies "officially" you are supposed to work for only one department.

Because this ultimately will be used in Central Access Rules and Policies, you'll want to use this field for authorization, so make sure it is checked.

4. Click OK when finished.

Side Task

For reference purposes, this task is the procedure for creating a resource property for which a claim type doesn't exist, for example, if you don't want to use the resource properties that Microsoft has provided or if they simply don't meet your needs. Another example would be if you created a custom attribute in Active Directory and wanted to use it as a claim type.

When you've completed the previous exercise, the New Resource Property window will open. Then follow these steps:

1. On the Dynamic Access Control screen, under Active Directory Administrative Center, Select Resource Properties, and in the Tasks list select New ➤ Resource Property.

2. In the Display name field enter **department_contoso_test**, and in the Value type field choose Single-valued Choice. You have different choices for value type and this is where your planning will come into play. Most companies allow an employee to be part of only one department at any one time, so in this case a single-valued choice is the most appropriate. See Figure 15.24.

FIGURE 15.25
Creating a new
resource property

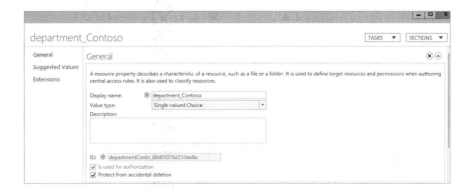

3. Take time to browse the options in the Value type field; notice you have quite a few to select from.

4. Scroll down to the Suggested Values section and add the suggested values as you did previously in creating the new claim type.

5. Click OK. You have now created your new resource property.

At this point you will return to the Resource Properties screen, as shown in Figure 15.26.

FIGURE 15.26
Resource Properties
screen

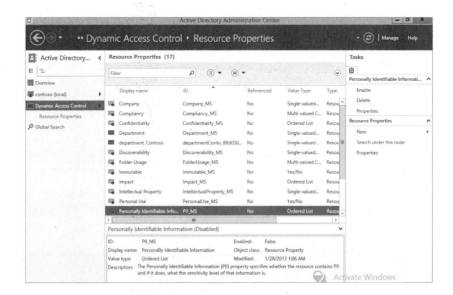

Remember when we mentioned that Microsoft has already done a lot of work to allow companies to deploy Dynamic Access Control quickly? Part of the overall goal was to make Dynamic Access Control quick to deploy, and although you have to put some thought into what rules/properties/claims types you need to create you will see from the next guide that there are a lot already done for you and all you have to do is select them.

1. Browse through the Resource Properties list to see what is configured and what you could potentially reuse rather than creating new properties.

   Now let's do a quick check:

   ◆ You've created a new claim type for Contoso departments.

   ◆ You've created a referenced resource property based on the Contoso Department claim.

   Next, you have to configure a resource property list. A resource property *must* be part of a resource property list. The resource property list will be downloaded by the file servers. As you can see in the main Dynamic Access Control window in Figure 15.27, the resource property list is of type Container.

FIGURE 15.27
Main Dynamic
Access Control
windows

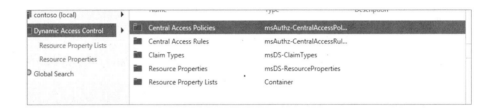

2. Double-click Resource Property Lists, and you will see the screen shown in Figure 15.28.

FIGURE 15.28
Resource Property
Lists showing the
Global Resource
Property List

The Global Resource Property List that is shown is the default list all file servers will receive.

3. For informational purposes, double-click the Global Resource Property List.

   Notice all the resource properties that are there by default, as shown in Figure 15.29.

FIGURE 15.29
The Global Resource
Property List screen

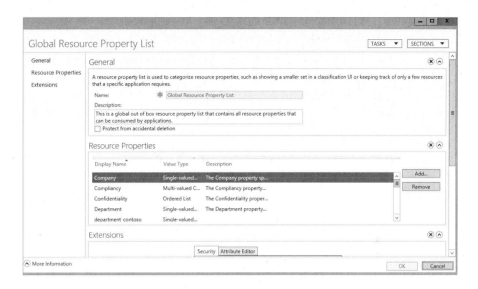

Let's add our resource property to the Global Resource Property List.

4. Click the Add button.

5. From the Select Resource Properties window, navigate to department_contoso and click the arrows pointing to the right to add it, as shown in Figure 15.30.

FIGURE 15.30
Adding a new resource
property to the Global
Resource Property
List

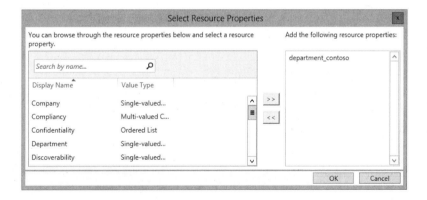

6. Click OK, browse the resource property list, and ensure that your resource property is now listed. Click OK on the main window to close it.

You have created a new claim type, a referenced resource property, and added it to the Global Resource Property List. Next, you need to create a Central Access Rule:

1. From the main Dynamic Access Control window again, click Central Access Rules, and in the Tasks menu select New ➤ Central Access rule.

2. In the Create Central Access Rule window, enter **Contoso_Demo_rule** in the Name field, as shown in Figure 15.31.

FIGURE 15.31
Create Central
Access Rule screen

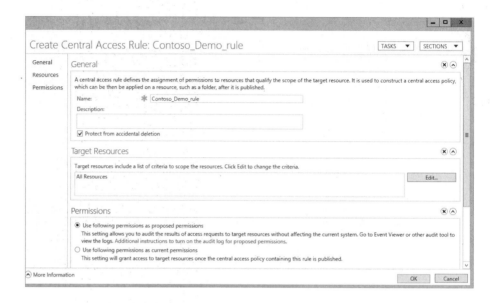

Under Target Resources, you can be more selective if you need to about the resources you want to control access to. For this example, leave it set to All Resources so that you can set up read-access for all authenticated users to all resources.

3. Now navigate to Permissions, and click "Use following permissions as current permissions," as shown in Figure 15.32.

FIGURE 15.32
Adding permissions
for a central access
rule

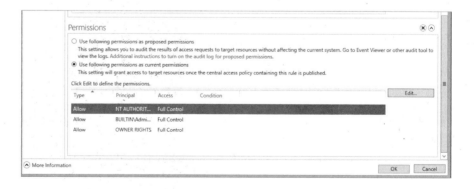

4. Click the Edit button.

This will open the Advanced Security Settings for Permissions window, as shown in Figure 15.33.

FIGURE 15.33
Advanced Security Settings for Permissions screen

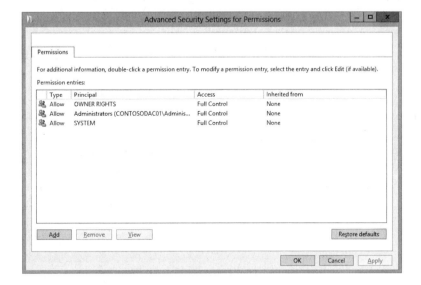

5. Click Add.

This will open the Permission Entry for Permissions window.

6. Click Select a Principle, and type in **Authenticated Users**; leave the Read and Read and Execute permissions as is; see Figure 15.34.

FIGURE 15.34
Permission Entry for Permissions screen

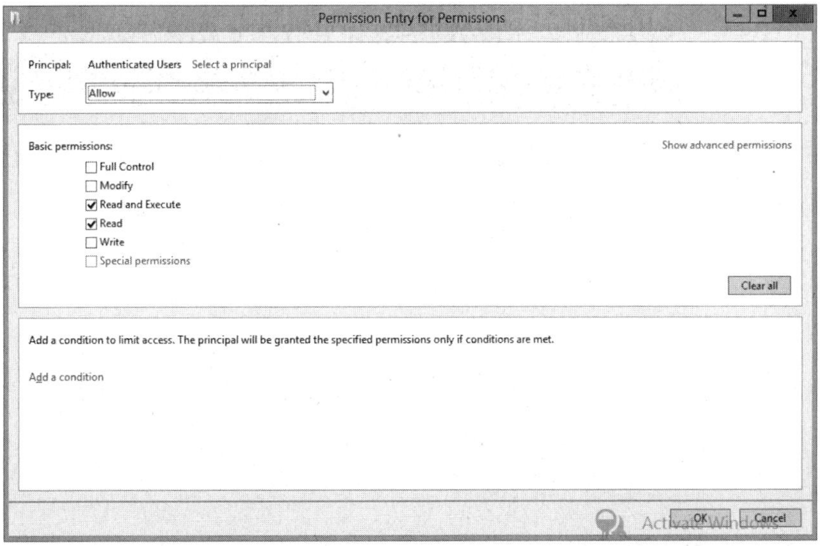

Next, as you did earlier in this chapter, you are going to add conditions.

7. Click "Add a condition."

This will bring up options for you to configure.

8. In the first box select User, in the second box select department_contoso, and in the final box select Accounts.

Notice that the drop-down list in the final box contains the options that you created earlier.

9. Repeat this step for the remaining departments. Use the "And" condition, as shown in Figure 15.35.

FIGURE 15.35
Adding conditions to a Central Access rule

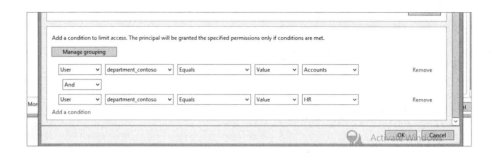

10. Click OK when you've finished adding conditions, and click OK twice more to close all windows.

Great! You are nearly finished, now you need to create a Central Access Policy that you will then use to deploy to your file servers:

1. From the main Dynamic Access Control window, select Central Access Policies, and in the Tasks menu select New ➤ Central Access Policy.

2. Enter **Contoso Test CAP** in the Name field when the new Create Central Access Policy window opens, as shown in Figure 15.36.

3. You need to add the rule you created earlier, so click Add under Member Central Access Rules.

This will open the Add Central Access Rules window.

4. Select Contoso_Demo_rule, click the arrows pointing to the right, and click OK, as shown in Figure 15.37.

5. Click OK to finish creating the policy.

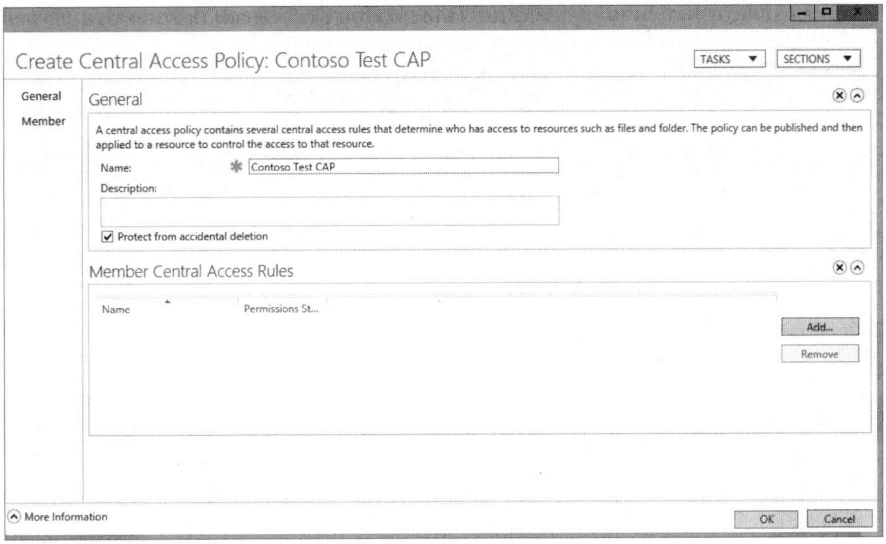

FIGURE 15.36
Create Central
Access Policy
window

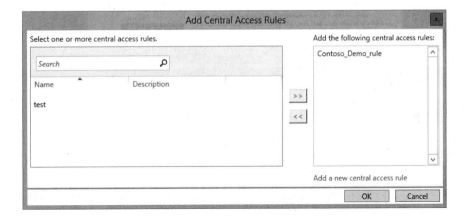

FIGURE 15.37
Adding a Central
Access rule to a
Central Access
Policy

APPLING DYNAMIC ACCESS CONTROL POLICIES

You have created a Dynamic Access Control policy, but you need to apply it to your servers in order for it to become effective. This is done via Group Policy. By deploying it via Group Policy you have amazing flexibility to start targeting specific server groups and roll it out further as necessary.

In Chapter 9 you would have become familiar with Group Policy; if not, skip back now and read it.

You need to use the Group Policy Management console to create a new group policy to roll out your Central Access Policy. To recap, the Group Policy Management console is located in Server Manager ➤ Tools.

In our example, our Group Policy Management console is located on our domain controller. (We assume at this point that you are familiar with this tool.)

You are now going to create a group policy just under the root level of the domain contoso.ie and target it to just your file servers. But before you start, here's some best practice advice:

◆ Create the necessary groups to properly target the file servers.

◆ Create organizational units in a structured hierarchal fashion and assign the group policy to the desired organizational unit and never at the root domain.

Let's begin:

1. Right-click contoso.ie, as shown in Figure 15.38, and select Create a GPO in this domain, and Link it here.

FIGURE 15.38
Creating a GPO
for Central Access
Policy deployment

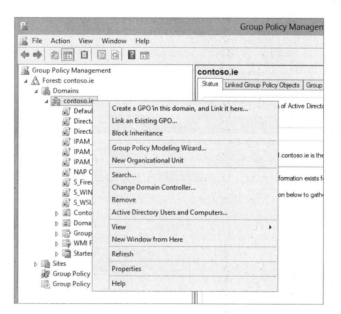

2. In the New GPO window, give it a name.

   In our scenario we're using **CAP-Contoso-Demo**.

3. Click OK, as shown in Figure 15.39.

   It should now appear in the list under contoso.ie.

4. Click the group policy, and under Security Filtering on the Scope tab of the Group Policy Management screen, as shown in Figure 15.40, select Authenticated Users and click Remove.

FIGURE 15.39
New GPO window

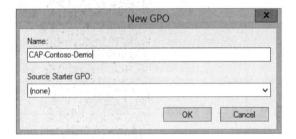

FIGURE 15.40
Removing
Authenticated
Users

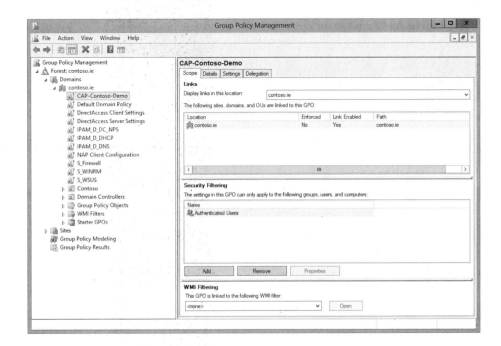

5. When prompted "Do you want to remove this delegation privilege?" click OK.

6. Click Add.

   This will bring up the Select User, Computer, or Group window.

7. Click the Object Types button and select Computer, since it is not checked by default, and click OK.

8. In the "Enter object name to select" field, type in the name of the file server you want to apply it to.

   In the example, we are using **contosofs01**.

9. Click Check Names, ensure that it resolves, and click OK. See Figure 15.41.

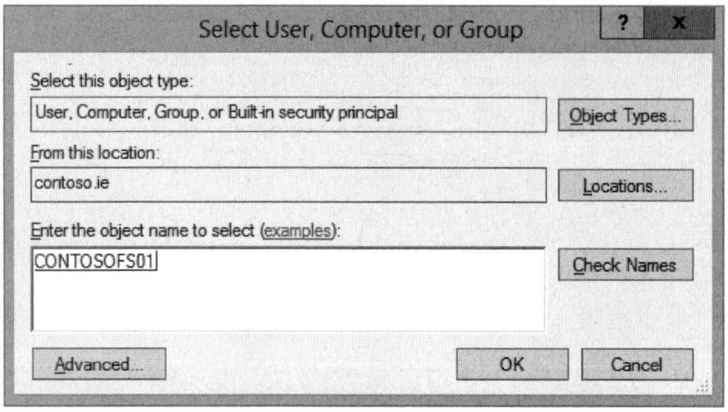

FIGURE 15.41
Ensuring the name
resolves in the
search window

In the Security Filtering field, you will see the full name of the computer account listed; this simply means that the policy will apply only to this computer, even though it is located at the root of the domain. See Figure 15.42.

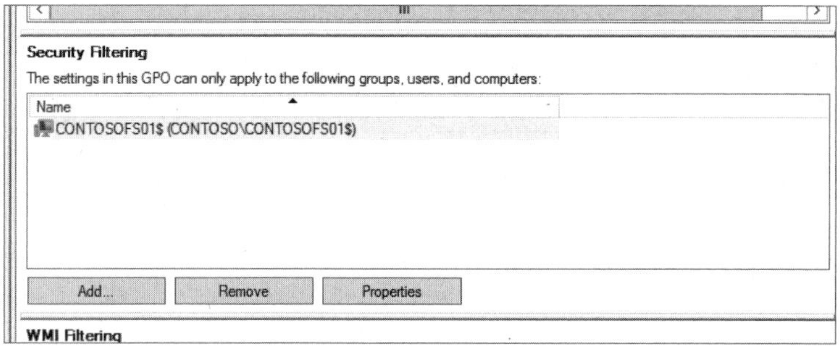

FIGURE 15.42
Computer account
added to Security
Filtering field

Next, you need to edit this group policy.

10. Right-click the CAP-Contoso-Demo group policy and click Edit.

This will open the Group Policy Management Editor window.

11. Navigate to Computer Configuration ➢ Policies ➢ Windows Settings ➢ Security Settings ➢ File System ➢ Central Access Policy, as shown in Figure 15.43.

Currently, nothing is configured.

12. Right-click Central Access Policy, and click Manage Central Access Policies, as shown in Figure 15.44.

FIGURE 15.43
Central Access Policy
location in Group Policy
Management Editor

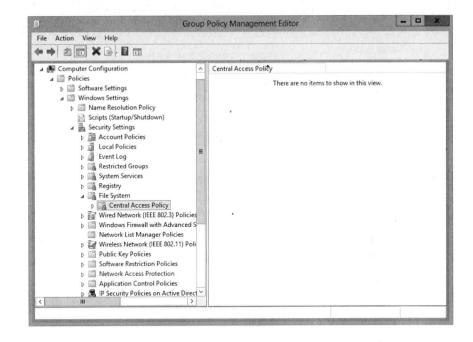

FIGURE 15.44
Manage Central
Access Policies

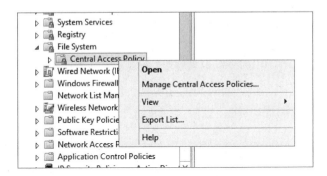

The Central Access Policies Configuration window will open, and you will see the Central Access Policies that you configured earlier listed.

13. Select the policy that you want to apply, and click Add. In this example, we are choosing Contoso Test CAP, as shown in Figure 15.45.

14. Click OK.

FIGURE 15.45
Selecting Central
Access Policies to
apply

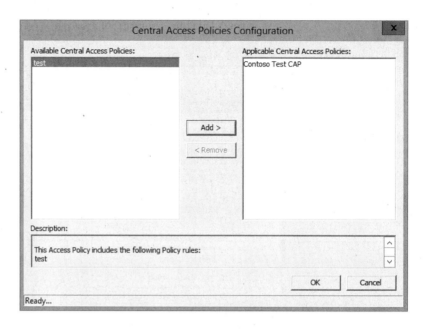

15. Next, scroll down in the Group Policy Management Editor to Advanced Audit Policy Configuration ➤ Audit Policies ➤ Object Access, and double-click Audit Central Access Policy Staging, as shown in Figure 15.46.

FIGURE 15.46
Enabling Central
Access Policy
Staging

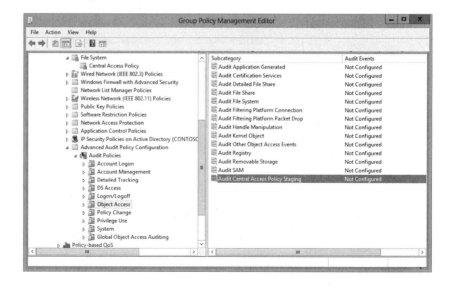

16. Select all the check boxes in the Audit Central Access Policy Staging Properties window, as shown in Figure 15.47, and click OK. Close the Group Policy Management Editor.

FIGURE 15.47
Configuring auditing

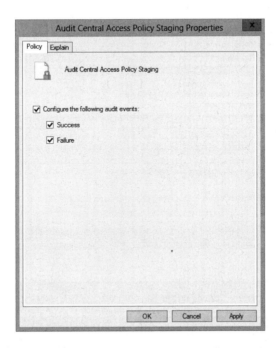

Now you need to ensure that the policy gets applied to the file server.

17. Log on to ContosoFS01 from our example, from an elevated command prompt run **gpupdate/force**.

This will apply the policy you have configured.

18. To confirm that it has been applied, look at a folder you have shared on ContosoFS01.

In our demo environment we have shared C:\share to \\contosofs01\share.

In Figure 15.48 and Figure 15.49 you can see that we have set up rules for NTFS security and share permissions.

Have you noticed the new tab? In Figure 15.49 you can see a new tab called Central Policy. By default, it applies no policy.

FIGURE 15.48
NTFS permissions

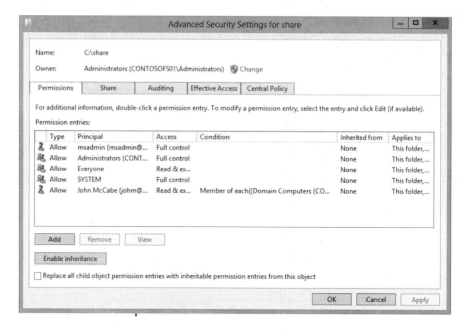

FIGURE 15.49
Share permissions

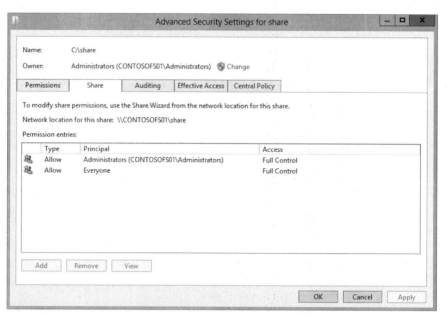

When you click on the Central Policy tab you will need to click the change hyperlink to access the drop-down list and you will find the policy we configured earlier that was assigned via Group Policy.

19. Select the policy Contoso Test CAP, and it will then display the Central Access rules you have configured for allowing/restricting access to resources.

20. Click the down arrow beside the Central Access rule, you will see the options you configured earlier.

TESTING THE NEW POLICY

You have now applied a preconfigured Central Access Policy to your file server share. If you look at Figure 15.48 and Figure 15.49 again. For the permissions, you will see that the Everyone group has been given read-acess to the folder and share after the Central Access Policy has been applied. This isn't really ideal, but it's a common problem in most environments.

Technically speaking anyone should be able to access this share and retrieve the valuable information contained within. So let's test it:

1. On Contosofs01 navigate to where your share is located.

In this example our share is located on C:\share.

2. Right-click C:\share and select Properties.

3. Click the Security tab, and then click Advanced to open the "Advanced Security Settings for share" window. See Figure 15.50.

FIGURE 15.50
"Advanced Security Settings for share" window

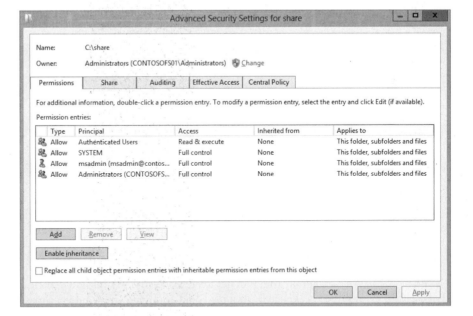

4. Click the Effective Access tab.

Effective access will allow you to test the permissions and Central Access Policies that are applied to a share for a user or device principal. For example, the Central Access Policy we have defined has one rule within, allowing only people from HR or Accounts access the share. In our lab environment we have two users configured: Tom, who is in the Accounts department, and Ken, who is in the IT department. Even though the NTFS permissions and share permissions allow Everyone to connect, the Central Access Policy will override this. The big question is, can you be sure?

Let's test it to find out. In the screen shown in Figure 15.51 you can select either a user or a device. In our example we are selecting a user because the claim type we set up was based on the user's department.

FIGURE 15.51

Effective Access tab

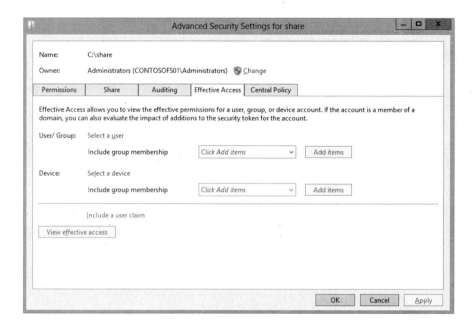

5. Click "Select a user" and type **Tom** in the Search field; click Check Names and then click OK. See Figure 15.52.

6. Now click "View effective access" at the bottom of the window.

We expect that Tom will get Read & Execute permissions. In Figure 15.53, you can see the results. As expected, Tom has Read and Read & Execute permissions as per the Central Access Policy we have configured.

FIGURE 15.52
Selecting a user
to test effective
access

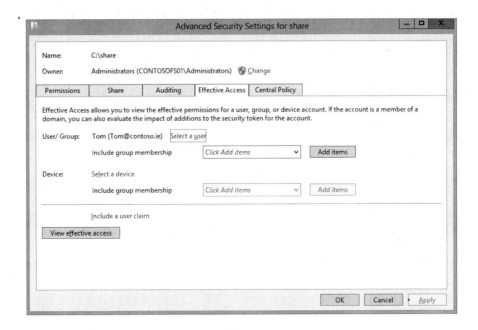

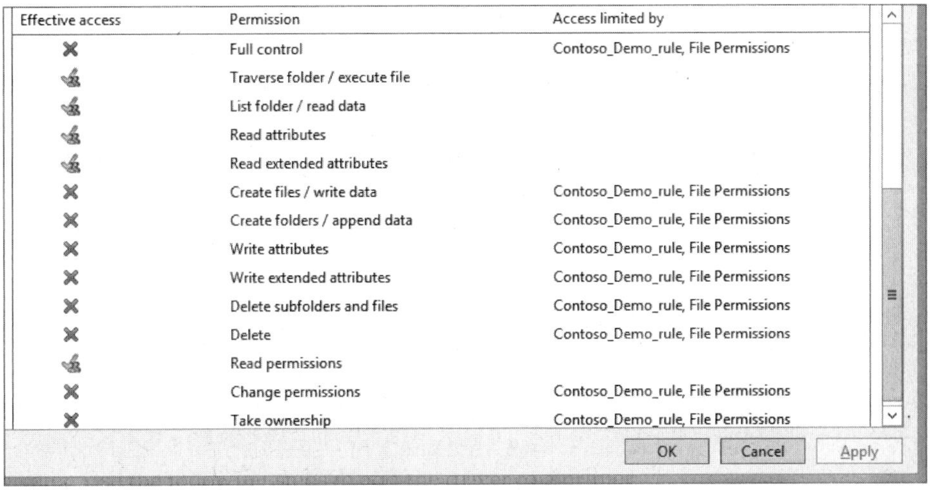

FIGURE 15.53
Effective access
results for Tom

7. Repeat the process for Ken.

Remember, Ken is part of IT, so according to our rules Ken should be denied access to the share completely. See Figure 15.54 for Ken's results; as expected, he is denied access.

FIGURE 15.54
Effective access
results for Ken

Effective access	Permission	Access limited by
✖	Full control	Contoso_Demo_rule, File Permissions
✖	Traverse folder / execute file	Contoso_Demo_rule
✖	List folder / read data	Contoso_Demo_rule
✖	Read attributes	Contoso_Demo_rule
✖	Read extended attributes	Contoso_Demo_rule
✖	Create files / write data	Contoso_Demo_rule, File Permissions
✖	Create folders / append data	Contoso_Demo_rule, File Permissions
✖	Write attributes	Contoso_Demo_rule, File Permissions
✖	Write extended attributes	Contoso_Demo_rule, File Permissions
✖	Delete subfolders and files	Contoso_Demo_rule, File Permissions
✖	Delete	Contoso_Demo_rule, File Permissions
✖	Read permissions	Contoso_Demo_rule
✖	Change permissions	Contoso_Demo_rule, File Permissions
✖	Take ownership	Contoso_Demo_rule, File Permissions

Try it out now on a Windows client, and see if you can access the share. For further fun, change your Department field in Active Directory. Then log off and log on and see if you have access.

Access Denied Assistance

On a daily basis in a large enterprise, the number of permissions that are being added and removed by help desk is astonishing. This is a manually intensive task, and it takes time to complete. Windows Server 2012 has introduced access-denied assistance to alleviate the burden and has put the responsibility of access control back on the data owner or requires the data owner at least give relevant information to the help desk to allow them to perform a quick turnaround on the access-denied problem.

Access-denied assistance can be configured in two ways:

◆ Via Group Policy

◆ Via File Server Resource Manager on an individual basis

First, we are going to show you how to configure it via Group Policy. Later in this chapter when we are dealing with classifications, we will demonstrate its configuration via File Server Resource Manager.

Let's configure a new GPO for access-denied assistance, which will be applied organization-wide:

1. On the machine (in our case ContosoDC01) that has your Group Policy Management console, open the tool and create a new group policy called **Global-Access-Denied-Assistance**.

2. As before, right-click the newly created GPO and click Edit.

   This will again bring you into the Group Policy Management Editor.

3. Navigate to Computer Configuration ➢ Policies ➢ Administrative Templates ➢ System ➢ Access-Denied Assistance, as shown in Figure 15.55.

4. On the right side of the screen, double-click the setting "Customize message for Access Denied errors."

FIGURE 15.55
Group Policy Editor
with Access-Denied
Assistance selected

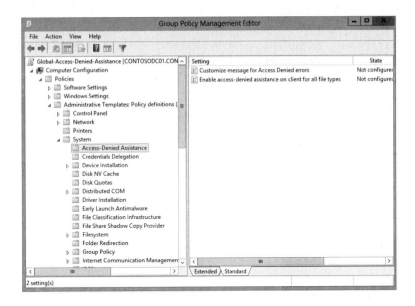

The "Customize message for Access Denied errors" window will appear, as shown in
Figure 15.56.

FIGURE 15.56
"Customize message
for Access Denied
errors" window

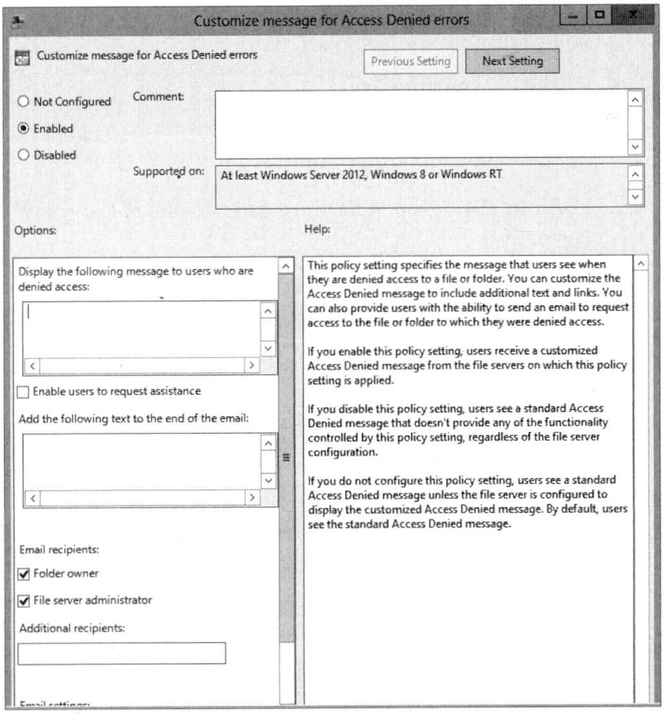

5. Click Enabled to configure the options in this new policy.

   In the Options section of the screen there are five different areas you can configure. In this example we are going to leave "Add the following text to the end of the email" and the "Email recipients" settings as configured by default. We will modify "Display the following message to users who are denied access" and "Enable users to request assistance."

6. Check the box for "Enable users to request assistance," and then you'll add a message that will be displayed when a user is denied access.

   One great thing in this area is the ability to use predefined macros to produce a really informative message for the user. The four macro's currently available are:

   ◆ [Original File Path]

   ◆ [Original File Path Folder]

   ◆ [Admin Email]

   ◆ [Data Owner Email]

   An example would be "Access is denied to [Original File Path]. Please contact [Admin Email] or click request assistance and provide business justification to access resources."

   This obviously is only a sample, but we already have two points of contact, and we can provide the complete file path to aid users in their troubleshooting.

7. Click OK when you have finished creating your message.

8. Now double-click "Enable access-denied assistance on client for all file types" and enable it.

9. Click OK when finished.

10. Now refresh the policy on your file server and client by running **gpupdate/force** from an elevated command prompt.

11. On your client, check for the existence of a registry key to ensure the policy has applied correctly.

    The key HKLM:\Software\Policies\Microsoft\Windows\Explorer should now exist and a new DWORD value called EnableShellExecuteFilestreamCheck with a Value of 1 should exist.

    Now from a user account (Ken in my example) that does not have access, try to connect to the share; the user will get a more informative message and the ability to request assistance, as shown in Figure 15.57.

FIGURE 15.57
Access-denied
custom message
from client

Notice that the [Data Owner Email] macro was replaced with the folder owner's email address and we have a nice customer-friendly message for the end user.

12. Click Request Assistance. The Request Assistance dialog is shown in Figure 15.58.

FIGURE 15.58
Request Assistance
window

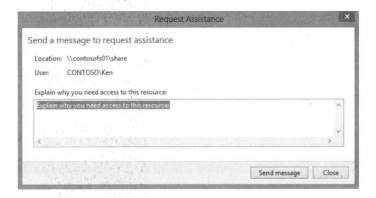

The user and the share they are trying to access are included in the message. They can now provide a business justification for the assistance if necessary.

13. Click "Send message" to send the request.

CONFIGURING EMAIL SETTINGS

You have to have email settings configured in File Server Resource Manager in order to send messages. And you must have a valid SMTP server in the domain that can relay your messages.

Claims—Using Different Attributes

We have walked you through a basic example of securing data using the Department field. Now we'll go one step further and secure data based on the office location and the job title. For this example, we are going to use our two users from the previous example, Tom and Ken. Both have become engineers, and Tom is located in the Empire State Building, while Ken is located in the Chrysler Building.

Our share on ContosoFS01 has two subfolders: Accounts and Engineering. We have applied our previous Central Access Policy to the Accounts folder to restrict access to Accounts and HR. We used an "Or" case for this, so if you were in either Accounts or HR, you would get access to the resource. In this case we want to ensure only engineers "And" staff in the Empire State Building get access to the Engineering resources.

Let's begin. First, we will summarize the steps we have to proceed through:

1. Create a claim type for title and office.

2. Create a resource property based on the claim types.

3. Add a resource property to the resource property list.

4. Create an access rule using the resource properties previously created.

5. Create a new access policy and deploy it to your file servers.

6. Apply the policy to the Engineering subfolder.

7. Test with effective access.

I would highly recommend trying this before we walk you through the scenario. Need the walk-through? No problem. Because we provided screenshots for the previous sample, we are going to omit them here to provide a little challenge.

First, as per our steps, we are going to create two new claims.

Step 1: Create the Claim

Perform the following steps to create a claim:

1. Open Active Directory Administrative Center, and on the left side click Dynamic Access Control.

2. Select Claim Types, and under Tasks choose New ➤ Claim Types.

3. In the search box under the Source attribute, type in **title**.

4. Scroll down to Suggested Values, and click "The following values are suggested."

5. Click the Add button, and enter the values in the following table:

VALUE	DISPLAY NAME
Engineer	Engineer
Accountant	Accountant
Reception	Reception
Director	Director

6. Click OK when finished.

Now, using these same steps, you need to create a new claim type of the following office buildings:

♦ Empire State Building

♦ Chrysler Building

It is often the case that the display field in an Active Directory user's account does not literally map to the attribute you expect. For example, in Figure 15.59 the Office field is listed.

FIGURE 15.59
Office field in the
Active Directory user
account properties

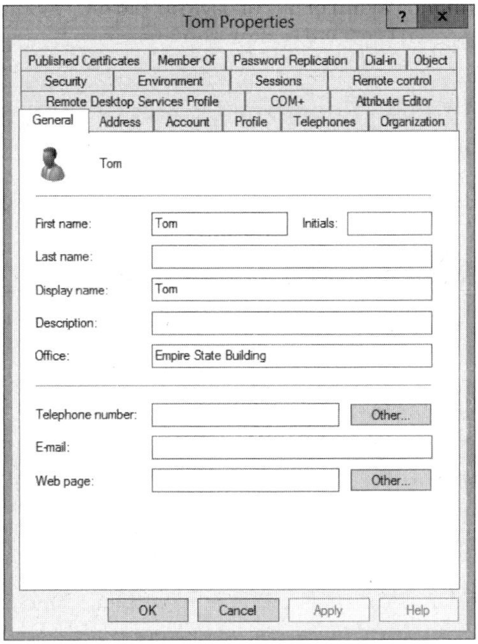

However, there is no Active Directory attribute called Office. The actual Active Directory attribute for the Office field is physicalDeliveryOfficeName; see Figure 15.60.

FIGURE 15.60
Actual Active
Directory attribute
for the Office field

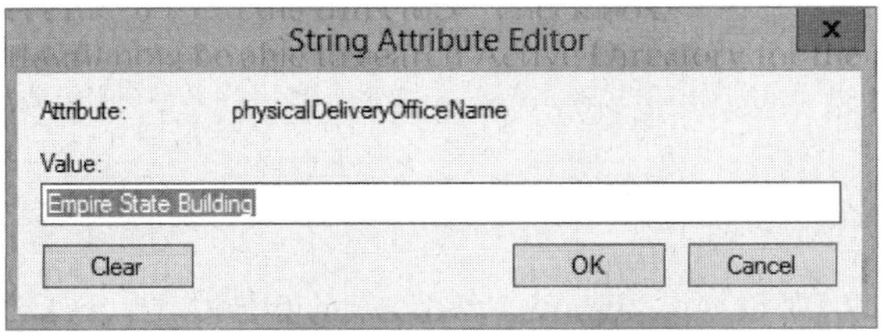

Step 2: Create the Resource Property

Perform the following steps to create the resource property:

1. From your Dynamic Access Control main window, select Resource Properties, and under Tasks choose New ≻ Referenced Resource Property.

Can you remember the difference? Referenced resource properties are for claim types you have already configured.

2. Under the referenced resource property select physicalDeliveryOfficeName, set its value type as Single-valued Choice, and click OK.

3. Repeat this for title.

Step 3: Add to the Resource Property List

This step is kind of a trick, because title and physicalDeliverOfficeName are already known attributes. You will find that they already exist in the Global Resource Property List. Verify that they exist before creating your rules.

Step 4: Create Central Access Rules

Perform the following steps to create Central Access rules:

1. From the main Dynamic Access Control window, select Central Access Rules, and under Tasks click New ≻ Central Access Rule.

2. For its name enter **Contoso-Title-Office-Secure**.

Leave the target resources as is, because you'll want to apply it to all resources that you will target later.

3. Under Permissions click Edit, and then click Add Users.

4. Click Select a Principal and type in **Authenticated Users**.

5. Click Check Names and then click OK.

6. Under Basic Permissions grant Full Control for this example.

7. Add the conditions shown in Figure 15.61, and click OK.

FIGURE 15.61
Securing conditions

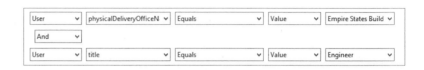

8. Click OK to close the Advanced Security Settings for Permissions window, and click OK again to finish creating your Central Access rule.

Step 5: Create a Central Access Policy and Deploy It via Group Policy

Perform the following steps to create a Central Access Policy:

1. From the main Dynamic Access Control window select Central Access Policies, and under Tasks choose New ➤ Central Access Policy.

2. Type **Contoso Secure By Title / Office** in the Name field.

3. In the Central Access Rules section click Add, and select the rule you created earlier.

4. Click OK to complete the policy.

5. Go to your machine that has the Group Policy Management console.

6. Open the Group Policy Management console. Right-click the CAP-Contoso-Demo group policy you created earlier, and click Edit.

7. Navigate to Computer Configuration ➤ Policies ➤ Windows Settings ➤ Security Settings ➤ File System.

8. Right-click Central Access Policy and click Manage Central Access Policies.

9. Add your new policy and click OK, and close the Group Policy Editor.

10. Run **Gpupdate/force** on your file server to receive the new policy.

Step 6: Apply the Policy to the Engineering Folder

Perform the following steps to apply the policy to the Engineering folder:

1. Navigate to the share, right-click it, and select Properties.

2. Click the Security tab and then click Advanced.

3. Click the central policy on the Advanced Security Settings for Engineering window.

4. Click Change and select the Contoso Secure By Title/Office policy.

5. Review the rules to ensure they are the correct rules.

Don't close the window!

Step 7: Test with Effective Access

Perform the following steps to test with effective access:

1. Click the Effective Access tab.

2. Click Select a User and type **Tom** in the search field.

3. Click Check Names and then click OK.

4. Click View Effective Access.

   Since Tom is an engineer and is located in the Empire State Building, he should get Full Control.

5. Now retry with Ken.

   Since Ken is an engineer but is not located in the Empire State Building, he should have no access to the folder.

IMPORTANT! NTFS PERMISSIONS—LEAST PRIVILEGE RULES

If you haven't noticed by now, Central Access Policies work with NTFS security permissions. The least privilege prevails in all cases. For example, if you are granted Full Access by a Central Access Policy and the maximum permission available from NTFS for a user is Read-Only, the rights you will see in the Effective Access tab will be Read-only!

The permissions are set as Central Access Policies logical "And" NTFS permissions. Try it out for yourself.

Classification

First, we'll quickly explain what is meant by *classification*. I am sure you are all familiar with army movies, and you've seen a file being opened with a big stamp on it saying "Top Secret." This is classification. Simple, eh? Essentially you are being up front with people about the contents of a file. In today's enterprise, documents can be classified based on what's important to the company. For example, for a hospital, patient information is highly sensitive and may be classified with the tag "Sensitive." A common scale consists of three classifications:

High Business Impact   Information that can damage a company's reputation or core business significantly to the point of closure or criminal investigation

Medium Business Impact   Information that would cause a company great embarrassment or would harm the company's future

Low Business Impact   Information that is generally available or of an insensitive nature

It is extremely important to understand the need to classify documents within an enterprise. Simply put: do you really want information leaking to outside the company that could, for example, expose a trade secret, causing irreparable harm to the company?

Classifying documents gives companies a chance to stop this type of data leakage. For example, with the Rights Management Service, which is part of Windows Server, you can detect that a document is top secret using different rules, and you can encrypt its contents or block it from being opened by unauthorized personnel.

The big problem, as you can imagine, is how to classify all the existing documents in an enterprise. Chances are it has not been the practice to write such information in the file's properties when saving the document. If an enterprise wants to retrofit classification onto their documents, it is a costly job in both time and money.

In Windows Server 2012 you have the ability to automatically classify documents, so you can secure the contents if necessary with RMS or block access with Dynamic Access Control. It is interesting to note that file classification has been available since Windows Server 2008.

Classifying a Document

It is possible to classify a document manually. In our lab environment under `C:\share\accounts` we have a file called `Finance.rtf`.

1. Right-click a file (in our case `Finance.rtf`) and click Properties.

You will see the Finance Properties screen with five tabs, as shown in Figure 15.62.

FIGURE 15.62
Finance Properties
screen

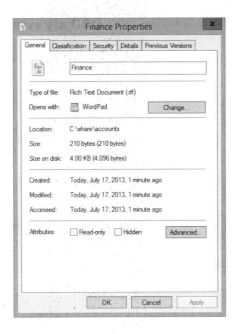

2. Click the Classification tab, and you will notice that it has some information already populated; see Figure 15.63.

FIGURE 15.63
Classification tab

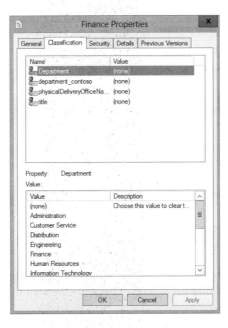

Do you notice something about the data? It's the resource properties we published earlier on in this chapter from Dynamic Access Control.

3. Click department_contoso and select Accounts.

Congratulations! You have just classified your first document.

As already mentioned, this would be a painful approach if you had to do this to all your documents. Windows Server 2012 includes a tool called File Server Resource Manager (not installed by default), located in Server Manager under Tools.

Take a quick look around the File Server Resource Manager for 2012. To open from Server Manager ➤ Tools ➤ Click File Server Resource Manager; this will open the MMC, as shown in Figure 15.64.

FIGURE 15.64
File Server
Resource Manager
MMC

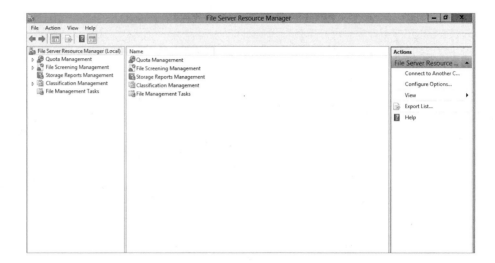

The left side lists Quota Management, File Screening Management, Storage Reports Management, Classification Management, and File Management Tasks. In this case we are interested in Classification Management.

Click the arrow beside it to show the sub-options, which are:

◆ Classification Properties

◆ Classification Rules

Classification Properties

Classification properties can be inherited via Dynamic Access Control or locally set. You can configure Authorization, File Classification, and Folder Management. You can also configure Access-Denied Assistance from here for the local file server only.

Note that you can't modify items with a scope of Global in this console because they are inherited from DAC.

Classification Rules

Classification rules allow you to set up conditions that will automatically classify documents for you. We are going to be diving deeper into this in our example. Over the next few steps we will show you how to create the appropriate rules to allow you to classify your documents and folders. We will walk you through all the steps required and demonstrate how automatic classification works.

To classify documents automatically you need to create a classification rule. First, to aid in the configuration and explanation of some items later on, you need to map your folders using Folder Usage:

1. In the File Server Resource Manager MMC, click Classification Properties.

2. Locate the Folder Usage property, as shown in Figure 15.65, and double-click it.

FIGURE 15.65
File Server Resource Manager showing the Folder Usage property

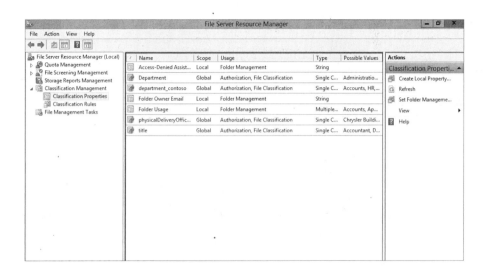

This will open the Edit Local Classification Property window, in the bottom part of the screen.

3. Scroll down to the bottom, click in an empty field, and type **Accounts**.

4. Repeat step 3 but enter **Engineering**, and click OK when you have finished, as shown in Figure 15.66.

FIGURE 15.66
Adding values to the
Folder Usage property

Now let's configure our folders:

1. In the Action menu on the right side of the MMC, click Set Folder Management.

   This will bring up the Set Folder Management Properties window.

2. In the Property box, select Folder Usage, as shown in Figure 15.67.

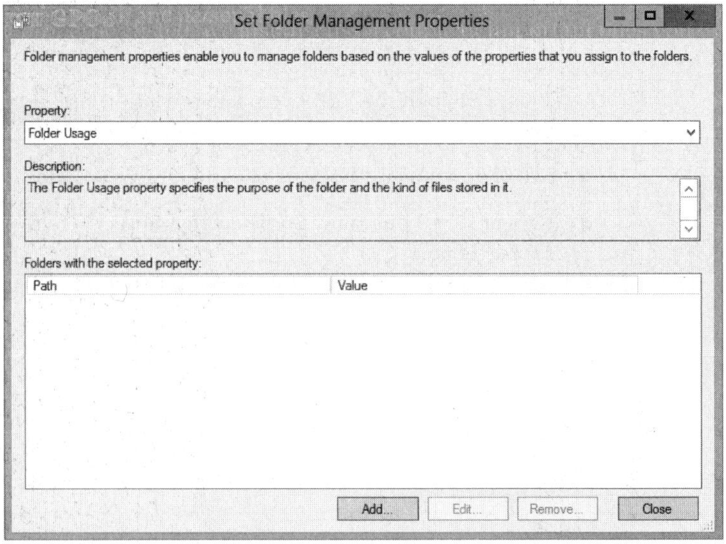

FIGURE 15.67
Set Folder Management
Properties screen

3. Click Add, browse to the path for the Accounts folder, and check the box for Accounts, as shown in Figure 15.68. Then click OK.

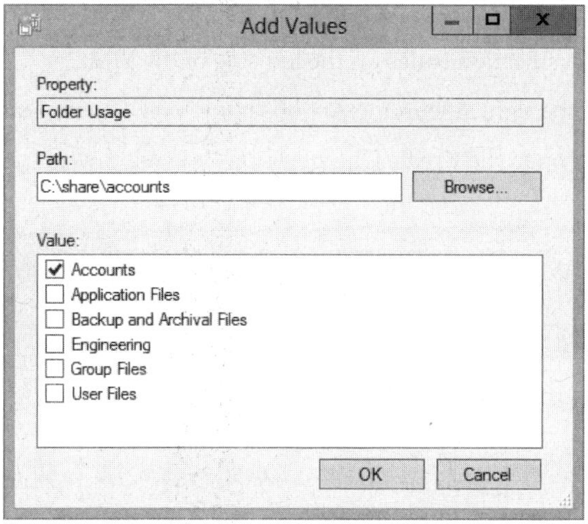

FIGURE 15.68
Adding a value to Accounts

4. Repeat step 3 for the Engineering folder, as shown in Figure 15.69.

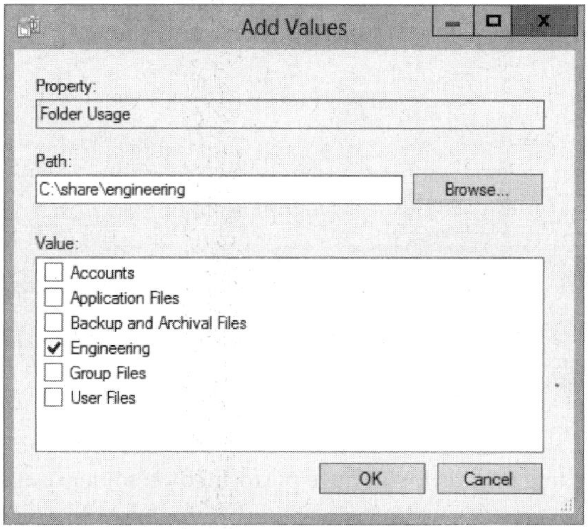

FIGURE 15.69
Adding a value to Engineering

5. Click Close.

This work will aid you later when creating your classification rules, because the properties that you have just confirmed will be available for selection during the building of a classification rule.

1. Click Classification Rules on the left side of the MMC.

2. Now on the right side in the Actions pane, click Create Classification Rule.

This will open the Create Classification Rule window, as shown in Figure 15.70.

FIGURE 15.70
Create Classification
Rule

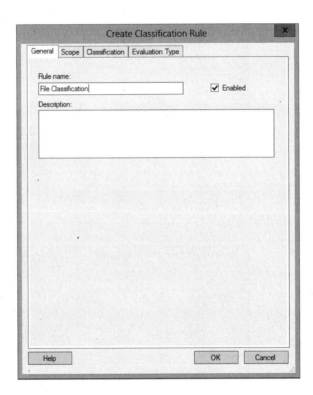

3. In the "Rule name" field, enter **File Classification**.

4. Next, click the Scope tab.

This is where the work you have performed on folder usage in the earlier steps comes into play.

5. Check the Accounts and Engineering check boxes.

Notice in Figure 15.71 that the folders in this scope are automatically populated.

FIGURE 15.71
Scope classification
rule

6. Next, click the Classification tab.

   In the Classification tab the first thing you need to choose is the classification method. There are three methods by default:

   Content Classifier Content Classifier allows you to set up patterns that you can detect within a file to autoclassify the document.

   Folder Classifier Folder Classifier automatically classifies all folders to the configured value.

   Windows PowerShell Classifier The PowerShell classifier allows you to write your own detection agent in PowerShell and execute it here. It's extremely powerful for advanced users.

7. In this exercise, select Content Classifier.

8. Next, in the Property field, select department_contoso and specify Accounts for its value, as shown in Figure 15.72.

FIGURE 15.72
Classification
configuration

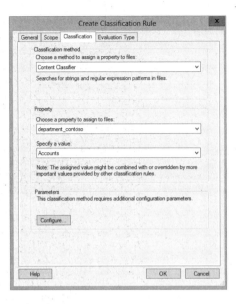

9. Click the Configure button under Parameters.

   This will open the Classification Parameters window, as shown in Figure 15.73. In the Expression Type drop-down menu there are three options:

   ◆ Regular expression

   ◆ String (case-sensitive)

   ◆ String

   These are explained in the next two sections.

FIGURE 15.73
Classification
Parameters
screen

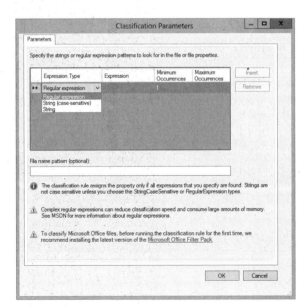

Expression Types

Regular expressions are used to identify patterns in data, similar to the Find option in Notepad, where you can press F3, type in a string to search for, and Find will find it. Regular expressions do the exact same thing. Traditionally, they are used in the programming world or in the telephony world for detecting patterns in data or manipulating telephone numbers. An example is that you can create a regular expression to detect a credit card number.

We are going to provide a quick primer on regular expressions in the next few pages because they are extremely powerful. But first, we are going to show you how to detect a simple string pattern called Finance and how upon detection of the Finance string within a document the regular expression will classify it appropriately:

1. For the purposes of this example, select String in the Expression Type field of the Classification Parameters dialog, because we are going to detect a string pattern within a document.

2. In the Expression field, type **Finance** and click OK.

CREATING MULTIPLE RULES

You can have multiple evaluation parameters of different types. However, the file you are evaluating must match all the criteria specified, and evaluation happens only once per file at runtime. If you need to search for and match multiple different patterns, you will need to create multiple rules.

---

3. Now select the Evaluation Type tab, as shown in Figure 15.74.

FIGURE 15.74
Evaluation Type tab

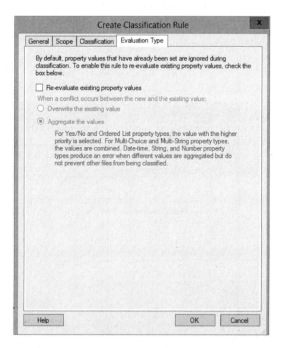

Here you have the ability to reevaluate the existing properties and when a conflict occurs either overwrite the previous value or merge values.

4. In our case we will reevaluate and overwrite the existing value.

5. Click OK when finished.

Your classification rule is complete. All you have to do now is either manually run it by selecting the rule, and in the Actions menu click Run Classification Rule or wait for the Task Scheduler to execute it.

When you manually run the classification you are prompted to choose to either run the task in the background or wait for it to complete, as shown in Figure 15.75.

FIGURE 15.75
Options for manually running the classification with all rules

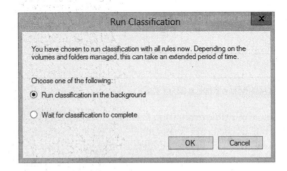

We'll choose the automatic option, which allows the Task Scheduler to execute the task on a scheduled basis. First, however, we need to configure the options for automatic file classification:

1. On the left side of the File Server Resource Manager MMC, navigate to the top of the tree to File Server Resource Manager (Local).

2. Right-click it and select Configure Options, as shown in Figure 15.76.

FIGURE 15.76
Configure Options for automatic file classification

3. When the Options window opens, select the Automatic Classification tab.

   As you will see, it is disabled by default.

4. Click Enable Fixed Schedule.

5. Set the "Run at" time to **01:00:00 AM.**

6. Choose Weekly and Sunday.

7. Check "Allow continuous classification for new files," and leave the rest of the options at their default. See Figure 15.77.

FIGURE 15.77
Options to configure for scheduling automatic file classification

8. Click OK when you have finished.

You can verify that the schedule has been set up in the Task Scheduler:

1. Open the Task Scheduler, and navigate to Task Scheduler Library ➤ Microsoft ➤ Windows ➤ File Server Resource Manager.

   Here you will see a new task named FciClassification with the options you configured.

2. Check what the task is running under Action—that's right, it's running PowerShell.

Since you want to run this right away and not wait until 1:00 a.m., you will want to run the manual classification and select Complete as a background task, but not yet.

1. First, you need to check the document for which you want to test if file classification is working correctly. Open the file that you want to use as a test.

In our lab environment we have under `C:\share\accounts` a single file called `Private Data.rtf`. The contents of the file are shown in Figure 15.78.

FIGURE 15.78
Contents of
Private
Data.rtf

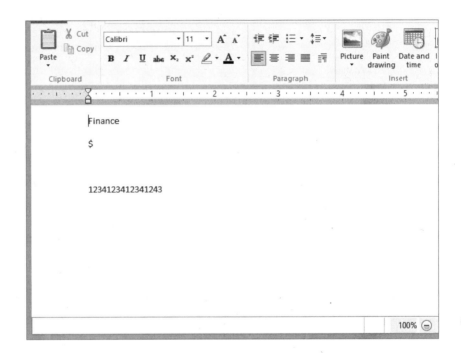

Remember that our classification rule is configured to classify on Content and on finding one instance of the expression Finance. This should classify the document as an Accounts document.

2. Next, check the existing classification of the document by right-clicking it and selecting Properties and then clicking the Classification tab.

As you can see in Figure 15.79, our file currently has no classification.

FIGURE 15.79
Private
Data.rtf
classification

3. Return to the File Server Resource Manager and run the file classification rule by select-ing the rule you want to execute and then in the right-hand side of the mmc under Actions select Run Classification With All Rules now. When prompted select Run Classification in the background.

4. Wait until it completes, and then recheck the file classification. As shown in Figure 15.80, the classification of department_contoso has been set to Accounts.

FIGURE 15.80
Private
Data.rtf
classification set

Before you start thinking that I am mad and that I also included the Engineering folder, let's check its contents and file classification. In our lab we included a file under `C:\share\engineering` called `Engineer Scope.rtf`, and as you can see in Figure 15.81, even after the File Classification Wizard has run, the classification of the file is not set. Why? Because we set no rules specifically for it.

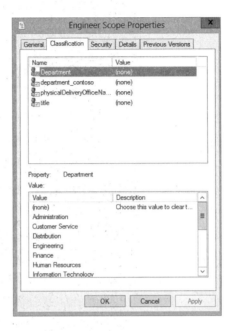

FIGURE 15.81
Engineer
Scope.rtf
classification

Try out different combinations and create new rules yourself now to really embed the principles of what we have covered so far.

Understanding Regular Expressions

I promised to give you a quick demonstration of regular expressions. This is something you should ask experienced programmers or telephony engineers about because they are wizards at this stuff and usually have a great ability to construct exceptionally complex but useful expressions.

Also, in your favorite search engine search for "Regular Expression Cheat Sheets." There are a few really cool links available that you can use as a reference.

As with most things, regular expressions won't make sense until you use them for something. So let's look at a basic example. Say you want to detect a credit card number. First, you should look at what characteristics a credit card number has, and to my thinking the simplest one to start with is that it always has 12 numbers. We'll start with that.

In order to detect a 12-digit number with regular expressions you would have a query like this:

"\d{12}"

If you break this down, very simply the \d means "detect a digit" and the {12} means "exactly 12 characters long."

Another way of writing this if the credit card number is stored like 1234-1234-1234-1234 is:

"\d{4}-\d{4}-\d{4}-\d{4}"

Simple, eh! Hopefully you won't have too many 12-digit numbers that are not credit cards in your environment that get classified unnecessarily with this basic rule. However, we can get a bit more focused. For example, let's say Visa cards start with the number 4 and then use a combination or 11 other digits. What would the regular expression for that look like?

"\d[4]{11}"

Here it is in standard credit card number format:

"{\d[4]{3}-\d{4}-\d{4}-{\d{4}"

Now let's look at a different example. Two things that come to mind that companies often do not want leaked to the public are intellectual property and payroll information. Hopefully you agree! To my mind these pieces of information need to be protected, and on that note let's build another regular expression. We will also reuse the following example later on when integrating this into our Dynamic Access Control configuration.

But first, what would a regular expression look for detecting the words *intellectual property*?
It can be as simple as this: "`intellectual.*property`"
Quick test: What do you think it might look like for *payroll*?
Think of a few more examples, like wages or pensions.
Here are a few useful links to regular expressions to get you going:

http://msdn.microsoft.com/en-us/library/ae5bf541(v=vs.80).aspx

http://www.solmetra.com/scripts/regex/index.php

http://www.regular-expressions.info/reference.html

http://www.cheatography.com/davechild/cheat-sheets/regular-expressions/

Been able to detect patterns like this and even more complex ones can give you great flexibility in the enterprise to classify data in the correct way so that you can secure it automatically with a range of other tools like Rights Management Server.

Securing Data Using DAC and File Classification

For the final piece of this chapter let's examine a real example you'll come across in the workplace. Most businesses now deal with credit card numbers at some point. And it is the company's responsibility to ensure that this data is secure. Hopefully these numbers are stored in encrypted databases in the real world, but in our example company, Contoso, they have been storing them in a Word document.

We need to safeguard not only the company but also the information so it isn't leaked. We don't want engineers logging on to the file share and being able to copy the credit card number file. That would be disastrous.

With all this in mind, here's what we are going to do:

◆ Create an RTF file with a credit card number in the content.

◆ Create an RTF file with the word *payroll* in the content.

◆ Create an RTF file with the words *Intellectual Property* in the content.

◆ Create a classification rule to detect these attributes using regular expressions and a string in the content.

◆ Create a Central Access Policy that will use the file classification to secure the resource.

Okay, let's go. First, create the three documents you need:

1. On your file server (using our example ContosoFS01) navigate to C:\share\accounts.

2. Right-click in the folder, and select New ➤ Rich Text Document; see Figure 15.82.

FIGURE 15.82
Creating a rich text document

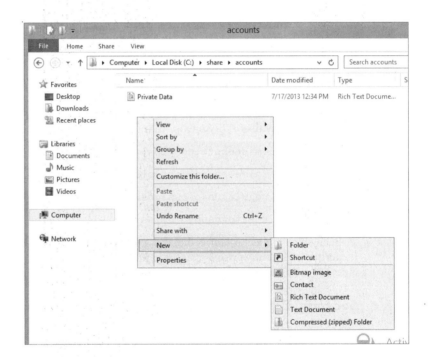

3. Type **File1** for its name.

We are using a generic name to ensure that it actually detects the content and classifies the document correctly.

4. Double-click File1 to open it and type a 12-digit number.

5. Save the document and close it.

6. Repeat this procedure using the names **File2** and **File3**.

7. In File2 put in random words and include the word *payroll*, and in File3 put in random words and then *Intellectual Property*.

8. Save all documents.

9. Quick test: Check the classification of each document and ensure that nothing is set.

Next, let's create the classification rules to automatically classify the documents:

1. On ContosoFS01 open the File Server Resource Manager.

   You will need to create three new rules, because you are looking for different patterns that won't necessarily be all in one file.

2. Click Classification Rules, and in the Action menu on the right, click Create Classification Rule.

3. Under the General tab, in the Rule Name section, type **Auto Classify For Credit Cards**.

4. Now click the Scope tab and click Accounts.

   Notice how the Accounts share gets autopopulated.

   Quick test: How did you get the folders included in the Accounts scope?

5. Now click the Classification tab.

6. For the classification method, select Content Classifier.

7. Under Property, choose a property to assign to the files.

8. Select department_contoso, and for "Specify a value" select Accounts.

9. Under Parameters, click Configure.

   Quick test: What does the regular expression look like for detecting a 12-digit number? Think of the pattern you are trying to match.

10. Click OK when you have finished.

11. Finally, click the Evaluation Type tab, check the "Re-evaluate existing property values" check box, and select "Overwrite the existing value."

12. Click OK when you have finished.

13. Create two more rules using the method previously described with the following information:

RULE NAME	TO SEARCH FOR	EXPRESSION TYPE	MIN OCCURRENCES
Auto Classify Payroll	Payroll	String	1
Auto Classify	Intellectual Property	Regular Expression	1

14. After you've created these, run the classification rules manually and wait for completion.

15. Finally, check that the rules have worked and that they have classified the documents correctly.

Your file-classification rules are in place and you have now verified that they work. It would make sense now to build a policy so that only Accounts or HR people can access these types of documents.

Prep time first! To ensure this is done correctly and you understand the flow, take some time to remove all Central Access Policies already applied to your folder:

1. Right-click the folder and choose Properties ➤ Security Advanced ➤ Central Policy ➤ Change ➤ No Central Policy Applied, and click OK.

2. Log on to the client machine with a non-Accounts user (in our examples it has been Ken), and ensure that the user can browse the Accounts folder and access the files.

3. If you can't access the files after removing the policy, check the permissions and assign the appropriate permissions, such as assigning the Domain Users group Full Control to the folder.

Now you'll need to re-secure your data with Central Access Policies:

1. From the Active Directory Administrative center, choose Dynamic Access Control ➤ Central Access Rules.

2. In the menu on the right, choose New ➤ Central Access Rules.

3. In the Name field of the new Central Access rule, type **Securing Auto Classified Accounts Data**.

4. Previously we told you to leave Target Resources alone, but now click Edit in that area.

Target resources will work with the classification of the file to protect it. The screen shown in Figure 15.83 is very similar to the other condition-based screens you have created in previous tasks.

FIGURE 15.83
Resource targeting

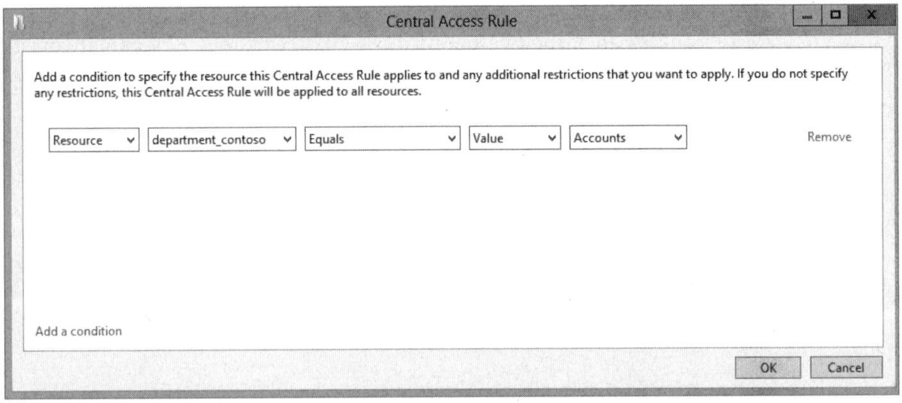

5. In this rule, mirror what is displayed in Figure 15.83, and click OK.

This will now target all files that have been classified for Accounts.

Now you need to set the permissions; you want only HR and Accounts staff to have Full Control over the documents:

1. In the Permissions section, click Edit and then click Add.

2. Select the principle Authenticated Users, and give them Full Control.

3. In the condition section, add the values shown in Figure 15.84.

4. Click OK twice to close all the screens.

5. Click OK to finish creating the Central Access rule.

Next, you need to create a Central Access Policy so you can then deploy this to your file servers:

FIGURE 15.84
Permissions and condition logic

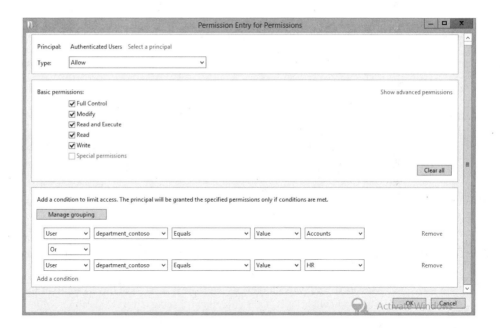

1. Click Dynamic Access Control in the menu on the left.

2. Right-click Central Access Policies, and choose New ➤ Central Access Policies.

3. Type **CAP-AutoClassify** for the name, and add the one that you created in the preceding set of steps.

4. Click OK to finish creating the policy.

5. Open the Group Policy Management console.

6. Locate the CAP-Contoso-Demo group policy you created earlier to deploy Central Access Policies to file servers.

7. Right-click it and select Edit.

8. Navigate to Computer Configuration Policies ➤ Windows Settings ➤ Security Settings ➤ File System ➤ Central Access Policy.

9. Right-click and select Manage Central Access Policies.

10. Add CAP-AutoClassify, and close the Group Policy Editor.

11. On your file server now run **gpupdate/force** from an elevated command prompt.

12. Apply the CAP-AutoClassify policy to the Accounts folder under C:\share.

13. Now on the client machine as a user who is not in HR or Accounts, try to access the information in Accounts.

    Can you see it?

14. If you can see it, try accessing it.

    If you can't see it, then you also have Access Based Enumeration turned on, and this hides files and folders for which it knows you don't have permissions.

15. Try logging on with a user in Accounts or HR, and experience the difference.

16. Finally, create a new RTF file called **file5** in the Accounts folder, and put any information inside that is not protected by your classification rules.

17. Now try to access it from the client with both an Accounts user and a non-Accounts user.

    How cool is that!

The Bottom Line

Secure your data using conditions.   Understand how you can secure your data without being a part of hundreds of groups. Using this knowledge, you will understand the building blocks of Dynamic Access Control.

    Master It   In your lab and using the examples we have shown at the start of this chapter, create a new share called **Projects**, and secure it so that only people in the Engineering and IT groups can access it. Make sure you test it. Do you remember how?

Create a new claim type and resource property.   As you move away from using groups and bloated Kerberos tokens, you need to understand how to ensure that only the right people can access your data. Using claim types and resource properties allows you to secure data with new elements.

    Master It   How can you ensure that only employees from Ireland can access the data located on your shares? What do you need to do in order to be able to use Country as an authorization token?

Secure hundreds of servers.   Dynamic Access Control is a powerful tool for securing data, but when you have a large server estate, you need to make this an easy technology to deliver to the organization to provide the maximum benefit.

> **Master It**   You need to secure all of your data across all of your files servers. How do you secure the data first so that only people in IT can have Full Control across all shares and Accounts and Engineering users have read-only access?

Classify and secure data without knowing what the data is.   Imagine a vast file server array with millions of files. As you know, it has not been common practice to properly classify documents as they are written. Knowing how to approach this and properly classify and secure this data is paramount to an organization.

> **Master It**   Across your file servers you have documents that contain sensitive information, including credit card numbers and payroll data. How can you automatically secure this data and ensure that only the Accounts and HR departments can access this information?

Chapter 16

Sharing Printers on Windows Server 2012 R2 Networks

If your company has unlimited funds, it can afford to purchase a print device for every user. Can you imagine that, a print device on every desk? Neither can we. Even in the best of times, profitable companies wouldn't be so wasteful.

Instead, a company will often identify a ratio of print devices to people such as one printer for every 5, 10, or 20 people. Not only do they save on the cost of the print devices, but they save on electricity and maintenance.

And, for better efficiency managing these printers, they are often hosted on print servers. A single print server can host hundreds of printers.

With Windows Server 2012 R2, you can add the Print and Document Services role, which comes with the Print Management console. Not only does this optimize the server to serve print jobs for end users, but the Print Management console allows you to manage multiple print servers from a central location.

In this chapter, you will learn to:

◆ Add the Print and Document Services role

◆ Manage printers using the Print Management console

◆ Manage print server properties

◆ Manage printer properties

Print Services Overview

Most of your users believe that a *printer* is the putty-colored box sitting within walking distance of their cubicles that they put paper into and create printed documents. But we all know that in the arcane world of systems administration, a printer is a logical software component that's an intermediary between user applications and the *print device*. All configuration settings apply to printers, not to print devices.

The ratio of printers to print devices is not necessarily one to one. You can have one printer and one print device, two printers for a single print device, or one printer and several print devices. We'll talk about *why* you might want to do any of these in the course of this chapter.

When you send documents to a printer, they become part of the printer's *queue*, the group of documents waiting to be printed. Documents wait in the queue until the print device is available to accept the print job.

Most people on your network won't have their own print device on their desk. Instead, users typically print to a network-accessible printer. This printer can be accessible directly on the network or available via a print server (the focus of this chapter).

Take a look at Figure 16.1 to see the different ways print devices can be configured on a network. Print device 1 is connected directly to a USB port on Sally's computer. This isn't considered a network printer unless Sally shares it. However, even if she shares it, the print device wouldn't be shared by the print server but instead by Sally's computer. In this context, Sally's computer is acting as a print server, even if she's just running Windows 7.

FIGURE 16.1

Print devices on a network

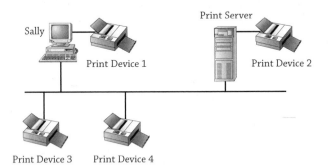

Print device 2 is directly connected to the print server and would be shared by the print server, so it is considered a network printer. Since print devices 3 and 4 are connected directly to the network, they are also considered network printers. Print devices 3 and 4 both must have NICs that can be assigned IP addresses to be accessible on the network.

What's not clear in Figure 16.1 is whether print devices 3 and 4 are being served by the print server. One could be, and the other could be a stand-alone network printer. Let's say that the print server is configured to serve print jobs for print device 3. All users would send their print jobs to the print server, and the print server would manage the queue for print device 3.

On the other hand, let's say that the print server is not configured to serve print jobs for print device 4. Users would instead need to configure the print device individually on each of their systems, and jobs would be sent directly to the print device instead of to the server. Print device 4 wouldn't have any of the benefits of the print server, such as, automatically downloading print jobs, controlling access to printers with permissions or schedules, or managing queues, unless this functionality is built into the device's software.

This chapter is focused on using a Windows Server 2012 R2 server as a print server. If the print devices are just connected to the network and not served by a printer, they are on their own.

The process of printing with Windows Server 2012 R2 is a bit more complex than it looks from the outside. The printing model uses several components to render application data for graphical output, get the data to a printer, and then help the printer manage multiple print jobs. Some of the following information on *how* printing works is background, but it's also helpful when it comes to troubleshooting.

The Print Spooler

Computers are much quicker than print devices. No surprise there. However, years ago, when print jobs were sent to print devices, the computer slowed to the speed of the print device until the entire print job was completed. During this time, the user wasn't able to do anything else with the computer.

WORKING WITHOUT A PRINT SERVER

We have spent a lot of time working in organizations that do not use print servers. Instead, print devices are placed directly on the network with an IP address, and each computer then needs to be configured to use the print device.

One of the significant drawbacks to this method is that users often have problems connecting to the print device and installing the correct driver. They'd have to learn the printer's IP address to connect, and even then, the wrong driver can be selected, resulting in useless printouts. The help desk is called, and unless the help-desk professional knows exactly what driver is needed, she often has to go on a driver hunt.

When a print server is used, users just need to use the universal naming convention (UNC) path of the printer (`\\serverName\shareName`) when adding it. The server will then automatically download the correct driver. As an example, a printer could be shared as Laser1 on a server named BF1, and users would only need to connect to `\\BF1\Laser1` to automatically download the correct driver for their operating system. Additionally, if the print device is moved to a different subnet, only the server needs to be reconfigured, not every client.

The trade-off is the cost of the print server and associated maintenance. However, since servers can easily share roles, file servers often act as print servers too.

You can bet this irritated many users, so the *print spooler* was developed. Now, when print jobs are sent by the user, the print spooler service accepts the print job and stores it in memory or on the hard drive until the print device can accept it. If you print a document, you can almost immediately begin working on something else, even if it takes 10 minutes for your document to print.

When users print documents to a printer served by a print server, two spoolers are actually involved. The spooler service on the user's computer spools the document (usually only to memory) and then sends the spooled job to the print server. When the print server receives the print job, it also spools it. Since the print server may be working on other jobs, it will usually spool print jobs to the hard drive.

The default folder for spooled documents is `C:\Windows\System322\Spool\Printers`. You'll see how you can change this later in this chapter.

The Printer Driver

Printer drivers are the software that enables the operating system to communicate with a printer and ultimately send the print job to the print device. Print drivers have been unified in recent years, making them a little easier to work with. You'll come across three primary print drivers:

Itanium	Type 3 – User Mode
x64	Type 3 – User Mode
x86	Type 3 – User Mode

Notice that each of these is referred to as a Type 3 – User Mode driver. Drivers before Windows 2000 were referred to as version 2 Kernel mode drivers. They would interact with the kernel of the operating system and had the potential of crashing the system if something went wrong.

Type 3 drivers work only in user mode and are isolated from the operating system. Itanium is a special 64-bit architecture used in high-end servers. x64 indicates a 64-bit architecture, and x86 indicates a 32-bit architecture. The good news about this is that you can install an x86 Type 3 – User Mode driver, and it will work with any 32-bit operating system—at least it should.

Thankfully, you can load all three print drivers onto a Windows Server 2012 R2 server, and when different systems connect, the correct driver will automatically be downloaded. However, you'll still need to ensure the correct drivers are loaded on the server. In other words, if you're supporting 32-bit Windows XP and 64-bit Windows 7 clients, you'll need to ensure you have both x86 and x64 drivers.

With the release of Windows Server 2012 R2 come the new v4 drivers. These drivers are not compatible with operating systems prior to Windows 8 and Windows Server 2012 R2, but—drum roll please—you can print to the v4 queue from the Windows Server 2012 R2 print server using the enhanced Point and Print Compatibility driver.

Since the v4 architecture supports the print-class driver framework, users can install printers without having to locate the driver for that printer. This addresses security and compatibility concerns found in v3 drivers.

PRINTER DRIVER HUNTS

Finding the correct print drivers (especially for new operating systems) is often very challenging. In a perfect world, as soon as a new operating system is released, every company would automatically have the correct driver so their hardware will work. However, a lot of things work against this scenario. Companies may create a print driver that works with the release candidate of an OS only to see that last-minute changes to the operating system result in their driver no longer working.

Of course, when a company realizes its driver no longer works, it tweaks and reengineers. And then it posts the new driver on its website as quickly as possible. However, the driver needs to be tested and validated before it's included with the operating system or available through Windows Update.

Meanwhile, users who have upgraded to a new OS realize that they can no longer print. They try Windows Update (which includes only those drivers that have gone through the lengthy submission and testing process) with no joy. Educated users (and administrators) know the best source in this situation is to go to the manufacturer's website.

They go to the manufacturer's website, which may or may not have the correct driver listed, and often a lengthy game of trial and error is started until the user (or administrator) either finds something that will work or gives up. This was very apparent when Windows Vista came out and resulted in a lot of complaints from users.

XML PAPER SPECIFICATION

XML Paper Specification (XPS) is based on Extensible Markup Language (XML), an industry standard that has been steadily creeping into many current technologies including databases, web services, and now printing. HTML (used for web pages) is based on XML. XML data is contained in a simple text document that can be read with simple applications such as Notepad, and it can be used to hold a significant amount of data and metadata.

XPS ON THE INTERNET

Microsoft has embraced XPS and has published a lot of material detailing how it is used in Microsoft products. The XPS home page is at www.microsoft.com/whdc/xps/default.mspx. Additionally, ECMA International is the driving force for standardizing XPS across multiple platforms. You can access details from meetings and available documents at www.ecma-international.org/memento/TC46-M.htm.

Metadata is used to describe the data. For example, metadata within a print document might be used to identify all the data on page 1, page 2, and so on. It could also be used to describe how the data should be displayed such as the font style or size.

Microsoft has embraced the XPS document format based on the Open XML Markup Compatibility specifications and Open Packaging Conventions (OPC). The vision is for much better efficiency, compatibility with more applications, and higher document quality when XPSDrv printer drivers are used.

XPS is similar in concept to the Portable Document Format (PDF) created by Adobe Systems for document exchange. We're betting that you've opened a few PDF documents during your travels since PDF documents are so widely used today. The cool thing about a PDF document is that the person who creates the document can control what it looks like when it prints. Compare this to a simple Word document that may print one way on one printer but another way on another printer.

You can create XPS documents from within Microsoft Office 2012, and these documents can be shared just as PDF files. Select Save As ➢ XPS Document to save your document in this format. Users who have an XPS view can view the documents, just as users can view PDF files if they have a matching version of Adobe Reader. In addition to saving files in the XPS format, documents can be translated to the XPS format so that they can be used by XPSDrv printer drivers.

XPSDRV: THE NEW PRINTER DRIVER MODEL

Print drivers created to take advantage of the new XPS format are referred to as XPSDrv printer drivers. These drivers provide greater flexibility than the older Graphics Device Interface (GDI) graphics processing functions that were used before XPSDrv printer drivers.

XPSDrv printer drivers use the XPS document format to provide a better what-you-see-is-what-you-get (WYSIWYG) output from printers. A greater range of colors can be used, and other graphic outputs such as transparent areas and gradients are possible.

Since the XPSDrv printer drivers use the XPS format and the XPS format produces smaller spooled files than the GDI format, the overall size of spooled printer files is reduced.

THE GRAPHICS DEVICE INTERFACE

GDI is the portion of the operating system that begins the process of producing visual output, whether that output is to the screen or to the printer. GDI has historically been used to produce WYSIWYG output to both the screen and the printed page. To produce screen output, the GDI calls the video driver; to produce printed output, the GDI calls the printer driver providing information about the print device needed and the type of data used.

Although GDI-based printer drivers are being replaced with XPSDrv-based printer drivers, you may still come across the older GDI-based printer drivers for a while.

Now that you have a little bit of an overview on print services, let's jump into the Print and Document Services role.

Installing the Print and Document Services Role

The Print and Document Services role is added to your server when you want it to become a print server. When you add this role, you'll have the option of adding several different services depending on what you want the print server to do:

Print Server The Print Server service includes the Print Management console that you'll use for the majority of management tasks on the print server. You can manage multiple printers and even multiple print servers through this snap-in. This is the primary service of a print server and is the focus of this chapter.

LPD Service If your organization includes Unix-based computers that will need to print to print devices served by your print server, you can add the Line Printer Daemon (LPD) service. The LPD service will allow any clients using the Line Printer Remote (LPR) service to print to printers shared on the print server.

Internet Printing The Internet Printing Protocol (IPP) can be used to allow clients that have the Internet Printing client installed to use a web browser to connect and print to printers shared on your server. Adding this service will also create a website where users can manage print jobs on the server instead of using the print console.

Distributed Scan Server This service allows the server to receive scanned documents from scanners on the network and route them to the correct destinations. When you add this service, it will also include the Scan Management snap-in.

Adding the Print and Document Services Role

The Print and Document Services role is fairly simple to install using Server Manager. The only choice you need to make is what services to add, and this will be decided based on what the clients are doing. You can use the following steps to add the Print and Document Services role to a Windows Server 2012 R2 server:

1. Launch Server Manager by selecting Server Manager from the taskbar.

2. Click Add Roles and Features.

3. Review the information on the Before You Begin page, and click Next.

4. Select Role Based Installation and click Next.

5. Select the server from the server pool and click Next.

6. On the Select Server Roles page, select Print and Document Services; then Click Next.

7. A popup will open asking you to add Role Administration Tools; click Add Features to continue.

8. You can skip past the features by clicking Next.

   You should be on the Print and Document Services summary, as shown in Figure 16.2. Click Next to continue.

FIGURE 16.2

Print and Document Services role summary

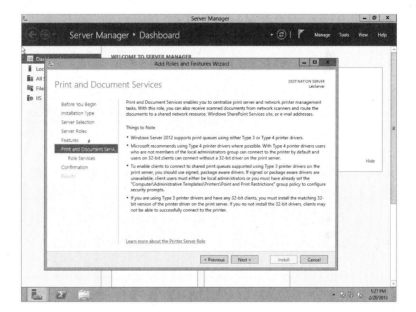

9. On the Role Services page Print Services will be selected by default; click Next to continue.

10. Click Install on the Confirmation page.

11. If everything was done correctly, you should see the installation progress, as shown in Figure 16.3.

FIGURE 16.3
Adding the Print
Server service

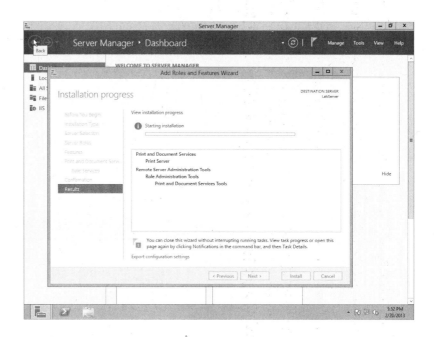

12. When the installation has completed, click Close.

Once you've added the Print and Document Services role, you can access the Print Services role in Server Manager. Print Services is your central source to manage all printing tasks.

Working in the Print Management Console

The Print Management console (PMC) is a great addition to the operating system interface, finally allowing you to do *everything* printer-related from a single console. It allows you to do just about anything with printers and other print servers, including the following:

- Add new drivers
- View printers using custom filters
- Manage printer settings and drivers
- Monitor printer status and configure alerts
- Connect to remote print servers so you can do all this for your entire enterprise

With the Print and Document Services role added to your server, you can launch the PMC by hitting the Windows key and clicking the Print Management Metro-style button. The PMC will look similar to Figure 16.4. It's also possible to view the PMC via Server Manager by clicking Tools ➢ Print Management.

FIGURE 16.4

Viewing the Print
Management
console

The PMC is divided into three main sections:

Custom Filters   The filters allow you to look at all the printers managed from this console, regardless of which print server they're connected to. If a print server hosts just five print devices, this is no big deal. However, if you have hundreds of print devices connected, the ability to search using the custom filters will make your job a lot easier. As you'll see later in this chapter, the tool comes with some default filters, but you can also create your own.

Print Servers   In Figure 16.4, one print server (LabServer) is added. However, if your organization has several print servers, you can manage them all through a single PMC. Each server would have its own drivers, forms, ports, and printers.

Deployed Printers   Printers that have been deployed using Group Policy are listed here. You'll see how to deploy printers with Group Policy later in this chapter.

Additionally, within each print server, you have four primary nodes. These nodes are used to manage the different print devices and printers served by the print server:

Drivers   You can add drivers that are needed for your printers here. Drivers have been simplified into three types: Itanium for high-end servers, x64 for 64-bit operating systems, and x86 for 32-bit operating systems.

Forms   The forms on a server show the various print layouts the installed printers can support. They define the paper size and the printer area margins. The majority of time most people use letter-size paper (8.5"×11"), and the letter form defines letter-size paper. However, there are many other forms that can be selected, and you can make your own. The forms are shown on a per-server basis, not a per-printer basis.

Ports   Ports are used to connect to print devices. The legacy ports are the serial ports (COM1 through COM4), parallel ports (LPT1 through LPT3), and FILE. If you plug in a USB printer, a

USB port will be automatically added. A new port is XPSPort and is used to create Microsoft XPS documents. You can also create standard TCP/IP ports to connect to any network printer using an IP address.

Printers When you add a printer, it will be listed here. Remember, the printer is the software interface that you can manipulate on the print server, and it will send print jobs to the print device. You can have multiple printers for any print device, depending on your needs.

ADDING NEW PRINTERS

You use the PMC to add new printers, and one piece of good news is that you can use it to automatically detect printers on the same subnet as the print server. If you right-click Printers and select Add Printer, your display will look similar to Figure 16.5. Notice that you have four choices:

FIGURE 16.5
Adding a new printer using the Network Printer Installation Wizard

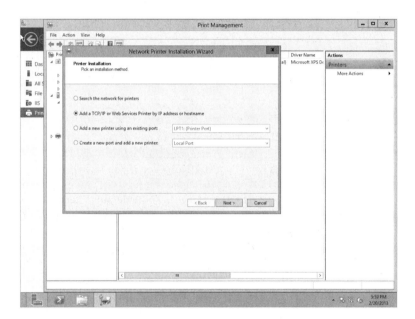

Search the Network for Printers This method allows PMC to automatically detect printers. It will work only with network printers on the local subnet, but if your printers are on the same subnet, it can save you a step.

Add a TCP/IP or Web Services Printer by IP Address or Hostname If the printer is on a separate subnet or configured as a web services printer (available from a web server), use this choice to manually add the IP address or hostname of the printer. If you use the hostname, you need to ensure that the name can be resolved by DNS or another name resolution method.

Add a New Printer Using an Existing Port   If a port already exists, you can use this method to add a printer to an existing port. A single printer would have one port configured for each print device. When printer pooling is enabled (you'll see how to enable printer pooling later), you can have multiple ports configured for a single printer; each port will be connected to a print device. You may also choose to add more printers for a single print device so that you can manipulate different properties such as printer permissions or schedules, as you'll see later in the chapter.

Create a New Port and Add a New Printer   This method allows you to create new ports and add printers to them. The wizard doesn't give as many choices, and you can achieve what you want using other methods, so you may never use this method.

Printers connected to the USB port of the server don't need any additional steps. Simply plug the printer into the USB port; it will be automatically sensed, and the driver will be added. It won't be shared by default, but you can access the printer properties sheet (covered later in the chapter) and share it from the Sharing tab.

DELETING A PRINTER

Sometimes you'll need to delete a printer from a print server. Most of the time this process is extremely simple: you open the Printers node of the Print Management console, right-click the printer about to be sent to that big network in the sky, and choose Delete from the context menu. The printer should disappear immediately.

If the printer you deleted *doesn't* disappear immediately, you may receive an error. Make sure that it's not in the middle of trying to print a document. Even if a printer never worked—for example, you were trying to set up a printer and specified the wrong port name—it can still have waiting print jobs. (Actually, this is *especially* likely if the printer never worked but you insisted on setting it up, damn the errors and full speed ahead.)

Check the print queue of the printer you're trying to delete. If it has waiting print jobs, select Printer ➢ Cancel All Documents, and then try to delete the printer. Rebooting the print server will not clear the list of spooled print jobs—you must explicitly cancel them.

AUTOMATICALLY DETECTING NETWORK PRINTERS

The "Search the network for printers" method of finding a printer is pretty cool but a little misleading. It will search the local subnet where the print server is located, but if your network includes multiple subnets, it won't search the entire LAN. In other words, it can't search for any printers that are accessible only through a router.

If you have a network printer on your local subnet, you can use the following steps to install it:

1. Launch the Print Management console, and select your print server.

2. Right-click the Printers node, and select Add Printers.

NETWORK MUST BE CONFIGURED AS PRIVATE

If your network is configured as a Public network in the Network and Sharing Center, you won't be able to automatically detect network printers. You'll need to change the configuration to Private, indicating this is a home or work network.

3. Select "Search the network for printers" and click Next.

   This will begin a broadcast search on the subnet. If you have any printers on the subnet, you'll see them appear, as shown in Figure 16.6.

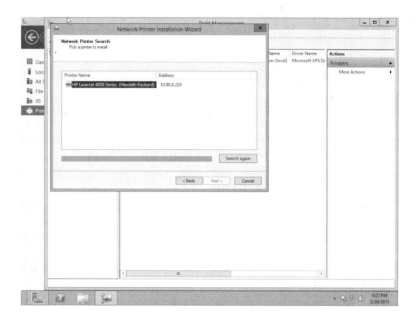

4. Once your printer has been located, select it, and click Next.

   Although it's not apparent here, this automatically creates a standard TCP/IP port with the IP address of your printer. You don't have to create the port as a separate step.

5. Windows will attempt to locate a driver for the printer. If it's successful, the printer driver will be selected on the Printer Driver page. If it can't find a driver, you'll need to install a new driver by selecting "Install a new driver" and clicking Next.

6. If the driver isn't found automatically, there are three choices for finding the driver at this point. All three are available from the screen shown in Figure 16.7.

   a. Select the manufacturer and printer model from the screen. However, since Windows didn't find the driver, it's unlikely this will be successful.

   b. If the server has access to the Internet, you can click Windows Update and search for a driver there.

   c. You can click Have Disk. Since 64-bit drivers aren't that common yet, you may need to go to the manufacturer's website, download the 64-bit version, and unzip it onto your system. After clicking Have Disk, you can browse to where you've unzipped the files, select the driver, and click OK.

   d. Once you've selected the driver, click Next.

FIGURE 16.7
Adding the printer
driver manually

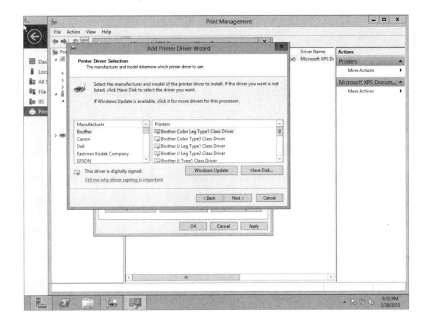

7. After you've loaded the driver, name and share it.

   The printer must be shared in order for users to be able to connect and send their print
   jobs to it. Figure 16.8 shows the Printer Name and Sharing Settings page. Feel free to give
   it a name that is more likely to be recognized by people using the printer.

FIGURE 16.8
Naming and sharing
the printer

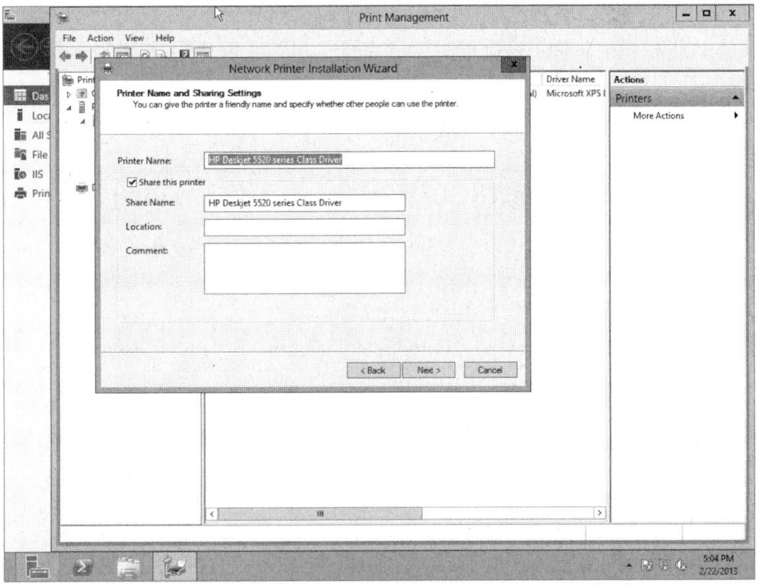

8. The Printer Found page will show the details you've selected. Click Next.

On the wizard completion page, the system will attempt to install the driver and then install the printer. If an incompatibility between the driver and the printer is discovered, it will show an error. Otherwise, you'll see the printer successfully added, as shown in Figure 16.9.

FIGURE 16.9
Printer successfully added

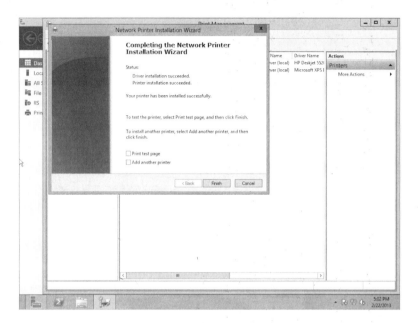

9. Select the "Print test page" box, and click Finish.

This provides a final check to ensure things are working properly.

USING (OR NOT USING) PRINTER LOCATIONS

Although you can enter "printer locations" in the add printer wizard, to allow users to search directly on this term, Printer Locations is also an advanced feature. However, it is usually not used because of its complexity.

When fully implemented, Printer Locations allows users to search for printers and returns a printer that is located close to them. For example, if a user searches for a printer that prints double-sided and there are 25 printers in the organization, only those printers that are close to them are used.

"Close to them," in this context means it's on the same subnet.

This requires subnets to be organized and implemented physically close together. For example, if an organization has multiple buildings, the buildings have multiple floors, and the floors have multiple wings, each wing of each floor of each building would need a separate subnet. If a single subnet spanned all floors of the east wing of a building, it wouldn't work because a user on the first floor could be referred to a printer on the third floor, which many users would not consider "close."

The Location property then needs to be accurately entered. First, it needs to be entered using Active Directory Sites and Services to add the location for each subnet. Second, it needs to be entered as the property for each printer. Spelling counts here. If the location for the subnet was entered as, "Bldg 1, Floor 3, West wing" but the location for the printer was entered as, "Bldg1, Floor 3, West wing" with no spaces between "Bldg" and "1," the location wouldn't match, and the printer wouldn't be found.

Although the idea of Printer Locations sounds good, we just don't see it being used. However, it still is possible to enter the location, and if users know what location to search, they can find it.

MANUALLY INSTALLING NEW PRINTERS

If you need to install a printer that isn't on your subnet, you can use the following procedure:

1. Right-click the Printers node within the PMC, and select Add Printers.

2. Select "Add a TCP/IP or Web Service Printer by IP address or hostname" and click Next.

3. Select TCP/IP Device as the type of device.

4. Type the IP address of the printer, or if DNS has been configured to resolve the printer's name, you can enter the printer's name.

5. Ensure that "Auto detect the printer driver to use" is selected. Your display will look similar to Figure 16.10. Click Next.

FIGURE 16.10
Adding the printer's
IP address

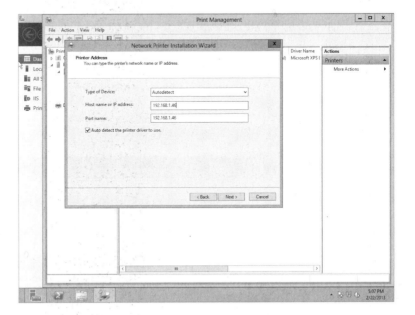

At this point, the wizard will complete just as it did in the automatic detection process. It will first try to detect the TCP/IP port. It will then try to find a driver. If it can't find a driver, do the following:

a. Select "Install a new driver."

b. Click Next, and browse to the correct driver.

c. Click Next.

6. After you've installed the driver, give the printer a name, share it, and give it a share name.

7. Click Next to review the details of your selections, and click Next again to install the driver and printer.

Notice that the only real difference here is that you're manually entering the IP address instead of allowing it to be found through a network search. As a reminder, you'll have to add it manually if the printer is on a different subnet.

CONFIGURING AND VIEWING SETTINGS AND RESOURCES

Installing a printer is the first step, but just installing the printer does not guarantee that it'll have the right drivers or the right forms available to users. In this section, we'll show you how the PMC organizes these settings to help you review and configure print server settings for drivers, ports, and available forms.

Managing Printer Drivers

If you want to add a printer to Windows Server 2012 R2 that users can print to, you'll need 64-bit drivers for it that are compatible with the print server. For end users to use the shared printers, the system needs drivers for their computers.

For example, if you are supporting clients running 32-bit operating systems, you'll need to add drivers to the print server for them. You can view a listing of all the drivers that are currently installed on your server by selecting the Drivers node in the PMC, as shown in Figure 16.11.

FIGURE 16.11
Viewing installed drivers

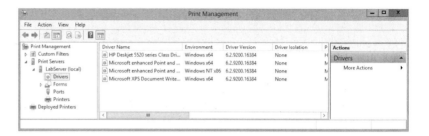

Notice in the figure that the printer drivers are x64 based. They won't be useful to any x86 (or 32-bit) clients.

Changing Printer Driver Views

The printer driver view shows a lot of information on drivers, but you may be interested in more information. You can change the view to show additional information or remove information as desired. As an example, you can add the URL for the manufacturer to identify the source for an update.

Figure 16.12 shows the Add/Remove Columns selection for the driver view. With the Drivers node selected, select View ➤ Add/Remove Columns to access this page.

FIGURE 16.12
Modifying the view for installed drivers

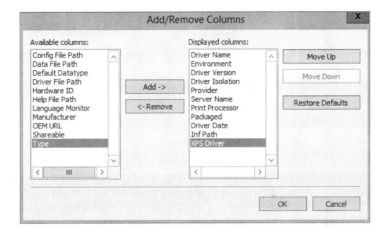

You can add any item in the "Available columns" list to the "Displayed columns" list by selecting it and clicking Add. Similarly, you can remove columns by selecting them from the "Displayed columns" list and clicking Remove. In the figure, we've added the URL for the driver to the view.

Installing New Printer Drivers

You can install additional printer drivers by using the Drivers node or by adding the driver to a specific printer. Use the following steps to add the driver to a printer:

1. Launch the Print Management console, and select your print server.

2. Browse to the Printers container. Right-click any printer, and select Properties.

3. Select the Sharing tab, and click the Additional Drivers button. Your display will look similar to Figure 16.13.

FIGURE 16.13
Viewing additional
drivers installed for
a printer

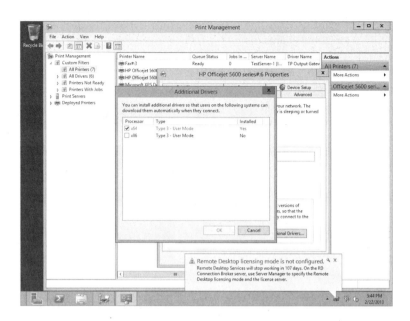

4. Select the x86 Type 3 – User Mode check box, and click OK.

   The server will search its internal driver store for a compatible driver. If it has a compatible driver, it will add it. If not, you'll be prompted to browse to the location of the driver. If the driver is not in the store, the best bet is to access the manufacturer's website to locate the driver and download and unzip it to a location you can browse to.

5. Browse the location, and click OK.

THE DRIVER STORE

All device drivers (including printer drivers in Windows Server 2012 R2) are installed in a secure folder referred to as the *driver store*. You can think of this as a regular store or mart where items can be purchased (except, of course, that the operating system doesn't charge you). When a driver is needed, the store is searched. If the driver is in the store, it's automatically installed. If the driver is not in the store, Windows can search additional locations (such as Windows Update) and may prompt the user for a path to the driver. Only signed drivers are stored in the driver store, making them a more secure option.

---

6. Click the Additional Drivers button to verify that the driver has been added.

   Instead of saying No for Installed, it will have changed to Yes.

Viewing and Editing Port Settings

Each printer server's ports are listed in its Ports folder. You can use this screen to identify which printers are connected to which port or which ports have printers attached.

Additionally, you can view or modify the properties of any port simply by right-clicking it and selecting Configure Port. Figure 16.14 shows the port configuration page.

FIGURE 16.14
Viewing available ports on a server

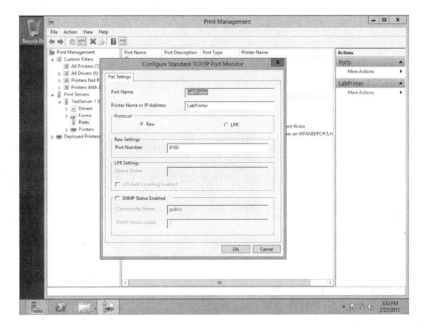

If necessary, you can change the IP address of the port number that the printer is using. Changing the IP address would be necessary if the printer was moved to a different subnet or assigned a different IP address for some other reason.

The Simple Network Management Protocol (SNMP) is often used for managing network devices, and although the default community name is Public, this will be changed in a production environment. If you want your ports to be able to communicate with an SNMP management system, you'll need to change the community name to match your environment.

Viewing Forms

The forms on a server show the various print layouts that the installed printers can support. The forms are shown on a per-server basis. In other words, all the forms on the server are available to all the printers.

If you right-click the Forms folder and choose Manage Forms, you'll open the printer server properties to the Forms tab. You can also access this tab via the server properties sheet. If there is a special need for a custom form with specific margins or sizes, you can create a custom form from this page.

Adding the Print Services Role to Server Core

Windows Server 2012 R2 supports the Print and Document Services role on Server Core. Server Core does not have a GUI but instead requires you to manage it from the command line—at least the initial management must be done from the command line.

If you're running Server Core on a server and want to make this a print server including the Print and Document Services role, you need to activate PowerShell. On the Server Core command line, type **PowerShell**. Notice that the command line now starts with PS to let you know you are in fact in the PowerShell application.

Then enter the following two commands on the PowerShell command line:

```
PS C:\Users\Administrator>ipmo ServerManager
PS C:\Users\Administrator>add-WindowsFeature Print-Server
```

After a moment, you will see the results of the installation, as shown in Figure 16.15.

FIGURE 16.15
Installing Print
Server on Server
Core using
PowerShell

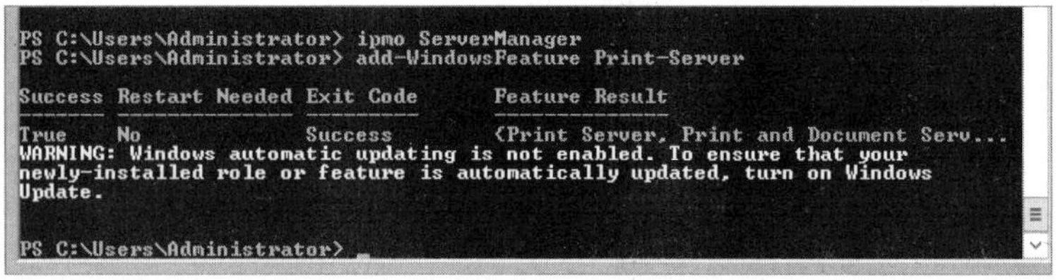

USE GET-WINDOWSFEATURE TO VIEW INSTALLED ROLES

You can use the Get-WindowsFeature cmdlet to provide configuration information on your Server Core installation. This also gives you the correct spelling and syntax of all the roles you want to add. For example, the printer role is identified as Print-Services.

At this point, you'll have a decision to make. Do you want to manage the Print-Services role from the command line or from a GUI? If you want to manage it from a GUI (which is much more intuitive), you can configure the Server Core server to be remotely administered. Chapter 17, "Remote Server Administration," covers how to do this.

Network Discovery needs to be enabled on the Server Core server for print server management. You can enable this with the following PowerShell command:

```
PS C:\Users\Administrator> netsh firewall set service fileandprint enable
```

You'll also need to enable the server to be managed by an MMC on a remote server with the following command. Even though it appears on two lines in the book, enter it as a single PowerShell command.

```
PS C:\Users\Administrator> netsh advfirewall firewall set rule group = "Remote
Administration"   new enable = yes
```

Once the Server Core server is configured for remote administration, you can then remotely administer it from a server that has the full operating system installed. For example, you may have 10 file and print servers all running Server Core but one central server with the full operating system installed that you'll use to remotely administer all the servers.

To add a print server to the PMC, right-click Print Servers, and select Add/Remove Servers. On the Add/Remove Servers page, enter the name of the remote server. You can also click

Browse. If Network Discovery is turned off, you'll be prompted to turn it on so that other computers can be located. Select your server, and click the Select Server button.

If you need to do any tasks from the Server Core command line, several tools can help.

PowerShell Cmdlets Reference

If you plan to use PowerShell on Windows Server 2012 R2, it will benefit you to have a quick reference of cmdlets to administer your Print Management tasks. Using these cmdlets will also relieve you of having to use scripts to manage printers and drivers.

Add-Printer   Adds a printer to the specified computer.

Add-PrinterDriver   Installs a printer driver on the specified computer.

Add-PrinterPort   Installs a printer port on the specified computer.

Get-PrintConfiguration   Gets the configuration information of a printer.

Get-Printer   Retrieves a list of printers installed on a computer.

Get-PrinterDriver   Retrieves the list of printer drivers installed on the specified computer.

Get-PrinterPort   Retrieves a list of printer ports installed on the specified computer.

Get-PrinterProperty   Retrieves printer properties for the specified printer.

Get-PrintJob   Retrieves a list of print jobs in the specified printer.

Remove-Printer   Removes a printer from the specified computer.

Remove-PrinterDriver   Deletes a printer driver from the specified computer.

Remove-PrinterPort   Removes the specified printer port from the specified computer.

Remove-PrintJob   Removes a print job on the specified printer.

Rename-Printer   Renames the specified printer.

Restart-PrintJob   Restarts a print job on the specified printer.

Resume-PrintJob   Resumes a suspended print job.

Set-PrintConfiguration   Sets the configuration information for the specified printer.

Set-Printer   Updates the configuration of an existing printer.

Set-PrinterProperty   Modifies the printer properties for the specified printer.

Suspend-PrintJob   Suspends a print job on the specified printer.

Deploying Printers to the Masses

Once you've added printers to the server, you'll want them to be available for the clients. You can accomplish this in three ways:

- Manually
- Through the Active Directory Search tool
- Through Group Policy

If your computers are in an Active Directory domain, you'll probably use the second or third choice to provide some automation. In the following sections, you'll learn how to deploy printers using each of the three methods.

Adding a Printer to a Client Manually

When you've added printers to a print server, it's relatively easy to add printers to the client (and have the proper drivers automatically installed). The following steps show how you can add a printer to a Windows 7 client:

1. With Windows 7 started, select Start ➢ Printers.

2. Click "Add a printer."

3. Select "Add a network, wireless, or Bluetooth printer."

    The system will search for available printers on the network.

4. Select "The printer that I want isn't listed."

5. Click "Select a shared printer by name," and enter **ServerName**\ to view a list of shared printers (but enter the actual server name).

    Figure 16.16 shows how we're connecting to a server named BF1.

FIGURE 16.16
Connecting to a shared printer from Windows 7

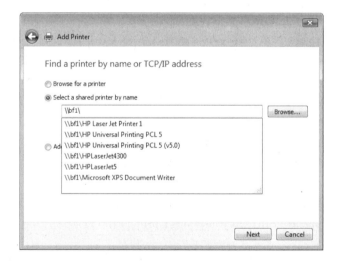

6. Select the desired shared printer, and click Next.

    The driver that was installed on the server is automatically downloaded and installed on the client. The name of the printer will be the same as that given on the client.

7. Click Next, and click Finish. That's it.

Of course, you may not want to do this for 500 clients in your organization. If not, you can configure the printer to be deployed automatically using Group Policy, as shown in the "Deploying Printers via GPO" section, later in this chapter.

Adding a Printer Using Active Directory Search

Active Directory is a huge database of objects that can be searched by both end users and administrators. Many objects are automatically published in Active Directory (such as users, computers, groups, and shares), allowing users to easily search for what they want. However, printers are not published in Active Directory by default. It's not hard to do so, and once they are listed in Active Directory, users can easily find them with a quick search.

Any printer that has been shared can also be listed in Active Directory as long as it is hosted on a server that is a member of the domain. In other words, network printers that aren't managed by a print server cannot be listed.

Open the Print Management console, browse to the Printers container, right-click the printer, and select List in Directory, as shown in Figure 16.17. That's it. The system will do the rest.

FIGURE 16.17

Listing a printer in Active Directory

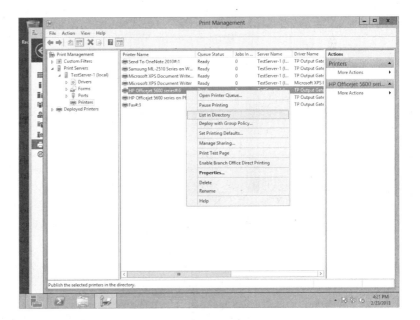

If List in Directory doesn't appear, double-check to ensure the printer is being shared by accessing the properties sheet of the printer and selecting the Sharing tab. You can also use this properties sheet to select the "List in the directory" check box.

Users in the domain will now be able to search Active Directory for the printer they want. For example, another Windows Server 2012 R2 server in the domain could locate this printer using the following steps:

1. Select Explorer ➤ Network.

2. Select Search Active Directory.

   The Search Active Directory choice is present only when the computer (including Windows 7 or 8 computers) is a member of a domain. Interestingly, it doesn't appear on

Network page for a domain controller, but it can be accessed through Active Directory Users and Computers on domain controllers.

3. In the Active Directory search box, select Printers in the Find box. Type **HP** in the Name text box, and click Find Now. Figure 16.18 shows the result.

FIGURE 16.18
Searching for a printer listed in Active Directory

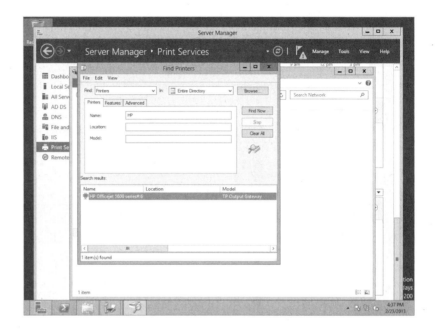

STRING SEARCHES

Notice that the full name of the model doesn't need to be entered. This is valuable since printer model names often have a length reminiscent of the names of minor royalty. Instead, the Active Directory Search tool looks for string matches, so any model starting with *HP* will be found. Although this example search worked, if all your models were HP, it wouldn't be as valuable.

Once the printer is located, a user could just double-click the printer to install it as an additional printer on their system. As long as the correct driver has been added to the print server, it will automatically be downloaded to the client, and the client doesn't need to take any additional steps to use the printer.

You can search for a printer based on just about any characteristic—or combination of characteristics—that you like. Searching for a printer by name doesn't seem very likely, since if you knew that much you'd probably know its domain and its server as well. However, you might know the printer's location. If the printer's location is entered when the printer is added, it can be used as a search term.

Since people may be using a printer's location to search Active Directory for that printer, keep printer locations short and consistent (such as Lab or Reception). As mentioned earlier, if you're using the full implementation of Printer Locations, you need to ensure that the printer location is entered exactly how it's entered in the Sites and Services subnet object.

Table 16.1 shows many of the common search criteria that can be used for finding printers in Active Directory.

TABLE 16.1:   Common Search Criteria for Finding Printers in Active Directory

PRINTER CHARACTERISTIC	LOCATION
Name	Printers tab
Location	Printers tab
Model	Printers tab
Double-sided printing	Features tab
Color printing	Features tab
Can staple	Features tab
Search on specific property	Advanced tab

FEATURE SEARCHES

Users often know enough about the printer to know they're looking for a color printer, one that can staple, or one that has some other features. Figure 16.19 shows the Features search tab. If a user is looking for a specific feature, they can select the desired feature and click Find Now.

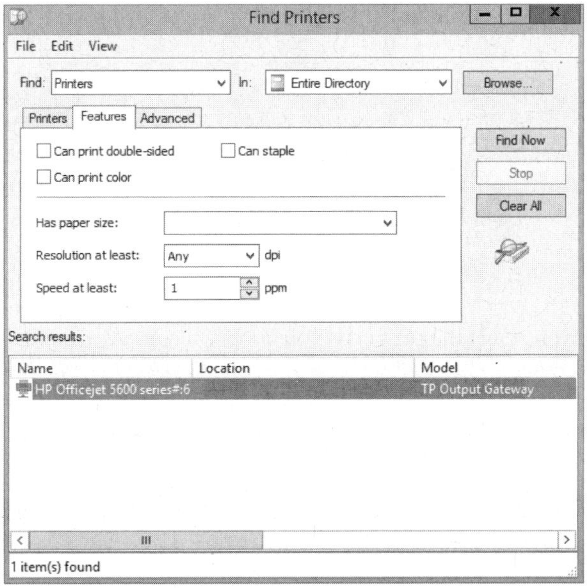

FIGURE 16.19
Searching for printers based on supported features

ADVANCED SEARCHES

The contents of the Advanced tab will be most suited to people who *really* know their printers, since the search criteria there are more granular than most people will need. Whereas the first two tabs allow you to describe a printer in terms of where it is, what it's called, and what you want it to be able to do, the Advanced tab allows you to describe the printer exactly.

Figure 16.20 shows the Field drop-down menu with the Paper Available property highlighted. Notice there are many different properties you can search on. If a printer property exists, you can select it.

FIGURE 16.20

Searching for printers using the Advanced tab

Once you select the property, you choose a condition such as "Starts with" and "Ends with" and then enter text in the Value field to match the property and condition. As an example, you could choose Server Name, select "Starts with," and enter **BF** in the Value field. After clicking Find Now, all printers hosted by any server that starts with *BF* will be shown.

Deploying Printers via GPO

You can also deploy printers using a Group Policy object. If you need to support Windows 8 clients and Windows Server 2012 R2 servers, there are a couple of warnings:

◆ Active Directory must be using a Windows Server 2012 R2 schema version. If you installed the first domain controller (DC) with Windows Server 2012 R2, you have the updated schema. If not, you'll need to run adprep to update the schema. You can find details on adprep at http://technet.microsoft.com/library/cc731728.aspx.

◆ Clients that are *not* running Windows 8 or Windows Server 2012 R2 must use the PushPrinterConnections.exe tool in a startup script or a logon script.

If your domain is completely Windows Server 2012 R2 or the schema has been updated with adprep, you can then follow these steps to deploy printers via GPOs:

1. Launch PMC and browse to the Printers node for the server.

2. Right-click the printer, and select Deploy with Group Policy.

   This selection is right under List in Directory, discussed in the previous section.

3. On the Deploy with Group Policy page, click Browse.

4. Click the Create a New Group Policy Object icon, and name it **Deploy Printers**. (If you hover over the icons, a tooltip will appear; you want the middle icon.)

   Your display will look similar to Figure 16.21.

FIGURE 16.21
Creating a Group
Policy object

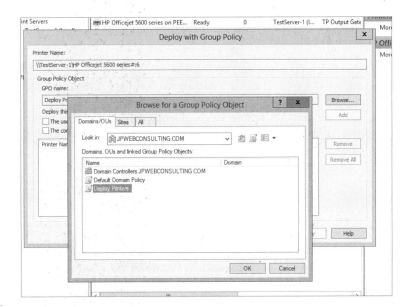

5. Select your Deploy Printers GPO, and click OK.

6. Select the "The computers that this GPO applies to (per machine)" check box.

   You could also select the "The users that this GPO applies to (per user)" check box if you wanted the GPO to apply to users without regard to who logged onto the computer or to the user no matter where they logged on.

7. Click Add. The settings you selected will be designated for the GPO.

8. Click OK to apply the settings.

   After a moment, a dialog box will indicate the printer deployment GPO has been successfully added, as shown in Figure 16.22.

FIGURE 16.22
Adding the settings to the GPO

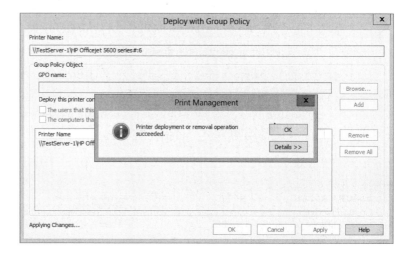

9. Click OK to dismiss the dialog box, and click OK again to dismiss the Deploy GPO screen.

   The previous step added the printer as a deployed printer in the Computer Configuration\Policies\Windows Settings\Deployed Printers node of the Deploy Printers GPO you created.

You can now go to any Windows 8 or Windows 2012 computer in the domain, type **gpupdate /force** at the command line to refresh Group Policy, and the printer will automatically appear with other devices and printers, with the correct driver.

If all your clients are running Windows 8 or Windows 2012, you'll be finished. However, if you have other clients such as Windows Vista and Windows XP, you'll need to configure the PushPrinterConnection.exe utility to run on each of them to have the printer deployed.

This utility is not on the default installation of Windows Server 2012 R2 or Windows 8 since they don't need it, but it is in the Windows\System32 folder of Windows Server 2008 and Windows Vista.

You can configure this utility to run on clients that need it with the following steps:

1. Launch the Group Policy Management console (GPMC) by pressing the Windows key and choosing Group Policy Management.

2. Browse to the Deploy Printers GPO in the domain, right-click, and select Edit, as shown in Figure 16.23.

FIGURE 16.23
Selecting a GPO
to edit

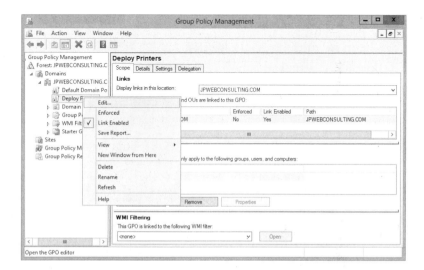

DEPLOYING VIA GPO DIRECTLY

You can also deploy printers from the Group Policy snap-in. Go to the Policies\Windows Settings\ Deployed Printers section, and right-click its folder. From the context menu, choose Deploy Printer, and browse to the desired printer.

---

3. Browse to the Computer Configuration\Policies\Windows Settings\Scripts (Startup/ Shutdown) node.

4. Double-click Startup, and click Show Files.

Notice that this is empty now. You need to copy the PushPrinterConnection.exe utility to this folder. Once the file is added, close Windows Explorer.

5. Click Add. Click Browse, and select PushPrinterConnections. Click Open.

Your display will look similar to Figure 16.24.

FIGURE 16.24
Adding
PushPrinterConnections
to the startup script

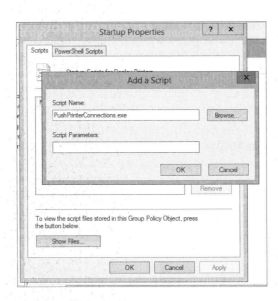

If desired, you can add `-log` to the Script Parameters text box to enable logging on computers where it runs. The log is located in the `%Windir%\temp\ppcMachine.log` file for computers or in the `%temp%\ppcUser.log` file for user connections.

6. Click OK to close the Add a Script dialog box, and click OK to close the Startup Properties dialog box.

That's it. A cool feature of the PushPrinterConnections utility is that if it attempts to start on a Windows 8 or Windows 2012 computer, it automatically detects the environment and exits. You don't have to worry about deploying this in a mixed environment.

BEING SELECTIVE WITH GPOS

Although these steps will deploy the GPO to all users in the domain, you could be more selective. For example, if you wanted this printer deployed only to users in the Sales OU, you could launch the Group Policy Management console, delete the link at the domain for the Deploy Printers GPO, and link the GPO to the Sales OU. As soon as domain clients refresh Group Policy (or it's forced with `gpupdate /force`) the printer will be removed for all clients that aren't in the Sales OU.

Viewing Deployed Printers

You can easily view all deployed printers from within the Print Management console by selecting the Deployed Printers container in the Print Management console. This will query Active Directory and show all the printers that are deployed via GPO.

Although you can't deploy additional printers from this view, you can remove the deployment option for printers using this view. Simply select any deployed printer, select Deploy with Group Policy, and remove the deployment option.

Adjusting Print Server Settings

Several settings apply at the server level and can be configured once to apply to all resources (drivers, forms, ports, and printers) managed by that server. You can also export and import printers to and from files and set notifications.

To edit server-wide printer settings, launch the Print Management console, browse to the Print Servers container, and right-click your server to view the context menu and access these choices.

Server Properties

If you select Server Properties from the context menu, you'll see that you can access five tabs. Figure 16.25 shows the Print Server Properties sheet with the Forms tab selected. You can also reach this page by selecting Forms under the server and selecting Manage Forms.

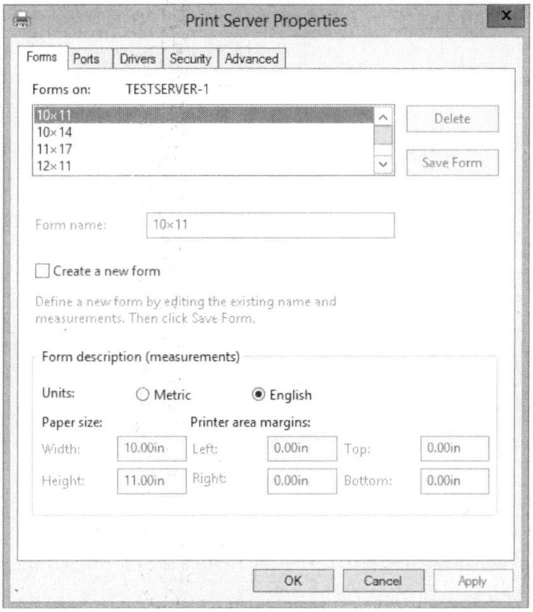

FIGURE 16.25
Viewing the Forms tab of system properties

As you can see, several tabs allow you to configure server properties:

◆   Forms

◆   Ports

◆   Drivers

◆   Security

◆   Advanced

CHOOSING FORM SETTINGS

Print jobs are arranged on the paper based on forms, which define a template for where text should appear. Print servers come with a long list of predefined forms you can choose from, but they also allow you to define your own form settings for customized needs such as printing to company letterhead.

Print servers are set up to print on blank 8.5″×11″ paper (the standard size). To choose a new form, find it in the list.

If you want to create a new form, select the "Create a new form" check box, edit the form description as desired, and click OK. Any forms that you've created can be modified by selecting it, making your modifications, and then clicking Save Form.

You can't delete the preexisting forms, but you can delete any forms you've created.

CONFIGURING SERVER PORT SETTINGS

You can select the Ports tab to view all the ports available on the server. Figure 16.26 shows the Ports tab. Notice that you can add ports, delete ports, and configure ports here, though most ports have very little configuration needed. You can also reach this page by selecting Ports under the server and selecting Manage Ports.

FIGURE 16.26
Viewing the Ports tab of Print Server Properties

You normally won't need to create a port by itself. Normally, when you add a network printer, you'll be adding the port as you saw earlier in the chapter. When you add a USB printer, the port will be added automatically. It's very rare to use LPT (parallel) or COM (serial) ports today, but if you do use them, several are already preconfigured.

If you're no longer using a port, you can simply select it and click Delete Port to delete it.

USB ports don't have any configurable options, and we covered the configuration of TCP/IP ports earlier in the chapter.

ADDING OR UPDATING THE PRINTER DRIVER ON A PRINT SERVER

Earlier, you saw how to add a printer driver to a printer. This is commonly done to support different clients. If you access the Drivers tab of the server properties, you can add printer drivers using a similar process.

Although most driver management will be done from within the printer, there may be times when you need to manage the drivers when the printer isn't installed on the server. For example, you may want to add drivers before adding the printer or remove unused drivers after the printer has been removed.

MANAGING PRINT SECURITY

You can manage permissions that apply to security for the entire server through the Security tab. There are differences in permissions that can apply to a server and permissions that apply to a printer.

Figure 16.27 shows the server permissions on the left and the printer permissions on the right.

FIGURE 16.27

Viewing the security tabs; server security is on the left, and individual printer security is on the right.

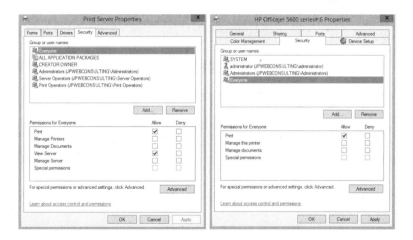

Just as NTFS and share permissions (covered in Chapter 10, "Active Directory Federation Services") can be set to Allow or Deny for any individual user or group of users, permissions on the print server or individual printers can be set to Allow or Deny.

For any of the permissions that are the same on the server and printer, setting them at the server level will cause all new printer installations to receive the same permissions. Existing permissions are not modified; only permissions for new installations are.

The print server permissions are as follows:

Print   Users can send print jobs to the printer. The Everyone group is granted this permission by default.

Manage Printers   Users can change printer properties and permissions. This is granted to the Administrators, Server Operators, and Print Operators groups by default.

Manage Documents   Users can control document-specific settings and pause, resume, restart, and delete spooled print jobs. This is granted to the Creator Owner, Administrators, Server Operators, and Print Operators groups by default. When a user creates a print job, they become a member of the Creator Owner group for that job, allowing them to manage their own documents.

View Server Users can view the server properties and settings. This does not give them permission to change the properties. The View Server permission is granted to the Everyone, Administrators, Server Operators, and Print Operators groups by default.

Manage Server The Manage Server permission allows users to modify any of the server properties and settings. It is granted to the Administrators, Server Operators, and Print Operators groups by default.

Special Permissions Individual permissions can be assigned at the granular level by clicking Advanced. If any granular permissions are assigned, the Special Permissions check box will be grayed out.

DELEGATION OF PERMISSIONS

Default permissions on Windows Server 2012 R2 do not allow non-administrative users to perform any administrative print operations. However, it is possible to grant any specific printer permission desired at the server without granting users full system administrative rights.

VIEWING THE SERVER ADVANCED PROPERTIES

The Advanced tab gives you a few additional options you can configure. Figure 16.28 shows the Advanced tab.

FIGURE 16.28
Viewing the
Advanced tab

The most common reason to access this tab is to change the location of the spool folder. As a reminder, any documents that can't be sent to the printer right away are spooled to the hard drive and then sent as the printer becomes available. On a dedicated print server, it's common to move the spool folder to another dedicated drive.

There are two reasons to move the spool folder:

To Give It More Disk Space   Since some print jobs can become quite large, they can consume the space available on the hard drive. Although a spooled job will be deleted after it's printed, if multiple jobs are spooled at the same time, you could run out of disk space.

To Get Better Performance   The default location will compete with the operating system for disk access. If performance is an issue, you can move the spool folder to a dedicated hard drive separate from the operating system.

Moving the spool folder is as simple as entering the path to the new location. If the path doesn't exist, it will be created. Beware, though. The change will occur immediately, and any documents that have been spooled will not print. You should wait until there are no active documents waiting to print before moving the spooler.

The other settings are minor. You can enable the system beep on errors from remote documents and show informational notifications for both local and network printers. Although it's not configurable here, a cool new feature is the ability to send notifications via email, which you'll see a little later in this chapter.

Printer Migration

Printer migration from one server to another is relatively easy using the Printer Migration Wizard. Imagine that you've been running a server as a print server for a period of time, and it is hosting 20 or more printers. You need to decommission this server, but before you do so, you want to have a new server host the printers. Manually re-creating all the printers on the new server could take a substantial amount of time.

You can export the printers to a file on the original server and then import the printers from that same file onto the new server. At this point, both servers will act as print servers for the same print devices. You'll then need to configure the clients to use the new print server before taking the old one down. If you've deployed them with Group Policy, you can just change the Group Policy settings to point to the new server, and you're finished.

To export the printers, simply right-click the server, and select Export Printers to a File, browse to a location, and save the file. You should then copy the file to a location accessible by the new server.

On the new server, right-click the server, select Import Printers from a File, and browse to the location of the exported file. The migration wizard gives you some import options, as shown in Figure 16.29.

FIGURE 16.29
Importing printers
to a new print server

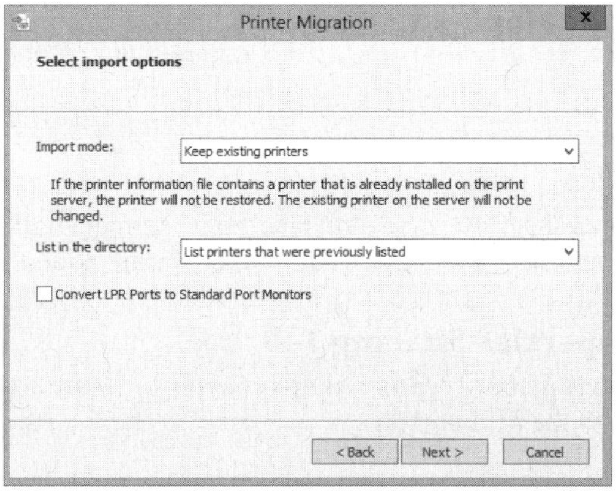

You can choose to keep existing printers or completely overwrite existing printers. You can also choose how the printers will be listed in Active Directory by choosing to list only the printers that were previously listed, list them all, or don't list any.

You can also use this method to restore your printer configurations to a previous time. If you have exported the printers to a file and they become corrupt, modified, or deleted, you can simply import the file to restore the configuration.

Managing Printer Properties

Just as the print server has several properties that can be managed, viewed, and manipulated, you can also manipulate properties for individual printers. Earlier in the chapter, you learned how to add printers. If you later need to modify any of the printers, simply right-click the printer, and select Properties.

Figure 16.30 shows the properties of a printer with the General tab selected. The General tab shows basic information on the printer such as the name, location, comments (if added), model, and features supported by the printer. This page will often include a Preferences button that can be used to modify specific user preferences for the printer. It also includes a button to print a test page that can be very useful to verify connectivity with the printer.

FIGURE 16.30
Viewing the General tab of printer properties

The properties sheet shows several tabs. Some printers will include more tabs depending on the capabilities of the printer. These additional tabs are added from the print driver package.

Printer Properties Sharing Tab

The Sharing tab was shown earlier in this chapter in Figure 16.8 when describing how to add printer drivers to the printer. You can also use it to share (or stop sharing) a printer by simply selecting the check box. This page includes the "List in the directory" check box that can be modified here or by right-clicking the printer and selecting List in Directory.

Printer Properties Ports Tab

The Ports tab allows you to add, delete, and configure ports used by the printer. Most printers can receive data to print and also send data to the server to report on conditions such as low toner, low paper, and paper jam conditions. This page includes the "Enable bidirectional support" check box, which is selected by default to enable the printer to send and receive.

The most common reason to access this tab is to enable printer pooling. Printer-pooling allows you to add multiple print devices to a single printer.

As we mentioned earlier in this chapter, the ratio of printers to print devices isn't always one to one. You'll see later how to create multiple printers for a single print device, but here you'll see how to have single printer support multiple print devices.

Why would you want to do this? It's mostly a matter of efficiency. Even with the fast print devices available today, busy offices may have more print jobs coming through than one print device can handle. To keep things running smoother and reduce delays, you can distribute print jobs among multiple print devices. Print clients will all send their print jobs to the same printer, but the jobs will go to the printer that's least busy at any given time. This is called *printer pooling*. Figure 16.31 shows the Ports tab with printer pooling enabled.

FIGURE 16.31
Enabling printer pooling from the Ports tab

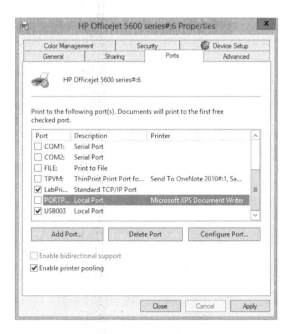

Notice in the figure that two ports are enabled. This is possible only when the "Enable printer pooling" check box is selected. You can add as many ports as you have print devices and your needs require.

There are a couple of catches to printer pooling. First, the print devices in the pool must use the same driver. Since many print devices use the same or similar internal parts, it's possible to have different print devices that use the same driver. However, if the devices require different drivers, they won't work in the same printer pool.

Second, we highly recommend putting the pooled print devices in the same physical location. Since users don't know which printer their job will print at, you don't want to have to wander from place to place looking for their print jobs.

SEPARATOR PAGES

Consider using separator pages with usernames in printer pools since users will not necessarily know which printer their job went to. Separator pages are explained in greater depth later in this chapter.

Printer Properties Security Tab

Those familiar with any current Windows-based operating system know that you secure the network by defining user rights for what people can *do* on the network and setting permissions for the resources that people can *use*. Printer security is controlled with permissions on a per-group or per-user basis. Permissions generally stack—that is, the most permissive set of permissions available to you applies—unless you're talking about denied access. Denied access overrides any allowed permissions.

You can use the Security tab to modify the permissions for the printer. You can assign four basic permissions to any user or group, as shown in Figure 16.32. Print permissions can be assigned as Allow or Deny just like other permissions in Windows.

FIGURE 16.32
Printer permissions shown on the Security tab

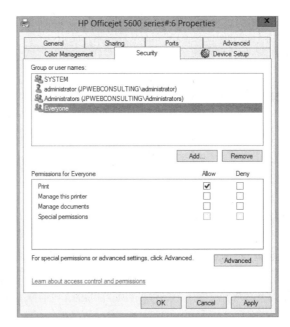

Although three basic permissions are showing, there are actually six granular permissions available.

You may remember from Chapter 10 that NTFS has basic permissions such as Read that map to granular permissions; the basic Read permission maps to the four granular permissions of Read Data, Read Permissions, Read Attributes, and Read Extended Attributes. By assigning the NTFS Read permission, you actually assign the four underlying permissions.

Print permissions work similarly, though they aren't as complex. There are three basic permissions and three additional granular permissions. The basic permissions are as follows:

Print The user can send jobs to the printer. Print includes Read Permissions. The Everyone group is granted Print Permissions by default.

Manage This Printer The user can change printer properties and permissions on the printer. Manage This Printer includes the following: Print, Read Permissions, Change Permissions, and Take Ownership. The Administrators, Server Operators, and Print Operators groups are all assigned the Manage This Printer permission by default.

Manage Documents User can control document-specific settings and pause, resume, restart, and delete spooled print jobs. This permission includes the following: Read Permissions, Change Permissions, and Take Ownership. The Creator Owner, Administrators, Server Operators, and Print Operators groups are all assigned the Manage Documents permission by default.

When users send print jobs to the printer, they become a member of the Creator Owner group for that print job and manage that document.

PERMISSIONS ARE CUMULATIVE

If a user is granted multiple permissions because the user is a member of multiple groups, that person will be granted the cumulative value of all the permissions. For example, if a user is a member of the Everyone group and is granted Print permission and is also a member of another group and is granted Manage This Printer permission, they have a combination of all the permissions.

The only exception is if Deny is used. If a user is a member of a group granted Print permission and a member of another group that is assigned Deny permission, Deny will always win. Just as Deny takes precedence in NTFS and share permissions, Deny takes precedence with printer permissions.

You can use the basic permissions to accomplish most, if not all, of your requirements. However, if you click the Advanced button on the Security tab and then click the Edit button, you'll see the advanced permissions, as shown in Figure 16.33.

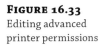

FIGURE 16.33
Editing advanced
printer permissions

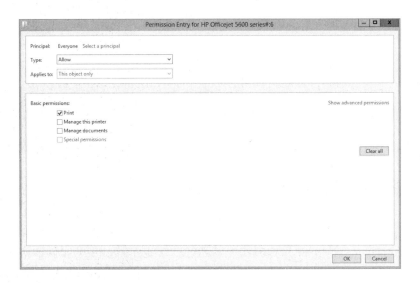

The advanced permissions include the basic permissions and these three additional permissions:

Read Permissions The user can view the permissions assigned to any users and groups for the printer. The Everyone group is granted Read Permissions by default.

Change Permissions The user can change the permissions all users and groups have for that printer. The Administrators, Server Operators, and Print Operators groups are all assigned Change Permissions by default.

Take Ownership The user can take ownership of the printer. As the owner, the user can grant himself any of the permissions.

The Administrators, Server Operators, and Print Operators groups are all assigned the Take Ownership permission by default.

To set or edit the permissions assigned to a printer, log in with an account that is granted Change Permissions, open the printer's properties sheets, and access the Security tab. If you want to add any user or group, click the Add button, and add the user or group just as you'd add a user or group for NTFS permissions (it's the same dialog box and procedure). With the user or group added, select Allow or Deny for the desired permission.

Now that you have a basic understanding of how print permissions work, we'll cover some common scenarios of how the permissions can be used.

USING PRINTER PERMISSIONS TO RESTRICT ACCESS

When a printer is created, the Everyone group is granted the Print permission. Although this often works just fine, there are some exceptions.

We once remember working in an organization where we had a very elaborate color printer used to produce some beautiful documents. It used special paper and special toner, and it was expensive to print each page. One day, the boss found several color pages printed out from a website using this printer and…well, let's just say he wasn't happy.

He wanted to change the permission so only a select group of users could print to this printer and so it wasn't available to everyone. We simply used the Security tab, removed the Everyone group, added a group that included the special users, and granted this group Allow for the Print permission.

If users don't have the Print permission (and when the Everyone group is removed, most users will no longer have the Print permission), they are not able to send print jobs to the print device.

Don't Deny Everyone

If you deny the Print permission to the Everyone group instead of removing the Everyone group, no one will be able to print. Remember, Deny takes precedence. Since everyone is in the Everyone group, everyone will be denied. It doesn't matter who is granted Allow; Deny takes precedence.

Using Printer Permissions for Delegation

It's common to delegate permission to someone located close to the printer to manage documents on the printer. This person can then administer the common problems associated with the printer without needing an administrator.

As an example, a printer could be located in an office with six people. Let's say that Joe sends a lengthy print job to the printer and then heads off to a meeting. Unfortunately, his job hangs up. Not only is his job not printing, but the other jobs behind his are held in a queue, waiting for his job to finish. Everyone is on hold until Joe comes back and cancels his job. Since the job is owned by Joe, only he can cancel it (or someone else with the Manage Documents permission).

A common solution is to assign someone responsible in the office the Manage Documents permission. If anyone's job gets hung up, this person can then pause, resume, restart, and delete spooled print jobs. Users in the office don't need to wait until Joe comes back or ask a busy administrator for help.

Auditing Printer Access

Curious to know who's doing what to the printers under your care? You can turn to the Auditing tab (accessible by clicking the Advanced button in the Security section of a printer's properties) to set up auditing. All auditable events will be recorded in the Security log.

It's relatively easy to enable auditing. The following steps will enable auditing of any successful printing to a printer:

1. Access the properties of the printer you want to audit, and select the Security tab.

2. Click Advanced, and select the Auditing tab.

3. Click Add, and then click the link "Select a principal."

4. Enter the name of the group you want to audit. If you want to audit all users, enter **Everyone**.

5. Select Check Names to ensure the group is recognized.

6. Your display will look similar to Figure 16.34. Click OK.

FIGURE 16.34
Enabling auditing
for Everyone

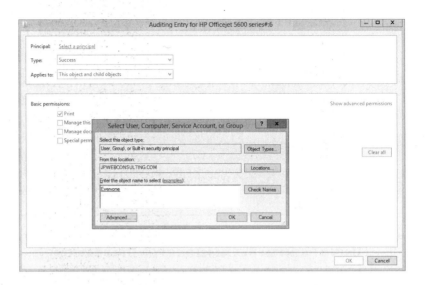

7. The permissions page will appear. Select Success from the Type drop-down.

8. Select the check box next to Print, as shown in Figure 16.35. Notice that it also selects Read Permissions automatically.

9. Click OK. Click OK to close the advanced settings.

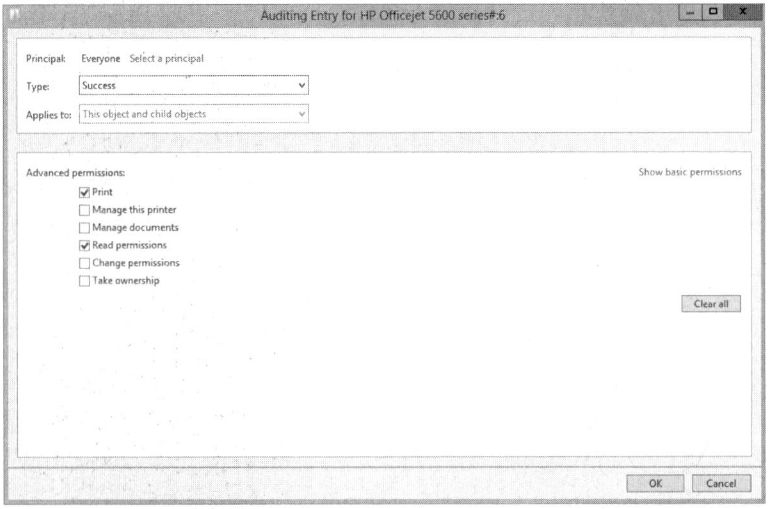

FIGURE 16.35
Auditing successful
printing attempts

You're not quite finished yet. Even though auditing has been enabled on the printer object, you still need to ensure that auditing is possible in the environment. This is typically done via Group Policy. You can use the Local Security Policy snap-in for a stand-alone server. If you're in a domain, you can create a new Group Policy object (GPO) or use an existing GPO such as the Default Domain Policy.

Follow these steps to enable auditing of object access in the Default Domain Policy:

1. Launch the GPMC by pressing the Windows key and choosing Group Policy Management.

2. Browse to your domain, and select Default Domain Policy.

3. Right-click Default Domain Policy, and select Edit, as shown in Figure 16.36.

FIGURE 16.36

Modifying Default Domain Policy using the GPMC

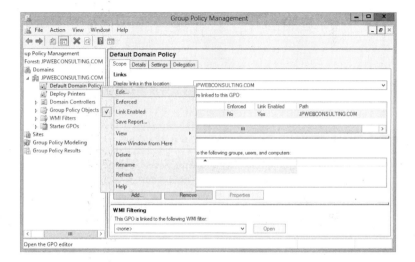

4. The Group Policy Management Editor will launch. Browse to the Computer Configuration\Policies\Windows Settings\Security Settings\Local Policies\Audit Policy node.

5. Double-click the "Audit object access" property.

6. Select the "Define these policy settings" check box and select the Success check box.

7. Your display will look similar to Figure 16.37. Click OK.

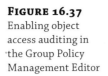

FIGURE 16.37
Enabling object
access auditing in
the Group Policy
Management Editor

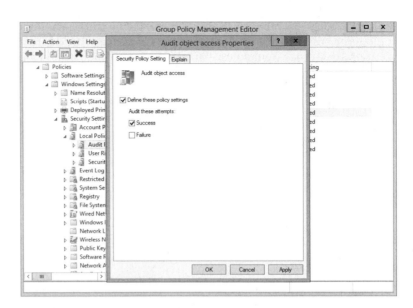

ENABLING OBJECT ACCESS AUDITING

Enabling object access auditing must be done before auditing on any individual objects will occur. In this context, objects are resources such as printers, files, and folders. Once object access auditing is enabled via Group Policy, auditing can be enabled on any individual objects. However, if auditing is enabled on the object but object access auditing is not enabled, then auditing doesn't occur at all. Both steps must be done.

---

8. Close all the windows, and you're finished.

Printer Properties Advanced Tab

The Advanced tab gives you the ability to set and configure a lot of different capabilities including adding a schedule for the printer, adding priorities for the printer, updating the driver, and doing some miscellaneous document management features and tasks.

Figure 16.38 shows the Advanced tab. Refer to this figure as we discuss the different capabilities.

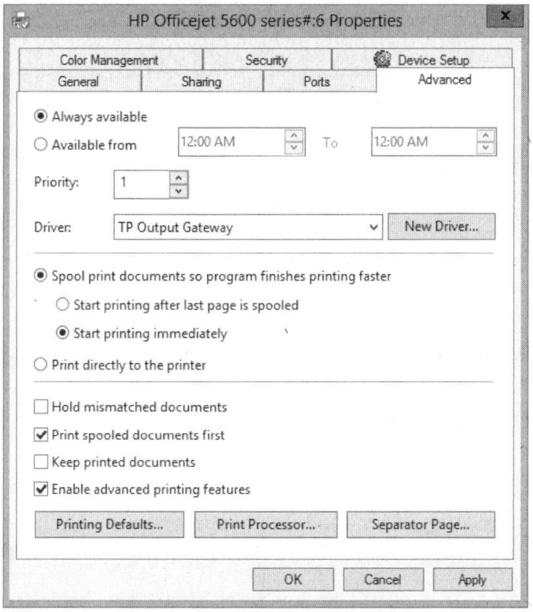

FIGURE 16.38

Printer properties
Advanced tab

SETTING AVAILABLE HOURS

You can make printers available all the time to everybody (which is the default), or you can pick and choose the times the printer will be available.

A printer will always accept print jobs, but you can manipulate the time when a printer will send jobs to the print device. If a print job is sent to a printer outside of these hours, the job will be queued and printed when the scheduled time arrives. Jobs queued in this manner won't prevent other jobs from printing.

As a simple example, suppose that Sally occasionally needs to print lengthy documents needed for the following day. Without a printer schedule, she'd print with everyone else. As her print jobs are printing, everyone else's print jobs will have to wait.

However, if you alter the printer schedule for Sally, her jobs could be set to print between the hours of 8 P.M. and 5 A.M.—when everyone else is gone.

There's an important point to grasp here, though. If you create a printer named LaserJet1 that everyone uses to print and then you alter the schedule for LaserJet1, you've just altered the schedule for everyone. What you must do is create a new printer.

Creating a Second Printer for a Single Print Device

You'd create a new printer using the procedures covered earlier in this chapter. Remember, the printer is the software component, and the print device is the physical device that creates the printed output. When creating the new printer, make sure you do two things:

◆ Give the new printer a different name and share name.

◆ Choose the same settings (port, printer manufacturer and model, and so on) you chose for the first printer.

Sending documents to the new printer will cause them to print on the same print device. The only difference will lie in the configuration options you set for the new printer.

In this example, you could name your printer **AfterHoursLaser**. All the settings would be the same, except you'd edit the printer's hours of availability.

Modifying the New Printer

Once you've created the second printer, you simply access the Advanced tab, select Available From, and select the desired time. You'd need to provide some training to the user to ensure the user understood that any jobs sent to this printer would not print until the scheduled time.

You can also modify the security settings so only Sally could print to this printer. And, if desired, you can modify the share settings so other users can't find the share. If you place a $ symbol at the beginning of the share name, it will be hidden. Users who know the printer name can still reach it, but it won't be visible.

SETTING PRINTER PRIORITIES

The default priority of a printer is 1, but you can choose different priorities between 1 and 99, where 99 is the highest priority. If several print jobs are waiting to be sent to a print device, they are queued. Print jobs with higher priorities (such as 99) will be placed in the queue ahead of print jobs with lower priorities (such as 1).

Print jobs that have a higher priority don't stop active print jobs. In other words, if a job with a priority of 1 is printing and a job with a priority of 99 is received, the priority 1 job will complete before the priority 99 job starts.

Let's state the obvious here, though. If everyone is using a printer named LaserJet1 and you change the priority of LaserJet1 to 50, you've just modified the priority for everyone. It doesn't matter what the priority is if it's the same for everyone.

Just as you need to create a new printer to assign a different schedule, you need to create a new printer to assign a different priority. It's also a good idea to modify the permissions so that only the person needing the higher-priority printer can use it; include the $ symbol at the beginning of the share name to hide it.

CONFIGURING SPOOLER SETTINGS

The different settings in the middle of the Advanced tab of the properties sheet affect how the spooler works. Spooling documents means the application you're printing from is tied up only for the time it takes to create the spool file, not to print the entire document. This is called *printing in the background*.

Normally, they will be set with the following settings:

◆ "Spool print documents so program finishes printing faster"

◆ "Start printing immediately"

You can configure it so that printing starts only after the last page is spooled. This could be used if the printer is quicker than your computer (not likely today).

If you can't use print spooling for some reason—perhaps if the print server's hard disk is so full that it can't create the spool file—then you can send documents directly to the printer port, without creating a spool file or using print server resources. Select "Print directly to the printer" on the Advanced tab.

Disabling spooling is not something you'll often want to do. Spool files allow you to print large and complex documents without running out of printer memory. They also allow users to regain control of their applications more quickly. Disable print spooling only if you can't print otherwise—it's something to tinker with if images aren't coming out properly.

MISCELLANEOUS SPOOLING SETTINGS

There are four additional miscellaneous settings close to the bottom of the Advanced tab of the printer properties:

Hold Mismatched Documents   A mismatched document is a print job sent to the print device that needs a different form or tray. Instead of printing it incorrectly or deleting the job, the spooler holds the print jobs until the printer is reconfigured.

Print Spooled Documents First   This is selected by default. It causes jobs that have completed spooling to print before jobs that are in the process of spooling—even if the job being spooled has a higher priority.

Keep Printed Documents   Normally documents are deleted from the queue after they're printed, but it is possible to keep a copy of the documents by selecting this option. This option allows you to easily reprint documents. Make sure your hard drive has enough space to store these documents if this is selected.

Enable Advanced Printing Features   Many printers have advanced printing features. By selecting this option, the advanced features will be available. If they're causing problems, you can simply disable the advanced features by deselecting the box.

USING SEPARATOR PAGES

When a lot of people are using the same printer, keeping print jobs organized can get complicated. To help you minimize the number of people who wander off with each other's print jobs, the operating system supports separator pages. These extra pages are printed at the beginning of documents to identify the person doing the printing, the time, the job number, or whatever other information is defined in the page. (We'll explain how you can tell what information a page will print and how you can create your own custom separator pages in a minute.)

SEPARATOR PAGES ARE ASSIGNED TO PRINTERS

Like other printer options, separator pages are assigned to printers, not to print devices, so you can use a different separator page for each printer.

CHOOSING A SEPARATOR PAGE

Printers don't use separator pages by default. However, several separator pages are included in Windows Server 2012 R2 and can be added to your printer.

With the printer properties open to the Advanced tab, click the Separator Page button, and click Browse. The "Separator page" field will open to the `Windows\System32` directory, and you can choose one of the four provided separator pages. Figure 16.39 shows the `sysprint.sep` separator page being added.

FIGURE 16.39
Adding a separator page

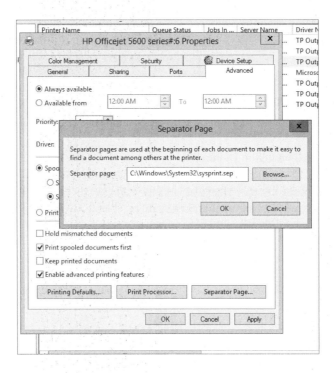

Table 16.2 describes the four built-in separator pages.

TABLE 16.2: Default Separator Pages

PAGE NAME	DESCRIPTION	COMPATIBILITY
sysprint.sep	Prints a separator page before print jobs	PostScript
pcl.sep	Switches a dual-language printer to PCL mode	PCL
pscript.sep	Switches a dual-language printer to PostScript mode	PostScript
sysprtj.sep	This is the same as the sysprint.sep page but with support for Japanese characters	PostScript

CREATING A NEW SEPARATOR PAGE

Given that the built-in separator pages are mostly necessary in specific instances, you'll probably want to create your own separator pages if you use them at all. Separator page files are just text files, so you can create the file in Notepad. You can also copy the original files and modify them to fit your needs.

On the first line of the new file, type a single character—any character will do—and press Enter. This character will now be the *escape character* that alerts the print server that you're performing a function, not entering text, so make it one that you won't need for anything else. Dollar signs ($) and pound signs (#) are both good escape characters, but the only rule is that you can't use the character as text.

Once you've picked an escape code, customize the separator page with any of the variables shown in Table 16.3. Be sure to include the escape character before each function, as we've shown in this table with a dollar sign.

TABLE 16.3:   Separator Page Functions

VARIABLE	FUNCTIONS
/B/S	Prints text in block characters created with pound signs (#) until you insert a $U. Be warned—printing text like this takes up a lot of room.
/D	Prints the date the job was printed, using the format defined on the Date tab of the Regional Options applet in Control Panel.
/E	Equivalent to a page break in Word; all further functions will be executed on a new page. If you get an extra blank separator page when you print, remove this function from the SEP file.
/Fpathname\filename	Prints the contents of the specified file to the separator page, starting on a blank line. Because separator pages are strictly text only, only the text will be printed—no formatting.
/Hnn	Sets a printer-specific control sequence, where nn is a hex ASCII code that goes directly to the printer. Look in your printer manual for any codes that you might set this way and for instructions on how and when to use them.
/I	Prints the job number. Each print job has a job number associated with it.
/Lxxx	Prints all the characters following (represented here with xxx) until it comes to another escape code. Use this function to print any customized text you like.
/N	Prints the login name of the person who submitted the print job.
/n	Skips n lines (where n is a number from 0 to 9). Skipping 0 lines just moves printing to the next line, so you could use that function to define where line breaks should occur.
/T	Prints the time the job was printed, using the format defined on the Time tab of the Regional Options applet in Control Panel.
/U	Turns off block character printing.
/Wnn	Sets the line width, where nn is a number of characters. Any characters in excess of this line width are truncated. The default (which you don't have to define) is 80 characters.

For example, you could use the following text in the SEP file:

```
/
/N
/n
/0
/D
/L This is a separator page. Only use these pages to organize
/L print jobs because they're otherwise a waste of paper.
```

It will produce this output:

```
Darril
10/31/09 This is a separator page. Only use these pages to organize print jobs
because they're otherwise a waste of paper.
```

Notice that there are line breaks only if you specifically include them. Without the /n codes, all output will be on a single line.

When you've finished, save the separator page file with a .sep extension to the %systemroot%\system32 folder if you want to store it with other separator pages. Otherwise, you can store the page anywhere on the print server. To use the new page, just load it as you would one of the defaults.

Managing Print Jobs

Managing print jobs is pretty straightforward. You can use the Print Management console and select Printers for the print server. You can then right-click the printer you're interested in and select Open Printer Queue.

Figure 16.40 shows the printer queue open for a printer named, HP Officejet 5600 series#:6. Notice in the figure that the Printers node also shows the queue status and the number of jobs in queue. We paused the printer so that the print jobs could build up as we sent several print jobs to the printer.

FIGURE 16.40
Viewing the print queue for a printer

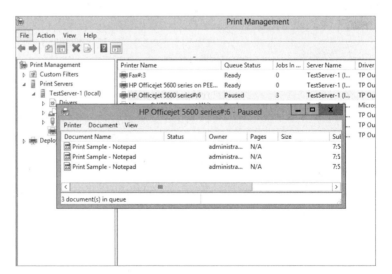

The print queue shows a list of all print jobs currently waiting to be printed and the following information:

♦ The filename of the document being printed

♦ The job's status (printing, spooling, paused, or blank if the printer is paused)

♦ Who sent the job to the printer

♦ How many pages are in the job and how many remain to be printed

♦ The file size of the print job

♦ The time and date the user submitted the job

When you select a job in the list, you can use the tools in the Document menu to pause a job, resume a paused job, restart a print job from the beginning, or cancel a print job. The only catch is that you have to do all this while the job is still spooling to the print device. You can't control the parts of the job that have already been sent to the print device.

If you pause a print job before it actually starts printing, you can edit its priority or printing times in the middle of printing. From the Document menu, choose Properties to open the dialog box shown in Figure 16.41.

FIGURE 16.41
Viewing the properties of a print job

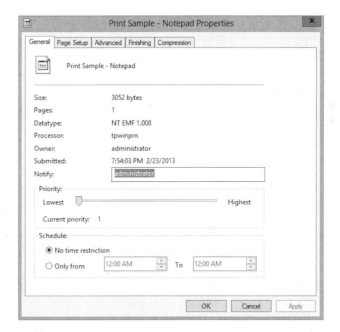

From here, you can view many properties inherited from the printer and passed to the job, and you can raise or lower the job's priority. The higher a job's priority, the higher its place in line, so you can use this feature to manipulate the order in which jobs print even if one job got to the printer before another did. This can be very useful on those occasions when the person printing the 200-page manual sends their job to the printer before the person creating a cover sheet for a FedEx package that has to be ready by 3:30 P.M.

Using Custom Filters

The Print Management console has several filters that can be used to assist with management of printers and print servers. If you have only three printers on one print server, you probably won't use these filters. But if you're managing 20 print servers and each print server has as many as 100 printers, these filters can be quite valuable.

The built-in filters are fairly straightforward:

All Printers   This shows all printers from all servers managed by the PMC. If the PMC is managing only a single server, this view will be the same as the Printers node within the Servers node.

All Drivers   This shows all drivers from all servers managed by the PMC. If the PMC is managing only a single server, this view will be the same as the Drivers node within the Servers node.

Printers Not Ready   If any printers are not reporting to the server because they are not ready (because of being offline, paused, out of paper, or any other reason), they will be listed here. Printers that aren't powered up or otherwise not reachable from the print server will not be listed here.

Printers with Jobs   If any printers have jobs that are either printing or in queue, they will be listed here.

You can also create custom filters to meet any specific needs. You can launch the wizard by right-clicking Custom Filters and selecting Add New Printer Filter or Add New Driver Filter. Give your filter a name and description, and then you can add your filter criteria. Figure 16.42 shows the filter criteria you can choose.

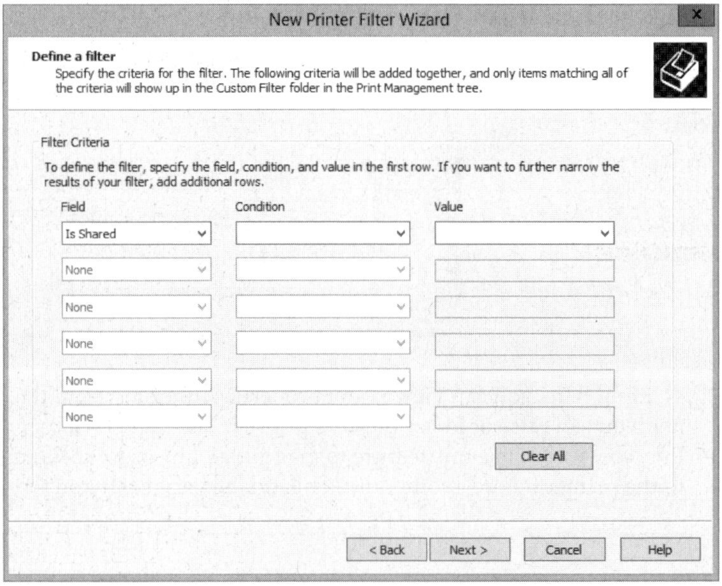

FIGURE 16.42
Defining a custom filter

Depending on which field you select, you'll have different conditions that can be selected (such as "is exactly" or "is not exactly") and you can then enter a value (such as **true** or **false**). It's possible to configure multiple conditions for any single filter. If all conditions are met, the filter will detect the printer or printers.

You also have the ability to configure notifications with your filter. Notifications can be configured to send an email or run a script. Figure 16.43 shows the notification page.

FIGURE 16.43
Configuring the notifications

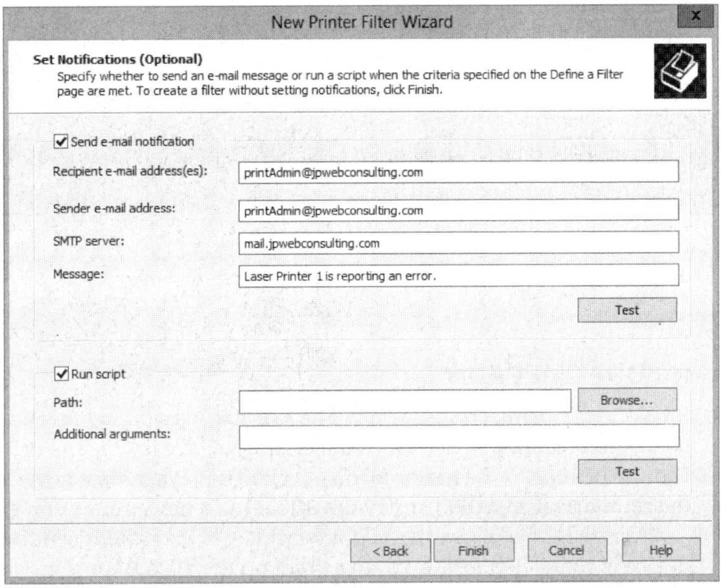

You wouldn't to do this for all your filters, or you'd start getting spammed by your print server. However, you could have a high-priority printer that needs to be fixed as soon as a problem is detected. You could create a filter with one condition to identify this printer and a second condition with a field of Queue Status, a condition of "is exactly," and a value of Error. Now whenever this filter detects this printer in error, it will send a notification. Or, if the solution is to run a script, you could configure the filter to automatically run the script.

Troubleshooting Printer Problems

Printing under Server 2012 R2 is usually pretty trouble-free—in the software, at any rate—but every once in a while you may run into problems. The remainder of this chapter describes some of the more common printing problems and tells you how to solve them.

Basic Troubleshooting: Identifying the Situation

First, try to figure out *where* the problem lies. Is it the printer? The application? The network? If you can tell where the problem lies, you'll simplify the troubleshooting process.

PAPER JAMS

The printing problem that frustrates us most is paper jams. Getting that last shred of jammed paper out of the print device can drive you to madness. To minimize paper jams, store paper somewhere with low humidity (curled paper jams more easily), don't overfill the paper tray, and keep paper neat before it goes in the tray. Furthermore, some paper is designed to be printed to a specific side; it is packaged with an arrow on the ream and should be loaded with the arrow pointing up.

There are also a lot of differences between paper types. As one of many examples, copy paper and printer paper have many different properties, and using paper designed for copying machines may impact the quality in addition to increasing the risks of paper jams.

Printing troubles can happen because of any combination of three different causes:

◆ Hardware errors

◆ Software errors

◆ User errors

NO ONE CAN PRINT

If no one can print, check the print device and network connection. Check the easy stuff first. Is the printer on and online? Does the cartridge have ink? Is the printer server up and running? Did the printer *ever* work, or is this its maiden voyage? If it never worked, make sure you have the right driver installed, or try downloading a newer one from the manufacturer's website.

From the console, check the port settings. Is the printer sending data to the port the print device is connected to? Make sure to set up the TCP/IP port for a network-connected printer properly.

Also, see whether you can print from the print server's console. There could be a network problem preventing people from reaching the print server.

Make sure there's enough space on the print server's hard disk to store spool files. If the print server can't create spool files, it can't print from a spool.

Make sure the printer is set up to use the proper print processor.

If you're using Internet Printing, make sure that this service is enabled.

SOME PEOPLE CAN'T PRINT

What do those people have in common? Are they all in a single subnet? In the same user group? Using the same application? Printing to the same printer? Find the element they have in common, and that's probably the element that's causing the printing problem. For example, if everyone who's printing from one subnet can print but users from another subnet cannot print, the problem is with the network, not the printer.

ONE PERSON CAN'T PRINT

If only one person can't print, try to narrow down the source of the problem. Can the person print from another application? Can the person print from another computer? If this person can't print at all, see whether someone else can print from their computer. If so, check the permissions attached to the person who can't print. They may be denied access to the printer altogether.

> ### REBOOTING SOLVES MANY ILLS
>
> If only one person is having printing problems, try rebooting the computer and retrying the print job. You can resolve many issues by rebooting the user's computer. You won't always know what the exact problem was, but it'll be solved, and both you and the user will be off doing more important things.

Restarting the Spooler Service

A common problem that occurs with print servers is that the print spooler service occasionally hangs. When this occurs, print jobs don't print and can't be canceled. The solution is to stop and restart the Print Spooler service.

You can restart the service in the Print Services role within Server Manager. Scroll down to the services window and find the Print Spooler service, right-click it, and select Restart. Sometimes you'll need to select Stop and then, after it stops, select Start.

Of course, you can also do the same thing from the command line with the following commands:

```
Net stop spooler
Net start spooler
```

Finally, here is the PowerShell cmdlet to stop, start, or restart the Spooler service.

```
Stop-Service "Spooler" -force
Start-Service "Spooler"
Restart-Service "Spooler" -force
```

Isolating Printer Drivers

A new feature available with Windows Server 2012 R2 is the ability to isolate printer drivers from the operating system. If you find that a printer driver is not playing well with others but still allows users to print, you can simply isolate it. Figure 16.44 shows a driver that has been configured in driver isolation mode.

FIGURE 16.44
Setting printer driver isolation

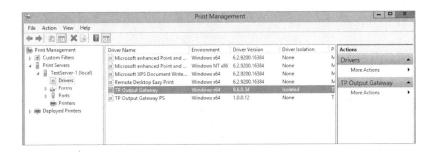

By isolating a printer driver, you can prevent a faulty driver from stopping all the print operations on a server. These are the three available choices:

None   Driver isolation isn't attempted.

Shared   Drivers operate in a shared process.

Isolated   The driver is isolated. This does take additional resources so it should be used only when necessary, and it can be useful for testing new drivers.

System Default (Shared)   This is used by default for all new drivers added to the server.

The Bottom Line

Add the Print and Document Services role.   Windows Server 2012 R2 servers can be configured to perform as print servers. One of the first steps you must take is to add the Print and Document Services role. There are different steps needed if you're adding the role to a full installation of Windows Server 2012 R2 vs. a Server Core installation.

Master It   What tool would you use to add the Print and Document Services role on a full installation of Windows Server 2012 R2? What tool would you use to add the Print and Document Services role on a Server Core installation of Windows Server 2012 R2?

Manage printers using the Print Management console.   After adding the Print and Documents Services role to the server, you can use the Print Management console to manage other print servers, printers, and print drivers.

Master It   Your company has purchased a new print device, and you want it to be hosted on a server that is configured as a print server. How would you add the printer to the print server?

Manage print server properties.   The spool folder can sometimes take a significant amount of space on the C drive, resulting in space problems and contention issues with the operating system. Because of these issues, the spool folder is often moved to another physical drive.

Master It   You want to move the spool folder to another location. How can you do this?

Manage printer properties.   Printers can be added to Active Directory so that they can be easily located by searching Active Directory. Printers must be shared first, but they aren't published to Active Directory by default when they are shared.

Master It   You want users to be able to easily locate a shared printer. What can you do to ensure the shared printer can be located by searching Active Directory?

Chapter 17

Remote Server Administration

The day-to-day administration of any server rarely occurs at the server. Instead, administrators commonly connect to servers remotely.

The servers are humming along smoothly in a cool (and sometimes downright cold) server room protected with physical security. Administrators are often in a comfortable office running a desktop system like Windows 7 or Windows 8. When administration is necessary, they connect to the servers remotely.

With this in mind, you need to know how to configure the servers for remote administration and connect to the servers from your desktop. Either that, or you will spend your time in the server room bundled up in a parka in the middle of the summer.

In this chapter, you will learn to:

◆ Configure Windows Server 2012 R2 servers for remote administration

◆ Remotely connect to Windows Server 2012 R2 servers using Remote Desktop Connection

◆ Remotely connect to Windows Server 2012 R2 servers using a Remote Desktop Protocol file

◆ Configure a server for Remote Assistance

◆ Install the Remote Server Administration Tools

Remote Desktop for Administration

Remote Desktop for Administration is the default implementation of Remote Desktop Services (RDS) on a Windows Server 2012 R2 server. In this mode, as many as two administrators can be remotely logged onto a server at the same time performing remote administration.

It's also possible to configure a server as a Remote Desktop Session Host server so that it can run desktops or desktop applications for remote users. However, configuring the server as a Remote Desktop Session Host server requires additional licenses and a licensing server. When using the server in the Remote Desktop for Administration mode, no additional licensing is required.

TERMINAL SERVICES RENAMED

If you've been working with previous versions of Windows, you're probably familiar with some of the RDS features but by a different name. In past versions, Remote Desktop Services was known as Terminal Services. It was renamed to RDS in Windows Server 2008 R2.

Remote Desktop for Administration allows you to connect to a server and do just about anything remotely that you could if you were physically at the server. You can access the Start menu, launch tools, install applications, install updates, and do much more when connected remotely. The two primary tools you'll use are Remote Desktop Connection and Remote Desktop.

The primary limitation you have is if the remote system needs a reboot or restart. Although it is possible to reboot the system remotely, when you do so, you will be disconnected. If something prevents the system from rebooting, you won't know what the problem is or be able to resolve it.

Configuring the Server for Remote Desktop

You can enable Remote Desktop on the server in several ways. You can access the advanced properties page of the server by one of the following methods:

◆ Click the link next to Remote Desktop, in the Server Manager local server properties window that appears when the system first boots.

◆ Click the Windows key on your keyboard, right-click the Metro-style box named Computer, and select Properties from the dynamic menu that appears at the bottom (see Figure 17.1). Click "Remote settings" to access the Remote tab of the System Properties dialog box.

FIGURE 17.1
Getting to the System Properties dialog box

Figure 17.2 shows the configuration choices you have on the Remote tab.

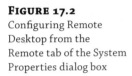

FIGURE 17.2
Configuring Remote Desktop from the Remote tab of the System Properties dialog box

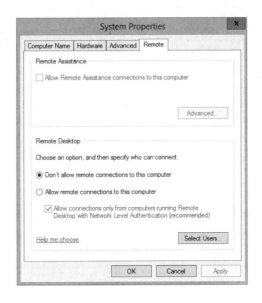

You can see that Windows Server 2012 R2 provides three choices for configuring the server for remote administration:

Don't Allow Remote Connections to This Computer   Remote Desktop is disabled.

Allow Remote Connections to This Computer   This will allow remote connections from clients.

Allow Connections Only from Computers Running Remote Desktop with Network Level Authentication (Recommended)   This supports connections from clients using RDC 6.0 or newer. RDC 6.0 and newer are available on Windows Vista and Windows 7. RDC 6.1 can be installed on Windows XP systems with at least SP2 installed.

When you enable Remote Desktop Connection, an exception is automatically created in the firewall on the local system. It's not necessary to add other exceptions on the local firewall. However, if you connect through a network firewall, port 3389 needs to be opened to allow the remote connections through. If opening port 3389 on your network firewall is not feasible in your network, you can create a Remote Desktop Gateway server as described later in this chapter.

Network Level Authentication (NLA) is a security feature available in Remote Desktop Services when the more secure setting is selected. NLA provides added security by completing the user authentication before the remote connection is established. If NLA is not used, the server is vulnerable to a denial-of-service attack.

NLA should be used whenever possible. The following are the requirements to support NLA:

◆   The client computer must be running at least RDC 6.0. RDC 6.0 is natively supported in Windows Vista clients.

◆   The client computer must support the Credential Security Support Provider (CredSSP) protocol.

◆   The server must be running Windows Server 2008 R2 or Windows Server 2012 R2.

RDC 6.1 FOR WINDOWS XP

The original version of RDC used in Windows XP doesn't support NLA. However, Microsoft later created RDC 6.1 for clients running Windows XP SP2 or SP3 that provides support for many of the features available in Windows Server 2012 R2 connections.

RDC 6.1 is available as a free download and is documented in KB article 952155 (`http://support` `.microsoft.com/kb/952155/`). RDC 6.0 is supported in Windows XP SP3.

Additionally, the CredSSP protocol can be enabled via a registry modification on Windows XP, as described in KB article 951608 (`http://support.microsoft.com/kb/951608/`).

Using Remote Desktop Connection

Remote Desktop Connection (RDC) is used to connect to a remote server. The version that works best with Windows Server 2012 R2 is RDC 6.0 or greater. Earlier versions don't support all of the features available, such as NLA.

You can launch RDC in Windows Vista, Windows 7, and Windows Server 2008 R2 by selecting Start ➢ All Programs ➢ Accessories ➢ Remote Desktop Connection. Once RDC is launched, you can click the Options button to view all the options available, as shown in Figure 17.3.

FIGURE 17.3

Remote Desktop Connection with Options expanded

Accessing RDC on Windows 8 and Windows Server 2012 R2 is a little different:

1. Hit your Windows key to get to your Metro-styled Start screen.

2. In the lower-right corner is a minimize icon. It's a hotspot you can mouse over. When the sidebar appears, simply type **remote** in the search box.

3. As you start to type in the search box, you will see Remote Desktop Connection appear on the left, as shown in Figure 17.4.

FIGURE 17.4
Getting to RDC on Windows Server 2012 R2

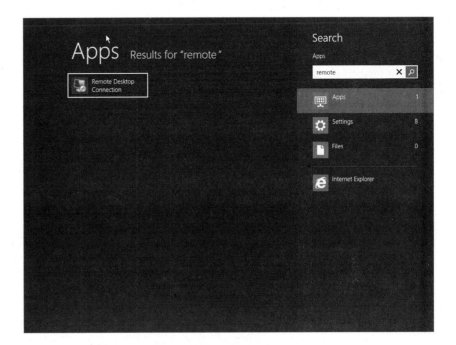

RDC includes six tabs that can be manipulated to provide different features, as detailed in the following sections.

RDC GENERAL TAB

The General tab is used to identify the remote computer you want to connect with and the user account you'll use to connect. Additionally, you can save your settings in a Remote Desktop Protocol file from this page.

By saving your settings in an RDP file, you can simply double-click the file to start the session. Follow these steps to save and use your RDP file:

REMOTE SESSIONS ARE POSSIBLE ON LOCAL COMPUTERS

If you have only one computer, you can still follow these steps. It's possible to log onto the remote session of a computer while logged on locally. You should use a different account with administrative permissions for the remote session. Although this wouldn't be very useful on the job, it does allow you to see the process in a test system.

---

1. Launch Remote Desktop Connection.

2. Click the Options button to expand the options.

3. Enter the remote computer's computer name in the Computer text box.

4. Enter a username that has permission to use RDC on the remote computer.

   If you want this username to be saved, select the "Allow me to save credentials" check box. You will be prompted for the password later.

5. Click Save As, and browse to the desktop. Rename the filename to **RDC.rdp**, and click Save.

6. Close the Remote Desktop Connection application.

7. Access your computer's desktop, and double-click the RDC.rdp file to launch it.

8. Review the warnings on this dialog box, as shown in Figure 17.5.

FIGURE 17.5
Remote Desktop
Connection unknown
publisher warning

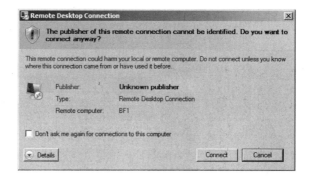

9. Click Details in the dialog box.

   This dialog box allows you to pick some local resources that you can bring to your remote session. You can also manipulate local resource settings on the Local Resources tab when the Remote Desktop Connection tool opens.

10. Since you created the RDP file, you can trust it and ignore the warnings. Click Connect.

    A dialog box appears allowing you to enter the password for your account or use another account.

11. Enter the password for an account with administrative privileges, and click OK.

    After a moment, another warning will appear similar to the one in Figure 17.6.

FIGURE 17.6

Remote Desktop Connection unknown certifying authority warning

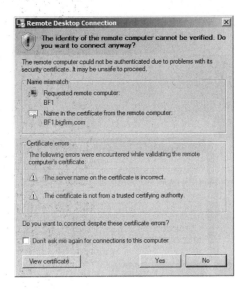

12. Click Yes to connect despite the warning.

   Your system will then connect to the remote session. Take your time looking around in the remote session.

   If you used the defaults in RDC, the connection bar will display across the top of the screen with the name of the server. If you click the X to close the screen, you will disconnect the session, but you won't close it. The session will remain open, consuming resources, either until you reconnect or log off, or until another administrator closes your session.

13. Click Start, and select Log Off to log off and close the session.

UNKNOWN PUBLISHER WARNINGS

When using an unsigned RDP file, you'll see two warnings indicating that the publisher of the remote connection cannot be identified and asking you whether you want to connect anyway. The first warning is shown at the top of the dialog box in Figure 17.5, and the second warning is shown in Figure 17.6.

RDP files can be signed using certificates for security. A signed RDP file has a signature within it indicating the identity of the client of the certificate authority (CA) that verified the identity. If you trust the CA, you'll trust this RDP file. When distributing RDP files to many clients, this added security feature can be quite valuable.

However, RDP files don't have to be signed. Since you are creating this RDP file, you can simply ignore the warnings.

The RDP file is associated with the Remote Desktop Connection application, so by double-clicking it, you will launch RDC. However, this RDP file is simply a text file. If you want to look at the contents, you can launch Notepad and browse to the file to see the contents.

RDC DISPLAY TAB

The Display tab allows you to configure the display for the remote desktop. You can configure the size of the desktop and the colors from this page. Figure 17.7 shows the Display tab.

FIGURE 17.7
Remote Desktop Connection Display tab

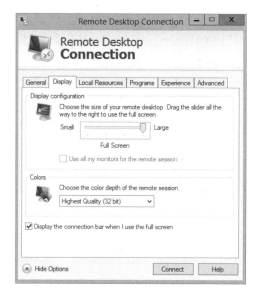

If you drag the slider all the way to the right, the remote desktop will display in full-screen mode. By default, a connection bar will be displayed across the top when in full-screen mode.

INCREASED PERFORMANCE OVER A WAN LINK

If you're accessing the remote server over a slow WAN connection, you can get increased performance by using a smaller screen or reducing the number of colors displayed. This isn't a problem in a well-connected network with a maximum of two remote sessions, but with a slow link, every bit helps.

The connection bar includes the name of the remote server, which can be useful if you have more than one instance of RDC running at a time. For example, if you're troubleshooting a problem and remote into three different servers using three different instances of RDC, you can quickly glance at the connection bar at the top of the window to remind yourself which server you're accessing.

When you remote into a server using RDC in full-screen mode, this connection bar is the only apparent difference you'll see. Everything else will look as if you're standing in front of the server.

At the left of the connection bar is a pushpin icon. It is selected by default and pins the connection bar to the top of the screen. You can deselect it to enable autohiding of the connection bar.

RDC LOCAL RESOURCES TAB

The Local Resources tab allows you to identify what resources you can bring to your remote session. For example, if you have a printer attached to your system and you want to print a log from the remote server, you can enable the local printer.

Microsoft introduced Easy Print in Windows Server 2008, which makes printer redirection easier with Remote Desktop Services and ensures that the client printers are installed in remote sessions. You don't have to install the print drivers on the server in order to print from an RDS session.

You can click the More button to enable additional resources during the remote session. Figure 17.8 shows the Local Resources tab and the additional resources that can be enabled after clicking the More button.

FIGURE 17.8
The Remote Desktop Connection Local Resources tab, with additional options

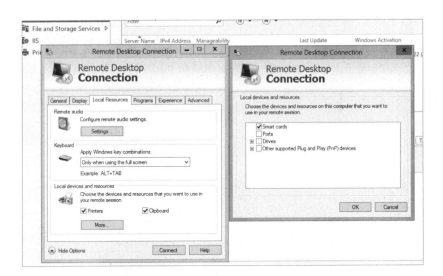

The primary reason why you'll access this tab is to enable or disable local devices and resources. Local printers and the local clipboard are enabled by default. The local clipboard allows you to copy text from your system (such as a script) and paste it into an application in the remote session.

Local drives are not enabled by default, but if you want to copy data from a local drive to the remote system, you can easily select the box. This does represent a security risk, though. If either the remote system or your local system is infected with malware, connecting the drives makes them accessible by the malware and susceptible to infection.

You can also configure the audio and keyboard settings. Audio settings include the following:

◆ "Play on this computer" (your local computer)

◆ "Do not play"

◆ "Play on remote computer"

If you're a fan of keyboard shortcuts, you may want to change the keyboard settings. The choices are as follows:

◆ "On this computer"

◆ "On the remote computer"

◆ "Only when using the full screen"

RDC PROGRAMS TAB

The Programs tab allows you to identify a program that will start when the remote connection is established. For example, you may always launch Server Manager when you start a specific server and want it to start automatically.

Figure 17.9 shows the RDC Programs tab. `ServerManager.msc` is entered in the text box, which will cause Server Manager to start when the connection is created.

FIGURE 17.9
Remote Desktop Connection
Programs tab

Since the path of Server Manager is already known by the system to be %systemroot%\System32, the path doesn't need to be included. However, if you wanted to launch a different program or script from an unknown path, you would need to include the full path.

SYSTEM PATH VARIABLE

You can identify what the known path of the system is by accessing the command line, typing **Path**, and pressing Enter. Any application in this path can be entered by just entering the name of the application.

You can modify this path by clicking Start, right-clicking Computer, selecting Properties, and then selecting "Advanced system settings." Select the Advanced tab of System Properties, and click the Environment Variables button. You can then select the Path system variable, and click Edit to modify it. You shouldn't delete any paths, but you can add paths by entering a semicolon and the additional paths.

RDC EXPERIENCE TAB

You can add or remove different features from the RDC Experience tab. Different features such as the desktop background, menu and window animations, and visual styles are available to enhance the remote connection's display or experience.

Figure 17.10 shows the RDC Experience tab with the connection speed set to "LAN (10 Mbps or higher)." These features take additional bandwidth, so default features are selected based on the connection speed selected on this page.

FIGURE 17.10
Remote Desktop Connection Experience tab

If you're connected in a local LAN, you have high-speed connectivity, so all of the features are available. If you see a decrease in performance, you can deselect some of the features. Additionally, if you connect using a modem over a 56 Kbps connection, you could select the Modem (56 Kbps) setting, and only persistent bitmap caching will be enabled by default.

The speed selection isn't automatically determined. When it is selected, default features are selected, but you can easily add or remove these features by selecting or deselecting the corresponding check boxes.

This page also includes the setting "Reconnect if the connection is dropped." This is useful on unreliable links. If the network connection is dropped, RDC will automatically try to reconnect.

RDC ADVANCED TAB

The RDC Advanced tab includes two sections: "Server authentication" and "Connect from anywhere."

Server authentication is a new security feature available when connecting to Windows Server 2008 or later servers. It provides verification that you are connecting to the computer that you intended to connect to, and it helps prevent the unintentional disclosure of confidential information.

You have three choices with server authentication:

Connect and Don't Warn Me   You can use this if you are consistently connecting to pre–Windows Server 2008 servers that don't support server authentication. Since these servers don't support server authentication, they will always give warnings.

Warn Me   This is the default. It would be used in a mixed environment of Windows Server servers and Windows 2003 (or older) servers.

Do Not Connect   If your environment is all Windows Server 2008 servers or newer, this setting will ensure that connections aren't created if the server can't authenticate.

Figure 17.11 shows the Remote Desktop Connection Advanced tab with the Remote Desktop Gateway (RD Gateway) settings expanded.

FIGURE 17.11
Remote Desktop
Connection
Advanced tab
and Remote
Desktop Gateway
settings

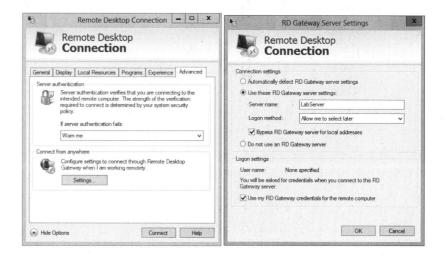

If you are connecting to a remote server through an RD Gateway server, you will configure the connection settings here. RD Gateway will be covered in more detail later in this chapter.

The important thing to realize is that the server name you enter here is that of the gateway server. RDC will connect to this RDC server first and then to the remote server identified on the General tab.

You will need to authenticate with both the RD Gateway server and the remote computer. If you use the same credentials for both, you can leave the "Use my RD Gateway credentials for the remote computer" check box selected. With this check box selected, you will be challenged only once. If you deselect it, you will be challenged at both servers, and you can enter different credentials for each.

Although knowing what each of the tabs within the Remote Desktop Connection can do for you is useful, you'll want to know some other details. For example, you can launch it from the command line, and with any command-line command, there are useful switches to master. Additionally, you can control several different limitations on remote connections.

MSTSC

You can launch the Remote Desktop Connection from the Run line or the command line using the `mstsc.exe` command. The name `mstsc` is derived from Microsoft Terminal Services Connection. Even though Terminal Services has been renamed to Remote Desktop Services, the `mstsc` command is still the same.

You can access the help screen for `mstsc` by entering **mstsc /?** at the command line. The following items show some of the common usages for `mstsc`:

Default Usage   Use the following command to launch Remote Desktop Connection (RDC):

`mstsc`

Identify a Server   Connect to a server named Srv1 using the `/v` switch:

`mstsc /v:Srv1`

Use an RDP File   Launch RDC using an RDP file located in the path `c:\data\srv1.rdp`:

`mstsc c:\data\Srv1.rdp`

Connect in Full-Screen Mode   Use the `/f` switch to launch RDC in full-screen mode after the connection is established:

`mstsc /f`

Use Multiple Monitors   If you want RDC to be able to span multiple monitors available on your local system, use the `/span` switch. This will cause the remote system to use the same width and height of your local desktop.

`mstsc /span`

Connect for Administrative Purposes   The `/admin` switch is used to connect to a Windows Server 2012 R2 server for administrative purposes. This is meaningful only if the server has the Remote Desktop Services installed. In other words, when the server is being used for Remote Desktop for Administration mode only, all connections are for administrative purposes, and this switch isn't needed. However, if the server is configured as a Remote Desktop Session Host server, you can use this switch to connect to one of the two administrator sessions.

You can also use the /admin switch to launch RDC in legacy console mode when connecting to Windows Server 2003 servers. Windows Server 2003 servers support a console session that isn't supported in Windows Server 2012 R2. The /admin switch will connect to the console session in Windows Server 2003.

CONNECTION LIMITATIONS

Only two connections are allowed to the server when it is used for normal administrative connections. In other words, only two administrators can be logged onto a single server at a time.

If the server is used to host desktops or applications for end users, then you can have as many connections as you need. Remote Desktop Services requires licenses for connections when used in Remote Desktop session host server mode. However, licenses are not required for the two administrator connections.

The two connections include either remote sessions or the session at the computer. Previous operating systems allowed you to connect to two remote sessions and the session at the computer. The session at the computer was referred to as the *console session* and you were even able to connect to this console session remotely, but the console session is no longer available.

Figure 17.12 shows the result if a third user tries to connect when two sessions are already active.

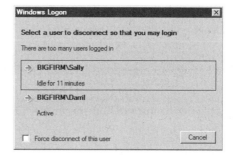

In the figure, a user named Darril is physically located at the server and logged on. Sally is connected via a remote session. Joe tries to log on, but since his session will be the third session, it is blocked. Notice that the dialog box also indicates whether these sessions are active or idle. In the figure, Sally's session has been idle for 11 minutes, and Darril's session is active.

If Joe selects the check box next to "Force disconnect of this user" and selects one of the users, that user will be immediately disconnected with a message saying this:

> *Your Remote Desktop session has ended. Another user connected to the remote computer so your connection was lost. Try connecting again, or contact your network administrator or technical support group.*

If Joe doesn't select the check box but instead just selects one of the users to disconnect the session, the user will get a notification. Figure 17.13 shows what appears on Darril's session when Joe tries to disconnect it without the check box selected. If Darril is working at the computer, he can see this connection attempt and click Cancel to block it. Otherwise, the request will automatically disconnect Darril's session after 30 seconds and allow Joe's session.

FIGURE 17.13
Disconnect request

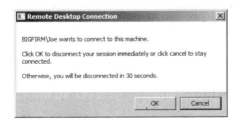

If Darril was active and clicked Cancel, Joe would receive a notification indicating that the logged-on user denied the disconnect request.

ACTIVE CONNECTIONS FOR INACTIVE SESSIONS

This method of closing an inactive administrator session provides a real-world solution to a common problem. We've worked in some large environments where administrators connect remotely to a server, but instead of logging off, they simply disconnect by closing the RDC application.

When this happens, the inactive session is left open on the server. If the server has reached the maximum number of sessions, other administrators can't log into a remote session. These inactive sessions would stay open until they timed out (if time-out settings were configured), the user logged back in and closed the session, or the session was closed in Remote Desktop Services Manager.

With the features now available in RDC, you can easily see who's connected, whether the session is active or idle, and even choose to disconnect the session.

INSTALLING REMOTE DESKTOP SERVICES WITH SESSION HOST SERVICE

For the next few sections of this chapter you will need the Remote Desktop Services role installed on the server.

To install this role, do the following:

1. Open the Server Manager Dashboard, and click Add Roles and Features.

2. Click Next to get past the "Before you begin" screen.

3. On the next screen (Figure 17.14) select "Role-based or feature-based installation."

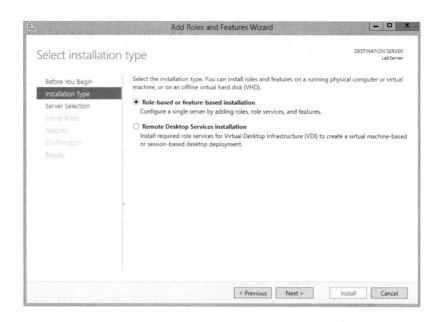

FIGURE 17.14
Select the type of
role installation

4. Next, select the server that you will install the role on.

   As you can see in Figure 17.15, we only have one server available to us. Select the server and click Next.

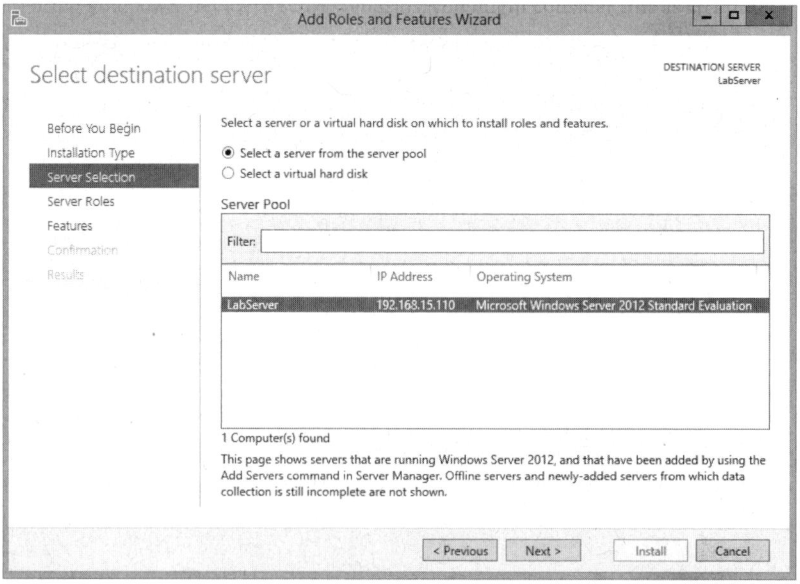

FIGURE 17.15
Select the server
on which to
install the RDS
role.

5. Select the Remote Desktop Services role, as shown in Figure 17.16, and click Next.

FIGURE 17.16
Selecting the
Remote Desktop
Services role

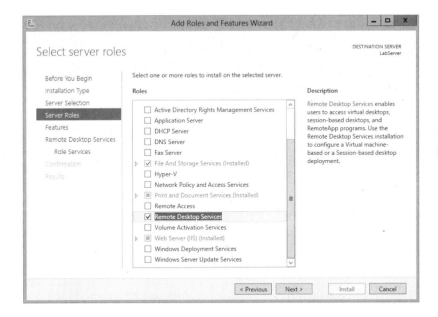

6. Since you do not need any features shown in the Features screen in Figure 17.17, just click Next to continue.

FIGURE 17.17
Features selection
screen

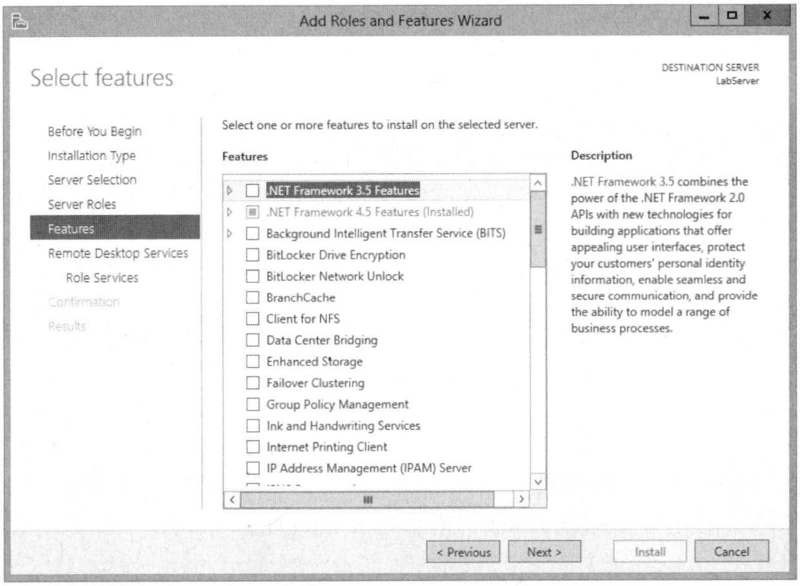

Figure 17.18 shows the summary screen explaining which role you are about to install. Seems like a waste to have this here. If you don't know what role you're installing by now, you should…never mind!

FIGURE 17.18
Role summary screen

7. In the next screen, shown in Figure 17.19, the following role services are available:

    Remote Desktop Connection Broker   Allows users to reconnect to their existing virtual desktops and session-based desktops. It also enables you to load-balance the pooled virtual desktops in a collection.

    Remote Desktop Gateway   Enables authorized users to connect to an internal corporate network from any Internet-connected device.

    Remote Desktop Licensing   Manages the licenses required to connect to a Remote Desktop Session Host server.

    Remote Desktop Session Host   Enables a server to host session-based desktops.

    Remote Desktop Virtualization Host   Integrates with Hyper-V to deploy pooled or personal virtual desktop collections within your organization by using Remote Desktop Connection.

    Remote Desktop Web Access   Allows users to connect via a web browser.

    Select Remote Desktop Session Host.

FIGURE 17.19
Selecting role
services

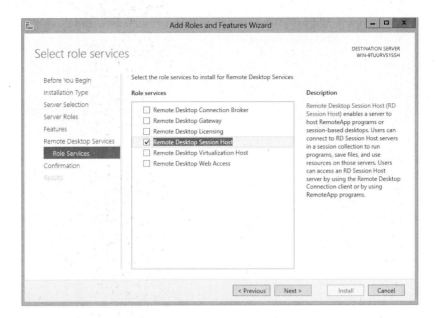

As you select the service you may get a pop-up screen asking you to install additional features to support your selections.

8. Select Add Features to install the supporting features.

Figure 17.20 shows the Network Policy and Access Services screen, letting us know we will need to also install this role service on the next screen.

FIGURE 17.20
Network
Policy and
Access Services
notification

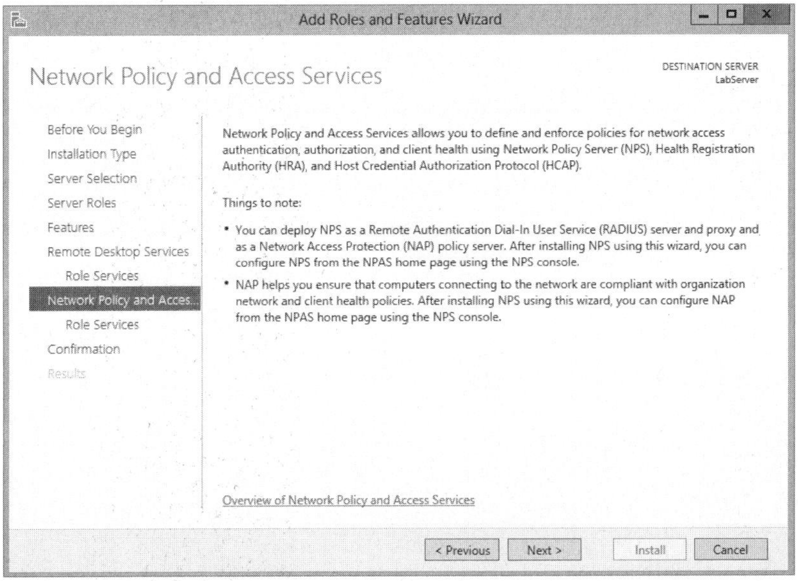

9. In Figure 17.21 you can see that the Network Policy Server is selected for us by default. Click Next to continue.

FIGURE 17.21
Network Policy
Server

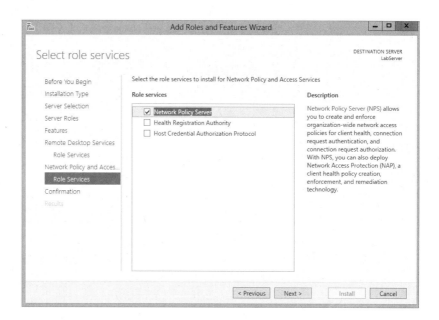

We are almost finished. In Figure 17.22 you see the confirmation page for the role we are about to install.

10. Check the box to restart the server after installation.

11. Click Install to begin the installation of the Remote Desktop Services and all its supporting features.

In Figure 17.23 you can see the progress of our installation.

12. After the server reboots, log in and you will see that the Server Manager menu has added the Remote Desktop Services option.

FIGURE 17.22
Role Confirmation
page

FIGURE 17.23
Installation
progress

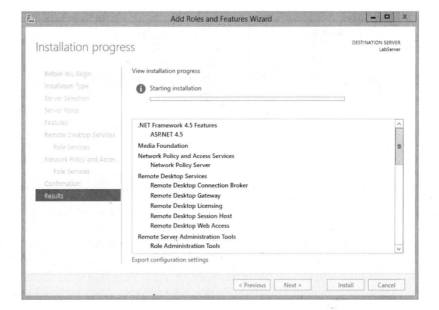

CONFIGURING HOST SESSION PROPERTIES

In Windows Server 2012 R2, you can no longer use the Remote Desktop Session Host Configuration Tool that you may have used in Windows Server 2008 R2.

You can configure session properties for remote sessions in the Remote Desktop Session Host from within Group Policy Management Editor. You can access this tool by hitting your Windows key and choosing Group Policy Management.

The primary configuration you'll use here when using Remote Desktop Services is the Remote Desktop Session Host. Figure 17.24 shows the properties available for Remote Desktop Session Host.

FIGURE 17.24
Using Group Policy
Manager to configure
Desktop Session Host

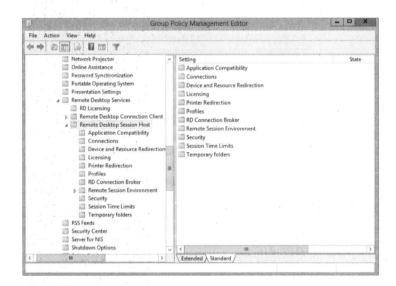

Since there are so many properties listed, we just discuss a couple of important ones you should be concerned with.

Security Since users will be remotely accessing the server, security properties should be an administrator's concern. The following are the security properties you can set:

Server Authentication Certificate Template This policy setting allows you to specify the name of the certificate template that determines which certificate is automatically selected to authenticate an RD Session Host server.

Set Client Connection Encryption Level This policy setting specifies whether to require the use of a specific encryption level to secure communications between client computers and RD Session Host servers during Remote Desktop Protocol connections.

Always Prompt for Password upon Connection You can use this setting to enforce a password prompt for users logging onto Remote Desktop Services, even if they already provided the password in the Remote Desktop Connection client.

Require Secure RPC Communications   You can use this setting to strengthen the security of RPC communication with clients by allowing only authenticated and encrypted requests.

Require Use of Specific Security Layer for Remote (RDP) Connections   This policy setting specifies whether to require the use of a specific security layer to secure communications between clients and RD Session Host servers during Remote Desktop Protocol connections.

Do Not Allow Local Administrators to Customize Permissions   You can use this setting to prevent administrators from making changes to the user groups allowed to connect remotely to the RD Session Host server. By default, administrators are able to make such changes.

Require User Authentication for Remote Connections by Using Network Level Authentication   If you enable this policy setting, only client computers that support Network Level Authentication can connect to the RD Session Host server.

Session Time Limits   The other properties you will probably find yourself changing will be the session time limits. The following are the session time limit properties with a short description of each.

Set Time Limit for Disconnected Sessions   You can use this policy setting to specify the maximum amount of time that a disconnected session remains active on the server. By default, Remote Desktop Services allows users to disconnect from a Remote Desktop Services session without logging off and ending the session.

Set Time Limit for Active but Idle Remote Desktop Services Sessions   If you enable this policy setting, you must select the desired time limit in the idle session limit list. Remote Desktop Services will automatically disconnect active but idle sessions after the specified amount of time. The user receives a warning two minutes before the session disconnects, which allows the user to press a key or move the mouse to keep the session active.

Set Time Limit for Active Remote Desktop Services Sessions   This policy setting allows you to specify the maximum amount of time that a Remote Desktop Services session can be active before it is automatically disconnected.

End Session When Time Limits Are Reached   This policy setting specifies whether to end a Remote Desktop Services session that has timed out instead of disconnecting it.

Set Time Limit for Logoff of RemoteApp Sessions   This policy setting allows you to specify how long a user's RemoteApp session will remain in a disconnected state before the session is logged off from the RD Session Host server.

By default, if a user closes a RemoteApp program, the session is disconnected from the RD Session Host server.

Although the Remote Desktop Connection is an extremely valuable tool to remotely administer servers within a controlled LAN, sometimes it won't meet your needs. For example, you may want to remotely connect to a server over the Internet, but the firewall administrators simply refuse to open the ports. Remote Desktop Gateway may be exactly what you need.

Remote Desktop Gateway

RD Gateway is used to allow connections to an internal network via the Internet. When RD Gateway is enabled, users can connect to resources on an internal network from any Internet-connected device. RD Gateway works the same way whether it's used to allow an administrator to access an internal resource or to allow a regular user to access a Session Host server, as covered in Chapter 29, "Installing, Using, and Administering Remote Desktop Services."

RD Gateway uses the Remote Desktop Protocol over HTTPS to establish a secure, encrypted connection between the remote users and the internal resource.

Figure 17.25 shows how RD Gateway could be configured. A Windows Server 2012 R2 server named BF4 is placed in the DMZ with the Remote Desktop Gateway role service installed. The client can connect to BF4 over the Internet using RDP over HTTPS.

FIGURE 17.25
RD Gateway providing access to an internal server

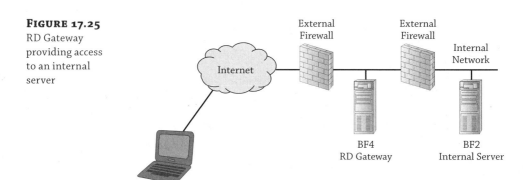

HTTPS uses Secure Sockets Layer (SSL) to encrypt the session and uses port 443. The external firewall needs port 443 open to support the HTTPS traffic.

BF4 will authenticate the client and act as the gateway to internal resources. RD Gateway can be configured with a resource authorization policy to restrict access to a single server (such as BF2 in the figure) or any resources in the network.

Remote Desktop Connection Authorization Policies (RD CAP) are used to restrict who can connect to the RD Gateway server. Remote Desktop Resource Authorization Policies (RD RAP) are used to restrict which servers can be accessed once a user connects.

TS GATEWAY RENAMED TO RD GATEWAY

RD Gateway was previously known as Terminal Services Gateway (TS Gateway). Since Terminal Services has been renamed to Remote Desktop Services, it has affected other names, including the RD Gateway.

In past versions of Windows, it was possible to remotely administer servers from the Internet. However, you had to open port 3389 on the firewall (or convince the firewall administrator to open the port). But every additional port opened on a firewall represents an additional vulnerability that needs to be managed.

From a security standpoint, it's much easier to simply leave the port closed. Even though remote administration through port 3389 was a useful feature, it was often blocked at the network firewall to mitigate the associated security risks.

Since RD Gateway uses RDP over HTTPS through port 443, the external firewall needs only port 443 open. Port 443 is commonly open to allow other HTTPS traffic through. If port 443 is open for other HTTPS traffic, you don't need to open additional ports to use RDP over HTTPS.

As an example, if a company was hosting a web server using HTTP and HTTPS, ports 80 and 443 would be open to support the web server. You can then implement RD Gateway on a server in the DMZ without modifying the firewall.

Even if port 443 isn't already open, the security of HTTPS is well understood by most administrators. It's easier for an administrator to weigh the risks of HTTPS and make a decision to open this port than it is to consider opening port 3389 for remote administration traffic.

REMOTE DESKTOP CONNECTION CLIENT

RD Gateway supports connections from Remote Desktop Connection 6.0 or greater. However, to support all the features available in RD Gateway in Windows Server 2012 R2, Remote Desktop Protocol 8.0 is recommended. This is natively provided in the RDC client supplied with Windows 8 and Windows 2012. The RDP 8.0 client is also available as an add-on for Windows 7 SP1 and Windows Server 2008 R2 SP1 (http://support.microsoft.com/kb/2592687).

Although these features are most useful when using Remote Desktop Services to host desktops and remote applications, administrators may find them useful too. These are some of the additional features that are available:

RemoteFX RemoteFX technologies enhance the user's visual user interface experience. There are a number of new improvements affecting RemoteFx:

- WAN support

- Network Auto Detect

- Adaptive Graphics

- Media Streaming

- USB Redirection for non-RemoteFX vGPU virtual desktops

Support for Nested Sessions You can now run a remote desktop session from within another remote desktop session.

Performance Counters for Monitoring the User Experience Performance counters let administrators monitor and troubleshoot user experience issues.

RD Gateway–Required Services and Features

RD Gateway requires the following additional role services and features on the Windows Server 2012 R2 server where it is hosted (which we had you install earlier in this section):

- Web Server (IIS) role:
    - Management Tools feature (to manage IIS)
    - Web Server services (support for HTML websites and ASP.NET)
- Network Policy and Access Services role: Network Policy Server services
- RPC over HTTP Proxy feature
- Remote Server Administration Tools feature

When you add the RD Gateway role, the wizard will prompt you to automatically install all the required roles, services, and features. You won't need to install them individually. However, if they are already installed, the wizard will recognize that they are active.

RD Gateway–Required Policies

Before users can connect through RD Gateway, you must have at least two policies:

RD Connection Authorization Policy (RD CAP)   RD CAP specifies the users who can connect to the RD Gateway server. For example, you may choose to give anyone in the Administrators group of the RD Gateway server permission to connect, or you could create a global security group (such as G RD Gateway Users) specifically for this purpose. You would then place any users for whom you want to grant connection access into this new global group.

RD Resource Allocation Policy (RD RAP)   RD RAP specifies the resources that users can access once they connect. For example, you may be creating this policy so that administrators can remotely administer a specific server. You would identify the server in RD RAP. Administrators could connect to this server but not to any other servers via the RD Gateway server.

It's also possible to configure RD RAP so that users can connect to any computer on the network without any restrictions.

Enabling Remote Desktop Gateway

Follow these steps to enable the Remote Desktop Gateway role service on a Windows Server 2012 R2 server. These steps will also lead you through adding the required roles, services, and features, as well as RD CAP and RD RAP:

1. Launch Server Manager from your taskbar.
2. Select Roles, and click Add Roles.
3. Review the information on the "Before you begin" page, and click Next.
4. Select the Role-Based Installation radio button and click Next.
5. Select the server to install it on, and click Next.
6. Expand the Remote Desktop Services role on the Select Server Roles page, and select Remote Desktop Gateway. Click Next.

7. You will be prompted that additional features may need to be installed. Click Add Features.

8. When the pop-up closes, click Next.

9. Click Next again on the features page.

10. Review the information on the Network Policy and Access Services page, and click Next.

11. Network Policy should be a selected role service; click Next.

12. Review the Confirmation page, select the check box to restart the server if needed, and click Install.

After a few minutes and a server reboot, you should have RD Gateway installed on your server. To access it you can hit your Windows key. You will see a new Metro-style button called Remote Desktop Gateway, as shown in Figure 17.26.

FIGURE 17.26
Remote Desktop Gateway

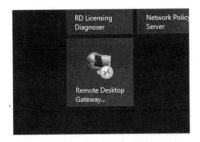

Once you get inside the RD Gateway Manager, you can see that it's very similar to the Group Policy Management tool. You can manage all aspects of the RD Gateway using this tool.

On the left window pane you will see your server with two folders underneath: Policies and Monitoring. If you click the server you will see current connection information and any outstanding configurations required, as shown in Figure 17.27.

As you can see in Figure 17.27, we still need to configure the Gateway certificate.

1. Click the link "View or modify certificate properties."

    The Choose a Server Authentication Certificate for SSL Encryption page will appear. You can install an existing certificate, create a self-signed certificate, or import a certificate.

    You can purchase a certificate from an external CA or obtain one from an internal CA.

2. For these steps, choose the option "Create a self-signed certificate for SSL encryption." Click "Create and Import Certificate."

3. In Figure 17.28 you see that we can create our self-signed certificate using the defaults. Click OK.

FIGURE 17.27
Gateway connection
information

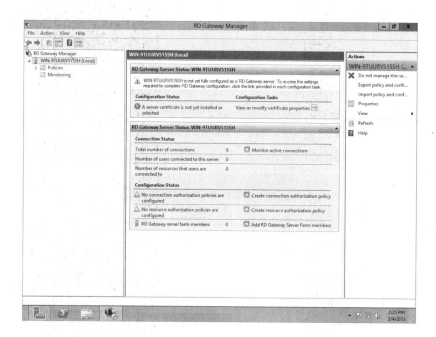

FIGURE 17.28
Create your
self-signed
certificate.

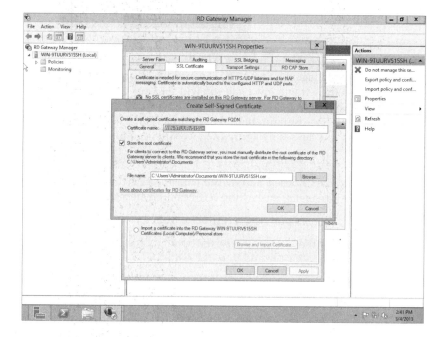

You can see in Figure 17.29 that our certificate has installed successfully.

FIGURE 17.29
Certificate installed
properly

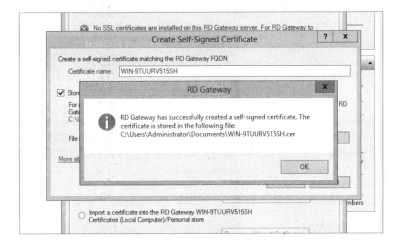

Figure 17.30 shows that we still have a few configuration items to attend to. The first one is Remote Desktop Connection Authorization Policy, and the other is Remote Desktop Resource Authorization Policies. For those of you familiar with Windows Server 2008 R2, you may have noticed that all three of these, starting with the certificate, are configured during the installation of the Remote Desktop Services role. In Windows Server 2012 R2 they get configured in Gateway Manager.

FIGURE 17.30
Requirements needed
to complete gateway
configuration

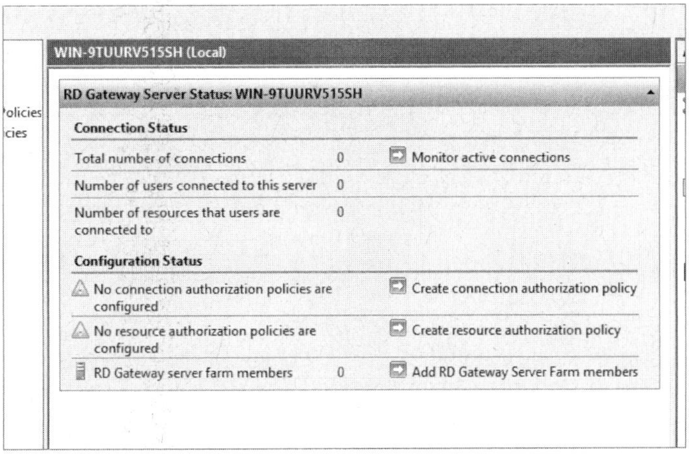

OBTAINING A CERTIFICATE FROM A CA

Self-signed certificates are useful for testing, but it is not recommended to use a self-signed certificate in a production environment. Instead, you should obtain a certificate from a certificate authority. Since a certificate used by RD Gateway for administration will be used only by administrators, you can use an internal CA to create a certificate instead of purchasing a certificate from an external CA.

---

1. Let's configure RD CAP by selecting the link "Create connection authorization policy," shown in Figure 17.30.

2. Under the General tab of the New RD CAP dialog box, enter a policy name, as shown in Figure 17.31.

FIGURE 17.31
Enter a policy name.

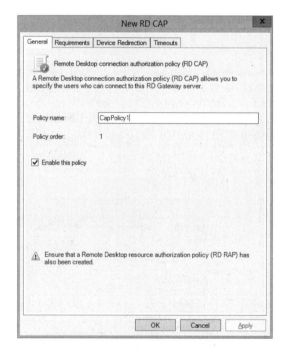

Under the Requirements tab, you can add permissions for groups and client computer membership. As you can see in Figure 17.32, we added Remote Management Users.

The next tab is Device Redirection, allowing or denying the use of these devices during the session.

FIGURE 17.32
Requirements tab

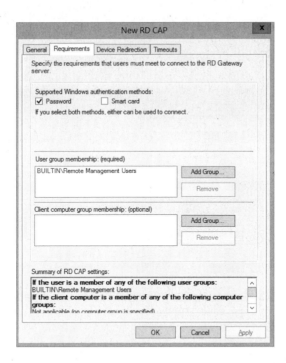

3. As shown in Figure 17.33, select the default to allow all devices on the client.

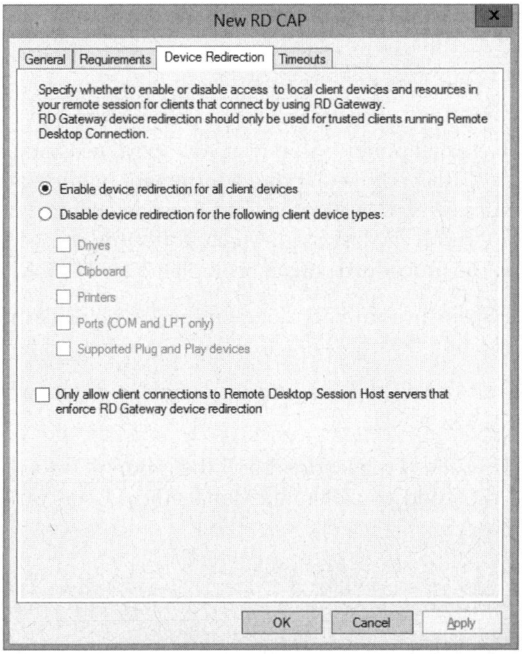

FIGURE 17.33
Device Redirection tab

4. The last tab is the Timeouts tab. Set your session timeouts as desired (see Figure 17.34).

FIGURE 17.34
Timeouts tab

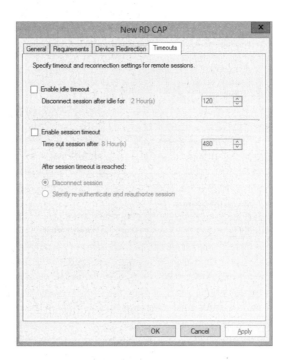

5. Click OK.

Your newly created policy will now show up in the Connection Authorization Policy window. You will also notice that the requirement on the Gateway property has been fulfilled.

As we mentioned earlier, we also need to set the Remote Desktop Resource Authorization Policy. This will fulfill the last requirement to setting up the Remote Desktop Gateway. This is very similar to the procedure you just completed for RD CAP:

1. On the Gateway summary page for the server, click the link Create Resource Authorization Policy. This will open the properties for the RD RAP.

2. Under the General tab, add a policy name and policy description, as we have done in Figure 17.35.

3. The User Groups tab is for adding the group permission for this policy. As shown in Figure 17.36, add your Remote Management Users group.

FIGURE 17.35
Add a policy name and description.

FIGURE 17.36
Add a group to the User Groups tab.

4. Under the Network Resource tab, add the network resource groups.

5. Select "Allow users to connect to any network resource," as shown in Figure 17.37.

6. The last tab is for selecting allowed ports; select to allow only port 3389, as shown in Figure 17.38.

FIGURE 17.37
Network Resource tab

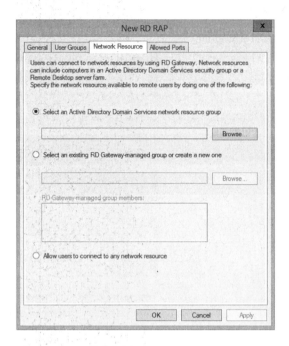

FIGURE 17.38
Allow Ports tab

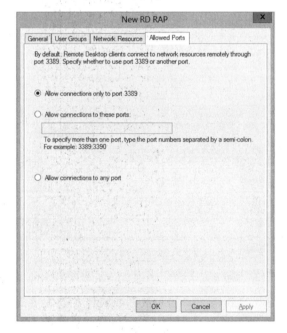

Congratulations! Your gateway is now configured and ready to allow connections.

Remote Desktop Connection and Remote Gateway are both valuable tools used to remotely administer servers. However, each of these will launch as single instances. There may be times when you're charged with managing multiple servers and you want to manage them through a single tool. Remote Desktops is your solution.

Configuring a Server for Remote Assistance

Remote Assistance is primarily a feature used on desktop systems and is not enabled by default on Windows Server 2012 R2. However, if you have a large organization with junior administrators in remote locations, it can be very useful to you.

For example, imagine you work at the main location of your company and your company has a remote office with only 20 people. One of these employees occasionally performs routine tasks on the server located in the remote office but may need some help. With Remote Assistance enabled, they can send you a request for assistance. You can then access the remote server's desktop and demonstrate how to perform a task.

The Remote Assistance check box in System Properties is grayed out and can't be enabled until the Remote Assistance feature is added to Windows Server 2012 R2. The following steps show how to enable Remote Assistance:

1. Launch Server Manager.

2. Select "Add roles and features."

3. Accept the defaults until you get to the features.

4. Select the Remote Assistance check box, and click Next.

5. Click Install on the Confirmation page.

6. When the wizard completes, click Close.

With the Remote Assistance feature added, Remote Assistance should now be enabled on the server. You can verify it with these steps:

1. Press the Windows key, right-click Computer, and select Properties from the taskbar.

2. Click Remote Settings.

3. Verify that the "Allow Remote Assistance connections to this computer" check box is selected.

4. Click the Advanced button. Verify that the "Allow this computer to be controlled remotely" check box is selected.

    The default lifetime of invitations is six hours, but it can be changed. After the time limit has passed, the invitation can no longer be used to connect.

This server is now configured for Remote Assistance. To start a Remote Assistance session, the user needs to send a Remote Assistance request.

SENDING A REMOTE ASSISTANCE REQUEST

The user who needs assistance should follow these steps to create a Remote Assistance request and begin the process:

1. Click Start, type **msra** in the Run box, and press Enter. The Windows Remote Assistance dialog box will appear.

2. Click "Invite someone you trust to help you."

3. Click "Save this invitation as a file."

4. Browse to a location on your hard drive. The invitation file is named Invitation .msrcIncident by default but can be changed if desired. Click Save.

5. A password is automatically created and can't be changed. You'll need to tell the helper this password.

6. Send the invitation to a helper as an email attachment, or place it on a share accessible to the helper.

At this point, the person needing help must wait for the response from the helper.

RESPONDING TO A REMOTE ASSISTANCE REQUEST

The helper can follow these steps with the person requesting assistance to begin a Remote Assistance session:

1. Double-click the invitation received from the person requesting help.

   This invitation could have been received via email or available on a share. It will take a moment for this invitation to open.

2. Enter the password in the Windows Remote Assistance dialog box, and click OK.

   If you enter an incorrect password, you will be notified immediately.

   The user requesting help will see a dialog box appear asking whether they want to allow the connection.

3. The user should click Yes.

   At this point, you will be able to see everything on the user's desktop, but you won't be able to interact with the desktop.

4. Click the Request Control button at the top of the Windows Remote Assistance window.

   The user will see a dialog box appear asking whether they want to allow the helper to share control of the desktop.

5. The user should click Yes.

   Note that the user has complete control and can deny the request. However, since the user requested assistance and gave the password, they would click Yes.

The helper can now control the mouse on the remote computer. Figure 17.39 shows the Windows Remote Assistance window viewed by the person being helped.

FIGURE 17.39
Remote Assistance
session on a
remote computer

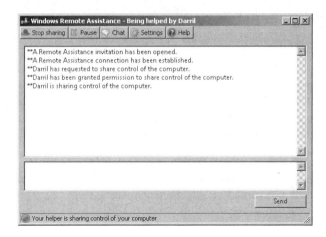

At this point, the helper can manipulate the mouse and keyboard of the remote desktop to demonstrate any tasks. This is shared control. In other words, both the helper and the user have control over the desktop.

It's useful if the helper and user are able to talk over the phone during this process, but it's not necessary. The Windows Remote Assistance dialog boxes include a Chat feature that allows each of the users to type questions and comments.

The helper could demonstrate a task and then simply type "now you try it" while observing the desktop. The helper could stop using the mouse, and the user could perform the same steps on their computer. Additionally, the user being helped can end the session whenever they want to by clicking Stop Sharing or Pause.

Windows Remote Management Service

The Windows Remote Management Service (WinRM) will allow you to issue any command-line command from one computer against a remote computer.

For example, you may be working on a Windows 7 or Windows 8 computer, but you want to query some information from a remote server. If the server has been configured with WinRM, you can execute a WinRS command-line command from the desktop system and get the results just as if you were at the computer or connected with RDC.

One of the benefits of this is that you don't need to consume one of the two remote sessions for a server or even launch RDC. You can simply enter the command at your command prompt.

The following are the two commands used by the Windows Remote Management Service:

WinRM The WinRM tool is executed on the remote server and enables the server to listen and respond to WinRS requests.

WinRS The WinRS tool is executed from the command line on a desktop or other server accessed by an administrator. It allows the administrator to execute any command-line commands against the remote server.

Enabling WinRM

WinRM is not enabled by default on Windows Server 2012 R2. You can use the following steps to enable WinRM on the server.

RD GATEWAY ENABLES WINRM

WinRM is not enabled to allow remote access for management by default. However, if you followed the steps to enable RD Gateway earlier in this chapter, you'll find that WinRM has been enabled on the same server. RD Gateway uses the Windows Remote Management service and enables it when the role service is installed. If you follow these steps, it will inform you that WinRM is already configured.

---

1. Select Power Shell and type **cmd** at the command prompt.

2. Type the following command, and press Enter:

   WinRM qc

   You will be promoted to allow the following changes to be made on your system:

   ◆ Create a WinRM listener on HTTP://* to access WS-Man requests to any IP on this machine.

   ◆ Enable the WinRM firewall exception.

   ◆ Configure LocalAccountTokenFilterPolicy to grant administrative rights remotely to local users.

3. Type **Y**, and press Enter to accept the changes.

   You will see a status message indicating the changes have been completed.

4. Type **WinRM /?** to see the help available for the Windows Remote Management command-line tool.

   WinRM includes a rich set of commands, and the help file can help you dig deeper if desired.

5. Type in the following command to enumerate (list) the properties for WinRM:

   WinRM enumerate WinRM/config/listener

   Notice that there is a space between WinRM and enumerate, and there is a second space between enumerate and WinRM, but no other spaces are used.

   This command will give you some of the details on how the service is configured and verification that it is enabled to listen on the HTTP transport using all the available IP addresses on your system. Notice that you can also type in the command with just the first letter of *enumerate* (e) as follows:

   WinRM e WinRM /config/listener

You can change the format of the output by modifying the -format switch. By default, the output is shown in text format, but you can output it as simple XML (using the -format:#XML switch) or formatted XML (using the -format:#pretty switch).

6. Try the following commands:

```
WinRM e WinRM /config/listener -format:#text
WinRM e WinRM /config/listener -format:#xml
WinRM e WinRM /config/listener -format:#pretty
```

Although there is more you can do with WinRM on the server, its primary purpose for remote administration is to enable the listener with the quickconfig command. Once this is done, you'll probably turn your attention to the client where you'll do the actual administration.

Using WinRS

The Windows Remote Shell (WinRS) is used to execute commands against a remote server that has been configured with WinRM. For example, you could use WinRS from a Windows 7 or Windows 8 system to execute commands against a remote server.

WinRS commands are primarily formatted as follows:

```
WinRS -r:servername command
```

The -r switch is used to identify the name of the remote server. Although other switches are available, the -r switch is the switch used the most.

ISSUING WMIC COMMANDS WITH WINRS

WinRS commands can be any command that you would issue from the command line. As an example, you can use the Windows Management Instrumentation Command-line (WMIC) tool to document the services running on computers.

Before using WinRS, you can use this command to show how WMIC can be used to document information on services running on any system. Launch a command line, and enter this command:

```
Wmic /output:services.htm /node:localhost service list brief /format:htable
```

This creates an HTML-formatted file named services.htm. You can view it by entering **services.htm** at the command prompt, which will launch Internet Explorer displaying the document. This lists all of the services on the system, as well as the start mode, the state, the status, and some additional details.

Now, use the same command to document the services of a remote computer that has been configured with WinRS. Substitute Srv2012 for the name of the server you have configured with WinRS, and change the name of the HTML file:

```
WinRS -r:Srv2012 Wmic /output:Srv2012services.htm /node:Srv2012 service list
brief /format:htable
```

You can view this file by entering the name of the file at the command prompt. In this example, it is Srv2012services.htm.

If you want more details on the services, change `list brief` to **`list full`**. This simple tool can easily give you some important documentation on multiple servers that you can easily print or save.

ISSUING POWERSHELL COMMANDS WITH WINRS

Although WMIC is certainly feature rich, it's not the only command you can use. Any command that you can enter at the server you can also enter remotely using WinRS. This includes PowerShell commands. The following link shows the PowerShell cmdlets:

```
http://msdn.microsoft.com/en-us/library/windows/desktop/ee309371(v=vs.85).aspx
```

PowerShell commands follow a verb-noun format. The verb specifies an action, and the noun identifies the object on which the action will take place.

The most popular verb is `get`, and if you enter **`get-`** at the PowerShell command prompt, you can tab through all the nouns associated with the `get` verb.

Other verbs include `set`, `copy`, `move`, and many more. You can do the same thing with any of the verbs; enter the verb with a hyphen (-), and tab through all the possible nouns associated with the verb. For a full list of the verbs, check out this MSDN page: `http://msdn.microsoft.com/en-us/library/ms714428(VS.85).aspx`.

For example, you can enter the following PowerShell command from the PowerShell prompt to check the status of services on a system:

```
Get-Service
```

You don't even need to type in the entire command. You can just type **`Get-S`** and press the Tab key.

This command will list all the services on the system with the status (running or stopped), name, and display name. Using this with WinRS, you can execute the same command remotely:

```
WinRS -r:SRV2012 PowerShell Get-Service
```

If you want to redirect this to a file, you can add the > redirect character as follows:

```
WinRS -r:SRV2012 PowerShell Get-Service > services.txt
```

The output will be stored in a file named `services.txt`. You can then open the file with Notepad from the command line with this command:

```
Notepad services.txt
```

Remote Server Administration Tools

The Remote Server Administration Tools (RSAT) are tools you need to manage roles and features on a Windows Server 2012 R2 server from your desktop operating system.

Although Remote Desktop Connection and Remote Desktops allow you to connect to the desktop of a server, sometimes you simply need to do a single task such as resetting a password on a user account or verifying that DNS is configured correctly.

RSAT includes tools like Active Directory Users and Computers (ADUC) and the DNS console. After installing RSAT on a desktop, you can launch ADUC to manipulate user accounts, or you can launch the DNS console to verify DNS configuration.

Users still need the appropriate permissions to run the installed tools. For example, a junior administrator who installs the tools on their desktop system won't be added to the Enterprise Admins role and suddenly be able to perform anything in the forest.

The tools available in RSAT can be used to Manage Windows Server 2012 R2 roles and features.

RSAT Compatibility Issues

RSAT is not compatible with the Administration Tools Pack used to remotely administer Windows Server 2000 and Windows Server 2003 servers. If you have these tools installed on your system, you must first uninstall them before installing RSAT.

Additionally, RSAT won't allow you to remotely manage a server with the Streaming Media Services role. There are separate Remote Server Administration Tools for the Streaming Media Services role you can download and install to manage a Windows Server 2012 R2 server hosting the Streaming Media Services role.

For more information on issues with a Streaming Media Services role server, check out the Microsoft KB article at http://support.microsoft.com/kb/934518. The RSAT information is located near the end of the article.

RSAT Tools

After installing RSAT on a desktop system, you'll have access to a full suite of tools that you'd find on a Windows Server 2012 R2 server with all of the roles and features installed. As long as the remote server has the appropriate role or feature installed, you can use the client-side RSAT tool to administer it.

In other words, if a server is running the DHCP role, you can use the DHCP console to remotely administer it. However, if the server isn't a DHCP server, you can't use the RSAT-installed DHCP console to make it a DHCP server.

The following list shows some of the more commonly used tools available with RSAT. This isn't meant to be an exhaustive list but instead a summary of some of the commonly used tools. For a complete list, check out the Microsoft KB article at http://support.microsoft.com/kb/941317.

Active Directory Domain Services Tools   The AD DS tools include Active Directory Users and Computers, Active Directory Domains and Trusts, Active Directory Sites and Services, and other snap-ins and command-line tools for remotely managing Active Directory Domain Services.

Active Directory Certificate Services Tools   These tools include the Active Directory Certification Authority tools used for enterprise certificate authorities and certificate authority tools used for stand-alone certificate authorities.

Dynamic Host Configuration Protocol Server Tools   The DHCP snap-in tool is included.

Domain Name System Server Tools   DNS tools include the DNS Manager snap-in and the Dnscmd.exe command-line tool.

File Services Tools   These tools include the Share and Storage Management snap-in, Distributed File System tools, and the File Server Resource Manager tools.

Network Policy and Access Services Tools   The Routing and Remote Access snap-in is included for network policy and network access.

Remote Desktop Services Tools   Remote Desktops and Remote Desktop Services Manager snap-ins are included.

BitLocker Drive Encryption Tools   The `Manage-bde.wsf` script is included for BitLocker Drive Encryption.

Failover Clustering Tools   These tools include the Failover Cluster Manager snap-in and the `Cluster.exe` command-line tool.

Group Policy Management Tools   The Group Policy Management Console, Group Policy Management Editor, and Group Policy Starter GPO Editor are all included.

Network Load Balancing Tools   The Network Load Balancing Manager utility and the `Nlb.exe` and `Wlbs.exe` command-line tools are included.

SMTP Server Tools   The SMTP snap-in is available.

Storage Manager for SANs Tools   The Storage Manager for SANs snap-in and the `ProvisionStorage.exe` command-line tool are both included.

Windows System Resource Manager Tools   The Windows System Resource Manager snap-in and the `Wsrmc.exe` command-line tool are included.

Installing RSAT

RSAT is available as a free download from Microsoft. You can download RSAT by going to the Microsoft download site at `www.Microsoft.com/downloads` and typing **RSAT**.

32-Bit and 64-Bit Versions of RSAT

Both 32-bit and 64-bit versions of RSAT are available. These need to match the platform where you're installing RSAT. In other words, if you're running 32-bit Windows 8 on your desktop, you need the 32-bit version of RSAT to remotely manage a 64-bit Windows Server 2012 R2 server.

Once you've downloaded RSAT, you can follow these steps to install and enable RSAT:

1. Use Windows Explorer to browse to where you saved the download.

2. Double-click the installation package, and follow the wizard to complete the installation.

3. When the installation completes, click Close.

   Normally you'd expect the installation to be complete at this point, but you need to take extra steps to enable RSAT on your system.

4. Select Start ➢ Control Panel to launch Control Panel.

5. Select Programs and then click "Turn Windows features on or off." If prompted by User Account Control, click Continue.

6. Select the Remote Server Administration Tools check box. Your display will look similar to Figure 17.40.

FIGURE 17.40
Adding the Remote Server
Administration Tools feature

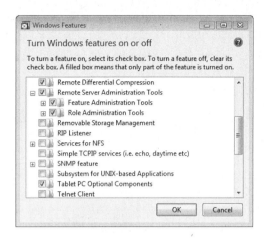

You can pick and choose individual feature and role administration tools if desired, or you can simply add them all by selecting the Remote Server Administration Tools check box.

7. Click OK. The tools will be configured to work on your system.

If Administrative Tools does not show on your Start menu, you can add the tools by following these steps:

1. Right-click the Start menu, and select Properties.

2. Ensure that the Start Menu tab is selected, and click Customize.

3. Scroll to the "System administrative tools" section close to the bottom of the customization window. Select "Display on the All Programs menu and the Start menu."

4. Click OK twice.

Once RSAT is installed on a system, you can use the tools in the same way you would use them on a server.

Remote Desktop and PowerShell

Before we close out this chapter, let's discuss how you can use PowerShell to remotely connect to another PowerShell session. If you do not plan on using PowerShell to remotely administer your server, then you can skip this section. If you plan on using PowerShell, then stick around and see how you can connect remotely using PowerShell cmdlets.

When you are sending cmdlets to the server, you will need to provide a username and password just like in the Remote Desktop UI. If you have to type several commands, you will have to enter this username and password for each command. To get around this you can assign the username and password to a session variable that will be hold the credentials for you.

When you enter the following command, you will see a login pop-up appear to enter your credentials (see Figure 17.41).

```
$cr = Get-Credential -Credential jpwebconsulting\administrator
```

FIGURE 17.41
Login credential pop-up screen

Now all your login information is stored in the $cr variable. You will see in the next cmdlet how this will be of use to you. The next cmdlet you will use is your connection to the remote system. You can now see the variable in use:

```
Enter-PSSession -ComputerName TestServer-1 -Credential $cr
```

You are now connected remotely to the server via PowerShell. You should see the following command prompt, and you will see that it switched over to TestServer-1. You can now administer the server as if you were sitting in front of it. I bet you didn't think it was that easy!

```
[TestServer-1]: PS C:\Users\Administrator\Documents>
```

The Bottom Line

Configure Windows Server 2012 R2 servers for remote administration. Servers must be configured to allow remote administration before administrators can connect remotely.

Master It Configure a server to allow remote connections by clients running RDC version 6.0 or greater.

Remotely connect to Windows Server 2012 R2 servers using Remote Desktop Connection. You can remotely connect to servers to do almost any administrative work. Servers are often located in a secure server room that is kept cool to protect the electronics. They can be in a different room, a different building, or even a separate geographical location, but they can still be remotely administered using either RDC or Remote Desktops.

Master It Connect to a server using RDC. Ensure your local drives are accessible when connected to the remote server.

Remotely connect to Windows Server 2012 R2 servers using a Remote Desktop Protocol file. If you regularly connect to a remote server using RDC, you can configure an RDP file that can be preconfigured based on your needs for this server. This RDP file will store all the settings you configure for this connection.

Master It Create an RDP file that you can use to connect with a server named Server1. Configure the file to automatically launch Server Manager when connected.

Configure a server for Remote Assistance. When your environment includes remote locations where junior administrators may occasionally need assistance, you can use Remote Assistance to access their session and demonstrate procedures.

Master It Configure a server for Remote Assistance.

Install the Remote Server Administration Tools. The Remote Assistance Server Administration Tools (RSAT) include the snap-ins and command-line tools needed to manage Server 2003, Server 2008, and Server 2012 servers from Windows Vista and Windows 7 and 8.

Master It Obtain and install RSAT on a Windows Vista or Windows 7 or 8 system.

Chapter 18

Connecting Windows and Mac Clients

You've built your server, created users, and shared network resources. Now you need to configure your client systems to connect to the network and use those resources. In this chapter, we'll show you how to set up various client systems with networking components, how to log on to the network, how to find and connect to shared resources, how to manage your passwords, and, when applicable, how to find and connect to Active Directory.

We also cover ways to connect your Mac clients to your Windows Server 2012 network and how to access various features such as file shares and printers from the Mac.

In this chapter, you'll learn to:

◆ Verify your network configuration

◆ Join a client computer to a domain

◆ Change user passwords

◆ Connect to network resources

◆ Prepare Active Directory for Mac OS X clients

◆ Connect a Mac to the domain

◆ Connect to file shares and printers

◆ Use Remote Desktop from a Mac client

What to Know Before You Begin

Before you connect workstations to the domain, you should know a few things about client computers and the network environment. If you are new to Microsoft networks, you may want to review some other chapters before attempting to configure clients:

◆ Chapter 2, "Installing and Upgrading to Windows Server 2012 R2," covers the basics of networking software and security.

◆ Chapter 4, "Windows Server 2012 R2 Networking Enhancements," and Chapter 20, "Advanced IP: Routing with Windows," deal with TCP/IP and infrastructure. Microsoft networks almost universally use TCP/IP.

◆ Chapter 8, "Creating and Managing User Accounts," shows you how to set up user accounts and computer accounts.

◆ Chapter 29, "Installing, Using, and Administering Remote Desktop Services," covers connecting clients to domain resources using Remote Desktop.

If you've read these chapters or are generally familiar with the concepts, then read on to learn more about the client networking stack and about the kinds of accounts you'll need.

Throughout this chapter, we'll connect to the same server, on the same domain, and with the same user account:

◆ The username is kevinb (if acting as a regular user) or bigadmin (if acting as a domain administrator).

◆ The domain name is bigfirm.com.

◆ There is a Windows Server 2012 domain controller on the network called bf1.bigfirm.com.

◆ There are several client machines on the network, representing the client operating systems we will deal with in this chapter. Their names are:

  ◆ WIN8CLIENT

  ◆ WIN7CLIENT

Understanding Client-side Software Requirements

In the past, for each client you would have to configure three basic software components: a *driver* for the network interface card (NIC), a *network protocol*, and a *network client*. The good news is that, these days, everything you need is built in except on a rare occasion you will need to install an NIC driver.

So that you will have a clear understanding of the underlining technology that makes all of this work, we will review these three basic components.

The NIC driver allows the operating system to communicate with the NIC. Before loading any network protocol or client software, the operating system must recognize the network card and load the appropriate driver. Because of the advancement of Universal Plug and Play (UPnP) and built-in driver libraries, most of the client systems discussed in this chapter can automatically detect the NIC and load a driver included with the OS. If the driver is not included with the OS or if your client system fails to detect the network card, you must use the driver and installation instructions for your OS that are provided by the manufacturer.

The network protocol, built into the operating system, allows nodes on the same network to communicate with each other. To communicate, the nodes must all use the same protocols. TCP/IP is the de facto standard for Microsoft networks today. Since most networks use IPv4, we'll use that version throughout this chapter. Having a good understanding of IPv6 is becoming much more relevant in today's networks and we recommend that you become knowledgeable on this subject.

WINDOWS RT

Outside of the overall networking components and protocols, the IT pro also needs to understand how to connect other versions of Windows, such as Windows RT and how connections in Windows RT work. These devices are designed as preconfigured versions of the Windows operating system, and any additions are done through the Microsoft Store.

Windows RT is an ARM-based system that was designed specifically for tablet devices that need to be light and sleek and have long battery life. (More information on ARM is available at `http://tinyurl.com/c18WinRTARM`.)

Since Windows RT devices have an operating system that cannot be changed, enterprises are unable to customize their Windows image on these devices and thus they cannot join a Windows domain. We will discuss some of the connection options of Windows RT as we move through this chapter. The following link will provide you with some additional information on Windows RT: `http://windows.microsoft.com/en-US/windows/rt-welcome`.

WINDOWS SERVER 2012 SUPPORT FOR IPV6

In Windows Server 2012 and Windows 8, IPv6 is installed and enabled by default. For more information on this protocol and configuring it for your environment, refer to Chapter 4, "Windows Server 2012 R2 Networking Enhancements."

The clients in the examples throughout this chapter will obtain a unique IP address and other necessary protocol configuration information from a Dynamic Host Configuration Protocol (DHCP) server on the network. Most servers in production will have a static IP address. Workstations, however, most often have dynamically assigned IP addresses. Not only does a DHCP server assign IP addresses to client workstations, but it can also supply all of the other values required in your particular TCP/IP environment (including a subnet mask, DNS servers to use, the default gateway to route through, and the domain suffix to apply to the connection). DHCP also keeps track of IP assignments and updates clients dynamically when you want to make IP configuration changes. (There will be cases where you won't use a DHCP server to assign address information to the client. This chapter will also cover how to set this information manually for each client operating system.)

The network client locates network resources and connects to them. For any given flavor of file-mounting, printer-sharing software that runs on a server, there is a client connection counterpart.

Domain Accounts and Local Accounts

Two kinds of accounts are key to using a client workstation and getting to network resources: domain accounts and local accounts. In general, domain accounts are used to authenticate access to shared domain resources, and local accounts are used to authenticate access to use or manage the local computer.

A *domain* is a logical grouping of computers, user accounts, and related network resources, all with a common security database called Active Directory. Domains provide centralized security, along with the resource grouping function of workgroups. Domain user accounts permit people to use a single login name to log on to any workstation and access resources on any server that belongs to the domain (provided that the user has permission to access the resources). All Microsoft operating systems can join domains with the exception of the Tablet RT version of Windows (http://windows.microsoft.com/en-US/windows/rt-welcome). A user account that is not a member of the domain or a member of a trusted domain cannot access network resources protected by domain security. For more information about domains, see Chapter 7, "Active Directory in Windows Server 2012 R2."

A *workgroup* is a logical grouping of computers with no central security database but organized under a single name. Although today's operating systems can join workgroups, this isn't common in production environments; even in smaller offices, domains are typically built for security purposes. It's much harder to manage access to workgroup resources, and they lack the discoverability that Active Directory provides.

Workgroup access is the method by which Windows RT devices access each other or broadcast out to the network. Since Windows RT devices can not join an Active Directory domain, they are left in a workgroup, which is the default.

Although domain membership is key to accessing centralized resources, local accounts also have their purposes: you need them for the local management of the workstation. All current Microsoft operating systems maintain local security databases. The configuration changes you are about to perform require administrative privileges, so you must log on using the local Administrator account (or an account in the local Administrators group) to make the changes.

GIVING USERS RIGHTS TO ADMINISTER A CLIENT COMPUTER

In the past, it was commonplace for administrators to add a user's Domain User account as a member of the local Administrators group on a client computer so they could perform certain tasks with elevated permissions.

These days, it is best practice to avoid giving users administrative access this way, and instead, you can take advantage of the new advanced security and delegation options (Dynamic Access Control, for example) in Windows Server 2012 R2 to give users the control they need. It's best to try to follow a least-privilege approach as opposed to giving users access to everything.

Verifying Your Network Configuration

The first step in joining a domain is to connect to the domain's network so the client computer can communicate with the domain controller. The steps for connecting to a network are basically the same for each of the client operating systems we discuss in this chapter:

1. Install a working network interface card and driver on the client computer.

2. Configure the NIC with the appropriate settings to communicate on the network.

We will address any UI (or other) differences between client operating systems as we go, but for now let's get ready to join a domain.

Log on to the system using a local Administrator account. Before trying to join the domain, it's good to verify that the NIC and its associated driver were installed correctly, and you'll need administrative rights to check everything.

Devices that your computer detects show up in Device Manager. To get there, go to Control Panel and open Device Manager (you can open the Start menu, start typing "Control Panel," as shown in Figure 18.1, and then select Control Panel, and it will open). The Computer Management console will open. The left side of your screen will show a list of all devices; expand the Network Adapters folder, and your NIC should be there.

FIGURE 18.1
Using the Windows 8 Start screen to access Control Panel

If you have problems with the NIC, such as a driver issue, you will know it clearly because the network adapter will be missing or could be "banged out" (the device will be there but will have a yellow exclamation point next to it). The NIC could also be banged out and located in the Other Devices folder. Refer to the NIC manufacturer's documentation and the operating system's Help and Support features to help you resolve hardware problems.

Verifying Local Area Connection Settings

If you accept the typical network settings during the installation, Setup will install and create a software representation of the NIC, called a *local area connection*. The installation will also install the following local area connection components:

TCP/IP   Allows the computer to communicate with other network nodes and devices.

Client for Microsoft Networks   Allows a computer to access resources on a Microsoft network.

QoS Packet Scheduler   The QoS (Quality of Service) Packet Scheduler provides network traffic control and prioritization services for data transmitted to and from the local device.

By default the local area connection will be configured to obtain the following configuration settings from a DHCP server:

IP Address Version 4 (TCP/IPv4)   The address of the computer as it relates to the network it is joining. Every node on the network must have a unique IP address.

IP Address Version 6 (TCP/IPv6)   This is the latest version of the Internet Protocol. It is slowly being adopted by larger organizations, and many Microsoft Server products and features require it to enable their functionality. The Microsoft Unified Access Gateway (UAG) is one of these products. Having IPv6 enabled for DHCP will not cause any issues in your configuration, and it is enabled by default. A typical IPv6 address looks like this: 2001:0db8:85a 3:0000:0000:8a2e:0370:7334.

Subnet Mask   A number that logically segments a larger network into separate subnetworks (the communication between these smaller subnetworks must be passed by a router).

Default Gateway   The IP address of the router that will route communications between nodes located in different subnetworks or other networks.

Domain Name System Server   The IP address of a DNS server on the network.

DNS Suffix (Optional)   The Active Directory domain name to which the computer is or will be joined (in this chapter it is bigfirm.com).

The fastest way to tell whether your NIC obtained the appropriate settings automatically is to open a command prompt and type the following:

```
ipconfig /all
```

You should get results similar to those shown in Figure 18.2.

FIGURE 18.2
ipconfig
command
results

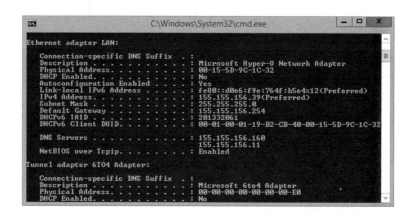

The lines from these results that will tell you that your NIC is configured properly are located in the Ethernet Adapter Local Area Connection Ethernet Adapter LAN section:

DHCP Enabled   If this is set to Yes, then the NIC is set to obtain IP address information from a DHCP server. If it is set to No, then you will need to manually configure an IP address for your local area connection.

Autoconfiguration Enabled   This is set to Yes and is present only if the NIC is set to obtain IP addresses automatically from the DHCP server.

IPv4 Address   This is the unique IP address assigned to the local area connection.

Subnet Mask   This is the subnetwork to which the node belongs.

Default Gateway   This is the router that will route traffic between your assigned subnet and other subnets and networks.

DNS Servers   DNS servers resolve IP addresses to computer names. You need to have a DNS server assigned, or you will not be able to join a domain. In most cases, the DNS server address is supplied by the DHCP server.

If the `ipconfig` results come up empty, then you may not have a DHCP server to allocate IP addresses, in which case you will need to configure your local area connection settings manually. To do this, you will need to open the local area connection associated with the NIC and enter the information by hand. For now, assume that the `ipconfig` results show that the NIC has the address information assigned.

Testing Network Connectivity with the *ping* Command

To be absolutely certain that your network card and TCP/IP are working properly and that the IP information assigned to the NIC is correct, open a command prompt, and use the `ping` command to test basic network connectivity.

If you are unfamiliar with `ping`, you can review the command and all the common switches here: `http://tinyurl.com/c18PingCommand`.

Here are typical `ping` commands that you can use to test network connectivity:

ping 127.0.0.1   This pings your computer (this address always specifies the node you are pinging from and is called the *loopback address*).

ping localhost -4   This pings your computer. It tells you that the local area connection is able to send and receive information. Use the -4 option to receive results in IPv4 format.

ping x.x.x.x   This pings another node (replace x.x.x.x with an IP address).

ping DNSNAME.DOMAIN.SUFFIX   This pings a node using its fully qualified domain name (the name stored in DNS that is mapped to an IP address). An example is `ping bf1.bigfirm.com`.

Verifying and Setting Local Area Connection Information Using the GUI

Knowing how to get to the client local area connection is important for these reasons:

 ◆ You can verify the local area connection configuration using the GUI.

 ◆ You can set the local area connection information manually if you do not have a DHCP server from which to obtain these settings automatically.

LOCAL AREA CONNECTIONS IN WINDOWS 8

To locate the local area connections on a Windows 8 client, select Start, type **Control Panel**, click Control Panel, and select Network and Sharing Center (shown in Figure 18.3).

The local area connection information will be the same on your Windows RT devices. The Windows networking interfaces are common across the Windows 8, RT, and Windows Server 2012 operating systems.

FIGURE 18.3
The Windows 8 Local
Area Connection icon
in the Network and
Sharing Center

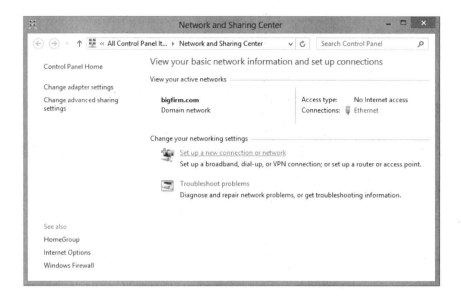

If you do not see a Local Area Connection icon in your active networks, your NIC may not have been properly detected. Use Device Manager to isolate the problem, or try to add the network adapter manually using the Add Hardware Wizard in Control Panel.

1. Click the Local Area Connection link to open the Local Area Connection Status window, as shown in Figure 18.4.

FIGURE 18.4
The Windows
8 Local Area
Connection
Status window

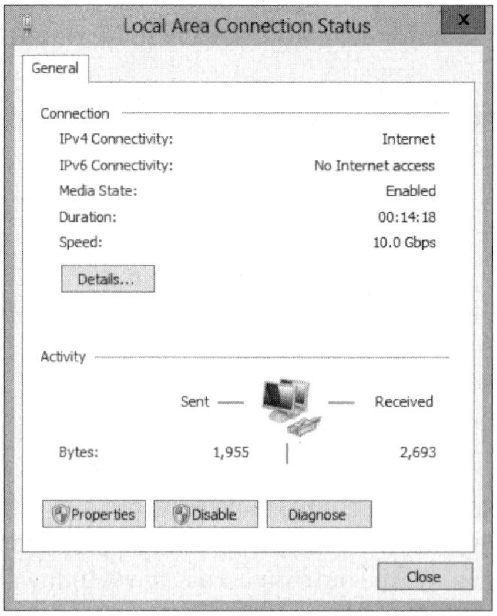

Here you can see that the connection is enabled (Media State is set to Enabled).

2. Click the Details button to open the Network Connection Details window, as shown in Figure 18.5.

FIGURE 18.5

The Windows 8 Network Connection Details window

Network Connection Details:	
Property	Value
Connection-specific DN...	bigfirm.com
Description	Microsoft Hyper-V Network Adapter
Physical Address	00-15-5D-01-85-01
DHCP Enabled	Yes
IPv4 Address	192.168.1.132
IPv4 Subnet Mask	255.255.255.0
Lease Obtained	Tuesday, April 30, 2013 10:23:21 PM
Lease Expires	Wednesday, May 8, 2013 10:23:21 PM
IPv4 Default Gateway	192.168.1.1
IPv4 DHCP Server	192.168.1.125
IPv4 DNS Server	192.168.1.125
IPv4 WINS Server	
NetBIOS over Tcpip En...	Yes
Link-local IPv6 Address	fe80::b5e9:a7da:2954:2f6d%12
IPv6 Default Gateway	
IPv6 DNS Server	

The data found here is a subset of the data retrieved by using the ipconfig command. The network connection details show that the local area connection is DHCP enabled, so you know it is getting its configuration from a DHCP server. The connection is configured with the DNS suffix bigfirm.com, the IP address 192.168.1.132, the subnet mask 255.255.255.0, the default gateway address 192.168.1.1, and DNS server address 192.168.1.125. You can also see when the DHCP information was given out (by the date in the Lease Obtained value) and when it will expire (the date in the Lease Expires value).

MANUALLY CONFIGURING LOCAL AREA CONNECTION SETTINGS IN WINDOWS 8

Close the Network Connection Details window and click the Properties button on the Local Area Connection Status page to open the Local Area Connection/Ethernet Properties page shown in Figure 18.6.

FIGURE 18.6
The Windows
8 Local Area
Connection
Properties page

The Local Area Connection Properties page shows which NIC it's associated with, as well as the components it uses. This is where you would manually give the local area connection a static IP address should you need to do so. Follow these steps:

1. Select Internet Protocol Version 4 (TCP/IPv4), and click Properties.

   The Internet Protocol Version 4 (TCP/IPv4) Properties page opens, as shown in Figure 18.7.

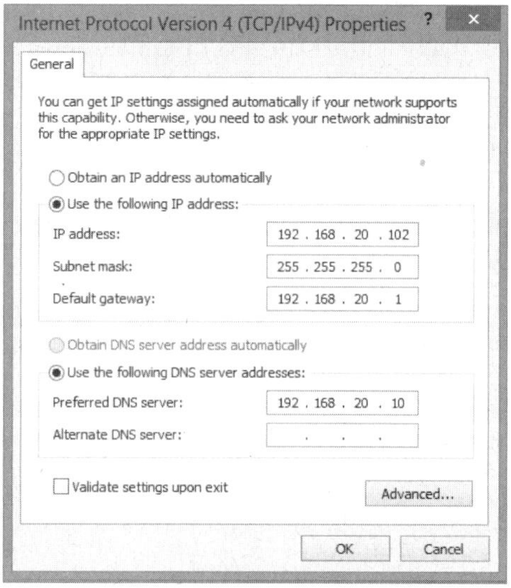

FIGURE 18.7
The Windows 8
Internet Protocol
Version 4 (TCP/
IPv4) Properties
page

2. Select "Use the following IP address."

3. Enter the IP address, subnet mask, and default gateway address.

4. Click "Use the following DNS server addresses," and enter the preferred and alternate DNS server addresses.

5. Click the Advanced button, click the DNS tab, and enter the DNS suffix you want appended to the name of this computer (to create the FQDN).

6. Select the "Validate settings upon exit" setting to run the Network Diagnostics applet.

   The applet will run when you exit the Local Area Connection Properties page and will validate your IP settings. If there is a problem, you will be notified and given information to help you solve the issue.

7. Click OK twice, and then close the remaining windows.

LOCAL AREA CONNECTIONS IN WINDOWS 7

To locate the local area connections on a Windows 7 client, select Start ➢ Control Panel ➢ Network and Internet, and go to the Network and Sharing Center (shown in Figure 18.8). To get there faster, type the word **Network** in the search area at the bottom of the Start menu, and then click Network and Sharing Center in the top portion of the Programs menu.

FIGURE 18.8
The Windows 7 Local Area Connection icon in the Network and Sharing Center

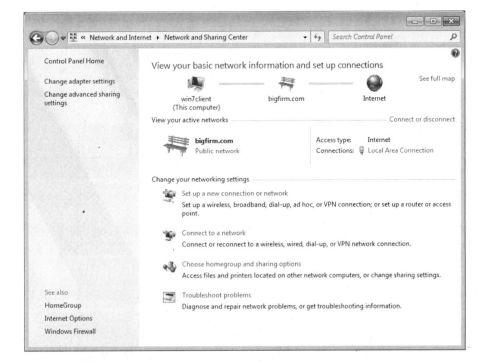

If you do not see a Local Area Connection icon, your NIC may not have been properly detected. Use Device Manager to isolate the problem, or try to add the network adapter manually using the Add Hardware Wizard in Control Panel.

1. Click the Local Area Connection link to open the Local Area Connection Status window, as shown in Figure 18.9.

FIGURE 18.9
The Windows 7 Local Area Connection Status window

Here you can see that the connection is enabled (Media State is set to Enabled).

2. Click the Details button to open the Network Connection Details window, as shown in Figure 18.10.

FIGURE 18.10
The Windows 7 Network Connection Details window

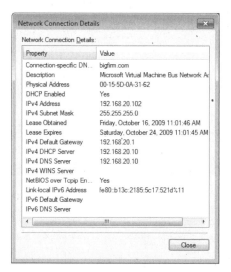

The data found here is a subset of the data retrieved from using the `ipconfig` command. The network connection details show that the local area connection is DHCP enabled, so you know it is getting its configuration from a DHCP server. The connection is configured with the DNS suffix bigfirm.com, the IP address 192.168.20.102, the subnet mask 255.255.255.0, the default gateway address 192.168.20.1, and DNS server address 192.168.20.10. You can also see when the DHCP information was given out (by the date in the Lease Obtained value) and when it will expire (the date in the Lease Expires value).

MANUALLY CONFIGURING LOCAL AREA CONNECTION SETTINGS IN WINDOWS 7

Close the Network Connection Details window and click the Properties button on the Local Area Connection Status page to open the Local Area Connection Properties page shown in Figure 18.11.

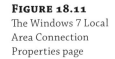

FIGURE 18.11
The Windows 7 Local Area Connection Properties page

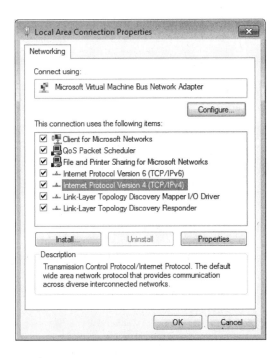

The Local Area Connection Properties page shows which NIC it's associated with, as well as the components it uses. This is where you would manually give the local area connection a static IP address should you need to do so. Follow these steps:

1. Select Internet Protocol Version 4 (TCP/IPv4), and click Properties.

The Internet Protocol Version 4 (TCP/IPv4) Properties page opens, as shown in Figure 18.12.

FIGURE 18.12
The Windows 7
Internet Protocol
Version 4 (TCP/IPv4)
Properties page

2. Select "Use the following IP address."

3. Enter the IP address, subnet mask, and default gateway address.

4. Click "Use the following DNS server addresses," and enter the preferred and alternate DNS server addresses.

5. Click the Advanced button, click the DNS tab, and enter the DNS suffix you want appended to the name of this computer (to create the FQDN).

6. Select the "Validate settings upon exit" setting to run the Network Diagnostics applet.

   The applet will run when you exit the Local Area Connection Properties page and will validate your IP settings. If there is a problem, you will be notified and given information to help you solve the issue.

7. Click OK twice, and then close the remaining windows.

Joining the Domain

To join a domain from any Windows operating system, you'll need the following information:

◆ The fully qualified domain name or NetBIOS name of the domain

◆ The name and password of an account with permission to join the domain

Joining a domain is easy. The main places you're likely to run into trouble are not knowing the right domain credentials and supplying the wrong computer name. Local administrators can't join computers to the domain, and you shouldn't join a computer to the domain using the same name as a different computer that previously joined and that has a computer account object in Active Directory. In replacement scenarios, utilizing the same computer account can be acceptable; for example, if a laptop has its hard drive replaced, the computer names are asset numbers, and you would want to use this name again. Using the Active Directory Users and Computers Snap-In to properly delete the old computer object is the best practice for this. Additionally, making sure you have given the system enough time to replicate the change to other domain controllers so you have no conflict in the name can be equally important. Make sure that the computer name is unique and that you have the right credentials to join the domain.

By default, Windows Server 2012 domains allow regular domain users to join up to 10 computers to a domain. Beyond that, domain admin accounts, of course, can add computers to a domain, and you can also delegate this right to other users via Group Policy. For information on how to delegate this right, see `http://technet.microsoft.com/library/dd392267(WS.10).aspx`.

Client computers always start out belonging to a workgroup called WORKGROUP. That's the beginning setting for all client operating systems discussed in this chapter.

ADDING DOMAIN ACCOUNTS TO LOCAL COMPUTER GROUPS

To log on and use a computer using a domain account, domain user accounts have to be added to a local group on the computer. This is true for all Windows 8, Windows 7, and older Windows versions back to Windows 2000/XP client computers that join a domain.

When a computer is joined to a domain, the Domain Admins group gets added to the local Administrators group on the computer. Domain admins are now administrators of the local computer and can fully manage the machine (can add or remove hardware, install software, and so on). Likewise, the Domain Users group gets added to the local Users group on the computer. Domain users are now afforded the normal local user rights on the computer (non-management tasks, such as using software, accessing network resources, and so on).

Joining a Domain from Windows 8

Typically, you'll join the domain from a computer connected to it, but Windows 7 and Windows 8 support both online joins and offline joins.

JOINING THE DOMAIN WHILE ONLINE

To join a domain from Windows 8 when connected to the network, follow these steps:

1. Open the System applet: To access this click the Start button and begin typing **Control Panel**. Once you reach Control Panel select System.

   You should see a dialog box like the one in Figure 18.13.

FIGURE 18.13
System information for the Windows 8 client

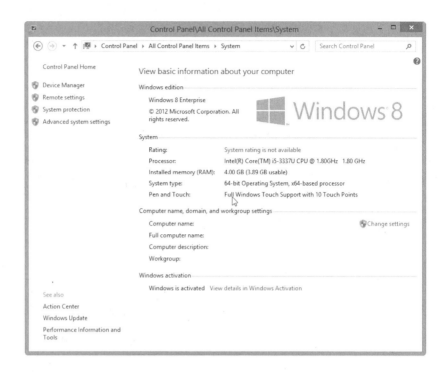

In this example, the computer hasn't yet joined the domain, so it's in the default workgroup (called WORKGROUP) that all Windows computers start in.

2. Click the "Change settings" link to open the System Properties dialog box, as shown in Figure 18.14.

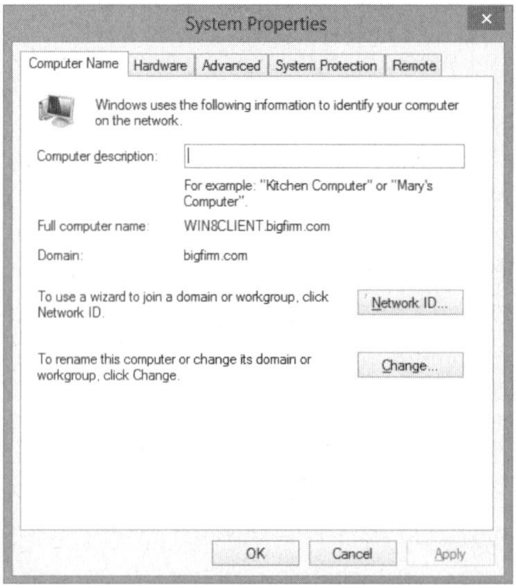

FIGURE 18.14
System Properties dialog box

3. The simplest way to join a domain is to click the Change button to open the dialog box shown in Figure 18.15.

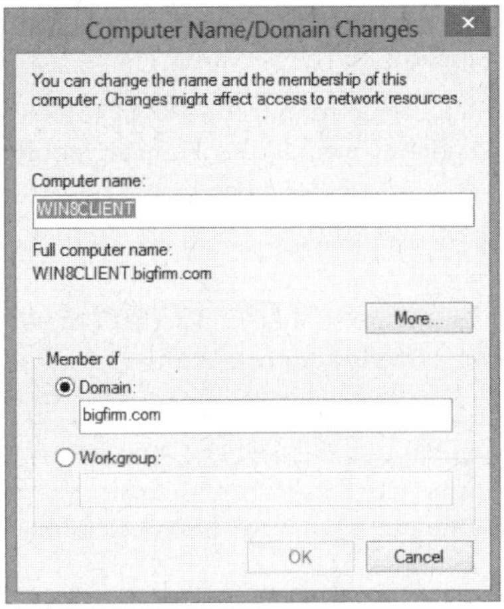

FIGURE 18.15
Type the domain name to join the domain.

4. Type the name of the domain (either the NetBIOS name or the FQDN), and click OK.

   When you click OK, you'll be prompted for the username and password of an account with permission to join the domain, as shown in Figure 18.16.

FIGURE 18.16
Provide credentials to join the domain.

5. Type the credentials. Remember, local administrators can't join computers to the domain. You must supply a domain account and click OK.

   You should see a dialog box welcoming you to the bigfirm domain.

6. Click OK, and you'll see first a warning that you'll need to reboot.

7. Click OK again. Then you will be prompted to reboot the computer.

8. Reboot to complete the join.

If you don't join successfully, check the credentials you used.

WINDOWS RT AND ACCESSING RESOURCES

Windows RT is a different type of operating system than Windows 8, but it carries many of the same feature sets and access capabilities. While you cannot join an Active Directory domain, as stated earlier, you can access resources on the network.

Microsoft's System Center Configuration Manager 2012 SP1 does support the management and configuration of Windows RT devices through its advanced mobile device management (MDM) services.

The more common way of accessing resources is via Windows File Explorer; you can use this tool to manage files and folders the same way you can on the non-RT desktop OSs. Through File Explorer you can map your network drives, access shares, and access enterprise storage devices. To access the network resources, Windows RT fully supports many connection types exactly the same way as Windows 8 devices do. Following are a few examples of accessing resources:

Wireless Networks You must manually set the connection and configurations on these networks, so having the appropriate SSID, connection accounts, and security details for that connection are imperative. Depending on your organization's security practices, you may have only have limited access to resources in your environment.

Wired Networks Many manufacturers provide an Ethernet port adapter. Most organizations utilize DHCP, so you will not be required to configure your network. If you do need to configure an IP address and subnet, you can do so following the same steps you would for Windows 8 via Control Panel.

Proxy Servers Since no group policies are applied because of the lack of domain joining, you have to manually configure your proxy settings. If you need to detect the presence of an internal proxy server you must enable the Web Proxy Autodiscovery Protocol on your corporate network. This involves configuring specific DHCP options as well as a web server, but as more companies move to bring-your-own-device (BYOD) scenarios, you might consider this as an option.

VPN Connectivity Windows RT devices can utilize VPN connections to establish a more domain-connected feel to your organization's network. Many IT pros like to utilize this option because it helps with security and access control. Since many VPN options are available for Windows RT, you should review the Windows RT VPN overview provided by Microsoft at `http://tinyurl.com/c18RTVPN`.

JOINING THE DOMAIN WHILE OFFLINE WITH *DJOIN.EXE*

Domain joining has one problem: what if you can't get to the domain controller to create the computer account or you can't write to it? You may also not be able to contact a domain controller if you're staging a group of client computers before deploying them or installing a client OS while offline.

Introduced in Windows 7 and available still in Windows 8 and Windows Server 2012 is the `djoin.exe` utility, which lets you join a computer to a domain even when the client computer can't communicate with the domain controller.

This section will show you how to use `djoin.exe` to join a new Windows 8 client computer (WIN8CLIENT) to the domain bigfirm.com when the client is offline.

In a nutshell, `djoin.exe` provisions a computer account in AD and then exports the data (called a *blob*, which is needed for the computer with that computer name to join the domain) to a text file. The offline computer then imports the blob and joins the domain. The blob can also be added to an unattended setup answer file in order to join a computer to a domain (offline) as part of the OS installation.

One thing about the blob: if you provision the computer account in AD using djoin.exe and then open the resulting text file expecting to read it, you will be disappointed because it's not human-readable. However, it contains sensitive data, such as the machine account password and other important domain information.

These are the steps to join an offline computer to the domain:

1. Run djoin on a Windows 8 or Windows Server 2012 machine that *can* communicate with the DC.

   This will create a computer account in AD for the computer name specified and create the text file used in step 3.

2. Move that file to the offline client computer (securely).

3. Run djoin on the offline machine, and import the text file.

djoin Requirements

You can run djoin only on Windows 7 and above and Windows Server 2012 computers. It's possible to use djoin to join a Windows 8 or Windows Server 2012 computer to a down-level DC (via the /downlevel parameter), but the example in this chapter will join a Windows 8 client to a Windows Server 2012 domain.

There are a few other general requirements as well. First, the user who runs djoin on the provisioning machine must have the right to add computers to the domain. Again, domain users have this permission although they can add only up to 10 computers to the domain by default.

You should also be familiar with the djoin parameters to understand the commands issued in the following example. Table 18.1 describes these parameters.

TABLE 18.1: djoin Parameters

PARAMETER	DESCRIPTION
/provision	Creates the computer account in Active Directory
/domain	Specifies the domain the computer will be joining
/machine	Specifies the name of the computer that will be added to ADDS and that you want to join the domain
/savefile <filepath>	Specifies the location and file to save the provisioning metadata
/dcname (optional)	Specifies the name of a specific DC you want to use to create the computer account
/reuse (optional)	Reuses an existing machine account (the machine account password will be reset)
/downlevel (optional)	Provides support for using a DC that runs Windows 2008 or older
/printblob (optional)	Creates a blob correctly encoded for use in an unattended answer file
/defpwd (optional)	Uses the default machine account password—not recommended

TABLE 18.1: djoin Parameters *(CONTINUED)*

PARAMETER	DESCRIPTION
/requestodj	Requests an offline domain join (ODJ) on reboot
/loadfile <filepath>	Specifies the file (created with the /savefile parameter) to be imported to the offline computer
/windowspath	Specifies the path of the Windows directory in an offline image, typically %systemroot% or %windir%
/localos	Specifies a local OS as opposed to an offline image (requires a reboot)

Adding the Computer to the Domain While Offline

To use djoin to join a computer to the domain, you will need to execute djoin commands on two different machines. In this example, they are as follows:

win8client.bigfirm.com This machine is already joined to the domain and can communicate with the DC. This machine will be used to provision the new computer account in AD (we refer to it as the *provisioning machine*).

win8client2 This is a newly created Windows 8 client that is in a workgroup and cannot communicate with a DC.

RUNNING DJOIN.EXE USING A REGULAR USER ACCOUNT

To avoid confusion, it's best to use an account that is a member of the Domain Admins group to run the djoin.exe command or to use an account that has been delegated the right to add computers to the domain. Regular users can run the djoin.exe command and create computer accounts, but only up to 10 times (because by default regular users are limited to joining no more than 10 computers to the domain). After that, the user will be denied, as shown in the following code:

```
Djoin djoin /provision /domain bigfirm.com /machine win7client11
/savefile c:\join.txt

Provisioning the computer account...

Failed to provision [win8client11] in the domain [bigfirm.com]: 0x216d.

Computer account provisioning failed: 0x216d.
Your computer could not be joined to the domain. You have exceeded
the maximum number of computer accounts you are allowed to create
in this domain. Contact your system administrator to have this
limit reset or increased.
```

From then on you will need to use a domain admin account or delegate this right to others (via Group Policy).

First, log onto the client computer win8client.bigfirm.com with a domain administrator account, and start an elevated command prompt. Then run the following command to create a computer account in Active Directory and also to create the provisioning text file:

```
C:\Users\bigadmin>djoin /provision /domain bigfirm.com
/machine win7client2 /savefile c:\join.txt
```

The results of this command are as follows:
```
Provisioning the computer account...

Successfully provisioned [win8client2] in the domain [bigfirm.com].
Provisioning data was saved successfully to [c:\join.txt].

Computer account provisioning completed successfully.
The operation completed successfully.
```

Active Directory Users and Computers on the DC (bf1) will now contain the computer account win8client2 stored in the default Computers folder, as shown in Figure 18.17.

FIGURE 18.17
Running djoin adds a computer account to AD DS.

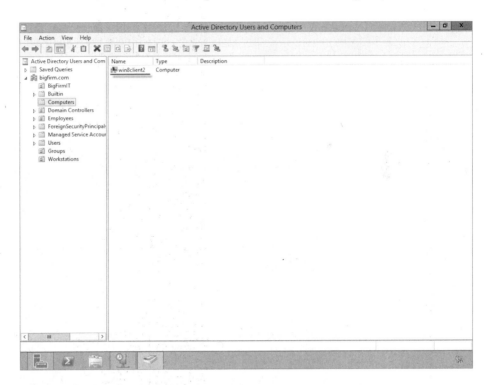

Next, move the resulting text file join.txt from the provisioning computer (win8client) to the computer you want to join (win8client2). In this example, the file is placed in the root of the C drive. Then on the client computer (win8client2), open a command prompt with elevated permissions, and type the following:

```
Djoin /requestODJ /loadfile c:\join.txt /windowspath %systemroot% /localos
```

Reboot the computer, and when it comes back up, it will be joined to the domain.

For more information on using djoin with unattended setups and delegating the right to join computers to the domain, refer to http://technet.microsoft.com/en-us/library/ff793312.aspx.

Joining a Domain with PowerShell

The additions to PowerShell in Windows Server 2012 and the fact that Windows 8 has a solid foundation everywhere PowerShell is used are very valuable to an IT pro. It is uncommon that you would be sitting at a client computer and joining it to the domain via PowerShell, but since you can run this command remotely and might want to have it as part of a script, we'll review the process.

To join a computer to the domain from PowerShell, you will be using the Add-Computer cmdlet:

1. Open a PowerShell console as an administrator.

2. Type in **Add-Computer -DomainName Bigfirm.com**.

3. Provide credentials with rights to join a machine to the domain (an example is shown in Figure 18.18).

For more information on the Add-Computer cmdlet see http://tinyurl.com/c18PSAdd.

FIGURE 18.18
Add-Computer
PowerShell cmdlet
and authentication
box

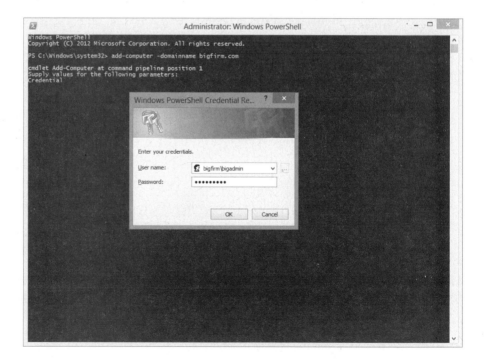

Changing Domain User Passwords

Good security practice demands that passwords be changed regularly and known only to the user. The operating system users employ to connect to a Windows Server 2012 domain requires user intervention to change the passwords.

Although most of this book is geared toward the administrator, this section has information that the administrator will need to convey to the user population so they can do it themselves. The good news is that changing passwords is extremely simple, and the UI gives all the guidance the user needs:

♦ If policy requires a user to change their password when they first use an account, they'll be prompted to do this.

♦ If policy demands a user to change a password because the password will soon expire, they'll be prompted to do so, told how to do it, and told how long they have until the password expires.

♦ If the password they type does not meet the security standards defined in Group Policy, they'll be told what those standards are so they can follow them.

If a user *forgets* their old password, they will not be able to change it themselves, and if the administrator has followed best security practices, they won't know the password either. The administrator will need to update the password on the domain user account and then set the password to be changed at first logon.

 Real World Scenario

PASSWORD POLICIES AND ADVANCED FEATURES

Windows Server 2012 provides the same user password policies that have existed since Windows Server 2008 and 2008 R2. Windows Server 2012 expands the available features such as fine-grained passwords.

Windows Server 2008 introduced fine-grained passwords to allow IT and security groups to have multiple security principals in the same domain or forest. Previously in Active Directory you could manage only one default password policy for your entire domain. Setting fine-grained passwords in Windows Server 2008 was quite a tedious task and wasn't very intuitive.

Windows Server 2012 has made this feature much more intuitive and allows you to perform configurations in Server Manager, or you can utilize the full-feature capabilities from PowerShell 3.0.

The Windows Server 2012 Default Domain Group Policy enforces regular password changes and password complexity rules. The Group Policy setting is located at Computer Configuration\Policies\Windows Settings\Security Settings\Account Policies\Password Policy.

The default password policy settings are as follows:

Enforce Password History This requires users to use a certain number of unique passwords before an old password can be reused. The default number is 24 passwords.

Maximum Password Age This is the number of days a password can be used before the user must change it. The default is 42 days.

Minimum Password Age This is the minimum number of days a password must be used before the user can change it. The default is one day.

Minimum Password Length This is the minimum number of characters a password must contain. The default is 7.

Password Must Meet Complexity Requirements Enabled by default, this setting enforces several rules about how a password must be created. For example, a password must not contain more than two consecutive characters that are part of the user's full name.

It's an even better idea to encourage users to use passphrases instead of mere passwords. A *passphrase* is a combination of words that together, in the exact right order, form the password. A passphrase as a whole still has to meet password policy complexity requirements but is generally longer and can contains spaces, so the passphrase can be much harder for the bad guys to figure out. Combined with vowel substitution (substituting some letters, namely vowels, for numbers), users can create very complex passphrases. For instance, a good passphrase could be My g00d d0g c4tch3s fr1sb33s! This is easy to remember but is long (29 characters long), complex (because of the use of multiple words, spaces, and vowel substitution), and would be difficult to crack.

See Chapter 9, "Group Policy: AD's Gauntlet and Active Directory Delegation," for an example of creating a complex password GPO.

Security considerations should require that you never allow two people to use the same account. Even if those two people never use the account at the same time (if they do, then doubling up on account usage will cause you all kinds of grief from lost profile changes), it's a bad idea. If more than one person uses an account, then you will never know who is using what on the network—or attempting to use resources that they're not authorized to touch. Security auditing requires a model of one account and one password for each user.

Incidentally, this advice about unique passwords for each user applies not just to ordinary users. To enable security auditing, all Windows Server administrators should have their own basic user account (instead of all administrators using the Administrator account). Best practice is to have a separate admin user account; here's an example:

Normal User Account: KevinB Kevin would use this user account to log in to all of his basic enterprise resources, email, and personal files.

Admin User Account: A-KevinB Kevin would use this account for logging in to servers, making domain changes, or performing any tasks that require escalated permissions.

You should also use Group Policy to require regular password changes. Although this model requires more account management, it allows you to track which server administrator did what and allows you to easily disable administrative access when someone leaves the company, without having to change the administrative passwords for everybody. Password policies are domain-wide, so it makes sense to follow best practices for everyone in the domain.

Changing Domain Passwords from Windows 8 and Windows 7

Most often, users will change passwords under two circumstances:

◆ When the administrator has just reset their domain account password and requires that it be changed

◆ When Group Policy is forcing the password to expire

Windows 7 and Windows Vista follow the same process and have the same GUI for this, so we'll combine the information about changing domain passwords for these two operating systems in the following sections.

CHANGING PASSWORDS AT FIRST LOGON

When the administrator forces a password reset (for security reasons or on a new account), the user will be prompted for the new password when they attempt to log on for the first time, as shown in Figure 18.19. The default password applied by the administrator is simply to prevent a user account from being unprotected before it's used.

When the user clicks OK, they'll be prompted for the new password, as shown in Figure 18.20.

FIGURE 18.19
Changing the password before logging on for the first time

FIGURE 18.20
Changing to the new password

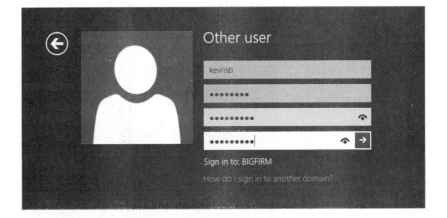

The user fills in the old password and types a new password. According to the Default Domain Group Policy the new password cannot be the same as the old password and must meet length and complexity requirements, or else the user will be nagged for a password that meets the security guidelines and told how to meet them. When the user has successfully changed the password, they'll see a message telling them that the password has been changed. When they click OK, they'll be able to log on with the new password. That's it. After the password is changed, the user can log on normally.

CHANGING PASSWORDS ON DEMAND

When a password is about to expire, users will start seeing messages a few days ahead of time telling them that their passwords are about to expire and telling them how to change them. A user might also want to change their password on demand. The simplest way to change a password is to press Ctrl+Alt+Del to open the Windows Security GUI and choose the "Change a password" option, as shown in Figure 18.21. You can also get to this screen from the Windows Security button located in the Start menu.

FIGURE 18.21
Changing a
password from
the Security GUI

When the user chooses to change a password, they'll see the Change a Password screen, as shown in Figure 18.22, prompting them to type the old password and the new one. Again, if the new password does not meet the security requirements, then they'll see an error message advising them of the password policies. Once the user enters their old and new password (twice) and clicks the arrow button, the password is changed.

FIGURE 18.22
The change
password form

AVOID REPEAT PASSWORD PROMPTS AFTER A PASSWORD CHANGE

If a user has more than one computer and is logged into both (for example, if they have both a laptop and a desktop computer), then they should log out and log back in on both computers after changing the password. The session will still work, but because their domain password will have changed, this can lead to repeated password prompts for network resources such as Exchange servers, SharePoint sites, and other applications requiring authentication. They can keep typing in their passwords when prompted, but it's simplest just to log in with the new password to avoid the prompts.

Connecting to Network Resources

One of the main reasons to join a domain is to access resources on the domain, such as the printer down the hall or some documents that you need to work on. You could access company photos, slide shows, and other media needed to make a marketing campaign. Whatever your need, the point is that you don't need to have these items and devices hooked or stored directly on your client machine. In fact, having them stored on the network is ideal because they are more secure there (access is centrally controlled, and ideally the files are backed up regularly). Examples of network resources include the following:

♦ Printers

♦ Shared folders and files

♦ Wireless devices (such as wireless printers)

♦ Services (such as Web Services)

♦ Company applications

Connecting to shared resources is easy for users, thanks to many of the changes in Active Directory and Group Policy. You can still use features like Network Discovery as a way for your computer to find resources on the network easily, although in most enterprises this is not recommended. With the introduction to Group Policy: Preference Policies, IT pros can now publish resources more easily for employees or departments through Group Policy objects and membership in domain groups. Users can continue to search Active Directory for published resources they may need. This means that the user doesn't need to know where the device is installed or contained. The user might not even know the exact name of a shared folder or printer or the server where it's stored. As long as the resource is published to Active Directory, with a little searching the user will most likely be able to find and utilize the resource.

There are several ways to access shared resources. This section will expand on these more common ways for each of the client operating systems addressed in this chapter:

♦ Resources are published to you through Group Policy objects.

♦ You can search for and access resources that are published in Active Directory.

♦ You can attach to shared network resources (for example, shared folders and printers) from the command line.

◆ You can create a mapped drive to network folder shares.

◆ You can use Windows Explorer to connect to uniform naming convention (UNC) paths that describe the path to a network location in the form of \\computername\sharename.

The following examples will access resources located on the bigfirm.com domain. Table 18.1 lists those resources and their locations on the network.

TABLE 18.1: Network Resources Used in This Section's Examples

NETWORK RESOURCE TYPE	NETWORK RESOURCE PATH	NETWORK RESOURCE MACHINE LOCATION
Marketing file share	\\bf1\BF_Marketing	bf1.bigfirm.com
Black-and-white printer	\\bf1\BF_Main_Printer	bf1.bigfirm.com

Publishing Resources with Group Policy Objects

Starting with Windows 2008's version of Active Directory, you are able to publish all the most common resources to client (and server) devices in a centralized way. The new feature as discussed in Chapter 9 is Group Policy: Preference Policies. These policies allow you to perform such operations as setting up drive mappings, creating shortcuts, and configuring environment settings, as shown in Figure 18.23. You can do this for both users and computers that are located in specific organizational units (OUs) or domain groups.

FIGURE 18.23
Group Policy Management Editor with Preference Policies

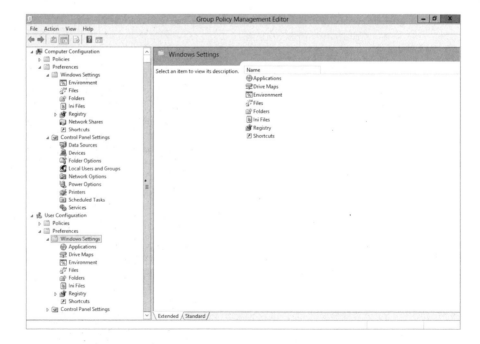

Configuration of resources in any organization should be managed centrally and controlled by the membership of Active Directory groups. Once you have these groups established, you can then manage the access to file shares, printers, and applications with policies. The approaches of the past of allowing Network Discovery and sharing resources on local computers have gone away because security and compliance requirements are audited in organizations. In the next section we will be walking through the creation and publishing of some resources to our workstations. In the next examples we will be focusing on the Marketing department of bigfirm.com and publishing the required resources to the WIN8CLIENT device that is used by the marketing team.

Usually, domain administrators keep company files in centralized, secure, and fault-tolerant locations that can be backed up easily (that is, not stored on individual computers). To gain access to these resources, you need to make sure that the appropriate Active Directory (AD) groups are applied to the file shares and begin to configure your Group Policy objects (GPO) for publishing.

PUBLISHING A NETWORK FILE SHARE

The following example will walk you through giving published resources to an end user. You'll begin this process by making a Groups OU and a Marketing Active Directory group. This example assumes you understand how to create organizational units and domain global groups. If you are unfamiliar with these processes, please see Chapter 7, "Active Directory in Windows Server 2012 R2."

1. Open Active Directory Users and Computers, and create an OU called **Groups**.

2. Select the Groups OU and create a new global group called **Marketing**. See Figure 18.24 for an example of what this would look like.

FIGURE 18.24
Active Directory
OU and group
setup

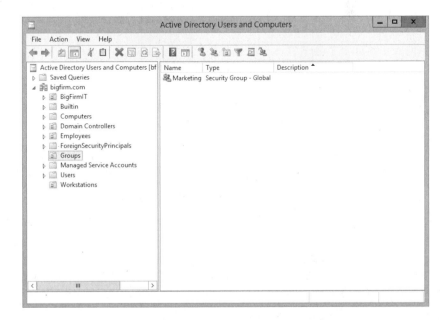

3. Open up your Marketing group and add employee **KevinB** to this group.

4. Click Apply and your Marketing user will be added, and you can start the configuration of your Group Policy object.

5. To create the GPO, first open Administrative Tools ➢ Group Policy Management.

6. Select the Group Policy Objects folder and right-click it. Create a new GPO, as shown in Figure 18.25.

FIGURE 18.25
Creating a new Group Policy object

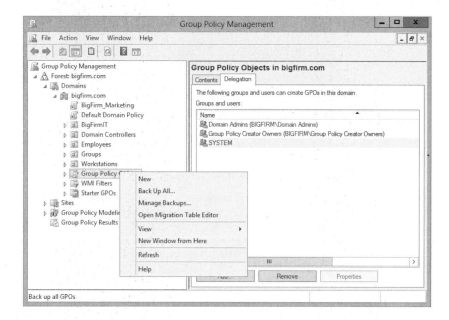

7. For this example, name the GPO **BigFirm_Marketing**.

8. Double-click the BigFirm_Marketing GPO.

You will see the first tab of the Group Policy dialog called Scope. In the Scope section you need to set the Marketing group to be applied to the GPO.

9. Click Add under the Security Filtering section, type in **Marketing**, and click OK.

10. Now select all other groups and then click Remove.

The only group that should have this GPO applied is the Marketing team.

11. Right-click the BigFirm_Marketing policy in the left pane and select Edit.

12. The Group Policy Management Editor will now open. Here select the User Configuration section.

13. Expand User Configuration\Preferences\Windows Settings. You will see all the basic preferences you can modify for a user.

14. Select Drive Maps, right-click, and select New, Mapped Drive.

The New Drive Properties dialog will open. Figure 18.26 shows the basics of this configuration.

FIGURE 18.26
Creating the new drive-mapping preference policy

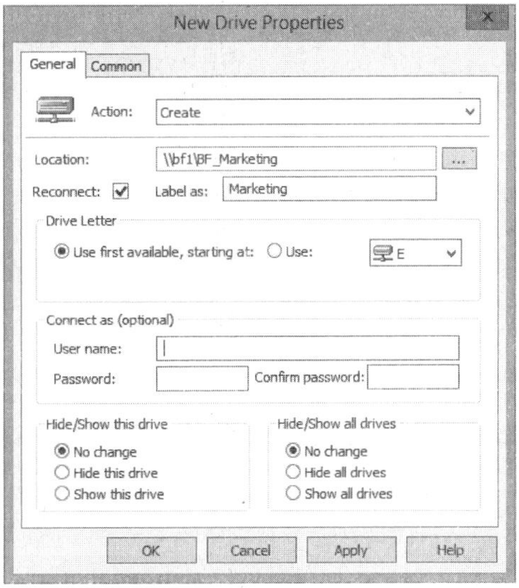

- In the Action field, select Create.

- In the Location field, enter your Universal Naming Convention (UNC) drive mapping: **\\bf1\BF_Marketing**.

- Check the Reconnect box.

- In the "Label as" field, enter how you want the drive to appear to your end users. We're using Marketing for our example.

- Click the "Use first available, starting at:" option for your drive letter. You can also click the Use: option and select a drive in the drop-down box.

- We are leaving all other options at their defaults, but you can modify these to fit your environment as needed.

15. Click Apply and OK to return to the Drive Maps section.

You should now see the E drive mapping appear in the right pane.

Now that you have the GPO created and a policy for drive mappings defined, you need to link it to bigfirm.com so you can start to use this policy, as shown in Figure 18.27. Having this Group Policy object linked to bigfirm.com allows Marketing users, no matter what child OU they are in, to have the policy applied to them.

FIGURE 18.27
GPO applied to
bigfirm.com

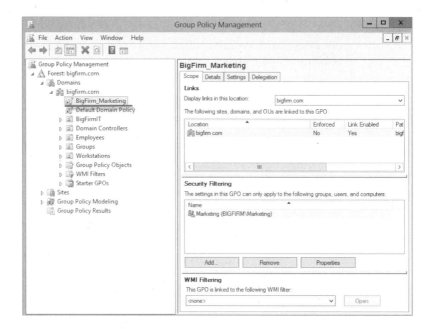

The next steps are all on the client side. You need to make sure that the Group Policy objects are applied to the user. Logging into WIN8CLIENT you can utilize the command prompt to force a Group Policy update. Follow these steps to update your policy on the workstation:

1. Open an elevated command prompt.

2. Type in **GPUPDATE.EXE /FORCE**.

You will be prompted to log off the computer because the settings you created are user specific. See Figure 18.28.

FIGURE 18.28
Group Policy
update with user
settings

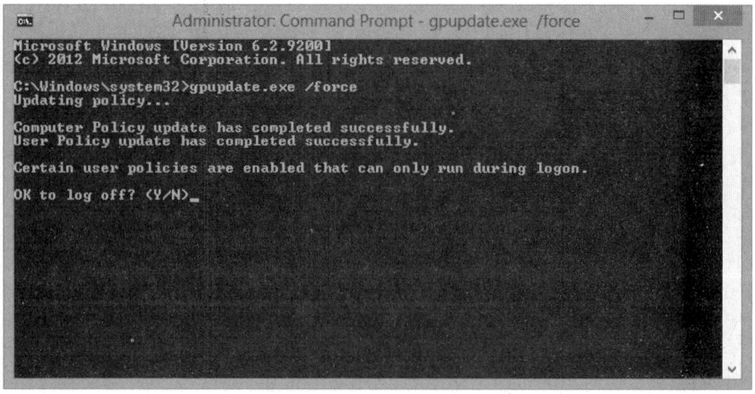

3. Type **Y** to say yes, and it will log you out of the system.

4. Log back in to the WIN8CLIENT to see the drive mapping appear on your computer, as shown in Figure 18.29.

FIGURE 18.29
Marketing drive mapped to Computer folder

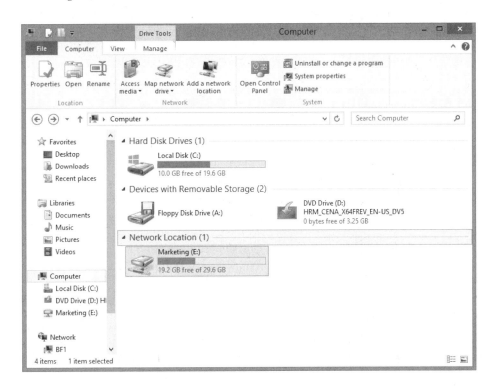

ADDING A NETWORK PRINTER

You can add a network printer by searching for a device from the GUI, using the command-line tools, or with the Network applet.

Finding a Printer by Searching for a Device

In Windows 8 searching for devices and media has been greatly simplified by the addition of the "Access media" icon in File Explorer. As shown in Figure 18.30, you can select "Access media" and it will search the network for any shared or published device, be it a printer or a media share.

FIGURE 18.30
"Access media" icon in File Explorer

In the Find drop-down list, choose Printers. If there are multiple domains on the network, you can make the search more specific by choosing your domain name from the drop-down list (located to the right of the Find drop-down list). If the list of printers is likely to be long, you can search by name or keyword or use the Advanced tab to search by other properties. Once you've set your search criteria, click Find Now. All printers published to Active Directory that meet your search criteria will appear in the Results window.

To add a found printer to your computer, right-click the printer and choose Connect. The printer will install, and you will see it in your Printers folder.

Adding a Network Printer from the Command Line

If you know the name of the printer you want and the print server it's attached to, you can add it from the command line with the `start` command. For instance, to add the printer called bf_main_printer located on server bf1 to a Windows 7 or Windows 7 client, open a command prompt and type the following:

```
start \\bf1\bf_main_printer
```

When the printer installs, the print queue for that printer will open, and the printer will be listed for use in the Devices and Printers applet.

Adding a Network Printer Using the Network Applet

To add a network printer to a Windows 8 or Windows 7 client machine, open the Network applet, and click the Add a Printer link on the toolbar of the Network Folder dialog box. Clicking the link will initiate the Add Printer Wizard. This is the same wizard you get when you add a printer from the Devices and Printers button (located on the Start menu in Windows 7) and the Printers applet (located in Control Panel in Windows Vista). Remember, you can get to operating system features in many ways.

Like all previous versions of the Add Printer Wizard, this version allows you to add local printers, Bluetooth printers, and printers that are located on the network. This section will concentrate on network resources, which comprise cabled or wireless network printers. To add a network printer, click "Add a network, wireless or Bluetooth printer," and click Next. As soon as you click this option, the wizard will search for printers on the network and return any it finds.

To add one of these printers, simply click the printer and click Next; then click Next again on the Results screen. The default configuration is to make this printer the default printer, but you can change this by deselecting the "Set as default printer" box. Click the "Print a test page" button to send a test page to the printer, and click Finish.

The options are to do the following:

◆ Search Active Directory for published network printers

◆ Enter a printer location and name (in the form of \\servername\printername)

◆ Specify a printer using its hostname or its TCP/IP address (often called a *TCP/IP printer*)

The option "Find a printer in the directory, based on location and feature" opens the Find Printers window. You search Active Directory for printers by specifying certain printer criteria (such as a name or a printer model) or a printing feature (such as the ability to print double-sided). Click the Find Now button, and the wizard returns printers that match the specified criteria, as shown in Figure 18.31. You can also enter no criteria, and the search will return all printers in Active Directory.

FIGURE 18.31

The Find Printers dialog box searches Active Directory for printers matching specified criteria.

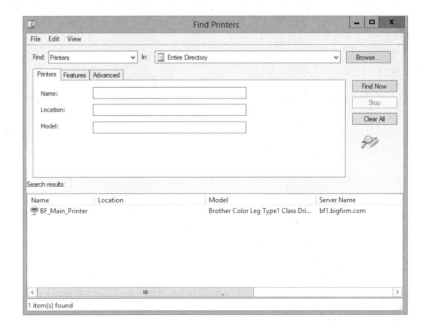

The wizard in our example returned one result. Once you find the printer, select it, click OK, and the wizard will add the printer. Click Next on the following Results screen. Click "Print a test page" to test printing to the printer, and then click Finish.

Instead of searching Active Directory for a printer, you can also add a shared printer by name. Select the option "Select a shared printer by name" and then either enter the network path and name of the printer in the form \\servername\printername or click the Browse button to locate a printer on a specific computer on the network. Once the printer name is added, click Next, click Next again on the information screen, and then click Finish.

Lastly, choose the option "Add a printer using a TCP/IP address or hostname" to add a TCP/IP printer. Enter the IP address of the printer in the "Hostname or IP address" input box. The port name will automatically mimic the IP address (you can change this if you want to use something more descriptive). The Device type defaults to AutoDetect. You should leave this setting alone unless you know the device type to specify. Click Next, and the wizard will attempt to locate the printer and install it.

ADDING WIRELESS DEVICES TO YOUR WINDOWS CLIENT COMPUTER

Windows 7 and Windows 8 have the ability to add wireless devices, such as Bluetooth keyboards and mice, wireless phones, Bluetooth modems, or Bluetooth printers. These aren't exactly network resources (ideally, your users don't have to share a mouse with someone else), but for the sake of completeness, we'll briefly discuss this option.

To add a wireless device to a Windows 7 or Windows 8 client computer, open the Network applet, and click the "Add a wireless device" link located on the toolbar. Clicking the link will initiate the Add a Wireless Device to the Network Wizard (in Windows 7 you can also invoke this wizard from the Devices and Printers applet). The wizard will automatically search for wireless devices for you.

If you have trouble adding a wireless network device to your client system, here are a few tips to help you:

◆ Make sure the wireless device is on and already connected to the wireless network.

◆ Check the network firewall to make sure it's not blocking the discovery process.

◆ Make sure Network Discovery is enabled on the client computer.

◆ Make sure you are not getting interference from other wireless appliances such as microwaves or cordless phones.

◆ Make sure the device is in wireless range of the computer (6 feet for Bluetooth devices, 100 feet for Wi-Fi devices).

MAPPING A DRIVE TO A SHARED FOLDER

Sometimes it's easier to use a drive letter than a UNC path to connect to a network share, especially if you're browsing from the command line. Some applications demand it; they won't save to or execute from UNC paths. Therefore, you can add network shares to drive letters—at least until you run out of letters. In Windows 7 and Windows 8, you can do this from the GUI, from the command line, or by creating network location shortcuts.

To map a drive to a shared network folder, follow these steps:

1. Open the Network applet, and click Search Active Directory.

2. In the Search Active Directory window, select Shared Folders in the Find drop-down menu.

3. Click Find Now, and shared folders that are published to Active Directory will appear in the Results window.

4. To connect to these shared folders, right-click the folder, and choose Map Network Drive, as shown in Figure 18.32.

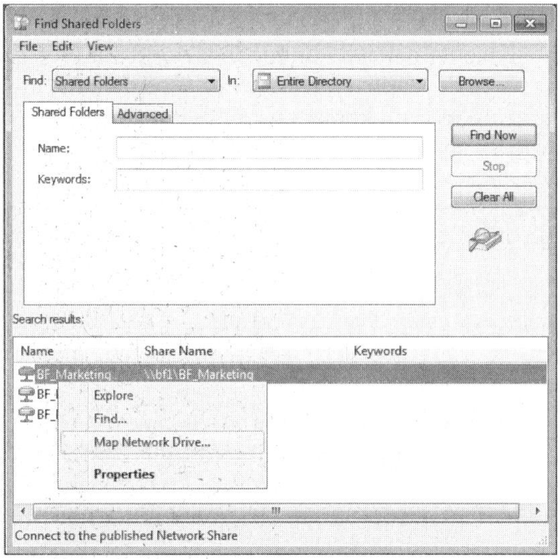

FIGURE 18.32
Mapping a drive to shared folders found in Active Directory

Every mapped drive needs to have a unique drive letter. The resulting Map Network Drive dialog box (shown in Figure 18.33) is already populated with an unused drive letter and automatically fills in the folder location. Mapped drives will be persistent unless you deselect the "Reconnect at logon" check box. By default, the current username and password will be used.

FIGURE 18.33
Map Network
Drive dialog box

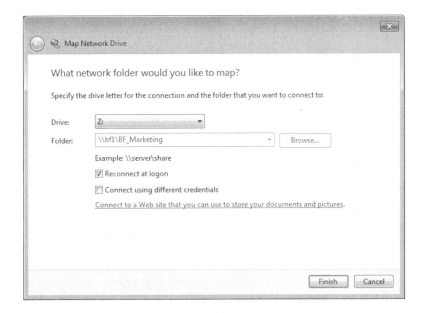

6. Click a different username link to specify a different account to use for the connection.

The link "Connect to a Web site that you can use to store your documents and pictures" opens the Add Network Location Wizard, which is discussed later in the "Adding Network Location Shortcuts" section.

6. Click Finish.

To access the mapped drive, select Start ➢ Computer, and double-click the mapped drive listed under the Network Location section of the main window. You can also click and drag a shortcut to the mapped drive and drop it on your desktop for fast access later. To disconnect from a mapped drive, simply right-click the drive and choose Disconnect.

Some shared folders might not be listed in Active Directory. To map a drive to an unpublished share on the network, follow these steps:

1. Open the Start menu, right-click Computer, and choose Map Network Drive.

2. Choose an unused drive letter from the Drive drop-down box.

3. Now you must give the location to the folder using one of these methods:

◆ Type in the UNC path to the share; for instance, type **\\BF1\BF_Marketing**.

◆ Click the Browse button, and visually locate shared folders by expanding the computer the share is located on, selecting the share, and clicking OK.

4. Click Finish, and the mapped drive will be listed in the Computer window under the Network Location section.

It's also possible to map drives from the command line with the net use command if you know the path to the share. In fact, administrators often create login scripts to automatically map drives for users when they log on to their computers. For instance, to map a drive to the bf_marketing share on server bf1, you would issue the following command:

```
net use M: \\bf1\bf_marketing /PERSISTENT:YES
```

Here's a breakdown of the parameters used in this example:

M: This represents the drive letter to which the drive will be mapped.

\\bf1\bf_marketing This is the UNC path to the share.

/PERSISTENT:YES This makes the mapped drive reconnect automatically each time the user logs on to this computer.

To get a full list of parameters for the net use command, open a command prompt and type **net use /?**.

But what if you don't know what's out there to connect to via CLI? No problem. You can use the net view command to get a list of shared resources on the network. Run it once, and you'll get a list of computers that are visible on the network. Now digging further, you can issue the net view command against a computer on the network to get a list of its shared resources. To delete a mapped drive from the command line, type **net use X: /delete**, where X is the drive letter of the mapped drive you want to delete.

CREATING A NETWORK FOLDER

You've learned how to map a drive in Windows 8 in ways very similar to older operating systems. But there is another way to access shared folders (and other network locations): by creating a *network folder* (basically a shortcut) to the shared location from within your Computer window. Why would you do this as opposed to just mapping a drive? There are both positive and negative differences between mapped drives and network location shortcuts. On one hand, a mapped drive acts like a local drive on the computer. Applications that need to access items from drives will treat the network location as a local drive. However, you can't map a drive letter to other kinds of locations such as FTP sites and web shares. So, there are reasons to utilize both access techniques.

A network location includes shared folders, web shares, FTP sites, and UNC paths. You can add links to these network places in your Computer window by using the Add Network Location Wizard. The Add Network Location Wizard is a menu option in XP's My Network Places. My Network Places has since been morphed into the Network and Sharing Center in Windows 7 and Windows 8—Network Location Wizard is no longer a feature of that applet.

To open the Add Network Location Wizard in Windows 7 and Windows 8, follow these steps:

1. Select Start ➤ Computer.

2. Right-click in the resulting window, and choose "Add a network location," as shown in Figure 18.34.

FIGURE 18.34
Starting the Add
Network Location
Wizard from the
Computer window

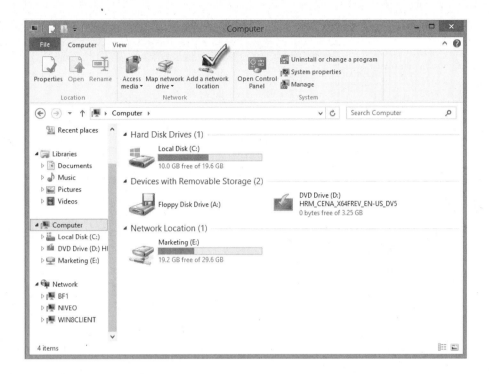

3. The Welcome screen will appear. Click the Next button, select "Choose a custom network location," and click Next.

4. Now you can either enter a location path if you know it (the UNC path to a network share, the FTP address of an FTP site, the URL of a web share), or you can click the Browse button to help you locate a folder share. (The Browse button will allow you to search the network only for folder shares, not other kinds of locations.)

5. Click Next. Figure 18.35 shows entering the URL for the bigfirm.com company FTP site: `ftp://ftp.bigfirm.com`.

By default, the wizard allows for anonymous access to the FTP site. If you want to change this, follow these steps:

1. Deselect "Log on anonymously," and then type in a username you want to use to log on.

2. Click the Next button, and name the location (for example **ftp.bigfirm.com**).

3. Click the Next button, and then click Finish.

The network location will open, and the network location will be listed in the Network Location section of the Computer window, as shown in Figure 18.36.

To disconnect a network location, simply right-click the network location, and select Delete.

FIGURE 18.35
Enter the path to the network location or browse the network to locate a network location.

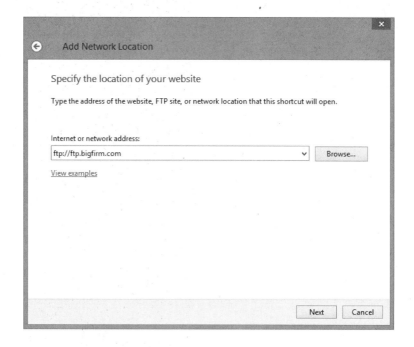

FIGURE 18.36
The network location is added to the Computer window.

Connecting Mac OS X Clients

More and more organizations are integrating Apple Macintosh computers into their Active Directory networks each year. This is being facilitated both by Apple, including better networking features, and by Microsoft adding federation services that make it easier for diverse network clients to take advantage of Active Directory.

In the past, the process of connecting a Mac client to a Windows Server machine required additional software to let the Mac understand the Server Message Block (SMB) file protocols used by Windows. In Mac OS X, all the necessary pieces are included with the operating system. This is because Apple has included a version of Samba with OS X. Samba lets Unix-like operating systems, such as Linux and OS X, speak the native SMB dialects that are used by Windows operating systems. So, the issue in connecting your Mac clients is more a matter of authentication than one of basic connectivity.

Even though Macs can speak SMB, Windows Server 2012 expects a certain default level of security for SMB communication that OS X cannot provide natively, namely, SMB packet signing. Packet signing helps a Windows server and client communicate more securely by digitally signing every packet that is sent by SMB. This technique can relieve some of the risk of the packets being intercepted and manipulated in a so-called man-in-the-middle attack.

To let your Mac clients communicate effectively with Windows Server 2012 Active Directory environments, you will need to disable the requirement for SMB packet signing. But in the interest of network security, you don't want to do away with packet signing altogether. Fortunately, the setting you want to use will enable SMB packet signing for clients that support it but not require it for clients (such as Macs) that don't.

To enable Mac clients running OS X to connect to your Active Directory domain, you must use the following Group Policy settings:

- Microsoft network server: Digitally sign communications (always).

- Set this policy to Disable: to turn off the requirement for SMB packet signing on client-to-server communications.

- Microsoft network server: Digitally sign communications (if client agrees).

- Set this policy to Enable: to allow Windows clients to still use SMB packet signing when communicating with Windows servers.

- Network security: LAN Manager authentication level.

- Set this policy to Send LM & NTLM; use NTLMv2 session security if negotiated. This policy will provide access to Mac clients while still permitting Windows clients to negotiate a higher security level.

You can set these policies in the local policies for domain controllers, which will enable access for Mac clients across the network. To set these policies, follow these steps:

1. Open Group Policy Management. You can do so in the following ways:

- Select Start ➢ Administrative Tools ➢ Group Policy Management.

- In Server Manager, expand Features, and then click Group Policy Management.

2. Open the Default Domain Policy.

3. In Server Manager, expand Group Policy Management, expand your forest, expand Domains, and expand your domain.

4. Right-click Default Domain Policy, and then click Edit.

5. If you are prompted at this point, click OK.

6. In the Group Policy Management Editor, go to Computer Configuration\Policies\Windows Settings\Security Settings\Local Policies\Security Options, as shown in Figure 18.37.

FIGURE 18.37
Using the Group Policy Management Editor

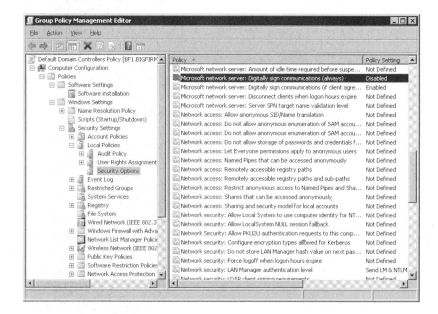

7. Scroll down to "Microsoft network server."

8. Double-click the "Microsoft network server: Digitally sign communications (always)" policy.

9. Click "Define the policy setting," and then select Disabled.

10. Click OK.

11. Double-click the "Microsoft network server: Digitally sign communications (if client agrees)" policy.

12. Click "Define the policy setting," and then select Enabled.

13. Click OK.

14. Scroll down to "Network security."

15. Double-click the "Network security: LAN Manager authentication level" policy.

16. Click "Define this policy."

17. Use the drop-down list to select "Send LM & NTLM; use NTLMv2 session security if negotiated."

18. Click OK.

Connecting a Mac to the Domain

Before you can bind your Mac OS X client to Active Directory, you must complete some preparatory steps. Some of them may be completed already if the clients receive their IP configuration through the Dynamic Host Configuration Protocol (DHCP). Before you try to bind your Mac client to Active Directory, ensure the following items are configured on your Mac:

- IP address

- DNS server address

- Default gateway

The Domain Name System (DNS) server address is the critical part. In most organizations using Active Directory, the DNS servers will likely be domain controllers, or at least they will be integrated with Active Directory. This is important because the Mac client will perform a DNS query to find the Lightweight Directory Access Protocol (LDAP) server responsible for the domain name. An Active Directory integrated DNS server will respond with the IP address of a domain controller, which is what you want in order to join the domain.

These are some additional bits of information you will need to provide during the bind process:

- User credentials with permission to add a computer to the domain

- Your Mac's computer name as it will appear in Active Directory

- Fully qualified domain name (such as bigfirm.com)

- Distinguished path to the organization unit where the computer account should be created

- Administrator account credentials for your Mac

With this information in hand, or at least in mind, you are ready to join your Mac client to your Active Directory domain. Log on to your Mac OS X computer, and perform the following steps:

1. Open System Preferences.

2. Select Users & Groups under the System section.

3. Select Login Options; if it is grayed out, you need to click the lock on the bottom to allow changes to the system to happen.

4. Click the Network Account Server: Join button.

5. Click Open Directory Utility.

You may be required to click the lock again to make changes.

6. The Directory utility will open. Enter your information in the following fields:

◆ Active Directory Forest

◆ Active Directory Domain

◆ Computer ID

7. In Active Directory Domain, type the fully qualified domain name, such as **bigfirm.com**.

8. In Computer ID, type the name for the Mac client computer; do not include dashes in the name.

9. Click Bind. When prompted, provide your Mac administrator name and password to permit the change. Click OK.

10. Provide the distinguished name for an account with permission to add the Mac client account to Active Directory, such as **administrator@bigfirm.com**.

11. Enter the password for the account.

12. Verify the distinguished path to the OU where this computer account will be created, as shown in Figure 18.38. Click OK.

FIGURE 18.38
Providing the
distinguished
path to the OU

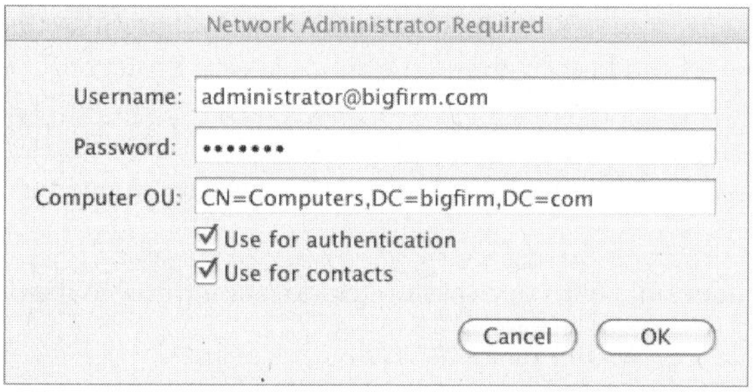

13. Click OK to save the Active Directory settings.

14. When prompted, enter your Mac administrator credentials, and click OK.

The Directory Services utility also allows you to configure and join Active Directory domains or forests from the command line. To configure your Mac from the command line, you need to use the dsconfigad utility to work through this example:

1. Open up Terminal.

2. Select a domain controller and type in the following command:

```
dsconfigad -preferred bf1.bigfirm.com -a "COMPUTERNAME" -domain bigfirm.com -u
administrator -p "password"
```

3. Select Login Options; if it is grayed out, you need to select the lock on the bottom to allow changes to the system to happen.

Once you have bound your Mac to the domain, you can use additional commands to get more advanced information. The next step is to use dsconfigad to set administrative options that are available via Active Directory.

4. In your Terminal session type in the following command:

```
Dsconfigad -alldomains enable -groups domain BigAdmin@Bigfrim.com, Enterprise
BigAdmins@bigfirm.com
```

The commands require you to use cleartext passwords, so if your Active Directory domain does not allow that, you will have to set this up to be enabled for Directory Services logging. Another tool that is commonly used is odutil. This command will look at the internal state of directory services and records, allowing you to enable logging and change your statistics.

5. Run the following command:

```
odutil set log debug
```

This command will set logging on the device to Debug mode, so if you have any issues connecting to your Active Directory domain, you can run debugging–event depth get detailed logs. The logs for odutil are stored at /var/log/opendirectoryd.log.

Connecting to File Shares

Once your Mac client is part of the Active Directory domain, connecting to shared folders is almost the same process as connecting to an OS X server. The single exception is that you must specify that the Finder will use the SMB protocol to connect to the share. Use the format smb://servername/sharename to define the path, similar to Figure 18.39.

FIGURE 18.39
Defining the path to the Windows server

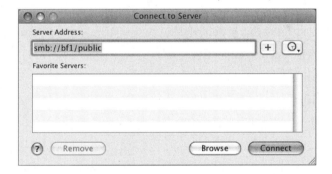

To connect your Mac client to a Windows Server 2012 shared folder, follows these steps:

1. In the Finder, click the Go menu, and then click Connect to Server.

2. Type the path to the shared folder using the format smb://servername/sharename.

3. Optionally, click the plus sign (+) to add this server to your list of favorite servers. If you do, you will be able to click the server name in the list, and then click Connect.

4. Click Connect.

5. Provide your Active Directory user credentials, and click OK.

Connecting to Printers

Like connecting to shared folders, connecting to network printers that are published in Active Directory is a relatively straightforward task. Once the Mac client has joined the Active Directory domain, published printers will be displayed on the Default tab when adding a printer on the Print & Fax page in System Preferences, similar to Figure 18.40.

FIGURE 18.40
Adding a printer from Active Directory

To add a printer that is published in Active Directory, follow these steps:

1. Open System Preferences.

2. Click Print & Scan.

3. Click the plus sign (+) to add a new printer.

4. On the Default tab, click the name of the printer you want to add.

5. Click Add.

To add printers in a Windows workgroup environment, the process is similar. You would still use the Print & Scan page of System Preferences to add the new printer, but instead of finding the Active Directory printers listed on the Default tab, you would use the Windows tab and browse for them.

Through the Print and Scan section of System Preferences you can also add IP-based printers and any fax machines that might be available to you.

Using Remote Desktop from a Mac Client

Now that you have added your OS X client to your Active Directory domain and you can access file shares and printers, how can you administer your network? Fortunately, Microsoft has created a Remote Desktop client for OS X that lets you access your Windows Server 2012 computers from your Mac. You can download the Remote Desktop Connection for Mac (RDC) for OS X for free from either Microsoft's (www.microsoft.com/downloads) or Apple's (www. apple.com/downloads) download sections. Search the sites for "Remote Desktop Connection."

To install the Remote Desktop Connection client, follow these steps:

1. Download the latest version of Remote Desktop Connection. The disk image package will automatically mount and start the setup. Click Continue.

2. Review the Read Me information, and then click Continue.

3. Review the license, and then click Continue. Click Agree if you accept the license.

4. Click Install to perform a standard installation, and the Remote Desktop Connection for the Mac 2 icon will be placed in your Applications folder on your primary hard disk.

   You can change the install destination by clicking Change Install Location.

5. Click Install. Figure 18.41 shows the Installation Type page.

FIGURE 18.41
Selecting the location to install RDC

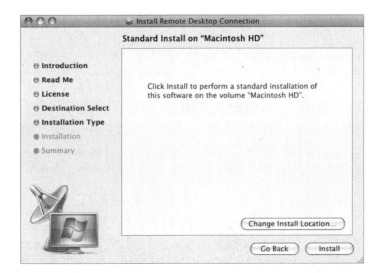

6. Provide your Mac administrator password to approve the installation, and then click OK.

7. When the installation process finishes, click Close to exit the installer.

Using the RDC is similar to using Remote Desktop in Windows, except that the interface has been changed somewhat to match the OS X style. The initial window contains only a space to enter the name of the computer to which you want to connect. To supply logon credentials and adjust any preferences, use the RDC menus at the top of the screen. Just like the Windows version of Remote Desktop, when you first connect to a remote computer, you will be prompted to provide your username, password, and domain name. RDC does save you some time by letting you store your Windows credentials in the Preferences screen and then save them in your Keychain. Having your Mac joined to an Active Directory domain is not a requirement to use the Remote Desktop client. If the Mac you are using is getting DHCP and DNS information from the network, you will be able to access servers and Windows workstations just as you would on any standard Windows Desktop.

Troubleshooting

In this section, we offer some troubleshooting tips that will come in handy if you experience these issues while trying to bind your Mac client to Active Directory:

You have an issue with AD domains ending in .local. Many people have reported issues connecting to an Active Directory domain that ends with .local (such as is often used with Windows Small Business Server networks). Bonjour, Apple's implementation of Multicast DNS, does not see .local as a valid top-level domain and assumes that it should be resolved through Bonjour. Because of this, the Mac client will not query the DNS server to retrieve an IP address for any host in a .local domain. You can enable your Mac to look up .local domain addresses by adding local to your list of search domains, as shown in Figure 18.42.

FIGURE 18.42
Adding local
to your search
domain order

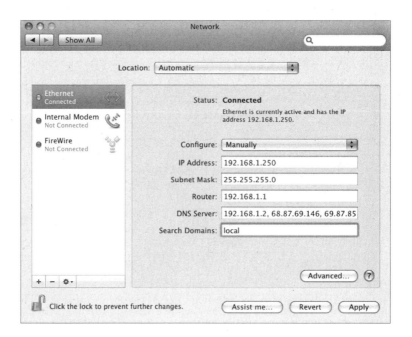

Active Directory does not respond when binding. If you receive an error that the Active Directory domain failed to respond when you tried to bind your Mac to the domain, there are a few things to check:

- Verify that your network settings specify a valid DNS server in the domain.
- Verify that SMB packet signing has been set correctly in Active Directory.

Active Directory stops responding. Various versions of OS X have had challenges connecting to Active Directory. Make sure you have the latest updates for the operating system. If your Mac client loses contact with Active Directory, try unbinding from the domain and then binding again.

The Bottom Line

Verify your network configuration. DHCP provides centralized IP address configurations, and all Windows clients understand DHCP without any additional installations required.

Master It You need to verify that a client machine has received the correct IP address configuration via DHCP for the network you are working on. Which of the following commands would return these results?

- `ipconfig /all`
- `ipconfig /refresh`
- `msconfig /show`
- `msconfig`

Join a client computer to a domain. Joining an Active Directory domain is key for workstations, because this provides centralized management from the Domain Admins group within the domain. Group Policy is centralized, security can be established, and even software can be controlled centrally.

Master It Is the following statement true or false? "When joining a computer to an Active Directory domain, the only way this can occur is if the user joining the computer to the domain is a domain admin."

Change user passwords. By default Windows AD provides a 42-day maximum password age limit. This limit is preceded by a 14-day reminder that you need to change your password. The 42-day maximum is designed to maintain a certain level of security for the enterprise, not allowing passwords to become stale.

Master It A user has become paranoid and wants to change his user account password right away. He does not know how to do this and calls the help desk. The computer he is using is running the Windows 7 operating system. What do you tell him?

Connect to network resources. Here's a typical scenario: a user wants to connect to a printer on the domain that does double-sided printing and also stapling. But the user does not know where the company keeps these printers. The user calls the help desk.

Master It Which of the following is the most efficient way for the user to find printers matching this description?

a. Tell the user to walk around the office complex and check each printer to see whether it has these features.

b. Tell the user to use the `net view` command to check for shared printers on a per-computer basis.

c. Tell the user to start the Add Printer Wizard and then select the Search Active Directory option.

Prepare Active Directory for Mac OS X clients. Although Mac OS X can join Active Directory domains, you must take some preparatory steps to ensure they can communicate with Windows Server 2012.

Master it You want your Active Directory users who have Mac clients to connect to your Windows Server 2008 R2 servers using a single Active Directory logon. What network security feature of Windows must you change to permit Mac clients to communicate with your Windows Server 2012 domain?

Connect a Mac to the domain. Mac OS X can connect to Active Directory and join domains. SMB protocol support is provided by a built-in version of Samba, letting OS X connect to Windows for file shares and printers.

Master it You want to add your Mac OS X client to your Active Directory domain. Which OS X utility should you use?

Connect to file shares and printers. OS X connects to Windows file shares and printers using the SMB support provided by Samba. Because support is integrated, you can use the Finder to connect to Windows resources directly rather than adding additional software.

Master It You are trying to access a network folder that is shared on a Windows Server 2012 computer from your domain-joined Mac client. How can you use the Finder to connect?

Use Remote Desktop from a Mac client. Microsoft created the Remote Desktop Connection for Mac to provide Remote Desktop connectivity for Mac clients. Using RDC, you can access the functionality of your Windows computer directly from your Mac clients.

Master It You are using RDC to connect to your Windows Server 2012 server computer and want to save your network credentials so that you don't have to enter them every time you connect. How can you do this?

Chapter 19

Web Server Management with IIS

The Microsoft Cloud OS initiative is in full swing, and Internet Information Services (IIS) has a front-row seat. Whether you're leveraging System Center 2012 R2 to manage your infrastructure, Windows Server Update Services to handle patching, or extending your infrastructure into the cloud with the Windows Azure Pack, IIS is a key component. With such an important role to play, Microsoft has made some major improvements in IIS, making it the fastest, most secure version of IIS ever, and yet it is still easy to use.

In this chapter, you'll learn to:

- ◆ Plan for and install IIS 8.5

- ◆ Manage IIS 8's global default

- ◆ Create and secure websites in IIS 8

- ◆ Manage IIS 8 with advanced administration techniques

What's New in IIS 8.0 and 8.5

Microsoft has made some exciting enhancements to IIS 8.0 and 8.5. There are improvements around virtualization, security, scalability, administration, and performance. The following is a brief description of each of these new features:

Dynamic IP Address Restrictions   IIS 8 takes IP address restriction to the next level by allowing administrators to configure the servers to blacklist access for IP addresses that exceed a specified number of concurrent requests or the number of requests over a period of time. IP filtering also adds a new proxy mode feature that will allow an IP address to be blocked not only by the client IP that IIS sees but also by the values received in the x-forwarded-for HTTP header. Administrators are also able to specify what ISS will do when an IP address is blocked, such as sending unauthorized, forbidden, or not-found messages or even aborting the connection.

FTP Login Attempt Restrictions   This feature is designed to help prevent unauthorized users from gaining access to your FTP site. It will let administrators configure the FTP servers to block access for the users who exceed a specified number of login requests over a period of time. This is different from dynamic IP address restriction in that it blocks only the offending user account, not the originating IP address.

App Pool CPU Throttling   Administrators can now control CPU load for each application pool, preventing one site from overwhelming the server and degrading performance of all other sites on that host. In previous versions of IIS, CPU throttling would disable the site once the configured threshold was reached, but that would prevent anyone from being able to access the site. IIS 8 will not disable the site, but it will continue to service requests at a reduced rate. IIS administrators can also configure CPU throttling to be active at all times or to kick in only when the host system is under an increased load.

Application Initialization   This feature allows web applications to be initialized in advance so that they are ready the first time a user accesses the application. This will help prevent the end user from having to wait for the web application to start up, but in the event the user is the trigger for the web application to start, IIS 8 can be configured to return static content until it has completed its initialization tasks. This can be combined with URL rewrite rules to create more complex static content while the application is initializing.

Centralized Certificate Store   Managing SSL certificates in web farms can be time consuming and tedious, from importing the certificates into each server to manually verifying the certificates are in sync. IIS 8 changes all of that with a centralized certificate store that allows you to store all of your web certificates on a network file share.

Server Name Indication   Previous versions of IIS have been able to leverage host headers so that administrators can assign multiple websites to a single IP address. IIS 8.0 brings that ability to Secure Socket Layer (SSL) protected sites. This ability does require that your client browsers support Server Name Indication (SNI). Most modern browsers do; however, no version of Internet Explorer on Windows XP will support SNI.

SSL Scalability   IIS 8 has had some significant improvements in the way certificates are handled. In previous versions, each SSL certificate needed to be loaded into memory the first time a client accessed the site and remained in memory indefinitely. In IIS 8, only the certificate that is needed at the time is loaded into memory, and it will unload after a configurable amount of time. In addition, SSL certificate enumeration and load times have been dramatically improved, allowing thousands of SSL sites per host.

Dynamic Site Activation   In previous version of IIS, when you hosted a lot of websites, you most likely experienced that it took a bit of time to load the IIS configuration file. That was because when the Windows Process Activation Service (WAS) runs, it loads the entire configuration for all websites hosted on the server. With Windows Server 2012 R2 and IIS 8.5, the process has been optimized to dramatically increase the performance. There is no specific user interface for this feature, but it can be configured via the Configuration Editor.

Idle Worker Process Page-Out   IIS 8.5 has improved the idle worker process. In previous versions of IIS, when a worker process would time out due to inactivity, IIS would terminate the process, freeing the resources associated with it. This was both good and bad because you would have the resources available to be used elsewhere, but when the worker process was requested again, you would have to wait for it to complete its startup process. In IIS 8.5 you can suspend the worker process. Using suspend will page out the process to disk, freeing up the memory, and when the process is requested again, the process will page in from disk without having to wait for the startup process. Using a combination of the idle worker process and the application-initialization feature, you can virtually prevent users from having to experience the startup time for any web application.

Logging Enhancements   IIS 8.5 now has more logging options. You now have the ability to perform logging of fields within the Request Header, Response Header, and/or Server variables. You have a slew of fields to choose from, or you can create a custom field.

ETW Events   IIS 8.5 now has event tracing built in. You can still use the standard logs, use Event Tracing for Windows (ETW), or both.

Installing IIS 8

Now that we have examined the new features of IIS, we'll take a deeper look at installing it. Windows Server 2012 comes in several editions and has new methods of employing different roles for the server. Without getting into a detailed analysis of those editions in this chapter, keep in mind that IIS 8.0 is available on all full Windows Server 2012 editions as well as Windows 8.

Although some IIS 8.x servers may be internally deployed as intranet servers or to support a web-based network application, others will be relegated to the perimeter TCP/IP network address space, sometimes called the *demilitarized zone* (DMZ), as public front-end web servers. Regardless of the IIS 8 server's intended purpose, the installation process is the same.

Adding the Web Server Role via Service Manager

Windows Server 2012 continues the concept of installing functionality into the OS by employing specific roles on the server. Assigning a role not only installs the corresponding services but also mandates dependency services and implies suggestions for hardening. To install IIS 8, you need to deploy the Web Server role on the server.

As with previous versions, IIS 8 consists of many modules. We cannot stress enough that you should add only the modules necessary to support your planned web content. Table 19.1 lists the roles and features available when using the Web Server role in the OS, along with their corresponding feature names in PowerShell. By installing no more modules than absolutely necessary, you can build a lean web server with a smaller resource footprint and reduced attack surface. Following this strategy will give you a more secure, better-performing web server.

TABLE 19.1:   OS Role Services for IIS 8 (in the Same Order as in the Server Manager Wizard)

SERVICE NAME (GUI)	POWERSHELL FEATURE NAME	DESCRIPTION	DEFAULT
Web Server	Web-WebServer	Publishes websites, web services, and web applications	Yes
Default Document	Web-Default-Doc	Configures a default file for websites to deliver when a page call is not specified in the URL	Yes
Directory Browsing	Web-Dir-Browsing	Autogenerates a list of all directories/files for websites to deliver when a page call is not specified in the URL and the default document is disabled or not configured	Yes

Continues

TABLE 19.1: OS Role Services for IIS 8 (in the Same Order as in the Server Manager Wizard) *(CONTINUED)*

SERVICE NAME (GUI)	POWERSHELL FEATURE NAME	DESCRIPTION	DEFAULT
HTTP Errors	Web-Http-Errors	Customizes error messages	Yes
Static Content	Web-Static-Content	Publishes static web file formats	Yes
HTTP Redirection	Web-Http-Redirect	Redirects one URL to another URL	No
WebDAV Publishing	Web-DAV-Publishing	Publishes files to/from a web server via HTTP	No
HTTP Logging	Web-Http-Logging	Provides logging of website activity	Yes
Custom Logging	Web-Custom-Logging	Creates custom log modules	No
Logging Tools	Web-Log-Libraries	Provides web server log management and automation infrastructure	No
ODBC Logging	Web-ODBC-Logging	Provides infrastructure to log web server activity to an ODBC-compliant database and retrieve it for web display	No
Request Monitor	Web-Request-Monitor	Provides infrastructure to capture IIS worker process information including HTTP request details	No
Tracing	Web-Http-Tracing	Provides infrastructure to capture defined events	No
Static Content Compression	Web-Stat-Compression	Provides infrastructure to compress static content for caching	Yes
Dynamic Content Compression	Web-Dyn-Compression	Provides infrastructure to compress dynamic content	No
Request Filtering	Web-Filtering	Filters incoming requests based on administrator-defined rules	Yes
Basic Authentication	Web-Basic-Auth	Supports basic authentication	No
Centralize SSL Certificate Support	Web-CertProvider	Supports centralized SLL certificates	No
Client Certificate Mapping Authentication	Web-Client-Auth	Supports client certificate authentication using Active Directory (one-to-one mappings across multiple web servers)	No
Digest Authentication	Web-Digest-Auth	Supports password-hashing authentication	No

TABLE 19.1: OS Role Services for IIS 8 (in the Same Order as in the Server Manager Wizard) *(CONTINUED)*

SERVICE NAME (GUI)	POWERSHELL FEATURE NAME	DESCRIPTION	DEFAULT
IIS Client Certificate Mapping Authentication	Web-Cert-Auth	Supports client certificate authentication using IIS (one-to-one or many-to-one mappings)	No
IP and Domain Restrictions	Web-IP-Security	Delivers content by originating requestor's IP address or domain name	No
URL Authorization	Web-Url-Auth	Supports rules-based content restrictions associated with users, groups, or HTTP header verbs	No
Windows Authentication	Web-Windows-Auth	Supports Windows account authentication	No
.NET Extensibility 3.5	Web-Net-Ext	Extends web server functionality in the request, configuration, or UI	No
.NET Extensibility 4.5	Web-Net-Ext45	Extends web server functionality in the request, configuration, or UI	No
Application Initialization	Web-AppInit	Performs expensive web application initialization tasks before serving web pages	
ASP	Web-ASP	Provides Active Server Page server-side scripting (both VBScript and JScript)	No
ASP.NET 3.5	Web-Asp-Net	Provides a server-side object model for managed applications based on the .NET Framework	No
ASP.NET 4.5	Web-Asp-Net45	Provides a server-side object model for managed applications based on the .NET 4.5 Framework	No
CGI	Web-CGI	Provides CGI support for CGI scripting to external programs	No
ISAPI Extensions	Web-ISAPI-Ext	Supports dynamic web content via ISAPI extensions engaged upon request	No
ISAPI Filters	Web-ISAPI-Filter	Supports files that filter requests to the web server in order to extend or change specific functionalities	No
Server-Side Includes (SSI)	Web-Includes	Provides script generation of dynamic HTML pages	No
WebSocket Protocol	Web-WebSockets	Supports applications that communicate over the WebSocket protocol	No

Continues

TABLE 19.1: OS Role Services for IIS 8 (in the Same Order as in the Server Manager Wizard) *(CONTINUED)*

SERVICE NAME (GUI)	POWERSHELL FEATURE NAME	DESCRIPTION	DEFAULT
FTP Server	Web-Ftp-Server	Provides infrastructure to build FTP sites that use FTP for uploading and downloading	No
FTP Service	Web-Ftp-Service	Enables FTP publishing	No
FTP Extensibility	Web-Ftp-Ext	Supports FTP extensibility features such as custom providers, ASP.NET users, or IIS Manager users	No
IIS Hostable Web Core	Web-WHC	Enables applications outside of IIS to serve HTTP requests using their own `.config` files	No
IIS Management Console	Web-Mgmt-Console	Provides GUI management of IIS 7.5 web services (not FTP or SMTP)	Yes
IIS 6 Management Compatibility	Web-Mgmt-Compat	Provides ABO and ADSI support for existing IIS 6.0 management scripts	No
IIS 6 Metabase Compatibility	Web-Metabase	Provides IIS 6.0 metabase query and configuration support for ABO and ADSI applications	No
IIS 6 Management Console	Web-Lgcy-Mgmt-Console	Provides infrastructure for administration of remote IIS 6 web servers and for administration of FTP and SMTP	No
IIS 6 Scripting Tools	Web-Lgcy-Scripting	Provides infrastructure to run IIS 6 scripts on IIS 7.5 including ADO and ADSI (requires WAS)	No
IIS 6 WMI Compatibility	Web-WMI	Provides WMI scripting interface for management and automation tasks using WMI CIM Studio, WMI Event Registration, WMI Event Viewer, and WMI Object Browser	No
IIS Management Scripts and Tools	Web-Scripting-Tools	Provides CLI and scripted management of IIS, which is valuable for automating administration	No
Management Service	Web-Mgmt-Service	Provides infrastructure for remote GUI management of IIS	No

A WEB SERVER FOR BIGFIRM

We will be using the Service Manager GUI to create two websites on a Windows Server 2012 R2 host running Microsoft IIS 8.5. Website 1 will be dedicated to apples and website 2 will focus on oranges.

To begin, launch Server Manager, and select Add Roles and Features from the Manage menu to add the Web Server role to the server, as shown in Figure 19.1. Alternatively, you could use PowerShell to install IIS and even write scripts for automatic or remote installation (more on PowerShell later).

FIGURE 19.1
Manage task list from the service manager dashboard

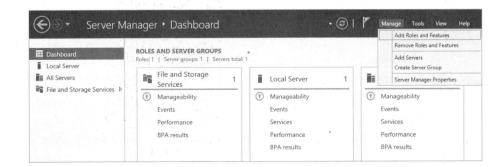

1. On the Before You Begin page, click Next.

2. On the Installation Type page, click Next.

3. On the Server Selection page, click Next to accept the server target as the local server.

4. Select Web Server (IIS) on the Select Server Roles page, and then click Next.

5. In the resulting pop-up, select Add Features to also install the IIS Management tools on the IIS server, and then click Next.

6. On the Web Server (IIS) page, click Next to advance the wizard.

7. On the Role Services selection list, select all of the role services, and click Next to continue (see Table 19.1 for an explanation of each).

8. On the Confirm page, review your selections and click Install.

9. On the Installation Progress page, confirm that the install was successful, and click Close.

Installing IIS 8 via PowerShell

As with all other features in Server 2012, you can install, configure, and remove IIS 8 using PowerShell. To install IIS from PowerShell, simply run the following command:

```
Install-WindowsFeature -Name Web-Server -IncludeManagemntTools
```

This will install the Web Server role with all of the default options, exactly like installing the Web Server role via the GUI. To add additional features to a running IIS server, run the `Install-WindowsFeature` cmdlet again with the name of the feature you wish to install. Table 19.1 contains a list of all the web server feature names, or you can run the following PowerShell command to see them:

```
Get-WindowsFeature -name web*
```

Renovating IIS Construction

Altering the construction of IIS is as easy as unplugging the A/C adapter of your laptop computer in favor of plugging in your mobile phone charger instead! Feel free to add or remove modules for exploration, testing, or actual production use. The addition of a feature to IIS is not a permanent decision. You can always remove the feature down the road by simply deselecting the check box.

If you did not perform a *full* installation of all Web Server role services in the OS when you initially installed IIS, then you will need to add the appropriate role service before that role service's associated native modules will be available to add to an IIS website. The "Adding Role Services to the Web Server Role for Bigfirm" section shows how to register a native module using the OS, allowing Windows Server 2012 to trust the code and give it unrestricted access to all resources. As with any escalated code, be careful to register only native IIS modules from trusted sources because they will have very privileged access to the system.

Adding Role Services to the Web Server Role for Bigfirm

In order to configure the websites in our example, you will need ASP page support on the Oranges website until you rewrite some of the content, and then you will use HTTP Redirection to port visitors to the new content once it is written. You can add role services to an already applied server role via the Server Manager GUI, AppCmd.exe, or PowerShell. For example, to add the ASP role service to an existing web server role on the BF1 server at Bigfirm via the Server Manager GUI, follow these steps:

1. Launch Server Manager.

2. Select the IIS role in the left tree pane.

3. Scroll down to the right details pane to reach the Role and Features Services section for a summary of the web server roles that are installed, as shown in Figure 19.2.

FIGURE 19.2
Installed roles and features

4. Click the Tasks drop-down menu on the right and select Add Roles and Features.

5. In the Add Roles and Features Wizard dialog box that pops up, advance to the Server Roles page, and select the ASP role service located under Web Server (IIS)\Web Server\ Application Development.

. Notice that already installed role services appear in gray and cannot be removed from this wizard. If you want to remove a role service, follow these steps:

a. Cancel this dialog box (confirm the cancellation).

b. Use the Remove Roles and Features option from the Tasks drop-down menu instead.

Because the newly added ASP role service requires the dependency role service titled ISAPI Extensions, which is not yet installed, an Add Role Services dialog box appears informing you of the requirement and giving you the chance to also install the dependency role service on the fly (see Figure 19.3).

FIGURE 19.3
Add roles and features wizard

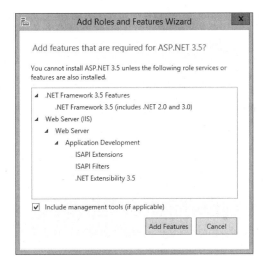

6. Click the Add Required Role Services button to allow the installation of the dependencies.

7. Click Next and advance through the features page.

The Confirmation dialog box will simply summarize your choices.

8. Just click Install to finalize the installation, returning you to Server Manager.

Notice that you do not get prompted for the Windows Server 2012 installation media. You no longer need to frantically search every software supply closet prior to administrating your IIS server!

Or if you prefer to use PowerShell to add role services to the Web Server role in the OS, the `Install-WindowsFeature` cmdlet will get the job done. Here's the PowerShell syntax for adding the HTTP Redirection role service:

```
Install-WindowsFeature Web-Http-Redirect
```

When the command runs, a progress bar will appear across the screen going from 0% to 100%, after which the PowerShell screen should contain the lines shown in Figure 19.4.

FIGURE 19.4
Completed role service installation via PowerShell

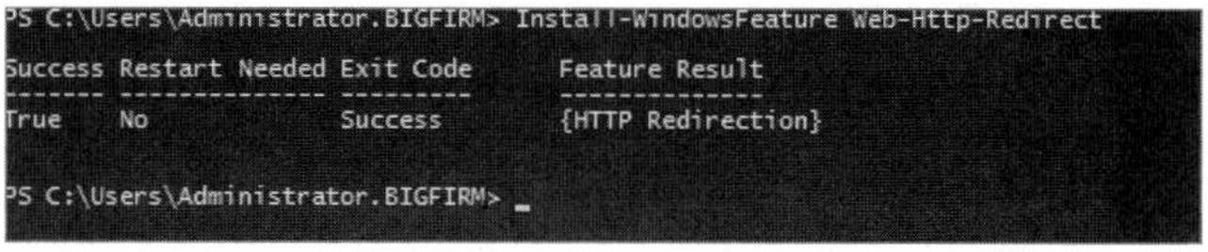
PS C:\Users\Administrator.BIGFIRM> Install-WindowsFeature Web-Http-Redirect
Success Restart Needed Exit Code Feature Result
True No Success {HTTP Redirection}
PS C:\Users\Administrator.BIGFIRM> _

REGISTERING NATIVE MODULES USING IIS MANAGER

When it comes to native modules, you could register a native module using the IIS Manager GUI. This is not as intuitive as using Server Manager, but if you are the kind of administrator who prefers to spend your whole day using one utility and IIS Manager is your preference, you can accomplish this very important task in IIS Manager as well. To register a native module on the fly, follow these steps:

1. Launch IIS Manager, and connect to or highlight a specific IIS server that you want to examine using the Connections pane on the left.

   The center page of IIS Manager reflects the categories of management tools by default.

2. Within the IIS category, click the Modules icon to see a list of modules installed at the server level.

3. Click the Configure Native Modules hyperlink from the modules-specific Actions pane on the right.

   This produces a dialog box listing the native modules currently installed (see Figure 19.5).

4. Click the Register button in the dialog box to manually register a native module on the fly.

   This, of course, requires that you know the actual filename of the native module.

5. Upon adding the native module to the list, select it to enable it at the server level.

FIGURE 19.5
Configure Native Modules dialog box

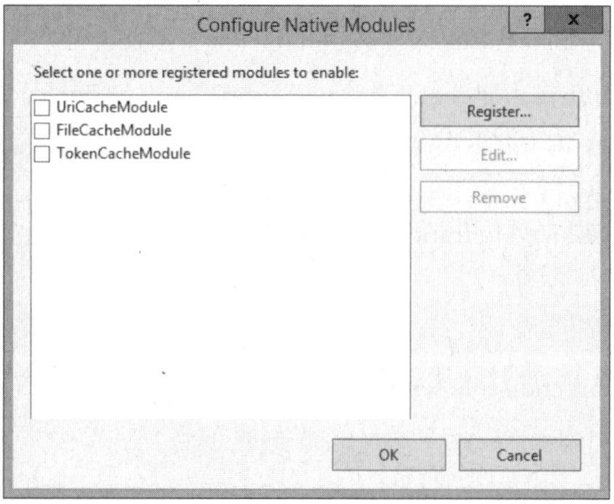
Configure Native Modules
Select one or more registered modules to enable:
UriCacheModule
FileCacheModule
TokenCacheModule
Register...
Edit...
Remove
OK
Cancel

MODULE MANAGEMENT VIA POWERSHELL

While you can still go in and edit the `applicationhost.config` file as in previous versions of IIS, you may find managing the modules available at either the server level or site level more convenient via PowerShell. Using PowerShell to install native modules at the server level will allow them to be automatically installed at every site, and the following commands will prove useful.

◆ To install a module, use this:

```
New-WebGlobalModule -Name {module name} -Image {module path}
```

◆ To uninstall a module, use this:

```
Remove-WebGlobalModule -Name {module name}
```

◆ To enable a module, use this:

```
Enable-WebGlobalModule -Name {module name}
```

◆ To enable a module for an individual site, use this:

```
Enable-WebGlobalModule -Name {module name} -PSPath "IIS:\sites\{SiteName}"
```

◆ To disable a module, use this:

```
Disable-WebGlobalModule -Name {module name}
```

◆ To disable a module for an individual site, use this:

```
Disable-WebGlobalModule -Name {module name} -PSPath "IIS:\sites\{SiteName}"
```

CONFIGURING MODULES AT THE SITE LEVEL

Once you have installed the necessary role services, the associated modules are available in IIS to process client requests properly. In fact, the native modules are automatically enabled on all websites that are inheriting their configuration from the parent `applicationhost.config` file. IIS modules can be configured or disabled at the site level by directly modifying the site's `web.config` file in a text editor, by using the `AppCmd.exe` utility, by using PowerShell, or by navigating the IIS Manager GUI. For example, beginning with the friendly GUI interface, follow these steps:

1. Launch IIS Manager, and connect to or highlight a specific IIS server that you want to examine using the Connections pane on the left.

   The center page of IIS Manager reflects the categories of management tools by default.

2. Within the IIS category, click the Modules icon to see a list of modules installed at the server level that are available to be managed at the site level.

   Note that any website set to inherit its feature structure from its parent will be inheriting these modules from the server level.

3. Navigate to Default Web Site under Sites in the Connections pane on the left, and highlight it.

Notice the Home icons available, particularly the ASP and HTTP Redirect icons, which are available now only because you installed the necessary role services at the server level (they did not appear here before).

4. Double-click the Modules icon, and peruse the list of installed modules, both native and managed, that are available for use on the Default Web Site.

Notice that ASP does not appear separately listed but rather is hidden within the IsapiModule.

5. To disable one of the inherited native modules here at the site level on the Default Web Site, such as IsapiModule, simply highlight the module, and click the Remove link in the Actions pane on the right.

Of course, the OS will prompt you to confirm the removal, so be ready to be sure. Notice that the module disappears from the list.

Enabling an already installed native module (one that is registered in `applicationhost .config`) at the site level isn't as obvious.

6. If you want to reenable the IsapiModule on the Default Web Site, click the Configure Native Modules hyperlink in the modules-specific Actions pane on the right.

This produces a dialog box, such as the one shown in Figure 19.6, that allows you to enable the IsapiModule by simply selecting its check box.

FIGURE 19.6
Configure Native Modules dialog box

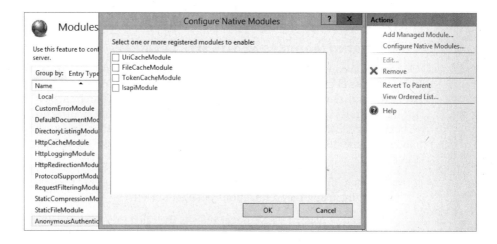

Remember, modules registered in the server-level `applicationhost.config` configuration file are automatically enabled on all sites that inherit their module structure from the server. There is no reason to enable the modules at every site in your IIS instance. And although there is much ado about the new site-specific `web.config` files, the reality is that a site doesn't even get a `web.config` file created for it until you make a configuration change to the site that disallows inheritance from the parent level. Once you make such a change, only the newly unique configuration setting is written into the site-specific `web.config` file, and the write happens immediately. So, 'in' or 'when' employing native modules by registering them at the server level, you have not yet caused any site-specific `web.config` file to be generated. We'll take a look at customizing websites in the next section.

Website Provisioning

Provisioning is the art of allocating resources and creating the structure for a new website. Several client access protocols are supported these days (HTTP, FTP, SOAP, and so on), so an accurate discourse on the subject of creating a website should clarify which type of traffic you expect the website to support. Vocabulary may again provide challenges when researching the best method of creating sites. Remember that a *site* in IIS is a logical entity that merely defines protocol handling and endpoint listening behavior in order to receive client requests and respond to them. For example, to create an HTTP site, you would configure the IP address, port number, and host header information that the server will recognize on an inbound request from a client in order to respond to it. Any client request bearing a destination IP address, destination port, or requested host header in the URL that matches your new site's configuration will immediately be directed to your new site as opposed to any other site existing on that same IIS server. These address, port, and header assignments are referred to in IIS as *bindings*.

Because each HTTP site's binding values must be unique in order to correctly route processing, IIS will throw an error if you attempt to create identical site protocol bindings on more than one site. However, there are many possible combinations of IP address, port, and host header that would allow you to build multiple sites on the same instance of IIS without conflict. We'll discuss hosting multiple sites in more detail in a bit.

Within a site, a smaller logical unit that represents part or all of the site's functionality is called an *application*. Multiple applications may exist within a single site and can be configured separately for performance and security reasons. Each application's URL namespace is mapped to a physical drive via a *virtual directory* configuration parameter. A site must contain a minimum of one application called the *root application*. This root application must be configured with a minimum of one virtual directory.

Before jumping into site creation, it is important to conceptualize the architecture in IIS. IIS is based on a distributed XML file configuration system. The server-level settings are held in the `applicationhost.config` file, and each site may have its own `web.config` file in which both site configuration and ASP.NET settings are defined. Given the architecture along with the continued binding uniqueness requirements, some of the justifications for creating new sites include the following:

- Supporting different domain names

- Supporting different authentication protocols

- Hosting multiple sites on a single instance of IIS

- Hosting separate ASP.NET applications on a single instance of IIS

- Maximizing performance by isolating applications into separate app pools

- Maximizing disk space utilization with separate virtual directories

- Delegating site administration

Understanding Global Settings

Before creating a new website, you should understand what global settings are defined at the server level in the three server configuration files:

Machine.config   Located in the %windir%\Microsoft.Net\Framework\Framwork_version\CONFIG directory. This file contains the global defaults for the .NET framework; it also contains some of the settings for ASP.NET.

Root Web.config   Located in the %windir%\Microsoft.NET\Framework\framework_version\CONFIG directory. This configuration file contains the remaining settings for ASP.NET.

applicationhost.config   Located in the %windir%\system32\inetsrv\config directory, which is a folder with very limited NTFS ACL access by default (see Table 19.2).

The applicationhost.config file is the root file of the configuration. It includes the definition of all sites, applications, virtual directories, and application pools, in addition to the global defaults.

Planning Bigfirm's Apples and Oranges Websites

One of the most popular protocols is still HTTP for delivery of static content, so let's concentrate on creating simple static HTTP websites. First, you will create an apples virtual directory within the Default Web Site, and then you will create a separate Oranges website using different protocol bindings. Since the Oranges site will need to support ASP pages, you should run it in a separate application pool. And given that both of your sites need to have different bindings and URLs, you should create the oranges pages as a new, separate website. However, the apples pages will use the same settings and application pool as the Default Web Site, so you can simply add the apples content as a new virtual directory into the Default Web Site.

When deciding between adding apples as a virtual directory to the existing Default Web Site root application versus creating a second application within the Default Web Site to support the apples content, the ultimate factor is code support. Recall that applications are designed to provide both content and code and thus give you the opportunity to assign a unique application pool to them. Since the apples pages are simply delivering static .htm content, creating a whole new application for these pages would be overkill for this illustration. However, when planning your own IIS implementation, you should plan for growth, scale, and development. If you think a set of pages will eventually need to include code, go ahead and build them an application at the beginning and grow into it down the road.

IIS 8 still offers the Default Web Site, which listens on TCP port 80 across all network interfaces and is not configured for any particular host header. If these dimensions are acceptable for your new website, feel free to direct the Default Web Site to your content directories instead of creating an additional site. This will work fine for the apples site.

TABLE 19.2:   NTFS Permissions on applicationhost.config

ACCESS CONTROL ENTRY	ALLOWED PERMISSION
Administrators	Full Control
SYSTEM	Full Control
TrustedInstaller	Full Control

To make server-level configuration changes, you can either edit the `applicationhost`
`.config` file directly or use the IIS Manager GUI, the `Appcmd.exe` utility, or PowerShell. If you
decide to alter the `applicationhost.config` file directly, pay close attention to the `%windir%\`
`system32\inetsrv\config\schema\IIS_schema.xml` file, which dictates the allowable
structure you can write into `applicationhost.config`. You may also decide to back up the
`applicationhost.config` file prior to making any changes, just in case. If you are going to
frequently edit the `applicationhost.config` file directly, it would be prudent to use a true
XML-editing application such as Microsoft's XML Notepad, available to download for free at
`http://tinyurl.com/MS2012XMLNotepad`.

IMPORTANT SECTIONS OF APPLICATIONHOST.CONFIG

There are so many elements in an `applicationhost.config` XML file that at first glance it may be
difficult to figure out which section of the file has what type of configuration settings in it. To help
you navigate this critical server-level configuration file, here are some descriptions of important
sections, indented to indicate their hierarchy level in the `applicationhost.config` XML schema:

> `<configuration>`: Root element

>> `<configSections>`: Registrations of non-nested sections organized into
groups

>>> `<Section>`: Building blocks of deployable, lockable, searchable settings

>> `<configProtectedData>`: Registrations of cryptography providers
(algorithms)

>> `<system.applicationHost>`: Site, web app, virtual directory, and app pool
configurations

>> `<applicationPools>`: Registrations of application pools of isolated
execution

>> `<customMetadata>`: ABO compatibility data (*Do not modify this!*)

>> `<listenerAdapters>`: Windows Process Activation Service (WAS) bindings

>> `<log>`: Binary and W3C log definitions

>> `<sites>`: Site definitions

> `<system.webServer>`: Global web defaults not found in `system`
`.applicationHost`

>> `<globalModules>`: Registrations of native modules

>> `<http…>`: HTTP compression, custom errors, custom headers, redirect, tracing,
ISAPI filters, and ODBC logging.

>> `<security>`: Server-level security settings

>> `<modules>`: Module-locking status for distributed management

There are many settings you may want to control from the server level. Registration and security of the modules come immediately to mind. And many of these settings are more easily managed in the IIS Manager GUI, AppCmd.exe, or PowerShell. We will cover more administration topics later, but suffice it to say that it would be a good idea to identify which settings from the server level you will be customizing on your new site and plan for disallowing inheritance once your new site is created.

Creating a Simple Website

You can use the GUI administration tools, the AppCmd.exe utility, or PowerShell to create new websites in IIS 8, depending on your comfort level and scripting needs. PowerShell will be covered in more depth later, so for now we will concentrate on the GUI. Before you can begin actually creating the site, planning is required to determine the appropriate settings for the new site:

- What IP address should be associated with the site?

- What TCP/IP port number should be associated with the site?

- Will the site use a custom host header in the URL?

- What application pools will the site's applications use?

- Where will the virtual directory point to locate content for the site?

To begin, you must become familiar with the new IIS Manager interface.

Site Setup via IIS Manager

Upon launching the new Internet Information Services Manager, you undoubtedly recognized that the snap-in has undergone an extreme makeover. Rest assured that this is still a preconfigured console file and that you can build the IIS Manager snap-in into any custom management console. The start page (see Figure 19.7) is mostly links to news and resources, although the "Recent connections" and "Connection tasks" panes can prove helpful when troubleshooting multiple IIS servers from a single management console.

FIGURE 19.7
Internet Information
Services Manager

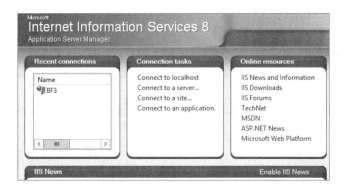

Once you're connected to a web server, you will notice that not much has changed in the navigation since IIS 7. The Connections pane on the left is still easily navigated vertically to expose the application pools and sites of various IIS servers the management console is currently connected to. This pane remains visible when using the console. The path across the top of the console has the familiar Forward, Back, Refresh, and Help buttons.

Once you highlight a connected server in the Connections pane, the start page disappears and is replaced with the server's Home page in Features view and grouped by area as the default. An Actions pane will also appear on the right, and the tasks hyperlinked in this pane will change relative to the Connections pane node being focused on (see Figure 19.8 for an example of the console pane's layout).

FIGURE 19.8
IIS Manager:
server focus

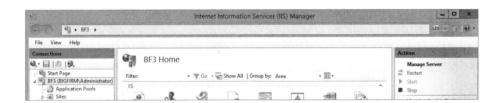

Performing administration via IIS Manager will be covered in greater detail throughout this chapter. For now, we will focus on creating a new website. Make note of the features listed at the server level, because you will be limited to only these functionalities for your new site. If there is a trick your new site must perform that is missing from the server, it is best to add the necessary feature to the server prior to creating your new site. You may also notice that the Actions pane offers many of the same configuration capabilities as the context menu would if you were to right-click the Connections node. Imagine that—more than one way to accomplish the same task in a Microsoft product! Regardless, you may want to take this opportunity to acquaint yourself with using the Actions pane instead of using context menus.

Constructing Bigfirm's Websites

For illustrative purposes, assume that the new Apples Rule!! pages will be part of the bigfirm.com domain and will serve static .htm content across all server network interfaces through TCP port 80. Also assume that the text and image content for these new pages is already stored in an Apples directory you created under the default IIS 8 content directory of %systemdrive%\inetpub.

To create the new Apples Rule!! web pages using IIS Manager, do the following:

1. Expand Server, and then expand the Sites node in the Connections pane.

2. Click Default Web Site, click View Virtual Directories in the Actions pane, and then click Add Virtual Directory in the Actions pane. The Add Virtual Directory dialog box opens, as shown in Figure 19.9.

FIGURE 19.9
Add virtual directory dialog box

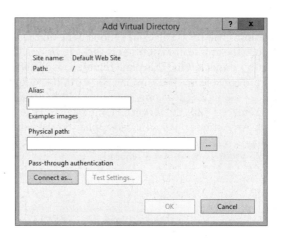

3. For the alias, enter a URL-friendly name that is descriptive but concise. In this case, the new name is **apples**.

4. For the physical path, enter `C:\inetpub\apples`.

   If the content is stored in a local folder on an IIS server that happens to also be shared, use the local path instead of the UNC path for maximum performance. As is always true when using UNC paths to remote folders, for performance or confidence reasons, you can always replace the hostname of the path with an IP address.

5. Click OK in the Add Virtual Directory dialog box.

   The new virtual directory should appear in the Virtual Directories list in the details pane of IIS Manager. From there you can manage the new virtual directory's properties and permissions.

Now that you have created a virtual directory that points to the Apples Rule!! content, you should test the new environment by browsing to the Apples Rule!! page. Without leaving IIS Manager, you can do either of the following:

1. Right-click the new virtual directory in the Connections pane, choose Manage Virtual Directory, and click Browse.

2. Click the new virtual directory in Virtual Directories list.

3. Click the Browse *.80 (HTTP) link in the Actions pane.

No matter which method you employ, a new instance of Internet Explorer will launch and navigate directly to the new Apples Rule!! page (as shown in Figure 19.10). Just a side note, Windows Server 2012 includes IE 8 with enhanced security engaged by default. If your new page will not display, consider either adding the URL to Trusted Sites or disengaging the IE Enhanced Security Configuration setting.

Now that the Apples Rule!! content is up, it is time to build the Oranges site. Remember, you plan to employ additional modules and some code on this site, so you need it to be completely separate from the Default Web Site and run in a separate application pool.

FIGURE 19.10
Apples homepage

To create the new Oranges website using IIS Manager, follow these steps:

1. Expand Server in the Connections pane, click the Sites node, and click Add Website in the Actions pane.

   The Add Website dialog box opens, as shown in Figure 19.11.

FIGURE 19.11
Add website dialog

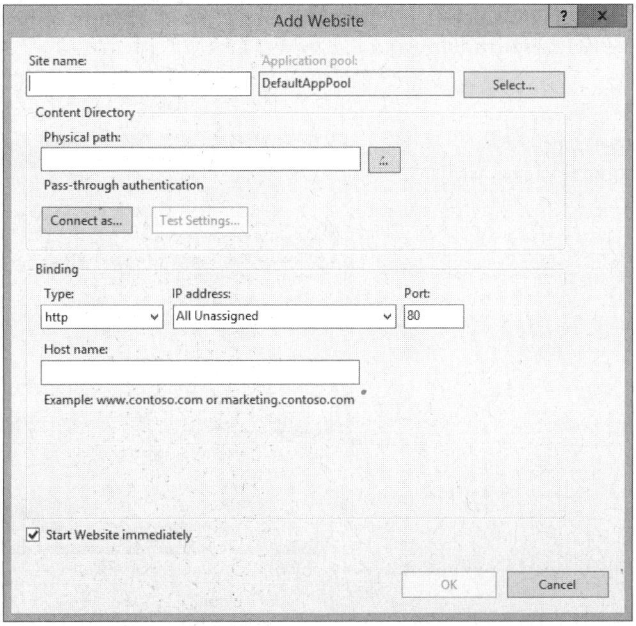

2. Enter a site name that is descriptive but concise; in this case enter **Oranges**.

   The value entered in this field will automatically generate a new .NET integrated-mode application pool by default and assign it to the new site unless you specify an existing application pool with the Select button. The new application pool will be created with the parameter settings defined using the Set Application Pool Defaults link available in the Actions pane when focused on the Application Pools node in Connections. Also, by default a new system-generated identity account will be automatically created with the same name as the pool for security purposes.

3. Enter the physical path of the website folder, `C:\Inetpub\Oranges`.

4. By default pass-through authentication credentials are used; should you need to change that to a specific account, click the "Connect as" button.

5. Select HTTP from the Protocol Type list.

6. Use the All Unassigned value for "IP address" to bind the new Oranges site to any and all IP addresses configured on all server network interfaces but not already assigned to other websites in IIS.

7. Leave the Port setting at 80.

   Note that customizing this value requires the clients to provide the chosen custom port number upon each request.

8. For the "Host name" setting, enter **oranges** to differentiate it from the apples pages within the Default Web Site.

To easily force all new sites created going forward to have specific settings, consider altering the Application Pool Defaults and Web Site Defaults settings to affect future site creations. Links to these dialog boxes appear in the Actions pane of IIS Manager when highlighting the Application Pools node or Sites node, respectively, in the Connections pane, as shown in Figure 19.12, Figure 19.13, and Figure 19.14.

FIGURE 19.12
Add roles and features task list

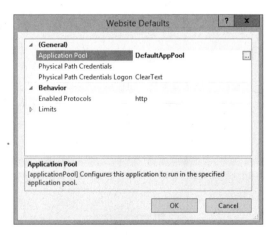

FIGURE 19.13
Add roles and features task list

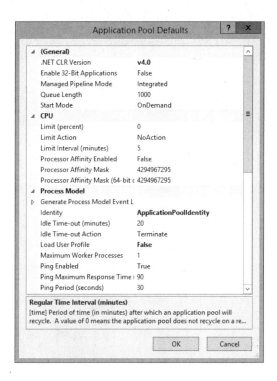

FIGURE 19.14
Add roles and features task list

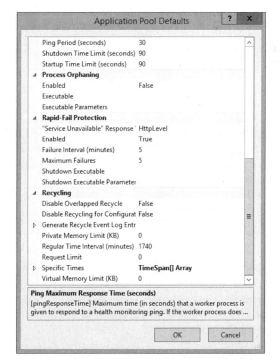

Now that the new Oranges site has been created, you can employ either of the two IIS Manager's navigation methods you learned earlier to test the new site by browsing to it (as shown in Figure 19.15). Remember to disengage the IE Enhanced Security Configuration setting or add the `http://oranges` URL to your list of trusted sites if necessary.

FIGURE 19.15
Oranges website

CREATING A SITE VIA POWERSHELL

Alternatively, you can use PowerShell to create a site on your web server. The beauty of PowerShell is that you can script sites for later use. In fact, the scripts could even be parameterized to allow the insertion of the site name and other values at runtime. Scripted creation helps you deploy a like-site structure and content across a network load-balanced web server farm as well as disaster recovery and documentation for change control.

The `New-WebSite` PowerShell cmdlet is the tool for PowerShell site creation. Here's the PowerShell syntax that would create a site called Oranges on TCP port 80 pointing to the assumed directory path ending in `\inetpub\oranges` and using a custom host header of `oranges`:

```
New-Website -Name Oranges -Port 80 -HostHeader Oranges -PhysicalPath
"$env:systemdrive\inetpub\oranges"
```

When creating a new site with PowerShell, if you omit the `-Id` parameter (as shown here), it causes IIS to simply assign the next-available ID number to the new site. Also, if you had failed to provide the `-PhysicalPath` parameter, then no applications or virtual directory would have been created for the new site, and you would have to manually add those settings to the new site once it was created.

PowerShell can also display existing sites for inventory or troubleshooting purposes with the following command:

```
Get-Website
```

When the command runs, the PowerShell screen should contain the lines shown in Figure 19.16.

Configuring Site Settings

Once a site has been created, you may need to refine the site's configuration prior to unleashing visitors on it. For example, the Oranges site needs to support ASP and HTTP redirection, but the apples pages do not. By default, a new website will immediately begin inheriting configuration settings from the applicationhost.config file. Right now both our apples and oranges pages are enabling all settings in the server-level file that have the enabled attribute set equal to true. Additionally, all modules listed in the <globalModules> section of applicationhost .config are also initiated on the Default Web Site that governs the apples pages as well as on the Oranges site.

Before you make any changes to the default build of a new site, you should know that it does not possess a web.config file. If, however, you were to alter a site, a new web.config file would appear in the site's root virtual directory. The new web.config file would contain only the changed parameter, and all else would continue to be inherited from the applicationhost .config file. However, it depends on the nature of the customization as to whether it warrants a web.config entry. For example, disengaging native modules does not generate a web.config entry. To disengage HTTP Redirection and ASP (the ISAPI module) on the Default Web Site, follow these steps:

1. Launch IIS Manager, and expand the IIS server in the Connections pane on the left.

2. Expand the Sites folder, and highlight Default Web Site.

   The center pane becomes the home page of the site in Features view by default.

3. Double-click the Modules icon to see a list of the enlisted native modules.

   Note that HttpRedirectionModule and IsapiModule are both listed.

4. Highlight both HttpRedirectionModule and IsapiModule, and click the Remove hyperlink in the Actions pane on the right.

5. Confirm the removal by clicking Yes to the prompt.

But what if the customization was not based on module employment but rather was simply the altering of a site setting? For instance, what if on a page currently being supported by the Default Web Site you decide to engage directory browsing? This change will construct a new web.config file in the \inetpub\wwwroot subfolder that contains the new directory-browsing behavior. To enable directory browsing on the Default Web Site, follow these steps:

1. Launch IIS Manager, and expand the IIS server in the Connections pane on the left.

2. Expand the Sites folder, and highlight Default Web Site.

   The center pane becomes the home page of the site in Features view by default.

3. Double-click the Directory Browsing icon.

4. Click the Enable hyperlink in the Actions pane on the right.

By enabling the directory-browsing setting, you have caused a new entry to be added to the web.config file for the Default Web Site:

```
<?xml version="1.0" encoding="UTF-8"?>
<configuration>
    <system.webServer>
        <directoryBrowse enabled="true" />
    </system.webServer>
</configuration>
```

What is nice about the web.config file is that now, regardless of what a server-level administrator might decide about directory browsing, the Default Web Site pages will allow browsing thanks to the custom web.config file. This is possible only because the applicationhost.config file is generously "allowing" the overrideMode on the directoryBrowse configuration. If the server-level administrator really wanted to control your site's behavior, they could modify the applicationhost.config file so that the site-level administrator could not change the directoryBrowse setting (by changing overrideModule="Deny"). There will be more about administration in a bit.

Hosting Multiple Websites

There are many reasons to host multiple sites on a single IIS server. Sometimes it is simply a matter of making the most of your hardware potential. Another strategy may be to host the same site on multiple servers in order to establish a workload-balanced web server farm. And then do the same for a second site, a third site, and on and on. When it comes to hosting multiple sites, you must make several decisions to assure smooth administration and delivery of the content:

◆ First, decide how many sites will be hosted on the web server.

   Dynamic Site Activation, by default, kicks in only if there are more than 99 sites, so if you have fewer than that but still want to leverage the speed enhancements, you will need to adjust its settings.

◆ Second, you will want to take website isolation into account.

   Separate the application pools and configure CPU throttling, so that no one site can inadvertently impact another site by consuming too many resources.

♦ Third, delegating administration allows distribution of duties so that administrators do not become overwhelmed with the responsibilities associated with multiple sites.

Distributed management may even be a political *requirement* of the environment.

♦ Fourth, if a site is going to be deployed to multiple servers (such as in a web server farm design), then settling on a preferred deployment method can streamline the process and enforce consistency.

Uniqueness of site bindings, application pool account assignment, and authentication processes round out some of the other points that should be settled before embarking on multiple-site hosting.

Deploying Sites

One of the benefits of the configuration design in IIS is that site configuration and content can be located in the same directory. The site-specific web.config file now contains both website configuration as well as ASP.NET configuration, so all necessary site settings are self-contained. The point here is that you can now port entire websites and their configurations between servers easily and efficiently!

In IIS 8 the IIS_IUSRS built-in group receives each process as a member at runtime, and it is through this membership that the process receives access to the website's configuration files and content. Since the IIS_IUSRS built-in group uses the same SID on all Windows Server 2012 operating systems, deploying sites to new servers no longer requires extensive redefining of directory permissions.

To disable automatic insertion of process identities as members into the IIS_IUSRS built-in group at runtime, enable manualGroupMembership by changing the following:

```
<applicationPools>
    <add name="DefaultAppPool">
        <processModel manualGroupMembership="true" />
    </add>
</applicationPools>
```

This is one of those defaults that needs to be edited directly in the applicationhost.config file, because it is not exposed in the IIS Manager GUI.

If you are a big fan of raw file copy, then the CLI utility xcopy.exe may be your choice for porting IIS websites between servers. But there may be a better way. Microsoft's Web Deploy 3.0 tool (msdeploy.exe) is available in 32-bit or 64-bit versions and fully supports IIS 7 and 8 for upgrading, synchronizing, or moving entire websites. In fact, the Web Deploy tool can be custom configured to migrate IIS supporting structure such as registry keys and ACLs as well. To investigate the Web Deploy tool beyond this book, see the following Internet sites:

♦ For a full dissertation on the Microsoft Web Deploy tool: http://tinyurl.com/MS2012WDTInfo

♦ To download the Microsoft Web Deploy tool: http://tinyurl.com/MS2012WDTInstaller

In addition to migrating or porting websites, the new Web Deploy tool also has the capability of producing a *snapshot*, or archive, of a website. Although this snapshot is no substitute for a dependable backup strategy, it can provide a quick copy of a website for troubleshooting, for recovery, or to be deployed onto another machine. The new Web Deploy tool can be installed in remote service mode or offline mode. Offline mode is nothing more than using msdeploy.exe to create a snapshot of a website and manually copying that snapshot to another server. Remote service mode allows msdeploy.exe to be executed from a destination server and request data from the source server running the dependency *Web Deployment Agent Service* that is listening on http://+:80/MSDEPLOYAgentService/ by default, but a custom URL can be specified during installation via the command line.

Before using msdeploy.exe to port a website, you may need to identify a list of any dependency components that would need to be in place on the target destination server in order for the site to function properly in its new habitat. The CLI syntax to view a list of dependencies is as follows:

```
Msdeploy -verb:getDependencies -source:apphostconfig="{site name}"
```

Once you have assured that all dependency objects have been successfully set up on the destination server, you can now use msdeploy.exe to migrate your site from an IIS 7.5 instance to your new IIS 8.5 instance:

1. Take an archive of the existing site on the destination (*if* any copying has been done in the past):

   ```
   Msdeploy -verb:sync -source:apphostconfig="{site name}"
   -dest:archivedir={path}
   ```

2. Run a mock synchronization to validate activity prior to actually copying data:

   ```
   Msdeploy -verb:sync -source:archivedire={path}
   -dest:apphostconfig="site name" -whatif > {filename}.log
   ```

3. Once the log file has been approved, synchronize the source site to the destination:

   ```
   Msdeploy -verb:sync -source:archivedire={path} -dest:apphostconfig="site name"
   ```

The aforementioned method will synchronize from an msdeploy.exe-generated archive or snapshot to your IIS 8.5 instance.

DYNAMIC HOST ACTIVATION

We previously talked about how Dynamic Host Activation will increase the startup performance of your IIS server. When you have a large number of sites, the Windows Process Activation Service will load each configured site on the server. Dynamic Host Activation will skip activating any sites when the service is started, instead activating them only if and when it receives a request. This will cause a delay in the initial load time of the first request, but after that the site should respond normally. The default number of configured sites for this to use Dynamic Host Activation is 100, but you can decrease or increase that number as follows:

1. In the IIS Manager console, select the server in the Connection pane and double-click the Configuration Editor.

2. Select the system.applicationHost/weblimits section.

3. Change the dynamicRegistrationThreshold value.

Site Uniqueness

Earlier in this chapter we discussed defining multiple sites within a single instance of IIS by employing unique site bindings, namely, selecting a particular IP address configured on one or more NIC interfaces, specifying a custom "non-80" TCP port number, or adding a custom host header to the new site. Although they assist in correctly routing requests, TCP/IP bindings are not the only way to differentiate a site from other sites on the same server.

Recall that by default the creation of a new website automatically creates a new application pool for the new site and spells the application pool name the same as the site's name. Keeping in mind that new application pools are created according to the application pool defaults mentioned earlier in this chapter, you can affect the identity of all new application pools by editing the Identity property in the Application Pool Defaults settings (Figure 19.17). The default Identity value in IIS 8 is the new Application Pool Identity Account (autogenerated during pool creation), but this can be altered to LocalService, LocalSystem, NetworkService, or a named account of your choice.

FIGURE 19.17
Application Pool Defaults dialog box

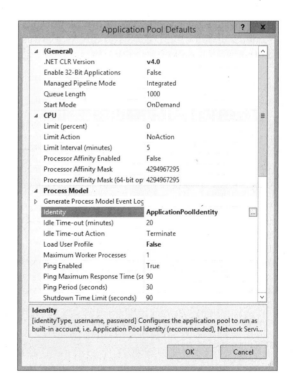

Setting Up an Anonymous Account

Now that we have discussed how you can apply a specific user account to an application pool either during creation (uniquely or via the application pool defaults), wouldn't it be nice to employ that same user account for more than simply application pool identity? It used to be that you would expect to see an IUSR_*machinename* account in Windows that is automatically assigned to all anonymous activity. However, IUSR_*machinename* was replaced with the IUSR account to avoid deployment issues in a multi–web server farm. You can still create an IUSR_*machinename* account for backward compatibility if you must, but beware that you will be limiting that account's capabilities in nontrusted domains.

Managing Multiple Sites for Bigfirm

Remember that the Oranges site needed the HTTP Redirection module because you plan to establish a new oranges site and eventually roll onto it. You cannot build the new oranges site with the same IP address, TCP port, and host header as the current Oranges site. That would just be wrong on so many levels!

Imagine you are auditing the Oranges site for I/O access and process initialization. Because the Oranges site can be configured to use a unique application pool and because each application pool can be configured to identify itself by a unique account credential, you can simplify narrowing a long log file to the exact website issuing the error by using application pool identities.

It may prove advantageous for developing ASP.NET applications on your new site or for differentiating between applications running in the same site to set the anonymous account to something other than IUSR. You can do so by assigning the user account of your choice to the authentication properties of the site:

1. Launch IIS Manager, and expand the IIS server in the Connections pane on the left.

2. Expand the Sites folder, and highlight Oranges.

   The center pane becomes the home page of the site in Features view by default.

3. Double-click the Authentication icon, and highlight Anonymous Authentication in the list of providers.

4. Click the Edit hyperlink in the Actions pane on the right.

5. Set the anonymous credential either to a specific user or to the application pool identity (see Figure 19.18).

The "Application pool identity" choice for the anonymous credential might come in handy on a website that supports multiple applications, each of which uses a unique application pool that is configured with a unique service account. Then your audit reports would show exactly which application within a site may be suffering abuse by anonymous visitors.

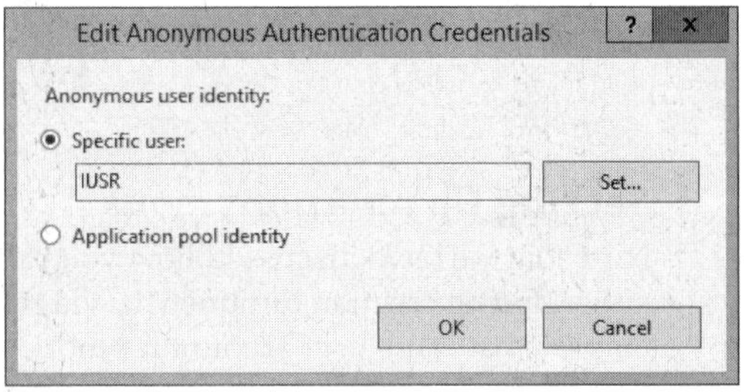

FIGURE 19.18
Edit Anonymous Authentication Credentials dialog box

FEATURE DELEGATION

Feature delegation is alive and well and the best solution for distributing administration of IIS 8 between the administrators and other users, for example, developers. Essentially, feature delegation is the practice of unlocking certain server-level configuration settings in the `appli cationhost.config` file so that other users, such as developers and site administrators, can override that setting's values on specific sites. However, planning efficient delegation can be like walking a tightrope—one false step and your IIS implementation could be left vulnerable to security threats. When it comes to configuring the delegation setting on each feature, consider carefully whom you trust enough to make resource utilization and security decisions for your web server. If you delegate a feature to an inexperienced site administrator, they may unwittingly expose the entire server to malicious code or content and compromise all the websites on your server. Governing and planning feature delegation should rank high on your priority list.

In essence, the effect of delegating a feature involves unlocking specific sections of one or more sites' `web.config` files. By allowing certain configuration settings to be Read-Write for a named finite group of users, you are allowing those users to make configuration changes to one or more websites without needing to contact you, the server administrator, but only so far as to configure the unlocked feature. For example, say you delegate the Digest Authentication feature but not the ASP feature. The users will be able to make configuration changes to the site that affect digest authentication, but they will not be able to alter any settings that affect ASP behavior. Feature delegation can be performed either at the server level to identify site defaults or at the site level to disallow inheritance of the server default and configure unique delegation site by site. In other words, if there is a conflict as to which features are delegated to whom, then the site-level delegation setting wins the conflict.

But wait, there's more. Which sites your chosen users can make configuration changes to also depends on the ACLs of the `web.config` files. Just because a feature has been delegated doesn't mean that your chosen users have anything beyond read permission to a site's `web.config` file. You now must grant your chosen users the write permission to their sites' `web.config` files to allow them to alter whatever feature configuration settings have been unlocked. Feature delegation and NTFS ACLs must be maintained in unison to achieve the most effective security for website configuration.

Delegating Administration

In a large IIS environment supported by a legion of IT administrators, it stands to reason that different personnel may be held responsible for managing different sites. On a single instance of IIS, delegating administrative responsibilities at the site level requires that the server-level administrator unlock specific aspects of the lower site levels.

In the server-level `applicationhost.config` file, the preferred method of unlocking specific configurable sections of lower website definitions so that they can be managed by website administrators is to add a `<location>` tag. For example, if you want to manage HTTP logging at the website by website level, you can alter the `applicationhost.config` file as follows:

```
<location path="Default Web Site" overrideMode="Allow">
        <system.webServer>
            <httpLogging />
        </system.webServer>
    </location>
```

Unlocking configurable settings can also be accomplished by using the `Remove-WebConfigurationLock` PowerShell cmdlet; however, as of the writing of this book it does not support removing an exclusive lock, and you would need to clear the whole section and then add the locks needed.

Of course, allowing override of server-level default settings at the lower website level does not guarantee that the lower website level administrator will actually take up the challenge and manage their own logs. The successful delegation of duties requires strong training and accountability management. But at least now the `applicationhost.config` file does not prevent editing of site settings via IIS Manager.

Installing and Configuring SMTP

Microsoft has deprecated the SMTP server as of Windows Server 2012. As of Windows Server 2012 R2, the SMTP service still works as it did back in Windows 2008 R2, with the exception of the management script, which has been removed. You can continue to use it as you have in the past, but administrators and programmers should start using System.Net.Smtp for sending mail. Information on System.Net.Smtp can be found online at `http://tinyurl.com/MS2012SMTP`.

The SMTP service in IIS 8 has not changed from previous versions but can still be a very useful tool. It's designed to send mail from the IIS server to another SMTP server, and although it sends and receives mail messages, it's not intended to provide mailboxes for end users. For that sort of functionality you will want to look at using Exchange Server or Office 365.

Getting Started

The SMTP server feature depends on the prior successful installation of the Internet Information Services (IIS) 6.0 Manager console *and* the IIS 6 Metabase modules from the IIS 6 Management Compatibility role service of IIS 8 (among others; more about installation in a bit) in order to load. These IIS 6.0 modules use an IIS 8 configuration file named `metabase.xml` (%systemroot%\System32\inetsrv), which gains several new entries upon SMTP installation. Some of the most noteworthy are as follows:

`<IISConfigObject Location="/LM…/DisplayName">` Sets the SMTP server feature's display name to SMTP Server

`<IISConfigObject Location="/LM…/BindingManagerMoniker">` Sets the event binding for the SMTP server to smtpsvc1

`<IISConfigObject Location="/LM…/Sources…/DisplayName">` Sets the bound service's OS object display name to smtpsvc1

`<IISSmtpService Location="/LM/SmtpSvc">` Contains all the settings for the SMTP services (such as time-outs, max connections, NTAuthenticationProviders, and options)

`<IISSmtpServer Location="/LM/SmtpSvc/1"…>` Contains mail settings for the SMTP services (such as directories, TCP port, and route settings)

You can manage the SMTP Server service by directly editing the `metabase.xml` file, but there is an easier way: the Internet Information Services (IIS) 6.0 Manager console (see Figure 19.19). This is basically the same console used by past administrators to configure the SMTP services that shipped with IIS 6.0. To expose the SMTP node, simply expand the server node of the SMTP hosting machine you want to configure in the tree pane on the left side of the console.

The first thing you might notice is that the SMTP service installs in a manual startup. To configure the startup parameters, you should configure the service itself using the Services console from the Administrative Tools program group (see Figure 19.20).

FIGURE 19.19

Internet Information
Services (IIS) 6.0
Manager console

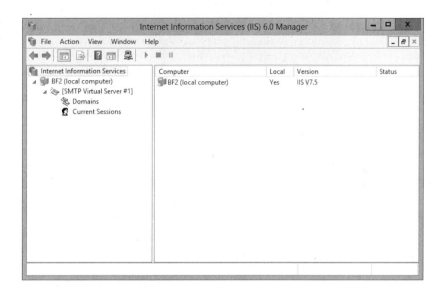

FIGURE 19.20

Simple Mail
Transfer Protocol
(SMTP) service
properties

If you install more than the prerequisite IIS 8 role services, the SMTP service startup behavior differs upon installation. Specifically, if you install all IIS 8 Web Server role services, then SMTP services will start immediately upon adding the SMTP feature, even though the service configuration has a startup setting of Manual. And although this may be helpful initially, the first time the web server gets rebooted, you'll be wondering why your SMTP services did not restart on their own as well. So, consider changing the startup setting of the service from Manual to Automatic.

Adding the SMTP Server Feature

In addition to IIS 8's role services of IIS 6 Metabase Compatibility and the IIS 6.0 Manager console, the SMTP feature also requires the SMTP Server Tools feature. Server Manager utilities, both GUI and CLI, are kind enough to install these dependencies during SMTP installation. The SMTP Server Tools feature provides the snap-in to the IIS 6.0 Manager console needed to administer SMTP services. To install this required SMTP Server Tools feature using the GUI, select SMTP Server Tools from the Feature Administration Tools group under the Remote Server Administration Tools group when running the Add Features Wizard. Could Microsoft have hidden it any deeper?

A WORD ABOUT OS SERVICE CONFIGURATION

The default OS name for the SMTP service is SMTPSVC with a display name of Simple Mail Transfer Protocol (SMTP), and it has a dependency on the IIS Admin service. By default it authenticates as the Local System account, is enabled for all hardware profiles, and has no recovery options configured. To protect SMTP services availability on your websites, consider configuring restart recovery options as you would any mission-critical service.

WHEN MINIMUM REQUIREMENTS AREN'T *REALLY* ENOUGH

The minimal installation of only the IIS 6.0 Metabase Compatibility and the IIS 6.0 Manager console role services for IIS 8 will not be enough to employ the IIS 8 feature named SMTP E-mail on your websites. In fact, not even a default installation of the Web Server role will provide enough role services to facilitate configuring SMTP support on your sites.

Microsoft's answer is a complete installation of all IIS 8 role services in order to incorporate SMTP into a website. Talk about a security concern! Thankfully, you can disable needless site features in the `applicationhost.config`, root `web.config`, or site-specific `web.config` files to harden the server.

To install the SMTP Server feature via the Server Manager GUI, simply select add roles and features from the Manage menu option. Then select SMTP Server from the features list. Should you instead decide to install the SMTP Server feature via PowerShell, use the following syntax to install both the prerequisite Web Server role services and the SMTP features:

```
Add-WindowsFeature SMTP-Server
```

Setting Up an SMTP Server

Once it's installed, you can customize the SMTP Server configuration and build additional domain support via the Internet Information Services (6.0) Manager console. Although the service itself is maintained in this console, embedding SMTP services into an IIS 8 website takes place elsewhere (we'll look deeper into that in a moment). Navigating the Internet Information Services (6.0) Manager console is a nostalgic trip down memory lane because the interface is the same console from IIS 6 in Windows Server 2003.

VIRTUAL SERVERS AND DOMAINS

The SMTP Server feature offers mail transfer capability per the configuration settings of an SMTP virtual server. By default, only one SMTP virtual server is created during SMTP installation, but you can create additional virtual servers if you will be hosting mail for different domain names and need them all to be configured separately. Within each SMTP virtual server, one or more domains must exist to associate the related file system directory for mail delivery to a particular fully qualified domain name (FQDN). By default, the initially created SMTP virtual server will house only one domain—that of the resident machine's FQDN.

Differing security and delivery limit requirements of additional domains may dictate that they be serviced by separate SMTP virtual servers. Before deciding which domains should be governed by which SMTP virtual server, you should know what virtual server settings will affect the domains. Each new virtual server will store its configuration settings in the IIS 6–compatible `metabase.xml` file under a separate `IIsSmtpServer` element with a `Location` attribute of `/LM/SmtpSvc/{number}` where `{number}` is a sequential integer assigned to new virtual servers in creation order. Feel free to create as many virtual servers as can be assigned to unique combinations of IP addresses and TCP port numbers supported by the server.

If instead you find that all email conforms to the same restrictions and limitations and can be serviced by a single virtual server, then using the default SMTP Virtual Server #1 constructed during feature installation is the easiest way to go. Simply add as many domains as must be supported for message routing to the Domains folder underneath the default virtual server. You can create a new domain in the folder by right-clicking the Domains folder and choosing to create a new domain via the New SMTP Domain Wizard. The wizard will identify the following:

Domain Type   Remote or alias

Domain Name   x400-compliant fully qualified address space of mail to be delivered by the new domain (be sure DNS is configured to resolve)

Upon completing the wizard, enter the new domain's properties to specify whether it must adhere to drop directory quota limits set forth in its resident virtual server's configuration settings. Each new domain will garner its own `IIsSmtpDomain` element in the `metabase.xml` configuration file.

SOME CHANGES REQUIRE SERVICE RESTART

Adding SMTP virtual servers and/or domains to Windows Server 2012 will not take effect until the SMTP services are stopped and restarted. The Internet Information Services (IIS) 6.0 Manager console offers a quick method of restarting all IIS services by right-clicking the computer name at the top of the tree pane, choosing All Tasks, and then selecting Restart IIS.

AUTHENTICATION

SMTP services can be configured to demand authentication from other SMTP hosts attempting to transfer messages to it for security. By default, only anonymous access is permitted, allowing any and all SMTP servers that want to push email messages for supported domain namespaces to flood the drop directory with items. In a secure environment and for auditing purposes, you may need to enforce an authentication method so that other SMTP hosts are required to identify themselves before being allowed to forward messages to your SMTP service.

Adding the SMTP E-mail Feature to an IIS 8 Website

Once both the SMTP feature and the entire Web Server role set of role services have been installed, the SMTP E-mail feature will appear in the Internet Information Services (IIS) Manager console for IIS 8 websites. Despite the SMTP virtual servers' state(s), the SMTP E-mail feature can be enabled or disabled for the entire IIS server or for only a few chosen sites or web applications. Global settings for SMTP defined at the server-level `applicationhost.config` file can be inherited by one or more websites.

The SMTP E-mail feature is listed at the server level under the area titled ASP.NET (see Figure 19.21). From the Features view, the Actions menu for the SMTP E-mail feature, like any other feature, offers quick links to open the feature's settings page, restarts/starts/stops the feature, views application pools that are configured to service the feature, views sites that have been configured to use the feature, or gets help with SMTP email.

Upon opening the SMTP E-mail feature's settings page (see Figure 19.22), you can set the configuration parameters shown in Table 19.3.

FIGURE 19.21
Server-level features for BF1 IIS 8 server

FIGURE 19.22
SMTP E-mail feature's settings page

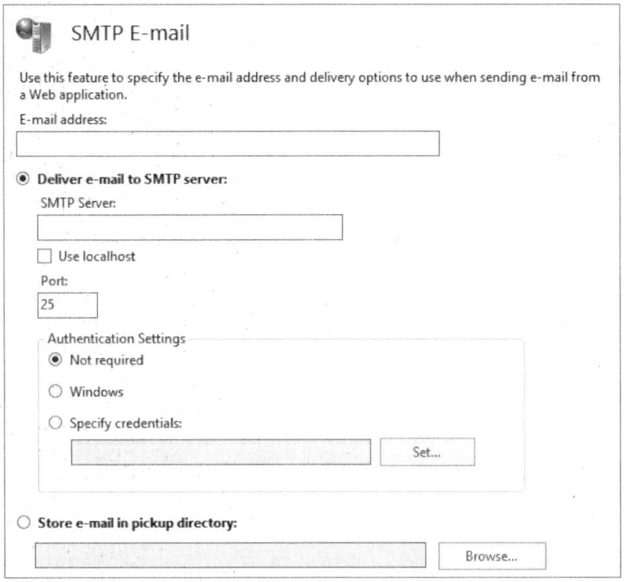

TABLE 19.3:   SMTP E-mail Feature Settings

SETTING	POSSIBLE VALUES	PURPOSE
E-mail address	A valid email box address from the sending domain	Declare the "sent from" email address that will be used when IIS sends email from a web application.
Deliver email to SMTP server: SMTP Server Note: Select the "Use localhost" check box to use the SMTP services on this same server.	A functioning SMTP server	Declare an SMTP server handling the domain declared on the "E-mail address" setting.
Port Default = 25	Any available TCP port number	Declare the TCP port on which the SMTP server will be listening for SMTP traffic.
Authentication Settings	Not required Windows Specify credentials	Declare the authentication method supported by the SMTP server. Enter a username and password for "Specify credentials."
Store email in pickup directory	Valid file system directory	An alternative to delivering email to the SMTP server. Holds email instead in a file system directory for later pickup by a mail retrieval application.

Once configured at the server level, individual websites and web applications can be modified to send email to alternate SMTP servers or support different domain namespaces in their email addresses. Simply click the SMTP E-mail feature icon at any website or web application to alter the mail behavior for that entity.

Integrating FTP into IIS 8 Web Pages

In the age of SkyDrive, Dropbox, and everything being cloud oriented, you might think that good-old FTP has become a thing of the past. But the tried-and-true act of a simple file transfer still holds a sentimental, if not functional, place in our hearts. And although it is true that many web applications developed in today's market make use of complex ASP.NET programming code to hide the actual movement of data between the server and client systems, sometimes the old adage "less is more" rings true when it comes to managing file transfers in a heterogeneous network.

Microsoft has made FTP more versatile than its previous version and has given you new security tools that will help protect data access and transport while keeping the user experience streamlined and easy. For example, FTP now supports restrictions to login attempts, as well as Windows Server 2012 disk quota integration for improved storage management. A deeper dive into the FTP services falls beyond the scope of this IIS chapter, so let's just take a quick look at incorporating FTP features into IIS 8 websites.

The FTP File Transfer Publishing Service

Because FTP is incorporated into IIS 8, you need only add the FTP role service to the Web Server role in order to take advantage of simple file transfers via your websites. Since we covered adding role services to IIS 8 earlier in this chapter, let's not digress. But as with all features, roles, and role services, do not add FTP to your web server unless you truly need to employ it on a website; otherwise, you could be introducing a security vulnerability. Once the FTP role service has been added, a host of new icons will be listed in the FTP area of the IIS Manager console (see Figure 19.23).

FIGURE 19.23
IIS Manager: FTP area

Adding FTP to an IIS 8 Website

One of the advantages of the FTP Publishing service is that you can add FTP functionality to an existing website in IIS 8 right alongside HTTP. From the Actions pane in the IIS Manager console, simply click the Add FTP Publishing link to kick off FTP configuration for the HTTP site. Before you add file transfer, however, you need to make some preliminary decisions.

First, because FTP is a separate protocol, you must identify a unique set of bindings for the services. Namely, the IP address, port number, and virtual host must be planned. Yes, we said *virtual host*. The FTP services can operate under a custom header name much like HTTP sites, making it easier for users to correctly connect to friendly named sites. Also, you must decide whether the FTP site starts automatically and whether to engage SSL. Figure 19.24 shows your SSL options. You can select Require SSL (thus alienating clients who are unable to participate in SSL), soften the security by choosing Allow SSL (which offers unsecure file transfer for those clients who cannot participate in SSL), or decide later by selecting No SSL (this will disable SSL connections).

FIGURE 19.24

Add FTP Site dialog box

Second, you must plan whether to allow the embedded FTP Publishing service to accept anonymous connections and support basic cleartext authentication strings. You can also limit access to anonymous users only or specific users/groups (see Figure 19.25). Additionally, you must decide whether allowed users may write or only read.

To prove that FTP Publishing services have been successfully embedded into the website, in the Connections pane you need expand the host to which FTP was added. A new group of icons for FTP management now appear in the Features view; some of the more notable features are:

◆ FTP authorization rules allow you to configure more rules that will either allow or deny a specific group of users a particular permission level of access to the FTP services on this site.

◆ FTP IP address and domain restrictions allow you to restrict FTP services to only a particular IP address, subnet range or domain name.

◆ FTP User isolation will allow you to prevent users from accessing other user's directories.

FIGURE 19.25
FTP site authentication
and authorization

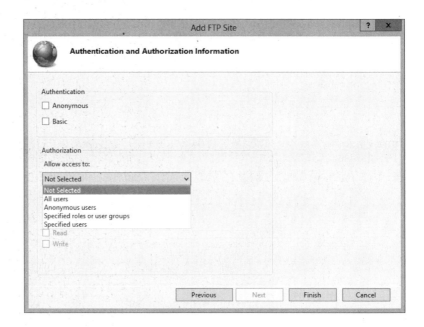

One notable feature that is not configured per-website is the FTP login attempt restrictions. This new feature will let you set a failed login attempt threshold that will lock out the IP address from where the failed logins are coming from or just make a note of the attempts in the log file. This setting is only configurable on the server level.

As an alternative method of creating a new FTP Publishing service site, you could use PowerShell. Some benefits of using PowerShell as the creation method include scripting, automation, and remote management. For example, to create a new FTP site named FTPTest with default parameters and using a custom port number of 2121 with an explicit physical directory of D:\FTPTest, the syntax would look something like this:

```
New-WebFTPSite -Name FTPTest -Port 2121 -PhysicalPath D:\FTPTest
```

Keep in mind that the new FTP site will be created with the next-available ID number since this syntax does not specify one. Also, the default authentication protocols and authorization entities will be configured.

Remember, FTP is a powerful role service in its own right, and there is much to consider when employing it on your web server. Entire chapters and short books have been written on the FTP product! Although a deeper dive into administration and security of FTP falls outside the scope of this IIS chapter, you would be wise to brush up on the protocol before you unwittingly open your websites to potential vulnerabilities.

Advanced Administration

So far, we have covered a great deal of information about installing and configuring IIS 8 as well as site creation and management. But there are still a few loose ends we need to tie up. The beauty of IIS 8 administration is all the tools Microsoft offers to accommodate a multitude of engineering tastes. For GUI aficionados, there is the very powerful IIS Manager. For engineers more comfortable in the command-line interface (CLI), there is Appcmd.exe or PowerShell. And for developers savvy in XML, there is always direct editing of the *.config files. The list doesn't seem to end.

And although it may be a comforting thought to believe that any time you need to manage IIS 8 or IIS 8.5, the server will be readily accessible and you can perform all of your maintenance from its keyboard, the reality is most administrators prefer the convenience of remote management over the reliability of local administration on the server itself. The Web Management Service (WMSVC) in IIS allows a remote connection into a Windows Server 2012 or Windows 8 installation of IIS by using the IIS Manager GUI console. Of course, the traditional remote administration and VPN approaches of remotely connecting to the operating system are still a possibility, but why introduce the extra bandwidth utilization if you don't have to? Considering that WMSVC uses a static TCP port assignment, punching the firewall for remote access from the beach seems easier than maintaining a VPN or RDP connection.

But if your heart is set on full OS access while remotely managing your IIS installation, Microsoft offers a robust remote management platform called Windows Remote Management (WinRM) that provides SOAP-based access to the Windows Server 2012 OS across commonly allowed firewall port calls. WinRM became available on Windows Server 2003 R2 but had to be added to the OS in Control Panel. Starting in Windows Server 2012, Windows Remote Management is installed, enabled, and ready to be used.

Using Web Management Services

Before you can sit at your desk in your comfy leather chair and launch an IIS Manager console that will connect to your IIS server down the hall, you must do some prep work. The basic tasks you need to perform to set up remote management services are the following:

1. Install WMSVC.

2. Enable remote connectivity.

3. Configure optional settings.

4. Start WMSVC.

Although the last task may seem to go without saying, the order of its execution is paramount. Try not to get overzealous and start the newly installed WMSVC service before configuring it. The service cannot be altered while it is running.

To install WMSVC onto the IIS server, add the Management Service role to the Web Server role in the OS. We covered different methods of adding role services earlier in this chapter. To enable remote connectivity on Windows Server 2012, follow these steps:

1. Launch IIS Manager, and click the IIS server to be remotely managed in the Connections pane on the left.

   The center pane becomes the home page of the server in Features view by default (see Figure 19.26).

2. Double-click the Management Service icon under the Management area.

3. Select the "Enable remote connections" check box (see Figure 19.27).

FIGURE 19.26
Server home in IIS
Manager

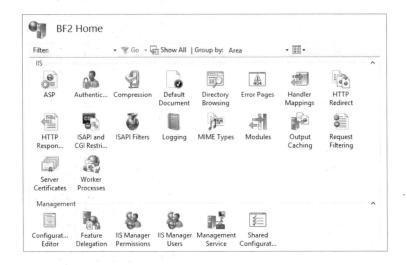

FIGURE 19.27
Management Service

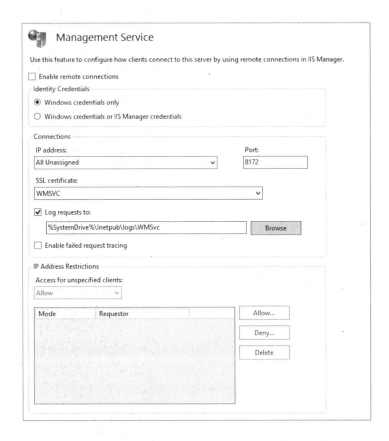

You can also enable remote connectivity by running the following PowerShell command:

```
Set-ItemProperty -Path HKLM:\SOFTWARE\Microsoft\WebManagement\Server -Name
EnableRemoteManagement -Value 1
```

Optional WMSVC settings you may want to configure include binding the service to a custom IP address or TCP port structure. By default, WMSVC listens on TCP port 8172 across all IP addresses on the server. Or you may want to explicitly list the IP addresses allowed to connect as well as whether WMSVC will accept both Windows credentials and IIS Manager credentials. To configure optional settings, follow these steps:

1. Launch IIS Manager, and click the IIS server to be remotely managed in the Connections pane on the left.

    The center pane becomes the home page of the server in Features view by default.

2. Double-click the Management Service icon under the Management area.

Once all configuration settings are complete, start WMSVC as you would any other service. For your convenience, there is a Start hyperlink in the Actions pane when IIS Manager is focused on Management Service. Once WMSVC is running on the IIS server, you can connect any IIS Manager console GUI to the IIS server by following these steps:

1. Launch IIS Manager on the remote computer.

2. On the Welcome page of IIS Manager, click the "Connect to a server" hyperlink under the "Connection tasks" section.

3. Provide the IIS server's name to which you want to connect.

4. Provide credentials for the connection.

BEWARE OF MULTIPLE CONNECTIONS

Allowing too many concurrent connections into WMSVC is a recipe for conflicting administration. Consider limiting WMSVC to receive connections from only specific administrators' machines, and train those administrators!

Connecting, Securing, Logging

In the grand scheme of securing a website, many factors play an important role in keeping the site content safe from harm:

♦ First, and most obvious, are visitor permissions while on the site.

♦ Additionally, there are encryption settings that protect data during transport and services that will help you keep the IIS server from overloading and crashing.

♦ Also, there is logging for when you want to know about every visit to your sites.

♦ Lastly, there is the small matter of backing up the site configuration and content to recover in the wake of a disaster.

IIS 8.0 includes some authentication parameters and failed-request tracing to assist administrators in becoming proactive toward user access needs. Windows Server 2012 can take advantage of the Windows System Resource Manager (WSRM) to manage resource utilization being usurped by IIS. Feature delegation restricts elevated privilege to site configurations, while user permissions dictate access to the content.

AUTHENTICATION

Several possible authentication mechanisms are available on an IIS 8 website. Table 19.4 outlines the differences between authentication methods.

TABLE 19.4: Authentication Methods

FEATURE METHOD	PURPOSE
AD Client Certificate	This maps AD users to client certificates.
Anonymous	The visitor doesn't need to supply credentials.
ASP.NET Impersonate	This runs ASP.NET applications under an alternative security context (instead of the default ASP.NET account).
Basic	The visitor must provide the username and password (transported in plain cleartext).
Digest	The visitor must provide an AD username and password (HTTP 1.1 browser required); the password does not traverse the medium.
Forms	The client-side redirection transparently forwards the user to an HTML form into which they enter credentials before transparently transferring back to the page requested.
Windows	NTLM or Kerberos authenticates the Windows username and password.

Choose the authentication method wisely for your site. If you select an authentication method that is less secure, unwanted visitors may get in. If you select an authentication method that is too strict, you may inadvertently alienate valid visitors.

PERMISSIONS

You can use the IIS Manager Permissions page in IIS Manager to grant IIS Manager user objects, Windows user accounts, or Windows group objects the permission to connect to a site or application for the purpose of managing it. Keep in mind that only features that have been delegated ("unlocked") at the server level will be available to the permission holders for site-level administration (see Figure 19.28).

Permission to access a site for browsing or uploading purposes revolves around the virtual directories of the site's applications. You can manage an individual virtual directory's permission structure by following these steps:

1. Launch IIS Manager, and expand the IIS server in the Connections pane on the left.

2. Expand the Sites folder, and highlight the particular site.

   The center pane becomes the home page of the site in Features view by default.

3. Click the View Virtual Directories link in the Actions pane on the right.

4. Highlight (single-click) the virtual directory of choice, and click the Edit Permissions hyperlink in the Actions pane on the right.

5. Set the permissions on the Security tab of the virtual directory's Properties dialog box.

FIGURE 19.28
IIS Manager
Permissions page

You can use either PowerShell or the IIS Manager GUI to specify which features are delegated and to what degree. To delegate a feature using IIS Manager, follow these steps:

1. Launch IIS Manager, and highlight the IIS server in the Connections pane on the left.

   The center pane becomes the home page of the site in Features view by default.

2. Click the Feature Delegation icon in the Management area.

3. Click the feature to be delegated, and click the hyperlink in the Actions pane on the right that denotes your intended level of delegation (Read Only, Read/Write, Reset to Inherited).

Keep in mind that delegating a feature at the server level makes it possible for that feature's configuration parameters to be altered on any and all websites throughout the server that are employing the delegated feature (depending on the individual site's web.config permissions, of course). This could endanger some sites, so use server-wide delegation cautiously. The PowerShell cmdlets to set, remove and display delegated features are listed here:

```
Add-WebConfigurationLock
Remove-WebConfigurationLock
Get-ConfigurationLock
```

CODE ACCESS SECURITY

You can configure the .NET trust levels to dictate a specific level of access that the .NET applications on a site will have to underlying content. You can edit the .NET trust levels in IIS Manager by clicking the .NET Trust Level icon or by editing the web.config file directly. Editing the .NET code's authority level will generate an entry into the site's web.config file. Table 19.5 outlines the possible settings for .NET trust levels and what they give away.

TABLE 19.5: .NET Trust Levels

TRUST LEVEL	PURPOSE
Full (internal)	Access to all resources pursuant to OS security
High (web_hightrust.config)	Cannot call code or services, write to event log, or access MSMQ, ODBC, OleDb
Medium (web_mediumtrust.config)	High restrictions, plus cannot access files outside the application directory hierarchy, access the registry, or make network/web service calls
Low (web_lowtrust.config)	High and medium restrictions, plus cannot write to file system and cannot call the Assert method
Minimal (web_minimaltrust.config)	Execute permissions only by default

INVOKING SSL

Secure Sockets Layer (SSL) protection has been around for many generations of the IIS product. By now, you likely realize that SSL is used to protect data that is passed to and from an IIS server. To invoke SSL on an IIS 8 website, you must first create an HTTPS binding on the site. To add bindings to a site, follow these steps:

1. Launch IIS Manager, and expand the IIS server in the Connections pane on the left.

2. Expand the Sites folder, and highlight the site requiring SSL.

3. In the Actions pane on the right, click Bindings.

4. Click the Add button in the Site Bindings dialog box.

5. Change the binding type from HTTP to HTTPS, and specify the certificate to be used.

Now that SSL has been bound to the website, you can fine-tune its behavior by double-clicking the SSL Settings icon on the home page of the site. Choose the bit level and whether client-side certificates will be required or even honored.

LOGGING

Previous versions of IIS logging were limited. You were restricted to a fixed set of standard fields, with no way to extend or customize them. Short of creating a custom logging module, you were stuck. With the release of IIS 8.5, all that has changed. To expand or customize your logging options, follow these steps:

1. Launch IIS Manager, select the site or server in the Connections pane, and double-click Logging.

   You have seven standard logging options in addition to those available by default.

2. Under Format, select W3C, and then click Select Fields.

3. In the W3C logging Fields page, click Add Field.

4. In the Add Custom Field page, enter a field name for your custom field within the log file.

   The field name cannot have any spaces.

5. For the source type, you can select from Request Header, Response Header, or Server Variable.

6. For the source, select the name of the HTTP header or server variable that contains a value that you want to log, or you can enter your own custom source string.

7. Click OK.

8. Click Apply in the Actions pane to apply your new settings.

Your new log file has "_x" appended to the filename to show that it contains custom fields. It is worth pointing out that the total size of the data collected from all of the custom fields cannot exceed 64 KB. If it does, IIS will truncate the data.

Backing Up and Restoring Data

No discussion of IIS 8 would be complete without at least mentioning disaster recovery. After all, no one ever anticipates corruption or system failures, but it's best to have a plan in place for the inevitable. Luckily, the architecture of IIS 8 makes it a rather simple network application to back up. We have already discussed taking snapshots of sites for porting; those same snapshots could be used to restore a site to a previous version. Also, the XML configuration files reside on NTFS and as such need only be backed up as part of the regular I/O backup strategy. It is worth pointing out that a system state backup will back up only the metabase and not the configuration files.

So, if it's all just a matter of backing up the configuration and content files, is there anything unique to IIS 8 about backing up? Just one thing—the PowerShell commands that can be used to create, restore, delete, and list backups:

◆ To generate a backup, use this:

```
Backup-WebConfiguration -Name {backup name}
```

◆ To restore a backup, use this:

```
Restore-WebConfiguration -Name {Backup name}
```

◆ To delete a backup (clean up), use this:

```
Remove-WebConfigurationBackup {Backup name}
```

◆ To list backups, use this:

```
Get-WebConfigurationBackup
```

These PowerShell commands can be written into a script and scheduled with the OS. But what if something goes wrong with the OS, and unbeknownst to the IIS administrator there has been no good backup created of the applicationhost.config file in weeks? Not to worry, IIS maintains a configuration history of applicationhost.config according to the default schedule found in the %windir%\system32\inetsrv\config\schema\iis_schema.xml file. These automatic backups will appear in the results of a Get-WebConfigurationBackup list PowerShell command along with manually generated backup files and can be restored with the Restore-WebConfiguration PowerShell command.

By default, IIS 8 stores the automatically generated historical versions of `applicationhost.config` in the history subdirectory under `%systemdrive%\inetpub`. This may not be the most secure location for these all important files. To redirect future history backups of `applicationhost.config` to another location, for instance, `D:\MyHistFiles`, execute the following PowerShell command:

```
Set-WebConfigurationProperty -Filter //System.ApplicationHost/ConfigHistory -Name
Path -Value "D:\MyHistFiles"
```

The Bottom Line

Plan for and install IIS 8.5.   Relatively lean by default, IIS 8.5 must be carefully and painstakingly planned so as not to install more modular functionality than you need. More than a resource concern, leaving unnecessary role services off the server is also a method of securing your websites. As always with Microsoft, there are multiple ways to install IIS 8.5, from an interactive GUI to PowerShell.

Master It   You are about to install IIS 8.5 on a Windows Server 2012 R2 with the GUI removed. You want to install only the default roles as well as the ASP.NET role and what that role requires. What is the PowerShell command need to accomplish this?

Manage IIS 8's global default.   IIS 8 modules are only one piece of evidence of the product's compartmentalization. Web applications and individual configuration settings per site can be independently managed as well. A hierarchical ladder of global, web, application, and page settings allows granular administration by multiple engineers.

Master It   What is feature delegation?

Create and secure websites in IIS 8.   Designing and generating new websites in IIS 8 can be accomplished via the GUI or CLI, allowing you to automate routine site creation. Permission structure can be copied from one site to another or managed from the upper layers of the settings hierarchy to simplify permission granting. IIS 8 eases site generation by packaging your website.

Master It   You need to create a new website that has all the characteristics of the Default Web Site but must also support ASP.NET pages. You do not want to add ASP.NET support to the Default Web Site for fear of adding vulnerability to existing web content. How would you implement this?

Manage IIS 8 with advanced administration techniques.   Day-to-day site maintenance and content posting may be the bulk of your IIS 8 administration. But additional higher-level management is what assures consistent and uninterrupted service of your web pages. Important configuring tasks, including recovering from disasters, monitoring performance, setting access or code security, and defining encryption, can be accomplished either locally or remotely.

Master It   Because of limited storage space, you are revising your disaster-recovery plan. You are considering delaying backups of the IIS `applicationhost.config` file to monthly. However, you are concerned that minor global configuration changes made throughout the month may get lost if a failure occurs before the monthly backup. How would you recover a mid-month edit?

Chapter 20

Advanced IP: Routing with Windows

Why route from Windows? The short answer is because you can, and it will open your eyes to a world previously unseen.

Over a decade ago routers were expensive and it was common for network-savvy companies to use cast-off PCs as cheap routers. For example, by putting a couple of network cards in the PC and installing a copy of Linux, a network engineer could save the company a lot of money on buying a huge chunk of metal from a major network vendor. Even now you can find these distributions lurking on the Internet and still in use in some ISPs.

Routing is a vital part of maintaining a network infrastructure (think about how many VLANs are in your network and how the traffic is routed among them!). It is important to understand how routing works in order to correctly manage your network and the hosts on it. Normally, this is beyond the control of a server administrator, but knowing a little about routing will also help you troubleshoot connection issues on your own hosts and network.

In this chapter, we will take you through the life of an IP packet as it is routed across your network, and we will explore the differences between class-based and classless routing (although these are relatively old concepts, looking at the differences still provides some insight). We will explain how network address translator (NAT) devices allow you to route TCP traffic, and in a brief history lesson, we'll show how the arrival of Winsock shaped the Internet boom.

We will walk you through the processes of installing the Remote Access role and then show you how to configure a router with NAT. (We will revisit the Remote Access role more in the next chapter.) We will cover how to configure a Windows Server 2012 R2 computer to route IP traffic, and we will discuss tunneling. Finally, you will learn how you can use the knowledge gained from this chapter, and a few common tools, to troubleshoot network communication difficulties.

In this chapter, you will learn to:

◆ Document the life of an IP packet routed through your network

◆ Explain the class-based and classless views of IP routing

◆ Use NAT devices to route TCP traffic

The Life of an IP Packet

The designers of the original Internet Protocol achieved something that goes beyond being merely clever: they made something that is just about as simple as it can be to achieve its purpose. As a result, you will notice that we are not going to tell you how to route UDP or TCP, because IP takes care of all that. We are also not going to tell you how to route Ethernet, because Ethernet doesn't route; it only communicates on a single subnet.

But this does mean that if you are to understand routing in TCP/IP, you have to know what makes an IP packet move through the system. To this end, we will describe the life cycle of a typical IP packet using a sample network, as illustrated in Figure 20.1.

FIGURE 20.1

A sample network

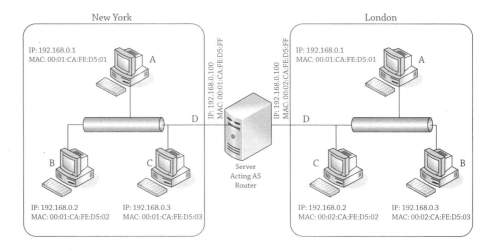

FIRST, A RECAP

Before we get into the nuts and bolts of routing with Windows, we'll start with a quick recap of what we expect you to know about TCP/IP for this chapter:

IP addresses identify individual interfaces. Each active interface on a TCP/IP host (whether it's a PC or a device such as a router or firewall) owns one or more IP addresses; these IP addresses are 32-bit numbers for IPv4 and 128-bit numbers for IPv6. IPv4 addresses are commonly written as "dotted quads"—four numbers from 0 to 255, separated by dots, such as 198.162.1.234. IPv6 addresses are written grouped as hex digits, representing 16 bits at a time, with colons to separate groups, such as 2001:db8::12af:d4f2:1cab:1002. (The double colon represents a string of zeros that has been removed for brevity, in this case, 32 bits' worth, or the equivalent of 0:0.)

IP is an inherently unreliable protocol. It makes no effort to guarantee delivery or to report on a failure of data to reach its destination.

UDP is an unreliable protocol built on top of IP. It adds the concept of ports to IP—one each for destination and source.

TCP is a reliable protocol built on top of IP. Apart from the size of addresses, there is no difference between TCP over IPv6 and TCP over IPv4. TCP adds to IP the concepts of *ports* for the destination and source, a *connection* lasting from initial greeting to end of life, a *handshake* protocol for opening and gracefully closing the connection, sequencing to maintain the order of each byte in the connection stream, and a way to abort a connection when either end detects an error condition.

In the example IP packet lifetimes in this section, we will be using the network diagram (we assume a subnet mask of 255.255.255.0 or /24 or class C) displayed in Figure 20.1.

First, the Simple Case: No Routing Required

The simple case is one where two computers that want to talk to each other are on the same Ethernet segment. Let's begin at the New York site and start some communication from computer A (IP address 192.168.0.1, MAC address 00:01:CA:FE:05:01) to computer C (IP address 192.168.0.3, MAC address 00:01:CA:FE:05:03). The procedure is as follows:

1. The application, or Network layer, sends an IP packet to the IP layer.

2. A's IP layer examines the header for the destination IP address.

3. A's IP layer finds B's MAC address using ARP (IPv4) or ND (IPv6).

4. A's IP layer creates an Ethernet packet and sends it.

5. C's Ethernet card recognizes the address, reads the packet, and forwards it to the IP layer.

6. C's IP layer examines the header and passes the payload to the protocol's handler.

That list of steps is something you'll refer to later when troubleshooting connectivity problems, but for now it needs some explanation.

If an IP packet had *parents*, they would be the source and destination IP addresses. Every IP packet has to know where it's starting and where it's going. Imagine getting into your car and not knowing your destination! In IPv4, the packet also needs a name, just in case it gets split into parts by an intermediate router. That way, the receiver will know which parts to put together. Finally, it needs a piece of information that tells the receiver how to treat its data (aka payload), whether it is to be handed to the TCP or UDP stack, or perhaps a different protocol, with abbreviations such as ICMP, IGMP, GRE, and so on. To IP, they are protocols 1, 2, 47, and so on. Most of the time you do not have to worry about this, but you can use tools like Wireshark or Network Monitor to dive into an IP packet to observe all this information.

When a packet is created, all this information—and perhaps some optional parts—is placed into the *IP header*, and the header and payload are sent to the IP layer of the network stack for forwarding.

The IP layer at any computer or router reads the source and destination addresses and uses them to determine where to send the packet. In this simple case, the source and destination addresses are clearly both on the same subnet, or local link. In that case, no routing is required for the packet.

The IP layer on the source computer has to tell the Network layer (in most cases, this would be the Ethernet driver) to put the packet onto the right network card, with the right network destination and source address, and to do that it must know the Ethernet address (the MAC address) corresponding to each IP address.

From Figure 20.1, it's clear that the MAC address for the source should be 00:01:CA:FE:D5:01 and that the MAC address for the destination should be 00:01:CA:FE:D5:03, but the source computer doesn't have this diagram, and since it's never spoken to C before, it has no idea of its MAC address. All it knows is that the IP address 192.168.0.3 is where this packet needs to go.

MAC ADDRESS EXAMPLES

Note that the examples we have chosen are example addresses. The Media Access Control (MAC) address is a globally unique identifier, expressed as a long string of hexadecimal digits, usually separated into pairs by dashes. These are generally assigned in pools to vendors by the Institute of Electrical and Electronics Engineers (IEEE).

IPv4: ADDRESS RESOLUTION PROTOCOL

This is where the Address Resolution Protocol (ARP) comes into the picture. ARP is an Ethernet broadcast. Technically, all Ethernet packets are broadcast across the whole subnet, but most of them carry a destination MAC address and are discarded by other Ethernet cards when they are received. An Ethernet broadcast packet is meant to be picked up by any Ethernet card.

The ARP packet contains the source MAC address of the requester and the IP address that is being searched for. Every Ethernet card on this segment will receive this request and has to forward it to its IP layer. The IP layer will check to see whether it owns the IP address being requested. The interface that does own this IP address will then respond affirmatively to the ARP request, with a unicast response that identifies itself as the owner of the requested address.

The requester receives this response and adds an association to its *ARP table* between the IP address and the Ethernet address. You can view this ARP table at any time in Windows using a number of different methods. The easiest to remember is probably the command arp -a, which shows the addresses that have been assigned to network cards, as you can see in Figure 20.2.

FIGURE 20.2
Displaying the ARP table

As with most network facilities, you can also see this table using a netsh command, netsh interface ipv4 show neighbors, as shown in Figure 20.3.

In this example, the IP layer at computer A will create a packet that says, "I am an ARP request packet from the machine at IP 192.168.0.1, and I want to know the MAC address for the interface with IP 192.168.0.3." Computer A will then "shout" that message to the whole New York segment, most of which will stop what they're doing, check their IP address to see whether they are 192.168.0.3, and only one (C) will send a response back to A, saying, "I am an ARP response packet from the machine at IP 192.168.0.3, and my MAC address is 00:01:CA:FE:D5:03."

Occasionally you have to clear a stale entry out of the ARP table; to do this use arp -d inet_addr (where inet_addr is the IP address you want to delete from the table) to resend the broadcast. You can explore further arp options using the help switch arp -?.

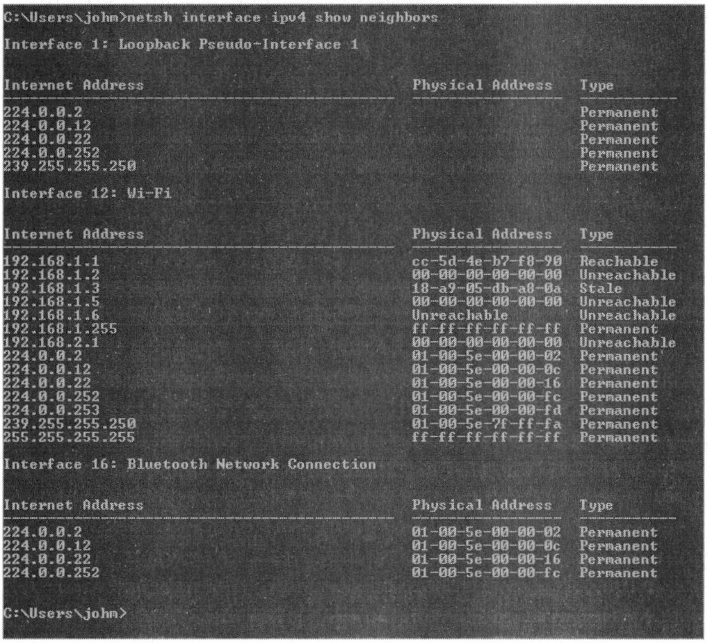

FIGURE 20.3
Using netsh
to show the
neighbors table

```
C:\Users\john>netsh interface ipv4 show neighbors

Interface 1: Loopback Pseudo-Interface 1


Internet Address                        Physical Address      Type
---------------------------------------------------------------------------
224.0.0.2                                                     Permanent
224.0.0.12                                                    Permanent
224.0.0.22                                                    Permanent
224.0.0.252                                                   Permanent
239.255.255.250                                              Permanent

Interface 12: Wi-Fi


Internet Address                        Physical Address      Type
---------------------------------------------------------------------------
192.168.1.1                             cc-5d-4e-b7-f8-90     Reachable
192.168.1.2                             00-00-00-00-00-00     Unreachable
192.168.1.3                             18-a9-05-db-a8-0a     Stale
192.168.1.5                             00-00-00-00-00-00     Unreachable
192.168.1.6                             Unreachable           Unreachable
192.168.1.255                           ff-ff-ff-ff-ff-ff     Permanent
192.168.2.1                             00-00-00-00-00-00     Unreachable
224.0.0.2                               01-00-5e-00-00-02     Permanent
224.0.0.12                              01-00-5e-00-00-0c     Permanent
224.0.0.22                              01-00-5e-00-00-16     Permanent
224.0.0.252                             01-00-5e-00-00-fc     Permanent
224.0.0.253                             01-00-5e-00-00-fd     Permanent
239.255.255.250                         01-00-5e-7f-ff-fa     Permanent
255.255.255.255                         ff-ff-ff-ff-ff-ff     Permanent

Interface 16: Bluetooth Network Connection


Internet Address                        Physical Address      Type
---------------------------------------------------------------------------
224.0.0.2                               01-00-5e-00-00-02     Permanent
224.0.0.12                              01-00-5e-00-00-0c     Permanent
224.0.0.22                              01-00-5e-00-00-16     Permanent
224.0.0.252                             01-00-5e-00-00-fc     Permanent


C:\Users\john>
```

IPv6: NEIGHBOR DISCOVERY

In IPv4, the IP layer of every computer on a subnet needs to pause what it's doing to inspect incoming ARP requests. If you can imagine how annoying it would be for everyone to stop their work every time someone called *anyone* in the company, that's roughly what it is like for IPv4 hosts. Switches help mitigate this a bit now, but if you are not careful, you can still have nasty broadcast storms that can bring down your network!

IPv6 discards the concept of broadcast-based protocols—they become multicast-based protocols—and the same is true of Neighbor Discovery (ND), which (among other things) takes over the resolution process from ARP, which is not supported on IPv6.

Rather cleverly, the IPv6 layer will take the last 24 bits of the IP address being queried for and will build a multicast address known as the *solicited node multicast address* by putting those 24 bits into the placeholder X bits of the destination address FF02:0:0:0:1:FFXX:XXXX. The Neighbor Solicitation message is sent to this address. Because there are more than 16 million possibilities for those last 24 bits, it's almost certain that this multicast message will interrupt only the Ethernet card and interface that own this IP address.

The Neighbor Advertisement message that comes back tells the requester what MAC address corresponds to the IP address requested—as with ARP, this is kept in a table that is always checked when sending an IP packet, so as to prevent repeatedly requesting the same Neighbor Solicitation message.

To show the neighbors table for IPv6, can you use the ARP command? No, because ARP is strictly for IPv4 only. The way to get the neighbor discovery table that is in use for your IPv6 layer is to run the netsh command, specifically, netsh interface ipv6 show neighbors; a sample output for the author's Local Area Connection is shown in Figure 20.4.

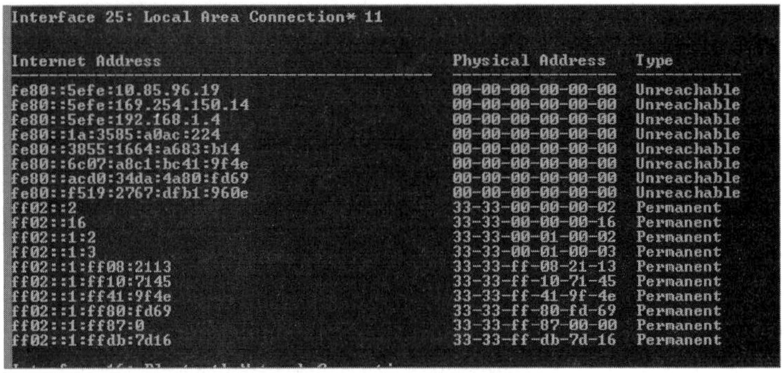
Interface 25: Local Area Connection* 11

Internet Address	Physical Address	Type
fe80::5efe:10.85.96.19	00-00-00-00-00-00	Unreachable
fe80::5efe:169.254.150.14	00-00-00-00-00-00	Unreachable
fe80::5efe:192.168.1.4	00-00-00-00-00-00	Unreachable
fe80::1a:3585:a0ac:224	00-00-00-00-00-00	Unreachable
fe80::3855:1664:a683:b14	00-00-00-00-00-00	Unreachable
fe80::6c07:a8c1:bc41:9f4e	00-00-00-00-00-00	Unreachable
fe80::acd0:34da:4a80:fd69	00-00-00-00-00-00	Unreachable
fe80::f519:2767:dfb1:960e	00-00-00-00-00-00	Unreachable
ff02::2	33-33-00-00-00-02	Permanent
ff02::16	33-33-00-00-00-16	Permanent
ff02::1:2	33-33-00-01-00-02	Permanent
ff02::1:3	33-33-00-01-00-03	Permanent
ff02::1:ff08:2113	33-33-ff-08-21-13	Permanent
ff02::1:ff10:7145	33-33-ff-10-71-45	Permanent
ff02::1:ff41:9f4e	33-33-ff-41-9f-4e	Permanent
ff02::1:ff80:fd69	33-33-ff-80-fd-69	Permanent
ff02::1:ff87:0	33-33-ff-87-00-00	Permanent
ff02::1:ffdb:7d16	33-33-ff-db-7d-16	Permanent

FIGURE 20.4 Showing the IPv6 neighbors table

FINALLY, YOU CAN SEND THE PACKET!

Now that you know who you are trying to talk to, the computer at interface A can finally send the data by building an Ethernet packet, whose payload is the IP packet (IP header and IP payload) and whose header contains the source and destination address, length, and type of protocol (in this case IP). This packet is then handed down to the Ethernet card, which sends it on.

ETHERNET TRIVIA

Did you know that although IP is an unreliable, "best-effort" protocol, which is free to lose packets of data for pretty much any reason, Ethernet itself is a reliable protocol? It's true: Ethernet uses electrical properties of the wire on which it runs to monitor whether a packet that it tried to send might have been confused with any other packet that was on the cable at the same time—if it finds this, it pauses a random length of time and tries again.

Now the Hard Case: With Routing

OK, it really isn't that hard, but we thought it best to approach you with as few confusing issues as possible, which is why we have separated the two parts of packet routing into different sections of this chapter.

EVERY HOST IS A LITTLE BIT ROUTER

Every computer with an IP address is part host, part router. It may not forward packets received from other hosts, as routers normally do, but it most certainly needs to keep a table of routes out from its own interfaces to the rest of the world, exactly as a router would do.

Just as with the ARP table, although you don't generally want to mess with the table's contents, you can always view them. Again, as with the ARP table, you can use a couple commands:

`route print` This command is the old standby for routing, and with no parameters other than `print`, it will display a list of interfaces and their MAC addresses, followed by a list of

IPv4 routes and then a list of IPv6 routes. If you just want the IPv4 routes, you can run `route -4 print`; for IPv6 routes, you can run `route -6 print`.

netsh The `netsh` command is designed to handle all network-related configuration settings and displays that will arise in the future. The command to display the routing table is `netsh interface ipv4 show route` or `netsh interface ipv6 show route`.

Each command displays the same routing table, but the information and presentation vary. The command `route print` displays a more class-based routing table and is familiar to many. You should feel comfortable by the end of this chapter with output such as that shown in Figure 20.5, which shows a sample of the IPv4 routing table.

FIGURE 20.5

Showing the IPv4 routing table with `route print`

```
IPv4 Route Table
===========================================================================
Active Routes:
Network Destination        Netmask          Gateway       Interface  Metric
          0.0.0.0          0.0.0.0      192.168.1.1    192.168.1.4     25
        127.0.0.0        255.0.0.0         On-link       127.0.0.1    306
        127.0.0.1  255.255.255.255         On-link       127.0.0.1    306
  127.255.255.255  255.255.255.255         On-link       127.0.0.1    306
      192.168.1.0    255.255.255.0         On-link     192.168.1.4    281
      192.168.1.4  255.255.255.255         On-link     192.168.1.4    281
    192.168.1.255  255.255.255.255         On-link     192.168.1.4    281
        224.0.0.0        240.0.0.0         On-link       127.0.0.1    306
        224.0.0.0        240.0.0.0         On-link     192.168.1.4    281
  255.255.255.255  255.255.255.255         On-link       127.0.0.1    306
  255.255.255.255  255.255.255.255         On-link     192.168.1.4    281
===========================================================================
Persistent Routes:
  None
```

The two `netsh interface ipvX show route` commands are a little more compact—if you don't need the interface index table, this format may be more what you need.

In both of the `netsh` outputs, the network destinations are in the newer Classless Inter-Domain Routing (CIDR) format, which we will describe in more detail shortly. Figure 20.6 shows the IPv4 routing table, and Figure 20.7 shows the IPv6 routing table. There is little difference between them except for the format and size of the prefix.

FIGURE 20.6

Using `netsh` to view the IPv4 routing table

```
C:\Users\john>netsh interface ipv4 show route

Publish  Type     Met  Prefix                Idx  Gateway/Interface Name
-------  -------  ----  ---------------       ---  ----------------------
No       Manual     0  0.0.0.0/0              12  192.168.1.1
No       System   256  127.0.0.0/8             1  Loopback Pseudo-Interface
1
No       System   256  127.0.0.1/32            1  Loopback Pseudo-Interface
1
No       System   256  127.255.255.255/32      1  Loopback Pseudo-Interface
1
No       System   256  192.168.1.0/24         12  Wi-Fi
No       System   256  192.168.1.2/32         12  Wi-Fi
No       System   256  192.168.1.255/32       12  Wi-Fi
No       System   256  224.0.0.0/4             1  Loopback Pseudo-Interface
1
No       System   256  224.0.0.0/4            16  Bluetooth Network Connect
ion
No       System   256  224.0.0.0/4            12  Wi-Fi
No       System   256  255.255.255.255/32      1  Loopback Pseudo-Interface
1
No       System   256  255.255.255.255/32     16  Bluetooth Network Connect
ion
No       System   256  255.255.255.255/32     12  Wi-Fi

C:\Users\john>
```

FIGURE 20.7
Using netsh to
view the IPv6
routing table

As you can see, that's a lot of confusing data to understand.

Let's pick one of those outputs and analyze it. Because it's new to everyone, let's go with the netsh output. This output has six columns—Publish, Type, Met, Prefix, Idx, and Gateway/Interface Name. Here is what each column represents:

Publish Is this route entry sent out in router advertisements to other computers? Usually this will be No on a machine that isn't acting as a router—only routers should be providing advertisements that they are routers!

Type This should show Manual for routes that have been statically added either by hand or by applications and should show Autoconf for routes that are added automatically by the IP layer. We have yet to see Autoconf in any of our routing tables.

Met This is an abbreviation for "metric." The metric is an arbitrary number that indicates the relative cost of using this route over another that will get to the same destination. When several routes match the same destination criteria, the one with the lowest metric is always used. We will look at this more in a moment.

Prefix This is the network prefix that will be matched against the destination address to find the shortest matching prefix.

Idx This is another abbreviation, this time for "interface index." This is a number indicating which interface this route entry refers to for outgoing traffic. The interface index can often be used in netsh commands to specify an interface without remembering its name.

Gateway/Interface Name For routes containing destination network prefixes outside the local subnet, this column contains the local subnet address of a router that can take packets and forward them. For routes whose destination network is on the local subnet, this column describes the name of the interface on which that local subnet lies.

How Is the Routing Table Used?

When an IP packet is assembled by an application and sent to the IP layer, its destination address is checked against the local subnet link address and mask of every network interface to see whether the destination address is local. You've already seen what happens if the address is indeed local—the ARP or ND table gets consulted and, if necessary, refreshed, and the packet is placed onto the appropriate NIC for transmission to its target.

If the address isn't local, you obviously have to send it through a router. You will find a router to send the packet to, and you will act as if the router's MAC address is actually the MAC address returned by an ARP query on your destination's IP address. In fact, in some very strange environments, this is exactly what the routers have been configured to do—respond to every ARP as if the router is indeed the host being searched for. That's a sign of a dysfunctional network, though, so we'll say no more about that.

How do you find the right route in the routing table? There are three simple criteria:

◆ *The routing table entry's destination network must be the closest match to the destination address of your packet*:

In the real world, this is analogous to saying that if you had two couriers offering to take your package and deliver it, you'd skip over the one who says, "I can get your package delivered to anyone in England," in favor of one who says, "I can get your package delivered to anyone in the town of Hadfield in England"—the latter will get your package there much faster, because he's already local.

◆ *If there are two possible routing entries, the one with the lowest metric is chosen*:

Metrics are rather arbitrary numbers, and their only purpose is to act as tiebreakers in this step of finding a matching route in the routing table. All that is necessary is to ensure that routes to the same destination can be sorted by metric to indicate the network designer's preference as to which router should be tried first.

◆ *If there is still more than one matching entry, the first one in the list is chosen*:

Note that "the first one in the list" is rather difficult to control accurately. As a result, you should be careful to choose metrics appropriately so that you can always predict which route gets chosen.

Once the IP layer has chosen a routing entry, as we mentioned earlier, it will send the IP packet to the router listed as the gateway in that entry. Of course, that means that the IP layer must use ARP to determine what MAC address corresponds to the IP address of the router. Note that the destination IP address in the IP packet that is eventually sent to the router is the original destination IP address, not that of the router.

Let's review our sample network again in Figure 20.8.

FIGURE 20.8
Sample network

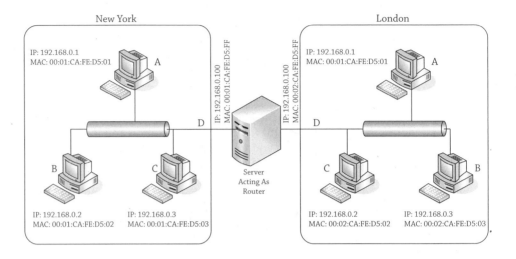

Now as you will see between the two different sites of London and New York, the IP addresses of the machines are on different subnets. So let us think for a second on how a host from the New York site would talk to or send a packet to a host located in the London site. To determine that, you need to know about network masks.

From Classes to Classless

We have deliberately chosen the `netsh` version of the router table, because it uses the more recent CIDR format, as opposed to the older `netmask` format that appears in the `route print` output in Figure 20.5.

Wherever you work with networks, you will encounter some people who were taught the new format and some who learned the old format; therefore, it's best to learn both, so you can be the interpreter between these two groups. The following description may not be entirely historically accurate, but it is logically accurate and will help you understand why the Internet is the way it is today.

In the Beginning Was the Class

When the Internet was young and the address space available to be assigned was plentiful, addresses were, well, not quite handed out like candy but were certainly assigned less strictly than they are today. Internet users were categorized into different classes, and along with them came different classes of address ranges to suit them.

The classes were named A through C, and they were each distinguished by the number of bits devoted to the network address and the number of bits devoted to the host address. With only 32 bits of IP address, a class A assignment would use 8 bits to signify the network address (i.e., a subnet mask of 255.0.0.0) and the remaining 24 to signify the host address, a class B assignment would use 16 bits for the network address (i.e., a subnet mask of 255.255.0.0) and 16 for the host address, and a class C assignment would use the first 24 bits for the network address (i.e., a subnet mask of 255.255.255.0) and 8 bits for the host address.

Classes are identified by reading the binary form to see how many of the most significant bits are set to 1, before reaching the first 0. Class A addresses start with 0, so the first octet is in the range 0000 0000 to 0111 1111 (or in decimal, 0 to 127). A class B address has a single 1 before the first 0, as in 1000 0000 to 1011 1111 (in decimal, 128 to 191). Class C addresses start with two 1s and then their first 0, so their range is 1100 0000 to 1101 1111 (or 192 to 223).

This all seemed very equitable, with class A users getting the ability to have nearly 2^{24} (16,777,216) hosts. Class B users received nearly 2^{16} (65,536) hosts, and class C users got nearly 256 hosts each.

Unusable Host Addresses

Why "nearly"? In every network range, a number of addresses are not available to be assigned to hosts. The only absolute, carved-in-stone (or at least, written in the RFCs, which are the Internet's equivalent of stone tablets) requirements are that in any network the top and bottom ends of the address ranges are reserved.

The top end of the address range—where all host bits are set to 1 (the *all 1s address*)—is reserved for directed broadcast. So, for instance, if your network was a class B assignment and had addresses starting with the sequence 192.168.*something.something*, the directed broadcast address would be 192.168.255.255, where the two 255 octets represent a binary sequence of 1111 1111. All 1s, see?

A packet sent to this address would reach every computer on the 192.168.*something.something* network. Every computer would pass that message up to its own IP layer, where something might be listening for that broadcasted traffic. (You will see this 192.168.*something.something* network appear in lots of documentation, and we will explain why in a few paragraphs.) Don't try this on your production network because you can flood your network very easily!

The bottom end of the address range—where all host bits are set to 0 (the *all 0s address*)—is technically reserved for broadcasting. Wait, we already said that the all 1s address was reserved for broadcasting, didn't we? Well, yes, that's true—and you won't find a system today that uses all 0s for broadcasting. But back in the Internet's equivalent of the Bronze Age, Internet developments were being made by several different groups at once. Apparently the broadcast was invented by more than one company. Sun chose to broadcast at all 0s, and everyone else chose to broadcast at all 1s. Much to Sun's surprise (because at the time, it was a major force in Internet development), everyone else won out.

But the all 0s address hasn't become available for use because it also represents another concept, that of the "network address." In router tables, as well as in network diagrams and other documentation, it refers to the network as a whole, so instead of talking about the 192.168.*something.something* network, you could now talk about the 192.168.0.0 network.

Internet addressing in IPv4 has an addressing concept—that all-all 1s and all-all 0s addresses, 255.255.255.255 and 0.0.0.0, represent something. All 0s' address 192.168.0.0 now represents the network of machines from 192.168.0.1 to 192.168.255.254, so what would 0.0.0.0 represent? It generally represents a network of one computer—"this" computer. By extension, 255.255.255.255 represents "broadcast to every computer out there."

Broadcast Gets Narrower: The First Unroutable Addresses

When the Internet was small, these broadcast addresses were great. If you wanted to know what computers a company had connected to the Internet, all you had to do was find that their network address was 192.168.0.0, and that meant you could enumerate their network by pinging

192.168.255.255. You would get a response from every machine they had (and you still can, but be careful!). Then you could try to connect to random machines and see which ones were interesting.

Similarly, if you wanted to enumerate the entire Internet, that was no problem either—you simply used ping 255.255.255.255, and you got in return a response from every machine that existed.

Because each of these actions had its own risks—the first, a risk of disclosure, and the second a risk of flooding your own network (or someone else's, if you could direct the responses to their directed broadcast address!)—pretty soon routers were being configured to disallow packets with these destinations from crossing them.

As a result, 192.168.255.255 could now be used only from inside the 192.168.0.0 network, so it became a directed broadcast that you could only direct at yourself, and 255.255.255.255 became a global broadcast that would only reach machines on your side of the router. Essentially, this meant that both broadcasts reached the same place—your local subnet—and since the 192.168.255.255 directed broadcast address required calculation but the 255.255.255.255 address could be hard-coded, pretty much nobody uses the directed broadcast form anymore. Unfortunately, this doesn't mean you can get that address back and use it for a host.

Routing the Unroutable, Part I: Private Addresses

The document that defines the all 0s and all 1s addresses (RFC 1122, "Requirements for Internet Hosts—Communication Layers") also defines a specific class A address as being reserved for the purpose of *loopback* communication. This is the network 127.0.0.0, but out of that 16 million address range, almost nobody ever uses anything other than the single address 127.0.0.1, which is usually given the alias *localhost*.

A useful convention that has grown over the years is to use the first address or last address in a network as the location for the default router. Note that this is only a convention, and nothing forces you to do this (in our example, for instance, the router does not follow this convention; it is set to 192.168.0.100 for New York and 192.169.0.100 for London). However, following this convention would make it simpler for the person who replaces you to find the router. An example would be that in the 192.168.0.0 network, you'd use 192.168.0.1 as the address of the default router following the first address convention.

There's that network again—192.168.0.0. Why do we keep using that network? Quite simply, it's because we know we won't get sued by the owners for accidentally directing traffic their way. How do we know this? This address is not owned by any one individual. Another RFC document (RFC 1918, "Address Allocation for Private Internets") lays out a series of network ranges that are reserved for private use. By default, these addresses are not routed—a public router will not forward an IP packet whose destination is in these ranges:

10.0.0.0–10.255.255.255

172.16.0.0–172.31.255.255

192.168.0.0–192.168.255.255

Those of you who can do binary math in your heads, or have memorized the class ranges, will have realized that the range 172.16.0.0–172.31.255.255 is not a network range that matches a class. It is, in fact, a supernetwork, or *supernet*, of 16 class B address ranges between 172.16.0.0 and 172.16.255.255 and 172.31.0.0 and 172.31.255.255. The 192.168.*.* range is also a supernet of 256 class C networks.

Of course, if you're in one of these networks, you'll realize that your packets do make it outside the router—what you may not realize is that they do so by virtue of a NAT, which alters the source address to something that the router will be willing to pass.

Originally, NATs would assume that only a certain number of internal users would be accessing the Internet at any one time so that number of external addresses was assigned to the NAT, and each time a user's traffic needed forwarding to the Internet, that user's internal address was mapped to a free, publically routable external address. For some organizations, this is still the way in which internal systems become accessible to the outside Internet.

SUBNETTING AND SUPERNETTING

Something that was realized early on in the design of the IP class system was that even a huge multinational corporation that might want a class A address would not actually have one physical Ethernet wire to which 16 million devices were attached. So, a scheme was developed whereby a larger network could be divided into several subnetworks, or *subnets*.

The way to do this was to say that class distinctions were no longer so important; every host would have its own notion of how many of its address bits defined "the network" and how many of its address bits defined "me on the network." Because this divided the binary address into two portions, not on an 8-bit octet boundary, they used a term borrowed from graphics processing and called it a *mask*. Specifically, this would be a *netmask*. You can imagine it as a sheet of paper with holes cut in it (just like a mask you might make for your kids at Halloween). The holes allow the network part of your address to show through and hide the host part, replacing those bits with 0s.

In Figure 20.9, we are looking at the effect of the netmask 255.252.0.0 on the address 192.168.143.8. The netmask is equivalent to the binary string 1111 1111 1111 1100 0000 0000 0000 0000—that's 14 bits set to 1 and 18 bits set to 0.

FIGURE 20.9
Demonstrating how a netmask works

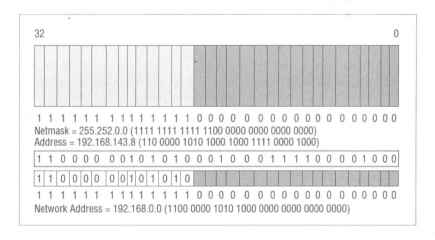

The address 192.168.143.8 is equivalent to the bits 1100 0000 1010 1000 1000 1111 0000 1000, and when you line this up underneath the netmask, you can see which bits to ignore when calculating the network address and which bits to count:

1111 1111 1111 1100 0000 0000 0000 0000: Netmask

1100 0000 1010 1000 1000 1111 0000 1000: Host address

1100 0000 1010 1000 0000 0000 0000 0000: Network address

In binary mathematics, this is equivalent to defining the mask as a number that's the same width as your address, with a 1 in every bit in the network portion, with a 0 in every bit in the host portion, and using the binary AND operation with your network address. The binary AND compares bits in the two inputs one position at a time—where the two bits are set to 1, the result will have a 1 bit; if any or both are set to 0, the result will have a 0 bit. Check our binary math, and make sure that we got it right!

As you've guessed from this section's heading, there were also organizations that bought a class C and then realized that they needed to use more than 254 addresses within their organization. They could buy another class C, of course, but if they could buy a class C that was next door to their existing one, they could "supernet" the two to create a network of 2^9-2 addresses—510 in all. The savings in number of addresses were not the main point, however—the savings that were important in supernetting were in the sizes of the routing tables on the way to this network.

You will see these network masks in the output from route -4 print, but they are a pain to calculate and to understand what number of bits each represents. The key to remember is that there are only nine values that can appear in any octet of a netmask: 255, 254, 252, 248, 240, 224, 192, 128, 0—that's 8, 7, 6, 5, 4, 3, 2, 1, and 0 bits, respectively. Add up the number of bits in each octet to come up with the total number of bits in a network mask to see how many bits of your host address are tied to the network.

Because a network might be subnetted at several different places, the netmask for an address depends on where you are in the network. The address 10.1.2.3, for instance, might be the third host in the network 10.1.2.0–10.1.2.255, or it might be the 66,051st host in the network 10.0.0.0–10.255.255.255.

Another casualty of subnetting and supernetting was the directed broadcast—even if the router allowed a directed broadcast to pass, how do you know how many bits to direct your broadcast at? This was yet another nail in the coffin of the directed broadcast, which now only truly exists as an annoying reason not to use the all 1s address in your network.

SUBNETTING BY RFC OR BY REALITY

Many of you may have already encountered a subnet range chosen from RFC 1918 (http://tools.ietf.org/html/rfc1918) values. Every time the you connect to a wireless device in a local coffee shop, you get an address in the 10.0.0.0 class A range that is reserved for private networking. But this netmask isn't 255.0.0.0. It's generally 255.255.255.0—allowing for only a maximum of 253 devices (the router takes up one address!) using wireless inside the coffee shop. Wherever you may be, it's a little optimistic to think that this limit won't be reached!

This 10.* range is also used frequently in home networks set up by broadband installers or those who follow the instructions for the default configuration of several brands of routers. If you use 10.0.0.0–10.0.0.255 with a netmask of 255.255.255.0 in your home, technically you're in violation of RFC 950, which says that you shouldn't use a subnet of all 0s or all 1s. But don't worry; the Internet police won't come knocking on your door.

If you're trying to take an exam based on this RFC and RFC 1122, you will want to trim off two subnets from your calculations—the all 0s subnet and the all 1s subnet.

CLASSLESS INTER-DOMAIN ROUTING: THE INTERNET LOSES ITS CLASS

As you can see from our assertion that the use of an all 1s or all 0s subnet address is no big deal, as well as from the widespread use of supernetting (which has no subnet part or perhaps a negative-length subnet part), it is pretty clear that the Internet's scheme of segregating network addresses by classes was becoming completely irrelevant.

Added to this was the sheer tedium of having to calculate the network masks. Network masks were always a string of some number of bits set to 1, followed by a number of bits set to 0, with the total number of bits being 32, which is the size of an IPv4 address. To save having to write network addresses as "10.0.0.0–10.0.255.255" or "10.0.0.0 with netmask 255.255.0.0," network administrators used a shorthand notation, writing a slash after the network number and then writing just the number of bits set to 1. So "10.0.0.0–10.0.255.255" would become "10.0.0.0/16." The default allocation of the 10.0.0.0 address as a class A network with netmask of 255.0.0.0 would be noted by describing it as "10.0.0.0/8."

The Internet is ruled by RFCs, as we've already mentioned, and this new shorthand notation was no exception. RFC 1519 defined the original solution as Classless Inter-Domain Routing (CIDR), and the name has held up.

In fact, the CIDR shortcut has been carried over into IPv6; you will see that IPv6 network prefixes throughout Windows Server 2012 R2 are specified in exactly this manner.

ROUTING TCP: NAPT AND PAT

Remember we told you early on in this chapter IP is the only layer that is routed—that Ethernet is a broadcast system and TCP doesn't need routing? That's a bit of a fib, we're afraid.

DECIPHERING THE ROUTER TABLE

Do you have enough information to read that router table in Figure 20.6? Let's look at the New York A router table again.

Reading from top to bottom and ignoring the Publish, Met, and Idx fields, you have the following routes:

New York A's Routing Entries

Prefix	Gateway/ Interface	Comments
0.0.0.0/0	192.168.1.1	The default route—this means "if you don't find a better match below, send the packet to 192.168.0.100, or New York D." 0.0.0.0/0 is a special value and should not be thought of as anything other than a placeholder meaning "default."
127.0.0.0/8 127.0.0.1/32 127.255.255.255/32	Loopback	Even the loopback address has to be routed! The first entry indicates that the entire loopback network can be reached through the loopback interface; the second entry indicates that the specific address 127.0.0.1 is on that interface, and the third entry indicates that directed broadcasts for this network can be sent there. Strictly speaking, the first entry should cover the others.
192.168.1.0/24 192.168.1.2/32 192.168.1.255/32	Wi-Fi	This indicates that any address on New York, even the router, can be reached through the Local Area Connection interface.
224.0.0.0/4	Loopback Bluetooth Network Connection Wi-Fi	These entries indicate that multicast traffic can be sent on either of the available interfaces.
255.255.255.255/32	Loopback Wi-Fi Bluetooth Network Connection	Again, these entries indicate that broadcasts can be sent on either interface.

As you can see, the table is displayed in order from least-specific route to most-specific route. You can think of the router inside this computer comparing the destination in the Prefix column against the destination of an IP packet:

"Hmm, I have a packet here for 192.168.0.2—where do I send it? Well, 0.0.0.0/0 matches anything, so if I don't find anything else, that entry will win out. What about the next few? They all start with 127, and the prefix hasn't masked that out. My destination address doesn't start with 127, so that won't work. 192.168.0.0/24 matches, because my destination address is 192.168.0.2, and if I zero everything past the first 24 bits (as the prefix says I should), I get 192.168.0.0, which is the same as the network address of the prefix for this entry. That's the match that I will choose instead of the less-specific match I have. No others match, so I am left with sending my packet through the Local Area Connection."

As long as the routing table is complete and correct, the computer will always follow this procedure of checking the prefix against the destination address, masking the destination address with the number of bits in the prefix first, and always discarding a less-specific match when a more-specific match is found. The metric is used only as a tiebreaker in case two entries have the same prefixes that are the closest match—the one with the lowest metric is chosen.

COMPLETING THE TABLE

How do you correct an incomplete router table? More to the point, how do you tell if a router table is incomplete?

You've already seen that the router table is consulted for every IP packet. So, a correct and complete router table must be able to tell you the right place to send every packet.

It must have at least one default route, with a prefix of 0.0.0.0/0 (or ::/0 for IPv6 routes); otherwise, there will be some packets it has no idea what to do with. Don't forget that the routing table may have more than one default route; in that case, there are several routers that volunteer for the task. Remember that the one with the lowest metric value will win.

Other than that, it must know exactly how to route to every destination address that does not go to the default router. In most home environments, this is not a problem. The default router is usually the one that connects to the DSL or cable router, and everything can be sent there.

In an enterprise environment, however, there are often several routers in your immediate subnet. Each leads to a different portion of your network. If you list the routers and the networks to which they lead, you should have a list that matches all the entries in your routing table.

If you find that you need to add a route to your routing table, that can be done very easily from the command line. There are two basic commands to use—the old `route` add and our good friend `netsh`. Suppose you wanted to add a route to the prefix 192.168.0.0/16 with a metric of 100 that leads to the router at 10.0.0.1. The command to do this could be any of the following:

```
route add 192.168.0.0 mask 255.255.0.0 10.0.0.1 metric 100
route add 192.168.0.0/16 10.0.0.1 metric 100
netsh interface ipv4 add route 192.168.0.0/16 "Local Area Connection" 10.0.0.1
```

The `netsh` command requires a little more typing than the `route` command, even if you abbreviate it to `netsh int ipv4 add ro 192.168.0.0/16 "Local" 10.0.0.1`.

Similarly, you can delete a route—though if it is one that is automatically added because of a router advertisement, it will come back as follows:

```
route del 192.168.0.0
netsh interface ipv4 delete route 129.0.0.0/8 "Local Area Connection"
```

It is certainly the original design that IP should be the only point that requires routing, and it was an original goal of IP. What was the original design for TCP that it didn't require routing, and how did that change over time?

WHY TCP: WHAT DOESN'T IP HAVE?

So, just what is wrong with IP that TCP needed inventing? IP doesn't have any concept of a connection—if we had to describe it as analogous to an existing system we're comfortable with, it would be the postal service. Every IP packet is like a postcard that goes through the system. Much like the postal service, some IP packets get lost in transit and if you send two IP packets, one soon after the other, they may arrive in the opposite order. Unlike the postal service, some IP packets get delivered twice!

An IP packet, just like a postcard, cannot contain a simple message like "Please ignore the previous message" because it is impossible to be certain that the sender and recipient will agree on what the previous message was. With occasional packet duplication, a recipient could even believe that they are to ignore the message that told them to ignore the previous message—very confusing!

So, for some kind of communications, these restrictions needed to be overcome—and a system of connected communications needed to be developed to allow for something more akin to a telephone conversation, with a start, an ordered exchange of information, and an end. This is what TCP provides.

Strictly speaking, TCP adds to IP the following attributes:

Handshaking   An exchange like, "How do you do?" "Fine, thanks. How are you?" "Oh, fine too," in TCP is known as the *three-way handshake* and consists of very short messages, known as SYN, SYN/ACK, and ACK. SYN is short for "synchronize," and ACK is short for "acknowledgment."

Sequencing   A counter of bytes sent/received is used to ensure that no two bytes are presented twice to the application and that bytes received out of sequence can be reordered. These sequences (one on each side of the connection) are set by the initial SYN and acknowledged with every ACK.

Flow Control   A clever system called *sliding windows* keeps traffic flowing without having to wait and without taking up too much memory in the sender or receiver.

Error Indication   An application that closes unexpectedly (akin to a hang up on a phone conversation) can be signaled to its communicating partner with a reset (RST) packet.

Ports   This is a little like having a switchboard that allows you to call a company at one number and be directed to any of thousands of extensions so that your conversation can be separated from other conversations with employees at that company.

Sockets, Ports, and Winsock

Almost no one actually writes applications that talk directly in IP. Fewer still write applications that directly control TCP, particularly on Windows, because various security measures prevent any application other than the network stack from creating TCP packets.

Instead, applications communicate to the TCP layer by using something known as a *socket*. Sockets are not unique to Windows; they have been around since some of the earliest days of the Internet.

A socket, in Internet terms, consists of five things—a source address, a destination address, a source port, a destination port, and a protocol (in this case, the protocol is TCP). A pair of matching sockets (where the source address and port of one socket are the destination address and port of the other, and vice versa) constitute a TCP connection. A socket is *unconnected* if its destination port and address are zero, and it is *unbound* if its source port and address are zero. An unbound socket is also unconnected.

Although you know what an address is, we have not yet told you what a port is. Quite simply, it's a number from 1 to 65,535, chosen to make sure that sockets can be distinguished from one another. The ports below 1024 are considered reserved, in that they are assigned to a particular protocol. For instance, ports 21 and 20 are assigned to FTP.

The life cycle of a connection starts in one of two states, depending on whether it is a server-side socket or a client-side socket. A server-side socket will start off in the LISTENING state, which requires a socket to be bound to a source address and port. The client-side socket, meanwhile, will start in the SYN-SENT state, when it starts its handshake with the server socket. This requires that the socket be bound and associated with a destination address and port. The server responds with its SYN-ACK, creating a new socket with the same source address and port as the listening socket, which it puts into the SYN-RECEIVED state. Ending the handshake, the client sends its ACK and puts its socket into the ESTABLISHED state. On the server side, when the initial ACK is received, the server too will put its socket into the ESTABLISHED state.

You can use the netstat command to get an idea of what is connecting to your machine and what state it is in. Figure 20.10 shows output from running the netstat command.

FIGURE 20.10

Sample netstat output

```
C:\Users\johm>netstat

Active Connections

  Proto  Local Address          Foreign Address        State
  TCP    192.168.1.2:15960      67:http                ESTABLISHED
  TCP    192.168.1.2:22235      JOHN-PC:ms-wbt-server  ESTABLISHED
  TCP    192.168.1.2:22247      77.67.4.56:https       CLOSE_WAIT
  TCP    192.168.1.2:28347      a77:http               ESTABLISHED
  TCP    192.168.1.2:28360      77.67.4.56:https       ESTABLISHED
  TCP    192.168.1.2:28381      channel-ecmp-06-frc1:https  ESTABLISHED
  TCP    192.168.1.2:46387      a92-123-72-41:http     ESTABLISHED
  TCP    192.168.1.2:46470      cds114:http            CLOSE_WAIT
  TCP    192.168.1.2:49658      64.4.27.55:https       TIME_WAIT
  TCP    192.168.1.2:49664      emea:https             TIME_WAIT
  TCP    192.168.1.2:49665      emea:https             TIME_WAIT
  TCP    192.168.1.2:49666      emea:https             TIME_WAIT
  TCP    192.168.1.2:49667      emea:https             TIME_WAIT
  TCP    192.168.1.2:49668      emea:https             TIME_WAIT
  TCP    192.168.1.2:49669      emea:https             TIME_WAIT
  TCP    192.168.1.2:49670      emea:https             TIME_WAIT
  TCP    192.168.1.2:49671      emea:https             TIME_WAIT
  TCP    192.168.1.2:49672      edge-star-ecmp-02-1hr2:https  ESTABLISHED
  TCP    192.168.1.2:49673      emea:https             TIME_WAIT
  TCP    192.168.1.2:49676      65.52.209.62:https     TIME_WAIT
  TCP    192.168.1.2:49678      65.52.209.62:https     TIME_WAIT
  TCP    192.168.1.2:49679      77.67.20.17:http       ESTABLISHED
  TCP    192.168.1.2:53378      157.55.236.112:https   ESTABLISHED
  TCP    192.168.1.2:58342      sipfed:https           ESTABLISHED
  TCP    192.168.1.2:58373      emea:https             ESTABLISHED
  TCP    192.168.1.2:58389      emea:https             ESTABLISHED
  TCP    192.168.1.2:58442      emea:https             ESTABLISHED
  TCP    192.168.1.2:58448      emea:https             ESTABLISHED
  TCP    192.168.1.2:58475      emea:https             ESTABLISHED
  TCP    192.168.1.2:58476      emea:https             ESTABLISHED
  TCP    192.168.1.2:58480      emea:https             ESTABLISHED
  TCP    192.168.1.2:58505      emea:https             ESTABLISHED
  TCP    192.168.1.2:63784      emea:https             ESTABLISHED
  TCP    192.168.1.2:63839      emea:https             ESTABLISHED
  TCP    192.168.1.2:63844      emea:https             ESTABLISHED
  TCP    192.168.1.2:63851      emea:https             ESTABLISHED
  TCP    [2001:0:cc9:ff10:243d:cfb5:a683:b14]:3982  [2001:4898:c8:604e:2e76:8aff
:fe50:15b8]:microsoft-ds  ESTABLISHED
  TCP    [2001:0:cc9:ff10:243d:cfb5:a683:b14]:49680  [2001:4898:4008:1008:fe:650
:5306:3073]:http  SYN_SENT
```

ONE PORT PER END MEANS TWO PORTS

It is not true to say that a connection to a listening socket creates a connection on a different port. This is an erroneous statement made by many who do not understand that there are two ports in play—one at each side. An example is a connection to a web server—say a client at 192.168.1.2 wants to connect to the web server at 10.20.30.40, and this is the client's first connection since it started.

We'll use some shorthand to describe the sockets. Each socket will be described as {source address, source port, protocol, destination address, destination port}. The web server is LISTENING at port 80, meaning it has a socket bound to source address 10.20.30.40, source port 80, protocol TCP, destination address 0.0.0.0, destination port 0—{10.20.30.40, 80, TCP, 0.0.0.0, 0}. The client creates a socket {192.168.1.2, 1025, TCP, 10.20.30.40, 80}. Huh? Where did 1025 come from? It's the first number above 1024, so it's the first port from the unreserved range, and it will be used as the source port for the first connection. The next connection will connect from port 8700. This is assigned randomly by applications and is very rarely in sequence. Consider it a security feature so traffic is not easily identified.

The client sends a SYN on its socket to start the handshake. When the LISTENING socket receives the SYN, the TCP layer creates a copy of the LISTENING socket and sets the destination address and port to match the incoming connection request, so it now has two sockets: {10.20.30.40, 80, TCP, 0.0.0.0, 0} in the LISTENING state and {10.20.30.40, 80, TCP, 192.168.1.2, 1025} in the SYN-RECEIVED state after the SYN-ACK is sent. This socket is paired with the client socket of {192.168.1.2, 1025, TCP, 10.20.30.40, 80} to form the connection. When the client receives the SYN-ACK and sends its ACK in response, both sockets can go to the ESTABLISHED state. A new socket, but not a new port, has been created at the server.

From now on, it is meaningless to call one socket the server and one socket the client; they are both on an equal footing. Each can send and receive data at any time. Although many protocols insist on strict synchronization between command and response, TCP is an asynchronous communications protocol, meaning that any side can send at any time.

To terminate the connection gracefully, one side of the communication (we'll call it the *closer*) will send a FIN and set its socket into the FIN-WAIT-1 state to indicate that it is waiting for an acknowledgment of its FIN, as well as for the other end (we'll call it the *closee*) to close the socket with a FIN. The closee can carry on sending data but will not receive more data from the closer after the FIN that it received.

At some point, usually pretty quickly after receiving the FIN, the closee will send an ACK that acknowledges the FIN. This will cause the closee to enter the CLOSE-WAIT state, indicating that it knows that it won't receive anything more but that it's still waiting for the application to finish sending and close. When the closer receives this ACK, it will enter the FIN-WAIT-2 state.

The closee will eventually finish sending data and will send a FIN to indicate that the application on its end is finished, too. After sending the FIN, the closee enters the LAST-ACK state (it's waiting for an ACK—the last ACK—from the closer), and when the closer receives the FIN, it will enter the TIME_WAIT state and send an ACK to the closee.

The closee will close its socket on receiving this ACK, at which point it is free to forget all about that connection. Technically, the socket is in the CLOSED state. The poor closer, on the other hand, has to keep its socket in the TIME_WAIT state for about four minutes, before it too can move the socket to the CLOSED state and forget about it. (This is to prevent packets that are still bouncing around in the network from being responded to with RST messages.)

Winsock: Why We Can All Use the Internet

Fortunately, even application developers don't need to handle this all for themselves. Wherever there is a network stack, there is an interface used for programming it. Back in the Iron Age of the Internet, there were as many different interfaces—or application programming interfaces (APIs)—as there were network stacks. There were about a dozen network stacks.

For the poor network programmers among us, that meant either we had to write a dozen different versions of our software or we had to pick one or two network stacks and hope we had backed the right horse. The "right horse" could change midstream, if you don't mind us mixing a metaphor, whenever the next "killer app" came along and its authors chose a different network stack than the one you had chosen.

Then in 1992 or 1993, the network stack vendors realized that this was constricting their market, because no one was producing applications for Windows networking. They banded together in what they called a spirit of "coopetition" and developed, over the course of several months, a common API that they would all stand behind. They called this Windows Sockets, because it was very similar to the BSD Sockets API on Unix systems. Everyone else quickly called it Winsock, because that's the name of the library with which you linked your network program.

It's some coincidence (but not much) that at this time the National Center for Supercomputing Applications released a hugely popular web browser called NCSA Mosaic that was available for Windows, among other platforms.

IMPORTANCE OF WINSOCK

Take a very common utility that can be found in most network administrators' toolboxes, WFTPD, an FTP server that is still going strong today and is available at http://www.wftpd.com/. Without Winsock this hugely popular tool could not have easily been created! Because of this utility, Winsock was a key component of the rise of the Internet around the world.

The graphical web browser from NCSA played a huge part in popularizing the Internet (fans of the musical *Avenue Q* will realize immediately why), as did the arrival of America Online (AOL) and its subsequent adoption of Winsock as the chief method of connecting applications to its dial-up stack.

Of course, these days, there are no "dozen network stacks" for Windows. For most of us, there is just one, and it comes from Microsoft. But it still supports Winsock, and developers can still write networking programs that they can feel reasonably certain will run on any Windows system.

Thanks, Winsock!

Routing the Unroutable, Part II: NAPT and PAT

So now that you know all about sockets and ports, we can explain the next big leap in technology for routing private networks to the Internet. With a plain NAT, we have shown that you could only have as many externally connected clients as you had external IP addresses—and this during a time when the number of available IP addresses is drying up.

The next bright idea, then, was to make possible the use of one external IP address for several internal IP addresses. This kind of NAT router would have to look beyond the IP layer into the TCP (or UDP) layer and use the IP address and port to map connections, rather than entire IP addresses, to external connections.

Such a router is called a *network address/port translator* (NAPT). Some people may also call it a *port/address translator* (PAT). We prefer NAPT, partly because this is what the RFCs refer to, but mostly because the "network" part of the job hasn't been lost, so the initial doesn't need to be tossed.

Because NAPT routers are so useful compared to NAT routers and because NAPT is a little harder to say, for the most part what you hear referred to as a NAT router is actually a NAPT router. Some enterprises still use a NAT router as an IP-level NAT router with no port translation, but that is somewhat of an oddity these days.

When a NAPT router sees a SYN crossing its bow from an internal address, it will assign an external IP address and a port (usually the same number as the internal port, but in case of conflicts, this can be assigned essentially at random) to that connection attempt. Then, whenever it sees the internal IP and port in a TCP-bearing IP packet coming from its inside edge, it will edit that packet and insert the external IP and port before forwarding the packet to the Internet. Likewise, when it sees an incoming TCP-bearing IP packet on its outside edge, it will find the matching internal IP address and port to replace that with, before forwarding the edited packet to its internal target.

NAPT's Unintended Consequences, Part I: An Accidental Firewall

For most applications, NAPT works really well. Indeed, it has an unexpected benefit to those of us who beg for security devices to "fail closed" and to "deny by default." Every NAPT device acts as a firewall, because by default a NAPT will not know where to send any incoming packet. Rather than guessing, the NAPT will either drop the packet or respond with a failure indication, such as an RST response.

Most NAPTs allow you to configure port mappings, for instance, to tell the NAPT that "we have a web server running at 192.168.230.21, port 80," in which case it will assign a static mapping from its external IP address, which is port 80, to its internal address 192.168.230.21, which is port 80.

You can also configure most NAPT devices to forward any unknown traffic to a particular IP address, sometimes known as the *DMZ host*. Try to resist the temptation to do this, because this will result in that host being bombarded with every network attack known to man. The Internet is a little hostile to those without a firewall.

NAPT's Unintended Consequences, Part II: App Killer

For some applications, however, NAPT devices have practically killed the protocols on which they rely. There are several protocols, such as FTP (file transfer), SIP (session initiation—for phone-like communication), and H.323 (again, for voice- and videophones), that send information about IP addresses and ports in their communication with their connection partners. Even IPsec, the secured protocol for IP that allows for authentication and encryption of IP traffic, will sometimes need to quote its IP address.

For instance, an FTP client will tell the FTP server "connect back to me at my address 192.168.230.21 on port 1025," with a command, such as PORT 192,168,230,21,4,1. The server can't connect to that address and port because it's a nonroutable address. This usually results in a time-out when the upcoming file transfer is attempted and makes FTP very hard to use from behind a firewall.

Routing the Unroutable, Part III: Application Layer Gateways

The developers of the NAPT specification (again, it's in an RFC—this time RFC 3022, "Traditional IP Network Address Translator") were aware of this kind of problem and suggested that Application Layer Gateways (ALGs) could be added to any NAPT router.

Such an ALG would inspect the contents of the TCP payloads for recognized protocols and commands, editing the TCP stream itself to change IP addresses and port numbers quoted there and opening up mappings to allow incoming connections as requested.

This works acceptably well except in the case where a protocol is unrecognized by the NAPT as belonging to a particular ALG. The cause of this can be as simple as the use of a different port or as complex as the use of encryption (IPsec, for instance, or FTP over SSL/TLS). In the former case, the NAPT doesn't know that you're sending FTP traffic because the server is not at port 21; in the latter case, the NAPT sees only encrypted data, which it can neither read nor modify.

NAPTs WILL SOMEDAY BECOME IRRELEVANT

IPv6 offers a new reality. There are so many addresses in IPv6 that we will never have the exhaustion problem that afflicted IPv4.

Yes, we know, we said that with IPv4, but this time we mean it. Really. Even if you gave an IPv6 address to every blade of grass in your lawn, you'd still have plenty of space in your own IPv6 address assignment to accommodate an address for each item in your refrigerator, every device you own, and every square inch of your house. Then there would still be room to spare between those addresses.

As a result of this huge address space, there will be no NATs or NAPTs for IPv6. If you need the "accidental firewall" feature of NAPTs, you will need to get a more "deliberate" firewall, one that operates only as a firewall.

Installing a NAT

Possibly the most likely use you will have for making a Windows Server 2012 R2 machine into a router is if you want to create a NAT over which you have finer control than you would get from a normal NAT device.

Installing NAT in Windows Server 2012 R2 is relatively simple, although it has many steps:

1. Install the Remote Access role.

   This consists of the routing components required.

2. Open Server Manager and click Manage ➢ Add Roles and Features.

   The familiar new Add Roles and Features Wizard appears, as shown in Figure 20.11.

FIGURE 20.11
Adding the server role for Remote Access

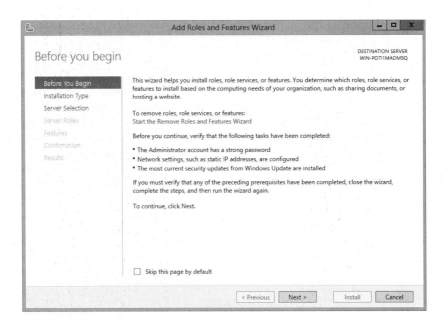

3. Click Next on the Before You Begin screen.

4. Next, select "Role-based or feature-based installation," as illustrated in Figure 20.12.

FIGURE 20.12
Selecting "Role-based or feature-based installation"

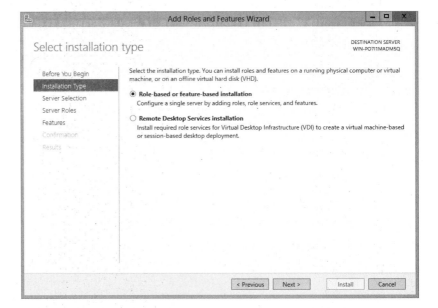

5. Select your server from the list and click Next. You will be on the Server Roles selection screen.

6. Scroll down until you locate Remote Access and select the check box, as illustrated in Figure 20.13.

FIGURE 20.13

Remote Access role selection

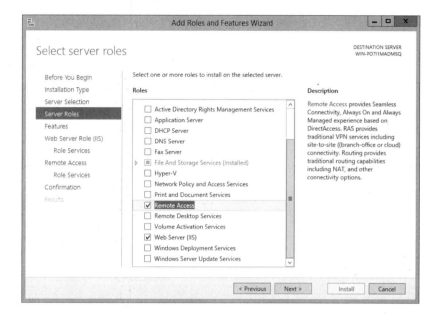

You will be prompted to install additional features.

7. Click Add Features, as illustrated in Figure 20.14.

FIGURE 20.14

Remote Access role additional features

Now that you have all the bits selected, you can continue with the installation.

8. Click Next.

9. On the Features page, click Next; there are no additional options required.

   Next, you will have the option to install additional elements of the roles that make up the prerequisites for the Remote Access role as well as the Remote Access role itself.

10. Because you don't need to install additional elements for the Web Server Role (IIS), just press Next until you get to the Remote Access preamble, as illustrated in Figure 20.15.

FIGURE 20.15
Remote Access preamble

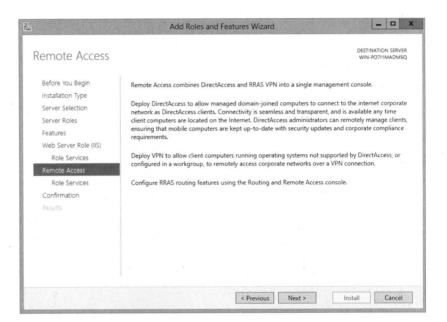

11. Now you're getting into the specifics. Click Next on the preamble screen and you will be brought to the Remote Access Role Services screen. Notice that Routing is not checked.

12. Select Routing, as illustrated in Figure 20.16.

13. Click Next, review the summary screen, and then click Install.

14. Allow the installation to complete and then click Close.

   One of the great things about Windows Server 2012 R2 is it follows up for you when post-configuration work is required. From Server Manager you will notice on the top part of the screen a flag symbol with a yellow exclamation mark.

1. Click the exclamation mark, and an additional screen appears, as illustrated in Figure 20.17.

   You will see Post-deployment Configuration for DirectAccess and the VPN (RAS) role.

FIGURE 20.16
Routing selection
in Remote Access
Role Services
screen

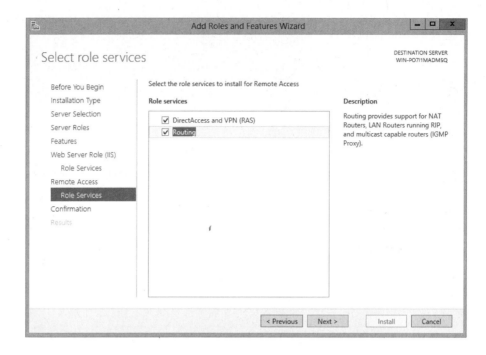

FIGURE 20.17
Post-deployment
Configuration

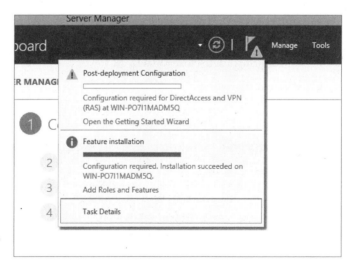

2. Click Open the Getting Started Wizard to complete the configuration.

This will launch the Configure Remote Access screen. As you can see from Figure 20.18, there are only options for configuring DirectAccess and VPN.

FIGURE 20.18
Configure Remote
Access Getting
Started Wizard

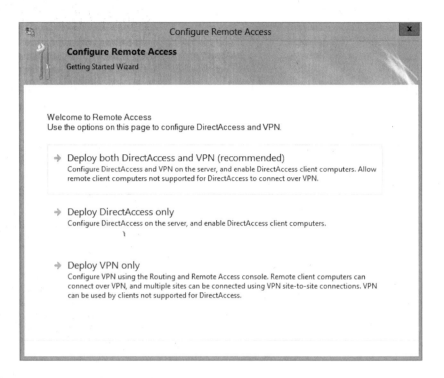

3. Since you are not configuring DirectAccess or VPN, just close the wizard. It will prompt you for confirmation to close the wizard.

4. Click OK when prompted.

   In order to complete configuration for just the routing and/or NAT elements, you need to use the traditional Routing and Remote Access console.

5. Open Server Manager, click Tools, and select Routing and Remote Access, as shown in Figure 20.19.

   As you will notice when the Routing and Remote Access console launches, it will be very familiar if you have used it in Windows 2008 R2. As you can see from Figure 20.20, the service is down (see the arrow pointing down at the server name).

6. Right-click the server name and select Configure and Enable Routing and Remote Access, as shown in Figure 20.20.

   This launches the Routing and Remote Access Server Setup Wizard. This experience should be very similar to that of Windows 2008 R2.

7. Click Next on the initial wizard screen to begin configuration.

   On the Configuration screen, as shown in Figure 20.21, you have several options.

FIGURE 20.19
Launching
Routing and
Remote Access

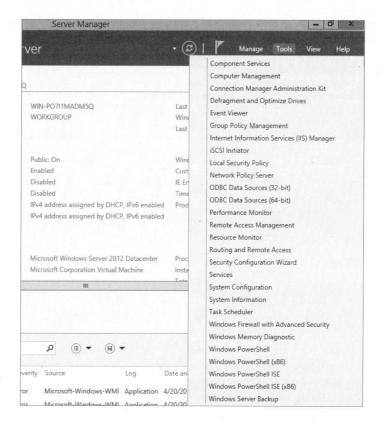

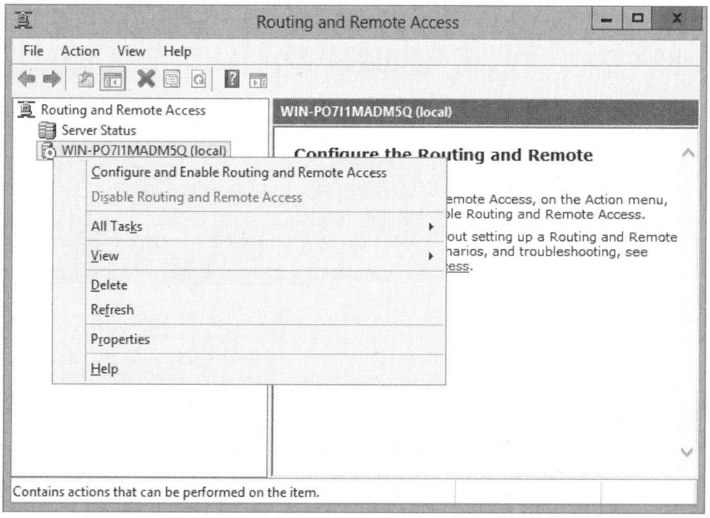

FIGURE 20.20
Configure and
Enable Routing
and Remote
Access

FIGURE 20.21
Configuration
screen of the
Routing and
Remote Access
Server Setup
Wizard

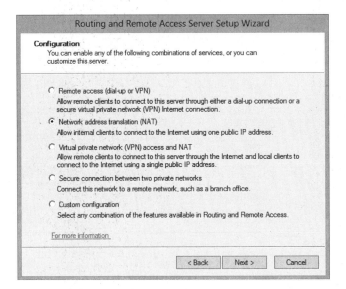

8. Because you want to configure NAT, select the option "Network address translation (NAT)" and click Next.

Remember, the purpose of NAT is primarily to allow you to route privately defined IP ranges across the Internet via a "masked" publically routable IP. Your next step in the configuration is to select the interface that will be the Internet-facing NIC. In our opinion it is a good idea before you continue to rename the NICs appropriately so that selecting the right interface is easy.

9. In this case, select the WAN interface, as shown in Figure 20.22.

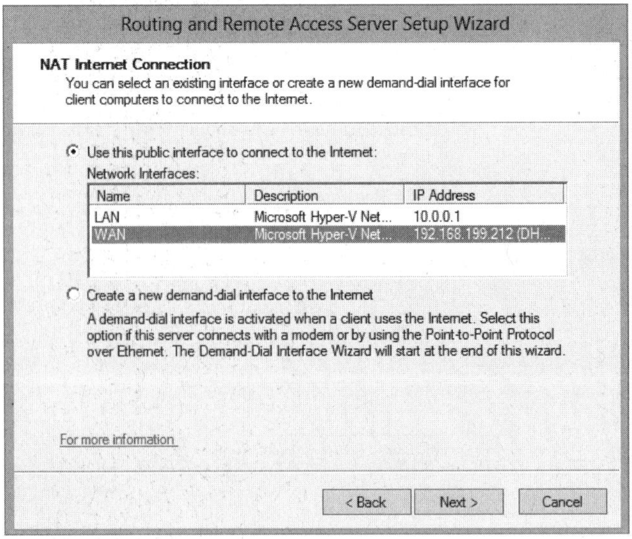

FIGURE 20.22
NAT Internet
Connection
screen—selecting
the interface

Next, you need to configure whether you want Routing and Remote Access to enable basic name and address services (DHCP and DNS). In most cases, if you already have Active Directory deployed, you generally have these services as part of it. The wizard tries to detect them. In general, these services are already deployed.

10. Select the option "I will set up name and address services later," and click Next. See Figure 20.23.

11. Click Finish to complete the configuration.

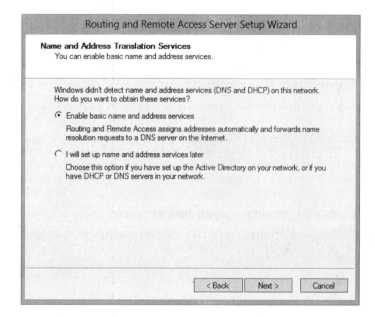

FIGURE 20.23
Name and Address Translation Services screen

There—you're finished! Now, any system configured with a default gateway or static route on the same network subnet connecting to the interface you've defined as internal (in our example, this was the New York subnet), will be configured to connect to the public Internet.

You've probably guessed that, like so many other NATs, the NAT in Windows Server 2012 R2 is really a NAPT, in that it will translate and map ports as necessary. There are also some built-in ALGs to support the use of FTP and PPTP.

CREATING A ROUTER

What is a router? A *router* is a multihomed machine (that is, one with more than one network interface) that has been set up to forward packets received from one network to another network.

The computer that sits between the New York and London networks, which we will call the Gateway computer, is well placed to be a router—it is multihomed, and each interface is on a different network. But is it a router yet? Not until it has been configured to forward.

By default, Windows Server 2012 R2 computers are not configured to forward. To cause a Windows Server 2012 R2 computer to forward IPv4 packets, you need to edit a registry setting. The setting is HKEY_LOCAL_MACHINE\SYSTEM\CurrentControlSet\Services\Tcpip\ Parameters\IPEnableRouter; it should already exist as a dword value set to 0, so set it to 1 in order to enable IP routing, and then restart the computer.

That's all you need to do to create a router between two local subnets. This computer will now automatically forward packets received on one interface to the interface corresponding with the network containing the destination address of the packets. Again, you can use the route add (or netsh, if you like typing) command to add any routes that are not already present in the router.

TUNNELING: NEARLY ROUTING

Network tunneling is a form of routing in which network traffic is encapsulated or transformed in some way by a tunnel endpoint so that it can reach another tunnel endpoint, at which point it is either de-encapsulated or transformed back.

In a way, NAT is a form of tunneling in which the transformation is to change the source and/or destination IP address and port along its travels. As with other tunneling methods, several NATs may be between the start of the packet's travel and its end.

CHEAT TUNNELING WITH PORTPROXY

The last netsh tunnel you'll visit is a very useful one, called portproxy. You can use it to cheat port restrictions by forwarding a "safe" port such as 80 (for the Web, using HTTP) to an "unsafe" port such as 119 (Network News Transfer Protocol—often blocked by enterprises to limit employees' access to this information source).

At the other end, forwarding port 119 to port 80, you begin by encapsulating the NNTP traffic from your newsreader into a connection that seems to the firewall to be a connection to a web server.

Assuming that your home computer is at address 10.20.30.40 and the news server you want to reach but can't is msnews.microsoft.com, these are the commands to use:

```
[At the work computer] netsh interface portproxy add v4tov4 119 10.20.30.40 80
[At the home computer] netsh interface portproxy add v4tov4 80 msnews.microsoft
.com 119
```

Connecting to systems at home using this method is probably going to get you into trouble, but there may be some work uses you can use this method for. Note that portproxy does not offer any kind of authentication, and it does not provide any encryption to protect your data in transit. You may find that a virtual private network (VPN) offers you more of what you need in this direction. Read Chapter 21 to find out how to configure Windows Server 2012 R2 as your VPN endpoint.

IPv6 TUNNEL COMMANDS

In the absence of native IPv6 support from your ISP, you may be testing IPv6 Internet access through the use of an IPv6 tunneling service, such as that provided by Hurricane Electric. We do this, and we set up our tunnel—IPv6 tunneling through IPv4—as follows:

```
netsh interface ipv6 add v6v4tunnel IP6Tunnel myIPv4Address 72.52.104.74
netsh interface ipv6 add address IP6Tunnel 2001:db8:1234:567:2
netsh interface ipv6 add route ::/0 IP6Tunnel 2001:db8:1234:567:1 publish=yes
netsh interface ipv6 set interface IP6Tunnel forwarding=enable
netsh interface ipv6 add route 2001:db8:fedc:ba98::/64 "Local Area Connection"
publish=yes
netsh interface ipv6 set interface "Local Area Connection" forwarding=enable
advertising=enable
```

The first command creates the tunnel itself from this server to the machine at 72.52.104.74, and the server on which you run this command is now capable of communicating in IPv6 through this tunnel. The second command creates an address and assigns it to the tunnel interface, while the third command creates a route that forwards traffic to the IPv6 tunnel if it has nowhere else more specific defined—::/0 is the IPv6 placeholder for a default destination in a routing entry.

The fourth command enables forwarding on the IPv6 tunnel so that any traffic coming through the tunnel for other machines on our network will be forwarded to them. The fifth command adds a route from this machine to other machines in our local network, and the sixth command enables forwarding and advertising for traffic on the local network so that we are able to forward packets received on that network and so that the computers on that network will know that we are willing to forward their traffic.

Another use for portproxy is to "IPv6-enable" an application that is able to use IPv4 traffic only. Again, picking on NNTP as the protocol in question, if you have an IPv4-only newsreader and an IPv6-only news server, you can connect the two with a portproxy command like this:

```
netsh interface portproxy add v4tov6 119 news6server.example.com 119
```

Then simply set your newsreader to point to localhost:119, and it will connect through the proxy to the IPv6 news server!

Testing and Troubleshooting

You will never need this section because with the information we have given you in this chapter you should understand routing in the context of a Windows Server 2012 R2 server. Oh, maybe that's a bit of an exaggeration—some basic troubleshooting will allow you to determine which machine beyond your control is administered by someone without your knowledge and is causing the problem you are experiencing.

Using the Application Itself

You can use many tools to debug the state of a network. Which you use, and when, will depend on the problem that you are trying to fix. The first tool, as ever, should be the one you actually plan to use. Let's say you're trying to make an FTP connection—first, read the errors that the FTP client is giving you.

If the FTP client says "Connection refused," then the client has received a TCP RST ostensibly from the IP address you tried to reach. This could be a sign of a firewall between you and the server, or the server application itself might not be running.

If the FTP client says "Timed out," then the client has received nothing in response to multiple requests to connect. This means either a "stealth" firewall is in between the client and the server or the server computer isn't reachable right now, either because there is no network route to it or because the computer is not currently running.

AVOID STEALTH FIREWALLS

Although some security proponents suggest using stealth firewalls, we do not. Stealth firewalls do not respond to unexpected incoming requests, preferring instead to remain silent. The appropriate TCP expression for "go away and don't talk to me" is a TCP RST; silence traditionally means "try again in a little while." Not only is an RST going to restrict accidental connections from retrying, but it will also prevent someone from using IP spoofing to pretend to be the server. If an IP spoofing session is under way, the genuine server will still receive a SYN, and the RST it sends in response will cause the client to abort its connection. In the absence of an RST, the client will continue to trust the spoofed server, which is a security risk.

Pinging a Remote Computer with ping

ping is the classic tool that many of us have used for decades. Its design has varied a little, but the basic principle is to send a packet to a remote machine that the remote machine is supposed to reply to and then wait for the reply and indicate whether it is successful. Windows Server 2012 R2 still uses the "classic" ping method of sending an ICMP echo request to the remote machine (with extra data consisting of "abcdefghijklmnopqrstuvwabcdefghi") and waiting for the ICMP echo reply to come back.

Thus, it is important to remember that ping tests only ICMP echo connectivity; it does not test the TCP connection to a server port. Only a TCP connection to the server port will do that (which is why we suggested earlier that your first debugging tool is the application you're trying to debug!).

Many firewalls block the ICMP echo service, so, as you can demonstrate by first pinging and then connecting with a web browser to www.microsoft.com, a failed ping does not necessarily mean a failed connection will result.

A successful ping, however, indicates that a machine somewhere is responding to your echo requests. You can also use the output from the ping command to ensure that you are resolving the name to the right IP address. The NsLookup tool allows you to query a DNS server, which makes it only a good tool for debugging the DNS server—to find out what the DNS client is going to do with a name, ping is as good as any other tool.

ping has a bewildering array of arguments. The most useful are the following:

◆ -t: This pings the host until stopped. It's useful for detecting when a downed server comes back up.

◆ -4 and -6: These are used to choose either IPv4 or IPv6, respectively. Note that this argument will affect the choice of DNS name resolution as well as the route used to send the ping packets.

For most troubleshooting, however, all the default parameters will generally be sufficient, and you can use `ping server.example.com` to give a rough-and-ready estimation of whether the server is resolvable and reachable.

Pinging a Remote Computer with traceroute

`tracert`, as Microsoft chose to abbreviate `traceroute` (does anyone still remember the days when eight-dot-three filenames were all we had?), is a tool whose purpose is to detail the route to a destination. As with `ping`, `tracert` is not necessarily an absolute indication that a TCP connection to a remote host will or will not work. But it's generally going to give you information that you can use.

`tracert` acts in a very similar way to `ping`, in that it sends an ICMP echo request and waits for an ICMP echo reply. How it differs is that `tracert` sets the TTL (hop count) on outgoing echo requests. The first three packets are sent with a hop count of 1, the next three are sent with a hop count of 2, and so on, up to a number you can specify (but that defaults to 30).

Since routers decrease the hop count on packets as they pass through, the first three packets will encounter an error at the first router on the way to the destination computer. Fortunately for `tracert`, this router reports that it discarded the packet, and the `tracert` program uses this information to display the address of the first router. Similarly, the second three packets will show where the second router is, and so on.

Some routers are not configured to respond with this information or are so busy that they don't have time to do so. These routers will be seen as a "time-out" in the `tracert` output. This may happen at one or two hops along a route. When you see several time-outs in a row, it usually indicates that the last router before the string of time-outs is unable to forward packets toward your destination or that your destination is not responding.

As you can see from the `tracert` output in Figure 20.24, the host for www.microsoft.com in this part of the world is `lb1.www.ms.akadns.net`. This may be different if you reproduce this test. We know already, from trying to `ping` this host, that it does not answer to ICMP echo requests, and for that reason, packets with hop counts of 14 or more are not replied to, either with echo replies or with errors.

FIGURE 20.24

Tracing the route to Microsoft's website

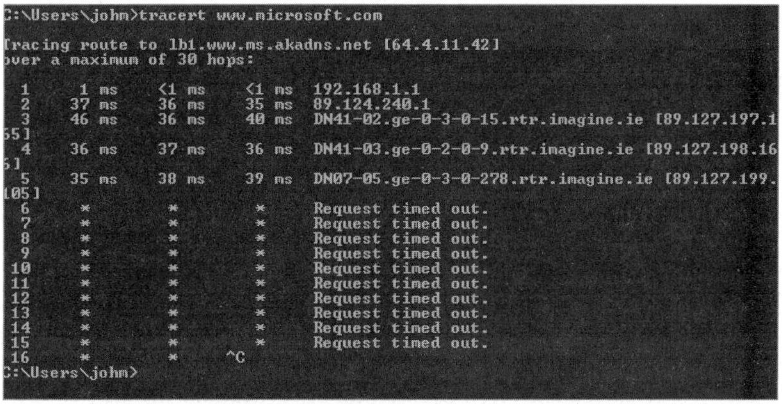

```
C:\Users\john>tracert www.microsoft.com

Tracing route to lb1.www.ms.akadns.net [64.4.11.42]
over a maximum of 30 hops:

  1     1 ms    <1 ms    <1 ms  192.168.1.1
  2    37 ms    36 ms    35 ms  89.124.240.1
  3    46 ms    36 ms    40 ms  DN41-02.ge-0-3-0-15.rtr.imagine.ie [89.127.197.1
65]
  4    36 ms    37 ms    36 ms  DN41-03.ge-0-2-0-9.rtr.imagine.ie [89.127.198.16
6]
  5    35 ms    38 ms    39 ms  DN07-05.ge-0-3-0-278.rtr.imagine.ie [89.127.199.
105]
  6     *         *         *    Request timed out.
  7     *         *         *    Request timed out.
  8     *         *         *    Request timed out.
  9     *         *         *    Request timed out.
 10     *         *         *    Request timed out.
 11     *         *         *    Request timed out.
 12     *         *         *    Request timed out.
 13     *         *         *    Request timed out.
 14     *         *         *    Request timed out.
 15     *         *         *    Request timed out.
 16     *         *       ^C
C:\Users\john>
```

However, this `tracert` output does give you a fairly good idea of the route toward Microsoft's website. Don't be put off by the * responses, it is quite common to block ICMP-based traffic to prevent probing.

Again, `tracert` has the parameters `-4` and `-6`, which you can use to force the trace to go over IPv4 or IPv6, respectively.

Checking Your Configuration with ipconfig

`ipconfig` will show information about the configuration of some or all of your network cards. `ipconfig /all` shows very detailed information, and `ipconfig` on its own shows a limited subset of that information. The best use of `ipconfig` is to ensure that your configuration matches what it is supposed to be, at least according to the network diagrams you're trying to match reality to.

Note that a number of virtual interfaces will show up in this listing. For instance, if you have enabled a VPN server or RRAS as a dial-up access point, an interface will be assigned for those connections to use.

For network interfaces that assign addresses through DHCP, it can be useful to run `ipconfig /renew` or `ipconfig /release` followed by `ipconfig /renew`. It may be just as quick, and require fewer privileges, to simply unplug and replug the associated network cable—that, too, causes a release and renew against the DHCP server.

Showing Routing and Neighbors

We have talked about the routing table in Windows Server 2012 R2 in this chapter, and you should find that analyzing the routing table as if you were the router can be constructive in tracing where a fault lies. If your routing table is very large and is not easily understood, that can be a fault in itself, in that no one thoroughly understands even a small section of the network enough to say that it is working as designed.

In addition to the routing table, using `arp -a` or `netsh interface ipv6 show neighbors` will let you know who this computer has recently been talking to on the local area link. If there are no entries in the table, except for those used by multicast addresses and loopback adapters, this indicates that the computer is probably not able to reach any of its neighbors on the local network link. This is often a sign of a faulty cable or switch port, and swapping out the cable or plugging it into a different port at the switch is a good option to try.

A lack of neighbors may also indicate an inability to negotiate network speeds with the switch. A recent case we worked on involved an old but generally serviceable 10/100 Mbps switch and a new computer with a Gigabit Ethernet card. The Ethernet card always negotiated down to 10 Mbps, and when we forced it to 100 Mbps, it would not see any other systems on the network—its ARP table would empty out. Replacing the switch with a new switch fixed that issue.

Using Network Monitor

Previously exclusively reserved for Windows Server administrators who knew where it was, and with its greatest features available only to users of Microsoft's System Management Server, Network Monitor is now a free commodity, available from the Microsoft download site. The current version, Network Monitor 3.3, is available from:

`http://www.microsoft.com/en-ie/download/details.aspx?id=4865`

Or you can simply connect to

`http://www.microsoft.com/downloads`

and search for *Network Monitor.*

It has gone through a significant rewrite, and if you have any developers in your enterprise, you can entice them to write protocol-analysis scripts in Network Monitor's own C/JScript-like language. Or you can use the scripts already there to analyze what traffic is present on your network. Additionally ensure you download the parsers from:

`http://nmparsers.codeplex.com/`

These give additional decoding abilities for protocols so you can better understand the messages on-screen.

As you can see from Figure 20.25, this capture, plus a simple filter `protocol.ICMP`, allows us to see all the traffic generated by our earlier use of the `ping` command.

FIGURE 20.25

Viewing a `ping` capture using Network Monitor 3.4

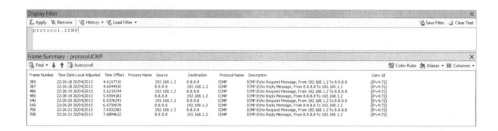

Which Card Do You Monitor?

If you want to capture data from only one card using Network Monitor, how do you decide which one to use? In most situations, this is relatively obvious because there is only one network card in most systems, and therefore there is no choice to make. However, one wrinkle comes out of the changes made between IPv4 and IPv6, and that is the topic of weak sends and weak receives:

Weak send   A *weak send* is one where the source IP address of the packet does not match an IP address belonging to the network interface to which it is sent.

Weak receive   A *weak receive*, by analogy then, is one where the destination IP address of the packet does not match an IP address belonging to the network interface on which it is received.

IPv4 for decades has confused network administrators with its behavior. Weak sends are enabled by default in IPv4 interfaces, which means that the interface that is chosen for sending an IP packet depends on the destination IP address, not the source IP address. The interface that is chosen is the one that is closest to the next-hop address in the route toward the destination.

That's *not* the case in Windows Server 2012 R2 and Windows 2008 R2, however. In Windows Vista and Windows Server 2008, Microsoft took the bold step of requiring that IP packets go out on the interface that matches their source address and, similarly, that IP packets will be discarded if their destination address does not match that of the interface on which they were received.

IPv6, by comparison, does not enable weak sends by default, so the packet will always be sent to the interface whose IP address matches the source IP address of the outgoing packet. No change there in Windows Server 2008.

The change, however, is that you can change this behavior. As with all new network configuration commands, you can achieve this through `netsh`:

```
netsh interface ipv4 set interface <NameOrIndex> weakhostsend=enabled
netsh interface ipv4 set interface <NameOrIndex> weakhostreceive=enabled
netsh interface ipv6 set interface <NameOrIndex> weakhostsend=enabled
netsh interface ipv6 set interface <NameOrIndex> weakhostreceive=enabled
```

Of course, you can set any of these values back to `disabled`, as the default, if you prefer that behavior.

Disabling weak host receives is a security feature for a multihomed computer, in that packets will be discarded if they are not received on the anticipated interface, but this may discard valid traffic that really should reach your computer, if the routing and the cabling send it to the wrong interface. If that is the case, then your network design needs revisiting. A local link, or subnet, should not find itself split across two network cards in a single computer.

In this chapter, we have given you a taste of some of the routing capabilities of Windows Server 2012 R2. You will shortly encounter a big routing ability in Chapter 21's description of virtual private networks.

The Bottom Line

Document the life of an IP packet routed through your network.   Understanding how the routing components work inside your hosts and routers will allow you to predict where network traffic will travel throughout your network. With this understanding comes the ability to troubleshoot network issues that appear perplexing.

Master It   In the New York/London network from Figure 20.1, use your understanding of the route taken by an IP packet from host A in the New York site to host C in the London site to determine which addresses you should ping in order to discover routing issues that are preventing packets from traveling between A and C.

Explain the class-based and classless views of IP routing.   When discussing routing with networking professionals, it is important to understand the old class-based terminology to allow for conversations and documentation that may still linger on these terms. Understanding how classless IP routing works is key to avoiding inefficiencies brought on by too strict an adherence to class boundaries in network addressing.

Master It   The address 172.24.255.255 lies inside class B, whose default netmask is 255.255.0.0. It also lies in the 172.16/20 RFC 1918 private network range, whose default netmask is 255.255.240.0. Given this information, is the address 172.24.255.255 a host address or a subnet broadcast address?

Use NAT devices to route TCP traffic.   Until we all switch to using IPv6, we will need to use NAT devices to route TCP traffic from our many networked hosts to the outside world, while using only a few of the increasingly rare public IP addresses. Understanding how NAT devices change the source and destination addresses of IP packets will allow you to read network packet traces and interpret which systems are intended as recipients of data.

> **Master It**   A user complains that when he tries to connect to an FTP site, the connection initially succeeds, but the first time that a file listing is attempted, his connection is severed, and the server states that it cannot connect to 192.168.0.10.
>
> What are likely causes of this problem, and how could this be addressed?

Chapter 21

Getting from the Office to the Road: VPNs

As mobile computing becomes more prevalent, an increasing number of users often need to remotely access their data located back in the office. Travelling salespeople, telecommuters, and IT consultants among others need to be able to securely connect and work as seamlessly as possible to ensure they stay productive while on the road. Virtual private networks (VPNs) are often used to meet this need.

A VPN is a private connection that is created over a public network, such as the Internet. If the users can access the Internet (there's hardly a café, airport, or public building these days that doesn't have some form of connectivity to it), they can then access the office over a VPN. Once connected, users can access any office resources just as if they were there—this includes email, shared folders, and more. The Windows Server 2012 R2 Remote Access role enables the traditional Routing and Remote Access Service (RRAS) features that you've become accustomed to in previous Windows Server iterations, but your remote connectivity options get a massive upgrade with the enhanced DirectAccess functionality that also comes bundled with this role. This is a clientless, always on and always managed, group policy–driven alternative VPN option that's based on the IP Security (IPSec) encryption protocol. DirectAccess provides support for Windows 7 Enterprise and Ultimate or Windows 8 Enterprise clients. For legacy clients, however, you still need to use RRAS for VPN connectivity.

In this chapter, you will learn to:

◆ Add the Network Policy and Access Services role

◆ Understand the Remote Access role

◆ Configure a VPN server

◆ Explore DirectAccess

Introducing VPNs

A VPN is used to provide access to a private network over a public network. The public network is often the Internet, but it could also be leased lines that are shared by different companies. Figure 21.1 shows a common example of a how a VPN server is configured.

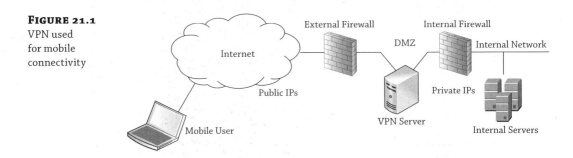

FIGURE 21.1
VPN used
for mobile
connectivity

The VPN server has at least two network interface cards (NICs). One NIC has a public IP address and can be reached by any user who has access to the Internet. The other NIC has a private address connected to the internal network.

VPN servers are often hosted in a *demilitarized zone* (DMZ), as shown in the figure. A DMZ would typically have two firewalls. One firewall provides a layer of protection to hosts in the DMZ from potential Internet attackers, and the second, internal firewall provides an extra layer of protection for internal clients. In other instances, a DMZ can be created by utilizing an interface on a single firewall and then using routing rules to create the segmentation between DMZ and LAN. Although the figure is simplified to show the VPN server, a DMZ can be configured with more than just a VPN server.

The mobile user can use the VPN connection to connect to the internal network by first connecting to the VPN server. Once connected, the user is able to access internal resources just as if they were physically located in the internal network. One drawback is that the connection is often slower.

First, the mobile user would gain access to the Internet. This could be via a broadband connection, a dial-up connection, or a wireless connection. How the user connects to the Internet isn't important, only that the user is connected. The VPN server then routes traffic between the mobile user and the internal network.

The specific role that supports VPNs in Windows Server 2012 R2 is the Remote Access role. The Routing and Remote Access Service within this role can be used for both VPNs and direct-dial connections. You can complement the Remote Access role by utilizing policy-driven network and client security through deployment of the Network Policy and Access Services role. Both of these roles will be discussed in detail later on.

Gateway-to-Gateway VPN

Although this chapter is focused on allowing mobile users to connect, it's also possible to configure VPNs to allow two different offices to connect. This is referred to as a *gateway-to-gateway VPN* and is shown in Figure 21.2.

In a gateway-to-gateway VPN, two VPN servers are connected over the public network. It's common for the public network in this situation to be semiprivate leased lines, but the Internet can also be used. This allows users in the branch office to easily connect to resources at the main office via the VPN. Users may notice that connectivity is slower, but otherwise the connection appears just as if the server were located in the remote office.

FIGURE 21.2
Gateway-to-gateway VPN

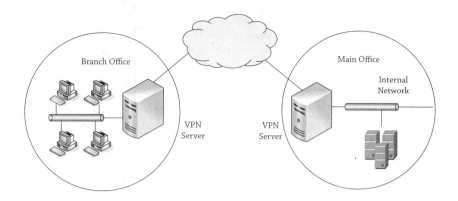

Understanding the Tunneling Protocols

When configuring a VPN, security is always a consideration. Data can't be sent across the Internet in cleartext without the risk of someone using a sniffer to capture it. To combat this risk, VPNs use tunneling protocols.

Currently, there are three primary tunneling protocols in use for Windows VPNs: Layer 2 Tunneling Protocol (L2TP), Secure Socket Tunneling Protocol (SSTP), and Internet Key Exchange version 2 (IKEv2). The Point-to-Point Tunneling Protocol (PPTP) has been used in the past but has known vulnerabilities and is being used less and less as administrators become even more concerned about security.

Both the VPN server and the VPN client must be configured to use the same tunneling protocol.

Layer 2 Tunneling Protocol

Layer 2 Tunneling Protocol is a popular tunneling protocol used with VPNs. It commonly encrypts traffic with IPSec (which is explained in depth later in this chapter), and you'll often see it expressed as L2TP/IPSec.

When used with IPSec, L2TP encrypts the data, providing confidentiality, and signs the data, providing integrity. However, IPSec has a weakness that prevents it from being used all the time—IPSec can't travel through a Network Address Translation (NAT) server.

NAT is commonly used to translate private IP addresses to public IP addresses and public back to private. However, because of the way that IPSec packets are put together, NAT affectively breaks IPSec packets. If you need to go through a NAT server, you simply can't use L2TP/IPSec.

In the past, if you had to go through a NAT server to connect to a Microsoft VPN server, you'd need to use Point-to-Point Tunneling Protocol. PPTP has security concerns, so you'll rarely see it being used today. However, if you need to go through a NAT server, you have another choice today—Secure Socket Tunneling Protocol.

Secure Socket Tunneling Protocol

Secure Socket Tunneling Protocol (SSTP) is a newer tunneling protocol that was introduced with Windows Server 2008 and is fully supported in Windows Server 2012 R2. It uses Secure Sockets Layer (SSL) over port 443 to secure VPN traffic.

This is actually a big deal. SSL is a well-respected, heavily used, and well-understood security protocol. Because of this, IT administrators and security professionals are willing to trust it much more than something new. That might not seem like much, but if you've ever tried to get a firewall administrator to open a port on an enterprise firewall, you know what we mean. Firewall administrators notoriously (and rightfully) want to ensure that only the necessary ports are open. And even if they're convinced a port must be open to perform a specific task, they need to be thoroughly convinced that it's safe to open the port.

However, since SSTP uses SSL over port 443, a firewall administrator is more willing to open the port (if it's not open already). They know SSL is secure, so as long as SSTP is being implemented for the business model, it's acceptable to the firewall administrator. Additionally, if the enterprise is already hosting a web server that uses HTTPS, port 443 is already open, and you won't need to beg or bribe the firewall administrator to open the port.

An SSTP session works by first creating an HTTPS session. This HTTPS session is encrypted with SSL, ensuring the session is secure before any data or authentication credentials are sent over the network. After the HTTPS session is established, the SSTP session sends authentication credentials and data over the encrypted channel.

A certificate must be installed on the VPN server from a trusted certificate authority to support SSL. When VPN clients connect, the certificate is sent to the client and used to create a secure session.

Internet Key Exchange Version 2

Internet Key Exchange version 2 was introduced in Windows Server 2008 R2 as a new VPN type and is now gaining a lot of traction in Windows Server 2012 R2. The biggest advantage of IKEv2 is its ability to support VPN Reconnect.

VPN Reconnect allows VPN clients to survive short interruptions in network connectivity without losing the entire connection. After the temporary loss of network connectivity, the VPN client is able to continue without starting the connection over from the start.

IKEv2 is useful in environments where clients may move from one wireless client to another or even move from a wireless to a wired connection. IKEv2 requires a certificate from a trusted certificate authority, but it can use the same certificate that is used by SSTP.

Using the Network Policy and Access Services Role

The Network Policy and Access Services role in Windows Server 2012 R2 enables you to create and enforce policies around your organization's network access, authentication, authorization, and client health. Deploying this role gives you access to the following services:

Network Policy Server Network Policy Server (NPS) is Microsoft's implementation of a Remote Authentication Dial-in User Service (RADIUS) server and includes network access policies, accounting, Network Access Protection (NAP), and more. NAP (also sometimes referred to as Endpoint Protection) can be used to ensure the "health" of clients before they are allowed access to network resources. Health is determined by examining the clients to ensure they meet certain conditions predefined by the administrator and can include items, such as being current with updates, having a firewall enabled, and having antivirus software running. These health policies can be applied to any clients—those within a wired network, those in a wireless network, or those connecting remotely.

Health Registration Authority   Health Registration Authority (HRA) is part of NAP and is used to issue health certificates for the NAP IPSec enforcement. If the client passes the health policy verification performed by NPS, the HRA will issue a clean bill of health in the form of a health certificate.

Host Credential Authorization Protocol   Host Credential Authorization Protocol (HCAP) is used to integrate Microsoft's NAP solution with Cisco's Network Access Control Server.

IS THIS ROLE A REQUIREMENT IF WE JUST WANT VPN?

Although it's not a prerequisite to deploy the Network Policy and Access Services role to create your VPNs, there's definitely an advantage to having this role installed alongside the Remote Access role to deliver the secure and granular network access that most organizations require with their VPNs. It's worth noting too that by default, all user accounts in Active Directory have been configured to control their dial-in access through the use of NPS Network Policy regardless of whether the role has been deployed or not.

Installing the Network Policy and Access Services Role

Before starting, we'll presume that you have an environment with at least one Windows Server 2012 R2 domain controller, a member server, and a Windows 8 client. Check out the earlier chapters in this book if you need assistance in setting up these servers before you attempt to deploy your remote access.

1. To begin, log on to your domain-joined Windows Server 2012 R2 installation with an account that has domain administrative permissions, and from the Server Manager ➤ Local Server ➤ Manage menu, choose the Add Roles and Features option.

2. In the "Before you Begin" dialog box, click Next.

3. Ensure that "Role-based or Feature-Based Installation" is selected in the Select Installation Type dialog box; then click Next.

4. In the Select Destination Server dialog box, leave the default option of "Select a Server from the Server Pool" checked, confirm that your server is highlighted in the Server Pool section, and then click Next to continue.

5. When you reach the Select Server Roles dialog box, scroll down until you find the Network Policy and Access Services option in the Roles list, and check the box beside it.

6. You'll then be prompted to add some required features here, such as the Remote Server Administration Tools (RSAT), so just click the Add Features button in the window that pops up.

7. Click Next again to continue.

8. Leave the features as they are in the Select Features dialog box; then click Next twice.

   When you reach the Select Role Services dialog box, you will be presented with three options to choose from in the Role Services pane, as shown in Figure 21.3.

FIGURE 21.3
Choosing the
role service

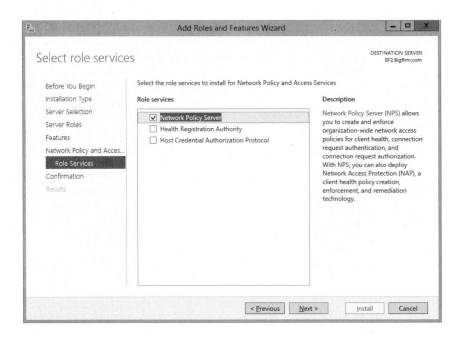

9. Check the box beside Network Policy Server, and then click Next.

10. In the Confirm Installation Selections dialog box, ensure that your settings have been chosen correctly; then click Install to begin.

11. After the installation completes, click Close.

Using the Remote Access Role

The Remote Access role includes much more than just the ability to create a traditional VPN server. The individual services within this role include the following:

Remote Access Service   The Remote Access Service (RAS) is used to host either a VPN server or a dial-up server and provides VPN support for older client computers. The server must have at least two NICs to be used as a VPN server.

Routing   The Routing service provides a software router to deliver support for routers with capabilities, such as Network Address Translation (NAT), Routing Information Protocol (RIP), and multicasting.

DirectAccess   With DirectAccess, users connect transparently to the corporate network every time their company-owned computer has an Internet connection. This delivers greater control and management back to the organization for mobile computers. We will discuss this technology in greater detail later.

Installing the Remote Access Role

Since you've already deployed the Network Policy and Access Services role, here are the remaining high-level steps you'll need to perform to configure your server as a VPN server and connect with a client:

1. Install the Remote Access role.

2. Configure Routing and Remote Access.

3. Add policies to allow connections.

4. Configure user dial-in permissions.

5. Configure the VPN client and connect.

The following sections will walk you through these steps to help you get your VPN server up and running.

Here's what you need to do to deploy the Remote Access role:

1. To begin, log on to your domain-joined Windows Server 2012 R2 installation with an account that has domain administrative permissions, and from the Server Manager ➢ Local Server ➢ Manage menu, choose the Add Roles and Features option.

2. In the "Before you Begin" dialog box, click Next.

3. Ensure that "Role-based or Feature-Based Installation" is selected in the Select Installation Type dialog box, and then click Next.

4. In the Select Destination Server dialog box, leave the default option of "Select a Server from the Server Pool" checked, confirm that your server is highlighted in the Server Pool section, and then click Next to continue.

5. When you reach the Select Server Roles dialog box, scroll down until you find the Remote Access option in the Roles list, and check the box beside it.

6. You'll then be prompted to add some required features here, such as the RAS Connection Manager Administration Kit (CMAK) and Web Server (IIS), so just click the Add Features button in the window that pops up.

7. Click Next again to continue.

8. Leave the features as they are in the Select Features dialog box, and then click Next twice.

    When you reach the Select Role Services dialog box, you will be presented with three options to choose from in the Role Services pane, as shown in Figure 21.4.

9. Check the box beside DirectAccess and VPN (RAS); then click Next three times, leaving the Web Server Role (IIS) selections at their defaults.

10. In the Confirm Installation Selections dialog box, ensure that your settings have been chosen correctly, and then click Install to begin.

11. After the installation completes, click Close.

FIGURE 21.4
Choose the role
service here, also.

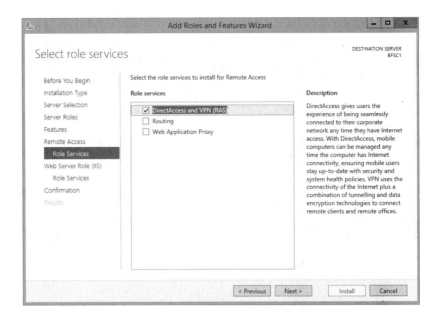

Although this adds the service, you'll still need to configure it and either add or modify policies before it can be used as a VPN server.

POWERSHELL TIP: INSTALLING THE REMOTE ACCESS ROLE

Use this simple line of PowerShell as a quick alternative to deploy the Remote Access role and its associated Remote Server Administration Tools:

```
Install-WindowsFeature RemoteAccess -IncludeManagementTools
```

Configuring Routing and Remote Access

Once you have installed the Remote Access role, the next step is to configure the Routing and Remote Access Service as a VPN server. You can manage this service via Server Manager or directly via an MMC snap-in. You should be logged on to the Windows Server 2012 R2 computer with an account with domain administrator permissions, not just local administrator permissions.

1. Click the Server Manager ➢ Remote Access menu and notice the warning bar that says "Configuration required for DirectAccess and VPN (RAS)."

2. Click the More link from the same warning bar to continue.

3. In the All Servers Task Details and Notifications dialog box shown in Figure 21.5, click the Open the Getting Started Wizard link.

FIGURE 21.5
Configuring
RRAS

When the Getting Started Wizard opens, you will be given the choice to deploy both DirectAccess and VPN together, DirectAccess only, or VPN only.

4. Select the Deploy VPN Only option.

   Later we'll discuss deployment of DirectAccess, but for now VPN is all you need.

5. In the Routing and Remote Access snap-in, right-click your server name and then choose the Configure and Enable Routing and Remote Access option from the context menu, as shown in Figure 21.6.

6. This opens the Routing and Remote Access Server Setup Wizard; click Next to continue.

FIGURE 21.6
Enabling the
RRAS server

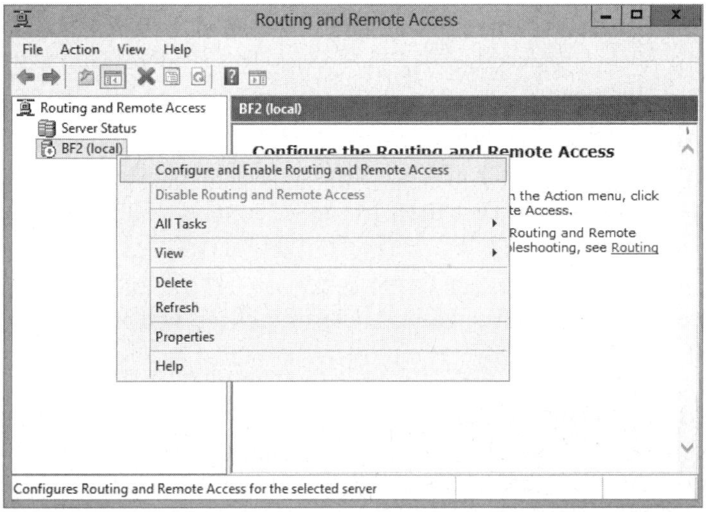

TWO NICS REQUIRED FOR VPN

As a reminder, two NICs are required to fully configure RRAS as a VPN server. However, if you have only one NIC, you can still configure RRAS so that you can explore both RRAS and NPS. Instead of choosing "Virtual private network (VPN) access and NAT" on the Configuration page, choose "Custom configuration," and select the VPN access and NAT options from the Custom Configuration page. Once this is complete, you'll also need to access the properties page of the server and add a static address pool from the IPv4 tab.

---

7. From the options presented in the Configuration dialog box, select "Virtual private network (VPN) access and NAT"; then click Next.

8. On the VPN Connection page, select the NIC that's connected to the Internet.

   On this example system we've renamed ours Internet Facing NIC, selected it, and simulated a public IP address by assigning it 74.1.2.3.

9. Once you're happy with your selections here, click Next.

10. On the IP Address Assignment page, select "From a specified range of addresses," and click Next.

11. Click New. Enter a starting IP address and an ending IP address.

    These will be assigned to VPN clients and should be chosen to allow access to the network. Here, we've chosen the range of 192.168.20.200 through 192.168.20.250 to be used as an example.

12. Click OK, and then click Next.

13. On the Managing Multiple Remote Access Servers page, accept the default of "No, use Routing and Remote Access to authenticate connection requests," and click Next. Click Finish.

    A dialog box will appear indicating that the DHCP relay agent must be added if DHCP is being used to give out IP addresses. This is not relevant with a static IP range as used in these steps.

14. Review the information and click OK to dismiss the dialog box.

15. If prompted, confirm the notification about the NPS connection request policy by clicking OK, and then click the Start Service button from the pop-up dialog box to start the RRAS service.

At this point, you have a VPN server joined to a domain with Routing and Remote Access Service installed and configured. However, clients will not be able to connect until a network access policy is configured.

Configuring Policies

Network access policies are an integral component in delivering secure and controlled VPN access. If a client doesn't meet the conditions of any policy, the client will not be able to connect. If the VPN server doesn't have any policies, clients can't meet the conditions of a policy and they can't connect. The Network Policy Server (NPS) service that you installed earlier is where these policies are managed in Windows Server 2012 R2.

NPS can be used to create and enforce network access policies throughout an organization. Although this chapter focuses on remote access, NPS can be used to create advanced policies to check any computers, including those in an internal network. Computers that don't meet the predefined conditions set by the administrator can be quarantined, and network access can be denied.

Policies are configured within the NPS console, and the NPS console can be accessed from two different methods. However, the console has different capabilities when accessed differently:

Launch from Routing and Remote Access Inside the Routing and Remote Access snap-in, you can right-click Remote Access Logging & Policies and select Launch NPS. When launched this way, NPS will show only the options that are directly related to RRAS. The top console in Figure 21.7 was launched from RAS and is the focus in this chapter.

FIGURE 21.7
Network Policy
Server consoles
when launched
from RRAS
(top) and when
launched from
Administrative
Tools (bottom)

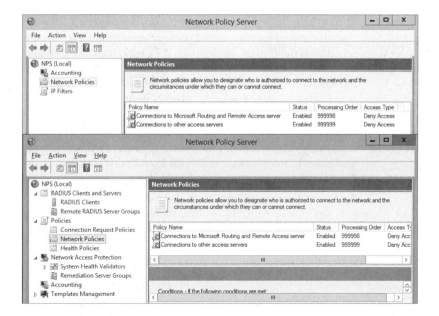

Launch via the Tools Menu When launched by selecting Server Manager ➤ Tools ➤ Network Policy Server, many additional tools are available. The bottom console shown in Figure 21.7 was launched from the Tools menu.

NPS includes two default policies in the Network Policies node. Each of these policies is set to Deny Access when created but can be changed if desired. The two policies are as follows:

Connections to Microsoft Routing and Remote Access Server Policy This includes a single condition that specifies that the RADIUS client must be a Microsoft client (specified as MS-RAS Vendor ^311$). This applies only to RADIUS clients.

Connections to Other Access Servers This includes a single condition of any time of the day and any day of the week. If no other conditions are met by previous policies, this policy will be used. Notice that the processing order of this starts with a default of 999999, which is the highest possible number that can be assigned. Although you can't assign the processing order directly, you can modify the order, such as which policy is processed first, second, and so on.

Policies have four important elements: conditions, permissions, constraints, and settings. For a big-picture perspective, here's an overview. In the following pages, we'll cover each of these elements in much more depth.

Conditions Each policy must have one or more conditions that must be met for the client to use the policy. If the condition is not met, the policy will not be used. Many conditions can be specified, such as being a member of a Windows group or connecting at a certain time of day or day of week.

If a user meets the condition of a policy, the policy will be used even if the policy prevents a user from accessing the VPN server. No other policies will be used. For example, consider a VPN server that has five policies. If a user meets the condition of the first policy and access is denied from this policy, the other four policies will not be checked.

Permissions Permissions help determine whether a user is granted access once it's determined that they will use this policy (by meeting the conditions of the policy). On the surface, permissions sound simple since they can be set to Grant Access or Deny Access. However, individual user account settings can override the permission of the policy, and the policy can be set to override the user account setting. As you dig in, you realize it isn't as simple as just Grant Access or Deny Access.

Constraints Constraints can be used to ensure that clients follow some specific rules for the connection. Constraints include authentication methods, time-outs for the session or idle time, and more. If a user meets the condition and is allowed permission but doesn't meet one of the constraints, the connection will be refused.

Settings Settings are applied if the policy meets the conditions and constraints of a policy. Settings include multilink and bandwidth-allocation options, encryption choices, IP settings, and IP filters.

POLICY CONDITIONS AND POLICY ORDER

The conditions are very important to set and understand for policies. Consider these basic rules that govern policies:

- A user must meet all the conditions of a policy to use a policy.

- A user will use only the first policy where all the conditions are met.

- If a user is denied access from a policy where conditions are met, additional policies are not evaluated.

- If a user doesn't meet the conditions of any policy, access cannot be granted.

- If there are no policies, conditions cannot be met, and access cannot be granted.

As a simple example, you may want to configure a policy for users in the Sales group. You can create a condition for the policy that includes the Sales group (assuming you have a Sales group in your domain). Any user who is a member of the Sales group will meet this condition and this policy will be used.

Understanding Policy Order

Policies are evaluated in a specific order, and when creating policies, it's important to consider the logic of each to determine which policy will be used. Imagine that after you've created the policy for the Sales group, you now have three administrative-created policies with the conditions and permissions shown in Table 21.1.

TABLE 21.1:   Evaluating policy conditions

POLICY NAME	CONDITIONS	PERMISSION
Domain Users	Member of Domain Users group	Deny Access
IT Admins	Member of IT Admins group in domain	Grant Access
Sales	Member of Sales group in domain	Grant Access

Figure 21.8 shows these policies. Notice in the figure that each of the policies includes a processing order. The Domain Users policy is at the top with a processing order of 1, the IT Admins policy has a processing order of 2, and so on. This identifies the order in which the policies will be evaluated and helps show a serious flaw with the current design.

FIGURE 21.8

Network access policies

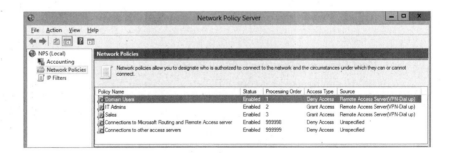

In this example, only the first policy (Domain Users) would ever be used. Anyone in either the IT Admins group or the Sales group is a member of the domain and would also be a member of the Domain Users group. Since these users are members of the Domain Users group, they would meet the conditions of the first policy and would use this policy. As shown, the IT Admins and Sales policies would never be used, and since the Domain Users policy is set to Deny Access, no one would ever be allowed access.

However, the problem is easy to fix. By right-clicking any of the policies, you can click Move Up or Move Down to change the processing order. Table 21.2 shows a more appropriate processing order. In general, policies should be ordered from most specific to least specific, but you also need to think through the logic.

TABLE 21.2:   Modifying policy order

POLICY NAME	CONDITIONS	PERMISSION	POLICY ORDER
IT Admins	Member of IT Admins group in domain	Grant Access	1
Sales	Member of Sales group in domain	Grant Access	2
Domain Users	Member of Domain Users group	Deny Access	3

It's possible to add more than one condition to a policy. If a policy includes more than one condition, all the conditions must be met in order to use the policy. The categories of the different conditions that can be used are Groups, Host Credential Authorization Protocol (HCAP), Day and Time Restrictions, Connection Properties, RADIUS Client Properties, and Gateway.

Employing the Groups Condition

You can use the Groups condition to restrict access to specific users or computers. Any valid group that is supported within a domain or any local group supported on individual systems can be added. Groups can include Windows groups, machine groups, and user groups.

Using groups can be an effective way to identify the user who is trying to access the VPN server. For example, if you want users in the IT Admins group to be able to dial in anytime but users in the Sales group to be able to dial in only at certain times, you can create two policies with one condition for each group. The constraints can then be configured to restrict access to a specific time.

Host Credential Authorization Protocol

HCAP can be used for communication between NPS and third-party network access servers. If all VPN servers are Microsoft, HCAP would not be used. However, HCAP allows you to support a hybrid environment with different types of VPN servers.

Day and Time Restrictions

Figure 21.9 shows the screen for Day and Time Restrictions. Imagine that you have reserved the hours of midnight to 4 a.m. for maintenance tasks on the server and want to ensure the server doesn't accept any connections during this time. You could configure the settings as shown.

The Day and Time Restrictions condition is one of the most often used to control access to the VPN server. You'll see later that you can also use Day and Time Restrictions as a constraint.

FIGURE 21.9
Restricting access using
Day and Time Restrictions

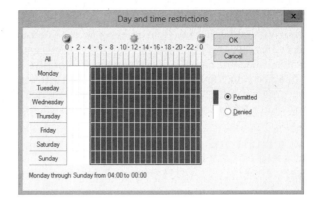

Connection Properties

The Connection Properties category includes several different protocols and specifics about the protocol that can be required by the client. The choices are as follows:

Access Client IPv4 and IPv6 Addresses   You can specify a specific IP address or IP subnet for the client. This can be useful in gateway-to-gateway VPNs where a remote office is connected to the main office via a VPN. If the remote office has a specific IP address that doesn't change, the condition can specify this IP address.

Authentication Type   Authentication protocols are used to allow the client to prove their identity. Many different authentication types can be used, and they can be identified in the condition or in the constraints section.

Allowed EAP Types   Extensible Authentication Protocol (EAP) is used to allow advanced authentication protocols. This allows the use of smart cards and other more secure methods of authentication.

Framed Protocol   Framed protocols include Point-to-Point Protocol (PPP) and Serial Line Interface Protocol (SLIP). The most common type is PPP and is used by the client for their initial connection to the Internet. For example, a client could dial into the Internet and then use a tunneling protocol to access the VPN server over the Internet. Several other less-used framed protocols are also supported.

Service Type   You can specify which service type a client is using, such as Callback Framed or Framed protocol.

Tunnel Type   The Tunnel Type setting can be used to specify the tunneling protocol used by the client. Tunnel types supported include L2TP, PPTP, and SSTP.

RADIUS Client Properties

RADIUS client properties can be used to identify specifics about RADIUS clients. Several conditions can be configured including the calling station ID, the RADIUS client's friendly name, the IPv4 or IPv6 address, and even the vendor of the client. These settings are used to configure a policy for a RADIUS server but not a VPN server.

Configuring a Gateway

If your VPN server has multiple points of access, you can configure a gateway to ensure that clients are accessing it in a specific way. The various gateway conditions include the phone number called, the name of the server, the IPv4 or IPv6 address, and the port type.

Imagine your VPN server has two NICs with different public IP addresses. One NIC may have a lot of bandwidth available, but another does not. You can restrict access to the higher-bandwidth NIC to a select group by combining a gateway condition with a Windows group condition.

SETTING POLICY PERMISSIONS

Policy permissions can be affected by several different elements. Figure 21.10 shows the Overview tab of a policy. The access permissions are identified in the center of the page.

FIGURE 21.10
Viewing access permissions in an access policy

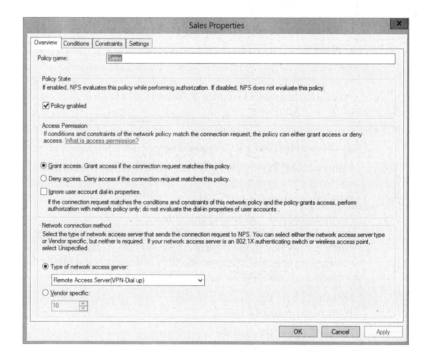

The Grant Access and Deny Access permissions mean access will be granted or denied if the condition of the policy is met, but only if the user account is configured to use the permissions of the policy and the "Ignore user account dial-in properties" check box is not selected. The user account properties are set on the user's Active Directory account.

🌐 Real World Scenario

RADIUS CLIENT VS. VPN CLIENT

The term *RADIUS client* is sometimes misunderstood. When RADIUS is used, the end user is not the RADIUS client, but instead the VPN server is the RADIUS client.

Imagine that you have several VPN servers. You could install NPS on another server to act as a RADIUS server and as a central point of authentication for all the VPN servers. Now, instead of each of these VPN servers authenticating the client, they could pass the authentication requests on to a RADIUS server.

Take a look at the illustration shown here. The end user is a VPN client and is accessing VPN Server 2. In this role, VPN Server 2 is acting as a server to the client. However, the VPN server then passes the authentication credentials on to the RADIUS server, and in this role, Server 2 is also RADIUS client.

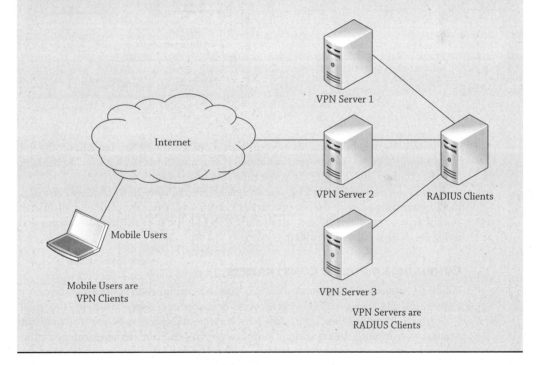

Figure 21.11 shows the properties of a user account with the Dial-in tab selected. The Network Access Permission area includes three settings: "Allow access," "Deny access," and "Control access through NPS Network Policy." As shown, the permissions of the policy will be used. However, if the permissions here are set to "Allow access" or "Deny access," the permissions of the policy will not take precedence unless you take an additional step.

FIGURE 21.11

Viewing user network access permissions in Active Directory Users and Computers

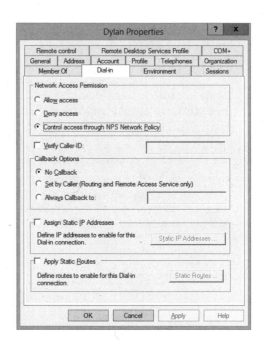

Alarm bells may be going off in your head. Wait a minute. You have to set the network access permission for every user in your network? If you have 5 users, that's no big deal, but if you have 5,000 users, this might take some time. There's an easier way.

If you look back at Figure 21.10, you can see a third choice in the Access Permission section: the "Ignore user account dial-in properties" check box. You can select it in addition to either "Grant access" or "Deny access," and when selected, the user setting for the user account shown in Figure 21.11 will be overridden.

CONFIGURING POLICY CONSTRAINTS

Policy constraints are additional elements you can configure to control the connections. Constraints can then be used to deny access or disconnect users based on other qualifiers.

Figure 21.12 shows the Constraints page for a network access policy. You may notice some crossover with the conditions and the constraints. Four elements can be configured as either conditions or constraints: Authentication Methods, Called Station ID, Day and Time Restrictions, and NAS Port Type.

A logical question is, "Should I use the element as a condition or a constraint?" The answer lies in the purpose of the condition—a condition is used to identify the policy to be used. Remember, all conditions of a policy must be met for the policy to be used, and then you set permissions, constraints, and settings to further restrict or control the connection.

As an example, you may want to allow Sales users to be able to connect any time of any day but members of the Domain Users group to connect only between 7 a.m. and 5 p.m. Monday through Friday. The following two policies could be created:

FIGURE 21.12
Configuring
constraints for a
network access
policy

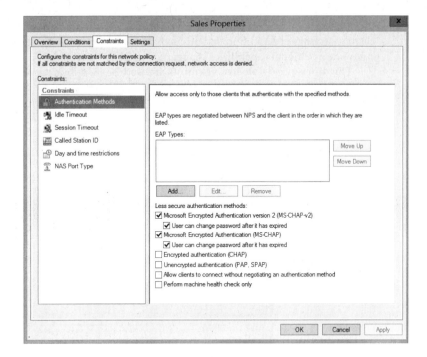

Policy 1

◆ Condition: Sales group, Allow access

◆ Constraints: None

Policy 2

◆ Condition: Domain Users group, Allow access

◆ Constraints: Day and time restrictions (7 a.m. to 5 p.m. Monday through Friday)

If users in the Sales group access the server, they will use Policy 1 based on the Sales group condition and the constraints won't restrict their access. If any domain user that's not in the Sales group accesses the server, they will use Policy 2 based on the Domain Users group condition. If they access the server between 7 a.m. and 5 p.m. Monday through Friday, the connection will complete. However, if they access it at any other time, they'll still use Policy 2, but the constraint will prevent the connection.

The two extra constraints are as follows:

Idle Timeout You can configure this to close the connection if the session is idle for a period of time, just as a screen saver can be configured to start if a system is idle.

Session Time-out The total connection time can be configured to control how long a user connects. For example, enabling this and setting it to 60 will disconnect users after they've been connected for 60 minutes.

CONFIGURING POLICY SETTINGS

Policy settings are additional settings that can be applied to the connection. The settings provide additional capabilities that can be used by the clients.

The difference between constraints and settings is subtle. Constraints are used to ensure a VPN client is using specific elements and will prevent the connection if the client does not use these elements. Settings provide additional capabilities that clients are free to use.

Figure 21.13 shows the Settings page for a policy. The RADIUS Attributes section applies only if the server is being used as a RADIUS server. The four Routing and Remote Access settings apply to a VPN server.

FIGURE 21.13
Configuring settings for a network access policy

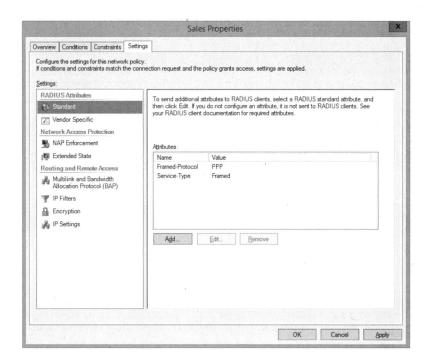

Multilink and Bandwidth Allocation Protocol

Multilink allows clients to use multiple lines for a connection. Although this isn't commonly used for a VPN, it can be valuable for dial-up connections. If a user connects via a single phone line, they are limited to a 56 Kbps modem, and even the modem is limited to speeds slower than 56 Kbps over a phone line.

However, if the client has two phone lines and two modems and the server also has at least two phone lines and two modems, the client is able to make a single shared connection over both phone lines and modems.

When Multilink is used, the Bandwidth Allocation Protocol (BAP) can also be used. It can be used to dynamically disconnect unused Multilink connections. In other words, if a user connected with two Multilink connections but was using only a small fraction of the bandwidth, BAP can disconnect the unused line so that it is available for another user.

Figure 21.14 shows the Settings page for Multilink and BAP with the default selections.

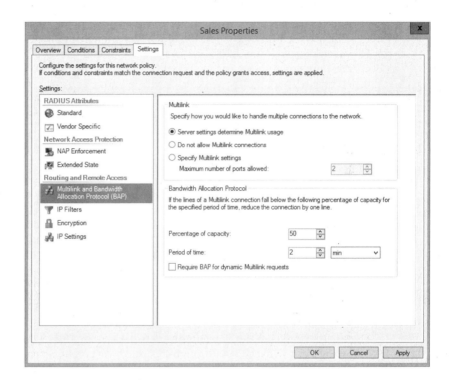

FIGURE 21.14
Configuring
multilink settings
for a network
access policy

IP Filters

You can use IPv4 and IPv6 input and output filters to control traffic going across the connection. The settings that can be configured are the same type of settings that can be configured on a basic packet-filtering router.

Packets can be filtered based on IP addresses, subnets, protocols, and ports. For example, if the VPN clients are supposed to have access only to a single subnet in the network, you could create a filter to grant access to this subnet and no others. Similarly, a filter could be granted to block access to a specific subnet while granting access to all others.

Encryption Settings

Encryption settings help determine what encryption will be used for the connection. Encryption will cipher the data so that it is not easily readable if intercepted. This page gives four encryption choices:

- Basic Encryption (MPPE 40-bit)
- Strong Encryption (MPPE 56-bit)
- Strongest Encryption (MPPE (128-bit)
- No Encryption

The actual encryption used is determined by other protocols. For example, if you're using PPTP, it will use Microsoft Point-to-Point Encryption (MPPE) with the bit lengths shown. However, if you're using L2TP, it will use IPSec instead of MPPE, and if you're using Secure Socket Tunneling Protocol (SSTP), it will use SSL instead of MPPE. Additionally, each of the different encryption techniques (MPPE, IPSec, and SSL) has different strengths of encryption.

When all four settings are selected, the client and the server will negotiate the strongest encryption that they both can use. It is not recommended to use the No Encryption setting.

IP Settings

The IP settings determine how the client receives an IP address that is used for internal connections. Although a VPN client typically has a public IP address used to tunnel through the Internet to the VPN server, it will also need an IP address that is local to the internal network after it is connected.

This internal IP address can be assigned through a range of addresses assigned by the VPN server, requested from an internal DHCP server, or assigned statically. For a gateway-to-gateway VPN connection (where the VPN server accepts only a single connection), a statically assigned address is used. If you followed the steps in the chapter to configure Routing and Remote Access, you configured a range of IP addresses that are assigned to VPN clients.

CREATING A NETWORK POLICY

Once you understand the elements of a network access policy, you can create your own. The following steps will lead you through the process of creating a network access policy to allow users in the Domain Users group to connect to your VPN server. These steps assume your VPN server is a member server in the domain so that the Domain Users group can be used:

1. Launch the Routing and Remote Access Server (RRAS) console by selecting Server Manager ➤ Tools ➤ Routing and Remote Access.

2. Launch the Network Policy Server console by right-clicking Remote Access Logging and Policies and selecting Launch NPS.

3. Select Network Policies in the Network Policy Server console. Right-click Network Policies, and select New.

4. Type **Domain Users** as the policy name.

5. Select Remote Access Server (VPN-Dial up) from the drop-down box as the type of network access server.

6. Your display will look similar to Figure 21.15. Click Next.

7. On the Specify Conditions page, click Add. Select Windows Groups, click Add, and then click the Add Groups button.

FIGURE 21.15

Specifying the network policy name and connection type for a policy

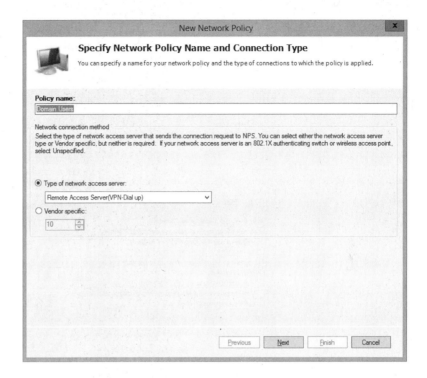

8. Enter **Domain Users** as the object name, and click Check Names.

9. If prompted, enter credentials for the domain. Click OK to accept the group on the Select Group page. Click OK on the Windows Groups page, and click Next on the Specify Conditions page.

   You can add as many conditions as you like on the Specify Conditions page. However, if more than one condition is added, all conditions must be met to use the policy.

   The Specify Access Permission page allows you to grant or deny access and override the user's dial-in properties.

10. Ensure "Access granted" is selected. Select the "Access is determined by User Dial-in properties (which override NPS policy)" box to ensure that dial-in user properties cannot override this policy. Click Next.

    On the Configure Authentication Methods page, you can identify what authentication methods the server and clients will use.

11. Click Add to view the extensible authentication protocols that can be added.

    Your display will look similar to Figure 21.16.

    You can add the additional EAP methods, but for now just leave the defaults.

FIGURE 21.16
Choosing from
the different
authentication
methods

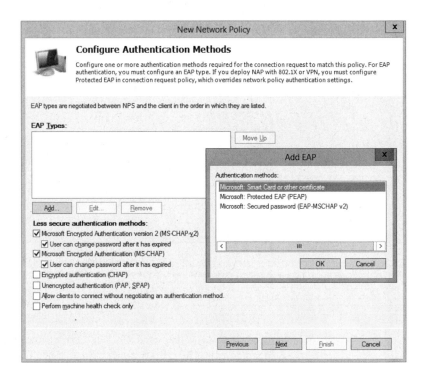

12. Click Cancel to dismiss the Add EAP dialog box.

    You'll explore the different authentication methods in greater depth in the next section.

13. Click Next.

14. On the Configure Constraints page, ensure Idle Timeout is selected, and select the "Disconnect after the maximum idle time" box.

15. Change the 1 to **15** to indicate 15 minutes. Feel free to click through the other constraints to view them. Click Next.

16. The Configure Settings page will appear. Select Encryption, and deselect "No encryption."

    Only "Basic encryption," "Strong encryption," or "Strongest encryption" should be selected. This will ensure that any connections will use some type of encryption.

17. Click Next.

18. Review the information on the Completing New Network Policy page, and click Finish.

At this point, you have created a VPN policy that can be used to grant access to any user who has a domain account.

You now have a domain controller (named BF1 in our example test bed) and a member server (named BF2 in our lab). The Network Policy and Access Services role and the Remote Access role have been added and RRAS configured on the server with an associated network access policy created too.

The next step is to configure a client to connect to the VPN server.

CONFIGURING AND CONNECTING WITH A VPN CLIENT

With your domain controller and VPN server created and configured, it's time to configure your client and connect. Although a VPN server would actually have one NIC connected to the Internet, a test bed will look more like Figure 21.17.

FIGURE 21.17
Connecting to a VPN server

Notice that the VPN server has two NICs. The backend NIC is connected to the network with an IP of 192.168.20.11/24, which is on the same subnet as the DC with 192.168.20.10/24.

The Internet-facing NIC has a public IP with a manually assigned IP of 74.1.2.3/8. The client will obtain any public IP from the Internet service provider (ISP), but for our lab we're manually assigning the NIC with an IP of 74.1.2.4/8, which is on the same subnet as the public IP.

One of the biggest challenges is getting a certificate to work with both the server and the client, so for initial testing, we'll do this without a certificate. Afterward, we'll show how to add a certificate and configure the server to use L2TP/IPSec.

Configure the RRAS server to use SSTP without SSL by following these steps:

1. Launch the Routing and Remote Access console.

2. Right-click the server and select Properties.

3. Select the Security tab and select the Use HTTP check box. This bypasses the need for a certificate.

   Your display will look similar to Figure 21.18.

Now all that's left is to configure the Windows 8 client and connect with a domain account. You can do so with the following steps:

1. Assign your Windows 8 client the IP address of 74.1.2.4/8 to simulate the public IP address that will reach the VPN server with these steps:

   a. From the Windows 8 Start screen, type the word **Network**, click Settings, and then launch the Network and Sharing Center.

   b. Select Change Adapter Settings. Right-click the Local Area Connection, and select Properties.

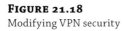

FIGURE 21.18
Modifying VPN security

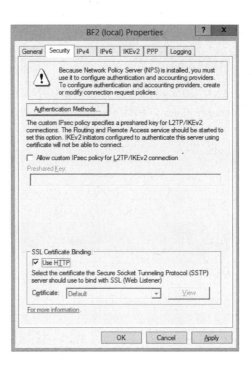

c. Select Internet Protocol Version 4 (TCP/IPv4), and select Properties.

d. Enter the IP address of **74.1.2.4** with a subnet mask of **255.0.0.0**.

e. Click OK to dismiss IPv4 Properties. Click Close to close the Local Area Connection Properties.

At this point, you should be able to access the command prompt and ping the IP address of the VPN server at 74.1.2.3. If you can't ping the server, you won't be able to connect with a VPN connection.

2. Click Back in the Explorer window to return to the Network and Sharing Center.

3. Create a VPN connection with these steps:

a. Click "Set up a new connection or network."

b. On the "Choose a connection option" page, select "Connect to a workplace." Click Next.

You'll be prompted to use an existing connection or create one.

c. Select "No, create a new connection." Click Next.

d. On the "How do you want to connect?" page, select "Use my Internet connection (VPN)."

You'll be prompted to identify how you want to connect to the Internet.

e. For this exercise, select "Let me decide later." Click Next.

f. Enter **74.1.2.3** as the Internet address. This is the IP address of the public-facing NIC on the VPN server. Click Create.

   Although a message indicates you must create an Internet connection, this isn't needed for the test bed. It would be needed for a client connecting over the Internet.

g. Click Close.

4. Connect to the VPN server with the following steps:

a. At the Networks pane that pops up, select the VPN connection you just created and then click Connect.

b. Enter the password of the domain account you entered when creating the connection. You can also enter a new username and password if desired. Your display will look similar to Figure 21.19.

c. Click OK.

FIGURE 21.19
Launching the VPN connection in Windows 8

The connection will try to connect to the server. It tries the SSTP connection first and then others if it's not successful.

Since SSTP is enabled without SSL, it will connect. Notice that both the Bigfirm VPN connection and the home network are shown as connected.

ADDING A CERTIFICATE

Now that you know the pieces are working, you can add a certificate to the server to secure the connection. There are several ways to obtain a certificate. You can purchase a certificate from a trusted root authority or add Active Directory Certificate Services and issue and install certificates for free.

We're taking the free route even though it does require the completion of several tasks. You'll need to do the following:

1. Install Active Directory Certificate Services.

2. Create the server authentication certificate.

3. Request and install the server authentication certificate.

4. Install the computer certificate on the VPN server.

5. Install the CA certificate on the client.

6. Reconfigure RRAS for a secure connection.

7. Connect with a secure connection.

The next few pages detail the steps needed to accomplish these tasks.

Step 1: Install Active Directory Certificate Services

Perform the following steps to install Active Directory Certificates Services onto your VPN server:

1. Log on to your domain-joined Windows Server 2012 R2 installation with an account that has domain administrative permissions, and from the Server Manager ➢ Local Server ➢ Manage menu, choose the Add Roles and Features option.

2. In the "Before you Begin" dialog box, click Next.

3. Ensure that "Role-based or Feature-Based Installation" is selected in the Select Installation Type dialog box, and then click Next.

4. On Select Destination Server page, leave the default option of Select a Server from the Server Pool checked, confirm that your server is highlighted in the Server Pool section, and then click Next to continue.

5. When you reach the Select Server Roles dialog box, check the box beside Active Directory Certificate Services and then click the Add Features button from the pop-up window.

6. Click Next three times to move to the Select Role Services dialog box.

7. On the Select Roles Services page, select Certification Authority and Certificate Authority Web Enrollment. When prompted to add additional role services, click the Add Required Role Services button. Click Next.

8. Accept all the defaults of the wizard. Review the information on the Confirm Installation Selections page, and click Install.

9. When the installation completes, click Close.

Step 2: Configure Active Directory Certificate Services

Before you can use the Certificate Services role, you need to complete some final configuration steps:

1. Click the Server Manager ➢ AD CS menu and notice the warning bar that says "Configuration required for Active Directory Certificate Services." Click the More link from the same warning bar to continue.

2. In the All Servers Task Details dialog box, click the "Configure Active Directory Certificate Services on the destination server" link.

    When the AD CS Configuration Wizard opens, you need to specify credentials for configuring the role.

3. Enter an account with administrative permissions (or leave the default domain admin in there); then click Next.

4. In the Select Role Services to Configure dialog box, choose the Certification Authority and Web Enrollment options, and then click Next.

5. Choose Enterprise CA from the next dialog box, and then click Next.

6. If you haven't previously deployed a CA into your environment or are running this in a lab, choose the Root CA option from the next dialog box; then click Next.

7. Click Create a Private Key, and click Next to move on.

8. On the Cryptography for CA page, leave the defaults and click Next.

9. Choose a name for your CA in the CA Name dialog box and then click Next.

10. Specify a validity period for your root certificate or just leave the default of 5 years, and click Next twice.

11. In the Confirmation dialog box, ensure that all of your settings have been input as you want, and when you've confirmed that all is good, click the Configure button.

CHANGING THE NAME OF YOUR CA

A word of warning here is that once you finalize this procedure, you cannot change the name of your CA and your only option will be uninstalling and reinstalling the role, so make sure you get it right the first time!

---

12. When the wizard has finished, click Close to exit.

Step 3: Create the Server Authentication Certificate

Perform these steps on the VPN server to create the server authentication certificate:

1. Select Server Manager ➢ Tools ➢ Certification Authority.

2. Browse to Certificate Templates. Right-click Certificate Templates, and click Manage.

3. Right-click the Web Server template, and select Duplicate Template.

4. In the Compatibility tab, leave the default setting of Windows Server 2003, and then click the General tab.

5. Change the Template display name to **VPN IPSec**.

6. Select the Request Handling tab, and select the "Allow private key to be exported" check box.

7. Select the Subject Name tab, and select "Supply in the request."

8. Select the Extensions tab. Select Application Policies, and confirm that Server Authentication is listed.

Your display will look similar to Figure 21.20.

FIGURE 21.20

Adding the Server Authentication application policy extension for the certificate

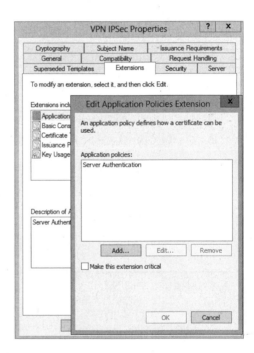

9. Click OK or Cancel to return to the Extensions tab.

10. Click OK to save the template.

11. Return to the Certificate Authority console.

12. Right-click Certificate Templates, and select New ➤ Certificate Template to Issue.

13. Select VPN IPSec, and click OK.

Step 4: Request and Install the Server Authentication Certificate

Perform these steps on the VPN server to install the server authentication certificate:

1. Use the following steps to configure Internet Explorer security so that you can use it to add the certificate:

   a. Launch Internet Explorer with administrative privileges (using Run As Administrator).

   b. Select Tools ➤ Internet Options, and select the Security tab.

   c. Select the Local intranet zone, and change the slider from Medium-low to Low. Click OK.

2. Enter **http://localhost/certsrv** in the address bar of Internet Explorer to connect to Certificate Services.

3. Click Request a Certificate. Then click Advanced Certificate Request.

4. Select Create, and submit a request to this CA. When prompted to allow an ActiveX control, click Yes.

5. Review the confirmation message, and click Yes again.

6. Select VPN IPSec as the certificate template. Enter the name of your server and the domain in the Name box. For the example exercise, this is BF2.Bigfirm.com.

7. Click Submit.

8. When prompted to allow the ActiveX control, click Yes, and click Yes again in the confirmation dialog box. At this point, the certificate has been created.

9. Click Install This Certificate, though you will need to take additional steps. Close Internet Explorer.

Step 5: Install the Computer Certificate on the VPN Server

Use the following steps to add the certificate on the VPN server to the certificate store:

1. From the Windows Server 2012 R2 Start screen, type **MMC**, and click the MMC option.

2. Select File ➤ Add/Remove Snap-in.

3. Select Certificates, and click Add.

4. Click Finish to add the "My user account certificate" snap-in. Click Add again, select Computer Account, and click Next.

5. Click Finish. Click OK.

6. Browse to the Certificates – Current User\Personal\Certificates container.

7. Export the server certificate with these steps:

   a. Right-click the server certificate, and select All Tasks ➤ Export.

   b. Click Next on the Welcome page.

   c. Select "Yes, export the private key," and click Next.

   d. Accept the default file format, and click Next.

  e. Enter a password in the Password and Confirm Password text boxes on the Password page, and click Next.

  f. Click Browse, and browse to the `C:\Certs` folder (create it if needed).

  g. Name the file **VPNIPsec**, and click Save.

  h. Click Next, click Finish, and click OK.

8. Back in the MMC, import the certificate using these steps:

  a. Browse to the Certificates (Local Computer)\Personal\Certificates container.

  b. Right-click Certificates, and select All Tasks ➤ Import.

  c. Click Next on the Welcome page.

  d. Click Browse, and browse to `C:\Certs`.

  e. Change the extension to All Files (*.*) so that the file you exported appears.

  f. Select your certificate, and click Open.

  g. Click Next on the File to Import page.

  h. Enter the password you used to protect the certificate, and click Next.

  i. Click Next to accept the default location of the certificate store, and click Next. Click OK.

9. Use the following steps to generate a trusted root certificate on the VPN server:

  a. Launch Internet Explorer using Run As Administrator.

  b. Enter **http://localhost/certsrv** in the address bar.

  c. Click "Download a CA certificate, certificate chain, or CRL."

  d. When the ActiveX warning appears, click Yes.

  e. Click Yes again on the confirmation dialog pop-up.

  f. Select "Download CA certificate," and click Save. Notice that the name is certnew.

  g. Browse to the `C:\Certs` folder, click Save, and then click Close.

You will install this root certificate on the client.

Step 6: Install the CA Certificate on the Client

When the client connects to the VPN server, the VPN server will pass the certificate to use to establish the session. However, the client won't trust this certificate as valid by default. Instead, the root CA certificate needs to be installed on the client so that the server's certificate is trusted.

 The following steps will install the root certificate on the client:

1. Copy the certnew certificate created in the previous steps from the server to the client in a folder named `C:\Certs`.

2. On the Windows 8 client, at the Start screen, type **MMC**, click the MMC.exe icon, and then press Enter.

3. If a User Account Control dialog box appears, click Yes to allow the action.

4. Select File ➢ Add/Remove Snap-in.

5. Select Certificates, and click Add.

6. Select Computer Account, and click Next.

7. Accept Local Computer, and click Finish. Click OK.

8. Browse to Certificates (Local Computers)\Trusted Root Certification Authorities\ Certificates.

9. Right-click Certificates, and select All Tasks ➢ Import.

10. Click Next on the Welcome page.

11. Browse to the `C:\Certs` folder, and select the `certnew.cer` certification file. Click Open. Click Next.

12. On the Certificate Store page, click Next to accept the default location. Click Finish. Click OK.

Step 7: Reconfigure RRAS for Secure Connection

You can now configure the RRAS server to use the certificate with the following steps:

1. If it's not open, launch the Routing and Remote Access console.

2. Right-click the server, and select Properties.

3. Select the Security tab.

4. Deselect Use HTTP in the SSL Certificate Binding area. Select the certificate you created earlier.

Step 8: Connect with a Secure Connection

At this point, you can connect using the same Windows 8 connection you created earlier. No changes are needed for Windows 8. It will automatically connect.

Connect to the VPN server with the following steps:

1. Access the Network pane on Windows 8.

2. Select the VPN connection you created earlier and click Connect.

3. Enter the password of the domain account you entered when creating the connection.

4. Click Connect, and you'll be connected with a secure connection.

In the previous steps, you accepted the defaults for authentication. However, you may choose to use different types of authentication methods. The following topic includes more details on the available authentication choices.

Authenticating VPN Clients

Authentication allows a client to prove who they are. Once that's been established, the network access policy is able to determine whether the client should be granted access. Obviously, authentication is very important. You wouldn't want just anyone to connect to your VPN server and have access to your network.

If an attacker can obtain another user's credentials, it's possible for the attacker to impersonate the legitimate user and gain access to the server. Because of this, authentication becomes a significant security concern and there are many different ways to authenticate individuals.

Since attackers have gotten better at attacks, IT pros have had to improve security to thwart the attacks. Then the attackers improve and the IT pros improve...it's never-ending. In the next page or so, you'll see many different authentication methods that show the progression and improvements with authentication.

The oldest authentication method of Password Authentication Protocol (PAP) sent passwords across in cleartext and was easily beatable with just a sniffer to capture the relevant packets. Today, the more-secure authentication methods are referred to as Extensible Authentication Protocol methods. They are extensions of the core authentication methods.

When more than one authentication method is chosen, the client and the server negotiate the most secure authentication method available to both of them. It's not uncommon for a VPN server to need to support multiple types of clients, so a VPN server will commonly support multiple authentication methods. You'll need to ensure your VPN server supports the authentication mechanisms for all the clients you choose to support.

On the other hand, you can choose to use only the most secure authentication mechanism. Clients will then need to ensure they can use this method, or they won't be able to connect.

You created the Domain Users policy earlier in this chapter using the default authentication methods. Authentication can be strengthened by adding the "Microsoft: Secured password (EAP-MS-MSCHAP v2)" authentication method to this policy by clicking Add and selecting the authentication method, as shown in Figure 21.21. This method does require adding a certificate from a certificate authority. If your users are issued smart cards, you can add the "Microsoft: Smart Card or other certificate" choice for the most secure authentication.

FIGURE 21.21
Modifying authentication methods for a policy

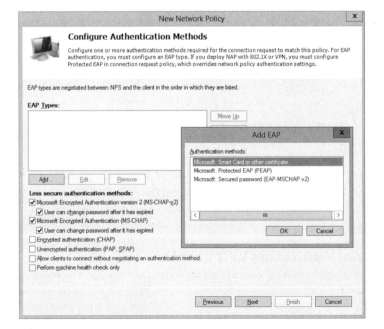

All the available authentication methods are listed here from the least secure to the most secure:

Perform Machine Health Check Only   If a network policy server is configured, this can be used to validate the health of the client. It isn't actually authentication since it validates only health but is listed in the authentication page.

Allow Clients to Connect without Negotiating an Authentication Method   No authentication is used. Any clients can connect without any proof of identity.

Unencrypted Authentication (PAP, SPAP)   Authentication is passed across the transmission lines in cleartext. A protocol analyzer (commonly called a *sniffer*) can capture the packets and read the credentials. This includes the generic Password Authentication Protocol and the proprietary Shiva Password Authentication Protocol (SPAP). We'd be surprised to see this being used in any production environment today.

Encrypted Authentication (CHAP)   Challenge Handshake Authentication Protocol was the first widely used encrypted authentication protocol. When a client connected, the client was challenged with a nonce (a number used once) that was combined with credential information, hashed, encrypted, and returned to the server. The server periodically sent a new nonce to the client and forced another challenge handshake during the session. CHAP has historically been used on Microsoft RRAS servers to support non-Microsoft clients, but the more secure EAP methods are recommended today instead of CHAP.

Microsoft Encrypted Authentication (MS-CHAP)   This was Microsoft's first improvement over CHAP. It worked only on Microsoft clients and has been replaced with MS-CHAP v2. MS-CHAP also encrypts the authentication to thwart sniffing attempts.

Microsoft Encrypted Authentication version 2 (MS-CHAP v2)   MS-CHAP v2 was created as an enhancement over MS-CHAP. It provided several improvements over MS-CHAP including mutual authentication. With mutual authentication, the server authenticates to the client before the client sends user credentials.

The following three authentication methods are referred to as Extensible Authentication Protocol methods. EAP is a security framework that can be used by any vendor and provides the strongest security with the most flexibility.

Microsoft: Secured Password (EAP-MS-CHAP v2)   EAP-MS-CHAP v2 uses certificates on the VPN server to provide better security. The certificate is issued by a CA that is trusted by the VPN client and is provided when the VPN client contacts the VPN server. Since the CA is trusted, the certificate provides authentication for the server to the client before the client-authentication process starts. TLS is used with public/private keys to create a secure channel for the MS-CHAP v2 authentication process.

EAP-MS-CHAP v2 is easier to deploy than EAP-TLS (smart card authentication) but still provides significant security enhancements over MS-CHAP v2.

Microsoft: Protected EAP (PEAP)   PEAP doesn't specify an authentication method but instead provides additional security for whatever authentication method is used. PEAP provides a protected channel that helps prevent an attacker from injecting packets between the client and the VPN server.

Microsoft: Smart Card or Other Certificate Certificate-based authentication is considered the strongest authentication method that a VPN server can use. Smart cards provide multifactor authentication because a user must have something (the smart card) and know something (an associated PIN). The smart card has an embedded digital certificate obtained from a trusted certificate authority (CA).

Smart cards can add significant expense. They require a CA to issue certificates, the hardware to create the smart cards with the embedded certificates, and the hardware to read the smart cards.

This method uses Transport Layer Security (TLS) and is sometimes referred to as EAP-TLS.

Configuring Accounting

Accounting is used in a VPN server to log details of who accesses the server and daily operations of the server. All the accounting is configured via the NPS console for a VPN server on Windows Server 2012 R2.

NPS includes a wizard that can be used to configure accounting and gives you four choices of how to store the accounting data:

- SQL Server database
- Text file
- SQL Server database and a local text file
- SQL Server database with text file logging for failover

If your network includes SQL Server and someone is familiar with how to configure SQL Server to provide the data, it is the best choice. However, if you don't have SQL Server running on your network, you should select to log the data to a text file.

Logging allows you to log several different types of data:

- Accounting requests
- Authentication requests
- Periodic accounting status
- Periodic authentication status

The authentication request and status information record all authentication events. These include both failed and successful authentication attempts. Although it's obvious that authentication occurs when a user first connects, it's not so obvious that the server periodically challenges the client. This is transparent to the user but ensures that the client's session isn't hijacked by a malicious attacker. A successful hijack attempt will disconnect the original user and allow the attacker access to data within the session.

Accounting requests and status comments record information that is often used for billing purposes, such as when a user connected, how long they stay connected, and activity during the connection.

You can use the following steps to configure accounting on a VPN server and to dump the information into a local text file:

1. Launch the Routing and Remote Access Services console by selecting Server Manager ➢ Tools ➢ Routing and Remote Access.

2. Launch the NPS console by right-clicking Remote Access Logging and Policies and selecting Launch NPS.

3. In the NPS console, select Accounting.

4. Click the Configure Accounting link in the middle pane.

5. Review the information on the Introduction page, and click Next.

6. On the Select Accounting Options page, select Log to a Text File on the Local Computer, and click Next.

   The Configure Local File Logging page allows you to pick and choose what type of information you want logged. Figure 21.22 shows the default selections.

7. If you want to select a different location, you can simply click Browse and browse to the new location.

FIGURE 21.22
Modifying authentication methods for a policy

An important selection is at the bottom of the screen: "If logging fails, discard connection requests." You need to know what's more important to you and your organization—the logging of accounting data or access to the VPN server. If it's more important for all access to be logged, select the box, and if logging fails, the VPN server won't allow any connections. If access to the VPN server is more important, deselect the box. If logging fails, users can still connect, but you won't have a record of the connections.

8. Accept the defaults and click Next.

9. Review the information on the Summary page, and click Next. Click Close.

At this point, you've added the Routing and Remote Access Service server, configured it to act as a VPN server, added a network access policy, and configured accounting. One thing you haven't done is explore the Routing and Remote Access console; you'll do so in the next section.

Exploring Routing and Remote Access

Once Routing and Remote Access has been added and configured using Server Manager, you can use the Routing and Remote Access console to modify the settings and view information on clients that have connected.

There are three primary areas you'll want to explore:

◆   Server properties

◆   Ports

◆   Remote access clients

CONFIGURING SERVER PROPERTIES

You can view the server properties by right-clicking the server within the Routing and Remote Access console and selecting Properties. This properties sheet includes several tabs that can all be viewed and changed for the server.

Server Properties General Tab

Figure 21.23 shows the properties sheet with the General tab selected. Since the server was configured as a VPN server, it includes both the Router and the "Remote access server" settings.

The IPv4 Router and "LAN and demand-dial routing" settings allow the VPN server to route packets from the public IP address (received from the VPN clients) to the internal LAN. At this point, both IPv4 and IPv6 are supported because the Internet is migrating to IPv6, so either IPv4 or IPv6 could be used. The bottom section has the "IPv4 Remote access server" check box selected to indicate that this is being used as remote access server and the internal network is using IPv4 addresses. From this page, you really can't tell whether it's being used as a VPN server or a dial-up server, but when you look at the ports available (shown later in this chapter), it becomes clear that this is being used as a VPN server.

Server Properties Security Tab

If you click the Security tab, you'll see a screen similar to Figure 21.24. In the figure, the Authentication Methods button was clicked to show the available authentication methods for the server.

FIGURE 21.23
General tab for RRAS server

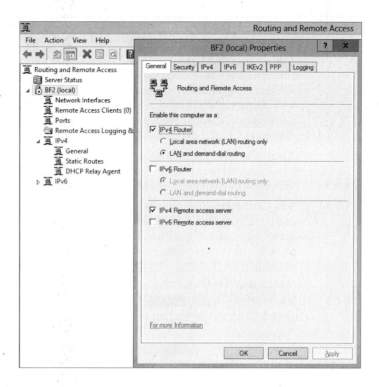

FIGURE 21.24
Security tab for
RRAS server

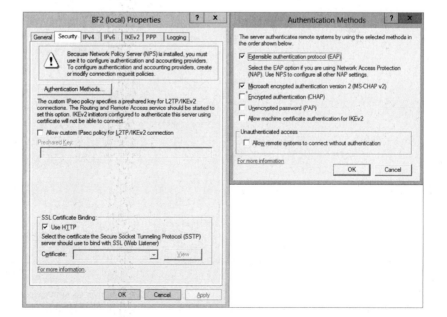

This tab has three main settings including authentication; however, if you have deployed the NPS role, then the Authentication settings are managed by that role instead:

Authentication Methods   If you have a single VPN server, this would be set to Windows Authentication, meaning that the VPN server will authenticate the client using typical Windows credentials. However, if your organization has multiple VPN servers, you very likely have a RADIUS server and you can choose RADIUS Authentication. Once you choose RADIUS Authentication, you'll need to click Configure to provide the information so that the VPN server can connect to the RADIUS server.

Allow Custom IPSec Policy   IPSec is commonly used with L2TP. If L2TP is used, you can configure a custom IPSec policy. When you select this, it requires a preshared key. Although a preshared key can be used, either Kerberos or a certificate is more secure.

SSL Certificate Binding   We covered SSTP earlier in this chapter. If you plan on using this, you need to add a certificate to the server so that the data can be encrypted with SSL. Once the certificate is added, you can select the certificate from the drop-down box. Certificates should be obtained from trusted certificate authorities.

Server Properties IPv4 Tab

Figure 21.25 shows the IPv4 tab. It includes the check box to enable IPv4 forwarding, IP address assignments for the VPN clients, and a check box to enable broadcast name resolution.

FIGURE 21.25
IPv4 tab for RRAS server

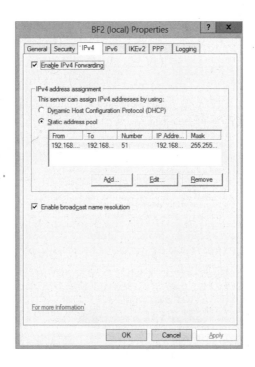

If you added the Routing and Remote Access Services server role and configured it using the steps in this chapter, you'll have a static address pool of 51 IP addresses (192.168.10.200 through 192.168.10.250) that can be assigned to VPN clients. It's also possible to use an existing DHCP server to assign the IP addresses.

The DHCP server doesn't need to be on the same server or even the same subnet as the VPN server. It can be any DHCP server that is reachable by the VPN server. However, since the VPN server must relay the DHCP requests from the VPN clients to the DHCP server, you must add the DHCP Relay Agent as an additional Routing and Remote Access service.

If "Enable broadcast name resolution" is selected (the default), clients are able to resolve names on the internal LAN using broadcasts. However, it's important to remember that broadcasts can't pass a router. In other words, broadcasts will only resolve names on the same internal subnet that the client's assigned IP address is on.

For example, if a client receives an IP address from the VPN server of 192.168.10.101 with a subnet mask of 255.255.255.0, broadcasts will only resolve IP addresses for clients on the 192.168.10.0 subnet. Clients on other subnets will need to be resolved using other means, such as DNS.

Server Properties IPv6 Tab

You can use the IPv6 tab if you're using IPv6 on your internal network. Although IPv6 is becoming much more common on the Internet, its usage hasn't been widely embraced on internal networks, so you may not need to touch this. This tab has three settings.

Select Enable IPv6 Forwarding if you want the VPN server to act as a router for IPv6 packets. Selecting Default Route Advertisement specifies whether a default route is advertised on the server. If the server is enabled to route IPv6 packets, this should be selected.

Last, you can specify an IPv6 prefix assignment to be compatible with IPv6 addresses on your internal network.

Server Properties IKEv2 Tab

Internet Protocol Security uses security associations to establish secure channels between the client and server. IKEv2 is used on Windows Server 2008 R2 to establish these security associations. Additionally, IKEv2 is used to establish a secure channel when using EAP-MS-CHAP v2 for authentication.

Figure 21.26 shows the IKEv2 tab for the RRAS server with the default settings. The settings can be modified to meet different needs or environments.

The settings are as follows:

Idle Time-out   This identifies how long (in minutes) the connection can be idle before IKEv2 will terminate the connection. The default value is 5 minutes.

Network Outage Time   This setting specifies how many minutes that IKEv2 packets can be retransmitted without receiving a response. This is useful if the network experiences network outages by allowing persistent connections. The default value is 30 minutes.

Security Association Expiration Time   When the expiration time has been reached, a new security association (SA) is negotiated and created before additional data can be transmitted. The default value is 8 hours (480 minutes).

Security Association Data Size Limit   When the data size limit has been reached, a new security association (SA) is negotiated and created before additional data can be transmitted. The default value is 100 MB.

Server Properties PPP Tab

The Point-to-Point Protocol is used for dial-up connections, and dial-up connections can be enhanced with various techniques, such as using multilink connections. Figure 21.27 shows the settings available on the PPP tab.

FIGURE 21.26
IKEv2 tab for RRAS server

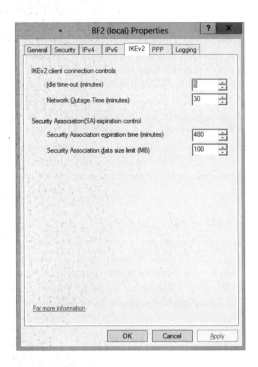

FIGURE 21.27
PPP tab for RRAS server

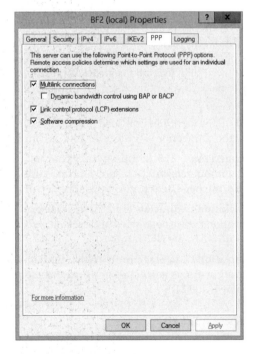

Settings configured on this tab won't necessarily apply to all users. Instead, these settings define what is possible on the server and individual network access policy settings define what can be used for the policy. As an example, you could configure these settings to allow multilink connections on the server. A policy defined for IT admins could be configured to allow multilink, while another policy defined for regular users could be defined so that multilink connections are not allowed. The available settings are as follows:

Multilink Connections   When enabled, remote access clients can combine multiple connections to increase the overall bandwidth available. This can also be used in demand-dial router connections used in gateway-to-gateway VPNs connecting a remote office with the main office. Two 56 Kbps lines could be connected to achieve a throughput of 112 Kbps.

Dynamic Bandwidth Control Using BAP or BACP   BAP and BACP allow lines to be dynamically added or deleted based on usage. For example, if a single user was using two lines but only using 10 percent of the bandwidth, the user's second line could be automatically dropped to make it available for other users.

Link Control Protocol (LCP) Extensions   LCP extensions are used to send additional traffic related to time remaining and identification used in accounting and logs. If this data is not needed, you can deselect this box to eliminate this extra traffic on the line.

Software Compression   With this box selected, the Microsoft Point-to-Point Compression (MPPC) protocol is used to compress data.

Server Properties Logging Tab

The Logging tab is used to control what events are logged and where they are logged. Figure 21.28 shows the details in the Logging tab. Although it's not apparent, these setting are actually for different logs.

FIGURE 21.28
Logging tab for RRAS server

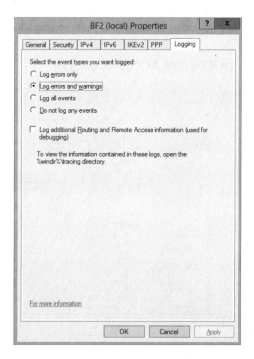

Events specified by the radio buttons are logged into the event log and can be viewed by Event Viewer. The choices are errors only, errors and warnings, all events, or no logging. For more information on how to view the event logs, check out Chapter 31.

The "Log additional Routing and Remote Access information (used for debugging)" check box is completely separate from the event log. This check box is used only when you're troubleshooting specific problems, but it can be quite valuable to help you find the source of problems.

Any time you come across trace or debug logs, you should keep an important consideration in mind—they should be enabled only long enough to troubleshoot a problem and then should be immediately turned off. Trace and debug logs have the potential to consume a significant amount of resources, including processing power, memory, and disk space. Yes, they are useful when troubleshooting, but they may impact normal operation if left on.

Trace logs are stored in the %windir%\tracing directory. By default, this directory is empty, but when you select it, several dozen files will be created in this directory.

%WINDIR% OFTEN = C:\WINDOWS

%windir% is an environment variable that points to where Windows is installed on a system. You don't have to install Windows on the C drive, and in older operating systems, the Windows folder could be called something else. However, the operating system always needs to be able to locate this directory, so when it boots, it populates the variable %windir% with the actual path to the Windows directory.

You can verify the value by going to the command line and typing **%windir%**. The command line will interpret the variable as C:\Windows (or wherever Windows is located). C:\Windows isn't a valid command, so it will give an error, but the first part of the error will tell you how %windir% is being interpreted. You can do this same procedure for any variables, such as %systemroot% or %programfiles%.

MONITORING REMOTE ACCESS CLIENTS

Once your VPN server starts hosting VPN clients, you'll occasionally need to view the activity. Figure 21.29 shows the Remote Access Clients node with a remote client connected.

FIGURE 21.29
Viewing active clients

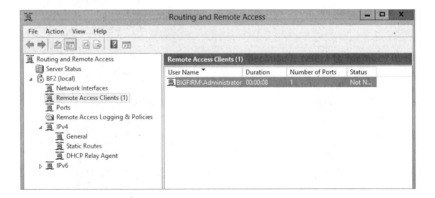

This view shows who is currently connected, how long they've been connected (duration), the number of ports they're using (if the connection is using multilink), and their current status (active or idle). You can disconnect any user by right-clicking the connection and selecting Disconnect.

CONFIGURING PORTS

When you create a VPN server, many ports are automatically created. These include 128 PPTP ports, 128 SSTP ports, 128 IKE v2 ports, and 128 L2TP ports. Figure 21.30 shows the ports that are created. Typically, you'll use only one type of port. In other words, if you're using SSTP for VPN connections, you wouldn't be using PPTP and probably wouldn't be using L2TP or IKEv2.

FIGURE 21.30
Viewing port properties on the RRAS server

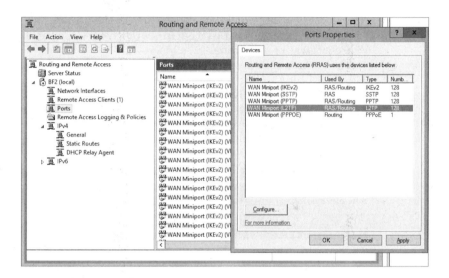

The number of ports that can be used is relative to how much bandwidth each user needs and the total amount of bandwidth for the server's connection. If the NIC is connected with a WAN connection with 100 Mbps (lucky you!), you can support a lot more than 128 connections for your chosen protocol, as follows:

1. Select the port.

2. Click Configure.

3. Change the number to allow more connections.

On the other hand, if your bandwidth is only about 1 Mbps, the performance will be dismal if all 128 connections are used simultaneously. In this situation, you'll likely reduce the number of possible connections.

Up to this point in the chapter, you've learned how to add and configure both the Network Policy and Access Services role and the Remote Access role and to then configure your server as a VPN server. Next up, we'll discuss DirectAccess and the benefits that can be gained by moving your remote access infrastructure and clients over to it.

Introducing DirectAccess

DirectAccess is a relatively new remote access functionality that was first introduced in Windows Server 2008 R2. Adoption of it was low, however, mainly because of the difficulty in getting it to work in the first place—you needed to be a wizard with IPv6 and a `netsh` command genius to figure it out! The fact that a true DirectAccess experience could only be achieved when you ran it with Microsoft's Unified Access Gateway (UAG) product meant that it definitely wasn't a cheap solution and was typically going to be available only to the larger enterprise customer.

With Windows Server 2012 R2 DirectAccess, though, this all changes. Microsoft has redesigned how it's deployed and managed, and by doing so, it means that this fantastic remote connectivity solution is now available to a much wider audience.

"Fantastic remote connectivity solution?" we hear you say. In this section we'll explain why we think so, and later we'll walk you through deploying and managing it. Once you understand what it can do and you've tried it out in your own environment, it'll be hard to go back to the old VPN client way of connecting.

DirectAccess enables remote users to securely connect back into the corporate environment without the need to use a traditional VPN client. I sometimes refer to this as a "hands-free VPN" solution because it has all the benefits of VPNs that we've become accustomed to but without the administrative overhead for end users and the requirement on IT administrators to configure and manage multiple authentication methods that come with third-party VPN clients. Whenever a computer that has been configured to connect with DirectAccess has an Internet connection and meets the policies set by the DirectAccess administrator, it will always get automatically connected to the internal office network—even before the user logs on. Users don't even have to think about connecting, and from the IT administrator's perspective, they will always have those remote computers under their control and management.

How DirectAccess Works

When you deploy DirectAccess, you get an always-on, IPSec-based remote connection to your office that's easy to manage and driven through Group Policy. As the person responsible for managing the remote-access solution for your company network, you'll most likely be familiar with employees constantly logging support calls related to not being able to log on remotely, forgetting their usernames or passwords, and so on.

All these issues go away when you give those same employees DirectAccess connectivity. The fact that all the data encryption, packet encapsulation, and authentication happen as soon as the TCP/IP protocol stack initializes on the client before they even log on, meaning that you still have the capability to push out your updates and group policies, is a win-win situation.

FEATURES

Here's a list of some of the DirectAccess features that you can take advantage of with Windows Server 2012 R2:

No PKI Prerequisite   In the earlier version of DirectAccess, it was a prerequisite to have a public-key infrastructure (PKI) deployed so you could make use of certificates for authentication. In smaller environments, configuring and managing a dedicated PKI was an administrative headache. With this release, you still use certificates for authentication in certain scenarios, but there's an option now to simply use a self-signed certificate as part of the configuration wizard.

Support behind a NAT Device   You can deploy DirectAccess either as an edge server in your DMZ or inside your main network and sitting behind a NAT device, such as a router or firewall. This is a welcome change to its predecessor, it means that you don't need to have a plethora of NICs and IP addresses at hand if you just want to get up and running quickly.

Load-Balancing Support   Windows Network Load Balancing (NLB) or third-party load-balancer solutions can be deployed with DirectAccess to provide high availability and scalability.

Multidomain Support   If you need to deliver remote connectivity to your users across multiple domains, then this functionality comes integrated and out of the box now.

NAP Integration   You can integrate DirectAccess with your Network Access Protection (NAP) deployments to ensure that remote clients are in a healthy state (all antivirus updates installed, BitLocker enabled, and so on) before gaining access to the internal network.

Monitoring and Diagnostics   A handy Monitoring dashboard is available that shows a summary of connected clients and inbound/outbound traffic metrics. You can also check out the health of your DirectAccess deployment from the Operations Status view in the main console.

IP-HTTPS Performance Improvements   One of the main reasons why using DirectAccess to connect to your network performs better than your traditional VPN clients is that it uses IPv6 as its core protocol stack for communications. IPv6 is a newer and ultimately faster stack than the older IPv4 stack that you're well accustomed to. One of the transitional technologies of IPv6 is IP-HTTPS, and there have been some significant performance gains in how it scales and reduces overhead.

Server Core and PowerShell Support   Windows Server 2012 R2 DirectAccess will work with Server Core installations of Windows Server 2012 R2 and also provides full Windows PowerShell support—unlike its predecessor, which supported neither.

REMOTE ACCESS POWERSHELL CMDLETS

As part of the new PowerShell support for the Remote Access role, you now have over 60 new cmdlets to work with. From a DirectAccess perspective, these new cmdlets allow you to add and remove configuration items, enable multisite deployment, and even provide help when troubleshooting clients. Check out the full list of cmdlets and their descriptions here: `http://tinyurl.com/ws2012racmdlets`.

Multisite Support   If you have responsibility for managing a large enterprise environment that's spread across multiple sites and geographic locations, then the new Multisite Support of DirectAccess should appeal to you. It allows you to deploy multiple DirectAccess server entry points across your networks to ensure that clients get the best remote connectivity performance, regardless of their location.

CLIENT SUPPORT

From the client computer side, if you want to connect to a DirectAccess server, you will need to be running Windows 7 Enterprise, Windows 7 Ultimate, or Windows 8/8.1 Enterprise editions. Because DirectAccess comes bundled as part of the Remote Access role in Windows Server

2012 R2, it comes as no surprise that it can coexist with your RRAS configurations (as discussed earlier in this chapter) to support any legacy clients that need VPN support and that aren't yet running a supported client operating system for DirectAccess connectivity.

DirectAccess Requirements

The following are the minimum requirements that you'll need to have in place to deploy DirectAccess:

Active Directory You'll need to have a working Active Directory environment up and running because DirectAccess uses security groups and Group Policy to push out its configuration changes to clients.

Domain Controllers At least one Windows Server 2008 R2, or higher, domain controller needs to be deployed to support DirectAccess.

DirectAccess Clients Security Group Create an Active Directory security group that will be used to hold the computer accounts of the computers that you will grant DirectAccess connectivity to. You can name it something similar to "DirectAccess Clients."

DirectAccess Server A Windows Server 2012 R2 virtual or physical computer is required to enable the Remote Access role, which comes bundled with the DirectAccess functionality.

A Single Internal IP Address If you deploy DirectAccess from inside your internal network (as opposed to your Edge/DMZ network), then you'll need to ensure that you have at least one NIC with a static IP address on your DirectAccess server and that you've configured Port 443 and IP Protocol 41 forwarding through your NAT device to that IP address.

An External DNS Record You'll need to have an external DNS A record configured that points a friendly name, such as directaccess.bigfirm.com to the public IP address that will connect NAT port 443 to your internal IP address. As an alternative to this, you could also use a dynamic DNS provider, such as Dyn DNS (http://dyn.com/dns) or FreeDNS (http://freedns.afraid.org).

Clients/Workstations As mentioned earlier, your client computers will need to be running Windows 7 Enterprise, Windows 7 Ultimate, or Windows 8/8.1 Enterprise to work with DirectAccess. They will also need to be part of the Active Directory domain to be able to receive the group policy updates from the DirectAccess server.

Client Computer Windows Firewall This is an absolute gotcha and something that catches a lot of people out when they go to deploy DirectAccess. Any clients that you want to connect to the DirectAccess server must have the Windows Firewall service enabled with the Domain and Public profiles set to On. When the group policy settings get pushed out to the clients, they create some rules and make some changes to Windows Firewall, and if it's been disabled, then DirectAccess won't work. It's best to configure and lock down this feature using a centralized group policy for all your users' computers.

Installing DirectAccess

In this section we'll walk you through the steps you need to get DirectAccess up and running in your environment. We'll be deploying our DirectAccess topology behind an edge device with a single network adapter to ensure that everyone can follow these steps with minimum effort and lab resources. We'll also presume that you have been working through the previous tasks in this chapter, have already deployed the Remote Access role with only RRAS configured, and have met the minimum requirements for DirectAccess as discussed in the previous section.

1. To begin, log on to your domain-joined Windows Server 2012 R2 installation with an account that has domain administrative permissions, and from the Server Manager ➤ Local Server ➤ Tools menu, choose the Remote Access Management option.

2. In the Remote Access Management Console shown in Figure 21.31, click Configuration from the navigation bar on the left.

FIGURE 21.31
Remote Access Management Console

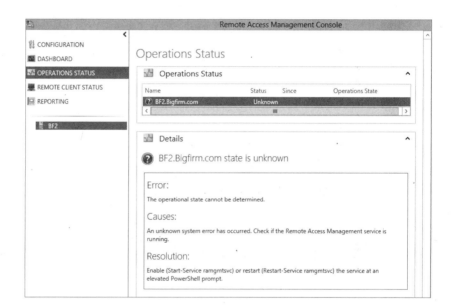

3. This should open the Enable DirectAccess Wizard. Click Next to begin the prerequisite check and initialize the configuration.

4. From the DirectAccess Client Setup dialog box, click Add, choose the security group that you configured earlier as part of the prerequisites, and then click Next.

5. In the Remote Access Server Setup dialog box shown in Figure 21.32, do the following:

   a. Choose the "Behind an edge device (with a single network adapter)" option.

   b. Type the public DNS name that your clients will use to connect to the Remote Access server (this should be the external DNS A record or Dynamic DNS record that you created as part of the minimum requirements to deploy DirectAccess).

   c. Click Next.

6. In the Infrastructure Server Setup and Configure Remote Access dialog boxes, leave the defaults selected and just click Next to move past them.

FIGURE 21.32
Configuring the
DirectAccess
topology and
public name

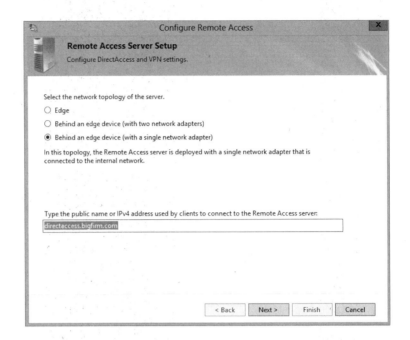

7. In the final dialog box, just click the Finish button.

   Don't worry too much at this point about making any changes to the default configuration because you'll do this at a more granular level from the Configuration dashboard once the initial setup is complete.

8. Once the DirectAccess server has been configured, click Close to exit the wizard.

9. Now open the Remote Access Management Console and click the Configuration link from the navigation bar again.

   This time you should see a diagram outlining the four steps that will help you configure your DirectAccess deployment, as shown in Figure 21.33.

10. Click the Edit button in Step 1, Remote Clients, to open the DirectAccess Client Setup Wizard.

11. Leave the default option of "Deploy full DirectAccess for client access and remote management" selected, and then click Next.

12. In the Select Groups dialog box, shown in Figure 21.34, ensure that the Active Directory security group you set up earlier as part of the minimum requirements is listed and any groups that aren't relevant have been removed.

    Notice the option here called "Enable DirectAccess for mobile computers only." If you select this, then a WMI query is performed to identify all computer objects that are mobile computers, such as laptops. Once identified, they are then enabled for DirectAccess and any non-mobile computers are ignored.

FIGURE 21.33
DirectAccess
configuration
diagram

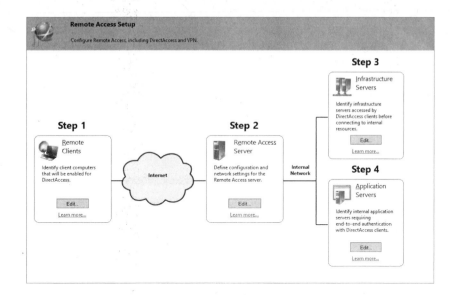

Be careful with this setting, though, because if you've selected it as part of your initial configuration and at a later date you decide to make DirectAccess available to some static remote branch office computers (i.e., not laptops), then you won't be able to get it to work until you uncheck this option.

13. When you've made your choice, click Next to move on.

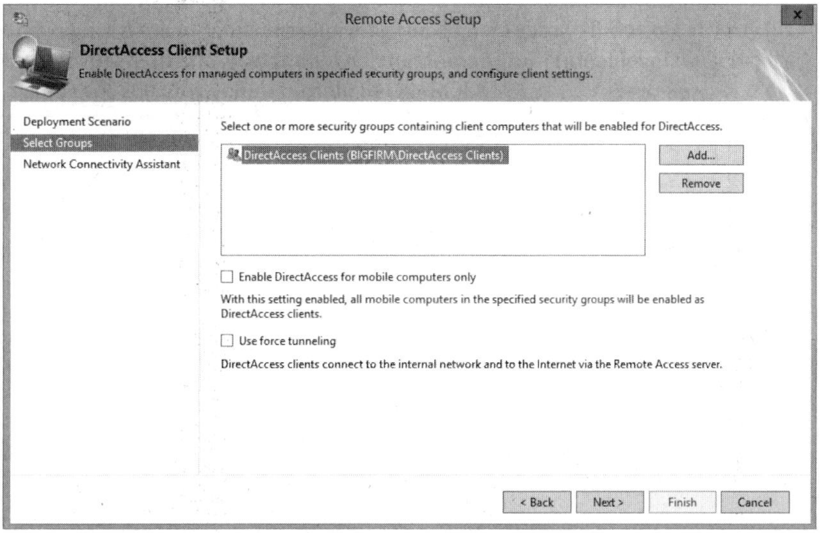

FIGURE 21.34
Selecting the
DirectAccess
Clients security
group

The final dialog box in Step 1 gives you the option of specifying resources that can be used with the Network Connectivity Assistant (NCA) to determine if the client is connected to the internal network or not. You can leave the default HTTP type resource here if you wish.

A very useful setting at this point to note is the "DirectAccess connection name." We recommend that you modify this to suit your own organizations needs because this will be the connection identifier that gets displayed in the network pane of each remotely connected DirectAccess client.

14. Click Finish once you've made your selections to complete the client configuration.

15. Now click the Edit button on Step 2, Remote Access Server.

The first dialog box you'll see here is Network Topology.

16. Confirm that your topology setting and public DNS name have been configured correctly, and click Next to continue.

In the Network Adapters dialog box you can see the adapter that you are using to connect DirectAccess to the internal network along with the certificate that's in use for all IP-HTTPS connections. This is where you can choose to use either a public trusted certificate or a basic self-signed one to authenticate any IP-HTTPS clients that are using DirectAccess.

17. Click Next to move on.

The next step is Authentication (as shown in Figure 21.35), and you have to pay particular attention to this if you want to connect any Windows 7 devices to your DirectAccess server.

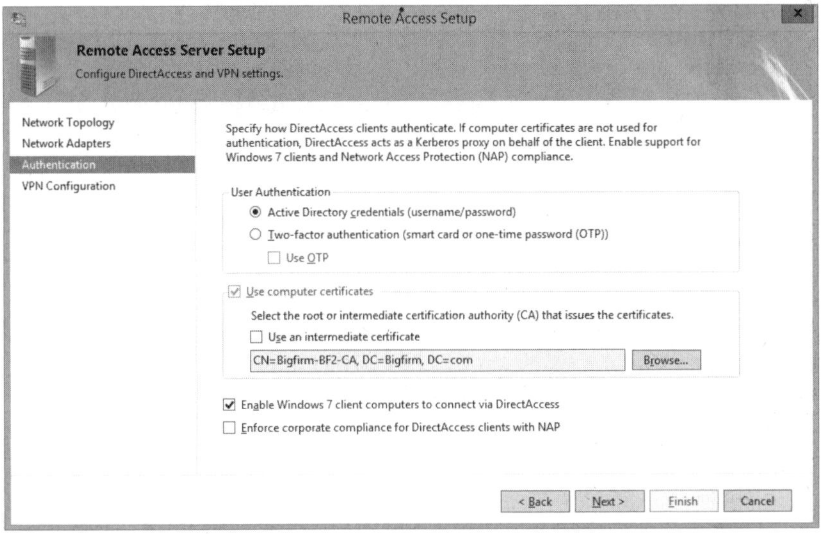

FIGURE 21.35
Enabling
Windows 7
clients

Notice the option "Enable Windows 7 client computers to connect via DirectAccess." This isn't enabled by default and is another gotcha that catches people. Make sure you've enabled it if you're planning on using any Windows 7 clients.

18. Click Next to move on.

Figure 21.36 shows the final step in this wizard, VPN Configuration. Here you can specify how remote clients connecting over a VPN are assigned their IP addresses. You can choose from a DHCP server or specify a static IP pool. The Authentication tab gives you the option to use a RADIUS server for client authentication.

FIGURE 21.36
VPN
Configuration
tab

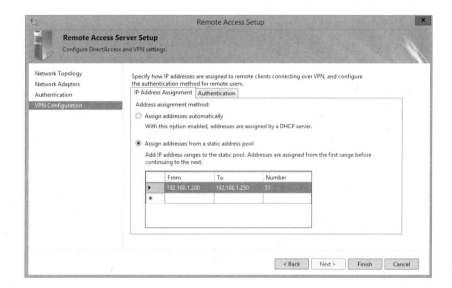

19. Click Finish after making your selection to complete the wizard.

20. Click the Edit button for Step 3, Infrastructure Servers, to open the Network Location Server dialog box.

Here you can modify the certificate that the network location server uses to authenticate clients. We'll leave it as its default self-signed certificate.

21. Click Next.

The DNS dialog box allows you to choose your local name-resolution options, and again, you can leave this at its default recommended setting.

22. Click Next.

The DNS Suffix Search List dialog box lets you specify which additional DNS suffix search lists will be used for the DirectAccess clients. This might come in useful in multidomain deployments, but for standard configurations there's no need to make any changes here.

23. Click Next to continue.

The Management dialog box gives you the option to specify management servers that can be used for updates and remediation of your remotely connected clients. You could specify a System Center 2012 R2 Configuration Manager server, for example.

24. Click Finish once you're happy with your changes.

25. At Step 4, Application Servers, click the Edit button to open the DirectAccess Application Server Setup dialog box.

Here you can choose to extend authentication between DirectAccess clients and specified application servers. You can also limit the servers that DirectAccess users can connect to by specifying security groups containing them. We'll leave this at the default option of "Do not extend authentication to application servers."

26. Click Finish.

Before you exit the console, you need to save your configuration changes and update the global Group Policy objects that DirectAccess uses to configure clients.

27. Click the Finish button at the bottom of the diagram beside the message that states "Some configuration changes have not yet been applied. Click Finish to apply the changes."

Configuring a DirectAccess Client

Now that you've installed DirectAccess on the server, you can go ahead and connect your clients. You'll test your connectivity on a Windows 8 Enterprise mobile computer. Here's all you need to do:

1. In Active Directory, add your Windows 8 Enterprise computer account to the security group that you specified in Step 1, Remote Clients, of the DirectAccess configuration diagram.

2. Ensure the Windows Firewall is turned on, as discussed in the "DirectAccess Requirements" section earlier.

3. With the Windows 8 computer connected to the corporate Active Directory environment, update Group Policy either by opening a command prompt and typing **gpupdate /force** or by simply restarting the computer and logging back onto the domain.

4. To quickly check that Group Policy has updated on your client, open Windows Firewall and click the Connection Security Rules view.

You should see the updated DirectAccess rules applied, similar to Figure 21.37.

5. If all of the requirements have been met and the GPOs have been updated to your computer, click the Charms bar in Windows 8 to see the new DirectAccess connection automatically connected alongside your normal Wi-Fi or LAN connection, as shown in Figure 21.38.

6. If you want to review your DirectAccess client configuration from Windows 8, open Windows PowerShell and type the following:

```
Get-DAClientExperienceConfiguration
```

7. To confirm that you're connected remotely to the corporate environment through the DirectAccess connection, in PowerShell type **Get-DAConnectionStatus**.

FIGURE 21.37
DirectAccess
Firewall rules

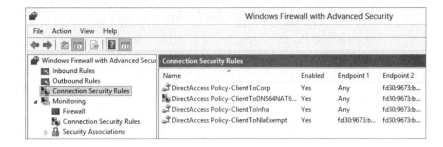

FIGURE 21.38
Windows 8 DirectAccess connection

A status of ConnectedRemotely means that you are connected using a DirectAccess connection.

That's all you need to do to enable DirectAccess on your Windows 8 Enterprise client. Now you should be able to browse resources on the remote network just as if you were sitting in the office and not have to worry about the administrative overhead from third-party VPN clients.

GETTING WINDOWS 7 CLIENTS TO WORK

Windows 8 clients will always be much easier than Windows 7 clients to configure with Windows Server 2012 R2 DirectAccess because of the new Kerberos Proxy feature, which allows for dual authentication of the user and client computer through Kerberos. Unfortunately, Windows 7 doesn't have this feature, and for that reason, the main difference in getting Windows 7 to work with DirectAccess is the need for workstation certificates delivered through a certificate authority. To meet this requirement, follow these steps:

1. Either create a new CA or use an existing one.

2. Create a new certificate template on it.

3. Enable auto-enrollment through Group Policy.

4. Check the "Enable Windows 7 client computers to connect via DirectAccess" option in Step 2 of the Remote Access Console diagram.

Here's a blog post to help you with the process: http://tinyurl.com/ws2012dawin7.

Managing DirectAccess

The Remote Access Management Console is the central user interface for DirectAccess. You can access it by opening the Server Manager ➢ Tools ➢ Remote Access Management menu. Once you open the console, you'll see five different navigation views that you can explore, as follows:

Configuration This view enables you to configure your DirectAccess environment in four easy steps (see "Installing DirectAccess" earlier in this chapter). From the Tasks pane on the right, you can also perform such actions as viewing your configuration summary, removing your configuration settings, reloading configurations, enabling multisite and load balancing, as well as launching the RRAS and VPN management consoles.

Dashboard The Remote Access Dashboard (shown in Figure 21.39) gives an overview of the Operations, Configuration, and Remote Client statuses.

FIGURE 21.39
Remote Access
Dashboard

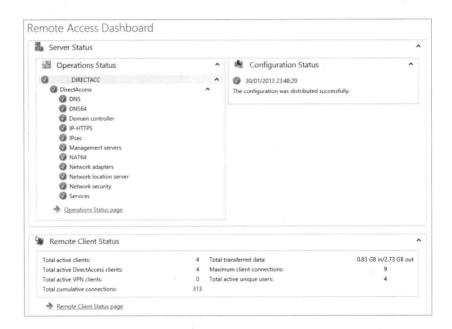

Operations Status Here, you can see the health state of the DirectAccess deployment. If you are having problems getting clients to connect via DirectAccess, then this is where you should look first to ensure that there are no warnings or errors. Essentially, what you're looking for here is the Details section to show a message of "Working Properly." You can also run the View Performance Counters task on the IP-HTTPS, IPSec, and Network Security components to get an insight into packet-level performance metrics.

Remote Client Status Clicking this view will show you a list of connected DirectAccess clients including their username, hostname, protocol, and the duration they've been connected for. Right-clicking a client and choosing Details will provide you with detailed statistics, should you need them.

Reporting The Remote Access Reporting section of the console is particularly interesting and useful when you need to generate reports on DirectAccess usage. All you need to do is input start and end dates and then click the Generate Report link. You can also use the Configure Accounting action in the Tasks pane to configure your Remote Access accounting and data logging, as shown in Figure 21.40. The accounting logs can be stored either on a remote RADIUS server or locally in a Windows Internal Database.

FIGURE 21.40
Configuring Remote
Access accounting

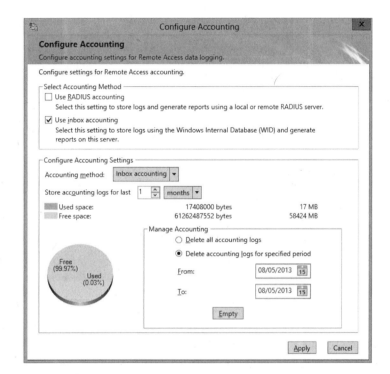

The Bottom Line

Add the Network Policy and Access Services role. The first step to create a VPN server is to add the Network Policy and Access Services role. Once the role is added, you can take additional steps to configure the VPN server.

> **Master It** You need to add the Network Policy and Access Services role to create a VPN server. How can you accomplish this?

Understand the Remote Access role. The Remote Access role includes much more than just the ability to create a traditional VPN server.

Master It Name the individual services within this role (choose three):

a. Remote Access Service

b. VPN Service

c. Routing

d. IPsec

e. DirectAccess

Configure a VPN server. You have added the Remote Access role and now want to configure your VPN server to accept connections from clients.

Master It What should you do to configure your VPN server?

Explore DirectAccess. DirectAccess enables remote users to securely connect back into the corporate environment without the need to use a traditional VPN client.

Master It What client operating systems are supported for Windows Server 2012 R2 DirectAccess?

Chapter 22

Adding More Locations: Sites in Active Directory

If all your domain controllers are located in a single physical location, you can skip this chapter. However, if you have some domain controllers that aren't in the same location, you'll need to teach Active Directory about the wide area network (WAN) links connecting the different locations.

Active Directory uses sites to identify different locations. However, Active Directory knows about only one site by default. This default first site is named Default-First-Site-Name. If your organization is in a single location, everything will work as expected without problems.

However, if you have more than one site, you will need to create additional sites, subnets, and site links. The sites represent the locations, the subnet objects represent the actual subnets that exist in the locations, and the site links represent the WAN links that connect the different locations.

This chapter covers creating sites and subnets, configuring intersite replication with site links, optimizing intersite replication by modifying site link properties, and configuring the next nearest site for clients.

In this chapter, you will learn to:

◆ Create a site

◆ Add subnets to sites

◆ Configure a site link to replicate only during certain times

◆ Configure Group Policy for the next nearest site

Mastering Site Concepts

Many organizations have more than one physical location. Production, sales, and other activities are often spread across a city, a country, or even the world. These organizations have to take extra steps to ensure that the day-to-day operations of Active Directory are optimized.

Consider Figure 22.1. It represents an organization named Bigfirm.com that has three physical locations: the headquarters (HQ), a crosstown office, and a remote office.

FIGURE 22.1
A multiple-location
company

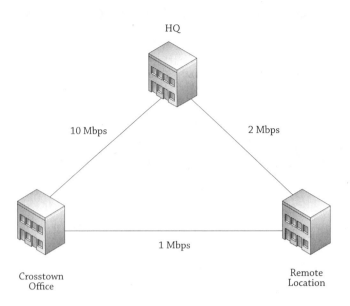

Each physical location is well connected. In other words, all the routers, switches, NICs, and cabling at HQ are capable of transmitting data at 1 Gbps, and all the components at the other two sites support 100 Mbps transfer rates. This is actually the basic definition of a *site*—a group of well-connected hosts or subnets.

Between the sites, the connection is something less than in the well-connected sites. In the figure, a 10 Mbps WAN link connects the HQ location with the crosstown office. The remote office is connected to HQ with a slower 2 Mbps connection, and a backup 1 Mbps connection connects the crosstown and remote offices.

Assume that each location has at least one domain controller, and consider these questions:

◆ When users log on in the remote office, what domain controller (DC) should authenticate them?

◆ If a domain controller in the remote office replicates Active Directory data with a domain controller at HQ, what path should it take?

◆ If the 10 Mbps line went down, how should a domain controller in HQ replicate with a domain controller in the crosstown office?

The answers are obvious when you look at Figure 22.1, shown previously:

◆ Remote office users should log onto a DC in the remote office.

◆ Replication between HQ and the remote office should occur using the 2 Mbps link.

◆ If the 10 Mbps link goes down, the replication path from HQ to the crosstown office should be through the 2 Mbps and then the 1 Mbps connections.

However, the answers aren't obvious to Active Directory. You have to teach Active Directory by configuring objects in Active Directory Sites and Services.

Remember, Active Directory is a huge database of objects such as users, computers, and groups that refer to real-world entities. When you create a user object in Active Directory, you aren't creating a person; instead, you're creating an object representing the user.

Similarly, when you create a site in Active Directory Sites and Services, you aren't creating a physical location. Instead, you're creating an object that refers to the physical location or physical site.

Sites and Replication

As a reminder, Active Directory replication is the replication of all the additions, deletions, and modifications to Active Directory. When a user account is added or a user changes their password, this change needs to be replicated to Active Directory.

Within a site, this replication occurs very quickly and uses a notification process. For example, consider a site with four domain controllers named BF1, BF2, BF3, and BF4, as shown in Figure 22.2.

FIGURE 22.2
Intrasite replication topology

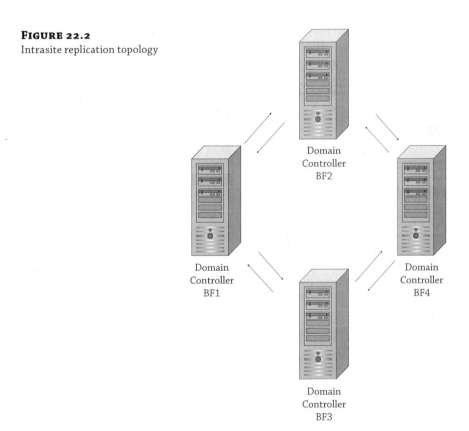

Domain
Controller
BF2

Domain
Controller
BF1

Domain
Controller
BF4

Domain
Controller
BF3

If a user account is added to BF1, BF1 will notify BF2 and BF3 of the change. BF2 and BF3 don't have this change, so they request it, and all three are up to date. Both BF2 and BF3 will send a notification to BF4 of the change. BF4 will request the change from the first notification it receives but not from both DCs.

Imagine that BF2's notification was received first. BF4 will request the change from BF2, but when it receives the notification from BF3, it will recognize that it already has the change, and the notification will be ignored. This notification process is called *propagation dampening*, and it prevents changes from endlessly being replicated to each other. DCs are more than happy to communicate through other DCs, but if the DC within the same site is more than three hops away, then the Knowledge Consistency Checker (KCC) will create a direct link to that DC. The KCC is responsible for creating and managing the replication topology between sites. It checks in with Active Directory every 15 minutes to create and delete connection objects throughout the forest.

Replication *between* sites is optimized by omitting this notification mechanism and by compressing the replicated data.

No Notification between Sites   Replication between sites is sent based on the schedule. All replicated data that has been collected since the last replication is sent without using a notification process.

Replication Compressed between Sites   Replicated data is compressed before being replicated. In a well-connected site, compression isn't needed. However, since WAN links have less bandwidth, this compression is quite valuable.

Understanding Site Terminology

You should understand several terms and concepts regarding sites before digging into the details. These are some of the key concepts related to sites:

Sites   A site is a group of well-connected hosts or well-connected subnets located together in a physical location.

The phrase *well-connected* is relative. One site may include all the network infrastructure components to run at 10 Mbps, and another site may be running at 1 Gbps. However, within each site, all the components are functioning in a well-connected LAN and referred to as a site even though there is such a disparity in their speeds.

Physical Locations   A physical location refers to the location of the LAN. A physical location could be a single remote office with 25 users or an entire building with thousands of users. If a physical location includes a domain controller, a site object should be configured in Active Directory representing the physical location.

TURNING OFF COMPRESSION

Occasionally, you may run across a situation where you have more bandwidth between sites than available processing power on the DCs performing the intersite replication. In this situation, you can consider turning off compression so that the DCs won't spend the processing time required to compress and decompress the replication.

Alternatively, you could add another DC to help share the processing load, or if by chance the DC in question is a VM, you could bump up the sockets and cores to increase performance if you have the resources available to do so. If these options are unavailable to you, turning off compression is one way to help reduce the used processing power of a DC.

This is an advanced procedure and requires modifying Active Directory settings using ADSI Edit, which should be done only when you're sure you have a good backup of Active Directory. If you've carefully weighed your options, you can turn off compression by following these steps:

1. Launch ADSI Edit from the Administrative Tools menu.

2. Right-click ADSI Edit, and select "Connect to."

3. Change the default naming context to Configuration.

4. Browse to the CN=Sites, CN=Intersite Site Transport, CN=IP container.

5. Double-click the site link you want to modify to access the properties.

6. Double-click the options property.

7. If this has a value of <not set>, change it to **4**, and click OK. You'll see that the value is now 0x4 = (DISABLE_COMPRESSION).

   If the options property has a value, you'll need to add 4 to it. For example, if it is set to 2, add 4 + 2 for a value of 6. You'd then enter **6**.

Subnets   Every LAN will have one or more subnets. These subnets already exist at each physical location. Site objects are added to Active Directory to represent physical locations, and subnet objects are added to the site objects to represent the actual subnets at these locations.

Site Links   Sites connect to other sites through slower WAN connections. For example, one site may connect to another through a fast T1 WAN link. Two other sites may connect using slower 128 Kbps WAN links. Site link objects are used to teach Active Directory about these WAN links, and site link properties are configured to provide details on the links such as which site link to use and when to use it.

Site Link Bridges   Site link bridges are automatically created within Active Directory, allowing replication between all sites. Even if a site doesn't have a direct path to another site, Active Directory *bridges* the sites together and provides connectivity through one or more other site links. Site link bridging can be disabled to exclude the use of specific site links.

ISTG   The Inter-site Topology Generator (ISTG) manages advanced replication management tasks. The ISTG designates the bridgehead server within the site and monitors it to ensure it is operational. If the bridgehead server fails, the ISTG will designate another domain controller as the bridgehead server.

Bridgehead Servers   A bridgehead server is the designated domain controller within a site that replicates Active Directory data to domain controllers in other sites. Each site has one bridgehead server designated by the ISTG. It's also possible to override the ISTG by identifying preferred bridgehead servers.

Preferred Bridgehead Servers Preferred bridgehead servers can be manually identified to prevent domain controllers with inadequate resources from being picked to act as a bridgehead server. Once one preferred bridgehead server is configured, any DCs that aren't configured as preferred bridgehead servers will not be designated as bridgehead servers.

Exploring Sites

Once you've built your TCP/IP infrastructure, you need to tell Active Directory about it. After Active Directory has the key information about your infrastructure, it can make intelligent decisions on how the bandwidth is used.

When replicating from one domain controller to another domain controller, each domain controller needs to know whether it's communicating via a high-speed link within a well-connected site or communicating with another domain controller over a 256 Kbps link and needs to take the time to compress the data. Intersite replication is compressed by default.

But the domain controller can't know what kind of link it is unless you help it. A DC knows that it can communicate at high speed with another DC if they're both in the same *site*. But it doesn't know that DCs are not in the same site unless you tell it.

How Sites Work

The obvious question is, "How can you tell AD that the DCs are in different sites?" The answer is, "By using the Active Directory Sites and Services snap-in."

DCs are located in the Servers container of one of the Sites containers of Active Directory. There is a separate container for each *site*. Remember, a site is defined as one or more subnets that communicate with each other at relatively high data rates. You define sites and then place domain controllers in sites.

Workstations and servers aren't added to AD Sites and Services. However, they still use the information here to identify DCs that are close to them when they log on. A process called the DC Locator service identifies which site a workstation is in based on the host's subnet. It then identifies a domain controller in the same site.

"But," you might wonder, "how did Active Directory figure out what sites it had, what subnets it had, and which subnets go into which sites?" *That's* the part that requires a little administrative elbow grease, so let's see how to apply that elbow grease using Active Directory Sites and Services.

You can launch it by selecting Server Manager ➢ Tools ➢ Active Directory Sites and Services. Figure 22.3 shows the Active Directory Sites and Services snap-in.

Notice that there's only one site, with the highly creative name Default-First-Site-Name. This example domain has four domain controllers (named BF1, BF2, BF3, and BF4), and they are all located in this default site.

When you create an Active Directory forest, AD creates this default site and assumes that everything is in it. If you have a single site, you can open Default-First-Site-Name, and you'll see that your domain controllers are in there.

FIGURE 22.3

Active Directory
Sites and Services

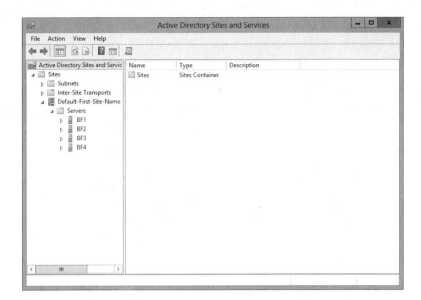

The following are the steps and requirements to set up AD's site topology:

1. Define each site.

A *site* refers to a well-connected location. The terms *site* and *location* are often used interchangeably. Within Active Directory, a site is an Active Directory object that refers to a well-connected location.

2. Define each subnet.

For each subnet that has been created in your physical environment, a subnet object needs to be created in Active Directory.

3. Assign each subnet to a site.

Each subnet is linked to the actual location by linking the subnet object with the site object.

4. Create site links to connect the sites.

Physical locations are connected with WAN links. These WAN links are represented by site link objects. Each site link object includes two or more sites.

5. Configure the site link properties.

Site links include three key properties that must be configured: cost, replicate every, and schedule. The cost property helps Active Directory decide whether the site link should be used using a lowest cost algorithm; the replicate every property identifies how often to replicate; the schedule property identifies when to replicate.

If you define the topology after you create your DCs, you'll need to move DCs to the correct site. However, if the topology is defined in Active Directory Sites and Services before promoting your DCs, the DC will automatically be added to the correct site.

Renaming Default-First-Site-Name

You can rename your first site from that goofy Default-First-Site-Name to something simple like HQ:

1. Open Active Directory Sites and Services.

2. Open the Sites folder to reveal the folder labeled Default-First-Site-Name.

3. Right-click the Default-First-Site-Name folder, and select Rename.

4. The name Default-First-Site-Name will be highlighted. Just overtype it with **HQ**, and click anywhere else on the screen.

This works best if you do it *early* in your AD creation. In fact, it's really best to rename Default-First-Site-Name when you create your first DC.

Defining a Site

Suppose you set up another site across town from the first site. Active Directory needs to know about that site. Right-click the Sites folder, and choose New Site; you'll see a screen like Figure 22.4.

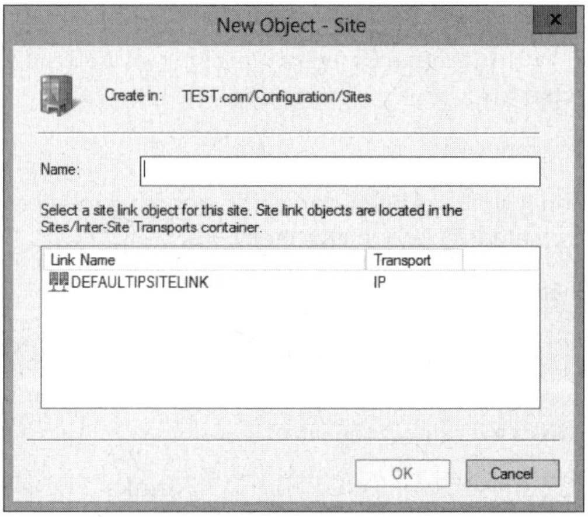

FIGURE 22.4
Creating a new site

Next, fill in a name for the new site (such as **Crosstown**), click the DEFAULTIPSITELINK object, and click OK. When you do, you get a message box like Figure 22.5.

FIGURE 22.5
Checklist for
hooking up the
new site

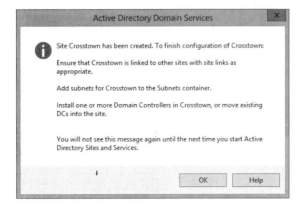

FIGURE 22.5
Checklist for hooking up the new site

You don't need to create a site for every location. In fact, the only reason you will create a site is if you plan on putting a domain controller into the location. If the location won't host a domain controller, don't create a site.

Deciding on DCs in Remote Locations

OK, if you should create a site only if the location will host a DC, you may be wondering when you should add a DC to a location. Good question.

Just because you have a separate location doesn't necessarily mean it needs a domain controller. For example, if a location has only five users connected via a WAN link, you probably won't add the expense of a domain controller at this location. The users can log on via the WAN link.

You should consider placing a DC into a location if one of the following situations exists:

100 Plus Users or Bandwidth Limitations In general, if there are more than 100 users at a location, you should place a DC there to manage all of the authentication requests. It's possible to place a DC in a site with fewer users, but beyond 100 users, you should a have DC there. The decision is easy.

Poor bandwidth is another good reason to place a DC at a remote site. You wouldn't want users in California to have to authenticate in against a DC in New York or even farther away like London. Office locations that are geographically dispersed should provide local authentication for their users. Fast connections crossing the country or even an ocean can get expensive.

WAN Link Unacceptably Slow If it's taking users too long to log on, a DC in the site will significantly reduce the logon time. Of course, *too long* is relative. In one environment, 10 minutes may be considered unacceptable, while another environment may consider it unacceptable when the logon time takes 2 minutes.

WAN Link Is Unreliable for Logon When Needed   If users can't reliably log on when they need to, consider placing a DC at the location. For example, if users need to log on between 8 A.M. and 5 P.M., Monday through Friday, but the WAN link is 100 percent utilized during this time, users won't be able to authenticate with the domain.

You should also consider whether remote users are accessing resources such as a file server in the remote site. If users can't authenticate with a DC, they won't be able to access resources that require their AD credentials. The "Cached Credentials" section later in this chapter provides a more thorough explanation of this scenario.

Frequent LDAP Traffic   If users or applications will frequently query Active Directory, a DC in the site will prevent these queries from using the WAN links. Lightweight Directory Access Protocol (LDAP) is used to query and/or modify data within Active Directory, and applications frequently query the global catalog. Frequent LDAP traffic often requires making the DC a global catalog (GC) server.

Windows Server 2012 R2 continues to offer the read-only domain controller (RODC) that can be deployed in smaller locations. RODCs store less data on the domain controller and can be used in remote locations. RODCs will be covered in Chapter 23, "The Third DC: Understanding Read-Only Domain Controllers."

DC AND DNS

If you place a DC in a site, you should seriously consider making it a DNS server. If it's the only DC, then you should definitely have DNS. When a user logs on, the `netlogon` service will query DNS to locate a domain controller in the user's site. If a DNS server isn't in the site, the WAN link will have to be used to query DNS.

Active Directory integrated (ADI) DNS is commonly used. ADI DNS is updated through regular Active Directory replication and doesn't require as much administration for the zones and zone transfer.

CACHED CREDENTIALS

You may remember that if a user has logged on to a system once before, then they can log on to the same system with the same domain credentials even if a domain controller is not available. Cached credentials are used.

Consider a user with a mobile computer. She plugs her laptop into a docking station at work and logs onto the domain. Later while waiting for a plane at the airport, she wants to use the same laptop computer to work on a report. She can use the same account to log onto her computer. However, the company's DC isn't available at the airport. Instead, she logs on using credentials that were cached on her laptop.

From the user's perspective, there is nothing different in the process. The user enters the same username and password, and the desktop appears.

This works the same way for users in remote locations without a DC and without reliable WAN links. If a user has logged onto their computer at the remote location over the WAN link before, they can log on again using the same credentials.

While a user is logged on using cached credentials, the system will periodically try to access a domain controller. If the WAN link becomes available, the system will log on, and they will be able to access resources normally.

CACHED CREDENTIALS AND THE GC

Cached credentials work a little differently if a DC is available but a DC hosting the global catalog is not available. The global catalog is the only location where universal group membership is held, and universal group membership must be identified for a successful logon.

When a user logs on, a token is built that includes the SIDs of any groups the user is a member of and the user's SID. However, if the GC isn't available, universal group membership can't be identified.

The reason is that access can be explicitly denied to members of a universal group. However, if universal group membership can't be identified and logon was allowed, it's possible that members of a universal group gain access to resources that should be denied.

Consider Figure 22.6. A user is logging on in the remote office. The WAN link is currently unavailable, but he can access BF2 in the remote office. Notice that BF1 is a global catalog server, but BF2 is not a global catalog server.

FIGURE 22.6

Logging on without access to a GC

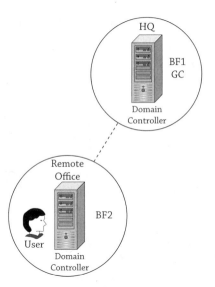

The `netlogon` service is able to validate his credentials on BF2, but since a GC can't be reached and universal group membership can't be identified, the logon is denied. The user isn't even logged on with cached credentials.

To avoid this problem, you should either make the DC at the remote site a global catalog server or enable universal group membership caching.

GC OR UNIVERSAL GROUP MEMBERSHIP CACHING

Once you've decided to place a domain controller into a site, you also need to decide whether you want to make the DC a global catalog server. A global catalog server will host the global catalog.

If you don't make the DC a GC, you should enable universal group membership caching on the site. When this is enabled, the domain controller will cache the user's universal group membership data the first time the user logs on and use it to create the user's token for subsequent logons.

Universal group membership for any users who have logged onto the DC is refreshed every eight hours. The DC can hold universal group membership cached data for as many as 500 users.

The primary reason why you wouldn't want to make a DC a GC in a remote site is that the replication of the global catalog will consume too much bandwidth. For example, if bandwidth utilization is already at 80 percent, making the DC a GC could cause utilization to peak at 100 percent.

You can make any DC a GC by modifying the NTDS Settings properties sheet of the server. Figure 22.7 shows this sheet with the Global Catalog check box selected.

FIGURE 22.7
Making a domain controller a global catalog server

To access the server's NTDS Site Settings properties sheet, locate the server object within the site in Active Directory Sites and Services. Right-click NTDS Settings, and select Properties.

You can enable universal group membership caching on a site by modifying the NTDS Site Settings properties sheet. Figure 22.8 shows this sheet with Universal Group Membership Caching enabled.

To access the site's NTDS Site Settings properties sheet, locate the site object within the Sites container in Active Directory Sites and Services. Right-click NTDS Settings for the site, and select Properties.

FIGURE 22.8
Enabling Universal Group
Membership Caching

Defining a Subnet and Placing It in a Site

Next, you need to describe the subnets in your enterprise. Suppose the original site has a single subnet of 192.168.20.0/24 and the Crosstown site has a subnet of 192.168.1.0/24. You need to tell Active Directory about these subnets: Always keep in mind that subnets have to be assigned to sites, so create the sites first, and then create the subnets.

1. Right-click the Subnets folder, and choose New Subnet.

2. Enter **192.168.20.0/24** to identify the subnet.

3. Select the HQ site to associate this subnet with HQ.

   Your display will look similar to Figure 22.9.

IPv4 OR IPv6

You can add both IPv4 and IPv6 subnets to Active Directory Sites and Services, but only one at a time. When adding the subnets, you need to identify the subnet mask using Classless Inter-Domain Routing (CIDR) notation. In CIDR notation, you identify how many bits a 1 is in the subnet mask. The /24 indicates the first 24 bits in the subnet mask are 1s; in other words, the subnet mask is 255.255.255.0.

FIGURE 22.9

Creating a new subnet

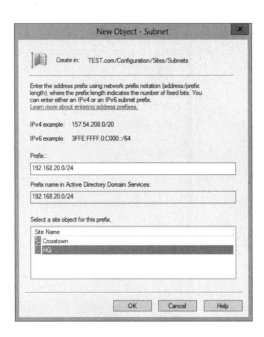

4. Add the 192.168.1.0/24 subnet, and associate it with the Crosstown site.

Your display will now look like Figure 22.10.

FIGURE 22.10

Sites and Services after adding subnets

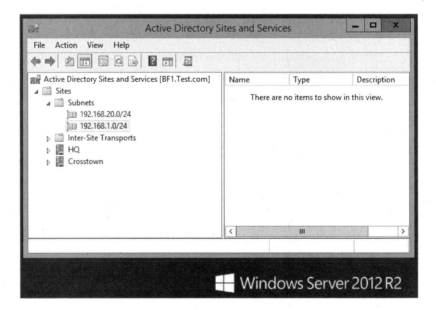

Placing a Server in a Site

Right now all four of the enterprise's DCs are in HQ. Suppose BF3 belongs in Crosstown. You could tell AD that BF3 is physically located in the Crosstown site by moving it there. Navigate to Sites ➤ HQ ➤ Servers, right-click BF3, and choose Move to see a dialog box like the one in Figure 22.11.

FIGURE 22.11

Moving a server

It's a little bit of work, but arranging your servers in Active Directory Sites and Services pays off if your enterprise includes multiple locations over WAN links.

Adding Site Links

Site links are used to identify the actual WAN links. Active Directory Sites and Services starts a default site link with another highly creative name: DefaultIPSiteLink. Just as you can rename the default site and add sites, you can rename the default site link and create other site links.

Consider Figure 22.12. It shows three sites within an enterprise: HQ, a crosstown office, and a remote office. This site diagram shows the three sites connected with three WAN links and different WAN link speeds. Later in this section, we'll show how to create site links to match these WAN links.

FIGURE 22.12

Three sites and three site links

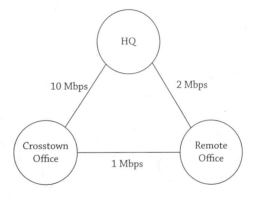

When creating site links, you have two choices: IP site links and SMTP site links. You will almost always use IP site links.

IP SITE LINK

IP site links use a remote procedure call (RPC) over IP transport connection. You will use IP site links almost all the time. One of the core requirements is that you have an IP connection available between the sites. If you can ping between the sites, you have an IP connection and should use an IP site link.

SMTP SITE LINK

If a direct IP connection isn't available and you aren't replicating domain data, you can configure an SMTP site link. On the surface, SMTP *sounds* like a great answer: it doesn't need to be running all the time, the link needn't be up that often, and—heck—you might even be able to send replication updates via Hotmail!

Unfortunately, it's not that useful. First, you can only replicate the forest-wide schema and configuration naming contexts, so you couldn't use SMTP to replicate updates between domain controllers in the same domain. In other words, simple tasks such as adding or modifying users, computers, or groups within a domain can't be replicated with SMTP.

Additionally, you can't use just any old mail server. You need a certificate issued from an enterprise certificate authority to ensure secure mail delivery before security-conscious AD will let you use it to replicate.

CREATING SITE LINKS

You can configure Active Directory Sites and Services to mimic the configuration shown previously in Figure 22.12 by following these steps:

1. Launch Active Directory Sites and Services.

2. Add a site named RemoteOffice using the procedure provided earlier in this chapter.

3. Add a 192.168.30.0/24 subnet to the RemoteOffice site using the procedure provided earlier in this chapter.

4. Browse to the Sites ➢ Inter-Site Transports ➢ IP folder. Right-click DEFAULTIPSITELINK, and select Rename.

5. Enter **CrossHQ** as the name.

   Crosstown, HQ, and RemoteOffice are added to this site link. You'll remove RemoteOffice in a moment.

6. Right-click IP, select New Site Link, and name the new site link **CrossRemote**.

7. Select the Crosstown and RemoteOffice sites, and click Add. Your display will look similar to Figure 22.13. Click OK.

FIGURE 22.13
Adding a site link

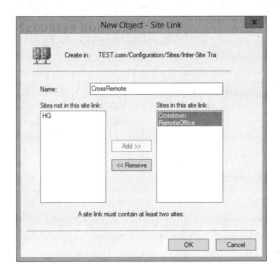

8. Right-click IP, and select New Site Link again.

9. Name the new site link **HQRemote.**

10. Select the HQ and RemoteOffice sites, and click Add. Click OK.

   When you created the RemoteOffice site, the only site link available was the DEFAULTIPSITELINK that you then renamed to CrossHQ.

11. Right-click CrossHQ, and select Properties.

12. Select RemoteOffice, and click Remove. Your display will look similar to Figure 22.14. Click OK.

FIGURE 22.14
Removing a site from a site link

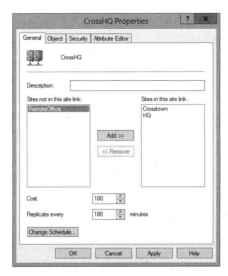

SITE LINK PROPERTIES

Site links include three important properties that are used by Active Directory to identify when the site link will be used. These three properties are the cost, how often replication will occur, and the replication schedule.

Cost Active Directory uses the cost to determine the lowest cost path to get from one site to another. If one path has a cost of 10 and another path has a cost of 100, the path with the least cost (10) will be used. When multiple site links are used to get to a site, each of the site link costs will be added together to determine the least cost. When you create a site link, the default cost is 100, but this can be changed to any value between 1 and 99,999.

Replicate Every This identifies how often replication occurs between sites. Initial replication within a site occurs every 15 seconds between domain controllers. However, replicating every 15 seconds over a WAN link is just too often. By default, replication over WAN links occurs every 180 minutes. You can change this value to anything between 15 and 10,080 minutes.

Schedule The schedule identifies when the link will be used. The default schedule is 24/7—24 hours a day every day of the week. However, you can limit when the link will be used for replication by modifying the schedule. For example, if the link has limited usage between midnight and 6 A.M. but is close to maximum use during normal hours, you can configure replication between sites to occur only between midnight and 6 A.M.

CALCULATING THE COST

You have a wide range of numbers (1 to 99,999) you can assign to the cost of your IP site links. Remember, these numbers will be used by Active Directory to determine which link to use to reach another site.

Real World Scenario

COST IS RELATIVE

When assigning cost, it's important to ensure that the costs accurately reflect the speed. For example, if one 10 Mbps line has a cost of 10, all 10 Mbps lines should have a cost of 10. Similarly, if a 10 Mbps line has a cost of 10, a 1 Mbps line should have a sufficiently higher number (such as 100); speeds between a 1 Mbps connection and a 10 Mbps connection would then have costs between 10 and 100.

You could also use different numbers and different ranges of numbers. For example, you could assign a cost of 1000 for a 1 Mbps connection and a cost of 100 for a 10 Mbps connection. However, we do not recommend using only low numbers with a very narrow range, such as a cost of 1 for a 10 Mbps line and 10 for a 1 Mbps line. If you added a 20 Mbps line in the future, you couldn't assign a cost lower than 1, so you'd need to redesign and reassign all the costs.

Consider Figure 22.15. It shows our three sites, with the site links and the speeds of the WAN links. Additionally, costs have been assigned to each link.

FIGURE 22.15

Three sites connected with three site links

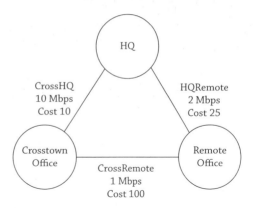

Since the CrossHQ link is connected with the fastest link (a 10 Mbps line), I have assigned it a cost of 10—the lowest cost of each of the links. The CrossRemote link is the slowest at 1 Mbps, and I have assigned it the highest cost of 100. CrossHQ has a 2 Mbps WAN link, and I have assigned it a cost of 25.

When HQ wants to replicate with the crosstown office, it sees that the direct path using CrossHQ has the lowest cost of 10 as compared to a cost of 125 (100 + 25) if it went through the remote office.

However, when the remote office wants to replicate with the crosstown office, the least-cost path is via HQ with a cost of 35 (10 + 25). The direct path using the CrossRemote link has a cost of 100, so it would be used only if one of the paths failed.

Configuring Intersite Replication

Now that you've seen how to create subnets, sites, and site links, you'll learn how to configure them to match your network infrastructure.

You already know that within a site AD replicates by building a replication topology between domain controllers. But the same topology across WAN links would be inefficient, so AD instead creates a minimal spanning tree, meaning that it creates a set of site-to-site replication paths that minimizes the load on your WAN bandwidth.

Take a look at the AD Sites and Services snap-in shown in Figure 22.16. It shows three sites with three IP site links.

Notice that the cost of each of the site links has been modified within Active Directory Sites and Services. You'll see how to do this in a moment.

This is a simple enterprise, but it'll serve fine to understand the issues in a multisite environment. You see, once you set up your sites, DCs figure out how to replicate all by themselves *within the site*. But across sites, they need a little help.

You tell AD about connections between sites by creating site links. You help AD identify which path to use for replication, when to perform replication, and how often to perform replication by configuring the site link properties.

If you double-click any site link object, you'll see a dialog box similar to Figure 22.17.

FIGURE 22.16
Active Directory Sites and
Services with three sites
and three site links

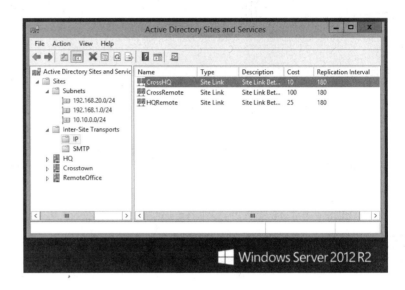

FIGURE 22.17
Site link properties page

This dialog box is *very* important for three reasons:

◆   The Cost spinner box is used to help AD identify which link to use. AD will choose lower-cost paths over higher-cost paths. It is set to a cost of 100 by default.

◆   The Replicate Every *xx* Minutes spinner box is used to control how often AD tries to replicate over this link. It is set to 180 minutes by default.

◆   Last, the Change Schedule button allows you to modify when replication occurs based on a schedule.

Click the Change Schedule button, and you'll see a dialog box similar to Figure 22.18. The schedule for this site link has been changed to allow replication only during the nonpeak hours of midnight to 6 A.M.

FIGURE 22.18

Setting the replication schedule

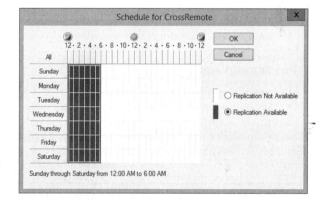

It could be that the HQ-to-Crosstown link is heavily used during the daytime hours, and you want replication to occur only during nonbusiness hours. Setting the schedule tells AD not to bother trying to replicate before 6 P.M. daily.

REPLICATE AT LEAST EVERY 180 DAYS

AD sites must replicate at least once every 180 days or less. AD throws away objects that have been inactive for 180 days, so if one site and another didn't talk for a few months, then they'd start deleting objects from their copies of AD that they weren't using but that other DCs in other sites were still using. This is only a problem if a DC goes down for a long period of time. Do not reconnect a DC to the network if it hasn't replicated to AD for more than 180 days.

This number was 60 days in previous operating system versions, based on the default tombstone lifetime. However, the tombstone lifetime was changed to 180 days in Server 2003 with SP1 and newer operating systems including Windows Server 2012 R2.

Once you tell AD all these things about sites, a souped-up version of the Knowledge Consistency Checker called the Inter-Site Topology Generator (ISTG) identifies what links to use and when to use them. One DC at each site is automatically designated as the ISTG.

You can identify which server is the ISTG by viewing the Site NTDS Site Settings properties sheet. Select the site, and double-click NTDS Site Settings to access this page. However, the ISTG needs very little oversight.

An important function of the ISTG is to assign bridgehead servers. Additionally, you can override the ISTG by assigning preferred bridgehead servers.

Bridgehead Servers

A *bridgehead server* is a DC within a site that will replicate to DCs in other sites. Every site will have only one active bridgehead server at any time.

The Inter Site Topology Generator designates a DC as a bridgehead server and periodically checks this DC to ensure it's still operational. If this DC crashes or is taken offline, the ISTG will automatically designate another server as the bridgehead server.

At least this is the way it works normally, assuming you haven't overridden the ISTG by assigning a preferred bridgehead server.

PREFERRED BRIDGEHEAD SERVERS

Occasionally, you may want to exclude a DC from becoming a bridgehead server. For example, a DC may be close to full capacity with the processing power hovering close to 80 percent and the paging file usage excessively high. When the ISTG designates this as the bridgehead server, the processing power could peak at 100 percent, significantly impacting the performance of other functions on the server.

USE PREFERRED BRIDGEHEAD SERVERS FOR EXCLUSION MANAGEMENT

Notice the subtlety here. You aren't picking a DC as a preferred bridgehead server because you want it to be the bridgehead server as much as you don't want *another* DC to be a bridgehead server. In other words, you select preferred bridgehead servers to exclude one or more DCs from the selection process. Once you designate any DC as a preferred bridgehead server, the ISTG will only pick preferred bridgehead servers to fill this role.

You can't directly exclude a DC as a preferred bridgehead server. However, you can designate other DCs as preferred bridgehead servers. For example, if you have four DCs and you don't want BF4 to be a bridgehead server, you'd designate BF1, BF2, and BF3 as preferred bridgehead servers.

This brings up a special consideration. If you ever designate a single DC as a preferred bridgehead server, you should also designate at least one more DC as a preferred bridgehead server. If only one is designated and it fails, the ISTG will not automatically switch the role to other DCs.

You can designate a server as a preferred bridgehead server by following these steps:

1. Launch AD Sites and Services.

2. Browse to the Servers container within the site you want to manipulate.

3. Right-click the server you want to add, and select Properties.

4. Select IP, and click Add.

   Your display will look similar to Figure 22.19.

FIGURE 22.19
Designating a server as a preferred bridgehead server

5. Click OK to close the properties sheet.

6. Repeat these steps for each server you want to designate as a preferred bridgehead server.

Forcing Replication

The repadmin command-line tool includes a neat feature that you can use to replicate data between two domain controllers even if it's outside the schedule. This can be useful when troubleshooting replication problems between sites. The repadmin switch is /replsingleobj.

USING COMMAND-LINE REPLICATION

In previous editions of Windows, the replsingleobject switch was used to replicate objects between DCs even if there wasn't a connection. However, this has been shortened to just replsingleobj (*obj* instead of *object*) in Windows Server 2012 R2. This shorter version was also available in Windows Server 2003 with the longer version, but in 2012 and 2008, only the shorter version is available. We can tell you from experience that no matter how many times you try it without shortening object to obj, it simply won't work.

This is the basic syntax for the `repadmin` tool:

```
repadmin <command> <arguments>
```

When using the `replsingleobj` command or switch, the syntax is as follows:

```
repadmin /replsingleobjc sourceDC destinationDC ObjectDN
```

Both the source and destination domain controllers can be identified with their name (such as BF1) or with their fully qualified domain name (such as BF1.Bigfirm.com).

The object distinguished name (DN) follows the LDAP DN rules. For example, a computer named TestCPU created in the Sales OU of the Bigfirm.com domain would have the following DN: `CN=TestCPU,OU=Sales,DC=bigfirm,DC=com`.

If the DN has any spaces in it, it must be enclosed in quotes.

To replicate the `TestCPU` object from BF1 to BF2, you can use the following command. Notice that the command wraps to multiple lines in the book, but it should be entered on a single line:

```
repadmin /replsingleobj BF1.bigfirm.com BF2.bigfirm.com
   CN=TestCPU,OU=Sales,DC=bigfirm.DC=com
```

Configuring Clients to Access the Next Closest Site

A great capability available with Windows Server 2012 R2 is the ability to teach clients what site to access if the domain controller in their site is down. Consider the Bigfirm.com enterprise shown in Figure 22.20.

FIGURE 22.20
Next closest site

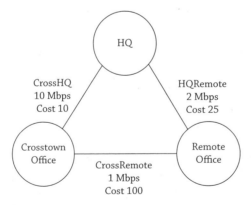

Each site has at least one domain controller, and normally users will log onto a domain controller in their own site. But what if the domain controller in the crosstown office site goes down?

You probably wouldn't want the users to have to use a slower connection and log onto DCs in the remote office site. However, this is exactly what might happen if the next closest site setting isn't enabled. The DC Locator service first tries to locate a DC in the same site as the client. If unsuccessful, it then looks for any DC regardless of the location unless the next closest site setting is enabled.

The term *closest site* is somewhat of a misnomer. Active Directory doesn't have any concept of distance, but it does understand the cost configured in the site link properties. Although it's likely that the closest sites will have the fastest WAN links and would be configured with the lowest cost, an organization could be configured differently.

As an example, the remote office could be one mile away from the crosstown office but five miles away from the headquarters location. The link between the remote office and HQ has a cost of 25, and the link between the crosstown office and the remote office is 100. If distance was used, the crosstown office would be considered closest, but since cost is considered, HQ would be identified as the next closest site since the cost is lowest.

NEXT CLOSEST SITE NOT AVAILABLE ON PRE-WINDOWS VISTA CLIENTS

The next closest site feature will work on only Windows 7, Windows 8, and Windows Server 2008 or greater clients and servers. This feature will not affect how Windows XP, Windows Server 2003, or previous clients behave.

You can configure Windows 7, Windows 8, and Windows Server 2012 R2 servers to use the cost to locate the next closest site. These are the two methods that can be used to configure this feature:

◆ Group Policy

◆ Registry modification

Configuring Next Closest Site with Group Policy

If you want to configure multiple clients to use the cost to determine which sites are the closest, you can modify Group Policy to do so. You can use the following steps to configure all clients in the domain.

SITE, DOMAIN, OR OU

The following procedure takes you through the steps to configure all the clients in the domain by modifying the default domain policy. However, you could slightly modify these steps to create or alter any GPO and link it to a site, domain, or organizational unit (OU) depending on which computers you want to affect.

1. Launch the Group Policy Management console by selecting Server Manager ➢ Tools ➢ Group Policy Management.

2. Browse to the Default Domain Policy object within the Forest ➢ Domains ➢ *Domain Name* folder.

3. Right-click Default Domain Policy, and click Edit.

4. Browse to the Computer Configuration ➢ Policies ➢ Administrative Templates ➢ System ➢ Net Logon ➢ DC Locator DNS Records Group Policy folder.

5. Double-click the Try Next Closest Site setting, and click Enabled. Your display will look similar to Figure 22.21. Click OK.

FIGURE 22.21
Configuring Try
Next Closest Site
through Group
Policy

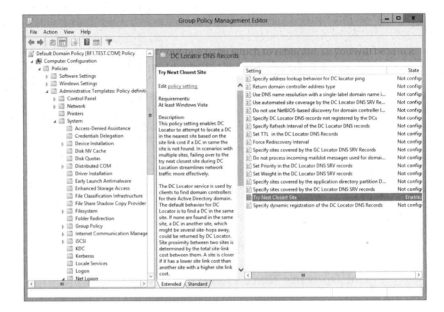

6. Close the Group Policy Management Editor and the Group Policy Management console.

You can wait until Group Policy is applied through the normal refresh cycle or use the gpupdate /force command from the command line to update any individual clients.

Configuring Next Closest Site through the Registry

Group Policy allows you to configure a setting once and affect multiple clients. However, if you want only a single client to use the next closest site capability, you can modify the registry.

BE CAREFUL WITH THE REGISTRY

You should be cautious any time you modify the registry. Incorrectly editing the registry may severely damage your system. It's recommended that you back up valuable data on your computer before modifying the registry.

You can use the following steps to enable the Try Next Closest Site setting for a single Windows 7 or Windows 8 client.

1. Launch the Registry Editor by clicking Start, typing **regedit** or **regedit32** in the Start Search box, and pressing Enter. Both commands launch the same Registry Editor.

2. Select the HKEY_LOCAL_MACHINE (HKLM) hive.

3. Browse to the System\CurrentControlSet\Services\Netlogon\Parameters folder.

4. Look for a registry key named Try Next Closest Site. If it doesn't exist, follow these steps to create it:

    a. Right-click Parameters, and select New ➢ DWORD (32-bit) Value.

    b. Rename the new key as **Try Next Closest Site** using spaces between each word.

5. Double-click the Try Next Closest Site key. Change the value to **1**. Your display will look similar to Figure 22.22.

FIGURE 22.22
Modifying the registry

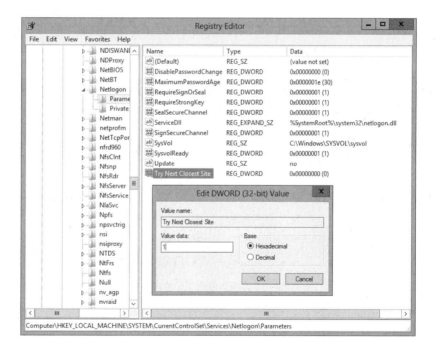

6. Click OK. Close the Registry Editor.

As a reminder, this setting is referenced only if a domain controller can't be contacted in the same site as the client.

If the value is 1 for this key, the DC Locator process will use the cost value of the site links to find a domain controller in the next closest site. If the value is 0, the DC Locator won't use the cost value and could contact any domain controller regardless of the location.

Using PowerShell

PowerShell cmdlets are covered in many chapters throughout this book, so you've probably already seen many. This section highlights a few cmdlets you can use and combine to retrieve information from Active Directory. It includes some basics on the Active Directory searcher tool built into PowerShell, which can be very useful if your organization is big enough to support multiple sites.

USING DISTINGUISHED NAMES

These steps talk about distinguished names (DNs), which were covered in much greater depth in Chapter 7, "Active Directory in Windows Server 2012 R2," and mentioned earlier in this chapter. It will take a little bit of practice before you can create a DN on the fly, but you'll find the ability to create and identify the DN useful, especially when scripting or digging into Active Directory details.

---

1. Launch an instance of Windows PowerShell.

2. Get some information about your environment by first creating a variable to represent the domain with the following cmdlet. It populates the variable $dom with the DN of the domain. Note that LDAP must be all caps:

   ```
   $dom=[adsi]"LDAP://RootDSE"
   ```

3. You can now query information about the domain using the $dom variable with these commands:

   a. View the naming context of the root domain:

   ```
   Write-Host $obj.RootDomainNamingContext
   ```

   Our result: DC=bigfirm,DC=com

   b. View the naming context of all domains in the forest:

   ```
   Write-Host $obj.NamingContexts
   ```

   Our result: DC=bigfirm,DC=com

   c. View the default naming context (or the partial DN of your domain):

   ```
   Write-Host $obj.DefaultNamingContext
   ```

   Our result: DC=bigfirm,DC=com

   d. Identify the number of the highest update sequence number (USN) used for replication:

   ```
   Write-Host $obj.HighestCommittedUSN
   ```

   Our result: 86051

There are times when you don't know the distinguished name of a user because you don't know what OU they're in. If you know some details about the account (such as the display name), you can retrieve the distinguished name using the built-in Active Directory searcher. This example assumes accounts use a display name of first name, period, last name (as in John .Smith). All you need to know are the user's first and last names to search.

1. First, create a variable for the filter (your search item) with this line:

```
$filter = "(&(ObjectCategory=User)(DisplayName=John.Smith*))"
```

The wildcard * is used to find all instances (such as John.Smith.2 and John.Smith.3).

2. Next, create an instance of the searcher using the filter with this line:

```
$Searcher = New-Object System.DirectoryServices.DirectorySearcher($Filter)
```

3. Last, find all instances with this command:

```
Searcher.Findall()
```

The DNs of all accounts matching this display name will be displayed.

You can even make the previous code into a script designed to accept a parameter (such as the username).

4. Type the following lines into any text editor (such as Notepad), and save it in the C:\Scripts folder as **FindUser.ps1.**

The first identifies the parameter that will be accepted, and the second line uses this parameter in the filter. The rest is the same:

```
Param($filterName)
$filter = "(&(ObjectCategory=User)(DisplayName=$filterName))"
    $Searcher = New-Object System.DirectoryServices.DirectorySearcher($Filter)
Searcher.Findall()
```

5. Execute the script with this line in PowerShell:

```
C:\Scripts\FindUser.ps1 John.Smith*
```

You may want to retrieve a list of group memberships for a user. If you know the DN, you can use these steps to do so:

1. First, create a variable for a user object in your domain using the DN.

In this code, we're using the Administrator account, but you can use any account (including computer accounts):

```
$user=[adsi]"LDAP://CN=Administrator,CN=Users,Dc=bigfirm,DC=com""
```

2. Retrieve the group membership for the user with this command:

```
Write-Host $user.memberof -separator " >>> "
```

This will show a list of groups in DN format. The separator switch makes it a little easier to see where one group stops and another starts.

The Bottom Line

Create a site. Site objects are added to Active Directory to represent well-connected physical locations that will host domain controllers. Once a decision has been made to place a DC in a physical location, you need to add a site.

Master It Create a site to represent a new business location in Virginia Beach.

Add subnets to sites. Active Directory uses clients' subnets to determine which site they are in. For this to work, subnet objects need to be created and associated with sites.

Master It Create a subnet object to represent the 10.15.0.0/16 subnet that exists in the Virginia Beach location. Associate the subnet object with the VB site.

Configure a site link to replicate only during certain times. It's often desirable to restrict when replication occurs between sites. If the defaults are used, replication will occur every 180 minutes. If the WAN link is heavily used during certain periods, you can configure the schedule so that it replicates only during certain times.

Master It Configure the Default-First-Site-Name site (or another site) to replicate only between midnight and 5 A.M.

Configure Group Policy for the next nearest site. If a domain controller can't be reached in a client's site, the client will look for any domain controller without regard to how close it is. This can negatively impact logons for enterprises with several locations connected with different speed WAN links. You can configure Windows Vista (and newer) clients to locate and log on to a DC in the next nearest site if a DC can't be located in their site. This can be done using Group Policy or the Registry Editor.

Master It Which of the following Group Policy settings can be manipulated to enable the next nearest site setting?

1. Computer Configuration ➢ Policies ➢ Administrative Templates ➢ System ➢ Logon ➢ DC Locator DNS Records

2. Computer Configuration ➢ Policies ➢ Administrative Templates ➢ System ➢ Net Logon ➢ DC Locator DNS Records

3. User Configuration ➢ Policies ➢ Administrative Templates ➢ System ➢ Logon ➢ DC Locator DNS Records

4. User Configuration ➢ Policies ➢ Administrative Templates ➢ System ➢ Net Logon ➢ DC Locator DNS Records

Chapter 23

The Third DC: Understanding Read-only Domain Controllers

Most domain controllers (DCs) hold a full copy of Active Directory, including all of the administrative accounts and their passwords. Also, most domain controllers enjoy a safe lifetime locked behind doors to a server room or server closet. As long as a DC is well protected with physical security, this arrangement works perfectly.

However, domain controllers sometimes need to be deployed to other locations to support users working in branch offices or remote locations. Ideally, these branch offices enjoy the same physical security as the main location, but in reality this just isn't true.

In the past, administrators have had to weigh the risk of a DC being stolen or attacked after it's been placed in a remote location against the benefit of providing better performance for users in the remote office. Today, administrators have another choice.

With the introduction of read-only domain controllers (RODCs) in Windows Server 2008, administrators could have it both ways. They could place their RODCs in a remote location to support the users, and they could significantly reduce the risks if the RODC is stolen or attacked. Windows Server 2012 R2 has made using RODCs even easier by improving the user-friendly deployment wizards and automation and management via Windows PowerShell.

In this chapter, you will learn to:

◆ Prepare a forest and a domain for RODCs

◆ Prepare the domain

◆ Allow passwords on any RODC

◆ Allow passwords on a single RODC

Introducing RODCs

Read-only domain controllers are a new type of a domain controller that was first introduced in Windows Server 2008. They're specifically designed to be used in remote office locations where physical security cannot be guaranteed.

THE THIRD DC

Any domain starts with a single writable domain controller. Companies often add a second DC for routine fault tolerance in case the first DC fails. Although you're not required to have two DCs before creating an RODC, this is what most companies will do. An RODC cannot be used for fault tolerance. If there's only one writable DC and it fails, the RODC can't be used to seize FSMO roles and won't hold the majority of passwords.

In Chapter 22, "Adding More Locations: Sites in Active Directory," you learned about adding sites in Active Directory for different geographical locations of your enterprise. As an example, imagine your company has a primary location and a remote office connected via a slow link, as shown in Figure 23.1.

FIGURE 23.1

Company with a remote site

Any users in the remote office would have to use the slow 256 Kbps WAN link to log onto their computers. You could improve their logon times by adding a domain controller to the remote office and configuring a site within Active Directory.

Moving the DC to the remote office will certainly improve the logon times for users there. However, it presents a significant security risk if the DC in the remote office is stolen or compromised.

A social engineer would probably not succeed if he came to your headquarters location and told people he was there to pick up the DC for its annual cleaning. However, employees at a remote office may be convinced by a cunning attacker that a DC does need to be taken away to be "cleaned."

If an attacker were able to gain unrestricted physical access to the DC, he could gain access to passwords of key accounts, including administrator accounts. However, if an RODC is placed at the remote location instead of a regular DC, the attacker will not be able to access all the passwords in the domain because the RODC holds only a limited amount of data that can be exploited.

Thanks to BitLocker, the drives themselves would be useless to someone who doesn't have proper access. Make sure to encrypt your RODCs using BitLocker to limit concerns of physical theft. Many small office locations that have only a limited number of personnel dedicated to tasks and duties unrelated to IT are known to have weak physical security policies. We've seen full-blown domain controllers and file servers siting on a shelf in the supply room where everyone has access. Control your environment whenever possible. Badge access or key control the room dedicated to IT infrastructure, encrypt your machines, and use RODCs instead of full-blown DCs when the situation allows.

Another great feature RODCs is Administrative Role Separation (ARS). ARS gives domain administrators the ability to delegate domain admin–like rights to any domain user or group in the environment. This comes in handy when no IT personnel are available at a remote office or remote DMZ to assist with the installation and management of an RODC. Having a site-based superuser or group allows for local management of the RODC. This person or persons can perform maintenance, patching, and upgrades for that individual RODC. One nice feature of ARS is that the user who is delegated with higher permissions only has rights to do admin-level procedures on that RODC. They will not have domain admin rights throughout the environment, so you won't have to worry about that user having too much control over the enterprise.

Making Changes on a Read-only Domain Controller

What does *read-only* really mean on a read-only domain controller? It doesn't mean that changes never occur on the RODC; instead, it means that changes cannot originate on the read-only domain controller. Changes can originate on a writable domain controller and replicate to the RODC.

A writable DC is any normal DC where additions, deletions, and modifications to Active Directory can be recorded. Normally when changes occur in Active Directory, such as adding an account or changing a password, they can occur on any DC in the domain. Changes are then replicated to other DCs.

RODCs are not writable DCs. This means that any changes that a user attempts while connected to an RODC are not made on the RODC. Instead, a writable DC is contacted, and the change is made on the writable DC after the credentials are checked. If appropriate, the change is then replicated back down to the RODC.

This prevents an attacker from taking over an RODC at a remote location, making changes to Active Directory, and having those changes replicate back to the writable DCs.

Even though an RODC will receive replicated data from a writable DC, it will not store all the same contents as a writable DC.

 Real World Scenario

STOLEN DOMAIN CONTROLLER

One company we know of had a remote office with about 15 users. They were separated from their main office by railroad tracks, and the railroad company would not allow cables to be run beneath the tracks. Users connected using a 256 Kbps dial-up modem that created a VPN between the main office and the remote office.

Not surprisingly, the users often complained that the logons were taking too long. Eventually, domain administrators created a domain controller and placed it in the remote office. Unfortunately, the remote office had very poor physical security.

About a month after they placed the DC in the remote office, it disappeared. Users weren't even sure exactly when it disappeared, though administrators were able to narrow down the time frame using logs. A lot of circumstantial evidence pointed to an employee who had access to the office after hours, but nothing was ever proven.

Since the DC had a full copy of Active Directory, including all the administrative accounts and their passwords, the IT department was soon in panic mode. They spent a great deal of time changing passwords and renaming accounts. They even seriously considered deleting their one-domain forest and starting over.

Management spent a lot of time evaluating the risk of not rebuilding the forest and weighing it against the business impact of deleting the forest and rebuilding it from scratch. Eventually they accepted the risk. It paid off. They never saw any evidence that anything was compromised from this theft.

If the DC were an RODC instead, the company would have lost the cost of the server, but the added risks that caused so much administrative and managerial headaches could have been avoided.

RODC Contents

An RODC holds all the Active Directory accounts and *most* of the attributes that can be found on a writable DC. A significant difference between an RODC and a writable DC is that an RODC holds very few passwords.

More specifically, the RODC will typically only hold the passwords of nonadministrator users who log on in the remote office. Other passwords are specifically blocked from being stored on the RODC.

Figure 23.2 shows the process if an RODC is placed in a remote office. Imagine Sally is logging onto the RODC for the first time. Her system will contact the RODC. The RODC doesn't have her account cached, so it will query the DC at the headquarters location.

FIGURE 23.2
RODC logon process

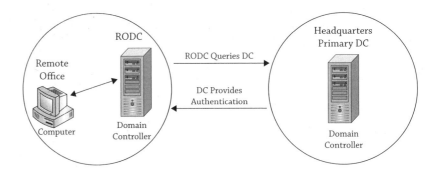

The DC at HQ will authenticate Sally's credentials and it will also check the password replication policy to determine whether her credentials can be cached on the RODC. By default, no passwords will be cached on the RODC. However, it's common to allow credentials for nonadministrator users working at the remote office location to be cached. Any passwords that aren't specifically allowed will not be cached on the RODC.

The next time Sally logs on at the remote site, her credentials are verified with the cached credentials on the RODC. The term *cached credentials* means that they are stored in a temporary location on the server's hard drive.

CACHED ON THE RODC HARD DRIVE

If you're a hardware guy or gal, you may be thinking of *cache* because it refers to memory used to improve performance. For example, L1 and L2 cache are additional memory to improve the performance of the processor. Memory is volatile, and its contents will be lost when the system is shut down or rebooted. However, credentials cached on an RODC are stored on the hard drive of the RODC. These credentials will be maintained even if the RODC loses power or is rebooted.

Most notably, passwords for users in the domain who have not logged on at the remote location are not stored or replicated to the RODC.

What if an administrator logs onto the RODC using an administrative account? The purpose of the RODC is to protect against a physical attack by not including administrator passwords on the server. But if an administrator logs on and the administrator password is cached, it defeats the purpose.

To specifically address this issue, a password replication policy is configured to ensure administrator accounts are not cached on the RODC. You can modify the password replication policy, and you can also identify specific groups that can have password replication allowed or denied.

PASSWORD REPLICATION POLICY

The password replication policy was added in Windows Server 2008 to support RODCs and continues to be an added benefit in Windows Server 2012 R2. It identifies which passwords will be cached on the RODC. By default, no passwords are cached on the RODC, so you will need to understand how this works so you can make some modifications.

Figure 23.3 shows the properties of an RODC with the Password Replication Policy tab selected. Each RODC has its own password replication policy.

FIGURE 23.3

Password Replication Policy tab

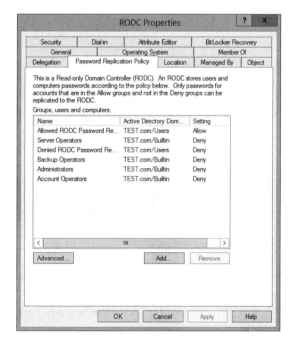

REPLICATION OR CACHING

You may notice the terms *replication* and *caching* are both used. Once a password is cached on an RODC, it will be replicated back to the RODC when changes occur through normal replication. Additionally, it's possible to designate specific user passwords to be replicated to an RODC even before a user logs on. Once the password is replicated to the RODC, it is considered cached on the RODC.

Notice that the following groups have a setting of Deny:

◆ Account Operators

◆ Administrators

◆ Backup Operators

◆ Denied RODC Password Replication

◆ Server Operators

Users with membership in any of these groups can log onto the RODC, but their credentials will not be cached on the RODC. The only group that has a setting of Allow by default is the Allowed RODC Password Replication group. Users in this group can have their passwords cached.

Windows Server 2012 R2 modifies the Active Directory schema to include several additional Active Directory attributes to support the password replication policy. These attributes are as follows:

msDS-Reveal-OnDemandGroup This is also known as the *allowed list*. It identifies which accounts can have passwords cached on an RODC. It includes only one value by default: the Allowed RODC Password Replication group. In other words, only users in the Allowed RODC Password Replication group (which is a domain local group) can have passwords cached on the RODC. The Allowed RODC Password Replication group starts empty, so by default no passwords will be cached on the RODC.

msDS-NeverRevealGroup This is also known as the *denied list*. It identifies which accounts cannot be cached on the RODC and includes the Account Operators, Server Operators, Backup Operators, and Administrators groups in addition to the members of the Denied RODC Password Replication group.

If an account is a member of the msDS-NeverRevealGroup and the msDS-Reveal-OnDemandGroup, the msDS-NeverRevealGroup will take precedence. In other words, if an account is both denied and allowed, Deny takes precedence.

msDS-RevealedList This is the list of accounts that have credentials cached on the RODC. You can view this list by clicking the Advanced button on the Password Replication Policy tab of the RODC properties sheet.

msDS-AuthenticatedToAccountList This list includes all accounts that have attempted to authenticate to the RODC. Administrators can occasionally look at this list to determine who is authenticating through the RODC and who may need to be added to the allow list. You can view this list by clicking the Advanced button on the Password Replication Policy tab of the RODC properties sheet.

The password replication policy works in conjunction with the Allowed RODC Password Replication group and the Denied RODC Password Replication group. The following are two important points to consider with the policy and the groups:

The Policy Is Specific to Each RODC   Any individual RODC can have specific users or groups allowed or denied, while another RODC can have different users or groups specifically allowed or denied.

Groups Apply to All RODCs Universally   The Allowed RODC Password Replication and Denied RODC Password Replication groups apply to all RODCs. For example, if a user is added to the Denied RODC Password Replication group, her credentials will not be cached on any RODC in the domain.

DENIED RODC PASSWORD REPLICATION GROUP

The Denied RODC Password Replication group is automatically added to Active Directory. Any users added to this group, or anyone who is a member of a group added to this group, will not have their passwords cached on any RODC in the domain.

For example, if Joe's account is added to this group, his account can't be cached on any RODC. If Sally is a member of the IT Admins group and the IT Admins group is added to the Denied RODC Password Replication group, Sally's account can't be cached on any RODC in the domain.

Figure 23.4 shows the group with the Members tab selected.

FIGURE 23.4
Denied RODC
Password
Replication group
members

This group is a domain local security group and includes the following members by default:

◆ Cert Publishers

◆ Domain Admins

◆ Domain Controllers

◆ Enterprise Admins

◆ Group Policy Creator Owners

◆ krbtgt

◆ Read-only Domain Controllers

◆ Schema Admins

KRBTGT AND KRBTGT123

Writable DCs use the krbtgt account with Kerberos. You can think of it as the Kerberos ticket-granting ticket account, and its password is known by all writable DCs. When tickets need to be created for authentication, they are encrypted with a symmetric key that is derived from the password. Since all DCs use the same password for this account, all DCs can decrypt tickets granted by other DCs.

The Kerberos ticket-granting ticket account works differently on RODCs. First, it has a different name such as krbtgt123 (or another semi-random string of numbers after krbtgt). Second, it has a different password. Writable DCs know the password of the RODC; however, the RODCs don't know the password of the krbtgt account used by writable DCs.

Users with accounts in any of these groups can still log onto the RODC. The only difference is that their credentials won't be cached, preventing the security risk if the RODC is stolen.

ALLOWED RODC PASSWORD REPLICATION GROUP

The Allowed RODC Password Replication group is also a domain local security group located in the Users container. Figure 23.5 shows the Allowed RODC Password Replication group.

Unlike the Denied RODC Password Replication group, which includes several members by default, the Allowed RODC Password Replication group does not include any members by default. Members added to this group can have their passwords replicated or cached to any RODC in the domain.

If a user is a member of both this group and the Denied RODC Password Replication group, the Denied RODC Password Replication group will take precedence.

FIGURE 23.5
Allowed RODC Password
Replication group

DELEGATING ADMINISTRATION FOR AN RODC

When you promote a server to an RODC, you will be prompted to identify a specific user or group that will administer the RODC or that may finish the promotion of the RODC. If a user at the remote office will be performing administration, this is the best way to delegate appropriate permissions to the user.

Whenever possible, it's recommended to use groups instead of users to designate permissions or privileges, and this is no exception. You should create a group and add the user (or users) to the group that will administer the RODC.

Users in this group will be able to complete the RODC installation at the remote site if needed and will also have specific permissions granted for administration of the RODC. They do not have any type of administrative permissions in the domain from this group.

Even though the group is granted specific permissions to the RODC, it is not added to the Allowed RODC Replication group by default. However, you probably will want to add this account to the allowed group so that the user's credentials will be cached on the DC and the user can perform local administrative tasks even if the WAN link is down.

RODC Requirements

Before an RODC can be deployed, Active Directory must meet some basic requirements:

At Least One DC Must Be Running Windows Server 2008 or 2012 The RODC needs to replicate with a Windows Server 2008 or Windows Server 2012 rewritable domain controller. If none of the domain controllers in the domain is running at least Windows Server 2008, you won't be able to install an RODC. If you are promoting the first Windows Server 2008 server to a domain controller in a preexisting domain (running Windows Server 2003, for example), you'll first need to prepare the domain and forest with adprep /forestprep and adprep /

domain prep. If the forest was built on Windows Server 2008 or Windows 2012 servers, it is not necessary to run adprep /forestprep and adprep /domain prep. Administrators upgrading from Server 2008 to Server 2012 will not need to worry about domain or forest prep when installing RODCs. Active Directory Domain Services will take care of any preconfiguration adprep tasks for you.

The Domain Functional Level Must Be at Least Windows Server 2003   The Windows Server 2003 domain functional level provides Kerberos-constrained delegation. This provides the necessary security for the RODC.

The Forest Functional Level Must Be at Least Windows Server 2003   The RODC requires linked value replication, which is available when the forest functional level has been raised to Windows Server 2003.

The Forest Must Be Prepared by Running adprep   You must run adprep /rodcprep before installing the first RODC.

DOMAIN FUNCTIONAL LEVEL

Different domain functional levels provide different capabilities. When all the domain controllers in a domain are upgraded to newer operating systems, you can upgrade the domain functional level to take advantage of the new capabilities.

FUNCTIONAL LEVELS CANNOT BE REVERSED

Although it's possible to raise a functional level from a lower level to a higher level, once you raise it, there's no turning back. This applies to both a domain functional level and a forest functional level. Since the higher functional levels provide extra capabilities, a logical question is, "Why not always choose the highest level?" The answer is that the domain functional level dictates the minimum operating system that must be running on domain controllers.

As an example, if you have an existing domain with Windows Server 2008 DCs, you can add a Windows Server 2012 R2 DC, but you won't be able to raise the level higher than 2008. Similarly, if you build a domain by promoting a Windows Server 2012 R2 server to a DC and select Windows Server 2012 R2 as both the domain and forest functional levels, you will never be able to promote anything less than a Windows Server 2012 server to a DC.

The different domain functional levels are as follows:

Windows Server 2003   Used when all domain controllers are running at least Windows Server 2003. As a reminder, this is the minimum domain functional level that will support RODCs.

Windows Server 2008   Used when all domain controllers are running at least Windows Server 2008.

Windows Server 2008 R2   Used when all domain controllers are running at least Windows Server 2008 R2.

Windows Server 2012   Used when all domain controllers are running at least Windows Server 2012.

Windows Server 2012 R2   Used when all domain controllers are running at least Windows Server 2012 R2.

You can verify (and upgrade if needed) the domain functional level that your domain is currently using with the following steps:

1. Log onto a domain controller.

2. Launch Active Directory Users and Computers by selecting Server Manager ➢ Tools ➢ Active Directory Users and Computers.

3. Right-click the domain name, and select Raise Domain Functional Level. Your display will look similar to Figure 23.6.

FIGURE 23.6
Verifying the domain functional level

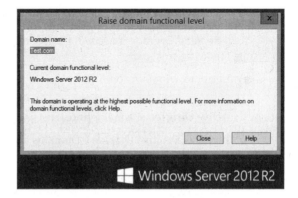

In the figure, the current domain functional level is Windows Server 2012 R2 and the domain is operating at the highest possible functional level until the next Windows Server release.

4. If the domain functional level is not at least Windows Server 2003, raise it to Windows Server 2003 by selecting Windows Server 2003 and clicking Raise.

   Recalling previous prerequisites for an RODC, the domain functional level must be at least Windows Server 2003 for you to be able to use RODCs.

You need to raise the domain functional level on only one domain controller in the domain. It will replicate to all domain controllers within a short period of time.

If all domain controllers aren't running at least Windows Server 2012 R2, you won't be able to raise the domain functional level to Windows Server 2012 R2. After you click the Raise button, you will receive an error. Domain controllers running older operating systems will need to be removed from the domain or upgraded.

FOREST FUNCTIONAL LEVELS

Just as domain functional levels provide different capabilities, different forest functional levels provide different capabilities. The different forest functional levels are as follows:

Windows Server 2003   Used when all domains are running at least Windows Server 2003 domain functional level. As a reminder, this is the minimum forest functional level required to support RODCs.

Windows Server 2008   Used when all domains are running at least Windows Server 2008 domain functional level.

Windows Server 2008 R2   Used when all domains are running at least Windows Server 2008 R2 domain functional level.

Windows Server 2012   Used when all domains are running at least Windows Server 2012 domain functional level.

Windows Server 2012 R2   Used when all domains are running at least Windows Server 2012 R2.

You can't raise the forest functional level higher than the lowest domain functional level. You must first upgrade all domain controllers in the domain so that you can upgrade the domain functional level. You can then upgrade the forest functional level.

To verify (and upgrade if needed) the forest functional level that your forest is currently using, follow these steps:

1. Log onto a domain controller.

2. Launch Active Directory Domains and Trusts by selecting Server Manager ➢ Tools ➢ Active Directory Domains and Trusts.

3. Right-click Active Directory Domains and Trusts, and select Raise Forest Functional Level.

   Your display will look similar to Figure 23.7. In the figure, the current forest functional level is Windows Server 2012 R2 and is operating at the highest forest functional level offered at this time.

FIGURE 23.7
Verifying the forest functional level

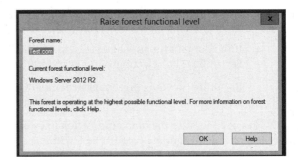

4. If the forest functional level is not at least Windows Server 2003, raise it to Windows Server 2003 by selecting Windows Server 2003 and clicking Raise.

If any of the domains are not raised to the selected forest level, it will fail. In other words, if any of the domains in your forest are currently set to Window Server 2008 R2 domain functional level and you try to raise the forest functional to Windows Server 2012, it will fail.

Once both the domain functional level and the forest functional level have been raised to at least Windows Server 2003, you can then run adprep to prepare your environment for read-only domain controllers if needed.

RUNNING ADPREP

You can use the command-line tool `adprep` to prepare Active Directory for different environments. It modifies the Active Directory schema and update permissions to prepare the forest and domain for different capabilities.

Remember, to support an RODC, you must have at least one Windows Server 2008 domain controller, but other domain controllers could be running Windows Server 2003. Since the domain functional level must be at least Windows Server 2003, all domain controllers must be running at least Windows Server 2003.

If the forest started with domain controllers running pre–Windows Server 2008 or Windows Server 2012 operating systems (such as Windows Server 2003), you need to run both `adprep /forestprep` and `adprep /domainprep`. However, if the forest started with Windows Server 2008 domain controllers or later, these two commands are not needed, but the `adprep /rodcprep` command is still required.

For best performance, you should run `adprep` on computers holding specific roles.

adprep /forestPrep   This should be run on the domain controller holding the Schema Master role. You must be a member of both the Schema Admins and Enterprise Admins groups to run this command.

adprep /domainPrep   This should be run on the domain controller holding the Infrastructure Master role. You must be a member of the Domain Admins group to run this command.

adprep /rodcPrep   This should be run on the domain controller holding the Infrastructure Master role. You must be a member of the Enterprise Admins group to run this command.

IDENTIFYING THE SCHEMA MASTER

If you're unsure which DC is holding the Schema Master or Infrastructure role, you can use one of these easy command-line queries: `dsquery server -hasfsmo schema` or `dsquery server -hasfsmo infr`. The `dsquery` command will return the distinguished name of the server holding the queried role. The distinguished name is a name that is used to uniquely identify objects using the Lightweight Directory Access Protocol (LDAP). For example, a DC named BF1 in the domain controller's organizational unit (OU) in a domain named TEST.com would have a distinguished name of CN=BF1,OU=Domain Controllers, DC=TEST,DC=Com.

`adprep` is available on both the Windows Server 2008 and Windows Server 2012 installation DVDs in the following locations:

Windows Server 2008   `adprep` is located in the `x:\Sources\Adprep` folder of the Windows Server 2008 installation DVD.

Windows Server 2008 R2   `adprep` is located in the `x:\Support\Adprep` folder of the Windows Server 2008 R2 installation DVD. This folder includes both a 64-bit version (named `adprep.exe`) and a 32-bit version (named `adprep32.exe`).

Windows Server 2012 and Windows Server 2012 R2   `adprep` is located in the `x:\Support\Adprep` folder of the Windows Server 2012 installation media. Unlike previous server editions, there is no 32-bit version of the utility available with this release.

Since you will be modifying the schema of the forest, you'll need to log on with an account that is in the Schema Admins and Enterprise Admins groups when running the adprep / forestprep command. For the adprep /domainprep command, you will need to be logged on with an account in the Domain Admins group. The adprep /rodcprep command requires membership in the Enterprise Admins group.

You can prepare your forest to install an RODC by following these steps:

1. Log onto the domain controller that is also the schema master with an administrative account in the Enterprise Admins group.

2. Insert the Windows Server 2012 R2 DVD.

3. From the Start screen type **cmd**, right-click Command Prompt, and select "Run as administrator."

4. Enter the drive letter of the DVD, enter a colon (**:**), and press Enter.

   For example, if the DVD is in the D drive, enter **D:**, and press Enter.

5. Change the path to the x:\support\adprep directory, where x is the actual name of your CD drive, by entering **cd \support\adprep** and pressing Enter.

6. Prepare the forest by following these steps:

   a. Type **adprep /forestprep**, and press Enter. If you are running adprep on a 32-bit version of Windows Server, you would substitute adprep32 for adprep.

   b. An ADPREP Warning dialog box will appear asking you to confirm that all DCs in the forest are running at least Windows Server 2003. Type **C**, and press Enter to continue.

FOREST ALREADY UPDATED ON WINDOWS SERVER 2008 AND WINDOWS SERVER 2012

If the first domain controller in your forest was Windows Server 2008 or later, the forest-wide information was up to date when the server was promoted to a domain controller. There is no harm in running it again and verifying that it is up to date. If it is, adprep will notify you that the forest-wide information has already been updated.

---

   c. adprep will complete several import commands and output the progress onto the screen. This will take a few minutes to complete. When adprep is completed, you will see the message "Adprep successfully updated the forest-wide information" and be returned to the drive prompt.

7. Prepare the domain with adprep by following these steps:

   a. Type **adprep /domainprep**, and press Enter.

      If you are running adprep on a 32-bit version of Windows Server, you would substitute adprep32 for adprep. Please note, there is no 32-bit version of adprep on WS2012. Server 2012 R2 is 64-bit only.

     b. adprep will update the domain and output the message "Adprep successfully updated the domain-wide information."

  8. Prepare the domain to create RODCs by following these steps:

     a. Type **adprep /rodcprep**, and press Enter.

       If you are running adprep on a 32-bit version of Windows Server, you would substitute adprep32 for adprep. Please note, there is no 32-bit version of adprep on WS2012. Server 2012 R2 is 64-bit only.

     b. adprep will update the ForestDnsZones partition, the DomainDnsZones partition, and the domain partition.

       You should see the message "Adprep completed without errors."

It will take time for the changes to replicate through the forest. Once the changes have replicated, you can then successfully promote a domain controller to an RODC.

RODC and Server Applications

Although some server applications will work normally on an RODC just as they would on a regular DC, you'll run into problems with applications that need to have much interaction with Active Directory. Considering that an RODC would be deployed to a remote office that doesn't have much IT support, it's possible that there aren't any other applications out there.

However, if you do have server applications that are deployed in the remote office or you want to install on the RODC, you'll need to do a little research.

Microsoft has posted an article titled, "Applications that are known to work with RODCs," that you can view at `http://technet.microsoft.com/library/cc732790.aspx`. The meat of the article covers what you need to do to make these applications work. Several server applications will work without any problems or with only minor preparation:

◆ Microsoft Internet Security and Acceleration (ISA) Server

◆ Microsoft Office Live Communications Server

◆ Microsoft Office Outlook

◆ Microsoft Systems Management Server (SMS)

◆ Microsoft Operations Manager (MOM)

◆ Windows SharePoint Services

◆ Microsoft SQL Server 2005

A big gotcha is when Exchange Server tries to interact with the global catalog (GC) on an RODC. An RODC can act as a GC but not enough of a GC to service a local Exchange Server instance.

The big message here is if you're trying to deploy an RODC to a remote office and the remote office is using other applications, you need to do some testing. Some will work with no problems, others require some minor tweaking, and others simply won't play with your RODC at all.

Installing the RODC

You can promote a Windows Server 2012 R2 server to a read-only domain controller by following these steps:

1. To start, ensure all of the following:

   ◆ The server has joined the domain.

   ◆ The server has the AD DS role installed.

   ◆ The domain is running at least the Server 2003 domain functional level.

   ◆ The forest is running at least the Server 2003 forest functional level.

   ◆ The forest and domain have been prepared with the following commands, if needed:

      ◆ adprep /forestprep

      ◆ adprep /domainprep

      ◆ adprep /rodcprep

   ◆ The changes from adprep have replicated through the forest.

WHEN IS ADPREP NEEDED?

In some situations adprep isn't needed. If your domain was built using Windows Server 2008 or Windows Server 2012 servers, the schema is already up to date, and adprep isn't needed.

However, if you're running a Windows Server 2003 domain, you'll need to run adprep /domainprep and adprep /forestprep before promoting the first Windows Server 2012 server (which is required before creating an RODC). You'll then need to run adprep /rodcprep before creating the RODC.

---

2. Create a site for your RODC in an existing domain by following these steps:

   a. Log onto a domain controller, and launch Active Directory Sites and Services by selecting Server Manager ➢ Tools ➢ Active Directory Sites and Services.

   b. Right-click Sites, and select New Site.

   c. Name the site **RemoteOffice**, and select a proper site link if you have any created within the domain. If you have not configured any custom site links on your domain yet, select DefaultIPSiteLink. Your display will look similar to Figure 23.8. Click OK.

   d. Review the information displayed in the dialog box, and click OK.

      Check out Chapter 22 in this book for a review of how to completely configure a site link.

   e. Close Active Directory Sites and Services.

FIGURE 23.8
Adding a site to Active
Directory Sites and Services

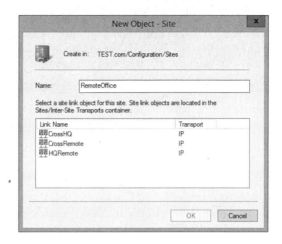

FIGURE 23.8
Adding a site to Active
Directory Sites and Services

3. Create a group that will be used to administer RODCs by following these steps:

   a. Launch Active Directory Users and Computers by selecting Server Manager ➢ Tools ➢ Active Directory Users and Computers.

   b. Right-click the Users container, and select New ➢ Group.

   c. In the New Object – Group dialog box, enter **Remote Office Admins** as the name of the group. Ensure "Group scope" is set to Global and "Group type" is set to Security. Your display should look similar to Figure 23.9. Click OK.

FIGURE 23.9
Adding a group for RODC
administration

4. Log onto the Windows Server 2012 R2 server that you want to promote to an RODC.

   This is a different server than you just used to create a site named RemoteOffice. To continue with the exercise of promoting this server to an RODC we will skip the step-by-step instruction of adding the AD DS role to this server. That step is assumed in this exercise. The same steps covered in Chapter 7, "Active Directory in Windows Server 2012 R2," are followed to promote an RODC that are used to promote primary or secondary domain controllers up to a certain point. We will instead pick up at the post-deployment configuration task first available to you upon the reboot of your server from adding the AD DS role.

5. After the reboot has completed, launch Server Manager, and click the Notifications button.

   You will notice there is warning icon telling you that the post-deployment task of promoting this server to a domain controller is available.

6. Click "Promote this server to a domain controller" to start the Active Directory Domain Services Configuration Wizard.

7. On the Choose a Deployment Configuration page, select the domain you wish to promote this RODC on, and ensure that "Add a domain controller to an existing domain" is selected.

   You will also want to change the credentials that you will use to connect this server to the domain.

8. Click Change and select a user who has rights to promote a server to a domain controller. Your display should look similar to Figure 23.10. Click Next.

FIGURE 23.10
Choosing a deployment configuration

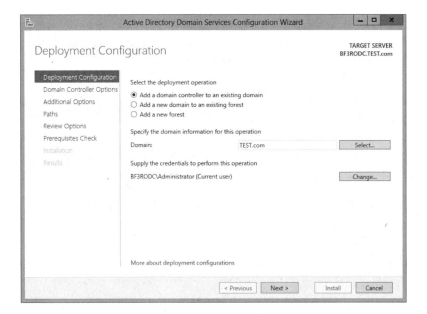

A Windows Security dialog box will appear. The name of the domain you have joined will automatically be prefilled.

9. Enter the credentials of an account that has permission to promote a server to a domain controller within your domain. Your display will look similar to Figure 23.11. Click OK.

FIGURE 23.11
Entering network credentials

10. The Domain Controller Options page will appear. Select the "Domain Name System (DNS) server" and "Read-only domain controller (RODC)" check boxes.

11. Deselect the Global Catalog check box.

12. Select the RemoteOffice site you created earlier in this exercise from the "Site name" drop-down list.

The last configuration option on this page has you create a Directory Services Restore Mode (DSRM) password. Click Next, and your display will look similar to Figure 23.12.

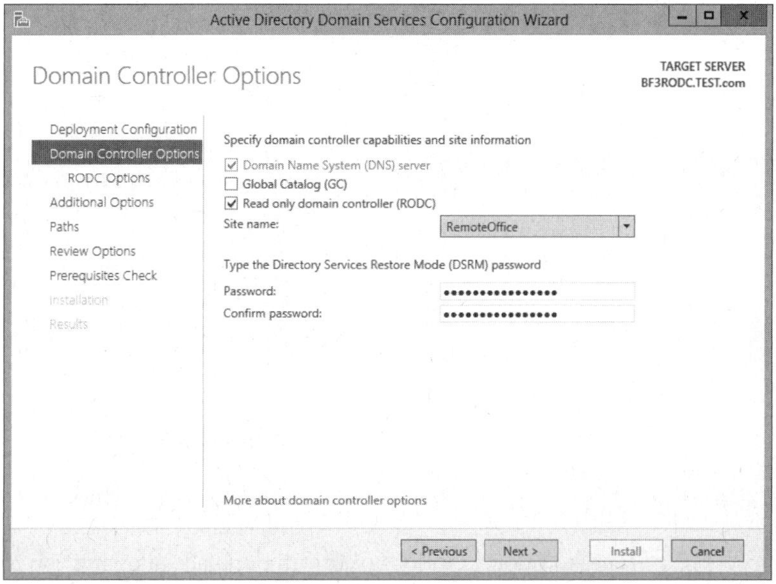

FIGURE 23.12
Domain
Controller
Options page

13. Click Next.

GLOBAL CATALOG OR UNIVERSAL GROUP MEMBERSHIP CACHING

When configuring an RODC in a site, you will need to consider whether to make it a global catalog server or enable universal group membership caching. Chapter 22 includes details that can help you decide what to use in a production site, but for a test lab, you can get away without either.

The RODC Options page will appear. This page will allow you to select a delegated administrator account or group for the RODC.

14. Select and apply the Remote Office Admins group you created earlier in the exercise.

Take note of both the accounts that are allowed to replicate passwords and the accounts that denied password replication abilities to the RODC. If you wish to make any changes to these default policies, simply click the Add button to either allow or deny replicated passwords. Remember that Deny always takes precedence, so if you have an account or group that lives in both columns, then password replication to the RODC will not occur. Your display will look similar to Figure 23.13.

FIGURE 23.13
RODC Options
page

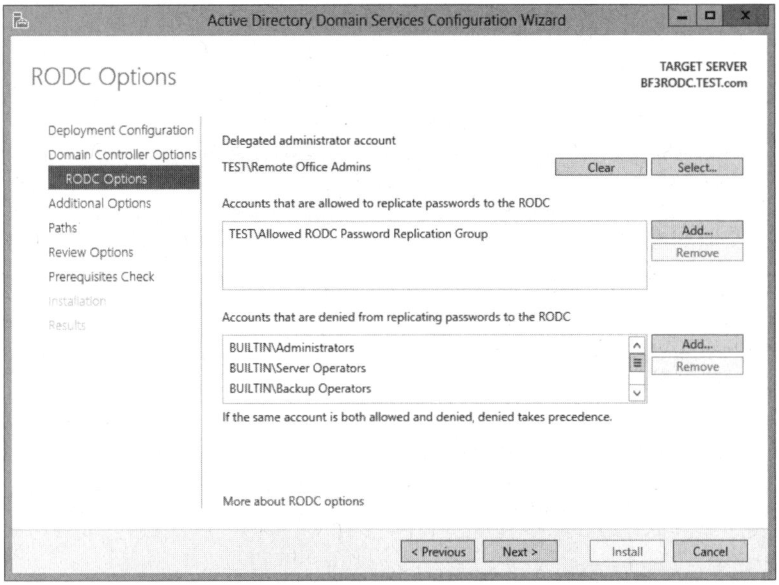

15. Click Next.

The Additional Options page will populate, allowing you to specify a path to install from media and choose a specific domain controller to replicate from if you want to.

16. Keep the defaults and click Next.

On the Paths page, default folder locations are provided for the AD DS database, log files, and SYSVOL. The ability to select a new path to a custom folder location is available to you here, but the default storage locations are more than sufficient for this exercise.

17. Keep the defaults, and click Next to continue.

The Review Options page provides a summary of all the configuration options that you have selected for the Active Directory Domain Services Configuration Wizard.

18. Review the information for accuracy and click Next to start the prerequisites check.

The wizard will run a prerequisites check of your configuration choices to validate and confirm that they are compatible with completing a proper installation of an RODC on the domain. In Figure 23.14 is an example of a successful prerequisites check. If any prerequisites fail, an error message describing what went wrong will be displayed in the "View results" pane. Errors will need to be fixed before the install can continue.

FIGURE 23.14
Prerequisites
Check page

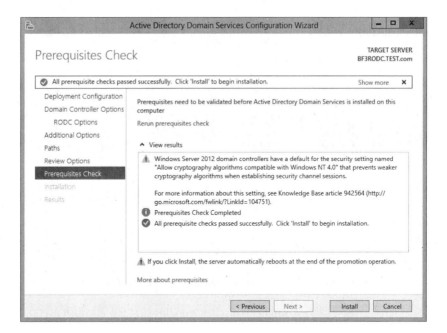

19. Click Install to create this RODC.

The install may take a few minutes to complete. After it has finished successfully, a Results page will be displayed confirming the installation.

20. Review for any warnings or errors, and click Close to complete the wizard.

Installing RODC on Server Core

Server Core will support the installation of an RODC. A new feature available in Windows Server 2012 is that an RODC can be built using the GUI, and then you can have the GUI removed by converting the server to Server Core from a full-blown instance of Windows Server 2012 R2. The same thing applies to servers that are running Server Core exclusively. Those machines can be upgraded to a full-blown GUI if you ever need the additional functionality. If you choose to install an RODC using just Server Core, remember that you will be given a command prompt only, so you'll need to run the AD DS configuration tasks with an unattend file.

You can create the unattend file in two ways:

◆ Run the AD DS configuration tasks on another member server with a full installation of Windows Server 2012 R2. When you get to the summary page, click the Export Settings button, and follow the wizard to save the file. (Chapter 7 showed this process, including how to run both the AD DS Installation and Configuration tasks with the unattend file.)

◆ Create the text file using Notepad. Here's a sample file:

```
[DCInstall]
InstallDNS=Yes
ConfirmGc=Yes
CriticalReplicationOnly=No
DisableCancelForDnsInstall=No
Password=P@ssw0rd
RebootOnCompletion=Yes
ReplicaDomainDNSName= DomainDNSName
ReplicaOrNewDomain=ReadOnlyReplica
ReplicationSourceDC=bf1.test.com
SafeModeAdminPassword=P@ssw0rd
SiteName=RemoteOffice
UserDomain=test.com
UserName=Administrator
```

Once you have the unattend file, you can promote a server to an RODC at the Server Core command prompt.

Viewing the RODC Properties

After you have promoted a server to an RODC, you can view and modify the properties of the server using Active Directory Users and Computers. You can do this on the RODC itself or on any other DC in the domain.

The following steps will show you how to view the different properties of the RODC:

1. Log onto a domain controller with administrative privileges.

2. Launch Active Directory Users and Computers by selecting Server Manager ➢ Tools ➢ Active Directory Users and Computers.

3. Browse to the Domain Controllers container in the domain, and select it. Locate the RODC you created. Right-click it and select Properties.

4. Select the Password Replication Policy tab.

Notice that the Allowed RODC Password Replication group has been granted Allow access, but all other groups are denied.

5. Click the Add button.

6. Select the "Allow passwords for the account to replicate to this RODC" radio button.

Your display will look similar to Figure 23.15.

Add Groups, Users and Computers

Choose the setting for the account you are adding to the password replication policy.

◉ Allow passwords for the account to replicate to this RODC

○ Deny passwords for the account from replicating to this RODC

[OK]   [Cancel]

7. Click OK.

8. Enter **Remote Office Admins** in the text box.

This is the name of a group created earlier in this chapter. If desired, you can also click the Advanced button, browse to locate a group, and add it here.

9. Once you've added a group, click OK. You'll see that your group has been added with the Allow setting.

Notice that you can add or remove any groups using this page. However, the setting of Allow or Deny can be configured only when you add the group. It's not possible to modify the setting directly. If you want to change the setting, you'll need to remove the group and then add it again using the different setting.

10. You should be back on the Password Replication Policy tab of the RODC properties sheet. Click the Advanced button. Your display should look similar to Figure 23.16.

This page has two selections. You can view any accounts that have been cached onto the RODC, and you can view any accounts that have been used to log onto the RODC.

You can use this page to identify any regular users who are logging onto the RODC who may need their accounts added to the password replication policy or the Allowed RODC Password Replication group.

11. Click the Prepopulate Passwords button.

Notice that this takes you to the Active Directory search tool. You can identify any user or computer accounts whose passwords you want to replicate to the RODC before the user actually logs on. This can be useful if the remote office has an unreliable WAN link and you want to ensure a user's account is cached on the RODC before they log on for the first time.

FIGURE 23.16
Viewing the Policy Usage tab

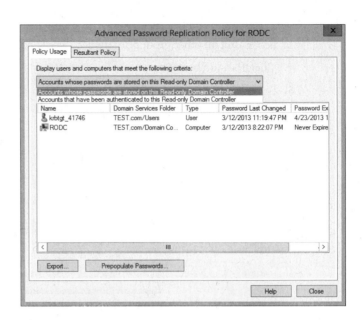

12. Click Cancel to close the Active Directory search page, click Close to close the Advanced Password Replication Policy page, and click OK to close the RODC's properties sheet.

Users or groups added to this page will be able to have their passwords replicated or cached onto this RODC. However, if you want a user or group to be able to have their passwords replicated or cached onto any RODC, you need to modify the Allowed RODC Password Replication group.

Modifying the Allowed List

If you want to allow users to be able to have their passwords replicated or cached onto any RODC instead of just a specific RODC, you can modify the properties of the Allowed RODC Password Replication group by following these steps:

1. Launch Active Directory Users and Computers.

2. Browse to the Users container.

3. Right-click the Allowed RODC Password Replication group, and select Properties.

4. Select the Members tab.

5. Click the Add button.

6. Enter **Remote Office Admins** in the text box.

   This is the name of a group created earlier in this chapter. If desired, you can also click the Advanced button and browse to locate a user or group. Your display will look similar to Figure 23.17. Notice that you can add or remove groups from this page.

FIGURE 23.17
Adding a group to the Allowed RODC
Password Replication group

7. Click OK to close the properties page.

You can follow a similar process to modify the members of the Denied RODC Password Replication group. The Denied RODC Password Replication group includes several groups by default. You can add or remove groups using this page.

SECURITY WARNING

Although it is possible to remove members from the Denied RODC Password Replication group, Microsoft recommends you don't modify any of the prepopulated groups. These groups help ensure that passwords for accounts with elevated permissions are not cached on the server. If a group is removed and a member of the group logs onto the RODC, it is possible their account credentials will be stored on the RODC and subject to compromise if the RODC is stolen or attacked.

Staged Installations

Normally, you need to be at least a member of the Domain Admins group to be able to promote a server to a domain controller. However, it's highly unlikely that a member of the Domain Admins group will be assigned to work at a remote office.

This may not be a problem in many scenarios, but situations may arise when it is difficult for a member of the Domain Admins group to travel to the remote office. With this in mind, you have several options:

Build the RODC at the Main Office and Ship It to the Remote Site This could be expensive and time consuming. If the server is a new purchase, it would be cheaper to ship it directly to the remote office and build it there.

Have a Domain Admin Travel to the Remote Site to Perform the Installation If the office is across the street, this would be an ideal solution. However, if the office is across the country, the cost of travel isn't justified.

Promote the Server Remotely Chapter 17, "Remote Server Administration," covers a lot of the remote administration technologies you can use to remotely administer a server. However, since promoting a server to a domain controller requires a reboot, conventional wisdom dictates that someone should be physically present.

Perform a Staged Installation A staged installation is performed in two steps. A domain administrator prestages the account (which you'll see how to do in the "Prestaging the RODC Account" section in this chapter), and an administrator with limited privileges at the remote location can then promote the server.

USING INSTALLATION MEDIA

Active Directory can be very large, and if the WAN link doesn't have a lot of available bandwidth, promoting a server to a domain controller can take a long time and may prevent other users from performing normal work with this link.

One way to avoid the problem is to create installation media that includes Active Directory. It can be stored on a CD and then shipped to the remote site.

To create the installation media, you need to run `ntdsutil` from the command line of a writable domain controller with the `ifm` command, which is short for "installing from media." The following steps will lead you through the process of creating the media:

1. Log onto a domain controller in the same domain where the RODC will be installed.

2. Launch a command prompt with administrative permissions.

3. Create an empty directory with the following command:

   `md c:\ifm`

   You can name your directory anything you desire and can also store it on a different drive if desired.

4. Type **ntdsutil** at the command prompt, and press Enter. The `ntdsutil` prompt will appear.

5. Type **Activate instance ntds**, and press Return.

   `ntdsutil` will connect to the instance of Active Directory on the domain controller and will output "Active instance set to ntds."

6. Type **ifm**, and press Enter. The `ifm` prompt will appear.

7. Type **Create rodc c:\ifm**, and press Enter.

A folder named Active Directory will be created in the ifm folder with a single file named `ntds.dit`. You can copy this file to installation media such as a CD and ship it to the remote office.

After the installation media is created, you can install it on the remote server using the Active Directory Domain Services Configuration Wizard. On the Paths page select the "Install from media" radio button and browse to the proper file location.

PRESTAGING THE RODC ACCOUNT

Prestaging an RODC account is just a fancy way of saying you create an account for the RODC before it is promoted. You must be a member of the Domain Admins group to prestage an RODC account.

Follow these steps to prestage an RODC account:

1. Launch Active Directory Users and Computers by selecting Server Manager ➢ Tools ➢ Active Directory Users and Computers.

2. Browse to the Domain Controllers OU. Right-click the Domain Controllers OU, and then select "Pre-create Read-only Domain Controller account," as shown in Figure 23.18.

FIGURE 23.18
Precreating an RODC account from Active Directory Users and Computers

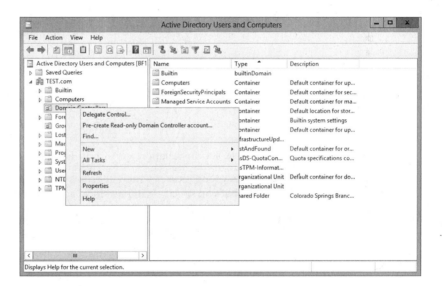

The Active Directory Domain Services Installation Wizard will start.

3. Review the information on the Welcome page and click Next.

4. On the Network Credentials page, click Alternate Credentials, and enter the credentials of an account in the Domain Admins group if the current logged-on credentials are not sufficient. Click Next.

5. On the Specify the Computer Name page, enter the name of the RODC. Your display will look similar to Figure 23.19. Click Next.

6. On the Select a Site page, select the site where the RODC will be placed. Click Next.

   The Additional Domain Controller Options page will appear with the DNS Server, Global Catalog, and Read-only Domain Controller (RODC) choices selected. You can deselect the DNS server or global catalog if desired, but the RODC selection is dimmed.

FIGURE 23.19
Specifying the name of the RODC

7. Click Next.

   The Delegation of RODC Installation and Administration page will appear.

8. Enter the name of a group or user who will promote the server to an RODC at the remote site. The account that you specify will have local administrative permissions on the RODC. Click Next.

9. Review the information on the Summary page and click next.

   The AD DS Installation Wizard will create the account for the RODC, assign appropriate permissions and settings, and report success.

10. Click Finish.

   Active Directory Users and Computers will show the RODC account in Domain Controllers, as shown in Figure 23.20.

Notice that the BF5RODC account has a down arrow indicating that it is not enabled. It will be enabled when the AD DS Configuration Wizard is run to promote it to an RODC. You can also see that the DC type is listed as Unoccupied DC Account (Read-only GC), which indicates it is a prestaged account.

With the account prestaged, the local administrator at the remote site can now run the AD DS Configuration Wizard to promote it.

FIGURE 23.20
A prestaged
RODC account

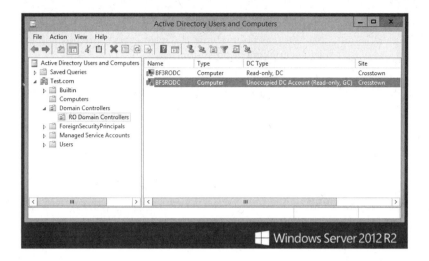

THE SECOND STAGE OF INSTALLING A PRESTAGED RODC

The local administrator can use the following steps to complete the installation of a prestaged RODC. The name of the computer where DCPromo is run must be the same name as the prestaged account.

DON'T JOIN THE DOMAIN

The prestaged account creates an actual computer account in the Domain Controllers OU. Since any computer can have only one account, the prestaged RODC cannot be a member of the domain before it is promoted. Instead, it starts as a member of a workgroup and is added to the domain as part of the AD DS Configuration process.

---

1. Log onto the server using the local Administrator account.

2. If not already installed, add the AD DS role and reboot the server.

3. After the reboot has completed, launch Server Manager, and click the Notifications button.

    You will notice a warning icon telling you that the post-deployment task of promoting this server to a domain controller is available.

4. Click "Promote this server to a domain controller" to start the Active Directory Domain Services Configuration Wizard.

5. On the Choose a Deployment Configuration page, ensure that "Add a domain controller to an existing domain" is selected.

You will notice that the required Domain field is blank.

6. Click the Select button and a Windows Security box will appear, requesting credentials for the deployment operation.

7. Enter the username and password of a user who is in the group that has been delegated permissions to complete the installation, and click Next to continue.

The Domain Controller Options page will display a notification that tells you that a prec- reated RODC account has been created that matches your hostname. The wizard defaults to the configuration option of "Use existing RODC account," as shown in Figure 23.21.

FIGURE 23.21
The AD DS Configuration Wizard detected the prestaged RODC.

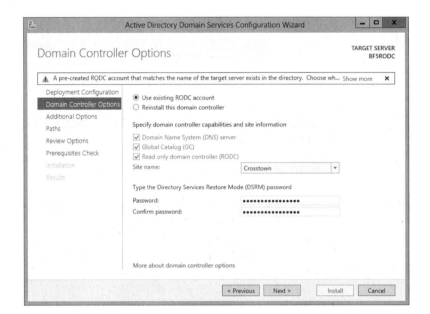

8. Keep the default and click Next to continue.

9. As discussed in earlier exercises, continue through the AD DS Configuration Wizard, making the appropriate selections on each page.

Promoting the RODC may take several minutes to run and requires a reboot upon completion. You can select the "Reboot on completion" check box to allow it to reboot automatically. After the installation has completed successfully, the RODC will be fully promoted to the domain and ready for use.

DNS on the RODC

It's strongly recommended that you install the DNS service on the RODC. In the steps used in this chapter, DNS was selected each time. It has very little overhead and provides significant gains.

If a DNS server isn't located in the branch office but a DC is located there, the users will still have to traverse the WAN link to query DNS to locate the DC. Additionally, normal DNS name resolution will still be required at the remote office.

Take a look at Figure 23.22 as you review the process of a normal logon.

FIGURE 23.22
DNS and the
logon process

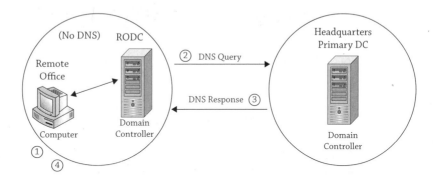

When a user logs on, the following actions are taken:

1. The user enters their credentials and the netlogon service takes over.

2. The netlogon process queries DNS to locate the name and IP address of a domain controller located in the same site as the user. Both the SRV and host record of the server need to be retrieved.

3. DNS responds.

4. The netlogon service passes the user's credentials to the RODC located in the site.

By configuring DNS on the RODC, the DNS queries over the WAN link will be avoided. The netlogon service queries the DNS service on the RODC and then passes the credentials to the RODC.

Active Directory Integrated DNS

If other DNS servers are configured as Active Directory integrated (ADI), then the RODC will also be set as an Active Directory integrated zone. ADI DNS takes advantage of Active Directory replication to replicate zone data and is strongly recommended in Windows domains.

When the sites are configured, Active Directory replication is significantly optimized.

◆ All replication traffic is compressed to about 10–15 percent of its original size.

◆ It can be scheduled to occur after hours or during nonpeak hours.

Read-only DNS

When DNS is added to the RODC, it will be a read-only DNS server. This is actually a new type of zone first introduced in Windows Server 2008 known as a *primary read-only zone*.

Normally, the Start of Authority (SOA) record for an ADI DNS server will list itself as the primary server. In other words, updates can occur on the server. However, an ADI DNS server on an RODC will hold a copy of an SOA record from a writable DNS server.

Traditional DNS works with a single DNS server hosting the primary zone data. You can then add multiple DNS servers hosting secondary zones. The secondary DNS servers are read-only and receive their updates from the primary DNS server.

A read-only ADI DNS server on an RODC works similarly to a primary/secondary DNS configuration. Updates can't occur on the RODC just as they can't occur on the secondary DNS server. However, the biggest difference is that you don't need to manage the DNS zone transfers as you would with traditional DNS servers. Zone transfers are managed through Active Directory replication.

The Bottom Line

Prepare a forest and a domain for RODCs.   RODCs are an excellent infrastructure asset in Windows Server 2012 R2 and can't be added until the forest and domain are prepared. The preparation will modify the schema and permissions.

   Master It   Identify the command that needs to be executed to prepare the forest to support RODCs.

Prepare the domain.   In addition to preparing the forest, you must also prepare the domain before RODCs can be added.

   Master It   Identify the two commands that need to be executed to prepare the domain to support RODCs.

Allow passwords on any RODC.   The RODC can cache passwords for users based on how it's configured. When a user's password is cached on the RODC, the authentication process doesn't have to traverse the WAN link and is quicker. However, a cached password is susceptible to an attack, so privileged accounts should not be cached on the server.

   Master It   What should you modify to allow users to have their passwords cached on any RODC in the domain?

   ◆ The Allowed RODC Password Replication group

   ◆ The Denied RODC Password Replication group

   ◆ The password replication policy

Allow passwords on a single RODC.   It's possible to configure the environment so members of a group can have their passwords replicated and cached to any RODC in the domain. It's also possible to configure the environment so that the passwords will be replicated or cached only to a single RODC.

   Master It   What should you modify to allow users to have their passwords cached on a specific RODC in the domain?

   ◆ The Allowed RODC Password Replication group

   ◆ The Denied RODC Password Replication group

   ◆ The password replication policy

Chapter 24

Creating Larger Active Directory Environments: Beyond One Domain

Throughout this book, we've been dealing with the plain-vanilla Active Directory (AD) implementation of one domain. Although Active Directory can support large enterprises with a single domain, IT shops are faced with administrating multiple domains for various reasons. Sometimes it is part of the plan, yet on occasion it is forced upon them by their company restructuring or acquiring other businesses.

Administrators need to understand the impact of multiple domains in an organization. They need to know the decision points that direct an organization to consider multiple domains. For the most part, growth is to be expected within a healthy organization. Always plan ahead of time by building a scalable infrastructure foundation, and be ready to expand and test the resource limitations of your environment in the future.

In this chapter, you will learn to:

- ◆ Explain the fundamental concepts of Active Directory with clarity

- ◆ Choose between using domains, multiple domains, or multiple forests with an Active Directory design

- ◆ Add domains to an Active Directory environment

- ◆ Manage function levels, trusts, FSMO roles, and the global catalog

The Foundations of Multiple-Domain Designs

Before you consider adding multiple domains to an Active Directory environment, you need to understand the essential concepts. Specifically, you need to understand the logical and physical components of Active Directory to help you plan the Active Directory design. Knowing the benefits and differences between a single domain, multiple domains in the single forest, and multiple forests will assist you in deciding on the proper implementation to meet the needs of your organization.

"Under-the-hood" processes—such as multimaster replication, the Kerberos authentication protocol, and programmed limitations of Active Directory—further define the structure of the Active Directory implementation. Each has pros and cons to consider.

Domains

The typical way to explain an AD domain is to say that it is a security boundary for users and computers in sharing resources and that it uses multimaster replication to distribute the information of these users and computers. That's true, but it's not very illuminating, so let's see what it means.

THE SECURITY BOUNDARY

Every network with any kind of security at all needs to keep a list of information about users—the names, passwords, and other information about people authorized to use the system. You also know that once you have more than one machine, you run into a problem—how do you share that list with all the machines in your company? Recall that you do that by setting up a small number of servers called *domain controllers* with a database of your users, called NTDS.DIT. This essential database file was named after "new technology directory services," and the file extension stands for "directory information tree," which is an industry-standardized format.

The member servers and workstations still have their lists of *local* user accounts, a list maintained in a security account management (SAM) database, but in most cases you won't make much use of these local accounts. Rather, you configure your workstations and member servers to *trust* the list of users on the domain controllers. When someone tries to sit down at a workstation and claims to be a member of your domain, then the workstation takes the name and password offered by the user and hands it to the domain controller (DC), saying, "Is this a valid username and password on your domain database?" And, again, if the DC says that the name/password combination is OK, then the workstation *trusts* that the DC is telling the truth.

The domain defines a security boundary. The domain provides a boundary to administer accounts and resource access. Members of the Domain Admins group are assigned full control over the domain's objects. The domain also controls application of GPOs to its users and computers.

In early versions of Windows Server, the domain was also a boundary for password policies and account lockout options. A great feature of Windows Server 2012 R2 is fine-grained password policies. These allow different password policies to be applied throughout a domain. Although Windows Server 2012 R2 provides this feature, existing Active Directory implementations may have included multiple domains to provide differing password policies prior to Windows Server 2008.

If you have one domain, access to resources is managed through the domain's groups and accounts. If there are multiple domains, a trust relationship is required that allows another domain's users and groups to be recognized by the domain's computers. The trust is similar to a gate in a fence that allows users in or out.

You must fully understand the security boundaries of the domain, forest, and physical domain controllers in order to design a secure Active Directory implementation.

MULTIMASTER REPLICATION

The second part of the domain's definition, *replication*, refers to the process that ensures that every copy of the domain database matches every other one. In other words, if you're sitting in the Topeka office and you create a user account, then that new record—the user account—exists only on the Active Directory domain controller in Topeka at that moment. Part of the job of AD's database engine is to get that new information to the other DCs as quickly as is reasonably possible—that's replication. The *multimaster* part comes from the fact that you can insert a change into the AD database from any DC.

NOT THE ONLY SECURITY BOUNDARY

The domain provides a security boundary for access and control to resources. Yet it is not the *only* security boundary. The domain is not an impenetrable wall where information is protected. Information about the domain is shared between other domain controllers within the Active Directory forest, and a group of domains has a built-in relationship among its members. So, another security boundary is the forest that protects information shared between domain controllers.

User and group information of the domain can be found in global catalog servers, which can be located in other domains. The domain controllers of the forest replicate additional information such as Active Directory configuration data.

The physical security boundary of Active Directory is the domain controllers. A domain controller contains the database on its physical disks and replicates changes to other domain controllers.

If any of these security boundaries are compromised, the Active Directory environment is compromised and subject to the whims of an evil hacker, who is commonly depicted as a black silhouette with a wool cap and trench coat.

When Microsoft became security conscientious, it discovered how damaging to an Active Directory environment the evil hacker can be. He could change configurations with administrative privileges in another domain, and the changes would be replicated to the rest of the domain controllers. With a physical domain controller, he could decrypt passwords for access. This was the primary impetus for Windows Server features of read-only domain controllers and password replication policies for caching passwords. If an evil hacker could get his hands on a domain controller in an unsecured area, at least the domain controller could not replicate changes to other domain controllers, and it would have a limited number of passwords to decrypt.

When you created your first domain by using the Active Directory Domain Services Configuration Wizard, the Active Directory database was created, which would be replicated using the multimaster replication process. The database is structured with three basic parts, or partitions:

Domain Partition   This contains the information of users, groups, and computers that are associated with accessing resources.

Configuration Partition   This contains replication parameters and other nifty configurations to the Active Directory environment like Exchange Server information.

Schema Partition   This contains the definition of objects. It tells Active Directory how to build a user account or a group, and it tells what data can be assigned to a user.

The domain partition is the largest portion of the database and is replicated to only domain controllers within the same domain. It will also be the growing portion of the database because organizations will create far more users, computers, and other domain-based objects than they will add data to the configuration or schema partitions.

If you want to limit the amount of replication across wide area network (WAN) links, you would consider segregating users and groups in one location from other locations by defining separate domains for each location.

That's basically how domains are structured. It is a security boundary administering access to resources and authenticating users. It is also a replication unit in that its information is shared with domain controllers in the same domain. Now let's look at options to expand Active Directory with more domains.

Forests

When considering additional domains in Active Directory, we get back to nature using familiar terms such as *forests* and *trees*. Although you can't start a forest without a tree, we'll begin with the concept of a forest.

After creating the first domain, you can create additional domain controllers for the same domain or create domain controllers for new domains in relation to this first domain. When additional domains are created in relation to this first domain, as you will do later in the "Creating Multiple Domains" section, not all the Active Directory database information is replicated to those domain controllers. The domain partition is not replicated to new domains' domain controllers. Configuration and schema partitions will be replicated to every domain controller in the forest. The phrase *in the forest* means a group of domains that replicate the configuration and schema partitions.

In addition, being *in the forest* means that the domains are built in relation to each other. The relation is the trust built between the domains when you add multiple domains to your forest. A nonconfigurable "two-way transitive" trust is built automatically between the new domain and another one in the forest. This means users and groups of one domain can access resources such as files and printers in the other domain, and vice versa. In fact, users in any domain could access resources in any other domain in the forest.

Getting back to nature, when you created the first domain on the first domain controller, you created a one-domain, one-tree forest. It is important to understand that building a domain from scratch, as you did in Chapter 7, "Active Directory in Windows Server 2012 R2," will create a stand-alone pristine forest that doesn't interact with anything else. It's just as you find in nature. A forest is a collection of trees. It is a security boundary for all the furry woodland creatures to remain hidden and safe. They can peacefully forage for food under the shade of the trees whose branches and roots are interconnected. The furry woodland creatures don't go prancing around to other forests. ("Don't go out into the meadow, Bambi. It's not safe.") So, separate forests don't share information unless manually configured to do so, and users don't venture into the other forests on their own. In addition, you can only add more trees to a forest. Roots of trees don't extend to the other forests. You can't transplant forests next to each other and expect them to be unified. The back-to-nature analogy works.

The security boundaries put in place by both domains and forests help you control object access and security within the environment. Each domain and forest acts as a security tollbooth for objects that want to traverse between entities and share information. These checks and balances help keep the environment secure. It's the forest's responsibility to be the overlying security umbrella for objects that live inside the forest. If you want to ensure one portion of your network is locked down, you may consider using a separate forest to prevent sharing resources with others.

Trees

When creating a new domain in an Active Directory forest, you have to name it. Primarily, a *tree* is a group of domains in the forest with the same last name, or namespace.

THE ROOT OF A FOREST

You would think we were finished with this back-to-nature analogy. However, we have to modify it. The root of a tree is the new namespace for a group of domains such as the Test.com namespace. The root domain of a forest of Active Directory domains is the first domain that you installed in the forest. Occasionally, it will be referred to as the *forest root*. It is commonly depicted at the top of the tree.

For example, the first domain or forest root domain was named Test.com. You can assign a name to the next child domain as Ecoast.Test.com. Thus, it shares the same namespace Test .com, and it is part of the same tree. If you create another domain named Consolidated.com, it doesn't have the same namespace. Ecoast.Test.com is considered a child domain to Test.com. Consolidated.com is a new tree within the forest. Consolidated.com is also a tree root even though it has no child domains.

In an Active Directory forest with just a couple domains, this doesn't make much difference, specifically when it comes to accessing resources through the trust relationships. Things are pretty much equal. With several domains, the effect of how the domains are named impacts the trust relationships. This is because of how the Kerberos authentication protocol works.

KERBEROS AND TRUSTS

Kerberos authentication is similar to dating in high school. Savvy guys learn that getting a date can't be done by simple pick-up lines or cute smiles; they learn to network. They have to get someone to vouch for them.

Say you see a cute potential date in the halls of your school, but you don't know her. You can't talk to her directly, and there's that security device named Mother who gets hot and bothered when you try to call her house. But your security device, Mom, knows the other security device; they're friends. So, you ask your mom to talk to her mother to initiate conversations between the user (you) and the resource (cute potential date).

When your mom isn't friends with the other security device, she knows of another friend who is. This friend is the forest root of the neighborhood; she's a friend to everyone. Now, your mom talks with her friend, who talks to the mother of the cute date. Ba-da-bing, you're there!

Logically, the trust relations between the domains are either parent-child or forest root–tree root. As we mentioned, Ecoast.Test.com is a child domain to Test.com, so it has a parent-to-child relation. Consolidated.com has a forest root–tree root relation. Figure 24.1 illustrates the trust relationship of the forest.

FIGURE 24.1
Active Directory
forest example

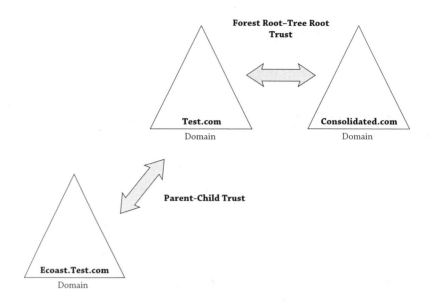

Kerberos works in this fashion across the domains' trust relations. A user account starts with its domain controller for a voucher (a *ticket*). If the resource is in another domain, it has to travel across the trust relations to the resource domain. It needs to go up the parent-child trust, across the forest root–tree root trust, and, if needed, down the other tree's parent-child trust path. If the user is in Ecoast.Test.com, this means the user must contact the Ecoast.Test.com domain controller. If the resource is in Consolidated.com, the Ecoast.Test.com domain controller contacts one in Test.com. Then the Test.com domain controller needs to contact a domain controller in Consolidated.com. It takes three jumps to get to the resource because that is the path the automatic trusts provide. Having taller trees means more jumps, more traffic, and more delay. If you find yourself within a large organization that houses many domains, instead of hopping from one domain trust to another, you could always create a shortcut trust, providing a direct link between two domains that live far away from each other within the domain hierarchy.

You Must Build Trees and Forests Together

Multiple domains sound great, and they of course have been a terrific improvement over the earlier Windows Server releases. But you cannot join existing domains into a tree. Remember, in nature, you can't transplant a forest next to another one. Nor can you join existing trees into a forest; transplanting trees is tough too. Just as the mighty oak comes from an acorn, the only way to build a forest is from scratch. You start with one domain, the forest root. Then you can add a domain to an existing tree (a child domain) or add a tree to an existing forest (a tree root). Other domains will remain outside your forest forever.

YOU CAN'T GRAFT OR PRUNE

So, suppose you were to create an AD domain named Test.com on one network. Then, on a completely separate network totally unconnected to Test.com's network, you create an AD domain named Eastcoast.Test.com. You cannot then attach the two networks and create a tearful reunion of parent and child domains. Nor could you build Consolidated.com and Test.com AD trees in isolation and then connect them, after the fact, to create a forest.

Attaching existing domains to existing trees or forests is called *grafting*, and it can't be done, at least not with the tools supplied by Microsoft. Thus, for example, if Exxon buys Mobil and Exxon already has a domain named Exxon.com and Mobil has a domain named Mobil.com, it's not possible to join them together in a tree with the supplied Microsoft Active Directory tools.

And don't get anxious if you aren't finding any third-party grafting tools. Microsoft just doesn't support it. One of the biggest deterrents from creating a solution that grafts a domain to a forest is the *schema*. The schema that defines objects within Active Directory can also be modified, which we'll discuss in the "FSMOs and GCs" section. If two companies modify their schemas in different manners, it would be impossible to develop a method to merge the differences. Another very important reason not to graft a domain to a forest is security concerns. In the example the names of the domain share the name "Test.com," but because they were not created together, the security identifiers don't match. If you allowed grafting of Test .com into Eastcoast.Test.com, then you'd have a significant hole in security.

Pruning can't be done either. If Consolidated.com is part of the forest and its company is spun off from Test.com, the domain can't run independently from the rest of the domains. There's no little check box to make this happen, and you would be missing all the security of the tree and hierarchy.

You Must Be an Enterprise Admin

Another factor to remember is you can't be just an average domain administrator to build another domain or two into your forest. You may have thought you could rule supremely with your domain admin credentials but you are mistaken. You need to be a member of the Enterprise Admins group.

If you create an AD domain named Test.com and want to create a child domain in its tree named Ecoast.Test.com, then you would log into the server that you wanted to be the first DC in Ecoast.Test.com and create the Ecoast.Test.com child domain. The process for creating the new child domain is very similar to the way your original domain was built. You will still use the Active Directory Domain Services Configuration Wizard for the creation, but you will make a few different selections along the way.

Before the wizard will let you add another domain, it demands the name and password of an all-powerful enterprise admin for the Test.com domain. AD DS configuration will refuse to create a child domain unless it can contact the parent domain right at that moment and get permission. In the same way, if you want to create a second tree in a forest, then the wizard will require that you tell it the name and password of an enterprise admin account for the first tree. (What about the third tree or fourth tree—what account do *they* need to provide? From the second to the millionth tree in a forest, you have to provide an enterprise admin account from the first tree in the forest.)

Planning Your Active Directory Environment

Before you promote the first domain controller, you need to consider the overall vision of the Active Directory network. In addition to the organizational unit structure, DNS namespace, domain controller placement, and replication, which are all part of a single-domain plan, you need to consider the need for multiple domains. Several factors lead to the correct decision. The following is a broad discussion of these factors.

Satisfying Political Needs

"That's *my* data, so I want it on *my* servers!" Because information has become the most important asset of many firms, occasionally parts of management have been reluctant to yield control of that information to a central IT group. And that isn't that irrational: if you were in charge of maintaining a five-million-person mailing list and if that list generated one half of your firm's sales leads, then you might well want to see that data housed on machines run by people who report directly to you.

Of course, on the other side of the story, there is the IT director who wants total control of all the servers in the building, and her reasoning is just as valid. You see, if a badly run server goes down and that failure affects the rest of the network, it's *her* head on the chopping block.

So, the department head or VP wants to control the iron and silicon that happens to be where his data lives, but the IT director who's concerned with making sure that all data is safe and that everything on the network plays well with others wants to control the data and network pieces. Who wins? It depends—and that's the "politics" part.

What does Active Directory do to help you deal with the political problems? Well, not as much as would be preferred—there is no "make the vice presidents get along well" wizard—but AD's variety of options for domain design gives the network designers the flexibility to build whatever kind of network structure they want. Got a relatively small organization that would fit nicely into a single domain but one VP with server ownership lust? No problem, give her an OU of her own within the domain. Got a firm with two moderately large offices with independent IT shops? Two domains and a trust relationship may be the answer. Because Windows Server 2012 R2 AD domain controllers don't need as much WAN bandwidth in comparison with earlier versions, you might find that a single domain makes sense because it's easier to administer than two domains, but it's not impossible from a network bandwidth point of view. And bandwidth utilization is our next consideration.

Connectivity and Replication Issues

More and more companies don't just live in one place. They've purchased another firm across the country, and what once were two separate *local* area networks are now one firm with a WAN need. The design of Active Directory is affected by the available bandwidth across the WAN. The decision point on a single domain or multiple domains is determined by how fast the WAN link is. *Fast* is a relative term. Some designs can tolerate links of 10 Mbps bandwidth, while others can't. This is primarily dependent on the size of the domain partition and how often it is modified.

If the WAN bandwidth can handle it, then you can hook the two offices up and create only one domain. A single-domain design is beneficial because it will be easier to administer. Each site will contain at least one domain controller that manages all the users and computers. If the WAN link is lost, the domain controller in each office can manage logins.

But those domain controllers must communicate with each other whenever something changes, such as when a user's password changes or when an administrator creates a new user account. This replication would occur across the WAN link.

If the link is not capable of supporting the replication traffic, you should consider multiple domains. Thus, the domain partition, the largest part of an Active Directory database, would be limited to the office location in which it resides. The configuration and schema partitions would be replicated across the WAN link, but they would not change frequently. This would greatly reduce the amount of replication traffic.

Active Directory allows you to tell it how it should replicate its information, but all parts of its database are subject to being replicated. So, organizations with multiple locations need to consider whether the available bandwidth can support the replication traffic.

While we're on the subject, the global catalog (GC), which contains objects from every domain, receives changes from domains across the forest. The GC is essential for the user login process and Exchange Server, so it must be located near the users. Thus, every domain will replicate information to GCs across the WAN links to other sites as well. The available bandwidth may not support this traffic; therefore, separate forests may be the ticket.

Multiple Domains: When They Make Sense

When, then, should you use one domain divided into OUs, and when should you have different domains or even different forests? A general rule of thumb is, "Don't use multiple domains unless you must." So, the real question is, "When do multiple domains make sense?" They make sense in a few cases:

Replication Problems Due to Poor Bandwidth   This is probably the best reason. All domain controllers in a domain really need to be online and available to each other all the time. Replication between domain controllers must be consistent; otherwise, the domain controllers will fail. If the WAN link can't support the replication traffic, it's better to implement multiple domains. Think of it this way: suppose you had one office in Chicago and another in Sydney (Australia) with an expensive link between the two. Suppose also that you had 20,000 people in the Chicago office and 150 in the Sydney office. Every time the Chicago people changed their passwords, you'd have to replicate all that traffic over the costly WAN link to the domain controllers in Sydney. That's not a great use of WAN links. It'd be better to just build two domains.

Legal Requirements   There may be legal considerations that would require separate domains and possibly separate forests. Although you don't initially think that multiple forests are part of Active Directory design, there are situations where they are necessary.

Since you can't prune a tree from a forest, you have to consider what the organization is thinking on the topic of restructuring. A spin-off would need to be a separate forest to ensure a clean separation from the main Active Directory forest.

Some national laws may prevent sharing of information across national boundaries. The Global Catalog role lists private information for everyone in the forest. It also includes contacts with their information. Some countries may have a problem with that. Thus, separate forests may be required.

Organizations may have similar regulations for users. Perhaps control of specific user accounts must be contained within four walls of a certain building, or resources must be segregated with tighter security control. Given the legal mandates, a separate domain or forest may be needed. With the potential security intrusions within a forest, separate forests may be required here as well.

Politics   We talked about this in the section, "Satisfying Political Needs."

We Just Found It This Way, Honest!   Your firm buys another firm, and you have to blend the two organizations. Third-party tools can help assimilate the new domain into your existing domain, but that'll be a big undertaking. You probably don't have the time to do that at the moment. In that case, you're living in a multidomain world for a while—multi*forest*, most likely. If you can, however, consider merging the two domains with a tool like the Active Directory Migration Tool, which we'll cover in Chapter 25, "Migrating, Merging, and Modifying Your Active Directory."

Some requirements for multiple domains have been alleviated by improvements in Windows Server 2008 and Windows Server 2012 R2. Password policies can now be set for different users within a domain. In the past, if you wanted that, you had to make separate domains. Branch offices dictated separate domains. For example, the security boundaries were threatened because the domain controller was sitting underneath someone's desk. The entire domain could be compromised if the domain controller was stolen. A separate domain would limit the amount of compromised information. The read-only domain controller and password-caching policies address this security threat.

The Case for an Empty Root

Refer again to Figure 24.1. In that figure, you see an extra tree root domain, Consolidated.com, in addition to Test.com, as well as Test.com's child domain, Ecoast.Test.com. We did that to make the diagram "look" right—but we're used to seeing hierarchies end up at a single point.

In a tree, it's simple to see which domain is the root or top-level domain—Consolidated.com is the top of the Consolidated.com tree, and Test.com is the top of the Test.com tree. But when you build two trees (Consolidated.com and Test.com) into one forest, then which domain is the top, or root, domain? Perhaps there isn't a root and all trees are equal?

In an Active Directory forest built of several trees, there *is* a single-forest domain root. It's just not obvious which one it is.

So, suppose you come across an AD forest that contains just three domains—Test.com, Apex .com, and Consolidated.com. Which domain is the forest root? The answer isn't obvious because the three domains seem to sit at the same level. We don't know of a quick way to find out which domain is the forest root, but here's a slightly slower one. Remember that only the forest root domain contains a group named Enterprise Admins; that's how you'll find the root.

Start Active Directory Users and Computers (Server Manger ➤ Tools ➤ Active Directory Users and Computers). In the left pane of the MMC snap-in, you'll see an icon representing a domain; it looks like three tower PCs clustered together. Right-click that icon, and choose Find. In the resulting dialog box, there's a drop-down list box labeled In, which lets you tell the program which domain to search in; click it, and you'll see that you have the ability to search any one of your forest's domains. Choose one of your top-level domains. Then notice the field labeled Name; enter **enterprise***, and press Enter. If the search finds a group called Enterprise Admins, then you've found the root. If not, open the In list box, and try another domain until you locate the one with Enterprise Admins.

Suppose Test.com turns out to be the root domain in our Test/Ecoast/Consolidated example. There are probably three domains because there are, or were at some time, three different business entities that for some reason are one firm now. Who *cares* if the Test guys happen to be the forest root?

The Consolidated and Ecoast guys do, that's who—whether they know it or not. You see, members of the Enterprise Admins group, which happens to live in the Test domain, have powers in *every domain in the forest*. They're not members of the Domain Admins group in those domains, but they might as well be, because Enterprise Admins have Domain Admin–like powers everywhere.

That means that although in *theory* Test, Ecoast, and Consolidated have separate domains with those nice, convenient security boundaries; in *practice* the Ecoast and Consolidated folks have to hope that the Test guys don't get the lust for power one day and decide to do something scary in the Ecoast or Consolidated domains. The answer? Don't create three domains; create four.

The first domain—the root domain—should be some domain that you're never going to use—e-gobbledygook.com or something like that. Create one administrative account in that domain, including Enterprise Admins in it. Let the CIO create it and then have her write down that account name and password, stuff the paper on which she's written them into her safe, and use the *Sopranos* personnel-termination procedure on anyone who knows the password besides you and her. (Just kidding. But this *is* a powerful account, and you don't want any nonessential people getting access to it.)

At the same time, create the other three domains. You'll need the CIO for a while. She'll have to type in the username and password for that Enterprise Admin account in order to create those three domains. Then you can put away the Enterprise Admin account, and you'll need it only now and then.

This idea of creating a first domain, populating it with only an account or two, and then doing nothing else with it, is called an *empty root* AD design.

Some firms create an empty root domain even if it's just a one-domain enterprise in case they acquire other companies at some time in the future. It's not a bad bit of bet-hedging, and we recommend it to some. Of course, the downside of it is that you need to have a DC or, better yet, two DCs, sitting around running, doing nothing to support the root domain, and each of them will need a copy of Server 2012 or a previous server edition depending on the forest level you want. But, again, it may not be a bad investment——an empty root is one case where we'd break our single-domain-preferred preference.

 Real World Scenario

THE CASE FOR TWO DOMAIN CONTROLLERS

It's a good practice in any environment to address availability and disaster recovery for services and systems. The multimaster replication model provided with Active Directory makes these concerns a piece of cake. All you need to do is install another domain controller in a site for availability or in another site for disaster recovery or both.

It's a *best practice* to add at least two domain controllers into an empty forest root domain. Although it may not have any users or resources in it, it still is an irreplaceable (literally) part of your Active Directory environment. It needs to be highly available and able to withstand a disaster. If it is supported by only one domain controller, that domain controller is going to do a lot of work. If you lose it and can't restore it, you probably will be calling Microsoft Premier Support and then polishing your resume.

Consider the impact of the solitary empty root domain controller:

◆ All Kerberos authentication traffic goes through the forest root domain. Remember, it is "friends with everyone," specifically, the root of each tree.

◆ Time synchronization is centralized on the PDC emulator of the forest root, which happens to be the first domain controller by default.

◆ Two FSMO roles, Domain Naming Master and Schema Master, reside in this domain and on that sole DC.

So, if that solitary empty root domain controller goes down, the rest of the forest will see the effect. You can't make a replica domain controller without one from which to replicate, so you will be stuck performing a cold-iron restore. You may have to rebuild the Active Directory environment from scratch and migrate users and computers to it if a restore is not available.

Active Directory Design Pointers

The purpose of this chapter is to give you an overall idea of how AD's pieces work. Earlier we discussed the primary decision areas for an Active Directory design. We strongly suggest that you peruse the rest of this book before starting to build your AD structure, because the AD *permeates* Windows-based networks. But the following sections provide a few hints on how to get started designing your AD structure.

EXAMINE YOUR WAN TOPOLOGY

Domain controllers in a domain must replicate among themselves in order to keep domain information consistent across the domain. DCs need not be connected exactly 24/7—you *could* just dial connections between branch offices and the home office every day or so and then try to force replication to occur, although that's not simple and may lead to problems down the road—but on the whole you'll find that domains work best if they have a constant end-to-end connection. If you have an area that's poorly or sporadically served by your WAN connections, perhaps it's best to make it a separate domain or a separate forest.

LAY OUT YOUR SITES

Once you know where the WAN connections are, list the sites that you'll have, name them, and figure out which machines go in which sites. Also, document the nature of their connections—speed and cost—to assist Active Directory in using the intersite bandwidth wisely.

FIGURE OUT WHICH EXISTING DOMAINS TO MERGE AND MERGE THEM

You'll probably want to reduce the number of domains in your enterprise. One way to do that would be to merge resource domains into a master domain. The idea here would be that you first upgrade the master domain to Server 2012 and then merge other domains into that master domain as organizational units using the Active Directory Migration Tool (ADMT) or whatever other migration tool you might buy. Merging domains and using the ADMT are topics discussed in detail in Chapter 25.

What Needs an OU, and What Needs a Domain?

As you read earlier, you can divide up enterprises by breaking them into multiple domains. In addition, you can create a single domain and use organizational units to parcel out administrative control, or you can do any combination of those.

This is partially a political question, but you can get a head start by looking at the perceived needs of the organization. Is administration centralized or decentralized? Who manages user accounts? Who manages the resources such as file servers? Do the company's divisions work together closely, or is there not very much collaboration?

The choice of OUs or multiple domains is to divide the network to the controlling forces so they can administrate it. OUs provide particular admins to control the computer, user, or group accounts that they are responsible for. So if admins have just this need, organizational units are the way to go. The multiple-domain choice is dependent on who will manage the domain controllers. If there is a separate group of admins who will control the domain controllers apart from the forest root domain, the additional domain would be justified.

From a technical point of view, there are really only a few reasons to use more than one domain, as you've read. The biggest reason is replication traffic. If you have two large domains connected only by a slow WAN link, then you may find that it makes sense to keep them as separate domains. But think carefully about it—Active Directory is very efficient at using WAN links for domain replication traffic.

Develop Names for Your Domains/Trees

Active Directory allows a wider variety of domain names, but sometimes you can have too much of a good thing with too *many* options. If you're going multidomain, how will the domains fit together? Do you divide geographically, by division, or by function? Where are the lines of control in the organization now?

It's important to understand that the names of domains are primarily political. With the exception of the parent-child trust relation, there is hardly any other technical impact concerning the name. The name will occasionally be reflected to the users through technology such as domain-based Distributed File Systems (DFSs) and depend on how they log onto computers. So, because the name will be seen by users, management might care what the domain is named.

Get the DNS Infrastructure Ready

Once you know the names of your domains, you need to map out the DNS infrastructure. Know which servers will support it. Plan how clients will be able to resolve internal names and external names. Remember the following:

◆ Plan a DNS zone whose name matches your AD domain name, and don't be afraid to use an imaginary top-level domain.

◆ It's recommended that you don't use your externally registered DNS names.

◆ Although Windows Server 2012 R2 sets up the DNS infrastructure automatically, it will be rare that you will be starting from scratch. If the DNS namespaces are already in place, ensure the DNS server supports dynamic DNS updates and service resource records. You needn't use a Microsoft DNS server, but it's not a bad idea, particularly with Active Directory integrated zones.

◆ If you have to use your company's registered DNS names, split-brain DNS is the *right* idea to protect your zones from external prying eyes for 99 percent of the AD.

OVERALL AD DESIGN ADVICE

There's a lot to consider in building your AD, and only you know what your organization needs and wants—we can't pass along a standard one-size-fits-all design for AD. But overall, remember the following:

◆ Use sites to control bandwidth and replication.

◆ Use organizational units to create islands of users and/or computers, which you can then delegate administrative control over.

◆ Use domains to solve replication, security, legal, and possible political problems.

Use forests to create completely separate network systems. If, for example, your enterprise had a subsidiary that wasn't completely trusted (in the human sense, not the AD sense) and you were worried that the automatic trust relationships (in the AD sense) created by common membership in a forest might lead to unwanted security links, then make them separate forests. The value of separate forests is that there is no security relationship at all between two forests unless you explicitly create the relationship using a trust relationship.

Creating Multiple Domains

After the hard thinking is accomplished and the boss buys the idea of how you want to implement Active Directory, it is high time to put your ideas on the street. If not in production, you can at least deploy your desired Active Directory structure in a lab. So you need to know the straightforward steps for building multiple domains.

The process of creating a new domain is similar to creating the first domain. Beforehand, the domain name must be determined. Since changing a domain name is a hugely intrusive process, it needs to be locked down, as in "There's no changing it." Like the initial domain, the new domain controller needs to be prepared to support Active Directory. It must also be able to resolve the forest root domain names through DNS. Then you'll promote the first server to a domain controller to create the new domain.

Naming Multidomain Structures

Real-world experience has shown that in large enterprises a hierarchy of domains works best. In Active Directory, we call this a *tree structure* despite the fact that computer trees tend to have their roots up in the air and their "leaves" at the bottom. (We know, some of the back-to-nature analogy isn't consistent.) Microsoft designed AD to use DNS as a naming system, and

DNS is hierarchical in nature anyway, so Active Directory exploits this happy coincidence and encourages you to build multidomain enterprises as hierarchies.

The multiple-domain namespaces must be supported by DNS. The preferred method is letting AD DS handle this via the Configuration Wizard. Child domains, since they have the same last name as an existing parent domain, have a DNS namespace. However, the Active Directory Wizard will automatically configure the new domain controllers to support the child domain's namespace. A new tree's namespace doesn't need to be created either because the domain controller promotion will automatically configure DNS to support it. However, the prospective domain controller needs to resolve names of the forest root domain to execute the new tree creation without error.

If the DNS environment is established beforehand, it will need to support service resource records and dynamic DNS updates.

You Can't Always Get What You Want

Although the domain's NetBIOS name's importance has been diminished, you will still see this name throughout the network. Prior to creating the domain, double-check to see if the NetBIOS name is available. The utility will do that too. If it isn't available, the utility will generate something else. If you are not aware of the name's availability, you could be stuck with a misnamed domain.

We have seen test domains assigned with the desired NetBIOS name. Thus when the real domain is built, the conflicting names become readily apparent and stop the process in its tracks.

Preparing the DC for the Second Domain

For our example, you'll now set up the first DC in another domain—Ecoast.Test.com. As we mentioned earlier, a big change from earlier server editions to Windows Server 2012 R2 is the requirement to set up DNS for a domain. In earlier Windows versions, you would need to get DNS ready prior to building the domain. The configuration of AD DS will identify the need to build DNS and run through the steps for you.

After the creation of the child domain, you will see the following:

◆ An Active Directory integrated zone on the new domain controller for the child domain name, such as Ecoast.Test.com

◆ A forwarder DNS server listing on this domain controller for the Test.com DNS servers

◆ A delegated DNS subdomain on Test.com to the new domain controller

First, set up a machine that will be the domain controller for Ecoast.Test.com. Name the server **EC1** to resemble the first domain controller in the Ecoast.Test.com child domain. It will need to be able to support Active Directory for the given number of users and computers in your organization. In a production environment, you should plan to build at least two domain controllers for the domain. The second domain controller will be a replica of the first one and provide fault tolerance of the domain database.

To use Active Directory, you need to install the Active Directory Domain Services role. Just as you did with the first domain controller for Test.com, the Add Roles and Features Wizard allows this role to be turned on. It will install all the binaries required to set up a domain controller including the .NET Framework and the DNS service.

Keep in mind, now that DCPromo has been deprecated, AD DS takes over with the process of promoting a server to a domain controller. This happens in a two-stage process; add the AD DS role to a server, and as a post-configuration task after a reboot, promote the server to a domain controller in the new domain using the Active Directory Domain Services Configuration Wizard.

Prior to promoting the server to a domain controller, ensure that you have the logon credentials for an account in the Enterprise Admins group.

Creating a Second Domain

After the role is installed, you can push on with installing the new child domain. Logged in as an administrator for EC1, run the post-configuration task for promoting the server to a domain controller. You can accomplish this by either selecting the option via Notifications in Server Manager or by navigating to the AD DS Management window pane in Server Manager and running the task.

The AD DS Configuration Wizard starts out as shown in Figure 24.2; you tell the wizard that you want to create a new domain in an existing forest but not to create a new tree. The "Select domain type" drop-down will default to Child Domain. Select the parent domain name to join (Test.com) and put in the name of your new domain (Ecoast). When you select the parent domain name to join, Windows Security will prompt for credentials from an Enterprise Admin–level account. Enter the appropriate information, and click Next to continue.

FIGURE 24.2
Choosing a deployment configuration for a new domain in an existing forest

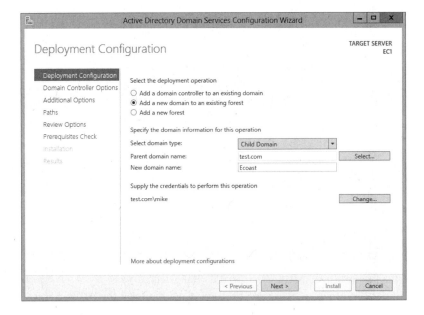

On the Domain Controller Options page, "Domain functional level" will be defaulted to the operating system used to deploy this primary domain controller for the new domain. In this example, the domain functional level is Windows Server 2012 R2. We will discuss domain functional levels in the next section. A few other options are available to you on this page of the wizard; make sure DNS server is selected, choose whether or not to make this domain controller a GC server, place the domain controller in the site created prior to this task, and set a Directory Services Restore Mode (DSRM) password. Your screen should look similar to Figure 24.3. Click Next to continue.

FIGURE 24.3
The Domain Controller Options page

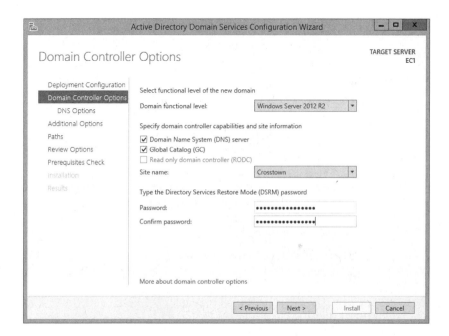

Verify that the "Create DNS delegation" check box and proper credentials are provided on the DNS Options page, and then continue on to the Additional Options page of this wizard. This page is an important one. Here you will assign the NetBIOS name of your new child domain, as shown in Figure 24.4. The name will be defaulted from the name you entered on the Deployment Configuration page. Ours reads ECOAST. Remember that since this is a child domain, it will take the suffix of the parent domain. Even though we only enter ECOAST here, the full domain name will read Ecoast.Test.com, and this domain controller's Fully Qualified Domain Name (FQDN) will read Ec1.Ecoast.Test.com.

FIGURE 24.4
The NetBIOS
domain name

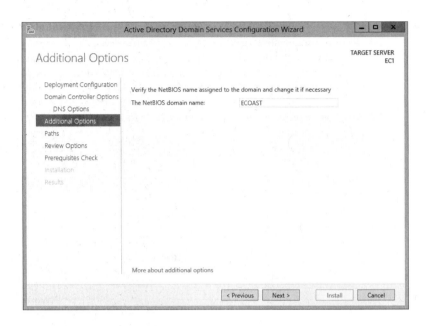

From this point on, you'll just answer the AD DS Wizard's questions as you did for the first domain, so we'll spare you the rest of the wizard pages.

Before leaving this topic, we'll make a few points about using AD DS to build domains. AD DS is kind of rigid about the order in which you create domains:

1. The first domain that you create in a forest is the forest root domain, and there's no changing that.

2. You should create at least one additional domain controller for the new domain. This provides fault tolerance for the domain.

3. You have to add domains by creating them through AD DS in relation to the existing domain.

   For example, you can't create a domain named Green.com and another named Yellow.com separately and then decide later to merge them into a forest. Instead, you must first create Green.com as the first domain in a forest and then create Yellow.com as the first domain in a new tree but in an existing forest.

After the reboot, you should examine your fully outfitted Ec1.Ecoast.Test.com. Check its IP configurations with **ipconfig /all**, and verify that it lists itself as the DNS server (::1 for IPv6 and 127.0.0.1 for IPv4). Open the DNS Manager console on the new domain controller, as shown in Figure 24.5. Look for the Ecoast.Test.com zone listing the domain controller Ec1 as the name server. The Ecoast.Test.com zone should have the DC's A record and the domain's SRV records registered in it.

Check the properties of the DNS server; you'll see there is at least one forwarder listing for BF1.Test.com or the domain controllers of the parent domain, as shown in Figure 24.6.

FIGURE 24.5
The DNS zone
for the new
domain

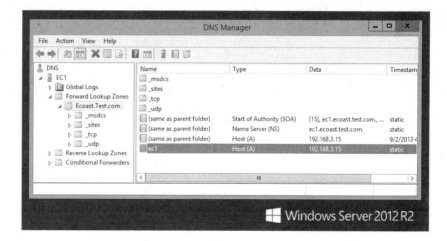

FIGURE 24.6
DNS forwarders
on the new
domain
controller

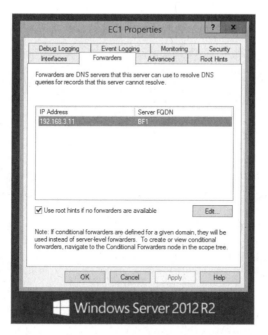

Also check BF1's DNS Manager console to make sure that delegation of the Ecoast subdomain is added, as shown in Figure 24.7. Additional checks include the same ones as for building any domain controller, such as the creation of database files, the folder, and services.

FIGURE 24.7
Delegation of
the subdomain

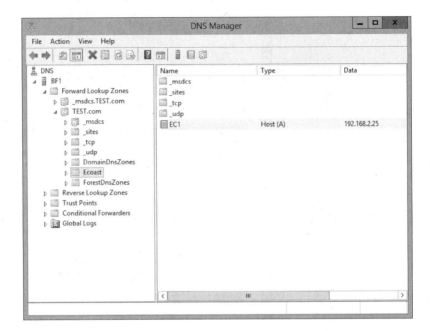

Once again, Windows Server 2012 R2 automatically configures the DNS infrastructure to support the new domains. If things aren't flying as expected, you may have to configure the DNS integration manually. Refer to Chapter 6, "DNS and Name Resolution in Server 2012 R2," for information about doing this and troubleshooting other DNS issues.

MISSPELLED DOMAINS

Misspelling a domain during this procedure is possible. In writing this book, we have created the Ecaost.Test.com domain and the Ecoast.Test.com.com domain in our virtual lab environment. Since we weren't paying attention, the wizard accepted the typing and got the "pencil" flying. So, when building a new domain in a production environment, have at least two sets of eyes on the monitor, and double-check what was typed in the summary screen.

Please note that there is a difference in renaming a misspelled domain name during creation and renaming a domain that has already been deployed and operational in the environment. It is much easier to get it right the first time. If you have to change a domain name at a later date, you have to run through a tedious and very intrusive process using random commands to complete the name change.

If the name is still misspelled after the creation of the first DC, you can run through AD DS Configuration Wizard again on the same server. In this case, it will identify that the server is a domain controller. It will assume you want to remove Active Directory from it. The only option it will provide is whether this is the last domain controller in the domain. For this case, it is. The eraser end of the pencil gets busy and cleanly removes the instance of Active Directory from this server and the environment.

Any other solution would be intrusive to Active Directory such as the domain rename process or destructive such as shutting down and removing the operating system.

Functional Levels

Functional levels are the configuration options used to manage legacy interoperability, and control which features are available in the domain or forest. They are also used for compatibility between multiple versions of Windows Server during operating system migrations and upgrades on domain controllers. Each Windows Server operating system has its own specific advanced features and unique functional level that integrates between various operating systems to provide you with the smooth operation of Active Directory Domain Services throughout the environment. We will explore the types of functional levels and the considerations in changing them.

Domain Functional Levels

In Windows 2000–based ADs, there were only two possible conditions: either a population of DCs that were all 2000-based or a population of DCs that included both 2000 and NT 4—that's why there were only two modes. But ADs that include Server 2003 through Server 2012 R2 can have several possible combinations of DCs, each with its own mode. The preferred term is *functional level*; we sometimes write it as *domain functional level* to distinguish it from *forest* functional levels that you'll meet soon.)

You change a domain's functional level by opening Active Directory Users and Computers and right-clicking the icon representing the domain. Choose Raise Domain Functional Level, and you'll see a dialog box like the one shown in Figure 24.8.

FIGURE 24.8
Viewing a domain's functional level

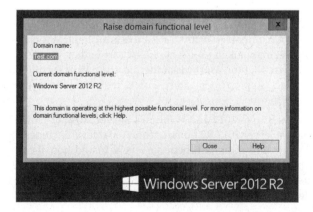

In this case, the domain is at the Windows Server 2012 R2 domain functional level, which is the highest domain functional level available at this time. Also, the dialog box doesn't provide the option of changing it. Functional levels can be changed upward but not downward. In this case, it's as far as we can go with this domain.

Changing the domain functional level should be performed with caution and consideration. Since it is a one-way operation, you need to ensure all domain controllers within the domain can meet that functional level. Otherwise, a legacy domain controller can be left out of the loop. It will not get the proper replication and end up with stale or incompatible data within its database.

Here's what you get from each functional level:

Windows Server 2003 Domain Functional Level To get here, you need to have all your DCs in the domain running Windows Server 2003. There are several exotic features here. These changes don't affect your job significantly. You may never see them working for you:

◆ Domain rename; see Chapter 25.

◆ User and computer containers can be redirected.

◆ Constrained delegation.

◆ Selective authorization. This is related to trusts.

◆ Logon timestamp update.

Windows Server 2008 Domain Functional Level Again, you need to have all your domain controllers on this version. However, there is a caveat in the Windows Server 2008 R2 help. Specifically, if you plan to add earlier versions such as Windows Server 2008 or 2003 as domain controllers, you could set the domain functional level to this value. Here are some features of this level:

◆ DFS replication support. In Chapter 14, "Creating and Managing Shared Folders," you read about the improved DDFS replication. These improvements can be applied to the folder as well.

◆ Advanced Encryption Services (AES 128 and 256).

◆ Track last interactive logon information for users on workstations.

◆ Password policies.

Windows Server 2008 R2 Domain Functional Level Yes, even this version has its own domain functional level. Its sole feature is authentication mechanism assurance. This modifies the security token for users passed to member servers for access to resources. Basically, it notifies you that the user was authenticated with a certificate instead of username/password credentials. Applications and resources then can be configured to grant permission based on this information.

Windows Server 2012 and Windows Server 2012 R2 Domain Functional Level The Windows Server 2012 R2 domain functional level includes all of the great features provided by the previous domain functional levels. In addition, it comes with a few extras that are worth mentioning. Now with Dynamic Access Control (D AC) in Windows Server 2012, Kerberos 5 authentication has changed quite a bit. Using the new Kerberos Key Distribution Center (KDC) support for claims, compound authentication, and Kerberos armoring, KDC administrative template policy settings give your domain controllers the ability to support claims and compound authentication for Kerberos armoring and Dynamic Access Control. This new policy setting is also available at the client level for Windows 8. Kerberos Authentication and Dynamic Access Control are discussed more in depth in Chapter 15, "Dynamic Access Control: File Shares, Reimagined."

There's another important reason to get to at least 2003 functional level or above. You can't upgrade your *forest* functional level until all the domains in the forest are at 2003 domain functional level. You also cannot take advantage of read-only domain controllers unless your environment is at least at the 2003 domain functional level.

Forest Functional Levels

When you upgrade DCs or domains in an existing forest or if you create a new forest, then 2012 assumes for safety's sake that not all DCs and domains are entirely 2012 based, and so it will not stretch its wings to use all the new capabilities that 2012 offers unless all the domain controllers in the forest are operating at domain functional level of 2012. Unless you are creating a brand-new forest using Windows Server 2012 R2 most organizations will need to go through an upgrade process from 2008 to 2012 R2 As part of that process, you will need to raise the forest's functional level.

You raise a forest's functional level with Active Directory Domains and Trusts (Server Manager ➢ Tools ➢ Active Directory Domains and Trusts). Right-click the icon in the left pane labeled Active Directory Domains and Trusts, and you'll see the dialog box shown in Figure 24.9. Notice that you don't right-click the domain icon. If you do right-click the domain icon, you'll see the Raise Domain Function Level option.

FIGURE 24.9
Raising a forest's functional level

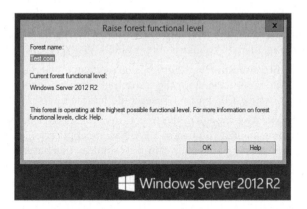

As shown in Figure 24.9, in this example, the forest functional level is as high as it can go just as with the domain functional level. In addition, you can't lower the functional level.

The nice thing is you can have domains running at a lower operating system functional level living in a forest that is operating on a higher operating system functional level. It's not uncommon to see a Windows Server 2008 R2 domain in a Server 2012 R2 forest. They work together and operate on different levels to leave room for migrations and interoperability between operating systems. As long as the domain functional level is Windows Server 2003 or higher, the domain can be part of a Windows Server 2012 R2 forest.

You can't go to the Windows Server 2012 R2 forest functional level unless every single DC in every single domain in the forest is running Windows 2012 R2 or higher. But think about that: doesn't that mean that all your domains must be in 2012 R2 domain functional level before Domains and Trusts lets you raise the forest functional level? No, it doesn't, as it turns out:

1. When you open the dialog box shown in Figure 24.9, the message displayed can vary depending on the current state of your environment. Since you built this test forest on Server 2012 R2 you'll notice that the message displayed is "This forest is operating at the highest possible functional level." If you were to try and raise the forest functional level to Windows Server 2012 R2 while still running DCs on Windows Server 2008, you'll get a message that says, "You can't go to 2012 R2 level," and tells you exactly which DCs must be upgraded before you can go to 2012 R2 forest functional level.

2. When you right-click AD Domains and Trusts, the forest does a quick census of its list of DCs:

    ◆   If they're all 2012-based DCs, then you get the option to raise the forest functional level.

    ◆   If not, you get the option to see which ones must be upgraded.

So, what do you get from this improved functional level? You get several items that we've discussed elsewhere but that we'll summarize here:

Windows Server 2003 Forest Functional Level   This contains the following:

Transitive Forest Trusts   One trust makes every domain in each of two forests trust each other—but only if both forests are at 2003 forest functional level.

More Flexible Group Membership Replication   Server 2000's old problem of "if you change a group's membership and I change that same group membership at about the same time, then one of our changes will be lost" goes away in a 2003-level forest.

Better Intersite Routing   Server 2003 saw a massive rewrite of the code that handles site-to-site replication, with the result that whereas 2000-based forests would fall apart at about 200 sites, 2003-based forests could handle up to 5,000 sites.

GC Fixes   Any change to the structure of the global catalog, such as the type that usually happens when you install an AD-aware application, causes GCs on a 2000-level forest to completely panic; they dump their entire databases and rebuild them from scratch, causing massive replication loads over the network. Server 2003–level forests are much smarter, because their GCs focus only on the changes to the database, rather than restarting from square one.

Schema Redefines   AD's somewhat inflexible schema structure loosens up a bit on a 2003-level forest. You still can't delete or undo schema changes, but the schema manages itself to ensure that you'll never have one AD-aware app accidentally step on another AD-aware app's schema changes.

Windows Server 2008 Forest Functional Level   There's actually nothing special about this level. So, there is no impetus to switch to this.

Windows Server 2008 R2 Forest Functional Level: Active Directory DS Recycle Bin   This offers the sweet ability to restore Active Directory objects while Active Directory DS is running. It's about time!

Windows Server 2012 and Window Server 2012 R2 Forest Functional Level   These levels include all the great features from all the other previous forest functional levels. No new addition features have been included at this time.

As anyone who lived through an initial AD rollout under Windows Server 2003 knows, the road to Windows Server 2008 R2 was sometimes long, and we're sure that'll be the case when moving a forest to Windows Server 2012 R2 But once there, it's worth it. As we've observed elsewhere, you *paid* for this stuff; you may as well get what you paid for.

FSMOs and GCs

Thus far, you've seen how to set up AD multiple domains, but there's more to AD planning than that. Making an AD run also requires knowing about the following:

Operations Masters and Global Catalogs   These are particular functions that some DCs must assume. Placement of these roles need to considered to ensure proper Active Directory functioning.

Time Synchronization   Believe it or not, AD simply will not run unless all the AD members and DCs all agree on what time it is to within five minutes. This is controlled by one of the operations masters, namely, the PDC emulator of the forest root domain.

In the next few sections, we'll take on this kind of intermediate-level AD planning and operation. First, we'll talk about operations masters.

Multimaster vs. Single-Master Replication

As we've mentioned, one of the things that differentiates AD domains and DCs from NT 4 and earlier domains is *multimaster* replication rather than *single-master* replication. Under multimaster, *any* DC can accept changes to the user account, so a local Tulsa admin could start up an administration tool such as Active Directory Users and Computers and make a change to a user's account on an available domain controller. Because any DC can accept changes, any DC is then a "master," which is why it's called *multimaster.*

But Not Everything Is Multimaster

In general, Active Directory tries to carry this notion of decentralized control throughout its structure. In general, all DCs are equal, but, to paraphrase George Orwell, some DCs are more equal than others. Those DCs are the ones that serve in any of five roles called either *Operations Master* or *Flexible Single Master of Operations* roles. By the way, no one says *Flexible Single Master of Operations*; it gets shortened to the acronym FSMO and is pronounced "fizz-moe." Strictly speaking, FSMO was the phrase that Microsoft used through most of Windows 2000's development process, but it renamed FSMOs to *Operations Masters* late in the beta process. As a result, you'll hear some people say *Operations Master*, but the FSMO name has stuck with many, even now in the days of Windows Server 2012 R2 probably because it's quicker to say "fizz-moe" (and more fun). So, for example, the phrases *Domain-Naming Operations Master* and *Domain-Naming FSMO* refer to the same thing.

Certain jobs in the AD just need to be centralized, and so we end up with FSMOs. For example, take the job of creating new domains. Suppose you have a Test.com domain, and someone decides to set up a new domain controller and thereby create a child domain, Ecoast

.Test.com. Creating a domain causes AD to build a lot of data structures—a domain for Ecoast.Test.com—causing more work for the global catalog, changes to the overall forest AD database, and so on. Now imagine that two people both try to create a new domain named Ecoast.Test.com at roughly the same time. That could be a nightmare—the parent domain would be receiving conflicting requests to modify the AD database, there might be potential security issues, and it might keep the whole forest from functioning.

Domain Naming: A FSMO Example

To avoid the situation of duplicate names and to oversee the forest structure, Microsoft developed one DC to act as a sort of central clearinghouse for new domain creation, and whenever you attempt to create a new child domain or new domain tree, AD DS stops and locates the one DC in the entire forest that is the "keeper of the domain names." That DC is said to be the domain-naming FSMO or domain-naming operations master. If AD DS on the new would-be DC cannot establish contact with the domain-naming FSMO, then it flatly refuses to go any further.

Remember, even if you have a worldwide enterprise with dozens of domains, hundreds of offices all around the world, thousands of domain controllers, and hundreds of thousands of workstations, there is one and only one computer that serves as the domain-naming FSMO. If it were, for example, in the Okinawa office and you were in the New York office sitting at a server trying to create a new domain in the forest, then your computer would be unable to proceed until it contacted the Okinawa computer and got its OK on building the new domain.

Why Administrators Must Know about FSMOs

In general, you won't think about the DCs that act as FSMOs in your forest much at all. However, you *do* need to do a little planning about which DCs will be FSMOs, and you need to know how to assign a particular FSMO role to a particular DC.

That reminds us, you *do* have to manage the FSMO roles by hand. The AD automatically picks a particular DC to act in each FSMO role—the first DC that you install—but it's not bright enough to move those roles around. So, for example, consider this scenario. Your company decides to play around with AD and sets up its first DC on a "junk" machine in a test lab—say, the old 1 GHz system with 1 GB of RAM. They see that AD works pretty well, so they start buying some "big guns" to be the production DCs. They roll out these big DCs, and things seem to work pretty well.

They work well until one Monday, folks come to work, and AD apparently still thinks it's the weekend because AD is not working. Administrators find that they can't create new user accounts or join machines to a domain. Someone tries to install Exchange Server, but it complains about not having the authorization to change something called the *schema*. The Cleveland office was scheduled to create a new child domain, but that's refused, too. The remaining domain controllers complain that they can't find the PDC, and account changes like password resets are clearly not getting to those backup domain controllers.

What happened? Well, someone was playing around in the lab that weekend and needed an extra machine with which to do some experimenting. The 1 GHz system was just sitting there, still running Server 2003 and acting like an AD domain controller. But it wasn't really relevant anymore, the weekend noodler reasoned, because the firm now has several dozen big DCs running. So, the experimenter wiped the hard disk on the 1 GHz system and put Linux on it.

You see, by default, AD assigns the FSMO roles to the first DC that you install. In this little story, that 1 GHz system quietly served a very important role. But now it can't. And AD isn't smart enough to figure that out and then nominate a new computer in that role. You might say that our "sparkling" forest has lost its "fizz-moe." It's now your job to transfer the FSMO roles to other DCs.

It's important to know where the FSMO roles live and operate in your environment. We have a few general recommendations on where certain roles should live in the domain and forest. Try not to spread roles across multiple domain controllers as much as possible. For the most part, the primary domain controller of the forest root domain should house the PDC, Schema Master, Domain Naming Master, and RID Master roles. Having them all centrally co-located makes them easier to manage. Technically speaking, the Infrastructure Master role can operate on any domain controller in an environment where every domain controller is a GC server. If you are in a multidomain environment where not all of your DCs are GCs, you must place the Infrastructure Master role on a domain controller that does not host the global catalog. We will take a look at each role in depth over the next few sections.

Global Catalogs

We've mentioned global catalog servers throughout the chapter. So, you might expect that with their hype they would fall into this FSMO category. They don't really, since they are not "single." Although you start out with one, you can enable other domain controllers to assume the role. However, like the FSMO roles, it is important to know which domain controllers have the role and where they are located.

 **Real World Scenario**

DECOMMISSIONING WITH DCPROMO & AD DS

This little story about the 1 GHz domain controller is not unrealistic. We've encountered situations where an uninformed admin wiped away the hard drives of a failed domain controller since they already had a couple replica domain controllers keeping the domain going. "It was old anyway." It just happened to be the first DC of the domain.

There is one case where AD automatically moves the FSMO role—when you use DCPROMO or AD DS to demote a domain controller that holds one or more FSMO roles into a member server. It finds another appropriate domain controller and moves the FSMO roles to that DC. In that case, decommissioning that old domain controller would have resulted in no problems. So, perhaps the best advice here is, "When you want to get rid of a domain controller, always use DCPROMO or AD DS to decommission it before fdisking it."

If you run into a disaster and can't recover the system, there are methods, discussed next, to move the FSMOs from that failed domain controller.

For starters, the first one is the first domain controller you build. Since all the necessary roles are required from the get-go, the FSMOs and the Global Catalog role are slammed onto that first server. So, with the previous example, the ghost of the 1 GHz workstation will rear its ugly head when the global catalog is needed in the logon process. Errors in the other domain controllers and workstation event logs will probably give you a subtle hint of this condition.

The global catalog has a little bit of everything. It has a subset of the properties or attributes for every object in the forest. Remember, an object includes users, contacts, groups, computers, and other entities described in Active Directory. So, all domain controllers that are GCs will have personal information for every user in the forest even if the global catalog isn't in the same domain as the user.

How many GCs are necessary? Typically it is dictated by how many sites you have. There are many uses for GCs. The most prominent is assisting in the logon process. If all users are assigned user principal names (UPNs) such as bdavis@test.com within a multiple domain forest, the domain controllers need to resolve to which domain they actually belong. The global catalog provides this information. So, it would be nice if a global catalog were in a site where the users are logging onto the domain.

Since a global catalog has all of this information, Active Directory–aware applications like Exchange Server love global catalogs. Exchange Server uses the GC to find all recipients and distribution group members in the organization. It would be nice if the Exchange Server instances had a GC in the same site.

You'll have to weigh this against the potential replication traffic that the servers will receive from the other domains. All domains will replicate their domain information to each global catalog. Typically, the importance of global catalogs for logon and Exchange Server significantly outweighs this consideration.

Once you have decided how many GCs are needed, you need to log on as an enterprise admin and enable domain controllers within the forest. This is done in the Active Directory Sites and Services console. Drilling down through Sites, to a specific site, and to the Servers object, you'll see that the properties of the NTDS settings have a Global Catalog check box with a lot of punch, as shown in Figure 24.10.

FIGURE 24.10
Enabling a global catalog

FSMO Roles

Active Directory has five FSMO roles:

- Schema Master

- Domain Naming Master

- Relative Identifier (RID) Master

- PDC Emulator

- Infrastructure Operations Master

There is only one Schema Master FSMO in the entire forest and similarly only one Domain Naming Master FSMO. Each domain in the forest, however, has its own RID, PDC, and Infrastructure Operations Master.

We look at each role's function and consider any requirements relating to its assignment on domain controllers.

Schema Master

Schema is the word for the structure of the AD database—the fields. It's the definition of things in the database, such as the usernames, passwords, and so on. In some senses, it's the directory to your Active Directory.

EXAMINING THE SCHEMA WITH THE SCHEMA SNAP-IN

You can look at the schema with the Active Directory Schema snap-in. It's not sitting in Administrative Tools, however; you'll have to follow these steps to run it:

1. Open a command prompt, and type **regsvr32 schmmgmt.dll**. You should get a message box that says "DllRegisterServer in schmmgmt.dll succeeded." Click OK to clear it.

2. Open up a Run dialog box, enter **mmc /a**, and then press Enter to start the Microsoft Management Console in Author mode.

3. Click File and then Add/Remove Snap-in.

4. Select the Active Directory Schema snap-in, click Add, and then click OK. The Active Directory Schema snap-in is now loaded and ready for use.

   You'll see a screen similar Figure 24.11.

   Here, we've highlighted the part of the schema that tells you that there's an attribute called userPrincipalName, which is one of the login names available to the user.

5. Double-click it, and you'll see a dialog box describing its properties, but they'll probably be grayed out, even if you're a member of the Enterprise Admins group.

   Recall that even enterprise admins can't modify the schema—you must be a member of the Schema Admins group to do that. But if you're a schema admin, then you'll see the properties page with everything enabled, as in Figure 24.12.

FIGURE 24.11
Active Directory
Schema snap-in

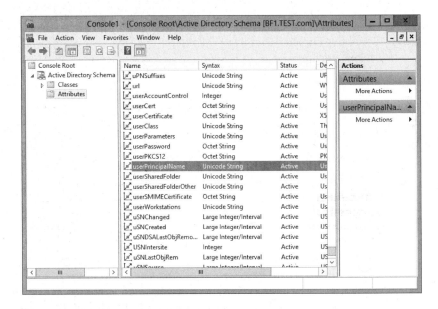

FIGURE 24.12
Properties page
for UPN

Like the enterprise admin, a schema admin is a user account that is a member of a group within the forest root domain. The group is named Schema Admins. By default, the Administrator account of this domain populates this group.

Notice the "Replicate this attribute to the Global Catalog" check box. You can, using this check box, control which attributes can replicate in the GC.

UNREGISTERING A DLL

To remove the Active Directory Schema snap-in from your server for security reasons, perform the following command:

```
REGSVR32 /u C:\Windows\System32\schmmgmt.dll
```

THE SCHEMA AND YOUR AD

Will you change the schema very much or very often? Probably not. But there are few things that you should bear in mind.

First, remember that there is only one schema for the entire forest; it's not meaningful to talk of changing the schema for a particular domain, because any changes to the schema are changes to the schema of an entire forest. So, a bit of innocent schema-dabbling will affect every domain controller in every domain in the forest, because all of those DCs will have to be notified of the changes and thus will have to make room for the new schema items in their copy of the schema, which burns up some CPU and disk time.

Second, when will you change the schema? Usually the only thing that you'll do that will cause the schema to change will be adding new server-based applications such as Exchange Server 2013 or other server-based apps that were designed with Active Directory in mind. Microsoft products will manage the schema update for you as part of the installation. You don't have to do it manually. In Chapter 25, you will read about using adprep for preparing earlier domains for Windows Server 2012 R2 This will modify the schema as well.

KEEPING SCHEMA CHANGES ORDERLY

Inasmuch as schema changes affect the whole forest, it's reasonable to say that the schema *does* change. You want it to change in an orderly fashion, and it'd be really bad if two people both modified the schema at the same time.

For that reason and because there's only one schema for the entire forest, there's only one computer that can approve schema changes in the entire forest. That computer is said to have the *schema FSMO* role. By default, the AD places the schema FSMO role on the first domain controller that you install in the first domain of the forest. So, the first DC that you set up should be a well-protected one!

You can see which computer is the schema FSMO computer like so:

1. Right-click the Active Directory Schema object.

2. Choose Operations Master to see a dialog box like the one shown in Figure 24.13.

You must be a schema admin to move the schema FSMO role.

FIGURE 24.13
Viewing the
schema FSMO

PLANNING FOR SCHEMA CHANGES...AND CONFLICTS

Before leaving the subject of the schema, we'll offer a thought about how it will affect your organization. There are very few AD-aware applications. But now let's consider what happens if conflicts arise within the schema. Let's imagine that you work at a big university with a lot of independent departments. The university's forest has many domains—Chemistry, English, Microbiology, Astronomy, Music, Geology, and others—that all live in a single forest and therefore have only one schema. Now imagine that Astronomy just got a cool new application that will aid its professors in researching something, and so they put it in AD. It adds a few dozen things to the schema, including a Magnitude field, which stores a star's brightness. Then suppose Geology buys some neat new application that will help them in seismology research, which also adds a few things to the schema—such as a Magnitude field, where they'd store information on earthquake power. What happens when Geology tries to install an application that wants to create a schema field whose name already exists? Well, to make a long story short, it depends...and not all possible outcomes are good.

Our point is this: Geology should have *known* when it first installed its app that the app would conflict with an existing one. But how could Geology have known? Well—and here's the part you won't like—every forest should consider keeping a testing lab up and running all the time, with a DC or two that run a working but independent version of your forest. Prior to rolling out any server-based apps, you should test them on the test lab to see whether they create schema changes that will make AD bellyache.

What's that you say? Astronomy and Geology are used to running things independently, not having to ask each other's permission to run applications? Yes, we can believe that—research and educational institutions have that tradition. But once you make the decision to stitch your organization together into a single forest, then your organizational components must communicate a bit more to keep things working. And *somebody* is going to have to keep that test lab up and running all the time, which means staffing it and finding space, machines, and software for it. Golly, that argument about how Windows lowers total cost of ownership doesn't seem quite as compelling now. At least Windows Server 2012 R2 offers Hyper-V. This test lab gives you a reason to buy it and play around with it.

Basically, in this case, AD is just another piece of software that says, "If you want to use me, you'll have to modify the way that you do business," and that seems awfully backward—sort of like a mouse manufacturer saying, "Gosh, we're sorry that our revolutionary mouse design doesn't fit your hand. Have you perhaps considered surgery?"

Domain Naming Master FSMO

You've already met this one—we used this FSMO as the example earlier of why you'd need an operations master in the first place. There is only one of these for the entire forest. As with the schema operations master, the AD places the Domain Naming Operations Master role on the first domain controller in the first domain.

DOMAIN NAMING MASTER PLACEMENT

The Domain Naming FSMO role should be placed *only* on a DC that is also a global catalog server. Apparently the AD developers got a little lazy and decided that, inasmuch as the global catalog knows about things from all over the forest, the Domain Naming FSMO could exploit the GC's knowledge.

RID Pool FSMO

One of the things that any native-mode AD domain controller can do is to create new accounts (user and machine) without having to go find some "central" or "primary" DC. In the Windows Server world, everything has a unique identifier, called its *security ID* (SID). SIDs look like this:

S-1-5-21-*D1-D2-D3-RID*

The 1-5-21 applies to all SIDs. What we've called *D1*, *D2*, and *D3* are actually three randomly generated 32-bit numbers. When AD first creates a domain, it generates these three unique 32-bit numbers, and they remain constant for any SID generated in that domain. And it's not just a matter of a separate D1/D2/D3 for a domain—the local SAM on a workstation or member server also has its own set of three unique 32-bit numbers.

So, for example, if you created a domain named Bigfirm.com and it happened to come up with D1=55, D2=1044, and D3=7, then every SID in Test.com would look like S-1-5-21-55-1044-7-*something*, where *something* is a 32-bit number. In other words, all SIDs in a domain are identical, save for the last 32 bits. Those last 32 bits are the only *relative* difference between SIDs; these bits are therefore called the *relative identifier* (RID). Some RIDs are fixed, such as the SID for the default Administrator account on a computer.

Anyway, if a DC needs to generate a new SID, then it *knows* what the first part of the SID will be. It just needs a unique RID. So, there's one DC in every domain that hands out pools of 500 RIDs at a clip. Each DC can then create up to 500 accounts before it has to go back to this one central DC, which then doles out 500 more RIDs. The computer that hands out the 500-RID bunches is called the *RID operations master*, or the RID FSMO. By default, it is the first DC installed *in a domain*. Note that there is an RID FSMO for each domain, not just one per forest.

You can view the RID FSMO assignment in the Active Directory Users and Computers snap-in. In the snap-in, right-click the domain object, and choose Operations Master from the context menu. The dialog box displayed in Figure 24.14 shows the RID Operations Master assignment as BF1.Test.com. The other tabs, PDC and Infrastructure, show the assignments of the PDC Emulator and Infrastructure Master roles for the domain.

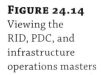

FIGURE 24.14
Viewing the
RID, PDC, and
infrastructure
operations masters

Infrastructure Operations Master

In a multidomain network, it is, according to the Microsoft folks, difficult to quickly reflect changes to group and user accounts across domains. So, you might rename a user or put a user in a group in the domain that you administer, but that change might not show up in other domains for a while. This period of time is based on the replication between domain controllers. With a single site with a couple domain controllers, it may be only 5 minutes. Within a single site with a large number of domain controllers, this period could be as long as 15 minutes. If the replication goes between sites, it is subject to the replication configurations of site links such as its interval and schedule. Something called the *infrastructure operations master* speeds this process up. You change its role in the same way that you'd change the RID FSMO. There is one infrastructure FSMO per domain.

INFRASTRUCTURE MASTER PLACEMENT

There's one oddity about the Infrastructure Operations Master role: don't make a DC that is a global catalog server into an infrastructure FSMO unless you have a single-domain forest. It is OK if all DCs in a domain are GCs. The very first DC that you set up assumes all five Operations Master roles, which means that initially your infrastructure master is on a global catalog server. That's OK so long as you have one domain, and of course that's true if you have only *one* DC. If you have a single-domain forest, the global catalog will have the same information as the single domain, so it's one and the same. When multiple domains become a reality, it's time to consider reassigning the role to another domain controller.

PDC Emulator FSMO

Finally, there's the PDC emulator FSMO. It's a very important one.

Arbitrarily dubbing one of an AD domain's DCs as the "primary" DC then makes sense. And although an AD domain is in mixed mode, the PDC emulator FSMO is more than just an emulator; it's the only DC that can accept account changes.

But does that mean that a PDC emulator becomes irrelevant once you're in native mode and have no pre-2000 boxes around? Not at all. The PDC emulator still serves two extremely important functions. Since we covered replication earlier in the book, you probably know that replicating AD changes can take time—sometimes a significant amount of time. So, suppose the following happens: you're working in St. Louis and need your password changed. You call the company help desk, which is, unknown to you, in Ottawa. The help-desk person changes your password, and it seems that all will be well.

But what DC did the help-desk person change your password on? Well, she probably did it on a DC that was physically close to her, in other words, a DC in Ottawa. So, an Ottawa DC knows your new password. But how long will it be before your local St. Louis DCs know your new password? Well, it could be hours. Does that mean that you'll have to just twiddle your thumbs for a few hours waiting for your new password to find its way to Missouri? Well, if you were talking about any other attribute besides a password, then the answer would be yes—but passwords are special.

When an admin changes a password on some DC somewhere, that DC immediately contacts the system acting as the PDC emulator FSMO for that domain. So, the PDC FSMO almost always knows the most up-to-date passwords. When you try to log into the domain, it is a local DC that tries to log you in. As you tell that DC your new password, the local DC is inclined at first to decline your logon, because the password that you offer doesn't match what the DC has. But before declining your logon, the DC connects to the PDC emulator FSMO for its domain and double-checks, and if the password that you gave your local DC matches the new one that the PDC has, then you're logged in.

This "high-priority replication" also occurs for one other user attribute—account unlocks. Thus, when a user forgets his password and retries to log on with the wrong password over and over, then not only does he need a new password but he probably also locks himself out of his account. So, when the administrator resets the user's password, the admin probably also has to unlock the account. Immediately replicating the new password without replicating the account unlock wouldn't be very helpful.

That's one important job for the PDC FSMO. What's the other one? We'll cover that in an upcoming section, "Time Sync."

Transferring FSMO Roles

If you want to move an FSMO assignment to another domain controller, you are going to transfer the role. This process is pretty simple. As you saw earlier, you can view the FSMO assignment in three different MMC snap-ins:

- ◆ The Active Directory Domains and Trusts snap-in manages the Domain Naming Master role.
- ◆ The Active Directory Schema snap-in manages the Schema Master role.
- ◆ The Active Directory Users and Computers snap-in manages the PDC Emulator, RID Master, and Infrastructure Operations Master roles.

So, to transfer the role, you can perform the following procedure:

1. Open the specific snap-in for the desired role.

2. Change the focus of the snap-in to your target domain controller, which will receive the role assignment:

   a. Just open the respective snap-in.

   b. Right-click the top object in that MMC snap-in.

   c. Choose Connect to Domain Controller.

      The dialog box displayed in Figure 24.15 is produced. Then you can select the target domain controller and click OK.

FIGURE 24.15
Changing the focus DC

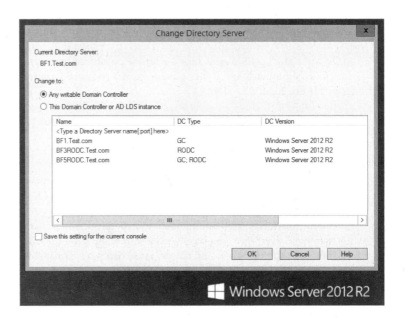

3. View the role by right-clicking the top object of the tree in the left panel and selecting Operation Masters.

   The new dialog box displays the current FSMO assignment. Figure 24.14, shown earlier, shows tabs for the domain-related roles (RID, PDC, and Infrastructure). Figure 24.13 shows the Schema role.

   In each of these dialog boxes, the bottom field displays the target domain controller.

4. To transfer the role to the target domain controller, click the Change button.

You must be a domain admin for a given domain to transfer the RID, PDC, or Infrastructure role for that domain. You must be an enterprise admin for transferring the Domain Naming Master role and a schema admin to transfer to Schema Master role.

Transferring FSMO roles is very simple via the GUI, as you've seen. But there's a catch: you can use the GUI to transfer an FSMO role *if the current FSMO is up and running*. If you fdisked the computer that was acting as your domain naming master, then there's no one around to "approve" transferring the role to another computer. In that case, you don't just *transfer* the Operations Master role—you must, using your best pirate accent, "Seize the master! Argh."

If your PDC emulator or infrastructure master goes offline, then it's perfectly safe to transfer those FSMO/Operations Master roles to another computer, and you can actually do it through the GUI. It'll tell you that the operations master is offline and that you can't transfer the role, but ignore it and click Change anyway.

But to seize the RID, domain naming, or schema FSMO, you'll need to use a command-line tool, ntdsutil. You can also transfer the FSMO roles with ntdsutil, but the GUI is so much easier. You could use this to administer Server Core installations. You start it from the command line by typing **ntdsutil**. Then do this:

1. Type **roles**; ntdsutil will respond by changing the prompt to fsmo maintenance:.

2. Type **connections** to point to the computer that you are going to transfer the FSMO role to. ntdsutil will respond by changing the prompt to server connections:.

3. Type **connect to server** *servername*, where *servername* is the target domain controller that you want to transfer the FSMO role to.

4. Type **quit** to return to FSMO maintenance.

5. You can use the question mark to list the possible commands. This will give you the correct spelling of the roles.

   ```
   fsmo maintenance: ?

   ?                              - Show this help information
   Connections                    - Connect to a specific AD DC/LDS instance
   Help                           - Show this help information
   Quit                           - Return to the prior menu
   Seize infrastructure master    - Overwrite infrastructure role on connected
   server
   Seize naming master            - Overwrite Naming Master role on connected
   server
   Seize PDC                      - Overwrite PDC role on connected server
   Seize RID master               - Overwrite RID role on connected server
   Seize schema master            - Overwrite schema role on connected server
   Select operation target        - Select sites, servers, domains, roles and
                                    naming contexts
   Transfer infrastructure master - Make connected server the infrastructure
   master
   Transfer naming master         - Make connected server the naming master
   Transfer PDC                   - Make connected server the PDC
   Transfer RID master            - Make connected server the RID master
   Transfer schema master         - Make connected server the schema master
   ```

6. Type **transfer** *fsmotype master*. You'll get a dialog box request for confirmation if ntdsutil finds that it cannot contact the current FSMO to get its approval. Confirm that you want to force a transfer.

7. If that works—if there are no error messages—then you're finished. But if the transfer fails, then type **seize *fsmotype* master**. That's a bit more drastic, but it always works.

8. Type **quit** twice, and you should be finished.

For example, here is a session where we seized the RID Master role from a computer called Bf2.Test.com to a computer named Bf1.Test.com (what we typed is in bold; the computer's responses are not bold):

```
C:\>ntdsutil
ntdsutil: roles
fsmo maintenance: connections
server connections: connect to server bf1.test.com
Binding to bf1.test.com ...
Connected to bf1.test.com using credentials of locally logged on user.
server connections: quitfsmo maintenance: transfer rid master
ldap_modify_sW error 0x34(52 (Unavailable).
Ldap extended error message is 000020AF: SvcErr: DSID-03210CB1, problem 5002
(UNAVAILABLE), data 1722

Win32 error returned is 0x20af(The requested FSMO operation failed.
The current FSMO holder could not be contacted.)
)
Depending on the error code this may indicate a connection,
ldap, or role transfer error.
Server "bf1.test.com" knows about 5 roles
Schema - CN=NTDS Settings,CN=BF1,CN=Servers,CN=Default-First-Site-Name,CN=Sites,
CN=Configuration,DC=test,DC=com
Naming Master - CN=NTDS Settings,CN=BF1,CN=Servers,CN=Default-First-Site-Name,
CN=Sites,CN=Configuration,DC=test,DC=comPDC - CN=NTDS Settings,CN=BF1,
CN=Servers,CN=Default-First-Site-Name,CN=Sites,
CN=Configuration,DC=test,DC=com
RID - CN=NTDS Settings,CN=BF2,CN=Servers,CN=Default-First-Site-Name,CN=Sites,
CN=Configuration,DC=test,DC=com
Infrastructure - CN=NTDS Settings,CN=BF1,CN=Servers,CN=Default-First-Site-Name,
CN=Sites,CN=Configuration,DC=test,DC=com

fsmo maintenance:
```

Hmmm, the transfer didn't work. Let's seize:

```
fsmo maintenance: seize rid master
Attempting safe transfer of RID FSMO before seizure.
ldap_modify_sW error 0x34(52 (Unavailable).
Ldap extended error message is 000020AF: SvcErr: DSID-03210CB1, problem 5002
(UNAVAILABLE), data 1722

Win32 error returned is 0x20af(The requested FSMO operation failed.
The current FSMO holder could not be contacted.)
)
Depending on the error code this may indicate a connection,
```

```
ldap, or role transfer error.
Transfer of RID FSMO failed, proceeding with seizure ...
Searching for highest rid pool in domain
Server "bf1.test.com" knows about 5 roles
Schema - CN=NTDS Settings,CN=BF1,CN=Servers,CN=Default-First-Site-Name,CN=Sites,
CN=Configuration,DC=bigfirm,DC=com
Naming Master - CN=NTDS Settings,CN=BF1,CN=Servers,CN=Default-First-Site-Name,
CN=Sites,CN=Configuration,DC=test,DC=com
PDC - CN=NTDS Settings,CN=BF1,CN=Servers,CN=Default-First-Site-Name,CN=Sites,
CN=Configuration,DC=test,DC=com
RID - CN=NTDS Settings,CN=BF1,CN=Servers,CN=Default-First-Site-Name,CN=Sites,
CN=Configuration,DC=bigfirm,DC=com
Infrastructure - CN=NTDS Settings,CN=BF1,CN=Servers,CN=Default-First-Site-Name,
CN=Sites,CN=Configuration,DC=test,DC=comfsmo maintenance:
```

SEIZE AND SLICK

If you seize an RID, domain naming, or schema master, make sure that the old master never comes online again, or AD havoc will result! If this domain controller comes up again, it will think it still has the FSMO role. So, contention between the old one and the new one will occur.

It is highly recommended that you remove the network cable and erase the hard drive. We recommend grabbing the installation CD and booting it up to delete the system partition for a clean installation.

Time Sync

When it comes to replication and trusts, the AD needs all of its domain controllers to pretty much agree about the current time and date. They don't have to be *exactly* the same, but they need to be close—Kerberos fails if a domain controller, and the system trying to use that DC to authenticate, disagree about what time it is by more than five minutes. Windows servers include a service called the Windows Time service that keeps all your Windows workstations and servers in good time sync.

Machines in AD stay in sync this way. The PDC emulator FSMO of the forest root—the first created domain's first domain controller—is the "Master Time Server Dude." All other servers automatically create a hierarchy, sort of like a "telephone tree," to distribute time synchronization information. Everyone below that top dog automatically gets time synced from someone above it in the hierarchy, specifically:

- Member servers and workstations synchronize to the DC that logged them in.

- DCs in a domain all look to the DC in their domain that holds the PDC Emulator Operations Master role.

- If there is more than one domain in the forest, then there will be more than one PDC emulator, because each domain has a PDC emulator.

The PDC emulators must agree on the time, so they choose one of their numbers to be "the source"—the PDC emulator for the *first* domain in the forest, the forest root. So, again, it's the PDC Emulator FSMO for the forest root domain that is the ultimate time authority.

But who syncs that top dog, the forest root domain's PDC FSMO?

First, odd as this sounds, you don't need to sync the FSMO. All that matters in AD is that all the servers think it's the same time. Sure, it'd be nice if it was the *actual* time, but that's not necessary. If your whole enterprise were 10 minutes early, that would constitute no problem for AD, as long as *all the* servers are 10 minutes early.

TIME ZONES AND TIME SYNC

But it's *very important* that you set the time zones correctly on all your systems! AD stores and syncs time in "universal time," so in its heart of hearts AD is always working on Greenwich, England, time. Windows operating systems use the time zones to understand the system clock's time and to display time that you'll understand. So, if you were to leave everyone's time zone set to Pacific and then just set the system clocks to whatever the local time was, each of those systems would think that the time in universal time was hours different, and synchronization would fail. Such a situation will drive you crazy, because you'll be looking at a DC and a workstation whose time *looks* identical—but unknown to you, their time zones are set differently—so, it's a mystery why they won't talk to one another. It wouldn't be if you could see their beliefs about what the *universal* time was! You can quickly check a system's time zone by opening a command prompt and typing: `w32tm /tz`.

But as long as we have this hierarchy, let's do it right and sync that root domain PDC somewhere reliable. You could purchase a Network Time Protocol appliance that syncs its time with the Global Positioning System (GPS). Or you could save a buck or two and just let the Internet set your time.

The suite of Internet standards includes a way of sharing time information called the Simple Network Time Protocol (SNTP); see RFC 1769 at www.faqs.org/rfcs/rfc1769.html. Many, many machines on the Internet serve as NTP servers and will provide up-to-date time information to any machine running an NTP client. Fortunately, Windows Server systems include an NTP client—in fact, it is *the* protocol that AD uses to synchronize its member systems. You can tell a Windows Server 2012 R2 machine to synchronize its clock from a given Internet time server with the `w32tm` command:

```
w32tm /config /computer:bf1 /update /manualpeerlist:time.windows.com
/syncfromflags:manual /reliable:yes
```

Let's parse out some of the strange parameters:

/computer The name of the computer. In this case, we would use the name of the forest root PDC emulator.

/Reliable Yes, it is a reliable time source for other computers.

/manualpeerlist This is the list of specific time servers you want to sync with.

/syncfromflags This is manual because you want to sync with only the servers in the manual peer list.

You can specify multiple time servers by separating them with spaces and surrounding them with double quotes, like so:

```
w32tm /config /computer:bf1 /update
/manualpeerlist:"time.windows.com AnotherTimeServer.com StillAnotherOne.com" /
syncfromflags:manual /reliable:yes
```

If you forget what server you told the clock to sync with, you can find out by typing this:

```
w32tm /query /computer:bf1 /source
```

By default, the forest root's PDC FSMO will try to synchronize with its time source once every six minutes until it successfully connects with the time source. Then it does it again in six minutes and again six minutes later. It keeps resynchronizing every six minutes until it has successfully synchronized three times in a row. Then it reduces its frequency to once every 100 minutes. You can change this with a registry entry, although we're not sure why you'd need to do so. (All Time service parameters are in HKLM\System\CurrentControlSet\ Services\W32Time\Config.) Alternatively, you can run the following command to view the configurations:

```
C:\Users\Administrator >w32tm /query /computer:bf1 /configuration
[Configuration]

EventLogFlags: 2 (Local)
AnnounceFlags: 10 (Local)
TimeJumpAuditOffset: 28800 (Local)
MinPollInterval: 6 (Local)
MaxPollInterval: 10 (Local)
MaxNegPhaseCorrection: 172800 (Local)
MaxPosPhaseCorrection: 172800 (Local)
MaxAllowedPhaseOffset: 300 (Local)

FrequencyCorrectRate: 4 (Local)
PollAdjustFactor: 5 (Local)
LargePhaseOffset: 50000000 (Local)
SpikeWatchPeriod: 900 (Local)
LocalClockDispersion: 10 (Local)
HoldPeriod: 5 (Local)
PhaseCorrectRate: 7 (Local)
UpdateInterval: 100 (Local)
```

But where do you find an SNTP server? Oddly enough, there are many around. Most ISPs' big DNS servers seem to act as SNTP servers. You can find out whether a particular machine is an SNTP server with a neat little free tool called ntpquery.exe from www.bytefusion.com/ products/fs/fs.htm. You just point it at a DNS name or IP address, and if that machine is a time server, you get a screen full of incomprehensible long numbers.

There doesn't seem to be a way to enable success/failure logging to the event log. But there is a diagnostic program that you can use to figure out whether you're connected to a useful time server. Shipped on all Windows machines, the program is called w32tm. Although it's not as pretty as ntpquery.exe, it's free and integrates with the Time service.

To find out whether a system's time server is working, open a command prompt, and type **w32tm /resync**. It'd look like this:

```
c:\>w32tm /resync
Sending resync command to local computer...
The command completed successfully.
```

Or, if it *didn't* work, you'd see this:

```
The computer did not resync because no time data was available.
```

This service requires that port 123 be open to the outside world, so set your firewalls appropriately.

Trusts

As discussed earlier in the chapter, computers within a domain allow users authenticated by the domain controllers to access to their resources. The computers trusted the domain controllers. For users outside the domain, an explicit trust was created between the domain controllers to authorize the users to access the computers' resources. This section will go into more detail on concepts behind these explicit trusts and how to administer them.

The trusts have characteristics that can be configured when they are created. They can have one direction or two. They can be transitive or nontransitive. Each of these characteristics is considered in the type of trust that will be created.

You can create and administer the trust using the Active Directory Domains and Trusts snap-in. In addition, the netdom utility can perform the same operations.

Defining the Domain: "Trust"

So, now you have a server that can authenticate a user, a DC. But for whom will it do this authenticating? Not just any system. A PC (whether workstation or server) can only use a domain's DCs to authenticate if that PC "joins" a domain to become a "domain member." Systems that are not members of any domain can authenticate using the user accounts in their local SAM database; systems that are domain members can either authenticate a user with those local SAM accounts or ask one of their domain's DCs to authenticate the user. In the world of Microsoft networking, we say that systems not in any domain *trust* only their local SAM but that systems in a domain *trust* their SAM and their domain's DCs. Joining a domain creates a *trust relationship* between the PC and the DCs. Before a workstation will trust a domain controller to provide it with logon services and before a domain controller will trust a workstation enough to *provide* those logon services, Microsoft software requires the agreement both of a domain-level administrator and of a workstation-level administrator.

When you join a machine to a domain, you are typically logged in using an account that workstation recognizes as a local administrator, but when you try to join the machine to a domain, you'll see that the domain then comes back and says, "Now I need to see an administrative account that the *domain* recognizes." Just as a treaty between two countries requires signatures from leaders of *both* countries, so also does trust between machines and domains require authorization from both local and domain-level admins.

But trusts can go further than that. As we discussed earlier, trusts occur between domains in the forest. You can also create trust relationships between forest domains and other domains. Thus, if your PC is a member of the Test.com domain and if the Test.com domain trusts the Apex.com domain, then your local DCs can authenticate information about not only user accounts in Test.com but also user accounts in Apex.com.

Trust Relationships in More Detail

If you want to connect an old domain and a new domain to do a clean and pristine migration, if you want domains in one forest to trust domains in another forest due to a corporate merger, or if you're even just sharing data between domains, then you must create a trust relationship. When a domain trusts another domain, then the first domain is saying that it once was only willing to accept authentications from its own DCs, but now it'll accept authentications from the second domain's DCs as well.

But how do you build one of those trusts? In the case of domain-to-domain trusts, you can use the GUI or a command-line tool named netdom.

Trusts Have Direction

To understand trusts in depth, the first thing to grasp is that trusts have direction. Trusts can be built to travel either one way or two. The language to describe the Windows Server trust relationship seems to muddle the concepts. Refer to Figure 24.16 to get this concept down and use it to remind yourself of the terminology to get the trust creation correct.

FIGURE 24.16
Trusts

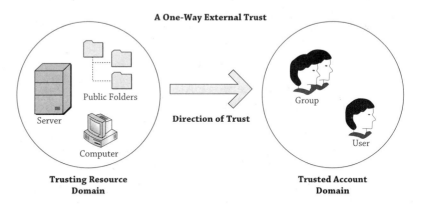

A One-Way External Trust

Public Folders

Server

Computer

Direction of Trust

Group

User

**Trusting Resource
Domain**

**Trusted Account
Domain**

Any trust between two domains has a trusting domain and a trusted domain. The *trusting* domain is willing to accept login information and authentications from the *trusted* domain. For example, suppose you have two domains—a domain named Factory.com and another domain named Workers.com. Suppose also that Factory.com is a domain that contains very few user accounts; instead, it contains the machine accounts for several hundred servers. People with user accounts in Workers.com need to get access to data in Factory.com's servers.

Or, in other words, you need the Factory.com domain to *trust* the Workers.com domain. "Resources" trust "accounts."

If you haven't messed around with trust relationships in the past, then read that again so you're clear on it. The primary goal is to give Worker.com people access to Factory.com's data. But Factory.com's servers will not, of course, let any users get to that data unless they can authenticate those users. But Factory.com can't authenticate the users; only their home domain's DCs can. Therefore, Factory.com must begin accepting authentication from Workers.com. That's the definition of "to trust" here: to accept authentications of another domain's DCs. So, Worker .com folks get to use Factory.com's data because Workers.com is *trusted*, and Factory.com lets them because it is *trusting*.

The automatically created trusts between domains within a forest are two-way in direction. Each domain trusts each other. Manually created trusts may have no need to allow the trust in both directions, so the option to create one-way trusts is still available.

Some Trusts Are Transitive

A neat thing about a forest is that all of its domains trust each other because of transitive trusts—even if domain A doesn't trust domain B directly, it might be that A trusts D, D trusts C, and C trusts B.

We illustrated how the trust relationships worked with the cute potential date earlier in the chapter in the "Kerberos and Trusts" section. If the cute potential date had an equally geeky brother as yourself and he considers your sister hot stuff, the trust relationship between Mother and Mom works in the opposite direction. It would work if there was a forest root of the neighborhood or even more motherly security devices to network through. As these trusts "flow through," there's a kind of "six degrees of Kevin Bacon" in that everyone trusts everyone.

This is the transitive nature of some trusts. The automatically built parent-child trusts and the forest root–tree root trusts are transitive. Shortcut trusts and forest trusts are transitive, but they are created manually. The transitive nature reduces the number of trusts needed to be created.

Trusts Do Not Remove All Security

People sometimes fear creating trusts between two domains, thinking that if domain A and domain B trust one another, then anyone with a user account in A can make mischief in B, and vice versa. That's not true at all. Establishing trusts between two domains just means that a system in the A domain can recognize a user in B, and B in A. To see why this isn't the end of the world, consider this question: can a user in domain A do anything that he wants on any system in domain A? Of course not—group policies, user rights, and permissions control all of those things.

People get that idea because they're used to working in networks running older versions of Windows Server that have been configured with default permissions and rights. Because earlier versions of Windows Server permissions were something like "Everyone in the world is welcome here," hooking up domain A and domain B meant that yes, anyone from A could do anything to any machine in B (and the other way around as well). But modern networks are tighter for two reasons. First, the default permissions and rights that a user has in a network running Windows 7 and later Windows operating systems and Windows Server 2008/2012–based domains are a lot more restrictive than the ones for a network running Windows XP or Windows 2003 workstations and domain controllers. Second, administrators are just plain more aware of security and so more likely to take a close look at how they secure their servers. Once a server in domain A is well protected from the users in domain A, then it'll be pretty much automatically protected from users in any other trusting domain.

Trusts Involve Administrators from Both Sides

The decision to let domain A accept authentications from domain B (to use a one-way trust example) isn't one that A can make unilaterally, and it isn't one that B can foist onto A. Creating a trust relationship is sort of like creating a treaty between countries; you need signatures from both sides to make it legal. Now, we realize that in many cases one person—probably you—will be the domain administrator on both sides, but you will nevertheless have to establish credentials on both domains before you'll be able to create that domain.

Four Kinds of Trusts

In a Windows Server 2012 R2 world, there are four kinds of trusts that can be created manually: external, shortcut, forest, and realm. These trusts were also available in Windows Server 2008. Only external and shortcut trusts were available on server editions prior to Windows Server 2003. You will probably work only with the external and, on rare occasions, forest trusts, but let's take a quick look at what they are:

External   External trusts are basically the kinds of trusts we've been mostly talking about when we talk about domain-to-domain trusts. Since they come directly from the NT trust technology, they're occasionally referred as *NT trusts*. If you want a domain in a forest to trust a domain *outside* the forest or, in Microsoft terms, an *external* domain, then you build an *external* trust. You'll use these for migration. For example, if you're migrating from a domain to a new empty Windows Server 2012 R2–based AD domain, then you must first create an external trust between the two domains so that you can copy the user accounts and other things to the new domain.

Shortcut   Shortcut trusts help speed up authentication in large forests. Remember the earlier discussion concerning the Kerberos and high-school dating? It would be nice to cut out the extra jumps between you and the cute date. The shortcut trust is like that. For our example, Ecoast.Test.com could pass around Test.com and directly contact Consolidated.com with this. This isn't a really impressive example. Only a forest with several trees or great-great-grand-child domains would actually benefit from this feature.

Forest   Forest trusts are the neat new-to-2003 trust that lets you build one trust relationship between two forests. Once done, every domain in the first forest trusts every domain in the second forest.

Realm   Realm trusts allow trust relationships with Unix systems that use Kerberos for authentication. (What we call domains, Unix Kerberos users call *realms*.)

We'll mostly use external trusts, but we'll show you how to build a forest trust also.

Understanding Transitive Forest Trusts

Since we can't graft forests together, we can't add a forest to another one. The best we can do is create a trust. The external trust is adequate for sharing resources across one domain. The forest trust is best for multiple domains. Forest trusts can only be utilized by domains running at least the 2003 forest functional level.

Like the automatic transitive trust relationships, the forest trust provides a gateway for all domains in one forest to trust the domains in the other. Thus, suppose Test.com buys Apex.com both of which have an existing forest. Test.com wants its forest to work well with Apex.com's, so it creates a single forest-to-forest root trust, and trust is universal.

This is good news, but there are a few reasons why this may not be all that Test.com and Apex.com wanted. Here's why:

- First, this is possible only if both Test.com and Apex.com are upgraded to at least the Windows Server 2003 forest functional level. Ideally you would want to upgrade all of your domains and domain controllers to Windows Server 2012 R2 so that you get to use all of the great features provided by the most up-to-date technology.

- Second, two trusting forests do not exactly equal a single forest as far as some AD-aware software is concerned. (Read: Exchange Server. Although it isn't the only one, it is the most important one.) That's because there is another very important bit of "glue" binding forests together in addition to their transitive trusts: the global catalog.

  Exchange Server sees your enterprise as one big firm no matter how many domains it has because Exchange Server thinks "all domains sharing a global catalog equal one enterprise." So, here's the problem: two separate trusting forests *still have two separate global catalogs*.

- Third, and this is probably a smaller issue, forest-to-forest trusts are, believe it or not, not transitive *across forests*. By that we mean if forest 1 trusts forest 2, then as you've seen, all of forest 1's domains trust all of forest 2's domains, and vice versa.

  But now let's say that you set up a transitive trust between forest 2 and forest 3. Now all of forest 2's domains trust all of forest 3's domains (and vice versa). But what about forest 1 and forest 3—what relationship do they have? None, as it turns out. Forest-to-forest trusts do not "flow through." You'd have to build a whole separate trust between forest 1 and forest 3 in order to have every forest around trust every other one.

You'll see the nuts and bolts of setting up trusts in the next section, "Manually Creating Trusts."

Manually Creating Trusts

The primary tool for managing trusts is the Active Directory Domains and Trusts (ADDT) console. Although those "old-school leatherneck admins" think wizards are for those "latte-sipping pencil-neck admins," the ADDT's New Trust Wizard gets the job done when you consider the complexity of the netdom command.

You can find the trusts of a domain on the Trusts tab of the properties of a listed domain within the console, as shown in Figure 24.17. This figure illustrates a one-way outgoing external trust for the Apex.com domain. Even using the "trusts" nomenclature, the idea of what the tab is telling you is thoroughly confounding.

FIGURE 24.17
The outgoing trust

Referring back to Figure 24.16, you can see that Apex.com is the domain with computers, printers, and files. The arrow is outgoing to the Test.com domain. On the Trusts tab shown in Figure 24.17, the top area, "Domains trusted by this domain (outgoing trusts)," lists the domains with the users and groups. In this case, users in Test.com can access files and printers in Apex .com. You can test this by creating a domain local group in the Apex.com domain's Active Directory Users and Computers snap-in. When you attempt to add members to the group, you can select users and groups from the Test.com domain. This domain local group can then be assigned permission to resources.

Figure 24.18 illustrates the incoming trust on Test.com. This is the same trust relationship discussed earlier and displayed on the Test.com domain controllers. Apex.com is in the bottom area, "Domains that trust this domain (incoming trusts)." Apex.com, the resource domain, trusts Test.com, which is the accounts domain.

FIGURE 24.18
The incoming trust

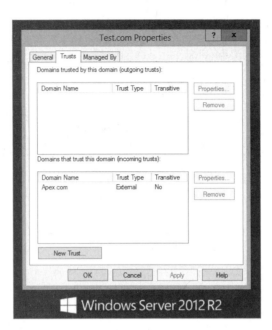

CREATING TRUSTS WITH THE NEW TRUST WIZARD

Let's cover forest trusts. As far as we can see, you can't get netdom to create the really cool transitive trusts between forests. For that, you'll need Active Directory Domains and Trusts (ADDT). However, in our experience, we've relied on external trusts. They're effective in getting the job done for trusts between one domain and another, which is the predominant requirement in Active Directory environments. The forest trust applies to much larger organizations than the typical IT shop.

Creating trusts with the ADDT's New Trust Wizard is the same for each of the trusts, and they require the same configurations and information.

1. First, as always, check DNS with a few NsLookup commands to see that the folks in each forest, realm, or domain will be able to find domain controllers in the other forest.

   Although there are different ways of setting up resolving the names with in a different domain, we prefer setting up DNS stub zones. The stub zone can be configured as Active Directory integrated, so it will be automatically replicated to other domain controllers in the domain. It doesn't require modifications of the primary zone like a secondary zone would. Conditional forwarders accomplish the same thing.

2. Then, make sure that both of the forests are at the Windows Server 2012 R2 forest functional level.

3. Finally, make sure that you have the name and password of an account that is either in Enterprise Admins or in Domain Admins for the forest root domain—and you'll need one of those accounts from each forest.

4. Start Active Directory Domains and Trusts (Server Manager ➤ Tools ➤ Active Directory Domains and Trusts).

5. Right-click the icon representing the forest root domain (you can't create a forest trust from any other domain), choose Properties, and on the resulting page click the Trusts tab. Refer to Figure 24.17.

   This figure shows how to create a forest trust between Test.com (which is, as you'll recall, a forest root domain) and Apex.com (which is the forest root of another forest). For the sake of this illustration, the trust in Figure 24.17 and Figure 24.18 was removed beforehand using the Remove button.

6. Click New Trust, and a Welcome to the New Trust Wizard screen appears; click Next, and you'll see something like the screen shown in Figure 24.19.

FIGURE 24.19
Who will you
trust?

We've filled in Apex.com. (This wizard is not case sensitive.)

7. Click Next to see the *important* choice, as shown in Figure 24.20.

   Recall that an external trust is a simple domain-to-domain trust, and a forest trust is the transitive trust that you want.

FIGURE 24.20
What kind of trust?

8. Choose "Forest trust," and click Next to see the screen shown in Figure 24.21.

FIGURE 24.21
Which way should the trust go?

As you've seen, at its heart a trust has two sides—the domain that trusts and the domain that is trusted. This page lets you choose who trusts whom and whether trusts should just run bidirectionally.

9. Choose Two-way, and click Next to see the screen shown in Figure 24.22.

FIGURE 24.22
Set up both sides
or just this one?

This is a real time-saver. As we said, one administrator can't create a trust for two domains; it takes admins from both sides. That used to mean that you'd first set up one side of the trust on one domain and then run over to a DC for the other domain and finish setting up the trust at the other domain. This, however, saves you the trouble. If you click "Both this domain and the specified domain," then the wizard will ask you for an administrator account and password on the other domain.

10. Fill in the administrative account and password and click Next, and you'll see the dialog box shown in Figure 24.23.

FIGURE 24.23
The other guy's
credentials

The next page will display the option for Forest-wide Authentication or Selective Authentication. In most cases, you create a forest trust because you want all the domains in one forest to trust all the domains in the other forest. If that's the case, then choose Forest-wide Authentication. If, on the other hand, you want to more finely tune the kind of authentication information that passes between the forests, then choose Selective Authentication. But if you do, you'll have a lot more work ahead of you!

11. Click Next, and the wizard will ask you the same question from the point of view of the other forest.

12. Select whatever you prefer, and click Next again.

You'll get two more information panels confirming what you've selected.

13. Click Next to get past them.

Then you'll be asked whether you want to confirm the link between forests. Then you'll end up at a final "This is what you did" page.

14. Click Finish, and it's done—Apex.com and Test.com are working as one, sort of.

Figure 24.24 shows the results on the Trusts tab. Apex.com is the added in both fields. If you select to view the properties of a trust, you can run through the validation of the trust. This is useful in troubleshooting.

FIGURE 24.24
Trusts tab after the wizard

NETDOM: THE SWISS ARMY KNIFE OF TRUST TOOLS

As we've said, the true, under-the-hood meaning of *trust relationship* extends beyond domain-to-domain trusts; it includes the connection between domain members and their DCs, meaning that even someone operating a one-domain enterprise deals with trusts. But there's a tendency for administrative tools to handle either domain-to-domain trusts or domain membership trusts; there's only one tool that we know of that envisages trusts in their entirety. It's called netdom. First introduced in the early days of Windows Server, netdom has become more powerful and useful with every version—and 2012's version is no exception. The sweet part of Windows Server 2012 R2 is that it is installed by default. No hunting for the support tools!

Most of netdom's options affect domain membership trusts. We don't want to devote too much space to this, because we're mainly interested in discussing domain-to-domain trusts, but it's worth listing some of the netdom options.

netdom add adds a machine account to a domain. It doesn't join the machine to the domain; it only creates the machine account on the target domain, and, if the domain is an AD domain, you can even tell netdom what OU to put the machine account in. This is useful because a machine's local administrator can join that machine to a domain, *if* a domain administrator has already created a machine account for that machine on the domain. Here's what its syntax looks like:

```
netdom add machine /domain:domainname
/userd:destination-domain-admin-account
/passwordd:destination-domain-admin-password
/server:dcname /ou:destination-OU /DC
```

That looks like a mouthful; let's pick it apart to make it easier to understand. If you wanted to create a machine account in a domain, then you'd need to know the following:

◆ The name of the machine for which you wanted to create a domain account. That's what the *machine* parameter supplies.

◆ Next, you'd need to know what domain you were joining that machine to. That's what the /domain:*domainname* parameter supplies. If you don't specify this, then the machine account gets created in your current domain.

◆ That domain is only going to let you add a machine account if you're someone with the permissions to do that on the domain. That's what the /userd and /passwordd parameters supply. Of course, if you're already logged on as someone with those permissions, then you needn't resupply them.

◆ You might want to force this operation to occur on a particular DC. The /server option lets you do that.

◆ You might want to place this new machine account in a particular OU; the /ou option accomplishes that. Unfortunately, you have to specify the OU in LDAP terminology.

◆ Finally, machine accounts for domain controllers are a bit different from the rest of the machine accounts, so netdom includes the /DC option for that eventuality.

So, if you wanted to create a machine account named Matterhorn in a domain named Apex.com and place its account in an OU named Workstations, you'd type the following:

```
netdom add Matterhorn /domain:apex.com /ou:"ou=Workstations,dc=apex,dc=com"
```

Again, that does not join Matterhorn—there needn't even be a system named Matterhorn for this to work. But now it'd be possible for a local administrator at Matterhorn to join Apex.com, and she would not have to fill in a domain account/password to satisfy her workstation OS. But what if you wanted to both create the machine account *and* join the machine to the domain? For that, there's netdom join. It looks like the following:

```
netdom join machine /domain:domainname
/userd:destination-domain-admin-account
/passwordd:destination-domain-admin-password
/usero:local-machine-admin-account
/passwordo:/local-machine-admin-password
/ou:ou /reboot
```

Most of those options will seem pretty familiar. As before, you need to tell netdom what machine to join, what domain to join it to, and perhaps what OU in that domain to place the machine account in. Because this creates a machine account on the domain, you'll need to present domain-level administrative credentials. But now because you're also joining the machine to the domain, you'll need the *machine's* permission as well, so you'll need to show that you have an account that the machine recognizes as a local administrator account—that's what passwordo and usero do. (Think of the o at the end as "object," as in "We're joining this object to the domain." The same for userd and passwordd—they're the user account with administrative privileges on the *destination* domain.) Finally, /reboot tells the workstation or member server to reboot to make the changes take effect. Interestingly enough, you don't need to be anywhere near the target machine to do this—it'll work remotely without a problem! So, for example, suppose you wanted to move a system named Saturn into a domain named Planets.com. The administrator account on the Saturn machine is named satadmin with password *hi*, and Planets.com has a domain administrator named planadmin with password *so*. The command would look like this:

```
netdom join Saturn /domain:planets.com
/usero:satadmin /passwordo:hi
/userd:planadmin /passwordd:so
/reboot
```

We told you that netdom could help with migration by letting you move a machine from one domain to another—that's the netdom move command. It'll need *three* sets of account names and passwords, because to move a machine from domain A to domain B, you'll need to demonstrate administrator credentials on domain A, on domain B, and on the machine that you're moving. As before, you specify userd, passwordd, usero, and passwordo. But now you'll need to specify userf and passwordf—an account name and password on the *former* domain. By now, all the options should be familiar:

```
netdom move machine /domain:destination-domainname
/userd:destination-domain-admin-account

/passwordd:destination-domain-admin-password
/usero:local-machine-admin-account
/passwordo:/local-machine-admin-password
/userf:former-domain-admin-account
/passwordf:former-domainadmin-password
/ou:ou /reboot
```

So, suppose you wanted to move a machine named saturn.planets.com from a domain named Planets .com to one named Cars.org. Say that you have an administrative account on Saturn named satadmin, a domain admin account on Planets.com called planadmin, and a domain account on Cars.org called caradmin. Finally, let's suppose that each of those admin accounts has the password *hi*. The command would look like this:

```
netdom move saturn.planets.com /domain:cars.org
/usero:satadmin /passwordo:hi
/userf:planadmin /passwordf:hi
/userd:caradmin /passwordd:hi
/reboot
```

Before moving to `netdom`'s domain-to-domain trust abilities, we'll mention that it can help out in other ways when maintaining domain member trusts:

netdom reset   Resets a machine's account. Sometimes you'll sit down at a system and be unable to log onto the domain because the machine has lost its domain account, or so it says. Sometimes just resetting it does the job.

netdom resetpwd   Resets a machine's domain password. You must be sitting at the machine for this to run. Sometimes if a machine has not connected to the domain for several weeks, then its account password expires; this can fix that.

netdom remove   Removes a system from a domain.

netdom renamecomputer   Renames a computer and its machine account. Be careful about doing this with certificate servers; they are installed to be name dependent.

BUILDING DOMAIN TRUSTS WITH NETDOM

Now you'll learn how to build a trust with `netdom`. Recall that you'll work with two kinds of trusts: external (domain-to-domain nontransitive) and forest (forest-to-forest transitive) trusts. `netdom` can create external trusts. By now, it'll be easy to guess how `netdom` does it. You need to specify who will trust whom and present domain admin credentials for each domain.

Here's the syntax:

```
NETDOM TRUST trusting_domain_name /Domain:trusted_domain_name
  [/UserD:user] [/PasswordD:[password | *]]
  [/UserO:user] [/PasswordO:[password | *]]
```

Remember that in the most basic trusts, there is a *trusting* and a *trusted* domain. The trusting domain accepts authentications from the trusted domain. You can choose to make it two-way, but even if you do, `netdom` insists that you call one domain the trusting and one the trusted. (Of course, if you're building a two-way trust, then it doesn't matter which you make the trusted and which you make the trusting.) As before, you present credentials, but this time you use the /uo and /po parameters to specify the username and password for a domain admin from the trusting "resource" domain, and you use /ud and /pd to specify the username and password for a domain admin from the trusted "accounts" domain. The /add parameter says to create the trust, and the /twoway parameter says to build it in both directions. That's optional—if you *do* want a one-way trust, then don't include /twoway./ enablesidhistory makes a trust that can support migration tools that create SID histories. We discuss this in further detail in Chapter 25.

So, for example, to make Apex.com and Test.com trust each other, let's suppose that Apex .com has a domain admin named apexAdmin with password @pex.c0m and Test.com has a domain admin named testAdmin with password T3$t.c0m. On the Test.com domain controller, the following command is used:

```
netdom trust apex.com /domain:test.com
/UserD:testAdmin /PasswordD:T3$t.c0m
/UserO:apexAdmin /PasswordO:@pex.c0m
/add /twoway /EnableSIDHistory
```

Trust relationships can fall apart for a variety of reasons, so if you create a trust, leave it for a few months, and then try to use it to migrate, you might find that it doesn't work. netdom can "refresh" a trust with the /reset option:

```
netdom trust apex.com /domain:Test.com
/UserD:testAdmin /PasswordD:T3$t.c0m
/UserO:apexAdmin /PasswordO:@pex.c0m
/reset
```

It's the same as the command that creates the trust, but instead of ending with /add /twoway /enablesidhistory, you just use /reset. Or, instead of /reset, use /verify to just check that the trust is working; if not, then try /reset. We *strongly* recommend that you verify a trust just to make certain it's working. You can also verify the Apex.com trust like this:

```
netdom query /d:apex.com
/ud:apexAdmin /pd:@pex.c0m
/verify  trust
```

Then, once the trust isn't needed any more, you can break it with this syntax:

```
netdom trust apex.com /domain:test.com
/UserD:testAdmin /PasswordD:T3$t.c0m
/UserO:apexAdmin /PasswordO:@pex.c0m
/remove /twoway
```

Once your trusts have been created, it is fairly easy to use Windows PowerShell to display all of the trusted objects within the forest. Use the following command to view existing AD Trusts:

```
C:\PS>Get-ADTrust -Filter *
```

The Bottom Line

Explain the fundamental concepts of Active Directory with clarity. The Active Directory environment gets back to nature with the forest and trees. The forest is the collection of domains built in relation to each other through AD DS. The trees are domains within a hierarchal DNS namespace with "the same last name." The key to the relation between domains is the automatic and nonconfigurable two-way transitive trust relation.

Master It When the first domain controller for the first domain is created, three partitions are created within the Active Directory database. What are these three partitions named, what is contained in them, and which are replicated to the other domain controllers of the forest?

Choose between using domains, multiple domains, or multiple forests with an Active Directory design.   In planning an Active Directory design, you might decide you need multiple domains instead of using organizational units within a single domain. Replication limitations, legal requirements, and political forces are the top reasons for considering multiple domains.

> **Master It**   What features of Windows Server 2012 R2 eliminate two security-related reasons for multiple domains?

Add domains to an Active Directory environment.   You have to use the Active Directory Domains Services Configuration Wizard whenever you are going to build a new domain or replica domain controller in an Active Directory forest. In previous versions of Windows Server, the DNS structure needed to be in place prior to the installation. With Windows Server 2012 R2, everything is done for you.

> **Master It**   Since DNS is now handled by Windows Server 2012 R2, it would be nice to know if it did it right. What four changes should you see if you add a new child domain?

Manage function levels, trusts, FSMO roles, and the global catalog.   Several forest-related configurations were discussed, which would be managed by enterprise admins. The functional levels for the forest and domains provide the availability of features of the latest Windows Server version. All domain controllers need to be upgraded to that level to benefit from these features. Although you can raise functional levels, you can't lower them. The five FSMOs are specific roles assigned to domain controllers within the domains and forest. The PDC Emulator, RID Master, and Infrastructure Master are domain-related roles. The Domain Naming Master and Schema Master are forest-related roles. Trusts are required to share resources between domains that are not part of the same forest. The exception is shortcut trusts, which reduce the trust path between two domains within the same forest.

> **Master It**   The placement of an FSMO role is dictated by the domain to which it is assigned and the Global Catalog role. Which two roles have rules concerning placement in regard to the global catalog?

Chapter 25

Migrating, Merging, and Modifying Your Active Directory

Active Directory has become the default and most common authentication and directory service in most major organizations. Active Directory controls access to the servers, computers, file and printer resources, email, databases, and applications throughout organizations.

Microsoft first released Active Directory with Windows 2000. It has had over a decade to become entrenched in organizations. Windows Server 2012 is the fifth major release of Active Directory. As an essential part of business operations, information technology and infrastructure becomes a discussion point when planning mergers, acquisitions, and spin-offs. Active Directory's design doesn't support domain grafting or pruning. In other words, you cannot add a domain or take away an existing domain from a forest. Thus, separating or adding business operations will impact the Active Directory environment, forcing you to manually migrate users, computers, and data while maintaining business continuity. It's important to talk intelligently about these operations to decision makers within management.

Since Windows Server 2008, the upgrade path has provided solid updates to the Active Directory functions. Microsoft spent the majority of the development cycles for Windows Server 2012 Active Directory advancing existing product features. For example, the Active Directory Recycle Bin has been given a GUI. Previously it was available only through PowerShell. Also, group Managed Service Accounts (gMSA) expands the Windows 2008 R2 feature to include support of Managed Service Accounts in things like clustering and load balancers.

Simple changes to the interface and performance tuning are always welcome, and I think you will like the refresh of basic items. Once you have upgraded your domain controller (DC), you can clone it with Hyper-V and use safe restore.

In this chapter, you will learn to:

♦ Introduce new versions of Active Directory into a network

♦ Migrate domain accounts from one domain to another

Upgrade and Migration Strategies

So far we've been talking like you were creating a new network where none existed before, but that's not likely these days. Instead, it's more likely that you already have an Active Directory domain and you want to move to a Windows Server 2012–based Active Directory domain. Or you might want to consolidate two AD infrastructures. Either way, that kind of work falls under the topic of *migration*.

As we start walking through migration strategies, we'll cover some basic review items and other considerations. If you're migrating, then you probably have a domain currently running and you want to convert or upgrade it to a functioning Windows Server 2012–based AD domain.

The major fear most IT administrators have is getting through the migration successfully. Having a domain that stops working or fails partially through the migration is not an option. Having an appropriate test plan in place and working through the migration in a test lab are absolute musts. It is common for companies to have a virtual infrastructure, either in production or at least in a test lab. The benefit of using your virtual infrastructure for testing is that you can use the Physical to Virtual (P2V) process to place your domain controller in a private network to test the upgrade process.

There are some specific things you need to do in order to work through this process, and I highly recommend that you build a test lab from your production environment; see `http://tinyurl.com/ch25p2v` for more information. The article describes how to take your current 2003, 2008, or R2 environment and build out a test lab. Because it may seem to be a bit outdated, the process is still the same, and can be followed.

There are three basic philosophies for migrating to a Windows 2012 domain:

In-place Domain Upgrade The process consists of installing the Windows Server 2012 operating system on top of an existing Windows domain controller.

Swing Migration A Windows Server 2012 member server is promoted as a replica domain controller of the existing domain. This is occasionally referred to as an Active Directory upgrade.

Domain Migration (Requires a New Forest or Domain) Some organizations prefer to set up a new AD as a way to build a pristine domain. This type of migration requires setting up a new namespace and moving over all objects. It is a very large undertaking and requires careful planning and precision execution. This topic is not discussed in detail in this chapter.

Upgrade Capabilities

Before we get too far along in the process of migrating and testing, we need to cover the basic question of which versions can be upgraded.

The forest functional level of Windows Server 2003 is the minimum requirement to be able to perform an in-place upgrade. If you are planning on upgrading Windows Server 2003 to Windows Server 2012, you first have to upgrade your domain to Windows 2008 or Windows 2008 R2. No direct path from Windows Server 2003 Active Directory to Windows Server 2012 R2 Active Directory exists.

Supported for upgrade:

◆ Windows 2008 (64-bit only)

◆ Windows 2008 R2

◆ Windows 2012

Not supported for upgrade:

◆ Windows 2008 32-bit

◆ Windows 2003 (any version)

◆ Windows 2000 (any version)

No Windows Server 2000 domain controllers can exist in the domain when you upgrade to Windows Server 2012. You will have to demote these Windows Server 2000 servers out of the Domain Controller role and let normal replication occur. (Validating the domain confirms that they are removed.)

Migrating with an In-place Upgrade

Moving your Active Directory Domain from previous (supported) versions of Windows Server to Windows Server 2012 is commonly done as a standard upgrade. Your production domain might have very few domain controllers or is clean and pristine. An in-place upgrade may seem like a quick and easy process.

In the in-place upgrade approach, you let Windows Server 2012's Setup program convert your domain's Active Directory database to a Windows Server 2012–based Active Directory. The process to do this is fairly painless and consists of installing Windows Server 2012 over the top of your previous supported versions of Windows Server. You run a couple preparatory procedures and then run the Setup program on the domain controller.

When the process is complete, everything within the domain is pretty much the same. Users and groups are the same. Computers are the same. No changes have been made to the users, and at this point the major benefits are specific to the tools available to the IT professional. This is an all-or-nothing option. Upgrades of applications and operating systems tend to be nonevents. Vendors go to great extents to ensure an upgrade is fail-safe and avoid costly support calls from customers. However, things can go wrong. If the upgrade of a domain controller were to bomb, the rollback would be very stressful and time-consuming.

UPGRADE PATHS

The available upgrade paths to Windows Server 2012 basically follow these guidelines: Windows Server 2008 x64 or later and the same or better edition (i.e., Datacenter or Standard Edition) Windows Server 2012 doesn't come with an x86 processor, so an in-place upgrade may not be an option for many organizations. Since a large majority of organizations are still using Windows 2003 for their Active Directory, it is extremely unlikely they are utilizing a 64-bit edition of Windows 2003.

If an organization has a Windows Server 2000 Active Directory, it must upgrade to Windows Server 2008 x64 first.

GETTING READY FOR THE UPGRADE

Before you start your upgrade, make absolutely sure you have your DNS infrastructure in place—perform the checks of the service resource records using NsLookup and DcDiag that we covered in Chapter 6, "DNS & Name Resolution in Windows Server 2012 R2."

And just to be certain that you have a fallback position, go to all domain controllers, synchronize them, and back them up. If the upgrade fails, you can perform a restore on the domain controller with its original system state data. (But let's hope it doesn't come to that.)

Having a domain controller offline is not an option as it was back in the old days, since the upgrade will need access to all domain controllers and roles.

Make sure your forest and domain functional levels are in at least 2003-mode.

PERFORMING AN IN-PLACE UPGRADE FROM A 2008 R2 (X64)–BASED AD

Performing an in-place upgrade involves these basic steps:

1. Prep the forest's schema to be compatible with Windows Server 2012.

2. Prep the domain for Windows Server 2012.

3. Run the Setup program to upgrade the domain controller.

These steps are described in detail in the following sections.

Prepping the Forest/Schema and Domain

When doing an in-place upgrade, not all of your domain controllers need to be the same version of Windows Server; a mix of Windows Server 2008 R2 and 2008 64-bit is acceptable (only 64-bit versions are supported for upgrades). However, some FSMO roles are required to be located on specific Windows Server 2008 or 2008 R2 domain controllers. The domain naming master of the forest, which by default is the first domain controller in the forest, must be at a minimum Windows Server 2008 64-bit. The PDC emulators of each domain within the forest are required to be at this minimum version as well. These by default are in the first domain controller in each domain.

Even if you're going to upgrade only one domain in your 2008-based forest to Windows Server 2012, you have to change your forest and domain's schema before 2012 can install on the target domain controller. All domains in a forest share the same schema, so you have to change your entire forest's schema. This task is done on the forest's schema operations master FSMO.

Microsoft has made some basic changes to the adprep tool, mostly to the areas where it writes data and indicates what objects are published. The following links are to TechNet articles that give you a breakdown of all entries. We recommend that you review these before running the adprep command in your production environment:

Forest-Wide Updates `http://tinyurl.com/c25AdPrepFW`

Domain-Wide Updates `http://tinyurl.com/c25AdPrepDW`

Read-only Domain Controller Updates No updates to read-only domain controllers (RODC)

Schema Updates `http://tinyurl.com/c25AdPrepSC`

Running adprep

Windows Server 2012 has adprep built into the default OS. If you are doing other migrations types (swing or domain migrations) when you add the Active Directory Domain Services role, they will run adprep as needed. You will need to access your CD/ISO to start this process for an in-place upgrade. In order to successfully run the adprep command, make sure you have the appropriate credentials to run the command:

adprep /forestprep requires membership in the following groups:

◆ Schema Admins

◆ Enterprise Admins

◆ Domain Admins

Adprep /domainprep (including /gpprep) requires membership in the following group:

◆   Domain Admins

ADPrep /rodcprep requires membership in the following group:

◆   Enterprise Admins

You will need to run the command manually, as follows:

1. Open an elevated command prompt on the Windows Server 2008 R2 domain controller you wish to upgrade.

2. Run adprep at the command prompt. Type (substituting your DVD/CD drive letter for d: if necessary) **d:\support\adprep\ adprep** and press Enter.

   This will show you all of the syntax options along with a small explanation.

3. To start the process of getting ready for the in-place upgrade, run adprep by typing **adprep /forestprep** and press Enter.

   You'll see something like this:

   ```
   D:\support\adprep>adprep /forestprep

   ADPREP WARNING:

   Before running adprep, all Windows Active Directory Domain Controllers
   in the forest should be upgraded to Windows 2003 or later.

   [User Action]
   If all domain controllers in the forest run Windows Server 2003 or later and
   you want to upgrade the schema, confirm by typing 'C' then press ENTER to
   continue. Otherwise, type any other key and press ENTER to quit.
   ```

   At this point, you might be tempted to skip reading the text and just hit Enter. This would abruptly end the command. We recommend that you read the text.

4. Type **c** and then press Enter to see adprep in action.

   This will produce a blur of text and innumerable periods.

   This continues while AD imports and installs a bunch of schema changes. Finally, it says the following:

   ```
   Adprep successfully updated the forest-wide information.
   ```

   A rollback after changing the schema requires restoring the system state data on the domain controller with the Schema Master role. The system state data will contain the latest backup of the Active Directory database. The schema master is the primary domain controller for schema replication, so restoring its Active Directory database will include the schema. This will be replicated to the other domain controllers.

Now you're ready to prep your domain.

5. Go to the infrastructure operations master FSMO, and get ready as before to run adprep.

6. Type **adprep /domainprep /gpprep**.

   DomainPrep prepares the domain for a Windows Server 2012 domain controller. GPprep modifies permissions on Group Policy objects for replication to Windows Server 2012 domain controllers. Once you run the command, you will see the following:

   ```
   D:\support\adprep>adprep/domainprep /gpprep

   Adprep successfully updated the domain-wide information.

   Adprep successfully updated the Group Policy Object (GPO) information.
   ```

   If you have not run adprep for read-only domain controllers, now is a great opportunity to do so. You may have already done this if you are running Windows Server 2008 Active Directory, and because this is the same schema, no changes will be made. I always recommend running it for future possible RODC and just to validate that it has been done previously.

7. Type **adprep /rodcprep**.

To summarize, before you can upgrade a Windows Server 2008/2008 R2–based AD domain to a Windows Server 2012-based AD domain, you must do the following:

1. All domain controllers must be the 64-bit version of the operating system.

2. Upgrade the forest by running adprep /forestprep on the schema FSMO computer for your forest, even if that machine is not in the domain that you're going to upgrade.

3. Upgrade the domain structure by running adprep /domainprep /gpprep on the infrastructure FSMO for each domain that you are going to upgrade.

4. Optionally, run /rodcprep to prepare for read-only domain controllers.

Running Setup

Now you're ready to run Setup:

1. Insert the DVD (or ISO).

2. Double-click it in My Computer if it doesn't autostart.

3. Select the Upgrade option.

Setup will warn you about anything that will change in this upgrade. It will also check that you've forest-prepped and domain-prepped properly. From there, Setup runs hands-off, and there's nothing to do until it's finished and you log onto your newly upgraded Windows Server 2012 DC for the first time. At this point, you're upgraded!

IN-PLACE UPGRADES: PROS AND CONS

The following factors are in favor of in-place upgrades:

◆ They don't typically require new machines.

◆ Your users keep their old SIDs, and the domain keeps its old trust relationships, so any servers in other domains—resource domains containing perhaps file and print servers or email servers, for example—will still recognize those users without trouble.

◆ The users keep their old passwords.

◆ It's a relatively simple, quick upgrade.

◆ If you're going from 2008-based ADs to 2012-based ADs, then the upgrade is basically trouble-free.

◆ In-place upgrades from Windows 2008 R2 are seamless and simple.

Some of the limitations are as follows:

◆ The upgrade path is somewhat limited. The Windows Server supported versions are 64-bit only. Many organizations deployed 32-bit domain controllers when Windows Server 2003 became available, so an in-place upgrade may not be an option.

◆ It is an all-or-nothing upgrade. You upgrade *all* the accounts, and it's a one-way trip—there's no AD rollback wizard. (However, you can, as we've suggested, restore the system state data.) We prefer more gradual approaches.

◆ Any leftover junk remains in your Active Directory database. I mention this because many people think an upgrade will clean out those old, stale objects. Some of the newer tools in Windows Server 2012 from the AD PowerShell modules can help you clean up these entries.

MIGRATING WITH A SWING MIGRATION

One gradual approach is the swing migration, also known as an *Active Directory migration.* This would involve adding a Windows Server 2012 domain controller into an Active Directory domain. The environment would remain essentially the same, but the existing domain controllers can be upgraded or replaced at the convenience of the administrators. Historically the drawback is the requirement for more hardware, but with today's virtualization such as Hyper-V, you can just create a virtual domain controller on Windows Server 2012.

You avoid the all-or-nothing nature of the server upgrade because the new domain controller doesn't threaten the integrity of the Active Directory database. The replica is just receiving a copy. This process still requires prepping the forest schema and domains, but these procedures are less intrusive than the upgrade.

A domain controller redeployment does involve complications that require some planning. The source domain controller is an important part of the environment. It may have FSMO roles and the global catalog assigned to it. It may have other services such as DNS, DHCP, file shares, and printers that users depend on regularly. There may be scripts and group policies that point to this domain controller. You need to find out what will happen when this server is removed from the network. You must determine resolutions to these gaps. Possibly, the new Windows Server 2012 can assume these roles and services.

The swing migration involves these basic steps:

1. Prep the forest's schema to be compatible with Windows Server 2012.

2. Prep the domain for Windows Server 2012.

3. Prep the original domain controller for possible decommission or change of configuration.

4. Prep the new member server and add the Domain Controller role, followed by running DCPromo.

5. Perform post-migration procedures considering FSMO placement, IP address changes, or other changes.

6. Redeploy the source domain controller as necessary.

PREPPING THE FOREST/SCHEMA AND DOMAIN

As with the in-place upgrade, the existing forest and target domain need to be prepped for Windows Server 2012's Active Directory changes. You must run ForestPrep, DomainPrep, and GPprep, but with Windows Server 2012 when you add the Active Directory Domain Services role it will run adprep automatically, similarly to what we discussed in the "Migrating with an In-Place Upgrade" section.

Rollback procedures at this point of the game are the same as for the in-place upgrade. You must restore the system state data on the schema master domain controller.

BUILDING A WINDOWS SERVER 2012 MEMBER SERVER

The new Domain Controller will start as a Windows Server 2012 member server in the original domain. In preparation, you need to install the Active Directory Domain Services role and DNS role prior to running the Active Directory Roles process.

VERIFYING DNS

Since the new domain controller will support DNS, you should add it as a name server to the applicable forward and reverse zones. Once the member server is promoted as a domain controller, the DNS zones will be replicated.

To ensure proper name resolution of the domain controllers, you should test DNS resolution. Perform checks of the service resource records using NsLookup and DcDiag that we covered earlier in this book, in Chapter 5, "IP Address Management (IPAM) and DHCP Fail-over."

PREPPING THE SOURCE DOMAIN CONTROLLER

You should plan for what will be done with the source domain controller prior to the operation. If the server is to remain in the domain as a domain controller, little needs to be done. If it will be redeployed, you must consider how to replace the network's reliance on this server.

You need to collect the following data for the source server in order to apply similar settings to the target member server after the domain controller promotion:

◆ Server name.

◆ IP addresses (IPv4 and IPv6).

◆ Assigned Active Directory site.

◆ Assigned OU.

◆ Applied GPOs and RSOP output. You can type **gpresult /scope computer >
GPOResult.txt** to push the results to a text file.

◆ Assigned FSMO roles. These will be transferred if the server will be decommissioned.

◆ Global catalog role.

◆ Additional services such as DHCP, File and Print Services, and Internet Authentication Services for VPN connections.

Finally, perform system state data backups for all domain controllers and file system backups for essential services to be migrated outside Active Directory Domain Services (AD DS).

Promoting the Member Server

Windows Server 2012 deprecates the DCPromo tool, and all of the features needed for the Active Directory Domain Services are provided through the Adding Roles and Features tool in Server Manager (shown in Figure 25.1). The installation will add all the required components for Active Directory Domain Services, including the PowerShell modules, command-line tools, and the Administrative Center.

FIGURE 25.1
Server Manager:
Add Roles and
Features

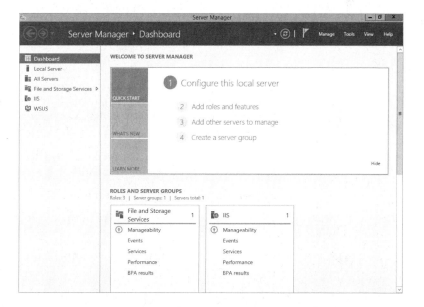

AD DS will walk you through the process just as DCPromo did previously in helping you connect to your DNS servers, namespaces, and domain controllers.

Before joining a domain, you must complete the basic feature installations that are required; the Add Roles and Features Wizard will walk you through this process. It will take a few minutes to get all of the components installed, and then you will be given the option "Promote this server to a domain controller," as shown in Figure 25.2.

FIGURE 25.2
Promoting a member server to a domain controller

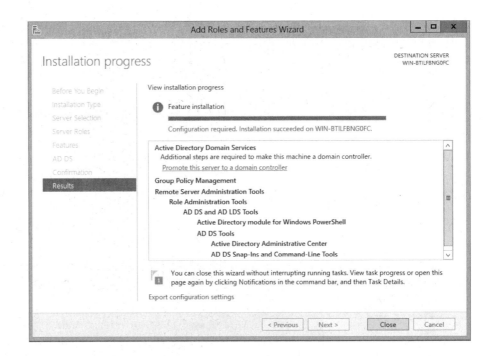

When you select this option, the AD DS Configuration Wizard will start. Follow these steps to work through the process of making your Windows Server 2012 member server a domain controller in an existing Windows Server 2008 R2 domain. The domain we will be working with in this example is called Oldfirm.com.

1. On the first AD DS Configuration Wizard screen, leave the default radio button selected, "Add a domain controller to an existing domain."

2. Under "Specify the domain information for this operation," set Domain to **Oldfirm.com**.

3. Under "Supply the credentials you need to perform this operation," enter **Oldfirm\ oldadmin**.

4. Once you have provided this information (shown in Figure 25.3), click Next.

FIGURE 25.3
Domain membership
information

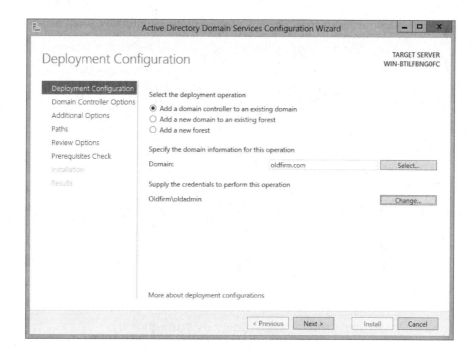

5. After your authentication has passed and the wizard continues, select the appropriate options for your domain controller:

   ◆ Domain Name System (DNS) server

   ◆ Global catalog (GC)

   ◆ Read-only domain controller (RODC)

   ◆ Site name: Select the appropriate site

   ◆ Directory Services Restore Mode Password (DSRM)

6. Click Next.

7. Specify your DNS delegation options and click Next.

8. Specify either "Install from Media" or "Replicate from a Domain Controller."

   You can replicate from any domain controller, or if you have a distributed network, you can select a high-speed one for this DC's location.

9. Specify the location of the AD DS database, log files, and SYSVOL. Click Next.

10. Review your options.

   This screen also has the View Script button. As with many of the Windows Server 2012 components, you can view and save the PowerShell script used to complete this operation.

11. After you have reviewed your selections, click Next.

12. Before promoting this server to a domain controller, you must validate the prerequisites.

If you have any issues or fail any section, the wizard will give you basic information on how to remediate it and will provide a web link with further detail.

13. Once all prerequisites are complete or the configuration has passed, click Install.

Typically this DCPromo task will take a few minutes to complete, but it will give you progress information if you leave the Configuration Wizard open during the install.

14. Reboot the system.

You will not have an option to restart; it will force you to do this.

Once the server has completed the restart, it will be a domain controller in the Oldfirm.com domain and ready to take on any FSMO roles and responsibilities you choose for it. One of the nice features of this swing migration process is that during your DC promotion tasks, Windows Server 2012 will do all of the database, SYSVOL, and log replication needed to be a fully functioning DC right after reboot. Since we are talking about swinging all domain controllers to Windows Server 2012, you can start looking at moving some of the FSMO roles to this domain controller.

MONITORING PERFORMANCE OF YOUR NEW DC

Typically you would leave this Windows Server 2012 domain controller online and make no other changes to the system for a few days to monitor its performance and see if any anomalies occur.

POST-MIGRATION PROCEDURES

After the migration you should verify the domain services. You can perform tool-based tests with the Event Viewer, DcDiag, and NetDiag to see if there are any initial problems. You should perform user acceptance tests as well, such as attempting to log on and accessing network resources with the new domain controller as the available authentication service.

Given the plans for the migration process, you should perform the following:

- FSMO role transfers and GC assignment.

- IP address reassignment.

- Network name reassignment. The domain controller can be renamed using the System applet (sysdm.cpl) in Control Panel or the netdom renamecomputer command.

- For DNS, the reassignment of the standard primary zones may be required.

Rollback is not complex. If the promotion process fails, running the Add Roles and Features Wizard again on the target domain controller should remove any record of the computer from the Active Directory database. If not, manual deletion of its computer object in Active Directory Sites and Services can help resolve this.

Repurposing Hardware

The swing migration provides the opportunity to redeploy an existing domain controller as a Windows Server 2012 domain controller. Remember, Windows Server 2012 comes in 64-bit only, so upgrading any 2003 or 2008 32-bit servers isn't possible.

This procedure requires an available virtual machine or hardware that can support Windows Server 2008 R2. This spare machine provides an intermediate phase between the two Active Directory states. Follow these general steps:

1. Prep the forest/schema and domain.

2. Build a Windows Server 2012 member server on the spare machine.

3. Verify that DNS is supporting Active Directory adequately.

4. Prep the source server.

5. Promote the spare member server.

6. Similar to the post-migration procedures, you will want to ensure everything is stable within the network and that users can access resources. Run DCPromo to uninstall Active Directory from the original domain controller. After that, it will be listed as a member server in the domain.

7. Build a Windows Server 2012 member server on the original hardware. You can use the same name and IP address as the original server as long as you delete the computer account in Active Directory.

8. Promote the member server as a domain controller.

9. Perform post-migration procedures including reviewing the FSMO placement. The spare domain controller may have FSMO roles assigned to it through the decommissioning of the source domain controller.

10. Once the domain and the domain controller services are validated, you can decommission the spare.

Swing Migrations from Windows Server 2003

Many organizations today are still actively running Windows Server 2003 as the primary Active Directory domain and could potentially be looking for Windows Server 2012's Active Directory to be the upgrade they have been waiting for.

In order for you to migrate an older system to Windows Server 2012 Active Directory, you will need to work through a process similar to the one in the previous section and build out a Windows Server 2012 member server and add the Active Directory Domain Services (AD DS) role to it. As stated before, it is highly recommended that you leverage your virtual infrastructure to build this out. After you have taken the appropriate steps to back up your domain controllers and schema, you will be ready to get started.

Transferring FSMO Roles

Starting the process for this is slightly different than if you are running Windows 2008 R2 since Windows 2003 is not supported. You need to move the FSMO roles over to your new Windows Server 2012 domain controller.

Open the Active Directory Domain and Trusts console and make the changes to your FSMO roles in this order:

1. Move the RID Master role to your new Windows Server 2012 DC.

2. Move the PDC Emulator role.

3. Move the Infrastructure Master role.

The tabs are in consecutive order on your server, so hopefully this isn't a big surprise. Once you've done this, you should consider doing a manual replication of your domain. It's always a good practice to give each of your domain-wide changes a couple minutes to settle and then manually synchronize them. Depending on how many domain controllers you have, this process can take some time when you take link speed and into consideration.

After you have made the changes and synchronized your domain, you can use the Active Directory Domains and Trusts console to change your current domain controller to the Windows Server 2012 domain controller; this might just be verification because it may already be utilizing that one, but you want to make sure. Now you will want to switch the Domain Naming Master role to the Windows Server 2012 domain controller.

CHANGING THE SCHEMA MASTER ROLE

The Schema Master role is held by one of the domain controllers and will do all updates and modifications to the Active Directory schema. The schema is the part of Active Directory that defines all objects and associated attributes for all items in the domain and controls the processing of the directory and all its objects. Since there is only one schema master per directory, it is not moved in the typical fashion.

To move the Schema Master role you will need to open an elevated command prompt and follow these steps:

1. At the command prompt type `regsvr32 schmmgmt.dll`.

   A pop-up will tell you if you succeeded or not.

2. If it succeeded, click OK and close the command prompt.

3. Open the MMC (which can be done from the Windows Server 2012 Start screen).

4. Choose Add/Remove Snap-In.

5. Choose and add the Active Directory Schema snap-in.

6. Click OK.

   This should now open your new MMC with the Active Directory schema loaded and ready to go.

A WORD OF CAUTION

Modifications to the schema should always be done with care. Even though you are not deleting or adding any records in this procedure, you always want to be careful.

Now within the Active Directory Schema tool you need to verify that you are connected to the appropriate domain controller. You want to be connected to your new Windows Server 2012 Active Directory DC for this. Once you have validated that you are, follow these steps:

1. Right-click Active Directory Schema and choose Operations Manager.

2. Select Change Schema Master.

3. Select Yes when it prompts you to validate if this is what you want to do.

4. Close the Change Schema Master section.

Now you need to replicate your domain controllers and give them a few minutes to update the AD database. Then you can move on to the next two tasks, which are removing your Windows Server 2003 server as a global catalog (GC) server and then removing the Windows Server 2003 server as a domain controller.

The process of removing the server as a GC server is simple. Open the Active Directory Sites and Services console on the new Windows Server 2012 domain controller, go to the appropriate site, and select Servers. In this folder you should see your Windows Server 2003 DC. Select that DC and do the following:

1. Right-click NTDS Settings and select Properties.

2. On the General tab that opens, uncheck the box that says Global Catalog.

3. Click Apply and then OK for this setting to take effect.

After a replication refresh you can use DCPromo to remove your Windows Server 2003 domain controller. But before jumping the gun, make sure you have run a tool like Netdom and queried your FSMO roles, and make sure that you have no errors showing up in your Event log, specifically under Directory Services.

SWING MIGRATION: PROS AND CONS

To summarize, these are the benefits of swing migrations:

◆ They are gradual in implementation. Once the first Windows Server 2012 domain controller is introduced, the rest of the domain controllers can be upgraded or replaced as necessary.

◆ Your users keep their old SIDs and the domain keeps its old trust relationships, so any servers in other domains—resource domains containing perhaps file and print servers or email servers, for example—will still recognize those users.

◆ The users keep their old passwords.

◆ The swing migration offers the opportunity to redeploy Windows Server 2012 on the original server.

There are few disadvantages of this method. These are the most common pain points:

◆ More preparation and planning are required to ensure a smooth delivery.

◆ Any leftover junk remains in your Active Directory database.

Active Directory Domain Migration

The third approach is characterized as *clean and pristine*. In this approach, you leave your existing domains (2003-based AD domains or 2008 R2–based AD domains) alone and create a new, empty AD domain. Then you use a program called a *migration tool* to copy user and machine accounts from the old domain (or domains) into the new AD domain.

The advantage of this method is that it is gradual. The migration can span a period of time where you can conduct testing and resolve issues. During this period, users still need access to their data. You can maintain access by reassigning permissions or relying on the capability of security identifier (SID) history.

DOMAIN MIGRATION IS GRADUAL

In specific cases, we prefer the domain migration approach. For one thing, it's gradual. With an in-place upgrade, you walk your domain through a one-way door. If you find later that Windows Server 2012–based ADs just aren't the thing for you, then too bad; you're stuck. But if you have a new domain and you copy some subset of your users over to that domain, then you tell just those users to log in to this new domain. If they start using the new domain and you find after a week or two that the AD is not the tool for you, then you can always tell those users to go back to their old domain accounts.

Although the swing migration approach is gradual as well, the process still leaves the artifacts that may have contributed to the poor performance and issues that instigated the migration in the first place. Over time, unknowledgeable administrators can configure Active Directory in some manner that confounds the wise folks who've read this book. These problems will still be there to work through after the domain is migrated to a later version.

The domain migration approach also provides an intermediate phase that is not available with the other two. During this phase, you have the opportunity to test the process, proving that users will be able to access their resources and uncovering some common issues that may arise with later production runs of the migration. This reduces the headaches that could arise upon crossing the threshold of the one-way door.

INTRAFOREST MIGRATIONS

Keep in mind that these same processes are applicable to intraforest migrations too. In Chapter 23, "The Third DC: Understanding Read-only Domain Controllers," you learned that the forest is a group of domains built in relation to each other.

Users, computers, and groups may need to be transferred to another domain within the forest. You migrate these objects from one domain to another domain in the forest using these procedures. The primary difference is that objects, like users and groups, must be moved rather than copied. The source user account is deleted after the target account is created. The Active Directory Migration Tool (ADMT) is used to migrate the accounts back to the source domain in a rollback. New computer accounts are created in the new domain, but the old computer account is disabled for rollback purposes.

There are two combinations of objects that need to be migrated together. These are referred to as *closed sets*.

Users and Global Groups   Global groups allow only users and other global groups from the same domain as members. When a user changes domains, it can't be a member of its original group. When a global group is moved, the members from the original domain are dropped as well. These need to be migrated together to maintain access within the limits of global group membership rules.

Resource Computers and Domain Local Groups   Resources cannot assign permissions to domain local groups from other domains. If the computer is migrated without the assigned domain local groups, the computer will not be able to see the group's SID on the user's security token to provide it access. As an alternative, you can opt to change the scope of the domain local group to universal, but this will impact the global catalog size.

Handling Permissions with the New Domain

Suppose you decide to go that domain migration route. Since there will be an intermediate phase, you can expect the users of the organization will be members of old domains or the new one. This will require users in the new domain to be able to access files and other resources in an old one. Straddling the two domains, the organization will be heavily dependent on the trusts between the domain controllers until all servers that hold the resources are on the same side as the users.

How will the users in the new domain maintain the same access to resources as they did in the old domain? Business continuity is big-ticket item for management; they need to ensure their people will be able to get to their data. A seamless migration will minimize any access outages.

There are two approaches to maintain access to the resources:

re-ACLing   ACL stands for *access control list*, a techie term for the security tab of a resource like a shared folder.

SID Histories   The SID is the security identifier, which is the unique number assigned to accounts to identify it within the permission structure.

If you don't blink after opening the security tab of a file, you may see the SID listed on the ACL before the computer resolves the SID to a friendly display name.

 Real World Scenario

The Domain Migration for Company Consolidations

A firm one of our authors worked at owned 11 smaller companies that ran and managed their own Active Directory infrastructure. In some places this may make the most sense or provide people the ability to do things within their own boundaries. One of the major problems this firm had was IT turnover. If one of the IT administrators left the company, that often would create a huge knowledge and support gap. They decided that along with moving toward an upgrade to Windows Server 2012 Active Directory, they would look to consolidate these domains into one. The management of the newly formed forest and domain wanted to merge the firms' Active Directory forests into one to provide a unified message system based on Exchange Server and reduce the administrative overhead and risks.

The network environment of many of the smaller companies seemed to be held together with duct tape and superglue. Unexplained system downtime was common, and performance slowed down after a few days of operations between reboots.

Too often they addressed issues in an aging and piecemeal environment; part-time administrators and IT professionals provided stop-gap measures, which became the long-term solutions. Similar solutions existed in Active Directory. The number of user accounts was triple the number of actual employees. The number of computer accounts surpassed the number of actual computers as well. The undocumented VPN solution that relied on the original domain controller could not be reconfigured. Thus, an upgrade or swing migration would potentially collapse the remote users' tunnel into the network. They decided that a full domain migration was the best approach and could provide the centralized management and support infrastructure they desperately needed.

Re-ACLing the Server

One approach is the obvious (and somewhat laborious) way: just walk over to all those old servers and add Sarah's new account to the permissions lists on those servers. This is called re-ACLing because the other name for a list of permissions on a network service is the access control list. It can be a real pain, but some migration tools will do the re-ACLing for you automatically.

Outside of the total excitement this process offers, especially when you may have to do this for 100+ shares for 100+ groups or users, the potential of error is high. The possibility of unintentionally removing access for one group, adding access to the wrong group, or forgetting to add another required group will make this a fun-filled adventure for all involved!

Using SID Histories

You know that every user has an SID. That's been true since NT 3.1. But since Windows Server 2000 native through Windows Server 2008 R2 domain functional levels, Active Directory lets users keep more than one SID. As migration tools create the new AD user accounts, those accounts get new SIDs. But the migration tools can tack the user's old SIDs onto the new user account as well, exploiting a feature called *SID history*. Then, when a user tries to access some resource that he had access to under his old account, his workstation tries to log him in to that resource using his new Active Directory account.

As with all domain logons, AD builds a *token* for the user that contains both his user SID and the SIDs of any global and universal groups to which he belongs. Here's the trick to SID histories: AD says, "Matthew is a member of a group with *this* SID" and sends along his old SID from the old domain.

Even though it's a user account's SID, the AD domain controller passes the SID along as if it were a global group SID, and apparently this is acceptable.

The resource, reviewing the token, says, "Hmmm…do I know any of these guys? Well, there's this user SID…nope, I don't know that Matthew guy…but wait, look, Matthew's a member of the 'Resource Group from the old domain' group. I have an ACL for that group, so I guess Matthew's in." Thus, even though Matthew is logged in as a person from the new group with a new SID, he's dragging the old SID around, and it gets him access to his old stuff.

This method is preferred over the re-ACLing method because the resources' permissions can remain unchanged. The key is ensuring that the SID history is recorded during the migration and the trusts do not filter them when the user is "crossing the trust" to access the resource.

WHAT YOU NEED TO CREATE SID HISTORIES

You need a migration tool that knows how to create SID histories. Microsoft's free Active Directory Migration Tool, which we'll cover a bit later in this chapter, can do that. Other migration tools are available, but you have to pay for them. Quest Software, for example, offers a suite of industry-approved migration tools.

Migration tools create SID histories as they copy user accounts from older domains to your new 2012 functional-level domain. Before a migration tool can work, you must create a trust relationship between the old and new domains. But no matter which migration tool you have, your migration tool cannot create SID histories unless you have created that trust relationship with `netdom` or with ADDT's New Trust Wizard. You can create SID histories only on domains with a functional level of Windows Server 2000 native or better. So, when you create that new clean-and-pristine AD domain, make sure that it's already shifted into Windows Server 2012 functional level—after all, you're building a fresh, new domain; you may as well get the most out of it—before creating the trust relationship and running the migration tool.

Please note that if you are planning on utilizing the ADMT tool, you will need to leave your domain functional level at Windows Server 2008 R2 because ADMT v3.2 does not currently support Windows Server 2012.

Windows Server 2012 also includes the ability to manage and configure SID history from PowerShell; the module in PowerShell allows you to make configuration changes and set token sizes. It is an absolute must for troubleshooting any issues that may occur. For more information about PowerShell and SID history, you can refer to `http://tinyurl.com/c25PSSIDHistory`.

ACTIVE DIRECTORY DOMAIN (CLEAN AND PRISTINE) MIGRATION: PROS AND CONS

Here are some migration advantages:

◆ Migrations let you do gradual upgrades.

◆ Migrations *copy* user accounts; they don't *move* them. The old accounts are still there if something goes wrong.

◆ Migrations let you build your DCs from clean installs, avoiding the extra complexity and potential issues of an in-place upgrade.

◆ Migrations are great for consolidating domains, collapsing a morass of many domains into just one or just a few.

◆ You can build a new domain structure in a virtual environment.

Although we've said that migrations have the advantage of reversibility, thus helping you manage your risk, they're not without some cons:

◆ You need more machines than you would if you were just upgrading. You'll need machines or virtual machines to act as domain controllers in the new domain.

◆ Most migration tools cannot copy passwords. ADMT provides a separate service to install on the source domain for this. Otherwise, the users will then have to create new passwords the first time they log in to the new AD domain. This isn't a showstopper, but for a large remote workforce, this would cause heartache.

◆ You have to buy a migration tool. There *is* ADMT, but it's really intended for small-scale migrations of 1,000 users at best. These tools aren't cheap, starting somewhere in the neighborhood of $10 per user. That's *per user*, not per administrator.

◆ You cannot create an Active Directory domain with the same NetBIOS name or FQDN as the original domain, because that would require you to be able to create two domains with the same name (since you don't decommission the old domains when you do a clean and pristine migration).

◆ It's more work. You have to worry about when to move any given set of users and groups, you may have to re-ACL or translate local profiles, and so on.

Using Microsoft's Free Migration Tool: ADMT

If you're thinking about a migration or domain consolidation, then you need a migration tool, and if you've priced migration tools, then you might be reconsidering a domain migration. But you needn't, because Microsoft offers a migration tool called the Active Directory Migration Tool, originally written for Microsoft by NetIQ. ADMT v3.2 maintains the ease of use of the first version and adds some nice features as well.

Version Incompatibility

At the time of this writing, ADMT 3.2 is not directly supported on Windows Server 2012 for migration. If you want to utilize ADMT, then you will need to configure a Windows Server 2008 R2 server that can act as the migration host. You will then need to have a Windows Server 2008 R2 domain controller in your new Windows Server 2012 domain. This will allow you to process the ADMT and Password Encryption Service (PES) programs properly.

Once you have migrated and completed all tasks, including moving the users and other components to being fully supported in your new Active Directory domain, you can then use DCPromo to remove the Windows Server 2008 R2 domain controller and move on.

If you have already placed your Windows Server 2012 Active Directory domain in a Windows Server 2012 domain functional level, you will need to utilize the following PowerShell commands to revert this:

To set your forest functional level back to Windows Server 2008 R2, run:

```
Set-AdForestMode -identify oldfirm.com -forestmode Windows2008 R2Forest
```

To set your domain functional level back to Windows Server 2008 R2, run:

```
Set-AdDomainMode -identity oldfirm.com -domainmode Windows2008 R2Domain
```

Considering that ADMT v3.2 is unsupported technically at this point, we are not going to dive into the steps to make this work. Many options exist in Windows Server 2012 Active Directory to help you clean up your current domain and offer great reporting and error checking. It is much better to utilize the in-place upgrade or swing migration approach to Active Directory than to do the Active Directory domain migration.

If you decide that you want to do the domain migration, you should highly consider seeking additional support from Microsoft or a private consulting company. In the next couple of sections we will go over the basics of trusts and how to enable some specific security policies and configurations to make tools like ADMT work. These are here as a guide for getting the new and old domains connected for whatever tool or updated version of the ADMT becomes available.

Establishing the Trust

Although we are not going through the ADMT v3.2 setup process, it is extremely important in any kind of Active Directory migration that you establish trust between the two domains. The quickest way to establish this trust is through the Active Directory Domains and Trusts console (domain.msc). Use the New Trust Wizard for the following:

◆ Specify the type of trust. An external trust is simple and effective for this procedure.

◆ Specify a two-way trust. Accounts from each domain will need to access each other's resources.

◆ Create the trusts on the other domain. This will require domain admin credentials on that domain.

◆ Validate the trust to make certain things are working correctly.

Once you have established the trust, you must test it—is the trust working, and are the permissions correct on the two domains? Since users and global groups from any domain can be members of domain local groups and member server local groups, you could now attempt to add a user from the opposite domain to a built-in group on the domain controller. This is a required step with any migration tool. So, you can search and add the Bigfirm administrator to the built-in Administrators group of Oldfirm in Active Directory Users and Computers.

But adding users to groups is not what you *really* want. You want the migrated accounts to be able to access resources in the other domain. This is where SID history comes into play. SID history is treated as another group on the security token that will be passed to the resource domain for access to the migrated accounts' resources.

SID filtering is disabled by default on trusts, and if you require that it be enabled, then you will have to do it manually. SID history can be exploited by a hacker in an elevated privilege attack. It is possible they could construct a security token with an SID of a domain administrator within the trusting resource domain. Since the SID is recognized as a domain administrator, this account would have the same level of access. SID filtering strips any SIDs that don't originate from the trusted user domain. Basically, your users' security token wouldn't buy a gumball in the source domain with SID filtering enabled because the SID history value would be stripped off. So, by following the useful hyperlink "Securing external trusts" in the window, you'll learn that you can use the netdom command to disable and enable SID filtering for migrations such as these.

The netdom command comes installed with Windows Server 2012, but be sure to search Microsoft's site for the latest version.

Run the following commands to disable SID filtering. The /quarantine:no parameter does the trick. You should be able to deduce how SID filtering would be enabled.

```
Rem performed on bf1.Bigfirm.com
Netdom trust oldfirm /domain:bigfirm /quarantine:No
/usero:administrator /passwordo:P@ssw0rd

Rem performed on the of1.oldfirm.com:
Netdom trust bigfirm /domain:oldfirm /quarantine:No
/usero:administrator /passwordo:P@ssw0rd
```

Getting Both Sides ADMT-friendly

ADMT can be an absolutely frustrating nightmare of a program because of its needs. It takes information that is fairly private and internal to a domain—user accounts and passwords—and reveals it to a completely different domain. Before ADMT can do that, you'll have to open a number of locked doors. Following are some of the things you have to do.

PUTTING A DOMAIN ADMIN IN EACH OTHER'S ADMINISTRATORS GROUPS

Tools like the ADMT utility need an account that is both a member of the Domain Admins group in the target domain, Bigfirm.com, and a member of local Administrator groups of servers and workstations in the source domain, Oldfirm.com. This will allow the migration utilities to make changes to permissions, user rights, and other nifty stuff that all administrators have the privileges to do. In this example, we created an account with the imaginative name of ADMT in the Bigfirm.com domain and assigned it to the Domain Admins group. Because of the trust relation between the two domains, it was also assigned to the built-in Administrators group in Oldfirm.com and the local Administrators group on OFIT1.

On the source domain, Oldfirm.com, there's a similar requirement for the Password Encryption Service. This is an additional service that will read the password of the migrating account, encrypt it, and then store it with the new account's properties. It needs to be a member of the Domain Admins group in the source domain, Oldfirm.com, and a member of the built-in Administrators group in the target domain, Bigfirm.com. We created an account with an equally imaginative name, PES, in Oldfirm.com. Over at Bigfirm.com, we opened Active Directory Users and Computers and drilled down to the Builtin folder to find the Administrators group. Then we made the PES account a member of that group.

TURNING ON AUDITING

ADMT has some specific auditing needs, presumably so that it can monitor how it's doing. The source domain—the one the users are being copied from, OldFirm.com—needs both success and failure audit enabled for user and group management.

On the target and source machines (Bf1.bigfirm.com and OF1.Oldfirm.com), you enable auditing by modifying a group policy called Default Domain Controller Policies. With Windows Server 2012, the Group Policy Management console is installed automatically. After opening this console, you drill down to the Group Policy Objects container. Then right-click the Default Domain Controllers Policy, and select Edit.

To get to the policy you're looking for, open Computer Configuration, then Windows Settings, then Security Settings, and then Local Policies; finally, inside Local Policies you see Audit Policy. Inside Audit Policy, double-click Audit Account Management, and make sure that Define These Policy Settings is selected, as is Success and Failure. Then click Close.

Now that those configuration changes are made, you can start to look at what domain migration tool you are going to use and know that you have successfully put in the appropriate policy.

Installing ADMT and PES

ADMT is available as a download from Microsoft. Installing the utility is straightforward for a clean and pristine installation since you will not be importing databases from previous versions. It does ask whether the database will be on SQL Express or a standard installation of SQL. In most cases, SQL Express will be the preferred option.

The Bottom Line

Introduce new versions of Active Directory into a network.   Upgrading to a new version of Windows Server means you also need to upgrade existing domain controllers. There are two basic methods to add a new version of Active Directory into an organization: Upgrading a domain controller or upgrading the domain by adding a new domain controller.

Master It   Both operations require you to modify the Active Directory database using the adprep.exe utility. What three options do you need to run? What option can you also run?

Migrate domains accounts from one domain to another.   The requirement to move users and groups from an existing domain to a clean and pristine domain often happens when companies merge or spin off. In addition, this can be required when a forest restructuring is justified. Microsoft offers the ADMT utility to perform domain migrations.

Master It   After a user account is migrated to the new domain, what gives the user access to resources within the original domain?

Chapter 26

Advanced User Account Management and User Support

You have already learned about the basics of user and group management. Now we're going to take user management to the next level in this chapter. You'll be utilizing some of the skills that you have developed while reading this book, such as managing file shares, Distributed File System (DFS) namespaces, and Group Policy objects (GPOs). Using these technologies, you can develop a flexible, fault-tolerant, and mobile working environment, something that Microsoft refers to as *dynamic IT*.

We'll cover how you can deploy solutions where a user's data and settings follow them around on the network using home directories and roaming profiles. You'll see how you can force a user to work in a locked-down environment using mandatory profiles. You'll then learn how you can use GPOs to change things up a little. You can control a user's personal profile using Group Policy settings. You can allow a user to have different roaming profiles for different locations or for Remote Desktop Services. You will also see where in a bring-your-own-device world you may choose to forgo the complications of roaming profiles in a mixed-device environment and leverage redirected folders instead. This technology allows you to take the folders on a device and move them to the server, invisibly to the user.

Redirected folders have existed for some time now, and Windows 2012 adds some more granular control. Windows Server 2012 and Windows 8 allow you to redirect more important folders to file servers so that users' personal working environments are available wherever they log in—all without the complications of roaming profiles.

You will also look at how Group Policy Preferences can be used to manage drive mappings and how you can run a set of commands whenever a user logs in or even when a user logs out, thanks to logon/logoff scripts. You'll learn about the best ways to connect users to the resources that you have invested time in preparing. We'll give you real-world situations that utilize these solutions for many of the scenarios that you will face when working with advanced user management.

In this chapter, you'll learn to:

- ◆ Deploy home directories to multiple users

- ◆ Set up mandatory roaming profiles

- ◆ Create logon scripts to automate administration

Experiencing the Flexible Desktop

The ideal scenario for a user's working environment is that the desktop, the laptop computer, or even the Remote Desktop server is nothing more than an appliance.

Consider the help-desk engineer who gets a call from a user having problems with one of their custom applications. For some reason, it won't work correctly. The legacy deployment of a desktop network would require that the engineer sit at that desktop until the problem is resolved. The desktop has a large collection of software installed. The user has all of their business data on a "data partition." The user's settings, including their mail archive, mail contacts, and web browser favorites, are all local on the PC. There is no alternative but to fix that application installation, no matter how long it takes.

Although there have been many improvements to the hardware in our devices to make them more reliable and less likely to fail, devices still fail. When that happens the users look to IT to recover their data that was stored on that device. Sure, Windows 8 and Windows 7 both have a backup tool, but do you really have the time or resources to manage backups for hundreds or tens of thousands of desktops and laptops? What would happen in these scenarios if the user's device was nothing more than an appliance? You could build the device using something like Windows Deployment Services, Microsoft Deployment Toolkit, or another paid-for cloning solution like System Center Configuration Manager (SCCM/ConfigMgr) 2012. That allows you to deploy an image of a configured operating system in minutes. Software deployment can be automated using solutions such as Group Policy, ConfigMgr 2012, or something like Microsoft's application virtualization solution, App-V. That configures the device to a previously known and managed standard in a few more minutes.

Patches are quickly deployed using Windows Software Update Services (WSUS) or ConfigMgr 2012. Group Policy configures the environment. Now the device is secured. This is all great because now the device is back to a healthy state and the custom application is working correctly for the user. This entire process probably took no more than 30 minutes. That's probably much less time than the help-desk engineer would have taken to resolve the issue.

But what about the data the user had on the device? Either you've formatted the disk by rebuilding the device or their data was lost during the hardware failure. Don't worry; the data was on a server all along. If they had a laptop, you made it available locally using a synchronized cache. The user will still have access to all their data when they log into their newly built device.

Using the practices we'll cover in this chapter, you will see how to do the following:

◆ Provide backups of the users' data

◆ Make data more available

◆ Allow the user to be mobile from one device to another or to a Remote Desktop server while maintaining access to data in a consistent manner

◆ Reduce time for troubleshooting

◆ Have happier users

◆ Create secure working environments where there is a shared computing solution

◆ Preconfigure the working environment to apply security policies or to even make the environment easier to use

Real World Scenario

WHEN TO REBUILD THE DEVICE

Here is a simple rule of thumb when you deploy this approach. If a problem is unique to the device (that is, not a network or shared services issue) and it looks like it will take more than 30 minutes to resolve, then you should rebuild the machine. It ends up being a time-saver for IT, the user, and the business. It also gives the user a long-term stable solution. You may even find that educated users will be able to rebuild the device for themselves in this scenario if you allow them.

Of course, this assumes you have used the techniques that are contained in this chapter to keep user data off the device and on the servers. You'll also need something like System Center Configuration Manager or similar to automatically deploy applications that are not contained within your standard images.

Configuring Home Directories

A *home directory* is a shared folder or a folder within a network share that is dedicated to a user. Each user has their own home directory on a file server. The concept is that you want users to store data on servers so that the data is easy to back up, audit, and archive. Some organizations will use company policy and Group Policy to prevent users from using the drives on their devices so that they are forced to use their home directories for their personal data. Organizations use home directories in two basic ways. The most common is that the directory's permissions are set up so that the home directory is private; in other words, the user is the only person with access to the contents. Local administrators and local systems on the server will also probably need access for administration, backup/recovery, and archive operations. An alternative you might see in some deployments is that there is no privacy on the home directory. It's treated as the user's personal share for sharing data with others on the network when the normal team, departmental, or company shares aren't appropriate.

This is where some people will argue that there is a lot of cheap disk space on every PC and that server storage is relatively expensive. Isn't it more economical to keep data on the device and distribute it via email? We'd argue that you're looking at the short-term costs. Email is a bad way to share files. Aside from the possibility that the file you're trying to share may be too large and get bounced back, everyone will end up with their own edited copies and there is no way to ensure any sort of version control. If you're using a mailbox-style server such as Exchange Server, then the file is being stored on the mail server. But most important, an organization must be able to ensure that its business data is being backed up or even archived to a secure store and retained for several years. These are legal requirements for many organizations, either public or private, around the world. How are you going to back up your devices? How are you going to archive files without user intervention? You'll find that it's a lot cheaper, easier to use, and much more reliable to centralize your data storage and perform one backup and manage one automated archive.

The other argument against home directories that we often hear comes from the HR/ personnel or accounting department. They don't want IT to be able to see their data, so they want to keep it on the device. We're sorry to burst their bubble, but if someone is a motivated administrator, then they can get into sensitive data no matter where it is. There was once an HR department that decided to store sensitive data on a USB-attached hard drive that they'd store in a safe. Can you imagine storing critical company payroll data on a non-fault-tolerant device with moving parts that are likely to fail? The best solution is to have independently monitored auditing of file server data access with clearly documented and communicated policies and actions that follow up any contravention of those policies.

We'll now cover how you can configure home directories for the users in your business.

Setting Up the Lab

In this example, you'll be working with two servers. BF1 is a Windows Server 2012 R2 domain controller for the BigFirm organization. BF2 is a Windows Server 2012 R2 file server. The network will also have a desktop called Win81 that is running...well, Windows 8.1. We strongly recommend that you do any work in a test lab and have everything documented before approaching your production system.

In this chapter you're going to see how to use DFS namespaces whenever you're using file shares. There are two reasons that you'll do this:

◆ You can abstract the physical location of the file shares:

Users and applications map to a logical name rather than to a physical server. This means that you can move the file shares from one server to another without having to change user configurations, logon scripts, or application configurations. This is very convenient when a server becomes obsolete or during a server failure when you need to recover data to an alternate location. You can quickly adjust the namespace without having to make many changes that you would otherwise have to make elsewhere.

◆ You can take advantage of DFS Replication (DFS-R) while maintaining the same drive mappings in user configurations, logon scripts, and application settings:

This means that you can replicate user data to another server in another site. If a disaster destroys your production server or even the site, then the data is available in an alternate location using the same drive mappings. You can also introduce more creative backup strategies. For example, you can use Volume Shadow Copy Service (VSS) for short-term operational backups in the production site and use the DR site for long-term backups that might otherwise interfere with network performance in the production site.

You should have already learned about how to set up a namespace and how to configure DFS-R. You are going to be using a namespace called \\bigfirm.com\BigFirmShares. You'll see later how you will add folders to this namespace that redirect to the shares that will contain the user's personal data.

Creating the Home Directories

You need to create a directory for each user and ensure that it is appropriately secured. You must ask the following questions when you are doing this:

◆ Who must be able to access each user's home directory?

The norm is to allow only the user, administrators, and System to access to the folder. Some organizations choose to treat the home directory as a personal folder that the user can use to share data with everyone else. We'll demonstrate the more usual private approach in this section.

◆ How will you name the folders?

Some people use something predictable. They name the folder after the user who owns the home directory. For example, the user Joe Bloggs has a username of JBloggs. His home directory will be called JBloggs. This makes it easier to perform automated tasks such as connecting the user to the share.

◆ How will you share the folder?

Some choose to share each and every home directory. That's a lot of work. Others prefer to create one generic share and create a folder underneath for each user. This suits the DFS approach discussed earlier because there's only one DFS link to alter if you need to restore or move the home directory share to a new location. The shared folder will be made available via a DFS namespace.

Let's start creating some home directories, but first we will need a few users. You have already learned about user and group creation back in Chapter 8, so I won't go over that again. For the rest of this chapter we will be using some users and groups named as follows:

Users

   ◆ Alexandra Garcia

   ◆ Joe Bloggs

   ◆ Joe Elway

Groups

   ◆ Accounts

   ◆ Home

   ◆ HR

   ◆ IT

   ◆ Profiles

   ◆ Senior Management

The users will be placed in the `\bigfirm.com\BigFirm\Users` organizational unit (OU), as shown in Figure 26.1. You'll be configuring a working environment for these users throughout this chapter.

FIGURE 26.1
The Joe Bloggs
test user

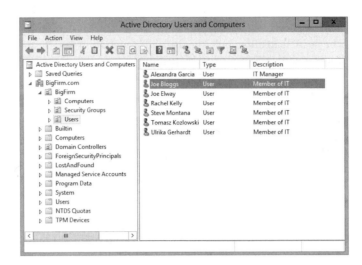

FIGURE 26.1
The Joe Bloggs
test user

You'll be creating a shared folder called Home on BF2. Some administrators like to create all of their shares in a single folder on the file server. This serves a couple of purposes:

◆ It keeps things tidy and the administrators can find all of their shares in one location.

◆ It makes automation tasks such as backup or directory replication much easier because there is only one folder to select.

Create a folder called Shares on the D drive, as shown in Figure 26.2.

FIGURE 26.2
The Shares
folder on BF2

Disable folder permission inheritance, and set the folder permissions as follows:

Group	Permission
BF2\Administrators	Full Control
System	Full Control

You're doing this because any folders you create in D:\Shares will inherit these permissions by default. This makes the new shared folders secure by default. It will be up to you and other administrators to assign access to the correct users or security groups. It will also prevent non-administrators from creating folders in here without permission. Now create a folder in D:\Shares called Home.

The Home folder will now be shared. This will mean that you can create subfolders for each user and only have to manage a single share. The aim of this is to simplify deployment and to make security management as easy as possible.

You are now going to use the File and Storage Services tool. The tool shown in Figure 26.3 will appear when you select File and Storage Services from the Server Manager Dashboard and then select the Shares tab.

FIGURE 26.3
File and Storage Services

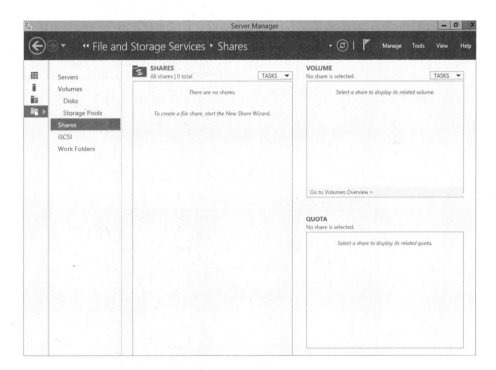

The wizard will prompt you to select a profile for the share, as shown in Figure 26.4. Select SMB Share - Quick to create a standard file share.

FIGURE 26.4
Share profile

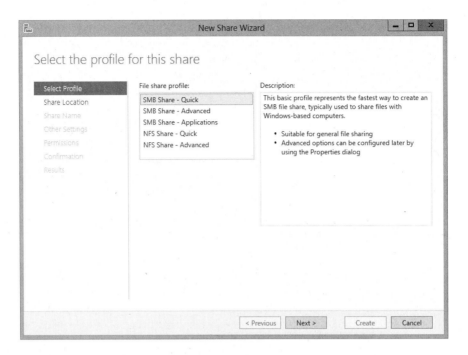

Here you specify the location of the folder that you want to share. Select the custom path radio button and browse out to the D:\Shares\Home folder you created earlier. Your screen should resemble Figure 26.5.

FIGURE 26.5
Share location

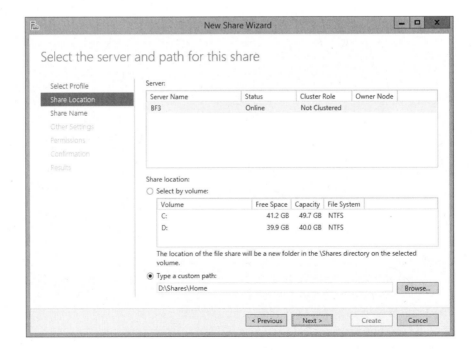

Click Next, and you will be on the "Specify share name" screen, as shown in Figure 26.6. The share name will be Home$.

FIGURE 26.6

Share description

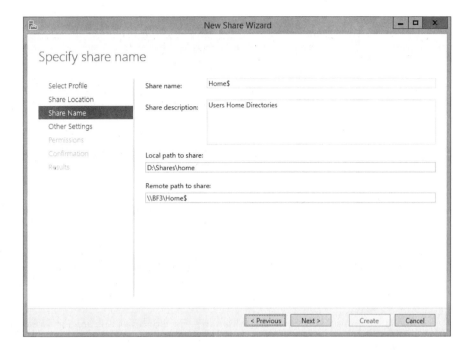

The screen also allows you to document the share. It makes sense to describe the shared folder for when someone else needs to diagnose or fix an issue and you're not around to help. Enter a description for the share.

The Other Settings screen provides some additional configuration options for your share. The "Allow caching of share" option will be enabled by default. You also have the options of encrypting the data access and enabling access-based enumeration.

It is best practice to lock down permissions on a shared folder in two ways. The first is to lock down the permissions on the NTFS folder; you have already done this. The second is to lock down permissions on the share. Click the Customize Setting button, select the Share tab, and set the share permissions as follows:

Group	Permission
BF2\Administrators	Full Control
Everyone	Read

Once completed, the share permissions will display as Custom, as in Figure 26.7.

FIGURE 26.7
Setting the SMB
permissions

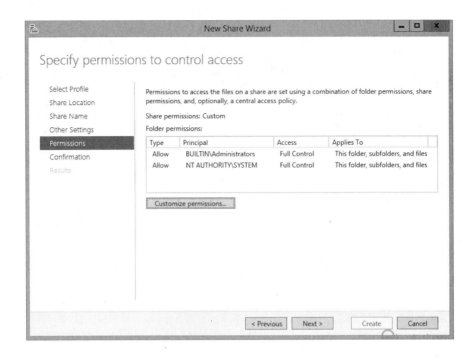

The combined effects of the folder and share permissions are as follows:

◆ Users will be able to pass through the Home$ share to folders beneath it. However, they cannot create anything here. This is thanks to the NTFS permissions in the folder.

◆ The user will be able to modify the contents of anything within Home$ *as long as they have permission*. This is required so that the user can create and modify files and folders within their home directory. As it stands, users can't do anything much on the Home$ share, but that will change when you create their personal home directories.

Once the wizard is complete, you will need to add the new share to DFS. This can be done through the DFS administration tool or in PowerShell. The folder will be set up within the BigFirmShares namespace with a new folder name of Home. This folder will be available on the network as \\bigfirm.com\BigFirmShares\Home. Here's how you can add the share to the DFS root with PowerShell. You'll be using the new-dfsnfolder cmdlet:

```
new-dfsnfolder -path "\\BigFirm.com\BigFirmShares\Home" -TargetPath "\\BF2\Home$"
-EnableTargetFailback $True -Description "Users home directory"
```

Now that the shares have been created, you should verify that the share is accessible. You can do this by browsing to the UNC path of the share within the DFS namespace. Check it with both administrator and non-administrator accounts to be sure that the permissions are correct.

You could use DFS to set up folder replication if you had a duplicate server in a disaster recovery (DR) site. If you do this and the DR plan is invoked, users can log into PCs or Remote Desktop servers in the DR site, and they'll still use the same UNC paths to browse to or connect to their home directories. No user objects or scripts need to be modified.

Thanks to the abstraction provided by DFS namespace, you can easily move the Home folder to another server. All it requires is a quick change of the mapping for the folder within the namespace. No user objects or scripts would need to be modified to reflect the move.

Administrators have used both of these approaches in the past and kept user disruption to a minimum. Administrators using the traditional file shares without DFS will find that there is some effort required to introduce DFS. However, the gains are worth the effort once the migrations are complete.

Creating Home Directories

It's time to create the folders for each user. You're really going to like how easy this can be.

Log into your domain controller and launch your preferred Active Directory administrative tool, either Active Directory Users and Computers (ADUC) or Active Directory Administrative Center (ADAC). For this example, log into BF1, launch ADUC, and navigate to where the users are in \BigFirm\Users.

Select all the users, right-click, and choose Properties. This opens the dialog box shown in Figure 26.8. This will allow you to configure all of these users with a home directory at the same time. You can see that we have configured the home directory to be mapped as Z:\ when the users log in. They will be mapped to \\bigfirm.com\BigFirmShares\Home\%Username%. The %Username% is where the magic is.

FIGURE 26.8
Setting home directories for many users

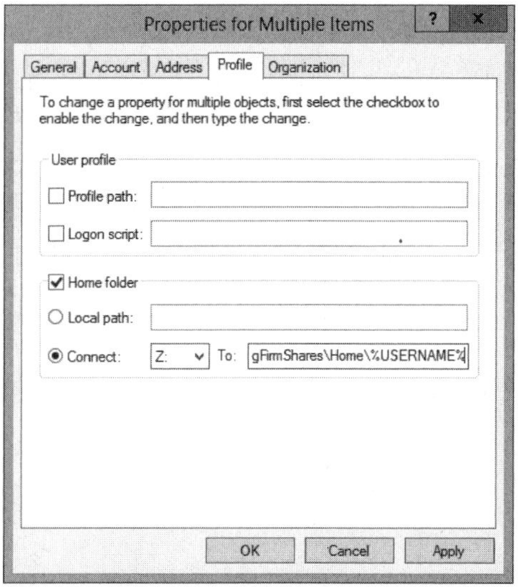

This automatically completes the path using the username of the account in question. For example, when you check the Home Folder setting in the JBloggs user object, you can see it has been mapped to \\bigfirm.com\BigFirmShares\Home\JBloggs. You can see this in Figure 26.9, where we have opened the properties of the JBloggs user account.

FIGURE 26.9
Checking the
user object home
directory setting

Here's the cool bit: Windows creates the folder and sets the correct permissions for you on
your file server. This is visible on the file server, as shown in Figure 26.10.

FIGURE 26.10
The automatically
created home
directories

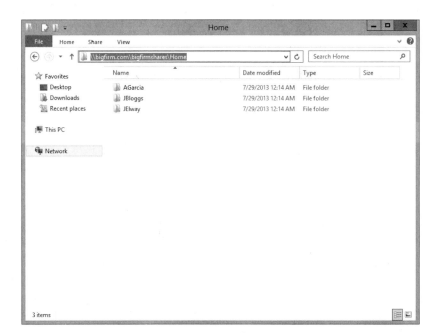

You can see in Figure 26.11 that the home directory for each user has inherited the permissions on the Home folder. Each user has been granted Full Control permissions over their own folder:

Group	Permission
BF2\Administrators	Full Control
System	Full Control
BigFirm\<User>	Full Control

FIGURE 26.11
The home directory's automatically created permissions

All of the work is done! It's that easy. You can now log on using one of those users. In our lab, JBloggs will log into Win8, and the Z drive will be mapped to JBloggs' own home directory. Thanks to the permissions that are on each folder, the user in question cannot access a home directory that is owned by somebody else.

SHARING HOME DIRECTORIES

We previously mentioned that some organizations choose to give users other than the owner access to the home directories. You can add that access quite easily by adding Authenticated Users to D:\Shares\Home. This permission will be inherited by every home directory. You can give them Read & Execute, for read-only access, or you can give them Change rights so that they can modify the contents of another person's home directory.

Some organizations choose to not configure the user object's Home Folder attribute. Their opinion is that it is easier to map the drive using a logon script. A logon script runs every time a user logs in and runs a set of commands. You'll look at them later. Alternatively, you can leverage Group Policy Preferences for drive mappings. If the drive moves to another server, then it's easy to change a single logon script command or group policy instead of changing hundreds or even thousands of users.

The counter opinion on this is that you have made your solution for home directories very dynamic by using a DFS namespace to abstract the physical location of the share. You can move the share, and all users will retain their mappings once you modify the single folder mapping in the DFS namespace. In addition to this, some environment variables for the user's home directory are available when you set up the Home Folder user attribute. These may be used by your scripts or by applications:

HOMEDRIVE   Represents the letter used to map the home directory, for example, `Z:`.

HOMEPATH   Represents the path within the HOMEDRIVE where the home directory is contained, for example, `\`. The total path is `%HOMEDRIVE%%HOMEPATH%` or `Z:\`.

HOMESHARE   This is the UNC path to the user's home directory, for example, `\\bigfirm .com\BigFirmShares\Home\JBloggs`.

Home Directory vs. Local Storage

You have given your users a centralized storage mechanism. You should consider communicating to your users that data should be stored on this drive and not on the local drive of the device. You can use Group Policy to enforce this policy. The following are keys to success:

◆   Communicate that home directories are backed up and that devices are not. There is no service-level agreement for data stored on devices.

◆   Enable the Volume Shadow Copy Service on your file servers, and educate users how to use the Previous Versions Client to recover their own files.

◆   Data on the device may not be secure. Educate the users about the need for data security.

◆   Use auditing where required to reassure users about sensitive files. Maybe even take a look at using Active Directory Rights Management Services to allow users to control at the file level who can see or edit a file.

You will look at some automated mechanisms a little later that will further encourage users to keep data on the server instead of on the device.

This section has discussed how to allow a user to make their personal data available to them no matter what server or device they log into. We'll now cover roaming profiles and discuss how they can do the same thing with their working environment.

Creating Roaming Profiles

A *profile* is a folder that contains all the settings pertaining to a user's working environment. By default, the profile is stored in the `C:\Users` directory. A *roaming profile* is stored on the network instead of the local drive of the machine where the user logs in. However, it is cached locally by default. The advantage of a roaming profile is that a user can log into any machine in the domain and have a consistent working environment. However, you have to watch out for the profile containing information that is specific to a computer, application, or operating system that won't apply to all machines that the user might log into.

A profile has two types of content:

♦ Files and folders

♦ ntuser.dat

A user's Windows and application settings are usually stored in HKEY_CURRENT_USER in the registry. This needs to be available to the user every time they log in. It is stored in a file called ntuser.dat.

Other types of content are stored as files in specially named folders in the profile, for example:

My Documents This is the default location where programs such as Microsoft Office look to store documents.

My Music This is where music players look to store and load music by default.

Favorites Internet Explorer keeps your Favorites link files here.

AppData Windows and other programs will store files and settings here that are configuration oriented but shouldn't be visible by default in order to simplify things for the user.

Desktop The user's desktop contents are stored here.

A new profile needs to be created for a user when they log into the machine for the first time. Out of the box, Windows generates one by copying the default profile. A new profile is created and is named after the user. You'll see a new folder in C:\Users that is named after the user, for example, C:\Users\JBloggs. That will be secured so that only System, Administrators, and the user have access to it. When the user logs in, the settings from the profile are loaded into the user's working session. When they log out, the changes are saved.

At this point, you may have noticed that the profile is a local resource by default. This means that the data and configuration that you have on one PC will be different on another PC. Imagine how ticked off your users will be if their browser favorites or their email contacts are missing when they log into a different machine. This problem will occur in different scenarios:

♦ Users log into a farm of Remote Desktop servers or virtual desktops. They never know which server they will be on, so their user configuration is different on every server.

♦ You have a hot-desk office where users sit down at different PCs every day. Their profile will be different on each machine.

♦ A user's PC fails or is replaced. They will lose their entire personal configuration. Think of the business data that might be permanently lost because PCs are not normally backed up.

You can see how all this conflicts with your desire for the appliance PC and dynamic IT. Users will rebel against IT as soon as they know that there is a risk of them losing their data or having an inconsistent working environment.

A solution to this problem is the roaming profile. The concept is that the user's profile is stored on a file share that is similar in structure to the one you've set up for home directories. The profile is downloaded from the file server whenever a user logs in. It is cached in C:\Users on the computer that the user is logged into. The contents of the profile that have changed are saved back to the file server when the user logs out. That can sound like a lot of files moving around the network. Potentially, it can be. However, Windows will download or upload only those files that need to be downloaded or uploaded. For example, when a user is logging into a PC with a roaming profile, only the files that are not already downloaded will be transferred. When the user logs out, only the files that have been changed will be uploaded.

Let's take a look at two ways to create roaming profiles. One is very quick and easy to set up. The second takes things a little further by increasing security, but it does require a little more work.

Creating a Roaming Profiles Share: The Easy Way

We'll now go through the process of configuring roaming profiles for the users in BigFirm. With this approach, you'll set up the profile settings in the user objects. Unlike the easy approach for setting up home directories, a folder will not be created for you once you set up the roaming profile attribute. Instead, the user's roaming profile will be set up automatically when the user logs in.

You'll start by using an approach often recommended by Microsoft that allows for the easy deployment of profiles. You'll create a file share on BF2, the file server.

1. Create a folder called Profiles in D:\Shares, as shown in Figure 26.12.

   Again, it's worth noting that in a production environment you would never place your user data on the system disk but on a separate dedicated volume.

FIGURE 26.12

The roaming Profiles folder on the file server

2. Disable inheritance of permissions on the folder, and configure the permissions as shown here (and Figure 26.13):

Group	Permission	Where
Creator Owner	Full Control	Subfolders and files
BF2\Administrators	Full Control	This folder, subfolders, and files
System	Full Control	This folder, subfolders, and files
Authenticated Users	List Folder/Read Data; Create Folders/Append Data; Read Attributes	This folder, subfolders, and files

FIGURE 26.13

The advanced permissions of the Profiles folder

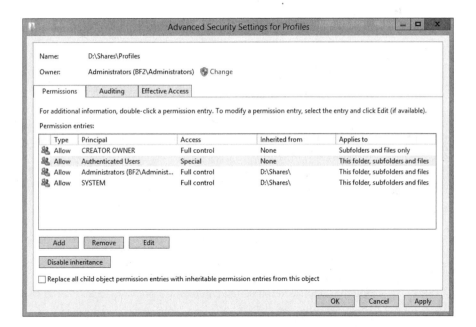

WHY READ ATTRIBUTES?

Notice that we've added that last permission for Read Attributes. It isn't documented in any Microsoft documentation that we have read. However, a user's profile will fail to completely save to the file server if this permission is not added to the profile folder.

These permissions will allow a user to create a folder within the share where their roaming profile will be stored. There is a downside to this approach. A user could create a folder within this share and then store data within it without approval. This is required because, with this approach, the user's rights are used to create their roaming profile. The user, unbeknownst to them, will be setting up their own roaming profile folder on the file server when they log in.

You're now going to share the Profiles folder and add it to the DFS namespace.

3. In the File and Storage Services dashboard, select Shares and choose New Share from the Tasks drop-down list to launch the New Share Wizard shown in Figure 26.14.

FIGURE 26.14
Profiles shared
folder location

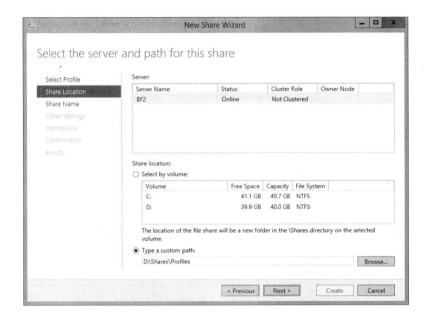

4. Then set the location as **D:\Shares\Profiles**; that's the location of the folder that you are going to use to store roaming profiles.

5. Share the Profiles folder as a hidden share called **Profiles$**, as shown in Figure 26.15.

6. Also set a description. In this example, enter **Users roaming profiles share** for the description of this share.

7. On the Permissions screen click the Customize Settings button, then select the Share tab, and set the share permissions as follows:

Group	Permission
BF2\Administrators	Full Control
Authenticated Users	Change

FIGURE 26.15
Profiles share name
and description

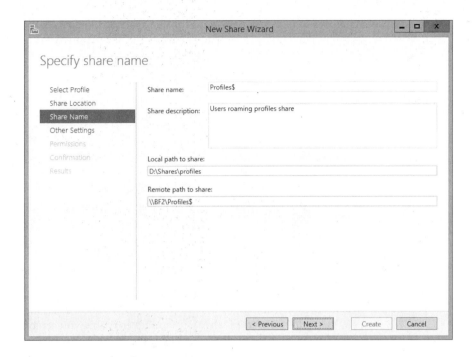

Once completed, the share permissions will display as Custom, as in Figure 26.16.

FIGURE 26.16
Setting the profile's
share permissions

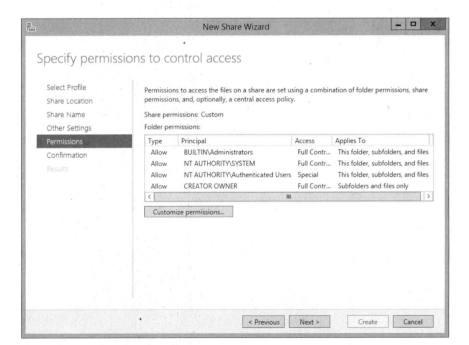

You'll be using PowerShell to make the profile share available in the DFS namespace. You can see this happening in Figure 26.17. You'll be using the `new-dfsnfolder` cmdlet:

```
new-dfsnfolder -path "\\BigFirm.com\BigFirmShares\Profiles" -TargetPath "\\BF2\
Profiles$" -EnableTargetFailback $True -Description "Users profile directory"
```

FIGURE 26.17
Adding Profiles$ to
the DFS namespace

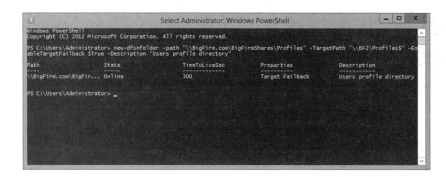

By using DFS you will be able replicate the folder or move it when you need to without having to make any huge adjustments when the system is in production.

When you've completed the wizard, you should verify that you can browse to `\\bigfirm .com\BigFirmShares\Profiles`. If you can, then you're ready to move on to the next step. If not, then you probably have an issue with permissions on the share, or you need to wait for or force the updated DFS namespace settings to replicate between domain controllers.

Deploying the folders for the profiles with this approach is easy. You simply configure the user account objects and let Windows do the rest. In Figure 26.18, we've selected all the user accounts at once and opened their properties to set the profile property.

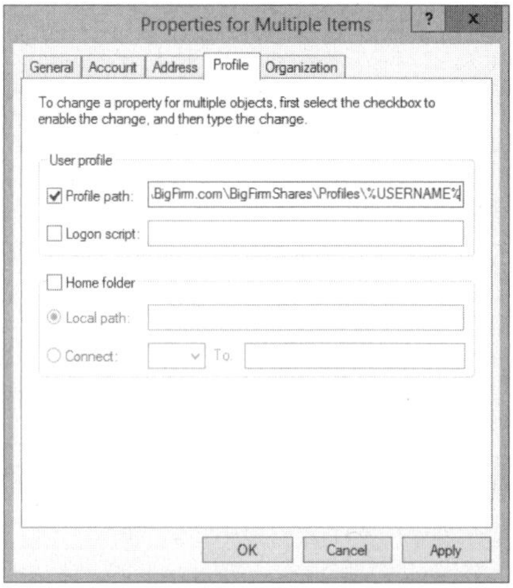

FIGURE 26.18
Configuring
many users with a
roaming profile

Alternatively, you can do this by editing a single user object, as you can see in Figure 26.19.

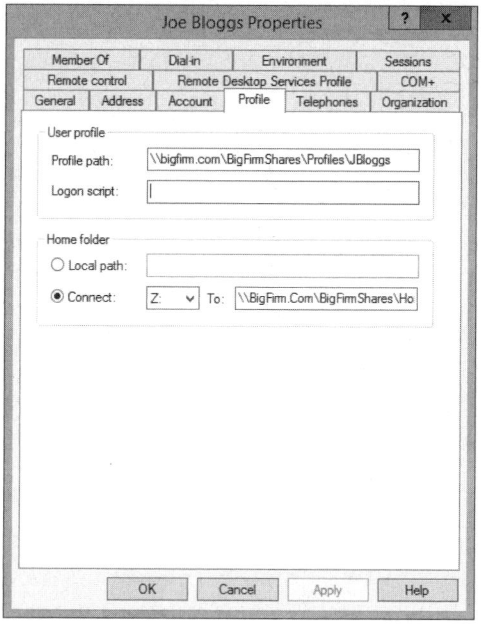

FIGURE 26.19
Configuring a single user with a roaming profile

When you do this, no folder is created. Remember that the folder will be created on behalf of the user when they log in. So, don't be surprised to find no new folders in the Profiles folder yet. You'll have to test it first.

You can also use PowerShell to configure a user's roaming profile attribute of the user object. You will use the set-aduser cmdlet:

```
set-aduser jbloggs -profilepath "\\bigfirm.com\bigfirmshares\Profiles\JBloggs"
```

You're now ready to test this, which is a necessary step before allowing your users to log in. You're going to notice a few things here.

A profile is created on the workstation (or Remote Desktop server) when the user logs in for the first time. You can see this in Figure 26.20.

A new, empty folder is created on the profile share for the user. Note that the name has a .V2 extension. This signifies that the profile is a *version 2* profile and was created by a Windows 7 or newer operating system. *Do not make the mistake of specifying* .V2 *in the profile path. It's an easy trap to fall into.* For example, specifying a profile as \\bigfirm.com\BigFirmShares\Profiles\ JBloggs.V2 will cause the profile to not load. Windows will automatically add that extension to the folder name as required.

Log your user out, and the user's profile is uploaded from the workstation to the file share. It is now possible for this user to roam from workstation to workstation and maintain the same working environment.

FIGURE 26.20
The cached profile
on the PC

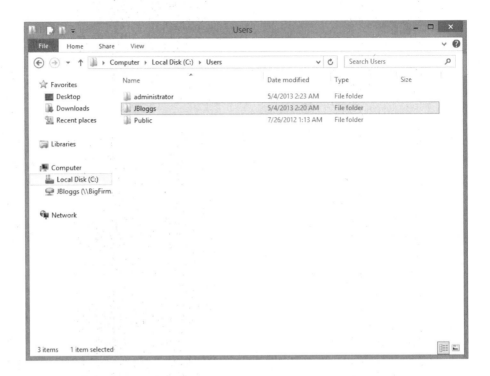

Hold on a second! How do you know if there's anything in that profile folder? You've probably just re-created this scenario and noticed that administrators don't have any access to the profile. That's actually the way this is meant to work. The user has created their own folder, and as Creator Owner they have full and *sole* access to it. That's a bit of a pain because it makes things like backup/recovery and helping the user nearly impossible!

It's messy to grant administrators to user profiles. Ideally, there would be a way to grant access as required. You can do this with a Group Policy setting that you can apply to the computers creating the profiles. However, this solution must be applied before the profiles are created. It has no retroactive effect.

1. Log into the domain controller, BF1, and launch the Group Policy Management console from Administrative Tools.

2. Create and link a new Group Policy object, as shown in Figure 26.21, to the Computers OU where Win8, the workstation, resides.

FIGURE 26.21

The new Group Policy object

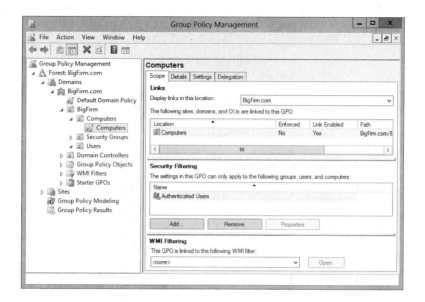

The policy that you will be enabling applies to the computer that the user will be logging into, not the user and not the file server where the profile is created. That's why the policy is linked to Computers, and not Servers, where the file server resides.

The policy that you are enabling is "Add the Administrators security group to roaming user profiles," which can be found in Computer Configuration \Administrative Templates\System\User Profiles. You can see it in Figure 26.22.

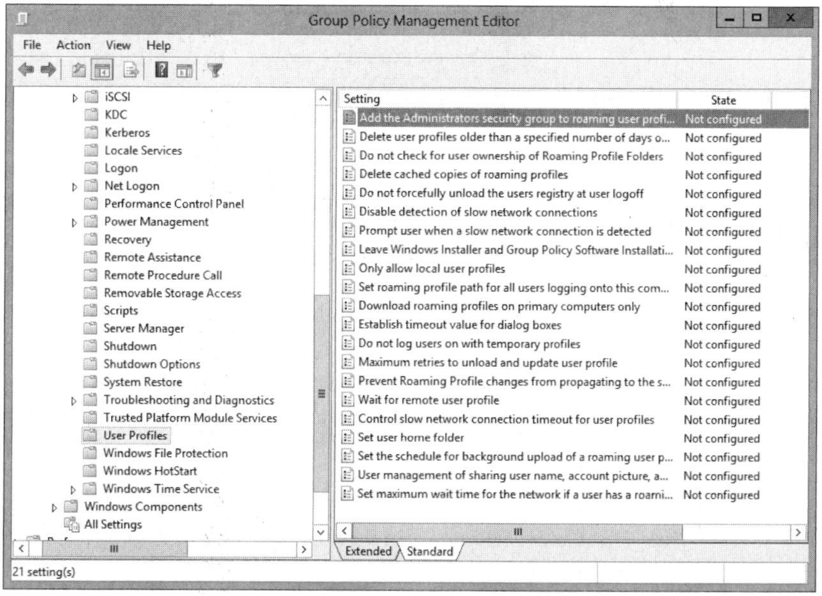

FIGURE 26.22

Configuring the Group Policy object

3. Set it to Enabled, and this policy will grant Administrators Full Control to any newly created profile.

   Remember that policies don't apply straightaway. In a production scenario, you will probably have to wait for the length of the refresh period.

4. In a test or lab scenario, run the following command to force a computer to apply a computer configuration from inherited GPOs:

```
gpupdate /target:computer /force
```

Figure 26.23 shows that when you test this, you will see that Administrators will have Full Control over the profile. This will make user management and troubleshooting a lot easier for administrative staff and allow services that run as an administrator user to access the contents.

FIGURE 26.23
Administrators have access to roaming profile folders.

You've managed to deploy roaming profiles just by creating a shared folder and configuring the user accounts. That was pretty simple. However, we did mention that the security of the Profiles folder isn't as tight as you might like thanks to the permissions required for this "self-service" technique. A sneaky user could start creating folders in the Profiles$ share and storing data there. You might want to look at an alternative way to deploy user profiles.

Creating a Roaming Profiles Share: The Hard Way

You can adopt this solution if you want 100-percent control over the contents of the folder containing the roaming profiles. You manually create every folder and set the permissions.

1. Create the Profiles folder in the same location as you did in the previous sections.

2. Disable inheritance, but do not copy the inherited permissions.

3. Now assign these permissions to the folder:

Group	Permission
BF2\Administrators	Full
System	Full
Authenticated Users	Read & Execute

Make sure that the Authenticated Users group does not have any special permission that allows the group to create folders in the Profiles folder.

4. Set up the Profiles$ share as shown here:

Group	Permission
BF2\Administrators	Full
BigFirm\Authenticated Users	Full

Don't worry about Authenticated Users having full permission on the share; they'll be restricted by the folder permissions to read everything. The user will be later granted additional permissions to their own profile folder. You can now link the Profiles$ share using a folder in the DFS namespace.

This is the extra step that requires much more work. You must manually create and set the permissions of a folder that will contain a user profile. A profile folder will not be automatically created when the user logs in because of the restrictive permissions set on the Profiles folder. For example, the user Joe Bloggs will require the folder `D:\Shares\Profiles\JBloggs.V2`. That folder must have permissions set on it as follows:

Group	Permission
BF2\Administrators	Full
System	Full
BigFirm\JBloggs	Modify

You'll note that you must disable permissions inheritance to get the previous permissions set. You can now configure the user accounts with their profile path. The total solution is this:

♦ The user can navigate through the Profiles$ share with read-only permissions.

♦ The user has Change permissions only on their profile, which is enough for complete functionality.

♦ The user cannot create folders or files in the Profiles$ share through any means without administrative rights.

When you test this, you'll find that nothing appears in the user's roaming profile folder on the file server until they log out. Make sure you do two things when you are testing:

1. Log in and out as a single user several times to make sure the profile loads and saves correctly. Be sure to make some changes when you are logged in.

2. Make sure that the non-administrator user cannot read other people's profiles and cannot create folders in the Profiles$ share outside of their own profile.

 Real World Scenario

HANDY TROUBLESHOOTING TIPS

You can delete locally cached roaming profiles on your Windows 8 machine by right-clicking the Start screen icon in the lower-left corner of the desktop and selecting System. That launches System from Control Panel (that's a handy shortcut). Then click Advanced System Settings. Click Settings in the User Profiles section of the Advanced tab. That dialog box will display the profiles that are cached on the PC. You can select one and delete it if required.

You shouldn't try to delete the profile of a logged-in user. Even if you log that user out and log in as an administrator, you still can't delete that cached profile because there's still an open or locked file or folder. You will have to resort to rebooting the PC.

If the PC gets a bit messy, it can be hard to find the user's cached profile folder in C:\Users. It's possible to have several versions of the profile whenever there's a corruption or access issue, with the user probably using the latest one. You can identify which folder the user is using by using regedit .exe, the registry editing tool. Browse to \HKEY_LOCAL_MACHINE\SOFTWARE\Microsoft\Windows NT\CurrentVersion\ProfileList. Here you'll see the security identifiers (SIDs) of the users. If this is a test machine, it won't be hard to identify which one to look at. Go into the key that is named after the SID of the relevant user. The ProfileImagePath value will contain the path to this user's locally cached profile.

While you test, take a look at the folders on the file server and the PC that you're testing. It's a good learning experience. You'll see that Windows caches the profile on the PC. That's handy for PC users, especially laptop users, whenever the file server is not available when the user logs in. Imagine if a laptop user goes home and can't download their profile. If there's no cache, then they get a temporary profile that doesn't contain their files and their settings. Thanks to the cache, they still have their files and settings.

It's worth doing some fun things in your test lab to re-create real-world scenarios. Change permissions on the Profiles folder so the user has no permissions. Rename the profile on the file server without changing the user object. You'll find that Windows will load a locally cached copy or will generate a temporary profile from the default user profile. Now you can try some troubleshooting.

You've now seen how to create roaming profiles in two different ways. This allows users to take their customized working environment around the network wherever they work. But what if your organization needs to lock down the user's working environment to maximize security and simplify the user interface? That brings us to mandatory profiles, a variation on roaming profiles.

Configuring Mandatory Profiles

Ask a veteran administrator what the cause of many problems is in a desktop environment, and you'll be sure to find that user configuration is not far from the top of the list. You may want a solution that provides users with a clean user configuration every time they log in.

The solution that we're talking about is a mandatory profile. This works by pre-creating a profile for users, configuring it as a mandatory profile, and making it available to all the required users as their roaming profile. No matter what changes the user makes, they will not be saved. Every time the user logs in, their profile will be reset to what the administrator had defined.

Other benefits include the following:

◆   You can provide the user with a preconfigured and consistent working experience.

◆   You can always ensure that the user has the required shortcuts for applications available.

◆   You will reduce the administrative workload and complexity associated with roaming profiles.

These are typical scenarios where you find mandatory profiles:

◆   Remote Desktop Services server farms

◆   Environments where there may be significant staff churn and where training time is minimal, for example, call centers

You'll now learn how to create a mandatory profile.

MANDATORY PROFILES ON WINDOWS 8

Creating mandatory profiles in Windows 8 is still a manual process. You will start by opening Windows Explorer and browsing to C:\Users, as shown in Figure 26.24. Here you can see the cached profiles on the PC. The one you're interested is C:\Users\JElway. You are going to copy this folder to the Profiles share on the file server, that is, \\bigfirm.com\BigFirmShares\ Profiles\.

FIGURE 26.24
The profiles on the
Windows 8 lab PC

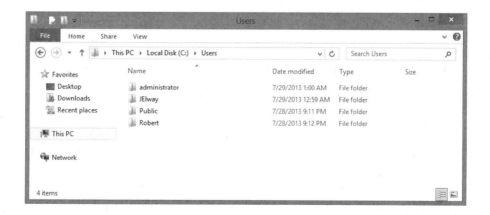

Once it has copied, you should rename it. Make sure that it has a `.V2` extension. We've renamed the profile folder to `Mandatory.V2`, as shown in Figure 26.25.

FIGURE 26.25
The copied profile on the file server

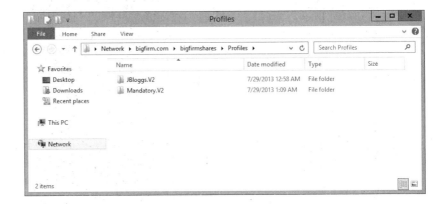

Figure 26.26 shows you the two folders that you need to delete from the roaming profile:

FIGURE 26.26
Deleting folders from the roaming profile

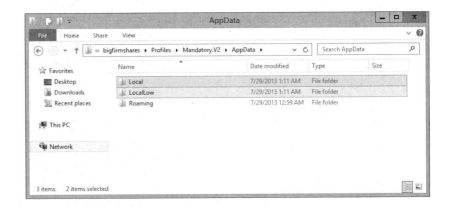

◆   `AppData\Local`

◆   `AppData\LocalLow`

Part of the profile is a file called `NTUSER.DAT`. It contains the `HKEY_CURRENT_USER` hive from the Windows registry. It has internal (not NTFS or file system) permissions. They protect the contents of the registry file so that only the assigned user (Joe Elway in this case) and administrators have access. You need to change that so users of the new mandatory roaming profile will have access to the contained `HKEY_CURRENT_USER` registry hive.

What you're going to do now is open up the `NTUSER.DAT` file in `regedit.exe`, the registry editor, and change the permissions of the `HKEY_CURRENT_USER` hive in that file.

1. Launch `regedit.exe` on the file server, and browse to `HKEY_USERS`, as shown in Figure 26.27.

FIGURE 26.27
Opening the registry editor

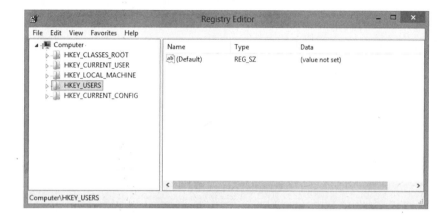

2. Select File ➢ Load Hive.

That opens the dialog box shown in Figure 26.28.

FIGURE 26.28
Load Hive in `regedit.exe`

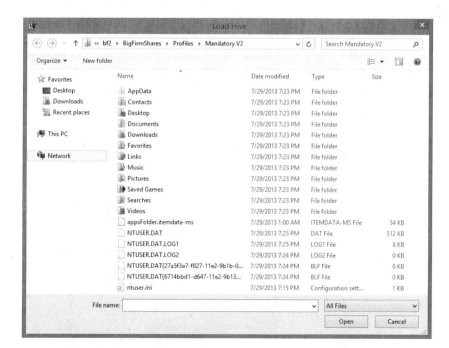

3. Browse to where the `NTUSER.DAT` file is contained on the file server.

   In our case, that is `D:\Shares\Profiles\Mandatory.V2\NTUSER.DAT`. Open that file.

4. You'll need to give the loaded hive a new name.

   You can't have a second `HKEY_CURRENT_USER`. Don't worry; this is only a temporary label that will be used while you're editing the opened `NTUSER.DAT` file. For the sake of simplicity, we've named the hive after the profile, that is, `Mandatory.V2`.

5. Browse to your loaded hive, for example, `Mandatory.V2` as shown in Figure 26.29, and right-click it.

FIGURE 26.29
Browsing to the loaded registry hive

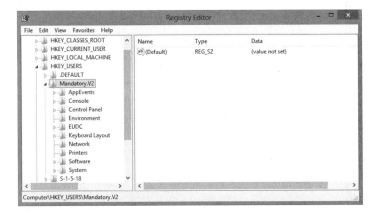

6. Select Permissions from the pop-up menu.

   What you see in Figure 26.30 is the permissions for `HKEY_CURRENT_USER` as contained within the `NTUSER.DAT` file in the new roaming profile.

FIGURE 26.30
Permissions for the loaded registry hive

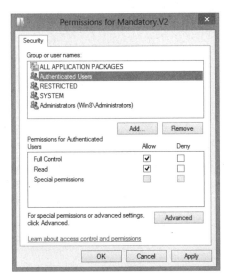

7. Do two things to the permissions:

   ◆ Remove the entry for the user that was used to create the profile, that is, JElway.

   ◆ Add an entry for a security group that will require access to the roaming mandatory profile. In this case, it is Authenticated Users from the domain. Grant this group Full Control over the hive.

8. Close the Permissions dialog box, and then select File ➢ Unload Hive in `regedit.exe`.

   You'll be asked whether you want to unload the key and its subkeys.

9. Say Yes to that, and your modified `NTUSER.DAT` is saved.

You cannot use this roaming profile until you unload the hive.

COMPLETING THE MANDATORY PROFILES

At this point, all you have done is create a roaming profile that could be used by anyone. You haven't made it a *mandatory* roaming profile. The conversion is quite easy. Navigate into the roaming profile you created, and rename `NTUSER.DAT` to `NTUSER.MAN`, as shown in Figure 26.31. The extension is what tells Windows that no changes should be saved to this profile; that is, it is a mandatory roaming profile.

FIGURE 26.31
Rename NTUSER
.DAT to NTUSER
.MAN

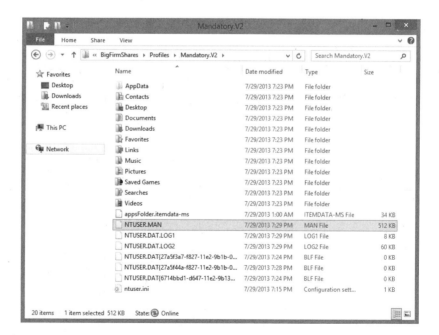

You need to correctly secure the mandatory roaming profile folder on the file server. Follow these steps:

1. Disable the inheritance of permissions from the parent folder, and set the mandatory profile's permissions as follows:

Group	Permission
BF2\Administrators	Full Control
System	Full Control
BigFirm\Authenticated Users	Read & Execute

You've granted access to the Authenticated Users security group.

2. Choose a group that matches the group to which you granted access to the NTUSER.DAT registry hive.

Setting the folder permissions does two things for you. It provides Authenticated Users (or whatever security group you choose to use) with access to the mandatory roaming profile but prevents members from changing it.

Now you need to test the mandatory roaming profile.

3. Simply navigate to a test user, and change the profile entry to \\bigfirm.com\ BigFirmShares\Profiles\Mandatory.

WHERE'S THE ".V2"?

Notice that you did not add the .V2 extension. Consider it to be silent; the newer versions of Windows will add it as required, as discussed earlier.

---

4. Log in as the test user and verify that the customizations to the mandatory roaming profile are loaded.

5. Make some changes, then undo the customizations, and make a few of your own.

6. Log out and log in again.

You should find that the loaded profile is reset to what was set up in the original mandatory roaming profile; no changes were saved. If that's what is happening, then you have a correctly functioning mandatory roaming profile.

You've configured JBloggs with \\bigfirm.com\BigFirmShares\Profiles\Mandatory.V2 as the path to his profile.

Joe Bloggs will now attempt to download the mandatory profile every time he logs in. If you log in now as JBloggs on a workstation, you will find that the entire profile is identical to that of JElway. You can still make changes. However, when you log out, those changes are not saved. You can log in again and get the same mandatory profile that you had before, without any of the previously made and unsaved changes.

Configuring Super Mandatory Profiles

There are some scenarios where you are using mandatory profiles but you cannot afford to allow anyone to be logged in if the mandatory profile cannot be downloaded for some reason, such as because of a network issue or a file server problem. When could this be a realistic option? We're probably talking about something like a kiosk or a publicly accessibly computer where it's better to have no service rather than a service that isn't tightly controlled.

So, it appears that you need to find a solution for this scenario. Luckily, you have one in the form of *super mandatory profiles*. Implementing this solution isn't all that different from implementing mandatory profiles.

Setting up a super mandatory profile is just an extension of setting up a mandatory profile. Follow the previously described steps for configuring a mandatory profile, and then do the following:

1. Rename the folder profile on the file server so it has a `.MAN.V2` extension; for example, rename `Mandatory.V2` to `Mandatory.MAN.V2`.

2. Configure the user's profile to include the `.MAN` extension.

3. Ignore the `.V2` component; for example, set the profile to `\\bigfirm.com\BigFirmShares\Profiles\Mandatory.MAN`.

That's it! You've just set up a super mandatory profile for the user. The profile will act like a normal mandatory profile, not allowing any changes to be saved to the file server. However, unlike a normal mandatory profile, this user will not be able to log in if the super mandatory profile cannot be downloaded.

There's an easy mistake that you can re-create to test this "no logon" functionality. Rename the `NTUSER.MAN` file in the super mandatory profile to **NTUSER.DAT**. Now try to log on as JBloggs. You'll be informed that the profile could not be downloaded and that the user cannot logon. Don't forget to rename the file back to **NTUSER.MAN** when you're finished!

Configuring a Default Network Profile

A *default profile* is used to build a user's profile if they don't already have one. Consider a user who has no roaming profile configuration and is logging into Windows 8 or Windows Server 2012. Their new profile is created by copying the contents of `C:\Users\Default` to the user's new profile folder in `C:\Users\<username>`.

There is a way for administrators to provide users with a customized default profile on the network. Domain member computers will automatically look for a default network profile. If one exists, then this is used instead of the default profile that is stored locally on the computer. You would use a default network profile when you want to provide a preconfigured working environment for users. This sounds like a mandatory profile, doesn't it? The difference is that the default network profile simply is copied to become the user's own profile. The user is free to save changes to their own profile.

The process for creating a default network profile is very similar to the one you used for creating a mandatory profile:

1. Create a template user.

2. Log in as that user on a test computer.

3. Configure the template user's profile, and log out.

4. Log into the computer as an administrator, and copy the template user's profile to
`\\<Active Directory Domain Name>\Netlogon\Default User.V2`.

   In the chapter's example, this would be `\\bigfirm.com\Netlogon\Default User.V2`.
   Notice the `.V2` extension. This signifies version 2 profiles for Windows 8 and Windows
   Server 2012 or newer.

5. Make sure that the Authenticated Users group is permitted to use this new profile when
you copy it.

6. Check out the process that you used to copy and assign permissions to profiles earlier in
this chapter.

This default network profile will now be copied to every new user on the network.

The flaw with this solution is in that last sentence. This default network profile defines
the user configuration for a user. This includes things such as regional settings. Consider an
organization where there are branch offices in foreign countries. Those users will probably need
different regional settings to match their keyboard and so on. It'll be a bit of a pain to change
these settings for the user when they first log in. You also need to be careful about keeping
location-specific settings in the profile. You don't want to save drive mappings for a file server in
New York and have someone logging in at the San Francisco office 3,000 miles away to find that
they have a file server that's appearing to be very slow.

You cannot have a "per-location" default network profile. The profile can be stored only in a
specific folder. And this folder is copied to all domain controllers via SYSVOL replication.

Default network profiles are fine for simple networks where everyone shares the same basic
configuration. You should think long and hard about deploying default network profiles in more
complex networks where users require different basic configurations such as regional settings.
Yes, the user can change those settings when they first log in, but that might generate lots of
help-desk tickets. You might want to look at an automated configuration. You could use a GPO
to define regional settings once a user has logged in, but this locks a user down. A common
experience is that not everyone shares the same configuration in an office in this environment.
Instead of default network profiles, consider a scripting or Group Policy solution that will make
those localized configurations when a user logs in for the first time. This allows those few users
who are not the norm to alter their own configuration and retain those settings.

Managing Roaming Profiles

Roaming profiles require considerable thought if you have different operating systems, users
roaming between branches with limited network links, and Remote Desktop Services. You can
do some advanced management of profiles by using Group Policy, as you saw earlier when you
granted rights to automatically generated profiles to administrators.

Let's look at a few examples where you might have issues. If you have a farm of Remote
Desktop servers, then a user could log into any one of them. If you have 1,000 users logging
into 10 servers, you could end up with 10,000 cached roaming profiles. That's a lot of disk space
being wasted.

Speaking of disk space, you might want to consider how big a roaming profile can get. For example, users could upload their entire MP3 collection into My Music. It might be an innocent action where they think they're only consuming local storage. But these are roaming profiles; 1,000 users all doing something like this soon adds up to terabytes of storage being consumed on the organization's file servers with nonbusiness data. Should the organization be paying for this?

The solution is to use machine and user Group Policy objects to control how roaming profiles behave in these and other circumstances.

Machine Settings

You'll now look at how you can control roaming profiles on a per-machine basis using Group Policy. Every user logging onto a machine inheriting the Group Policy settings that you configure will be subject to these settings.

CLEANING UP THOSE PROFILES

If you look, you'll find that a locally cached copy of the mandatory profile is created and *kept* on the workstation on the Remote Desktop server. When you think about it, it probably makes no sense to keep a copy of it in environments where you are using a mandatory profile.

Even if you're not using mandatory profiles, you might want some way to clean up older profiles when a computer reboots. Group Policy gives you some tools to do this (see Table 26.1).

TABLE 26.1   Cached user profiles GPO

PATH	ENTRY	DESCRIPTION
Computer Configuration \Administrative Templates\System\User Profiles	Delete cached copies of roaming profiles	Locally cached copies of a roaming profile will be deleted when the user logs out.
Computer Configuration \Administrative Templates\System\User Profiles	Delete user profiles older than a specified number of days on system restart	Profiles older than a specified number of days will automatically be deleted when a computer restarts.

MULTIPLE SITES AND ROAMING PROFILES

What do you do with a user who has a roaming profile and that user travels between branch offices across the world? By default, the computer that the user is logging into will measure the network speed between itself and the location where the profile is stored. If the link is considered too slow, then the profile will not be downloaded. Instead, the user will be offered a temporary local profile. However, remember that this won't work with super mandatory profiles. You can control how this measurement process works using GPO (see Table 26.2).

TABLE 26.2   Slow Networks and User Profiles GPO

PATH	ENTRY	DESCRIPTION
Computer Configuration \ Administrative Templates\ System\User Profiles	Disable detection of slow network connections	You can prevent a computer from detecting whether a profile download will take too long. Be very careful with this because a user logon could take a *very* long time and flood a branch-office WAN link.
Computer Configuration \ Administrative Templates\ System\User Profiles	Prompt user when a slow network connection is detected	If a slow network connection is detected, the user can be prompted. This allows the user to choose to download their roaming profile despite the network issue. Again, be very careful with this.
Computer Configuration \ Administrative Templates\ System\User Profiles	Control slow network connection time-out for user profiles	This allows you to define what "slow" means when measuring the link to the file server hosting the user's profile. This is done using kilobits per second and latency measured in milliseconds.
Computer Configuration \ Administrative Templates\ System\User Profiles	Wait for remote user profile	This directs the system to wait as long as it takes for a roaming profile to download. It is ignored if "Do not detect slow network connections" is enabled.

This gives you a pretty crude mechanism for giving users a roaming profile when the users travel to other locations. You have some other ways to make the environment flexible to business needs.

If your users have a predictable travel pattern, then you might be able to take advantage of DFS Replication (DFS-R). Now you're seeing why we like to use DFS for hosting home directories and user profiles. You can choose to replicate selected folders to servers in other branch offices. You'll find that this could get difficult to manage, so you will want to manage things very carefully.

An alternative is to allow users to have different roaming profiles in each site. This would mean that their roaming profile wouldn't actually roam between sites, only between computers within a site. You can configure this using the following GPO settings:

Path   The path is Computer Configuration\Administrative Templates\System\User Profiles.

Entry   The entry is "Set roaming profile path for all users logging onto this computer."

Description   You can specify a path for roaming profiles for any users logging into the computer. Use the %username% variable to have different profiles for users. This takes precedence over the profile specified in the user object.

REMOTE DESKTOP SERVICES

There are several complications to consider when dealing with Remote Desktop Services and roaming profiles:

◆ It is a bad idea to mix a user's desktop roaming profile with the profile that will be used on a Remote Desktop server/virtual desktop because registry settings and shortcuts from the different systems will be mixed together.

◆ You may employ the concept of "application silos" in a Remote Desktop server farm; in other words, Server1 and Server2 might have BizzApp installed, but Server3 might not. You don't want shortcuts for BizzApp to appear when a user is logged into Server3 with a roaming profile.

◆ A common use for Remote Desktop servers is to share applications from a central site with users in branch offices. You do not want branch-office roaming profiles to load across the WAN, but you do want some sort of roaming profile solution.

You can apply this Group Policy object to disable roaming profiles on the machine:

Path The path is Computer Configuration\Administrative Templates\System\User Profiles.

Entry The entry is "Only allow local user profiles."

Description Disable the usage of roaming profiles on this computer.

This is a rather crude solution. It turns off the ability to download a roaming profile and returns you to a scenario where the user does not have a consistent working environment.

Alternatively, you might configure users with specific roaming profiles for farms of machines. For example, when a user logs into a Remote Desktop server farm, they will use a dedicated profile from a Remote Desktop server roaming profile share. When they log into their PC, they will use a dedicated profile from a PC roaming profile share. When they log into a virtual desktop, they will use a dedicated profile from a virtual desktop roaming profile share. Table 26.3 shows the settings required to do this.

TABLE 26.3   Remote Desktop Services Profile GPO

PATH	ENTRY	DESCRIPTION
Computer Configuration \ Administrative Templates\Windows Components\Remote Desktop Services\Remote Desktop Session Host\Profiles	Set path for Remote Desktop Services roaming user profile	You can specify the path of a profile for a user account when logging in via Remote Desktop Services. This takes precedence over all other profile settings. You can use %username% to allow multiple profiles or simply use one folder for all users.
Computer Configuration \ Administrative Templates\Windows Components\Remote Desktop Services\Remote Desktop Session Host\Profiles	Use mandatory profiles on the Remote Desktop session host server	When enabled, this turns the profile specified in the previous GPO setting into a mandatory profile.

The second set of settings in Table 26.3 allows you to tell the computer to treat any roaming profile as a mandatory profile, that is, to never save any changes made by the user. This is an alternative to the previously described method for creating a mandatory roaming profile.

For Windows Server 2012, you'll find these GPO settings in `Computer Configuration \ Administrative Templates\Windows Components\Remote Desktop Services\Remote Desktop Session Host\Profiles`.

SPECIFYING A REMOTE DESKTOP SERVICES PROFILE

There is an option in the user account to specify a Remote Desktop Services profile. That's a rather simple solution that implies that there will only ever be one possible profile for that user that is suitable for all Remote Desktop servers. This might be suitable for smaller organizations with one or maybe two Remote Desktop servers. We recommend that you think long term and adopt the GPO approach to manage Remote Desktop Services roaming profiles.

You will need to clean up cached profiles (covered earlier in the chapter) if you're using roaming profiles on your Remote Desktop servers. They can quickly eat up a lot of space on your system drive if left unmanaged.

ADDITIONAL ROAMING PROFILE GPO SETTINGS

You've seen only about half of the GPO settings you can use to configure roaming profiles. Table 26.4 shows the rest.

TABLE 26.4 Miscellaneous GPO settings for roaming profiles

PATH	ENTRY	DESCRIPTION
Computer Configuration \ Administrative Templates\System\ User Profiles	User management of sharing user name, Account pictures and domain information with apps	Allows app to have access to the user-name, account picture, and domain information.
Computer Configuration \ Administrative Templates\System\ User Profiles	Set user home folder	You can configure the user's Home folder here instead of on the user account.
Computer Configuration \ Administrative Templates\System\ User Profiles	Set the schedule for background upload of a roaming user profile's registry file while user is logged on	You can configure a schedule to regularly upload the NTUSER.DAT file to the file server in the background while the user is logged in.
Computer Configuration \ Administrative Templates\System\ User Profiles	Do not check for user ownership of Roaming Profile Folders	By default Windows checks for user own-ership of the profile before downloading it. This policy can reverse this practice.

TABLE 26.4   Miscellaneous GPO settings for roaming profiles *(CONTINUED)*

PATH	ENTRY	DESCRIPTION
Computer Configuration \ Administrative Templates\System\ User Profiles	Do not forcefully unload the user's registry at user logoff	When a user logs off, their applications should close and release their open file handles on the registry. Faulty applications may not do so. Windows will then force the registry to close. There may be scenarios when this is undesirable.
Computer Configuration \ Administrative Templates\System\ User Profiles	Do not log on users with temporary profiles	This has the same effect as the super mandatory profile. When the user's assigned profile cannot be loaded, then the user will be immediately automatically logged out after their login attempt.
Computer Configuration \ Administrative Templates\System\ User Profiles	Leave Windows Installer and Group Policy Software Installation Data	It is possible to install applications for a user via Group Policy. This stores data in the user's profile. Deleting the profile causes this data to be deleted and thus causes applications to be installed again. This policy prevents nonrequired repeat installations.
Computer Configuration \ Administrative Templates\System\ User Profiles	Maximum retries to unload and update user profile	This allows an administrator to specify how many times Windows will try to save the NTUSER.DAT file to the file share. You might need to increase this if faulty applications are slow to update it at logoff. By default Windows tries it a maximum of 60 times over 60 seconds.
Computer Configuration \ Administrative Templates\System\ User Profiles	Prevent Roaming Profile changes from propagating to the server	Any changes made to the user's profile on this machine are not saved to their roaming profile.
Computer Configuration \ Administrative Templates\System\ User Profiles	Set maximum wait time for the network if a user has a roaming user profile or remote home directory	Windows will wait up to 30 seconds if the file server with those shares is unavailable. You can override that setting. You might use this on wireless networks when you notice roaming profiles are not downloaded and home directories are not connected, and the only issue is timing.
Computer Configuration \ Administrative Templates\System\ User Profiles	Establish time-out for dialog boxes	Windows will pop up a dialog box when it needs human interaction to make a decision. The default is 30 seconds. You can change this from between 0 and 600 seconds.

These are all settings for a machine; that is, they will affect all users who log into the machine that the policy is applied to. You can also apply policies to user objects to control roaming profiles.

User Settings

You can use some settings to manage roaming profiles on a per-user basis. You might want to control the contents of the roaming profile or even control the size of the roaming profile itself with the settings shown in Table 26.5.

TABLE 26.5   Roaming Profile Contents GPO settings

PATH	ENTRY	DESCRIPTION
User Configuration \ Administrative Templates\ System\User Profiles	Exclude directories in roaming profile	You might find some folders that you do not want to make available on all computers. You can specify them here. The `Appdata\Local` and `Appdata\LocalLow` folders and their contents are not replicated to a file server by default.
User Configuration \ Administrative Templates\ System\User Profiles	Limit profile size	You can determine a quota for roaming profiles. Operating systems prior to Windows Vista simply refused to allow a user to log out if the quota was exceeded. Vista allows the user to log out without saving the profile to the file server. Users can be notified of an issue and reminded using a set message at set times.

Be careful of the Limit Profile Size policy. Remember that folders like My Documents and Desktop are contained within it. You'll need to find a way to move them to another location—you'll be looking at that soon.

Redirecting Folders

Roaming profiles have been pretty common practice in the Windows world. They work, but they are far from perfect.

Roaming profiles are prone to complications with files being loaded, unloaded, and corruptions. Things can get very complicated. That brings us to *folder redirection*.

Folder redirection allows you to move special folders within the user profile to another, more suitable location. For example, instead of storing these folders in a roaming profile, you could store them in the user's home directory. Folder redirection will allow you to move the following folders:

- AppData (Roaming)
- Desktop
- Start Menu

- Documents

- Pictures

- Music

- Videos

- Favorites

- Contacts

- Downloads

- Links

- Searches

- Saved Games

ORIGIN OF FOLDER REDIRECTION

Folder redirection was introduced as part of IntelliMirror in Windows 2000. The concept of IntelliMirror was to provide the user with a mobile working environment that followed the user wherever the user moved. The brand name seems to have slipped by the wayside over the years, unfortunately.

When you look at that list, it appears to be everything that is important within a profile. If you can store these folders in some special folder, why would you even want to have roaming profiles?

That's a very good question. In fact, many organizations don't bother deploying roaming profiles anymore. You've seen that deploying a roaming profile in addition to a home directory doubles the amount of administration that you must do. By storing them in the user's home directory, you could halve the amount of file share administration on the network. That simplifies deployment, backup/recovery, security, auditing, archiving, and disaster recovery planning/implementations. There are many complications with roaming profiles such as their mobility between machines with different software configurations and between machines with different operating systems.

So, what exactly does folder redirection do? Quite simply, you configure each of these listed special folders to point to an alternate location outside the profile. This location would be a file share unique to the user. Such a folder probably already exists—you've probably created home directories for each of your users so you can configure folder redirection to map there instead of to the profile. For example, My Documents normally exists as Documents in the profile. Using folder redirection, it could exist as Documents in the home directory. This accomplishes a number of things:

- You can redirect all the required folders to the home directory so that a user can have a consistent working environment on current and legacy operating systems; that is, the data exists outside the restrictions of profile versions.

◆ By redirecting folders that contain user data, you can reliably apply profile size quotas without impacting business data contained in folders such as My Documents.

◆ You can probably eliminate the need for profiles altogether by redirecting all the folders that are important to the organization. Roaming profiles can be a source of trouble and are considered an obsolete technology by some administrators.

Before you move on, we should quickly address a question that might be popping up at this point. What use is something like My Documents if it is redirected to a file server and you're a user who travels around with a laptop? By default, redirected folders are replicated to the local computer using Offline Files. Offline Files creates a secure cache of the files on the computer. When connected to the network, the computer will synchronize the Offline Files cache with the shares on the file server(s).

Basic Folder Redirection

You're probably itching to see how to do this right about now. We won't delay any longer. Folder redirection is controlled using Group Policy settings that are applied to users. Say all your users reside in \bigfirm.com\BigFirm\Users. You've created and linked a policy called User Folder Redirections to this OU.

1. Edit the policy object that will be applied to the user accounts for which you want to redirect folders.

2. Create and link a policy to the Users OU, as shown in Figure 26.32.

FIGURE 26.32

A new GPO object for user folder redirection

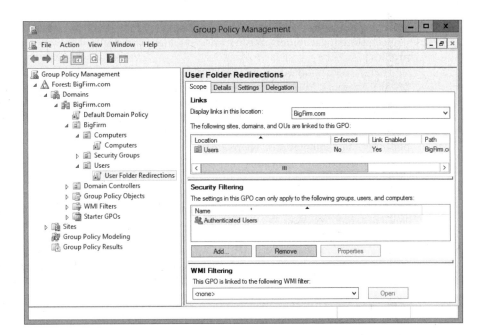

3. Navigate into User Configuration\Windows Settings\Folder Redirection.

   It is here that you can see all the folders that you can redirect on a current Windows operating system computer, as shown in Figure 26.33.

FIGURE 26.33
The folder redirection policies

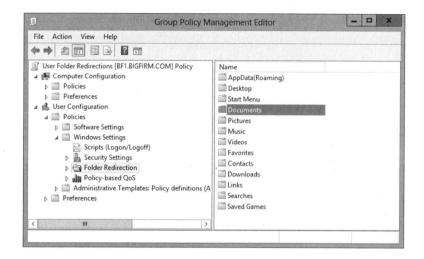

You are going to start out by redirecting Documents to the user's home directory.

4. Right-click Documents, and select Properties.

   This opens a dialog box where you can configure the redirection of the folder. You have three choices here:

   Not Configured   This disables folder redirection.

   Basic – Redirect Everyone's Folder To The Same Location   This allows you to configure all users to redirect to a common location. For example, all users have their home directory in a common file share, so redirect all folders to \\bigfirm.com\BigFirmShares\ Home. It's a "one-size-fits-all" policy that usually is the appropriate choice.

   Advanced – Specify Locations For Various User Groups   This allows you to specify unique paths for different groups. You'll go with this one when your OU layout doesn't match up with your desired folder redirection design.

   We'll cover the simple approach that you are most likely to apply, that is, basic redirection.

5. Select Basic, as shown in Figure 26.34.

   Target Folder Location offers you a number of choices depending on which folder you are redirecting:

FIGURE 26.34
Redirecting folders
to the user's home
directory

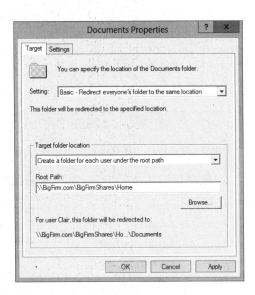

Redirect To The User's Home Directory   This very simple solution will redirect the folder to the user's home directory. It does not create a subfolder for the redirected folder. Instead, it just dumps contents to the root of their home directory. Things will get impossible for users if you redirect many folders.

Create A Folder For Each User Under The Root Path   This will create a folder named after the redirected folder within the path you specify; for example, Documents will be created in \\bigfirm.com\BigFirmShares\Home\JBloggs if you specify \\bigfirm .com\BigFirmShares\Home. Do you see how it intelligently adds the username? This will solve the previous confusion problem we mentioned.

Redirect To The Following Location   This is a simple redirection where all users will share a common folder. This might be suitable if redirecting a Start menu for a Remote Desktop server farm.

Redirect To The Local User Profile Location   This forces the folder back to the local profile.

6. As shown in Figure 26.34, select to redirect Documents to a subfolder within the user home directory.

Remember that you set up the home directories in a DFS namespace. You can move the physical storage location of the folders, and you won't have to change this policy. You just need to update the link in the DFS namespace. You can do this with additional folders knowing that the user will see a distinct folder within their home directory for each redirected folder—nice and simple and fewer help-desk tickets!

7. Click the Settings tab to see how Windows will handle the redirection.

We'll go through the settings in Figure 26.35 in a moment.

FIGURE 26.35
Default Documents
folder redirection
settings

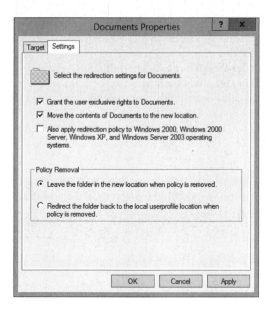

By default, the user will get exclusive rights to any folders created during folder redirection. Note that this doesn't apply when redirecting Documents to the home directory itself (and not a subfolder). You can change this by deselecting "Grant the user exclusive rights to Documents." You will probably want to do this so that you can perform administrative tasks with Documents to assist the user or if you use administrator accounts for services such as archiving or backup/recovery. We've done this in Figure 26.36.

FIGURE 26.36
Configured
Documents
folder redirection
settings

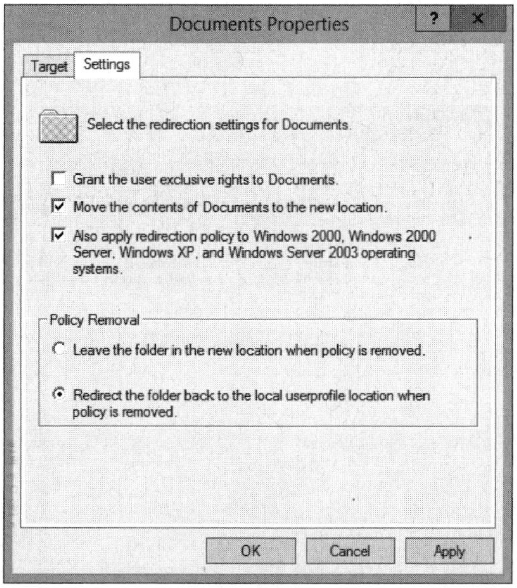

You can move all contents of Documents in the profile when the redirection policy applies. This is on by default and is probably what you will want to do. However, you do have the option to turn this behavior off.

You can change what will happen when the policy you are now configuring no longer applies to a user. The default is that the redirected folder and contents are left where they are when redirection is disabled. You can redirect the folder and its contents back to the profile in this situation.

Figure 26.36 shows disabling exclusive access to the folder, moving the contents, and turning on legacy support. The folder will also be redirected back to the profile when the policy no longer applies.

You'll now want to test this:

1. Log into your test workstation using a user account that is inheriting the new policy.

   Use JBloggs to log into Win8; JBloggs is configured to not use a roaming or mandatory profile.

2. In a lab, you won't want to wait for policies to refresh, so run the following on your test workstation:

   ```
   gpupdate /target:user /force
   ```

   You use the /force flag here because some GPO settings can take two refreshes to apply.

   You will be told that you need to log out to apply new policy settings. This is a sign that your folder redirection is working—it applies only during logon. Log back in, and check out where Documents is now located.

3. Log in as JBloggs, and open the properties of the Documents folder.

   The location of Documents shows you that the folder has been redirected to the user's home directory. You can see in Figure 26.37 that in this example it has been moved to a folder called Documents in the user's home directory on the file server.

FIGURE 26.37
Checking the redirected folder properties

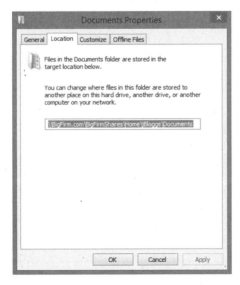

4. Open Windows Explorer and browse to JBloggs's home directory to see that a special folder called My Documents has been created for the user.

Interestingly, browsing into My Documents shows you that the following folders are automatically redirected as subfolders of Documents, as shown in Figure 26.38. That's a time-saver!

FIGURE 26.38
The contents of the redirected Documents

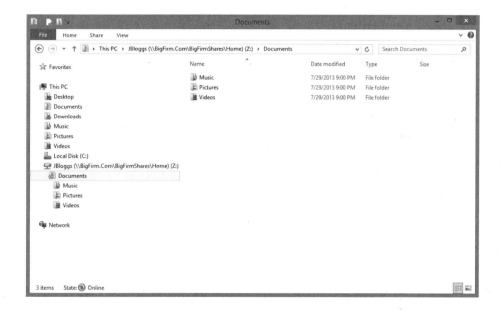

◆   My Music

◆   My Pictures

◆   My Videos

This is because the default Group Policy setting for these folders is that they should follow My Documents to wherever it is redirected to. There's actually enough of the user's data here that you can consider completely abandoning the concept of profiles!

COST-AWARE SYNCHRONIZATION

With Windows 2012 and Windows 8 you now have the ability to disable the background synchronization of data under the following conditions:

◆   A user is on a metered network connection, like a 4G mobile network, and they are near or over their limit.

◆   A user is roaming on another provider's network.

> Windows 2012 and Windows 8 both automatically monitor bandwidth usage and roaming on metered connections. This gives them the ability to know when to switch to offline mode and prevents data synchronization. It does not stop the user from manually synchronizing, and this feature can be overridden for specific users, such as executives.
>
> This feature is controlled by the Computer Configuration\Administrative Templates\Network\ Offline Files\Enable file synchronization on costed networks GPO.

This example of basic folder redirection will suit organizations where the OU design is similar to how you want to handle folder redirection. You'll now move on to doing some more advanced folder redirection.

Advanced Folder Redirection

Basic folder redirection configures everyone who received the policy to redirect their folders in a similar way. This is probably fine in most situations, but there are times when you might want to apply a single policy where users redirect to different locations depending on their group membership rather than just OU location. Here are a few examples:

- ◆ You apply different security policies to home directory shares to different groups in the organization. This means that user A might have her profile in a different share than user B.

- ◆ You control DFS replication of home directories on a per-share basis.

- ◆ You have been forced to deploy multiple servers for home directory file shares.

You can use advanced folder redirection to apply your policy to security groups. Each security group will receive a different configuration for the folder redirection policy. This will become a little clearer when you look at it in action.

Open the GPO and properties of the folder that you want to redirect. In the previous example of folder redirection, you selected basic folder redirection. This time you are going with "Advanced – Specify locations for various user groups." You can click Add to specify a user group and a location for the folder redirection.

The dialog box shown in Figure 26.39 allows you to do the following:

- ◆ Select a security group to apply this policy to.

- ◆ Define where the folder will be redirected. This has an identical set of options as Target Folder Location in basic folder redirection.

- ◆ Specify the path where the redirected folder will reside.

You can see in Figure 26.40 that you can configure folder redirection of a single folder for security groups differently using a single GPO.

FIGURE 26.39
Setting up
advanced folder
redirection
under a root
path

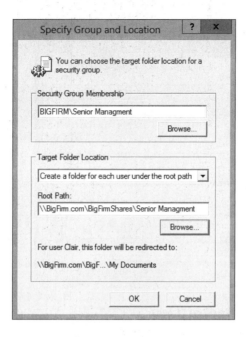

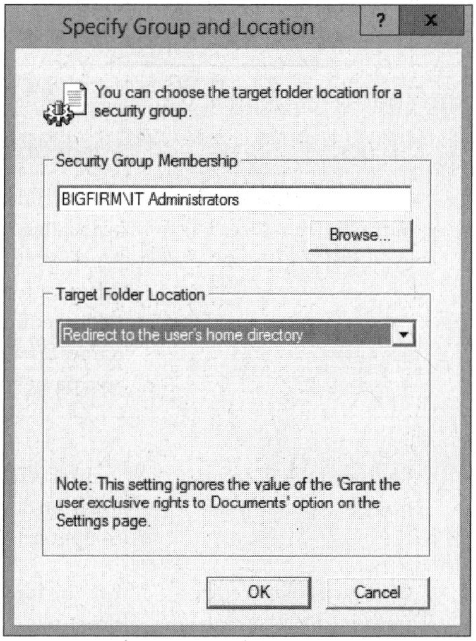

In Figure 26.41, we have configured three different security groups to redirect Documents using various methods within a single Group Policy object. This demonstrates how flexible folder redirection can be and how it can adjust to the needs of the organization.

FIGURE 26.40
Advanced folder
redirection to
the user's home
directory

Managing Folder Redirection

You use Group Policy to configure folder redirection (see Table 26.6). You can use other Group Policy settings to manage how folder redirection is processed.

TABLE 26.6 Folder Redirection Management GPO

PATH	ENTRY	DESCRIPTION
Computer Configuration \ Administrative Templates\ System\Folder Redirection	Use localized subfolder names when redirecting Start and My Documents	The special folders in a profile will normally be localized; for example, what you see in an American English version of Windows will be different from a German version. By default, folder redirection does not maintain these names. Enabling this policy will allow localized names on a per-system basis.
Computer Configuration \ Administrative Templates\ System\Folder Redirection	Redirect folders on primary computers only	Redirects folders only if the computer has been designated as the user's primary computer.
Computer Configuration \ Administrative Templates\ System\Group Policy	Configure folder redirection policy processing	You can force folder redirection to work over slow links (off by default). You can also configure a folder redirection policy to process even if the policy has not changed.

TABLE 26.6 Folder Redirection Management GPO *(CONTINUED)*

PATH	ENTRY	DESCRIPTION
User Configuration \ Administrative Templates\ System\Folder Redirection	Do not automatically make redirected folders available offline	Redirected folders automatically are synchronized using Offline Files. You can disable this behavior.
User Configuration \ Administrative Templates\ System\Folder Redirection	Do not automatically make specific redirected folders available offline	Allows you to prevent redirected shell folders from being available offline.
Computer Configuration \ Administrative Templates\ System\Folder Redirection	Redirect folders on primary computers only	Redirects folders only if the computer has been designated as the user's primary computer.
User Configuration \ Administrative Templates\ System\Folder Redirection	Use localized subfolder names when redirecting Start and My Documents	Provides the same functionality as the computer setting but on a user basis.
User Configuration \ Administrative Templates\ System\Folder Redirection	Use localized subfolder names when redirecting Start and My Documents	The special folders in a profile will normally be localized; for example, what you see in an American English version of Windows will be different from a German version. By default, folder redirection does not maintain these names. Enabling this policy will allow localized names on a per-user basis.

PRIMARY COMPUTER SUPPORT

Windows 2012 and Windows 8 have added Primary Computer, or user device affinity support to roaming profiles and folder redirection. What does this mean for you? You now have the ability to control what computers can access your user's redirected folders and/or roaming profiles. Using this feature can be beneficial in many ways:

◆ Reduces the login time when not logging onto the user's primary computer.

◆ Reduces the risk of sensitive data being left behind on a non-primary computer the user has logged onto, such as a conference room or kiosk computer.

◆ Prevents corruption of the users' profiles when using computers with different hardware configurations, such as x86 and x64 systems.

In order to take advantage of primary computer support, you will need to designate at least one primary computer for each user, following these steps:

1. Get the distinguished name of the user's computer.

This can be accomplished using Active Directory Users and Computers using the advanced view. Open the properties window of the computer object, scroll down to the distinguishedName attribute, and copy it.

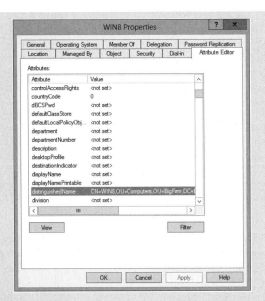

2. Open the properties window of the user to whom you wish to assign a primary computer. Scroll down to the msDS-PrimaryComputer attribute and paste in the distinguished name that you just copied.

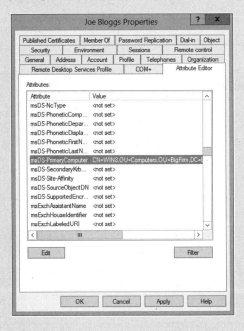

3. Create and link a GPO listed in Table 26.6 that controls the primary computer support.

Work Folders

Another new feature in Windows Server 2012 R2 is Work Folders. This feature allows end users to have their work data synchronized across all of their devices. When a user saves the files in their work folders on their workstation in the office, the workstation will sync with their devices. Sound familiar? That's what SkyDrive, SkyDrive Pro, or any number of other consumer products do, so why would you use Work Folders? For an enterprise solution, SkyDrive Pro is the way to go; it integrates into SharePoint, it allows users to share and collaborate on documents, and it is available on mobile devices. But if you want to leverage your existing file servers and just want to extend the ability to sync the users' files, Work Folders is the answer.

So now that you know a little about why you would use Work Folder, let's install it so you can see just how easy it is to add this feature into your environment.

Installing Work Folders

Log on to the BF2 file server. Open the Service Manager console and add the Work Folders role; it can be found under the Files and Storage Services section. Or you can install the role by using the following PowerShell command:

```
Install-WindowsFeature FS-SyncShareService
```

This will install Work Folders and its dependency on the IIS Web Server role with the IIS Hostable Web Core. I should also point out that Work Folders clients communicate to the Work Folder servers only via SSL, so you will need to configure a public certificate or a self-signed certificate and make sure it's installed on all your clients. You will also need to make the server available on the Internet, possibly via a reverse proxy or network gateway.

Sync Share Configuration

The Work Folders interface is very simple and easy to use; you will find it as a node under the Files and Storage Services dashboard. To create a new sync share, simply right-click in the Work Folders window and select New Sync Share, or select New Sync Share from the Tasks drop-down list. The New Sync Share Wizard will open and guide you through the process.

1. The Server and Path screen will display all servers that have been added to your Server Manager dashboard with Work Folders enabled. You have option of selecting an existing share from one of these servers or specifying a local path. Enter a local path of **D:\ITSyncShare**, as shown in Figure 26.42, and click Next.

    The User Folder Structure screen that appears next will have two options: you can accept the default of "User alias" or choose "User alias@domain." "User alias" creates the user folders as you currently do with folder redirection and home folders, whereas "User alias@domain" appends the @domain of each account to the folder name, which is useful if you have multiple domains with names that have the potential to conflict; see Figure 26.43. You also have the ability to single out a specific folder to be synced, omitting all the others that appear in the share. This could be useful for folder redirection, giving you the ability to sync the Documents folder but leave all of the other redirected folders alone.

2. For now, just accept the default settings.

FIGURE 26.42
New Sync Share
Wizard - Server
and Path

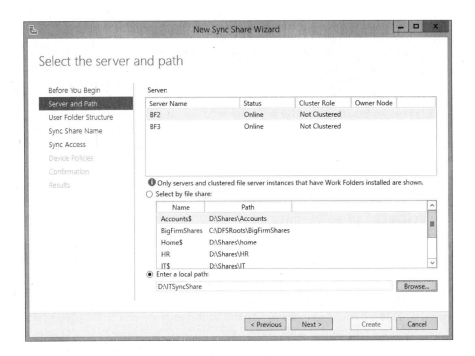

FIGURE 26.43
New Sync Share
Wizard - User
Folder Structure

3. On the Sync Share Name screen, you can rename the share and provide a description. The description is optional, but six months or a year down the road it can prove to be very helpful when you are trying to figure out what each sync folder was being used for.

4. The next screen, Sync Access, is where you will be granting access to the share. You can do this by user or security group. Click Add and select IT Administrators. By default, administrators will not have access to the users' data on the server; should you want to give admins access to this data, uncheck the "Disable inherited permissions" check box.

   The Device Policy screen is where you can enforce polices on the device that the data will be synced to.

5. Select both check boxes and move on to the next step.

6. Review your settings and then create the share.

The Work Folders screen will now show your newly created share, the users who have access, the volume information, and any quotas that have been defined for the users, as shown in Figure 26.44. That's it! The server side has been configured and is ready for the users to start syncing their files. Alternatively, you could have configured Work Folders via PowerShell with the following command:

```
PS C:\>New-SyncShare ITSyncShare –path D:\ITSyncShare –User "BigFirm\IT
Administrators" –RequireEncryption $true –RequirePasswordAutoLock $true
```

FIGURE 26.44
Work Folders
configured

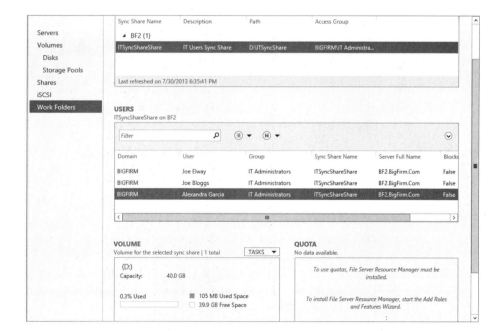

Client Configuration

Now that the server is set up, the clients will need to know where to connect to and agree to the device settings that are being applied in order to start synchronizing files.

Users can configure their Work Folder settings by choosing Control Panel ➢ System and Security ➢ Work Folders. Once there, they will see a link to set up Work Folders, as shown in Figure 26.45.

FIGURE 26.45
Manage Work Folders

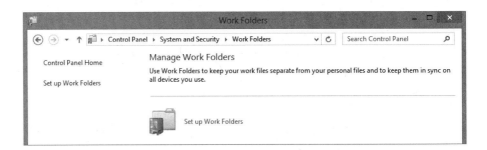

After the user clicks the setup link, they will be prompted for their email address. If the workstation is not joined to the domain, they will be prompted for their domain credentials. The user will also be asked to agree to the data policies that have been placed on the files stored in Work Folders, as shown in Figure 26.46.

FIGURE 26.46
Security policies

Once they agree to the policies, Work Folders will be set up. The user will be able to view their sync settings in the Work Folders control panel, and Work Folders will be displayed under My Computer/This PC, as shown in Figure 26.47.

FIGURE 26.47

Work Folders control panel

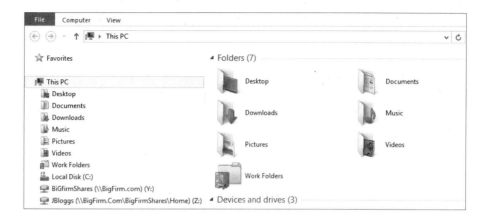

Having all the users configure their own Work Folders settings isn't practical, so you can also configure the Work Folders settings via Group Policy. Table 26.7 breaks down the two policies that control Work Folders settings.

TABLE 26.7   Work Folder management with Group Policies

PATH	ENTRY	DESCRIPTION
Computer Configuration \ Administrative Templates\Windows Components\Work Folders	Force automatic setup for all users	This policy forces the configuration of Work Folders for all users. No settings are defined here, so this policy must be used along with the "Specify Work Folders settings" user policy.
User Configuration \Administrative Templates\Windows Components\ Work Folders	Specify Work Folders settings	This policy defines which Work Folders server the users should be connecting to.

Work Folders is easy to set up and can be combined with other technologies, such as Workplace Join and RMS Protection. Leveraging these features together will help you secure your data while giving the users the flexibility of using whatever devices they would like to use.

As of the time of this writing, Work Folders is limited to syncing Windows 8.1 devices but is expected to expand this functionality to Windows 7 and 8 shortly after the release of Windows 8.1. Don't be surprised if in a couple of versions this becomes the standard for synchronizing users' data.

Managing the Desktop Using Group Policy

Mandatory profiles allow administrators to provide a consistent working experience for users when they log in. No changes can be saved. However, what if you do not want to allow users to make any changes at all? Mandatory profiles can't be considered a security solution because they don't stop users from doing what they want. Consider the following scenarios:

- A Remote Desktop server where you want to restrict users to a locked-down experience where they can start only certain programs

- A kiosk where only one program can be run and there is no other interaction with the system

- A PC in a security- or regulatory-conscious organization where administrators need to tie down what a user can do

All of these types of problems require a solution where the user cannot make changes. Clearly, mandatory profiles aren't the complete solution.

Windows provides the ability to lock down the desktop using registry edits. A wide variety of options are available to administrators, such as these:

- Restricting what is on the Start menu

- Disabling browsing on the C drive

- Restricting access to Control Panel

You probably don't want to deploy your security solution using registry edits because of the excessive amount of work involved. Luckily, a number of built-in Group Policy settings are included in the administrative templates in Windows Server 2012. You can use these to configure Group Policy for those users and/or computers that you need to secure. We'll now take a look at a *few* of those that you can use to tie down your computers or Remote Desktop server desktops. There are *many* more settings available, but these are ones that you might find more important to start working with.

Using the settings in Computer Configuration\Administrative Templates\Network\Offline Files, you can manage offline files on a per-system basis; that is, the settings you apply here will affect all users who log onto the targeted computers (see Table 26.8).

TABLE 26.8   Computer Configuration: Offline Files

ITEM	DESCRIPTION
At logoff, delete the local copy of user's offline files	Use this option if you decide that you need to remove all offline files from a computer when the user logs off.
Encrypt the offline files cache	Data on a computer is vulnerable to attack if not encrypted. Enabling this setting forces the offline files cache to be secured by encryption. Users cannot turn this off.
Prohibit "Make Available Offline" for these files and folders	You can specify certain folders that must not be made available offline. There may be certain information that you cannot risk being on laptop computers because of the risk of theft if you allow access to that information.

TABLE 26.9 Computer Configuration: Internet Explorer *(CONTINUED)*

ITEM	DESCRIPTION
Synchronize all offline files before logging on	All marked files and folders are synchronized before a user is logged on. This guarantees that changes made by a user while traveling with their laptop are copied to the file server.
Synchronize all offline files before logging off	This guarantees that the user will have the latest copy of all files when they take their laptop away from the office.
Prohibit user configuration of offline files	Users are often the cause of problems on computers. You can configure offline files using a GPO and prevent users from tampering with that configuration.

Computer Configuration\Administrative Templates\Windows Components\Internet Explorer contains a nested set of GPO settings for controlling how a user can manage Internet Explorer on a computer (see Table 26.9).

TABLE 26.9 Computer Configuration: Internet Explorer

ITEM	DESCRIPTION
Disable automatic install of Internet Explorer components	By default, users are prompted to download components when a web page requires them. You can prevent this behavior using this policy.
Make proxy settings per machine (rather than per user)	You can configure proxy settings for the machine and force those settings on all logged-in users.
Security Zones: Do not allow users to add/delete sites	A zone in Internet Explorer changes the permissions for the sites in that zone and how IE will behave. Adding or deleting sites to or from a zone changes how IE will handle those sites. Enabling this setting forces a per-system configuration on all users to prevent them from editing zone memberships.
Internet Control Panel\Disable the connections page	This prevents users from being able to alter the way IE connects to the Internet, for example, via proxy settings.

A number of settings for controlling applications are built into Windows. You might need to do the following:

- Preconfigure these applications.
- Lock down their configuration.
- Prevent access to them.

Some applications such as Microsoft Office allow you to add templates to do these tasks. Windows Messenger (see Table 26.10) is an example of a built-in template, and you can manage it on a per-system basis using the settings in Computer Configuration\Administrative Templates\ Windows Components\Windows Messenger.

TABLE 26.10   Computer Configuration: Windows Messenger

ITEM	DESCRIPTION
Do not allow Windows Messenger to be run	This prevents Windows or users from starting Windows Messenger.
Do not automatically start Windows Messenger initially	This turns off the default setting to start Windows Messenger when a user logs in. However, this setting can be overridden if a user chooses to do so.

That's just a small sample of the munitions that are available in an administrator's arsenal to lock down a user's desktop experience on a per-system basis. Let's look at what you can do on a per-user basis.

One of the things that you will probably need to do is preconfigure Internet Explorer. You can do this on a per-user basis using the settings contained within User Configuration\ Preferences\Windows Settings\Internet Explorer (see Table 26.9). The Preferences settings have replaced Internet Explorer Maintenance and will allow you to define settings from IE 5 to the most current version. Should the Preferences settings not provide all of the functionality your environment requires, you can customize Internet Explorer by using the Internet Explorer Administration Kit (IEAK). For more information on using IEAK, you can visit `http://tinyurl.com/c26IESettings`.

Control Panel is one of those places where a user can really get into trouble. You can remove a user's ability to access the components of Control Panel or even their ability to open it (see Table 26.11.) This is controlled in User Configuration\Administrative Templates\Control Panel.

TABLE 26.11   User Configuration: Control Panel

ITEM	DESCRIPTION
Hide specified Control Panel items	You can list specific modules from Control Panel that should be made unavailable to a user.
Show only specified Control Panel items	It might be easier to reveal only certain items in Control Panel than to list almost all of them. This setting allows a user to access only the modules listed.
Prohibit access to Control Panel	You can prevent a user from being able to see or use Control Panel.
Personalization\force specific screen saver	This forces a specific screen saver to be selected by the user.

TABLE 26.11   User Configuration: Control Panel   *(CONTINUED)*

ITEM	DESCRIPTION
Personalization\screen saver time-out	This configures a timer for the screen saver; in other words, it will be activated after *x* seconds of inactivity.
Personalization\Enable screen saver	This enables the screen saver. It requires the previous two entries to be configured.
Personalization\Password protect the screen saver	This forces the user to enter their password to unlock the screen saver.

 Real World Scenario

TAKE CARE WHEN IMPLEMENTING SCREEN SAVER SECURITY

Be careful with forcing policies such as screen saver configuration. Best practice in terms of security is that the screen saver should be active for everyone and require a password to unlock it. A common experience is that the people who most require this security are the ones who will hate it the most. Directors and sales staff hate things like screen savers with password locking. You should find the balance between IT security and sustained employment—it's good to get guidance on something like this from your employer after presenting a considered briefing on best-practice security before going gung-ho and applying policies by yourself.

File Explorer is locked down to some extent in most GPO deployments. You can configure File Explorer in User Configuration\Administrative Templates\Windows Components\File Explorer (see Table 26.12).

TABLE 26.12   User Configuration: File Explorer

ITEM	DESCRIPTION
Do not track shell shortcuts during roaming.	This disables a computer from trying to track back to the original remote target of a shortcut if a local target cannot be found.
Remove CD burning features.	File Explorer includes the ability to create CDs. You can disable this ability using this setting.
Hide these specified drives in My Computer.	You can hide a combination of the local drives or all drives on a computer in File Explorer. This does not restrict access to resources on those drives, for example, programs. You can bypass this using tools other than File Explorer.
Prevent access to drives from My Computer.	You can prevent access to a combination of the local drives or all drives on a computer using File Explorer. This does not restrict access to resources on those drives; you can still launch programs installed there via the normal shortcuts. You can bypass this using tools other than File Explorer.

As you can see, many options are available for per-user configuration. You will likely use a mixture of per-user and per-system configurations. For example, an OU containing Windows kiosks can be efficiently locked down using Computer Configuration policies. An open office plan featuring "hot-desking" will probably rely more on the use of User Configuration policies. The reason is that a per-system policy will not suit the wide variety of users who may use a single computer. It would be better to configure the users rather than the computers.

What method you use to test and develop your lockdown policy will determine the success of your deployment and how easy it will be to manage. You've seen just a very small sample of the available settings. There are many more included with Windows Server 2012. More still can be added via templates for applications, for example, for Microsoft Office. You can also implement custom templates by editing them yourself or by using third-party utilities.

Our advice is that you build a lab environment that is as identical to your production network as you can afford. This can be a virtual network, which would give you an opportunity to deploy Hyper-V! Building your policies should be a very gradual and deliberate process. Add one policy setting at a time. Only then can you test to see what the true effect of the policy is. If you implement many policies at once, how can you truly know which one is causing a problem? You should test to see when the policy applies, for example, at every logon, after a second logon, or during a normal policy refresh. We recommend logging on several times because we have seen complex scenarios where a policy implementation can be inconsistent. You can use the Group Policy Management console to document your policies once they are complete and to export them for implementation in your production network.

Managing Users with Group Policy Preferences and Logon Scripts

So far in this chapter you have seen how to set up network resources for a user, such as a profile, a home directory, and redirected folders. Other resources are available on the network, such as file shares, DFS namespaces, and printers. How do you connect a user to those? The more traditional solution is to use logon scripts that run each time the user logs in to map drives, use printers, and adjust registry settings, but there is a better way, Group Policy Preferences. Group Policy Preferences allows you to do all the things you used to use scripts for but with better control and faster processing, and it's the preferred method for managing the user settings in Server 2012.

Managing Drive Mappings

One of the most common jobs for a network administrator is to manage the drive mappings for the various users and departments. Traditionally, login scripts were leveraged to accomplish this, but they can require complex scripts that take more time to test and debug. Group Policy Preferences removes a lot of those challenges and makes it easy to tie your drive-mappings to security groups via item-level targeting.

Earlier in this chapter we deployed a DFS namespace called \\bigfirm.com\BigFirmShares, shown in Figure 26.48. We have since added a number of file shares to allow users to work with each other on a team or departmental basis. Say you want to automatically map this namespace for all users of the Senior Management group as the Y drive on their computers. This means all members of that group will see all file shares using a single drive letter.

FIGURE 26.48

BigFirm's populated
DFS namespace

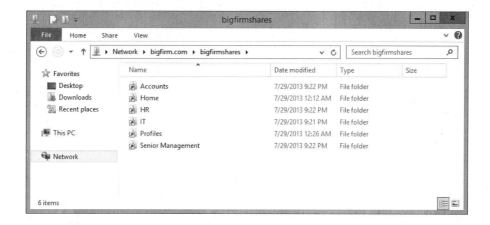

We've already covered the basics of creating and linking Group Policy objects back in Chapter 9, so we will skip ahead to the meat of what the drive-mapping preferences are all about. In a newly created group policy called Drive Mappings, select the Drive Maps preference item and create a new mapping.

Your first option will be to select what action you want your drive mapping to perform. As shown in Table 26.13, you have four possible choices. It is also worth noting that these same four choices will appear again and again throughout most of the Group Policy Preferences.

TABLE 26.13   Drive-mapping actions

ITEM	DESCRIPTION
Create	This will create a new drive mapping if one does not exist. If there is a drive mapping already in place with that drive letter, it will do nothing.
Replace	Deletes the existing mapped drive and then creates a new one.
Update	Modifies the settings of an existing mapped drive. If no mapped drive exists, then it will create a new one.
Delete	Deletes the mapped drive.

We are going to select Replace, because we want to ensure that the drive will be mapped to our DFS file share as Y. Next, you will want to enter the location of the DFS file shares and set your drive letter to Y, as shown in Figure 26.49.

The next step will be to make sure that only the members of the Senior Management group get this drive mapping. To do this you will use item-level targeting. With the New Drive Properties window still open, select the Common tab, check the "Item-level targeting" box, and click the Targeting button. As Figure 26.50 shows, you can select a multitude of options for applying the preference, everything from the type of network connection you have to the time of day. In our scenario we will select Security Group, apply the BigFirm\Senior Management group, and link the group policy to the root of BigFirm.

FIGURE 26.49
New Drive
Properties

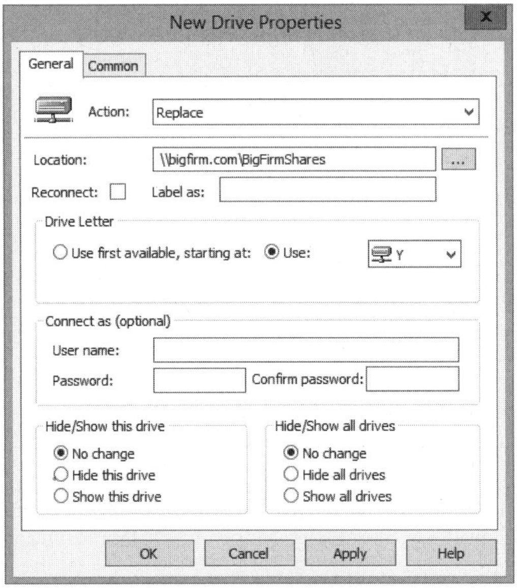

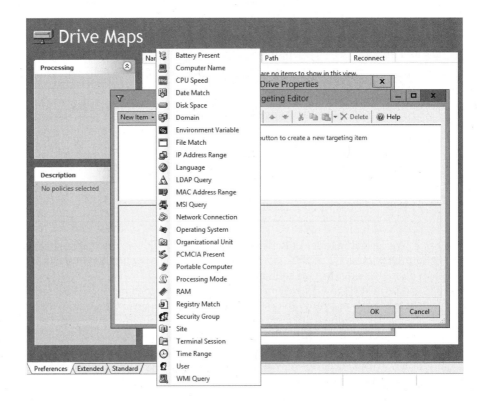

FIGURE 26.50
New Drive
Properties
options

Item-level targeting not only allows you to select a condition, such as if a user is a member of a group (Inclusive), but also allows you to choose to apply the policy if the user is not a member of a security group (Exclusive). You have the ability to mix and match conditions, such as if the user is a member of a security group and has a particular application installed as well.

As you can see in Figure 26.51, when you log in as one of the test users in the Senior Managers group, the user inherits the Group Policy object, and the Y drive mapping preference has been applied.

FIGURE 26.51
Drive mapping via Group Policy Preferences

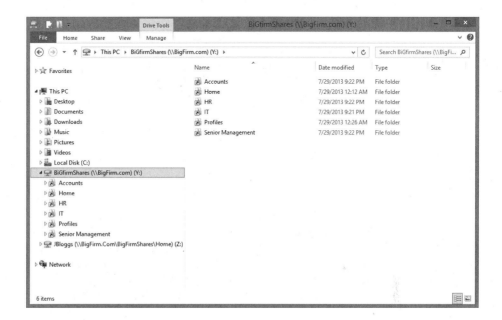

Executing Commands at Logon

Login scripts still have a place in the Windows 2012 world. They are still very useful, such as when needing to execute a series of commands at logon.

Say you've also deployed an antivirus application that you will run a command for every time a user logs in. The command is `MyAVApp -configure`. The script that you want everyone to run when they log in is as follows:

```
MyAVApp -configure
```

Launch Notepad, type in the previous commands, and save this as **Logon.bat** on your workstation. That's the logon script, and you want it to run every time a user logs in. That will cause the contained commands to run every time the user logs in. You could use Visual Basic Scripting (VBS) or PowerShell instead. You need to make this logon script available to all users in the domain in all locations where they can log in. Fortunately, there is a share on every domain controller that is part of Active Directory and hence is replicated for you. This share is called NETLOGON and can be found in \\bigfirm.com\SYSVOL\bigfirm.com\ scripts as well as \\bigfirm.com\Netlogon. You can also find it on every domain controller in \\<servername>\NETLOGON, such as \\bf1\NETLOGON. Copy all your logon scripts in here.

You'll want to think about the name of your logon script if you have a large domain and will have many logon scripts. A naming standard that describes the role of the script and who it will be associated with will simplify keeping track of the script.

You need to decide how this logon script will be linked to your users. There are several ways you can do this.

The simplest solution is to define the logon script on a per-user basis, which you can see in Figure 26.52. The "Logon script" field in the user object allows you to specify a script that is contained within the NETLOGON share on your domain controllers. The logon script *must* be contained in NETLOGON.

FIGURE 26.52

Configuring the user object "Logon script" attribute

This method is fine if there are only a few users or if the user has a unique script. However, you will want a different mechanism if there are many users to configure.

A much better way to configure users with a logon script is to use a GPO. Think about this for a moment:

◆   A single GPO can apply to many users.

◆   A GPO can be linked to an OU; that is, a logon script can be linked to a unit of the logical structure of the organization.

◆   A GPO can be linked to an Active Directory site; that is, a logon script can be linked to a unit of the physical structure of the organization. For example, maybe certain things should be done when anyone logs into specific local networks in a site.

◆   You can use loopback policy processing to associate a different logon script with a user when they log onto certain computers.

Create and link a GPO, and open it for editing. Navigate to \User Configuration\Windows Settings\Scripts (Logon/Logoff).

You cannot argue that this isn't a more powerful approach. Some organizations have chosen to use per-user configuration. Their reasoning was that each user had a unique logon script. Any reasoning for this approach can be eliminated by utilizing OUs, security groups, and decision-making in your logon script. You'll now use it to deploy a script using a GPO. Double-click Logon in the GPO to edit the logon script settings.

This opens the dialog box where you can add a logon script:

1. Click Add.

This opens the dialog box shown in Figure 26.53.

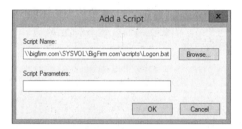

2. Select a specific logon script.

3. Feed parameters to the logon script that will change its behavior.

This is an example of how you can use decision-making in your scripts to reduce the number of scripts you need to implement.

4. Click Browse to open a wizard in order to select an existing logon script.

The default location that it chooses is a folder (`\User\Scripts\Logon`) within which the GPO that you are editing is contained. This is a nasty location to find when you aren't editing the GPO. That's why we didn't recommend it as a place to keep your logon script! However, its entirety is available to everyone as a share, so you might consider using this default location for your logon scripts in very complex AD deployments.

5. Navigate to the DFS namespace folder that represents NETLOGON in your domain.

Our domain is bigfirm.com. This is in `\\bigfirm.com\SYSVOL`. The NETLOGON share is in `\\bigfirm.com\SYSVOL\bigfirm.com\scripts`. In this folder you will find the logon script that you previously copied to NETLOGON.

The logon script is now displayed in the Add a Script dialog box.

6. Click OK in the Logon Properties dialog box shown in Figure 26.54, and you will have finished deploying your logon script via a GPO.

You should test this now, by logging in and verifying that your command is executed before configuring users.

FIGURE 26.54
The configured
logon script
using Group
Policy

Multiple Logon Scripts

You can associate multiple logon scripts with a user if you use Group Policy assignment. Each of these scripts will run for the user.

Figure 26.55 shows where we have added multiple logon scripts using a single GPO. You can change the ordering of the logon scripts using the Up and Down buttons. The script that is listed on top is the first to be executed.

FIGURE 26.55
Configuring many
logon scripts
using Group
Policy

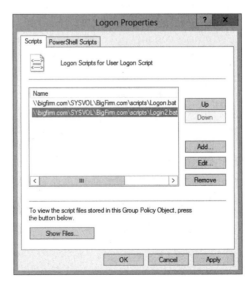

You may have a situation where you have multiple logon scripts assigned by multiple Group Policy objects. Figure 26.56 shows an example in the Group Policy Results.

FIGURE 26.56
Group Policy
Results showing
multiple logon
scripts

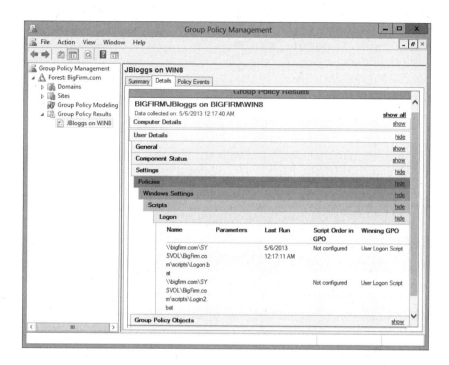

This is an example where a logon script performs tasks that are common for all users underneath the bigfirm.com domain. Another logon script performs tasks for the Users OU. The members of the Users OU will run both logon scripts. Normal policy execution order (site, domain, OU, child OU) is maintained. In this example, the logon script for bigfirm.com runs before the Users logon script.

Managing Logon Scripts with Group Policy

You can use a number of Group Policy settings to manage how logon scripts are processed (see Table 26.14). You can do this on a per-system or per-user basis.

TABLE 26.14   Logon Script GPO

PATH	ENTRY	DESCRIPTION
Computer Configuration \ Administrative Templates\ System\Scripts	Maximum wait time for Group Policy scripts	This defines the number of seconds that Group Policy processing will allow a script to run before terminating the process. The default is 600 seconds.

TABLE 26.14   Logon Script GPO   *(CONTINUED)*

PATH	ENTRY	DESCRIPTION
Computer Configuration \ Administrative Templates\ System\Scripts	Run logon scripts synchronously	Enabling this setting forces Windows Explorer to wait until all logon scripts have run before allowing the user to do anything.
User Configuration \ Administrative Templates\ System\Scripts	Run logon scripts visible	The default is that users cannot see the logon script running. Enabling this setting allows users to see the commands running in a window.
User Configuration \ Administrative Templates\ System\Scripts	Run Windows PowerShell scripts first at user logon, logoff	PowerShell scripts run before non-PowerShell scripts. You can reverse this policy. Must be at least Windows 7, Server 2008 R2.
User Configuration \ Administrative Templates\ System\Scripts	Run Windows PowerShell scripts first at computer startup, shutdown	PowerShell scripts run before non-PowerShell scripts at startup and shutdown. Must be at least Windows 7, Server 2008 R2.

Managing Shutdown Tasks with Logoff Scripts

While you were setting up a logon script using Group Policy, you likely saw an option for logoff scripts.

A logoff script runs every time a user logs off. This allows administrators to define some tasks that can be run every time a user logs off. It is set up identically to how you set up a logon script. You can see an example of a configured logoff script in Figure 26.57.

FIGURE 26.57
A configured logoff script in Group Policy

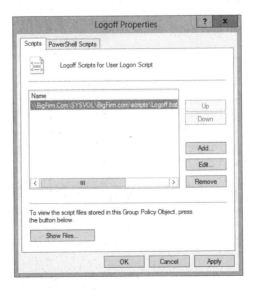

Note that a logoff script will not run if a user just turns off their PC without going through a clean shutdown. It also doesn't run if a user puts their machine into hibernation or disconnects a Remote Desktop Services session.

The Bottom Line

Deploy home directories to multiple users.   Home directories allow a user to have a personal store of information stored on a file server. This makes their data available to them no matter where they log in on the network.

Master It   You've been tasked with deploying home directories to many users in the OU that you manage. You want to do this as quickly as possible. Your backup application uses an administrator user account, so you need to ensure that it has access to the users' home directories on the file server. How will you set this up?

Set up mandatory roaming profiles.   Mandatory roaming profiles can be used to provide users with a preconfigured working environment and to prevent them from saving changes to it.

Master It   Your manager has asked you to set up a mandatory roaming profile for users of Windows 8. You're also asked to see whether there is a way to prevent users from logging in if the mandatory roaming profile cannot be loaded.

Create logon scripts to automate administration.   Administrators can use logon scripts to run a series of commands to preconfigure the working environment for a user when they log in. Administrators can use scripting languages such as command-prompt command, VBScript, or PowerShell.

Master It   You are designing an Active Directory for a large multisite organization. You need to be able to set up logon scripts for different scenarios:

- There are global commands that must be run for everyone.

- Anyone in the Accounts OU must have access to certain resources.

- Anyone, including visitors, logging in at the Dublin Active Directory site must connect to a local shared drive.

You are asked what the running order will be for any user who will run all of the logon scripts.

Chapter 27

Server Virtualization with Hyper-V

In Windows Server 2012 R2, Microsoft has raised the bar with Hyper-V, their out-of-box virtualization offering. When they first introduced Hyper-V to the world in Windows Server 2008, it was clear they had a long way to go to match what the long-established competition in the virtualization world was giving their customers. That all changed at the TechEd North America 2013 conference in New Orleans; there Microsoft announced a huge number of new feature enhancements and additions to Hyper-V in Windows Server 2012 R2 that offer far greater possibilities and deliver higher performance results than ever before.

Virtualization is a huge subject. Typically, server virtualization is a game of big iron that lends itself extremely well to cloud computing: many large multiprocessor servers, loads of memory, SAN and clustering technologies, virtual hard disks, software-defined networking, management software, and so on. In one chapter of a general-purpose book on Windows Server 2012 R2 such as this one, it would be impossible to cover everything. If you want a deep dive into Windows Server 2012 Hyper-V, check out *Windows Server 2012 Hyper-V Installation and Configuration Guide* by Sybex, which was authored by some of the best Microsoft Most Valuable Professionals (MVPs) in the virtualization world.

In this chapter, you can expect an introduction to Hyper-V, including an overview of the new Windows Server 2012 R2 capabilities with sufficient information to get you to first base and enable you to build your own small environment using only native Windows software. We address topics such as what server virtualization is and what it's used for, how to install and use Hyper-V, as well as the constituent components of Hyper-V and how they work together in a newly created virtual machine.

In this chapter, you will learn to:

- ◆ Understand server virtualization

- ◆ Explore what's new in Hyper-V 2012 R2

- ◆ Understand Hyper-V architecture

- ◆ Install and configure a Hyper-V host

- ◆ Configure and install a virtual machine

Understanding Server Virtualization

The term *virtualization* is used for a lot of different things nowadays. It is used in association with applications, storage, network, servers, screen presentation, and so on. In this chapter, *virtualization* means the ability to run a full operating system on a software platform in such a way that the OS thinks it is running on a "real" computer. This type of virtualization is called *hardware virtualization* or *server virtualization*. So, why would you want to have that?

Chances are that you are a system administrator, responsible for a number of servers in your organization. If you've been in the business a while, you will have noticed that server power tends to grow faster than the resource requirements of applications.

In the past, if a company needed to host a new line of business application, they would most likely go out and purchase a new server for it. That server would typically be a low-end server with at least 4 GB of RAM and probably 8 GB or more. Moreover, because Windows Server requires 64-bit capable hardware, they'd purchase a machine that supported this. This process was then repeated frequently when new applications were brought online; a consequence of this is that most such servers are just idling away with 5 percent CPU usage, have multiple gigabytes of free memory, and have I/O bandwidth to spare. Clearly, this is a waste of resources, and that's where virtualization starts to make a lot of sense.

With virtualization, you can consolidate many servers on the same hardware. Not only will these servers make more effective use of the hardware, but because you have fewer physical servers, you will consume less power and rack space. Even better, with the right software, you can move virtual servers between physical servers easily, giving you a flexible configuration.

To illustrate the principle, Figure 27.1 shows one physical server running Windows Server 2012 R2 with Hyper-V virtualization software and a number of virtual machines (VMs) with different guest operating systems such as Linux, Windows 8.1, Windows Server 2008 R2, and Windows Server 2012. The machine running Hyper-V is known as the *host*.

FIGURE 27.1

Hyper-V on Windows Server 2012 R2 running multiple VMs

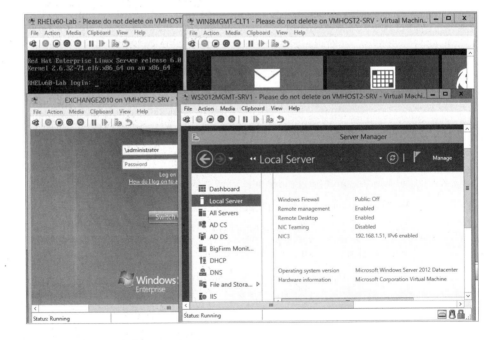

How does this work, generally speaking? Clearly, you cannot have two operating systems accessing the same hardware at the same time. One has to be in charge (that would be the host), and the other (the VM) will need to access that hardware through emulation, synthetic drivers, or some other means. In principle, the same goes for the execution of CPU instructions and even memory access.

Modern dedicated virtualization systems like Hyper-V go out of their way to use system resources as efficiently as possible. They use real memory and the CPU directly executes the code of the VM—with some exceptions that we will discuss later. The same argument holds for high-performance devices such as network, disk, or video interfaces. Emulation where existing hardware behavior needs to be simulated will cost you performance. Sometimes this is unavoidable, but Hyper-V takes a different route. It uses its own driver architecture for each type of device to reduce such overhead as much as possible. This design tightly integrates with the computer architecture.

What Use Is Server Virtualization?

Now that you have some idea of what virtualization is about, let's discuss what to use it for. Some important applications are testing and development, consolidation of servers, and disaster recovery. These all benefit from the high degree of flexibility that virtualization offers.

The technology really took off in the beginning as a test bed for administrators and consultants in need of hardware for a quick test and who were only too happy to use an existing machine with virtualization software to run a couple of VMs. Larger organizations usually have multiple testing environments for various purposes. With virtualization, you can quickly add and remove VMs as required. Whenever a new application comes along or a new infrastructure component needs to be integrated, a new virtual environment is all that you need to deploy for the project to use.

Many administrators have a couple of VMs for their own private use so that they can quickly test and research changes before actually applying them in a production network. For instance, as an Active Directory specialist, you might run four or five DCs plus a Windows 8.1 workstation in VMs on a normal 8-GB desktop that's running Windows Server 2012 R2 with Hyper-V. You might use this to research the fine points of Active Directory replication or the effects of a Group Policy change on the client.

Similarly, virtualization is great for giving technology demos. Because of the low-performance requirements for demos, you can run multiple VMs on a powerful laptop and show people how it actually works.

Away from using virtualization for testing and delivering demos, the largest deployments of server virtualization are in datacenters where numerous servers are consolidated for mainstream and private cloud service usage. Also, huge numbers of organizations (big and small) are migrating their physical IT estates to virtual platforms to reap the cost-saving and flexibility benefits. A virtualized environment offers the following advantages:

Conserves Resources and Saves Costs   One host running multiple VMs saves rack space, electrical power, and cooling capacity. It would not be unreasonable to consolidate 20 or 30 lowly utilized physical machines to one highly spec'd physical host machine.

Shares Hardware   A host offers the same "virtual" hardware to each VM. In other words, all VMs share common hardware. This makes them predictable and makes the maintenance of drivers easy. Deploying VMs is much easier than deploying physical machines, mainly because drivers are no longer a factor.

Increases Flexibility   The same feature of identical virtual hardware makes for a high degree of flexibility. You can move VMs between hosts for load distribution or maintenance. If your company is thinking of moving to the cloud (either public or private), then virtualization plays a major role in cloud elasticity.

Joins Legacy Operating Systems   Many organizations run a mix of operating systems—not only Windows Server 2012 R2 but likely also older systems running Windows 2008 or even Windows 2003. Chances are that those older systems require little computing power on modern hardware. This makes them ideal candidates for consolidation. One host will have enough power for many older operating systems, which will also benefit from the uniform virtual hardware.

In large environments with large storage area network (SAN) deployments, mirrored datacenters, and similar infrastructure, server virtualization is an asset for disaster recovery. Not only is server consolidation a benefit here, but all virtual machines have the same type of virtual hardware. You will have *no* driver or HAL issues when restarting a virtual machine on a new Hyper-V host.

Each technology has its downside and virtualization is no exception. Some of these disadvantages may impact you more than others:

Increases Complexity   Virtualization adds a layer of complexity to the existing environment. You now need to know whether a given server is a VM or a physical server, or perhaps a host for VMs. For example, SQL Server administrators previously would be responsible for all aspects of SQL Server: software, hardware, and configuration. If SQL Server is virtualized, they must depend on the administrators of the host server to keep their VMs running. Any impact on the host will also impact the SQL Server VMs.

Places Demands on Infrastructure   A full-blown VM environment will need additional infrastructure: a SAN solution is mandatory in large environments, as are dedicated management software and a dedicated high-speed IP network.

Can Cause Large-scale Failure   If you are not specifically designing for service availability, a host is a single point of failure. If it goes down unexpectedly, for instance, because the CPU overheats and shuts down, it will take all running VMs down with it. Think of the phrase "putting all your eggs in the same basket!"

Requires Special Maintenance   If you have a library of offline VMs, you will need to do some form of maintenance on those as well, such as applying patches.

Creates Unique Security Issues   There are some non-obvious security considerations related to virtualization. For instance, in a SAN-based environment, you will have two additional groups of administrators who can access data in a VM: the administrators responsible for the host machines and the SAN administrators. A SQL Server administrator responsible for a VM may not be aware that those other administrators can, in principle, access his data at will, assuming they have the desire and knowledge to do so.

Another example would be a scenario where multiple security domains are located on the same virtualization infrastructure, such as an organization's DMZ and LAN located on the same host, or a multi-tenant cloud scenario that runs completely different customer environments.

Requires a Learning Curve   When you deploy a new technology, you need to learn it. While you are learning it, you will make mistakes. Some of those will impact your production environment. That's nothing new, but it's still a factor to consider.

Clearly, it's a balancing act. For most organizations (but not all), the advantages will far outweigh the disadvantages. The main point is that server virtualization is here to stay. If your organization has not deployed it yet, chances are that it will soon. Another compelling point is that because Hyper-V comes bundled as part of the Windows Server 2012 R2 operating system license, if you've purchased Windows Server 2012, then you already own the virtualization piece and don't need to purchase any other software to get up and running.

Getting Started with Hyper-V

Not surprisingly, there are hardware and software requirements for running Hyper-V. In addition, there are some intricate licensing issues involved, which we'll discuss later in this chapter.

HARDWARE REQUIREMENTS

The base requirements for running Hyper-V are quite simple, and this section outlines what you need:

CPU and BIOS　You need an x64-based CPU and a BIOS that supports both CPU-assisted virtualization and Data Execution Prevention (DEP). A common problem is that although these features are offered by the system, they are not typically enabled in the BIOS of older server hardware. Make sure these features are turned on. If you need to change the DEP or virtualization settings, be aware that a cold boot is required: the computer must be turned completely off. A reset or software reboot is not sufficient. Note that any applicable server hardware purchased from 2008 or earlier may need a BIOS upgrade as well to enable access to these settings. Just about all modern servers now have these features enabled in the BIOS by default, but it's something to double-check before you get started with Hyper-V.

Certified for Windows Server 2012　If you want to be really sure that the servers you buy can run Hyper-V, you should check directly with your vendor. They are responsible for testing that Hyper-V actually runs on their hardware. Most large vendors also participate in the "Certified for Windows Server 2012" program, which requires them to test their hardware using Microsoft-standard procedures. After the server passes the test, the vendor can submit the configuration to Microsoft for inclusion in the public catalog. However, not all vendors submit all of their hardware. That's why you should ask them directly. The Microsoft catalog is available at http://windowsservercatalog.com. You can specifically search for *Hyper-V compatible systems.*

Now that you know generally what features to look for, let's talk about the specifics. There are several things to keep in mind when selecting hardware for virtualization. For your VMs to run optimally, they like a lot of memory (RAM) and disk I/O bandwidth, and the more NICs you have, the better.

RAM　When deploying Hyper-V, you must first ensure that your server has met the minimum requirements for running Windows Sever 2012 R2 as outlined in Chapter 2. Once you have enough RAM to keep the host operating system running smoothly, you need to work out how much additional memory is needed for each of your virtual machines. For a low-end personal testing system dedicated to virtualization, you should probably select something with at least 8 GB of memory and a single- or dual-socket CPU motherboard with quad-core CPUs.

Disks   Get as many disk spindles as you can reasonably afford. Four independent medium-capacity disks will be faster than two large-capacity disks when using multiple VMs. SATA disks are OK for testing and non-demanding applications. For better performance go for SCSI or SAS disks, but if you have the money for it, invest in high-speed solid-state disks for optimal performance. Avoid a RAID-5 configuration because it's slow on write operations. RAID 0 and RAID 1 combinations are fine for low-end systems—remember that RAID 0 has no fault tolerance though. For high-end applications, consider RAID 10.

NICs   For Hyper-V networking, the general recommendation is to have at least two NICs, one to manage the host and another for the VMs to access the network. Preferably, you should have four or more NICs if you want to make use of the built-in NIC Teaming, Converged Networking, and Failover Cluster features of Windows Server 2012 R2. If you expect high network throughput or have iSCSI connections that require dedicated NICs, you will need even more.

SOFTWARE REQUIREMENTS

Now that you have your hardware requirements sorted, we'll discuss the software side. Table 27.1 summarizes the different Hyper-V options and their virtualization rights based on the number of Virtual Operating System Environment (VOSE) instances you can run on them. VOSE is a licensing term for a guest operating system running on a host.

TABLE 27.1:   Windows Server 2012 Editions and Hyper-V

WINDOWS 2012 EDITION	CPU SOCKETS	VIRTUALIZATION RIGHTS
Windows Server 2012 R2 Datacenter	Two	Unlimited free VSOEs
Windows Server 2012 R2 Standard	Two	Two free VSOEs
Hyper-V Server 2012	N/A	No free VSOEs
Windows Server 2012 Essentials	N/A	Hyper-V not available
Windows Server 2012 Foundation	N/A	Hyper-V not available

Note the specific edition named Hyper-V Server 2012. This is basically a scaled-down version of Server Core with the Hyper-V role enabled by default. Its main benefit is that it's available as a free download and can only be used for basic virtualization. The remaining editions differ in their virtualization capabilities and licensing models. Briefly, Datacenter and Standard edition licenses cover two CPU sockets. So if your server has four sockets, you'll need two licenses. The unlimited VSOE is on condition that the sockets are licensed correctly. Hyper-V Server 2012 has valid use when customers already have existing licenses that can cover the VMs. In the other two editions of Windows Server 2012 (Essentials and Foundation), the Hyper-V role is not available.

Hyper-V in Client Operating Systems

Although Table 27.1 lists only server editions of Windows that can run Hyper-V, it's worth mentioning here that you can also deploy the Hyper-V role as part of the Windows 8 and Windows 8.1 client operating systems. Known as *Client Hyper-V*, this feature is the same technology that you get in Windows Server without the enterprise clustering, disaster recovery, and scalability functionality.

A primary use for Client Hyper-V is to provide IT pros and developers with a basic virtualization environment on their laptops or PCs that they can use for test and demonstration purposes. It's not designed to run any production server guest instances or workloads.

If you want to learn more about Client Hyper-V, then check out "Using Windows 8 Client Hyper-V" from Microsoft here: http://tinyurl.com/win8clienthyperv.

What's New in Hyper-V 2012 R2?

It's fair to say that as part of the development of Windows Server 2012 R2, Microsoft put a huge amount of resources and budget into making Hyper-V even better than its Windows Server 2012 (RTM) predecessor. It's also fair to say that Microsoft used what their competition (VMware) was offering to their customers as a baseline for where to begin with R2 and then delivered a plethora of new enhancements and features that left their competitors trailing behind. For us IT pros, consultants, and administrators, this can only be a good thing because it means we have a much easier job convincing our customers or bosses to use Hyper-V inside the business.

In this section we'll first give you an overview of what's new and exclusive to Hyper-V in Windows Server 2012 R2. After that, we'll discuss the bigger and better numbers you can expect out-of-box to truly deliver enterprise-class scale and performance to the datacenter.

New VHDX Format   Windows Server 2012 (RTM) introduced Microsoft's new virtual hard disk format (.vhdx) as the replacement for the long-standing original virtual disk format (.vhd) that had been in use since the old virtual PC days. With VHDX, Microsoft broke away from the VHD limitation of a maximum storage capacity of just under 2 TB and moved into new realms of possibility with 64 TB virtual disks. The physical sector size of VHDs was limited to 512 bytes, but with VHDX that has changed to a far superior 4 KB. Also, with Windows Server 2012 R2 you can now leverage the VHDX format to resize your virtual hard disks while the VM is online, as shown in Figure 27.2.

Resizing wasn't possible in Windows Server 2008 R2 or even Windows Server 2012 RTM without shutting down the VM first, thus creating downtime. All you need to do to avail of this cool and pretty useful feature is to have your VHDX attached to a virtual SCSI controller on your VM.

Shared VHDX   Staying with the new VHDX format in Windows Server 2012 R2, you can now share virtual disks to provide commodity shared storage for Hyper-V guest clusters. Essentially, this means that you no longer need to complicate your designs with iSCSI, Fibre Channel, or SMB 3.0 file shares when you want to create failover clusters using virtual machines. You can configure VHDX sharing either through the GUI or with just a few simple lines of PowerShell code. For more information, check out this post from Hyper-V MVP Didier van Hoye: http://workinghardinit.wordpress.com/2013/06/06/shared-virtual-disks-in-windows-server-2012-r2-hyper-v-maximizes-tcoroi/.

FIGURE 27.2
Online VHDX
resizing

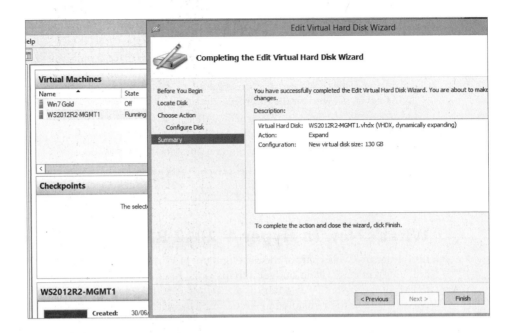

CONVERT VHDs TO VHDX

After reading all about how cool the new VHDX format is in Windows Server 2012 R2, you might be interested to know that you can easily convert those old VHD files that are currently running on your VMs inside your Windows Server 2008 environments. You can do this either through the Hyper-V Manager console by clicking the Edit Disk link from the Actions pane and choosing the Convert action from the wizard or by using the following PowerShell command (substituting the path and disk names of your own configurations):

```
Convert-VHD –Path E:\VirtualMachine1\DataDisk.vhd –DestinationPath E:\
VirtualMachine1\DataDisk.vhdx
```

Gen2 Virtual Machines   With earlier versions of Hyper-V, virtual machines had a number of limitations concerning architecture and capability, such as the requirement for emulated devices—COM ports, legacy NICs, and floppy disk drives, for example—and the restriction to allow booting only from IDE. Windows Server 2012 R2, however, now uses Generation 2 (or Gen2) virtual machines. These new VMs allow booting from virtual SCSI adapters, remove the dependency on emulated devices, and come with a new Unified Extensible Firmware Interface (UEFI) BIOS that delivers secure-boot functionality. Figure 27.3 shows a setting comparison of a Gen1 VM (on the left) and a Gen2 VM (on the right). Notice that the Gen2 VM boots from SCSI and doesn't have the emulated hardware components that the Gen1 VM has.

FIGURE 27.3
Gen1 and Gen2
VM settings

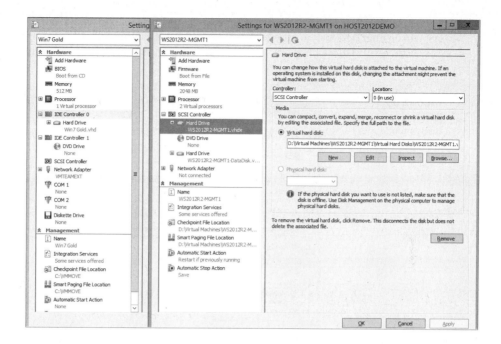

Enhanced Session Mode (VM Direct Connect) This is a simple enhancement on the surface of things, but speaking as a consultant who's worked with Hyper-V for years, I find it to be one of my favorite features of Hyper-V in Windows Server 2012 R2. With earlier versions of Hyper-V, rich copy and paste between the host server and a VM wasn't possible. You could copy and paste into a VM if you had a network connection configured, but no network connection meant no copy and paste. This made even simple tasks like inputting a product key into a new VM cumbersome. It also meant that if you had no network connection to the VM, you had to use the Hyper-V console to manage it, and performance was never optimal doing this long-term.

With enhanced session mode, though, you can now easily copy and paste directly to and from a VM—even without a network connection being configured. It's the same experience you get with a remote desktop connection to a machine but minus the need to worry about networking. Enhanced session mode leverages the VMBus via the Hyper-V integration components to deliver this experience; we'll discuss the VMBus in more detail later. This feature must be enabled and disabled on a per-host basis, and by default it's turned off. To turn it on, all you need to do is to open Hyper-V Manager, click the Hyper-V Settings link from the Actions pane, select the Enhanced Session Mode Policy option, and then check the "Allow enhanced session mode" box, as shown in Figure 27.4.

Turbo-charged Live Migration Live migration has been around since Hyper-V 2008 R2, and it enables you to migrate your VMs between hosts while staying online. A big problem was that this could be quite time-consuming depending on factors, such as how much memory was allocated to the VM and which way you configured your cluster networks. If you wanted to power down a host in a Hyper-V 2008 R2 cluster and you had a large number of VMs waiting to be migrated off it to another host, you had to wait while each VM migrated one-by-one. It was painful to watch, particularly if you had only a small maintenance window to perform the reboot of the host.

FIGURE 27.4
Enabling enhanced session mode

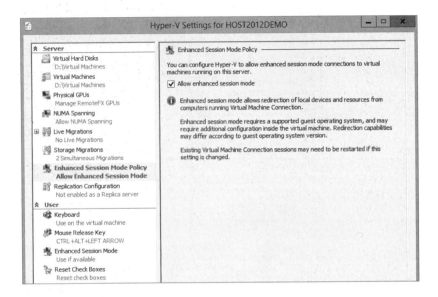

Windows Server 2012 R2 Hyper-V has several enhancements to live migration. First, you no longer need to wait for your VMs to migrate individually because you can do unlimited live migrations at the same time. Obviously, this could have an impact on the performance of your host depending on your network and CPU configuration, so it's wise to not try to migrate 100 VMs of substantial size at the same time. You can tweak the number of migrations that you can do simultaneously by opening Hyper-V Manager and clicking the Hyper-V Settings link from the Actions pane. Once there, click the Live Migrations option, check the "Enable incoming and outgoing live migrations" box, and then input the number you want to migrate at any given time. Figure 27.5 shows an example of this.

Microsoft didn't stop there, though, and with Hyper-V 2012 R2, they've introduced (and enabled by default) *live migration compression*. When you migrate your VMs with compression, you'll get at least twice the speed of migration that you had with earlier versions of Hyper-V. You can leverage live migration compression even further if you have the budget for some high-end networking equipment and make use of the new live migration over SMB functionality. Essentially with this, you can use either *SMB Multichannel*—where multiple NICs are automatically used to get more overall bandwidth—or *SMB Direct*—where you've purchased dedicated 10 Gbps RDMA NICs and DCB-capable switches for your live migration networks. With SMB Direct, you can reduce the time to migrate a VM from minutes to literally seconds! If you want to configure Live Migration over SMB, then open Hyper-V Manager, click the Hyper-V Settings link, expand the Live Migrations option, and choose the Advanced Features option. Figure 27.6 shows the Advanced Features screen, where you can choose from the built-in compression or the optional SMB setting.

FIGURE 27.5
Specifying the number of simultaneous live migrations

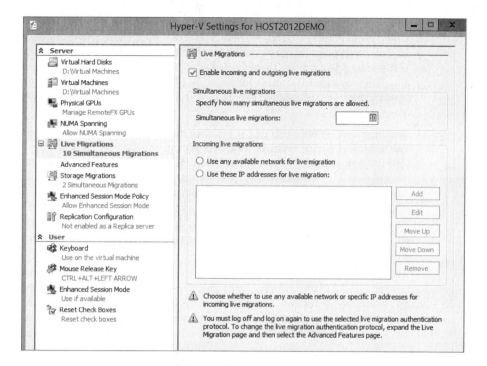

FIGURE 27.6
Configuring Live Migration compression and SMB

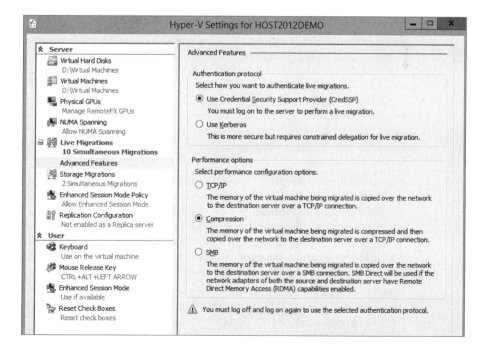

Online Checkpoint Merging   What you knew as snapshots in Hyper-V 2008 R2 are now called checkpoints in Windows Server 2012 (RTM) onward, and they allow you to take a point-in-time checkpoint image of your VM while it's still running. Hyper-V 2008 R2 created a new differencing disk (.avhd) that was linked to the original VHD but was a completely separate file. This was a useful feature, for example, when you wanted to apply a new service pack or hotfix to a server and needed to ensure you could quickly roll back to its original state if things went wrong.

The negatives far outweighed the benefits, though, and before Windows Server 2012, if you wanted to delete that point-in-time checkpoint, you had to shut down the VM and wait for the AVHD file to merge back into the parent VHD. This could take a considerable amount of time to complete if the AVHD was large—all with downtime on the VM. Thankfully, you can now perform online checkpoint merging with Windows Server 2012 R2, so if you need to create checkpoints for your VMs, you can safely merge them back without any downtime. There will be a small performance overhead on the VM while the online checkpoint is being merged, so be aware that this will have an effect on your production systems and might be best carried out after business hours.

Windows Server Gateway   Windows Server Gateway (WSG) is a new addition in Windows Server 2012 R2 to the already comprehensive Hyper-V networking stack that is available in the Windows Server 2012 release. It operates as a virtual machine software router that enables datacenter and cloud service providers to route traffic between their physical and virtual network environments as well as the Internet. It integrates into Hyper-V networking and utilizes the Network Virtualization Generic Routing Encapsulation (NVGRE) standard that delivers true datacenter address space isolation for multi-tenant environments. Deep diving into this technology is out of scope for this book, but you can get more information here: `http://technet.microsoft.com/en-us/library/dn313101.aspx`.

Enhanced Linux VM Support   If you are running Linux VMs in your Hyper-V 2012 R2 environment, you can now make use of dynamic memory support, which allows you to configure how much startup RAM is allocated to the VM and how much it can dynamically expand in times of high utilization. Also, if you've ever tried to manage a Linux VM from older versions of the Hyper-V management console, you'll recall that the performance and mouse support weren't up to scratch. Hyper-V 2012 R2 provides enhanced drivers to improve video and mouse performance and, ultimately, your management experience. Finally, for Linux VMs, Windows Server 2012 R2 enables online backups with no pause, as was the case with previous versions of Hyper-V.

Extended Hyper-V Replica   Windows Server 2012 (RTM) introduced Hyper-V Replica. This is essentially used as a disaster-recovery solution that replicates existing VMs from a host on one site to a host on a second site. In Windows Server 2012 R2, Hyper-V Replica is extended to allow you replicate your VMs to a third site. This functionality brings additional flexibility to how you manage your offline replicas for disaster recovery or even basic backup. For example, you might want to have one replica copy in your own local site and another one up in the cloud or with a third-party service provider.

Also, the previous release of Hyper-V Replica had an update interval restriction of no less than 5 minutes, and although this was more than sufficient for most organizations, in Server 2012 R2, you can now configure an update interval of 30 seconds, as shown in Figure 27.7. We'll discuss Hyper-V Replica in the next chapter in more detail.

FIGURE 27.7
Configure the
update interval

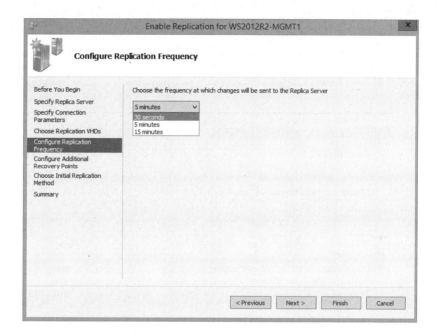

Automatic Virtual Machine Activation   With Windows Server 2012 R2 Datacenter edition, you have unlimited virtualization rights for your Hyper-V hosts. This means that once you're licensed, you can run as many VMs as you like on each host, but with that benefit also comes the hassle of having to activate the product key on each one. Although not a massively arduous task, activating a lot of VMs can get repetitive, and if you're running VMs with no Internet connectivity, it then becomes a problem.

Now you have the capability with Automatic Virtual Machine Activation (AVMA) to configure the Windows Server 2012 R2 Datacenter edition Hyper-V host to automatically activate any guest VMs that are running on it. All you need to do to use this handy new feature is to first deploy a guest VM with a Windows Server 2012 R2 Datacenter, Standard, or Essentials edition (any operating system below 2012 R2 won't work with AVMA) and then install the AVMA key inside the guest VM using the following command:

```
slmgr /ipk <AVMA_key>
```

Once you run this command (substituting the <AVMA_key> option with the actual key you get with your Windows Server 2012 R2 Datacenter purchase), the guest VM automatically activates itself against its host. If you're deploying your VMs using an unattended setup file, then adding the AVMA key to it will give you the hands-free approach to activation.

Hyper-V Scalability   With Windows Server 2012 R2, the only difference between the Standard and Datacenter editions is based on virtualization rights. In the past you had access to only certain roles and features depending on the edition of Windows Server you purchased. Now, regardless of the edition you deploy, you will always have full access to all the roles and features available, making it far easier to understand what you are entitled to from the beginning.

Since Hyper-V was first released back in Windows Server 2008 SP1, there have been some quiet changes in certain limits, such as the number of supported processor cores or number of running virtual machines. Although this information is correct at the time of writing, those limits may well change again, so check the Microsoft site for the current feature set. For now, see Table 27.2.

TABLE 27.2:   Windows Server 2012 R2 Hyper-V Scalability List

FEATURE	WINDOWS SERVER 2012 R2 STANDARD AND DATACENTER
Maximum host physical memory	4 TB
Maximum host logical processors	320
Maximum number of running VMs per host	1,024
Maximum virtual processors running per host	2,048
Maximum VM memory	1 TB per VM
Maximum VM virtual processors	64 per VM
Maximum hosts in a single cluster	64
Maximum number of VMs in a single cluster	8,000
Maximum number of live migrations	Unlimited

Understanding the Hyper-V Architecture

By this time, you should have a feeling for the basic functionality of Hyper-V. You've learned what server virtualization is used for and also what's required from a hardware and software perspective to get it up and running. However, to understand what's going on and to be able to troubleshoot problems, you need a deeper understanding of how Hyper-V was designed. In this section, you will learn more about the software architecture of Hyper-V.

CPU capabilities play an essential role in the implementation of server virtualization. The Intel/AMD model for processors has a number of privilege levels, known as *rings*. In the traditional model, ring 0 has the highest privilege. The Windows kernel and device drivers use this level. Processes in ring 0 are able to access any hardware in the system. Ring 1 and ring 2 are not normally used in current versions of Windows. Ring 3 has the lowest privilege level. It runs normal "user" programs. In practice, this should mean any code that does not require kernel privileges. The trick here is that the CPU forbids any code running in a higher ring to write data or code belonging to a lower ring. In other words, it's a hardware security feature.

When you deploy the Hyper-V role to your computer, you're creating a hypervisor architecture. A *hypervisor* is a software layer between the hardware and the operating systems running on the host. This is known as the *bare-metal* approach: virtualization at the lowest possible level. The main purpose of the hypervisor is to create isolated execution environments (partitions) for all operating systems. In line with that function, it is responsible for arbitrating access to the hardware. During the Hyper-V role deployment, the host restarts a couple of times to accommodate the placement of Hyper-V on top of the hardware that is located at *ring -1*, as shown in Figure 27.8.

FIGURE 27.8
With a hypervisor, the host operates on the same level as the VMs: atop a hypervisor layer.

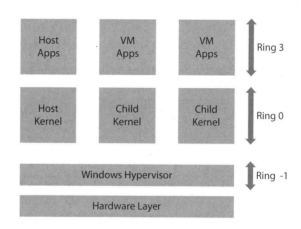

Let's take a look at the ring structure. Ring -1 is not a mandatory feature of a hypervisor, but most modern hypervisors use it. This ring is the main feature of the Intel VT and AMD-V CPU virtualization additions. It's a relatively new access level of even higher priority than ring 0. It allows all kernels to really run on ring 0 without the tweaking that is required in older hybrid models that didn't include a hypervisor. This makes for a cleaner architecture, implying fewer bugs in code and ideally better performance.

The diagram illustrates that all VMs are created equal but that one is more equal than the others: the *Host* or *Management OS* that is responsible for the management and high-level arbitration of all VMs. It's the default owner of all hardware resources and controls the startup and shutdown of the *child* partitions.

The Hyper-V hypervisor is *microkernelized*. As the term suggests, it was written to be as lean and mean as possible. It contains no GUI code and just enough intelligence to do its main job: manage memory and regulate access to the hardware. Other (non-Microsoft) hypervisors may take a different approach. In the monolithic approach, the hypervisor contains drivers and takes more responsibility for inter-VM communication. One advantage of a monolithic hypervisor is that it theoretically can deliver a higher maximum performance because of its tighter integration with drivers to access the hardware. On the other hand, if this hypervisor has no drivers for your specific hardware, you are out of luck. For mature products, this shouldn't be a real problem. In the microkernel hypervisor, the drivers actually reside in the parent partition, which in the case of Hyper-V must be a Windows 2012 server. The parent partition has the drivers, so if your hardware has drivers for Windows 2012, it can work with Hyper-V.

Let's step away from the generalities and take a look at the specifics of Hyper-V in Windows Server 2012. Microsoft designed it with the following goals in mind:

◆ The hypervisor should be as lean and mean as possible.

◆ It should be manageable using open APIs.

◆ Reliability and performance should be maximized.

◆ It should be a built-in feature of the Windows server.

What they came up with is an implementation roughly along the lines of Figure 27.9.

FIGURE 27.9
Hyper-V architecture: the hypervisor, the virtual machines, and their relationship

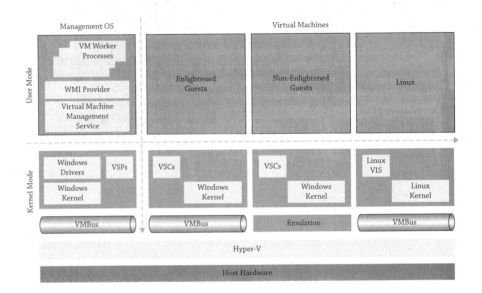

The bottom of the diagram shows the by-now familiar layers of the hardware and the hypervisor. Kernel mode is where the kernel of the Management OS is running along with three different virtual machine *(Guest OS)* partitions. Let's start with the Management OS partition.

The Management OS Partition

This partition really has two parts. The lower block runs in ring 0, or kernel mode. It contains four blocks, three of which are new in this discussion: the VMBus, the Windows drivers, and the virtualization service providers (VSPs). The upper block corresponds to ring 3 code, or user mode. Shown here are only the components that are relevant to Hyper-V. The Management OS partition must run at a version of Windows Server that can run Hyper-V (which means Windows Server 2008 or higher) in order to support the hypervisor. Depending on your needs, this can be a full GUI version or the Server Core edition.

INSTALLATION AND BOOT PROCESS OF THE HYPERVISOR

You may wonder about this chicken-and-egg problem: the hypervisor needs a Windows Server with Hyper-V parent to manage it, but the parent needs the hypervisor before it can do anything. What happens is this: You first install the Windows Server 2012 R2 edition with Hyper-V, such as Standard or Datacenter. At this point, there is no hypervisor. When you enable the Hyper-V role, Windows will install all required software components such as the VMBus and the VSP but not the hypervisor.

Instead, Windows installs the device driver Hvboot.sys, which will load the actual hypervisor on next boot. This can be either the %Systemroot%\System32\Hvax64.exe hypervisor for AMD processors or %Systemroot%\System32\Hvix64.exe for Intel. These files are both less than 1 MB in size, illustrating their microkernel nature. Once loaded, the hypervisor uses the virtualization extensions of the CPU to insert itself as a ring -1 process, taking over control of the hardware. It proceeds to load the Windows 2012 R2 kernel of the parent partition, prepared with the VMBus and VSP.

Coming back to the ring 0 part of the Management OS partition, you see the VMBus component at the lowest level. As the name suggests, the VMBus is used for data communication. It is 100 percent virtual, meaning that it has no hardware components. It is a point-to-point connection between partitions. It does not communicate with the hypervisor directly and uses shared memory and inter-process communication (IPC) mechanisms to share data. The point to note here is that data is shared and not copied for obvious performance reasons. The VMBus is an important differentiator compared to the older hybrid model.

The Windows drivers live on top of the VMBus, but only in the Management OS partition. This illustrates that you install no external drivers in the child partitions. The Windows drivers in this context are the usual drivers that are supplied with every version of Windows: disk drives, SCSI bus, RAID, network, video, and so on.

Key to the performance of Hyper-V is the combination of the VSP in the Management OS partition and the virtualization service client (VSC) in the virtual machine partition. The parent VSP component is responsible for translating data between the VMBus and the Windows drivers. The VSP is actually a combination of multiple modules for each hardware type: storage, networking, video, input devices, and so on. This makes sense, because each of these has very different requirements regarding the transaction speed and the amount of data to be processed. Table 27.3 shows an overview of the most important hypervisor files.

TABLE 27.3:   Relevant Hypervisor Files

FUNCTION	PATH TO FILE
Hypervisor boot driver	%systemroot%\system32\drivers\hvboot.sys
Hypervisor (for AMD)	%systemroot%\system32\hvax64.exe
Hypervisor (for Intel)	%systemroot%\system32\hvix64.exe
Virtual Machine Management service	%systemroot%\system32\vmms.exe
VM worker process	%systemroot%\system32\vmwp.exe

These VSP modules are paired with corresponding VSC modules. For example, the storage module of the VSC will communicate with the storage module in the VSP. Where the VSC communicates only with the VSP in the parent partition, the VSP communicates with all VSC components. It's possible for non-Microsoft developers to design and build their own modules since the relevant APIs are open to all.

With the kernel mode part of the Management OS partition covered, now we'll progress to the user mode components. The Virtual Machine Management (VMM) service is responsible for managing all virtual machine partitions. Whenever a virtual machine partition is started, the VMM service starts a new virtual machine worker (VMW) process for this guest. This process doesn't really do any work, except for monitoring, starting up, shutting down, and so on.

WHAT PROCESS "RUNS" THE VM?

Contrary to similar worker processes in the hybrid model, the VMW process does not really "run" the virtual machine partition. It just controls it. You can't tell from the CPU usage of the VMW process if the guest is doing anything, with the exception of data transfer by legacy (non-enlightened) devices.

In fact, all virtual machine partitions may be running up to 100 percent CPU without anything showing up in the Management OS partition directly. To find out what the guest is doing, you need to either connect to the guest directly using normal server management tools, Performance Monitor counters, or accessing the WMI provider in the Management OS partition.

The final component in the Management OS partition is the WMI provider. Years ago Microsoft decided that WMI would be the preferred way to manage and monitor system resources, and Hyper-V is no exception. The WMI provider is publicly documented on MSDN and provides the following functionality:

◆ Status reporting on mouse and keyboard

◆ Access to the VM BIOS

◆ Managing and reading the configuration of networking, serial devices, storage, guest partitions, and so on

◆ Reading current CPU properties

◆ Managing power state

From this feature set you can see that the WMI provider has all the functionality required to manage the Hyper-V environment. In fact, most management systems for Hyper-V are expected to use WMI. Unfortunately, the WMI interface is a little too involved to use directly for most daily management activities. Only people with extensive WMI programming experience will be able to work productively with this, and as more and more functionality has been introduced into PowerShell to help ease management and administration, this is surely the way forward.

> ### THE TWO HYPER-V APIS
>
> Hyper-V actually has two built-in APIs. Besides WMI, it has the Hypervisor interface. The Hypervisor API is a low-level interface capable of configuring the hypervisor, managing partition states, handling inter-partition communication (VMBus), handling the scheduler, and so on. The Hypervisor interface is really meant for those writing their own VSP/VSC modules and other system-level coding. As an administrator, you will most likely never touch the Hypervisor API directly.

To complete the Management OS partition overview, you should have an idea of the services running in the Hyper-V parent partition, and they are shown in Table 27.4.

TABLE 27.4:   Hyper-V Services

SERVICE	STARTUP TYPE	DESCRIPTION
Hyper-V Data Exchange Service	Manual	Provides a mechanism to exchange data between the VM and the operating system running on the physical computer.
Hyper-V Guest Service Interface	Manual	Provides an interface for the Hyper-V host to interact with specific services running inside the VM.
Hyper-V Guest Shutdown Service	Manual	Provides a mechanism to shut down the operating system of the VM from the management interfaces on the physical computer.
Hyper-V Heartbeat Service	Manual	Monitors the state of the VM by reporting a heartbeat at regular intervals. This service helps you identify running VMs that have stopped responding.
Hyper-V Remote Desktop Virtualization Service	Manual	Provides a platform for communication between the VM and the operating system running on the physical computer.
Hyper-V Time Synchronization Service	Manual	Synchronizes the system time of this VM with the system time of the physical computer.
Hyper-V Virtual Machine Management	Automatic	Management service for Hyper-V, provides a service to run multiple VMs.

Virtual Machine (Guest) Partitions

With most of the Hyper-V architecture picture explained, we have just the virtual machine partition left to discuss, and we have actually already covered some elements of that. The first child partition in Figure 27.9 runs an operating system that is aware of the hypervisor. Microsoft refers to such an OS as an *enlightened guest*, while others may call it *paravirtualized*. As such, it has a VMBus interface and a Virtualization Service Client. The question is, how does the virtual machine partition become enlightened in the first place? In the Management OS, you installed the Hyper-V role, but clearly you need to do something else in the guest to supply the required software components. The Hyper-V software for VMs is commonly called the Integration Components and is also referred to in Microsoft documentation as Virtualization Service Clients (VSCs). The VSC version of a virtual machine must match the Hyper-V server version of the host.

ENLIGHTENMENT COMES IN TWO FLAVORS

Enlightenment exists in two variants, a general flavor and a more specific one. Generally speaking, an operating system that works with the VMBus interface is considered an enlightened guest. Older systems, such as Windows XP and Windows 2003 that need the VSCs to be first installed, are considered non-enlightened guests. The specific variant applies to the kernel: if the kernel natively knows about the hypervisor, the operating system is said to have an *enlightened kernel*. This would include any guest running Windows 2008 or higher for server Guest OSs and Vista SP1 and higher for client Guest OSs. The advantage of an enlightened kernel is that it can further optimize access to the VMBus. For instance, Windows 2012 can bypass some internal software layers for network and disk access when it realizes the data is intended for a virtual device.

Only guests running Windows Server 2008 and higher have a version of the VSCs built in, although that version will need to be upgraded to match the current Hyper-V version of your host; running a Windows Server 2008 guest VM on a Windows Server 2012 R2 host would be an example of this. For other operating systems, you will need to install the VSCs explicitly. One of the ways to do this is to insert an ISO file with the VSCs into the VM. This ISO file comes bundled with Hyper-V.

The VSCs are actually a set of modules installed in `%systemroot%\Virtualization\<version>` in the virtual machine partition. There is one `<version>` folder for each update of VSCs. Taking a deeper look at its functionality, you can see that it is really split into two parts. On one hand, there are drivers for storage, video, and network. Another driver directly integrates with the kernel to optimize its performance running as a VM. On the other hand, there is a multipurpose service (`vmicsvc.exe`) executable that is started four times with different arguments to provide the following functionality:

Operating System Shutdown Service   On request of the parent partition, this service will shut down the VM in an orderly manner.

Heartbeat Service   The parent needs a way to tell whether the child is still alive. If the parent can no longer hear the heartbeats, it is safe to assume the child has a severe problem.

Time Synchronization Service   A child partition has no direct access to the hardware clock. This service offers an alternative. Don't use this feature in an Active Directory domain environment, because that has its own time-synchronization infrastructure.

Data Exchange Service   This service is the only way for user (ring 3) processes in the parent and child services to communicate outside of the regular devices. It works through certain registry keys.

Backup (Volume Snapshot) Service   This service will work with a backup service on the parent to provide consistent backups for both the parent and the child partitions, using VSS technology.

Guest Services   This is a new VSC that is available only with Windows Server 2012 R2 Generation 2 virtual machines. It's disabled by default, but when you enable it, you then have the ability to copy files to a running virtual machine without utilizing a network connection.

It's worth noting that the VSCs cannot be configured from the virtual machine partition. The only (proper) way to do it is through the Management OS partition, either using the Hyper-V management console, through PowerShell, or by using the WMI interface.

Continuing the discussion of virtual machine partitions, let's look at the second child partition in Figure 27.9. It's labeled "Non-Enlightened Guests." What this really means is that the operating system is not enlightened. This may be because the VSCs are not installed or are not available. For instance, you can have Windows 2003 installed both as a legacy system and as enlightened. For older unsupported systems such as Windows 2000 or Windows NT 4 (hopefully you're not still running any of these), Microsoft obviously has not written any VSCs, although in principle a third party could do so if need be. Lack of VSCs doesn't mean that the VM won't install or run, but it does imply that it will never reach a high level of performance or be supported if you run into any problems. On the other hand, many legacy operating systems should perform just fine on modern hardware, even if virtualized. The diagram shows that a non-enlightened system has no VMBus or VSC provider and instead is using emulation.

The third and final type of virtual machine partition runs a non-Microsoft operating system, such as Linux using the Linux Virtual Integration Services (VIS). These are kernel-level drivers that provide access to the VMBus component and offer nearly all the functionality of the VSCs for Microsoft VMs delivery. These Linux VIS components are written specifically for that operating system by Microsoft, so they are fully supported should you run into any difficulties running these types of VMs in Hyper-V. You may expect near-native performance from such an enlightened system.

Installing and Configuring Hyper-V

In this walk-through, you will learn how to install Hyper-V on Windows Server 2012 R2, and we'll discuss the different options in the management console. Along the way, you'll pick up some practical tips to help you when dealing with Hyper-V.

Since you have gotten this far in the book, you should know how to install a server, join it to a domain, and so on. For this reason, we'll skip the details for the base installation and get straight into the Hyper-V piece. Table 27.5 shows the suggested configuration for a test setup. Feel free to vary the instructions as you see fit. This walk-through uses Windows Server 2012 R2, but there is hardly any difference in the installation experience if you use Windows Server 2012.

TABLE 27.5: Hyper-V Host System

SETTING	CONFIGURATION
Internal memory	8 GB; 4 GB is the practical minimum.
Hard disks	Two 200 GB or more. One disk is acceptable for a test system, but expect low performance.
Partitions	Disk 1: System on C:\.
	Disk 2: Reserved for Hyper-V on D:\.
Network	Two 1 Gbit NICs minimum for production. One NIC is acceptable for a test system but not production.
Operating system	Hyper-V–enabled editions of Windows Server 2012 R2 or Windows Server 2012.
Installation type	Full GUI is required to follow the examples.
Hostname	HOST2012DEMO if you want to follow the examples; anything you like is fine.
IP configuration	Address: 192.168.1.54/24.Gateway: 192.168.1.1.DNS: 192.168.1.51.
Active Directory	Domain-joined recommended for production. Workgroup is workable for testing, although configuring remote management is difficult and far easier if you just use Active Directory.

Just about the only thing you need to decide before you install the Hyper-V role is which NIC to use for managing the Hyper-V host. The idea is to have at least two NICs in the host, although you can make do with one if you really must. Expect no performance miracles in that case. With two NICs available, dedicate one to managing the host and the second for VM network traffic. To make this obvious, one trick is to rename the network connections, as shown in Figure 27.10.

FIGURE 27.10
Renaming the network connections to reflect their role in the Hyper-V host

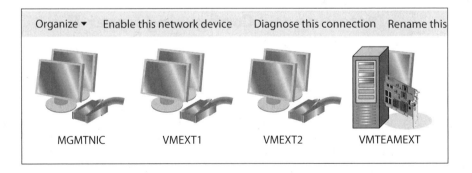

Organize ▾   Enable this network device   Diagnose this connection   Rename this

MGMTNIC   VMEXT1   VMEXT2   VMTEAMEXT

Let's start with the installation of the Hyper-V role:

1. Install the server using the parameters in Table 27.5 as a guide for the version, server name, IP configuration, and so on.

   Make sure to have dedicated disks or partitions for Hyper-V data.

2. Join the computer to the domain if you want to follow some of the later examples.

   The domain bigfirm.com is used throughout this book.

   After you install the Hyper-V host server operating system, you are ready to install the Hyper-V role. During the installation, the network connection will be broken once or twice because of upgraded network components.

3. Log on to your Windows Server 2012 R2 installation with an account that has domain administrative permissions, and from the Server Manager ➤ Local Server ➤ Manage menu, choose the Add Roles and Features option.

4. In the Before You Begin dialog box, click Next.

5. Ensure that Role-Based or Feature-Based Installation is selected in the Select Installation Type dialog box; then click Next.

6. Under Select Destination Server, leave the default option of Select a Server from the Server Pool checked; confirm that your server is highlighted in the Server Pool section and then click Next, to continue.

7. When you reach the Select Server Roles dialog box, scroll down until you find the Hyper-V option from the Roles list, and check the box beside it.

   You'll then be prompted to add some required features here such as the Hyper-V Management Tools.

8. Click the Add Features button from the window that pops up.

9. Click Next to continue.

10. Leave the features as they are in the Select Features dialog box; then click Next twice.

11. In the Create Virtual Switches dialog box shown in Figure 27.11, choose the NIC for a virtual switch that you are going to use with your VMs.

    You'll find the details later in this chapter, but briefly, for each NIC that you select here, one virtual switch will be created. If you have two NICs or more, you should leave one blank—we're leaving our MGMTNIC unselected here. An unselected NIC will not have a switch associated with it and can be used to manage the host. If you have only one NIC, select it. If you don't select any NIC, your VMs have no easy way to communicate with the outside world, although you could correct this later. Because we remembered to give sensible names to the network connections, it's now easy to select the one we will use for VM network traffic.

FIGURE 27.11
Select one NIC to use for VM traffic. The unselected NIC is used to manage the Hyper-V host.

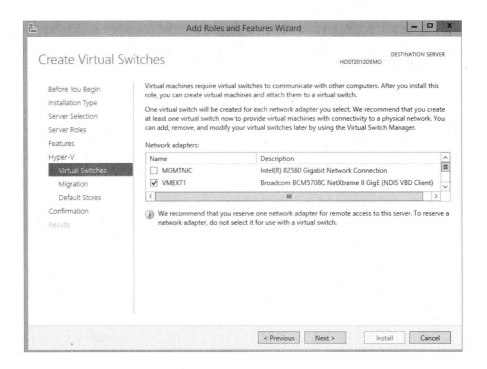

12. Click Next, and you'll be presented with the Virtual Machine Migration screen.

13. Leave the option here unselected (we'll come back to this later in the chapter) and click Next.

14. Be careful in the Default Stores dialog box shown in Figure 27.12. It's here that you need to specify where your virtual hard disks and VM configuration files will be stored on your host.

    If you have more than one disk or volume available, then it's best practice to modify the default locations here to store these files on a volume that has enough disk space to host your VMs. Even in a test or lab environment, you don't want your system C:\ partition running out of disk space as your virtual machines grow.

15. Click Next, confirm your installation selections, and then click Install.

16. Once the installation is finished, reboot the server; this shouldn't take longer than a few minutes.

17. When it comes back, log on using an administrator account.

   After Server Manager initializes, the configuration process will resume and finalize what it needs to do. Give it a minute or two and then you should see the Hyper-V role on the Server Manager dashboard light up green for healthy, indicating the installation was successful.

FIGURE 27.12
Choosing the
default store for
your VM files

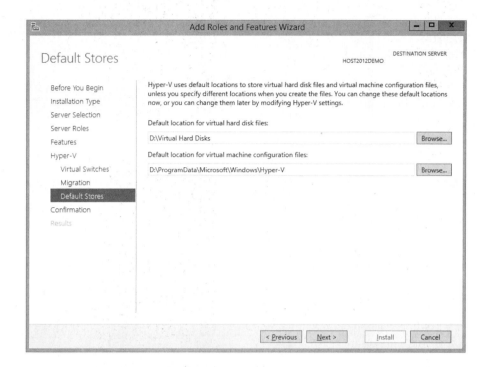

FIGURE 27.12
Choosing the
default store for
your VM files

HYPER-V BEST PRACTICES CHECKLIST

If you want to ensure that you're building your Hyper-V environments in accordance with best-practice recommendations, take a look at this useful blog post by Microsoft PFE Roger Osborne that I normally use as a checklist guide for the customer deployments I'm involved in: `http://blogs.technet.com/b/askpfeplat/archive/2013/03/10/windows-server-2012-hyper-v-best-practices-in-easy-checklist-form.aspx`.

Working with the Console

Take a look at what you have now. Start the console from Server Manager ➢ Tools ➢ Hyper-V Manager. You have a console that allows you to manage your virtualization environment settings, as shown in Figure 27.13. The left pane holds the Hyper-V host you want to manage. Shown is the current server HOST2012DEMO, but you can have more than one server listed if you want to manage multiple hosts from one console.

The middle pane has three regions:

Virtual Machines This section lists the VMs on this host with some relevant parameters such as their current state (running, off, saved, and so on).

FIGURE 27.13
The Hyper-V
management
console

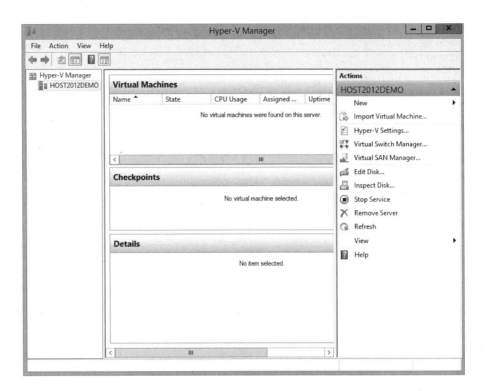

FIGURE 27.13
The Hyper-V
management
console

Checkpoints   As mentioned earlier, these are point-in-time disk images, including memory and CPU states. You might create a checkpoint of a server if you want to be able to roll back to such an image after deploying a service pack or hotfix that could break more things than it fixes or if you use that particular VM for demo purposes and want to reset it to its original state.

Details   This section contains extra information on the currently selected VM (if any), such as summary, memory, networking, and replication.

The Actions pane on the right is the most interesting for now. It allows you to manage various aspects of your Hyper-V environment. Some actions are pretty obvious, such as stopping or starting the Hyper-V Virtual Machine Management service or removing the current server from the console. Others such as the Virtual Switch Manager, Virtual SAN Manager, Edit Disk, and Inspect Disk are not so obvious if you're new to the virtualization game.

Exploring the Actions Pane

If you want to competently manage Hyper-V through the GUI with native tools, then you'll need to utilize the Actions pane of the Hyper-V management console. The New Wizard and the Import Virtual Machine Wizard deal with creating VMs and virtual disks, so we'll leave them for the next sections.

Clicking the Hyper-V Settings option opens the dialog box shown in Figure 27.14, which allows you to set parameters for Hyper-V such as virtual disk and VM configuration store locations, live and storage migrations, enhanced session mode, and replication.

FIGURE 27.14
The Hyper-V Settings
dialog box

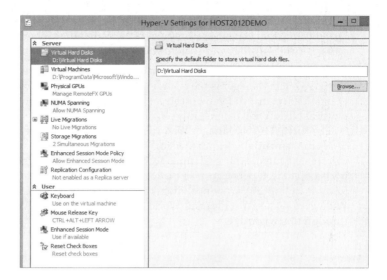

Each parameter shows its current setting. As we mentioned earlier in the Hyper-V installation section, two of the most important parameters are the default paths for virtual hard disks and for virtual machine configurations. In the Hyper-V philosophy, the files for virtual disks are separate from the virtual machine settings. Make sure you set them to something sensible and different from each other. We've already discussed the Enhanced Session Mode Policy option, and in the next chapter, we'll dive into the options related to live migrations, storage migrations, and replication.

Physical GPUs   This option is enabled only when you have installed the Remote Desktop Virtualization Host role. It allows you to choose from physical graphics processing unit (GPU) cards, such as NVIDIA, and use them with the advanced remote desktop (RDP) solution called RemoteFX.

NUMA Spanning   This option is enabled by default and allows virtual machines to span Non-Uniform Memory Architecture (NUMA) nodes. If the host has NUMA nodes to use, then enabling this option gives your VMs additional performance benefits and allows you to run many more VMs at the same time than on a host without NUMA.

The remaining settings here are all related to the way you use Hyper-V and access the VMs:

Keyboard   Specify how Windows special keys (Alt+Tab, for example) should behave in the VM console.

Mouse Release Key   Specify what keyboard combination should be used to release input focus from a VM console in a situation where the integration components or virtual machine drivers aren't installed. Pressing Ctrl+Alt+left arrow is the default here.

Enhanced Session Mode   Similar to (but dependent on) the Enhanced Session Mode Policy in the Server settings discussed earlier and shown in Figure 27.4, the user version of this setting determines whether or not to use an enhanced session mode connection when it's available inside a guest operating system. Supported guest operating systems are Windows Server 2012 R2 and Windows 8.1 or later.

Reset Check Boxes At various points in the Hyper-V console you can select check boxes indicating that you never want to see a particular dialog box again. This option brings them all back to the way they were before you starting changing things.

Continuing the overview of the Actions pane, we have three more wizards to discuss briefly. Virtual Switch Manager is the central management point for virtual switches (or *networks*). Using this wizard, you view, create, and edit networks. External switches can be assigned to physical NICs. We'll discuss this wizard in detail later on.

The Virtual SAN Manager Wizard is where you get to configure your virtual Fibre Channel SANs that essentially group physical HBA ports together and present them to your VMs. You can create a virtual Fibre Channel SAN only if the wizard detects physical Fibre Channel ports on your Hyper-V host, so make sure they're up and running and accessible to the host prior to attempting to connect them to your VMs. As you can see in Figure 27.15, World Wide Port Name (WWPN) and World Wide Node Name (WWNN) addresses can be defined through this wizard too.

FIGURE 27.15
The Virtual SAN Manager Wizard

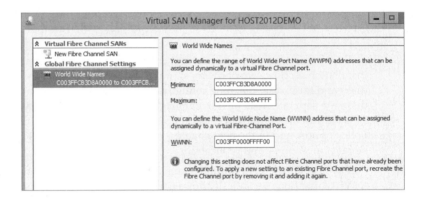

Surprisingly perhaps, the Edit Disk Wizard cannot be used to create virtual disks. That activity is reserved for the New Wizard. The Edit Disk Wizard does allow you to change a disk from VHD to VHDX and from dynamic to fixed, as you'll learn in the next section. It also allows you to expand its size and to remove blank space from the virtual disk file. Finally, the Inspect Disk dialog box inspects a virtual disk for consistency and will display properties, such as format, type, location, name, and size.

Now that you have an understanding of how to install and configure the Hyper-V service, we'll discuss the virtual disk options that you can configure to run with your VMs.

Understanding Virtual Disks

When you create a virtual machine, you assign virtual devices for network, video, and so on. Your VM also needs a virtual disk, of course. The question is, what type of disk? The physical disks are in use by the host! The solution is simple and obvious: because you are virtualizing and emulating already, use a file instead and present that to the VM as a disk. A virtual disk is nothing more than a very large file—don't forget that it can scale up to 64 TB if required!

Hyper-V has multiple flavors of virtual disk systems to offer to a VM and different scenarios where you might want to use each one:

Dynamically Expanding Disk   A virtual disk in this format will allocate the physical disk space it needs and no more. For instance, you might allocate 127 GB for a Windows Server 2012 VM, which uses less than 10 GB after a basic install. Every time the VM needs more disk space, the file expands. The expanding virtual disk makes the best use of the available disk room on the host. But as you can imagine, there can be a performance cost involved when an expansion is needed, and you run the risk of fragmentation.

Also, a clear disadvantage is that you may run out of disk space on the host when the dynamic virtual disk expands beyond available room. When that happens, Hyper-V freezes all VMs, and the event log turns red—not a nice situation to find yourself in! This issue is not isolated to Hyper-V and is the same when using thin provisioned disks in VMware.

Fixed-size Disk   To get rid of the overhead of dynamically expanding disks, you can choose to use a fixed-size disk. The full size of the virtual disk will be allocated when the disk is created, so you can easily work out how much physical space you are using for your VMs. This is generally the recommended format for most production loads.

When you create such a disk, a file is created with the full size that you specify. During creation, the file is filled with binary zeros. This may take quite some time, depending on the size you specify. A fixed-size disk is widely recommended to be your default for any production systems.

Differencing Disk   This is an interesting feature where you have a parent-child relation between two virtual disks. The parent disk is a static, read-only reference. The differencing disk (child) stores all changes with respect to the parent. The point of this feature is to save disk space on the host and be able to create a new VM quickly. However, if the VM using the differencing disk is writing a lot of new data, the advantage of saving disk space will disappear quickly. Clearly, this feature is suitable only for test purposes.

Pass-through Disk   The last flavor is a pass-through disk, where you assign a physical disk for dedicated use by a VM. This is possible when this disk is not used by the host. Pass-through disks enable you to connect a VM directly to a SAN or to an iSCSI target. To dedicate a physical disk to a VM, it must appear as a physical disk to the Windows host machine. This may be a local disk, a disk on a SAN, an iSCSI disk, and so on. It can't be a partition. It really must be a full disk, as visible in Disk Manager. Also, to be able to use the disk in a VM, it must be offline in the host to prevent the host from using it. You can set a disk offline or online in Disk Manager.

Generally speaking, you'll use a pass-through disk only in certain clustering scenarios where you need a volume greater than 64 TB or if you have a paranoid IT admin or manager who insists on running their workloads on physical storage. If you don't need to use pass-through disks, stick with normal fixed or dynamic virtual disks and let the host mount disks on the SAN or iSCSI target.

Virtual Disks and Their Controllers

As you learned earlier in "What's New in Hyper-V 2012 R2," you have a new a *virtual disk* file format to work with. In Windows Server 2012, its normal extension is .vhdx, and earlier versions of Microsoft's virtualization products use the .vhd format for their virtual disks. Even more important, this structure is published and freely usable by anyone. The specification is low level from a disk point of view, meaning that it does not assume any type of file system in the VM. The VM may run Windows with NTFS and FAT32 or run Linux with EX2, ReiserFS, or whatever will be developed in the future. The open specification of VHDX and VHD files means that they can be used for virtualization products from other companies and that anyone can write tools to handle them.

Windows accesses disks through controllers and a VM running on Hyper-V is no different. The two usual types are present: IDE and SCSI. In a physical machine, SCSI systems generally perform better on a server. Not only are SCSI disks faster than IDE disks (very generally speaking!), but the SCSI interface was designed to handle multiple I/O requests at the same time. In an enlightened VM, both IDE and SCSI data transfers are quickly translated to VMBus requests that in turn depend on the storage system of the host. In fact, the .vhdx file has no knowledge of its controller. This means that the same .vhdx file can be used with an IDE and SCSI controller.

FIXED OR DYNAMIC VHDX: WHICH VIRTUAL DISK TYPE IS BEST?

If you're familiar with Hyper-V, and you've carried out your research on virtual disk types in Windows Server 2012 R2 and can't make your mind up as to whether to use fixed, dynamic, or even pass-through disks, then you're not alone. In earlier versions of Hyper-V and with the legacy VHD format, the general consensus was that if you wanted the best performance, then you absolutely had to use fixed disks. Dynamic VHD disks were the cause of untold performance issues, but when Windows Server 2012 was released, Microsoft was encouraging people to use dynamic disks with their new VHDX format since the performance issues of the past had been resolved.

There's still a bit of a divide, though, inside the Hyper-V community as to the performance gains or losses between fixed and dynamic VHDX disks and the practicality of using each one. You only have to look at this blog post from Irish Hyper-V MVP Aidan Finn, http://www.aidanfinn. com/?p=13230, to see that fixed-type VHDX is his preference above all else. Or for a different perspective, see this post from another well-regarded Hyper-V MVP, Thomas Maurer, http://www .thomasmaurer.ch/2012/11/windows-server-2012-hyper-v-virtual-disk-vhd-vhdx-recommendations/, who prefers using dynamic VHDX disks for the majority of environments.

My own personal preference with Windows Server 2012 R2 is to use dynamic VHDX disks for all low-utilization VMs (such as domain controllers, print servers, and so on) and fixed VHDX disks for any VM that requires a higher level of I/O (such as SQL and Exchange Server). That way, I get the best of both worlds in terms of performance and storage maintenance.

Creating a New Virtual Disk

You can create a new virtual disk during the deployment of a new VM, while editing the configuration of a VM, or just as a stand-alone disk whenever you want. In this section we'll walk you through the process of creating a new fixed-size, stand-alone VHDX virtual disk by making use of the New Virtual Hard Disk Wizard in the Hyper-V console.

1. To begin, open Hyper-V Manager, click New from the Actions pane, and then choose Hard Disk from the resulting menu to start the New Virtual Hard Disk Wizard.

2. Click Next.

3. In the Choose Disk Format dialog box shown in Figure 27.16, select the VHDX format option. Click Next.

FIGURE 27.16
Choosing your
new virtual disk
format

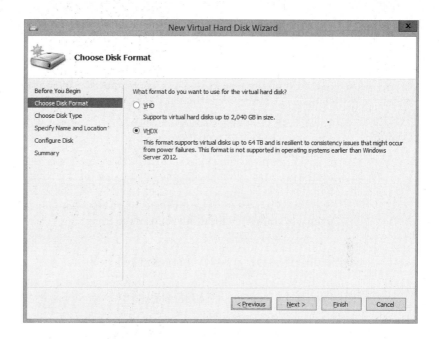

The Choose Disk Type dialog box opens, allowing you to select from either "Fixed size," "Dynamically expanding," or "Differencing disks."

4. Select the "Fixed size" option, as shown in Figure 27.17.

Click Next.

FIGURE 27.17
Different disk type
options

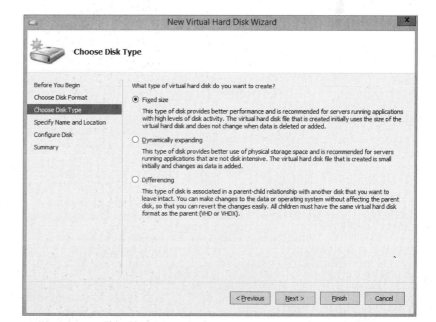

5. From the Specify Name and Location dialog box, give your new disk a name and specify where it's going to be located.

   Click Next.

6. In the Configure Disk dialog box, specify the size of your new virtual disk; you can also copy the contents of a particular physical or other virtual disk.

   The default size suggested for new blank virtual disks is 127 GB, and you can scale up to a maximum of 64 TB here if required.

   If you're creating a new fixed-size disk, then remember that whatever size you specify for the new disk, you need to ensure you have at least that amount in free space on the location you specified in the previous step. Also, the bigger the fixed-size disk, the longer you'll have to wait for it to finish creating—that would be a pretty long wait if you were to go with the 64 TB limit! As you can see from Figure 27.18, we've modified the default value to 50 GB.

   Click Next when you're ready to move on.

7. In the Summary dialog box, ensure that you've configured everything as it should be; then click Finish to kick off the virtual disk creation.

FIGURE 27.18
Specifying a size for your virtual disk

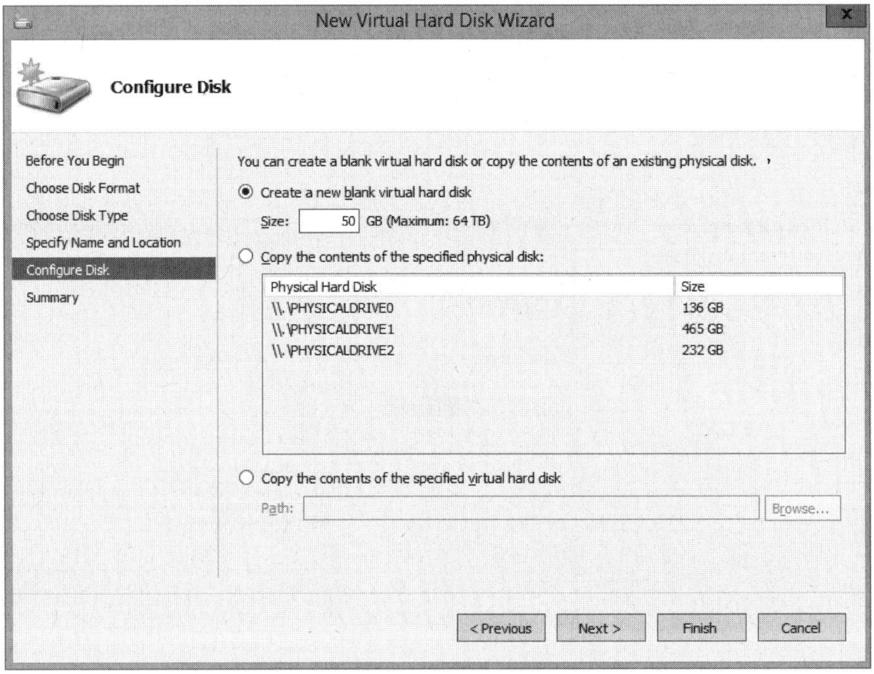

Real World Scenario

VMs Mysteriously Running Slow

Bigfirm has deployed a number of Hyper-V host servers as a test environment. Each server has 128 GB of internal memory and 12 TB in usable disk space. The Hyper-V hosts are run by the IS department. Other departments use and manage the VMs.

One day, complaints start coming in that certain VMs are slow to respond, although there is no obvious load on the VMs. The IS department takes the complaints and investigates. None of the VMs show any sign of trouble. The CPU usage is normal, all applications are running, the OS is not swapping, and there is no memory pressure. In short, there is no obvious cause. One pattern emerges: most "slow" VMs share the same host.

The IS department starts running performance counters on the host, including the CPU and Logical Disk objects. After an hour of measuring, they note that some counters are consistently high: the counter disk seconds/read averages 30 milliseconds, and the counter disk seconds/write is mostly over 50 milliseconds. The average disk queue length counter of the disk hosting the VMs often peaks at more than 20. Compared to other hosts, these are really high values. Clearly, the host has trouble delivering the required disk I/O.

An inspection of the host shows that the disk on which the VMs are located is a RAID 5 configuration, which is good at reads but slow at writes. The combined disk I/O of all VMs has pushed the host capacity over the limit. The problem is solved by rearranging the disks in a RAID 10 configuration and adding more disks to increase the maximum I/O throughput.

This case illustrates the added complexity of managing a virtualized server environment. The combined VMs may put the host in trouble if the underlying physical disk hardware has not been configured for optimal performance.

Disk Maintenance

The most essential parts of a VM are its disks. Not only do they contain the data, but they determine in large part the performance of the VM. In this section, you will learn how to maintain virtual disks.

When using dynamic and differencing disks, if you create a lot of data and then remove it (such as copying large ISO files onto it and then deleting them), you'll leave a lot of empty space on the disk. In other words, the virtual disk is larger than it needs to be. Hyper-V can remove this empty space with an operation called *compaction*. To do that, it mounts the virtual disk in the parent partition. If the file system on the virtual disk is NTFS, the parent can inspect its data structures to figure out where the empty space is. It uses this information to reduce the size of the file representing the virtual disk. To compact a virtual disk, the corresponding VM cannot be running. You must shut it down or save its state. Once you've done that, it goes like this:

1. From the Actions pane in the Hyper-V management console, start the Edit Virtual Hard Disk Wizard.

2. Locate the virtual disk you want to compact, such as the one you created earlier, and then click Next.

As shown in Figure 27.19, the Choose Action dialog box presents you with three options that can be applied to your virtual disks.

FIGURE 27.19
Compacting your
virtual disk with
the Edit Virtual
Hard Disk Wizard

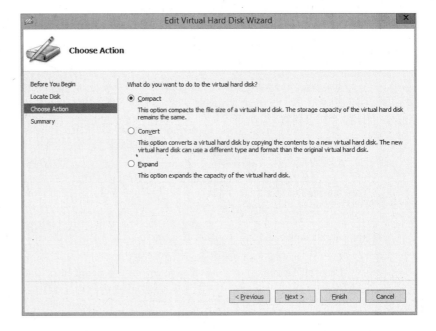

3. Select the default action Compact and then click Next.

4. Click Finish.

The actual process may take a while.

You might find yourself in a situation where you want to change the type of disk you're working with. For instance, you may decide that a dynamic disk wasn't a great choice and that you would prefer to have a fixed-size disk instead. Or, you may have a differencing disk that you would like to disentangle from its parent. Hyper-V offers a number of disk-conversion operations when you choose the Convert option from the Edit Virtual Hard Disk Wizard, as shown in Table 27.6.

TABLE 27.6:   Disk Convert Operations

TYPE OF DISK	POSSIBLE OPERATIONS
Dynamically expanding disk	Create a new fixed-size disk, compact, or expand.
Fixed-size disk	Create a new dynamic disk or expand.
Differencing disk	Merge with parent disk, compact, or reconnect to a parent disk that was moved to a different path.

These options are all accessed from the Edit Virtual Hard Disk Wizard. If you do a lot of testing using differencing disks, you will at some point want to create stand-alone disks, because a much-used differencing disk will be larger than its parent—exactly the situation you wanted to avoid. We'll show an example. Say you have a differencing disk called differencing.vhd, and you want to create a new, independent virtual disk. Again, for such a procedure, the VM must be turned off.

1. From the Actions pane on the Hyper-V management console, start the Edit Virtual Hard Disk Wizard.

2. Locate the disk you want to merge, which is differencing.vhd in this example.

   The wizard will determine that it's a differencing disk and present you with the relevant options only.

3. From the Choose Action dialog box, select the Merge option.

   A sub-dialog box appears giving you two basic options. Do you want to merge the differencing disk into its parent, or do you want a new dynamic or fixed differencing disk? Be really careful when merging a disk into its parent because any other child disks will be invalidated.

4. For testing, you will want to create a new dynamic disk: Choose a suitable name, such as servername-dynamic.vhd, as shown in Figure 27.20.

5. Click Next, and then click Finish to start the actual procedure.

6. To use the new disk, edit the virtual machine properties and replace the current differencing disk.

FIGURE 27.20
Merging a differencing disk and its parent to a new (dynamic) virtual hard disk

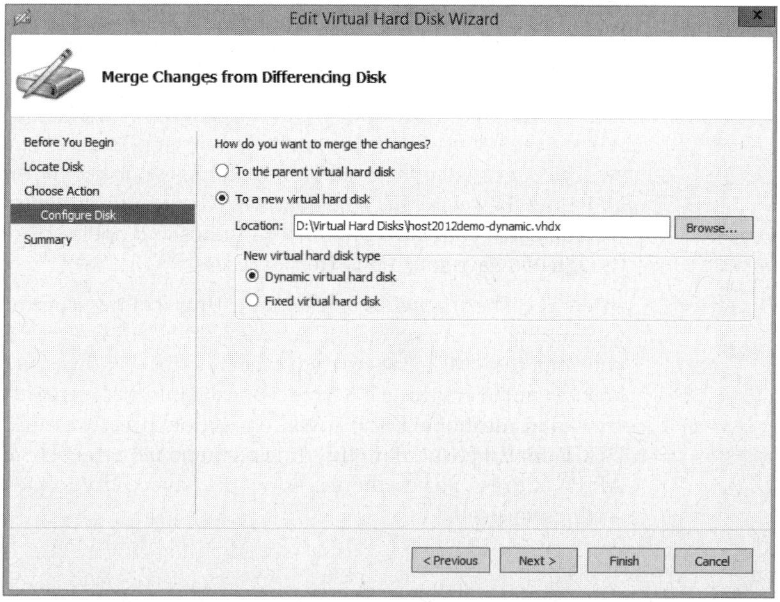

If you look at the Actions pane of the Hyper-V management console, you will see one additional menu related to disks: Inspect Disk. As we discussed earlier, this is a simple menu option that does nothing more than to open a virtual disk and tell what type it is with some additional information. It has one useful feature for differencing disks, though: if the parent disk is missing, it will tell you. It will give you the option to reconnect it to its parent, which you can do by browsing to it.

From the discussion you have seen that virtual disks come in various types, and the .vhdx extension doesn't tell the whole story at first glance.

Understanding Virtual Switches

As you learned in Chapter 4, the enhancements to networking delivered in Windows Server 2012 have been the area with the biggest investments and improvements compared to its predecessors. This version of Hyper-V introduces the concepts of converged fabric, storage QoS, and extensible switches. In this section we'll help you to understand some of these concepts and explain how you can use them in your Hyper-V deployments going forward.

In earlier versions of Hyper-V, you had a reasonably simple method of getting your VMs connected with three different types of basic virtual networks that you could configure through the Virtual Network Manager. In Windows Server 2012, the virtual network concept was replaced with the *virtual switch*, and at a glance, it comes with the same type of behavior. When you dig into the capabilities of the virtual switch, however, it soon becomes apparent that you can do a whole lot more with your virtual networking than before.

Virtual switches are 100 percent software defined, and they deliver high-speed connections between VMs that are configured with one or more virtual NICs. Like in the physical world, on a virtual switch, you "plug in" virtualized NICs of VMs.

Choosing a Virtual Switch

With Hyper-V, you can choose from the following virtual switch types:

External This is full network access. A VM connected to an *external* connection can communicate through the physical NIC of the host with the outside world. Any other network device will see the VM as if it were a normal computer. The only exception is the (physical) network switch connected to the host. This switch sees one host with two MAC addresses and two IP addresses. Be aware that some older network environments may not allow this. The symptom would be that your VM can talk to your host but not to any other machine on the network even though you have specified external access.

Internal The *internal* switch is interesting. It allows communication between all VMs with the host but not directly to the outside world. This is suitable for most test installations where you want the VMs to talk to each other and to be allowed to transfer files and folders from the host but not to anything external. For each internal virtual switch that you create, Hyper-V creates an additional Local Area Connection directly connected to the new switch. There is no DHCP on that particular NIC (unless you put it there), so everything on that switch will get an APIPA address. So yes, there is network connectivity, but to use it you need to configure the IP settings yourself.

Private   With *private* virtual switches, VMs are connected to each other but cannot see the host. Effectively, they are completely isolated from the physical network. Again, this is ideal for testing. For instance, when you test the DHCP features of Windows Server 2012 R2, you wouldn't want to try this on the physical network. In some companies, that could get you fired! When in doubt, a private virtual switch is the safest option for testing.

A useful feature of virtual switches is that you can change their scopes and functionality. You might start a switch as internal and connect it to a physical external NIC later.

Using virtual switches brings a great deal of flexibility to your VMs, and you can generate quite complicated networks inside the host. Using three virtual switches, you could, for instance, build a classic DMZ setup: one switch for the outside interface connected to a physical NIC, one switch for the DMZ hosts, and one switch for the internal LAN.

Creating a Virtual Switch

There are two parts to configuring virtual networking: virtual NICs and virtual switches. The virtual NICs are managed through the VM settings window, which we'll discuss later, and the virtual switch is configured through the Virtual Switch Manager.

To create a new virtual switch, you need to follow these steps:

1. Open Hyper-V Manager and click Virtual Switch Manager in the Actions pane.

2. As shown in Figure 27.21, click to select the "New virtual network switch" option.

3. In the "Create virtual switch" section, choose the type of virtual switch you want to create (External, Internal, or Private), and then click the Create Virtual Switch button.

   In Figure 27.22, the virtual switch VMEXT1 is selected. This switch was created when we installed the Hyper-V role and told the wizard which NICs to use for VM traffic. Look back to Figure 27.11 to see this again.

FIGURE 27.21
The Virtual Switch Manager dialog box, which you open from the Actions pane of the Hyper-V management console

FIGURE 27.22
The Virtual Switch
Manager after
setup

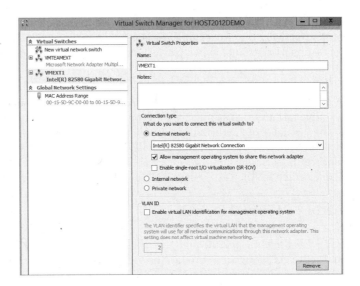

Also enabled by default here is the "Allow management operating system to share this network adapter" option. Leaving this enabled means the host can access this switch, meaning that traffic between the VMs and their host operating system is shared. In a lab or non-production environment where you might have just one NIC available, leaving this option enabled should suffice, but if you have more than one NIC or are running a production Hyper-V environment, then it's recommended to disable this option by simply unchecking the box and clicking Apply.

4. If you want to create a new external virtual switch instead of using the one that you created during Hyper-V setup, then in the Virtual Switch Properties pane, give the switch a name and then from the drop-down menu choose the physical NIC that you will connect to.

   An annoyance here if you have a number of different physical NICs is that you're presented with a list of NIC device names only instead of the friendly description that you might have given your NICs in the Network Connections applet. This makes it difficult to identify which NIC you want to assign to the new virtual switch, but if you use the Get-NetAdapter | Format-Table -Autosize cmdlets in PowerShell, you can see a list of NIC device names mapped to their more descriptive friendly names.

5. Once you've selected your virtual switch type and configured it, click the OK button to finish the process.

POWERSHELL TIP

You can create a new virtual switch that isn't sharing connectivity with the Management OS using the following in PowerShell:

```
New-VMSwitch -Name "VMEXT1" -AllowManagementOS $false -NetAdapterName "Local
    Area Connection 2"
```

When you connect your virtual NICs to your virtual switches, they get an automatically assigned unique media access control (MAC) address. Each NIC's MAC address is assigned from a pool of addresses that can be defined in Virtual Switch Manager under the Global Network Settings section, as shown in Figure 27.23.

These virtual switches are a powerful concept. Using them, you can create an internal network as complex as you like. This is great for testing and exploring new technology! We're only getting started though, there's so much more to explore in the coming sections.

FIGURE 27.23
Defining the MAC address range

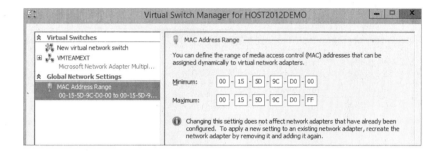

Getting Started with Virtual Machines

At this point, you have the Hyper-V service deployed and have an understanding of virtual disks and virtual switches. Now you're ready to start configuring a VM. Before you get started, check that you have all that you need:

♦ An ISO containing the operating system you want to install. An ISO image is required here because Windows Server 2012 R2 Hyper-V no longer offers a physical CD/DVD as a means to install an operating system into a VM (you could add a DVD option manually later, but it isn't part of the New Virtual Machine Wizard). We've configured the server HOST2012DEMO with a share hosting our ISO files: \\host2012demo\ISO.

♦ A name for the new server.

♦ An idea of which type of virtual switch (external, internal, or private) you want to use with the VM and an IP address to go with it.

♦ How much memory to use. Make sure you're not too conservative with this. If the VM needs to start swapping its memory, it puts a heavy load on the disk I/O capacity of the host—capacity that would be better used to accommodate more VMs. For a base install of Windows Server 2012 R2, use a minimum of 512 MB but preferably more, depending on workload.

♦ The virtual disk type to use: dynamic or fixed.

Conceptually, it takes two steps to create a VM from scratch. First, you configure the virtual hardware of the VM, then you boot the VM and start installing the operating system. The New Virtual Machine Wizard takes care of configuring the VM.

1. Open the Hyper-V management console and select New ➢ Virtual Machine.

Figure 27.24 shows the Before You Begin screen of the wizard, telling you briefly what a VM is for.

2. Use the check box to skip this screen in the future.

At this point, you could even click Finish to create a VM with the default settings, but that's not a good idea. Generally, no two VMs are the same.

FIGURE 27.24
The start of the New Virtual Machine Wizard. Select the check box to never see this opening screen again.

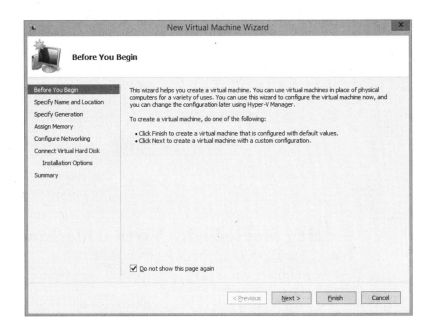

3. Enter a name for the VM, as shown in Figure 27.25.

Note that this is the friendly name used in the management console, not the actual hostname. Of course, it would make sense to make those names at least almost the same so as to be able to easily identify them later in the Hyper-V console.

4. Once you've entered a name for the VM, choose a location to store the VM or just leave the default location as it is (this would have been specified during the host installation process earlier). Click Next.

As shown in Figure 27.26, the Specify Generation dialog box is where you can choose the legacy Generation 1 VM type (which is compatible with older versions of Hyper-V), or you can select Generation 2 to take advantage of all the latest features and enhancements that Hyper-V 2012 R2 delivers.

5. Choose your generation type.

Notice the warning once you've chosen your generation type, *it can't be changed*. Click Next to continue.

The Assign Memory page asks you to specify the amount of memory for the VM.

FIGURE 27.25
Give the new VM
its name.

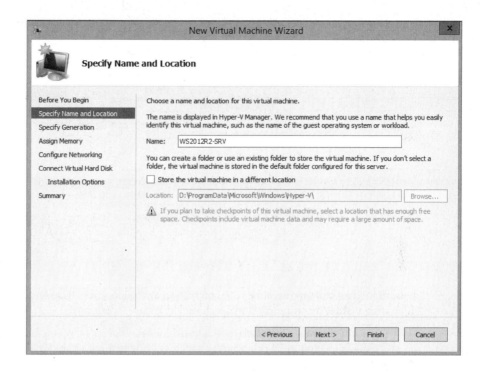

FIGURE 27.26
Choosing the
generation type
for your VM

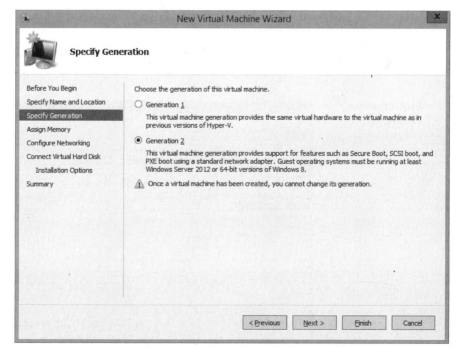

FIGURE 27.27
Assigning startup and
Dynamic Memory settings

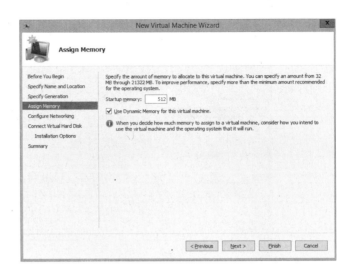

6. Specify a startup memory value of 512 MB and choose the "Use Dynamic Memory for this virtual machine" option, as shown in Figure 27.27.

   Dynamic Memory is a feature that optimizes how physical memory from the Hyper-V host is allocated to VMs by the management operating system. We'll explain this feature in a little more detail later. Click Next, to continue.

   The Configure Networking dialog box is used to specify the virtual switch to use. The default is Not Connected, which is a safe but not very useful option.

7. Select the virtual switch you created earlier (VMEXT1 in our example) to connect to.

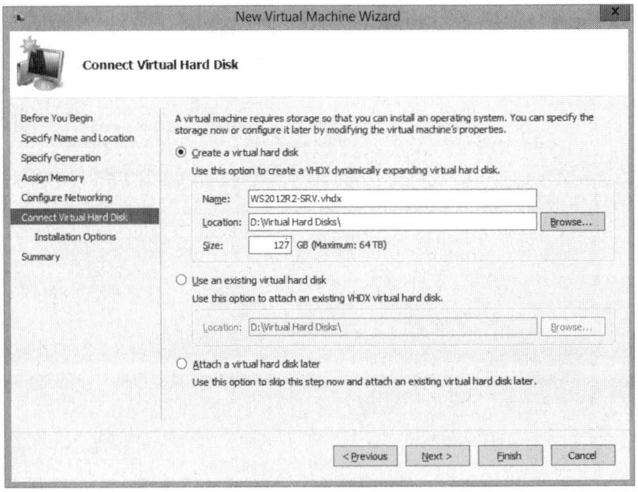

FIGURE 27.28
The new virtual
disk is dynamic.

Remember, this switch is external and allows the VM to talk to the outside world directly. Click Next.

8. In the Connect Virtual Hard Disk dialog box shown in Figure 27.28, you can create a new virtual disk or assign an existing one.

   The defaults are good here for a test setup: a new virtual disk in the default location, 127 GB in size. Although the dialog box doesn't show it, this disk is dynamic, which means that its real-world size is roughly as large as the data it contains, usually much less than 127 GB. If you want a fixed-size disk, you must build one before you create the VM or attach it afterward. The wizard proposes a default name for the virtual disk (which is the same as the friendly name you specified for the VM earlier).

   Click Next when you're ready to move on.

9. The Installation Options dialog box basically allows you to install an operating system later or right now. Here you can set the initial installation media: an ISO or something from the network. In this example, you install using an ISO file.

10. Use the radio button "Install an operating system from a bootable image file" to get started.

11. Browse to the spot where you have stored the ISO for Windows Server 2012 R2, select the ISO, and then click Next.

12. Review the summary of your VM configuration; click Finish to let the wizard start working.

FIGURE 27.29
Select a VM to see the actions that apply to it.

FIGURE 27.30
Managing all VM
parameters from
the Settings dialog
box

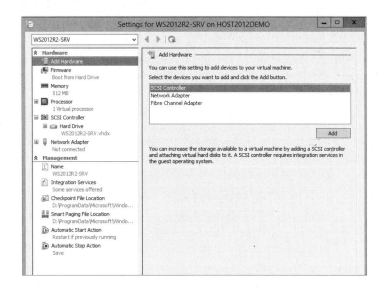

After a couple of seconds, you will have a new VM. In the Hyper-V Manager, you should now see your first VM.

13. Select this VM, and the Actions pane extends to display specific options for the VM (named WS2012R2-SRV in our example), as shown in Figure 27.29.

   This menu varies, depending on the power state of the VM among other things.

14. Click the Settings option to take a look at the VM configuration, as shown in Figure 27.30.

The Settings dialog box is one you will see a lot in the future. The left pane has two sections, Hardware and Management.

The Hardware section manages all virtual hardware. Here's an explanation of each option that you will see on a Generation 2 VM:

Add Hardware   Here you can add an SCSI controller that you can use to add virtual SCSI drives. As we discussed earlier, with this release of Hyper-V, you can now boot your VMs directly from a SCSI controller, and this is the only controller option available to you when configuring Gen2 VMs.

Firmware   This is where the new Unified Extensible Firmware Interface (UEFI) BIOS feature delivers the ability to enable or disable secure-boot functionality. You can also select the order of boot devices: DVD drive, network adapter, or hard drive.

Memory   Figure 27.31 shows the Memory section of the VM Settings window. In the figure, you can see we've selected a startup RAM value of 512 MB and have enabled the Dynamic Memory feature to manage the amount of RAM our VM gets allocated by the host depending on its utilization.

The Minimum RAM setting allows you to specify an amount of memory that is lower than the actual startup RAM (which, of course, is the minimum required to start up the VM in the first place), and this can be useful in VMs that are left running idle with very low utilization over long periods of time.

FIGURE 27.31

Configuring
Dynamic Memory
settings

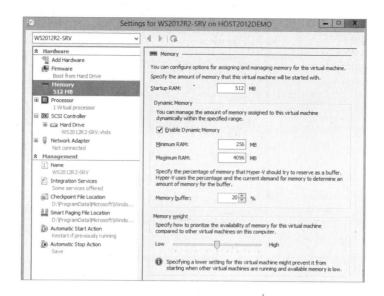

With the Maximum RAM setting you can determine the amount of memory that gets allocated to a VM from the host with a top-level limit of 1 TB. It's useful to know that you can modify this value while the VM is running so as to maintain availability, but you can never allocate more RAM than is available on the physical host.

You can learn much more about Dynamic Memory by reading Hyper-V MVP Aidan Finn's whitepaper on the subject here: http://www.aidanfinn.com/?p=11289.

Processor Here you can specify the number of virtual processors configured for this particular VM, up to a maximum of 64. On boot, the VM will see that number of processors. Of course, they are not by default reserved for that particular VM. The hypervisor is the sole owner of the processors and decides which VM gets how much time. The host itself is under the control of the hypervisor in this aspect. To say this another way, you can have many more virtual CPUs in total than the number of real CPU cores.

In Figure 27.32, you can see the "Resource control" settings, where you specify what percentage of the selected processors should be reserved for this VM. The grayed-out boxes tell you how much this is in terms of the full host capacity. This is a lower limit that's always available. The upper limit is set by the virtual machine limit. The VM will never use more than this particular percentage. This feature is very useful to limit misbehaving applications that use CPU resources for no good reason.

In the figure, you can see two additional processor options that you need to consider for processor functionality:

Compatibility This gives you the "Migrate to a physical computer with a different processor version" option and is used in a situation where you have Hyper-V hosts with slightly different physical CPUs from the same manufacturer. The feature works by disabling certain CPU instructions whose functionality varies between processors. The price you pay is potential lower performance, depending on your workload, and for that reason this feature is disabled by default.

FIGURE 27.32
Configuring
processor set-
tings inside your
VMs

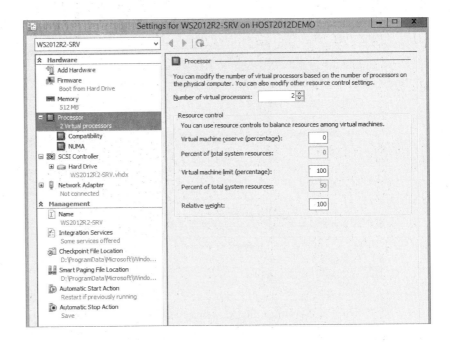

NUMA Non-Uniform Memory Access delivers scalability for your multiprocessor VMs through the way compatible processors access different banks of memory on the motherboard. This setting works in conjunction with the NUMA Spanning option inside Hyper-V settings to control how Dynamic Memory spans across multiple NUMA nodes.

SCSI Controller The next item on the Hardware list is SCSI Controller. The first SCSI controller is automatically used for booting the virtual hard disk that you configured as part of the New Virtual Machine Wizard. You can add up to four SCSI controllers to a virtual machine, and each of these controllers can have up to 64 virtual hard disks attached, each virtual disk having a storage capacity of 64 TB. If you do the math on this, you'll see that a virtual machine in Windows Server 2012 R2 can have over 16 petabytes of storage!

Under the SCSI Controller section, you can also attach a DVD drive to use for mounting ISO files. Unlike in earlier versions of Hyper-V, the DVD drive is no longer attached by default to Gen2 VMs, and this is why it's not available as an option to use when first running the New Virtual Machine Wizard.

When you have a virtual hard drive attached to an SCSI controller, you can click the plus sign beside the drive to expand and access the Advanced Features area. Here you can turn on Quality of Service management for a specific virtual hard disk, where you can determine minimum and maximum values for IOPS measured in 8 KB increments. You can also enable virtual hard disk sharing here to allocate a specific disk to be used as shared storage to facilitate clustering scenarios with your virtual machines. These advanced options are shown in Figure 27.33.

FIGURE 27.33
Advanced virtual
hard disk features

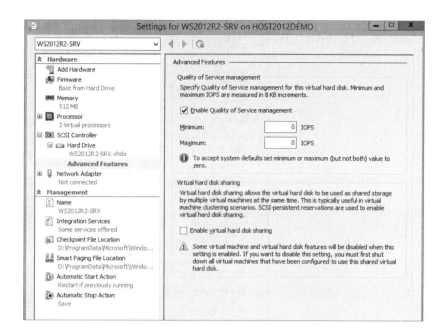

Network Adapter Virtual network connections are managed from the Network Adapter dialog box. For each NIC, you can select any virtual switch you like from the drop-down menu. You can change this binding while the VM is running too, which can be quite a handy feature to have. From the VM point of view, this is like pulling the cable from one switch and plugging it into another. One use for it is to install the operating system, patch it on Windows Update, and then connect it to an internal switch for testing.

Expanding the Network Adapter option gives you the following two options, as shown in Figure 27.34:

Hardware Acceleration This is where you can specify different tasks to be offloaded to a physical network adapter. First up here is "Virtual machine queue," which binds the MAC address of a virtual NIC to a queue on a physical NIC, optimizing network traffic for your VMs.

Next in the list is "IPsec task offloading." This allows you to offload the processing of your IPsec traffic encryption and decryption to hardware to free up resources on the host.

The final (and possibly most intriguing) hardware acceleration option is "Single-root I/O virtualization" (SR-IOV). To take advantage of this feature, you'll need dedicated hardware, but the rewards can definitely be worth it if you take the time and money to invest. The idea of SR-IOV is to replace the virtual switch in your VM connectivity designs and to route traffic directly to a special SR-IOV physical NIC connected to the host. This means far greater improvements in CPU utilization, network latency, and network throughput. You can enable SR-IOV, as shown in Figure 27.34, and if you want to learn more, check out this blog post series from Microsoft's John Howard: `http://tinyurl.com/WS2012SRIOV`.

FIGURE 27.34
Enabling SR-IOV
in a VM

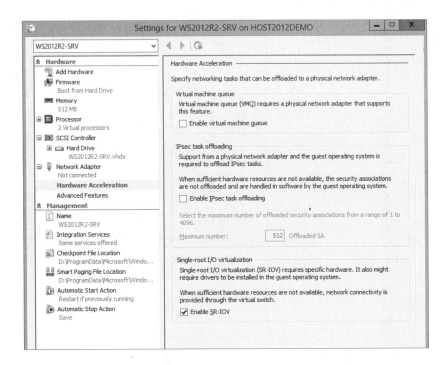

Advanced Features   In the Network Adapter Advanced Features section shown in Figure 27.35, you have the option to use a dynamic or static MAC address. Hyper-V manages its own pool of MAC addresses, so unless you encounter a MAC conflict, you should probably leave this setting at Dynamic.

Then there's the option "Enable MAC address spoofing." That sounds like a bad thing, doesn't it? Well, it was the only behavior available when Hyper-V was first released. One compromised VM could start flooding the switch or impersonate another VM. These days, Hyper-V is far more secure. The virtual switch learns which MAC address corresponds to which VM and doesn't allow it to change its MAC address anymore. Usually this isn't a problem, except for those situations where you really do need multiple MAC addresses. Can't think of one? Consider network load balancing or failover clustering.

If you have problems in your production environment with administrators deploying unauthorized DHCP servers, then you don't need us to tell you that it can lead to an administrative nightmare of invalid IP addresses. That's where the "DHCP guard" option comes in useful. If you enable it here, your VM will stop answering DHCP clients through this specific network adapter.

"Router guard" is pretty similar to "DHCP guard," and it will prevent your VMs from sending out router redirection to the network from this specific virtual network adapter.

If you're running a Hyper-V failover cluster and you enable the "Protected network" option here, your VMs will move to another cluster node if they detect a network disconnection, therefore ensuring network availability for your services.

FIGURE 27.35
Network adapter
advanced features

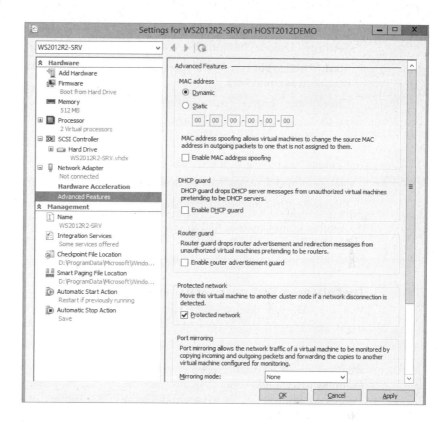

"Port mirroring" can be used for network traffic analysis between two VMs connected to the same virtual switch. One of the VMs can have the diagnostic tools to perform the analysis, and the other one might be part of a locked-down environment whereby these analysis tools can't be installed into it. Mirroring the port of the VM without the tools to the VM with the tools enables the analysis required.

The final advanced option here is "NIC teaming." Not to be confused with the NIC teaming functionality of the host that we spoke about in Chapter 4, the "Enable this network adapter to be part of a team in a guest operating system" check box does exactly what it says on the tin! If you want to create an NIC team inside your VMs that stays up if one of the physical NICs stops working, then ensure that you have this option enabled.

Continuing the discussion of the left pane, we come to the Management section. Normally you don't need to change any settings here, since the defaults are sensible. You can change the name of the VM here, configure the Integration Services components (discussed earlier in "Virtual Machine (Guest) Partitions"), specify the checkpoint file (discussed later when we fully discuss checkpoints) and smart paging file locations, and decide what should happen when the host starts up or shuts down.

We haven't finished discussing the Actions pane in Figure 27.29 yet. With a VM selected, you have these additional options:

Connect   Used to start the virtual console.

Settings   Used to configure the VM, as discussed in previous sections.

Start   Used to boot the VM. Depending on the state of the VM, you will have more options here, such as Shutdown.

Checkpoint   Used to create a point-in-time image of the VM.

Move   Used to move a virtual machine or its storage.

Export   Used to save the entire VM, including configuration and virtual hardware.

Rename   Used to give the VM another name.

Delete   Used to remove the VM configuration but not its virtual hard disks.

Enable Replication   Used to replicate the entire VM to another Hyper-V host.

Another point to note is that the exact items in the Actions pane vary with the power state of the VM. The previous options assume that the VM is still turned off. When a VM is running, you have additional items to turn the VM off, reset, shut down, and so on.

Installing a Virtual Machine

With the VM configured, the hard part is done. The next step is to install the operating system in the VM. You are used to dealing with physical servers, but the details of installing in a VM are a bit different.

The first question is how to connect to the console of the VM. After all, you want to see what's going on. To do that, open Hyper-V Manager, select the VM (WS2012R2-SRV in our example) you want to connect to, and click Connect in the lower-right corner. A Virtual Machine Connection console opens, as shown in Figure 27.36. Another way to do this is to double-click the thumbnail at the bottom.

FIGURE 27.36
Connecting to a
VM shows you
its console.

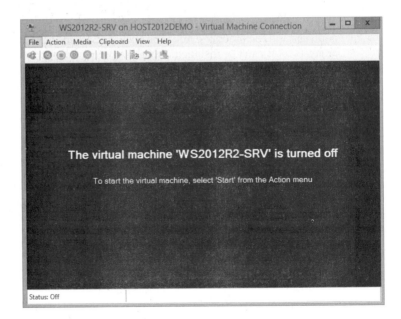

The virtual console has a menu bar and a button bar. Most of the functions have duplicates in the Hyper-V management console that you are already familiar with. The black screen telling you that the VM named WS2012R2-SRV is turned off is your virtual screen. When you boot the VM, this will show you the familiar messages of Windows progressing from boot to full GUI. Before you go ahead and boot the VM, there is something you need to be aware of. It's clear how the screen works, but what about the keyboard and mouse?

The console can "capture" the keyboard and mouse. You allow it to do so by clicking the virtual screen. When the keyboard and mouse are captured, all input from them is sent to the VM. Initially, you can't release control from the VM by just moving the mouse. You press the key sequence Ctrl+Alt+Left arrow to release control. In a fully running VM with Integration Services installed, the experience is much better: you can move the mouse out of the virtual screen onto the desktop, and when that happens, the host has control of the keyboard and mouse again. There is one special case: the Ctrl+Alt+Del sequence. Even when the VM has control, the host will process it. To send the Ctrl+Alt+Del sequence to a VM, you can either press Ctrl+Alt+End or use the console menu action (Ctrl+Alt+Del).

THE VIRTUAL CONSOLE UNDER THE HOOD

The Hyper-V virtual console uses the Remote Desktop Protocol (RDP) to talk to the VM; this is the same protocol that is used for Remote Desktop Services. The difference is that it does not use the default RDP port but instead uses TCP port 2179. When you start the virtual console from Hyper-V Manager, it starts a client application called vmconnect.exe, located in %programfiles%\hyper-v. This application is similar to the Remote Desktop Client but additionally allows you to select the VM you want to connect to. The Virtual Machine Management Service is the listening service. When you connect to it using vmconnect.exe, it tells the client which VMs are available and makes sure the RDP traffic goes to the correct VM. In other words, this service acts as an RDP multiplexer.

Using RDP and client code means that VMConnect shares a number of keyboard shortcuts with RDP and introduces some of its own. Table 27.7 lists the most relevant ones.

TABLE 27.7: Hyper-V Virtual Console Keyboard Shortcuts

HYPER-V KEY	WINDOWS KEY	EXPLANATION
Ctrl+Alt+End	Ctrl+Alt+Del	The well-known three-finger salute to display the logon screen or security dialog box
Alt+Page Up	Alt+Tab	Switches to next program
Alt+Page Down	Shift+Alt+Tab	Switches to previous program
Ctrl+Alt+Left arrow		Releases keyboard and mouse focus from the VM
Ctrl+Alt+Pause		Toggles full-screen mode

If you attached a DVD to an SCSI controller and specified an ISO with it as discussed earlier, you can then open the Media menu from the virtual console, from which you can open the DVD Drive menu. From here, select DVD Drive and you'll see that the ISO file for Windows Server 2012 R2 is mounted. With the DVD ready for booting, you're ready to go. You can find Start under the Action menu, but the quickest way is to just push the green power-on button. The console will display a few messages and then quickly show the familiar boot screen of Windows Server 2012 R2. Click the virtual console to let it capture the keyboard and mouse. Don't forget: to release the mouse, just press Ctrl+Alt+Left arrow.

Now follow the onscreen prompts and configure the operating system as normal. After the installation and final reboot, you end up with a fully running Windows Server 2012 R2 VM. If you have DHCP on the LAN connected to its virtual switch, it will be fully network enabled as well.

USING POWERSHELL TO CREATE A NEW VM

You can create a new VM using the GUI in a couple of minutes, but using the New-VM cmdlet in PowerShell will enable you to do it in seconds! Try it for yourself by simply opening an elevated PowerShell window, typing **New-VM**, and hitting Enter. This will instantly create a Gen1 blank virtual machine called New Virtual Machine with 512 MB of RAM and one CPU.

By adding a few simple additional switches to the New-VM cmdlet you can customize configuration settings, such as the description, RAM, CPU, and virtual disk. As is the case with all PowerShell cmdlets, typing Get-Help before the cmdlet will display all the available options that you need to start rapidly deploying VMs into Hyper-V. Here's a useful three-part series of blog posts that goes into this cmdlet in detail: http://blogs.technet.com/b/heyscriptingguy/archive/2013/06/14/ create-a-new-virtual-machine-with-windows-powershell-part-1.aspx.

With your new VM installed, the work is not quite done yet. Unless your VM runs the same OS and service pack as the host system, its Integration Services will not match those of the Hyper-V host. Upgrading the Integration Services is easily done, however, using the built-in ISO file of the Integration Services software. The details may vary a bit, depending on the OS version and/or previously installed versions of Integration Services:

1. Log on to the VM using an administrator account.

2. From the VM console, select Action ➢ Insert Integration Services Setup Disk.

    After a short while, the Autoplay dialog box should offer to run Setup, as shown in Figure 27.37. If this does not happen, perhaps because Autoplay is disabled, you can run Setup directly from the virtual DVD drive in the VM.

3. Run Setup.

    After this, you know the drill. One or more reboots may be required. If the Integration Services are already up to date with the latest version, you will be presented with a dialog box stating so.

FIGURE 27.37
Autoplay dialog box
for setting up
Integration Services

KEEPING YOUR INTEGRATION SERVICES UPDATED

It's recommended that you keep your Guest OS Integration Services up to date in the same way that you keep your host OS updated with the latest patches and fixes from Microsoft. The Integration Services don't automatically update themselves with a newer version when you update the host, so you'll need to manually update them or automate the process using something like System Center 2012 - Orchestrator. To determine if your Integration Services need to be updated, you can check their version using this excellent script from Hyper-V MVP Didier Van Hoye: `http://workinghardinit.wordpress.com/2012/12/07/checking-host-integration-services-version-on-all-nodes-of-a-windows-server-2012-hyper-v-cluster-with-power-shell/`.

A final word on the power states of a VM: you can boot, shut down, hibernate, suspend, and reset a physical machine. But a VM has an additional power state: it can be in a *saved state*. This feature is very nice to have in a test environment. It's similar to a hibernated state but initiated from the host. This means that it always works, no matter what OS is installed in the VM. The Save action can be found in the usual place in the Hyper-V management console or the VM virtual console, and when you click it, you'll see a status of Saving with a percentage counter showing its progress. Start the VM again and the saved stated will be reloaded to resume exactly where you left off.

For some tests, it's useful to freeze the VM in place. This is different from a saved state because no data is saved to disk. A freeze (or *pause*, as Hyper-V calls it) just stops the VM in its tracks, instantaneously. This is another feature that is hard to find on a physical machine. Figure 27.38 shows the power state buttons on the Hyper-V console.

From left to right, you can do the following with these buttons:

◆ Send a Ctrl+Alt+Del sequence to the VM.

◆ Start the VM after a shutdown or saved state.

FIGURE 27.38

Virtual machine
power state buttons
on the console

◆ Turn off the VM directly. Windows will ask you whether you are sure you want to do this. It is the equivalent of pulling the plug.

◆ Shut down the VM. This works only with properly installed Integration Services. The Hyper-V host will work with the VM to initiate a normal shutdown sequence. It's quite useful! There's no need to log on to the console anymore.

◆ Save the current state of the VM. For testing, this is probably the one we use most.

◆ Pause (or freeze) the VM. Click the button again to resume.

◆ Reset the VM, similar to a hardware reset on a physical host.

◆ Checkpoint the VM: save all current state and configuration and bookmark it. The VM continues running, but you can revert to the saved snapshot later. This is very useful, but it's potentially dangerous, as you will see later.

◆ Revert to a saved checkpoint.

◆ Revert to a basic session: If you've enabled enhanced session mode for your VM, clicking this button will change it back to a basic session similar to what was available in earlier versions of Hyper-V.

Working with VLANs

Earlier we discussed virtual switches and Hyper-V networking. Now that you understand how to configure and install a new virtual machine, it's a good time to go into some more detail about how you can connect your VMs to different network subnets. In the physical networking world, if you wanted to isolate different subnets for security or scalability reasons, you would most likely make use of virtual LAN (VLAN) technology. A VLAN is created on the network device (usually a switch or router), and it delivers isolation of networks through network ID tagging.

VLANs operate on the OSI network layer 2. The exact protocol definition is known as 802.1Q. Each network packet belonging to a VLAN has an identifier. This is just a number between 0 and 4095, with both 0 and 4095 reserved for other uses. Let's assume a VLAN with an identifier of 100. A NIC configured with the VLAN ID of 100 will pick up network packets with the same ID and will ignore all other IDs. The point of VLANs is that switches and routers enabled for 802.1Q can present VLANs to different switch ports in the network. In other words, where a normal IP subnet is limited to a set of ports on a physical switch, a subnet defined in a VLAN can be present on any switch port—if so configured, of course.

With a Hyper-V virtual switch, you can leverage VLAN connectivity and ID tagging by assigning the IDs to virtual NICs. The physical NIC in the host needs to be connected to the VLAN trunk port on the physical switch (or whatever physical network device manages the VLAN), and a Hyper-V external virtual switch is created and assigned to the physical NIC. Once you've configured your networking in this way, all you have to do is follow these steps:

FIGURE 27.39
VLAN ID tagging

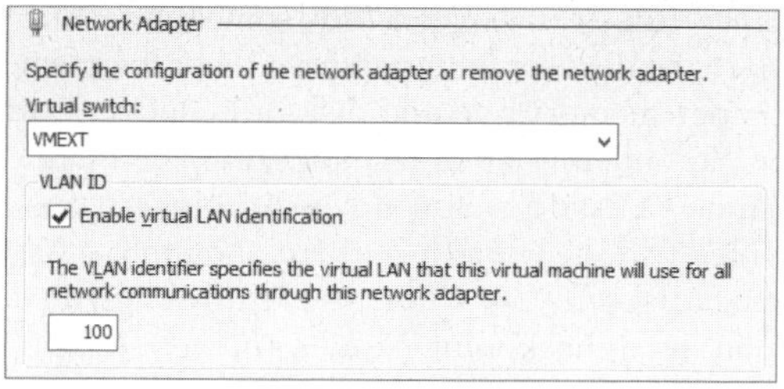

🔌 Network Adapter	

Specify the configuration of the network adapter or remove the network adapter.

Virtual switch:

VMEXT ▾

VLAN ID

☑ Enable virtual LAN identification

The VLAN identifier specifies the virtual LAN that this virtual machine will use for all network communications through this network adapter.

100

1. From the settings of the virtual machine, select Network Adapter in the Hardware pane.

2. Connect your VM to the external virtual switch you created by choosing it from the drop-down Virtual Switch menu.

3. In the VLAN ID section, check the "Enable virtual LAN identification" box, and then enter the specified VLAN ID tag in the box below, as shown in Figure 27.39.

4. Click OK to close the dialog box and save the VLAN ID settings.

Time Travel with Checkpoints

As you have seen, many features of Hyper-V can be very helpful when you are running labs or test environments either at home or in your organization. Dynamic disks save you valuable disk space and differencing disks allow you to quickly deploy new VMs. But wouldn't it be nice if you could prepare a VM for testing and save it easily so that you can revert to it when things go wrong? This—and more—is what checkpoints offer you.

A *checkpoint* is best understood as a point-in-time copy of a VM. The copy includes virtual disks, memory, processor state, and configuration of the VM. The VM may be turned off, may be running, or may be in a saved state—it doesn't matter. Of course, the entire VM isn't really copied. Hyper-V is efficient about it. When you checkpoint a VM, Hyper-V does the following:

1. For each virtual disk connected to the VM, it creates a new differencing disk.

2. It decouples the virtual disks from the VM and replaces them with the corresponding differencing disks.

   From this point on, you will start to see slow degradation in performance of the VM.

3. It copies the files containing the configuration of the VM.

4. Hyper-V allows the VM to resume. Usually at this point you have less than a second of downtime.

5. While the VM is running, it writes its memory to disk. If the VM writes to memory, Hyper-V intercepts the write action, and the original memory is quickly written to disk. Then it allows the write action to succeed. In this way, it preserves all the memory at the time of the snapshot, while allowing the VM to keep running.

6. When it completes the memory dump, the checkpoint is done.

If you look at this carefully, you can conclude some interesting things. First, Hyper-V allows a true undo. Not only are the disk contents preserved, but the memory and even the configuration are too. You could change memory and add disks and networks and still be able to revert to the original situation. Second, in a lab or test environment, there is no reason why you couldn't repeat this process. You can have a chain or even multiple chains of checkpoints up to a maximum of 50 (you really don't want to go there, though!). A limitation of this process is that it works only with virtual disks. If your VM uses pass-through disks, you can't checkpoint it.

Finally, although taking a checkpoint is quick and very tempting in a lot of scenarios, we highly recommend you use this feature with care and diligence and preferably in the confines of your lab or test environment. Anyone using a VM in production with large checkpoint files would notice a definite performance hit until the checkpoints were removed.

Taking a checkpoint can be done in various ways, similar to changing power states. To do it from the Hyper-V management console, right-click the VM and select Checkpoint from the context menu. Figure 27.40 illustrates the Checkpoints section of Hyper-V Manager. The base checkpoint is Base OS Install and it has two subtrees called After Domain Join and Before Service Pack.

FIGURE 27.40
A VM with multiple checkpoint trees

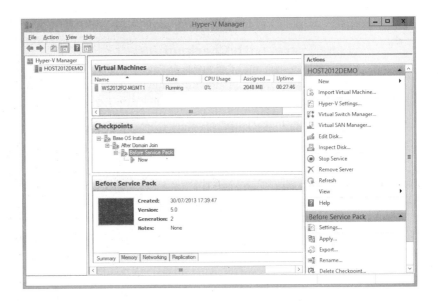

This example already has a number of checkpoints. The current checkpoint is highlighted. Its icon is different from the others. The default name for a new checkpoint is the current time and date, but renaming it immediately makes more sense.

CHECKPOINTS WITH POWERSHELL

If you need to script your checkpoints, then the new Checkpoint-VM cmdlet is where you start. Type the following to create a new checkpoint of a virtual machine with a custom name:

```
Checkpoint-VM -Name "WS2012R2-SRV" -SnapshotName "Before Service Pack Install"
```

It's not hard to move around between checkpoints. However, if you want to preserve the current state, you need to take a new checkpoint first. If you don't, the latest preserved state is that of its latest checkpoint. So, to go to a different checkpoint while the current one is running, you do the following:

1. Select the checkpoint you want to move to.

You can select any one you like, even the ones in the middle of a chain.

2. Use the Apply action from the Checkpoint menu.

You get a dialog box with three choices: Create Checkpoint and Apply (the default), Apply, and Cancel.

3. Make your choice, and after a couple of seconds, the selected checkpoint starts running.

In the same way, you can also delete any checkpoint you want. From the management console, this seems simple, but under the hood there is more going on. The key to checkpoints is the use of differencing disks. So what happens if you remove a checkpoint in the middle of a chain? In that case, the differencing disks of the removed checkpoint are preserved, keeping the disk chain intact. Just the configuration files are removed. In Hyper-V 2012, you can delete checkpoints while the VM is still running and the host will merge the orphaned differencing disks into their parents without downtime. The Hyper-V management console will show a status of Merging (and will indicate the percentage completed). There are more scenarios to consider here, but the key point is that Hyper-V is aware of them and will do the right thing.

One particular example is when you remove a VM that has checkpoints. The dialog box will tell you that it will not remove the associated virtual disks. That's only partially true. When you do delete the VM, it will take longer than you might expect. A dialog box stays onscreen telling you that it is Destroying (and will indicate a percentage) and counting. It is not removing the disks; it is merging the active checkpoint with its parents, leaving you with just one .vhdx file. That's probably the right thing to do, because it leaves you with just one .vhdx representing all the data of the VM you just deleted.

As a testing feature, checkpoints are just great. You can mess up your environment all you want and you have your get-out-of-jail-free card ready to bail you out. Always? No, not always. There are some situations where applying an earlier checkpoint can get you into serious trouble. For a stand-alone computer without relations to others, checkpoints are perfectly safe. For any situation where computers share some configuration, you need to be careful. The best example of this is Active Directory.

In fact, there are a number of ways that checkpoints can get you into trouble with Active Directory. The most obvious example is where you have a checkpoint of a member server taken 40 days ago. As you know, a server that is a member of a domain changes its password every 30 days. Since 40 days ago, that server has changed its password in Active Directory at least once and maybe twice. In its local database, it stores two passwords, the current and the previous. If it has changed its password two times, the checkpointed server no longer has a matching password in Active Directory. In other words, it is no longer a member of the domain and needs to be rejoined. This problem is the same as with regular backups. However, there is a more subtle and dangerous problem that affects any domain controller with a version of Active Directory earlier than Windows Server 2012 (RTM).

For domain controllers to replicate, they need some administration that tells them what information they've already received from their partners and what they are still missing. This administration depends on the update sequence numbers (USNs) that each DC generates with each modification of its database. Any change has a unique USN associated with it. The point is that when you restore a snapshot of a DC, you also restore the USN configuration of that time. The problem is that the other DCs don't know this has happened! When they look at the DC that had a snapshot restored, they see that they've already processed the current USN of that DC. So the replication partners of that DC see no need to replicate any data. Effectively, that DC will not replicate until its USN is finally higher than its partners have administered. All data that the affected DC generates in that period will never leave the DC.

This complicated but very serious problem affecting legacy DCs, known as *USN rollback*, is documented in Microsoft's Knowledge Base article 875495 (`http://support.microsoft.com/kb/875495`). Luckily, if the DC detects that this is going on, it will immediately stop all Active Directory activity and log the problem in the Directory Services event log. The point is to make you aware that using checkpoints can lead to unexpected problems, even in systems you think you know well. The best way to avoid such problems is to checkpoint computers as a group after shutting them down and to restore them as a group. You may wonder why such problems don't occur when you do a regular backup of a DC and restore it. The reason is that the Windows restore operations are aware of the Active Directory replication administration and reset it. When a restored domain controller comes online after a non-authoritative restore, it signals to its partners that it should be treated as if it has never replicated before. As mentioned, this USN rollback issue affects DCs running versions of Active Directory earlier than Windows Server 2012 (RTM). In the next chapter, we'll discuss the advances in virtualization with Hyper-V that prevent this issue from occurring with Windows Server 2012 DCs.

To finish up this section on Hyper-V checkpoints, the two key summary points are these:

- Checkpoints are a great testing feature that can make your life a lot easier.

- Checkpoints should not be used in production networks unless you are completely aware of the risks associated with their use and even then you should avoid them if possible.

The Bottom Line

Understand server virtualization.   You are buying new servers whose main role will be to run Hyper-V. However, you are concerned that the new servers may not be capable of running Hyper-V because they do not meet the minimum requirements.

> **Master It**   What are the base CPU and BIOS requirements to run Hyper-V?

Explore what's new in Hyper-V 2012 R2.   Microsoft has released a large number of new features and enhancements with Hyper-V 2012 R2 that should give IT pros, administrators, and consultants a much easier job in convincing their customers and bosses to use Hyper-V inside the business.

> **Master It**   In earlier versions of Hyper-V, rich copy and paste into VMs could be achieved only by using a Remote Desktop connection and didn't work at all if there was no network connection present. What's the name of the new feature that enables copy and paste into a VM with no network connection by utilizing the VMBus?

Understand Hyper-V architecture. When you deploy the Hyper-V role to your computer, you're creating a hypervisor architecture. A *hypervisor* is a software layer between the hardware and the operating systems running on the host. This is known as the *bare-metal* approach: virtualization at the lowest possible level. The main purpose of the hypervisor is to create isolated execution environments (partitions) for all operating systems. In line with that function, it is responsible for arbitrating access to the hardware.

> **Master It** During the Hyper-V role deployment, the host restarts a couple of times to accommodate the placement of Hyper-V on top of the hardware, which is located at which ring level? (Choose one.)
>
> **a.** RING 3
>
> **b.** RING 0
>
> **c.** RING -1
>
> **d.** RING 2

Install and configure a Hyper-V host. Just about the only thing you need to decide before you install the Hyper-V role is which NIC to use for managing the Hyper-V host. The idea is to have at least two NICs in the host, although you can make do with one if you really must. Expect no performance miracles in that case. With two NICs available, dedicate one to managing the host and the second for VM network traffic.

> **Master It** If you have two or more NIC's available for your Hyper-V environment, which option that's enabled by default should you uncheck on the virtual NIC?

Configure and install a virtual machine. Conceptually, it takes two steps to create a VM from scratch. First you configure the virtual hardware of the VM, then you boot the VM and start installing the operating system. Once these two steps have been completed, you can use either Hyper-V Manager or PowerShell to manage the VM.

> **Master It** When using the GUI to manage your VM, the console can "capture" the keyboard and mouse. You do so by clicking the virtual screen. When they've been captured, all input from the keyboard and mouse are sent to the VM. Initially, you can't release control from the VM by just moving the mouse. What keyboard combination is configured by default to release control of the keyboard and mouse back to the host OS?

Chapter 28

Managing Virtual Machines

In the previous chapter, you learned the main points of Hyper-V: how to install it, its software architecture, and the ins and outs of virtual disks and networks. We also discussed how to get started with virtual machines and what's required to configure and install them. There's still a lot more to talk about with Hyper-V, and in this chapter we will discuss topics such as virtualizing domain controllers, live migration, managing your virtual machines, and disaster recovery. Some of these topics we'll briefly discuss just for awareness, and others we'll dive into in more depth.

In this chapter, you will learn to:

◆ Virtualize domain controllers

◆ Understand how to move your VMs around

◆ Manage your VMs

◆ Understand disaster recovery with Hyper-V

Domain Controllers and Hyper-V

While virtualization has taken most parts of server computing by storm, it's always been just a bit dangerous to virtualize domain controllers (DCs). Let's be honest, though; with the flexibility and cost savings of virtualization, the temptation for most of us to have virtualized DCs was just too much, and there are plenty of them out there sitting on various hypervisor platforms. Prior to Windows Server 2012, if you virtualized your DCs, then you had to jump through a number of hoops and cut through some red tape to ensure Active Directory maintained its integrity.

When you virtualize your DCs, due to the dependency that Kerberos authentication has on reliable timekeeping, issues such as maintaining accurate time synchronization inside the VM become paramount to the health of your overall Active Directory.

To illustrate what might go wrong, consider a real-world example of a VM running an Active Directory domain controller. It's running on a stand-alone Hyper-V host that is not joined to a domain. Instead, it takes its time from a network component, a centrally located switch, for example. During maintenance, the switch gets a new firmware update and accidentally sets the time a year ahead. The host picks this up and also sets its time a year ahead. Then the virtual DC does the same. At that point, it stops replicating with its peers because Kerberos authentication is broken, and pretty soon your phone will start ringing off the wall with users complaining of logon issues.

Another problem with bad time synchronization inside virtual DCs is that the internal Active Directory administration for deleted objects goes badly wrong if the time jumps ahead too far. Some objects will be permanently deleted; others won't. The result is a badly corrupted forest. The list goes on and on, if you start thinking about it.

Bottom line: in a production environment, make sure to really have a correct time synchronization configuration, especially for VMs.

SHOULD I DISABLE THE TIME SYNCHRONIZATION SERVICE?

To tackle the time synchronization problems with virtual DCs, a lot of people thought disabling the Time Synchronization service—part of the integration components—for the VM through the Hyper-V console would solve their problems. Unfortunately, this wasn't the case, and doing this would cause more problems than it fixed in the long run.

It's best practice to never disable the Time Synchronization service and to instead just augment its functionality with an external time source. This post from Hyper-V Program Manager Ben Armstrong explains the best way to manage time synchronization: `http://blogs.msdn.com/b/virtual_pc_guy/archive/2010/11/19/time-synchronization-in-hyper-v.aspx`.

Once you've read through Ben's post, check out this link from Microsoft to automatically configure an external authoritative time source by clicking the Microsoft Fix It button halfway down the page under the "Configuring the Windows Time service to use an external time source" section: `http://support.microsoft.com/kb/816042`.

Time synchronization isn't the only thing to be aware of when dealing with virtual DCs. In Chapter 27, "Server Virtualization with Hyper-V," we discussed the USN rollback issue that affected DCs running versions of Active Directory prior to Windows Server 2012 when using checkpoints. Another problem you might have encountered if you had a virtual DC running on a Hyper-V failover cluster in Windows Server 2008 was that unless you deployed it in a *very* specific way, you needed to make sure you had at least one physical DC sitting outside the cluster to ensure everything started up again after cluster reboots! This KB article from Microsoft nicely sums up some of these issues and Microsoft's support policy with virtual DCs: `http://support.microsoft.com/kb/888794`.

Now at this point, you would be forgiven for thinking to yourself, "Why bother virtualizing DCs if they cause so many problems?" Thankfully, Hyper-V and Active Directory in Windows Server 2012 R2 go a long way toward resolving a lot of these issues, as you'll learn in the next section.

Virtual DCs That Just Work

Starting with Windows Server 2012, virtual DCs got a new built-in identifier called *VM-Generation ID*. The purpose of this new identifier is to provide a safety net to protect against scenarios whereby a virtual DC is rolled back in time through the use of checkpoints, therefore initiating an unwanted update sequence number (USN) rollback situation, as described here: `http://tinyurl.com/USNRollback`.

When the virtual Windows Server 2012 DC is deployed, the VM-Generation ID gets stored as an attribute in the Active Directory database under the *msDS-GenerationID* attribute of the newly created computer account (shown in Figure 28.1). A Windows driver inside the VM ensures that the VM-Generation ID is independently tracked at all times.

FIGURE 28.1

The msDS-GenerationID attribute

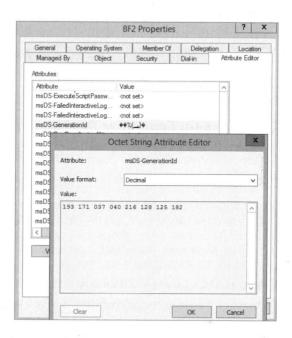

If the virtual DC is rolled back to a previous point through an old checkpoint, for example, the VM-Generation ID value of the checkpoint instance is cross-referenced with the current VM-Generation ID value that's stored in the Active Directory database. If the two values don't match, then another unique identifier known as the InvocationID gets reset, which, in turn, prevents the USN from being reused, therefore avoiding USN rollback. This is definitely a welcome change from earlier versions of Active Directory and something that should serve as encouragement to safer virtualization of your DCs.

Another neat idea behind the VM-Generation ID design was to make it hypervisor vendor independent, meaning that its benefits aren't limited to virtual DCs running on Hyper-V. This feature works even with virtual DCs running on a VMware host!

CLUSTER BOOTSTRAPPING MEANS NO MORE PHYSICAL DCS

If you've configured a Hyper-V failover cluster in the past with Windows Server 2008 R2, you're probably acutely aware of the requirement to have a physical DC or at least a DC located on a stand-alone virtual host that wasn't part of the cluster. The reason for this requirement was that the failover cluster needed to be able to authenticate with a DC before it could boot up. If the only DC that you had in your environment was a virtual machine located on the cluster that was trying to boot, then you were caught between a rock and a hard place, so to speak.

With Windows Server 2012 failover clusters, Microsoft introduced *cluster bootstrapping*, which is a new feature that allows the cluster to boot without the need to authenticate with Active Directory first. It does this by allowing the cluster node that boots first to create the cluster and then attempt to gain quorum. Once this happens, the remaining cluster nodes will boot up, all without needing authentication to a DC.

Cluster bootstrapping happens by default without the need for you to preconfigure anything in the failover cluster. But be aware that it doesn't mean you don't need to have an Active Directory environment in place to begin with. AD is still required to create the original cluster object and when any new nodes are added to the cluster.

Quick Domain Controller Deployment

Windows Server 2012 includes a new method of deploying any number of virtual DCs very quickly through *virtual domain controller cloning*. This gives administrators a supported solution to rapidly spin up replica domain controllers using an existing template DC for reference. Virtual DC cloning can be beneficial to organizations that want to quickly deploy multiple DCs into new domains. It's also a helpful feature in private cloud environments to meet scalability requirements.

It's quite possible, though, that the most frequent use of this feature will be in test and demo environments, where you can deploy numerous configurations of DCs to try out new features and capabilities before rolling them into production.

VIRTUAL DC CLONING PREREQUISITES

This section discusses the prerequisites that you need to have lined up to get started with virtual DC cloning:

◆ A user account that is a member of the Domain Admins group in Active Directory.

◆ At least one Hyper-V host (VMHOST1-SRV in our example) running Windows Server 2012 or higher.

◆ Local admin rights on the Hyper-V host server.

◆ An existing Windows Server 2012 or higher DC hosting the PDC emulator FSMO role (WS2012R2-DC1) needs to be already deployed.

 You can type **netdom query fsmo** into a command prompt to see which server hosts this role in an existing Active Directory. This server won't be touched as part of the cloning process and is used primarily for authentication and security auditing.

◆ A virtual DC running Windows Server 2012 or higher (WS2012R2-DC2) in the same domain as the PDC emulator we just mentioned.

 This will be the template DC that you will use for cloning. This template DC shouldn't have the DHCP, Active Directory Certificate Services, or Lightweight Directory Services roles installed because none of them are supported for cloning. It can have the DNS server role installed hosting Active Directory integrated zones, but be aware that your cloned DC will then also get deployed as a DNS server.

◆ Ensure that you eject the virtual floppy drive (VFD) on your template virtual DC because leaving it connected can cause issues when trying to import the new VM.

> **MULTIPLE HOST REQUIREMENTS FOR CLONING**
>
> If you are cloning a DC from one Hyper-V host and placing it on another one, then you need to ensure that the virtual network switch names are exactly the same on each node that you will be exporting and importing on. For example, if you have a virtual switch named VMEXT1 on Host1, then you will need to have a virtual switch named VMEXT1 on Host2 as well. Also, if your hosts have different processors, make sure to select the "Migrate to a physical computer with a different processor version" option on the virtual DC you plan to export first.

CLONING A VIRTUAL DC

Once you have all the prerequisites in place, you're ready to work through the steps in this section and get your first virtual DC cloned:

1. Log on to the DC hosting the PDC Emulator role with a domain administrator account and choose Server Manager ➤ Tools ➤ Active Directory Users and Computers.

2. Expand the domain root object and then click the Users organizational unit.

   You should see the Cloneable Domain Controllers security group, as shown in Figure 28.2.

FIGURE 28.2
Cloneable Domain
Controllers security
group

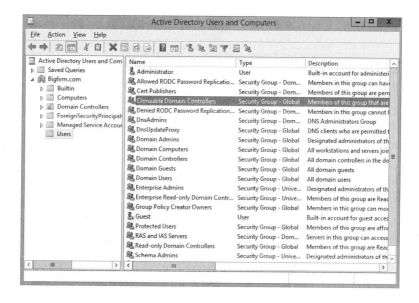

This group is managed by the Active Directory administration team and is used to control which DCs are to be cloned. Typically in a low-privilege security environment, the Active Directory and virtualization teams would be separate entities, thus ensuring that authorization to clone a critical server such as a DC is managed by the AD team. If you don't see this group, then you aren't using a Windows Server 2012 DC to host the PDC Emulator role, as mentioned earlier.

3. Double-click the Cloneable Domain Controllers group, choose the Members tab, and then click the Add button.

4. Change the Object Types option to search for objects of type Computers; then enter the name of your template virtual DC (WS2012R2-DC2), and click the Add button.

5. Click OK to close the window and confirm that the template virtual DC is added to the group.

   With the template virtual DC now authorized for cloning, you need to ensure that all applications (if any) that are running on it can be safely cloned.

6. To do this, log on to the template virtual DC with an account that has administrative permissions and run the `Get-ADDCCloningExcludedApplicationList` PowerShell cmdlet.

7. From the resulting list of applications, check with the relevant software vendor to ascertain if they are supported for cloning (if applicable).

8. To provision these applications, from an elevated PowerShell prompt, run `Get-ADDCClon ingExcludedApplicationList -GenerateXML`.

   This creates a new XML file located by default in `%windir%\NTDS` called `CustomDCCloneAllowList.xml`, as shown in Figure 28.3.

9. Staying with PowerShell on the template virtual DC, you now need to run the `New-ADDCCloneConfigFile` cmdlet with all relevant parameters required for the new clone DC (hostname, TCP/IP info, and so on).

   Running this cmdlet will create the `DCCloneConfig.xml` file that will be used to trigger and ensure successful cloning. You can get the full syntax options of this cmdlet here: `http://technet.microsoft.com/en-us/library/jj158947.aspx`

FIGURE 28.3
Provisioning applications for cloning

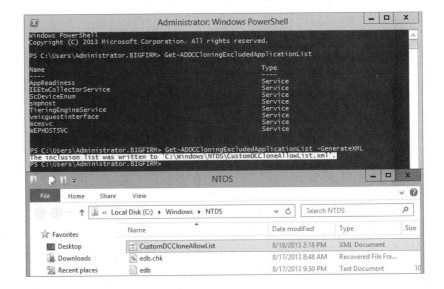

10. Type the following to create the `DCCloneConfig` file (substituting parameters that are relevant to your own environment):

```
New-ADDCCloneConfigFile –Static –IPv4Address "192.168.0.210" –IPv4DNSResolver
"192.168.0.100" –IPv4SubnetMask "255.255.255.0" –CloneComputerName "WS2012R2-
DC3" –IPv4DefaultGateway "192.168.0.254" –SiteName "DUBLIN"
```

11. Now shut down the template virtual DC (WS2012R2-DC2 in our example) and delete any checkpoints that you might have made previously before continuing.

12. From Hyper-V Manager, highlight the shutdown virtual template DC, click Export from the Actions menu to open the Export Virtual Machine dialog box, choose a location to export the VM to, as shown in Figure 28.4, and then click the Export button.

When the export process has completed, you can choose to either copy the exported files to another Hyper-V host (if you want to deploy the new clone DC there) or simply leave them where they are if you have only one host to work with.

13. Wherever you choose to locate the exported files, on the Hyper-V host, deploy the new clone DC, open Hyper-V Manager, and choose the Import Virtual Machine option from the Actions pane.

FIGURE 28.4
Exporting the virtual template DC

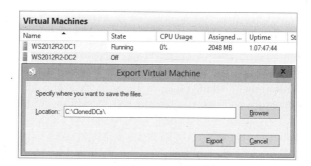

14. At the Import Virtual Machine wizard, click Next to move on to the Locate Folder dialog box, and then browse to the location of the exported files.

15. Click Next.

16. In the Select Virtual Machine dialog box, ensure that the template virtual DC name is selected as the virtual machine to import; then click Next.

17. In the Choose Import Type dialog box, you need to select the "Copy the virtual machine (create a new unique ID)" option, as shown in Figure 28.5; then click Next.

The next two dialog boxes allow you to choose folders to store your imported VMs and if you want to create multiple clone DCs from within the Hyper-V Manager UI.

18. Specify a new folder location here each time you import from the template virtual DC.

19. Click Next to move on through the wizard; then click Finish to begin the import.

20. When the import process completes, start up the template virtual DC (WS2012R2-DC2) again, and when that's up and running, start the newly imported VM (WS2012R2-DC3).

FIGURE 28.5
Creating a
unique ID for the
imported VM

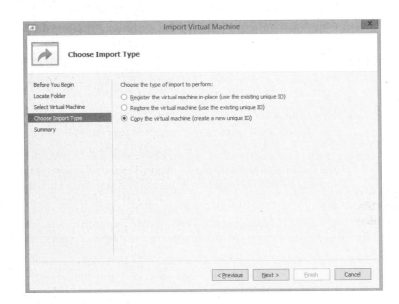

As the new DC starts up, you should see a message indicating the progress of the DC cloning similar to Figure 28.6.

After the new virtual DC cloning has finished, you will see that the cloned domain controller has been added as a member of the Cloneable Domain Controllers security group. This is because it copies its membership from the original template virtual DC. As a best practice, Microsoft recommends that you leave this security group empty until you are performing cloning operations and that you remove members after cloning has been completed.

FIGURE 28.6
Newly imported
virtual DC cloning
status

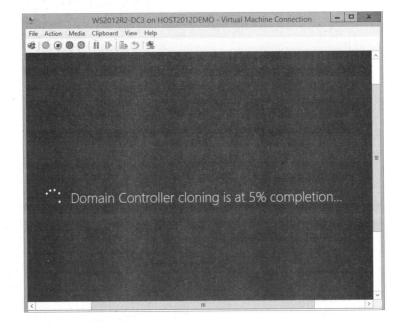

Moving VMs: Export and Import

One great advantage of server virtualization technology is that because your VMs are essentially just a bunch of files (made up of virtual disks and XML files), you can easily move them between physical hosts—not too different from how you would cut, copy, or paste your traditional files and folders.

As we discussed earlier in "Cloning a Virtual DC," Hyper-V in Windows Server 2012 gives you the option to *export* and *import* VMs between hosts with relative simplicity. This is made possible by the fact that all Hyper-V hosts offer almost identical hardware to their VMs through the integration components and synthetic drivers. If you wanted to move OS installations in the physical server world, you would at the very least need to move the physical disks, which works only if the hardware is similar enough, and it isn't a guaranteed success. With dissimilar hardware, you would probably have to reinstall the whole machine. In this section we will discuss Hyper-V export and import in more detail, this time between two hosts. All you need is a regular high-speed network between them because of the amount of data you are moving. A SAN is not required.

A VM has three parameters: configuration, current state, and data. When moving a VM to another Hyper-V host, you need to make sure that all of these come along. The Hyper-V management console has the Export Virtual Machine Wizard, which collects all relevant data, including checkpoints, and copies it to a target folder. This feature has been around since the first iteration of Hyper-V, but the cool thing about exporting your VMs in Windows Server 2012 is that you can run the export while the VM is still online—as opposed to having to first shut down the VM in earlier versions. This is a really useful feature that delivers the flexibility to quickly take a copy of a running server in a production environment and bring it into a test lab to validate any software updates or troubleshoot application problems.

On the Hyper-V host where you want to run the VM, you run the Import Virtual Machine Wizard, and that's all there is to it—well, almost.

The first point to be aware of is that an export operation simply copies all the VM configuration, state, and data. The import operation is different. You have some decisions to make:

◆ Should you keep the old virtual machine unique ID (default) or generate a new one?

◆ Should you use the export files directly to run the VM or copy them first? If you do not copy the files, you can import only once.

VIRTUAL MACHINE IDS

As most experienced Windows administrators know, many objects in the Windows world have multiple names. A well-known example is an Active Directory object. Its true name is a *globally unique identifier* (GUID), but we prefer to use human-readable names such as *display name* or *common name*. It's the same with VMs. Their true name is also a GUID, which does not change, even if you rename the server. The display name can be anything you like. Other objects in the VM world also have GUIDs, such as virtual switches and NICs.

An interesting property of VMs is that their IDs need to be unique, but the display names may be identical. This typically happens when you import a VM on the same host that you used for export. As long as you use a different ID on import, this will work fine.

A second, more subtle point is that of the virtual network configuration. How does the VM know which virtual switches to use on the new host? Internally, each virtual switch is known by its GUID, allowing you to give the switch any name you like without interfering with its relations to virtual NICs. But if you create a virtual switch on another host, it will have a different GUID. Hyper-V has one little trick to get around this. On import, it looks for virtual switches with exactly the same display name (including character case) as the ones included in the export files. If it finds them, the virtual NICs are connected. If not, the imported VM will have disconnected NICs.

Let's walk through an example where you export and import a VM. Any VM will do, but in this case we will use WS2012R2-SRV1. Ideally you should have a second Hyper-V host for import, but the example works with one host.

Assume you have a second host; we'll use one called VMHOST2-SRV as our target for importing. Create a shared folder with a descriptive name like ImportedVMs. The required share permissions for this folder are a bit tricky. The export process runs as SYSTEM, not as you. So, the share should have permissions for the host computer account to write data. Use either the computer account of the source host (VMHOST1-SRV in our example) or the Everyone security principal to give write access. Then, start the export process on the source host:

1. On the Hyper-V management console, select the VM you wish to export, which is WS2012R2-SRV1 in this example.

2. With the VM still running, choose the Export option from the Actions pane.

3. Enter a destination path for your export.

   This can be a local drive, USB drive, or a remote network location. This time, we will export directly to another Hyper-V host: \\vmhost2-srv\ImportedVMs. If the path does not exist, the wizard will create it. Whatever path you specify here, the wizard will create a subdirectory with the name of the VM.

After the export procedure is finished, you will import the VM. You can do this from the Hyper-V management console on the source server by adding the target host as an additional managed machine, but for the example you will log on directly to the target:

1. Log on to VMHOST2-SRV with an administrative account and open the Hyper-V management console.

2. If you want the virtual NICs to connect automatically on import, make sure there are virtual switches on both hosts with exactly the same names.

   In our example, we use MGMTNIC for management and VMEXT1 for external network connectivity.

3. From the Actions pane in the Hyper-V management console, select Import Virtual Machine; then click Next.

4. In the Locate Folder dialog box, input or browse for the path where the exported VM is stored such as D:\ImportedVMs\WS2012R2-SRV1 and then click Next.

5. In the Select Virtual Machine dialog box, ensure you select the correct version of the VM to import; then click Next to move on.

The default settings in the Choose Import Type dialog box (as shown earlier in Figure 28.5) deserve some attention:

Register   If you register the VM, then Hyper-V will bring the VM online and presume that you are content with the stored location of your VM files. This isn't always ideal because most likely you will have your files located in a folder such as ImportedVMs, and maybe you want to keep all your VMs together in a library or on a particular volume. Before selecting this option, ensure you have your VM files where you want them.

Restore   When you choose the Restore option, you get to select a location to store the VM files, as shown in Figure 28.7.

FIGURE 28.7
Choosing the Restore import type allows you to select locations for your VM files.

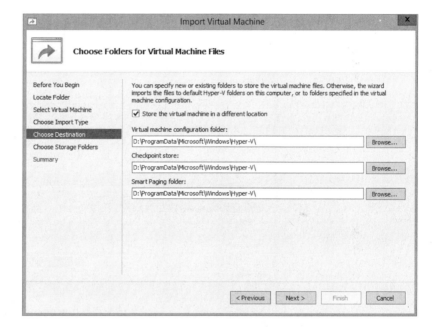

Copy   The Copy option allows you to import the VM multiple times from a template and will create a new unique ID for each copied VM.

6. Make your decision; then click Next to move on.

7. In the Summary dialog box, click Finish to begin the import process.

It will take just a few seconds and come back with a status update. If there was a problem, you need to search the event log. A common issue is that no matching virtual switch was found, leaving the NICs unconnected.

8. Select the newly imported VM.

You will see that any checkpoints you had have also been imported.

9. Check the VM properties, and note the paths to the virtual disks.

10. Verify the connection state of the NICs.

11. When ready, click Start from the Actions pane to bring the VM back online.

Just remember, though, that you have now effectively cloned the old VM. If the old one is still running on another host and you bring this newly imported one online, you'll have two identical machines on the network, which will certainly cause you problems!

You may be interested to know how Hyper-V keeps track of VM configuration. The actual VM configuration is the easy part. When you create a VM, you tell it where to put the top-level folder containing the VM configuration. Figure 28.8 shows the configuration of VM1 on Hyper-V host VMHOST1-SRV.

FIGURE 28.8
VM configuration files

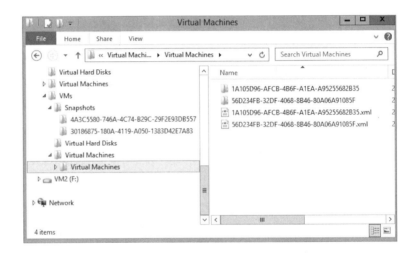

The screenshot shows three folders: Snapshots, Virtual Hard Disks, and Virtual Machines. There are two virtual machines registered here. Each has one folder named after its GUID, which is the real name of the virtual machine. For instance, the folder name 1A105D96-AFCB... corresponds to WS2012R2-SRV1. This folder contains the current memory state if you save its state. Each VM also has an XML document, again named after the GUID of the VM. This document is fully readable, although you probably should not edit it manually. If you look through it, you will find the entire configuration of the VM. As an illustration, the XML file has all the virtual switches the VM is connected to listed by the GUID of the virtual switch, not by the friendly name.

The Snapshot (this is a reference to the old term used for a checkpoint) folder contains GUID subfolders, containing state information of each checkpoint: the current configuration of the processes and virtual hardware in a .vsv file and all virtual memory in a .bin file. The difference files of the checkpoints are saved as .avhdx files in the Virtual Hard Disks folder.

When creating a VM or virtual disk, you can put it basically any place you like. So, how does Hyper-V know where to find everything? It uses *symbolic links*, which are very small files that refer to other files in a way that is transparent to applications. In this case, all relevant symbolic links are in the central configuration location for Hyper-V: `%systemdrive%\ProgramData\Microsoft\Windows\Hyper-V`. The folder ProgramData is hidden; it's visible only if you tell Windows Explorer not to hide hidden and system files. Starting with Windows Server 2008 R2, you can actually view symbolic links such as from Explorer.

In Figure 28.9, you can see from the description in the Type column that these are symbolic links, not ordinary files. Also, the file size of 0 bytes gives it away. In earlier versions of Windows Server, you would need to revert to the command prompt to tell the difference between symbolic links and normal files.

FIGURE 28.9

The starting point for Hyper-V configuration files. All files here are symbolic links, pointing to the physical location of the XML files that define virtual machines.

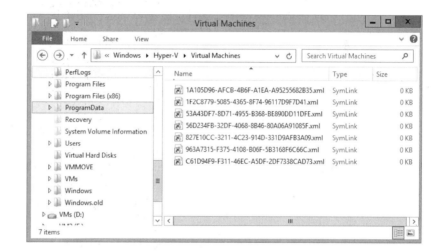

Knowing how this reference mechanism works can be quite useful for repairing the Hyper-V configuration after a disaster. Keep it in mind!

Quick Migration and Live Migration

It's impossible to have a full discussion of server virtualization without mentioning quick migration and live migration. These are related but different technologies to move virtual machines between hosts. In previous versions of Hyper-V, you had to use shared storage with shared high-speed networks, but with Hyper-V 2012 R2, you have the option to use nonshared storage and networks. In this section, we'll introduce you to quick migration and traditional live migration, and later, we'll discuss the new Shared Nothing Live Migration functionality.

Quick Migration   Quick migration works by saving the state of the VM, transferring control to another node, and restarting it on that node. This process is predictable and reliable but not so fast that it passes unnoticed. Time is lost during saving and restoring the VM state, which may take a number of minutes for VMs with a lot of memory.

Live Migration   The second technology is live migration, called that because it is fast enough to move a VM to another node without loss of service. In Chapter 27, "Server Virtualization with Hyper-V," we discussed some of the new enhancements to live migration in this release of Windows Server, including unlimited simultaneous live migrations, out-of-box compression, SMB Multichannel, and SMB Direct. Its key feature is that the unavailability of the VM during the actual move is very short and can be measured in subsecond time frames. This time is short enough to keep TCP/IP sessions alive. In other words, anyone using that VM will at most notice a subsecond delay, but everything keeps working.

Live migration works roughly like this:

1. The migration is initiated. The VM configuration is transferred to the destination host, which builds a skeleton VM.

2. The memory store of the VM is locked, and a different file is started. All memory changes are written to this file.

3. The memory store of the VM is transferred to the destination node using the shared network.

   Clearly, this network should be as fast as possible. The destination node starts loading this memory into the skeleton VM.

4. The first difference file is locked, and a second one is started. The first difference file is transferred to the destination node. This process repeats until the difference files become small.

5. Up to now, the VM has kept running, but at this point, the VM is frozen, and the final difference file is transferred as well.

6. Control of the VHDX files of the VM is transferred to the destination node. This happens quickly.

7. The VM configuration is removed from the original node and registered on the destination node.

8. The VM starts running on the destination.

For obvious reasons, live migration is the more frequently used of the two migration technologies. The ability to move VMs quickly between hosts this way opens up some interesting scenarios:

VM Drain on Shutdown   If you are running a Hyper-V cluster, then you will find this feature useful. Any time you need to do something on a host that requires downtime, you can move all VMs away without downtime for those VMs with a new feature enhancement to Hyper-V 2012 R2 called Virtual Machine Drain on Shutdown. This is extremely useful when carrying out hardware maintenance like adding memory, patching, and so on. Essentially, when you shut down a Hyper-V host that is part of a failover cluster (even without putting it into maintenance mode), all the VMs hosted on that node will automatically live-migrate across to another host.

On-demand Resource Allocation   You may have VMs that are running "hot" and are using a lot of CPU or disk I/O resources. With live migration, you can quickly move these VMs to a lightly loaded host or, alternatively, get other VMs out of the way. If you deploy System Center 2012, you can configure it to move these VMs automatically at times of heavy load.

Enabling Green IT   With live migration, you have the potential to shut down lightly used hosts, although in the real world you would need additional tooling to pull this off, such as System Center 2012. The idea is that you move VMs away from lightly used hosts, putting them all on a few hosts that are well utilized—say, up to 60 percent average CPU time or whatever you prefer. You can shut down the hosts without VMs until they are needed again, with corresponding power savings.

All the major server virtualization vendors offer similar features but may use different names. However, shared storage implies SANs, iSCSI, and other storage technologies that we won't fully discuss here. Still, we'll cover the basic principles and show you a brief walk-through, assuming that you are able to set up the basic storage infrastructure yourself. If you have never worked with remote storage before, we will offer some hints to help you along.

Live migration relies on the Failover Clustering role in Windows Server 2012 R2. *Failover clustering* is the ability to transfer running applications between hosts, including all their data and current state. This transfer (also known as *failover event*) can be initiated by the user, but usually a number of conditions are set that should trigger the failover. Dependencies of the application are good examples of such a condition: disks, networks, certain services that should be running, and so on. If any of these goes missing, failover clustering will trigger a failover. An application needs to know that it's running on a cluster and take action when requested. Well-known examples of failover clusters other than Hyper-V are SQL Server, Exchange Server, File and Print Services, and so on. You can see where the shared storage comes in: a data disk for an application running on one node needs to go to another node if the application fails over.

In a traditional live migration scenario, you would need to have at least two Hyper-V hosts both using a shared storage and networking configuration similar to what is shown in Figure 28.10.

FIGURE 28.10
Moving VMs between hosts using live migration requires a high-speed network and shared storage.

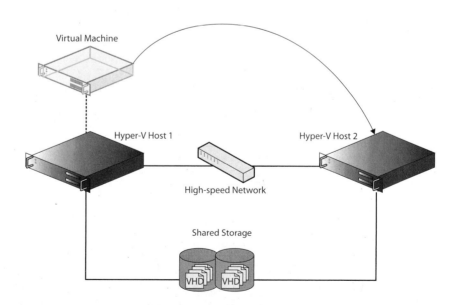

Each host server taking part in a clustering setup is a node. In Windows Server 2012 R2, the maximum number of nodes has been pushed to 64, a massive increase from the 16-node limitation in Windows Server 2008 R2. The main point of failover clustering is to provide high availability: if one host goes down, either planned or unexpectedly, the clustering services ensure that the application is restarted on another node.

How to Choose between Live Migration and Quick Migration

Why would you ever want to use quick migration when you can have live migration? One reason is that live migration can sometimes fail. If you look at how it works, you can see its theoretical weak spot: it needs to transfer memory faster to the destination host than the VM is changing it. If you have an application that writes a lot of data to memory very quickly and keeps doing this, it could make live migration impossible. Clearly, a fast network is required to make live migration reliable.

But this does show the advantage of quick migration: it is deterministic because it saves and restores the VM state between migrations. So, if live migration ever fails for a particular VM, try using quick migration.

Cluster-free Live Migrations

As we mentioned earlier, Windows Server 2012 has an enhancement whereby you can migrate running VMs between hosts with no downtime and—crucially—no shared cluster configurations! This capability is known as *Shared Nothing Live Migration*. All you need is two hosts and a high-speed network cable, as shown in Figure 28.11.

FIGURE 28.11
Moving VMs with
Shared Nothing Live
Migration

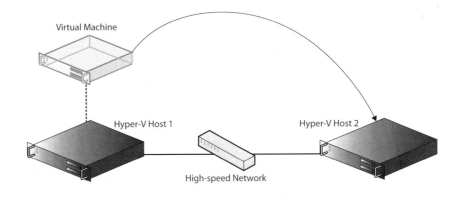

It's made possible using a process very similar to the online VM export functionality we discussed previously and another new feature in Windows Server 2012 R2 called *Live Storage Migration*.

With Live Storage Migration, you can choose to move the storage (virtual disks) of your VM to another location, such as a new folder structure on the local host or onto storage located on a remote host. This feature alone is a very welcome addition to Hyper-V since it was noticeably lacking from previous releases, which meant you always had to plan for downtime if you wanted to migrate VM storage in the past.

After all this explaining, let's get on with the walk-through. The following steps presume that you have access to two hosts (one will be the source and one will be the destination) running Windows Server 2012 R2 with the Hyper-V role installed. These two hosts should be part of the same Active Directory domain.

1. Log on to the source Hyper-V host server with an account that has administrator permissions.

2. Open Hyper-V Manager, ensure that the source host is selected in the left pane, and then click Hyper-V Settings in the Actions pane.

3. Click Live Migrations and then check the "Enable incoming and outgoing live migrations" check box to turn on the feature, as shown in Figure 28.12.

FIGURE 28.12
Enabling Shared Nothing Live Migration

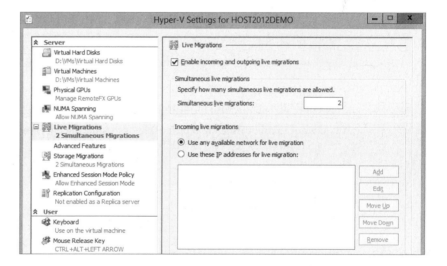

4. Input the number of simultaneous live migrations you want to run on this server, or just leave it at the default of 2.

5. If you want to use a specific network for live migration, then select it in the "Incoming live migrations" section, as shown in the figure.

6. From the Server pane on the left, expand the Live Migrations link and click Advanced Features.

   Figure 28.13 shows that the default authentication protocol is set to Use Credential Security Support Provider (CredSSP) and that Compression is the default performance option enabled. You might also notice the warning message here telling you to log off and then log on again to allow use of CredSSP—now would be a good time to do that.

FIGURE 28.13

Live Migration Advanced Features

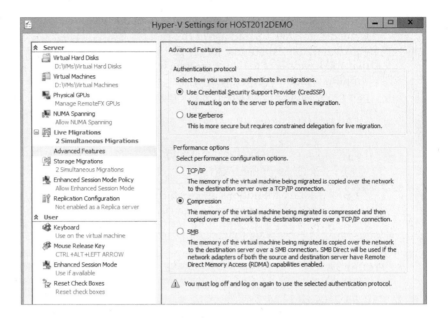

7. Repeat these steps on the destination Hyper-V host, making sure to log off and back on again at the end of the configuration process.

If you want to mix things up a bit, instead of using the GUI, you could use the following PowerShell commands to carry out the same process:

```
Enable-VMMigration
Set-VMHost –UseAnyNetworkForMigration $true
```

REMOTELY TRIGGERING SHARED NOTHING LIVE MIGRATION

If you want to kick off a live migration of a VM between two hosts using Shared Nothing Live Migration from a remote server or workstation (not the source or destination hosts), then you will need to enable Kerberos Constrained Delegation through the Active Directory Users and Computers snap-in and then choose the Kerberos authentication option from the Live Migrations ➢ Advanced Settings screen in Hyper-V Settings. Check out this link for more information: http://technet .microsoft.com/en-us/library/jj134199.aspx#BKMK_Step1.

When you have your live migration settings configured on both the source and destination hosts, it's time to put it to the test and move a VM between the two of them.

1. Log on to the source Hyper-V host server with an account that has administrator permissions.

2. Right-click a running VM and then choose the Move option from the context menu.

In the Choose Move Type dialog box shown in Figure 28.14 you have the option to move the whole virtual machine or move just the virtual machine's storage.

3. Leave "Move the virtual machine" selected; then click Next.

4. Specify the name of the destination host; then click Next.

FIGURE 28.14
Choosing the move type

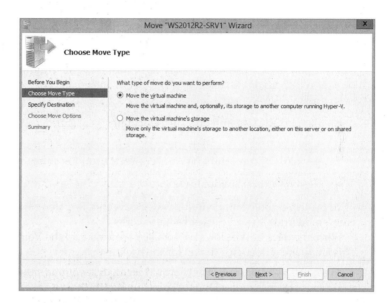

5. In the Choose Move Options dialog box, decide where you want to locate the virtual machine data (or just leave the default setting here) and click Next.

6. If you accepted the default option in the previous step, you now need to specify the location on the destination host server where the migrated VM will be placed. Click Next.

7. In the Summary screen, confirm the settings you have configured, and then click Finish to begin the Shared Nothing Live Migration of your VM to the destination host.

TAKING LIVE MIGRATION TO THE NEXT LEVEL

Using SMB 3.0, RDMA, and Multichannel in Windows Server 2012 R2, you can really enhance your continuous availability offering and remove limitations on VM mobility in the datacenter—if you have the budget for it! Didier Van Hoye (Hyper-V MVP) has written a blog post on this subject that's well worth checking out: http://workinghardinit.wordpress.com/2013/06/04/ complete-vm-mobility-across-the-data-center-with-smb-3-0-rdma-multichannel- windows-server-2012-r2/.

When you've finished reading Didier's post, have a read over this one from Aidan Finn (Hyper-V MVP) on setting SMB 3.0 bandwidth limits in Windows Server 2012 R2: http://www.aidanfinn .com/?p=15262.

VM Maintenance

Although virtualization brings a lot of new features and flexibility to the table, you still need to consider some of the more traditional maintenance tasks for your VMs such as backing them up, managing malware protection, and keeping them up to date with the latest patches. This section will discuss your options for these maintenance tasks.

Backing Up and Restoring Virtual Machines

From a systems-management point of view, you should treat VMs as if they are physical machines, with some exceptions. When it comes to backup and restore, there are some special issues to consider. If you look at a Hyper-V host machine running a number of VMs, you may wonder whether you can back up all of that in one go. In the ideal world, you could do the following:

♦ Back up all VMs, and do so incrementally.

♦ Make all VMs aware of the backup so that they can do the right thing on restore. This is particularly important for Active Directory and Exchange Server.

♦ Restore VMs individually.

In principle you could do it this way. The reality is different, however. We'll review briefly how a modern Windows Server backup works.

Since the days of Windows Server 2003, we have had the Volume Shadow Copy Service (VSS). This component does two things for the backup process:

Freeze a Disk Volume   First, it can freeze a disk volume, take a snapshot, and unfreeze the disk again (this works along the same lines as the host-level checkpoint that we can take of a VM, which we discussed in Chapter 27). The snapshot stays on the volume. It works using a differencing algorithm and takes little space.

Interact with Applications   Second, VSS interacts with applications during the backup to allow them to clean up and prepare, such as flush buffers, stabilize data structures, and so on. You can see how this benefits complex applications. VSS allows them to be backed up quickly and with data structures intact. Such applications would be Active Directory, SQL Server, Exchange Server, and, of course, Hyper-V.

So, to make VSS work in a virtual environment, you need a VSS provider for Hyper-V and a component in the VM that integrates with this provider. How else would the applications in the VM be aware that a backup is in progress? In other words, it's a two-stage rocket: the VSS process in the host needs to trigger the VSS process in the VM during backup, using the Hyper-V VSS provider as the communication channel. In the VM itself, Integration Services takes care of the coordination. This is an important point to note: without working Integration Services, you cannot have a real backup from the host. Yes, using VSS you can back up the .vhdx files that make up the VM, but the VM will not be aware of the backup. It would be nothing better than a live image backup with all its limitations and lack of application-aware functionality.

Let's recap. You have two options to back up operating systems and applications in a VM:

◆ Run a backup from the host, using a backup tool that is VSS aware such as Windows Server Backup or System Center 2012 Data Protection Manager. Integration Services in the VM is required.

◆ Treat the VM as a physical machine, and run backup software from inside the virtualized OS.

Both options have their merits:

Backing Up from the Host   If you run a host-level backup of your VMs, then you are ensuring that you have a full and complete backup of the entire VM should you need to recover it—no more bare-metal recoveries and reinstallation of applications in the event of a server failing. This option also slots nicely into an offsite disaster-recovery scenario where the entire VM is replicated offsite. One downside of host-level backups, though, is that depending on the size of the VM, they can take a lot longer to back up, even with an incremental backup plan. You also need to ensure that you have a large-capacity disk solution to use because a tape-only backup is deemed legacy now and in any case wouldn't be practical if you had a large number of VMs to back up in their entirety. Something else to consider is the potential for a performance hit on the host as multiple VMs get backed up, but you can easily avoid this with proper planning and design.

Backing Up in the Virtualized OS   This will fit right in with your existing backup system, it won't break anything, and you know how to do it. You would most likely need to deploy a backup agent to each VM's guest operating system and back up the system state along with files, folders, and applications. This way, the host can be a black box that can be replaced at will, although if you lose a host with all your VMs running on it and all you have are these in-machine backups, be prepared to spend a long time recovering them all to another host. Something else to be aware of is that a backup initiated from inside a VM generates a lot of disk I/O. If you have 10 VMs on one host all doing their backup at the same time, you will generate 10 times the load on the host. It takes pretty good hardware to keep up with that!

If you want to have the full gamut of options available for Hyper-V backups, then we recommend deploying System Center 2012 - Data Protection Manager (DPM), but if that's not an option, then as mentioned earlier, the built-in tool for backing up Hyper-V is Windows Server Backup (WSB). Chapter 32, "Windows Server 2012 and Active Directory Backup and Maintenance," discusses this tool in greater detail, but for the purpose of getting an understanding of how it backs up your VMs, we'll take a quick walk-through here. First up, you need to install WSB, and a nice and simple way to do this is to open up a PowerShell command with an administrative account and then type the following:

```
Install-WindowsFeature Windows-Server-Backup
```

After you have WSB installed, you can then carry on with backing up a VM:

1. From Server Manager ➢ Local Server ➢ Tools, click Windows Server Backup to open the MMC snap-in.

2. Right-click Local Backup in the left tree pane; then click Backup Schedule from the context menu to open the Backup Schedule Wizard.

3. Click Next in the Getting Started dialog box.

4. Select Custom for the backup type; then click Next.

5. Click the Add Items button to open the Select Items dialog box.

6. Expand Hyper-V and then choose the VM that you wish to back up, as shown in Figure 28.15.

FIGURE 28.15
Backing up VMs with WSB

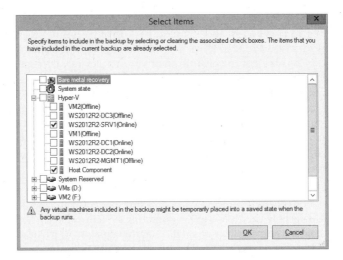

Note that we have also selected the Host Component because this protects the virtual switches, resource pools, and Windows Authorization Manager on the host.

7. Back in the Select Items for Backup dialog box, click the Advanced Settings button, and then select the VSS Settings tab.

8. Choose "VSS full backup" if you're not using any other backup product to protect your VMs or "VSS copy backup" if you are using another backup solution and want to retain the application log files.

9. Click OK to close the dialog box; then click Next to continue.

10. Set the time of day to start the backup.

   Your options include:

   ◆ "Once a day," for which you select the time of day to start the backup

   ◆ "More than once a day," where you select an available time

11. Click Add to move it to the "Scheduled time" list.

   Using the "More than once a day" option lets you schedule as many backups as you want, with the caveat that you want to leave enough time between backup operations so that they are able to complete before the next backup is triggered.

12. Click Next.

13. Select the option "Back up to a hard disk that is dedicated for backups (recommended)."

   To use this option, you must have at least one disk attached to the server computer that has no existing volume. The disk should be raw, with no partition or file system.

14. Click Next.

15. Select the disk to use for the backup volume and click Next.

   You will be warned that finishing this wizard will cause the selected disks to be formatted, losing any existing data on the disks.

16. If you are certain you want to use the selected disks, click Yes to proceed.

17. Review your selected options; then click Finish to format the disks and schedule the backup.

It may have occurred to you to use the Export feature as a backup. Still, an exported VM is not equivalent to a normal backup because there is no VSS integration. When you import a VM, it doesn't know it has been "restored." The downsides of using exports are that you typically do them one by one and importing them may require you to delete the current VM first (if it still exists). If you know what you are doing, an export/import will do in a pinch. Otherwise, it's not a backup solution and doing it at scale isn't an option either.

Malware Protection and Patching

It goes without saying that having some type of malware protection on your servers is a good idea. The question is more to what extent you need protection. Do you need continuous scanning, or can you get away with daily or weekly scans? As long as you are in a position to counter new threats, you are probably OK.

A possible complication with virtualization may have occurred to you. Not only do you have the host to consider, but disk I/O is a precious resource on a virtualization platform. If you have a host with 10 VMs, all of them performing continuous malware scanning, the I/O system of the host gets 10 times more load because of scanning than a single server would have. In practice, this is not often a limiting factor. Modern antimalware software, certainly the server-class kind, knows how to be careful with I/O bandwidth. So, for VMs, the advice is clear: install malware scanners in all of them. Treat a VM the same way as a physical server, and ensure that you have implemented the documented antivirus exclusions relevant to the workload.

But what about the Hyper-V host? If it runs no services except Hyper-V, what is the need for malware scanning? Especially on Server Core, there is little for malware to attack. Although that's true, that's not quite the point. Any operating system connected to a network is potentially vulnerable to attacks. Even a flaw in the TCP/IP stack could lead to a compromise of the system. So if you want full protection, you need to scan the host as well. Consider that by far the most disk activity will be performed by the VMs, and you see that the performance impact of a malware scanner on the host will be low. Clearly, you will need to exclude the virtual disks and the Hyper-V processes from scanning. To be precise, exclude the default VM Configuration folder, the VHD folder, the Snapshot folder, VMMS.exe, and VMWP.exe. Without excluding these from an online access malware scanner, you might well find that some of your VMs don't start up or even disappear from Hyper-V Manager!

Although malware scanning is a direct form of protection, keeping up to date with patches is indirect but just as important. There's no need to tell you that you should patch the VMs and the host—if you don't, you're just asking for trouble. Patching the host may require a reboot, taking all the VMs offline. That requires planning and may cause problems if you cannot shut down VMs reliably. That's why Integration Services is so important. One of its functions is to initiate the save-state procedure in the VM when the host asks for it. The default action configured on each VM is to save its state when the stand-alone host shuts down. Having more than one host will help here, though, because you could use Shared Nothing Live Migration to keep the VMs online.

If you have a Hyper-V failover cluster environment running Windows Server 2012 or higher, then you can leverage the *Cluster-Aware Updating* (CAU) feature, which will allow you to patch your servers with minimal downtime while the updates are being deployed. CAU integrates with the built-in Windows Update Agent and Windows Server Update Services (WSUS) to download and install the updates. When you want to patch a Hyper-V cluster node running Windows Server 2012 R2, all you need to do is shut down the host and the new VM Drain feature (discussed earlier in this chapter) will kick in, which will migrate all the VMs over to any other available hosts. If you're running Windows Server 2012 (not R2), then you will first need to pause the host using Failover Cluster Manager and choose the Drain Roles option to get the same result. To learn more about CAU, check out this TechNet document: `http://tinyurl .com/ws2012cua`.

Disaster Recovery

These days, the sheer volume of information and news from around the world that you have access to through the Internet can be mind boggling. Nearly every day you can pick out a news story where some form of natural or human-made disaster has befallen a country, city, town, or business. An example of such a disaster happened in April 2011 when the west coast of Japan was hit by a tsunami, which left untold damage across the region. Countless relief efforts and charity campaigns around the globe sprang up, and one of the ways that global IT providers extended a helping hand to the people of Japan was by opening their datacenters and cloud offerings for free. As the Japanese started to rebuild their livelihoods and businesses, they used the cloud platform as a way of going forward and were able to get back up and running in a very quick and simple fashion. Once these organizations had rebuilt their offices and local infrastructure, the majority of them chose to maintain a presence in the cloud instead of moving everything back in-house so as to mitigate against another possible disaster.

Virtualization is a key pillar of cloud computing, and with the evolution of technologies such as Hyper-V, disaster recovery (DR) has become far easier and cheaper to deliver than ever before.

It's a good time to mention that the concepts of DR and high availability (HA) are not the same thing. They share some characteristics but serve different purposes. HA focuses on the persistent availability of your environment, and in Hyper-V terms that means your VMs. You deliver HA for your VMs through Hyper-V Failover Clustering and provide redundancy for the hosts by ensuring you've deployed enough physical servers in the cluster to maintain uptime in the event of a host failure. The purpose of DR, on the other hand, is to ensure that the organization can maintain running their IT systems (and ultimately their business) through offsite replication and fault-tolerant DR sites. Think of DR as a Plan B option that kicks in when a disaster strikes.

In this section we will look at a new DR feature in Windows Server 2012 called Hyper-V Replica.

Cheap DR with Hyper-V Replica

Hyper-V Replica (HVR) is a feature available since Windows Server 2012, and it allows for host-based replication of VMs without the need for any shared cluster components. Essentially, you can take a VM running on a Hyper-V host in one site and simply replicate it over to another site, up to a maximum of two additional sites. Microsoft designed HVR to work with commercial broadband connections, so the need to have expensive high-speed fiber-optic connectivity to the DR site isn't essential for replication to occur. Figure 28.16 shows a basic HVR scenario.

FIGURE 28.16
A basic Hyper-V
Replica scenario

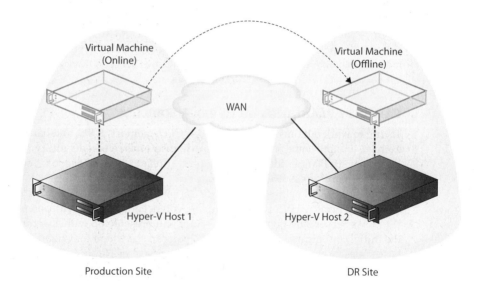

HVR uses either Active Directory or certificate-based authentication between hosts for security. You can select which virtual disks in a VM are to be replicated and which ones you don't need (a virtual disk containing a large paging file, for example). When you configure replication for the first time, a "seed" synchronization takes place between the source and destination hosts, and once this has completed, asynchronous replication kicks in. The replicated VM will be powered off on the destination host, and you must manually carry out a planned or unplanned failover to power it up if required. A neat feature of HVR is that if you needed to invoke your DR plan and had failed over all your replicated VMs to the DR site, once your production site comes back online, you can reverse the replication process back over to the original site with relative ease.

HYPER-V REPLICA PREREQUISITES

Your source and destination hosts need to be running Hyper-V on one of the following operating systems:

◆ Windows Server 2012 Standard/Datacenter edition

◆ Windows Server 2012 R2 Standard/Datacenter edition

◆ Hyper-V Server 2012 (this is the free one)

◆ Hyper-V Server 2012 R2

Both hosts must have the same version of Hyper-V running for HVR to work, and you cannot replicate a VM running on a host with Windows Server 2012 R2 to a host with Windows Server 2012, for example. For authentication purposes, you need to ensure that both the source and destination hosts are in the same Active Directory forest. If not, then you will need to manually import X.509 v3 certificates with the requirements outlined here: `http://blogs.technet.com/b/virtualization/archive/2012/03/13/hyper-v-replica-certificate-requirements.aspx`.

Once you have met the host requirements for HVR, all you need for the guest VMs is to ensure that they are running an operating system that is supported on Hyper-V 2012. This means that you are not restricted to just Windows Server 2012 or higher VMs for HVR, making it a very attractive DR feature for older VMs.

CAPACITY PLANNING FOR HYPER-V REPLICA

Trying to work out the impact of HVR on CPU, memory, IOPS, and bandwidth can be a tricky exercise without some additional help. Microsoft has released a utility that does just that called the "Capacity Planner for Hyper-V Replica" (`http://www.microsoft.com/en-us/download/details.aspx?id=39057`).

This utility will help you design the server, storage, and network infrastructure required to maintain a healthy HVR deployment. All you need to do is download and run the tool from a Windows Server 2012 Hyper-V host, and it will present you with a wizard to walk you through the initial configuration. In Figure 28.17, you can see where the wizard prompts you to enter hostnames for your primary and secondary servers or Hyper-V Replica Broker Client Access Point (CAP) if you're using a failover cluster configuration. You also need to supply an estimated WAN bandwidth and collection duration metric here.

When you've given the utility your HVR host and bandwidth specifics, you then select a temporary location for the planner to create and replicate a test VM. This test VM is used to calculate the network deployment requirements between the primary and replica servers. After you've entered all your information, the utility will start calculating the capacity required and will present you with a report similar to the one shown in Figure 28.18.

SUPPORTED SCENARIOS FOR HYPER-V REPLICA

Not only can Hyper-V Replica replicate between two non-clustered hosts, but it can also replicate from a non-clustered host to a node in a Hyper-V cluster and vice versa. This can be useful if you want to ensure that a specific clustered VM gets shipped out to a non-clustered host in your DR site.

FIGURE 28.17
HVR Capacity
Planner

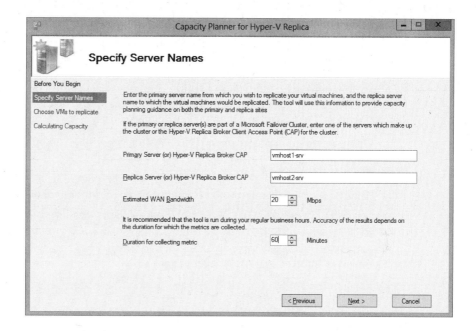

FIGURE 28.18
Capacity report

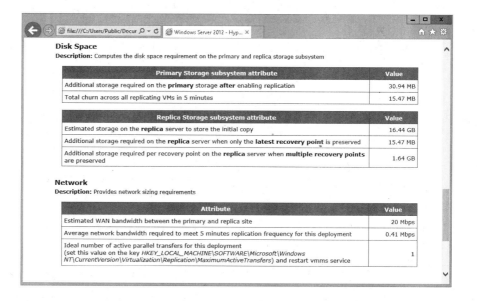

ENABLING HYPER-V REPLICA

Now that you have an understanding of what HVR is, in this section we will walk through configuring a replication of VM between two non-clustered Hyper-V hosts running Windows Server 2012 R2. We will use VMHOST1-SRV as our source server and VMHOST2-SRV as the replica destination server. Both hosts in this example are part of the same Active Directory forest and can resolve each other's DNS names across the WAN. By default, HVR is disabled, and you will need to first enable it on the destination server.

1. On the destination server, open Hyper-V Manager with an account that has administrative permissions, right-click the host, and then select Hyper-V Settings from the context menu.

2. Click Replication Configuration from the Server column; then select the "Enable this computer as a Replica server" check box, as shown in Figure 28.19.

   Notice the two different authentication options here for Kerberos and certificate-based authentication: because we are using Active Directory to authenticate, Kerberos is fine in this case.

FIGURE 28.19
Enabling HVR on the destination host

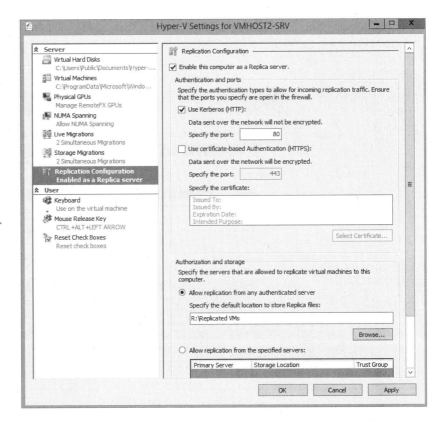

3. Enable the "Allow replication from any authenticated server" option, and choose a location on the destination host to store the replicated VMs (ensuring you have enough free disk space there to support the replicas).

4. Click OK to close the Hyper-V Settings window.

5. Acknowledge the pop-up dialog box that warns you about configuring inbound firewall rules to support replication, and then verify that you have enabled the relevant Hyper-V Replica Listener rule in Windows Firewall on the destination host, as shown in Figure 28.20.

FIGURE 28.20
Hyper-V Replica
Firewall rules

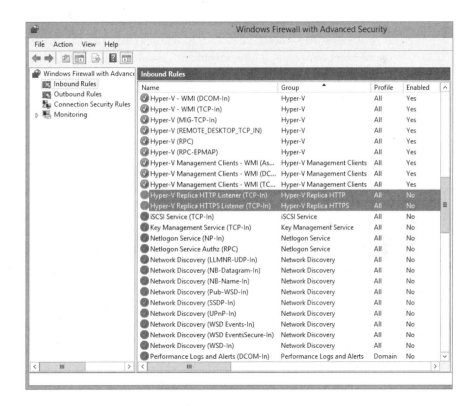

You will need to create custom rules if you've modified the HTTP and HTTPS port settings from their defaults.

CONFIGURING VM REPLICATION

Once you have enabled HVR, you then need to configure VM replication. This is enabled on an individual VM basis. When you initially enable replication for a VM, you need to choose how the initial "seed" copy will be created. Since this initial copy will be quite large (depending on the size of the VM being replicated), you have three different synchronization methods to choose from:

Send Initial Copy over the Network   This is the most straightforward option to choose for your initial copy, but it's dependent on having a pretty good upload link from your production site to the DR site. If you don't have a dedicated WAN connection for replication between sites, then this may not be the best option to choose. This method is popular, though, if you are creating the Hyper-V Replica configuration while both the production and DR hosts are on the same site—possibly as a temporary measure to support the initial copy process.

Send Initial Copy Using External Media   With this option, you can create an online export of a VM and then store it on external media such as a USB drive. You then bring the external media to the DR site and import the copy onto the destination host. This is a great option for organizations that have WAN links with bad upload speeds and that would otherwise need to spend weeks copying the replicas over to the DR site.

Remember to encrypt your removable drives before creating the copy and transporting them because they will contain very sensitive data that you don't want falling into the wrong hands.

Use an Existing Virtual Machine on the Replica Server as the Initial Copy   An intriguing final choice for your initial copy is the potential to use an existing VM that might be restored from an offsite backup solution such as DPM and import that into the destination server. When you enable replication on the restored VM, HVR synchronizes it with the source host across the WAN.

Be very careful with this option, though, because if you restore a VM from your backups and bring it online at the same time as the original VM in the production site, you'll quickly run into problems.

In the following steps, you'll use the first option to create your initial copy over the network.

1. On the source server (VMHOST1-SRV), open Hyper-V Manager with an account that has administrative permissions, right-click the VM that you want to replicate, and select the Enable Replication option from the menu.

2. In the Specify Replica Server dialog box, type the name of (or browse for) the destination server that you previously enabled HVR on.

3. Choose the authentication type for your VM replica or leave the default settings in place here; then click Next.

4. From the Choose Replication VHDs dialog box shown in Figure 28.21, select the VHDs that you want to be replicated and deselect any that you don't need, such as dedicated paging file VHDs; then click Next.

   The next dialog box allows you to choose the frequency at which changes will be sent to your destination server. Your options here are 30 seconds, 5 minutes, and 15 minutes.

5. Click Next when you've made your choice.

6. In the Configure Additional Recovery Points dialog box, choose to store only the latest recovery point of the replicated VM, or create additional recovery points to have the option of recovering the VM to an earlier point.

7. Click Next to continue.

FIGURE 28.21
Choosing VHDs
to be replicated

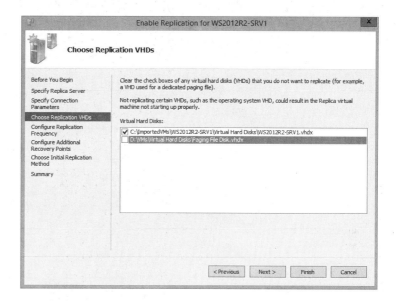

The penultimate dialog box in this wizard is shown in Figure 28.22, and it's where you choose an initial replication method (as discussed earlier) and a time when the initial copy will be carried out.

8. Click Next to move on when you've made your choices.

9. Confirm your configuration settings in the Summary dialog box, and then click Finish to complete the wizard.

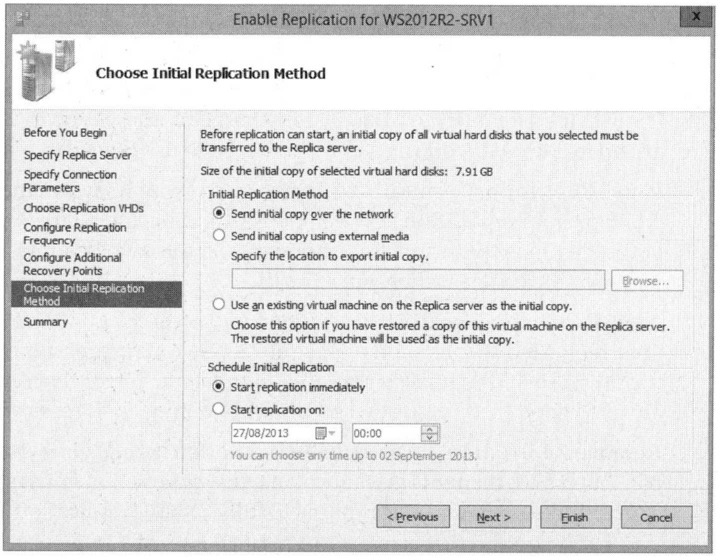

FIGURE 28.22
Choosing the
initial replication
method

MANAGING VM REPLICAS

With your VM replicas configured, you can perform a number of actions by right-clicking the offline replicated VM located on the destination host and choosing the Replication menu, as shown in Figure 28.23.

FIGURE 28.23
VM replication options on the destination host

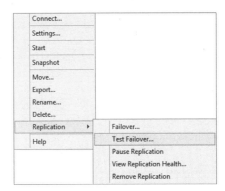

From this menu, you can perform the following failover tasks:

Unplanned Failover   An *unplanned failover* is not to be carried out lightly, and it presumes that the production VM cannot be contacted anymore as a result of an unexpected outage or disaster. You can simulate an unplanned failover by turning off the production VM, right-clicking the replica VM located on the destination host, and selecting the Failover option. From there you can choose the relevant recovery point to use. When you've chosen the recovery point, the replica VM will power up on the destination host.

Test Failover   A *test failover* creates a copy of the VM by cloning it and storing the clone on a differential virtual disk using the replica VM's storage as its parent. Because it uses the replica VM's storage, it will save the differential disk in the same volume as the replica; so ensure you have enough disk space free on this volume if you intend to keep the test VM up and running for an extended period of time. This test process allows you to verify if your recovery points are up to date and working should you need to use them in a real DR situation.

Pause Replication   This option does exactly what it says on the tin. You will use this if you want to pause replication between the destination and source hosts for a particular VM. When you've paused replication, this option then changes to Resume Replication, which you can use to restart the process when you're ready.

View Replication Health   This option will present you with statistics based on the health of your replicated VM, as shown in Figure 28.24. You can get some really useful information here including such things as average data size, latency, errors encountered, and last sync time. It's always a good place to start when troubleshooting HVR replicas.

Remove Replication   Another obvious option here. If you wish to remove replication for a particular VM, then this is what you need to choose. You must select this option on both the source and destination VM replicas to fully remove replication.

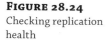

FIGURE 28.24
Checking replication
health

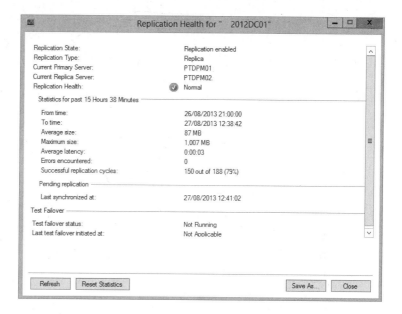

If you right-click the production VM located on the source host and choose the Replication option from the context menu, you don't get the Failover and Test Replication choices, but instead you get the Planned Failover option, as shown in Figure 28.25.

FIGURE 28.25
Replication options from
the source host

Planned Failover   If you wanted to carry out a *planned failover,* you would need to ensure the production VM is first shut down, and then you would right-click the production VM on the source host and choose Failover from there. This would then kick off a prerequisite check to verify that the production VM is indeed turned off and that replication can be reversed once the planned failover is completed. When this check has completed, the Hyper-V Replica log files are pushed out to the replica destination host and applied. Finally, the replica VM will be automatically powered up on the destination host ready for use.

Online Resources for Hyper-V

This section provides an invaluable list of online resources that you can refer to and use when working with Hyper-V in Windows Server 2012 R2. These references include official Microsoft links, community blogs, and social networking references.

Ben Armstrong is the Hyper-V Program Manager at Microsoft, and his Virtualization Blog is where you'll find all manner of really useful Hyper-V-related posts:

```
http://blogs.msdn.com/b/virtual_pc_guy/
```

Aidan Finn's blog is one of the most visited Hyper-V websites on the Internet. Aidan is an Irish Hyper-V MVP and has written numerous books, whitepapers, and articles on all versions of Hyper-V. He was lead author of *Hyper-V Installation and Configuration Guide* published by Sybex, and if you want to go really deep into Hyper-V, then this book is a must-have. You can check out his blog from this link:

```
http://www.aidanfinn.com
```

Didier Van Hoye is a Belgium-based Hyper-V MVP whose blog posts break down the barriers of deploying and managing Hyper-V in large organizations. Some of his benchmark tests with Hyper-V and enterprise storage solutions have proven to be extremely popular and well worth a read:

```
http://workinghardinit.wordpress.com/
```

Another MVP who certainly knows his way around Hyper-V is Hans Vredevoort. Hans regularly blogs about complex troubleshooting solutions and integrations with Hyper-V and System Center. He can be found online at:

```
http://hyper-v.nu/
```

If you search for Windows Server 2012 R2 Hyper-V–related content on the Web, you'll most likely come across a blog post or two from Switzerland's Thomas Maurer (Hyper-V MVP). Take a look at some of his posts here:

```
http://www.thomasmaurer.ch/
```

Finally, when you find yourself needing help understanding Hyper-V network virtualization and things, such as converged fabric, NVGRE, and virtual gateways, then you will definitely want to read of Damian Flynn's (Cloud and Datacenter MVP) blog. Damian was a co-author of *Hyper-V Installation and Configuration Guide,* and he's the go-to man outside of Microsoft on these subjects. You can read his blog posts here:

```
http://www.damianflynn.com/
```

The Bottom Line

Virtualize domain controllers.   Windows Server 2012 includes a new method of deploying any number of virtual DCs very quickly through *virtual domain controller cloning*. This gives administrators a supported solution to rapidly spin up replica domain controllers using an existing template DC for reference. Virtual DC cloning can be beneficial to organizations that want to quickly deploy multiple DCs into new domains as well as a helpful feature in private cloud environments to meet scalability requirements.

Master It   What is the minimum supported version of Active Directory that you can use with virtual DC cloning?

Understand how to move your VMs around.   Hyper-V in Windows Server 2012 gives you the option to *export* and *import* VMs between hosts with relative simplicity. This is made possible by the fact that all Hyper-V hosts offer almost identical hardware to their VMs through the integration components and synthetic drivers. If you wanted to move OS installations around in the physical server world, you would at the very least need to move the physical disks, which works only if the hardware is similar enough and isn't always a guaranteed success.

> **Master It**   When moving a VM to another Hyper-V host, which three parameters need to be moved?

Manage your VMs.   Although virtualization brings a lot of new features and flexibility to the table, there are still some of the more traditional maintenance tasks that you need to consider for your VMs, such as backing them up, managing malware protection, and keeping them up to date with the latest patches.

> **Master It**   If you are running a Hyper-V failover cluster on Windows Server 2012 R2, what technology would you use to patch your production VMs?

Understand disaster recovery with Hyper-V.   Hyper-V Replica (HVR) is a feature available in Windows Server 2012 and higher. It allows for host-based replication of VMs without the need for any shared cluster components to support disaster-recovery scenarios.

> **Master It**   How many sites outside of your production site can you replicate your VMs to if you are running Hyper-V Replica on Windows Server 2012 R2?

Installing, Using, and Administering Remote Desktop Services

Remote Desktop Services (RDS)—formerly known as Terminal Services—is a role in Windows 2012 R2 that allows users to connect to session-based desktops, applications, and virtual desktops.

Applications that run on the RD Session Host server are called RDS RemoteApp applications. From the end-user perspective, these applications look and feel as though they are running on their local system. The user's keystrokes and mouse movements are sent to the server. Images are sent back to the user's system. Even thin clients can easily run sophisticated applications with ease, although RDS RemoteApps are most commonly run on regular desktop systems.

The old Terminal Services came in two flavors: TS for Administrators and TS in application mode. TS for Administrators is now known as Remote Desktop for Administration, and TS in application mode is known as Remote Desktop Services with an RD Session Host server. Remote Desktop for Administration was covered in Chapter 17, and this chapter covers Remote Desktop Services with an RD Session Host server.

In this chapter, you will learn to:

◆ Limit the maximum number of connections

◆ Add an application to an RD Session Host server

◆ Add a RemoteApp for Web Access

Who Needs Remote Desktop Services?

Remote Desktop Services can be used to enable end users to run a Windows-based program on a remote server from their desktop computer. The server hosting the application is called a *Remote Desktop Session Host (RD Session Host)* server. It's also possible for the end users to access a full desktop session on the RD Session Host server, and if that isn't enough, you can now use the Remote Desktop Services Virtualization Host for Virtual Desktop Infrastructures.

As an administrator, you can do the following:

◆ Deploy and manage applications on a few RDS servers instead of on hundreds or thousands of client computers.

◆ Provide applications to end users whom you cannot easily support because they're in another office—or another country.

◆ Reduce the impact of client hardware failures by keeping all applications on a central server. If a client's computer dies, plug in a new one, and they're back to work.

◆ Avoid misconfigured computers, for example, if an application requires a specific set of binaries to run correctly but people install other apps that overwrite these binaries.

◆ Get out of the hardware rat race that constantly requires updates to support the latest and greatest software.

◆ Use computers in environments that are not compatible with desktop computers; for example, industry manufacturing where air pollution is an issue can break PCs.

◆ Simplify help-desk and training support.

If any of these tasks are important to you, then you should seriously consider using Remote Desktop Services with a Session Host server.

Centralized Deployment of Applications

One great benefit of Remote Desktop Services is how it simplifies application deployment. Instead of deploying an application to all the clients using Group Policy or Microsoft System Center Configuration Manager (SCCM), you can install it once on the RD Session Host server.

As an example, your company may have a line-of-business application that 100 users need to access. Instead of installing the application on all 100 desktop computers, you could use an RD Session Host server. The application could be installed once on the server, and each user could then access the application remotely. Even better, when the application needs to be upgraded or patched, you need to do it only once—on the RDS server.

Supporting Remote Users

You can use Remote Desktop Services for remote access or branch-office access. Some applications have difficulty performing over low-speed connections or need special ports opened on the firewall. Instead of running the application over the low-speed connection, you can host the application on the RDS server within a well-connected network.

Clients can still connect via a VPN or low-speed dial-up connection. However, since the application is running on the RD Session Host server in a well-connected network, its performance isn't impacted by the slower connections.

More and more people are telecommuting at least a couple of days a week. Many U.S. government agencies have a legal requirement to support telecommuters, and many telecommuters often don't even have offices or desks in the facility. Rather than trying to maintain desktop computers for all the staff, many companies are giving users computers to take home and providing their applications via remote servers.

Supporting PC-unfriendly Environments

The dream of "a PC on every desktop" will remain a dream, if for no other reason then in some environments the conditions are bad for the desktop PC or the desktop PC is bad for the conditions. In other words, it's not feasible to put a desktop PC anywhere.

Some environments are bad for PCs. PCs don't like dust, excessive heat, or vibration, and you won't like maintaining the PCs if you try to use them in an environment that has any of these characteristics. Of course, PCs can be built to work in extreme conditions, such as temperatures as high as 120 degrees or even underwater. And for the companies and people who must have them in these extreme environments, engineers have designed solutions—but at a cost. When cost is an issue and a thin client will work, Remote Desktop Services can be a good solution.

We've also seen terminals in health club cafes and coffeehouses set up so that only the monitor is visible, thus reducing the chances of someone dropping a strawberry-banana low-fat smoothie with a shot of wheatgrass juice down the vents. For that matter, if someone does drop the smoothie down the terminal's vents, then because the applications are installed on and running from the RDS server, replacing the device to provide an identical environment is as simple as unplugging the sticky terminal and plugging in a new one. If you drop a smoothie down a computer's vents, then restoring an identical working environment is significantly more complicated.

What about PCs being bad for the conditions? Clean rooms where chips and boards are made are good candidates for Windows terminals. You can't have dust in a clean room, and the fans in a PC kick up dust. Additionally, becoming sanitized to enter a clean room is neither simple nor inexpensive; you don't want to put devices that need care and feeding from the IT staff in there. Another factor applies to many situations, not just clean rooms: anyplace where space is at a premium is a good candidate for a Windows terminal.

Clients can be running thin clients or just about any desktop operating system including Windows, Linux, and Macintosh (though security is optimized on Windows Vista or Windows 7/8).

This section isn't to sell you on the idea of Windows terminals but to point out that sometimes they're useful, even required—and you can't use them without an RDS server.

 **Real World Scenario**

POWER STRUGGLES

Another aspect of the environment-unfriendly PC applies to the power a desktop PC uses. Several studies have been published on the cost savings of thin clients versus desktop PCs. With the cost of power these days, the savings can be significant.

One study located at the following URL (www.thinclient.net/pdf/Thin_Client_Benefits_Paper.pdf) shows some of the possibilities. It is an old study but the principles still stand true for today. For example, a single thin client averaged about 10 watts a day while a desktop PC averaged 69 watts. This doesn't include the monitor, but both thin clients and PCs can use low-power LCD monitors instead of the power-hungry CRTs of the past.

The study estimated the cost of power at 0.10 per kWh and 0.20 per kWh, which is a good range of power costs within the United States. For 100 clients, this equated to savings of between $3,000 and $6,000 annually.

Saving on power costs isn't the only reason to use Windows terminals, but if you're tossing around the idea of replacing PCs with terminals, it's a compelling argument in favor of it.

Reducing Hardware Refreshes

Does it take a Core i5 2.5 GHz processor with 4 GB of RAM installed to check email, do accounting, and poke around on the Web a bit? Of course not, but as of mid-2013 that's not an unusual hardware profile for a desktop computer. Not that these computers are too expensive in absolute terms, but we are amused that every time we buy a new computer, we pay less for a system more powerful than the last one we bought.

Still, even though they're not too expensive in absolute terms, the new computers aren't always worth it because what you're doing doesn't demand all that much from your hardware. Ironically, unless your job is something demanding, such as computer-assisted design, you're more likely to need a powerful computer at home than at work because game hardware requirements are so high. It takes more computing power to play a few swift rounds of the most recent version of Warcraft than it does to write this chapter. (Fighting orcs is hard work!)

The trouble is, sometimes you do need those more powerful computers if you're planning to keep up with existing software technology. True, you don't need the world's fastest computer to do word processing. You may, however, need a computer faster than the one you have if you're going to keep up with the latest and greatest word processing package that everyone is using. If you want to be able to read all those charts and graphs, you can't always do it when the word processor you're using is six years old, even if it still suits your in-house needs. And you can't always run that new word processor if your computer is six years old.

You must also take into account the modern devices that are now available. Power consumption is paramount in these devices in order to make them light, portable, and last for a decent amount of "use" time. In order to reduce the power consumption manufacturers have also had to reduce the processing power of devices, so now in order to perform more intense functions, an RDS server becomes more important. This also holds true if a company adopts a BYOD strategy; for almost every platform a Remote Desktop client is available. This gives users the flexibility of purchasing and using the devices that they require while the corporate administrators maintain a control over the corporate system and desktop applications.

In summary, if you're using Remote Desktop Services with an RD Session Host server, the client only displays applications running on the RDS server rather than running them locally. You don't have to concern yourself with whether the applications will run on the client computer; your concern is just the server. If the application will run on the RD server and the client can get to the RD server, then the application will display on the client regardless of the platform.

Simplifying the User Interface

Another potential benefit to Remote Desktop Services is that it can simplify the user interface (UI). Using a computer isn't as easy for everyone as the marketing world would have you believe. Experienced users find it easy to customize their interface, but those who are less experienced find all sorts of pitfalls when it comes to using their computers: there are so many options that they get confused and there are too many ways to break something. Colorful icons with rounded corners do not a simple UI make.

If the people you're supporting need only a single application, then you can save yourself and them a lot of grief by providing a connection that runs this application in a remote desktop and nothing else. This is particularly true with Windows-based terminals, which are little more than a monitor, a box, a keyboard, and a mouse.

Or, if the users are already running a desktop operating system, you can use RemoteApp applications. RemoteApp applications deployed via RDS are as easy to use as any other applications on the end user's computer. RemoteApp applications can be launched from the Start menu, from a desktop icon (of an .rdp file), or from a web page.

Providing Help-desk Support

Finally, Remote Desktop Services can make application support easier, not just in terms of installing new applications and applying fixes but in terms of helping people learn to use those applications. *Remote Desktop Shadowing* (previously called Remote Control) lets help-desk personnel or administrators connect to another person's remote session either to watch what they're doing or to interact with the session. This doesn't happen automatically and requires some sort of input from an administrator and user. Also, you can control some of its behavior using a GPO.

When you have remote control of another user's session, you can either watch what they're doing and coach them (perhaps over the telephone) or actually interact with the session so that you can demonstrate a process. This beats standing over someone's shoulder saying, "Click the File button at the top left. No, File. The FILE button," or trying to figure out what they're doing when your only information comes from their description of the screen.

Deploying RDS RemoteApp

RemoteApp programs are applications that are running on the RD Session Host server but appear to the end user to be running on their desktop. This is often easier for an end user to conceptualize. They don't have to manage multiple desktops but instead can simply launch another application from their main desktop.

Windows Server 2008 introduced RemoteApp programs, and they've been improved in every generation of Windows since, including Windows 2012 R2. Here are some of the new enhancements brought into this release:

RemoteApp Rotation   Faster resolution and rotation on client machines including changing the remote session's resolution.

Monitor Hot-add/subtract   If you add a monitor, it will allow you to move the app to it and readjust if you remove it.

Click Once App Support   Users can now install apps directly from the browser, rather than having an administrator distribute and deploy them as in previous versions.

Hi-fi RemoteApp   This enables Windows RT to support apps that use Desktop Window Manager. You also now get transparent toast notifications with fadeaway effects.

Do take into account that it requires a bit of configuration to support RemoteApp programs. However, once you've configured all the pieces, users can access RemoteApp applications via the following methods:

Through a Web Browser   If RD Web Access is configured, users can access the web page and click a link to launch the application.

Using a Remote Desktop Protocol File   Users can simply double-click a properly configured .rdp file to launch the RemoteApp application.

Through the Start Menu or a Program Icon   RemoteApp applications can be installed using traditional Windows Installer (.msi) packages (also called Microsoft Installer packages). Once they're installed, users can launch the applications just like any other installed application. Or they can use the new Click Once deployment method.

You'll learn how to install all the components and deploy RemoteApp applications for each of these methods in the section "Adding Remote Desktop Services" later in this chapter.

Understanding the Remote Desktop Services Processing Model

Thin-client networking or *server-based computing* (same thing, different emphasis) refers to any computing environment in which most application processing takes place on a server enabled for multiuser access, instead of a client. The terms refer to a network by definition, so that doesn't include stand-alone small computing devices, such as smartphones and tablet computers, although you can add thin-client support to some of these devices.

What makes thin-client networking and computing "thin" is neither the size of the operating system nor the complexity of the apps run on the client but how processing is distributed. In a thin-client network, most if not all processing takes place on the server. Instructions for creating video output travel from server to client, mouse clicks and keystrokes pass from the client to the server, and all video output is rendered on the client.

Son of Mainframe?

You may have heard thin-client networking described as "a return to the mainframe paradigm." (We have heard this less politely phrased as "You just reinvented the mainframe, stupid!") This comparison is partly apt and partly misleading. It's true that applications are stored and run on a central server, with only output shown at the client.

TABLET AND THIN CLIENTS

Tablets have exploded on the scene, and you may be wondering how they fit in here. In case you've just gotten off a desert island, a tablet is a small (7- to 10-inch screen) portable computer designed for communication on the Internet primarily but has also evolved to be a device for all sorts of purposes in our daily lives. They usually have more resources than a thin client but significantly less than a full-blown desktop PC. Because of their size, they are highly mobile. They use less processing power, less RAM, and simpler graphics (but they are catching up at an unparalleled rate), which all contribute to using less power and to a longer battery life.

It's entirely possible to use these devices as part of a Remote Desktop solution. These devices could connect to the Remote Desktop server either directly over the Internet using RD Gateway or via a VPN. The applications or desktops can be executed on the Remote Desktop server so that the netbook's hardware resources aren't overly taxed.

However, the applications being run in the thin-client environment are different from those run in a mainframe environment; mainframes didn't support word processing or slide show packages, and the video demands on the graphical Windows client are necessarily greater than they were with a text-based green-screen terminal. Yet the degree of control that thin-client networking offers is mainframe-like, and we've heard one person happily describe thin-client networking and the command it gave him over his user base as "a return to the good-old mainframe days."

Why the move from centralized computing to personal computers and back again? Business applications drove the development of PCs—the new applications simply couldn't work in a mainframe environment. Not all mainframes were scrapped, by any means, but the newer application designs were too hardware intensive to work well in a shared computing environment. But those applications came back to a centralized model when it became clear that the mainframe model had some things to offer that a PC-based LAN did not:

♦ Grouping of computing resources to make sure none are wasted

♦ Centralized distribution and maintenance of applications

♦ Clients that don't have to be running the latest and greatest operating system with the latest and greatest hardware to support it

♦ Client machines that don't require power protection because they're not running any applications locally

All in all, reinventing the mainframe has its advantages. Just as PCs didn't replace mainframes, server-based computing isn't replacing PCs. However, it's nice to have the option to use server-based computing when it makes more sense than installing applications on the desktop.

Anatomy of a Thin-client Session

A thin-client networking session has three parts:

The RDS Server Runs a multiuser operating system

The Remote Desktop A multichannel protocol that allows for separate channels to carry a variety of information (including presentation data, control info, license info, and so on)

The Client Can be running any kind of operating system that supports the terminal client

These are explained in detail in the following sections.

THE RDS SERVER

Remote Desktop Services is one of the optional components you can choose to install on Windows Server 2012 R2. If you've added the Remote Desktop Services role, RDS begins listening at TCP port 3389 for incoming client connection requests as soon as the server boots up and loads the core operating system. Remember to configure the firewall to allow the port in.

Understanding Sessions

When a client requests a connection to the server and the server accepts the request, the client's unique view of the RDS server is called its *session*. In addition to the remote sessions, a special client session for the console is created.

DESKTOP PCS CAN'T RUN RDS

Some have asked whether there's any way to make Windows XP, Windows Vista, Windows 7, or Windows 8 into a multiuser server (of sorts). Nope—no Microsoft desktop operating system includes full-fledged Remote Desktop Services, and there is no way to add it. Windows XP, Windows Vista, Windows 7, and Windows 8 all include the Remote Desktop feature that allows someone to connect to the computer via the RDP display protocol. However, only one connection is supported at a time. The Remote Desktop Services feature we discuss in this chapter is solely a server-class feature.

All sessions have unique session IDs that the server uses to distinguish the processes running within different RDS sessions on the same computer. In this context, processes are roughly equivalent to executable files. When a client connects to the RDS server, a session ID is created for the session.

Figure 29.1 shows the Remote Desktop Services console in Server Manager monitoring sessions running on an RDS server.

FIGURE 29.1
Remote Desktop
Services Manager

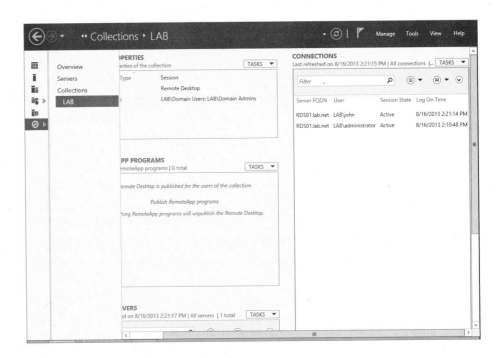

Every desktop session has several base processes running within it to support the user. Additional processes in the session will depend on the applications the user is running.

EXECUTABLES, IMAGES, AND THREADS

In Windows operating systems, an executable file is internally known as an *image*. This is because, technically speaking, an application isn't the piece getting processor cycles but instead is a collection of commands called *threads* that get processor time to do whatever they need to do. The threads have an environment called the *process* that tells them where to store and retrieve their data. The part of the process that does something is collectively called the *image* or *executable*. For the sake of consistency with the interface, we'll refer to programs running on the RDS server as *processes*.

The session keeps per-session processes from corrupting each other or viewing each other's data. However, although the sessions are allowed to ignore each other, they still have to coexist. All sessions use the same resources—processor time, memory, and operating system functions—so the operating system must divide the use of these resources among all the sessions. To do so, the RDS server identifies the processes initiated in each session not only by their process ID but by their session ID as well.

Each session has a high-priority thread reserved for keyboard and mouse input and display output, but ordinary applications run at the priority they'd have in a single-user environment. Because all session threads have the same priority, the scheduler processes user input in round-robin format, with each session's input thread having a certain amount of time to process data before control of the processor passes to another user thread. If the sessions are very active, there'll be much more competition for processor time.

The number of sessions an RDS server can support depends on how many sessions the hardware (generally memory but also processor time, network bandwidth, and disk access) can support and how many licenses are available. When a client logs out of their session, the virtual channels to that client machine close, and the resources allocated to that session are released.

THE REMOTE DESKTOP PROTOCOL—UNDER THE HOOD

You can run all the sessions you like on the RDS server, but that won't do you any good unless you can view the session output from a remote computer and upload your input to the terminal server for processing. The mechanism that allows you to do both (and many other things) is the *Remote Desktop Protocol.*

How the Remote Desktop Protocol Works

The Remote Desktop Protocol (RDP) downloads instructions for rendering graphical images from the RDS server to the client and uploads keyboard and mouse input from the client to the server. Remote Desktop Services natively supports the Remote Desktop Protocol. RDP provides a point-to-point connection dependent on TCP/IP that displays either the desktop or a single application on the desktop of a client running RDP.

The processing demands placed on the client are reduced by a feature called *client-side caching* that allows the client to "remember" images that have already been downloaded during the session. With caching, only the changed parts of the screen are downloaded to the client during each refresh. For example, if the Microsoft Word icon has already been downloaded to the client, there's no need for it to be downloaded again as the image of the desktop is updated. The hard disk's cache stores data for a limited amount of time and then eventually discards data using the least recently used (LRU) algorithm. When the cache gets full, it discards the data that has been unused the longest in favor of new data.

RDP, as previously mentioned, has had many changes over the years. The following article will allow you to get a full understanding of the Remote Desktop Protocol:

```
http://support.microsoft.com/kb/186607
```

AUTOMATIC REFRESH TIMING

The image on the screen is updated at very short intervals when the session is active. If the person logged in to the session stops sending mouse clicks and keystrokes to the server, then the RD server notes the inactivity and reduces the refresh rate until client activity picks up again.

Note that in addition to each client session, there's also a session for the server's use. All locally run services and executables run within the context of this server session.

RDP Protocol Versions

RDP has been around since NT 4.0 days (the first version was RDP 4.0) and has had a lot of upgrades. The current version available with Windows Server 2012 R2 is version 8.1.

Although there have been many incremental changes to the protocol, the core focus in Windows Server 2012 and R2 is on WAN optimization, providing easier administration over all components, reduced storage and network costs using online Data Deduplication (Dedup), and full support for storage spaces and tier storage. As you can see, RDP has come a long way since NT 4.0.

THE CLIENT

The client improvements are in line with what we have discussed for the Remote Desktop Protocol. You should make sure that the client supports the latest RDP version that the RDS server supports. Otherwise, you will not get all the nice features and benefits of the later protocols.

Server and Client Requirements

The computing model for thin-client networking means that the horsepower is concentrated on the server end, not the client end. Because the server will be supporting dozens of people—maybe hundreds—this is not the time to skimp on power.

Server Hardware

The notion of using a bigger server so that you can skimp on client-side hardware isn't new. That's all a file server is: a computer running a big, fast hard disk so that you don't have to buy big, fast hard disks for everyone in the office. RDS servers are designed on a similar principle—if most of the processing takes place in a single location, you can concentrate the hardware resources needed to support that processing in a single location and worry less about power on the client end.

USE A POWERFUL RD SESSION HOST SERVER

Since an RD Session Host server will be serving applications or full desktops to clients, you'll need to purchase or build a powerful server. (Although good practice would be to have multiple less-powerful hosts, so you can distribute the load.)

Processing power and RAM are the most important resources. Depending on the types and number of sessions you're supporting, you may also want to consider boosting disk access and network bandwidth.

On the surface, calculating the needs seems straightforward. Just follow these steps:

1. Calculate the resources needed for the operating system.

2. Calculate the resources needed for a small number of sessions (such as 5).

3. Multiply the resources needed for your sessions based on the total number of sessions you plan to support.

> If you plan to support 100 sessions, for example, and you measured 5 sessions, you'd multiply by 20 to get to 100 sessions ($20 \times 5 = 100$ sessions). So if you need 4 GB of RAM to support 5 Sessions you need 4 GB $\times$ 20 which will require you to have 80 GB of RAM to support 100 sessions. By the way, the multiplier 20 is obtained by dividing the total number of sessions you want (100 in this case) by the sample number of sessions (5 in this case).
>
> **4.** Add the total session resources needed for sessions to the resources needed for the operating system.
>
> Although this seems like simple math, it never seems to work out that way. Synergy is often hard to predict. Synergy (where the whole is greater than the sum of its parts) often results in something unexpected. Additionally, if the deployment is successful and users are happy with what they can do, they may end up using it much more than you anticipated.
>
> You don't need to tell this to the budget people, but it's best to add a buffer for the unknowns and to plan for expansion. Several vendors publish "reference architectures" for their hardware platforms that you can also use to help you decide on the resources for the platform.

CORE HARDWARE RESOURCES

For the purposes of running an efficient RD Session Host server, the bare minimum required to run Server 2012 R2 won't cut it. Although there are no hard-and-fast specifications for an RDS server, some general guidelines for server sizing follow:

Processor   Faster is better to a point. More important than a fast processor is one with enough cache so that it doesn't have to reach out to the (slower) system memory for code and data. Faced with a choice between more cache and more speed, go with more cache. Most RDS servers these days have multiple processors, and these processors have multiple cores. Although only multithreaded applications will actually use more than one processor at a time, if there are multiple processors, the threads needing execution can line up at both.

Memory   RDS servers tend to be memory bound, not processor bound. Get high-speed, error-correcting memory; get plenty of it; and be prepared to add more as you add more users or applications to the RDS server. However, sometimes adding another box to reduce the load is better because there is only so much memory you can add before it negatively impacts the system. The amount of memory you'll need depends on the applications that people use, the number of concurrent sessions, and the memory demands of the files opened in those sessions—computer-aided design (CAD) programs will stress the system more than, say, Notepad. Thankfully, the 64-bit operating system goes well beyond the 4 GB limit. Start your calculations with at least 8 GB of RAM for the server, and start adding based on the number of users and memory required by the applications they'll run on the server. Windows Server 2012 R2 will support up to 4 TB of RAM.

Disk   Consider using Serial Computer System Interface (SCSI) disks on an RDS server if at all possible. An SCSI disk controller can multitask among all the devices in the SCSI chain. Most people believe that SCSI performs much better than both Serial Advanced Technology Attachment (SATA) and Enhanced Integrated Drive Electronics (EIDE) disks, although some people are starting to find that high-end SATA solutions perform better than low-end SCSI solutions. Disk performance is an important capability in any server but especially in an RDS server.

Additionally, consider a Redundant Array of Inexpensive Disks (RAID) solution to increase the performance and/or fault tolerance of the drives. For a high-end RDS server, a RAID 1+0 solution provides both performance gains and redundancy. If you're deploying in a virtualized environment, consider the underlying storage tier as well. Use high-performance SSD when possible and Fixed VHDX for the operating system.

Network   On a busy RDS server, consider NIC-teaming for high-speed network cards, which can assign multiple NICs to the same IP address and thus split the load of network traffic. An alternative is a multihomed server with one NIC dedicated to RDS session traffic. As far as network *speed* goes, sending application output and client-side input back and forth requires little bandwidth, but client print jobs sent to mapped printers can take quite a bit of bandwidth. Mapped drives may also increase the load by making it possible to copy files back and forth across the RDP connection.

USING PERFORMANCE MONITOR

Performance Monitor can help you get an idea of how RDS sessions are stressing the server. Server load should scale closely with the number of people using the server; therefore, as long as you pick a representative group of about five people, you should be able to extrapolate your needs for larger groups. The key objects and counters introduced for measuring general server stress can be found in a free tool called Performance Analysis of Logs (located at `http://pal .codeplex.com`); these will help you size your RDS servers. But a couple of Performance Monitor objects are worth examining to give you detailed information for your RDS server.

PERFORMANCE MONITOR OBJECTS STILL CALLED TERMINAL SERVICES

Although the name of Terminal Services has been changed to Remote Desktop Services since Windows Server 2008 R2, it's still called Terminal Services in Performance Monitor. It might look like a typo, but the two objects are called Terminal Services and Terminal Services Session.

First, the Terminal Services object has counters representing the number of active sessions (sessions where the user has connected to the RD Session Host server and successfully logged on), inactive sessions (where the user is still logged onto the RDS server but has stopped using the session), and the total combined.

Besides simply monitoring activity, you could use this to alert you when the number of active sessions reaches a certain threshold. Say you wanted to know when a server hosts more than 100 sessions. You could do this with a data collector set.

In Performance Monitor, it's possible to set up a simple user-defined data collector set with an alert. This is done by creating the user-defined data collector set manually (not with a template), selecting Performance Counter Alert, and then setting the threshold for the active sessions. You can then set a task for the alert to notify you with a basic script or log the event to a file.

Although you can get some session-level information from the Remote Desktop Services Manager, a performance object called Terminal Services Session provides quite a bit more data. Use the Remote Desktop Services Manager to find the session you want to monitor—sessions are identified in Performance Monitor by their session numbers, not user login name—and then add counters to monitor that session. Each session object has processor and memory counters that should look familiar to anyone who's used Performance Monitor, but it also has session-specific counters such as the ones in Table 29.1. We haven't included all the counters here, just the ones that show you the kind of information that will be useful when you're calculating the load on the server and looking at the kind of performance the sessions are getting.

TABLE 29.1:   Key Terminal Services Session Performance Monitor Counters

COUNTER	DESCRIPTION	SEE ALSO
% Processor Time	Percentage of time that all of the threads in the session used the processor to execute instructions. On multiprocessor machines the maximum value of the counter is 100 percent times the number of processors.	
Total Bytes	Total number of bytes sent to and from this session, including all protocol overhead.	Input Bytes, Output Bytes
Total Compressed Bytes	Total number of bytes after compression. Total Compressed Bytes compared with Total Bytes is the compression ratio.	Total Compression Ratio
Total Protocol Cache Hit Ratio	Total hits in all protocol caches holding Windows objects likely to be reused. Hits in the cache represent objects that did not need to be re-sent, so a higher hit ratio implies more cache reuse and possibly a more responsive session.	Protocol Save Screen Bitmap Cache Hit Ratio, Protocol Glyph Cache Hit Ratio, Protocol Brush Cache Hit Ratio
Working Set	Current number of bytes in the working set of this session.	Virtual Bytes, Page Faults/Sec

---

WAIT ON THE LICENSE SERVER

When experimenting with Remote Desktop sessions to find out how many users you'll be able to support for each session, do not set up a license server; let the RDS server issue its temporary 120-day licenses for this purpose. Although this sounds counterintuitive, using the temporary licenses prevents you from unwittingly assigning per-device licenses to test equipment. See the "Licensing Mode" section for an explanation of how licensing and license allocation works.

Client Hardware

When connecting to an RD Session Host server via a native RDP client, you'll most often use a PC with a Windows operating system loaded, a Windows terminal.

NATIVE RDP CLIENT

In this context, a native RDP client means one available from Microsoft and thus implies Windows. Although Microsoft does not support other platforms (except for its OS X Macintosh client, available for download at www.microsoft.com/mac/products/remote-desktop/default.mspx), Hobsoft sells a cross-platform (Windows, Mac, Linux, DOS) Java client at www.hobsoft.com/products/connect/jwt.jsp, and there is a free Linux RDP client available at www.rdesktop.org.

WINDOWS TERMINALS

In its narrowest definition, a *Windows terminal* is a network-dependent device running Windows CE that supports one or more display protocols such as RDP or Independent Computing Architecture (ICA), the display protocol used to connect to Presentation Server servers. Many Windows terminals also support some form of terminal emulation.

For this section, think of a Windows terminal as any terminal device designed to connect to a Windows RD Session Host server; it can run any operating system that has an RDP client. A Windows-based terminal (WBT) is such a device that's running a Windows operating system locally and follows the Microsoft system design requirements for WBTs.

The main thing defining a Windows terminal is its thin hardware profile: because the main job of most Windows terminals is to run a display protocol, they don't need much memory or processing power, and they don't use any storage. A Windows terminal includes a processor; some amount of memory, network, and video support; and input devices such as a keyboard (or equivalent) and mouse (or equivalent). The terminals don't generally have hard disks, CD-ROMs, or DVD players. The operating system is stored in local memory. Beyond those similarities, Windows terminals range physically from a "toaster" form factor to a pad to a small box that can attach to the back of a monitor—or even be part of the monitor itself. Some models of Windows terminals are wireless tablets, intended for people (such as doctors and nurses) who would ordinarily use clipboards and folders to store information.

Although most Windows terminals are entirely dependent on their RDS server, a small set of them can run applications locally. The devices still don't have hard disks; the applications are stored in ROM like the operating system. The types of applications available depend on the terminal's operating system, since locally stored applications must run locally instead of just being displayed. Generally speaking, however, it's more common for Windows terminals to depend on an RDS server for applications.

Windows terminals are most popular in environments where people are using a single application, where supporting PCs would be logistically difficult, or anywhere else that PCs aren't a good fit. However, PCs still outnumber Windows terminals as thin clients. Part of this is because many environments can't depend totally on server-based computing. Companies already have PCs, and unless they're refreshing the desktop entirely, taking away a powerful PC to replace it with a less-powerful terminal doesn't really make sense.

PC CLIENTS

At this point, people are using more than twice as many PCs as Windows terminals for RDS server client machines. This isn't surprising.

♦ First, unless they're starting fresh, people already have the PCs. Even though WBTs are a little less expensive than low-end PCs (not much, though), they're still an added cost.

♦ Second, not all applications work well in an RDS server environment. It's often best to run some applications from the RDS server and some locally.

Unless you're buying new hardware and don't anticipate any need to run applications locally, you're likely to have to work with PCs for at least some of your terminal clients.

To work with Remote Desktop Services, the PCs must be running a Windows operating system, have the RDP display protocol installed, and have a live network connection using TCP/IP and a valid IP address.

TABLETS

We're not surprised that tablets are so commonplace today, given how handy they are. They're a terrific substitute for a laptop—inexpensive, lightweight, and thrifty with their power so that travelers can actually use them during the entire flight instead of having to give up two hours after takeoff. (You can also use one on a plane without worrying that the person in front of you will suddenly recline their seat and crack your laptop's display.) Usually, they run Windows or Android or Apple IOS. You can use wired or wireless LAN connections to connect to an RDS server with VPN or without.

What a tablet looks like depends on who makes it. Some tablets look like a laptop's baby brother, like Microsoft Surface. Others fold into a little portfolio shape or are a flat tablet. Some are small pocket-sized deals that are too small to really work on. Some—the ones we prefer—have keyboards; others have only styluses. What all this comes down to is that a tablet isn't generally in a position to replace a desktop PC, although there are some exceptions like the Microsoft Surface Pro, which is a tablet with a keyboard that has the power of a desktop. A tablet is usually used in cooperation with a primary machine which it's partnered with in some way, using OneNote or SkyDrive, for example.

Adding Remote Desktop Services

You can add the Remote Desktop Services role to any domain-joined Windows Server 2012 R2 server using Server Manager. Server Manager includes wizards that allow you to add many roles, and you've probably already used it.

When adding the RDS role, the Add Roles and Features Wizard first gives you a dedicated menu (see Figure 29.2). Then it will ask you further RDS-specific questions.

The following sections provide the knowledge you need to answer these questions and successfully add the role. Topics related to an RD Session Host server installation include the following:

♦ Additional role services

♦ Network Level Authentication

♦ Licensing mode

♦ Local Remote Desktop Users group membership

♦ Adding applications

FIGURE 29.2
Add Roles and
Features Wizard

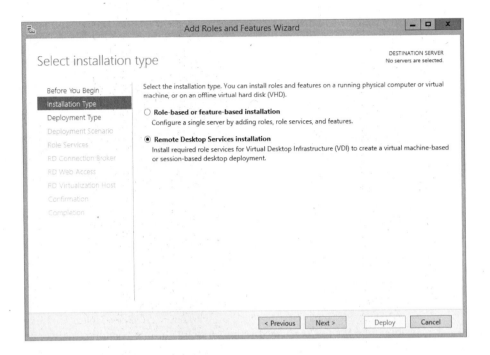

After you install the role, you'll need to configure the server. This section will guide you through the decision-making process and the steps to add and configure the server.

REMOTE DESKTOP SERVICES NOT NEEDED FOR ADMINISTRATOR CONNECTIONS

Remote Desktop Services is not needed to connect to a server for administrator connections. Chapter 17, "Remote Server Administration," covers remotely connecting to a server using Remote Desktop Connection (RDC) or Remote Desktops. To use these tools, you don't need to install Remote Desktop Services. Instead, you only need to enable Remote Desktop connections on the server.

A significant difference between remotely connecting for administrator purposes and using an RD Session Host server is that licenses aren't needed for administrator connections. Any server can support as many as two remote administrator connections without a license. However, licenses are required for RD Session Host server connections on one-to-one basis. In other words, you'll need a license for every connection.

Required Role Services

Remote Desktop Services is a server role and includes several role services. All of the services aren't required for every installation. You'll need to evaluate what you're trying to accomplish to determine which services to add.

Remote Desktop Session Host   The RD Session Host service enables the server to host Windows-based programs or a full Windows desktop. This is a required service for the role.

Remote Desktop Virtualization Host   The RD Virtualization Host service is integrated with Hyper-V to allow users to connect to a virtual machine on a server hosting Hyper-V. It can be configured so that users will connect to their own unique virtual machine and allow users to run multiple operating systems simultaneously. This service requires the Hyper-V role service and is needed if you are using the Hyper-V role service.

Remote Desktop Licensing   The RD Licensing service manages the Client Access Licenses (RDS CALs) that are needed to connect to an RD Session Host server. It's possible to run Remote Desktop Services without licenses for a limited grace period of 120 days. This allows you time to deploy, configure, and test the server.

Remote Desktop Connection Broker   The RD Connection Broker service is used for session load balancing and session reconnection in an RD Session Host server farm. It's also required to support RDS RemoteApp applications that allow users to launch applications on the RD Session Host server via Internet Explorer.

If you are using multiple RD Session Host servers, the RD Connection Broker can redirect connections to the servers that are the least busy, which provides load balancing. Additionally, if a user is disconnected, the RD Connection Broker will ensure they are reconnected to the same server where their session is active.

Remote Desktop Gateway   The RD Gateway service is used to allow users to connect to RD Session Host servers and remote desktops over the Internet. This service requires additional role services including Web Server (IIS), Network Policy and Access Services, RPC over HTTP Proxy, and Remote Server Administration Tools.

We covered Remote Desktop Gateway in much greater depth in Chapter 17, including how to add the required services and enable it.

Remote Desktop Web Access   The RD Web Access service allows users to access RemoteApp and Remote Desktop Connection through a web browser. If the clients are running Windows 7, they can access these through the Start menu on their system. This service requires additional supporting role services including Web Server (IIS) and Remote Server Administration Tools. IIS is short for Microsoft's Internet Information Services.

APPLICATION COMPATIBILITY

If you plan on using the RD Session Host server to host applications for end users, you should *first* install RDS before installing the applications. Applications that are installed before adding the RD Session Host role may not work correctly in a multiple-user environment.

Although some applications will work in multiuser mode even if they've already been installed, many will not. If you've already installed applications that you want to use with the RD Session Host server, you should consider uninstalling the applications before adding the Remote Desktop Services role.

Easy Print

A neat new feature available since Windows Server 2008 is called Easy Print. Easy Print ensures that client printers are always installed in remote sessions without requiring printer drivers to be installed on the terminal server. There have been no updates to Easy Print since Windows 2008 R2.

This might not seem like much, but in the past, you were required to install printer drivers on the terminal server for all the printers used by clients. If you have just 50 clients and they were using 10 different print devices, you'd then need to install printer drivers for all 10 print devices on the server even if they were already installed on the client's systems.

Now you may be wondering what you need to do to support Easy Print. The answer is almost nothing. The support is there automatically as long as Remote Desktop Services is installed on Server 2008 R2 and above.

Clients need to be running RDC 6.1 and the Microsoft .NET Framework 3.0 with SP1. RDC 6.1 is backward compatible to XP SP3 with a download, as mentioned earlier. Microsoft .NET Framework 3.0 with SP1 is available for download for XP clients from Microsoft's download site: www.microsoft.com/downloads. Search for "Microsoft .NET Framework 3.0 Service Pack 1."

Single Sign-on

Single sign-on (SSO) is the ability for users to provide their credentials once and use these credentials for the entire session. As long as these credentials have adequate permissions, users aren't asked to provide them again. Without single sign-on, users can be queried several times to provide the same username and password.

You can implement single sign-on for users who access the RDS server using Windows XP SP3, Windows Vista, and Windows 7 clients or from Windows Server 2008 or 2008 R2 servers.

Two settings are required in the RDP TCP/IP Connection properties. You'll see graphics of these later, but here are the two settings:

- Ensure that the Security layer is set to either Negotiate or SSL (TLS 1.0) on the General tab of the RDP TCP/IP Connection properties.

- Ensure that "Always prompt for password" is not selected in the "Log on" settings of the RDP TCP/IP Connection properties.

In Windows Server 2008, SSO was quite difficult to set up. In Windows Server 2012 (including R2), SSO has been simplified to work almost out of the box. There is a small pitfall to this ease of enablement: the accessing client must support RDP 8.0, the virtual desktop infrastructure must be Windows 8, and the servers must be 2012 and above. If you still require a mixed environment, you must configure SSO the traditional way.

Here are two links to help you further in the quest of enabling SSO:

http://blogs.msdn.com/b/rds/archive/2009/08/11/introducing-web-single-sign-on-for-remoteapp-and-desktop-connections.aspx

http://blogs.msdn.com/b/rds/archive/2012/06/25/remote-desktop-web-access-single-sign-on-now-easier-to-enable-in-windows-server-2012.aspx

Network Level Authentication

Network Level Authentication (NLA) can be used in Remote Desktop sessions to provide better security. When adding the Remote Desktop Services role, you need to specify whether NLA is required. Your decision is based on the clients the RD Session Host server will support.

NLA ensures that the authentication is completed before a full Remote Desktop connection is established. Without NLA, there is a small window of opportunity for a malicious user or malicious software to attack, even if authentication is unsuccessful.

NLA is available by default in Windows Vista, Windows 7, and Windows 8. It relies on the Credential Security Support Provider (CredSSP). If all the clients are running Windows Vista, Windows 7, or Windows 8, then you should require Network Level Authentication on the RD Session Host server.

Windows XP doesn't natively support NLA. However, if you upgrade to SP3 and enable CredSSP, you can use NLA. You need to modify the registry to use CredSSP in Windows XP SP3. Check out these two Microsoft Knowledge Base articles for more information:

♦ KB article 951608, "Description of the Credential Security Support Provider (CredSSP) in Windows XP Service Pack 3": http://support.microsoft.com/kb/951608/

♦ KB article 951616, "Description of the Remote Desktop Connection 6.1 client update for Terminal Services": http://support.microsoft.com/kb/951616

If your clients are older than Windows XP SP3, they cannot connect using NLA, and NLA should not be enabled.

Licensing Mode

You'll be required to select the licensing mode when you configure Remote Desktop Services. The licensing mode specifies what type of Remote Desktop Services Client Access Licenses (RDS CALs) you'll use. You have three choices:

Configure Later   You'll have a grace period of 120 days to configure licensing and select a licensing mode. It's common to choose this option early in the deployment cycle and then configure the RDS CALs once you've worked out the kinks in your RD environment.

Per Device   A per-device CAL is issued to a client computer or device. If the licensing mode is set to Per Device and a licensing server has been configured, the licensing server will issue the device a temporary license the first time the device connects. The second time the device connects, the licensing server will attempt to issue it a permanent license.

The licensing server will enforce per-device CALs. In other words, if a per-device CAL doesn't exist for the device and an RDS CAL isn't available to be issued, the connection will be blocked.

You should use per-device CALs if multiple users will use the same device to connect to an RD Session Host server.

Per User   A per-user CAL allows a user to connect to an RD Session Host server from any number of devices. Interestingly, the license server doesn't track the per-user CALs. This can make things both easier and more difficult. It's easier to manage on a day-to-day basis because the RD Session Host server won't stop users from connecting. However, administrators still have a responsibility to ensure that appropriate CALs have been purchased, which does take some extra administration.

You should use a per-user CAL if users will connect to an RD Session Host server from multiple devices.

A Remote Desktop Services Licensing server needs to be configured to install, issue, and track RDS CALs. Clients won't be able to connect to the RD Session Host server if RDS CALs haven't been purchased and added to the licensing server after the grace period.

Remote Desktop Users Group

Users need to be members of the local Remote Desktop Users group in order to connect to the RS Session Host server. You can add them when you add the role or add them later. The Administrators group is added to the Remote Desktop Users group by default.

Two Remote Desktop Users groups exist: one in the domain and a local group on the RD Session Host server. You need to add users and groups into the *local* group to grant access for them to connect.

It's not uncommon for an administrator to incorrectly add users to the domain Remote Desktop Users group thinking this will grant access to the RD Session Host server. After a little bit of head banging or hair pulling, the little word *local* is noticed. Once users are added to the local group, things work just as advertised. This can all be avoided through proper planning and placement and at installation.

Adding the Remote Desktop Services Role

You can use the following steps to install Remote Desktop Services. A word of warning, though: you really need to install this on a computer that isn't a domain controller. In our example environment, we're using one server as a DC (named AD-01) and two other servers as the RDS servers (named RDS01 and RDS01) in a domain named lab.net.

1. Log onto a member server.

2. If Server Manager doesn't launch automatically, launch it by selecting Start ≻ Administrative Tools ≻ Server Manager.

3. In Server Manager, click Manage and then Add Roles and Features.

    This will invoke the Add Roles and Features Wizard.

4. Click Next to continue.

    As we mentioned earlier in this chapter, rather than selecting the role as you did in previous versions of Windows, you can select the option for Remote Desktop Services installation.

5. Select that and then click Next.

    You then need to choose the deployment type. There are two options: a standard deployment, which will allow you to deploy across multiple servers, or a quick start.

6. Choose the standard deployment and click Next.

7. Now you need to choose the deployment scenario.

    In this instance we are selecting session-based desktop deployment. Later in this chapter we will demonstrate the virtual machine–based desktop deployment options.

As part of a standard deployment three roles are installed:

◆ Remote Desktop Connection Broker

◆ Remote Desktop Web Access

◆ Remote Desktop Session Host

8. Click Next to continue.

Over the next few steps, you will be required to add the relevant servers you want to configure.

9. Repeat step 8 for each role.

10. Review the information in the Confirmation screen.

You will need to check the "Restart the destination server automatically if required" box before you can click the Deploy button.

The server will restart as part of the deployment (unfortunately the installer does not set up autologon, so you will have to pay attention and log on again to complete the installation).

After you log on, it's normal to get informational messages related to the Remote Desktop Services Server License server since it has not yet been installed or configured (if there is one already in the enterprise).

The Add Roles and Features Wizard will relaunch, and the installation will finish.

11. Verify that all roles installed successfully.

In Windows Server 2012 (including R2) you now configure Remote Desktop Services directly from Server Manager.

12. Click Remote Desktop Services from within Server Manager.

This will bring you into the Overview screen, as shown in Figure 29.3.

Configuring RDS in Windows Server 2012 (R2) is a little different than in previous versions, and the options that you would have normally configured as part of the wizard are now configured separately.

13. Click the Tasks button beside Deployment Overview and select Edit Deployment Properties.

The deployment properties include several options, but the one of most interest is the configuration of the licensing. This is where you choose between per-device and per-user CALs.

14. For this example choose Per User; see Figure 29.4.

Next, in order to allow users to connect and configure parameters (including allowed groups), you must create a collection.

15. From the Deployment Overview window shown in Figure 29.3, scroll to the bottom where RD Session Host is listed. Right-click and select Create Session Collection.

FIGURE 29.3
Overview of
Remote Desktop
Services

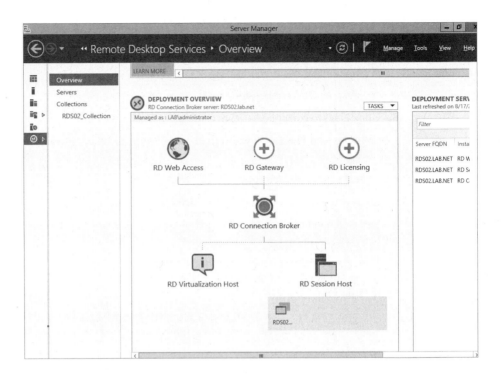

FIGURE 29.4
Deployment
properties

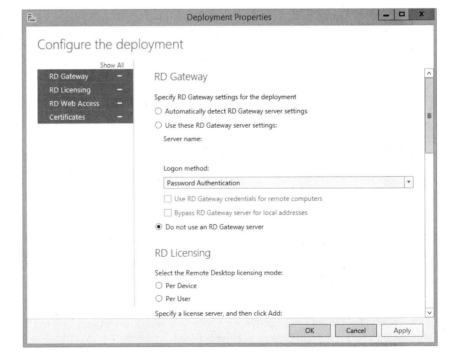

This will invoke the Collection Wizard.

16. Bypass the Begin screen, and enter a descriptive name for the Collection Name.

In our example we are entering RDS02_Collection.

17. Select the RDS servers to deploy this collection to.

In our case we are selecting RDS02.

18. Select the group for which you want allow access to the RDS server.

In our case we are leaving the default of Domain Users (but it could be any group).

19. Select the location and size limit of users' profiles on the RDS server.

This was a huge problem in previous versions since everything usually got stored on the System drive.

20. Because it's a demo environment, turn it off for now.

21. Confirm your choices and create the session collection.

That completes a basic configuration for allowing users to connect.

You may have noticed by now that you traditionally had to configure and review a significant number of settings before committing the server to production. In Server Manager, under Remote Desktop Services, you will now see a Collections menu, and under the Collections menu, you will now see the collection you just configured, as shown in Figure 29.5.

FIGURE 29.5
Collection
configuration

On the Properties section of this screen click Tasks ≻ Edit Properties. This will allow you to configure additional groups, session options, and a range of other items. See Figure 29.6 for a sample of the options you can configure.

FIGURE 29.6
Collection
properties

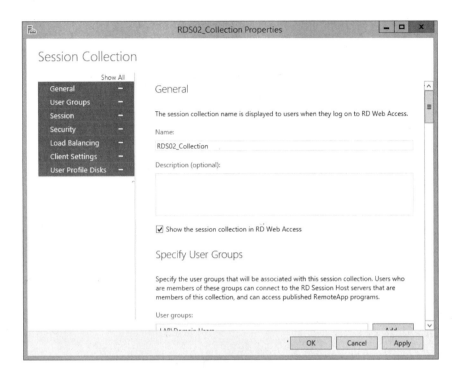

Adding Applications

Although many applications will work automatically in multiuser mode (such as Paint, Calculator, and Notepad), other applications need to be installed. Previous versions of Remote Desktop Services (called Terminal Services) required extra steps to install the applications, but the process is much simpler with RDS.

After the role has been added, you can install any application using an .msi (Windows Installer) file or via the Control Panel's Add/Remove Programs Wizard. If the application will install via one of these methods, that's all that's necessary.

However, if you have a legacy application that won't install via one of these methods, you'll need to use the Change User command. The three-step process is as follows:

1. Execute the Change User /install command from the command prompt.

This puts the RDS server into installation mode.

2. Install the application.

3. Execute the Change User /execute command from the command prompt.

This returns the RDS server to the normal mode of operation.

Connecting to an RDS Session

After adding the RDS role, clients who are members of the Domain Users group can access desktop sessions on the RD Session Host server. During configuration, we added the Domain Users group, which in turn got added to the Remote Desktop Users group. Be careful if you manually edit this group because the changes are not reflected in the Remote Desktop Services UI. Now let's connect to the newly created RD Session Host and collection.

1. Click Start, type **MSTSC** in the Search box, and press Enter.

   This will launch the Remote Desktop Connection console. For a full description of all the options available in this tool, you can check out Chapter 17.

2. Click the Options button.

3. Enter the name of the computer hosting RDS in the Computer box, and enter the user-name of a user in the local Remote Desktop Users group.

   Your display will look similar to Figure 29.7.

FIGURE 29.7

Connecting with Remote Desktop Connection

4. Click Connect.

   A Windows Security screen will appear, and you will be prompted to enter the password for the user.

5. Enter the password, and click OK.

   Security will be negotiated, and after a moment, you will be connected to the desktop. Depending on how MSTSC was configured, the connection may start as a window on the desktop or in full-screen mode. Figure 29.8 shows the connection. Notice it has a Windows 8 look and feel.

FIGURE 29.8
Connected to
the RD Session
Host server using
Remote Desktop
Connection

Although this verifies that you have successfully installed RDS and can connect to RDS sessions, the sessions are still plain desktops. You can install applications on the RD Session Host server and make them available to all users, or you can use RD RemoteApp applications to allow users to run the applications in Windows on their desktops.

Adding an RDS RemoteApp Application

Remote Desktop RemoteApp applications are a neat feature with RDS. Once added and configured, they will run in their own window on the end user's computer. Instead of a user launching a full desktop of another operating system, the RemoteApp application appears just like another application.

RemoteApps have become part of configuring a collection, compared to previous versions where a significant number of steps were required in order to get them working. This is now a relatively easy task to accomplish. We will show you in the next few steps how to publish Calculator, which is in the default list for publishing, and the command prompt, which is not in the default list, but the process we will go through will demonstrate how to add an app. Remember that you have to install the app you want to publish first. Ensure that you install it in multiuser mode; otherwise it may not work.

1. Open Server Manager, and navigate to Remote Desktop Services.

2. Click Remote Desktop Services ➢ Collections.

3. Select RDS02_Collection.

   You now have a RemoteApp Programs screen, which can be used to easily add new RemoteApps and publish them to the users' collections.

4. Click Publish RemoteApp Programs in the center of the RemoteApp Programs screen.

This will invoke the wizard to publish a new RemoteApp.

5. From the Publish RemoteApp Programs Wizard shown in Figure 29.9, select Calculator as an app to publish.

FIGURE 29.9
Selecting an app
to publish

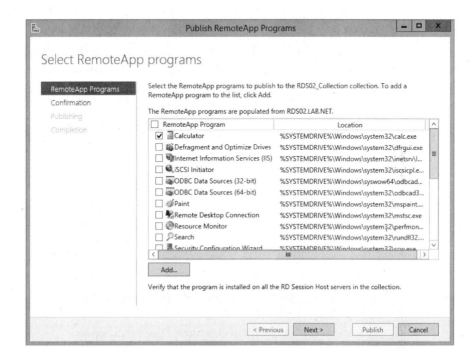

6. Confirm the path and the RemoteApp program name, and click Publish.

You have finished publishing the app; this is considerably easier than it was in previous versions of RemoteApp.

Now let's take another example, say users have a requirement to be able to launch programs from the command prompt on the server. Here we show you how to publish the command prompt. All of these are just examples of course and you can publish any app on the server.

1. If you want to add a program that is not in the list, click Tasks (beside RemoteApp Programs in Server Manager; see Figure 29.5) and click Publish RemoteApp Programs.

2. Click Add on the Select RemoteApp Programs screen.

3. Navigate to the executable you wish to publish and select it.

In our demo we are publishing the command prompt, which is located at c:\windows\ system32\cmd.exe.

4. Finish publishing the app as detailed in the earlier steps.

By default when you publish a RemoteApp it is published to everyone who is authorized in the collection; in our case the entire lab Domain Users group has access. You may want to restrict a RemoteApp to a single user or another group, as follows:

1. Right-click a RemoteApp from the RemoteApp Programs list.

2. Edit its properties.

3. Modify the user assignment.

LAUNCHING A REMOTEAPP FROM INTERNET EXPLORER

You can launch a RemoteApp from Internet Explorer using the following steps. You can do this from your RDS server, or you can do it from another computer in your network.

1. Launch Internet Explorer.

2. Enter the following URL into the address bar: `https://localhost/rdweb`.

   If you're accessing this from a remote host, enter the name of the server in place of `localhost`. For example, our server name is RDS02, so we would enter it as `https://rds02/rdweb`.

   Since the server is using a self-signed certificate, you'll see an error.

3. Click the Continue to This Website (Not Recommended) link.

4. If prompted by the Internet Explorer Enhanced Security Configuration, click Add to indicate that you trust this website.

5. Click Add again, and click Close.

   The RemoteApp and Desktop Connection page will appear.

6. Enter a username in the format of *domain\user name* and a password for an account that is in the local Remote Desktop Users group of the RDS server.

   We've created an account named John in the lab domain, so we have entered it as **lab\ john**, as shown in Figure 29.10.

   Notice that you can also select whether you're accessing the RemoteApps from a public or private computer. The private setting allows a longer period of activity before logging you off. It's strongly recommended that users close the session as soon as they are finished to flush any remnant data from the session.

7. Enter the user's password, and click "Sign in."

   The RemoteApp programs that have been published to the server are listed, as shown in Figure 29.11.

8. Click the Calculator application.

   A warning will appear saying that the RemoteApp program is starting.

9. Click Connect.

FIGURE 29.10
Logging into
the Enterprise
Remote Access
website

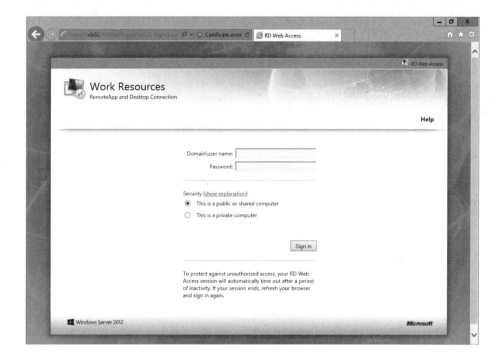

FIGURE 29.11
Accessing
RemoteApp
programs
using Internet
Explorer

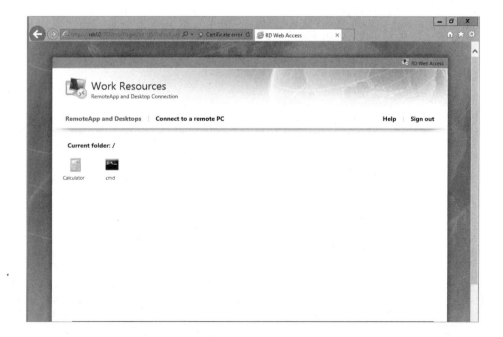

Notice that you don't have to enter any credentials (in previous versions you would have had to enter multiple credentials to launch the application).

10. Launch the cmd application as well, and click Connect when prompted.

11. In the command prompt enter **hostname**, and it should return the name of the RDS server it is running on.

12. Close all apps and close Internet Explorer.

In previous versions of RemoteApp you were able to package the application into an RDP file or an MSI file for distribution. This feature has been deprecated in 2012 R2.

Virtual Desktop Infrastructure

Virtual Desktop Infrastructure (VDI) has been around a long time. There are many different implementations and approaches as to how to implement it. VDI is a pooled collection of client operating systems (usually Windows XP, Windows Vista, Windows 7, or Windows 8) hosted on a virtualization platform. Connections to this pool are controlled by a broker service. This allows clients to extend the asset's lifecycle throughout their enterprise and centralize their core applications in the datacenter. In Windows Server 2012 this is considered part of the Remote Desktop stack with a mix of Hyper-V.

A key improvement in Windows Server 2012 R2—which has more to do with storage but benefits VDI as well—is Storage Deduplication. If you have multiple identical images from copies of a master VHDX file, you can use Dedup and save space without impacting performance. Dedup is supported only with VHDX scenarios.

In the previous section you learned about the roles that you can select when deploying Remote Desktop Services. In our discussion of VDI we will be focusing on three roles:

◆ RD Virtualization Host

◆ RD Connection Broker

◆ RD Web Access

Given that we have discussed what these roles do already, we'll discuss some prerequisites you need to take into account before proceeding. In Windows Server 2012 R2 the first thing you need to decide on is the client OS that you will operate in your VDI infrastructure. Microsoft currently supports Windows 7 SP1 and Windows 8 (8.1 when released will also be supported). When you choose the client OS, you will have to build a template; the template should be a standard build of the OS with the applications you require on it (for example, Office, Adobe Reader, and so on). Once all the applications are installed and you have tuned the OS appropriately, you then need to run sysprep on the image. We will be showing you how to do this over the next few pages.

First, we'll show you how to configure VDI on Windows Server 2012 R2 and deploy two types of collections: a pooled collection (where everyone shares the resources) and a personal virtual desktop collection (where you can dedicate a VDI machine to just one user). The image in our lab will be of Windows 8. In the lab environment we also have a domain controller called AD-01 and a host that is virtualization capable running Windows Server 2012 called VDIHOST02. On VDIHOST02 we have also copied the Windows 8 ISO for later use. The following are the steps required:

1. Log on to VDIHOST02 and open Server Manager.

2. Choose Manage ➢ Add Roles and Features.

3. Click Next on the Before You Begin screen of the Add Roles and Features Wizard.

4. Choose Remote Desktop Services Installation and click Next.

5. Select Standard Deployment for the deployment type and click Next.

6. For the deployment scenario, select "Virtual machine based desktop deployment."

   A standard deployment will deploy the following roles:

   ◆ Remote Desktop Connection Broker

   ◆ Remote Desktop Web Access

   ◆ Remote Desktop Virtualization Host

7. For the Remote Desktop Connection Broker and Remote Desktop Web Access roles, add VDIHOST02 and click Next.

8. For the Remote Desktop Virtualization Host role, select VDIHOST02 again, but ensure "Create a new virtual switch on the selected servers" is checked, as shown in Figure 29.12.

FIGURE 29.12
Remote Desktop Virtualization Host options

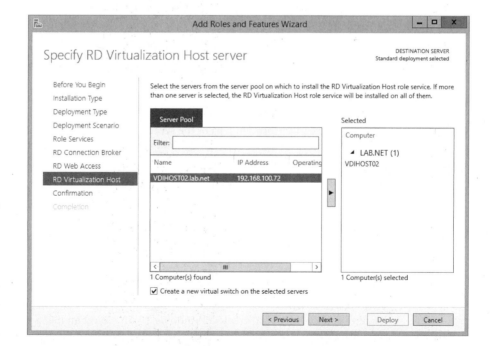

9. Confirm the settings you have just configured, check the "Restart the destination server automatically if required" check box, and then click Deploy.

   The server will deploy these roles and will reboot once or twice; this is because it is also adding the Hyper-V role. It can take about 10–15 minutes for the installation to complete, so you have time to grab a cup of coffee.

10. When the reboots are complete, log back on to VDIHOST02, and the Add Roles and Features Wizard will relaunch and complete.

    As with the installation of the session host earlier, ignore the license messages for now.

    Next, on AD-01 you need to create an organizational unit (OU) where the VDI computer accounts will be stored.

11. Log on to AD-01, and launch Active Directory Users and Computers.

12. Create an OU for storing the VDI computer accounts.

    In our lab we have created an OU called VDI Computers.

13. Choose View ➢ Advanced Features.

14. Right-click the VDI computers OU, and select Attribute Editor.

15. Scroll down to the distinguishedname attribute and copy its contents.

    For this lab the distinguishedname is OU=VDI Computers,OU=LAB,DC=lab,DC=NET.

16. Log back on to VDIHOST02; if Server Manager has closed, reopen it and click Remote Desktop Services.

17. In the Deployment Overview section, choose Tasks ➢ Edit Deployment Properties.

18. Click Active Directory, and then select "Specify the distinguished name of the organizational unit."

19. Populate the OU as recorded in step 15 and as shown in Figure 29.13.

    Did you notice in the bottom part of the screen that it warns you that the permissions have not been correctly configured and that it will correct them for you when you click Apply?

20. Click Apply, and it will attempt to set the permissions.

    The message should change to inform you the settings have been applied and the appropriate permissions are now in place.

    We need to take a small sidestep now to create the image that will be used for the VDI deployment.

21. Open Hyper-V Manager on VDIHOST02.

    Since you have worked with virtual machines and Hyper-V in Chapters 27 and 28, we assume you know how to create a Windows 8 VM, mount an ISO, and install an operating system. In our lab we called our VM Win8-Gold. We also placed it locally on the C drive in a folder called VMSTORE.

FIGURE 29.13
Specify the AD
OU properties.

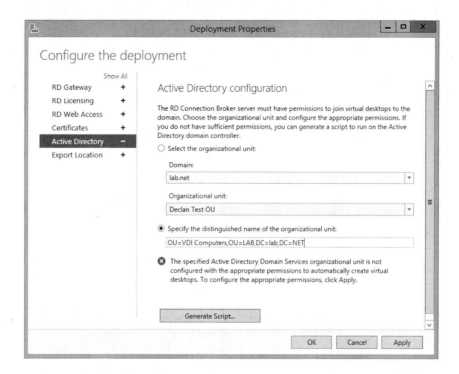

22. Once the operating system is installed and you have deployed the applications you want, open an elevated command prompt and type **c:\windows\system32\sysprep\sysprep**.

23. Select the options illustrated in Figure 29.14.

FIGURE 29.14
Sysprep options

24. Once the VM has turned itself off in Hyper-V, right-click the VM and select Export.

    You will be asked to specify a path. By default VDI on Windows Server 2012 R2 requires you to place it in the path c:\RDVirtualDesktopTemplate.

25. Configure this path via PowerShell using the `Get-RDVirtualDesktopTemplateExportP` `ath` and the `Set-RDVirtualDesktopTemplateExportPath` cmdlets.

26. Allow the export to complete, and then delete your VM.

27. Import the VM you just exported from `C:\RDVirtualDesktopTemplatePath\Win8-Gold`.

28. Return now to Server Manager ➤ Remote Desktop Services ➤ Collections.

29. Choose Tasks ➤ Create Virtual Desktop Collection.

30. Click Next on the Before You Begin screen.

31. Enter a collection name, and then click Next.

In our lab we entered Win8-VDI- Pooled.

32. Select Pooled Virtual Desktop Collection and click Next.

The template you configured earlier now appears in the list.

33. Click Next to continue.

34. Select "Provide unattended installation settings" and click Next.

You can choose use an existing `sysprep` answer file if your organization has one prepared.

35. Set the time zone to the region where you are located, and then specify the `distinguishedname` you recorded earlier and click Next.

36. Add the groups you will authorize to access the VDI pool. Define the number of VDI desktops that you need in your pool (remember to size appropriate to the hardware as well), and finally specify a prefix.

See Figure 29.15 for the options we selected in our lab.

37. Select the correct server (if you have more than one in the environment), but take a second to review the information on memory and processor and any existing virtual machines. Click Next when finished.

You can configure where you want to place the new VDI desktop virtual hard disks.

38. In this case, select the default because we have only one hard disk in the demo server.

In production you would consider the other options depending on the infrastructure. At the very least, if you choose the "Specify a separate path on which to store the parent disk," you will be following best practices and allowing for optimal storage performance.

39. Uncheck "Enable User Profiles Disk" because we won't be using it in our environment.

Note that most enterprises considering VDI generally have the users profile redirected to a file share, so this option is not required.

40. Confirm all the settings and click Create.

Depending on your hardware, this process can take 5–30 minutes on average.

41. Click Close so that you can create your second collection for personal connections.

42. Create a new virtual desktop collection.

FIGURE 29.15
Specifying users
and user groups

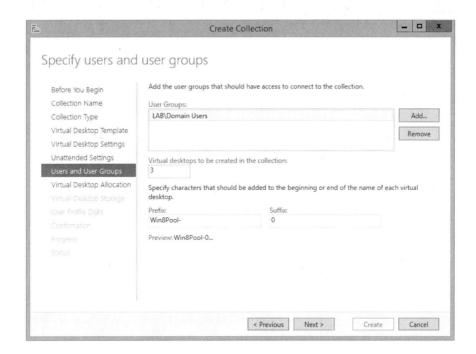

43. Name the collection **Win8-VDI-Personal**.

44. Select Personal Virtual Desktop Collection and click Next.

45. Select the Win8-Gold image again.

    You will be notified that it is in use by other collections. Because this is a personal desktop collection, you can choose Automatic Assignment or Disable Automatic Assignment.

46. To alleviate overhead choose Automatic Assignment.

    Automatic assignment is best, but there could be times where you need to manually assign a user to a VM.

    As before, you can provide a `sysprep` answer file if the organization has one.

47. In this case, select "Provide unattended installation settings."

48. Set the time zone and the appropriate OU as before.

49. Configure the appropriate group for access and assignment to the virtual desktop. Configure the number of desktops you wish to deploy and the prefix.

    Figure 29.16 shows you the options we selected in our lab.

50. Review the allocation screen as you did previously, and click Next.

    For the virtual desktop storage, notice how the default option has changed and that you now have less to select from.

FIGURE 29.16
Configured
options for
personal VDI

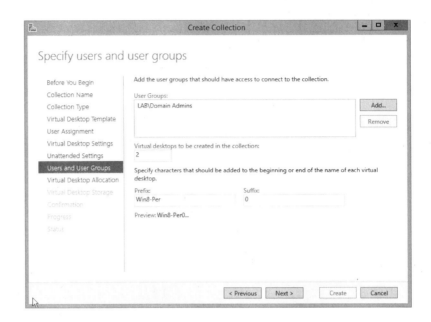

51. For the lab choose Store on Each RD Virtualization Host Server.

52. Review and confirm the settings and click Create.

53. Close the screen and monitor the deployment progress.

54. From a remote client, log on to `https://vdihost02.lab.net/rdweb` (this is our URL).

    Ignore the certificate errors, since by default it deploys a self-signed certificate.

55. Enter the credentials of a domain user, in this case **lab\john**.

    Figure 29.17 shows you the sample web page we get when we log on.

56. First, test the Win8-VDI-Pooled connection by clicking it.

    You will be prompted to confirm the connection.

57. Click Connect.

    This will log you onto a pooled VDI VM.

58. Sign out after you have verified your apps and network connectivity.

59. Second, test the Win8-VDI-Personal connection by clicking it.

60. Again, click Connect when prompted.

    Essentially it should be the same experience, but now every time you log on you will get the same VM.

FIGURE 29.17
RD web access
page for VDI

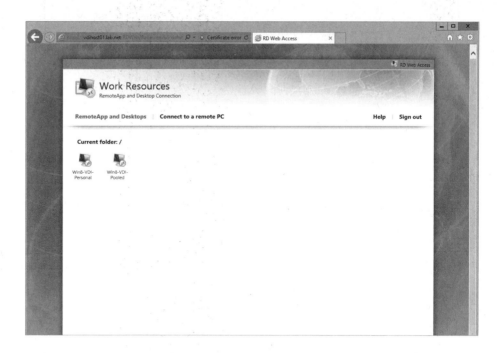

Figure 29.18 shows you the VMs related to the VDI deployment. Notice how one is in Saved state; this happens automatically, preserving resources on the box when they are not in use.

FIGURE 29.18
VM view of a VDI deployment

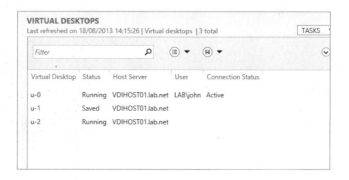

Now it's a fully working VDI solution. We mentioned earlier that VDI has now been optimized to work with storage Dedup in Windows Server 2012. To give you a quick idea, when we created our gold image we had an 8 GB VHDX file. When we created the two pools, a copy of the gold image for each pool was created. This totals to about 24 GB of storage just in VHDX files, making it a prime candidate for storage Dedup. You would save nearly 60 percent of the storage costs just by enabling Dedup. Remember, though, not to place your VDI files on the root volume because you cannot enable Dedup on it. From step 25 onward, we showed you how to configure the path to ensure it is not the root volume.

Monitoring Remote Desktop Services

Once Remote Desktop Services is up and running, you'll need to monitor and manage it. In previous versions of Windows several RDS tools were available:

◆ Remote Desktop Services Manager

◆ Remote Desktop Session Host Configuration

◆ RemoteApp Manager

◆ Remote Desktop Web Access Configuration

◆ Remote Desktop Licensing Manager

◆ Remote Desktop Connection Manager

◆ Remote Desktops

In Windows Server 2012 R2 all the administration tools except for two are located directly within the Server Manager UI under Remote Desktop Services. The two that are still located under Start ➢ Administrative Tools ➢ Remote Desktop Services are as follows:

◆ Remote Desktop Licensing Manager

◆ RD Licensing Diagnoser (new)

The RD Licensing Diagnoser does exactly what it says: it helps you figure out if you will have problems in your environment with licensing. In Figure 29.19 we show the output for an environment where we have not published licenses yet and are still within the grace period.

FIGURE 29.19
RD Licensing
Diagnoser

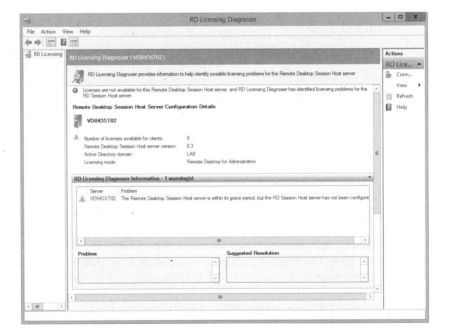

The Remote Desktop Licensing Manager has not really changed and still performs the same functions as before. The requirement to activate the licensing server on the Microsoft Clearinghouse first is still in place, and you still need to install the appropriate CALs. A nice report feature on CAL usage is now available, but beside that the feature set is the same as in previous generations.

Common Tasks and How to Do Them

As we mentioned, all the legacy tools prior to Windows 2012 for monitoring and even configuring Remote Desktop Services exist inside the UI (except PowerShell, obviously). During deployment of both Remote Desktop and VDI we provided screenshots of where you can access certain pieces of information you commonly need in a deployment. In the next couple of pages we will talk about some of the more common areas required.

Example 1: Configure licensing for RD Session Host or Virtualization Host

1. In Server Manager under Remote Desktop Services, click Overview.

2. Navigate to Deployment Overview, and choose Tasks ➤ Edit Deployment Options.

3. Click the plus sign beside RD Licensing.

   This lets you configure Per Device or Per User licensing mode for this host, as shown in Figure 29.20.

FIGURE 29.20
Configuring RD
Licensing mode

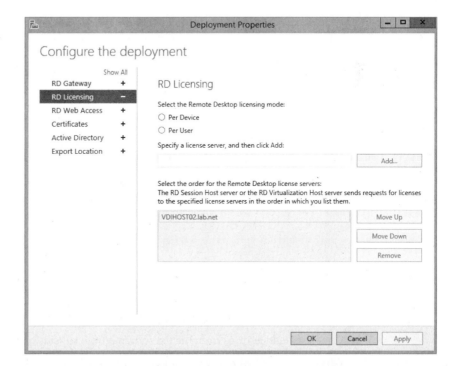

Example 2: Modify the virtual desktop template export location

1. Review Figure 29.20 and at the bottom of the left column you will see Export Location. This refers to the template location.

2. Open an elevated command prompt and type **net share**.

   This will allow you to quickly map the share to the physical path.

3. Simply point it to another path that you have configured.

Example 3: Change the RDS encryption level to FIPS Compliant

1. Open Server Manager ➤ Remote Desktop Services ➤ Collection ➤ "Name of your Collection."

2. Look at the properties window, and click Tasks ➤ Edit Properties.

3. Choose Security from the list on the left, and under Encryption Level from the drop-down list, select FIPS Compliant; see Figure 29.21.

FIGURE 29.21
Changing the
RDS encryption
level

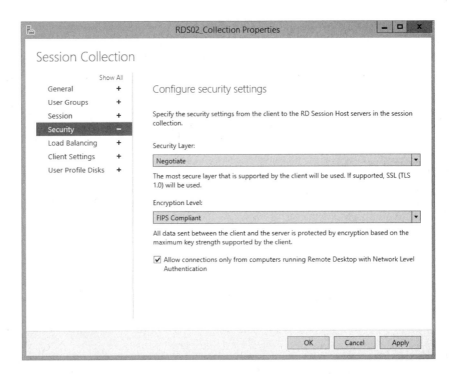

Example 4: Change client settings for RD Session Host

1. Choose Client Settings from the list shown on the left side of Figure 29.21.

   Observe that now that you can turn on and off different options to affect the client experience.

2. Map the drives through RDS from the local machine.

3. Copy things to and from the clipboard.

4. Disable audio and video playback.

Example 5: Find out who is logged on to what

1. Open Server Manager ➤ Remote Desktop Services ➤ Collections ➤ "Name of your collection."

2. Look at Figure 29.22.

FIGURE 29.22
Who is logged on to what

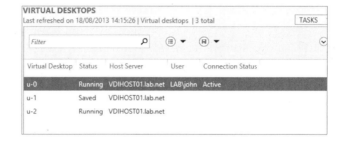

You see a sample output of who is logged onto what VM in a personal VDI pool.

These are just some examples of how to perform some common tasks that you would normally do when deploying Remote Desktop Services. They are applicable for both VDI and RDS scenarios.

All these options are available in PowerShell as well. You can review the full list of cmdlets available on your machine by using the following cmdlet:

```
get-command -module RemoteDesktop
```

There are 73 cmdlets to play with in Windows Server 2012 R2. For a complete list and reference to all the cmdlets, please check out the following link:

```
http://technet.microsoft.com/en-us/library/jj215451.aspx
```

Remote Desktop Licensing Manager

Although you have a grace period during which RDS will function normally, after the grace period ends, RDS will no longer accept connections if licensing is not configured. The grace period lasts for 120 days or until the first permanent RDS CAL is issued by a license server, whichever occurs first.

As mentioned previously, you can choose between per-user or per-device Remote Desktop Services Client Access Licenses. The licensing server must be activated before you can install the licenses.

After you've configured your RDS environment, you'll want to configure the license server. The RD Licensing Manager is used to install, issue, and track the availability of RDS CALs on a

Remote Desktop license server. Licenses are purchased through a variety of different methods, depending on your company's relationship with Microsoft, such as the following:

◆ Enterprise Agreement

◆ Campus Agreement

◆ School Agreement

◆ Services Provider License Agreement

◆ Other Agreement

If you have one of these agreements with Microsoft, the best way to obtain licenses is through this agreement. It's also possible to purchase licenses through retail channels by purchasing a license pack. For detailed information on how to purchase licenses, check out this page:

```
http://www.microsoft.com/en-us/server-cloud/windows-server/buy.aspx
```

The license server can be on the same server as the RD Session Host server, or for larger implementations of Remote Desktop Services with multiple servers, a single-license server will manage licenses for multiple RDS servers.

Older Terminal Services license servers used a discovery scope to allow TS servers to locate the license server. If you're installing the license server on Windows Server 2012 R2, this is not needed. Instead, you should use the Remote Desktop Session Host Configuration tool to specify a license server for the RD Session Host server to use. This is done on the Licensing tab of the RDP-TCP Connections Properties dialog box, where you identify the type of RDS CALs used for the server (per user or per device).

You can configure the RD Licensing Manager by following these steps:

1. Launch the RD Licensing Manager by selecting Start ➢ Administrative Tools ➢ Remote Desktop Services ➢ Remote Desktop Licensing Manager.

2. Click the plus sign (+) to expand All Servers.

You'll see your server marked with a white *X* in a red circle.

3. Select your server; right-click it, and select Activate Server.

4. Review the information on the wizard's Welcome page, and click Next.

5. On the Connection Method page, accept the default of Automatic Connection (Recommended).

Use this method if the RDS server has access to the Internet. If the server doesn't have access to the Internet, you can connect with another computer over the Internet or via a telephone.

6. Click Next.

The Company Information page will appear.

7. Enter your first name, last name, company, and country.

This information is used if you need help from Microsoft.

8. Click Next.

9. Enter the additional information requested on the Optional Company Information page. Click Next.

A dialog box will appear with a progress bar. The server is connecting to the Microsoft Clearinghouse and is being activated. When it completes, the completion page will appear.

10. Deselect the Start Install Licenses Wizard Now check box, and click Finish.

At this point, the licensing server is activated, but there aren't any RDS CALs installed.

SET PER USER OR PER DEVICE

It may be necessary to return to the Remote Desktop Session Host Configuration console and set the Remote Desktop licensing mode. After launching the console, double-click the Remote Desktop licensing mode to access the property page. Select Per Device or Per User depending on what type of licenses you have purchased, and enter the name of the license server.

---

11. Right-click your server, and select Install Licenses.

This will launch the wizard to install your licenses. There are multiple paths this can take, depending on what type of licenses you've purchased and where you've purchased them from.

The Bottom Line

Limit the maximum number of connections.   You can change the licensing mode of a server to help ensure you remain compliant with the licensing agreement and allocations you have.

Master It   You want to know what licensing mode the server is in. How do you do it?

Add an application to an RD Session Host server.   Once the RDS role is added and the RD Session Host server is configured, you can add applications to make them available to the server.

Master It   Your company has purchased an application that supports multiuser access. You want to install it on the RD Session Host server. What should you do?

Add a RemoteApp for Web Access.   RemoteApp applications can be configured so that they are accessible to users via a web browser. Users simply need to access the correct page and select the application to launch it.

Master It   Assume you have already configured your environment to support RemoteApp applications. You now want to add a RemoteApp application. What should you do?

Chapter 30

Monitoring Windows Server 2012 R2

The best time to know about a problem is before it happens. This is as true in the IT world as anywhere else. If you want to know about potential problems with servers before they morph into a full-blown crisis, you have to monitor them.

With just a bit of proactive monitoring and the right tools, you can identify minor errors and negative trends before they bloom into hardcore problems.

In this chapter, we will first discuss some of the basic tools that come built into Windows Server 2012 R2 that help you gain an understanding of any errors or performance issues. These monitoring tools are the Server Manager console, Best Practices Analyzer, Event Viewer, Performance Monitor, and Resource Monitor. Once you understand how to use these, we will talk about two additional (and little-known) external tools—PAL and PerfView—that can be used to deliver deeper performance analysis. Finally, we'll discuss Microsoft's recommended monitoring solution—System Center 2012 R2 Operations Manager—and how it can help you quickly analyze the root cause of problems on your Windows Server 2012 R2 workloads.

In this chapter, you will learn to:

- ◆ Use Server Manager to monitor multiple servers
- ◆ Understand how to use Event Viewer
- ◆ Explore Performance Monitor
- ◆ Explore the PAL and PerfView tools
- ◆ Understand System Center 2012 R2 Operations Manager

Using Server Manager to Monitor Multiple Servers

The new Server Manager console in Windows Server 2012 R2 delivers out-of-box monitoring and health checks of your local and remote server infrastructure. In the "Troubleshooting Roles and Features" section from Chapter 2, you learned how Server Manager can monitor a single server and its associated roles. This section will elaborate on that information and will discuss how to utilize Server Manager to monitor multiple servers and the roles they are responsible for, all from one central console.

Adding Servers to Manage

You can add additional servers to manage and monitor with Server Manager by following these steps:

1. Log on to your Windows Server 2012 R2 computer with an elevated account that has administrative permissions.

2. Click Server Manager ➤ Dashboard.

3. Choose the "Add other servers to manage" option from the Quick Start tab.

4. From the Add Servers dialog box and in the Active Directory tab, filter by location and operating system; then either type the beginning of a name for the servers that you want to add or just click the Find Now button to display all servers for your chosen options.

5. Double-click (or Ctrl+click) each server that you want to add to the Selected column; then click OK.

   Now in the Dashboard view, you should see the "Servers total" value under the Roles and Server Groups view reflect the number of servers you've added for monitoring.

6. Click the View menu button from Server Manager, then choose 75% to see a compressed view of all the roles from your chosen multiple servers now under your monitoring control within Server Manager, as shown in Figure 30.1, with each individual server role and its relevant health state (green for healthy and red for unhealthy).

FIGURE 30.1
Monitoring
multiple servers

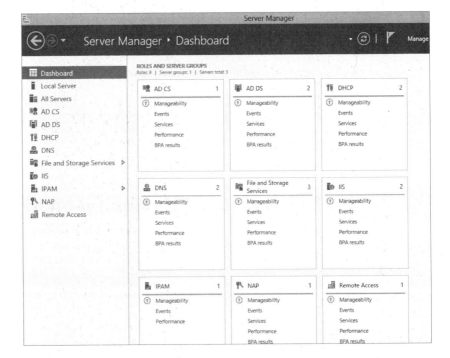

Creating a Server Group for Monitoring

When you add multiple servers to the Server Manager console, you are presented with a segmented view for each server role, as you saw in Figure 30.1. You might, however, need to have a collated health state for the collective roles on multiple servers and this is where server groups in Server Manager can come in handy. To create a server group that contains all the servers you wish to monitor from within the console, do the following:

1. Log on to your Windows Server 2012 R2 computer with an elevated account that has administrative permissions.

2. Click Server Manager ➤ Dashboard.

3. Choose the "Create a server group" option from the Quick Start tab.

4. In the Create Server Group dialog box, type a server group name in the top field; select multiple servers to add to the group from the Server Pool, Active Directory, DNS, or Import tabs (we used the Server Pool tab, as shown in Figure 30.2); then click OK.

FIGURE 30.2
Adding multiple servers to a group

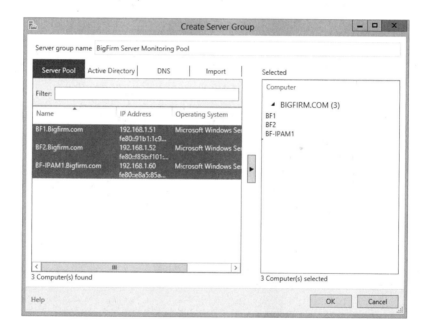

Now at the Dashboard view again, you can see a new server group that shows a rolled-up health state of all the servers contained within, as shown in Figure 30.3.

Monitoring with Server Groups

When you have configured your server groups in the Server Manager console, you can then quickly identify if there's a problem with any servers contained in those groups from the following key areas:

FIGURE 30.3
New server group

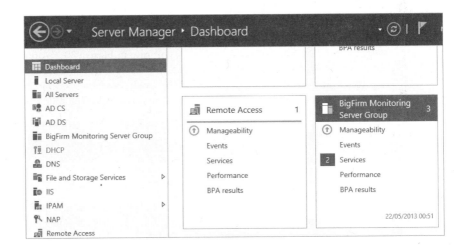

Manageability   Here you can see some standard monitoring metrics that determine if a server's manageability error criteria have been met.

Events   This area gives you a centralized view of all the Critical, Error, and Warning events that occur on your servers.

Services   Here you get an overview of the services that are running (or not running) on your chosen servers.

Performance   The Performance area gives you a monitored view of the CPU and memory resource types on your chosen servers.

BPA Results   This area shows the different security levels (Information, Warning, and Error) that are generated after the Best Practices Analyzer (BPA) has been run.

From the server group that we created in the previous section, you can see that we have a number of issues that need to be addressed, as shown in Figure 30.4.

FIGURE 30.4
Server group with problems

Clicking one of the problem areas highlighted will quickly show you which servers are having problems and what's generating the alert in the Server Manager console. If we click the Services area of our Server Group tile, the Services Detail View dialog box opens, where we can clearly see that there's a problem with two services being stopped on two different servers, as shown in Figure 30.5.

FIGURE 30.5
Identifying the problem

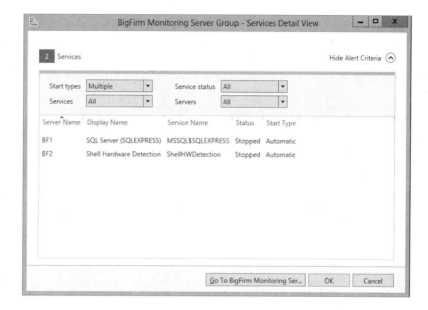

THE SERVER GROUP VIEW

If you want to get a more granular view of your server group from within Server Manager instead of using the Dashboard view, simply click the server group name from the navigation bar on the left side. This will present you with a single scrollable window containing a number of dialog boxes for each of the key areas we discussed earlier. Each dialog box has a Tasks button that will give you different tasks depending on the area you have chosen.

Utilizing the Best Practice Analyzers

For a number of years the Solution Accelerator team of Microsoft would periodically release Best Practices Analyzer tools to complement some of their key product offerings. One of the best known of these was the Microsoft Exchange BPA (ExBPA), this tool enabled system administrators and consultants around the world to ensure they had configured their environments optimally and to the best-practice recommendations of Microsoft. Back then, the BPAs were separate tools from the application, and because of the massive success of the ExBPA, Microsoft made a design decision to start including BPAs in Windows Server (from the 2008 release onward) to analyze each role deployed in the operating system. A nice benefit of this is that the BPAs get updated through Windows Update in the same way that the operating system does, ensuring that you always get up-to-date recommendations when you need them.

The fact that you have so many new roles and so much functionality out of the box with Windows Server 2012 R2 makes the case for understanding when to use these BPAs as part of your troubleshooting and consulting toolkit all the more compelling. The BPAs in Windows

Server 2012 R2 can be easily launched from the Server Manager console under each specific role. Here's how to do it:

1. Log on to your Windows Server 2012 R2 computer with an elevated account that has administrative permissions.

2. Open Server Manager and then click a specific role in the navigation bar on the left. We'll use DNS for this example.

3. Scroll down to the Best Practices Analyzer pane, click the Tasks button, and then choose Start BPA Scan, as shown in Figure 30.6.

FIGURE 30.6
Running the BPA

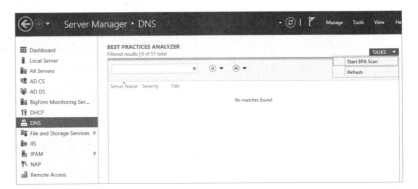

4. Choose the server (or multiple servers) that you want to scan; then click the Start Scan button to begin.

Once the scan has completed, you will be presented with the results giving you an insight into any errors, warnings, or informational items that Microsoft deems to not be concurrent with their best practices. The results of our BPA scan on the DNS role are shown in Figure 30.7.

FIGURE 30.7
BPA scan results

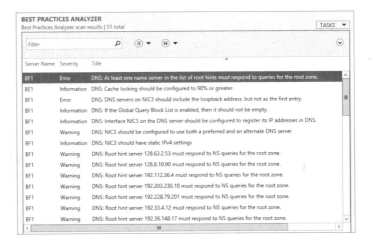

Monitoring Your System with Event Viewer

Event Viewer in Windows Server 2012 R2 is one of the essential tools used to monitor your system. Often, it's one of the first places you'll look once you realize your server has a problem, but it can also be used to proactively monitor servers. Event Viewer can help you to quickly identify the source of a problem or at least gain enough knowledge to know where to look next.

You can launch Event Viewer from the Windows Server 2012 R2 Start screen by typing **eventvwr** and then pressing Enter or via Server Manager ➤ Tools ➤ Event Viewer.

Figure 30.8 shows Event Viewer and some of the available event logs that you will come across.

FIGURE 30.8
Event Viewer

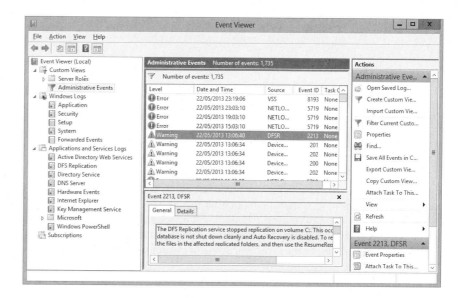

The left pane shows all the selectable logs. The center pane shows the events from the selected log and it also displays information from the selected event at the bottom. The right pane shows all the available actions for the selected log or event.

Note that all the logs aren't necessarily used all of the time and some may be used only for a specific purpose. As a simple example, the Setup log is used to log events only during installation. If this log is cleared, you won't ever see events here again. If you dig into some of these lesser-used logs, you may see that they are empty, but that doesn't indicate a problem exists.

Viewing an Event

You can double-click any event in the center pane and a dialog box will appear providing all the details on the event. Details in many of the events include some handy information to help you troubleshoot and resolve the reason the error was raised in the first place. Figure 30.9 shows an example of an error event.

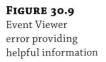

FIGURE 30.9
Event Viewer
error providing
helpful information

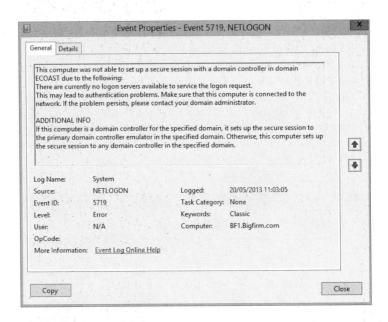

In Figure 30.9, the information contained in the General tab for this event clearly informs you that there was an issue setting up a secure session with a domain controller in the ECOAST domain. It goes on to offer some advice on what to do to resolve the problem along with additional information about how the secure session connectivity works.

You can also click the Event Log Online Help link from the General tab. If the server has access to the Internet, it will transmit information on the error and bring up a Microsoft TechNet page related to the error. For some of the common errors, this online check can be useful.

A neat extra feature is the ability to click the Copy button to copy all the details to the clipboard. You can then paste them into a document to easily review them or even paste them into a troubleshooting log or database.

Understanding Event Levels

Events are categorized by their level. These levels have both names and numbers associated with them. You'll see the level identified by its name and icon when looking at events, but if you're configuring custom views, you can use the level numbers in the XML file.

Information Events: Level 0 and Level 4 These entries are used to indicate a change has occurred or to describe the successful completion of an operation. The icon used to represent Information events is an *i* in a circle.

Critical Events: Level 1 A Critical event is one that an application or component cannot automatically recover from. Critical events are the most serious. The icon used to represent Critical events is a white *x* in a red circle.

Error Events: Level 2 Error events indicate a problem occurred external to the application or component that might impact the functionality of the application or component. The icon used to represent Error events is a white exclamation point in a red circle.

Warning Events: Level 3   Warning events indicate events that may lead to a problem in the future. The event isn't necessarily significant. Sometimes you can trace back from critical or error events to identify a preceding warning. The icon used to represent Warning events is a black exclamation point in a yellow triangle.

Verbose: Level 5   Verbose logging provides more details in the log entry. If the log entry supports verbose logging, these additional details will be recorded in the log when this check box is enabled in the Create Custom View dialog box.

The event levels are shown by default in all logs except the Security log. The Security log is focused more on audit success and audit failure so it lists these audit keywords instead of the levels.

Creating and Using Custom Views

Often when you're looking at the logs, you're looking for specific events, or at least events related to a specific issue or problem. The Custom Views node of Event Viewer provides predefined focused views of the events and allows you to create your own views. This is helpful because you don't have to re-create the view each time you want to look at these events.

Some custom views are automatically created:

Server Roles   Each time you add a server role, an associated custom view is automatically created. For example, if you promote a server to a domain controller, a custom view named Active Directory Domain Services will be added below the Server Roles node to show system events for Active Directory Domain Services.

Administrative Events   The Administrative Events custom view shows Critical, Error, and Warning events from all the administrative logs. In other words, it shows everything except for the informational events. This view includes the basic administrative logs (Application, Security, and System) found on any system. It also includes logs in the Applications and Services Logs node and some of the logs in the Applications and Services Logs ➤ Microsoft ➤ Windows node.

When the server is configured with a new role or feature and additional logs are added, the Administrative Events custom view is modified to include these additional logs.

Although you can't modify these predefined custom views, you can create your own custom views and modify them. The next section will show you how to create your own modifiable custom views.

PREDEFINED CUSTOM VIEWS CAN'T BE FILTERED

Neither the Administrative Events custom view nor any of the server role custom views can be filtered. If you want to filter these logs, you'll need to create a copy of the custom view first.

CREATING A COPY OF A CUSTOM VIEW

You may like one of the predefined custom views but want to make a slight modification. Instead of starting from scratch, you can create a copy of the custom view and modify it.

As an example, you may want to use the Administrative Events log as a template but add information events and filter it so only the last 24 hours are viewable. The following steps will show you how to create this log:

1. Launch Event Viewer from the Windows Server 2012 R2 Start screen by typing **eventvwr** and then pressing Enter or via Server Manager ➤ Tools ➤ Event Viewer.

2. Right-click the Administrative Events custom view, select Copy Custom View.

3. Change the name to **Today's Core Log Events**.

4. Click New Folder. Type **My Custom Views** in the Name text box and click OK.

5. Click OK to create the copy of the Administrative Events custom view in the My Custom Views folder.

6. Right-click the Today's Core Log Events log, and select Properties.

7. Click the Edit Filter button.

   Notice that the properties are the same as the original Administrative Events custom view, but you can edit them.

8. Select the drop-down box for Logged, and select Last 24 Hours.

9. Select the Event Level check box for Information.

   The check boxes for Critical, Warning, and Error should already be checked.

10. Select the Event Logs drop-down box.

    The Application and Services Logs item has the check box dimmed indicating that some of the logs are selected.

11. Select it once to select all the logs. Click it again to deselect it, and all of the logs will be deselected.

    Your display will look similar to Figure 30.10. In the figure, we have clicked the plus sign to show all the available logs, but only three of the Windows logs are actually selected.

12. Click OK twice to save your new custom view.

CREATING A NEW CUSTOM VIEW

You can also create custom views from scratch. This is useful if you're troubleshooting specific issues. For example, you may need to monitor the starting and stopping of services.

You can use the following steps to create a custom view that allows you to quickly view all the events related to a service starting or stopping:

1. Launch Event Viewer from the Windows Server 2012 R2 Start screen by typing **eventvwr** and then pressing Enter or via Server Manager ➤ Tools ➤ Event Viewer.

2. Right-click Custom Views, and select Create Custom View.

3. Select the Critical, Warning, Error, and Information check boxes.

4. Select the By Source radio button.

FIGURE 30.10
Modifying a
custom view

5. Select the Event Sources drop-down box, scroll down, and click the check box next to Service Control Manager and Service Control Manager Performance Diagnostic Provider.

    Notice that two logs are automatically selected: the System log and the Microsoft-Windows-Services/Diagnostic log.

6. Click OK. Enter **Monitor Services** as the name of the custom view. Click OK.

    This custom view will show only those events related to the Service Control Manager.

FILTERING A CUSTOM VIEW

Custom views can be filtered just as any regular event log can be filtered. A log could contain hundreds or thousands of events. If you're looking for a specific event, it may take you hours to comb through the events one by one, but you can use a filter to quickly narrow your search.

FILTERING LOGS

Although this section covers how to filter a custom view, you can follow the same steps to filter any log within Event Viewer.

The following steps show how to filter a log. These steps use a log created earlier in this chapter (named Today's Core Log Events); however, you can use these steps as a guideline to filter any log:

1. Launch Event Viewer from the Windows Server 2012 R2 Start screen by typing **eventvwr** and then pressing Enter or via Server Manager ➤ Tools ➤ Event Viewer.

2. Open the Custom Views node.

3. Select a custom view that you've created, such as the Monitor Services view created in the preceding section.

4. Create a filter to show different event levels:

   a. Right-click the log and select Filter Current Custom View.

   b. Deselect the Event Level check boxes for Warning, Error, and Information. This will leave only the Critical level selected.

   c. Click OK. Your log will now show only Critical events.

   d. Right-click the log and select Clear Filter.

5. Create a filter to show specific event sources:

   a. Right-click the log and select Filter Current Custom View.

   b. Select the Event Sources drop-down box, and select the check box next to Service Control Manager. You can select as many event sources as desired.

SELECTING BY LOG OR BY SOURCE

The By Log and By Source radio buttons are a little misleading. Radio buttons are usually used to choose only one option, so these buttons imply that you can filter only by log or by source, but you can actually choose both.

When the By Log radio button is chosen, you can select the event logs and then narrow the search by selecting specific event sources in the Event Sources drop-down box.

If you select the By Source radio button and select an event source in the Event Sources drop-down box, the available logs in the Event Logs drop-down box change, showing only the logs that include this event source.

---

   c. Click OK. Your log will now show events related to services.

   d. Right-click the log and select Clear Filter.

6. Create a filter to show only specific event IDs:

   a. Right-click the log and select Filter Current Custom View.

   b. Click in the text box that shows <All Event IDs>.

   c. Enter **7000-7999, 8224** to select Event ID 8224 and all events between 7000 and 7999.

SELECTING EVENT IDS

You can select ranges of event IDs by using a hyphen (as in 7000-7999). You can add multiple ranges by separating each range with a comma (as in 7000-7999, 8050-8059). You can filter for any specific event IDs by separating each one with a comma (as in 7036, 7042). You can also combine any of these methods (as in 7000-7999, 8050-8059, 8042, 636).

---

    d. Click OK to view the filtered log.

    e. Right-click the log and select Clear Filter.

These steps lead you through modifying the filter for specific reasons, but you can filter based on other criteria depending on your needs.

EXPORTING AND IMPORTING CUSTOM VIEWS

A pretty cool tip to remember is that custom views created on one server can be exported and then imported onto another server. Although it's certainly possible to manually create the custom view on another system, it may be difficult, or at least time-consuming, to reproduce the filter without any errors. However, the export and import process will be reproduced quickly and exactly.

XML-BASED LOGS

All event logs since Windows Vista share a common XML-based infrastructure. A great strength of XML is that it's a common format stored in a simple text file. Custom views are exported as an XML file and can then be copied just as you'd copy any file.

Use the following steps to export a custom view. These steps export the predefined Administrative Events custom view, but you could just as easily use the same steps for any custom view you have created:

    1. Launch Event Viewer from the Windows Server 2012 R2 Start screen by typing **eventvwr** and then pressing Enter or via Server Manager ➢ Tools ➢ Event Viewer.

    2. Open the Custom Views node.

    3. Right-click the Administrative Events custom view, and select Export Custom View.

    4. Browse to a location on your computer where you want to save the file. Type in the name of the file, such as **ExportedCustomView**, and click Save.

The XML file can be copied to another server or a share that is accessible by another server. It can even be imported on the same server if the original file has become corrupt. Use the following steps to import the XML file:

    1. If Event Viewer is not open, launch it from the Windows Server 2012 R2 Start screen by typing **eventvwr** and then pressing Enter or via Server Manager ➢ Tools ➢ Event Viewer.

    2. Right-click the Custom Views node, and select Import Custom View.

3. Browse to the location of the exported XML file.

4. Select the XML file, and click Open.

5. Enter a different name for the imported view.

   Your display will look similar to Figure 30.11.

FIGURE 30.11
Importing a custom view

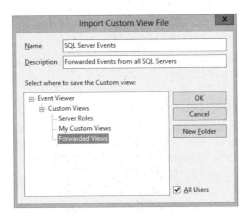

You can give the file a new description if desired. You can also organize your custom views by creating folders.

Once you've imported a custom view, you can manipulate the filter just as you can manipulate any other custom views. The original XML file used to import the custom view won't be affected if the custom view is modified.

Understanding Windows Logs

The Windows logs are the traditional logs that have been available in past versions of Windows plus the Setup and Forwarded Events logs:

Application   The Application log is used to log events from applications. The application developer can choose to log events in this log or create an additional application log specifically for the application. As an example, SQL Server will log applications into this log, but the Windows PowerShell application will log events into the Windows PowerShell log in the Applications and Services Logs section.

Security   The Security log will show all audited events. Audited events include logons, files, and other object usage, as well as any other auditing events the administrator has enabled. Audited events can be specified to include both success and failure events. Windows Server 2012 R2 does enable auditing of specific events by default, so these logs will have events even if the administrator hasn't modified auditing.

The Setup log includes events related to the setup of the operating system or installed applications. These logs include the addition or removal of any roles or features.

System   The System log records events related to the operating system. It includes information related to system drivers and system services.

Forwarded Events   If subscriptions are enabled, the Forwarded Events log will show all events forwarded to this computer. Event subscriptions must be configured before events show in this log.

Understanding Applications and Services Logs

The Applications and Services Logs folder includes logs for specific applications or components. Event log views are dynamically added here as different roles and features are added to Windows Server 2012 R2 and custom views are added into the Server Roles node.

As an example, when a server is promoted to a domain controller, additional logs are added to this folder including the Active Directory Web Services log, the DFS Replication log, and the Directory Service log.

The intent of these types of logs is to provide important relevant information to targeted personnel, instead of generic information that everyone uses.

You can also access a slew of useful Windows logs from this folder that historically couldn't be accessed from Event Viewer and instead were only available as text or XML files. These logs are available under the Microsoft\Windows view. Logs in this particular folder fall into one of four categories:

Admin   Admin logs are targeted at administrators and support personnel. The goal is to identify issues and include a solution that an administrator can take to resolve a problem.

Operational   Operational logs are intended to be used to analyze or diagnose a problem or occurrence of an event.

Analytic   Analytic logs are used to log and describe the details of operation of a program or component. An analytic log will typically have a large number of events that log each step.

Debug   Debug logs are intended to be used by application developers with troubleshooting programs during the development phase.

Configuring Event Log Properties

Every event log has a properties page that identifies details on the log. You can configure where the log is located, the maximum size of the log, and what to do when the maximum size is reached from this page.

Figure 30.12 shows the properties page of the System log. You can access this page by right-clicking the log file and selecting Properties.

CUSTOM VIEW LOG SIZES CAN'T BE CONFIGURED

You can't configure the maximum log size on a custom view. This is because a custom view isn't actually a file. Instead, it's simply a filtered view of one or more existing files. Each time you select a custom view, it retrieves the data from the original log files.

The log path shows the location of the log file. Moving the location of the log file is as simple as typing in a new path.

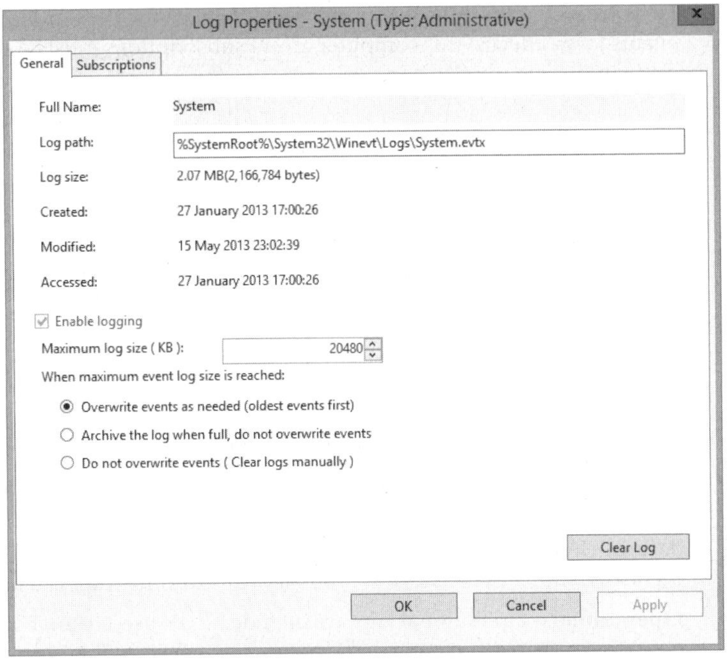

FIGURE 30.12
System log
properties page

Interestingly, when you move the log file, the existing events are retained in the original location. All new events are logged in the new location. However, Event Viewer remembers where the original events are and displays events from both locations. You can click the Clear Log button after moving it and you will be prompted to save the contents of the log file.

You can set the maximum log size from this page. Different log files have different default sizes. For example, the System log defaults to 20 MB and the Security log defaults to about 130 MB. Set the maximum log size to a size that won't consume too much of the hard drive space but that also will allow you to view the events.

Last, you can determine what to do when the maximum log size is reached. The choices are as follows:

♦ "Overwrite events as needed (oldest events first)"

♦ "Archive the log when full, do not overwrite events"

♦ "Do not overwrite events (Clear logs manually)"

SAVING A LOG FILE

Many organizations have policies in place that require log files to be archived. Once archived, the original file is saved and can be viewed later, new events won't overwrite archived events.

If you right-click a log file in Event Viewer and select Clear Log, you will be prompted to save the contents of the log file. Click the Save and Clear buttons. You can then give it a name and browse to a location where you want to save the file.

You can also right-click the log file and select Save All Events As. Again, you'll be able to give the file a name and browse to a location where you want to save it. The difference is that if you click Save As instead of Clear Log, the saved events will remain in the log.

You may also be prompted to save display information. If you work in a bilingual environment, this ensures the data can be displayed properly on other computers with a different default language.

DISPLAYING A SAVED LOG FILE

You can open any saved log from Event Viewer. Right-click any node in Event Viewer, and select Open Saved Log. You can then browse to the location of the saved log, select it, and click Open.

The default location to display the saved log is a new folder aptly named Saved Logs. You can use this as the location to display the saved log or you can create a new folder to display the new logs.

If you use the default location, a new folder named Saved Logs will appear. You can go back and forth between the live log and the saved log just by pointing and clicking.

Subscribing to Event Logs

Event log subscriptions allow you to configure a single server to collect copies of events from multiple systems. The single server collecting the events is called the *collector computer,* and events are forwarded to the collector computer from source computers.

Figure 30.13 shows how the source and collector computers work together with event subscriptions. In the figure, the collector computer is collecting copies of event log events from several source computers.

FIGURE 30.13
Source and collector computers

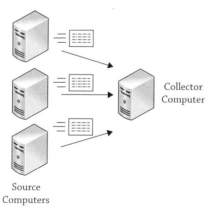

Collector
Computer

Source
Computers

Having a central server monitor events can make it a lot easier to maintain and administer several servers. As an example, you may administer multiple Microsoft SQL Server instances. You can create subscriptions to forward events from each of the SQL Server instances to a central monitoring server.

Once the events are captured on the collector computer, you can manipulate and filter them just like any other events on the computer. You can also create custom views for forwarded events.

Understanding Subscription Types

Subscriptions can be either collector initiated or source computer initiated. A collector-initiated subscription identifies all the computers that the collector will receive events from and will normally pull events from these computers. In a source computer–initiated subscription, source computers push events to the collector.

COLLECTOR-INITIATED SUBSCRIPTIONS

Collector-initiated subscriptions list all the computers that will forward events (event sources). This is the most common type of subscription used by server administrators.

Figure 30.14 shows the configuration page for a collector-initiated subscription named CollectSQLEvents.

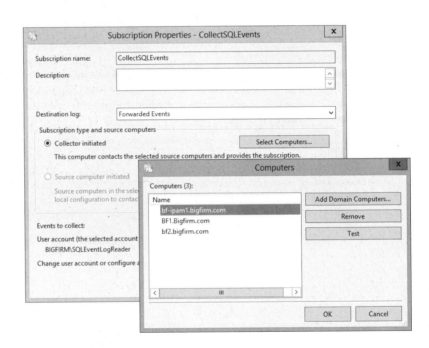

FIGURE 30.14
Creating a collector-initiated subscription

When configuring a collector-initiated subscription, you need to add the source computers by clicking the Select Computers button. If the source computers stay the same, the collector-initiated subscription is the best choice. You identify the list of computers once and you'll need to reconfigure it only if you want to add or remove a computer to/from the subscription.

Collector-initiated subscriptions also need to be configured with the credentials of an account that has Read permissions on the source logs. Since subscriptions will include events from multiple computers, you should use a domain account that can easily be granted read permission on multiple computers.

In the figure, you can see that a domain account named SQLEventLogReader was created. This account was added to the Event Log Readers group.

EVENT LOG READERS GROUP

The easiest way to grant Read permission on the source logs is to add a user account to the Event Log Readers group. You can add an account to this group on each computer, or you can add a user account to the domain Event Log Readers group located in the built-in container.

SOURCE COMPUTER–INITIATED SUBSCRIPTIONS

In a source computer–initiated subscription, the source computers push the subscriptions to the collector computer. The source computers can be identified individually or by using a global group within Active Directory.

Source computer–initiated subscriptions work best when the list of source computers changes frequently. The subscription can be created once using a global group, then the groups can be added and removed from this global group in Active Directory.

Figure 30.15 shows the configuration page for a source computer–initiated subscription. In the figure, a global group named Event Monitored Computers from the Bigfirm domain is added to the subscription. This global group includes a list of computers that will act as source computers in the subscription.

FIGURE 30.15
Creating a source computer–initiated subscription

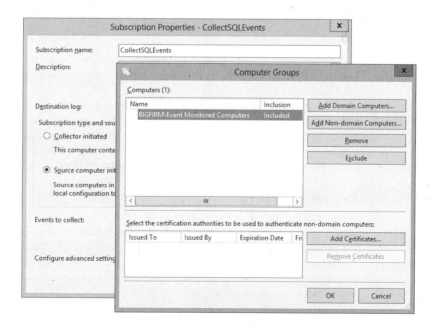

Additional configuration of the source computers is done through Group Policy. Specifically, you would configure the Computer Configuration ➤ Policies ➤ Administrative Templates ➤ Windows Components ➤ Event Forwarding node.

The Group Policy setting to configure is "Configure target Subscription Manager."

You must add the fully qualified domain name of the collector computer as the subscription manager. Once you enable the setting, you can click Show and then add the name of the server on the Subscription Managers page.

As an example, a server named BF2 in the Bigfirm.com domain would be identified with a value of Server=BF2.BigFirm.com, as shown in Figure 30.16.

FIGURE 30.16
Configuring Group Policy for a source-initiated subscription

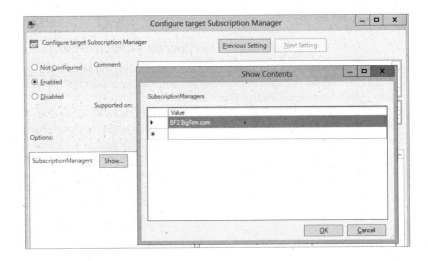

As a reminder, Group Policy objects (GPOs) can be linked to sites, domains, and organizational units (OUs). For this scenario, it makes sense to place all the servers you want to manage in an OU and then link the GPO to the OU.

It's also possible to configure this setting on each of the source computers manually if they aren't in a domain. If your computers are in a workgroup instead of a domain, you also need to use certificates issued from a certificate authority for authentication.

Given the additional requirements for source-initiated subscriptions within a workgroup, you'll probably stick with collector-initiated subscriptions in non-domain environments.

Selecting Events

When configuring an event subscription, you need to identify which events will be forwarded. Selecting events works the same for both collector-initiated and source computer–initiated subscriptions.

You can choose to forward all events for specific logs or forward only specific events. When you click the Select Events button, you will see the same page you use to filter any Event Viewer log or create a custom view.

It's also possible to create the subscription from the command line. When using the command line, the events are selected using an XML query.

Setting Advanced Options

Advanced options include the user account, the event delivery optimization settings, and the protocol and port. The user account is configurable only in a collector-initiated subscription. The other advanced options are available in both types of subscriptions.

CONFIGURING USER ACCOUNTS

The collector-initiated subscription will actually read the logs on the source computers and need to have at least read permission on the logs. You have to configure the account on the subscription and ensure the account has the appropriate permission on each of the source computers.

The easiest way to meet the requirements within a domain is to create a domain account and add this account to the Event Log Readers built-in domain local group.

User accounts are not configurable on source computer–initiated subscriptions.

OPTIMIZING EVENT DELIVERY

When configuring subscriptions, you can optimize them for environments with different bandwidth capabilities or different latency requirements. These settings can be configured for both collector-initiated and source computer–initiated subscriptions.

Figure 30.17 shows the Advanced Subscription Settings dialog box for a collector-initiated subscription. Notice that there are three Event Delivery Optimization options: Normal, Minimize Bandwidth, and Minimize Latency.

FIGURE 30.17
Advanced Subscription
Settings dialog box

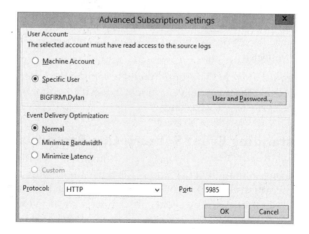

A source-initiated subscription has the same Event Delivery Optimization choices but omits the user account settings. The collector computer doesn't read the logs on the source computer in a source-initiated subscription but instead just receives them, so an account with appropriate permissions isn't required.

Normally, the servers will all be in a well-connected environment within the same LAN and use Normal mode. Events are forwarded within 15 minutes and don't require excessive bandwidth. However, if your servers are separated by WAN links or you need the events sent to the collector more quickly, you can optimize delivery of the events.

The different delivery modes use batches and batch time outs. Before you can understand the delivery modes, you need to understand the basics of batches and batch time outs.

Batches Events can be sent one at a time, but they are usually sent in batches. A batch is simply several events grouped together for transmission. Different optimization modes have thresholds of how many events are included in a batch. For example, Normal mode waits until five events are received and sends them as a batch of five items.

Batch Time out A batch time out specifies the maximum amount of time a system will wait before sending the events, even if the batch threshold isn't reached. For example, Normal mode has a batch time out of 15 minutes. If the subscription specifies five items per batch but only three items are received in 15 minutes, these three items will be sent as a batch after 15 minutes.

Each of the three Event Delivery Optimization options uses batches and batch time outs a little differently. The Event Delivery Optimization options are as follows:

Normal Normal mode is used in a typical well-connected LAN. It doesn't attempt to conserve bandwidth and sends events often. The default threshold for batches is five events, and the default batch time out is 15 minutes.

Minimize Bandwidth The Minimize Bandwidth option significantly limits how often events are sent no matter how many events are collected. It doesn't use a batch threshold, and the default batch time out is six hours. In other words, it will send all the collected events only every six hours.

Use this option if the source computers are connected to the collector computer via a WAN link.

The trade-off with this option is that messages on the collector computer have a high degree of latency. Events occurring on the source computer may take as long as six hours to appear on the collector.

Minimize Latency This option sends events to the collector computer every 30 seconds by default using the push delivery mode. It doesn't monitor the batch threshold but instead uses the batch time out of 30 seconds.

Understanding Event Subscription Protocols

Subscriptions use HTTP for unencrypted transmissions and HTTPS for encrypted transmissions. Although HTTP and HTTPS use the default ports of 80 and 443 on the Internet, event subscriptions use different ports for these protocols.

The default ports used by event subscriptions are as follows:

◆ HTTP: 5985

◆ HTTPS: 5986

The only reason to change the default ports is if there is a conflict with another application on your network. In other words, if port 5985 or 5986 is already in use on your network, you could use another port.

If you do change the ports in the subscription configuration, the servers involved in the subscription will need to be reconfigured using the `WinRM` command. This is the format of the `WinRM` command:

```
Winrm set winrm/config/listener?Address=*+Transport=HTTP @{Port="8888"}
```

Since event subscriptions use different ports than are typically used with HTTP and HTTPS, event subscriptions won't conflict with an installed IIS server.

Configuring Event Subscriptions

These are the overall requirements to configure event subscriptions:

- Ensure the required services are enabled on source and collector computers.

- Configure the source and collector computers.

- Configure the subscription.

ENABLING REQUIRED SERVICES

Two services are needed to support event log subscriptions. Both of these services must be running on both the source and collector computers:

Windows Event Collector (`wecutil`) Service   Wecutil is the primary service used to manage subscriptions. It should be set to Automatic or Automatic (Delayed Start). Wecutil supports the WS-Management protocol that is implemented in Windows with the WinRM service.

Windows Remote Management (WinRM) Service   WinRM uses web services over HTTP and HTTPS to implement remote software and hardware management. It should be set to Automatic or Automatic (Delayed Start). WinRM doesn't depend on the Web Services (IIS) role and can coexist if this role is installed on the same server.

CONFIGURING THE COMPUTERS

Before event subscriptions can be created, you must configure both the source and collector computers. Use the following steps to configure the source computer to receive events. These steps will configure Windows Remote Management (WinRM) on the source server:

1. Launch a command prompt with administrative permissions.

2. Enter the following command:

   ```
   Winrm quickconfig
   ```

WINDOWS EVENT COLLECTOR SERVICE

The first time you select the Subscriptions node of Event Viewer or the Subscription tab of any log, a dialog box will appear stating that the Windows Event Collector service must be running and configured. It then asks whether you want to start and configure the service. If you click Yes, it starts the service and changes the startup type from Manual to Automatic (Delayed Start), causing it to start each time Windows starts.

If WinRM hasn't been configured yet, you will be prompted to do the following:

◆ Create a WinRM listener on HTTP://* to accept WS-Man requests to any IP on this machine.

◆ Enable the WinRM firewall exception.

If it has already been configured, then you will see a message stating that the service is up and running and is configured for remote management.

3. Type **Y** and press Enter to make these changes.

The system will respond indicating that WinRM was updated for remote management. Use the following steps to configure the collector computer to receive events. These steps will configure the Windows Event Collector (`wecutil`) service on the collector server:

1. Launch a command prompt with administrative permissions.

2. Enter the following command:

```
Wecutil qc
```

It will reply with a message indicating the service startup mode will be changed to Delay-Start and prompt you to type Y or N.

3. Type **Y** and press Enter to make these changes.

The system will respond indicating that the Windows Event Collector service was configured successfully.

CREATING A COLLECTOR-INITIATED SUBSCRIPTION

Use the following steps to create a collector-initiated subscription within a domain environment:

1. Launch Event Viewer from the Windows Server 2012 R2 Start screen by typing **eventvwr** and then pressing Enter or via Server Manager ➤ Tools ➤ Event Viewer.

2. Right-click Subscriptions, and select Create Subscription.

3. Enter **Collector Initiated** as the Subscription Name.

Notice that Forwarded Events is selected as the destination log.

4. Ensure that Collector Initiated is selected, and click Select Computers.

5. Click Add Domain Computers. Enter **LocalHost** as the computer name, and click OK.

LocalHost will be resolved to your actual computer name. In a live environment, there would be no need to create a subscription for your own computer. However, this does allow you to follow the steps to create a subscription.

6. Add other computers if desired.

7. Click the Test button. This verifies that you have connectivity to the server.

FQDN OR LOGON NAME

When you add the server, the system attempts to reach it, and if it can, it displays the fully qualified domain name (FQDN) of the server (as in BF1.Bigfirm.com). If it can't reach it, it will display the name in the logon format of domain\account (as in Bigfirm\BF3). If the server doesn't exist in Active Directory, it can't be added.

8. Click OK to dismiss the Connectivity Test Succeeded dialog box. Click OK in the Computers dialog box.

9. Click the Select Events button. Click the check boxes for Critical, Warning, Error, and Information. You can choose different event levels to meet your needs.

10. Select the drop-down box next to Event Logs.

11. Select the plus (+) sign next Windows Logs, and select the Application and System logs.

    You can also choose any logs in the Application and Services Logs node.

SELECT FEWER THAN 10 LOGS

Any time you select more than 10 logs, a warning appears indicating this isn't a wise action. Selecting too many logs can consume a large amount of server resources and affect system performance. Avoid the temptation to monitor everything, instead identify exactly what you want to monitor.

12. Click OK to close the Query Filter selection.

13. Click the Advanced button.

    Notice that the machine account is selected by default. It will not have read access to the source logs on any remote server.

14. Use the following steps to create a domain account, and grant it read access to the source logs on remote systems:

    a. Launch Active Directory Users and Computers.

    b. Right-click the Users node, and select New ➤ User.

    c. Type **EventLogReader** in the First Name and User Logon Name text boxes. Click Next.

    d. Enter a password that meets the complexity requirements of your domain in the Password and Confirm Password text boxes.

    e. Deselect the User Must Change Password at Next Logon check box.

    f. Select the User Cannot Change Password and Password Never Expires check boxes.

EVENT LOG READER ACCOUNT

You should treat the event log reader account as a service account. Service accounts are often configured so that the password does not expire. However, service accounts (and the event log reader account) should still be managed. In other words, you should have a process in place to periodically change the passwords of these accounts, or better yet, use the Managed Service Accounts feature available with Windows Server 2012 R2.

      g. Click Next, then click Finish to create the account.

      h. Double-click the EventLogReader account to access the properties.

      i. Click the Member Of tab, and click Add.

      j. Type **Event Log Readers**, and click OK to add the account to the Event Log Readers group.

15. Return to the Advanced Subscription Settings page, and select Specific User.

16. Click the User and Password button.

17. Enter the username and password of the account you just created in the Credentials dialog box. The username should be entered in the format of domain\username. Click OK.

18. Review the Event Delivery Optimization choices, ensure that the Normal option is selected.

19. Review the protocols and ports. The default port for HTTP is 5985 and the default port for HTTPS is 5986. You can view the port for HTTPS by selecting HTTPS in the Protocol drop-down list box.

20. Click OK to accept your changes.

21. Click OK to complete the creation of your subscription.

ERRORS WHEN CREATING SUBSCRIPTION

If you receive any errors when creating the subscription, verify that the computers that you've added to the subscription are operational and reachable by your server. You can easily verify this by clicking the Select Computers button, selecting each of the computers, and clicking Test.

After a subscription is created, you can right-click it and select Properties to reconfigure most of the properties of the subscription. You can't change the subscription type (collector initiated or source computer initiated) or the subscription name, but you can modify any of the other properties.

Troubleshooting Event Forwarding

The most common problems associated with event forwarding errors are that the servers involved in the subscription aren't accessible in the network, the subscription is configured incorrectly, or the user account doesn't have the right permissions.

Checking the Runtime Status

A useful check is the runtime status of the event subscription. You can access it by right-clicking the subscription and selecting Runtime Status.

Figure 30.18 shows the runtime status of a subscription created with an account problem. When the error is selected, the details of the error are displayed in the bottom pane.

FIGURE 30.18
Viewing the runtime status

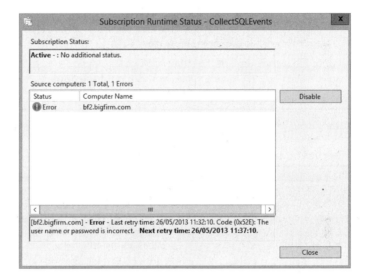

In this case, the error message is "Logon failure." The account used for the subscription doesn't have permission to read the logs on the remote computer due to an incorrect username or password. This can be resolved by verifying that the correct username and password have been input and ensuring that the user account has been added to the Event Log Readers group.

Using the Windows Event Collector Utility

You can also run the Windows Event Collector utility at the command line to configure and troubleshoot event forwarding.

You can accomplish most of the same tasks using either the Event Viewer GUI or the `wecutil` commands. So, you may be asking why you'd really need the `wecutil` commands. There are two reasons:

◆ The first and most important reason is that `wecutil` commands can be executed remotely using the `WinRS` command. If `WinRS` is configured, any of the `wecutil` commands can be executed from the command line of a remote computer.

◆ The second reason is that the `wecutil` commands can be scripted. Any commands you can enter at the command line can be put into a batch file or PowerShell script and easily executed. For example, if you created a subscription using a batch file, you could easily re-create it by simply rerunning the batch file. Table 30.1 shows the various switches available with `wecutil`.

The most common way to use these commands for troubleshooting event subscriptions is to first list the subscriptions with this command:

`Wecutil es`

This will list the event subscriptions with their name. For example, if you did the earlier steps to create a collector-initiated subscription named Collector Initiated, the output would be `Collector Initiated`.

With the name of the subscription known, you can now retrieve the runtime status of the subscription with the following command:

`Wecutil gr "Collector Initiated"`

Note that the name of the subscription has a space in it so it must be enclosed in quotes. If the subscription doesn't have a space, you can omit the quotes.

TABLE 30.1: Wecutil commands

Wecutil COMMAND	COMMENTS
Wecutil /?	Help. Shows the basic commands.
	You can ask for additional help on any command by using the /? switch after the command, as in `wecutil es /?`.
Wecutil es	Enumerate subscription. You can list all the subscriptions on your system. Use this command to get the subscription ID to use with other commands.
Wecutil gs <subscription id>	Get subscription. The gs command will list all the parameters and options for a created subscription.
Wecutil gr <subscription id>	Get subscription runtime status. This command is useful when troubleshooting subscriptions. If the subscription isn't work-ing, it will include details of the last error message. You can also access this information by right-clicking the subscription in Event Viewer and selecting Runtime Status.
Wecutil ss	Set subscription. You can use this command to set the param-eters of a subscription. There is a lot of additional help on this command. Use the following command to pipe it into a text file named `sshelp.txt`:
	`Wecutil ss /? > sshelp.txt`.
	Open the help file with this: `Notepad sshelp.txt`

TABLE 30.1:   Wecutil command *(CONTINUED)*

Wecutil COMMAND	COMMENTS
Wecutil cs	Create subscription. You can use this command to create a subscription. You can get a lot of additional help on this command by using the /? switch.
Wecutil ds <subscription id>	Delete subscription.
Wecutil rs <subscription id>	Retry subscription. This command will attempt to establish a connection and send a remote subscription request. You can follow it with a gr command to get the current status after the retry attempt.
Wecutil qc	The quick configure switch is used to configure the Windows Event Collector service.

Monitoring Performance

Performance Monitor has been a mainstay in Windows operating systems since Windows 2000 and has become an essential component of the IT toolkit for administrators around the world. It can be used to watch your system in real time or create log files that you can use to identify changes in performance.

Figure 30.19 shows the Performance Monitor window. The left pane shows all the tools available to you from this snap-in. In the center pane is the system summary that appears by default. The four core resources (memory, network interface, physical disk, and processor) are monitored in real time, with counters showing you details of their performance.

FIGURE 30.19
Performance
Monitor

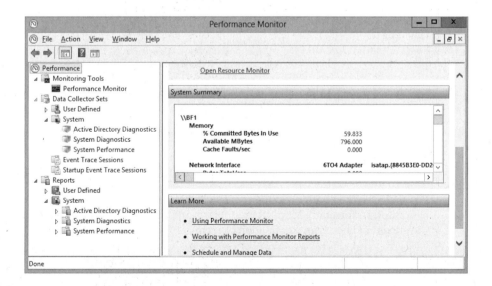

A core functionality of Performance Monitor is the data collector sets, which allow you to collect and view key performance data on your system grouped by diagnostic and performance category.

IS IT CALLED "PERFORMANCE" OR "PERFORMANCE MONITOR"?

In different versions of Windows, this tool has been called both Performance and Performance Monitor. In Windows Server 2012 R2, it's called both. When you launch it, you launch Performance Monitor (open the Start Screen, type **perfmon**, and then click the Performance Monitor icon). You can also launch it by entering **perfmon** from PowerShell or a command prompt.

Once it's launched, the title bar names it, "Performance Monitor."

However, the top node in the navigation bar on the left is titled, "Performance." Within the Monitoring Tools node, you'll see the familiar Performance Monitor you may have used in previous editions of Windows. The point we're trying to make is that Performance Monitor has evolved into a suite of tools that are more than just the traditional Perfmon.exe tool that was available in earlier iterations of Windows. In this chapter we refer to the full suite of tools as *Performance Monitor* and the older Performance Monitor (in the Monitoring Tools node) as the *legacy Performance Monitor*.

Using Monitoring Tools

This section includes the legacy Performance Monitor, Resource Monitor, and a system reliability report.

The legacy Performance Monitor is displayed by default, but if you right-click the Monitoring Tools node, you'll also have the Resource Monitor and "View system reliability" options to choose from, as shown in Figure 30.20.

FIGURE 30.20
Accessing the additional monitoring tools

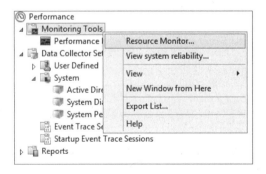

PERFORMANCE MONITOR

If you've worked with previous versions of Windows, you've probably worked with Performance Monitor. Performance Monitor uses objects and counters to deliver real-time monitoring of your systems, and here's an explanation of each:

Objects   Performance Monitor objects are specific resources that can be measured. Some commonly measured objects are Processor, Memory, Network Interface, and Physical Disk.

Counters   Counters are the individual metrics within an object. For example, the Processor object includes counters, such as % Processor Time, % User Time, and Interrupts/Sec.

Counters monitored in this Performance Monitor are used throughout the entire suite of Performance Monitor tools including the data collector sets.

RESOURCE MONITOR

Resource Monitor is constantly running and capturing counters on the four core resources of your system. You can access it by right-clicking Monitoring Tools and selecting Resource Monitor. You can also access it via Task Manager. Select the Performance tab and click the Resource Monitor button.

Figure 30.21 shows Resource Monitor with the Overview tab selected. The left pane shows details on each of the resources and the right pane shows a graphic of each of the resources.

FIGURE 30.21
Accessing the additional monitoring tools

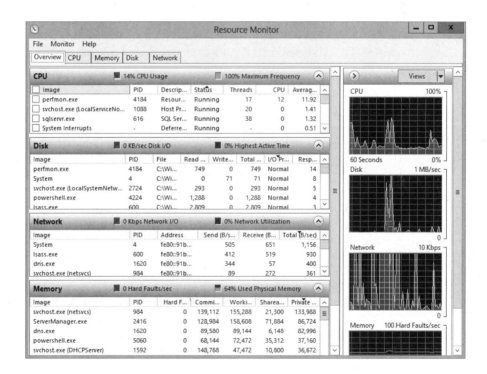

You can select the tab for any of the four resources to drill into additional details on the performance of the processor, memory, disk subsystem, or network interface.

One of the primary benefits of Resource Monitor is the ability to filter the results according to specific processes or services. For example, if you want to identify the load a specific application is placing on your system, you can select only that application's processes.

You can also use Resource Monitor to help you identify what process may be locking a file or DLL. As an example, malware will often prevent a file from being deleted by locking it. If you try to delete the malware file, the system balks because it claims the file is locked. However, you can use Resource Monitor to get some more details on what's happening.

Select the CPU tab and open the Associated Handles section. You can type in the name of the file in the text box and click the Search button. Details on the handle will be displayed. You can right-click the result and select End Process, and you should be able to delete the file.

BE CAREFUL WITH ENDING PROCESSES

Ending processes may result in system instability. You should end a process only as a last resort. It's sometimes a good solution but not a good first solution. Additionally, some processes are resilient, and if stopped, they'll automatically be restarted. This happens with some system resources and some malware.

Sometimes you may need to dig a little deeper. Identify the process ID (in the PID column), click the Overview tab, and look at the CPU section. The second column is labeled PID, and if you click it, you can sort the processes in ascending or descending order to easily find the process. When you click it once, an up arrow will indicate ascending order, and when you click it again, a down arrow will display.

Once you've found the process, you can right-click it and end it here or gather more information. If you select Analyze Wait Chain, it will show all the processes using or waiting to use the same resource.

VIEWING SYSTEM RELIABILITY

System reliability is tracked by Reliability Monitor. It uses a stability index to assess the system's stability on a scale of 1 to 10, with 10 indicating perfect reliability.

Reliability Monitor monitors hardware failures, application failures, Windows failures, and other miscellaneous failures and warnings. When a failure occurs, the stability index is reduced depending on the severity of the problem. The longer the system runs without any failures, the higher the stability index.

Data is displayed on a graph that shows icons for information, warnings, and failures. You can select any of the icons to view details on the failure.

Reliability Monitor can be useful in identifying trends of systems. Most of your servers should have similar stability indexes. However, if you identify a server that has a significantly lower index, it could be because of problems with incompatible hardware or buggy applications.

Using Data Collector Sets

Data collector sets are an exciting feature available within the Performance Monitor suite that first appeared in Windows Server 2008. Each data collector set is a predefined set of performance counters, event trace data, and configuration information used to monitor key elements within a system.

Performance Monitor includes prebuilt system data collector sets you can use to monitor your system. You can also use these system data collector sets as templates to create your own data collector sets.

Membership in the Administrators group is required on the local system to run or access data collector sets. Although the Performance Log Users group exists in Windows Server 2012 R2, these users have only minimal access to tools within the Performance Monitor suite.

SYSTEM DATA COLLECTOR SETS

The two prebuilt data collector sets are System Diagnostics and System Performance. If you promote a server to a domain controller, the Active Directory Diagnostics data collector set is added.

Unlike Resource Monitor, which is constantly running, the data collector sets are not configured to automatically run. You can start them by right-clicking any data collector set and selecting Start.

Data collected from these data collector sets is stored in the `c:\Perflogs` folder:

System Diagnostics   The System Diagnostics data collector set provides details on local hardware resources, system response times, and processes on the local computer. It includes system information and configuration data. The resulting report includes suggestions to maximize performance and streamline the system's operation. It will run for 10 minutes after being started.

System Performance   The System Performance data collector set can be used to identify possible causes of performance issues. It includes information on local hardware resources, system response times, and processes. It will run for one minute after being started.

Active Directory Diagnostics   The Active Directory Diagnostics data collector set collects Active Directory–related data, including performance counters, trace events, and registry keys that can be used to troubleshoot Active Directory performance issues. It will run for five minutes after being started.

The configuration details and properties of each of the prebuilt data collector sets can be viewed, but they can't be modified.

Use the following steps to run the System Performance and System Diagnostics data collector sets and view their results:

1. Launch the Performance Monitor suite from the Windows Server 2012 R2 Start screen by typing **perfmon** and then pressing Enter or via Server Manager ➢ Tools ➢ Performance Monitor.

2. Browse to the Data Collector Sets ➢ System node to access the prebuilt data collector sets.

3. Right-click the System Performance data collector set, and select Start.

   The data collector set will run for one minute. When it completes, you can view the report.

4. After the data collector set completes, right-click the System Diagnostics data collector set, and select Start.

This will run while you're viewing the System Performance data collector set report.

5. Browse to the Reports ➤ System ➤ System Performance node within Performance Monitor. Select the report.

   Your display will be similar to Figure 30.22.

FIGURE 30.22

Data collector set report

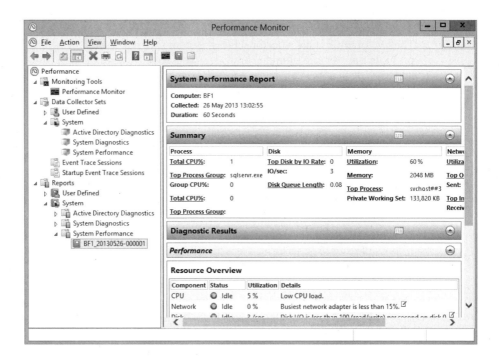

6. Browse through the details of the report.

   It includes details on the overall performance of your system and the CPU, network, disk, and memory resources. At the end of the report are overall report statistics.

7. Right-click the report, and select View ➤ Performance Monitor.

   Your display will look similar to Figure 30.23. This shows the same report data from step 6 but this time within the legacy Performance Monitor. As you can see, it's quite a mess and not easy on the eye at all! Although a picture is worth a thousand words, a thousand data points on the legacy Performance Monitor graph don't easily tell you a story. Microsoft has done a great job in cleaning up this data and displaying it in the report format.

FIGURE 30.23
Data collector set
report viewed in
graph mode

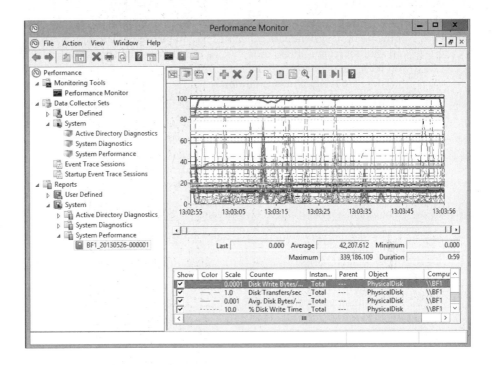

8. Right-click the report, and select View ➤ Folder.

   This shows you the actual Windows Explorer view of the files used to create the report. System Performance data collector sets are stored in the `c:\Perflogs\System\Performance` folder by default. Each report will be contained within a separate folder.

9. When the System Diagnostics data collector set finishes, right-click it, and select Latest Report.

10. Browse through this report.

   Notice that the Warnings section includes the symptoms, cause, details, and a suggested resolution for each error. Additionally, it often includes a link to a website in the Related section where you can look for information related to the error.

USER-DEFINED DATA COLLECTOR SETS

You can create your own data collector sets to meet specific needs. Unlike the prebuilt data collector sets, you can modify any of the properties of a user-defined data collector set. These include the length of time it runs and the schedule used to launch it.

When creating a user-defined data collector set, you typically start with a template, and each of the prebuilt system data collector sets can be used as a template. You can also create a data collector set from scratch, though it's a little like re-creating the wheel. The templates provide you with a good starting point.

These are the two most common reasons to create a user-defined data collector set:

To Create a Baseline A baseline will document the system operation at a point in time. If the performance degrades later, you can easily identify which resource or which application is causing the problem.

To Schedule a Data Collector Set A user-defined data collector set can be scheduled to run on a regular basis. For example, you could create two data collector sets from the System Diagnostics and System Performance built-in templates and then schedule them to run once a day. You can review the reports on a regular basis, and if a problem appears on your server, you'll have a history you can easily reference.

The next two procedures will lead you through the steps to create a baseline and to schedule a data collector set to run on a regular basis.

Use the following steps to create a data collector set that can be used as a baseline:

1. Launch the Performance Monitor suite from the Windows Server 2012 R2 Start screen by typing **perfmon** and then pressing Enter, or via Server Manager ➤ Tools ➤ Performance Monitor.

2. Browse to the Data Collector Sets ➤ User Defined node to access the prebuilt data collector sets.

3. Right-click User Defined, and select New ➤ Data Collector Set.

4. Enter **Baseline** as the name for your data collector set.

5. Ensure that Create From a Template (Recommended) is selected, and click Next.

6. Select the System Performance template, and click Next.

7. Accept the default location for the data to be stored by clicking Next.

   On a production server, you may want to change this path to a different partition that won't compete with the operating system.

8. On the Create the Data Collector Set page, you can designate another account to run the data collector set.

   The default user account is the built-in System account and will work for the local system.

9. Click Finish.

10. Right-click the Baseline data collector set, and select Start.

    It will run for a minute and then complete. An icon similar to a Play button appears while it is running. When the schedule completes, the icon will disappear.

11. Browse to the Reports ➤ User Defined ➤ Baseline node. Select the report from your baseline, and view it.

    At this point, there's no difference between your user-defined data collector set and the System Performance data collector set.

12. Right-click your Baseline data collector set, and select Properties.

13. Click the Stop Condition tab.

14. Change the Overall Duration Units from Minutes to Weeks.

Your display will look similar to Figure 30.24.

FIGURE 30.24
Modifying data
collector set
properties

15. Click the Directory tab.

Notice that you can modify where the report is stored and the format of the report's name. By default, the reports are named with the following convention: ServerName_dateyyyymmdd-sequential number. As you modify the settings on this page, the example directory is shown at the bottom of the page.

16. Select each of the tabs in the properties of your data collector set.

Notice that you can configure many properties, but the sample interval isn't available on any of the property pages.

17. Click OK to save your changes.

MODIFY THE DEFAULT SAMPLE INTERVAL

The default sample interval is set to 1 second, meaning that the data collector set will capture all the metrics every second. When capturing the data for 60 seconds, sampling every second is useful. However, if you're capturing data for a full week as part of a baseline, you only need to capture the samples every 30 to 45 minutes to get an accurate picture of the system's performance.

18. With the baseline data collector set selected, right-click the Performance Counter element, and select Properties.

You can add or remove performance counters from this page. For example, if you are monitoring a server hosting SQL Server, you may want to add some of the SQL Server performance counters in addition to the core resource counters.

19. Change Sample Interval from 1 to 45, and change Units from Seconds to Minutes.

Your display will look similar to Figure 30.25.

FIGURE 30.25
Modifying
Performance
Counter
properties

20. Click OK.

At this point, you have a data collector set that will run for a week and will capture samples every 45 minutes. It can be manually started, or you could modify the properties to add a schedule to start it on a specific date. Either way, it will run for seven days and create a baseline report of your system.

You can also manually stop any data collector set. Right-click the data collector set that is running, and select Stop.

ONLY ONE DATA COLLECTOR SET AT A TIME

Data collector sets require exclusive access to some system resources. Because of this, you can run only one data collector set at a time. If one is running and you try to start another, you will receive an error. Once the first data collector set finishes, another can be started, but they aren't queued.

If you've created the baseline in the preceding exercise and started it, you'll need to stop it before you can run the data collector set created in the following exercise.

Use the following steps to create a system diagnostics data collector set and schedule it to run once a day:

1. Launch Performance Monitor by selecting Start ➢ Administrative Tools ➢ Performance Monitor.

2. Browse to the Data Collector Sets ➢ User Defined node to access the prebuilt data collector sets.

3. Right-click User Defined, and select New ➢ Data Collector Set.

4. Enter **Routine Diagnostics** as the name for your data collector set. Ensure that Create From a Template (Recommended) is selected. Click Next.

5. Select the System Diagnostics template, and click Next.

6. Accept the default location for the data to be stored by clicking Next.

7. Select the "Open Properties for this Data Collector Set" option, and then click Finish.

8. Click the Schedule tab, and click Add to add a schedule.

   Notice that a schedule isn't created by default. However, you can add schedules to occur any day of the week, to occur any time of the day, to start on any date on the calendar, and to expire on any date.

9. Click OK to accept the default schedule starting at midnight for each day of the week.

10. Click OK to complete the creation of the Routine Diagnostics data collector set.

You now have a user-defined data collector set that will run daily.

REPORT MAINTENANCE

After creating reports to run on a regular basis, the only other thing you need to consider is the data-retention policies. The worst-case scenario is that the reports consume the disk space and the system shuts down—which of course you don't want to happen! Thankfully, there are built-in protections that will prevent this from occurring. However, these protections can delete reports you may want to keep.

Reports are grouped together for each data collector set and managed by individual data-retention policies. Each time you run a data collector set, another report is created in the same node or folder, and other reports are examined to determine whether they should be deleted or archived.

The data-retention policy is managed using the Data Manager tab and the Actions tab of the report properties sheet.

Figure 30.26 shows the Data Manager tab for a user-defined data collector set named Routine Diagnostics. You can access this page by right-clicking the report group and selecting Properties. The report group will have the same name as the data collector set. In this example, you can locate the report group at Reports ➢ User Defined ➢ Routine Diagnostics.

FIGURE 30.26
Managing reports

The Data Manager tab provides details on when reports will be deleted based on disk usage. These settings are used to prevent the reports from consuming the entire disk:

Minimum Free Disk and Maximum Folders   If the amount of free disk space drops below the minimum threshold (200 MB by default) or the number of folders exceeds the maximum threshold (100 reports by default), the policy will delete reports until the amount no longer exceeds the threshold. Each report is contained within a folder, so for this context, a folder is the same as a report.

Resource Policy   When a threshold is reached, you can choose to delete the largest reports (the default) or the oldest reports.

Apply Policy Before The Data Collector Starts   Selecting this box will cause data to be deleted before the data collector starts. If this check box is deselected, the Data Manager limits will be ignored. Data retention will be managed exclusively by the rules defined on the Actions tab.

Maximum Root Path Size   This refers to all the report data in this common path. For example, the common path by default is c:\Perflogs. If all the report data exceeds 1 GB, then this policy will cause files to be deleted or archived. This setting will override the Minimum Free Disk and Maximum Folders settings.

PERFLOGS FOLDER

If required, you can access the reports directly using Windows Explorer. If you browse to the c:\Perflogs folder, you'll see two folders: Admin and System. The Admin folder holds report data from all the user-defined data collector sets. The System folder holds report data from all the system data collector sets. It's also possible to choose a different path including a different partition for any user-defined data collector sets.

The Actions tab provides details on how reports are archived and deleted even if the disk usage doesn't exceed the defined thresholds. Clicking the Add or Edit button here opens the Folder Action window, which is used to create conditions for any scheduled action. Reports that have been created from templates have three default folder actions:

1 Day After a day, a cabinet file will be created and the source data will be deleted. A cabinet file is an archive format that can be used by a user to retrieve the original data. Data must first be extracted from the cabinet file before it can be viewed in a report. Data archived into a cabinet file will disappear from the Reports view in Performance Monitor. However, you can extract the data into a different folder and double-click the report.html file to view the report.

8 Weeks The cabinet file will be deleted. A report.xml file will remain that holds the raw data from the report.

24 Weeks The report will be deleted. This rule will also check for the original data and the cabinet file. If either of these exists, it will also be deleted.

SAVE YOUR REPORT

If you want to save any report and ensure it's not deleted as part of the data-retention policies, you should copy the entire folder and save it in a different location using Windows Explorer. Any time you want to view the report, open the folder and double-click the report.html document. The entire report is viewable in Internet Explorer. You can also modify the data-retention policy so that it doesn't automatically remove it.

PAL and PerfView

Now that you have a handle on using the Performance Monitor suite of built-in tools to gain insight into how your Windows Server deployments are running, it's time to kick things up a gear and delve into some additional external tools that can be useful in providing deeper performance insight than what you get out of the box.

The Performance Analysis of Logs (PAL) and PerfView tools are two such offerings that can help you simplify the collection and analysis of your performance data as well as create comprehensive performance baselines for your applications that are running on Windows Server 2012 R2.

Introducing PAL

The PAL tool was developed around 2007 by Microsoft's Clint Huffman and is a free download available here: http://pal.codeplex.com/. Running on PowerShell, it allows you to analyze existing performance counter logs and generate reports to give you baselines using thresholds that have been defined by Microsoft and that are relevant to the performance of your applications and systems. PAL can be very useful when used in conjunction with the counter logs (*.blg files) generated by the Performance Monitor data collector sets that we discussed earlier.

The next section will discuss the prerequisites for PAL and provide a walkthrough of its installation.

PREREQUISITES

Before you install PAL, make sure that you are running it on a client with at least Windows 7 64-bit edition—this is the only client OS that the latest release of this tool was tested on by its developer, but we've successfully run it on Windows 8 and Windows Server 2012 R2 without issue. You'll also need to ensure you have the following products installed on the computer running it:

◆ PowerShell v2.0 or greater

◆ Microsoft .NET Framework 3.5 Service Pack 1

◆ Microsoft Chart Controls for Microsoft .NET Framework 3.5

INSTALLATION

Once you've met the prerequisites and downloaded the tool, follow these steps to get it installed:

1. Log on to the computer where you wish to install PAL with an administrative account.

2. Browse to the location where you've downloaded the binaries, right-click setup.exe, and choose "Run as administrator" to begin the installation.

3. Acknowledge the initial warning message at the Welcome dialog box about the PowerShell execution policy setting, and then click Next.

4. Choose the installation folder location; then click Next twice.

5. From the Installation Complete dialog box, click the Close button to finish the wizard.

USING PAL

Now that you've installed PAL, it's time to put it to good use! This section will walk you through the initial configuration steps required to generate your first report. If you haven't worked through the tasks in the "System Data Collector Sets" section, then now would be a good time to go through them because we'll use the performance counter log file that's generated as a target for the PAL tool.

1. Log on to the computer where you've installed PAL with an administrative account, and launch PAL from the Start screen or menu.

    When the tool runs, you will be presented with the PAL Wizard, as shown in Figure 30.27. This wizard will take you through the configuration of the tool in no time.

2. Click Next to begin.

3. At the Counter Log tab, specify the location of the counter logs that you want to use for analysis.

    We're going to use the System Performance counter log that we generated earlier, which is located at c:\Perflogs\System\Performance. Figure 30.28 shows an example of what it should look like. You can also choose the date and time range that the report will focus on from here.

FIGURE 30.27
The PAL Wizard

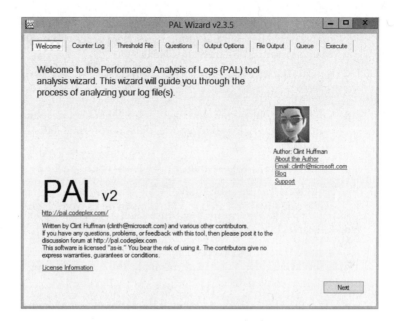

FIGURE 30.28
Specifying the
counter log

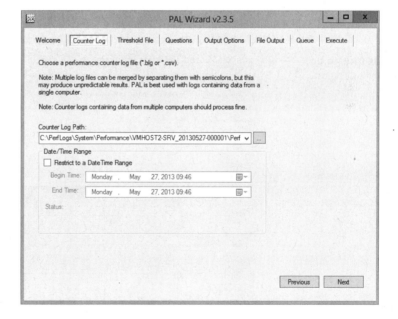

4. Click Next when you're ready to move on.

5. From the Threshold File tab choose System Overview as the file title, and then click Next.

6. On the Questions tab, click each question and then input the requested information based on the computer that the counter logs were generated on (Number of Processors, Total Memory, and so on); then click Next.

7. Choose the Analysis Interval option from the Output Options tab (or just leave it as AUTO); then click Next.

8. On the File Output tab, you have a number of choices to make about such things as the output directory for your reports, the report format (either HTML or XML), and the filename.

9. Click Next to move on when you've made your selections.

    The Queue tab essentially shows you an overview of your selections through the wizard so far and gives you an option to remove items from the running order queue.

10. Click Next.

11. On the Execute tab, you can choose to execute the analysis immediately, to add more items to the queue, or to execute analysis before restarting the wizard with the same settings for convenience.

12. Clicking Finish here will kick off the script that works with the counter logs specified to generate your report.

    After a number of minutes of PowerShell running, you should see your analysis containing content similar to that shown in Figure 30.29.

FIGURE 30.29

Analysis report

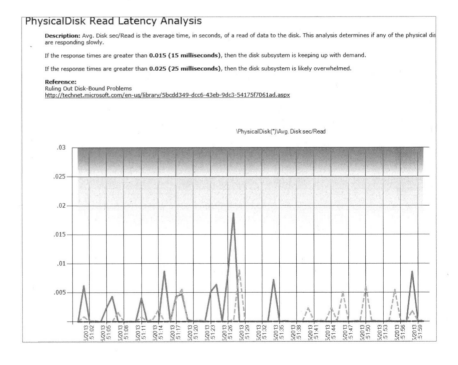

This report is just one example of the depth of information that you can get when you use PAL in conjunction with the built-in Performance Monitor suite in Windows Server 2012 R2. If you want to learn more about PAL, then check out Clint Huffman's blog and in particular this post on his PAL collector script: `http://tinyurl.com/ws2012pal`.

PerfView

PerfView is another interesting analysis tool that can be used to simplify the collection and analysis of your performance-related data. This runs at a deeper level than Performance Monitor or PAL and utilizes the Event Tracing for Windows (ETW) feature of Windows Server 2012 R2 to collect information. Ordinarily, this type of ETW information can seem like complete jargon to you and me, but to performance-monitoring ninjas, such as the Windows Performance group inside Microsoft who use this tool, it's translated into an understandable and easy-to-use format. In Figure 30.30, you can see an example of the PerfView tool in action.

FIGURE 30.30
The PerfView tool

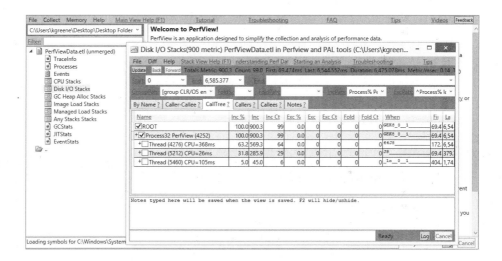

This flexible tool allows you to dig deeply into the likes of your CPU and Disk I/O stacks—if you're inclined that way! Because of the developer-oriented nature of this tool, a walk-through of the deployment and usage of it is out of scope for this book, but nonetheless it's a worthwhile weapon to add to your performance-analysis toolkit. You can download PerfView for free from the Microsoft Download Center here: `http://tinyurl.com/ws2012perfview`. Be sure to check out the associated user guides and sample use cases.

Advanced Monitoring with System Center 2012 R2

If you've worked through each of the chapters in this book and have moved your deployments of Windows Server, Failover Clustering, Hyper-V, and so on out of your lab and into an enterprise production environment, you'll most likely need to complement those deployments with an enterprise-level management and monitoring solution. Microsoft has delivered on this requirement with their System Center 2012 R2 suite of tools.

System Center 2012 R2 comprises the following eight core products:

- Operations Manager (monitoring)

- Virtual Machine Manager (fabric management)

- Service Manager (incident, change, and service management)

- Orchestrator (automation)

- Data Protection Manager (backup)

- App Controller (hybrid cloud management)

- Configuration Manager (device management)

- Endpoint Protection (malware and antivirus)

Each of these products has a different role inside the Microsoft cloud OS story that brings together private and public cloud management. The product that you're going to learn about in this section is Operations Manager, because you can leverage it to deliver full monitoring transparency of your Windows Server 2012 R2 deployments and their associated service-level agreements (SLAs).

Operations Manager is quite a big product to come to grips with initially, and we can't cover all of its features and functionality. If you want to learn much more about Operations Manager than the high-level overview you will get here, then check out *Mastering System Center 2012 Operations Manager* (Sybex, 2012, Bob Cornelissen, Kevin Greene et al).

Introduction to Operations Manager

Operations Manager (also known as OpsMgr or SCOM) is an end-to-end monitoring solution that covers Microsoft and 19 different cross-platform environments. With it, you can centrally monitor servers, applications, hardware, and operations for many computers from a central console. You can use it to map out all of the components of your individual IT services and then roll them up into a holistic and easy-to-manage single monitoring view. Think of it as an advanced take on the server groups functionality we spoke about earlier in this chapter, except instead of just grouping servers together, you're putting all of your service components in one place.

As an example of what it can do, take the email service in any organization. The IT department needs to be able to monitor not just the Microsoft Exchange servers that handle the emails for their company but also such things as the SAN, the Hyper-V hosts, the Windows Server operating system, the network switches, and routers. All of these components make up the overall email service, and if any of them go down, the whole service is potentially down. Operations Manager helps the IT department see them all as a single entity. This is called *IT service modeling* or *IT as a service.*

When you can manage and monitor your service as a single entity, you can get a view of the overall health of that service and have the service display green for healthy, red for critical, and yellow for warning. This leads to significantly quicker root-cause analysis of your IT services when compared to some of the more traditional monitoring methods. Figure 30.31 shows an example of IT as a service using Operations Manager.

FIGURE 30.31

IT as a service

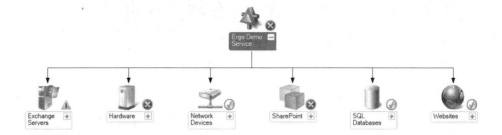

MANAGEMENT PACKS OVERVIEW

Unlike some of the other monitoring solutions on the market that attempt to monitor everything from the start, when you first deploy Operations Manager and decide to push an agent out to a server, it will only see that server as an entity that is either up or down. Operations Manager won't know that the agent has been deployed to a Windows Server 2012 R2 computer or that the agent is running on a server that has the Hyper-V role deployed, for example.

Operations Manager understands what it has to monitor on each agent through specific management packs that have been developed and made available by either the application/product vendor or the general System Center community. These management packs throw light on the Operations Manager infrastructure and allow the agents to understand the components that need to be brought under monitoring control.

WINDOWS SERVER 2012 R2 MONITORING

Microsoft has released a large number of management packs (MPs) for Windows Server 2012 R2 that cover nearly all of the essential roles that you can deploy inside the operating system. Here are some examples:

- Windows Server Active Directory MP

- Windows Server Base Operating System MP

- Windows Server Cluster Management MP

- Windows Server DNS 2012 MP

- Windows Server DHCP 2012 MP

- Windows Server File and iSCSI Services MP

- Windows Server Group Policy MP

- Windows Server Hyper-V 2012 MP

- Windows Server Internet Information Services MP

- Windows Server Network Load Balancing MP

- Windows Server Print Server MP

- Windows Server Remote Desktop Services 2012 MP

- Windows Terminal Services MP

Each of these management packs contains its own alerts, monitors, rules, tasks, diagrams, dashboards, and even reports that are based on the associated technology that it was designed to monitor. The fact that each one was developed in association with the actual Microsoft product group that designed the original role or feature means that you're getting a best-of-breed monitoring solution that contains all of the best-practice recommendations that you would typically have to get from Internet searches when you need help.

For a full list of all the available Microsoft management packs for Operations Manager, check out this TechNet Wiki page: `http://tinyurl.com/ws2012scom`.

Exploring the Windows Server Base OS MP

If you're new to Operations Manager, then before you deploy any management pack you should read the associated MP guide. These guides are like user manuals, and you can garner a huge amount of information about what the MP can and can't do. The Windows Server Base OS MP is just under 60 pages long, but if you take the time to read through it, you will learn about all of the different Windows Server components that it can discover and monitor, such as disks, CPU, memory, and network adapters.

In addition, a large number of reports come with this MP that allow you to run performance baselines and check utilization and configurations, and they help you keep on top of day-to-day situations such as low disk space on all your servers. Figure 30.32 shows all of the different views pertaining to health state and performance monitoring available when you monitor Windows Server 2012 R2 with Operations Manager.

FIGURE 30.32
The Windows
Server MP

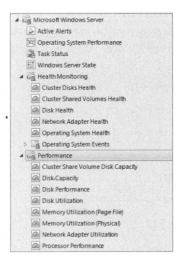

Monitoring Performance

Operations Manager uses a data warehouse SQL database that retains monitoring and performance data for one year. This amount of data means that it's one of the larger SQL databases that you'll have to deal with in your time as an IT administrator. However, it also means that you can very quickly create dashboards and baseline views spanning any period you wish over the last year. Having access to this depth of information is an excellent way of getting an insight into how your critical business applications and services have been performing.

The dashboard functionality in Operations Manager makes it easy to surface this data and present it on-screen to deliver maximum visualization of the environment being monitored. Figure 30.33 shows an example of a performance-monitoring dashboard in action.

FIGURE 30.33
Performance-
monitoring
dashboard

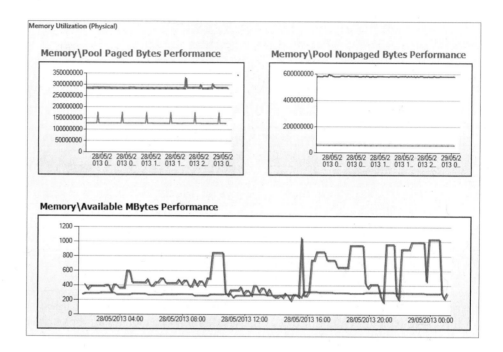

REPORTING WITH OPERATIONS MANAGER

A key function of Operations Manager is taking all of the information that it stores in its data warehouse about your computers, applications, and hardware devices and then letting you quickly run all manner of reports to help reinforce your role as an IT administrator. You can configure these reports to run as needed or on a scheduled basis to be sent via email. This scheduling feature is a great way to keep your different business unit owners and senior management happy by ensuring that they get the information they require all nicely laid out, as shown in Figure 30.34, and delivered straight to their inbox.

FIGURE 30.34
Operations
Manager
reporting

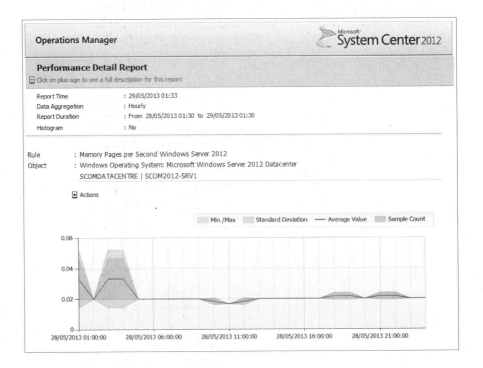

The Bottom Line

Use Server Manager to monitor multiple servers. The new Server Manager console in Windows Server 2012 R2 delivers out-of-box monitoring and health checks of your local and remote server infrastructure. It can be utilized to monitor multiple servers and the roles they are responsible for—all from one central console.

Master It You need to have a collated health state for the collective roles on multiple servers and want to manage them through Server Manager. What do you need to deploy? (Choose one.)

a. Security groups

b. Server groups

c. Distribution groups

d. Administrative groups

Understand how to use Event Viewer. Event Viewer in Windows Server 2012 R2 is one of the essential tools used to monitor your system. Often, it's one of the first places you'll look once you realize your server has a problem, but it can also be used to proactively monitor servers. Event Viewer can often help you to quickly identify the source of a problem or at least gain enough knowledge to know where to look next.

Master It You've just deployed the Hyper-V role to your Windows Server 2012 R2 computer. Where would you find the associated event log for this role?

Explore Performance Monitor. Data collector sets can be used to measure and monitor the performance of a server. Performance Monitor includes built-in data collector sets that can be run on demand, and you can also create your own data collector set.

Master It Run the System Performance data collector set and view the resulting report.

Explore the PAL and PerfView tools. Performance Analysis of Logs (PAL) and PerfView are two external tools that can help you simplify the collection and analysis of your performance data, as well as create comprehensive performance baselines for your applications that are running on Windows Server 2012 R2.

Master It PAL can be very useful when used in conjunction with Performance Monitor counter logs. What file extension is used with these counter logs? (Choose one.)

a. .chk

b. .perf

c. .blg

d. .evnt

Understand System Center 2012 R2 Operations Manager. Operations Manager (also known as OpsMgr or SCOM) is an end-to-end monitoring solution that covers Microsoft and 19 different cross-platform environments. With it, you can centrally monitor servers, applications, hardware, and operations for many computers from a central console. You can use it to map out all of the components of your individual IT services and then roll them up into a holistic and easy-to-manage single monitoring view.

Master It When you first deploy Operations Manager and decide to push an agent out to a server, it will only see that server as an entity that is either up or down. How do you get Operations Manager to see the different roles and applications on your servers?

Chapter 31

Patch Management

Patch management has been the process of minimizing your organization's threat and vulnerability surface by managing and deploying software updates, but over time it has moved to support feature updates and overall product updates. Updates can be deployed and managed by a number of different products and tools; an example of this is System Center Configuration Manager. In this chapter we will focus on the toolset built into the Windows Server 2012 R2 framework and its capabilities out of the box. Software updates have become an everyday task in today's online and collaborative world. The frequency at which you deploy and validate updates can mean the difference between having compromised or damaged computers or enjoying the weekend with your family and friends.

Software updates seem like a never-ending cycle, and unless you enjoy walking around to every computer to install updates, you need tools to help you do the job. Beyond the tools, you also need a sound patch-management process. You need to know whether each update is applicable to computers on your network, whether it is compatible with your existing applications, and how urgent it is to deploy this update.

In this chapter we walk through install and configuration of the Windows Server 2012 R2 Windows Server Update Services role and what you need to consider when you are deploying this patch-management process. After that, we analyze security updates and then take a detailed look at Windows Server Update Services (WSUS), which is now integrated into the operating system as a server role. We then cover how to migrate from Windows Server 2008 R2 WSUS to Windows Server 2012 R2 WSUS, and finally we present an overview of the available PowerShell cmdlets. In this chapter, you will learn to:

◆ Use Windows Automatic Updates to check for new updates on a computer running Windows 8

◆ Use the Windows Update Standalone Installer to silently install a security update

◆ Identify the four phases of patch management

What's New in Windows Server 2012 R2 Windows Server Update Services

Windows Server Update Services (WSUS) is now integrated into Windows Server 2012 R2. This new role allows administrators to use the Server Management tool to configure and manage updates; the same rich reporting and status updates are included with some new features and changes to the past functionality.

New Features of WSUS v6 in Windows Server 2012 R2

Several new features have been added to WSUS v6; the following is a basic list of these features:

◆ Services can be added or removed by using Server Manager.

◆ PowerShell cmdlets are available to manage the 10 most important tasks in WSUS.

◆ SHA256 hash capability has been added for additional security.

◆ Client and server separation is provided. Versions of the Windows Update Agent (WUA) can ship independently of WSUS.

Software Requirements for WSUS Servers and Clients

Before installing WSUS in your environment, you must ensure that both the WSUS server(s) and clients meet the minimum software requirements.

The WSUS servers must have at least the following installed:

◆ Windows Server 2012 R2

◆ Internet Information Services (IIS)

◆ .NET Framework 4.0 or newer

◆ If you are using a separate database server, you must have a computer installed that is running SQL Server 2012 R2 or 2008 R2 with Service Pack 1 or newer.

WSUS endpoints need to be on the version 7.8 (WUAgent 7.8) of the Windows Update Agent. WSUS clients must be running one of the following operating systems:

◆ Windows 8

◆ Windows RT

◆ Windows 7

◆ Windows Server 2008 R2

◆ Windows Server 2008

◆ Windows Server 2003 with Service Pack 1

◆ Windows Vista

These are the WSUS supported databases:

◆ Windows Internal Database (WID)

◆ Microsoft SQL Server 2012 R2 Standard Edition

◆ Microsoft SQL Server 2012 R2 Enterprise Edition

◆ Microsoft SQL Server 2012 R2 Express Edition

◆ Microsoft SQL Server 2008 R2 SP1 Standard Edition

♦   Microsoft SQL Server 2008 R2 SP1 Enterprise Edition

♦   Microsoft SQL Server 2008 R2 SP 1 Express Edition

SQL Server Express 2012 and SQL Server Express 2008 R2 have a database limit of 10 GB; this database size might be sufficient for many environments but is something to take into serious consideration when determining the appropriate limit for your system. The considerations in sizing should always begin with how many clients are you going to support and how many platforms.

Deployment Scenarios

The Windows Server 2012 R2 version of WSUS has been modified for deployment scenarios to focus not so much on the business size but on the requirements for capacity and location. The three main deployments are single WSUS server, multiple WSUS servers, and disconnected WSUS server. For medium to large organizations or a complex infrastructure, you should consider a product from the System Center family (www.microsoft.com/systemcenter).

A single-instance deployment is one primary WSUS server that synchronizes directly with Microsoft Update. The WSUS clients can be spread across different geographical areas but are all behind the same firewall, as shown in Figure 31.1.

FIGURE 31.1
Single WSUS
server deployment

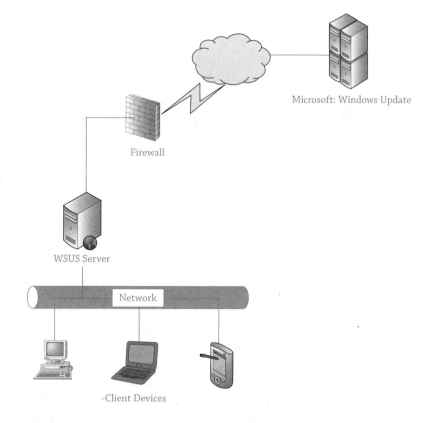

Many medium to large organizations utilize the multiserver infrastructure comprising more than one WSUS server serving clients that are geographically spread out. One WSUS server may synchronize with the other (shown in Figure 31.2), or they may get their updates separately from Microsoft Update. In this configuration only one server is exposed to the Internet, and the rest of the WSUS servers are set up as downstream servers to synchronize with the first. An advantage of having only one server synchronizing with Microsoft Update is that the other WSUS servers are not exposed to the Internet.

FIGURE 31.2
Multi-WSUS server deployment with one WSUS server synchronizing with another WSUS server

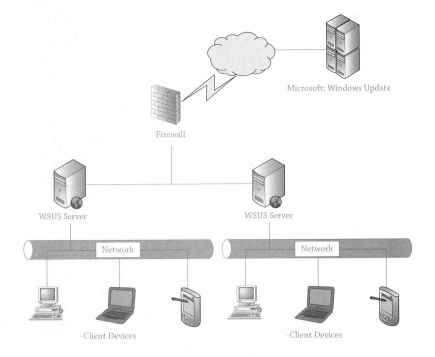

The disconnected infrastructure scenario is for computers that are not allowed access to the Internet or that have limited access to it. You can obtain updates for computers connected to this isolated network by setting up a WSUS server in that disconnected network. Once you have processed all patches to your production network, they can then be exported to devices such as a USB drive. The basic steps for this process are as follows:

1. Export patches from the WSUS console to a USB drive. You will need to use the WSUTIL.exe command to export these.

2. Import the patches into your disconnected WSUS server.

3. Approve the schedule and deploy the patches.

Once the patches are exported, they can be imported onto the disconnected WSUS server, as shown in Figure 31.3, and deployment can happen on that WSUS server's schedule.

FIGURE 31.3
Disconnected
WSUS server
deployment

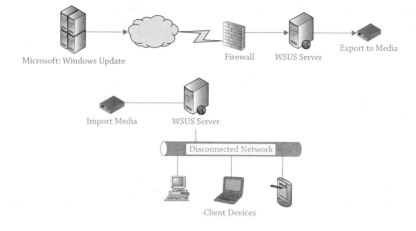

FIGURE 31.4
Autonomous
mode in a
multisite
environment

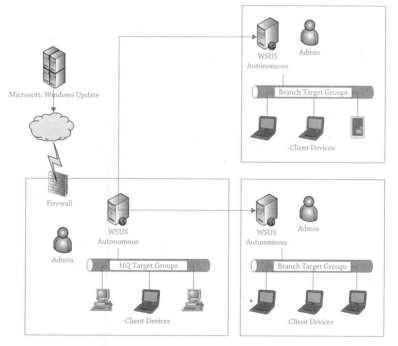

Complex Hierarchies with WSUS

Depending on the server deployment type and the needs of your organization, there are a few additional advantages to using the newer version of Windows Server. Doing so can greatly help minimize the server hardware (or virtual) deployments required to manage your environment. Building on the capabilities of Windows Server 2012 R2 and WSUS, you can configure Autonomous mode, Replica mode, as well as branch-office and roaming clients.

Autonomous mode, commonly called distributed mode, is the default installation option for WSUS. In this configuration (shown in Figure 31.4), you are using an upstream server to share updates with one or multiple downstream servers, and by leveraging access controls you can give local administrators the ability to manage their own environments.

FIGURE 31.5
Replica mode
in a multiple
branch-office
scenario

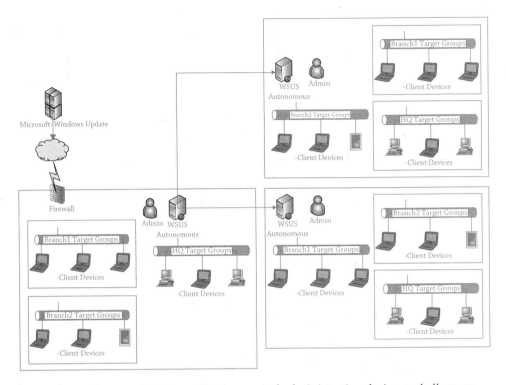

Replica mode, as diagramed in Figure 31.5, is a central administration design and allows an upstream server to share its updates, client groups, and other components with downstream servers. The replica servers are just downstream servers that are managed via the primary upstream server. This configuration is handiest when central IT is managing updates in a multisite or branch-office scenario.

Branch offices are one of the newer scenarios first introduced in Windows Server 2008 R2. In this configuration you leverage Windows Server 2012 R2 BranchCache; see http://tinyurl.com/c31BranchCache. Using this and the Branch Office feature in Windows, you can help reduce WAN link utilization and improve responsiveness.

Installation and Configuration of Patch Management

Installing updates on the computers on your organization's network is critical to protect the security of the network and to keep the organization's client computers performing optimally. How updates are rolled out on your network requires planning and testing to ensure a successful installation. Microsoft recommends a phased approach to patch management; each of the phases is discussed in detail on the Microsoft TechNet website at http://tinyurl.com/c31updateprocess.

Installing the WSUS Role on Windows Server 2012 R2

One of the new features of Windows Server 2012 R2 is the ability to install a server role and have it automatically add all of the required components as part of the installation. In previous versions of Windows Server, you would have to configure many of the roles and features as separate tasks.

To install the WSUS role on Windows Server 2012 R2, follow these steps:

1. Open the Server Manager dashboard, and select "Add roles and features," as shown in Figure 31.6.

FIGURE 31.6
Adding roles in
Windows Server
2012 R2

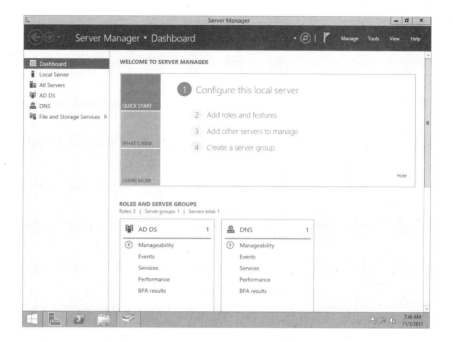

2. Log onto the computer as a member of the local Administrators group or as a domain admin.

3. Select Server Manager (this autostarts with Windows Server 2012 R2 by default).

4. In the "Configure this local server" section, click "Add roles and features."

5. On the Before You Begin page, click Next.

6. Choose "Role-based or feature-based installation" as your installation type.

7. On the "Select destination server" page, leave the default as on your server and click Next.

8. Scroll down to Windows Server Update Server, click the check box, and click Next.

9. You will be prompted to add the additional components for this installation to continue, as shown in Figure 31.7.

10. Select Add Features. You will now see Web Server (IIS) also selected; click Next.

The Features window will now open, and the following items will be preselected for this installation:

FIGURE 31.7
Required components for the Windows Server Update Services role

◆ Remote Server Administration Tools

◆ Windows Internal Database

◆ Windows Process Activation

11. Review your selections and click Next.

12. Windows Server Update Services loads; click Next.

Role Services by default has the WID Database (Windows Internal Database) and WSUS Services check boxes selected. The Database option is available in case you plan to use SQL on another server; it will provide additional options.

13. Leave this blank and click Next.

The next section lets you choose the location of the Windows Update files (if you chose to have them available locally); for the purposes of our example, uncheck this box. Doing so gives you the ability to store all updates on Microsoft Update and apply them when needed.

14. Once you have unchecked the box "Store updates in the following location," click Next.

15. The Web Server Role (IIS) loads; click Next.

The Role Services window will now open and the following items will be preselected for this installation:

◆ Common HTTP Features

  ◆ Default Document

  ◆ Static Content

◆ Performance: Dynamic Content Compression

- ◆ Security
  - ◆ Request Filtering
  - ◆ Windows Authentication
- ◆ Application Development
  - ◆ .NET Extensibility 4.5
  - ◆ ASP .NET 4.5
  - ◆ ISAPI Extensions
  - ◆ ISAPI Filters
- ◆ Management Tools
  - ◆ IIS Management Console
  - ◆ IIS 6 Management Compatibility
  - ◆ IIS 6 Metabase Compatibility

16. Review your selections and click Next.

17. Confirm your installation selections, and click Install.

Windows Server 2012 R2 will allow you to select and export any configuration settings you have made during role and feature installation, as shown in Figure 31.8. You will find this option at the bottom of the "Confirm installation selections" page, which is very handy when you are doing multiple, identical server configurations or you have made customizations to a specific configuration that you want to save.

FIGURE 31.8
Export configuration settings

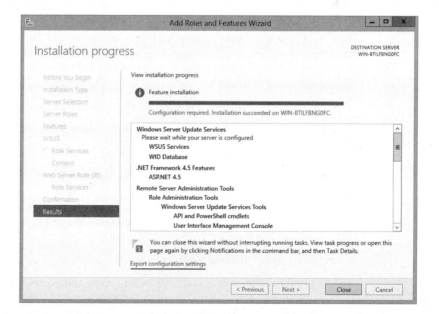

Configuring WSUS for Deployments

Once the installation of the WSUS server role is complete, you can launch Windows Server Update Services (shown in Figure 31.9) from the Start screen and begin your configuration.

FIGURE 31.9
Windows Server
Update Services on
your Start screen

To begin the configuration of your WSUS server you need to configure the updates required for your environment. Once the Update Services console has opened, you will be presented with the Windows Server Update Services Configuration Wizard; this wizard will walk you through the steps to get updates configured for deployment. As the wizard starts, the first screen you will see is Before You Begin; this has a couple of items you need to make sure of before starting this process:

◆ Is the server firewall configured to allow clients to access the server?

◆ Can this computer connect to the upstream server (such as Microsoft Update)?

◆ Do you have user credentials for the proxy server, if needed?

After you have validated that you have the appropriate items set up, follow these steps:

1. Begin the initial configuration of Windows Update Services by clicking Next.

You will be prompted to join the Microsoft Update Improvement Program—you can leave the check box set to Yes if you so desire.

2. Once you've decided whether to join the program, click Next to continue.

You'll need to choose your upstream server, and you will utilize Microsoft Update if this is your first server. Any additional servers you add later can point to this server to synchronize with. For this example we will be utilizing Microsoft Update as our synchronization partner.

3. Accept the default and click Next.

4. Specify a proxy server. If your organization uses a proxy server, fill in all the required fields, as shown by the example in Figure 31.10, and click Next.

FIGURE 31.10
Proxy server
configuration

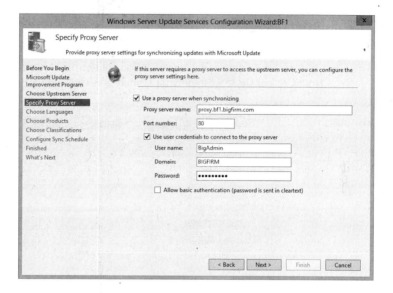

You will now connect to the upstream server so that you can start getting the available products, languages, and types of updates for your update server.

5. Click the Start Connecting button (shown in Figure 31.11) to begin this process.

FIGURE 31.11
Connecting to
your upstream
server

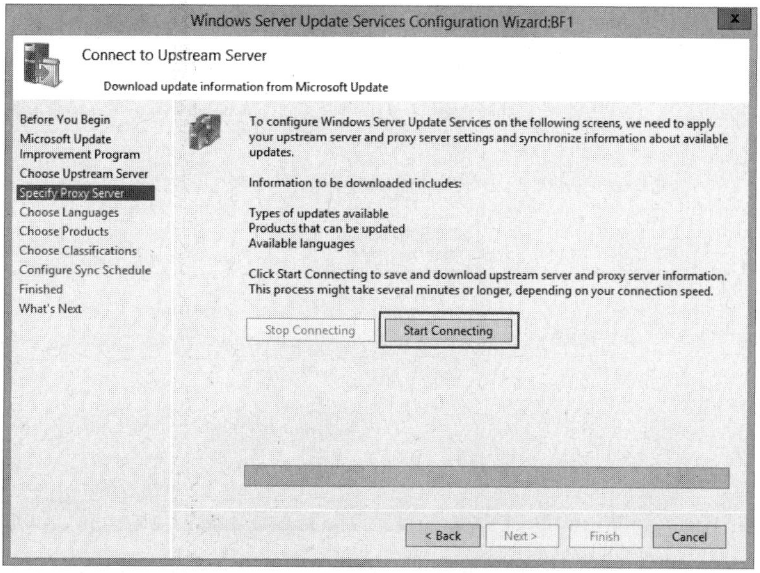

The process of connecting to your upstream server the first time can take a few minutes.

6. Once the process is complete, click Next.

The Product Updates screen will give you a list of all the products available on your upstream server. You have the choice to select an entire product or a specific version.

7. In this example (shown in figure 31.12), we have selected only Office 2013 and all versions of Silverlight. Choose the products you want, and click Next.

Next, you will choose the classifications of your updates to synchronize. This list ranges from Critical Updates to normal Updates, as shown in Figure 31.13.

FIGURE 31.12
Choosing your products to update

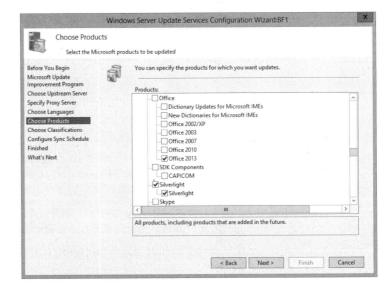

FIGURE 31.13
Selecting your update classifications

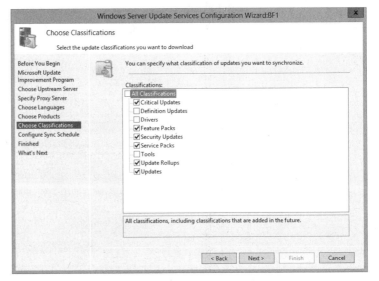

8. After making your selections, click Next.

The next screen lets you set up your sync schedule. You have two options here, the first being a manual sync, which you can do via the Update Services console, and the second lets you set up automatic synchronization at a specific day and time. (You can also have multiple syncs per day.)

9. Once you have decided your sync schedule, click Next.

10. Finishing up, you can now select to begin initial synchronization by checking the box and selecting Finish.

Alternatively, you can click Next, to be brought to the What's Next section in this area, where you can work through more advanced configuration items such as SSL (Secure Sockets Layer) and assigning your computers using Group Policies. (Group Policies are covered in the next section.)

The Windows updates will start getting synchronized with Microsoft Update and will begin to populate your Update Services console.

Before getting into deploying updates and configuring Group Policy objects (GPOs), let's review a few other options in the console that you should consider in the final steps of your configuration.

The first one we want to look at is computers. How do you want your devices to be added to WSUS? By opening the Options section of the Update Services console (see Figure 31.14), you can choose the Computers object, and it will allow you to either use the Update Services console to assign computers to groups or use Group Policy (or registry settings) to assign computers.

FIGURE 31.14
Update Services
console options

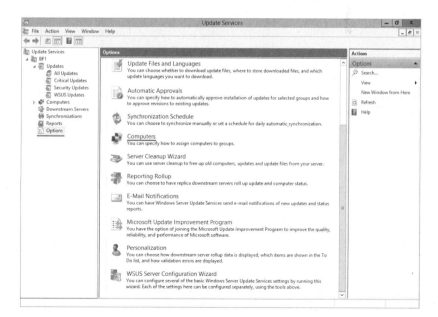

In the Synchronizations section you should validate that you have a successful sync, but if it has not started, you can manually kick off this sync yourself by selecting the Synchronize Now task in the Actions pane. See Figure 31.15 for more details.

FIGURE 31.15
Update Services console, synchronization settings, and tasks

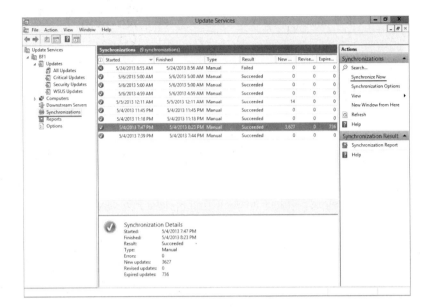

Deploying Updates and Migration for Windows Server Update Services

You must be running one of the following operating systems to receive WSUS updates: Windows 8, Windows 7, Windows Server 2012 R2, Windows Server 2008 R2, Windows Vista, Windows Server 2008, or Windows Server 2003. Windows 8 RT is also supported in a limited capacity.

Configuring Group Policies for Windows Update

Utilizing Group Policy objects is the most common and recommended approach for managing Windows Server Update Services. In this section you will be configuring the required settings to push out Windows updates with a GPO. For this example we are creating a brand-new GPO and applying it to the Workstations Organization Unit in Active Directory. This newly created GPO is called BigFirmUpdates, as shown in Figure 31.16.

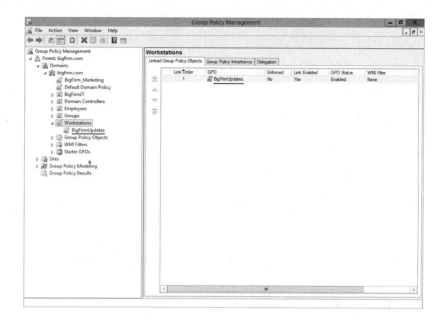

To configure Windows automatic update settings, follow these steps:

1. Right-click the Group Policy object and select Edit to open the Group Policy Management Editor, as shown in Figure 31.17.

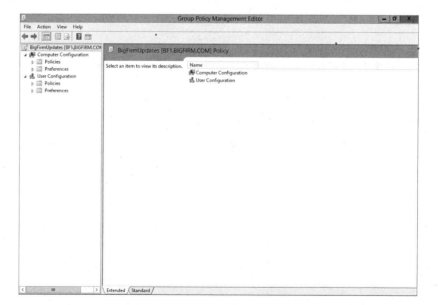

2. In the Group Policy Management Editor, navigate to Computer Configuration\
Administrative Templates\Windows Components\Windows Update.

3. Double-click Configure Automatic Updates, and then select the Enabled option, as shown
in Figure 31.18.

a. For the "Configure automatic updating" box, select the appropriate setting. The choices
are "Notify for download and notify for install," "Auto download and notify for
install," "Auto download and schedule the install," and "Allow local admin to choose
setting."

b. If you choose "Auto download and schedule the install," you must enter the day and
time for which the updates are scheduled.

FIGURE 31.18
Configuring
automatic
updates

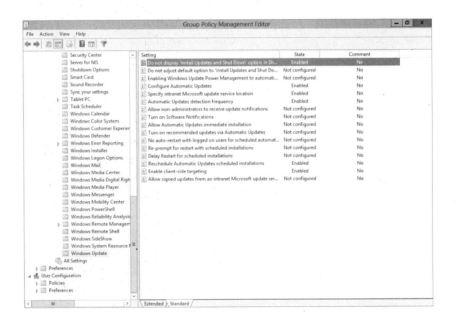

4. Next, choose the "Specify intranet Microsoft update service location" option. Here you
are going to point the WSUS clients to the WSUS server:

a. Select the Enabled option.

b. In the "Set the intranet update service for detecting updates" and "Set the intranet statistics server" boxes, type the name of the WSUS server, as shown in Figure 31.19.

c. Click OK.

These are the requirements to get updates pushed out to your client devices and utilize
the WSUS infrastructure you have just built.

FIGURE 31.19
Configuring the
WSUS server

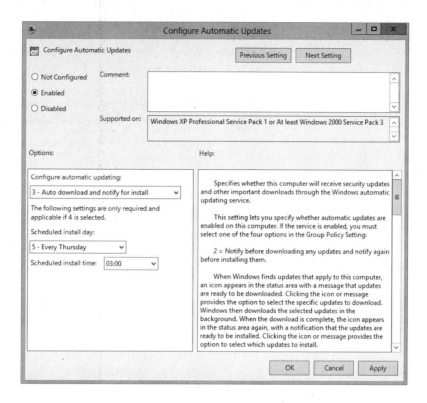

As you can see in the Windows Update section of your Group Policy Object Editor (shown in Figure 31.20) a few other options exist to help make the Windows Update experience and administration much more affective, giving you the ability to reschedule automatic updates, enable client-side targeting, and disable the display options clients have when updates are available.

Configuring Clients for Windows Updates

In this section we will cover configuration and validation that a Windows 8 computer (called WIN8CLIENT) is getting updates from our Windows Server 2012 R2 WSUS server. The client-side setup is very simple and only requires the updates or configuration of the Group Policy object to receive updates. If you have upgraded to a new Windows Server 2012 R2 WSUS server, then you only need to modify the Group Policy objects from the previous section.

Modification of the GPOs is really the only major task to configure your clients to get updates from your new WSUS server. This section will cover some of the basics to check and make sure your client is getting its updates and is pointed to the right server.

FIGURE 31.20
Windows Update
Group Policy
options for further
customization

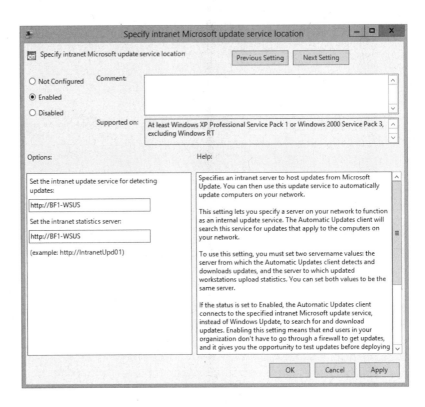

The Group Policy update that happens once you have pointed clients to a new WSUS server can take 90 to 120 minutes to do a refresh. The default GPO update takes 90 minutes for a refresh. If you want to test a client, you can do the following:

1. From your Windows client open a command prompt.

2. Type in **wuauclt.exe /detectnow /reportnow**.

   This will force the client to go to the WSUS server right away, check its updates, and report to it, basically validating its existence.

To validate and check on any errors or issues with a local client, you can use the local system's Event Viewer and open up the following location: \Applications and Services Logs\ Microsoft\Windows\Windows Update Client\. Here you will see (as shown in Figure 31.21) the information, errors, and warnings your client system has regarding updates.

FIGURE 31.21
Windows
Applications
and Services log
for client-side
updates

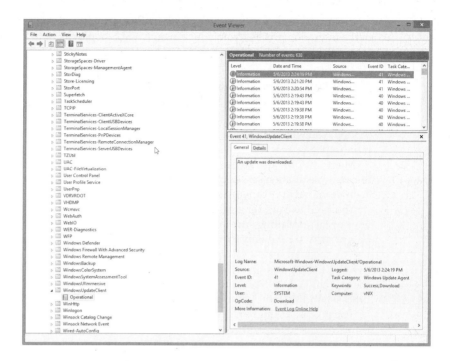

Or you can always open up Windows Update from the client Control Panel and validate that it's receiving its updates. Windows Update will show you (as shown in Figure 31.22) when it most recently checked for updates, updates that were installed, and how updates are managed.

FIGURE 31.22
Windows Update
in Windows 8

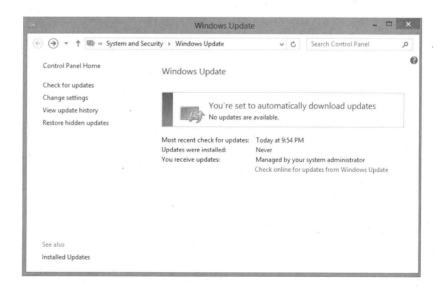

In the next section we are going to shift away from the client settings and look at an overview of the migration process from your current WSUS deployment to Windows Server 2012 R2 and the built-in role for Windows Server Update Services.

Migration from WSUS 3.0 to Windows Server 2012 R2

WSUS 3.0 is packaged as a stand-alone installer available from the Microsoft Download Center, whereas WSUS v6 (or 4.0 as some refer to it) is a built-in role in Windows Server 2012 R2. In this section, you will learn the basics of how to migrate from your WSUS 3.0 installation to the new built-in platform of Windows Server 2012 R2.

Microsoft provides an outline for a four-step process to migrate from your existing WSUS to a new destination server running Windows Server 2012 R2. You can find this outline on TechNet at http://tinyurl.com/c31wsusmigrate.

You need to consider many different things before doing any migration in your production environment. Making sure you have a solid review and inventory of all servers should always be a priority second only to a review of the possible migration scenarios.

Windows Server 2012 R2 Standard and Datacenter editions are supported as destination servers, and migrating from a physical to a virtual OS is supported. The upgrade will support the migration from SQL or the Windows Internal Database (WID) as a part of this migration process. Additionally, you can migrate from WID to SQL Server.

The process to migrate from your WSUS 3.0 SP2 into a Windows Server 2012 R2 WSUS infrastructure does require a bit of effort, and it is critical that you have a backup/back-out plan if something does not work as expected. When starting your migration process, the initial effort requires taking all of your WSUS updates and moving them from your old source server to the new Windows Server 2012 R2 destination server. Utilizing tools like XCopy or Robocopy is a viable option, but having a better understanding of the PowerShell cmdlets and management is far more important to master. Utilizing PowerShell to move things like your binaries is explained in full detail here: http://tinyurl.com/c31PSBackup.

Backing Up Your WSUS Database

Before tackling any major migration task, you should always have a solid backup of the configuration, patches that have been applied, and databases. Always make sure that you have tested the backup-and-restore process before any major upgrade or migration tasks.

Part of the best practices migration strategy is to back up your WSUS 3.0 SP2 database and then restore that data on the new destination server. Once you have restored the WSUS 3.0 SP2 database to your new Windows Server 2012 R2 WSUS v6, things should transition pretty smoothly and with no worry of lost reports, compliance data, or superseded patches.

Backups for the WSUS information and database will depend on the type of backup that you are doing. There is one process for backup and restore of the Windows Internal Database and a series of different steps if you are leveraging SQL Server as your database server. You can review the backup of SQL here: http://tinyurl.com/c31sqlbackup.

The WID is stored in the Object Explorer; once you expand the databases it will be labeled in all instances SUSDB.

For more in-depth information about WSUS backups and step-by-step guidance for this, refer to http://tinyurl.com/c31widbackup.

Review Additional Considerations

Outside of making sure you have a backup plan for your new WSUS environment and confirming that all the clients in your organization are getting updates from the new Windows Server 2012 R2 WSUS server, you want to make sure you have developed solid documentation on all of the settings defined for your organization. Taking the time to include PowerShell scripts, links to any components, and prerequisites.

Major considerations as you have seen from many of the previous examples are the heavy utilization of PowerShell and how many of the new processes are executed from this command line. Make sure you have a solid test plan and some form of task list to help you establish checkpoints along the way of your migration.

Another major consideration is building out your own migration plan and documentation so that you have a defined process with all the basic prerequisites and a diagram of your infrastructure. Having this documentation becomes extremely useful when you need to migrate to a larger server in the future, or if you decide to migrate from a WID to SQL.

Operational Management and Tools

Client computers use the Windows automatic updating client to receive WSUS updates and can be configured by using a Group Policy object. A GPO drastically reduces the administrative overhead because one GPO can be deployed to all computers in an Active Directory installation at once. Configuring Windows automatic updating through a GPO is done by using the Group Policy Object Editor.

PowerShell and WSUS

Managing everything from your WSUS can be done via PowerShell, and it offers a great set of tools you can use in your everyday management of updates. A really great example of things you can do and the capabilities of PowerShell in WSUS is that you can go from installing the WSUS role on your Windows Server 2012 R2 server, as shown here,

```
...\Install-WSUSServ.ps1 -ComputerName BF1 -StoreUpdatesLocally
-ContectDirectory "E:\Packages\WSUS -InstallDatabasePatch "E:\"
-CreateDatabase -Verbose
```

to manipulating your client and registry settings with Get-WSUSClientSettings and Set-Client WSUSSettings. You can obtain more details on either of these commands by running Get-Help or by looking online. The Microsoft Scripting Guys have a great blog post on WSUS and PowerShell management here: http://tinyurl.com/c31pswsus.

Cluster-Aware Updating

Windows Server 2012 R2 offers a new cluster feature called Cluster-Aware Updating (CAU). This feature allows you to update clusters without loss of availability during your patch window. When your update window starts CAU, it puts the first node in maintenance mode and fails over the workloads to other servers in the cluster while it installs updates and reboots if necessary. Once the first node comes back up, CAU takes that particular server out of maintenance mode, fails back the original roles, and moves on to the next node.

As an example, if you have a two-node cluster, all the roles or servers from Node 1 will migrate to Node 2. Once Node 1 has been patched and rebooted, it will fail back its original roles, and then once that has completed, it will take the roles that are living on Node 2. Node 2 will send the job to put itself in maintenance mode and fail its servers over to Node 1.

The Cluster-Aware Update tools can be installed on both Windows Server 2012 R2 and Windows 8 clients. After the tools are installed, you configure the CAU scenario you want; examples of these scenarios can be found at `http://tinyurl.com/c31cluster`.

As you will see from the Cluster-Aware Update scenario guides, the CAU works in two basic modes:

Self-Updating   This configuration is run on the cluster node you want to update, and you just build an update schedule and let CAU update the cluster.

Remote Updating   You run the CAU from a stand-alone server or client that is not clustered; an example would be your Windows 8 desktop with the CUA tools installed. You then utilize the tool to connect to the specific cluster you want and update the cluster on your schedule.

During your installation and management of Cluster-Aware Updates you will find a series of PowerShell cmdlets that can help you check if a server is ready, launch the process, and check the overall status of the clusters. Once you have chosen the method for how you want to

---

ADDITIONAL PATCH MANAGEMENT TOOLS PROVIDED BY MICROSOFT

Although we're focusing on WSUS in this section, Microsoft has several other tools that can assist you in managing updates in your organization:

Microsoft Update   Microsoft Update is now included in your Control Panel, and from there you can view your current settings, when updates are applied, and the action that is taken when updates are found.

Microsoft Update Catalog   All files available on Microsoft Update are available in the Microsoft Update Catalog, including drivers, updates, security, and other updates to Microsoft products. One nifty thing about the Microsoft Update Catalog is the ability to add multiple files to your shopping basket and download them all at once. You can find the Microsoft Update Catalog at `http://catalog.update.microsoft.com`.

Windows Server Update Services Cmdlets in PowerShell   Windows Server 2012 R2 offers an extensive library of PowerShell cmdlets that you can utilize to take on common and repeatable tasks in your WSUS infrastructure. You can get a full list of these cmdlets on TechNet (`http://tinyurl.com/c31pscmdlets`). Being able to manage components and patch classifications from PowerShell gives you the ability to further automate the management of multiserver infrastructures and gives you the granularity you may need to do things like deny a specific patch for a particular deployment.

Microsoft Security Tools   The MBSA has been replaced with the Security Assessment Tools for Windows Server 2012 R2 and Windows 8 clients; it covers the support of Windows 7, Windows Server 2008, Windows XP, Windows Vista, and Server 2008 R2.

> Multiple tools are available: Microsoft Security Assessment Tool 4.0, Microsoft Baseline Security Analyzer 2.2, and Microsoft Security Compliance Manager. You can find all of these tools and more details at *http://tinyurl.com/c31mst*.
>
> **Microsoft Security Response Center Blog**   The Microsoft Security Response Center (MSRC) is in charge of issuing security updates for Microsoft. The site also issues advisories for problems that haven't been disclosed but that it's investigating. The MSRC blog is a good way to get current information. See http://blogs.technet.com/b/msrc/.
>
> Following the team on Twitter @MSFTSecResponse is a great option to keep you current on updates.

use CAU and get your schedule set, you can take advantage of both Windows Server 2012 R2's advanced features and your new WSUS v6 role!

System Center Configuration Manager

System Center Configuration Manager (SCCM) is a centralized management tool built on Microsoft's System Center suite of software. The focus area of SCCM includes client (server and workstation) management, patching, endpoint protection, application deployment, and automated operating system delivery. A breakdown of SCCM 2012 SP1, the most current version of the product, can be found at http://www.microsoft.com/en-us/server-cloud/system-center/configuration-manager-2012.aspx.

System Center Configuration Manager offers advanced reporting and compliance capabilities over WSUS. A typical recommendation is that any midsize to large organization utilize SCCM as their primary patching tool. Some additional benefits are as follows:

- Centralized ability to roll back a patch that was already deployed.

- Compliance assessment, which allows you to scan for software or updates that are needed for compliance.

- One unified client—you can leverage the SCCM client to install updates, manage or throttle your updates, and make one-off deployments much easier.

- Advanced reports and the ability to define subscriptions that come out of the box to help measure compliance.

- You can define maintenance windows for pushing your patches out; using Group Policies provides only strict "all or nothing" for patching your systems. With SCCM and maintenance windows, you can have patches applied to subgroups of computers only during specific hours of the day.

- System Center Update Publisher allows you to gather downloads of vendor patches from Adobe, Java, and hardware manufacturers. These patches get integrated into the deployment and schedule with ease.

♦ Offline servicing provides you the ability to update a WIM (Windows Image File Format) after you have saved it, saving you from deploying and updating the image manually. This ensures that your OS deployment images are always deployed with the latest patch.

The Bottom Line

Use Windows Automatic Updates to check for new updates on a computer running Windows 8.   Windows Automatic Updating is a Control Panel item used to check the Microsoft Update site to see whether any updates are available for your computer.

Master It   On a Windows 8 computer, use Windows Automatic Updating to see whether any new updates are available for your computer.

Use the Windows Update Standalone Installer to silently install a security update.   The Windows Update Standalone Installer is used to install security updates on all Windows operating systems since Windows Vista and Windows Server 2008.

Master It   Install a security update in quiet mode and defer a required reboot by using the Windows Update Standalone Installer.

Identify the four phases of patch management.   According to Microsoft, there are four phases in planning a patch-management strategy.

Master It   Which of the following is not one of the four phases of patch management?

1. Identify

2. Troubleshoot

3. Evaluate and Plan

4. Assess

5. Deploy

Chapter 32

Windows Server 2012 R2 and Active Directory Backup and Maintenance

Backup and recovery are familiar tasks to most server administrators. Protecting data and applications is important enough, but recovering your Active Directory can be even more vital to continued operations.

In this chapter, we'll cover the various types of backup and recovery available in Windows Server 2012 R2 as well as how they apply to Active Directory. You will also learn about the Active Directory Recycle Bin, Microsoft System Center 2012 R2 Data Protection Manager, and a new online backup option for Windows Server 2012 R2 that allows you to back up to the cloud with Microsoft's Windows Azure offering.

In addition, we'll describe some Active Directory maintenance tasks, such as the ability to stop and restart Active Directory without having to restart the server computer. The ability to stop Active Directory lets you perform offline maintenance of the Active Directory database, such as defragmentation and integrity checks.

In this chapter, you will learn to:

◆ Use Windows Server Backup to back up and restore a Windows Server 2012 R2 computer

◆ Defragment AD DS offline

◆ Install the Active Directory Recycle Bin

◆ Create and recover a system state backup for Active Directory

Introducing Windows Server Backup

Backup has long been part of Windows Server, and in Windows Server 2012 R2 the backup tasks are performed by Windows Server Backup. Although Windows Server Backup may not provide every feature you might want in an enterprise environment, it does a very good job of backing up and restoring a Windows Server 2012 R2 server and can be a viable solution for small- to medium-size environments. Windows Server Backup can be used to back up remote computers, but it's most suited to backing up the local server.

The Windows Server Backup tool included with Windows Server 2012 R2 has some notable improvements over the previous version in Windows Server 2008 R2. Here's a list of them:

◆ Backing up and restoring individual virtual machines from a Hyper-V host server is now supported.

◆ Managing backup versions and backup retention has now been improved, and you can specify deletion policies to help manage your used space.

◆ The limitation of only backing up volumes with a capacity of no more than 2 TB and sector size of 512 bytes has been removed. Large volumes or drives such as the new 64 TB virtual hard disk (.VHDX) format can now be backed up, and sector sizes of 4 kilobytes are supported.

◆ Cluster Shared Volumes (CSVs) are now supported although there are a few limitations, such as virtual machines hosted on CSVs can't be backed up and full CSV volume recovery isn't available.

◆ Neater configuration of System State component reporting means that the System Writer now only reports Win32 service files to be part of the Windows 8 client operating system and not Windows Server 2012 R2. This means a more efficient system state backup.

BACKING UP TO TAPE WITH WINDOWS SERVER BACKUP

Windows Server Backup does not support tape backups (this has been the case since Windows Server 2008 R2). If your organization requires the more traditional backup-to-tape method, then you will need to deploy a product, such as Microsoft's System Center 2012 R2 Data Protection Manager.

Installing Windows Server Backup

Windows Server Backup is installed as a feature within Windows Server 2012 R2 and comprises three distinct components:

◆ Microsoft Management Console (MMC) snap-in

◆ Command-line tools (Wbadmin.exe)

◆ Windows PowerShell cmdlets

Windows Server Backup is not installed by default, so here's what you need to do to get it up and running:

1. To begin, log on to your domain-joined Windows Server 2012 R2 installation with an account that has domain administrative permissions, and from the Server Manager ➢ Local Server ➢ Manage menu, choose the Add Roles and Features option.

2. In the Before You Begin dialog box, click Next.

3. Ensure that Role-Based or Feature-Based Installation is selected in the Select Installation Type dialog box; then click Next.

4. In the Select Destination Server dialog box, leave the default option of "Select a Server from the Server Pool" checked, confirm that your server is highlighted in the Server Pool section, and then click Next to continue.

5. When you reach the Select Server Roles dialog box, just click Next again to continue.

6. When you reach the Select Features dialog box, scroll down the list until you find Windows Server Backup, check the box, and then click Next.

7. At the Confirm Installation Selections dialog box, click the Install button to start the installation, and click Close once the wizard has finished.

Backing Up and Restoring a Full Server

The biggest difference between storing backups in a network shared folder versus using a local disk is that Windows Server Backup will store multiple versions of backups on a local disk but will store only the most recent version of a backup in a remote location. Having multiple backups for a specific server computer means that you can recover from changes made on those dates as well as recover from a complete data loss. This is most useful when restoring files that may have been changed or deleted prior to the most recent backup.

When backing up to disks, consider using some type of removable disk, such as an external USB or eSATA hard disk. A better implementation would include multiple removable disks that could then be rotated to off-site storage to provide a higher level of disaster-recovery protection. Windows Server Backup can identify disks to be used for backup and automatically use whichever disk is present, deleting the oldest backup on the disk to make room for the current backup operation.

Performing a full server backup is one of the easiest types of backup to perform and is also one of the best types in terms of recovery. A full server backup includes the following parts:

◆ All local volumes (virtual disks hosted on local volumes will not be backed up if they are online)

◆ Critical volumes

◆ System state

With a full server backup, you can recover individual files and folders and entire volumes in case of disk failure. You can also perform a "bare-metal" recovery in which you have replaced the entire server computer (or at least the hard disks containing the operating system and system state) and there is no operating system installed. The drawbacks to a full server backup are the size of the backup and the time required to perform the backup.

PERFORMING A FULL SERVER BACKUP

These steps assume that you will be performing a full server backup to a local disk and defining a schedule for the backup operation to be automatically repeated:

1. From Server Manager ➢ Local Server ➢ Tools, click Windows Server Backup to open the MMC snap-in.

2. From here, right-click Local Backup in the left tree pane, and then click Backup Schedule from the resulting menu to open the Backup Schedule Wizard.

3. Click Next in the Getting Started dialog box.

4. Select "Full server (recommended)" for the backup type, as shown in Figure 32.1; then click Next.

5. Set the time of day to start the backup, as shown in Figure 32.2.

FIGURE 32.1
Selecting the
backup type

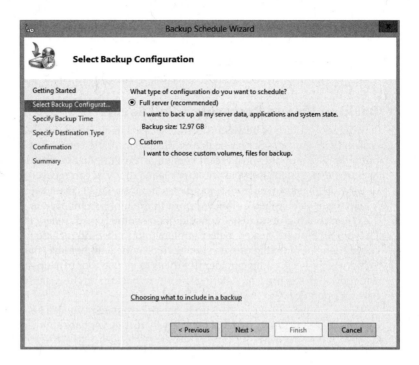

FIGURE 32.2
Selecting the
time of day

Your options include "Once a day," for which you select the time of day to start the backup, and "More than once a day," where you select an available time and click Add to move it to the "Scheduled time" list. Using the "More than once a day" option lets you schedule as many backups as you want, with the caveat that you want to leave enough time between backup operations so that they are able to complete before the next backup is triggered.

6. Click Next.

WHEN TO BACK UP

Remember that performing a backup requires heavy disk activity and processor cycles. Because of this, backups should be performed only when user activity on the server is low, such as overnight during off-hours. If you perform backups during peak usage times, your users may complain of slow access, and their activities on the server may delay the backup.

---

7. Select the option "Back up to a hard disk that is dedicated for backups (recommended)," as shown in Figure 32.3.

FIGURE 32.3
Selecting the type of disk

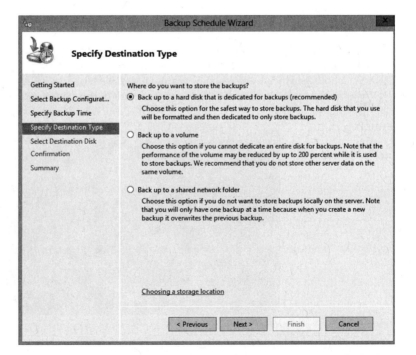

To use this option, you must have at least one disk attached to the server computer that has no existing volume. The disk should be raw, with no partition or file system.

8. Click Next.

9. Select the disk to use for the backup volume. To use off-site disk rotation, specify multiple disks on this page. Click Next.

   You will be warned that finishing this wizard will cause the selected disks to be formatted, losing any existing data on the disks.

10. If you are certain you want to use the selected disks, click Yes to proceed.

11. Review your selected options for the scheduled full server backup. If you are satisfied with the options, click Finish to format the disks and schedule the backup.

PERFORMING A FULL SERVER BACKUP FROM THE COMMAND LINE

Windows Server Backup's command-line component, Wbadmin.exe, can be used in cases where you want to script backup operations or when you prefer to use the command line to maintain a server computer. These steps assume that you will be creating a scheduled full server backup using the command line:

1. Open an elevated command prompt. You must be a member of either the Administrators or Backup Operators group to perform these steps.

2. Enter the following command:

   ```
   Wbadmin.exe enable backup -vssFull -schedule:02:00 -addtarget:E: -include:C:\
   ```

   The -vssFull switch indicates a full server backup, and -addtarget defines the destination path to store the backup as the E drive. -include:C:\ indicates that the C drive should be included. Whenever you use a drive letter with -include, you must include the final backslash. Figure 32.4 shows the result of this command.

FIGURE 32.4
Creating a new scheduled backup

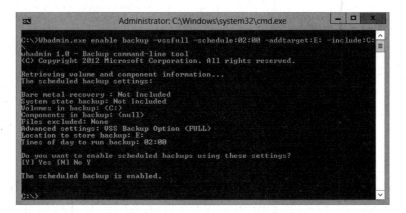

3. Enter the following command to start the backup you just created:

   ```
   Wbadmin.exe start backup
   ```

PERFORMING A BACKUP WITH POWERSHELL

In Chapter 27, "Virtualization with Hyper-V," you learned how to create virtual machines on your Windows Server 2012 R2 host. Here we're going to discuss how to back up a Hyper-V virtual machine using PowerShell as an alternative to wbadmin.exe. You can utilize PowerShell cmdlets for Windows Server Backup to create your backup policy (New-WBPolicy), specify where you want it backed up to (New-WBBackupTarget), add the virtual machine (Add-WBVirtualMachine), and then configure the schedule you want it to run on (Set-WBSchedule).

1. Open an elevated PowerShell window. (You must be a member of either the Administrators or Backup Operators group to perform these steps.)

2. Configure your script execution policy to allow untrusted scripts by typing the following and choosing Yes when prompted:

   ```
   Set-ExecutionPolicy Unrestricted
   ```

3. Now input the following PowerShell script while making sure to change the values for New-WBBackupTarget and Get-WBVirtualMachine to something that's relevant to your own environment:

   ```
   # Create a New Backup Policy

   $BackupPolicy = New-WBPolicy

   # Specify a Target

   $BackupTarget = New-WBBackupTarget -VolumePath F:

   # Add the target to your policy

   Add-WBBackupTarget -Policy $BackupPolicy -Target $BackupTarget

   #  Specify your virtual machine name

   $VMs = Get-WBVirtualMachine | where vmname -like "ws2012r2*"

   Add-WBVirtualMachine -Policy $BackupPolicy -VirtualMachine $VMs

   # Configure the schedule

   $BackupTime = [datetime] "23:00"

   Set-WBSchedule -Policy $BackupPolicy -Schedule $BackupTime


   # Activate the policy

   Set-WBPolicy -Policy $BackupPolicy -AllowDeleteOldBackups
   ```

4. Once the script runs, your backup policy will be configured to run at the scheduled time, and you can view the job from inside the Windows Server Backup console, as shown in Figure 32.5.

FIGURE 32.5
Viewing the
PowerShell-created
backup job

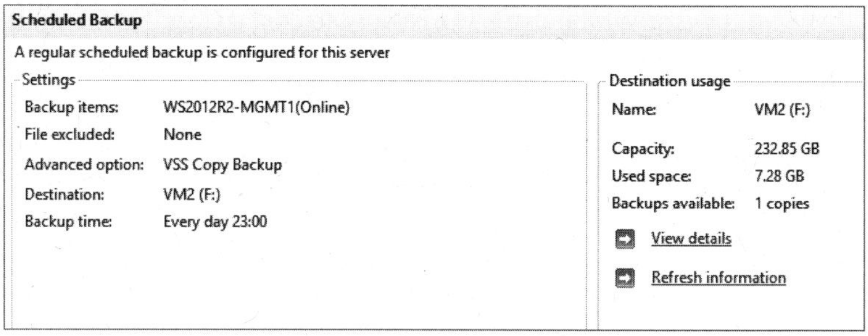

Scheduled Backup				
A regular scheduled backup is configured for this server				
Settings			Destination usage	
Backup items:	WS2012R2-MGMT1(Online)		Name:	VM2 (F:)
File excluded:	None			
Advanced option:	VSS Copy Backup		Capacity:	232.85 GB
			Used space:	7.28 GB
Destination:	VM2 (F:)		Backups available:	1 copies
Backup time:	Every day 23:00			
			➡ View details	
			➡ Refresh information	

POWERSHELL CMDLETS FOR WINDOWS SERVER BACKUP

For a full list and description of all the Windows Server Backup PowerShell cmdlets, check out this link: http://tinyurl.com/ws2012R2wsb.

PERFORMING A FULL SERVER RESTORE

You can recover your server using different methods depending on the amount of data that must be recovered and the time you want to spend on the recovery. Consider the worst-case scenario of complete data loss on the server, either from hardware failure or from data corruption. In this case, you could choose to reinstall the Windows Server 2012 R2 operating system and then perform a full server restore using Windows Server Backup. Or you could choose to perform a bare-metal restore using the Windows Server 2012 R2 installation media and the full server backup. This process is targeted at smaller environments and isn't feasible if you're managing a large organization with a number of domain controllers.

The following steps assume that your server computer has suffered total data loss and that you have resolved the hardware issues, replacing the failed hard disks. Make sure that the new hard disks are at least equal in capacity to the disks being replaced. Be sure to attach the drive containing the backup that will be restored so that Windows Setup will be able to locate it. Alternatively, you can access a backup located in a shared folder on the network.

1. Boot the computer with your Windows Server 2012 R2 media.

2. In the Windows Setup dialog box, select the correct language options, and click Next.

3. Now click the "Repair your computer" option at the bottom left.

4. At the Choose an Option screen, click the Troubleshoot option to continue.

5. From the Advanced Options screen, choose the System Image Recovery option, as shown in Figure 32.6.

FIGURE 32.6
Advanced recovery
options

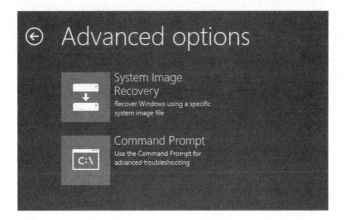

Windows Setup will attempt to identify any existing Windows installations on the hard disks and, if found, offer to repair them. If you are restoring onto a fresh hard disk, you'll get an error stating that a system image can't be located.

6. Click Next.

7. In the "Re-image your computer" wizard, select either, "Use the latest available system image" or, "Select a system image."

If you choose "Select a system image," you will be shown a list of images the wizard detects that can be used to recover your server. Clicking the Advanced button here gives you an option to search for an image on the network as well as allowing you to install a driver for the new computer that may not have been included in the backed-up image.

8. Click Next to move on when you've made your selections.

9. Choose the available backup set in the "Select the date and time of system image to restore" dialog box; then click Next.

10. On the "Choose additional restore options" screen, select the appropriate options:

   ♦ Select the "Format and repartition disks" box to repartition and format the disks you are recovering to. When you select this option, the option "Exclude disks" becomes available, and you can choose to exclude some disks from the formatting. This is particularly important when you are only recovering the disk containing the operating system and do not want to affect data stored on other volumes.

   ♦ If you do not see all the disks installed in the computer, you may need to install drivers. Click "Install drivers."

   ♦ In the Advanced options, specify whether the computer will automatically be restarted and whether to check for disk errors upon restart.

11. Review your selected options, and then click Finish to begin the recovery.

If you are restoring from a network location, be aware that your server is not functioning as a domain computer while being recovered. The server containing the backups must be available to non-domain computers in order to be accessible during the recovery. For this reason, it is often easier to perform a recovery from a locally attached external drive.

A full server restore is most useful on a server computer that requires a complete restore of the operating system and all data on each disk. If you are restoring only the operating system or everything on the critical drives (such as operating system and registry files), restoring from Windows Setup works well provided you are careful to exclude disks where the data is not being recovered.

 Real World Scenario

WHEN THINGS GO WRONG

As a server administrator, you take steps to protect your data just in case something goes wrong. As a case in point, we recently heard from a client who had done everything right in preparing for data recovery. The domain controller for this small office housed not only Active Directory for the domain but also several important applications and user data. The operating system, applications, and user data were all stored on a RAID 5 set comprising four physical disks. Backups were scheduled to run every night, and they ran full manual backups at least once a month to be stored off-site.

RAID 5 sets are resilient enough to lose a single hard disk without downtime. You can add a new disk to replace the failed disk and tell the RAID 5 set to rebuild, all on the fly. The client's domain controller, however, suffered the loss of two physical disks in the set on the same night. It was a freak occurrence, but it was something they weren't able to recover from.

After discovering the problem the next morning, the administrator was able to recover the domain controller by replacing the failed disks, establishing a new RAID 5 set, and then performing a full server restore. The process included booting the computer using the installation media with the backup drive attached and then using the backup to perform a bare-metal restore. The server was up and running in a few short hours.

RECOVERING THE SYSTEM STATE

You can also recover the server by reinstalling the operating system and then using Windows Server Backup to restore the system state. This might be the preferred method if the backup is stored on a domain computer that cannot be accessed through Windows Setup.

To use Windows Server Backup to recover the system state of your server, follow these steps:

1. Open Windows Server Backup by either choosing Server Manager ➤ Local Server ➤ Tools ➤ Windows Server Backup, or from the Windows Server 2012 R2 Start screen simply typing the word **backup** and then clicking the Windows Server Backup icon.

2. From here, right-click Local Backup in the left tree pane, and then click Recover from the resulting menu to open the Recovery Wizard.

3. In the Getting Started dialog box, select one of the following options:

◆ "This server": The local server will be recovered.

◆ "A backup stored on another location": You will be restoring data to a remote server. If you select this option, you will be prompted to select the location of the backup files to use, either on the local computer or on a network shared folder.

4. In the Select Backup Date dialog box, use the calendar control to select the date of the backup to restore, and select the time if there was more than one backup made on that date.

5. When finished, click Next to move on.

6. In the Select Recovery Type dialog box, choose the System State option, and then click Next.

7. Select the location to restore to, either "Original location" or "Alternate location."

If you choose to restore to another location, either type the path to the restore location or use the Browse button to specify the location.

8. Review your settings, and then click Recover to begin the restore.

In Windows Server 2012 R2, you can also restore the system state from the command line using the Wbadmin.exe tool or with PowerShell using the Start-WBSystemStateRecovery cmdlet. This section gives an example of using WBadmin.exe to perform a system state recovery:

```
Wbadmin.exe start systemstaterecovery -version -backupTarget
-machine -recoveryTarget -authsysvol -autoreboot
```

-version Defines the date and time of the backup. For example, to specify the backup made on May 12, 2013, at 11 p.m., use -version:05/12/2013-23:00.

-backupTarget Defines the computer where the backup file is stored, for example: -backupTarget:\\server1\share.

-machine Defines the name of the computer being recovered; use this switch with -backupTarget if there are backups for multiple computers stored in that location, for example: -machine:Server1.

-recoveryTarget Defines the destination of the backup if not being restored to the original location.

-authsysvol Indicates that the restore should perform an authoritative restore of the system volume shared folder.

-autoreboot Tells the recovery to automatically restart the computer once the system state restore has completed.

CAUTION REQUIRED

Once you start a system state recovery, you must not stop it or restart the computer until it has completed. If the system state recovery is interrupted, the server computer may be left in an unbootable state.

Backing Up and Restoring Files and Folders

In addition to full server and system state backups, Windows Server Backup lets you back up and restore individual files, folders, and volumes. This is the method to use when you are more concerned about recovering data than recovering the operating system itself or when performing interim backups of important data that changes frequently. Backing up data folders can be useful for recovery scenarios where the operating system can be restored through imaging and then the data is restored through backup.

PERFORMING A MANUAL BACKUP OF FILES AND FOLDERS

Data backups (of files and folders) either can be scheduled or can be manual operations in Windows Server Backup. One common backup configuration for a server that houses important data would be for a full server backup each night with an additional file and folder backup of data during the day.

These steps assume that Windows Server Backup is installed as discussed earlier in this chapter and that you have folders containing data to be backed up:

1. Open Windows Server Backup by either choosing Server Manager ➤ Local Server ➤ Tools ➤ Windows Server Backup or from the Windows Server 2012 R2 Start screen typing the **backup** and then clicking the Windows Server Backup icon.

2. From here, right-click Local Backup in the left tree pane, and then click Backup Once from the context menu to open the Backup Once Wizard. Click Next.

3. In the Select Backup Configuration dialog box, select Custom, as shown in Figure 32.7, and then click Next.

FIGURE 32.7
Selecting Custom to perform a backup of specific files and folders

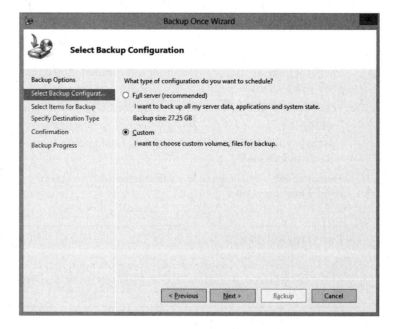

4. In the Select Items for Backup dialog box, click Add Items to select the files and folders you wish to back up.

5. Once you've made your selections, click OK.

6. Now click the Advanced Settings button.

   On the Exclusions tab, you can add file exclusions to omit certain files from the backup. This is very useful if you're backing up volumes with files, such as MP3 and or large video files that don't need to be backed up.

   On the VSS Settings tab, you can modify the behavior of Windows Server Backup regarding backup history flags. Select VSS Full Backup if Windows Server Backup is the only backup software you will use with these files and folders. Otherwise, if you use additional backup software and want the backup flags to remain unchanged after this manual backup, select VSS Copy Backup.

7. Click OK, and then click Next.

8. Specify the backup destination type, either a local disk or a network location. Click Next.

9. Specify the location for the backup.

   This page will vary depending on the type of destination you selected previously. If you selected a network location, you can also determine whether the created backup file will inherit the permissions of the shared folder destination or maintain specific permissions. If you select "Do not inherit," you will be prompted to provide user credentials to assign permissions to the file.

10. Click Next.

11. Review the settings for the backup, and then click Backup to begin the operation.

The Backup Progress page shows the progress of the backup, including any errors encountered and the completion.

RECOVERING A FOLDER FROM A BACKUP

Recovering individual files and folders is a rather common task for many administrators. Consider how many times a user has said that they accidentally deleted a presentation or spreadsheet that they need to have for an important meeting. You can easily accomplish this task with a custom recovery in Windows Server Backup (provided the backup files are accessible):

1. Open Windows Server Backup by choosing Server Manager ➤ Local Server ➤ Tools ➤ Windows Server Backup or from the Windows Server 2012 R2 Start screen typing the **backup** and then clicking the Windows Server Backup icon.

2. From here, right-click Local Backup in the left tree pane, and then click Recover from the context menu to open the Recovery Wizard.

3. Select the location of the backup file that you will use for this recovery (we'll choose "This server" here).

   If you select a remote location, you must provide the type of location and the location path in subsequent steps.

4. Click Next.

5. Select the backup date and time that you want to use.

   If there is only one backup present, the date and time will default to that backup. If there are multiple backups, it will default to the most recent one.

6. Click Next.

7. In the Select Recovery Type dialog box, choose Files and Folders; then click Next.

8. Use the tree view under "Available items" to locate the folder you want to recover.

9. If you are trying to restore individual files, select the files in the "Items to recover" pane, and click Next.

10. In the Specify Recovery Options dialog box, select the recovery location, permissions for the recovered files and folders, and what to do if there are existing copies of the files in the location you are restoring to. Click Next.

11. Review the settings for accuracy, and then click Recover.

You can also recover a single folder from the command line. The following example recovers the C:\Library folder:

```
Wbadmin.exe START RECOVERY -version:05/12/2013-18:39
-items:C:\Library -itemtype:File -backupTarget:E: -recursive
```

START RECOVERY This switch tells **Wbadmin.exe** to begin a restore operation.

-version The -version switch defines the backup version to use for the restore. It is specified in a MM/DD/YYYY-HH:MM format. You can use the Wbadmin.exe GET VERSIONS command to list all available backup versions.

-items This switch provides a comma-delimited list of items to restore.

-itemtype This option specifies the type of objects in the **-items** list and can include FILE, APP, and VOLUME. Use separate switches to specify more than one type in a restore operation.

-backupTarget This specifies the location of the backup file you want to use for the restore operation.

SYSTEM CENTER 2012 R2 DATA PROTECTION MANAGER

As you learned in Chapter 30, System Center 2012 R2 is Microsoft's premier systems management solution. Data Protection Manager (DPM) is the backup offering of the System Center 2012 R2 suite, and it's a best-of-breed solution for backing up Microsoft workloads. With DPM, you can back up entire virtual machines or just standard file and folder workloads. It can integrate into applications such as SQL, SharePoint, and Exchange and offer high-speed backup and recovery of the data contained within them.

Its primary backup media is to disk, and there's also an option to back up to an external tape drive if you require long-term retention of your data (remember that Windows Server Backup doesn't support tape backups). For disaster recovery (DR), you can configure a primary DPM server on your production site and a secondary DPM server in your DR site and have the backup sets (known as protection groups) replicated across the WAN to safeguard your data.

DPM backs up Windows Server 2012 R2 with the help of an agent, and all management is provided through the DPM Administrator Console, as shown in the following illustration:

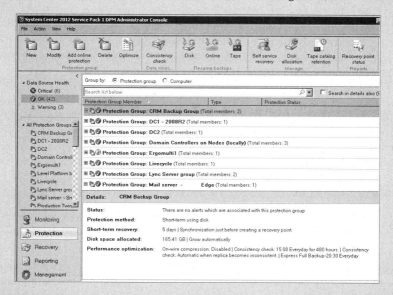

If you want to learn more about Data Protection Manager, you can download the trial from here: `http://www.microsoft.com/systemcenter`.

Backing Up to the Cloud

A complementary disaster recovery solution to DPM for your Windows Server 2012 R2 backups is Windows Azure Backup. This add-on provides a route into Microsoft's Azure cloud offering and enables you to back up and restore files, folders, and even virtual machines located on Windows Server 2012 R2 computers. It can be used side-by-side with Windows Server Backup or integrated into DPM, and once deployed, it can be launched from inside the same management snap-ins.

You do, of course, need to have a decent Internet connection—if you're still accessing the Web on a 1 MB DSL line, then you can forget about cloud backup! Also, you will need to create an Azure online account ID. Take a look at the official TechNet documentation here: `http://tinyurl.com/ws2012R2wab`. If you want a walk-through on getting it up and running, then this blog post will point you in the right direction: `http://tinyurl.com/ws2012azurebackup`.

Stopping and Restarting Active Directory

Restartable Active Directory Domain Services (AD DS), introduced in Windows Server 2008, lets you stop AD DS to perform maintenance on the server without requiring you to restart the server in Active Directory Restore Mode (ADRM). The benefits of being able to stop and restart AD DS include offline defragmentation and the application of server updates without requiring a restart of the computer. However, performing a system state recovery is not supported without restarting the server computer in ADRM.

Once you stop AD DS on the server, users can continue to log on to the domain if other domain controllers are available. In addition, you will be able to log on to the server using your domain administrator account to perform tasks on the server if there is another domain controller available to process your logon. Otherwise, if you have stopped AD DS on the only domain controller, you must log on to the server using the ADRM administrator credentials. To enable this option, you must modify the DSRMAdminLogonBehavior registry value to either 1 (the Directory Services Restore Mode administrator account can log on when AD DS is stopped on the server) or 2 (the Directory Services Restore Mode administrator account can always log on to the server). The option to allow the Directory Services Restore Mode (DSRM) administrator account to always log on to the server, whether AD DS is stopped or not, is not a good idea since the credentials are not checked against any password policies. The registry value is located here:

```
HKLM\System\CurrentControlSet\Control\Lsa\DSRMAdminLogonBehavior
```

Stopping and Starting AD DS

Stopping AD DS is carried out exactly the same way as stopping any service in Windows, by using the Services snap-in in Server Manager ➤ Tools or from command line.

You must be a member of the Domain Administrators group to perform these steps:

1. Open the Server Manager ➤ Tools menu and choose Services.

2. Right-click Active Directory Domain Services in the details pane, and click Stop on the context menu.

   You will be prompted to approve a list of other services on which AD DS depends.

3. Accept the list, and those services will also be stopped.

   They will be restarted when you start AD DS again.

4. To start AD DS, right-click Active Directory Domain Services, and then click Start.

Defragmenting Active Directory Offline

In earlier versions of Windows Server, you had to restart a domain controller in DSRM to perform an offline defragmentation and integrity check of the AD DS database. Although having to perform an AD defragmentation isn't all that common, in certain cases it can be useful when you're looking to clean up the AD database file and reclaim some disk space on your system drive as well as potentially helping with AD performance in larger environments. With Windows Server 2012 R2 you have the ability to perform these tasks without having to restart the computer and enter DSRM. Instead, you can stop AD DS and then use Ntdsutil.exe from an elevated command prompt to perform the offline defragmentation and integrity check.

Before performing an offline defragmentation, it would be wise to back up the system state and critical drives of the domain controller to be sure you can recover from any serious errors that might occur. You should verify that there is ample free space on the volume that contains the AD DS database (Ntds.dit) for temporary space. Microsoft recommends free space equal to at least 15 percent of the Ntds.dit file size for temporary space needs.

Active Directory automatically performs online defragmentation to optimize the storage of data within the Ntds.dit file part of the daily garbage-collection process. This does help optimize the database, but it does nothing to reduce the size of the database file. Offline defragmentation is the only effective way to reduce the size of the database.

PERFORMING OFFLINE DEFRAGMENTATION OF NTDS.DIT

These steps assume that you have stopped the Active Directory Domain Services service, as discussed earlier, and that you will be compacting the Ntds.dit file to a local folder. If you plan to defragment and compact the database to a remote shared folder, map a drive letter to that shared folder before you begin these steps, and use that drive letter in the path where appropriate.

1. Open an elevated command prompt.

2. Type **ntdsutil**, and then press Enter.

3. Type **Activate instance NTDS**, and press Enter.

4. At the resulting ntdsutil prompt, type **Files** (case sensitive), and then press Enter.

5. At the file maintenance prompt, type **compact to** followed by the path to the destination folder for the defragmentation, and then press Enter.

   If there are spaces in your path to the destination folder, enclose the entire path in double quotation marks (such as **"c:\temp folder\"**). Ntdsutil.exe will display a progress indicator. Upon completion, it will instruct you to perform an immediate backup of the original and the compacted files.

6. Copy the new Ntds.dit file to your %systemroot%\NTDS\ directory (for example, c:\Windows\NTDS\Ntds.dit).

7. Delete all the log files in the NTDS folder (for example, type **del C:\Windows\NTDS*.log**).

8. Type **quit** and press Enter to exit file maintenance mode, and then type **quit** and press Enter again to exit Ntdsutil.exe.

9. After you complete all these steps, restart AD DS.

It's interesting to note that you will not be able to access files and folders on the server computer after stopping AD DS without providing the DSRM administrator credentials.

Checking the Integrity of an Active Directory Database

Active Directory uses the same indexed sequential access manager (ISAM) database engine that is used in Exchange Server, and the version used in Windows Server 2012 R2 is called the *Extensible Storage Engine* (ESE).

There might be times when you need to check the integrity of your AD database—maybe to rule out any corruption issues and also to generate reports on the number of deleted or phantom records that are referenced in it. You can check the integrity of the Ntds.dit file in two ways; the first uses the Files subcommand of Ntdsutil.exe, and the second uses the Semantic database analysis subcommand of Ntdsutil.exe. Microsoft warns that the Semantic database analysis subcommand should not be used as part of normal database management because improper use can result in severe data loss for Active Directory; instead, it is used only as part of troubleshooting when working with Microsoft product support. Even though Microsoft warns against using Semantic database analysis, each time you use the integrity and recover subcommands under Files, it will prompt you to also run Semantic database analysis.

PERFORMING AN INTEGRITY CHECK OF NTDS.DIT

Using the Files subcommand in Ntdsutil.exe lets you verify the integrity of the database file and repair any corruption that is found. You should always use the recover command before performing an integrity check. The recover command flushes all transactions to the database file, ensuring that the file has the most up-to-date information. It uses the Esentutl.exe program to perform a soft recovery of the Ntds.dit database and commits all outstanding transactions.

Perform these steps after stopping the AD DS service to check the integrity of Ntds.dit:

1. Open an elevated command prompt.

2. Type **ntdsutil**, and press Enter.

3. Type **Activate instance NTDS**, and press Enter.

4. At the resulting ntdsutil prompt, type **Files** (case sensitive), and then press Enter.

5. At the file maintenance prompt, type **recover**, and press Enter.

6. Type **integrity**, and then press Enter.

7. Type **quit** and press Enter to exit file maintenance mode, and then type **quit** and press Enter again to exit Ntdsutil.exe.

8. After you have completed these steps, restart AD DS.

USING SEMANTIC DATABASE ANALYSIS

The Files subcommand of Ntdsutil.exe checks the Ntds.dit file for normal file corruption, using the Semantic database analysis subcommand checks the internal structure of Ntds.dit to ensure it complies with the normal semantics of Active Directory and outputs a report of the number of records currently in the database, including deleted and phantom records. The report is named dsdit.dmp.x, where x is a number that is incremented each time you run the report.

Perform these steps after stopping the AD DS service:

1. Open an elevated command prompt. Click Start, right-click Command Prompt, and select Run as Administrator.

2. Type **ntdsutil**, and press Enter.

3. Type **Activate instance NTDS**, and press Enter.

4. Type **Semantic database analysis** (case sensitive), and then press Enter.

5. At the semantic checker prompt, type **Go** to start the analysis. Use **Go Fixup** to run the analysis and repair semantic errors in the file.

6. Type **quit** and press Enter to exit semantic checker mode, and then type **quit** and press Enter again to exit Ntdsutil.exe.

7. After you have completed these steps, restart AD DS.

The report file generated by the Semantic database analysis subcommand is in the current folder from which you ran Ntdsutil.exe, typically c:\Users%username%. The system variable %username% will be automatically replaced with the name of the currently logged-on user.

Capturing Active Directory Snapshots

In Windows Server 2012 R2 you can use the Volume Shadow Copy Service (VSS) to create a snapshot of the AD DS database. You can then use this snapshot as an offline copy to view data, or it can be processed to be used as a Lightweight Directory Access Protocol (LDAP) directory database. Snapshots can be used to view current objects in AD DS without risking the current state of the database. An easier method for recovering deleted objects in AD DS in Windows Server 2012 R2 is the Active Directory Recycle Bin, which is described in the "Recovering a Deleted Object with the Recycle Bin" section, later in this chapter.

Creating an Active Directory Snapshot

You can create AD DS snapshots with the Ntdsutil.exe tool from an elevated command prompt. Because you do not have to stop AD DS before creating a snapshot, snapshots are ideal for viewing objects from a domain controller without taking it offline.

1. Open an elevated command prompt. Click Start, right-click Command Prompt, and select Run as Administrator.

2. Type **ntdsutil**, and press Enter.

3. Type **Snapshot**, and then press Enter.

4. At the snapshot prompt, type **Activate instance NTDS**, and then press Enter.

5. Type **Create**, and then press Enter.

The snapshot will be created, and the GUID of the snapshot will be displayed, as shown in Figure 32.8.

FIGURE 32.8
Creating an Active
Directory snapshot

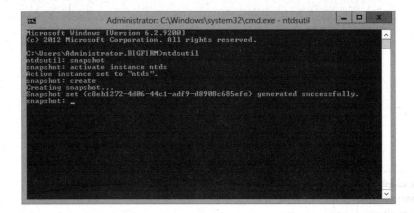

6. Type **quit** and press Enter to exit snapshot mode, and then type **quit** and press Enter again to exit Ntdsutil.exe.

Mounting an Active Directory Snapshot

You won't be able to work with an AD DS snapshot until you have mounted it. Mounting takes the snapshot and makes it available as a local path on the server computer. Once it's mounted, you can access the AD DS files in the NTDS folder under Windows.

1. Open an elevated command prompt.

2. Type **ntdsutil**, and press Enter.

3. Type **Snapshot**, and then press Enter.

4. At the snapshot prompt, type **Activate instance NTDS**, and then press Enter.

5. Type **List All**, and then press Enter.

   This will display all the snapshots currently on the server computer. Each entry will have an index number and then display the GUID of the snapshot.

6. Type **mount x**, where x is either the index number or the GUID of the snapshot you want to mount, and then press Enter.

   If the command completes successfully, it will return the local mount path of the snapshot, typically a folder off the C drive root. The result should be similar to Figure 32.9.

7. Type **quit** and press Enter to exit snapshot mode, and then type **quit** and press Enter again to exit Ntdsutil.exe.

Working with Mounted Active Directory Snapshots

After you have created and mounted an Active Directory snapshot, you need to make it available by using the Dsamain.exe command. Dsamain.exe is installed on Windows Server 2012 R2 with the AD DS role or the Active Directory Lightweight Directory Services (AD

LDS) role, and it requires that you be a member of the Domain Administrators or Enterprise Administrators group to use it.

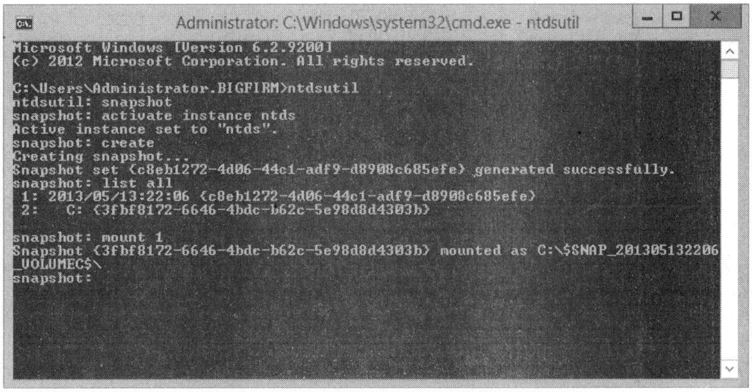

FIGURE 32.9

Mounting an Active
Directory snapshot

USING DSAMAIN.EXE

`Dsamain.exe` makes a copy of the AD DS database available through the LDAP from the server computer. Using LDAP, you can access this version of AD DS using a variety of tools, such as `Ldp.exe` or any of the Active Directory snap-ins in Windows Server 2012 R2.

These steps assume that you have created and mounted a snapshot using the previous procedures:

1. Use Windows Explorer to browse to the `Ntds.dit` file in the mounted snapshot. The path will be similar to `c:\$SNAP_200906191422_VOLUMEC$\Windows\NTDS\Ntds.dit`.

2. Hold down the Shift key, and right-click `Ntds.dit`. Click "Copy as path."

3. Open an elevated command prompt.

4. Type **dsamain /dbpath <path> /ldapPort 10389**. For the <path> value, right-click the command prompt, and select Paste, to paste in the copied path.

   The result should be similar to this:

   ```
   Dsamain /dbpath "C:\$SNAP_200906191422_VOLUMEC$\Windows\NTDS\Ntds.dit"
   /ldapPort 10389
   ```

5. If the command completes successfully, leave the command prompt open while you work with the mounted snapshot.

   Once you close the command prompt, you will close the `Dsamain.exe` session.

6. To quit `Dsamain.exe`, press Ctrl+C.

Now that you have the snapshot mounted and have made it available as an LDAP instance, you can view it with any tool that can connect to LDAP, such as `adsiedit`.

1. From an elevated command prompt, type **adsiedit**, and then press Enter.

2. On the Action menu, click "Connect to."

3. Click Advanced.

4. In the Port field, type the port number you assigned previously in the Dsamain.exe command line. Click OK.

5. Click OK to connect to the LDAP instance.

You can use adsiedit to view the contents of the snapshot, such as when verifying that objects have been created.

Backing Up and Restoring Active Directory

Active Directory is backed up as part of the system state on a domain controller whenever you perform a backup using Windows Server Backup, Wbadmin.exe, or PowerShell. As described earlier in this chapter, Windows Server Backup must be installed through features in Server Manager before you can use it to back up or recover your server computer.

The type of backup you select for your domain controllers will depend on the frequency of changes to Active Directory and the data or applications that might be installed on the domain controller. The bare minimum you need to back up to protect AD DS on a domain controller is the system state. The system state includes the following list plus some additional items depending on the roles that are installed:

- Active Directory database (Ntds.dit)
- Registry
- COM+ registration database
- Active Directory Certificate Services database
- Boot files
- SYSVOL folder
- Cluster service information
- Any system files that are protected by Windows Resource protection
- Microsoft Internet Information Services metadirectory

The next level of backup protection is provided by a critical volumes backup, which includes the following:

- Volume containing the boot files, including the Bootmgr and Boot Configuration Data (BCD) store
- Volume containing the Windows operating system and registry
- Volume containing the folder structure
- Volume containing the AD DS database (Ntds.dit) and log files

These backup types can be run manually on demand, or they can be scheduled either using Windows Server Backup or using `Wbadmin.exe` and Scheduled Tasks.

LIMITATIONS OF ACTIVE DIRECTORY BACKUPS

You can use either Windows Server backup or `Wbadmin.exe` to perform a system state backup of a domain controller to back up Active Directory. Microsoft recommends using either a dedicated internal disk or an external removable disk such as a USB hard disk to perform the backups. External disks have the advantage of being easily rotated for off-site storage as part of your normal disaster-recovery planning; however, they don't travel well in comparison to the more traditional tapes, so make sure you have a solid transportation plan in place.

You must have administrative credentials to schedule a system state backup or restore; backup operators do not have privileges required to schedule backups. System state backups will back up Active Directory integrated DNS zones but will not back up file-based DNS zones. File-based DNS zones must be backed up as part of a volume-level backup, such as a critical volumes backup or full server backup.

Introducing the Active Directory Recycle Bin

If you have ever had the misfortune to accidentally delete an object from Active Directory and then had to recover that object from your backups, you know that it's not one of the most pleasant tasks that you've ever had to carry out in your IT career. Thankfully, in Windows Server 2008 R2, Microsoft introduced the Active Directory Recycle Bin to provide protection for deleted objects much in the same way as you would utilize the standard Windows Recycle Bin for your files and folders.

A downside for some people with the Windows Server 2008 R2 version of the Recycle Bin, though, was that it had to be managed fully through PowerShell. In Windows Server 2012 R2, you now have GUI management of the Recycle Bin through the Active Directory Administrative Center (ADAC), which ultimately makes managing deleted objects an easier task.

AD RECYCLE BIN OR SYSTEM STATE?

If you're wondering about the need to even have a system state backup if you've configured the AD Recycle Bin, then think again. The AD Recycle Bin should be a supplementary offering to your normal AD backups and should not be used as the primary recovery method. This is because you might have a situation where the Recycle Bin isn't reachable. To reach the Recycle Bin, you need to be able to log on to the domain, and if the domain has fallen over, there's no Recycle Bin!

Without the Active Directory Recycle Bin and in earlier versions of Windows Server that didn't support it, when you deleted an object, it was flagged for deletion (*tombstoned*) rather than being immediately deleted. Tombstoned objects are permanently deleted when the garbage-collection process runs.

With the Active Directory Recycle Bin installed on Windows Server, however, the process changes. Now when an object is deleted, it is flagged as a deleted object for the span of time determined by the msDS-DeletedObjectLifetime property in AD DS, which defaults to null. Once the deleted object lifetime expires, the object is flagged as a recycled object and is stripped of most of its attributes. It still resides in the Deleted Objects container and can be recovered for the duration of its lifetime, which is defined by the tombstoneLifetime attribute in AD DS.

WHAT ABOUT OLD TOMBSTONED OBJECTS?

When you install the Active Directory Recycle Bin, any preexisting tombstoned objects automatically become recycled objects, but they cannot be recovered like any other recycled objects from that point on. To prevent this situation, you should check that you have recovered any tombstoned objects you might want to save prior to installing the Active Directory Recycle Bin.

ACTIVE DIRECTORY RECYCLE BIN PREREQUISITES

Before we discuss enabling the Active Directory Recycle Bin, there are a few prerequisites that you need to have in place. You will need to ensure the following:

◆ You have deployed at least one domain controller running Windows Server 2012 R2 with the Active Directory Administrative Center enabled.

◆ All other domain controllers in the domain are running a minimum of Windows Server 2008 R2 or higher.

◆ Your Active Directory forest must be running a functional level of Windows Server 2008 R2 or higher.

ENABLING THE ACTIVE DIRECTORY RECYCLE BIN

The Active Directory Recycle Bin is disabled by default. This process will walk you through enabling it through the GUI. Be aware, though, that once you enable this feature, it cannot be disabled:

1. From Server Manager, choose Local Server ➢ Tools ➢ Active Directory Administrative Center, and click your (local) domain from the navigation pane on the left.

2. Now, in the Tasks pane on the right, click Enable Recycle Bin, as shown in Figure 32.10.

3. In the Enable Recycle Bin Confirmation dialog box, acknowledge that this change cannot be reversed; then click OK.

4. Click OK in the dialog box that opens up informing you that the Recycle Bin won't be available until all domain controllers have replicated, and then refresh the Active Directory Administrative Center.

FIGURE 32.10
Enabling the
Recycle Bin

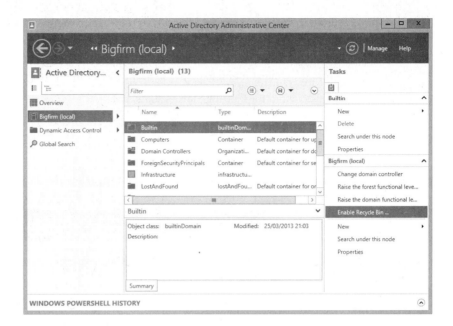

ENABLING THE AD RECYCLE BIN WITH POWERSHELL

Use the following PowerShell script as an alternative method to enable the AD Recycle Bin:

```
Enable-ADOptionalFeature -Identity 'CN=Recycle Bin Feature,CN=Optional
Features,CN=Directory Service,CN=Windows NT,CN=Services,CN=Configuration,DC=BigF
irm,DC=COM' -Scope ForestOrConfigurationSet -Target 'BigFirm.com'
```

RECOVERING A DELETED OBJECT WITH THE RECYCLE BIN

If you've accidentally deleted an object in your Active Directory but you have the AD Recycle Bin enabled, follow these steps to quickly recover it. (For our example, we've deleted a user called Sally and now need to get it back):

1. From Server Manager, choose Local Server ➢ Tools ➢ Active Directory Administrative Center, and click your (local) domain from the navigation pane on the left.

2. Double click the Deleted Objects container in the central pane.

3. Locate the deleted object, right-click it, and then choose a restore option from the context menu, as shown in Figure 32.11.

Creating an Active Directory Backup

This process will walk you through backing up just the system state of your computer, which contains the Active Directory structure and database:

1. From the Server Manager ➢ Local Server ➢ Tools menu, click Windows Server Backup to open the MMC snap-in.

2. From here, right-click Local Backup in the left tree pane, and then click Backup Schedule from the context menu to open the Backup Schedule Wizard.

3. Click Next in the Getting Started dialog box.

4. Select Custom for the backup type, and then click Next.

5. Click the Add Items button, check the box beside System State, and then click Next.

6. Keep moving through the wizard while choosing your backup schedule time and storage options, and then click Finish to exit the wizard.

FIGURE 32.11
Recovering an object with the AD Recycle Bin

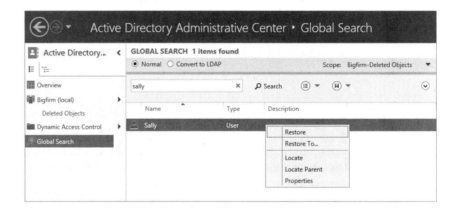

Be careful to maintain appropriate security for your Active Directory backups because they contain complete copies of your domain's security objects and credentials. Remember that a system state backup is the safest way to back up Active Directory. If you ever need to call Microsoft for support on a failed Active Directory environment, then having a working system state backup is essential.

If you've used a third-party backup product to get your system state backed up, then you'll have to use that third-party vendor for support in recovering it. It's good practice to always have a recent copy of your system state backed up to disk and then use the other non-Microsoft backup product to back up to a remote disk or tape.

Restoring an Active Directory Backup

There are two types of restore operations for Active Directory: authoritative and non-authoritative. An authoritative restore allows you to recover objects that have been deleted from Active Directory, but in this case, it won't allow replication to overwrite the restored objects. What happens instead is that the restored objects replicate authoritatively to the other DCs in the domain. With a non-authoritative restore, a DC is restored to the state that it was in at the time of the backup. Once it's restored, you then allow replication to update the DC to the current state of the rest of Active Directory. In this section we will discuss the non-authoritative restore. Both methods are performed in Directory Services Restore Mode, which require restarting the server computer and using the F8 option menu to select DSRM.

1. Power on the server computer, and after POST, press the F8 key to bring up the Windows Server 2012 R2 boot options screen.

2. Select Directory Services Repair Mode, and then press Enter.

3. Hit Ctrl+Alt+Del to log on, enter your DSRM username and password, and then press .Enter.

   This is a quicker and easier process than what you had to do for earlier versions of Windows Server because it logs you directly onto the desktop with Active Directory services disabled.

4. Now open a command prompt.

5. At the prompt, type **wbadmin get versions -backuptarget:<drive>:-machine:<computername>**, where <drive> is the drive letter of the drive where the backup is located, and <computername> is the name of the computer being restored.

   The -machine switch is required only if there are backups from multiple computers on the backup disk.

6. Press Enter.

   Note that the version ID of the version that you want to restore must be entered exactly to work.

7. At the prompt, type **wbadmin start systemstaterecovery -version:<MM:DD:YYYY-HH:MM> -backuptarget:<drive>: -machine:<computername> -quiet**.

   The -quiet parameter suppresses prompts to verify that you want to start the restore and that the system state has not changed. The command should look similar to Figure 32.12.

FIGURE 32.12
Restoring the system state

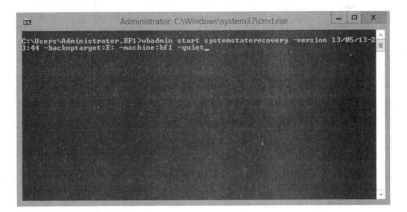

If you will be performing an authoritative restore after the non-authoritative restore completes, do not restart the server. Once you restart the domain controller, AD DS and Active Directory Certificate Services detect that a restore has occurred, and they run automatic integrity checks of their databases.

METADATA CLEANUP

Something else to consider is that if you lose a domain controller because of hardware failure or OS corruption, sometimes it's faster to use the `ntdsutil metadata clean up` command to remove the failed DC and then just install a fresh one with the same name and let Active Directory replication do its thing.

This link has some additional information on cleaning up server metadata in Active Directory: `http://tinyurl.com/ws2012ntdsutil`.

Performing an Authoritative Restore

The purpose of an authoritative restore is to recover deleted AD DS objects by marking the restored objects as authoritative or by marking the new copy that should be replicated to the other domain controllers. Every time a change is made to AD DS, the version number of the database is incremented. Making an authoritative restore of deleted objects involves setting the version number higher than the currently replicated version of the AD DS database.

Wherever possible, authoritative restores should be made on the global catalog server so that group information can be fully recovered. If you can isolate the global catalog server before it receives replication of the deletion you are trying to recover, you can restore the objects without first performing a non-authoritative restore. In other words, if you are quick enough, you can unplug the network cable from the global catalog server and avoid having to recover from a backup.

To perform an authoritative restore before the change has replicated, do the following:

1. Isolate the server either by disconnecting the network cables or by typing the **repadmin / options \<servername\> +DISABLE_INBOUND_REPL** command.

2. Stop AD DS either by using Services from the Tools menu in Server Manager, as described earlier in this chapter, or by typing the **net stop ntds** command at an elevated command prompt.

3. At an elevated command prompt, type **ntdsutil**, and press Enter.

4. At the `ntdsutil` prompt, type **authoritative restore**, and press Enter.

5. Type the appropriate command for the type of object being restored:

   ◆ To restore a subtree, such as an entire OU, type **restore subtree \<DN\>**, where \<DN\> is the full distinguished name of the object being restored. For example, to restore the HR OU in Bigfirm.com, type **restore object "OU=HR,DC=bigfirm,DC=com"**.

   ◆ To restore a single object, such as a user account, type **restore object \<DN\>**, where \<DN\> is the full distinguished name of the object.

6. Make a note of any `.txt` or `.ldif` files that are generated because they can be used to re-create any back links for the objects being restored:

   ◆ Back links contain the information for group memberships.

   ◆ The `.txt` files can be used to re-create group memberships in other domains for the restored user accounts using the `create ldif file from` command in `Ntdsutil` in the other domains.

◆ The .ldif files can be used to restore group memberships in the local domain using the Ldifde.exe utility.

7. Type **quit** to exit authoritative restore mode, and then type **quit** again to exit Ntdsutil. Restart the server normally.

Performing an authoritative restore where the changes have already replicated will require a non-authoritative restore from backup first and then the same steps to perform authoritative restores of the deleted objects.

The Bottom Line

Use Windows Server Backup to back up and restore a Windows Server 2012 R2 computer. Windows Server Backup is installed as a feature in Windows Server 2012 R2 and can be used to create various types of backups to protect your server computer. Full server backups contain the operating system, critical volumes, and all data on the server; while critical volume backups protect all volumes the operating system depends on, but not necessarily the additional data stored on the server.

Master It Your server contains two hard disks; the first contains the operating system, and the second contains user data. How can you use Windows Server Backup to protect the operating system and the user data?

Defragment AD DS offline. Windows Server 2012 R2 gives you the ability to perform an offline defragmentation and integrity check of the AD DS database without having to restart the computer and enter DSRM. Instead, you can stop AD DS and then use Ntdsutil.exe from an elevated command prompt to perform the offline defragmentation and integrity check.

Master It You want to defragment your AD DS database but do not want to shut down the server and restart it in DSRM. How do you do that?

Install the Active Directory Recycle Bin. A downside for some people with the Windows Server 2008 R2 version of the Recycle Bin was that it had to be managed fully through PowerShell. In Windows Server 2012 R2, you now have GUI management of the Recycle Bin.

Master It You want to install the Active Directory Recycle Bin without using PowerShell. How do you achieve this?

Create and recover a system state backup for Active Directory. Because domain controllers contain all the database information for Active Directory, recovering a failed domain controller server is critically important. When using Windows Server Backup or the command-line utility Wbadmin.exe, perform backups containing the system state at a minimum to preserve Active Directory.

Master It You want to protect your Active Directory data from the possibility of complete hardware failure of the server computer. Which types of backup will provide this protection?

Appendix

The Bottom Line

Each of The Bottom Line sections in the chapters suggests exercises to deepen skills and understanding. Sometimes there is only one possible solution, but often you are encouraged to use your skills and creativity to create something that builds on what you know and lets you explore one of many possibilities.

Chapter 2: Installing and Upgrading to Windows Server 2012 R2

Upgrade your old servers. Microsoft has provided several upgrade options for Windows Server 2012 R2.

> **Master It** You have a Windows 2008 x86 file server. What will your upgrade path be to Windows Server 2012 R2?
>
> **Solution** Windows Server 2012 R2 is available only as an x64 build. You will have to prepare a new machine with Windows Server 2012 R2. You will then migrate the services and data from the Windows 2008 machine to the Windows Server 2012 R2 machine.

Configure your server. Windows Server 2012 R2 allows you to use Server Manager and PowerShell to add or remove roles, role services, and features.

> **Master It** You have started to deploy Windows Server 2012 R2. You are planning on automating as much of the build process as possible. What tool will you use to add or remove roles, role services, and features?
>
> **Solution** Import-Module will add the following PowerShell cmdlets. Get-WindowsFeature will list the install status of every role, role service, and feature. Add-WindowsFeature will allow you to install a component, and Remove-WindowsFeature will allow you to uninstall a component. You can write PowerShell scripts to automate your configuration changes.

Build a small server farm. Installing Windows Server normally requires that you sit in front of the machine and answer a number of questions. This is time-consuming and distracts administrators from other engineering or project tasks that they could be working on. A number of alternative techniques can be employed.

Master It You have been instructed to build four new servers with Windows Server 2012 R2. This will be the first time your organization will deploy Windows Server 2012 R2. Your department is short-staffed because a number of your colleagues are on vacation. You want to do this job quickly and efficiently. How will you do it?

Solution If you had more time, you could look into preparing a server with Windows Deployment Services (WDS). However, you need to work quickly. You can download and install the latest Windows Automated Installation Kit (ADK) from Microsoft's website. You use Windows System Image Manager (WSIM) to prepare an unattended answer file called `autounattend.xml`, copy that file onto a USB stick, insert the Windows Server 2012 R2 DVD into each server, and boot the server from the DVD. Insert the USB stick in the server, and the Windows Installer will load the answer file from the USB stick and automate the installation of Windows. Your next step on the server is to change the Administrator password and log in.

Chapter 3: Introduction to Server Core

Use the new functionality in Server Core. The Windows Server 2012 Server Core operating system is a trimmed-down version of its full installation. The removed code reduces the profile for security threats and also reduces performance demands. The primary administration interface is the command prompt. It can perform several but not all of the roles available with the full installation.

Master It The Windows Server 2012 Server Core version differs from the original release in Windows Server 2008. What are those key differences, and how does that impact the roles the server can perform?

Solution The original version did not allow you to switch between the GUI version and Server Core. Windows Server 2012 allows you to set up you server in GUI mode then just switch it over to Server Core.

Install and configure Server Core. The installation of Server Core is the same as installing a full installation of Windows Server 2012. The full installation provides a list of initial configuration tasks such as joining the domain, initiating automatic updates, and installing features. Each of these operations has a command associated with it.

Master It Server Core has a specific script to perform several common tasks that edit the registry. What is this script's name? What parameter can provide a list of additional commands to perform many of the common configuration tasks?

Solution The `SCRegedit.wsf` script located in `c:\windows\system32` performs several configurations, such as enabling automatic updates and enabling Remote Desktop. The `/cli` parameter lists the additional commands for performing the initial configuration tasks.

Set up Server Core for a branch-office deployment. The branch-office deployment is one possible scenario for the Server Core implementation. The infrastructure roles of Active

Directory Domain Services, DNS, DHCP, File Services, and Print and Document Services would be installed and configured on a server, which would provide these basic services to the users within a small office environment. The configurations of these services could be performed remotely.

Master It   To configure Active Directory Domain Services and DNS, the Active Directory Domain Services Installation Wizard (DCPromo) is run from the command line. What is needed to enter the parameters for the command?

Solution   DCPromo requires an answer file to install on Server Core. Since many of the graphic capabilities have been removed from the installation, the utility cannot be run interactively. The command to use the answer file is dcpromo /unattend:answerFile .txt.

Remotely manage the operating system.   Server Core can be remotely managed by three options. Remote Desktop administration is available, but only the command prompt and provided GUIs with Server Core can be used. The MMC snap-ins can connect to the server's services to manage with the standard Windows tools. Finally, a new service, Windows Remote Shell, provides single-command connections to the server.

Master It   The Windows Remote Shell offers a quickconfig option. What security concerns should system administrators be aware of when using this option? What can be done to address these concerns?

Solution   The Windows Remote Shell quickconfig option sets up the service to listen for requests on TCP port 5985 using HTTP. This means the command and results will be transmitted unencrypted. In addition, the server is unauthenticated, which could result in configuring the wrong server. One way to resolve this is to set up IPSec between the server and clients. Another way is to configure the service to use HTTPS with TCP port 5986, which would encrypt the transmissions and authenticate the server.

Chapter 4: Windows Server 2012 R2 Networking Enhancements

Understand IPv6.   The journey from IPv4 to IPv6 will definitely not happen in a short time frame, and it became apparent to the designers of IPv6 that both protocols would have to coexist and work together on the same infrastructure. The caveat is that IPv4 and IPv6 cannot natively talk to each other, and for the duration of this transitional period a solution was required to address the communication barriers between these two protocols.

Master It   Which of the following is not an IPv6 transitional technology?

a. ISATAP

b. DirectAccess

c. 6to4

d. Teredo

Solution   b. DirectAccess is not an IPv6 transitional technology.

Use PowerShell for better networking manageability.   Windows Server 2012 R2 has nearly 2,500 PowerShell cmdlets to work with, and from this enormous pool there are literally hundreds that can be used to view, configure, and monitor all of its different networking components and services. You can perform a wide variety of tasks using these cmdlets, ranging from simple IP address configuration to more specialized functions like configuring Quality of Service and virtualization networking parameters.

   Master It   Which new cmdlet is built into Windows Server 2012 R2 that is a real contender to replace the traditional ping command?

   Solution   The Test-NetConnection cmdlet comes built into Windows Server 2012 R2 and will give you far greater information than the traditional ping command ever could.

Implement NIC Teaming.   In today's always-connected world, it's essential that the network connections on your servers remain fault tolerant and that they can maintain uptime in the event of a failed adapter. Windows Server 2012 R2 helps to deliver this fault tolerance through the use of NIC Teaming and negates the need to purchase any additional (and potentially expensive) hardware or software.

   Master It   If you want to create your NIC team using PowerShell, how would you go about it?

   Solution   To create a new NIC team from a command, open a PowerShell window with an account that has administrative permissions and type the following (make sure to substitute the team and NIC names to match your own environment): **New-NetLbfoTeam Team1 NIC3,NIC4**.

Understand the new QoS features.   Quality of Service (QoS) allows administrators to configure and deploy policies that predetermine which applications or services should be prioritized when it comes to allocating bandwidth. Administrators can determine critical interactive services, such as Voice over IP (VoIP) and line-of-business (LOB) applications, that must have acceptable levels and bandwidth available to them whenever they seek it.

   Master It   In earlier operating systems, you could use QoS only to enforce maximum bandwidth consumption, also known as rate limiting. Instead of a bandwidth-reservation system, it was more like a bandwidth-throttling solution. What QoS feature can you use in Windows Server 2012 R2 to solve this problem?

   Solution   To solve this problem, Minimum Bandwidth was introduced as a new feature to QoS in Windows Server 2012. Minimum Bandwidth provides the bandwidth-reservation solution that was missing with previous iterations and gives you the ability to ensure different types of network traffic get the granular bandwidth configurations they require.

Manage network performance.   Understanding how to manage the performance of your Windows Server 2012 R2 networking environment is paramount to ensuring that your business can maintain an optimal level of productivity.

Master It   Which of the following tools can be used to manage network performance in Windows Server 2012 R2? (Choose two.)

a. `Ipconfig.exe`

b. `Perfmon.exe`

c. `Dfsrmon.exe`

d. Server Performance Advisor

e. `Networkview.exe`

Solution   b) `Perfmon.exe` and d) Server Performance Advisor are both tools that can be used to manage network performance in Windows Server 2012 R2.

Chapter 5: IP Address Management and DHCP Failover

Implement IPAM.   IPAM is an integrated suite of tools to enable end-to-end planning, deploying, managing, and monitoring of your IP address infrastructure, with a rich user experience. IPAM automatically discovers IP address infrastructure servers on your network and enables you to manage them from a central interface.

Master It   IPAM has some specific prerequisites that need to be in place before you can deploy it. What are the requirements for Active Directory that you should be aware of?

Solution   An IPAM server must be a member of an Active Directory domain; non-domain-joined IPAM server deployments are not supported. The IPAM server can operate only within the confines of a single Active Directory forest, but inside that forest you can have a mix of trusted and untrusted domains that can all be managed by the IPAM server. Also, you can manage only domain-joined servers; any servers that are not members of an Active Directory domain will not be supported with IPAM.

Effectively use IPAM components.   IPAM is made up of three different feature components that integrate to deliver holistic management of your IP address infrastructure. These three components deliver functionality for Multi-Server Management, Address Space Management, and Network Auditing.

Master It   Which feature of IPAM enables you to perform simultaneous updates to all of your DHCP and DNS servers? (Choose one.)

a. Multi-Server Management

b. Address Space Management

c. Network Auditing

Solution   a. The Multi-Server Management feature of IPAM delivers the automated discovery of manageable DHCP and DNS servers and provides centralization of the resources they serve. If you don't want to use the automatic discovery method, you can still choose to add or remove your DHCP and DNS servers manually. If you want to perform simultaneous updates to all of your DHCP and DNS servers, this is where that functionality stems from.

Integrate IPAM with System Center 2012. With all the focus on datacenter and cloud management, it's here that Microsoft has invested the most in enhancing IPAM for Windows Server 2012 R2. The Virtualized IP Address Space section of the IPAM console streamlines the management of your physical and virtual address spaces through a new integration connection with VMM. This integration opens up IP address-management capabilities between your on-premise and cloud-based IP address schemes.

Master It What version of Windows Server and VMM do you need to be running to enable IPAM integration?

Solution You need to be running Windows Server 2012 R2 with System Center 2012 R2 Virtual Machine Manager if you want to use the IPAM integration feature to manage your physical and virtual addresses seamlessly.

Manage IPAM delegation. When you install the IPAM server role, the installation process automatically creates a number of local security groups that can be used to deliver Role-Based Access Control of your IPAM environment to designated users and administrators. Depending on the type of administrative privileges that you want your users to have, all you need to do is to add their accounts to the appropriate security group.

Master It There are five local security groups that IPAM creates to deliver RBAC. Which group from the following list *is not* one of them? (Choose one.)

a. IPAM Administrators

b. IPAM IP Audit Administrators

c. IPAM ASM Administrators

d. IPAM Advanced Users

e. IPAM MSM Administrators

f. IPAM Users

Solution e) The IPAM Advanced Users group *is not* one of the five local security groups created by IPAM for RBAC and access delegation.

Understand DHCP Failover. The beauty of DHCP Failover is that there is now no need for any expensive shared storage, such as a Storage Area Network device, between your DHCP servers. Instead, the IP address lease data is replicated between each server continuously. With both DHCP Failover servers containing a copy of the latest IP address assignment and scope information, you will always be able to sustain a failure of one DHCP server without losing any DHCP functionality.

Master It The new DHCP Failover functionality allows you to configure two different types of failover relationships. What are these relationships called? (Choose two.)

a. Failover clustering (active/active)

b. Hot standby (active/passive)

c. Split-scope (active/passive)

d. Seeded (active/active)

e. Load balanced (active/active)

Solution   b. Hot standby (active/passive) and e) load balanced (active/active) are the two different types of DHCP Failover relationships that you can choose from when creating a failover between servers.

Chapter 6: DNS and Name Resolution in Windows Server 2012 R2

Explain the fundamental components and processes of DNS.   DNS relies on integrated servers that manage a hierarchical naming structure. On the Internet, this structure starts with root servers and then top-level domain servers, which delegate subdomains to other DNS servers. Within a DNS server, the database of records is known as a *zone*, and it can be replicated between other DNS servers to provide distributed query resolution for a given namespace.

Master It   Several common DNS records were discussed in this chapter. The SRV and MX records both have a parameter named priority. If there were two SRV records for the same service with a priority parameter of 10 and 20, which SRV record would be selected first?

Solution   The priority parameter can have a value from 0 to 65535 on SRV records. However, the lowest number has the highest priority. Therefore, the record with the priority parameter of 10 would be selected first.

Configure DNS to support an Active Directory environment.   Active Directory requires a DNS namespace to be available to support the assigned name of the domain. Windows Server 2012 R2 provides an automatic capability to create the required DNS structure through the domain controller promotion process. The DNS zones can be stored in the Active Directory database, which provides multimaster replication of the DNS records. With the use of SRV records and DDNS update, the domain controllers can register their services in DNS for clients to access them.

Master It   The DNS service on DCs can create Active Directory integrated zones. In which locations within the Active Directory database can the zones be placed? What scope do these locations provide?

Solution   There are four locations that can be chosen when creating a new zone:

◆ Domain partition accessible by all domain controllers in the domain including Windows 2000 domain controllers.

◆ Domain DNS application partition accessible by all domain controllers in the domain.

◆ Forest DNS application partition accessible by all domain controllers in the forest.

◆ A custom DNS application partition that can be accessed by all domain controllers in the forest. They must enlist in the replication of the partition before supporting it.

Manage and troubleshoot DNS resolution for both internal and external names. Internal and external name resolution relies on the connectivity between DNS servers. Forwarding and root hints are the primary methods to allow DNS servers to send queries between them. Several tools are available to assist troubleshooting and monitoring DNS configurations and performance, including `NsLookup`, PowerShell, and `DcDiag`.

Master It The SRV record registration for domain controllers is performed by the `netlogon` service. It is a very complex and demanding task to attempt to perform this manually. What tests can be performed to verify whether SRV records are correctly registered within a domain?

Solution The `DcDiag` utility provides tests to verify whether SRV records are available within the specified domain. `Dcdiag /registerindns` validates that the domain controller can perform updates to the domain zone using DDNS updates.

Chapter 7: Active Directory in Windows Server 2012

Create a single-domain forest. Any Windows Server 2012 server can be promoted to a domain controller to create a single-domain forest. A DC hosts an instance of Active Directory Domain Services.

Master It You want to promote a server to a DC and create a single-domain forest. What should you do?

Solution Install the Active Directory Domain Services role and then run the Active Directory Domain Services Configuration Wizard. Follow the wizard to create a new forest.

Add a second DC to the domain. A single DC represents a potential single point of failure. If it goes down, the domain goes down. Often, administrators will add a second DC to the domain.

Master It You want to add a second DC to your domain. What should you do?

Solution Install the Active Directory Domain Services role and then run the Active Directory Domain Services Configuration Wizard. Follow the wizard to an existing domain.

Decide whether to add a global catalog. A global catalog server hosts a copy of the global catalog. Any domain controller can become a GC, but only the first domain controller is a GC by default.

Master It You are promoting a second server to a domain controller in your single-domain forest. Should you make it a GC?

Solution   Yes. In a single-domain forest, all domain controllers should also be global catalog servers. This provides redundancy in the domain without any additional overhead.

Create accounts.   Any domain needs to host user and computer accounts representing users and computers that will access the domain. There are several ways to create user and computer accounts.

Master It   What are four methods that can be used to create a user account? Two have a GUI and the other two are command-line tools.

Solution   The four methods are Active Directory Users and Computers, Active Directory Administrative Center, the DSAdd command-line tool, and PowerShell using the New-ADUser cmdlet.

Create fine-grained password policies.   Windows Server 2012 introduced the ability to create multiple password policies within a domain by using fine-grained password policies. You can use a fine-grained password policy to assign a different password policy to a user or group within the domain.

Master It   You want to create a fine-grained password policy for a group of administrators in your network. What should you create and what tool should you use?

Solution   Create a password-settings object with the Active Directory Administrative Center GUI. You can also apply the PSO to users or groups using Active Directory Users and Computers.

Understand the Windows Server 2012 forest functional level.   Each forest functional level has traditionally offered new functionality to Active Directory. For example, the Windows Server 2008 R2 forest functional level brought support for the Recycle Bin feature.

Master It   What new feature is offered in the Windows Server 2012 forest functional level?

Solution   There are no new features in the Windows Server 2012 forest functional level.

Upgrade your domain to Windows Server 2012.   You currently have a Windows Server 2008 single-forest domain, and you are figuring out how to upgrade this forest. You want to have a Windows Server 2012 forest.

Master It   What methods for upgrading or migrating your forest make the most sense?

Solution   You probably want to perform in-place upgrades or a swing migration depending on your flavor. A migration using ADMT probably does not make sense.

Chapter 8: Creating and Managing User Accounts

Manage local users and groups.   Local users and groups are stored on a computer and cannot be used to log into or access resources on other computers.

Master It You have 25 PCs with 25 users on a workgroup network, in other words, a network with no Active Directory or Windows domain. You are installing two file servers. You want to provide authorized-only access to shared resources on the file servers. How will you do this?

Solution You will need to create a user account for each of the 25 users. However, because there is no domain, you will need to create the user account on the users' PCs and on each of the two servers. The username and password will have to be identical on their PCs and each of the two servers. You can speed the process up by using a scripted option, such as using the net user command in a script.

Manage users and groups in Active Directory. Users and groups can be stored in Active Directory. That means administrators can create a single copy of each user and group that is stored in a replicated database and can be used by member computers across the entire Active Directory forest. You can use Active Directory Users and Computers, the command prompt, PowerShell, and Active Directory Administrative Center to manage users and groups on Windows Server 2012.

Master It List the different types of Active Directory group types and scopes. Why would you use each of them?

Solution There are two Active Directory group types:

◆ The *distribution group* type is used to collectively communicate with the group members via a single mail address that is associated with the group.

◆ The primary purpose of the *security group* type is to manage assigned permissions for a collection of members.

The members of an Active Directory group may be users or other group objects. There are three group scopes:

◆ A *domain local group* can be used only within the domain that it was created in. It can contain user/computer accounts, global groups, and universal groups from any domain in the forest and domain local groups from the same domain.

◆ The default scope when you create a group in Active Directory is the *global group*. A global group can be used by computers within the domain that it is a member of and by members of other domains in the Active Directory forest. It can contain user/computer accounts from the domain that the global group is created in.

◆ The *universal group* is the third and final group scope. A universal group is stored on domain controllers that are configured as global catalogs. The universal group is replicated to domains across the entire forest. That allows a universal group to not only be able to be used by all computers in the forest but also to contain members from any domain within the forest. Universal groups can contain user/computer accounts, global groups, and other universal groups from any domain in the forest.

Manage users and computers in Windows Server 2012. You can manage users and computers using either PowerShell or the new Active Directory Administrative Center. ADAC makes it quicker and easier for administrators to perform day-to-day operations such as resetting passwords, unlocking user accounts, and finding objects in the forest that they want to manage. The Active Directory module for Windows PowerShell offers a command-line interface and way to script Active Directory management tasks. You can use this to automate repetitive tasks using scripts or to perform complex and large operations that would consume too much time using an administrative console.

Master It   You are managing the Windows Server 2012 Active Directory forest for an international corporation. The directors have announced that a new call center with 5,000 employees is to be opened soon. The human resources department will be able to produce a file from its database with the names of the new employees thanks to some in-house developers. You want to create the user objects as quickly as possible with minimum human effort. How will you do this?

Solution   You can work with the in-house developers so that the new employee export from the human resources application will be a CSV file. The header row will describe the entries in the following rows. Each of the following rows will contain the values that you would use in the PowerShell New-ADuser cmdlet, for example:

```
Name,SamAccountName,GivenName,Surname,DisplayName,
Path,UserPrincipalName,
AccountPassword
Rachel Kelly,RKelly,Rachel,Kelly,Rachel Kelly,"OU=Users,OU=BigFirm,DC=bigfirm,
DC=com",RKelly@bigfirm.com,NewPassw0rd
Ulrika Gerhardt,UGerhardt,Ulrika,Gerhardt,Ulrika Gerhardt,"OU=Users,OU=BigFirm
,DC=bigfirm,DC=com",UGerhardt@bigfirm.com,
NewPassw0rd
Tomasz Kozlowski, TKozlowski,Tomasz,Kozlowski,Tomaz Kozlowski,"OU=Users,OU=Big
Firm,DC=bigfirm,DC=com",TKozlowski@bigfirm.com,
NewPassw0rd
```

You will then run a PowerShell command that reads each line of the CSV file and runs the New-ADuser cmdlet using the values in each row to create the new user objects, for example:

```
PS C:\Users\Administrator> Import-CSV c:\users.csv | foreach {New-ADUser -Name
$_.Name -SamAccountName $_.SamAccountName -GivenName $_.GivenName -Surname
$_.Surname -DisplayName $_.DisplayName -Path $_.Path -UserPrincipalName
$_.UserPrincipalName -AccountPassword (ConvertTo-SecureString -AsPlainText
$_.AccountPassword -Force) -Enabled $true -ChangePasswordAtLogon 1}
```

This command will rapidly read the file and create each of the 5,000 user objects in the organizational unit(s) of your choice. Instead of spending days creating objects using a console, you will spend one minute typing this command.

Delegate group management.   Part of the power of Active Directory is the ability to delegate administrative rights. You can grant permissions to users or groups to manage any organizational unit or object in the domain. You can limit those rights so people only have permissions to do what they need to do for their role in the organization.

Master It   You are a domain administrator in a large organization. Your network contains several file servers. File shares are secured using domain-based security groups.

You have delegated rights to help-desk staff to manage these groups. The organization is relying on the help desk to know who should have read, read/write, and no access to the file shares. Mistakes are being made and changes are taking too long, causing employees to be unable to access critical information. You've considered a paper-based procedure where the business owners of the file shares document who should have access. This has proven to be unpopular because it slows down the business. You have been asked to implement a solution that ensures the business is not delayed and where only authorized people have access to sensitive information.

Solution Perform the following steps:

1. Create a Read Only and Read and Write domain-based security group for each file share.

2. Grant each of these groups the appropriate permissions on the shares.

3. Create an additional Owners domain-based security group for each file share.

4. Add the business owners of the information in the shares to each Owners group.

5. Edit the properties of the Read Only and Read and Write groups.

6. Add the appropriate Owners groups as managers of the Read Only and Read and Write groups on the Managed By tab.

The result of this solution is that anyone who is a member of the Management Owners group for the Management share will be able to manage the membership of the Management Read Only and the Management Read and Write groups. The business owners know who should have access to their file shares. The help desk cannot know this. The business owners are now empowered to make the appropriate changes in the group memberships. IT is no longer involved in the process. This reduces the communication process and allows employees of the organization to access information without delay.

Deal with users leaving the organization. It is important to understand that Windows tracks users, groups, and computers by their security identifier and not by their visible friendly name. When you delete and re-create an object, the new object is actually a different object and does not keep the old object's rights and permissions.

Master It The personnel department has informed you that an employee, BKavanagh, is leaving the organization immediately under bad circumstances. The security officer informs you that there is a security risk. You have been asked to deal with this risk without any delay. What do you do? Two hours later you are told that the personnel department gave you the wrong name. The correct name is BCavanagh. BKavanagh has called the help desk to say that she cannot do any work. What do you do to rectify the situation?

Solution When you originally disabled BKavanagh, you should have disabled the user account. This prevents the account from being usable. When you get the call that this was the wrong user account, you can simply reenable the account, and BKavanagh can start working again.

If you have a Windows Server 2012 Active Directory and you deleted the BKavanagh account, then you should reanimate it from the Active Directory Recycle Bin.

If you deleted the user account and don't have a Windows Server 2012 Active Directory, then you will have to re-create it and add the user to all the groups that she was in before. This is a time-consuming process.

You should disable the BCavanagh account to comply with the security officer and the personnel department. You can delete the account after a predetermined time has passed and the user has not returned to the organization.

Chapter 9: Group Policy: AD's Gauntlet and Active Directory Delegation

Understand local policies and Group Policy objects.   Every Windows computer from Windows 2000 Professional and up has a local group policy. Windows 8 has many local group policies, which can accommodate for various situations where the computer might be located. There are Group Policy objects stored in Active Directory too, which allow for central administration of computers and users who are associated with the domain.

Master It   Which of the following is not a local group policy?

◆ Local Computer Policy

◆ Administrator

◆ Non-Administrator

◆ All Users

Solution   All Users is not a local group policy.

Create GPOs.   Group Policy objects can and should be created within your Active Directory domain. These additional GPOs will allow you to control settings, software, and security on the different users and computers that you have within the domain. GPOs are typically linked to OUs but can be linked to the domain node and to AD sites as well. GPOs are created within AD by using the Group Policy Management console.

Master It   Create a new GPO and link it to the HRUsers OU.

Solution   To create the GPO and link it to HRUsers OU:

1. Create the HRUsers OU under the domain.

2. Within the GPMC, right-click the HRUsers OU, and select the option to create and link a GPO.

3. Give the new GPO a name of HRUserSecurity.

Troubleshoot group policies.   At times a GPO setting or group policy fails to apply. There can be many reasons for this, and you can use many tools to investigate the issue. Some tools, such as the `rsop.msc` tool, are presented in a resulting window, and other tools, such as `gpresult`, are used on the command line. Regardless of the tool you use, troubleshooting Group Policy is sometimes required.

Master It Which tool would you use to ensure that all settings in all GPOs linked to Active Directory have applied, even if there have not been any changes to a GPO or a setting in a GPO?

Solution The tool to use to ensure all settings have been applied to active directory is `gpupdate /force`.

Delegate control using organizational units. Delegation is a powerful feature in Active Directory that allows domain administrators to delegate tasks to junior administrators. The idea is that the delegation granted is narrow in scope, providing only limited capabilities within Active Directory and the objects contained within.

Master It Establish delegation on the HRUsers organizational unit such that the HRHelpDesk security group can reset the passwords for all users in the HRUsers OU.

Solution

1. Create the HRHelpDesk security group under the Users container.

2. Create the HRUsers OU under the domain.

3. Run the Delegation of Control Wizard by right-clicking the HRUsers OU.

4. Grant permissions to the HRHelpDesk group.

5. Grant the Reset Password permission.

6. Complete the delegation.

Use advanced delegation to manually set individual permissions. There are thousands of individual permissions for any given AD object. Advanced delegation provides the ability to set any of these permissions to give a user or security group access to the object for the specified permission. The Delegation of Control Wizard is a useful tool to grant common tasks, but when the wizard does not provide the level of detail required, you must grant delegation manually.

Master It *Delegation* is another term for which of the following?

◆ Replicating AD database

◆ Read-only domain controller

◆ Setting permissions on AD objects

◆ Using Group Policy to set security

Solution Delegation is another term for setting permissions on AD objects.

Find out which delegations have been set.   It is unfortunate, but the Delegation of Control Wizard is a tool that can only grant permissions, not report on what has been set. To find out what delegations have been set, you have to resort to using other tools.

Master It   Name a tool that you can use to view what delegations have been set.

Solution   dsacls is a command-line utility that comes with Windows Server 2012 R2 for viewing detailed delegation settings.

Chapter 10: Active Directory Federation Services

Install the AD FS role on a server.   Installing the AD FS role on a server is one of the first steps in implementing an AD FS infrastructure. Windows Server 2012 R2 has made it easier than ever to install and use AD FS. AD FS provides you with single sign-on access within your corporate network, to a partner organization, and to websites and applications hosted on the Internet.

Master It   How do you install AD FS on a server?

Solution   Install the AD FS roles and features using Server Manager.

Configure the first federation server in a server farm.   A federation server serves as part of a federation service that can issue, manage, and validate requests for security tokens and identity management. Multiple federation servers provide much-needed functionality like high availability and network load balancing in a large AD FS infrastructure. For proper SSO user access between your organization and a partner organization, federation servers must be deployed in the partner's organization as well as your own.

Master It   How do you create the first federation server in a federation services server farm?

Solution   Using the AD FS Management snap-in, launch and complete the AD FS Server Configuration Wizard.

Configure AD FS performance monitoring.   AD FS includes its own dedicated performance counters to help you monitor the performance of both federation servers and federation server proxy machines. This is a nice little addition that helps you manage AD FS more easily. Generated reports provide AD FS–specific details that show you how well it is running in the environment. Monitoring performance is an essential part of planning for growth and scalability. High utilization could mean that you need to deploy another federation server to balance the load more proficiently.

Master It   How would you monitor the performance of your AD FS infrastructure?

Solution   Using Performance Monitor, create a new AD FS data collection set.

Chapter 11: Shared Storage and Clustering Introduction

Use the available storage options for clustering.   With the release of Windows Server 2012 R2, many more storage options are available for your clustering and high-availability solutions.

Master It   You want to build out a JBOD solution and need the most effective type of disk capacity. The failover doesn't matter as much as space and speed. What technology should you consider?

Solution   You must build out a Storage Spaces solution utilizing simple volumes; this volume type is designed for throughput and size. Maximize the disks and access to the disks to make the solution fast and effective.

Use quorums to help in clustering.   A quorum is "the minimum number of members required to be present at an assembly or meeting before it can validly proceed to transact business." This definition holds true for the use of a quorum in clustering.

Master it   You have chosen to deploy an odd-numbered cluster with five nodes, and you will use one node as a file share witness for quorum. Once the cluster is up and running, you host an application. But after the install the application has a major memory leak and starts seizing up the servers and shutting them down. How many nodes will go down before the cluster is completely offline?

Solution   Since you have an even number of quorum nodes and a spare witness node, the cluster will remain online until the very last node is about to go down. With proper monitoring and alerting, you would never let anything get this far, would you? Hopefully not, but the benefit of a witness node is that you can keep your application up and active while you get those other servers either back online or rolled back to a different version of the application.

Build out host and guest clusters.   Clustering is a mix of software and hardware and can be hosted on physical servers or virtual machines. Windows Server 2012 R2 has the components and tools built in to help you deploy your clusters, including a handy prerequisites wizard to validate that you have all the components and configurations in place to successfully set up a cluster.

Master it   When planning your host- and guest-based clusters, excluding the Hyper-V role, what is the difference between the two in setting up a cluster?

Solution   There is no difference; once you start to plan your hardware and networks, the requirements on both the VM and host sides of the cluster process are exactly the same. The process is simple and easy to step through.

Chapter 12: Windows 2012 R2 Storage: Storage Spaces, SANish Abilities, and Better Tools

Create a storage pool on a virtual disk.   Storage is an ever-growing business requirement. If you were constantly buying SAN solutions to meet this need, it would prove very costly. Also, it is very hard to predict what you may need in a year's time. How would you manage your storage to get the most out of it and to meet your future storage needs?

Master It   In your lab create a storage pool using the GUI with three disks. Create a virtual disk three times the size of the total usable capacity of the disk. Format it and get it ready to use.

Solution   In Server Manager, under File and Storage Services, navigate to Volumes ➤ Storage Pools. From the primordial pool, right-click and select a new storage pool. Enter a name and then select three physical disks (note their individual capacities and add them up). Select your storage pool from the Storage Pool window, and create a new virtual disk from it. Give it a useful name and select Parity as the storage layout. Select Single Parity and Thinly Provision the Disk. For its size use the total storage capacity you worked out times three. Create a volume on that virtual disk and copy some files into it.

Create additional storage on a virtual disk.   A common occurrence in enterprises today is last-minute requests for provisioning of applications that require large amounts of storage. Often the storage available locally in the server is not large enough to meet the need. How can you get additional storage onto the server without adding local storage?

Master It   In your lab deploy an iSCSI target, create a virtual disk, and then connect your server to use the newly created storage.

Solution   New in 2012/2012 R2 Microsoft has introduced a variety of new cmdlets to help you configure the iSCSI target and client software. The steps you would take to configure this solution via PowerShell are listed as follows:

1. From PowerShell on the server you have selected as your iSCSI target server, run the following cmdlet:

   ```
   Add-windowsfeature FS-iSCSITarget-Server -IncludeManagementTools
   ```

2. Create a new iSCSI target as follows:

   ```
   New-IscsiServerTarget -TargetName TestTarget01 -InitiatorID iqn.1991-05.
   com.microsoft:server01.contoso.com
   ```

   (Change the iqn to that of your remote server.)

3. Add a new virtual disk using the following cmdlet:

   ```
   New-IscsiVirtualDisk -path e:\newdisk.vhdx -SizeBytes 20GB
   ```

4. Add the disk to the previously created iSCSI target, as shown here:

   ```
   Add-IscsiVirtualDiskTargetMapping -TargetName TestTarget01 -path e:\
   newdisk.vhdx
   ```

5. On the remote server where you need the extra storage, from an elevated PowerShell prompt run the following:

   ```
   Set-Service -Name msiscsi -StartupType Automatic
   Start-Service msiscsi
   ```

6. Type:

   ```
   New-iscsitargetportal -targetportaladdress TestTarget01
   ```

7. Then type:

```
Get-IscsiTarget | Connect-IscsiTarget
```

8. Check Disk Manager for newly added disks, and then initialize them and bring them online.

Use deduplication techniques to reduce file size. Part of the reason behind data growth in today's environments is the availability of storage, but storage will become a problem sooner rather than later. A high percentage of these files contain a large degree of identical data patterns, but using deduplication techniques can dramatically reduce the disk space required and make better overall use of the storage in place.

Master It In your lab copy an ISO multiple times into different shares, and repeat for office documents that are not located on your System volume. Enable Deduplication on the data drive, and exclude a share of importance in your environment.

Solution Deduplication in Windows Server 2012 R2 can be managed via PowerShell. Here we outline the steps you will take to work with deduplication and some of the cmdlets you would use.

1. From PowerShell type,

```
Enable-DeDupVolume -Volume E:
```

where E: is the volume you are trying to dedup.

2. Exclude a folder using PowerShell:

```
Set-DedupVolume -Volume E: -ExcludeFolder E:\shares
```

3. Verify all the information using:

```
Get-DeDupVolume -Volume E: | fl *
```

4. Change the file age field to 0 days so all files are immediately considered for dedup:

```
Set-DedupVolume -Volume E: -MinimumFileAgeDays 0
```

5. Start an optimization job:

```
Start-Dedupjob -Type Optimization -Volume E:
```

6. Verify that space savings have been made:

```
Get-DeDupStatus -Volume E:
```

Chapter 13: Files, Folders, and Basic Shares

Install additional File and Storage Services roles on a server. The File and Storage Services role includes services designed to optimize serving files from the server. A significant addition is the File Server Resource Manager role, which can be used to manage quotas, to add file screens, and to produce comprehensive reports.

Master It How do you add FSRM to the server?

Solution Install the File Server Resource Manager role service using Server Manager.

Combine share and NTFS permissions.   When a folder is shared from an NTFS drive, it includes both share permissions and NTFS permissions. It's important to understand how these permissions interact so that users can be granted appropriate permission.

Master It   Maria is in the G_HR and G_HRManagers groups. A folder named Policies is shared as Policies on a server with the following permissions:

NTFS: G_HR Read, G_HR_Managers Full Control

Share: G_HR Read, G_HR Change

What is Maria's permission when accessing the share? What is her permission when accessing the folder directly on the server?

Solution   Maria's permission when accessing the share is Change. You can determine the result of combined NTFS and share permissions in three steps:

◆ *Determine cumulative NTFS permissions:* She has Read and Full Control, so her cumulative NTFS permission is Full Control.

◆ *Determine cumulative share permissions:* She has Read and Change, so her cumulative share permission is Change.

◆ *Determine which of the two provides the least access (or is the most restrictive):* Change is more restrictive than Full Control.

If the folder is accessed directly, share permissions do not apply. So, she would have Full Control permission.

Implement BitLocker Drive Encryption.   BitLocker Drive Encryption allows you to encrypt an entire drive. If someone obtains the drive that shouldn't have access to the data, the encryption will prevent them from accessing the data.

Master It   What are the hardware requirements for BitLocker Drive Encryption, and what needs to be done to the operating system to use BitLocker?

Solution   BitLocker requires Trusted Platform Module 1.2, which is a hardware component and is typically included in the motherboard on systems that have it. It is possible to use BitLocker without TPM using either a password or a smart card and a PIN. BitLocker needs to be added as a feature using Server Manager before it can be implemented.

Chapter 14: Creating and Managing Shared Folders

Add a File and Storage Services role to your server.   Before you can create and use DFS or NFS, share files and folders, or perform any other file-related function across the domain in Server 2012, you will need to install the additional File and Storage Services roles.

Master It   Go into Server Manager, and add the server roles DFS and NFS.

Solution   Perform the following steps:

1. Open Server Manager and click Tools ➤ Add Roles and Features.

2. In the Add Roles and Features Wizard, drill down to the roles and features you wish to install, and then click the Install button.

3. After the wizard completes, go back into Server Manager, click Manage, and you should see the additional roles and features installed.

If done correctly, your server will show that the DFS and NFS roles are installed.

Add a shared folder using NFS.   Once the proper File and Storage Services roles have been added, you can then share folders, such as a folder called APPS.

Master It   Create a shared folder called APPS on your Windows Server 2012 R2 server; when you have finished, the wizard should show a successful share.

Solution   Once you set up the permissions on your share, click Next to see the final screen of the Share a Folder Wizard, which lists the results and gives you the option to run the wizard again.

1. Select Control Panel ➤ Administrative Tools ➤ Computer Management ➤ Shares ➤ New ➤ Share.

2. Follow the wizard, and browse to the folder you want to share. Click Next, and then set the kind of permissions you want for the shared folder. Click Finish.

Add a DFS root.   If your organization ends up with a lot of file servers created over time, you may have users who do not know where all the files are located. You can streamline the process of finding and using multiple file servers by creating a DFS root and consolidate the existing file servers into common namespaces.

Master It   Create a new namespace called **MYFIRSTNS** on your Windows Server 2012 R2 server; when you have finished, the wizard should show a new namespace called MYFIRSTNS.

Solution   In the upper-right side of the DFS Management screen, click New Namespace. You will then see the Namespace Server Wizard. Follow the steps through to completion:

1. Select Server Manager ➤ Tools ➤ DFS Management.

2. In DFS Management, click the Action drop-down, and select New Replication Group.

3. In New Replication Group Wizard, select the group type. Enter the name of the replication group (MYFIRSTNS), add any descriptions, and click Next.

4. Add the servers, and then click Next.

5. Select the topology, and then click Next.

6. Add the hub members, and click Next.

7. Select the replication group schedule, and click Next.

8. Set whether it is a primary member, and click Next.

9. Now add the folders to replicate, and click Next.

10. Review the settings, and click Finish.

Chapter 15: Dynamic Access Control: File Shares, Reimagined

Secure your data using conditions. Understand how you can secure your data without being a part of hundreds of groups. Using this knowledge, you will understand the building blocks of Dynamic Access Control.

Master It In your lab and using the examples we have shown at the start of this chapter, create a new share called **Projects**, and secure it so that only people in the Engineering and IT groups can access it. Make sure you test it. Do you remember how?

Solution Using Advanced Security on the folder, add in a condition for the Authenticated Users principal that selects the IT or Engineering group. Refer to Figure 15.5, which will show you the fields you need to modify.

Create a new claim type and resource property. As you move away from using groups and bloated Kerberos tokens, you need to understand how to ensure that only the right people can access your data. Using claim types and resource properties allows you to secure data with new elements.

Master It How can you ensure that only employees from Ireland can access the data located on your shares? What do you need to do in order to be able to use Country as an authorization token?

Solution Using the Dynamic Access Control Configuration Tool in Active Directory Administrative Center, create a new claim type that is based on the Country Active Directory attribute, and add in different values including Ireland. Once you have created a new claim type, create a new referenced resource property, which should be based on the claim type you just configured.

Secure hundreds of servers. Dynamic Access Control is a powerful tool for securing data, but when you have a large server estate, you need to make this an easy technology to deliver to the organization to provide the maximum benefit.

Master It You need to secure all of your data across all of your files servers. How do you secure the data first so that only people in IT can have Full Control across all shares and Accounts and Engineering users have read-only access?

Solution First, you need to create Central Access rules, which will contain the permissions for securing your data. Then you need to add in authenticated users and set the permissions to Read Only and Read and Execute. Then modify the condition for users from the Accounts and Engineering departments. Then add authenticated users again, and add Full Control and a condition for users from the IT department.

Create a Central Access Policy and add the Central Access rule to the policy. When you have finished, create a new GPO and add the new Central Access Policy. Apply the group policy to the appropriate OU so it gets applied to the correct file servers.

If necessary, run **GPUPDATE** on the relevant file servers, and then on a share you want to apply the policy to, select the correct Central Access Policy.

Classify and secure data without knowing what the data is.   Imagine a vast file server array with millions of files. As you know, it has not been common practice to properly classify documents as they are written. Knowing how to approach this and properly classify and secure this data is paramount to an organization.

Master It   Across your file servers you have documents that contain sensitive information, including credit card numbers and payroll data. How can you automatically secure this data and ensure that only the Accounts and HR departments can access this information?

Solution   First, create classification rules; the credit card rules should use regular expressions to detect credit card number patterns. The next set of rules should detect strings that are relevant to payroll, for example, monthly pay or salary. Configure the options in File Server Resource Manager to run on a schedule so it will retroactively apply to the entire server. Finally, using Dynamic Access Control, create a new access rule and policy that will target the resources that have been classified by department, and secure them using conditional access to the Accounts and HR departments.

Chapter 16: Sharing Printers on Windows Server 2012 R2 Networks

Add the Print and Document Services role.   Windows Server 2012 R2 servers can be configured to perform as print servers. One of the first steps you must take is to add the Print and Document Services role. There are different steps needed if you're adding the role to a full installation of Windows Server 2012 R2 vs. a Server Core installation.

Master It   What tool would you use to add the Print and Document Services role on a full installation of Windows Server 2012 R2? What tool would you use to add the Print and Document Services role on a Server Core installation of Windows Server 2012 R2?

Solution   Use Server Manager to add the Print and Document Services role on a full installation of Windows Server 2012 R2. Use the PowerShell command-line utility to add the Print and Document Services role on a Server Core installation of Windows Server 2012 R2. The actual command is as follows:

```
add-WindowsFeature Print-Service
```

Manage printers using the Print Management console.   After adding the Print and Documents Services role to the server, you can use the Print Management console to manage other print servers, printers, and print drivers.

Master It   Your company has purchased a new print device, and you want it to be hosted on a server that is configured as a print server. How would you add the printer to the print server?

Solution   You can add printers through the Print Management console. Right-click the printer's node within the desired server, and select Add Printer to start the Add Printer Wizard.

Manage print server properties.   The spool folder can sometimes take a significant amount of space on the C drive, resulting in space problems and contention issues with the operating system. Because of these issues, the spool folder is often moved to another physical drive.

Master It   You want to move the spool folder to another location. How can you do this?

Solution   Launch the PMC, and browse to the server. Right-click the server, and select Properties. Change the location of the spool folder on the Advanced tab. Any spooled documents will be lost, so you should ensure users aren't currently printing to any printers hosted by the server.

Manage printer properties.   Printers can be added to Active Directory so that they can be easily located by searching Active Directory. Printers must be shared first, but they aren't published to Active Directory by default when they are shared.

Master It   You want users to be able to easily locate a shared printer. What can you do to ensure the shared printer can be located by searching Active Directory?

Solution   Launch the PMC, and browse to the printer. Right-click the printer, and select List in Directory, or access the Sharing tab of the printer's properties, and select List in Directory.

Chapter 17: Remote Server Administration

Configure Windows Server 2012 R2 servers for remote administration.   Servers must be configured to allow remote administration before administrators can connect remotely.

Master It   Configure a server to allow remote connections by clients running RDC version 6.0 or greater.

Solution   Click Start, right-click Computer, and select Properties. Click Remote Settings. Select "Allow connections only from computers running Remote Desktop with Network Level Authentication (Recommended)." Click OK.

Remotely connect to Windows Server 2012 R2 servers using Remote Desktop Connection.   You can remotely connect to servers to do almost any administrative work. Servers are often located in a secure server room that is kept cool to protect the electronics. They can be in a different room, a different building, or even a separate geographical location, but they can still be remotely administered using either RDC or Remote Desktops.

Master It   Connect to a server using RDC. Ensure your local drives are accessible when connected to the remote server.

Solution   Launch RDC by selecting Start ➢ Accessories ➢ Remote Desktop Connection. Alternatively, you could enter **mstsc** from the command line or Run line. Enter the name of the remote server in the Computer text box. Click Options. Select the Local Resources tab. Click More, and select Drives.

Remotely connect to Windows Server 2012 R2 servers using a Remote Desktop Protocol file.   If you regularly connect to a remote server using RDC, you can configure an RDP file that can be preconfigured based on your needs for this server. This RDP file will store all the settings you configure for this connection.

Master It   Create an RDP file that you can use to connect with a server named Server1. Configure the file to automatically launch Server Manager when connected.

Solution   Launch RDC by selecting Start ➢ Accessories ➢ Remote Desktop Connection. Click Options, and select the Programs tab. Select the "Start the Following Program on Connection" check box, and enter ServerManager.msc in the text box. Click the General tab, and enter Server1 in the Computer text box. Click Save As, and save the file.

Configure a server for Remote Assistance.   When your environment includes remote locations where junior administrators may occasionally need assistance, you can use Remote Assistance to access their session and demonstrate procedures.

Master It   Configure a server for Remote Assistance.

Solution   Launch Server Manager, select Roles and Features, and add the Remote Assistance feature. Once the wizard has completed, ensure Remote Assistance is enabled. Click Start, right-click Computer, select Properties, and select Remote Settings. Verify that the Remote Assistance check box is selected.

Install the Remote Server Administration Tools.   The Remote Assistance Server Administration Tools (RSAT) include the snap-ins and command-line tools needed to manage Server 2003, Server 2008, and Server 2012 servers from Windows Vista and Windows 7 and 8.

Master It   Obtain and install RSAT on a Windows Vista or Windows 7 or 8 system.

Solution   Obtain RSAT by going to Microsoft's download site at www.Microsoft.com/downloads and typing in RSAT. Install RSAT by double-clicking the downloaded file and following the wizard. Enable the tools by adding the Remote Server Administration Tools feature via Control Panel ➢ Programs ➢ Turn Windows Features On or Off.

Chapter 18: Connecting Windows and Mac Clients

Verify your network configuration.   DHCP provides centralized IP address configurations, and all Windows clients understand DHCP without any additional installations required.

Master It   You need to verify that a client machine has received the correct IP address configuration via DHCP for the network you are working on. Which of the following commands would return these results?

◆   `ipconfig /all`

◆   `ipconfig /refresh`

◆   `msconfig /show`

◆   `msconfig`

Solution   The `ipconfig /all` command returns local area connection configuration information including the following:

◆   IP address

◆   DNS IP addresses

◆   DHCP server IP address

◆   Domain name suffix

Join a client computer to a domain.   Joining an Active Directory domain is key for workstations, because this provides centralized management from the Domain Admins group within the domain. Group Policy is centralized, security can be established, and even software can be controlled centrally.

Master It   Is the following statement true or false? "When joining a computer to an Active Directory domain, the only way this can occur is if the user joining the computer to the domain is a domain admin."

Solution   It is false. Domain users can also add computers to the domain, but they can only do so up to 10 times. Users can also be delegated the right to add computers to the domain.

Change user passwords.   By default Windows AD provides a 42-day maximum password age limit. This limit is preceded by a 14-day reminder that you need to change your password. The 42-day maximum is designed to maintain a certain level of security for the enterprise, not allowing passwords to become stale.

Master It   A user has become paranoid and wants to change his user account password right away. He does not know how to do this and calls the help desk. The computer he is using is running the Windows 7 operating system. What do you tell him?

Solution   Tell the user to open the Start menu, click the Windows Security button, and then click "Change a password." He will need to input his old password and his new password and then click the arrow button.

Connect to network resources.   Here's a typical scenario: a user wants to connect to a printer on the domain that does double-sided printing and also stapling. But the user does not know where the company keeps these printers. The user calls the help desk.

Master It Which of the following is the most efficient way for the user to find printers matching this description?

a. Tell the user to walk around the office complex and check each printer to see whether it has these features.

b. Tell the user to use the `net view` command to check for shared printers on a per-computer basis.

c. Tell the user to start the Add Printer Wizard and then select the Search Active Directory option.

Solution c. The user should search Active Directory using the Add Printer Wizard. Using this wizard, the user can specify specific printer feature criteria and see all the printers that are published to Active Directory that have the feature set the user needs.

Prepare Active Directory for Mac OS X clients. Although Mac OS X can join Active Directory domains, you must take some preparatory steps to ensure they can communicate with Windows Server 2012.

Master it You want your Active Directory users who have Mac clients to connect to your Windows Server 2008 R2 servers using a single Active Directory logon. What network security feature of Windows must you change to permit Mac clients to communicate with your Windows Server 2012 domain?

Solution You must change the local policy for domain controllers to not always require SMB packet signing.

Connect a Mac to the domain. Mac OS X can connect to Active Directory and join domains. SMB protocol support is provided by a built-in version of Samba, letting OS X connect to Windows for file shares and printers.

Master it You want to add your Mac OS X client to your Active Directory domain. Which OS X utility should you use?

Solution Use Directory Access in your Utilities folder to configure and connect to Active Directory and create a computer account in the domain.

Connect to file shares and printers. OS X connects to Windows file shares and printers using the SMB support provided by Samba. Because support is integrated, you can use the Finder to connect to Windows resources directly rather than adding additional software.

Master It You are trying to access a network folder that is shared on a Windows Server 2012 computer from your domain-joined Mac client. How can you use the Finder to connect?

Solution In the Finder, click the Go menu, and select Connect to Server; then type the path using the format `smb://servername/sharename`.

Use Remote Desktop from a Mac client. Microsoft created the Remote Desktop Connection for Mac to provide Remote Desktop connectivity for Mac clients. Using RDC, you can access the functionality of your Windows computer directly from your Mac clients.

Master It You are using RDC to connect to your Windows Server 2012 server computer and want to save your network credentials so that you don't have to enter them every time you connect. How can you do this?

Solution Enter your Active Directory credentials in Preferences under the RDC menu, and select the option to save the credentials in your Keychain.

Chapter 19: Web Server Management with IIS

Plan for and install IIS 8.5. Relatively lean by default, IIS 8.5 must be carefully and painstakingly planned so as not to install more modular functionality than you need. More than a resource concern, leaving unnecessary role services off the server is also a method of securing your websites. As always with Microsoft, there are multiple ways to install IIS 8.5, from an interactive GUI to PowerShell.

Master It You are about to install IIS 8.5 on a Windows Server 2012 R2 with the GUI removed. You want to install only the default roles as well as the ASP.NET role and what that role requires. What is the PowerShell command needed to accomplish this?

Solution The PowerShell command is `Install-WindowsFeature -Name Web-Server`, `Web-ASP-Net45`.

Manage IIS 8's global default. IIS 8 modules are only one piece of evidence of the product's compartmentalization. Web applications and individual configuration settings per site can be independently managed as well. A hierarchical ladder of global, web, application, and page settings allows granular administration by multiple engineers.

Master It What is feature delegation?

Solution Feature delegation is the art of allowing site administrators to configure a specific IIS feature at their own sites rather than accepting the feature behavior dictated by the global settings on the server. Delegation is enabled by unlocking specific sections of the `web.config` files on one or more sites.

Create and secure websites in IIS 8. Designing and generating new websites in IIS 8 can be accomplished via the GUI or CLI, allowing you to automate routine site creation. Permission structure can be copied from one site to another or managed from the upper layers of the settings hierarchy to simplify permission granting. IIS 8 eases site generation by packaging your website.

Master It You need to create a new website that has all the characteristics of the Default Web Site but must also support ASP.NET pages. You do not want to add ASP.NET support to the Default Web Site for fear of adding vulnerability to existing web content. How would you implement this?

Solution   Create a new website, and add the ASP.NET module to the new site. Use a custom TCP/IP port number or host header to differentiate the new site from existing sites. Consider configuring a unique application pool identity for the site to isolate ASP.NET activity during troubleshooting.

Manage IIS 8 with advanced administration techniques.   Day-to-day site maintenance and content posting may be the bulk of your IIS 8 administration. But additional higher-level management is what assures consistent and uninterrupted service of your web pages. Important configuring tasks, including recovering from disasters, monitoring performance, setting access or code security, and defining encryption, can be accomplished either locally or remotely.

Master It   Because of limited storage space, you are revising your disaster-recovery plan. You are considering delaying backups of the IIS `applicationhost.config` file to monthly. However, you are concerned that minor global configuration changes made throughout the month may get lost if a failure occurs before the monthly backup. How would you recover a mid-month edit?

Solution   IIS 8 maintains a configuration history of `applicationhost.config` according to the default schedule found in the iis_schema.xml file. Previous versions of the file can be restored with the `Restore-WebConfiguration` PowerShell command. By default, the automatically generated historical versions of `applicationhost.config` are stored in the history subdirectory under `%systemdrive%\inetpub`.

Chapter 20: Advanced IP: Routing with Windows

Document the life of an IP packet routed through your network.   Understanding how the routing components work inside your hosts and routers will allow you to predict where network traffic will travel throughout your network. With this understanding comes the ability to troubleshoot network issues that appear perplexing.

Master It   In the New York/London network from Figure 20.1, use your understanding of the route taken by an IP packet from host A in the New York site to host C in the London site to determine which addresses you should ping in order to discover routing issues that are preventing packets from traveling between A and C.

Solution   When using the ping tool to track traffic from one host to another, it is important to realize that you are tracking return traffic. If a route is broken, it may well be in the return journey. Having said that, when debugging router issues from system A (New York) to system C (London), you should ping, in order, the following IP addresses:

A—192.168.0.1—To ensure that IP is configured on host A (New York)

D—192.168.0.100—To ensure that the router is on the network

D—192.169.0.100—To ensure that the router is routing traffic

B—192.169.0.3—To ensure that host B (London) is receiving, and responding to, traffic

Explain the class-based and classless views of IP routing.   When discussing routing with networking professionals, it is important to understand the old class-based terminology to allow for conversations and documentation that may still linger on these terms. Understanding how classless IP routing works is key to avoiding inefficiencies brought on by too strict an adherence to class boundaries in network addressing.

Master It   The address 172.24.255.255 lies inside class B, whose default netmask is 255.255.0.0. It also lies in the 172.16/20 RFC 1918 private network range, whose default netmask is 255.255.240.0. Given this information, is the address 172.24.255.255 a host address or a subnet broadcast address?

Solution   The information given is insufficient to determine whether the address 172.24.255.255 is a host address or a subnet broadcast address. The default netmask is not relevant; only the netmask that is actually in use is relevant. If this is a network built by a network designer who was not thinking about supernetting or CIDR, this address may very well be treated as a subnet broadcast address. It is more likely, given that RFC 1918 talks about supernetting this address range, that this is a simple host address.

Use NAT devices to route TCP traffic.   Until we all switch to using IPv6, we will need to use NAT devices to route TCP traffic from our many networked hosts to the outside world, while using only a few of the increasingly rare public IP addresses. Understanding how NAT devices change the source and destination addresses of IP packets will allow you to read network packet traces and interpret which systems are intended as recipients of data.

Master It   A user complains that when he tries to connect to an FTP site, the connection initially succeeds, but the first time that a file listing is attempted, his connection is severed, and the server states that it cannot connect to 192.168.0.10.

What are likely causes of this problem, and how could this be addressed?

Solution   FTP, like SIP and several other protocols, often includes the IP address of the host in its communication.

Whenever an RFC 1918 address such as 192.168.*.* is seen as part of an error, your first thought should be that there may be a problem with a NAT router between the two hosts. With FTP, there are a number of possible causes and fixes:

◆ The FTP ALG in the NAT should be changing the IP address and port in the control channel—the usual cause for it not doing so is that the FTP server is running on a port other than the default port, 21. If possible, moving the server back to port 21 will allow the ALG to work correctly.

◆ If the FTP server is on port 21, it is possible that encryption is being used on the control channel, using FTP over SSL or FTP over GSSAPI. In this case, the ALG cannot see or modify the traffic.

◆ Many FTP clients allow the user to select "passive mode" communications for data transfers, in which case it is the server's IP address that needs to pass through the NAT, and this may allow for data to travel between client and server.

◆ If this is not possible, the use of an FTP proxy service may prove necessary to ensure that data connections can flow correctly.

Chapter 21: Getting from the Office to the Road: VPNs

Add the Network Policy and Access Services role.   The first step to create a VPN server is to add the Network Policy and Access Services role. Once the role is added, you can take additional steps to configure the VPN server.

Master It   You need to add the Network Policy and Access Services role to create a VPN server. How can you accomplish this?

Solution   Launch the Server Manager ➢ Local Server ➢ Manage menu, choose the Add Roles and Features option, and then add the Network Policy and Access Services role.

Understand the Remote Access role.   The Remote Access role includes much more than just the ability to create a traditional VPN server.

Master It   Name the individual services within this role (choose three):

a. Remote Access Service

b. VPN Service

c. Routing

d. IPsec

e. DirectAccess

Solution   a, c, e Remote Access Service, Routing, and DirectAccess are the three individual services that make up the Remote Access role.

Configure a VPN server.   You have added the Remote Access role and now want to configure your VPN server to accept connections from clients.

Master It   What should you do to configure your VPN server?

Solution   Launch Routing and Remote Access by selecting Server Manager ➢ Tools ➢ Routing and Remote Access. Right-click the server, and select Configure and Enable Routing and Remote Access. Use the wizard to complete the configuration.

Explore DirectAccess.   DirectAccess enables remote users to securely connect back into the corporate environment without the need to use a traditional VPN client.

Master It   What client operating systems are supported for Windows Server 2012 R2 DirectAccess?

Solution   Only Windows 7 Enterprise and Ultimate and Windows 8 Enterprise are supported client operating systems for DirectAccess.

Chapter 22: Adding More Locations: Sites in Active Directory

Create a site.   Site objects are added to Active Directory to represent well-connected physical locations that will host domain controllers. Once a decision has been made to place a DC in a physical location, you need to add a site.

Master It   Create a site to represent a new business location in Virginia Beach.

Solution   Launch Active Directory Sites and Services. Right-click Sites, and select New Site. Name the site **VB,** select an existing site link, and click OK.

Add subnets to sites.   Active Directory uses clients' subnets to determine which site they are in. For this to work, subnet objects need to be created and associated with sites.

Master It   Create a subnet object to represent the 10.15.0.0/16 subnet that exists in the Virginia Beach location. Associate the subnet object with the VB site.

Solution   Launch Active Directory Sites and Services. Right-click Subnets, and select New Subnet. Enter **10.15.0.0/16** as the prefix, and select the VB site. Click OK.

Configure a site link to replicate only during certain times.   It's often desirable to restrict when replication occurs between sites. If the defaults are used, replication will occur every 180 minutes. If the WAN link is heavily used during certain periods, you can configure the schedule so that it replicates only during certain times.

Master It   Configure the Default-First-Site-Name site (or another site) to replicate only between midnight and 5 a.m.

Solution   Launch Active Directory Sites and Services. Right-click the DefaultIPSiteLink site link, and select Properties. Click the Change Schedule button. Click Replication Not Available to change the schedule so that replication isn't scheduled. Use your mouse to highlight the hours 5 a.m. to midnight for all seven days of the week. Click Replication Available, and click OK.

Configure Group Policy for the next nearest site.   If a domain controller can't be reached in a client's site, the client will look for any domain controller without regard to how close it is. This can negatively impact logons for enterprises with several locations connected with different speed WAN links. You can configure Windows Vista (and newer) clients to locate and log on to a DC in the next nearest site if a DC can't be located in their site. This can be done using Group Policy or the Registry Editor.

Master It   Which of the following Group Policy settings can be manipulated to enable the next nearest site setting?

1. Computer Configuration ➢ Policies ➢ Administrative Templates ➢ System ➢ Logon ➢ DC Locator DNS Records

2. Computer Configuration ➢ Policies ➢ Administrative Templates ➢ System ➢ Net Logon ➢ DC Locator DNS Records

3. User Configuration ➢ Policies ➢ Administrative Templates ➢ System ➢ Logon ➢ DC Locator DNS Records

4. User Configuration ➢ Policies ➢ Administrative Templates ➢ System ➢ Net Logon ➢ DC Locator DNS Records

Solution Computer Configuration ➤ Policies ➤ Administrative Templates ➤ System ➤ Net Logon ➤ DC Locator DNS Records. The setting applies to computers, not users. Additionally, it affects how the `netlogon` service (not the logon process) locates domain controllers.

Chapter 23: The Third DC: Understanding Read-Only Domain Controllers

Prepare a forest and a domain for RODCs. RODCs are an excellent infrastructure asset in Windows Server 2012 R2 and can't be added until the forest and domain are prepared. The preparation will modify the schema and permissions.

Master It Identify the command that needs to be executed to prepare the forest to support RODCs.

Solution The adprep command needs to be executed from the command line. The following command will prepare the forest: `adprep /forestprep`.

Prepare the domain. In addition to preparing the forest, you must also prepare the domain before RODCs can be added.

Master It Identify the two commands that need to be executed to prepare the domain to support RODCs.

Solution The adprep command needs to be executed from the command line. The following two commands should be executed after `adprep /forestprep`:

◆ `adprep /domainprep`

◆ `adprep /rodcprep`

If a forest is created with all Windows Server 2008 or later servers as domain controllers, it's not necessary to execute `adprep /forestprep` and `adprep /domainprep`, but `adprep /rodcprep` still must be executed.

Allow passwords on any RODC. The RODC can cache passwords for users based on how it's configured. When a user's password is cached on the RODC, the authentication process doesn't have to traverse the WAN link and is quicker. However, a cached password is susceptible to an attack, so privileged accounts should not be cached on the server.

Master It What should you modify to allow users to have their passwords cached on any RODC in the domain?

◆ The Allowed RODC Password Replication group

◆ The Denied RODC Password Replication group

◆ The password replication policy

Solution   You should modify the Allowed RODC Password Replication group. Members of this group can have their passwords replicated or cached on any RODC in the domain.

Allow passwords on a single RODC.   It's possible to configure the environment so members of a group can have their passwords replicated and cached to any RODC in the domain. It's also possible to configure the environment so that the passwords will be replicated or cached only to a single RODC.

Master It   What should you modify to allow users to have their passwords cached on a specific RODC in the domain?

◆ The Allowed RODC Password Replication group

◆ The Denied RODC Password Replication group

◆ The password replication policy

Solution   You should modify the password replication policy. Each RODC has a Password Replication Policy tab that can be modified to allow users to have their passwords cached or replicated onto that RODC.

Chapter 24: Creating Larger Active Directory Environments: Beyond One Domain

Explain the fundamental concepts of Active Directory with clarity.   The Active Directory environment gets back to nature with the forest and trees. The forest is the collection of domains built in relation to each other through AD DS. The trees are domains within a hierarchal DNS namespace with "the same last name." The key to the relation between domains is the automatic and nonconfigurable two-way transitive trust relation.

Master It   When the first domain controller for the first domain is created, three partitions are created within the Active Directory database. What are these three partitions named, what is contained in them, and which are replicated to the other domain controllers of the forest?

Solution   The three partitions are the domain partition, the schema partition, and the configuration partition. The domain partition contains objects pertaining to the domain such as computer and user accounts and is replicated to domain controllers of the domain. The schema partition defines the objects of Active Directory and which data values are assigned to each object. The configuration partition holds data concerning Active Directory replication and other forest-related configurations. The schema and configuration partitions are replicated throughout the forest.

Choose between using domains, multiple domains, or multiple forests with an Active Directory design.   In planning an Active Directory design, you might decide you need multiple domains instead of using organizational units within a single domain. Replication

1618 | **APPENDIX** THE BOTTOM LINE

limitations, legal requirements, and political forces are the top reasons for considering multiple domains.

Master It   What features of Windows Server 2012 R2 eliminate two security-related reasons for multiple domains?

Solution   The two security-related reasons for multiple domains were password policies and poor security at branch offices. The feature of fine-tuned password policies that can be applied to users through the use of GPOs relieved the need for creating separate domains for differing password policies. The read-only domain controller with password caching reduces the risk of a stolen domain controller getting into the hands of an evil hacker and retrieving passwords from the Active Directory database or replicating corrupt changes to the rest of domain controllers.

Add domains to an Active Directory environment.   You have to use the Active Directory Domains Services Configuration Wizard whenever you are going to build a new domain or replica domain controller in an Active Directory forest. In previous versions of Windows Server, the DNS structure needed to be in place prior to the installation. With Windows Server 2012 R2, everything is done for you.

Master It   Since DNS is now handled by Windows Server 2012 R2, it would be nice to know if it did it right. What four changes should you see if you add a new child domain?

Solution   You should see these changes:

♦ In the IP configurations, the domain controller is listed as the DNS server using loopback addresses for IPv4 and IPv6.

♦ The DNS zone for the new child domain is supported on the domain controller as an Active Directory integrated zone.

♦ The parent domain controller is listed as the forwarder for the DNS service.

♦ The child domain's DNS domain name is delegated to the new domain controller in the parent DNS zone.

Manage function levels, trusts, FSMO roles, and the global catalog.   Several forest-related configurations were discussed, which would be managed by enterprise admins. The functional levels for the forest and domains provide the availability of features of the latest Windows Server version. All domain controllers need to be upgraded to that level to benefit from these features. Although you can raise functional levels, you can't lower them. The five FSMOs are specific roles assigned to domain controllers within the domains and forest. The PDC Emulator, RID Master, and Infrastructure Master are domain-related roles. The Domain Naming Master and Schema Master are forest-related roles. Trusts are required to share resources between domains that are not part of the same forest. The exception is shortcut trusts, which reduce the trust path between two domains within the same forest.

Master It   The placement of an FSMO role is dictated by the domain to which it is assigned and the Global Catalog role. Which two roles have rules concerning placement in regard to the global catalog?

Solution   The Domain Naming Master, which is located in the forest root domain, has to be placed on a domain controller with the Global Catalog role. The Infrastructure Master role, which is located in each domain, cannot be located on a domain controller with the Global Catalog role. However, in a single-domain Active Directory environment, this doesn't apply.

Chapter 25: Migrating, Merging, and Modifying Your Active Directory

Introduce new versions of Active Directory into a network.   Upgrading to a new version of Windows Server means you also need to upgrade existing domain controllers. There are two basic methods to add a new version of Active Directory into an organization: Upgrading a domain controller or upgrading the domain by adding a new domain controller.

Master It   Both operations require you to modify the Active Directory database using the adprep.exe utility. What three options do you need to run? What option can you also run?

Solution   /forestprep modifies the schema of the Active Directory forest to support Windows Server 2008 R2's Active Directory.

/domainprep prepares the domain for a Windows Server 2008 R2 domain controller.

/gpprep modifies permissions on Group Policy objects for replication to Windows Server 2008 R2 domain controllers.

/rodcprep prepares the forest for deploying the read-only domain controllers. This is optional and can be run at another point.

Migrate domains accounts from one domain to another.   The requirement to move users and groups from an existing domain to a clean and pristine domain often happens when companies merge or spin off. In addition, this can be required when a forest restructuring is justified. Microsoft offers the ADMT utility to perform domain migrations.

Master It   After a user account is migrated to the new domain, what gives the user access to resources within the original domain?

Solution   Resources in the original domain have permissions assigned, allowing access to listed security principles such as user accounts. The permissions, also named ACEs, list the user's SID. After a user account is migrated, its SID changes. However, the original SID is saved as SID history. When the user authenticates in the other domain, the SID history will identify with the permission on the resource.

SID filtering, which is enabled by default on domain trusts, will prevent this action from happening. You must manually disable this security feature.

Chapter 26: Advanced User Account Management and User Support

Deploy home directories to multiple users.   Home directories allow a user to have a personal store of information stored on a file server. This makes their data available to them no matter where they log in on the network.

Master It   You've been tasked with deploying home directories to many users in the OU that you manage. You want to do this as quickly as possible. Your backup application uses an administrator user account, so you need to ensure that it has access to the users' home directories on the file server. How will you set this up?

Solution

1. Create a file share on the file server to contain your home directories, and set the permissions appropriately.

2. Configure a Group Policy object for your OU. Enable "Add the Administrators security group to roaming users' profiles," which can be found in Computer Configuration\Administrative Templates\System\User Profiles.

3. Navigate to the OU in Active Directory Users and Computers. Select all of the user objects in the OU, right-click, and select Properties. Enter the path of the home directory file share, and add \%username to the end.

Your home directories will be created automatically and administrators on the file server will have access to them.

Set up mandatory roaming profiles.   Mandatory roaming profiles can be used to provide users with a preconfigured working environment and to prevent them from saving changes to it.

Master It   Your manager has asked you to set up a mandatory roaming profile for users of Windows 8. You're also asked to see whether there is a way to prevent users from logging in if the mandatory roaming profile cannot be loaded.

Solution   You need to configure a super mandatory roaming profile:

1. Log in as a sample user on a PC. Configure the working environment as required.

2. Log back into the PC as an administrator, and copy the sample user's profile onto the network. You need to ensure that the required Active Directory security group has Full Control over the registry hive in the profile using regedit.exe.

3. Rename NTUSER.DAT in the profile to **NTUSER.MAN.** This will cause the profile to become a mandatory profile.

4. Rename the profile to something like Mandatory.V2 knowing that the .V2 is required for Windows 8 users.

5. To make this roaming mandatory profile into a super mandatory profile, you can rename the profile folder to `Mandatory.MAN.V2.`

Create logon scripts to automate administration. Administrators can use logon scripts to run a series of commands to preconfigure the working environment for a user when they log in. Administrators can use scripting languages such as command-prompt command, VBScript, or PowerShell.

Master It You are designing an Active Directory for a large multisite organization. You need to be able to set up logon scripts for different scenarios:

♦ There are global commands that must be run for everyone.

♦ Anyone in the Accounts OU must have access to certain resources.

♦ Anyone, including visitors, logging in at the Dublin Active Directory site must connect to a local shared drive.

You are asked what the running order will be for any user who will run all of the logon scripts.

Solution Write the three logon scripts, and save them into the NETLOGON folder on your domain controller. Create three Group Policy objects. Link the first GPO to the domain, and edit it to run the logon script for everyone. Link the second GPO to the Accounts OU, and edit it to run the logon script for the Accounts OU. Link the third GPO to the Dublin Active Directory site, and edit it to run the Dublin logon script.

The running order for GPOs is site, domain, OU, child OU. The running order of the logon scripts for a user inheriting all of the policies will be as follows:

♦ Dublin

♦ Domain

♦ Accounts

Chapter 27: Server Virtualization with Hyper-V

Understand server virtualization. You are buying new servers whose main role will be to run Hyper-V. However, you are concerned that the new servers may not be capable of running Hyper-V because they do not meet the minimum requirements.

Master It What are the base CPU and BIOS requirements to run Hyper-V?

Solution You need an x64-based CPU and a BIOS that supports both CPU-assisted virtualization and Data Execution Prevention (DEP). A common problem is that although these features are offered by the system, they are not typically enabled in the BIOS of older server hardware. Make sure these features are turned on. If you need to change the DEP or virtualization settings, be aware that a cold boot is required: the computer must be turned completely off. A reset or software reboot is not sufficient.

Explore what's new in Hyper-V 2012 R2. Microsoft has released a large number of new features and enhancements with Hyper-V 2012 R2 that should give IT pros, administrators, and consultants a much easier job in convincing their customers and bosses to use Hyper-V inside the business.

Master It In earlier versions of Hyper-V, rich copy and paste into VMs could be achieved only by using a Remote Desktop connection and didn't work at all if there was no network connection present. What's the name of the new feature that enables copy and paste into a VM with no network connection by utilizing the VMBus?

Solution Enhanced session mode allows you to easily copy and paste directly to and from a VM, even without a network connection being configured. It's the same experience you get with a Remote Desktop connection to a machine but minus the need to worry about networking. Enhanced session mode leverages the VMBus via the Hyper-V integration components to deliver this experience.

Understand Hyper-V architecture. When you deploy the Hyper-V role to your computer, you're creating a *hypervisor* architecture. A hypervisor is a software layer between the hardware and the operating systems running on the host. This is known as the *bare-metal* approach: virtualization at the lowest possible level. The main purpose of the hypervisor is to create isolated execution environments (partitions) for all operating systems. In line with that function, it is responsible for arbitrating access to the hardware.

Master It During the Hyper-V role deployment, the host restarts a couple of times to accommodate the placement of Hyper-V on top of the hardware, which is located at which ring level? (Choose one.)

a. Ring 3

b. Ring 0

c. Ring -1

d. Ring 2

Solution c. Ring -1 is where Hyper-V is placed on top of the hardware.

Install and configure a Hyper-V host. Just about the only thing you need to decide before you install the Hyper-V role is which NIC to use for managing the Hyper-V host. The idea is to have at least two NICs in the host, although you can make do with one if you really must. Expect no performance miracles in that case. With two NICs available, dedicate one to managing the host and the second for VM network traffic.

Master It If you have two or more NIC's available for your Hyper-V environment, which option that's enabled by default should you uncheck on the virtual NIC?

Solution It's recommended to uncheck the "Allow management operating system to share this network adapter" option from your virtual NIC once the Hyper-V setup wizard has completed. Leaving this enabled means the host can access this switch, meaning that traffic between the VMs and their host operating system is shared, thus causing performance issues in heavily utilized environments. In a lab or non-production environment where you might have just one NIC available, leaving this option enabled should suffice, but if you have more than one NIC or are running a production Hyper-V environment, then it's recommended to disable this option by simply unchecking the box and clicking Apply.

Configure and install a virtual machine. Conceptually, it takes two steps to create a VM from scratch. First you configure the virtual hardware of the VM, then you boot the VM and start installing the operating system. Once these two steps have been completed, you can use either Hyper-V Manager or PowerShell to manage the VM.

Master It When using the GUI to manage your VM, the console can "capture" the keyboard and mouse. You do so by clicking the virtual screen. When they've been captured, all input from the keyboard and mouse are sent to the VM. Initially, you can't release control from the VM by just moving the mouse. What keyboard combination is configured by default to release control of the keyboard and mouse back to the host OS?

Solution You press the key sequence Ctrl+Alt+left arrow to release control. In a fully running VM with Integration Services installed, the experience is much better: you can move the mouse out of the virtual screen onto the desktop, and when that happens, the host takes control of the keyboard and mouse again. There is one special case: the Ctrl+Alt+Del sequence. Even when the VM has control, the host will process it. To send the Ctrl+Alt+Del sequence to a VM, you can either press Ctrl+Alt+End or use the console menu action (Ctrl+Alt+Del).

Chapter 28: Managing Virtual Machines

Virtualize domain controllers. Windows Server 2012 includes a new method of deploying any number of virtual DCs very quickly through *virtual domain controller cloning*. This gives administrators a supported solution to rapidly spin up replica domain controllers using an existing template DC for reference. Virtual DC cloning can be beneficial to organizations that want to quickly deploy multiple DCs into new domains as well as a helpful feature in private cloud environments to meet scalability requirements.

Master It What is the minimum supported version of Active Directory that you can use with virtual DC cloning?

Solution A virtual DC running Windows Server 2012 or higher that is a member of the same domain that a PDC emulator also running Windows Server 2012 or higher is required for virtual DC cloning.

Understand how to move your VMs around. Hyper-V in Windows Server 2012 gives you the option to *export* and *import* VMs between hosts with relative simplicity. This is made possible by the fact that all Hyper-V hosts offer almost identical hardware to their VMs through the integration components and synthetic drivers. If you wanted to move OS installations around in the physical server world, you would at the very least need to move the physical disks, which works only if the hardware is similar enough and isn't always a guaranteed success.

Master It   When moving a VM to another Hyper-V host, which three parameters need to be moved?

Solution   The three parameters of a VM that need to be moved to another host when performing a VM move are configuration, current state, and data.

Manage your VMs.   Although virtualization brings a lot of new features and flexibility to the table, there are still some of the more traditional maintenance tasks that you need to consider for your VMs, such as backing them up, managing malware protection, and keeping them up to date with the latest patches.

Master It   If you are running a Hyper-V failover cluster on Windows Server 2012 R2, what technology would you use to patch your production VMs?

Solution   If you have a Hyper-V failover cluster environment running Windows Server 2012 or higher, then you can leverage the *Cluster-Aware Updating* (CAU) feature, which will allow you to patch your servers with minimal downtime while the updates are being deployed.

CAU integrates with the built-in Windows Update Agent and Windows Server Update Services (WSUS) to download and install the updates. When you want to patch a Hyper-V cluster node running Windows Server 2012 R2, all you need to do is shut down the host and the new VM Drain feature will kick in, which will migrate all the VMs over to any other available hosts.

Understand disaster recovery with Hyper-V.   Hyper-V Replica (HVR) is a feature available in Windows Server 2012 and higher. It allows for host-based replication of VMs without the need for any shared cluster components to support disaster-recovery scenarios.

Master It   How many sites outside of your production site can you replicate your VMs to if you are running Hyper-V Replica on Windows Server 2012 R2?

Solution   Using Hyper-V Replica, you can take a VM running on a Hyper-V host in one site and easily replicate it over to another site, up to a maximum of two additional sites.

Chapter 29: Installing, Using, and Administering Remote Desktop Services

Limit the maximum number of connections.   You can change the licensing mode of a server to help ensure you remain compliant with the licensing agreement and allocations you have.

Master It   You want to know what licensing mode the server is in. How do you do it?

Solution

1. Launch Server Manager.

2. Click Remote Desktop Services.

3. Choose Tasks ➢ Edit Deployment.

4. Choose RD Licensing.

Add an application to an RD Session Host server. Once the RDS role is added and the RD Session Host server is configured, you can add applications to make them available to the server.

> **Master It** Your company has purchased an application that supports multiuser access. You want to install it on the RD Session Host server. What should you do?

> **Solution** Install the application using the .msi (Windows Installer) file or using the Control Panel Add/Remove Programs Wizard.

> If the application can be installed via one of these methods, it is not necessary to use the Change User command that was required in older versions of Terminal Services. If it can't be installed using the .msi file or Add/Remove Programs, you must use the Change User /install command before installation and the Change User /execute command after the installation.

Add a RemoteApp for Web Access. RemoteApp applications can be configured so that they are accessible to users via a web browser. Users simply need to access the correct page and select the application to launch it.

> **Master It** Assume you have already configured your environment to support RemoteApp applications. You now want to add a RemoteApp application. What should you do?

> **Solution**

> **1.** Open Server Manager.

> **2.** Click Remote Desktop Services.

> **3.** Choose Collections.

> **4.** Select your collection.

> **5.** Click Tasks on the RemoteApp window and select Publish RemoteApp.

> **6.** Select your app from the list or by navigating to the binary.

> **7.** Click Publish.

> **8.** Click Close.

Chapter 30: Monitoring Windows Server 2012 R2

Use Server Manager to monitor multiple servers. The new Server Manager console in Windows Server 2012 R2 delivers out-of-box monitoring and health checks of your local and remote server infrastructure. It can be utilized to monitor multiple servers and the roles they are responsible for—all from one central console.

Master It   You need to have a collated health state for the collective roles on multiple servers and want to manage them through Server Manager. What do you need to deploy? (Choose one.)

a.   Security groups

b.   Server groups

c.   Distribution groups

d.   Administrative groups

Solution   b. Server groups are used when you need to have a collated health state for the collective roles on multiple servers and want to manage them through Server Manager.

Understand how to use Event Viewer.   Event Viewer in Windows Server 2012 R2 is one of the essential tools used to monitor your system. Often, it's one of the first places you'll look once you realize your server has a problem, but it can also be used to proactively monitor servers. Event Viewer can often help you to quickly identify the source of a problem or at least gain enough knowledge to know where to look next.

Master It   You've just deployed the Hyper-V role to your Windows Server 2012 R2 computer. Where would you find the associated event log for this role?

Solution   The Applications and Services Logs folder includes logs for specific applications or components, and this is where you'd find the associated log for the Hyper-V role.

Explore Performance Monitor.   Data collector sets can be used to measure and monitor the performance of a server. Performance Monitor includes built-in data collector sets that can be run on demand, and you can also create your own data collector set.

Master It   Run the System Performance data collector set and view the resulting report.

Solution   Launch the Performance Monitor suite via Server Manager ➤ Tools ➤ Performance Monitor. Right-click the System Performance data collector set, and select Start. When it completes, right-click the data collector set, and select Latest Report.

Explore the PAL and PerfView tools.   Performance Analysis of Logs (PAL) and PerfView are two external tools that can help you simplify the collection and analysis of your performance data, as well as create comprehensive performance baselines for your applications that are running on Windows Server 2012 R2.

Master It   PAL can be very useful when used in conjunction with Performance Monitor counter logs. What file extension is used with these counter logs? (Choose one.)

a.   .chk

b.   .perf

c. `.blg`

d. `.evnt`

Solution   c. `.blg` file extensions are used with Performance Monitor counter logs.

Understand System Center 2012 R2 Operations Manager.   Operations Manager (also known as OpsMgr or SCOM) is an end-to-end monitoring solution that covers Microsoft and 19 different cross-platform environments. With it, you can centrally monitor servers, applications, hardware, and operations for many computers from a central console. You can use it to map out all of the components of your individual IT services and then roll them up into a holistic and easy-to-manage single monitoring view.

Master It   When you first deploy Operations Manager and decide to push an agent out to a server, it will only see that server as an entity that is either up or down. How do you get Operations Manager to see the different roles and applications on your servers?

Solution   Operations Manager understands what it has to monitor on each agent through specific management packs that have been developed and made available by either the application/product vendor or the general System Center community. These management packs throw light on the Operations Manager infrastructure and allow the agents to understand the roles and applications that need to be brought under monitoring control.

Chapter 31: Patch Management

Use Windows Automatic Updates to check for new updates on a computer running Windows 8.   Windows Automatic Updating is a Control Panel item used to check the Microsoft Update site to see whether any updates are available for your computer.

Master It   On a Windows 8 computer, use Windows Automatic Updating to see whether any new updates are available for your computer.

Solution   Follow these steps to see if updates are available:

1. Click Start, and then type **Control Panel.**

2. Click Windows Update.

3. Click "Check for updates."

If updates are available for your computer, you will be prompted to install them.

Use the Windows Update Standalone Installer to silently install a security update.   The Windows Update Standalone Installer is used to install security updates on all Windows operating systems since Windows Vista and Windows Server 2008.

Master It   Install a security update in quiet mode and defer a required reboot by using the Windows Update Standalone Installer.

Solution Run *executable* /quiet /norestart at an elevated command prompt where *executable* is the filename of the security update.

Identify the four phases of patch management. According to Microsoft, there are four phases in planning a patch-management strategy.

Master It Which of the following is not one of the four phases of patch management?

1. Identify

2. Troubleshoot

3. Evaluate and Plan

4. Assess

5. Deploy

Solution Troubleshoot is not one of the four phases of patch management. The four phases in order are as follows:

1. Identify

2. Evaluate and Plan

3. Assess

4. Deploy

Following a standardized, documented process helps bring order to the chaos of patch management.

Chapter 32: Windows Server 2012 R2 and Active Directory Backup and Maintenance

Use Windows Server Backup to back up and restore a Windows Server 2012 R2 computer. Windows Server Backup is installed as a feature in Windows Server 2012 R2 and can be used to create various types of backups to protect your server computer. Full server backups contain the operating system, critical volumes, and all data on the server; while critical volume backups protect all volumes the operating system depends on, but not necessarily the additional data stored on the server.

Master It Your server contains two hard disks; the first contains the operating system, and the second contains user data. How can you use Windows Server Backup to protect the operating system and the user data?

Solution Perform a full server backup, which will by default back up both volumes.

Defragment AD DS offline. Windows Server 2012 R2 gives you the ability to perform an offline defragmentation and integrity check of the AD DS database without having to restart the computer and enter DSRM. Instead, you can stop AD DS and then use `Ntdsutil.exe` from an elevated command prompt to perform the offline defragmentation and integrity check.

Master It   You want to defragment your AD DS database but do not want to shut down the server and restart it in DSRM. How do you do that?

Solution   Stop AD DS, and then use `Ntdsutil.exe` from an elevated command prompt to defragment the `Ntds.dit` database.

Install the Active Directory Recycle Bin.   A downside for some people with the Windows Server 2008 R2 version of the Recycle Bin was that it had to be managed fully through Power-Shell. In Windows Server 2012 R2, you now have GUI management of the Recycle Bin.

Master It   You want to install the Active Directory Recycle Bin without using PowerShell. How do you achieve this?

Solution   From the Active Directory Administrative Center, click your (local) domain from the navigation pane on the left, and then in the Tasks pane on the right, click Enable Recycle Bin.

Create and recover a system state backup for Active Directory.   Because domain controllers contain all the database information for Active Directory, recovering a failed domain controller server is critically important. When using Windows Server Backup or the command-line utility `Wbadmin.exe`, perform backups containing the system state at a minimum to preserve Active Directory.

Master It   You want to protect your Active Directory data from the possibility of complete hardware failure of the server computer. Which types of backup will provide this protection?

Solution   Use a system state backup at a minimum. Critical volume and full server backups also include all the information necessary to recover Active Directory.

Index

Numbers

32-bit applications, WOW32 system and, 22
4K sector, on hard disks, 591
64-bit support, 20, 22
6to4 tunneling, 149
802.1Q protocol, 1392–1393
802.IX authentication, 165

A

A (host) records, 230, 242, 1035
access control
    dynamic. *See* DAC (Dynamic Access Control)
    role-based, 199–203
access control lists. *See* ACLs (access control lists)
access-based enumeration, creating shares and, 659
access-denied assistance
    classification properties, 806
    in DAC (Dynamic Access Control), 796–799
    in FSRM (File Server Resource Manager), 688
account lockout policies
    managing, 435–436
    setting, 504
account partner component, of AD FS, 534
accounting, configuring for VPNs, 1100–1102
accounts
    computer accounts. *See* computer accounts
    creating and managing, 285
    creating with ADAC, 292–293
    groups. *See* groups
    prestaging RODC account, 1179–1181
    user accounts. *See* user accounts
ACK message, TCP and, 1044
ACLs (access control lists)
    filtering policies with, 482–486
    re-ACLing the server following migration, 345–346, 349, 1260
    share/NTFS permissions using, 668
ACT (Application Compatibility Toolkit), 84
Actions pane, Hyper-V console
    options in, 1388
    overview of, 1364–1366
activation
    of KMS server, 143–144
    of Windows Server 2012 R2, 42, 45–46
Active Directory
    adding DC to forest, 279
    adding server to Server Manager, 663
    administering trusts, 1229
    administrative center. *See* ADAC (Active Directory Administrative Center)
    analyzing semantic database, 1572–1573
    attributes, 765–766, 1158

benefits of single domain, 261–262
building forests, 1190
certificate services. *See* AD CS (Active Directory Certificate Services)
changes in Windows Server 2012, 3–4, 76
changes to Power Shell, 6–7
changes to RMS (Rights Management Services), 7–8, 79
checking database integrity, 1571–1573
clean and pristine migration. *See* C&P (clean and pristine) migration
configuring server for single-domain forest, 263–264
connecting to printers, 974
connectivity and replication issues in planning, 1192–1193
creating accounts, 292–293
creating accounts with PowerShell, 293–294
creating and naming trees, 1188–1189
creating groups, 294–295
creating groups with PowerShell, 296
creating OUs, 286–288
creating OUs with PowerShell, 288–289
creating second domain, 1200–1204
creating single-domain forest, 262
creating snapshots, 1573–1574
creating trusts manually, 1230–1232
creating trusts with netdom, 1239–1240
creating trusts with New Trust Wizard, 1232–1236
decommissioning DCs, 299–300
defining domain trust, 1226–1227
defragmenting offline, 1570–1571
delegating control using OUs, 297
delegation, 297, 518
deploying printers, 849–851
deployment configuration for forests, 264–265, 281
design pointers, 1196–1198
DFS-R (Distributed File System Replication) and, 317–318
DirectAccess requirements, 1112
directionality in trust relationships, 1227–1228
DNS integration with, 239, 266
domain functional levels, 266–269, 1205–1207
domain migration. *See* C&P (clean and pristine) migration
Domain Naming Master role, 1217
domain services. *See* AD DS (Active Directory Domain Services)
domain-based DFS and, 737–738
domains and trusts. *See* AD DT (Active Directory Domains and Trusts)
DSRM (Directory Services Restore Mode) and, 273–274
empty root design, 1194–1195

federation services. *See* AD FS (Active Directory Federation Services)
fine-grained password policies, 310–313
forest functional levels, 269–270, 1207–1209
FRS (file replication service) and, 313–317
FSMO role, 1210–1211
GCs in, 1211–1212
grafting and pruning forests not supported, 1190–1191
Group Policy. *See* Group Policy
groups. *See* groups
HVR (Hyper-V Replica) and, 1423
Hyper-V checkpoints and, 1395–1396
Infrastructure Operations Master role, 1218
installing DNS and GC for DCs and forests, 265, 281–282
IPAM requirements, 177
joining domains and, 298–299
location of files and SYSVOL shared folder, 270–272
maintaining domains, 297–298
managing domain time, 306–308
managing FSMO roles, 308–309
managing with GPOs, 285
migrating. *See* migration, of Active Directory
mounting and working with snapshots, 1574–1575
multimaster vs. single-master replication, 1209–1210
multiple-domain design, 1198
multiple-domain designs, 1185
namespace for multiple-domain design, 1198–1199
naming root domain, 265–266
netdom domain manager, 304–306
overview of, 257–260
path to forest function level following migration, 367–368
PDC Emulator role, 1219
in-place upgrade, 335–339
planning, 1191–1192
PowerShell and, 289–292
PowerShell History Viewer, 297
preparing DC for second domain, 1199–1300
publishing shares, 664–666
raising domain functional levels, 302–304, 321–322
raising forest functional levels, 302–304
recycle bin improvements, 4–5, 1577–1579
ReFS file system and, 265
Replication Status tool, 337
RIDs (relative IDs) and, 1217–1218
Schema Master role, 1213–1217
searching for shares, 674
security and trusts, 1228–1229

sites. *See* sites, AD
swing migration. *See* swing migration
SYSVOL and, 313
time sync and, 1223–1226
transferring FSMO roles, 1219–1223
transitive forest trusts, 1230
transitive trusts, 1228
troubleshooting DNS, 301–302
troubleshooting Mac OS X issues, 976–977
upgrade strategies, 80
upgrading domain to Windows Server
   2012, 334–335
upgrading schema to Windows Server
   2012, 331–334
when to use multiple domains, 1193–1194
in Windows Azure. *See* WAAD
   (Windows Azure Active Directory)
Workplace Join and, 374–375
Active Directory backups
   AD recycle bin and, 1577–1579
   authoritative restore, 1582–1583
   creating, 1579–1580
   limitations of, 1577
   overview of, 1576–1577
   recycle bin and, 1577–1579
   restore operations, 1580–1581
Active Directory Certificate Services. *See* AD
   CS (Active Directory Certificate Services)
Active Directory Diagnostics, 1511
Active Directory Domain Services. *See* AD DS
   (Active Directory Domain Services)
Active Directory Domain Services
   Configuration Wizard
   adding installation media, 1178
   building domains and forests, 1191
   creating first domain, 1187
   creating second domain, 1200–1204
Active Directory Domain Services Installation
   Wizard
   adding AD DS role, 239
   prestaging RODC account, 1179–1181
   promoting Windows Server 2012 R2 to
      RODC, 1170
Active Directory Domains and Trusts. *See* AD
   DT (Active Directory Domains and Trusts)
Active Directory Federation Services. *See* AD
   FS (Active Directory Federation Services)
Active Directory Integrated (ADI) zones, DNS,
   224–226, 299, 1183
Active Directory Lightweight Directory
   Services (AD LDS), 1574–1575
Active Directory Lookup, NFS services, 751
Active Directory migration. *See* swing migration
Active Directory Migration Tool. *See* ADMT
   (Active Directory Migration Tool)
Active Directory Restore Mode (ADRM), 1570
Active Directory Schema snap-in
   examining schema with, 1213–1215
   managing Schema Master role, 1219
Active Directory Sites and Services snap-in
   configuring intersite replication, 1141–1144
   creating site links, 1138–1139
   enabling a global catalog, 1212
   renaming sites, 1130
   working with sites, 1128

Active Directory Users and Computers.
   See ADUC (Active Directory Users and
   Computers)
Active Directory Web Services (ADWS), 448
Active screening, file screens, 684
AD CS (Active Directory Certificate Services)
   adding certificates to certificate store, 1095
   changes in Windows Server 2012, 8, 78–79
   configuring for VPN server, 1093
   creating server authentication certificate,
      1093–1095
   installing certificate on client, 1096–1097
   installing on VPN server, 1092
   RSAT tools, 923
   setting up WinRS for HTTP, 122–124
AD DS (Active Directory Domain Services)
   adding roles and features, 117
   changes in Windows Server 2012, 4, 76–78
   copying database with dsamain.exe,
      1575–1576
   creating domain controller, 132
   creating second domain, 1202
   creating snapshots of database, 1573–1574
   defined, 258
   defragmenting Active Directory offline,
      1570–1571
   federation between AD DS systems, 533
   installing role for, 280
   mounting and working with snapshots,
      1574–1575
   preparing for in-place upgrade,
      1246–1247
   promoting member server during swing
      migration, 1251–1254
   prompting for location of files and
      SYSVOL folder, 270
   restartable, 273
   RSAT tools, 923
   running configuration wizard for first
      DC, 275–278
   running configuration wizard for forest
      with second DC, 282–284
   selecting domain functional level,
      267–268
   stopping and restarting, 1570
   upgrading schema to Windows Server
      2012, 332–334
AD DT (Active Directory Domains and Trusts)
   creating trusts, 1226
   establishing trust between domains prior
      to migration, 349–351
   managing Domain Naming Master role,
      1219
   New Trust Wizard, 1232–1236, 1263
   raising forest functional levels, 302,
      1207–1209
   transferring FSMO roles between DCs,
      1256
   verifying/upgrading forest functional
      level, 1164
AD FS (Active Directory Federation Services)
   adding proxy server role, 557–558
   adding servers to server farm, 556–557
   adding token-signing or token-
      decrypting certificates, 551–552

adding trusted relying party, 549–551
administering from command line, 547–548
automating client configuration, 559–560
certificates, 536–537
configuring, 551
configuring on server, 544–547
configuring performance monitoring,
   552–555
creating SSL certificates with IIS, 543–544
installing roles and features, 539–543
logon flavors and, 372
overview of, 533
planning deployment of, 537–539
SSO (single sign-on) and, 368
terminology, 534–535
AD LDS (Active Directory Lightweight
   Directory Services), 1574–1575
ADAC (Active Directory Administrative
   Center)
   adding locations to tree view, 441–442
   configuring DAC (Dynamic Access
      Control), 767–768
   configuring group properties, 447–448
   configuring user properties, 444–445
   creating accounts, 285, 292–293, 443–444
   creating groups, 285, 295, 445–447
   creating home directory for each user,
      1277
   creating OUs, 285–288
   creating PSOs, 310
   navigating tree view, 440–441
   overview of, 285–286, 437–440
   PowerShell History Viewer and, 448–451
   raising domain functional levels, 303, 322
   raising forest functional levels, 303–304
   tips for working with, 448
   viewing PSO rules, 311–312
Add Printer Wizard, 962
Add Roles and Features Wizard. *See also* roles
   and features
   adding AD DS role, 280, 283
   adding DNS role, 216–217
   adding File and Storage Services role,
      653–656
   adding Hyper-V role, 1361
   adding NAT role, 1047–1050
   adding RD Virtualization Host role, 1465
   adding RDS role, 1449–1450, 1454–1458
   adding Remote Desktop Services role,
      897–903
   adding services to Web Server role, 987
   adding SMTP Server Tools feature, 1010
   adding Web Server role, 984–985
   adding WSUS role, 1537–1539
   changes in Windows Server 2012, 12
   configuring servers, 56–57
   enabling Remote Server Administration
      Tools, 120
   installing IPAM client features, 182
   installing IPAM server features, 180–181
   overview of, 45
   promoting member server during swing
      migration, 1251–1254
Add-Printer cmdlet, setting up print server, 142
address hashes, NIC Teaming options, 153

Address Resolution Protocol (ARP), 1028–1029
Address Space Management. *See* ASM (Address Space Management)
ADI (Active Directory Integrated) zones, 299, 1183
ADK (Assessment and Deployment Kit)
    installing, 82–85
    replaces WAIK (Windows Automated Installation Kit), 81
    selecting features, 85–87
ADM templates. *See* administrative templates
Admin logs, 1493
ADMIN$ share, connecting to, 675
administration
    changes in Windows Server 2012, 5–6
    delegating administration of Group Policy, 518–521
    of IIS 8.0, 1016–1017
    separation of roles and, 383–384
    of trusts in multiple-domain design, 1229
Administration Tools Pack, RSAT compatibility issues and, 923
administrative events, custom views by, 1487–1488
Administrative Role Separation (ARS), in RODCs, 1154–1155
administrative shares
    ADMIN$ share as, 675
    defined, 675
administrative templates
    controlling behavior of Group Policy, 480
    overview of, 499–500
    preventing editing of registry, 501
    preventing installation or use of unauthorized software, 501–502
    restricting Internet Explorer, 500–501
Administrator account
    connecting to administrative shares, 675
    overview of, 378–379
Administrator and Non-administrator LGPOs, 471–473
administrators
    changing password of, 110–111
    enabling remote administration, 55–56
    FSMOs and, 1210–1211
    granting access to roaming profile folders, 1290
    logging in as, 31
    resetting passwords, 505–508
    setting password of, 30
    uses of RDS, 1435–1436
    viewing or changing delegation, 530–531
Administrators group
    Allow and Deny permissions, 715
    assigning Full Control permissions, 138–139
    creating for RODC, 1169
    preparing for migration between domains, 1264
    share permissions, 710
ADML files. *See also* administrative templates, 499
ADMT (Active Directory Migration Tool)
    auditing and, 351–352, 1264–1265
    Domain Admins group and, 351, 1264

downloading and installing, 353–354
enabling cryptographic settings on target domain, 352
establishing trust between domains, 349–351, 1263–1264
installing, 1265
interface options, 356–357
merging domains, 1196
migrating computer accounts, 354–355, 366–367
migrating users and groups, 354–355, 357–362
overview of, 347–349, 1262
preparing for use of, 352
preparing workstation for, 354
rollback of C&P migration, 367
testing resource access for migrated groups, 363–364
translating profiles, 364–366
version compatibility issues, 1262–1263
working with ADMT command-line utility, 363
ADMT.exe, 363
ADMX files. *See also* administrative templates, 499
adprep
    preparing environment for RODC, 1165–1167
    preparing for in-place upgrade, 338, 1246–1248
    promoting Windows Server 2012 R2 to RODC, 1168
    upgrade strategies and, 80
    upgrading schema to Windows Server 2012, 331–332
ADRM (Active Directory Restore Mode), 1570
ADUC (Active Directory Users and Computers)
    Administrative Center and, 437
    Advanced Features view, 396
    built-in users and groups, 384
    changing domain functional level, 1205–1206
    creating accounts, 285, 292
    creating Administrators group, 1169
    creating groups, 285, 295, 426
    creating home directory for each user, 1277
    creating OUs, 285
    decommissioning DCs, 300
    managing FSMO roles, 1219
    managing user accounts, 922–923
    manually setting permissions, 526–529
    prestaging RODC account, 1179–1181
    raising forest functional levels, 302
    synchronizing domain time, 306–308
    verifying/upgrading domain functional level, 1163
    viewing network access permissions, 1082
    viewing RODC properties, 1174–1176
Advanced Encryption Standard (AES)
    AES-CMAC (Advanced Encryption Standard-CMAC), 691
    logon settings, 400

advanced searches, printer deployment and, 852
Advanced share profile options, 658
Advanced tab, RDC (Remote Desktop Connection), 894–895
ADWS (Active Directory Web Services), 448
AES (Advanced Encryption Standard)
    AES-CMAC (Advanced Encryption Standard-CMAC), 691
    logon settings, 400
ALGs (Application Layer Gateways), 1047
alias (CNAME) records, DNS, 230
all zone transfers (AXFR), 223
Allow permissions
    assigning, 667–668
    comparing shares and NTFS, 667
    Deny taking precedence, 668–669
    folder sharing and, 715
allowed list, password replication policy and, 1158–1159
Allowed RODC Password Replication group
    attributes supporting password replication policy, 1158–1159
    modifying, 1176–1177
    overview of, 1160–1161
    viewing RODC properties, 1174–1175
Always Offline Mode, Offline Files, 698
analytic logs, Applications and Services Logs folder, 1493
anonymous accounts, 1005–1006
answer file
    adding components to, 92–97
    applying, 100–101
    creating, 91–92
    saving, 97–98
    viewing in Notepad, 98–100
App Controller, in System Center 2012 R2, 1524
app killer, NAPT as, 1046–1047
AppCmd.exe, 994
AppData folder, in user profile, 1281
Apple Macintosh. *See* Mac OS X clients
Application Compatibility Toolkit (ACT), 84
Application Layer Gateways (ALGs), 1047
application logs
    checking for error in, 1288
    types of Windows logs, 1492
application partitions, creating in Active Directory, 240
application pools, websites and, 1005
applicationhost.config, global settings of web sites and, 992–993
applications
    32-bit, 22
    ACT (Application Compatibility Toolkit), 84–85
    adding RemoteApp applications, 1460–1462
    adding to RDS, 1458
    centralizing deployment of, 1436
    connecting to network resources, 955–956
    controlling user access to, 487
    deploying, 1269
    deploying RemoteApp applications, 1439
    initialization in IIS 8.0, 980

launching RemoteApp application, 1462–1464

managing Windows built-in applications, 1325–1326

Reliability Monitor and, 1510

RemoteApp applications on RD Session Host, 1435

server applications compatible with RODCs, 1167

website, 991

Applications and Services Logs folder, 1493

apps, app CPU throttling, 980

ARP (Address Resolution Protocol), 1028–1029

ARS (Administrative Role Separation), in RODCs, 1154–1155

ASM (Address Space Management)

  IPAM components, 179

  managing IP address space, 191–193

  managing virtual IP address space, 193–196

Assessment and Deployment Kit. *See* ADK (Assessment and Deployment Kit)

atomic permissions

  list of, 716–717

  overview of, 717–719

Attribute editor, for domain user accounts, 404

attribute store, component of AD FS, 534

attributes

  access control using, 765–766

  attribute or property editor for domain accounts, 404

  editing multiple AD objects, 408–410

  securing data by, 766–767

  supporting password replication policy, 1158–1159

Audit Policy, 1264

auditing

  migration between domains and, 351–352, 1264–1265

  printer access, 867–870

authentication

  adding trusted relying party to AD FS, 549

  benefits of replication with FRS, 315

  configuring host session properties, 904–905

  configuring NFS authentication, 753

  of DCs (domain controllers), 265

  DHCP failover and, 207

  of FTP sites, 1016

  Kerberos service for, 241, 1189–1190

  managing multiple websites, 1006

  NLA (Network Level Authentication), 1453

  of RODC logon, 1156

  of servers, 894–895, 1093–1095

  setting up NFS shares and, 633–634

  of SMTP services, 1011

  two-factor, 400

  of VPN clients, 1097–1100

  VPN connections and, 1079

  of websites, 1020

authoritative restore

  overview of, 1580–1581

  performing, 1582–1583

authorization

  classification properties, 806

  of FTP sites, 1016

  user accounts and, 769

Automatic Classification, in FSRM (File Server Resource Manager), 688

automatic file classification, in DAC (Dynamic Access Control), 769

Automatic Updates

  enabling, 116

  setting up during upgrade install, 43

Automatic Virtual Machine Activation (AVMA), 1351

autonomous (distributed) mode, WSUS configuration, 1535

availability setting, printers, 871–872

AVMA (Automatic Virtual Machine Activation), 1351

AXFR (all zone transfers), 223

B

background zone loading, DNS, 244

backup domain controller (BDC), 221

Backup Operators, connecting to administrative shares, 675

backups (and restore)

  of Active Directory. *See* Active Directory backups

  to Cloud, 1569

  creating policy for, 144–145

  flexibility of desktop and, 1268

  of GPOs (Group Policy Objects), 511–513

  Hyper-V backup service, 1359

  of IIS data, 1023–1024

  overview of, 1555

  of VMs (virtual machines), 1418–1421

  with VSS (Volume Copy Service), 1270

  Windows Server Backup. *See* Windows Server Backup

  of WSUS database, 1550

bandwidth

  capacity planning for HVR, 1424

  deciding on DCs in remote locations and, 1131

  editing DFS bandwidth, 747–748

  optimizing event subscriptions, 1500

  QoS Minimum Bandwidth feature, 161

BAP (Bandwidth Allocation Protocol)

  VPN clients and, 1084–1085

  VPN servers and, 1107

bare-metal approach, to deploying Hyper-V, 1352–1353

baseline, user-defined data collector sets and, 1514–1516

batches, optimizing event subscriptions, 1500

BDC (backup domain controller), 221

Best Practices Analyzers

  launching for specific roles, 1483–1484

  monitoring with server groups, 1482

  scanning server, 72–74

BIOS

  boot configuration and, 24

  hardware requirements for Hyper-V, 1343

UEFI (Unified Extensible Firmware Interface) BIOS, 592, 1382

BitLocker encryption

  BitLocker To Go, 697

  enabling, 695–697

  encrypting drives, 1154

  hardware requirements for, 693–694

  implementing, 692–697

  installing for role services, 655–656

  recovery key, 694–695

  RSAT tools, 924

  what's new, 692–693

blobs, joining domains while offline with djoin.exe, 946–947

Bluetooth, adding wireless devices to Windows clients, 963–964

boot menu, POST (Power-On Self Test) and, 24

boot process

  GPT (GUID Partition Table) and, 592

  in Hyper-V, 1355

branch offices, WSUS configuration modes, 1536

BranchCache

  advanced sharing with, 706

  changes in Windows Server 2012, 14–15, 166–167

  creating shares, 659

  File and Storage Services role and, 653

  installing for role services, 655–656

  managing storage, 565

  modes, 166

  overview of, 165

  PowerShell networking modules, 151

  SMB Directory Leasing using, 689

  WAN optimization, 165–167

bridgehead servers

  defined, 1127

  ISTG designating, 1144–1145

bring-your-own-device (BYOD), Workplace Join and, 374–375

broadcast addresses, 1035–1036

BYOD (bring-your-own-device), Workplace Join and, 374–375

C

C$ share, connecting to, 675–676

C&P (clean and pristine) migration. *See also* ADMT (Active Directory Migration Tool)

  for company consolidations, 1259–1260

  defined, 1244

  gradual nature of, 344, 1258

  handling permissions in new domain, 345, 1259

  overview of, 335, 343, 1258

  pros/cons of, 347, 1261–1262

  re-ACLing the server, 345–346, 1260

  rollback of, 367

  SID histories and, 346–347, 1260–1261

cached credentials

  AD sites and, 1132–1133

  attributes supporting password replication policy, 1158

  RODC logon and, 1156

caching
  creating shares, 659
  enabling Offline Files on server, 699–701
  how Offline Files work, 698
  remotely with BranchCache, 699
caching-only DNS servers, 220
CALs (client access licenses)
  RD licensing manager and, 1475–1477
  RDS licensing modes, 1453–1454
  upgrade install and, 33
CAP (Client Access Point), HVR (Hyper-V Replica), 1424
capacity planning, HVR (Hyper-V Replica), 1424–1425
CAs (certificate authorities), 122–124
catalog file, creating, 90
CAU (Cluster-Aware Updating), 567–568, 1422, 1551–1552
CD drives, as removable storage, 101
CEIP (Customer Experience Improvement Program), Microsoft, 83
Central Access Policies
  Central Access Rule for, 781–784
  claim type in, 775–777
  creating, 784–785, 803
  defined, 768
  deploying, 786–793, 803
  enforcing Full Control permission with, 823
  overview of, 774–775
  removing, 822–823
  resource property for, 777–781
  testing, 793–796, 803
Central Access Rules
  creating, 781–785, 802
  defined, 768
  overview of, 771
certificate authorities (CAs), 122–124
Certificate Services. See CS (Certificate Services)
certificate Services. See AD CS (Active Directory Certificate Services)
certificate store, centralization in IIS 8.0, 980
certificate templates, 904
certificates
  AD FS (Active Directory Federation Services) and, 536–537
  adding to certificate store, 1095
  adding token-signing or token-decrypting, 551–552
  automating AD FS client configuration, 559–560
  creating server authentication certificate, 1093–1095
  creating SSL certificate with IIS, 543–544
  domain user account settings, 404–405
  getting, 122–124
  HVR (Hyper-V Replica) and, 1423
  installing on VPN client, 1096–1097
  installing/configuring AD CS, 1092–1093
  setting up WinRS for HTTP, 122–124
  VPNs (virtual private networks) and, 1092
Certified for Windows Server 2012, hardware requirements for Hyper-V, 1343

Challenge Handshake Authentication Protocol (CHAP), 1099
change permissions
  NTFS permissions, 667
  share permissions, 713
  types of advanced permissions, 866
Change User command, adding legacy applications, 1458
CHAP (Challenge Handshake Authentication Protocol), 1099
chat tunneling, with portproxy, 1056–1057
checkpoints, Hyper-V
  creating with PowerShell, 1394
  online checkpoint merging, 1350
  for point-in-time copy of VM, 1393–1396
  working with Hyper-V console, 1364
CHKDSK
  new options in, 593–594
  online self-healing, 592
chunk stores, data deduplication and, 637
CIDR (Classless Inter-Domain Routing)
  defining and placing subnets in AD sites, 1135
  overview of, 1039
CIFS (Common Internet File System), 688
Citrix XenServer, testing Windows Server 2012 R2, 34
claims
  as components of AD FS, 534
  creating, 800–801
  DAC policy and, 775–777
  overview of, 770
  types of, 768
classes, IP address
  overview of, 1034–1035
  unusable host addresses, 1035
classification of data
  automatic file classification, 769
  checking, 816–818
  configuring automatic file classification, 814–815
  detecting string pattern with regular expression, 813–814
  documents and, 804–806
  n rules, 807–812
  overview of, 804
  properties, 806
  securing data using DAC and file classification, 819–824
Classless Inter-Domain Routing (CIDR)
  defining and placing subnets in AD sites, 1135
  overview of, 1039
clean and pristine migration. See C&P (clean and pristine) migration
clean install
  choosing installation type (clean or upgrade), 27
  choosing language, time, currency, and keyboard settings, 24–25
  creating a laboratory or test network, 102
  EULA (end user license agreement), 26–27, 38
  installation media (DVD or ISO image), 24

  installation types, 26
  logging in as administrator, 31
  overview of, 23
  setting administrator password, 30
  setting up drives, 27–29
CLI (command-line interface)
  adding Mac OS X client to domain, 972–973
  adding network printers, 962
  administering IIS 8.0, 1017
  ADMT interface options, 356
  creating Active Directory groups, 432–433
  creating local user accounts, 382
  managing domain user accounts, 410–412
  migration from, 363
  recovering system state of server, 1565
Client Access Point (CAP), HVR (Hyper-V Replica), 1424
Client for Microsoft Networks, 933
Client for NFS, 752
clients
  activating and pointing clients to KMS, 143–144
  adding printers to manually, 848
  automating client configuration using Group Policy, 559–560
  CALs (client access licenses), 33, 1453–1454
  configuring access to closest AD site, 1146–1147
  configuring for Work Folders, 1322–1323
  configuring for WSUS, 1547–1550
  configuring WINS and NetBIOS clients, 236
  connecting to NFS shares from client side, 635
  DHCP client, 238
  DirectAccess requirements, 1112
  DNS clients. See DNS clients
  Group Policy for accessing closest AD site, 1147–1148
  Hyper-V in client OSs, 1345
  installing IPAM client feature, 182
  Mac OS X clients. See Mac OS X clients
  managing DNS clients, 232
  PC clients. See PC clients, RDS and
  RDP support, 1444
  RDS clients. See RDS clients
  registry for accessing closest AD site, 1148–1150
  thin-clients. See thin-clients
  VPN. See VPN clients
  VSC (virtualization service client), 1355–1356, 1358–1359
  Windows 7. See Windows 7
  Windows 8. See Windows 8
  WSUS clients and operating systems, 1532
clients, connecting to network
  adding network printer for Mac OS X client, 974
  adding network printer for Windows clients, 961–964

changing domain user passwords,
951–953
changing passwords at first logon,
953–954
changing passwords on demand, 954
checking local area connections in
Windows 7, 939–941
checking local area connections in
Windows 8, 935–937
connecting Mac OS X clients to network,
969–971
connecting to file shares, 973
connecting to network resources, 955–956
creating network folder, 966–968
domain and local accounts, 931–932
joining domains from Windows OSs,
942–945
joining domains while offline with
djoin.exe, 946–950
joining domains while with PowerShell,
950
joining domains with Mac OS X client,
971–973
manually configuring local area
connections in Windows 7, 941–942
manually configuring local area
connections in Windows 8, 937–938
mapping drive to shared folder, 964–966
overview of, 929–930
publishing network file shares, 957–961
publishing resources with GPOs, 956–957
testing connectivity with ping command,
935
troubleshooting, 976–977
understanding client software
requirements, 930–931
using Remote Desktop from Mac OS X
client, 974–976
verifying local area connection settings,
933–935
verifying network configuration, 932–933
clients, DirectAccess
configuring, 1118–1119
managing, 1120
support for, 1111–1112
client-side caching
enabling, 700–701
Remote Desktop Protocol and, 1443
using BranchCache, 699
Cloneable Domain Controllers security group,
1403–1404
cloning, for rapid deployment, 77
cloud
backing up to, 1569
as storage service, 595
cluster bootstrapping, 1402
Cluster Shared Volumes (CSVs), 568–569, 1556
Cluster-Aware Updating (CAU), 567–568,
1422, 1551–1552
clustering
adding first node to cluster, 575–585
adding second node to cluster, 585–587
BitLocker encryption for clustered
shared volumes, 693

configuring, 574–575
CSVs (Cluster Shared Volumes), 568–569
functionality of, 567–568
HA (high availability) and, 571
with NFS, 652
overview of, 566
quorums, 570–571
requirements, 566–567
setting up guest-based cluster, 587–588
SMB scale out for, 688
SMB transport failover for, 688
storage options of, 575
virtualization and, 569–570
in VMs, 573
vs.split scope in DHCP failover, 205
CMC (Computer Management Console)
creating local user accounts, 378–381
creating shares remotely, 707–710
defining share permissions, 712–714
CNAME (alias) records, DNS, 230
code access security, 1021–1022
cold spots, disk assignment categories, 590
collector computer
collector-initiated subscriptions,
1496–1497
creating collector-initiated subscription,
1502–1504
event log subscription and, 1495–1496
COM+ settings, domain user accounts and,
403–404
command-line interface. See CLI (command-
line interface)
commands/cmdlets, PowerShell
activating and pointing clients to KMS,
143–144
adding computers to domain, 950
adding first node to cluster, 575
adding members to groups, 460–461
adding services to Web Server role,
987–988
adding share to DFS root, 1276
adding/configuring data deduplication,
637
administering AD FS, 547–548
administering DNS server, 249–250
administering IIS 8.0, 1017
administering printers, 847
administering remote servers, 925–926
backing up/restoring IIS data, 1023–1024
bringing offline disks online, 618–619
changing administrator password, 110–111
changing default settings of command
prompt, 108
checking for corrupt volumes, 646
cloning virtual DCs, 1404–1405
closing command prompt, 110
command reference, 112
configuring data deduplication,
641–645
configuring DHCP service, 133–135
configuring Server Core, 113–116
creating checkpoints, 1394
creating domain controller and
managing DNS, 132–133

creating folders and assigning
permissions, 137–139
creating groups, 296, 459–460
creating multiple user accounts
simultaneously, 455–457
creating NIC team, 159
creating OUs, 288–289
creating PowerShell scripts, 290–292
creating primary partition, 136–137
creating shared folders, 710–711
creating SMB files shares, 710
creating storage pools, 604–605
creating user accounts, 452–453
creating users and AD objects, 293–294
creating virtual disks, 612–614
creating virtual switches, 1376
creating VMs, 1390
creating websites, 1000–1001
DCB (Data Center Bridge) and, 162–163
decommissioning DCs, 299
enabling firewalls, 143
enabling iSCSI target service, 623–624
enabling recycle bin, 1578–1579
enabling user accounts, 459
enabling write-back cache, 622
getting certificates, 124
getting Windows features, 846
installing DCs, 277–278
installing IIS 8, 985
installing IPAM server, 181
installing NFS server role, 754
installing Remote Access role, 1072
installing roles, 64–66
installing roles of multiple servers, 66–69
installing Windows Server Backup,
1419–1421
issuing with WinRS, 922
joining computers to domain, 306
listing available partitions, 226
making profile share available in DFS
namespace, 1286
managing deployment, 78–79
managing modules, 989
managing RDS, 1475
managing updates, 1551–1552
managing website permissions, 1021
managing Windows Backup Server,
144–145
new in NFS, 652
overview of, 64
performing backup with, 1561–1562
provisioning storage, 186, 597–598
quick setup of NFS shares, 632–635
raising forest functional levels, 302, 304
rebooting and shutting down server, 112
recovering system state of server, 1565
removing groups, 464
removing members from groups,
462–463
removing roles, 69–70
for replication, 1145
retrieving AD information, 1150–1151
reverting domain functional levels, 1262
setting passwords, 453–455

setting up File Server role, 135
setting up print server, 142
for Shared Nothing Live Migration (cluster-free), 1416–1417
sharing folders, 139
for testing, 301
unlocking user accounts, 457–459
updating help files, 452
viewing available roles and features, 118
Windows Backup Server and, 1556
working with networking modules, 150–151
comma-separated values (CSV) file, in creating user account, 455–457
Common Internet File System (CIFS), 688
compaction, of virtual disks, 1371–1372
company consolidation, domain migration for, 1259–1260
compatibility
    ACT (Application Compatibility Toolkit), 84–85
    RSAT (Remote Server Administration Tools), 923–924
    SMB 3.0 and, 689–690
    upgrade install and, 38–40
compression
    benefits of replication with FRS, 315
    compression algorithm in DFS-R, 317
    live migration feature in Hyper-V and, 1348–1349
    site replication and, 1126–1127
computer accounts
    creating domain accounts, 1237–1239
    migrating between domains, 366–367
Computer Configuration
    controlling behavior of Group Policy, 480
    Group Policy and, 487–488
    specifying logon/logoff scripts with Group Policy, 488–490
Computer Management Console (CMC)
    creating local user accounts, 378–381
    creating shares remotely, 707–710
    defining share permissions, 712–714
computers
    configuring Server Core, 113, 115
    migrating between domains, 354–355
    renaming, 50–53
    roaming profiles and machine settings, 1301
    securing data by machine attributes, 766–767
    setting up during upgrade install, 43
concurrency, setting user limits on shares, 662–663
conditional forwarders, DNS server, 219–220
conditions
    assigning permissions with Security tab of DAC, 761–764
    day and time restrictions, 1078–1079
    Groups condition applied to network access, 1078
    network access policies and, 1076
    rules governing network access policies, 1076–1077

Conficker virus, troubleshooting DNS and, 250
ConfigMgr. *See* SCCM (System Center Configuration Manager)
configuration database, component of AD FS, 534
configuration files, website global settings and, 992
Configuration Manager. *See* SCCM (System Center Configuration Manager)
configuration partition, AD database, 1187
configuration passes, unattended installation and, 87–88
configuring servers, with Server Manager
    activating Windows, 45–46
    adding roles and features, 56–63
    Best Practices Analyzer, 72–74
    changes to Server Manager, 45
    changing network properties, 46–50
    common tasks, 45
    diagnosing problems with events tool, 71–72
    enabling remote administration, 55–56
    installing roles of multiple servers using scripts, 66–69
    installing roles using PowerShell, 64–66
    joining domains, 53–54
    overview of, 43–45
    removing roles, 69–70
    renaming servers, 50–53
    troubleshooting roles and features, 70–71
    viewing list of installed servers, 71
    viewing role performance, 75
    viewing roles and associated features, 75–76
    viewing services, 72
Confirmation page, New Share Wizard, 660
conflict resolution
    ADMT migration and, 362
    FRS replication and, 315
connection limits, remote server administration, 896–897
connectivity
    benefits of IPv6, 148
    planning Active Directory, 1192–1193
    testing with ping command, 935
constraints, network access policies and, 1076, 1082–1083
containers, Active Directory, 288
continuous availability, clustering and, 567
continuous replication, FRS (file replication service), 315
Control Panel
    accessing in Windows 8, 933
    searching, 695
    troubleshooting profiles in System settings, 1292
    user configuration with, 1326–1327
controllers, virtual disk, 1367–1368
cost, site link properties, 1140–1141
counters. *See* performance counters
CPUs
    app CPU throttling, 980
    capacity planning for HVR, 1424
    configuring CPU throttling, 1002

hardware requirements for Hyper-V, 1343
    in implementation of server virtualization, 1352
    managing virtual hardware and, 1383–1384
    PerfView and, 1523
    for RDS Server, 1445
    VMs supporting on-demand allocation, 1412
    Windows Server 2012 requirements, 21
create, read, update, and delete (CRUD), REST and, 370
credential conflicts, when connecting to shares, 674
CredSSP (Credential Security Support Provider), 1453
critical events, event levels, 1486
CRUD (create, read, update, and delete), REST and, 370
cryptography. *See* encryption
CS (Certificate Services). *See also* AD CS (Active Directory Certificate Services)
    certificate settings for domain accounts, 404–405
    changes to, 78–79
    changes to Active Directory, 8
    integration with Server Manager, 78
    managing deployment with PowerShell, 78–79
CSV (comma-separated values) file, in creating user account, 455–457
CSVs (Cluster Shared Volumes), 568–569, 1556
cumulative permissions
    combining share/NTFS permissions, 671–672
    overview of, 668
currency, choosing settings during installation, 24–25
custom filters
    in managing printers and print servers, 878–879
    working with Print Management console, 835
Customer Experience Improvement Program (CEIP), Microsoft, 83
customizing servers
    adding roles and features, 117–118
    configuring firewall, 118–119
    enabling Remote Desktop, 118

D

D$ share, connecting to, 675–676
DAC (discretionary access control), 668
DAC (Dynamic Access Control)
    applying policy, 785–793, 803
    checking classification, 816–818
    classification properties, 806
    classification rules, 807–812
    classifying data, 769, 804
    classifying documents, 804–806
    configuring access denied assistance, 796–799

configuring automatic file classification, 814–815

creating Central Access Rule, 781–785, 802–803

creating claim type, 775–777, 800–801

creating policy, 774–775

creating resource property, 777–781, 802

detecting string pattern with regular expression, 813–814

enabling, 771–774

groups and user attributes in, 765–766

overview of, 759–760

regular expressions and, 818–819

securing data, 819–824

securing data by machine attributes, 766–767

securing file shares, 760–764

templates for centralized control of permissions, 767–768

testing policy, 793–796, 803

troubleshooting access control, 769

user rights and, 932

users, devices, resources, and claims, 769–771

verifying schedule set up in Task Scheduler, 815–816

DACL (discretionary access control list), 668

data

   Hyper-V data exchange service, 1359

   reports on data retention, 1517–1519

   retrieving server data with IPAM, 189

   transfers using SMB Direct, 689

Data Center Bridge. *See* DCB (Data Center Bridge)

data collector sets

   overview of, 1510–1511

   for routine diagnostics, 1517–1519

   system data collector sets, 1511–1513

   user-defined data collector sets, 1513–1517

data deduplication

   checking for corrupt volumes and, 646

   configuring with PowerShell, 641–645

   configuring with Server Manager, 638–641

   File and Storage Services role of, 651–652

   managing storage with File and Storage Services, 565

   overview of, 636–637

   support for, 569

Data Manager tab, of report properties sheet, 1517–1519

Data Protection Manager. *See* DPM (Data Protection Manager)

Database Managers group

   permissions, 722

   viewing user rights, 725

databases

   AD FS configuration database, 534

   backing up WSUS database, 1550

   checking integrity of Active Directory database, 1571–1573

   copying AD DS database, 1575–1576

   creating security database, 497–498

of DNS zones, 211

IPAM support for, 178

planning deployment of AD FS and, 538

WSUS supported, 1532–1533

Datacenter Edition

   overview of, 2

   setting up DCs and, 262

DCB (Data Center Bridge)

   Hyper-V QoS and, 163

   managing, 161–163

   overview of, 161

DcDiag

   checking system with, 321

   performing post upgrade tasks, 342

   preparing for in-place upgrade, 337

   troubleshooting DNS, 253–254

   verifying DNS service, 340

   verifying domain services, 1254

DCPromo

   installing Active Directory and, 257

   prestaging RODC account, 1181

   promoting member server, 1251–1254

   removing server following swing migration, 1257

   uninstalling Active Directory, 343

DCs (domain controllers)

   Active Directory upgrade strategies, 80

   ADAC tips and, 448

   adding to forest, 279

   authentication and, 265

   cached credentials, 1132–1134

   case for three DCs, 1154

   case for two DCs, 1195–1196

   changes to Active Directory, 4

   choosing Windows Server 2012 version when setting up, 262

   comparing RODC with, 1156

   creating, 132–133

   decommissioning, 299–300

   Default Domain Controllers Policy, 260

   deployment configuration, 264, 281

   DirectAccess requirements, 1112

   DNS and, 1132

   forests and, 1188

   Hyper-V checkpoints and, 1396

   installing DNS and GC for domain with single DC, 265

   installing with PowerShell, 277–278

   location relative to sites, 1128

   migrating to DFS-R, 318–319

   optimizing, 272

   in-place upgrade and, 335–336

   preparing for second domain, 1199–1300

   preparing for swing migration, 341, 1250–1251

   primary and backup controllers, 221

   read-only. *See* RODCs (read-only domain controllers)

   in remote locations, 1131–1132

   renaming with netdom command, 305

   requirements for RODC deployment, 1161–1162

   restarting in DSRM mode, 273

   risks of stolen, 1155

running AD DS for, 275–278, 282–284

as security boundary, 1187

server configuration, 263–264

setting up site topology and, 1130

sites and, 1124

transferring FSMO roles between, 1219–1223

verifying health during in-place upgrade, 336–337

virtualizing. *See* virtual DCs (virtual domain controllers)

DDNS (Dynamic DNS)

   configuring stand-alone DNS server, 214

   hostnames and, 228

   netlogon service performing DDNS requests, 241

   registering SRV records, 253–254

   updating DNS dynamically, 237–239

debug logs

   administering DNS server, 248–249

   Applications and Services Logs folder, 1493

deduplication. *See* data deduplication

Default Domain Controllers Policy, 260

Default Domain Policy, 260

default gateway, 934–935

default network profile, 1299–1300

Default Web Site, 992

defragmenting Active Directory offline, 1570–1571

delegation

   Active Directory, 297, 518

   best practices, 525–526

   controlling access to user accounts, 407

   of DNS servers, 214

   of DNS subdomains, 240

   of Group Policy administration, 518–521

   of IIS 8.0 features, 1007

   of IPAM (IP Address Management), 199–203

   for managing OUs in different departments, 425

   manually setting permissions, 525–529

   methods for name resolution, 217–219

   OUs in delegation of control, 297, 521–525

   of permissions, 860

   of printer administration, 867

   of RODC administration, 1161

   viewing or changing, 530–531

   of website administration, 1007–1008

Delivery tab, Storage Reports, 685–687

demilitarized zones. *See* DMZ (demilitarized zones)

denied list, password replication policy and, 1158–1159

Denied RODC Password Replication group, 1158–1160

Deny permissions

   assigning, 667–668

   default permissions of Users group, 727

   file and directory permissions, 728–730

   network access permissions, 1080–1082

   share and NTFS similarities, 667

shared folders and, 715
taking precedence over Allow, 668–669
deployment
of AD FS, 537–539
centralizing application deployment, 1436
cloning for rapid deployment, 77
configuring patch deployment, 1540–1544
DISM (Deployment Image Servicing and Management), 85
flexibility of desktop and, 1268
IPAM topology options, 179–180
of RemoteApp program, 1439
of software via Group Policy, 487
of virtual DCs, 1402
of websites, 1003–1004
of WSUS server, 1533–1535
deployment, printer
adding to clients manually, 848
adding using Active Directory search, 849–851
advanced searches, 852
overview of, 847–848, 862
searching for printer features and, 851
via GPOs, 853–856
viewing deployed printers, 856
working with Print Management console, 835
deployment configuration, DCs (domain controllers) and, 264–265, 281
Deployment Image Servicing and Management (DISM), 85
deprecated items, in Windows Server 2012, 10
DES encryption, 400
design pointers, for planning Active Directory, 1196–1198
desktop
changes in Windows Server 2012, 3
controlling Windows built-in applications, 1325–1326
managing Internet Explorer, 1325
managing offline files, 1324–1325
managing with Group Policy, 1323–1324
named folders in user profile, 1281
policies for creating consistency across organization, 502
restricting features with Group Policy, 487
user configuration from Control Panel, 1326–1327
user configuration with File Explorer, 1327
device drivers
client-side requirements, 930
driver store, 844
printers. *See* printer drivers
updating during upgrade install, 36
Device Manager, verifying network configuration, 933
devices, access control, 769–771
DFS (Distributed File System). *See also* DFS-R (Distributed File System Replication)
adding links to DFS root, 743–744
adding shares, 1276–1277

configuring replication, 745–747
consolidating enterprise resources, 750
creating DFS root, 739–743
editing replication schedules and bandwidth, 747–748
enabling/disabling replication, 748–749
File and Storage Services role of, 650–651
file shares and DFS namespaces, 1270
FRS and, 314–316
life-cycle management, 750–751
making shares available in DFS namespace, 1286
managing drive mappings, 1328–1329
overview of, 734–736
sharing/publishing replicated folders, 749–750
stand-alone vs. domain-based, 737–738
terminology, 736
understanding DFS replication, 747
DFS links
adding to DFS root, 743–744
defined, 736
DFS management tool
adding links to DFS root, 743–744
configuring DFS replication, 745–747
creating DFS root, 739–743
enabling/disabling replication, 748–749
installing, 323
running Health and Propagation reports, 324–325
sharing/publishing replicated folders, 749–750
DFS Namespaces
creating, 736, 739–743
managing storage with File and Storage Services, 565
overview of, 734
DFS root
adding links to, 743–744
creating, 739–743
overview of, 736
DFS-R (Distributed File System Replication)
advantages of, 1270
compared with FRS, 313–317
configuring replications, 745–747
editing replication schedules and bandwidth, 747–748
enabling/disabling replication, 748–749
migrating to DFS-R, 322–325
migrating to eliminated state, 328–331
migrating to redirected state, 326–328
overview of, 317–318, 735
raising domain functional levels, 321–322
roaming profiles and, 1302
service, 747
sharing/publishing replicated folders, 749–750
steps in migration to, 318–319
transition states in migration to, 320
understanding, 747
dfsrmig command
migrating to DFS-R, 319, 322–325
migrating to eliminated state, 328–331
migrating to redirected state, 326–328

DHCP (Dynamic Host Configuration Protocol)
adding Mac OS X clients to domain, 971
adding roles and features, 117
checking local area connections, 937
client-side requirements and, 931
configuring DHCP service, 133–135
IPAM support, 177
managing DHCP scope, 196–197
managing DHCP service, 121–122
in-place upgrade and, 335
RSAT server tools, 923
tracking DHCP configuration events, 198–199
verifying local area connection settings, 934
DHCP client, dynamic DNS updates and, 238
DHCP failover
installing, 206–209
overview of, 204–205
requirements, 205–206
DHCP server
dynamic DNS updates and, 238–239
scope options, 196–197
Diagnostic Report Wizard, DFS Manager, 324–325
dial-in, local user account settings, 395
differencing disks, types of VHDs, 1367
Differentiated Services Code Point (DSCP), 164
DIG (Domain Information Groper), 254
digital signatures, SMB 3.0 security improvement, 691
DirectAccess. *See also* VPN (virtual private networks)
client support, 1111–1112
configuring clients, 1118–1119
configuring RRAS, 1073
features, 1110–1111
installing, 1112–1118
managing, 1120–1121
overview of, 1110
requirements, 1112
services provided by Network Policy and Access Services role, 1070
Directory Leasing, SMB, 689
directory permissions, assigning, 720–725
DirSync tool, synchronizing objects to Windows Azure, 372
discretionary access control (DAC), 668
discretionary access control list (DACL), 668
disk deduplication. *See* data deduplication
disk drives
4K sectors and, 591
answer file installation, 94
checking for corrupt volumes, 646
connecting to common shares, 675–676
HA (high availability), 571
hard disks. *See* HDDs (hard disk drives)
managing drive mappings, 1328–1331
mapping to shared folders, 964–966
parallelized repair, 591
for RDS Server, 1445
report on free disk space, 1518

setting up during clean install, 27–29
solid state. *See* SSDs (solid state drives)
types of removable storage, 101
viewing in storage pools, 603–604
virtual hard disks. *See* VHDs (virtual
hard disks)
Windows Server 2012 requirements, 21
write-back cache and, 590–591
disk I/O
PerfView and, 1523
VMs supporting on-demand allocation,
1412
Disk Manager (Disk Management Console)
creating volumes from virtual disks,
614–617
DiskPart command as alternative to,
136–137
viewing disk drives in storage pools,
603–604
disk space
BitLocker encrypting, 693, 696
monitoring, 687
disk volumes. *See* volumes
DiskPart command
bringing offline disks online, 618
creating primary partition, 136–137
creating volumes from virtual disks, 614
DISM (Deployment Image Servicing and
Management), 85
Display tab, RDC (Remote Desktop
Connection), 890–891
displays
allowing RDC to span multiple monitors,
895
Windows Server 2012 requirements, 21
distinguished names. *See* DNs (distinguished
names)
Distributed Cache mode, BranchCache, 166,
699
Distributed File System Replication. *See* DFS-R
(Distributed File System Replication)
Distributed Scan Server, 832
distribution groups, Active Directory, 424
djoin.exe
adding computer to domain while
offline, 948–950
overview of, 946–947
requirements, 947
DMZ (demilitarized zones)
installing IIS 8 and, 981
NAPT as accidental firewall, 1046
RD Gateway and, 906–907
VPN servers hosted in, 1066
DNs (distinguished names)
creating, 1150
finding, 1151
identifying server roles by, 1165
LDAP and, 287–288
obtaining, 390
retrieving group membership by, 1131
DNS (Domain Name Services)
Active Directory and, 239, 266
adding Mac OS X client to domain and,
971

adding roles and features, 117
adding server to local Server Manager,
663
ADI (Active Directory Integrated) zones,
224–226
administering DNS server, 248–250
background zone loading, 244
changes in Windows Server 2012, 11
checking local area connections, 937, 939
configuring automatically, 239–241
configuring clients, 235–237
configuring stand-alone DNS server,
214–217
creating DNS zone for second domain,
1202–1203
DcDiag tool and, 253–254
DCs (domain controllers) and, 1132
DirectAccess requirements, 1112
DNSSEC (DNS Security Extensions), 244
dynamic updates, 237–239
forwarders, 1203
FRS requirements and dependencies, 317
global query block list, 242
GlobalNames feature, 242–244
hostname resolution, 232–235
installing, 214
installing for domain with single DC, 265
installing for forest with second DC,
281–282, 284
integrating DNS servers, 217–220
IPAM support, 177
joining domains and, 53–54
managing, 132–133
managing clients and name resolution,
232
managing SRV records, 143
manually configuring local area
connection, 942
mapping DNS infrastructure to AD
domains, 1197–1198
monitoring DNS zones, 197–198
multiple-domain design and, 1198–1199
namespace management, 221
NsLookup tool and, 250–252
in-place upgrade and, 335
post upgrade tasks, 342
preparing for in-place upgrade, 1245
preparing for swing migration, 340, 1250
record types, 228–232
resolving external names, 246–248
reverse lookup zones, 226–228
on RODCs (read-only domain
controllers), 1182–1184
RSAT server tools, 923
split-brain scenario, 245–246
standard primary zone, 221–222
standard secondary zone, 222–224
stub zones, 226
suffix, 215
support for external DNS domains, 245
troubleshooting, 301–302
troubleshooting links for, 254–255
trust anchors, 244–245
understanding DNS server role, 211–214

understanding SRV records and clients,
241–242
verifying configuration, 922–923
verifying local area connection settings,
934–935
DNS clients
changes in Windows Server 2012, 11
configuring, 235–237
hostname resolution, 232–235
managing, 232
SRV records and, 241–242
DNS Security Extensions (DNSSEC)
overview of, 244
trust anchors, 244–245
DNS servers
administering, 248–250
caching-only servers, 220
changes in Windows Server 2012, 11
configuring stand-alone server, 214–217
integrating servers, 217–220
monitoring DNS zones, 197–198
NsLookup tool for querying, 1058
understanding server role, 211–214
dnscmd, promoting member server, 341–342
DNSSEC (DNS Security Extensions)
overview of, 244
trust anchors, 244–245
documents
adding Print and Document Services
role, 832–834
managing printer security, 859–860
Security tab and print permissions, 865
domain accounts
certificate settings, 404–405
COM+ settings, 403–404
connecting clients to network, 931–932
group membership settings, 405–406
managing from command line, 410–412
object settings, 406–407
security settings, 407–408
telephone settings, 401–402
Domain Admins group
full control permissions granted to, 1186
preparing for migration between
domains, 351, 1264
prestaging RODC account, 1179–1181
RODC install when group member
unavailable, 1177–1178
domain controllers. *See* DCs (domain
controllers)
domain functional levels
migration to DFS-R and, 321–322
for multiple-domain designs, 1205–1207
overview of, 266–267
raising, 302–304
reverting, 1262
in RODCs, 1162–1163
selecting, 267–268
upgrade paths and, 367–368
in Windows Server versions, 268–269
Domain Information Groper (DIG), 254
domain local groups
creating, 294–295, 427
creating from command line, 432

Denied RODC Password Replication group, 1159–1160
membership settings, 429–430
nesting, 430–431
scope of, 425
domain migration. *See* C&P (clean and pristine) migration
domain names, FSMO example, 1210
Domain Naming Master role, 1217
domain partition, AD database and, 1187
domain policies, auditing printer access, 868
Domain Services. *See* AD DS (Active Directory Domain Services)
domain user accounts
adding to local computer groups, 943
capabilities of, 932
domain-based DFS
creating DFS root, 739–743
stand-alone DFS, 737–738
domain-based GPOs
for applying security templates, 498
creating, 474–479
DomainPrep, 340
domains
ADAC tips and, 448
adding computers to, 950
adding servers to, 53–54
applying GPOs to, 468
building forests, 1190
cached credentials, 1132–1133
changing domain user passwords, 951–953
choosing OU vs. domain, 1197
configuring membership, 43
configuring Server Core, 115–116
creating second domain, 1200–1204
cryptographic settings on target domain, 352
DCHP failover requirements, 206
Default Domain Policy, 260
defined, 258, 932
DNS naming structure, 212
establishing trust between domains prior to migration, 349–351, 1263–1264
FSMO domain name example, 1210
grafting and pruning not supported, 1190–1191
joining, 298–299
joining while offline, 946–950
linking GPOs to, 285, 1147
Mac OS X clients joining, 971–973
maintaining, 297–298
managing with Netdom, 304–306
mapping DNS infrastructure to AD domains, 1197–1198
merging, 1196
migrating users and computers between, 354–355
multimaster replication, 1186–1187
naming, 1197
overview of, 1186
in-place upgrade. *See* in-place upgrade
preparing DC for second domain, 1199–1300

preparing for in-place upgrade, 337–338, 1246
preparing for RODC with adprep, 1166–1167
preparing for swing migration, 340, 1250
root domain, 265–266
security boundaries, 1186
support for external DNS domains, 245
synchronizing of domain time, 306–308
in trees, 1188
troubleshooting, 976
trusted and trusting, 1226–1228
upgrading Active Directory and, 334–335
Windows OSs clients joining, 942–945
domains, multiple
creating second domain, 1200–1204
namespace for, 1198–1199
overview of, 1185, 1198
preparing DC for second domain, 1199–1300
when to use multiple domains, 1193–1194
domains, with single DC
Active Directory and, 262
benefits of, 261–262
deployment configuration, 264–265
DNS and, 266
domain functional levels, 266–269
DSRM (Directory Services Restore Mode), 273–274
forest functional levels, 269–270
installing DNS and GC, 265
location of files and SYSVOL shared folder, 270–272
naming root domain, 265–266
ReFS file system and, 265
running AD DS configuration wizard, 275–278
server configuration, 263–264
domains, with two DCs
deployment configuration, 281
installing AD DS role, 280
installing DNS and GC, 281–282
overview of, 279
running AD DS configuration wizard, 282–284
Domains and Trusts. *See* AD DT (Active Directory Domains and Trusts)
downloading updates, during upgrade install, 36–37
DPM (Data Protection Manager)
backing up and restoring VMs, 1419
core product in System Center 2012 R2, 1524
overview of, 1568–1569
DR (disaster recovery). *See also* HVR (Hyper-V Replica)
benefits of single domain and, 262
clustering and, 573
DPM servers and, 1569
folder replication and, 1276
VMs (virtual machines) and, 1422–1423
drivers. *See* device drivers
drives. *See* disk drives

DS (Domain Services). *See also* AD DS (Active Directory Domain Services)
changes to Active Directory, 4
cloning for rapid deployment, 77
fine-grained password policies, 77
PowerShell History Viewer, 78
rapid deployment with cloning, 77
recycle bin and, 76–77
simplified management, 77–78
dsadd
creating AD groups, 432–433
creating new user, 387–388
creating users and objects, 293–294
Dsamain.exe
copying AD DS database, 1575–1576
mounting and working with snapshots, 1574
dsconfigad utility, 972–973
DSCP (Differentiated Services Code Point), 164
dsmod
managing domain accounts, 410–411
resetting passwords, 435
dsquery
identifying server roles, 1165
managing domain accounts, 410, 412
DSRM (Directory Services Restore Mode)
authoritative and nonauthoritative restores, 1580–1581
creating password for, 273–274, 1171
restarting DC in, 273
setting password for, 1201
dsrm, managing domain accounts, 412
DVD/DVD-ROM
as installation media, 24
types of removable storage, 101
Windows Server 2012 requirements, 21
Dynamic Access Control. *See* DAC (Dynamic Access Control)
Dynamic DNS. *See* DDNS (Dynamic DNS)
Dynamic Host Activation
configuring, 1004
hosting multiple sites and, 1002
Dynamic Host Configuration Protocol. *See* DHCP (Dynamic Host Configuration Protocol)
dynamic IP addresses, 979
dynamic IT, 1267
dynamic load balancing, 154
Dynamic Memory, 1380
dynamic updates, DNS, 237–239
dynamic virtual disks
disk conversion operations, 1372–1373
types of VHDs, 1367–1368

E

EAP (Extensible Authentication Protocol)
authenticating VPN clients, 1098–1099
VPN connections and, 1079
EAP-MS-CHAPv2, 1098–1099
EAP-TTLS (Extensible Authentication Protocol with Tunneled Transport Layer Security)
802.IX authentication, 165
changes in Windows Server 2012, 11

Easy Print
    overview of, 1452
    printer redirection with, 891
editions of Windows Server 2012
    choosing, 37
    overview of, 2–3
    software requirements for Hyper-V and, 1344
    upgrade install, 39
effective permissions
    NTFS permissions, 730–732
    troubleshooting access control, 769
EIDE (Enhanced Integrated Drive Electronics), 1445
eliminated state, migrating to DFS-R, 319, 328–331
e-mail, adding SMTP e-mail to website, 1012–1013
E-mail Message tab, quota templates
    configuring new quota, 681
    working with, 678–679
Email Notifications, FSRM (File Server Resource Manager), 687
empty root design, planning Active Directory, 1194–1195
Enable-ADUser, 459
encryption
    benefits of FRS, 315
    certificate settings for domain accounts, 404–405
    configuring host session properties, 904
    creating shares and, 659–660
    enabling cryptographic settings on target domains, 352
    legacy algorithms and, 265
    logon settings and, 400
    PES (password encryption file), 353–354, 1262, 1265
    SMB Encryption, 689, 691–692
    storing passwords and, 503–504
    VPN settings, 1085–1086
end user license agreement. *See* EULA (end user license agreement)
Endpoint Protection, in System Center 2012 R2, 1524
Enhanced Integrated Drive Electronics (EIDE), 1445
enhanced session mode, in Hyper-V, 1365
Enhanced Storage, installing for role services, 655–656
enlightened guest. *See also* guest (virtual machine) partition, 1357–1358
enlightened kernel, 1358
Enterprise Admins group
    building domains and forests, 1191
    in root domain, 1195
enterprise resources, DFS consolidating, 750
ERP (enterprise resource planning), 752
error events, 1486
ESE (Extensible Storage Engine), 1571–1572
Essentials Edition, 3
Ethernet, reliability of, 1030
ETW (Event Tracing for Windows)

new features in IIS 8.0, 981
PerfView and, 1523
selecting ADK features, 85
SPA (Server Performance Advisor) and, 169
EULA (end user license agreement)
    answer file installation and, 96
    clean install and, 26–27
    installing ADK (Assessment and Deployment Kit), 83–84
    upgrade install and, 38
Event Catalog view, IPAM
    tracking DHCP configuration events, 198–199
    tracking IP addresses, 199
    tracking IPAM configuration events, 198
event forwarding
    checking runtime status, 1505
    troubleshooting with `Wecutil`, 1505–1507
Event Log tab, quota templates
    configuring new quota, 681
    working with, 679–680
event logs. *See also* logs/logging
    administering DNS server, 248
    in Applications and Services Logs folder, 1493
    checking for error in application log, 1288
    collector computer and, 1495–1496
    configuring, 1493–1494
    displaying saved, 1495
    saving, 1494–1495
    selecting events to log, 1498–1499
    subscribing to, 1495–1498
    Windows logs, 1492–1493
event subscription
    advanced options for, 1499–1500
    collector-initiated subscriptions, 1496–1497
    configuring, 1501–1502
    creating collector-initiated subscription, 1502–1504
    protocols, 1500–1501
    source-initiated subscriptions, 1497–1498
    troubleshooting event forwarding, 1505–1507
Event Tracing for Windows. *See* ETW (Event Tracing for Windows)
Event Viewer
    advanced options for event subscription, 1499–1500
    Applications and Services Logs folder and, 1493
    checking for error in application log, 1288
    configuring event logs, 1493–1494
    configuring event subscriptions, 1501–1504
    creating custom views, 1488–1489
    displaying saved log files, 1495
    exporting/importing custom views, 1491–1492
    filtering custom views, 1489–1491
    IPAM troubleshooting and, 203
    overview of, 1485

post upgrade tasks, 342
protocols for event subscription, 1500–1501
saving log files, 1494–1495
scrubbing logs, 646
selecting events to log, 1498–1499
subscribing to event logs, 1495–1498
troubleshooting event forwarding, 1505–1507
troubleshooting Group Policy, 517
understanding event levels, 1486–1487
verifying domain services following migration, 1254
viewing events, 1485–1486
Windows logs, 1492–1493
events
    creating custom views, 1488–1489
    exporting/importing custom views, 1491–1492
    filtering custom views, 1489–1491
    monitoring with server groups, 1482
    selecting event IDs, 1491
    selecting events to log, 1498–1499
    understanding event levels, 1486–1487
    viewing, 1485–1486
events tool, diagnosing problems with, 71–72
Everyone group, share permissions and, 710, 712
Exchange Server, 1212
executables
    permission to execute, 666–667
    Windows OSs and, 1442
Experience tab, RDC (Remote Desktop Connection), 893–894
Export Virtual Machine Wizard, in Hyper-V management console, 1407
exporting
    custom event views, 1491–1492
    patches to USB, 1534
    pros/cons as backup solution, 1411
    roles to configuration XML file, 67–68
    VMs (virtual machines), 1407–1410
Extended Protection for Authentication, 539
Extensible Authentication Protocol. *See* EAP-TTLS (Extensible Authentication Protocol with Tunneled Transport Layer Security)
Extensible Markup Language (XML)
    paper specification, 831
    XML-based logs, 1491–1492
Extensible Storage Engine (ESE), 1571–1572
external trusts, 1229
external virtual switches, 1374

F
failover
    events, 1413
    LBFO (load balancing and failover), 152
    managing VM replicas and, 1430–1431
failover clustering
    adding first node to cluster, 575–585
    BitLocker encryption for, 693
    CAU (Cluster-Aware Updating), 1422
    CSVs (Cluster Shared Volumes), 568–569

Hyper-V and, 1401–1402
live migration relying on, 1413–1414
RSAT tools, 924
fault tolerance
benefits of replication with FRS, 315
DCs and, 1154
DFS and, 744
HA (high availability), 571
SMB Multichannel, 689
Favorites, named folders in user profile, 1281
FC (Fibre Channel)
choosing disk type by storage needs, 590
not supported in storage pools, 602
options for shared storage, 575
overview of, 563
SANs (Storage Area Networks) over, 562
Virtual SAN Manager Wizard and, 1366
FCP (Fibre Channel Protocol), 563
features. See roles and features
federation metadata
adding trusted relying party to AD FS, 549
as key component of AD FS, 534–535
federation server farms, 535
federation server proxy
adding proxy server role to AD FS server, 557–558
as key component of AD FS, 535
networking requirements and, 539
federation servers. See also AD FS (Active Directory Federation Services)
adding proxy server role to AD FS server, 557–558
adding to AD FS server farm, 556–557
configuring, 544–547
deploying, 538
installing AD FS role, 540–543
networking requirements and, 539
overview of, 535
requirements for, 536
verifying functionality of, 557
Federation Services. See AD FS (Active Directory Federation Services)
Fibre Channel. See FC (Fibre Channel)
Fibre Channel Protocol (FCP), 563
file and directory permissions. See NTFS permissions
file and print sharing
changes in Windows Server 2012, 14–15
preparing workstation for ADMT migration, 354
File and Storage Services role
adding roles to, 653–656
configuring data deduplication, 638–641
configuring quota, 680–682
creating file shares, 1273
creating shares with Server Manager, 657–660
creating storage pools, 599–602
managing file servers and storage options, 564–566
overview of, 595–597
quick setup of NFS shares, 632–635
role services/features, 651–653

sharing profiles folder and adding to DFS namespace, 1284
Sync Share configuration, 1319–1321
understanding, 650–651
File Explorer
configuring users, 1327
creating shared folders, 705–706
defining share permissions, 712–714
File Screen Audit, FSRM (File Server Resource Manager), 688
file screens
configuring policies for, 682–684
defined, 682
File Server Resource Manager. See FSRM (File Server Resource Manager)
File Server VSS Agent Service, 653
file servers. See also DAC (Dynamic Access Control)
File and Storage Services role, 651
managing shares, 565
roaming profiles folder, 1282
securing mandatory profile folder on, 1297–1298
setting up File Server role, 135
file services, RSAT tools, 923
file shares. See also NFS (Network File System); shared folders
abstracting physical location of, 1270
accessing, 111
basics of, 704
connecting to network resources, 955–956
creating for roaming profile, 1283–1286
creating manually, 1290–1291
creating SMB files shares with PowerShell, 710
Mac OS X clients connecting to, 973
making available in DFS namespace, 1286
publishing, 957–961
securing with DAC (Dynamic Access Control), 760–764
Server Core and, 111
setting folder permissions, 1291–1292
file systems
distributed. See DFS (Distributed File System)
network. See NFS (Network File System)
NT. See NTFS (NT File System)
resilient. See ReFS (Resilient File System)
VMs and, 1367
File Transfer Protocol. See FTP (File Transfer Protocol)
files
assigning permissions, 761–764
backing up and restoring, 1566
classification properties, 806
configuring permissions, 1283
connecting to shares, 672–676
default NFS permissions, 754
implementing BitLocker, 692–697
location in Active Directory, 270–272
manual backup, 1566–1567
overview of, 649
in profiles, 1281

understanding SMB 3.0, 688–692
using Offline Files/Client-Side Caching, 697–701
filters
events and logs, 1489–1491
filtering policies and ACLs, 482–486
managing printers and print servers, 878–879
working with Print Management console, 835
FIM (Forefront Identity Manager), 533
FIN message, TCP (Transmission Control Protocol), 1044
fine-grained password policies
changes to Active Directory, 4, 77
overview of, 310–313
security boundaries and, 1186
firewalls
avoiding stealth firewalls, 1058
configuring patch deployment, 1540
creating inbound firewall rule, 126–131
DirectAccess requirements, 1112
enabling, 143
installing NFS and, 755–756
NAPT as, 1046
preparing workstation for ADMT migration, 354
RD Gateway and, 907
firmware, UEFI (Unified Extensible Firmware Interface) BIOS, 592, 1382
fixed provisioning, disk storage and, 572
fixed-size virtual disks
creating virtual disks, 1369
disk conversion operations, 1372
types of VHDs, 1367–1368
Flexible Single Master Operations roles. See FSMO (Flexible Single Master Operations) roles
flow control attributed, TCP adding to IP, 1042
folder management, classification properties, 806
folder redirection
applying advanced, 1314–1316
applying basic, 1308–1312
with Group Policy, 490–492
managing, 1316–1318
overview of, 1306–1308
testing, 1312–1314
folders
assigning permissions, 137–139, 761–764
backing up and restoring, 1566
configuring permissions, 1283
creating, 137–139, 1277–1280
creating shared, 1272–1276
default NFS permissions, 754
deploying for profiles by editing single user object, 1286–1287
File Server role added when sharing, 653
manual backup, 1566–1567
naming and sharing, 1271
in profiles, 1281
recovering from a backup, 1567–1568
securing mandatory profile folder on, 1297–1298

sharing, 139
sharing profiles folder and adding to
DFS namespace, 1284
Forefront Identity Manager (FIM), 533
forest functional levels
list of supported, 269
for multiple-domain designs, 1207–1209
path to forest function level following
migration, 367–368
raising, 302–304
in RODCs, 1162–1164
selecting based on Windows Server
version, 269–270
upgrade paths and, 367–368
forest root, 1189
forest trusts
creating with New Trust Wizard, 1234
types of trust relationships, 1229
understanding transitive forest trusts, 1230
ForestPrep, 340
forests
ADAC tips and, 448
adding second DC. *See* domains, with
two DCs
building, 1190
creating single-domain forest. *See*
domains, with single DC
defined, 260
grafting and pruning not supported,
1190–1191
intra-forest migration, 344
overview of, 1188
preparing for in-place upgrade, 337–338,
1246
preparing for RODC with adprep, 1166
preparing for swing migration, 340, 1250
transitive forest trusts, 1230
formats, selecting for reports, 684–685
forms
choosing form settings for print jobs,
857–858
viewing print layout forms, 845
working with Print Management
console, 835
forward lookup zones, DNS zones, 226
forwarded events, types of Windows logs,
1493
forwarders, DNS server
adding, 240
overview of, 219–220
forwarding
DNS servers, 214
methods for name resolution, 217, 220
Foundation Edition, 2
FQDN (Fully Qualified Domain Name)
configuring clients, 236–237
defined, 212
DNS record types and, 230
recursion in resolving, 213
reverse lookup zones and, 226–228
root domain and, 266
troubleshooting DNS and, 251
FRS (file replication service). *See also* DFS-R
(Distributed File System Replication)

benefits of, 315–316
DFS (Distributed File System) and,
314–315
future of, 317
monitoring, 321
overview of, 313–314
requirements and dependencies, 316–317
FS (Federation Services). *See* AD FS (Active
Directory Federation Services)
FSMO (Flexible Single Master Operations)
roles
decommissioning DCs and, 299
Domain Naming Master role, 1217
Infrastructure Operations Master role,
1218
list of, 308, 1213
moving, 309
multimaster vs. single-master replication,
1209–1210
overview of, 1210–1211
PDC Emulator role, 1219
post upgrade tasks, 342–343
preparing for in-place upgrade, 337–338
RID FSMO role, 1217–1218
Schema Master role, 1213–1217
transferring FSMO roles to another DC,
1219–1223, 1255–1256
FSRM (File Server Resource Manager)
changes in Windows Server 2012, 15
classification of data and, 769
configuring access denied assistance, 796
configuring automatic file classification,
814–815
creating classification rules, 807–812
creating file screen policies, 682–684
creating quota, 680–682
creating quota policies, 676–680
File and Storage Services role of, 652
generating reports, 684–687
managing classification, 806
managing storage with File and Storage
Services, 565
modifying options, 687–688
testing classification rules, 816–818
verifying schedules, 815–816
viewing installed roles and features, 656
FTP (File Transfer Protocol)
adding FTP Publishing service to
websites, 1014–1016
adding FTP role, 1014
anonymous access and, 967
changes in Windows Server 2012, 17
integrating FTP into web pages,
1013–1014
logon attempt restrictions in IIS 8.0, 979
Full Control permissions
assigning to Administrators group,
138–139
enforcing, 823
granting to Domain Admins group, 1186
in list of molecular permissions, 719
NTFS and, 667
setting folder permissions, 1279
share permissions and, 667, 713

full server backup and restore
overview of, 1557
performing backup, 1557–1560
performing backup from command line,
1560
performing restore, 1562–1564
Fully Qualified Domain Name. *See* FQDN
(Fully Qualified Domain Name)
functional levels
domain. *See* domain functional levels
forest. *See* forest functional levels
overview of, 1205

G

gateways
configuring for VPN server, 1080
verifying local area connection settings,
934
gateway-to-gateway VPNs, 1066–1067
GCs (global catalogs)
cached credentials and, 1133
compatibility with RODCs, 1167
defined, 260
installing for domain with single DC,
265
installing for forest with second DC,
281–282, 284
looking up data in, 241
in multiple-domain design, 1211–1212
post upgrade tasks, 342
replicating across WAN links, 1193
role placement, 1209
swing migration and, 1257
universal group membership and,
1133–1135
GDI (graphics device interface)
comparing XPSDrv printer driver model
with, 831
printer drivers and, 832
Get-ADUser, for creating accounts, 457–458
Get-Command, administering AD FS, 548
Get-Help, administering AD FS, 548
Get-WindowsFeature, viewing installed
roles, 846
global catalog. *See* GCs (global catalogs)
global groups
ADMT migration and, 354–355
creating, 294
creating command line, 433
intra-forest migration and, 344
scope of, 425
Global Positioning System (GPS), time
synchronization and, 1224
global query block list, 242
Global Search tool, 439–440
global settings, for websites, 992
globally unique identifier (GUID), 1407–1408
GlobalNames feature, DNS, 242–244
GPC (Group Policy container), storing GPOs
in, 468
GPMC (Group Policy Management console)
backing up and restoring GPOs, 511–513
configuring client access to closest site
with Group Policy, 1147–1148

connecting Mac OS X client to domain, 969–971
delegating administration of policies, 518–521
getting RSOP results with, 514–516
managing domain-based GPOs, 474–479
modeling policies with, 516
overview of, 509–510
Starter GPOs, 510–511
GPME (Group Policy Management editor)
auditing object access, 868–869
non-local settings, 470–471
publishing network resources with GPOs, 956–957
user and computer configuration settings, 487–488
GPOs (Group Policy Objects)
applying security templates, 498
associating multiple logon scripts, 1334–1335
backing up and restoring, 511–513
bottom-up execution of policies, 481–482
for cached user profiles, 1301
changes in Windows Server 2012, 14
computer and user configuration in, 468
configuring users with logon script, 1332–1334
controlling behavior of Group Policy, 480–481
creating, 474–479
creating and linking to sites, domains, and OUs, 285
creating for Central Access Policy deployment, 786
delegating administration, 518–521
deploying printers, 853–856
enforcing or blocking inheritance, 486
filtering policies with ACLs, 482–486
granting access to roaming profiles, 1289–1290
how it works "under the hood," 469–470
importing security templates, 498–499
inability to selectively apply, 468–469
inherited and cumulative nature of, 469
linking to sites, domains, or OUs, 1147
local policies and. See LGPOs (local group policy objects)
managing Active Directory, 285
provisioning in IPAM, 186–189
publishing network resources, 956–957
redirecting folders, 1308, 1316–1318
refresh intervals, 481
roaming profiles and, 1302, 1304–1306
setting password and account lockout policies, 502–504
slow networks and user profiles GPO, 1302
Starter GPOs, 510–511
user settings for roaming profiles, 1306
GPP (Group Policy preferences)
computer and user configuration and, 468
eliminating logon scripts, 509

item-level targeting with, 508
overview of, 504
publishing network resources with GPOs, 956–957
resetting passwords, 505–508
settings, 504–505
GPPrep, 340
gpresult.exe, troubleshooting Group Policy, 516–517
GPS (Global Positioning System), time synchronization and, 1224
GPT (Group Policy template), 468
GPT (GUID Partition Table), 592
gpupdate.exe, 960
GPUs (graphics processing units), 1365
Grant Access, setting network access policy permissions, 1080–1082
Graph API, in Windows Azure, 371
graphics device interface (GDI)
comparing XPSDrv printer driver model with, 831
printer drivers and, 832
graphics processing units (GPUs), 1365
Green IT, live migration and, 1413
group nesting, 425, 430–431
Group Policy
administrative templates, 499–500
Administrator and Non-administrator LGPOs, 471–473
applying DAC policies, 785–793
applying security templates with domain-based GPOs, 498
automating AD FS client configuration, 559–560
automating deployment, 1268
backing up and restoring GPOs, 511–513
changing domain user passwords, 951–953
cleaning up older profiles with, 1301
configuring access denied assistance, 796–799
configuring access to closest AD site with, 1147–1148
configuring clients for WSUS, 1547–1550
configuring IPAM provisioning, 182–184
connecting Mac OS X client to domain, 969–971
creating and deploying Central Access Policies, 803
creating GPOs, 474–479
creating security database, 497–498
defined, 259
disabling roaming profiles, 1303
eliminating logon scripts, 509
enabling/managing BranchCache, 699
enforcing or blocking inheritance, 486
enforcing storage preference, 1280
executing policies from bottom up, 481–482
filtering policies with ACLs, 482–486
generating Kerberos authentication tickets, 771–774
getting RSOP results with GPMC, 514–516

granting access to roaming profiles, 1288–1290
how it works "under the hood," 469–470
importing security templates, 498–499
inability to selectively apply policies, 468–469
inherited and cumulative nature of policies, 469
item-level targeting with, 508
local and non-local policies, 470–471
management console for. See GPMC (Group Policy Management console)
managing desktop, 1323–1324
managing domain time, 307
managing drive mappings, 1328–1331
managing logon scripts, 1335–1336
managing OUs, accounts, and groups, 285
managing shutdown with logoff scripts, 1336–1337
managing updates with, 1544–1547, 1551
managing Work Folders, 1323
modeling policies, 516
modifying default behavior, 479
overview of, 467–468
policy-based QoS, 164–165
possible applications of, 486–487
preferences. See GPP (Group Policy preferences)
preventing installation or use of unauthorized software, 501–502
RDS as alternative for deploying applications, 1436
redirecting folders, 490–492, 1316–1317
refresh intervals, 469
restricting Internet Explorer, 500–501
RSOP (Resultant Set of Policy), 513–514
security settings, 492–493
security templates, 493–494
setting password and account lockout policies, 502–504
settings, 480–481
specifying scripts with, 488–490
Starter GPOs, 510–511
troubleshooting, 513
troubleshooting with Event Viewer, 517
troubleshooting with gpresult.exe, 516–517
user and computer configuration settings, 487–488
user-specific LGPOs, 473–474
working with security templates, 494–496
Group Policy container (GPC), storing GPOs in, 468
Group Policy Management console. See GPMC (Group Policy Management console)
Group Policy Management, RSAT tools, 924
Group Policy Manager, 904–905
Group Policy Objects. See GPOs (Group Policy Objects)
Group Policy preferences. See GPP (Group Policy preferences)

Group Policy Results Wizard, 515–516
Group Policy template (GPT), 468
Group Policy tool (gpedit.msc), 470
groups
    access control using group attributes,
      765–766
    adding domain user account to local
      computer groups, 943
    adding members, 419–422
    adding members with PowerShell,
      460–461
    Administrators group for RODC, 1169
    ADMT migration and, 354–355
    configuring, 427–432
    configuring file and folder permissions,
      1283
    configuring with ADAC, 447–448
    creating, 294–295, 413–418, 426–427,
      522–523
    creating from command line, 419,
      432–433
    creating with ADAC, 445–447
    creating with PowerShell, 296, 459–460
    default permissions, 723
    domain user membership in, 405–406
    intra-forest migration and, 344
    local, 413
    logging in with new group membership,
      418
    managing, 412–413
    migrating between domains, 357–362
    naming standards, 428
    nesting, 425–426, 430–431
    new in Windows Server 2012, 334
    removing groups with PowerShell, 464
    removing members, 422–423
    removing members with PowerShell,
      462–463
    removing permissions, 728
    Schema Admins group, 1214
    scope of, 425
    security templates controlling
      membership in, 494
    testing resource access for migrated
      groups, 363–364
    tools for creating, 285
    types of, 424
    viewing user rights, 725–727
guest (virtual machine) partition
    deploying Hyper-V and, 1354
    overview of, 1357–1359
Guest account, 378–379
guest services, Hyper-V services, 1359
guest-based cluster, 587–588
GUI
    accessing Task Manager, 109–110
    administration of IIS 8.0, 1017
    ADMT interface options, 356
    choosing installation type, 26
    configuring NIC Teaming, 155–159
    switching to/from Server Core, 105, 109
GUID (globally unique identifier),
    1407–1408
GUID Partition Table (GPT), 592

H

HA (high availability)
    clustering and, 571, 573
    compared with disaster recovery, 1422
    DHCP failover and, 204
handshake protocols, 1026
handshaking, attributes TCP adds to IP, 1042
hard disks. *See* HDDs (hard disk drives)
hard disks, virtual. *See* VHDs (virtual hard
    disks)
hard quota limit
    configuring, 681
    defined, 677
hardware
    64-bit support, 22
    BitLocker requirements, 693
    disk drives. *See* disk drives
    HA (high availability), 571
    Hyper-V requirements, 1343–1344
    managing virtual, 1382–1388
    for RDS client, 1447
    for RDS server, 1444–1446
    reducing refresh rates, 1437–1438
    Reliability Monitor and, 1510
    repurposing following swing migration,
      342, 1255
    requirements for in-place upgrade, 336
    sharing via virtualization, 1341
    troubleshooting printers, 880
Hardware Compatibility List (HCL), 603
hardware virtualization. *See* server
    virtualization
hash, SMB 3.0 security improvement, 691
HBA (host bus adapters)
    Fibre Channel and, 563
    SANs and, 562
HCAP (Host Credential Authorization
    Protocol)
    for communication between NPS and
      network access servers, 1078
    services provided by Network Policy
      and Access Services role, 1069
HCL (Hardware Compatibility List), 603
HDDs (hard disk drives)
    backing up to, 1559
    BitLocker encryption of, 693, 1154
    bringing offline disks online, 618–619
    choosing disk type by storage needs, 590
    creating storage pools, 620–621
    creating storage tiers and, 620–621
    creating virtual disks, 608–612
    determining layout of virtual disks,
      607–608
    hardware requirements for Hyper-V,
      1344
    limitations of storage pools and, 602
Health Registration Authority (HRA), 1069
heartbeat service, Hyper-V services, 1358
help desk, RDS support for, 1439
hidden shares, 732–734
high availability. *See* HA (high availability)
HKEY_CURRENT_USE hive
    creating mandatory profiles and,
      1295–1297

ntuser.dat file, 1281, 1295–1297
HMAC SHA-256, 691
home directories
    advanced folder redirection, 1314–1315
    creating folders for each user, 1277–1280
    creating shared folders, 1272–1276
    overview of, 1269–1270
    questions to ask when creating,
      1270–1271
    redirecting folders to, 1310
    sharing, 1279
    vs. local storage, 1277–1280
host (A) records, 230, 242, 1035
host bus adapters (HBA)
    Fibre Channel and, 563
    SANs and, 562
Host Credential Authorization Protocol
    (HCAP)
    for communication between NPS and
      network access servers, 1078
    services provided by Network Policy
      and Access Services role, 1069
host sessions
    configuring RDS host sessions, 904–905
    support for nested sessions, 907
Hosted Cache mode, BranchCache, 166, 699
hostname
    adding new printers by, 836
    DDNS (Dynamic DNS) and, 228
    defined, 212
    resolving, 232–235
HOSTS file, 212
hosts/hosting
    computers with IP address act as host
      and router, 1030–1033
    Hyper-V, 1340, 1353
    multiple sites on single server, 1002–1003
hot spots, disk assignment categories, 590
HRA (Health Registration Authority), 1069
HTTP
    event subscription protocols, 1500
    Windows Azure and, 370–371
HTTPS
    creating inbound firewall rule, 126
    DirectAccess and, 1111
    optimizing event subscriptions, 1500
    RD Gateway using, 906–907
    setting up WinRS for, 122
HVR (Hyper-V Replica)
    capacity planning, 1424–1425
    configuring VM replication, 1427–1429
    enabling replication between two hosts,
      1426–1427
    managing VM replicas, 1430–1431
    overview of, 1423
    prerequisites, 1424
    what's new in Hyper-V, 1350
Hyper-V
    Actions pane, 1364–1366
    backing up and restoring VMs,
      1418–1421, 1561
    best practices checklist, 1363
    checkpoints, 1393–1396
    choosing virtual switch type, 1374–1375

in client OSs, 1345
  creating and configuring VMs, 1377–1382
  creating virtual disks, 1368–1371
  creating virtual switches, 1375–1377
  disaster recovery, 1422–1423
  failover clustering, 1401–1402
  hardware requirements, 1343–1344
  improvements in Windows Server 2012,
    8–10
  installing and configuring, 1359–1363
  installing VMs, 1388–1390
  keeping track of VM configuration,
    1410–1411
  maintaining virtual disks, 1371–1374
  malware protection, 1421–1422
  management OS partition, 1354–1357
  managing virtual hardware, 1382–1388
  migration options, 1411–1414
  moving VMs via export/import,
    1407–1410
  networking QoS, 163
  online resources for, 1431–1432
  overview of, 1339
  services, 1357
  Shared Nothing Live Migration (cluster-
    free), 1414–1417
  software architecture of, 1352–1354
  software requirements for, 1344
  support for AD FS, 537
  testing Windows Server 2012 R2, 34
  upgrading Integration Services for
    virtual machine, 1390–1392
  virtual disks and, 1366–1367
  virtual disks and controllers, 1367–1368
  virtual disks for shared storage, 568
  virtual machine (guest) partition,
    1357–1359
  virtual machines, 1377
  virtual switches, 1374
  virtualization of DCs. *See* DCs (domain
    controllers), virtualizing
  what's new, 1345–1352
  working with console, 1363–1364
  working with VLANs, 1392–1393
  write-back cache and, 591
Hyper-V port, NIC Teaming options, 153
Hyper-V Replica. *See* HVR (Hyper-V Replica)
hypervisor. *See also* Hyper-V
  boot process of, 1355
  deploying Hyper-V and, 1352–1354
  files, 1355–1356
  hypervisor, 1357
  interface, 1357

I

ICA (Independent Computing Architecture),
  1448
ICMP echo
  ping and, 1058
  traceroute and, 1059–1060
IDE controllers, for virtual disks, 1368
idle worker processes, new features in IIS
  8.0, 980
IDs (identifiers), VMs, 1407–1408

IEAK (Internet Explorer Administration Kit),
  1326
IEEE (Institute of Electrical and Electronics
  Engineers), 165
IETF (Internet Engineering Task Force), 147
IIS (Internet Information Services)
  adding services to Web Server role,
    986–988
  adding SMTP Server Tools feature,
    1009–1010
  adding Web Server role, 981–985
  advanced administration with, 1016–1017
  altering, 986
  authentication of SMTP services, 1011
  backing up and restoring data, 1023–1024
  changes in Windows Server 2012, 15–17
  code access security, 1021
  configuring modules at site level,
    989–991
  creating SSL certificates, 543–544
  creating web pages, 995
  delegation of administrations,
    1007–1008
  installing and configuring SMTP,
    1008–1009
  installing IIS 8, 981
  installing IIS 8 with PowerShell, 985
  integrating FTP into web pages,
    1013–1016
  logs, 1022–1023
  managing modules with PowerShell, 989
  overview of, 979
  permissions, 1020–1021
  registering native modules, 988
  remote management services, 1017–1019
  setting up anonymous accounts,
    1005–1006
  setting up SMTP Server, 1010
  setting up web server, 58–59
  virtual SMTP Servers and domains,
    1010–1011
  what's new, 979–981
  WMSVC (Web Management Services),
    1017
IIS Manager
  configuring modules at site level,
    989–991
  configuring websites, 1001–1002
  constructing websites, 995–1000
  installing and configuring SMTP,
    1008–1009
  invoking SSL protection for websites,
    1022
  managing logging options, 1022–1023
  managing multiple websites, 1006
  permissions, 1020–1021
  registering native modules, 988
  setting up websites, 994–995
IKEv2 (Internet Key Exchange version 2)
  configuring VPN ports, 1109
  configuring VPN servers, 1105–1106
  overview of, 1068
images, Windows OSs, 1442
IMAGEX command, managing WIM files, 95

implicit deny
  defined, 668
  overview of, 669
  share and NTFS supporting, 667
Import tab, adding server to local Server
  Manager, 663
importing
  custom event views, 1491–1492
  security templates, 498–499
  VMs (virtual machines), 1407–1410
incremental zone transfers (IXFR), 223
Independent Computing Architecture (ICA),
  1448
indexed sequential access manager (ISAM),
  1571–1572
information events, event levels, 1486
Infrastructure Operations Master role
  identifying, 1165
  placing, 1218
inheritance
  configuring file and folder permissions,
    1283
  Group Policy and, 469
  of permissions, 720
  policies for enforcing or blocking, 486
Initial Configuration Tasks utility, 45
in-place upgrade
  defined, 1244
  overview of, 334, 1245
  preparing for, 1245
  prepping forest, schema, and domain
    for, 337–338
  pros/cons of, 339, 1249
  repadmin command for verifying DC
    health, 336–337
  requirements, 336
  running Setup, 338
  steps in, 337
  upgrade paths by Windows Server
    version, 335
  from Windows 2008 R2, 1246–1248
input devices
  setting up during clean install, 24
  Windows Server 2012 requirements, 21
install image, WSIM (Windows System Image
  Manager), 88
installation media
  DVD or ISO image, 24
  for RODCs, 1178
Installation Type page, Add Roles and
  Features Wizard, 653
installation types
  choosing during clean install, 27
  choosing during upgrade install, 37, 39
  overview of, 26
installing
  Active Directory, 257
  AD CS role, 1092
  AD DS role, 280
  AD FS role, 539–543
  ADK (Assessment and Deployment Kit),
    82–85
  ADMT (Active Directory Migration
    Tool), 353–354, 1265

BranchCache, 655–656
certificate on VPN clients, 1096–1097
DCs (domain controllers), 277–278
DFS management tool, 323
DHCP failover, 206–209
DirectAccess, 1112–1118
DNS (Domain Name Services), 214
DNS and GCs for domains, 265, 281–282, 284
encryption features for role services, 655–656
GPMC (Group Policy Management console), 509
Hyper-V, 1359–1363
IPAM client features, 182
IPAM server features, 180–181
NAT (network address translator), 1047–1050
Network Policy and Access Services role, 1069–1070
NFS server role, 754
OSs (operating systems), 23
printer drivers, 843–844
Remote Access role, 1071–1072
Remote Desktop Services role, 897–903
RODCs (read-only domain controllers), 1174, 1181–1182
roles, 64–66
roles using scripts, 66–69
RSAT (Remote Server Administration Tools), 924–925
Server for NFS, 753
Sever Core, 106–108
SMTP (Simple Mail Transfer Protocol), 1008–1009
SPA (Server Performance Advisor) 3.0, 170–172
updates, 116–117
VMs (virtual machines), 1388–1390
Windows Server Backup, 1419–1421, 1556–1557
WMSVC (Web Management Services), 1017–1019
Work Folders, 1319
WSUS role, 1537–1539
installing IIS 8
adding Web Server role, 981–985
overview of, 981
with PowerShell, 985
installing Windows Server 2012
64-bit support, 22
clean install. *See* clean install
installation requirements, 20–21
OS installation, 23
overview of, 19
unattended installation. *See* unattended installation
upgrade install. *See* upgrade install
what has changed, 19–20
Institute of Electrical and Electronics Engineers (IEEE), 165
Integrated Scripting Environment (ISE), 290–292
Integration Services
guest (virtual machine) partition and, 1358

save-state procedure for VMs, 1422
upgrading for VMs, 1390–1392
IntelliMirror, 1307
internal virtual switches, 1374
Internet
support for external DNS domains, 245
Windows Server 2012 requirements, 21
Internet Engineering Task Force (IETF), 147
Internet Explorer
customizing, 1326
Group Policy restricting, 500–501
launching RemoteApp application, 1462–1464
managing, 1325
Internet Explorer Administration Kit (IEAK), 1326
Internet Information Services. *See* IIS (Internet Information Services)
Internet Key Exchange version 2. *See* IKEv2 (Internet Key Exchange version 2)
Internet Printing Protocol (IPP), 832
Internet Small Computer System Interface. *See* iSCSI (Internet Small Computer System Interface)
Internet Small Computer System Interface (iSCSI)
File and Storage Services role of iSCSI Target Server, 653
options for shared storage, 575
overview of, 562–563
Inter-site Topology Generator (ISTG)
defined, 1127
functions of, 1144
Intra-site Automatic Tunnel Addressing Protocol (ISATAP)
global query block list and, 242
transitioning to IPv6 and, 149
IP (Internet Protocol). *See also* TCP/IP
reliability of, 1026
site links and, 1138
VPN settings, 1086
IP Address Management. *See* IPAM (IP Address Management)
IP addresses
adding Mac OS X client to domain and, 971
adding new printers by, 836
benefits of IPv6, 148
blocks of IP address spaces, 191
changing network properties, 48–50
checking local area connections, 938–939
classes, 1034–1035
client-side requirements and, 931
computers acting as host and router, 1030–1033
configuring DHCP service, 134–135
DirectAccess requirements, 1112
dynamic IP address restrictions in IIS 8.0, 979
identifying active interfaces, 1026
inventorying, 193
managing IP addresses with IPAM, 191–193
managing virtual IP addresses with IPAM, 193–196

manually adding printers, 841–842
manually configuring local area connection, 941–942
post upgrade tasks, 342
server configuration for single-domain forest, 263
tracking, 199
verifying local area connection settings, 933–934
VPN settings, 1086
weak send and weak receive, 1061–1062
when no routing required, 1027–1028
IP filters, 1085
IP headers, 1027
IP packets
overview of, 1025–1027
when no routing required, 1027–1028
IP routing
ALGs (Application Layer Gateways), 1047
broadcast addresses and, 1035–1036
chat tunneling with `portproxy`, 1056–1057
checking configuration with `ipconfig`, 1060
CIDR (Classless Inter-Domain Routing), 1039
computers acting as host and router, 1030–1033
creating routers, 1055–1056
debugging, 1057–1058
installing NATs, 1047–1050
IP address classes and, 1034–1035
IP packets and, 1025–1027
NAPT and PAT and, 1045–1047
overview of, 1025
post-configuration work on NATs, 1050–1055
private addresses, 1036–1037
routing tables, 1033–1034
showing routing and neighbors, 1060
subnetting and supernetting, 1037–1038
subnetting by RFC, 1038–1039
TCP and, 1040–1042
TCP sockets and ports, 1042–1044
testing remote computer with `ping`, 1058–1059
testing remote computer with `traceroute`, 1059–1060
troubleshooting with Network Monitor, 1060–1062
tunneling and, 1056
Winsock, 1045
IP Security (IPSec)
DirectAccess and, 1110
L2TP and, 1067, 1086
IPAM (IP Address Management)
adding server groups, 198
changes in Windows Server 2012, 11
choosing servers for managing, 185–189
components, 178–179
configuring events, 198
configuring provisioning methods, 182–184

configuring server discovery, 184–185
delegation, 199–203
installing client feature, 182
installing server feature, 180–181
managing DHCP scope, 196–197
managing IP address space, 191–193
managing virtual IP address space, 193–196
monitoring DNS zones, 197–198
overview of, 175–176
Overview view, 190
requirements, 177–178
retrieving server data, 189
Server Inventory view, 190–191
topology deployment options, 179–180
tracking IP Addresses, 199
troubleshooting, 203–204
IPAM administrators, 200
IPAM ASM Administrators, 200
IPAM IP Audit Administrators, 200
IPAM MSM Administrators, 200
IPAM users, 200
IPC$ share, 675
ipconfig
checking configuration, 1060
checking local area connections, 937
displaying/flushing DNS cache, 234–235
IPP (Internet Printing Protocol), 832
IPSec (IP Security)
DirectAccess and, 1110
L2TP and, 1067, 1086
IPv4
ARP (Address Resolution Protocol) and, 1028–1029
changing network properties, 48–50
checking local area connections, 938
client-side requirements, 930
configuring VPN server properties, 1104–1105
creating private address block, 191–192
creating public address block, 192
defining and placing subnets, 1135
filtering VPN connections, 1085
managing IP address space, 176
manually configuring local area connection, 941–942
showing routing table, 1031
transitioning to IPv6, 148–150
verifying local area connection settings, 933–934
VPN connections and, 1079
weak send and weak receive, 1061–1062
IPv6
benefits of, 148
client-side requirements, 930–931
configuring VPN server properties, 1105
defining and placing subnets, 1135
DHCP failover and, 205
filtering VPN connections, 1085
history of, 147–148
managing IP address space, 176
neighbor discovery in, 1029–1030
transition technologies, 148–150

tunnel commands, 1057
verifying local area connection settings, 934
VPN connections and, 1079
weak send and weak receive, 1061–1062
ISAM (indexed sequential access manager), 1571–1572
ISATAP (Intra-site Automatic Tunnel Addressing Protocol)
global query block list and, 242
transitioning to IPv6 and, 149
iSCI Initiator, 623
iSCI Target Server, 565, 623–624
iSCSI (Internet Small Computer System Interface)
adding iSCSI Target server, 623–624
connecting to iSCSI virtual disk from client side, 628–631
creating iSCSI virtual disk, 624–628
File and Storage Services role of iSCSI Target Server, 653
managing storage with File and Storage Services, 565
not supported in storage pools, 602
options for shared storage, 575
overview of, 562–563, 623
ISE (Integrated Scripting Environment), 290–292
ISO images
creating VMs and, 1381
as installation media, 24
ISTG (Inter-site Topology Generator)
defined, 1127
functions of, 1144
IT service modeling, 1524–1525
item-level targeting, with GPP settings, 508
iteration, in name resolution, 214, 217
IXFR (incremental zone transfers), 223

J

JBOD (just a bunch of disks), 589

K

KCC (Knowledge Consistency Checker), 1126
KDC (Kerberos Distribution Center), 771
Kerberos
authentication service, 241
benefits of replication with FRS, 315
enabling DAC and, 771–774
FRS requirements and dependencies, 317
logon settings, 400
setting up NFS shares, 633–634
synchronizing domain time, 306
trusts and, 1189–1190
using ticket-granting ticket account on RODCs, 1160
virtualizing DCs and, 1399
Kerberos Distribution Center (KDC), 771
Key Management Service. See KMS (Key Management Service)
keyboards
capturing for use with VMs, 1389
choosing settings during installation, 24–25
working with Hyper-V Actions pane, 1365

keywords, locating published shares by adding, 664–666
KMS (Key Management Service)
activating, 143
managing licenses with, 142–143
pointing clients to, 144
Knowledge Consistency Checker (KCC), 1126
krbtgt account, 1160

L

L2TP (Layer 2 Tunneling Protocol)
configuring ports for VPNs, 1109
IPSec for encryption, 1086
overview of, 1067
laboratory, creating, 102
LACP (Link Aggregation Control Protocol), 153
language settings
adding components to answer file, 93
choosing during installation, 24–25
LANs (local area networks), 1392–1393
laptops, using Offline Files/Client-Side Caching, 697–701
law/legality, when to use multiple-domains, 1193
Layer 2 Tunneling Protocol. See L2TP (Layer 2 Tunneling Protocol)
layout, viewing print layout forms, 845
LBFO (load balancing and failover), 152
LCP (Link Control Protocol), 1107
LDAP (Lightweight Directory Access Protocol)
adding Mac OS X clients to domain, 971
deciding on DCs in remote locations, 1132
DNs (distinguished names) and, 287–288, 1165
looking up data in global catalog, 241–242
WAAD and, 370
LGPOs (local group policy objects)
Administrator and Non-administrator LGPOs, 471–473
local and non-local policies, 470–471
overview of, 470–471
user-specific LGPOs, 473–474
licenses
configuring licensing for RD session host or virtualization host, 1473
managing with KMS, 142–143
RDS licensing manager, 1475–1477
RDS licensing mode, 1453–1454
setting user limits on shares, 662
life-cycle management, of DFS, 750–751
Lightweight Directory Access Protocol. See LDAP (Lightweight Directory Access Protocol)
Line Printer Daemon (LPD), 832
Line Printer Remote (LPR), 832
line-of-business (LOB), networking QoS, 160
Link Aggregation Control Protocol (LACP), 153
Link Control Protocol (LCP), 1107

Linux
    enhanced support for Linux VMs in
        Hyper-V, 1350
    NFS shares and, 631
List Folder Contents permissions
    default permissions of Users group, 724
    in list of molecular permissions, 720
    NTFS permissions, 667
listeners, creating, 124–126
live migration
    benefits of, 1412–1414
    clustering benefits, 570
    enhancing, 1417
    overview of, 1412
    Shared Nothing Live Migration (cluster-
        free), 1414–1417
    vs. quick migration, 1414
    what's new in Hyper-V, 1347–1348
Live Storage Migration, 1414–1415
LMHOSTS file
    configuring DNS clients, 235
    hostname resolution and, 233
load balancing
    DHCP failover and, 207
    dynamic, 154
    LBFO (load balancing and failover), 152
    network load balancer. See NLB (network
        load balancer)
    round-robin approach, 229
LOB (line-of-business), networking QoS, 160
local area connection
    checking in Windows 7, 939–941
    checking in Windows 8, 935–937
    manually configuring in Windows 7,
        941–942
    manually configuring in Windows 8,
        937–938
    verifying, 933–935
local area networks (LANs), 1392–1393
local group policy objects. See LGPOs (local
    group policy objects)
local groups
    adding domain user account to, 943
    adding members to, 414–418, 419–422
    creating, 413–414
    creating from command line, 419
    overview of, 413
    removing users from, 422–423
Local Resources tab, RDC (Remote Desktop
    Connection), 891–892
local storage, home directories vs., 1277–1280
local user accounts
    configuring, 388
    connecting clients to network, 931–932
    creating from command line, 382
    creating with Computer Management,
        378–381
    dial-in settings, 395
    environment settings, 391–392
    membership settings, 389
    profile settings, 389–391
    remote control settings, 393–395
    session settings, 392–393
localhost, class A addresses and, 1036

lockout policies. See account lockout policies
logical unit numbers (LUNs), iSCSI and, 623
logoff scripts, 1336–1337
logon
    as administrator, 31
    changing passwords at, 953–954
    controlling with Group Policy, 487
    domain user settings, 397–401
    executing commands at, 1331–1334
    local user settings, 380
    processing with NETLOGON share,
        675–676
    to RODCs, 1156
    trusts and, 1226
    user names and, 386
logon scripts
    associating multiple logon scripts with
        users, 1334–1335
    eliminating, 509
    for executing commands at logon,
        1331–1334
    managing with Group Policy, 1335–1336
    specifying with Group Policy, 488–490
logs/logging
    Applications and Services Logs folder,
        1493
    checking for errors in application log,
        1288
    configuring event logs, 1493–1494
    configuring VPN server properties,
        1107–1108
    displaying saved log files, 1495
    filtering, 1489–1490
    IIS (Internet Information Services) and,
        981, 1022–1023
    online logging, 593
    operational logs, 517
    saving log files, 1494–1495
    selecting events to log, 1498–1499
    subscribing to event logs, 1495–1498
    verifying swing migration, 1257
    Windows logs, 1492–1493
    XML-based logs, 1491–1492
loopback communication, class A addresses
    and, 1036
LPD (Line Printer Daemon), 832
LPR (Line Printer Remote), 832
LUNs (logical unit numbers), iSCSI and, 623

M

MAC (Media Access Control) addresses
    creating virtual switches, 1377
    Neighbor Advertisement message and,
        1029
    when no routing required, 1027–1028
Mac OS X clients
    adding network printer for, 974
    connecting to file shares, 973
    connecting to network, 969–971
    joining domains, 971–973
    using Remote Desktop from, 974–976
machine. See also computers
    roaming profiles and machine settings,
        1301

    securing data by machine attributes,
        766–767
mail exchanger (MX) records, DNS, 230
maintenance, of domains, 297–298
malware protection, VMs (virtual machines),
    1421–1422
Managed Service Accounts (MSA), 415
management OS partition, Hyper-V
    hosting function of, 1353
    overview of, 1354–1357
management packs (MPs), 1525
mandatory profiles. See also profiles
    changing permissions HKEY_CURRENT_
        USE hive, 1295–1298
    cleaning up older profiles with Group
        Policy, 1301
    configuring, 1297–1298
    creating, 1293–1294
    local user settings, 394
    overview of, 1293
    securing folder for, 1297–1298
Map Network Drive dialog, 965
mapping drives, 673, 964–966
masks, subnet, 1037–1038
member servers
    preparing for swing migration, 1250
    preparing to promote, 340
    promoting, 341–342, 1251–1254
    security boundaries and, 1186
membership
    in AD groups, 429
    creating groups with ADAC and, 447
    domain users, 405–406
    in local groups, 414–418
    local users, 389
memory
    capacity planning for HVR, 1424
    for RDS Server, 1445
message authentication, DHCP failover and,
    207
metadata
    federation metadata, 534–535
    print documents and, 831
metrics, performance, 167
microkernelization, of Hyper-V, 1353
Microsoft
    Better Together marketing campaigns,
        690
    CEIP (Customer Experience
        Improvement Program), 83
    NIC Teams. See NIC Teaming
    patch management, 1552–1553
    synchronizing updates, 1543
Microsoft Baseline Security Analyzer, 1553
Microsoft CHAP (MS-CHAP), 1098–1099
Microsoft Deployment Toolkit 2012
    cloning solutions for unattended
        installations, 81
    flexibility of desktop and, 1268
Microsoft Point-to-Point Encryption (MPPE),
    1086
Microsoft Security Assessment Tool,
    1552–1553
Microsoft Security Compliance Manager, 1553

Microsoft Security Response Center (MSRC), 1553
Microsoft Update, 1543, 1552
Microsoft Update Catalog, 1552
migration
    live migration feature in Hyper-V, 1347–1348
    options for VMs, 1362, 1411–1414
    of printers from one server to another, 861–862
    Shared Nothing Live Migration (cluster-free), 1414–1417
migration, of Active Directory. *See also* ADMT
  (Active Directory Migration Tool)
    to DFS-R, 318–319
    domain migration, 354–355, 1258–1261
    intra-forest migration, 344
    moving computer accounts, 366–367
    moving users and groups, 357–362
    overview of, 1243
    in-place upgrade, 1245
    post swing migration tasks, 1254
    preparing for upgrade, 1245
    prepping domain controller for swing migration, 1250
    prepping forest, schema, and domain for swing migration, 1250
    promoting member server for swing migration, 1251–1254
    pros/cons of in-place upgrades, 1249
    repurposing hardware following swing migration, 1255
    strategies, 1243–1244
    swing migration, 1249–1250
    swing migration from Windows Server 2003, 1255–1257
    testing resource access for migrated groups, 363–364
    transition states in migration to DFS-R, 320
    upgrade capabilities, 1244–1245
    upgrading from 2008 R2, 1246–1248
migration of Active Directory, to DFS-R
    to eliminated state, 328–331
    overview of, 318–319
    process of, 322–325
    raising domain functional levels, 321–322
    to redirected state, 326–328
    transition states in, 320
Minimum Bandwidth feature
    DCB (Data Center Bridge) and, 163
    networking QoS and, 161
mirroring, determining layout of virtual disks, 607–608, 610
MMC (Microsoft Management Console)
    snap-ins
      accessing LGPOs, 471–472
      administering firewall from, 119
      managing DHCP service, 121–122
      managing remotely with, 120–122
      monitoring and managing DHCP and DNS servers, 196–197
      Windows Backup Server and, 1556
Modify permissions
    applying, 723

    in list of molecular permissions, 719
    NTFS, 667
modules, PowerShell
    Active Directory module, 289–290, 451
    configuring at site level, 989–991
    managing, 989
    networking module, 150–151
    registering native, 988
molecular permissions
    list of, 716–717
    overview of, 719–720
monitoring
    DNS server, 248–249
    RDS (Remote Desktop Services), 1472–1473
Monitoring Windows Server 2012 R2
    adding servers for management by Server Manager, 1480
    with Best Practices Analyzers, 1483–1484
    creating server group, 1481
    monitoring with server group, 1481–1483
    overview of, 1479
    performance monitoring. *See* performance monitoring
    system monitoring. *See* Event Viewer
mouse
    capturing for use with VMs, 1389
    working with Hyper-V Actions pane, 1365
MPIO (Multipath Input/Output), 571
MPPE (Microsoft Point-to-Point Encryption), 1086
MPs (management packs)
    exploring Windows Server Base OS MP, 1526
    overview of, 1525
    for Windows Server 2012 R2, 1525–1526
MSA (Managed Service Accounts), 415
MS-CHAP (Microsoft CHAP), 1098–1099
msra command, sending Remote Assistance request, 918
MSRC (Microsoft Security Response Center), 1553
mstsc command, launching RDC with, 895–896
multicast addresses, in IPv6, 1029
multiforest domains. *See* domains, with two DCs
Multilink
    VPN clients and, 1084–1085
    VPN servers and, 1107
multimaster replication
    overview of, 1186–1187
    vs. single-master replication, 1209–1210
Multipath Input/Output (MPIO), 571
multiple-domain design, in Active Directory
    creating second domain, 1200–1204
    namespace for multiple-domain design, 1198–1199
    overview of, 1198
    preparing DC for second domain, 1199–1300
    when to use, 1193–1194
Multi-Server Management and Monitoring, IPAM components, 178–179

MX (mail exchanger) records, DNS, 230
My Documents
    folder redirection and, 1313
    named folders in user profile, 1281
My Music, named folders in user profile, 1281

N

name resolution. *See also* DNS (Domain Name Services)
    hostname resolution, 232–235
    managing, 232
    methods for, 217
    resolving external names, 246–248
name server (NS) records, DNS, 232
name servers. *See also* DNS servers, 212
named pipes, IPC$ share used by, 675
namespace
    defined, 212
    managing with DNS zones, 221
    for multiple-domain designs, 1198–1199
naming standards
    AD groups, 428
    new shares, 659
NAP (Network Access Protection)
    DirectAccess and, 1111
    services provided by Network Policy and Access Services role, 1068–1069
NAPT (network address/port translator)
    ALGs (Application Layer Gateways) and, 1047
    overview of, 1045–1046
    unintended consequences, 1046–1047
NAS (Network Attached Storage), 561
NAT (network address translator)
    capabilities of Routing service, 1070
    DirectAccess and, 1111
    installing, 1047–1050
    L2TP/IPSec and, 1067
    NAPT (network address/port translator) and, 1046
    post-configuration work, 1050–1055
    routing TCP traffic, 1025
    tunneling and, 1056
navigation nodes, ADAC navigation pane, 441–442
neighbor discovery
    in IPv6, 1029–1030
    showing routing and neighbors, 1060
net share command
    migrating to eliminated state and, 329–330
    migrating to redirected state and, 327–328
    sharing folders, 139
    verifying sharing of SYSVOL, 321, 323
net stop ntds, stopping AD DS, 1582
.NET trust levels, 1021–1022
net use command
    handling credential conflicts for shares, 674
    searching for shares in Active Directory, 674
    using on WAN, 674–675
net user command, changing administrator password, 110–111

`net view` command, accessing file shares, 111
NetBIOS Naming System
    configuring clients, 236
    configuring stand-alone DNS server, 214
    GlobalNames feature and, 242–243
    hostname resolution and, 232–234
    joining domains and, 942
    name conflicts and, 1199
`NetDiag` command
    post upgrade tasks, 342
    verifying domain services following migration, 1254
`netdom` command
    adding servers to domains, 53–54
    creating machine account in domain, 1237–1239
    creating trusts, 1239–1240
    joining computers to domain, 305
    managing domains, 304–306
    options, 306
    querying FSMO roles, 309
    renaming computers, 305
    renaming servers, 53
    verifying swing migration, 1257
`netlogon` service
    connecting to, 675–676
    DDNS requests, 241
    executing commands at logon, 1331–1334
    troubleshooting DNS and, 302
    validating credentials, 1133
netmasks
    netmask ordering, 229
    subnets and, 1037–1038
`netsh` command
    configuring DHCP service, 133–135
    configuring firewall for NFS, 756
    managing IPv6, 150
    `netsh advfirewall firewall set rule`, 118–119
    overview of, 1031
    showing IPv6 routing table, 1032
    showing neighbors table, 1029–1030
`netstat` command, 1043
Network Access Protection (NAP)
    DirectAccess and, 1111
    services provided by Network Policy and Access Services role, 1068–1069
network adapters
    managing virtual hardware, 1385–1387
    PowerShell networking modules, 151
network address translator. *See* NAT (network address translator)
network address/port translator. *See* NAPT (network address/port translator)
Network applet, adding network printer with, 962
Network Attached Storage (NAS), 561
Network Auditing, IPAM components, 179
Network Connectivity Status module, PowerShell, 151
Network File System. *See* NFS (Network File System)
network folder, creating, 966–968

network interface cards. *See* NICs (network interface cards)
Network Level Authentication (NLA), 885–886, 1453
network load balancer. *See* NLB (network load balancer)
Network Load Balancing Manager, RSAT tools, 924
Network Monitor
    determining which network card to monitor, 1061–1062
    viewing `ping` capture with, 1060–1061
Network Policy and Access Services role
    installing, 1069–1070
    notification, 901, 908
    RSAT tools, 923
    services provided by, 1068–1069
Network Policy Server. *See* NPS (Network Policy Server)
Network Printer Installation Wizard, 141
network printers
    adding for Mac OS X clients, 974
    adding for Windows clients, 961–964
    automatically detecting, 837–840
    connecting to, 955–956
network protocols, client-side requirements, 930
network resources
    connecting clients to network resources, 955–956
    publishing network resources with GPOs, 956–957
Network Security module, PowerShell, 151
Network Switch Team module, PowerShell, 151
Network Time Protocol (NTP)
    synchronizing domain time, 307
    synchronizing server clocks, 206
Network Transition module, PowerShell, 151
Network Unlock, BitLocker, 693
networking
    802.lX authentication, 165
    BranchCache and, 165–167
    changes in Windows Server 2012, 11
    changing network properties, 46–50
    client-side requirements, 930
    configuring connectivity, 43
    configuring network settings, 114–115
    configuring NIC Teaming, 155–159
    connecting clients to network. *See* clients, connecting to network
    creating network folder, 966–968
    DCB (Data Center Bridge) and QoS, 161–163
    default network profile, 1299–1300
    detecting network printers, 837–840
    Group Policy and QoS, 164–165
    Hyper-V and QoS, 163
    IPAM support, 178
    IPv6 and, 147–148
    managing performance, 167–168
    Minimum Bandwidth feature, 161
    NIC Team configuration options, 152–154
    Offline Files reducing traffic on, 698

    overview of, 147
    `Perfmon.exe` tool, 168–169
    planning deployment of AD FS and, 539
    PowerShell modules, 150–151
    publishing network resources with GPOs, 956–957
    QoS (Quality of Service) enhancements, 160
    RDS Server and, 1446
    searching for network printers, 836
    SPA (Server Performance Advisor), 169–172
    transitioning to IPv6, 148–150
    verifying configuration, 932–933
New Share Wizard, 657–660, 699–701
New Trust Wizard
    ADDT (Active Directory Domains and Trusts), 1230, 1232–1236, 1263
    establishing trust between domains prior to migration, 349–351
`New-ADUser` command
    assigning CSV values to user account, 456
    creating user accounts, 448, 452–453
NFS (Network File System)
    connecting to NFS shares from client side, 635
    creating NFS shares with Server Manager, 658
    creating shared folders, 753–754
    File and Storage Services role of, 652
    installing NFS server role, 753–754
    managing storage with File and Storage Services, 565
    new PowerShell cmdlets for, 652
    overview of, 751
    quick setup of NFS shares, 632–635
    services of, 751–752
    setting up firewall, 755–756
    when to use NFS shares, 631
NFS shares
    connecting to from client side, 635
    creating shared folders, 753–754
    creating with Server Manager, 658
    quick setup, 632–635
    when to use NFS shares, 631
NIC Teaming
    changes in Windows Server 2012, 11
    configuration modes, 152–154
    configuring, 155–159
    online resources for, 154
    overview of, 152
    PowerShell networking modules, 151
NICs (network interface cards)
    changing network properties, 46–47
    client-side requirements, 930
    continuous availability and, 567–568
    creating virtual switches, 1375–1377
    hardware requirements for Hyper-V, 1344
    installing Hyper-V and, 1360–1362
    SANs and, 562
    supported by NIC Teaming, 154
    verifying network configuration, 932–933
    virtual switches, 1374

VPN servers, 1066
    working with VLANs, 1392–1393
NLA (Network Level Authentication),
    885–886, 1453
NLB (network load balancer)
    AD FS networking requirements, 539
    DirectAccess and, 1111
    key components of AD FS, 535
nodes, cluster
    adding first, 575–585
    adding second, 585–587
    overview of, 566
Non-Uniform Memory Architecture (NUMA)
    scalability of multiprocessor VMs, 1384
    working with Hyper-V Actions pane,
        1365
Notepad, editing text files, 112
Notification Limits, File Server Resource
    Manager, 687
notifications (warnings), viewing post-
    deployment tasks, 1170
NPS (Network Policy Server)
    configuring network access policies,
        1074–1076
    creating network policy, 1086–1089
    HCAP and, 1078
    services provided by Network Policy and
        Access Services role, 1068–1069
NS (name server) records, DNS, 232
NsLookup tool
    querying DNS servers, 1058
    reverse lookup of network names, 227
    testing resolution of global name, 243
    troubleshooting DNS, 250–252
    verifying DNS during swing migration,
        340
NT File System (NTFS). See NTFS (NT File
    System)
ntdsutil.exe
    creating installation media, 283–284, 1178
    creating snapshots of AD DS database,
        1573–1574
    decommissioning DCs and, 300
    defragmenting Active Directory offline,
        1570–1571
    moving FSMO roles, 309
    stopping AD DS, 1582
NTFS (NT File System)
    choosing file system when creating
        volumes, 616–617
    data deduplication support, 637
    FRS requirements and dependencies, 317
    ReFS compared with, 265
NTFS permissions. See also permissions ·
    assigning, 720–725, 761–764
    atomic permissions, 717–719
    combining share permissions and, 671–672
    comparing with share permissions, 667
    conflicts among permissions, 728
    creating shares with Server Manager, 660
    Deny permissions, 728–730
    deploying DAC policies and, 792
    detailed interface for working with,
        728–732

effective permissions, 730–732
folder permissions, 1275–1276
inherited permissions, 720
least privilege rules, 804
managing, 666–667
modifying, 669–671
molecular permissions, 719–720
overview of, 715
ownership of, 732
removing users or groups, 727
security templates and, 493
types of, 715–717
viewing atomic permissions, 726
viewing user rights, 725–726
website global settings and, 992
NTP (Network Time Protocol)
    synchronizing domain time, 307
    synchronizing server clocks, 206
ntuser.dat file
    configuring super mandatory profiles,
        1297–1298
    HKEY_CURRENT_USE hive, 1281, 1295–1297
NUMA (Non-Uniform Memory Architecture)
    scalability of multiprocessor VMs, 1384
    working with Hyper-V Actions pane, 1365

O

objects
    Active Directory, 259
    auditing access to, 868–869
    deploying profiles by editing single user
        object, 1286–1287
    domain account settings, 406–407
    editing attributes of, 408–410
    Group Policy. See GPOs (Group Policy
        Objects)
    local GPOs. See LGPOs (local group
        policy objects)
    password-settings. See PSO (password-
        settings objects)
    Performance Monitor, 1509
    recovering from recycle bin, 1578–1579
    renaming or deleting, 411–412
    searching for, 438–440
Office 365, 595
offline files
    creating shares with Server Manager, 659
    enabling on server, 699–701
    how it works, 698–699
    managing, 1324–1325
    overview of, 697–698
    using BranchCache, 699
online self-healing, 592
online verification, with Spot Verifier service,
    592–593
OPC (Open Packaging Conventions), 831
operating systems. See OSs (operating
    systems)
operational logs
    Applications and Services Logs folder,
        1493
    troubleshooting Group Policy, 517
Operations Manager. See SCOM (System
    Center Operations Manager)

Operations Master roles. See FSMO (Flexible
    Single Master Operations) roles
OpsMgr. See SCOM (System Center
    Operations Manager)
Orchestrator, core products in System Center
    2012 R2, 1524
organizational units. See OUs (organizational
    units)
OSs (operating systems)
    checking OS version and build, 35
    Hyper-V in client OSs, 1345
    installing, 23
    legacy OSs and virtualization, 1342
    OS Role Services in IIS 8.0, 981–984
    ReFS (Resilient File System) and, 265
    SMB version in relation to OS version, 690
    WSUS clients and, 1532
    WSUS support for, 1544
OUs (organizational units)
    ADMT migration and, 359
    applying GPOs to, 468
    choosing OU vs. domain, 1197
    creating for groups, 385, 522–523
    creating for users, 385
    creating with ADAC, 286–288
    creating with PowerShell, 288–289
    defined, 259–260
    delegating ability to reset passwords,
        523–525
    delegating control using, 297, 521–522
    DNs (distinguished names) and, 288
    linking GPOs to, 1147
    managing with Group Policy, 285
    moving user accounts to, 522
    restoring, 5
Overview view, IPAM, 190
ownership, NTFS permissions, 732

P

P2V (Physical to Virtual), testing upgrade
    process, 1244
Packet Scheduler, QoS (Quality of Service),
    933
PAL (Performance Analysis of Logs)
    overview of, 1519
    prerequisites and installation, 1520
    working with, 1520–1523
PAP (Password Authentication Protocol),
    1098–1099
parallelized repair, 591
paravirtualized guest. See also guest (virtual
    machine) partition, 1357
parity
    determining layout of virtual disks,
        607–608, 610
    RAID and, 572
partitions
    of AD database, 1187
    answer file installation and, 94
    COM+ settings, 403–404
    creating application partitions, 240
    creating primary partition, 136–137
    implementing BitLocker on, 694
    installing Server Core and, 107

listing available, 226
setting up disk drives during clean install, 27–29
Passive screening, file screens, 684
passphrases, 381
pass-through disks, types of VHDs, 1367
Password Authentication Protocol (PAP), 1098–1099
password encryption service (PES), 353–354, 1262, 1265
password replication policy, for RODCs
  Allowed RODC Password Replication group, 1160–1161
  Denied RODC Password Replication group, 1159–1160
  modifying Allowed RODC Password Replication group, 1176–1177
  overview of, 1157–1159
  viewing RODC properties, 1174–1176
passwords
  ADMT migration and, 359
  changes to Active Directory, 77
  changing administrator password, 110–111
  changing at first logon, 953–954
  changing domain user password, 951–952
  changing in BitLocker, 693
  changing on demand, 954
  configuring host session properties, 904
  creating accounts and, 380, 444
  delegating ability to reset, 523–525
  DSRM (Directory Services Restore Mode) and, 273–274, 1171
  enabling BitLocker, 696
  enabling BitLocker To Go, 697
  fine-grained policies, 310–313
  improvements to AD password policy, 4
  logon settings, 399–400
  managing account lockout policies and, 435–436
  managing from command line, 382
  passphrases as alternative to, 381
  PES (password encryption file), 353–354, 1262, 1265
  policies, 951
  replication settings for domain user accounts, 406
  resetting administrator passwords, 505–508
  resetting user passwords, 434–435
  resetting with ADAC, 438
  RODCs and, 1156–1157
  security boundaries and, 1186
  setting administrator password, 30
  setting password policies, 502–504
  setting with PowerShell, 453–455
  unlocking BitLocker-protected drive, 693–694
password-settings objects. *See* PSO (password-settings objects)
patch management
  CAU (Cluster-Aware Updating) and, 1551–1552

deploying patches, 1268
  as malware protection, 1422
  Microsoft tools for, 1552–1553
  overview of, 1531
  SCCM (System Center Configuration Manager), 1553
  WSUS (Windows Software Update Services). *See* WSUS (Windows Software Update Services)
PC clients, RDS and
  hardware, 1447
  overview of, 1448–1449
  support for, 1436–1437
PDC (primary domain controller)
  migrating to DFS-R, 318
  synchronizing domain time and, 306–308
  types of domain controllers, 221
PDC Emulator role
  overview of, 1219
  time synchronization for multiple-domain designs, 1223–1226
PDF (Portable Document Format), 831
PEAP (Protected EAP). *See also* EAP (Extensible Authentication Protocol), 1098–1099
perfmon command. *See also* Performance Monitor
  accessing Performance Monitor, 1508
  networking and, 168–169
performance
  BitLocker provisioning for, 692–693
  NFS services and, 751
  viewing role performance, 75
performance, network
  managing, 167–168
  perfmon command, 168–169
  SPA (Server Performance Advisor), 169–172
Performance Analysis of Logs. *See* PAL (Performance Analysis of Logs)
performance counters
  configuring performance monitoring for AD FS, 552–555
  disk performance and, 272
  list of AD FS counters, 555
  network performance and, 168–169
  performance counter log as PAL target, 1520
  in Performance Monitor, 1509
  RDC (Remote Desktop Connection) features, 907
Performance Monitor
  creating baselines, 1514–1516
  data collector sets, 1510–1511
  networking and, 168–169
  overview of, 1508–1509
  system data collector sets, 1511
  viewing RDS sessions, 1446–1447
performance monitoring
  configuring AD FS for, 552–555
  data collector sets, 1510–1511
  overview of, 1507–1508
  with PAL, 1519–1523
  with Performance Monitor, 1508–1509

with PerfView, 1523
  with Reliability Monitor, 1510
  reports and data retention and, 1517–1519
  with Resource Monitor, 1509–1510
  with server groups, 1482
  with System Center 2012 R2, 1523–1528
  system data collector sets, 1511–1513
  tools, 1508
  user-defined data collector sets, 1513–1517
PerfView, 1523
permissions
  for accessing printers, 866–867
  ADAC tips and, 448
  Allow and Deny, 667–668, 715
  assigning folder permissions, 137–139
  assigning NTFS permissions, 720–725
  atomic, 717–719
  C&P migration and, 345
  centralizing control of, 767–768
  changes to RMS (Rights Management Services), 7–8
  combining share and NTFS permissions, 671–672
  comparing share and NTFS permissions, 667
  configuring access denied assistance, 796–799
  configuring host session properties, 905
  creating share permissions, 711–712
  creating share permissions manually, 1290–1291
  cumulative nature of, 668, 865
  default file and folder permissions, 754
  defining share permissions, 712–714
  delegating printers, 867
  delegating RODCs, 1161
  delegation of, 407, 860
  Deny taking precedence, 668–669
  deploying DAC policies and, 792
  detailed interface for working with, 728–732
  enforcing Full Control permission, 823
  handling in new domain, 1259
  IIS, 1020–1021
  implicit deny, 669
  inherited, 720
  managing printer security, 859–860
  modifying, 669–671
  molecular permissions, 719–720
  multiple, 668
  for network access policies, 1076
  NTFS permissions, 666–667
  removing users or groups, 728
  Security tab and print permissions, 864–866
  setting folder permissions, 1273, 1279, 1291–1292
  setting manually, 525–529
  setting network access permissions, 1080–1082
  setting up NFS shares and, 635
  share permissions, 667, 1284–1285

troubleshooting access control with
effective permissions, 769
types of, 715–717
understanding, 666
viewing user rights, 725–727
for websites, 1020
personal identification numbers (PINs)
changing in BitLocker, 693
logon settings, 400
PES (password encryption service), 353–354,
1262, 1265
physical disks. *See also* HDDs (hard disk
drives)
bringing offline disks online, 618–619
cmdlets for working with, 597–598
storage pools, 572
in Storage Spaces, 597
viewing, 603–604
physical locations, site terminology, 1126
physical security, BitLocker enhancing, 692
physical server, NIC Teaming on, 154
Physical to Virtual (P2V), testing upgrade
process, 1244
ping command
arguments of, 1058
testing connectivity, 50, 935
testing DNS server, 234
testing remote computer, 1058–1059
viewing ping capture with Network
Monitor, 1061
PINs (personal identification numbers)
changing in BitLocker, 693
logon settings, 400
planning Active Directory
case for two DCs, 1195–1196
connectivity and replication issues in
planning, 1192–1193
design pointers, 1196–1198
empty root design, 1194–1195
overview of, 1191–1192
political issues in planning, 1192
when to use multiple domains, 1193–1194
planning websites, 992–994
PMC (Print Management console)
adding new printers, 836–837
automatically detecting network
printers, 837–840
deleting printers, 837
listing printers in Active Directory,
849–851
managing print jobs, 876–878
manually adding printers, 841–842
setting up print server, 140–142
viewing deployed printers, 856
working with, 834–836
pointer (PTR) records, DNS, 230
Point-to-Point Protocol (PPP)
VPN connections and, 1079
VPN servers and, 1105–1106
Point-to-Point Tunneling Protocol. *See* PPTP
(Point-to-Point Tunneling Protocol)
policies. *See also* Group Policy
configuring file screen, 682–684
creating backup policy, 144–145

creating quota policy, 676
Default Domain Controllers Policy, 260
fine-grained password policies, 310–313
policy-based QoS, 164–165
RD Gateway and, 908
Remote Desktop and, 906
storage usage monitoring vs. quota,
676
policies, DAC
applying, 785–793, 803
Central Access Rule, 781–785, 802–803
creating claim type, 775–777, 800–801
creating resource property, 777–781, 802
overview of, 774–775
testing, 793–796, 803
policies, network access
configuring, 1074–1076, 1084
creating, 1086–1089
rules governing policies and policy
order, 1076–1080
setting constraints, 1082–1083
setting permissions, 1080–1082
political issues, in planning Active Directory,
1192
pools. *See* storage pools
Port tab, printer properties, 863–864
Portable Document Format (PDF), 831
portproxy, chat tunneling with, 1056–1057
ports
attributes TCP adds to IP, 1042
configuring for VPNs, 1109
creating inbound firewall rule, 126–131
creating listeners, 124–126
opening firewall port for NFS, 755–756
RD Gateway and, 907
setting up print server, 140–141
TCP, 1042–1044
ports, printer
adding new printers, 837
managing settings, 844–845
print servers and, 858
working with Print Management
console, 835–836
POST (Power-On Self Test), 24
power supplies, HA (high availability) and,
571
PowerShell
Active Directory and, 289–292
Active Directory module for, 451
applying. *See* commands/cmdlets,
PowerShell
BranchCache and, 166
creating scripts, 290–292
DirectAccess support, 1111
improvements in Windows Server 2012,
6–7
networking and, 150–151
NFS and, 652
RMS and, 79
SMB Windows and, 689
switching between Server Core and
GUI, 109
version 4.0 in Windows Server 2012
R2, 292

PowerShell History Viewer
accessing, 448
fields of, 297
overview of, 78
working in background of ADAC,
448–449
PPP (Point-to-Point Protocol)
VPN connections and, 1079
VPN servers and, 1105–1106
PPTP (Point-to-Point Tunneling Protocol)
configuring ports for VPNs, 1109
MPPE (Microsoft Point-to-Point
Encryption), 1086
overview of, 1067
preferred bridgehead servers
defined, 1128
ISTG designating, 1144–1145
prepared (state 1), migrating to DFS-R,
319
prestaging RODC account
installing prestaged RODC, 1181–1182
overview of, 1179–1181
Primary Computer support, Windows 8 and
Windows 2012, 1317–1318
primary domain controller. *See* PDC (primary
domain controller)
primary read-only zones, DNS, 1183–1184
Print and Document Services role
adding, 117, 832–834
adding print services role to Server Core,
845–847
setting up print server, 140–142
print devices. *See* printers/printing
print jobs, 876–878
Print Management console. *See* PMC (Print
Management console)
print queues, 877–878
print servers
adding/updating drivers, 859
configuring, 857–858
custom filters in managing, 878–879
form settings, 857–858
migration of printers from one server to
another, 861–862
port settings, 858
Print Server service, 832
security management, 859–860
Server Properties, 857
setting up, 140–142
viewing advanced properties, 860–861
working with Print Management
console, 835
working without, 829
print spooler
moving spool folder, 860–861
overview of, 828–829
restarting spooler service as
troubleshooting step, 881
settings, 872–873
PRINT$ share, connecting to, 675
printer drivers
adding/updating, 859
custom filters and, 878
GDI (graphics device interface) and, 832

hunting for correct driver, 830
installing new, 843–844
isolating as troubleshooting step, 881–882
managing, 842–843
overview of, 829–830
setting up print servers, 140–142
working with Print Management console, 835
XPSDrv driver model, 831
Printer Migration Wizard, 861–862
printers/printing
  adding network printer for Mac OS X clients, 974
  adding network printer for Windows clients, 961–964
  adding new printers, 836–837
  adding Print and Document Services role, 832–834
  adding Print and Document Services role to Server Core, 845–847
  adding printers manually, 841–842, 848
  adding printers using Active Directory search, 849–851
  administering with PowerShell cmdlets, 847
  advanced properties, 870–871
  advanced searches, 852
  auditing access to, 867–870
  automatically detecting network printers, 837–840
  availability settings, 871–872
  changes in Windows Server 2012, 14–15
  configuring print servers, 857–858
  connecting to network resources, 955–956
  custom filters in managing printers and print servers, 878–879
  deleting printers, 837
  deploying printers, 847–848
  deploying printers via GPOs, 853–856
  Easy Print feature, 1452
  form settings, 857–858
  GDI (graphics device interface), 832
  managing port settings, 844–845
  managing print jobs, 876–878
  managing print security, 859–860
  managing printer properties, 862
  migrating printers from one server to another, 861–862
  overview of print services, 827–828
  permissions for access control, 866–867
  permissions for delegation, 867
  pooling printers, 863–864
  Port tab, 863–864
  print spooler and, 828–829
  print spooler settings, 872–873
  printer redirection with Easy Print, 891
  priority settings, 872
  searching for printer features, 851
  Security tab, 864–866
  separator pages, 873–876
  Sharing tab, 862–863
  troubleshooting, 879–882
  viewing deployed, 856
  viewing print layout forms, 845

viewing print server advanced properties, 860–861
working with Print Management console, 834–836
priority settings, printer, 872
private addresses, routing and, 1036–1037
private virtual switches, 1375
processors. See CPUs
product key, configuring Server Core, 114
profiles
  changing permissions HKEY_CURRENT_USE hive, 1295–1298
  cleaning up older profiles with Group Policy, 1301
  comparing profile types, 1280
  configuring default network profile, 1299–1300
  configuring super mandatory profiles, 1297–1298
  creating mandatory profiles in Windows 8, 1293–1294
  creating shares with Server Manager, 658
  domain user settings, 401
  local user settings, 389–391, 394
  mandatory, 394, 1293
  redirecting folders to local profile, 1310
  roaming. See roaming profiles
  securing mandatory profile folder on file server, 1297–1298
  translating during ADMT migration, 364–366
programs
  deploying RemoteApp applications via program icon, 1439
  restricting features with Group Policy, 487
Programs tab, RDC (Remote Desktop Connection), 892–893
promoting servers
  to DC, 283
  preparing to promote member server, 340
  promoting member server for swing migration, 1251–1254
  promoting member servers, 341–342
  promoting Windows Server 2012 R2 to RODC, 1168–1173
  to RODCs, 1168–1173
propagation dampening, site replication and, 1126
properties
  changing network properties, 46–50
  classification properties, 806
  configuring group properties, 447–448
  configuring host session properties, 904–905
  configuring new quota, 681
  configuring user properties, 444–445
  configuring VPN server properties, 1102–1108
  enabling offline files on server, 699–701
  File Server Resource Manager, 687–688
  property editor for domain accounts, 404
  RADIUS client for VPNs, 1079

resource, 768, 777–781
RODCs, 1174–1176
setting user limits on shares, 662–663
site link, 1140–1141
system log, 1494
viewing RRAS server port properties, 1109–1110
properties, print servers, 857, 860–861
properties, printer
  advanced properties, 870–871
  auditing access, 867–870
  availability settings, 871–872
  overview of, 870–871
  permissions for access control, 866–867
  permissions for delegation, 867
  Port tab, 863–864
  priority settings, 872
  Security tab, 864–866
  separator pages and, 873–876
  Sharing tab, 862–863
  spooler settings, 872–873
Protected EAP (PEAP). See also EAP (Extensible Authentication Protocol), 1098–1099
provisioning
  BitLocker, 692–693
  IPAM (IP Address Management), 182–184, 186–189
  storage, 186, 572, 597–598
  websites, 991
proxy servers
  accessing with Windows RT, 946
  adding proxy server role to AD FS server, 557–558
  federation server proxy, 535, 539
PSO (password-settings objects)
  creating, 310–311
  improvements to AD password policy, 4
  precedence setting, 312–313
  viewing PSO rules, 311–312
PTR (pointer) records, DNS, 230
Publish RemoteApp Programs Wizard, 1461
publishing
  network resources, 956–957
  Publish RemoteApp Programs Wizard, 1461
  shares, 664–666
  unknown publisher warning, 889

Q

QoS (Quality of Service)
  benefits of IPv6, 148
  DCB (Data Center Bridge), 161–163
  enhancements to networking, 160
  Group Policy, 164–165
  Hyper-V, 163
  Minimum Bandwidth feature, 161
  Packet Scheduler, 933
  PowerShell networking modules, 151
quick migration
  overview of, 1411
  vs. live migration, 1414
Quick share profile options, 658

quorums, clustering and, 570–571
quotas
    configuring file screen policies, 682–684
    creating, 680–682
    generating storage reports, 684–687
    policies for, 676
    templates, 677–680

R

RADIUS (Remote Authentication Dial-In User
    Service)
    comparing RADIUS clients with VPN
        clients, 1081
    configuring network access policies, 1075
    NPS implementation of, 1068
    setting RADIUS client properties for
        VPNs, 1079
RAID (Redundant Array of Independent
    Disks)
    backups (RAID 5), 1564
    hardware requirements for RDS Server,
        1446
    hot spares and parallelized repair, 591
    mirroring (RAID 1), 572
    overview of, 563
RAM
    hardware requirements for Hyper-V, 1343
    managing virtual hardware and,
        1382–1383
    Windows Server 2012 requirements, 21
range, IP addresses, 193
RAS (Remote Access Service). *See also* RRAS
    (Routing and Remote Access Service)
    overview of, 1070
    security groups and, 199–203
RBAC (Role-Based Access Control), 199–203
RD (Remote Desktop) Gateway
    adding RDS services, 1451
    administering remote server, 906–907
    enabling, 908–917
    overview of, 900
    policies, 908
    RD Gateway Manager, 909
    Remote Desktop Connection client, 907
    services and features, 908
    WinRM and, 920
RD CAP (Remote Desktop Connection
    Authorization Policies)
    configuring authorization policies,
        911–916
    overview of, 906
    RD Gateway required policies, 908
RD Connection Broker
    adding RDS services, 1451
    overview of, 900
RD Licensing
    adding RDS services, 1451
    RD Licensing Diagnoser, 1472–1473
    RD Licensing Manager, 1476–1477
RD RAP (Remote Desktop Resource
    Authorization Policies)
    configuring authorization policies,
        911–916
    RD Gateway required policies, 906

RD Session Host
    adding RDS services, 1451
    centralizing deployment of applications,
        1436
    changing client settings, 1474–1475
    configuring licensing, 1473–1474
    connecting to sessions, 1459–1460
    deploying RemoteApp applications, 1439
    overview of, 900, 1435
    RemoteApp applications on, 1435
    using powerful server for, 1444–1445
    Windows terminal and, 1448
RD Shadowing, 1439
RD Users group, 1454
RD Virtualization Host
    adding RDS services, 1451
    adding role for, 1465–1470
    configuring licensing for, 1473–1474
    overview of, 900
    VDI (virtual desktop interface) and,
        1435, 1464
RD Web Access, 1451
RDC (Remote Desktop Connection)
    Advanced tab, 894–895
    allowing connections, 885
    connecting to remote server, 886–887,
        1450
    Display tab, 890–891
    Experience tab, 893–894
    General tab, 887–890
    launching, 895–896
    Local Resources tab o, 891–892
    Mac OS X client using, 974–976
    Programs tab, 892–893
    Remote Desktop Connection Broker,
        900
    Remote Desktop Connection client, 907
RDC (Remote Differential Compression), 317
RDP (Remote Desktop Protocol)
    anatomy of thin-client session, 1441
    communicating with VMs via Hyper-V,
        1389
    configuring host sessions, 905
    deploying RemoteApp applications, 1439
    enabling remote administration, 55–56
    how it works "under the hood,"
        1443–1444
    saving remote connection settings,
        887–890
    unknown publisher warning, 889
    versions, 1444
RDS (Remote Desktop Services)
    adding applications, 1458
    adding RDS role, 1449–1450,
        1454–1458
    adding RemoteApp application,
        1460–1462
    administrative uses of, 1435–1436
    Advanced tab of RDC, 894–895
    centralizing application deployment,
        1436
    changes in Windows Server 2012, 13–14
    changing client settings for RD session
        host, 1474–1475

    configuring host session properties,
        904–905
    configuring licensing for RD session host
        or virtualization host, 1473
    configuring server for Remote Desktop,
        884–885
    connecting to sessions, 1459–1460
    deploying RemoteApp program, 1439
    Display tab of RDC, 890–891
    Easy Print and, 1452
    enabling, 43
    environment settings for local accounts,
        391–392
    Experience tab of RDC, 893–894
    General tab of RDC, 887–890
    hardware for RDS clients, 1447
    hardware for RDS Server, 1444–1446
    installing Remote Desktop Services role,
        897–903
    launching RDC with mstsc command,
        895–896
    launching RemoteApp from Internet
        Explorer, 1462–1464
    licensing manager, 1475–1477
    licensing mode, 1453–1454
    Local Resources tab of RDC, 891–892
    local user settings, 393–395
    managing servers, 119–120
    modifying virtual desktop template
        export location, 1474
    monitoring, 1472–1473
    NLA (Network Level Authentication),
        1453
    overview of, 883–884, 1435
    PC clients, 1448–1449
    Performance Monitor for viewing
        sessions, 1446–1447
    Programs tab of RDC, 892–893
    providing help desk support, 1439
    RDS Server, 1441
    reducing hardware refresh rates,
        1437–1438
    Remote Desktop Protocol and,
        1443–1444
    Remote Desktop Users group, 1454
    roaming profiles and, 1303–1304
    RSAT tools, 924
    selecting among RDS services, 1450–1451
    sessions, 1441–1443
    simplifying UI (user interface) with, 1438
    SSO (single sign-on), 1452
    supporting non-PC environments,
        1436–1437
    supporting remote users, 1436
    tablet clients, 1449
    thin-client approach in, 1440–1441
    viewing who is logged in, 1475
    Windows terminal and, 1448
RDS clients, 1447, 1474–1475
RDS servers
    anatomy of thin-client session, 1441
    hardware for, 1444–1446
    managing, 119–120
    sessions, 1441

re-ACLing the server
    ADMT migration and, 349
    C&P migration and, 345–346
    following migration, 1260
Read & Execute permissions
    default permissions of Users group, 724
    defined, 666–667
    in list of molecular permissions, 719
Read permissions
    default permissions of Users group, 724
    in list of molecular permissions, 719
    NTFS, 666
    share permissions and, 667, 713
    types of advanced permissions, 866
read-only DNS, 1183–1184
read-only domain controllers. See RODCs
    (read-only domain controllers)
realm trusts, 1229
rebooting Server Core, 112
Receive Segment Coalescing (RSC), 167
Receive-Side Scaling (RSS), 168
record types, DNS, 228–232
recover command, for integrity checks, 1572
recovery. See restore
recovery key
    enabling BitLocker, 696
    enabling BitLocker To Go, 697
    overview of, 694–695
recursion
    DNS names and, 212–213
    methods for name resolution, 217
recycle bin
    changes to Active Directory, 4–5, 76–77
    enabling, 1578–1579
    overview of, 1577–1578
    prerequisites, 1578
    recovering deleted objects, 1578–1579
redirected state, migrating to DFS-R, 319,
    326–328
Redundant Array of Independent Disks. See
    RAID (Redundant Array of Independent
    Disks)
refresh intervals, Group Policy, 469
ReFS (Resilient File System)
    choosing file system when creating
        volumes, 616–617
    does not support storage of AD
        component, 271
    overview of, 265
    support for, 569
Registered I/O (RIO), 167
registry
    configuring access to closest AD site
        with, 1148–1150
    preventing editing of, 501
    verifying AD and, 321
registry editor
    changing permissions HKEY_CURRENT_
        USE hive, 1295–1298
    locking down desktop, 1324
    verifying SYSVOL entry, 321
regular expressions
    detecting string pattern with, 813–814
    overview of, 818–819

relative IDs (RIDs), 1217–1218
Reliability Monitor, 1510
relying party trust
    adding to AD FS, 549–551
    key components of AD FS, 535
Remote Access Dashboard, 1120
Remote Access role
    configuring, 1072–1074
    installing, 1071–1072
    installing with PowerShell, 1072
    monitoring remote access clients,
        1108–1109
    NAT and, 1047
    NICs required for VPN server, 1074
    services provided by, 1070
Remote Access Service. See RAS (Remote
    Access Service)
Remote Assistance
    configuring server for, 917
    responding to request, 918–919
    sending request, 918
Remote Authentication Dial-In User Service.
    See RADIUS (Remote Authentication
    Dial-In User Service)
Remote Control, 1439
Remote Desktop Connection. See RDC
    (Remote Desktop Connection)
Remote Desktop Connection Authorization
    Policies. See RD CAP (Remote Desktop
    Connection Authorization Policies)
Remote Desktop Gateway. See RD (Remote
    Desktop) Gateway
Remote Desktop Protocol. See RDP (Remote
    Desktop Protocol)
Remote Desktop Resource Authorization
    Policies. See RD RAP (Remote Desktop
    Resource Authorization Policies)
Remote Differential Compression (RDC), 317
remote locations, benefits of RODCs, 1153
remote management
    connecting to administrative shares, 675
    creating shares with Server Manager,
        660–661
    IIS (Internet Information Services) and,
        1017–1019
    managing Windows Server 2008 from
        Server 2012 R2, 661–664
Remote Procedure Call. See RPC (Remote
    Procedure Call)
remote server administration
    Advanced tab of RDC, 894–895
    compatibility issues with RSAT, 923–924
    configuring firewalls, 118
    configuring host session properties,
        904–905
    configuring server for Remote
        Assistance, 917
    configuring server for Remote Desktop,
        884–885
    connection limits, 896–897
    creating inbound firewall rule, 126–131
    creating listeners, 124–126
    Display tab of RDC, 890–891
    enabling, 55–56

enabling Remote Desktop Gateway,
    908–917
enabling WinRM, 920
Experience tab of RDC, 893–894
General tab of RDC, 887–890
getting certificates, 122–124
installing Remote Desktop Services role,
    897–903
installing RSAT, 924–925
issuing PowerShell commands with
    WinRS, 922
issuing WMIC commands with WinRS,
    921–922
launching RDC with mstsc command,
    895–896
Local Resources tab of RDC, 891–892
managing remotely with MMC snap-ins,
    120–122
managing servers with Remote Desktop,
    119–120
overview of, 119, 883
PowerShell and, 925–926
Programs tab of RDC, 892–893
RDC (Remote Desktop Connection),
    886–887
RDS (Remote Desktop Services), 883–884
Remote Desktop Connection client, 907
Remote Desktop Gateway, 906–907
Remote Desktop Gateway policies, 908
Remote Desktop Gateway services and
    features, 908
responding to Remote Assistance
    request, 918–919
RSAT (Remote Server Administration
    Tools), 279, 922–923
sending commands remotely with
    Windows Remote Shell, 122
sending Remote Assistance request, 918
staging RODC install, 1178
testing service with with WinRS, 131
WinRM (Windows Remote
    Management), 919
WinRS (Windows Remote Shell), 921
Remote Server Administration Tools. See
    RSAT (Remote Server Administration
    Tools)
Remote tab, System Properties dialog, 884–885
remote tools, changes in Windows Server
    2012, 13
remote users, RDS support for, 1436
RemoteApp program
    adding RemoteApp application, 1460–1462
    deploying, 1439
    launching from Internet Explorer,
        1462–1464
    RemoteApp applications on RD Session
        Host, 1435
RemoteFX technologies, 907
Remove-ADUser command, 464
repadmin command
    authoritative restore, 1582–1583
    forcing replication, 1145–1146
    verifying DC health, 336–337
    verifying replication, 321, 336–337

Replica mode, WSUS configuration, 1536
replication
    from command-line, 1145
    configuring intersite replication,
        1141–1144
    defined, 258–259
    DFS replicas, 736
    distributed file system replication. *See*
        DFS-R (Distributed File System
        Replication)
    file system replication. *See* FRS (file
        replication service)
    forcing, 1145–1146
    frequency of, 1143
    of GPOs, 470
    multimaster replication, 1186–1187
    planning Active Directory, 1192–1193
    problems due to poor bandwidth, 1193
    site link properties, 1140
    sites and, 1125–1126
    verifying AD replication, 321
    of VMs (virtual machines). *See* HVR
        (Hyper-V Replica)
Report Locations, File Server Resource
    Manager, 688
Report tab, quota templates
    viewing for new quota, 681–682
    working with, 680
reports
    data retention and, 1517–1519
    generating storage, 684–687
    managing DirectAccess, 1121
    System Center 2012 R2, 1527–1528
Representational State Transfer (REST), 370
requirements
    ADAC (Active Directory Administrative
        Center), 448
    cloning virtual DCs, 1402–1403
    clustering, 566–567
    DCHP failover, 205–206
    DirectAccess, 1112
    djoin.exe, 947
    federation servers, 536
    FRS, 316–317
    hardware requirements for BitLocker
        encryption, 693–694
    hardware requirements for Hyper-V, 1343
    hardware requirements for RDS Server,
        1445–1446
    IPAM (IP Address Management),
        177–178
    network client-side, 930
    networking, 539
    in-place upgrade, 336
    RODCs, 1161–1162
    Windows Server 2012 installation,
        20–21
    WSUS software, 1532–1533
Reset Password dialog, 434–435
resetting passwords, 523–525, 531
Resilient File System. *See* ReFS (Resilient File
    System)
Resource Monitor, 1509–1510
resource partner, key components of AD FS, 535

resources
    accessing with Windows RT, 946
    connecting clients to network resources,
        955–956
    creating resource policy, 1518
    publishing network resources, 956–957
    VMs supporting on-demand allocation,
        1412
resources, DAC
    access control and, 770
    creating resource property, 777–781, 802
    resource lists, 768, 802
    resource properties, 768
REST (Representational State Transfer), 370
restore. *See also* backups (and restore);
    Windows Server Backup
    Active Directory, 1580–1581
    authoritative, 1582–1583
    directory services. *See* DSRM (Directory
        Services Restore Mode)
    files and folders, 1566
    GPOs, 512
    performing full server restore, 1562–1564
    recovering folders, 1567–1568
    recovering system state of server,
        1564–1565
Resultant Set of Policy. *See* RSOP (Resultant
    Set of Policy)
reverse lookup zones, DNS, 226–228
RFCs
    IPv6 transition technologies and, 148–149
    subnetting by, 1038–1039
RIDs (relative IDs), 1217–1218
Rights Management Services. *See* RMS (Rights
    Management Services)
RIO (Registered I/O), 167
RMS (Rights Management Services)
    changes to, 79
    changes to Active Directory, 7–8
    Work Folders and, 1323
roaming profiles
    applying advanced folder redirection,
        1314–1316
    applying basic folder redirection,
        1308–1312
    changing permissions HKEY_CURRENT_
        USE hive, 1295–1298
    cleaning up older profiles, 1301
    configuring super mandatory profiles,
        1297–1298
    creating mandatory profiles in Windows
        8, 1293–1294
    creating share for, 1283–1286
    creating shares and setting permissions
        manually, 1290–1291
    deploying folders for profiles by editing
        single user object, 1286–1287
    folder redirection and, 1306–1308
    GPO settings, 1304–1306
    granting access with Group Policy,
        1288–1290
    machine settings, 1301
    making share available in DFS
        namespace, 1286

    managing, 1300–1301
    managing folder redirection, 1316–1318
    mandatory profiles, 1293
    multiple sites and, 1301–1302
    overview of, 1280–1282
    RDS (Remote Desktop Services) and,
        1303–1304
    securing mandatory profile folder on file
        server, 1297–1298
    testing, 1292
    testing folder redirection, 1312–1314
    user settings, 1306
RODCs (read-only domain controllers)
    Allowed RODC Password Replication
        group, 1160–1161
    attribute or property editor for, 404
    certificate settings, 404–405
    COM+ settings, 403–404
    configuring, 396–397
    contents of, 1156–1157
    creating, 382–388
    delegating administration of, 1161
    Denied RODC Password Replication
        group, 1159–1160
    DNS on, 1182–1184
    domain functional levels, 1162–1163
    editing multiple accounts
        simultaneously, 408–410
    forest functional levels, 1163–1164
    general settings, 397
    group membership settings, 405–406
    installation media for, 1178
    installing on Server Core, 1174
    installing prestaged RODC, 1181–1182
    logon settings, 397–401
    makes changes to, 1155
    managing from command line, 410–412
    modifying Allowed RODC Password
        Replication group, 1176–1177
    not allowed as first DC, 265
    object settings, 406–407
    overview of, 1153–1155
    password replication policy, 1157–1159
    password replication settings, 406
    postal address settings, 397
    prestaging RODC account, 1179–1181
    profile settings, 401
    promoting server to, 1168–1173
    requirements for deploying, 1161–1162
    running adprep for, 1165–1167
    security settings, 407–408
    server applications on, 1167
    staged installation scenarios, 1177–1178
    telephone settings, 401–402
    viewing properties of, 1174–1176
Role Health Service, 587
Role-Based Access Control (RBAC), 199–203
roles and features
    AD DS role, 239, 280, 283
    AD FS role, 539–543
    Add Roles and Features Wizard, 12
    adding, 43, 56–63
    adding services to Web Server role, 986–988
    adding SMTP Server Tools feature, 1010

adding VHDs (virtual hard disks), 58–59
comparing roles and features, 655
configuring, 131–132
creating domain controller and
    managing DNS, 132–133
custom views by server role, 1487
customizing servers, 117–118
DNS role, 216–217
DNS server role, 211–214
Domain Naming Master role, 1217
exporting to configuration XML file, 67–68
File and Storage Services role, 653–656
File Server role, 135
FSMO roles, 308–309, 1213
FTP role, 1014
Hyper-V role, 1361
identifying server roles with dsquery, 1165
IIS 8.0 and feature delegation, 1007
Infrastructure Operations Master role, 1218
installing encryption features for role
    services, 655–656
installing IPAM client features, 182
installing IPAM server features, 180–181
installing roles of multiple servers using
    scripts, 66–69
installing with PowerShell, 64–66
Network Policy and Access Services role,
    1068–1070
NFS server role, 754
PDC Emulator role, 1219
placement in GCs, 1209
Print and Document Services role,
    832–834, 845–847
promoting member server during swing
    migration, 1251–1254
proxy server role, 557–558
RD Virtualization Host role, 1465
RDS role, 1449–1450, 1454–1458
Remote Access role, 1065, 1071–1074
Remote Assistance, 917
Remote Desktop Services role, 897–903
Remote Server Administration Tools, 120
removing, 69–70
RID FSMO role, 1217–1218
role services, 62
Schema Master role, 1213–1217,
    1256–1257
searching for printers by, 851
separation of roles, 383–384
transferring FSMO roles, 1219–1223,
    1255–1256
troubleshooting, 70–71
viewing available, 118
viewing role performance, 75
viewing servers roles, 71
viewing services associated with roles,
    72, 75–76
viewing with FSRM (File Server
    Resource Manager), 656
Web Server role, 981–985
WSUS role, 1537–1539
rollback, of C&P migration, 367
root application, website, 991
root domain

empty root design, 1195
    naming, 265–266
round-robin, network load balancing, 229
route print command, 1031
routers. *See also* IP routing
    computers with IP address act as host
        and router, 1030–1033
    creating, 1055–1056
routing, configuring RRAS, 1072–1074
Routing and Remote Access Server Setup
    Wizard, 1052
Routing and Remote Access Service. *See* RRAS
    (Routing and Remote Access Service)
Routing and Remote Access snap-in, 1075
Routing service. *See also* RRAS (Routing and
    Remote Access Service), 1070
routing tables
    deciphering, 1039–1041
    how they are used, 1033–1034
    showing IPv4 routing table, 1031
RPC (Remote Procedure Call)
    configuring host session properties, 905
    FRS requirements and dependencies, 317
    FRS using encrypted RPCs, 315
    RD Gateway required services, 908
    WinRM replaces, 13
RRAS (Routing and Remote Access Service).
    See also Remote Access role
    authentication options, 1099
    configuring, 1072–1074
    configuring RRAS server properties,
        1102–1108
    configuring RRAS server to use SSTP,
        1089
    launching, 1075, 1086
    Remote Access role and, 1065
    securing connections, 1097
    viewing RRAS server port properties,
        1109–1110
RRAS servers
    configuring, 1102–1108
    using SSTP, 1089
    viewing server port properties, 1109–1110
RSAT (Remote Server Administration Tools)
    ADAC requirements, 448
    administering Windows Server 2012
        remotely, 279
    compatibility issues, 923–924
    installing, 924–925
    installing IPAM client feature, 182
    overview of, 120, 922–923
    RD Gateway requirements, 908
RSC (Receive Segment Coalescing), 167
RSOP (Resultant Set of Policy)
    getting RSOP results with GPMC,
        514–516
    gpresult.exe and, 516–517
    overview of, 513–514
RSS (Receive-Side Scaling), 168
RST, TCP (Transmission Control Protocol), 1058

S

SAM (security account management), 1186
Samba, 969

SANs (Storage Area Networks)
    bringing offline disks online, 618–619
    options, 575
    overview of, 562
    shared storage and, 561
    Storage Manager for, 924
    Virtual SAN Manager Wizard, 1366
SAS (Serial Attached SCSI)
    choosing disk type by storage needs, 590
    enclosures, 563
    options, 575
    shared storage and, 561
SATA (Serial Advance Technology
    Attachment)
    choosing disk type by storage needs, 590
    hardware requirements for RDS Server,
        1445
sc config command, 663
scalability, of Hyper-V, 1345–1351-14
scale out, SMB, 688
Scale-Out File Servers (SOFS), 567
scanners, Distributed Scan Server, 832
SCCM (System Center Configuration
    Manager)
    core products in System Center 2012
        R2, 1524
    deploying applications, 1269
    flexibility of desktop and, 1268
    patch management, 1553
    RDS as alternative for deploying
        applications, 1436
    virtualization and, 1268
Scheduled reports, Storage Reports, 686–687
schedules
    site link properties, 1140
    Task Scheduler, 622–623, 815–816
schema
    Active Directory, 259
    changes to, 1215–1216
    examining, 1213–1215
    planning for changes and conflicts, 1216
    preparing for in-place upgrade, 337–338,
        1246
    preparing for swing migration, 340, 1250
    preventing grafting of trees or forests,
        1191
    upgrading Active Directory and, 331–334
Schema Admins group, 1214
Schema Master role
    identifying, 1165
    moving during swing migration,
        1256–1257
    in multiple-domain design, 1213–1217
schema partition, AD database, 1187
SCOM (System Center Operations Manager)
    monitoring DNS zones, 198
    monitoring performance, 1526–1527
    MPs (management packs), 1525–1526
    overview of, 1524
    for performance monitoring and
        management, 169
    reports, 1527–1528
    upgrade install and, 34
scope, of Active Directory groups, 425

Scope tab, Storage Reports, 685–686
scripts
    associating multiple logon scripts with
        users, 1334–1335
    creating PowerShell scripts, 290–292
    eliminating logon scripts, 509
    installing roles of multiple servers with
        PowerShell, 66–69
    managing logon scripts, 1335–1336
    managing shutdown with logoff scripts,
        1336–1337
    specifying with Group Policy, 488–490
    VBScript, 356–357
SCSI. *See also* iSCSI (Internet Small Computer
    System Interface); SAS (Serial Attached
    SCSI)
    controllers for virtual disks, 1368
    hardware requirements for RDS Server,
        1445
    managing virtual hardware, 1384
SCSI Enclosure Services (SES), 597
Search Active Directory
    connecting to shares, 674
    locating published share, 665–666
searches
    Control Panel, 695
    for network printers, 836
    for objects, 438–440
    for printer features, 851
    Search Active Directory, 665–666, 849–851
    for shares, 672–674
Secure Socket Tunneling Protocol. *See* SSTP
    (Secure Socket Tunneling Protocol)
Secure Sockets Layer. *See* SSL (Secure Sockets
    Layer)
security
    benefits of IPv6, 148
    code access security, 1021–1022
    configuring VPN server properties,
        1102–1104
    domain user account settings, 407–408
    Group Policy settings, 492–493
    managing print servers, 859–860
    SMB 3.0 improvements, 691–692
    trusts and, 1228–1229
    virtualization and, 1342
security account management (SAM), 1186
security boundaries, domains and forests and,
    1186–1188
Security Configuration and Analysis snap-in,
    497–498
security database, 497–498
security groups
    ADAC navigation node for, 445
    Cloneable Domain Controllers,
        1403–1404
    Denied RODC Password Replication
        group, 1159–1160
    DirectAccess requirements, 1112
    RBAC (Role-Based Access Control),
        199–203
    types of Active Directory groups, 424
Security GUI, changing passwords on
    demand, 954

security identifiers. *See* SIDs (security
    identifiers)
security identifiers (SIDs). *See* SIDs (security
    identifiers)
security logs
    auditing printer access, 867–868
    types of Windows logs, 1492
security principal, 411, 424
Security tab, printer properties, 864–866
security templates
    creating security database, 497–498
    domain-based GPOs for applying, 498
    importing, 498–499
    overview of, 493–494
    working with, 494–496
Security Translation Wizard, 364–366
Semantic database analysis, Active Directory,
    1572–1573
separation of administration, 383–384
separator pages
    choosing, 873–874
    creating, 874–876
    overview of, 873
sequencing, attributes TCP adds to IP, 1042
Serial Advance Technology Attachment
    (SATA)
    choosing disk type by storage needs, 590
    hardware requirements for RDS Server,
        1445
Serial Attached SCSI (SAS). *See* SAS (Serial
    Attached SCSI)
Serial Line Interface Protocol (SLIP), 1079
Server Core
    accessing file shares, 111
    accessing Task Manager, 109–110
    activating and using KMS server,
        143–144
    adding print services role to, 845–847
    administering remotely, 119
    changing administrator password,
        110–111
    choosing installation type, 26
    closing command prompt, 110
    command line reference, 112
    configuring, 113–116
    configuring DHCP service, 133–135
    configuring roles and features, 131–132
    creating DCs, 132–133
    creating folders and assigning
        permissions, 137–139
    creating inbound firewall rule, 126–131
    creating listeners, 124–126
    creating primary partition, 136–137
    customizing servers, 117–119
    DirectAccess support, 1111
    editing text files and Registry, 112
    enabling firewalls, 143
    getting certificates, 122–124
    installing, 106–108
    installing RODCs on, 1174
    managing DNS, 132–133
    managing licenses with KMS, 142–143
    managing remotely with MMC snap-ins,
        120–122

    managing servers with Remote Desktop,
        119–120
    managing SRV records, 143
    protecting data with Windows Backup
        Server, 144–145
    rebooting and shutting down, 112
    sending commands remotely with
        Windows Remote Shell, 122
    setting up file server, 135
    setting up print server, 140–142
    sharing folders, 139
    supported upgrade scenarios, 32–33
    switching to/from GUI, 109
    testing service with with WinRS, 131
    updating server, 116–117
    what's new, 105
Server for NFS, 752–753
server groups
    adding, 198
    creating, 1481
    monitoring with, 1481–1483
Server Inventory view, IPAM, 190–191
Server Manager
    AD FS Management, 549
    adding new machines, 663
    adding Print and Document Services
        role, 832–834
    adding roles, 653–654
    adding servers for management by, 1480
    adding servers to AD FS server farm,
        556–557
    adding services to Web Server role,
        986–988
    adding Web Server role, 984–985
    adding/removing WSUS services, 1532
    Best Practices Analyzers, 1483–1484
    changes in Windows Server 2012, 12–13,
        45
    configuring data deduplication, 638–641
    configuring servers. *See* configuring
        servers, with Server Manager
    creating custom event views, 1488–1489
    creating server groups, 1481
    creating shares, 657–661
    creating virtual disks, 608–612
    dashboard, 42
    deploying RMS for, 79
    exporting/importing custom views,
        1491–1492
    File and Storage Services tool, 595, 1273
    installing AD FS, 539–543
    installing GPMC, 509
    integration of CS (Certificate Services)
        with, 78
    joining domains, 298–299
    launching RRAS, 1086
    login and, 44
    modifying permissions, 669–671
    monitoring and checking health, 1479
    monitoring with server groups,
        1481–1483
    performing full server backup, 1557
    performing manual backup of files and
        folders, 1566–1567

promoting server to DC, 283
recovering deleted objects from recycle bin, 1578–1579
recovering folder from a backup, 1567–1568
server group view, 1483
stopping and restarting AD DS, 1570, 1582
upgrade install and, 40–41
viewing post-deployment tasks, 1170
Server Message Block. *See* SMB (Server Message Block) 3.0
Server Performance Advisor. *See* SPA (Server Performance Advisor) 3.0
Server Properties, print servers, 857
Server Roles page, Add Roles and Features Wizard, 654–655
Server Selection page, Add Roles and Features Wizard, 653
server virtualization. *See also* Hyper-V
overview of, 1339–1341
uses of, 1341–1343
server-based computing. *See also* thin-clients, 1440
servers
adding to sites, 1129
administering remote. *See* remote server administration
authentication of, 894–895
configuring for Remote Assistance, 917
configuring for Remote Desktop, 884–885
configuring for single-domain forest, 263–264
configuring VDI on, 1464–1470
configuring with Server Manager. *See* configuring servers, with Server Manager
connecting to remote, 886–887
custom views by server role, 1487
customizing, 117–119
DNS. *See* DNS servers
federation servers. *See* federation servers
file. *See* file servers
installing IPAM server feature, 180–181
installing Remote Desktop Services role, 897–903
IPAM managing, 185–189
managing with IIS. *See* IIS (Internet Information Services)
managing with Remote Desktop, 119–120
name servers, 212
placing in AD sites, 1137
print. *See* print servers
promoting. *See* promoting servers
proxy. *See* proxy servers
RDS. *See* RDS servers
RRAS. *See* RRAS servers
server applications on RODCs, 1167
server discovery, 184–185
SMTP, 679, 924
SQL Server. *See* SQL Server
updating, 116–117
viewing server roles, 71
VPN. *See* VPN servers
web. *See* web servers (IIS)
Windows. *See* Windows Servers

service (SRV) records. *See* SRV (service) records
service communication certificate, 536
Service Manager, in System Center 2012 R2, 1524
service-level agreements (SLAs), Hyper-V QoS and, 163
services
adding to Web Server role, 986–988
connecting to network resources, 955–956
monitoring with server groups, 1482
selecting among RDS services, 1450–1451
services tool, viewing services associated with roles, 72
SES (SCSI Enclosure Services), 597
sessions, local user settings, 392–393
sessions, RDS
changing client settings for RD session host, 1474–1475
connecting to, 1459–1460
overview of, 1441–1443
Performance Monitor for viewing, 1446–1447
RDS Server and, 1441–1443
Set-ADAccount, 448
Set-ADAccountControl, 448
Set-ADAccountPassword, 448, 457
Set-ADUser, 448
Setup program
installing Server Core, 106
running in-place upgrade, 338, 1248
share permissions. *See also* permissions
Allow and Deny permissions, 715
assigning file and directory permissions, 720–725
assigning with Security tab of DAC, 761–764
atomic permissions, 717–719
combining NTFS permissions and, 671–672
creating, 711–712
defining, 712–714
deploying DAC policies and, 792
detailed interface for working with, 728–732
inherited permissions, 720
managing, 667, 711
modifying, 669–671
molecular permissions, 719–720
similarities to NTFS permissions, 667
shared folders. *See also* file shares
Allow and Deny permissions, 715
assigning file and directory permissions, 720–725
atomic permissions, 717–719
connecting to file shares, 973
connecting to network resources, 955–956
creating from File Explorer, 705–706
creating NFS shared folder, 753–754
creating remotely, 707–710
creating with PowerShell, 710–711
defining share permission, 712–714
detailed interface for working with permissions, 728–732

hidden shares, 732–734
home directories and, 1272–1276
inherited permissions, 720
mapping drive to, 964–966
molecular permissions, 719–720
NTFS permissions, 715–717
overview of, 703–704
removing users or groups, 728
share permissions, 711–712
viewing user rights, 725–727
Shared Nothing Live Migration (cluster-free), 1414–1417
shared storage
adding first node to cluster, 575–585
adding second node to cluster, 585–587
clustering and, 566
clustering functionality, 567–568
clustering requirements, 566–567
clustering with VMs, 572
clusters and virtualization, 569–570
configuring clusters, 574–575
CSVs (Cluster Shared Volumes), 568–569
File and Storage Services, 564–566
HA (high availability) and, 571
overview of, 561–562
quorums, 570–571
SANs (Storage Area Networks), 562
setting up guest-based cluster, 587–588
storage options of clusters, 575
Storage Spaces, 571–572
technologies, 562–564
virtual disks for, 568
shares
connecting to, 672–676
creating, 657–660
creating on remote computers, 660–661
enabling offline files on server, 699–701
File Server role added when sharing folders, 653
files. *See* file shares
folders. *See* shared folders
linking to network resources, 955–956
managing Windows Server 2008 from Server 2012 R2, 661–664
mapping drives to, 650–651
net share command, 139
publishing in Active Directory, 664–666
setting user limits, 662–663
Sharing tab, printer properties, 862–863
shortcut trusts, types of trust relationships, 1229
shutdown of OS, Hyper-V services, 1358
shutdown of Server Core, 112
SID histories
ADMT migration and, 348, 350–351, 354–355, 360–361
C&P migration and, 346–347
domain migration and, 1260–1261
testing resource access for migrated groups, 363–364
SIDs (security identifiers)
caution in use of, 424
filtering, 1263
RIDs (relative IDs) and, 1217–1218

share/NTFS permissions using, 668
understanding use of, 411
simple layout, of virtual disks, 607, 610
Simple Mail Transfer Protocol. *See* SMTP
(Simple Mail Transfer Protocol)
Simple Network Time Protocol (SNTP),
1224–1225
Simple Object Access Protocol (SOAP), 122
single-master replication. *See also* replication,
1209
sink link bridges, 1127
site links
adding, 1137–1138
calculating cost of, 1140–1141
creating, 1138–1139
defined, 1127
properties of, 1140
types of, 1138
sites, AD
adding site links, 1137–1138
applying GPOs to, 468
bridgehead servers and, 1144–1145
cached credentials, 1132–1133
calculating cost of site links, 1140–1141
configuring client access to closest site,
1146–1147
configuring client access to closest site
with Group Policy, 1147–1148
configuring client access to closest site
with Registry, 1148–1150
configuring intersite replication,
1141–1144
creating site links, 1138–1139
DCs and, 1131–1132
defining, 1124, 1130–1131, 1135–1136
design pointers for Active Directory, 1196
forcing replication, 1145–1146
global catalogs and, 1133–1135
how they work, 1128–1130
linking GPOs to, 285, 1147
mastering concepts related to,
1123–1125
overview of, 258, 1123
placing servers in, 1137
placing subnets in, 1135–1136
properties of site links, 1140
renaming, 1130
replication and, 1125–1126
retrieving AD information with
PowerShell, 1150–1151
roaming profiles and, 1301–1302
terminology, 1126–1128
types of site links, 1138
SLAs (service-level agreements), Hyper-V QoS
and, 163
sliding windows, attributes TCP adds to IP,
1042
SLIP (Serial Line Interface Protocol), 1079
smart cards
authenticating VPN clients, 1098, 1100
enabling BitLocker, 696
logon settings, 400
unlocking BitLocker-protected drive,
693–694

SMB (Server Message Block) 3.0
changes in Windows Server 2012, 15
compatibility with SMB 2.0 and 1.0,
689–690
creating shares with PowerShell, 710
creating shares with Server Manager, 658
features, 688–689
Mac OS X client and, 969
new features, 564
options for shared storage, 575
protocol specification, 689
security, 691–692
set up requirements, 563
setting permissions, 1275–1276
SMB Direct, 689, 1348–1349
SMB Multichannel, 689, 1348–1349
SMS (System Management Server), 1060
SMTP (Simple Mail Transfer Protocol)
adding SMTP e-mail to website, 1012–1013
adding SMTP Server Tools feature,
1009–1010
authentication of SMTP services, 1011
delegation of administrations, 1007–1008
installing and configuring, 1008–1009
MX records and, 230
setting up SMTP Server, 1010
site links, 1138
virtual SMTP Servers and domains,
1010–1011
SMTP server
configuring FSRM to send email, 679
RSAT tools, 924
SMTP Server Tools, 1009–1010
SMTPSVC, 1010
snapshots, Active Directory
creating, 1573–1574
mounting and working with, 1574–1575
SNTP (Simple Network Time Protocol),
1224–1225
SOA (Start of Authority) records
DNS, 231–232
dynamic updates and, 237
read-only DNS and, 1183–1184
SOAP (Simple Object Access Protocol), 122
sockets, TCP, 1042–1044
SOFS (Scale-Out File Servers), 567
soft quota limit, 677
software
deploying via Group Policy, 487
Hyper-V architecture, 1352–1354
Hyper-V requirements, 1344
preventing installation or use of
unauthorized software, 501–502
requirements for in-place upgrade, 336
troubleshooting printers, 880
understanding client software
requirements, 930–931
WSUS requirements, 1532–1533
solid state drives. *See* SSDs (solid state drives)
source computer
event log subscription and, 1495–1496
source-initiated subscriptions, 1497–1498
SPA (Server Performance Advisor) 3.0
installing, 170–172

networking, 169–172
overview of, 169
Special Permissions, in list of molecular
permissions, 720
split-brain DNS, 245–246
split-scope, vs. clustering in DHCP failover, 205
spooler. *See* print spooler
Spot Verifier service, online verification with,
592–593
SQL Server
configuring AD FS and, 546
planning deployment of AD FS and, 538
storing VPN accounting data in SQL
Server database, 1100
SQL Server Express, 85
SRV (service) records
Active Directory and DNS and, 266
DNS clients and, 241–242
installing DNS for forest with second
DC, 281
managing, 143
overview of, 230–231
registering with DDNS, 253–254
troubleshooting DNS and, 301
SSDs (solid state drives)
choosing disk type by storage needs, 590
creating storage pools, 620–621
creating storage tiers, 620–621
SSL (Secure Sockets Layer)
configuring AD FS, 545
creating certificate for AD FS, 543–544
in HTTPS, 906
new features in IIS 8.0, 980
protecting websites, 1022
RDP (Remote Desktop Protocol) and, 1452
required by federation servers, 536
SSTP (Secure Socket Tunneling Protocol)
and, 1067, 1086
SSO (single sign-on)
AD FS (Active Directory Federation
Services) and, 533
automating client configuration using
Group Policy, 559–560
logon flavors and, 372
RDS (Remote Desktop Services) and, 1452
testing SSO capabilities before turning
on, 537
Windows Azure and, 368
SSTP (Secure Socket Tunneling Protocol)
configuring RRAS server, 1089
configuring VPN ports, 1109
encryption provided by SSL, 1086
overview of, 1067–1068
stand-alone DFS
creating DFS root, 739–743
vs. domain-based, 737–738
Standard Edition
overview of, 2
setting up DCs and, 262
Standard Primary zone, DNS zones, 221–222
Standard Secondary zone, DNS zones,
222–224
start (state 0), migrating to DFS-R, 319
start button, in Windows Server 2012, 44

start menu
    deploying RemoteApp applications, 1439
    policies for creating consistency across organization, 502
Start of Authority. *See* SOA (Start of Authority) records
Starter GPOs, 510–511
startup/shutdown, controlling with Group Policy, 487
static IP addresses
    configuring stand-alone DNS server, 214–215
    installing second DC and, 280
static teaming, NIC Teaming options, 152
stealth firewalls, avoiding, 1058
storage
    4K sector support, 591
    adding mass storage controller driver during clean install, 29
    bringing offline disks online, 618–619
    CHKDSK improvements, 592–594
    cloud services, 595
    creating SSD and HDD pools, 620–621
    creating storage pools, 599–602
    creating storage pools with PowerShell, 604–605
    creating storage spaces, 598
    data deduplication. *See* data deduplication
    File and Storage Services tool, 595–597
    home directories vs. local storage, 1280
    iSSCI. *See* iSCSI (Internet Small Computer System Interface)
    limitations of storage pools, 602–603
    NFS shares. *See* NFS shares
    online features and, 592–593
    optimizing storage tiers, 622–623
    overview of, 589
    parallelized repair, 591
    PowerShell cmdlets, 597–598
    quota policies vs. usage monitoring, 676
    sharing. *See* shared storage
    tiered approach, 590
    UEFI BIOS support, 592
    viewing disk drives in storage pools, 603–604
    write-back cache, 590–591, 622
Storage Area Networks. *See* SANs (Storage Area Networks)
storage fabric, SANs (Storage Area Networks), 562
Storage Manager for SANs, RSAT tools, 924
storage pools
    accessing from File and Storage Services, 596–597
    allocating to virtual disk, 606–607
    cmdlets for working with, 597–598
    configuring JBOD into, 589
    creating, 599–602
    creating virtual disks, 608–612
    creating with PowerShell, 604–605
    limitations of, 602–603

physical disks, 572
    viewing disk drives, 603–604
Storage Reports, File Server Resource Manager, 688
Storage Reports Management node, 685–687
Storage Services role. *See* File and Storage Services role
Storage Spaces. *See also* storage
    clustering requirements, 567
    HA (high availability), 571
    overview of, 571–572
storage tiers
    creating, 620–621
    optimizing, 622–623
Storage Tiers Management Services, 590
Streaming Media Services role, 923
stub zones, DNS zones, 226
subdomains
    delegating, 240
    DNS hierarchical naming structure, 212
subnets/subnetting
    defining and placing subnets in AD sites, 1135–1136
    overview of, 1037–1038
    by RFC, 1038–1039
    sites and, 1127
    verifying local area connection settings, 934–935
subscription
    advanced options for, 1499–1500
    collector-initiated, 1496–1497
    configuring, 1501–1502
    creating collector-initiated, 1502–1504
    protocols, 1500–1501
    source-initiated, 1497–1498
    troubleshooting event forwarding, 1505–1507
superbar, Server Manager in, 43
supernetting, 1038
Support tools, 351
swing migration
    defined, 1244
    overview of, 334, 339, 1249–1250
    post upgrade tasks, 342, 1254
    preparing for, 340–341, 1250
    promoting member server, 341–342, 1251–1254
    pros/cons of, 1257
    repurposing hardware, 342, 1255
    steps in, 340
    from Windows Server 2003, 1255–1257
switch-independent teaming, NIC Teaming options, 152–153
symbolic links, Hyper-V, 1411
SYN message, TCP (Transmission Control Protocol), 1044
Sync Share configuration, for Work Folders, 1319–1321
synchronization
    DirSync tool for synchronizing objects to Windows Azure, 372
    of Microsoft updates, 1543

    of offline files, 699
    of time. *See* time synchronization
System Center 2012 R2
    Configuration Manager. *See* SCCM (System Center Configuration Manager)
    core products in, 1524
    monitoring performance with, 1526–1527
    MPs (management packs), 1525–1526
    Operations Manager. *See* SCOM (System Center Operations Manager)
    overview of, 1523
    reports, 1527–1528
System Center Configuration Manager. *See* SCCM (System Center Configuration Manager)
System Center Operations Manager. *See* SCOM (System Center Operations Manager)
system data collector sets, 1511–1513
System Diagnostics, 1511, 1517
system logs
    properties, 1494
    types of Windows logs, 1492
System Management Server (SMS), 1060
system monitoring. *See* Event Viewer
System Performance, 1511
System Properties dialog, Remote tab, 884–885
system settings
    controlling with Group Policy, 487
    troubleshooting profiles, 1292
system state
    AD recycle bin and, 1577
    recovering, 1564–1565
System Writer, 1556
SYSVOL
    connecting to SYSVOL share, 676
    FRS and, 314–315
    FRS requirements and dependencies, 316–317
    location in Active Directory, 270–272
    migrating to DFS-R, 318–319
    migrating to eliminated state, 328–331
    migrating to redirected state, 327–328
    old and new features, 313
    ReFS vs. NTFS and, 265
    verifying AD and, 321

T

tablet computers
    RDS and, 1449
    thin-client approach and, 1440
take ownership permissions, 866
tape backups, 1556
target, DFS, 736
Target Server, iSCSI, 653
Task Manager, 109–110
Task Scheduler
    optimizing storage tiers, 622–623
    verifying schedule set up in, 815–816
TCP (Transmission Control Protocol)
    attributes TCP adds to IP, 1042
    built on IP, 1026
    in the history of IPv6, 147

IP routing and, 1040–1041
RST, 1058
setting up print server on TCP port, 140–141
sockets and ports, 1042–1044
TCP/IP
  adding new printers by IP address or hostname, 836
  client-side requirements and, 930–931
  in the history of IPv6, 147–148
  IP routing. *See* IP routing
  manually configuring local area connection, 941
  planning deployment of AD FS and, 539
  verifying local area connection settings, 933
telephone settings, domain user accounts, 401–402
templates
  administrative, 499–500
  for centralized control of permissions, 767–768
  file screen, 682–684
  security. *See* security templates
templates, quota
  creating quota, 681
  E-mail Message tab, 678–679
  Event Log tab, 679–680
  overview of, 677–678
  Report tab, 680
Teredo tunneling, 150
Terminal Services
  environment settings for local accounts, 391–392
  history of, 119–120
  MTSC (Microsoft Terminal Services Connection), 895
  Performance Monitor and, 1446
  replaced by RDS, 883, 1435
Terminal Services (TS) Gateway, 906
test network, creating, 102
Test-NetConnection cmdlet, 151
text files, editing with Notepad, 112
thin provisioning, disk storage and, 572
thin-clients
  anatomy of thin-client session, 1441
  overview of, 1436
  in RDS, 1440–1441
  tablets and, 1440
threads, Windows OSs, 1442
tickets, Kerberos, 1190
time limits, configuring host session properties, 905
time settings, choosing during installation, 24–25, 42
time synchronization
  Hyper-V services, 1358
  multiple-domain designs and, 1223–1226
  overview of, 306–308
  virtual DCs and, 1399–1400
time zones
  configuring Server Core, 114
  setting during upgrade install, 42

time synchronization for multiple-domain designs, 1224–1226
token-decryption certificate
  adding to AD FS, 551–552
  federation server requirements, 536
token-signing certificate
  adding to AD FS, 551–552
  federation server requirements, 536
TPM (Trusted Platform Module) 1.2, 693–695
tracert/traceroute, 1059–1060
transaction logs, Active Directory, 271–272
transition states, in migration to DFS-R, 320
transitive trusts
  forests and, 1230
  overview of, 1228
Transmission Control Protocol. *See* TCP (Transmission Control Protocol)
Transmission Control Protocol/Internet Protocol. *See* TCP/IP
transport failover, SMB, 688
trees
  Active Directory, 260
  building forests and, 1190
  creating and naming, 1188–1189
  domain hierarchy and, 1198–1199
  grafting and pruning not supported, 1190–1191
  naming, 1197
  tree view in ADAC navigation pane, 440–442
troubleshooting
  client connection to network, 976–977
  IPAM (IP Address Management), 203–204
  printers/printing, 879
troubleshooting DNS
  Active Directory and, 301–302
  DcDiag tool, 253–254
  helpful links, 254–255
  NsLookup tool, 250–252
troubleshooting Group Policy
  Event Viewer, 517
  getting RSOP results with GPMC, 514–516
  gpresult.exe, 516–517
  minimizing troubleshooting time, 517–518
  modeling policies with GPMC, 516
  overview of, 517–518
  RSOP (Resultant Set of Policy), 513–514
troubleshooting IP routing
  ipconfig for checking configuration, 1060
  Network Monitor, 1060–1062
  overview of, 1057–1058
  ping for testing remote computer, 1058–1059
  showing routing and neighbors, 1060
  traceroute for testing remote computer, 1059–1060
trust anchors, DNS, 244–245
trust levels, .NET, 1021–1022
trusted domain, directionality in trust relationships and, 1227–1228

Trusted Platform Module (TPM) 1.2, 693–695
trusting domain, directionality in trust relationships and, 1227–1228
trusts, between domains. *See also* AD DT (Active Directory Domains and Trusts)
  administering, 1229
  creating manually, 1230–1232
  creating with netdom, 1239–1240
  creating with New Trust Wizard, 1232–1236, 1263
  defined, 260
  defining domain trust, 1226–1227
  directionality in trust relationships, 1227–1228
  establishing prior to migration, 349–351
  Kerberos and, 1189–1190
  managing with netdom, 304
  security and, 1228–1229
  setting up for ADMT migration, 354
  transitive, 1228
  transitive forest trusts, 1230
TS (Terminal Services) Gateway, 906
TTLS (Tunneled Transport Layer Security). *See* EAP-TTLS (Extensible Authentication Protocol with Tunneled Transport Layer Security)
tunneling
  6to4 tunneling, 149–150
  chat tunneling with portproxy, 1056–1057
  EAP-TTLS (Extensible Authentication Protocol with Tunneled Transport Layer Security), 11, 165
  Intra-site Automatic Tunnel Addressing Protocol (ISATAP), 242
  IPv6 commands, 1057
  L2TP (Layer 2 Tunneling Protocol), 1086, 1109
  overview of, 1056
  PPTP (Point-to-Point Tunneling Protocol), 1086, 1109
  specifying supported protocols, 1079
  SSTP (Secure Socket Tunneling Protocol), 1086, 1089, 1109
  types of tunneling protocols, 1067–1068
  VPN tunneling, 395
two-factor authentication, 400
Type 3 printer drivers, 830

U

UAC (User Account Control), 90, 383–384
UAG (Unified Access Gateway), 1110
UDP (User Datagram Protocol), 1026
UEFI (Unified Extensible Firmware Interface), 592, 1382
UI (user interface), 1438
Ultrasound tool, monitoring FRS, 321, 323
unattended installation
  adding components to answer file, 92–97
  adding Windows image to WSIM, 89–90
  applying answer file, 100–101
  configuration passes and, 87–88
  creating answer file, 91–92
  creating catalog file, 90

creating unattend file for RODC installation, 1174
installing ADK (Assessment and Deployment Kit), 82–85
overview of, 81
saving answer file, 97–98
selecting ADK features, 85–87
selecting components, 90–91
viewing answer file in Notepad, 98–100
WSIM (Windows System Image Manager) and, 88
unauthorized software, preventing installation or use of, 501–502
UNC (universal naming convention)
connecting to shares with, 672–673, 675–676
mapping drive to shared folder, 964–966
Unified Access Gateway (UAG), 1110
Unified Extensible Firmware Interface (UEFI), 592, 1382
universal groups
creating from command line, 433
creating groups, 295
scope of AD groups, 425
universal naming convention (UNC)
connecting to shares with, 672–673, 675–676
mapping drive to shared folder, 964–966
Universal Plug and Play (UPnP), 930
Unix
NFS for Unix clients, 658
NFS services and, 751
NFS shares and, 631
update sequence numbers (USNs)
DCs (domain controllers), 1396
virtual DCs and, 1400–1401
updates. *See also* patch management
downloading and installing, 116–117
downloading during upgrade installation, 36–37
enabling automatic, 116
manually forcing, 43
upgrade install
capabilities, 1244–1245
choosing edition and installation type, 37, 39
compatibility report, 38–40
creating a laboratory or test network, 102
downloading updates during, 36–37
final steps, 41–42
in-place upgrade, 1245
in-place upgrade from 2008 R2, 1246–1248
preparing for, 33–34
preparing for in-place upgrade, 1245
pros/cons of in-place upgrades, 1249
strategies for upgrading Active Directory, 1243–1244
supported upgrade scenarios, 32–33
testing in virtual lab, 34
upgrade paths and, 1245
when to use, 31–32
from Windows 2008 R2 x64 to Windows Server 2012 R2, 35

upgrading Active Directory
C&P (clean and pristine) migration approach, 343–347
migration tool. *See* ADMT (Active Directory Migration Tool)
in-place upgrade, 335–339
strategies, 80
swing migration, 339–343
upgrading domain to Windows Server 2012, 334–335
upgrading schema to Windows Server 2012, 331–334
UPN (user principal name), 386, 1212
UPnP (Universal Plug and Play), 930
USB memory stick
enabling BitLocker To Go, 697
types of removable storage, 101
User Account Control (UAC), 90, 383–384
User Account Migration Wizard, ADMT, 357–362
user accounts
access control, 765–766
Active Directory groups, 424–426
adding members to groups, 419–422
adding members to groups with PowerShell, 460–461
Administrator and Guest accounts, 378–379
authorizing users, 769
certificate settings for domain accounts, 404–405
COM+ settings for domain accounts, 403–404
configuring domain accounts, 396–397
configuring for event subscriptions, 1499
configuring groups, 427–432
configuring groups with ADAC, 447–448
configuring local accounts, 388
configuring with ADAC, 444–445
connecting clients to network, 931–932
creating domain accounts, 382–388
creating groups, 413–418, 426–427
creating groups from command line, 419, 432–433
creating groups with ADAC, 445–447
creating groups with PowerShell, 459–460
creating local user account, 379–381
creating local user account from command line, 382
creating multiple accounts simultaneously, 455–457
creating with ADAC, 443–444
creating with PowerShell, 452–453
DAC (Dynamic Access Control), 769–771
dial-in settings for local accounts, 395
editing domain accounts, 404
editing multiple accounts simultaneously, 408–410
enabling/disabling with PowerShell, 459
environment settings for local accounts, 391–392
general settings for domain accounts, 397

group membership settings for domain accounts, 405–406
listed in SAM (security account management), 1186
local groups, 413
logon settings for domain accounts, 397–401
managing domain accounts from command line, 410–412
managing groups, 412–413
managing lockout policies, 435–436
managing with ADUC, 922–923
membership settings for local accounts, 389
migrating users between domains, 354–355
migrating users between domains with ADMT, 357–362
moving to OUs (organizational units), 522
new features for managing, 437
object settings for domain accounts, 406–407
overview of, 377–378
password replication settings for domain accounts, 406
postal address settings for domain accounts, 397
profile settings for domain accounts, 401
profile settings for local accounts, 389–391
remote control settings, 393–395
remote control settings for local accounts, 393–394
removing groups with PowerShell, 464
removing members from groups, 422–423
removing members from groups with PowerShell, 462–463
removing permissions, 728
resetting passwords, 434–435
roaming profiles and, 1306
running djoin.exe, 948
security settings for domain accounts, 407–408
session settings for local accounts, 392–393
setting passwords with PowerShell, 453–455
setting up anonymous accounts, 1005–1006
share permissions, 710
telephone settings for domain accounts, 401–402
tools for creating, 285
UAC (User Account Control), 90
unlocking with PowerShell, 457–459
user accounts, advanced management
associating multiple logon scripts with users, 1334–1335
configuration from Control Panel, 1326–1327
configuration with File Explorer, 1327
configuring home directories. *See* home directories
controlling Windows built-in applications, 1325–1326
executing commands at logon, 1331–1334

flexibility of desktop and, 1268
managing desktop with Group Policy, 1323–1324
managing drive mappings, 1328–1331
managing Internet Explorer, 1325
managing logon scripts with Group Policy, 1335–1336
managing offline files, 1324–1325
managing shutdown with logoff scripts, 1336–1337
overview of, 1267
roaming profiles. *See* roaming profiles
Work Folders. *See* Work Folders
User Configuration
controlling behavior of Group Policy, 480
folder redirection and, 490–492
option in Group Policy, 487–488
specifying logon/logoff scripts with Group Policy, 488–490
User Datagram Protocol (UDP), 1026
user error, troubleshooting printers, 880
user interface (UI), 1438
user limits, for shares, 662–663
user principal name (UPN), 386, 1212
user-defined data collector sets, 1513–1517
USMT (User State Migration Tool), 85
USNs (update sequence numbers)
DCs (domain controllers), 1396
virtual DCs and, 1400–1401

V

VAMT (Volume Activation Management Tool), 85
VBScript, 356–357
VDI (virtual desktop interface)
configuring on server, 1464–1470
improvements in Windows Server 2012, 10–11
overview of, 1464
VDS (Virtual Disk Service)
automatically starting with sc config, 663
managing Windows Server 2008 from Server 2012 R2, 661
verbose logging, event levels, 1487
VHDs (virtual hard disks)
adding roles and features and, 58–59
bringing offline disks online, 618–619
configuring VM replication, 1428–1429
configuring VMs, 1381
connecting to iSCSI virtual disk from client side, 628–631
controllers, 1367–1368
converting to VHDX format, 1346, 1366
creating, 1368–1371
iSCSI and, 623
maintaining, 1371–1374
overview of, 1366–1367
sharing, 570
virtual disks compared with, 597
VHDX format
backups and, 1556
clustering and, 573
converting VHDs to, 1366
creating virtual disks, 1368–1371

fixed vs. dynamic virtual disks and, 1368
open specification, 1368
for shared storage, 568
what's new in Hyper-V, 1345–1346
virtual DCs (virtual domain controllers)
cloning, 1403–1406
overview of, 1399
quick deployment of, 1402
requirements for cloning, 1402–1403
VM-Generation ID, 1400–1401
virtual desktop interface. *See* VDI (virtual desktop interface)
virtual directory, mapping URL namespace to physical drive, 991
Virtual Disk Service (VDS)
automatically starting with sc config, 663
managing Windows Server 2008 from Server 2012 R2, 661
virtual disks
allocating storage pool to, 606–607
bringing offline disks online, 618–619
cmdlets for working with, 597–598
creating volumes from, 614–617
creating with GUI, 608–612
creating with PowerShell, 612–614
determining layout of, 607–608
overview of, 597
for shared storage, 568
storage pools, 572
virtual domain controller cloning
overview of, 1402
prerequisites, 1402
process of, 1403–1406
virtual domain controllers. *See* virtual DCs (virtual domain controllers)
virtual hard disks. *See* VHDs (virtual hard disks)
virtual IP addresses, 193–196
virtual lab, for testing upgrade install, 34
virtual LANs (VLANs), 1392–1393
Virtual Machine Drain on Shutdown, 1412, 1422
virtual machine (guest) partition
deploying Hyper-V and, 1354
overview of, 1357–1359
Virtual Machine Management (VMM) service, 1356
virtual machine manager. *See* VMM (virtual machine manager)
virtual machines. *See* VMs (virtual machines)
Virtual operating System Environment (VOSE), 1344
virtual private networks. *See* VPN (virtual private networks)
Virtual SAN Manager Wizard, 1366
virtual SMTP Servers and domains, 1010–1011
Virtual Switch Manager, 1375–1377
virtual switches
choosing switch type, 1374–1375
connecting VM to, 1380–1381
creating, 1361, 1375–1377
overview of, 1374
working with VLANs, 1392–1393

virtualization
changes in Windows Server 2012, 8
clustering and, 569–570
server virtualization with Hyper-V. *See* Hyper-V
support for AD FS, 537
VDI (virtual desktop interface), 10–11
virtualization service client (VSC), 1355–1356, 1358–1359
virtualization service providers (VSPs), 1354–1356
VLANs (virtual LANs), 1392–1393
VM Direct Connect, 1347
VMBus
guest (virtual machine) partition and, 1358
in Hyper-V management OS partition, 1354–1355
VM-Generation ID, 1400–1401
VMM (Virtual Machine Management) service, 1356
VMM (virtual machine manager)
core products in System Center 2012 R2, 1524
improvements in Windows Server 2012, 9
managing virtual IP addresses and, 193–196
VMs (virtual machines)
AVMA (Automatic Virtual Machine Activation), 1351
backing up, 1418–1421, 1561
benefits of clustering, 570
benefits of server virtualization, 1341–1343
checkpoints, 1393–1396
clustering with, 572
configuring, 1410–1411
creating, 1377–1382
CSVs (Cluster Shared Volumes), 568–569
data deduplication and, 637
disaster recovery, 1422–1423
enhanced support for Linux VM in Hyper-V, 1350
file systems, 1367
Gen2, 1346
Hyper-V and, 1377
installing, 1388–1390
malware protection, 1421–1422
managing virtual hardware, 1382–1388
migration options, 1411–1414
moving via export/import, 1407–1410
NIC Teaming in, 154, 158
QoS (Quality of Service) and, 160
replication with HVR. *See* HVR (Hyper-V Replica)
server virtualization and, 8
setting up guest-based cluster, 587–588
Shared Nothing Live Migration (cluster-free), 1414–1417
troubleshooting slow running, 1371
upgrading Integration Services for, 1390–1392
working with Hyper-V console, 1363

VMware
  Hyper-V and, 1345
  support for AD FS, 537
  testing Windows Server 2012 R2, 34
VoIP (Voice over IP), 160
Volume Activation 3.0, 142
Volume Activation Management Tool
  (VAMT), 85
Volume Copy Service. *See* VSS (Volume Copy
  Service)
volumes
  answer file installation and, 94
  checking for corrupt, 646
  creating from virtual disks, 614–617
  setting up disk drives during clean
    install, 27–29
  snapshots, 1418
VOSE (Virtual operating System
  Environment), 1344
VPN (virtual private networks)
  accessing with Windows RT, 946
  adding certificate to certificate store,
    1095
  adding certificates, 1092
  authenticating VPN clients, 1097–1100
  configuring accounting, 1100–1102
  configuring AD CS, 1093
  configuring clients and connecting via,
    1089–1091
  configuring network access policies,
    1074–1076
  configuring policy settings, 1084
  configuring ports, 1109
  configuring RRAS, 1072–1074, 1097
  configuring server properties, 1102–1108
  creating network policy, 1086–1089
  creating server authentication certificate,
    1093–1095
  encryption settings, 1085–1086
  gateway-to-gateway, 1066–1067
  hands free solution. *See* DirectAccess
  installing AD CS, 1092
  installing certificate on client, 1096–1097
  installing Network Policy and Access
    Services role, 1069–1070
  installing Remote Access role, 1071–1072
  IP filters, 1085
  IP settings, 1086
  monitoring remote access clients,
    1108–1109
  Multilink and Bandwidth Allocation
    Protocol and, 1084–1085
  overview of, 1065–1066
  rules governing policies and policy
    order, 1076–1080
  services provided by Network Policy and
    Access Services role, 1068–1069
  services provided by Remote Access
    role, 1070
  setting policy constraints, 1082–1083
  setting policy permissions, 1080–1082
  tunneling protocols and, 1067–1068
VPN clients
  authenticating, 1097–1100

comparing RADIUS clients with VPN
    clients, 1081
  configuring and connecting to, 1089–1091
  installing certificate on, 1096–1097
  monitoring remote access clients,
    1108–1109
  Multilink and Bandwidth Allocation
    Protocol and, 1084–1085
VPN servers
  authenticating VPN clients, 1097–1100
  configuring accounting, 1100–1102
  configuring AD CS for, 1093
  configuring and connecting clients to,
    1089–1091
  configuring ports, 1109
  configuring server properties, 1102–1108
  creating server authentication certificate,
    1093–1095
  gateway configuration for, 1080
  installing AD CS on, 1092
  monitoring remote access clients,
    1108–1109
  NICs (network interface cards), 1066, 1074
  secure connection to, 1097
VPN tunneling, 395
VSC (virtualization service client), 1355–1356,
  1358–1359
VSPs (virtualization service providers),
  1354–1356
VSS (Volume Copy Service)
  backing up and restoring VMs, 1418–1421
  backing up with, 1270
  creating snapshots of AD DS database,
    1573–1574
VSS for SMB File Shares, 653

W

W32tm (Windows Time Service), 307–308
WAAD (Windows Azure Active Directory)
  interacting with, 370–371
  logon flavors, 372–374
  overview of, 368–370
  synchronizing, 371–372
WAIK (Windows Automated Installation
  Kit), 81
WAN (wide area network)
  bandwidth in planning Active Directory,
    1192–1193
  deciding on DCs in remote locations and,
    1131–1132
  design pointers for Active Directory, 1196
  increasing performance over WAN
    connections, 890
  links. *See* site links
  setting up site topology and, 1129
  sites and, 1123
  SMB Directory Leasing over, 689
  using new use on, 674–675
warning events, event levels, 1487
Wbadmin.exe
  performing full server backup from
    command line, 1560
  recovering system state of server, 1565
  Windows Backup Server and, 1556

WBT (Windows-based terminal), 1448
weak send/weak receive, IP addresses,
  1061–1062
web access, Remote Desktop services and, 900
web browsers
  deploying RemoteApp applications, 1439
  planning deployment of AD FS and, 539
Web Deploy tool, for deploying websites,
  1003–1004
Web Management Services. *See* WMSVC (Web
  Management Services)
Web Proxy Automatic Discovery Protocol
  (WPAD), 242
Web Server role
  adding, 981–985
  services, 986–988
web servers (IIS)
  changes in Windows Server 2012, 15–17
  RD Gateway required services, 908
  setting up web server, 58–59
web services
  adding new printers by IP address or
    hostname, 836
  changes in Windows Server 2012, 15–17
websites
  adding FTP Publishing service to,
    1014–1016
  adding SMTP e-mail to, 1012–1013
  authenticating, 1020
  configuring, 1001–1002
  configuring modules at site level,
    989–991
  constructing, 995–1000
  creating, 994
  creating with PowerShell, 1000–1001
  deploying, 1003–1004
  differentiating, 1005
  dynamic site activation, 980
  global settings, 992
  hosting multiple, 1002–1003
  invoking SSL protection for, 1022
  links for troubleshooting DNS, 254–255
  managing multiple, 1006
  permissions, 1020–1021
  planning, 992–994
  provisioning, 991
  securing, 1019–1020
  setting up, 994–995
Wecutil (Windows event collector) service
  event subscription and, 1501–1502
  troubleshooting event forwarding,
    1505–1507
WID (Windows Internal Database)
  configuring AD FS and, 546
  planning deployment of AD FS and, 538
wide area network. *See* WAN (wide area
  network)
Windows 2000, upgrading to Windows Server
  2012 R2, 33–34
Windows 2012, Primary Computer support,
  1317–1318
Windows 7
  adding network printer, 962–964
  adding wireless devices, 963–964

checking local area connection, 939–941
creating network folder, 966–968
DirectAccess support and, 1119
joining domains, 942–945
joining domains while offline, 946–950
manually configuring local area
connection, 941–942
NLA (Network Level Authentication),
1453
VDI (virtual desktop interface) and, 1464
Windows 8
accessing Control Panel, 933
adding network printer, 961–964
adding wireless devices, 963–964
checking local area connection, 935–937
configuring clients for VPN server,
1089–1091
creating mandatory profiles, 1293–1294
creating network folder, 966–968
DirectAccess support and, 1119
joining domains, 942–945
joining domains while offline, 946–950
manually configuring local area
connection, 937–938
new ADK release with, 82
NLA (Network Level Authentication),
1453
Primary Computer support, 1317–1318
VDI (virtual desktop interface) and, 1464
Windows applications, controlling built-in
applications, 1325–1326
Windows Azure
Active Directory. See WAAD (Windows
Azure Active Directory)
backing up to Cloud, 1569
improvements in Storage Spaces and,
595
Windows Backup Server, 144–145
Windows Deployment Services
cloning solutions for unattended
installations, 81
flexibility of desktop and, 1268
Windows drivers, in Hyper-V management
OS partition, 1354–1355
Windows event collector (Wecutil) service
event subscription and, 1501–1502
troubleshooting event forwarding,
1505–1507
Windows Firewall
answer file installation and, 96
configuring, 43
creating inbound firewall rule, 126–131
DirectAccess requirements, 1112
enabling firewalls, 143
upgrade install and, 34
Windows Internal Database (WID)
configuring AD FS and, 546
planning deployment of AD FS and, 538
Windows Management Instrumentation.
See WMI (Windows Management
Instrumentation)
Windows Management Instrumentation
Command-line (WMIC) tool, 921–922
Windows Messenger, user configuration, 1326

Windows Network Virtualization module,
PowerShell, 151
Windows OSs
NLA (Network Level Authentication),
1453
VDI (virtual desktop interface) and, 1464
Windows 7. See Windows 7
Windows 8. See Windows 8
Windows PE (Windows Preinstallation
Environment)
configuration passes and, 88
selecting ADK features, 85
Windows Performance Toolkit, 85
Windows Remote Management. See WinRM
(Windows Remote Management)
Windows Remote Shell. See WinRS (Windows
Remote Shell)
Windows RT
accessing resources and, 946
overview of, 931–932
Windows Server 2003, swing migration from,
1255–1257
Windows Server 2008 R2
managing from Server 2012 R2, 661–664
in-place upgrade from, 1246–1248
Windows Server 2012, what's new
Active Directory changes, 3–8
desktop changes, 3
editions, 2–3
file and print sharing, 14–15
GPOs (Group Policy Objects), 14
Hyper-V, 8–10
management tools, 12
networking changes, 11
overview of, 1–2
Remote Desktop Services, 13–14
remote tools, 13
Server Manager, 12–13
VDI (virtual desktop interface), 10–11
virtualization features, 8
web-based services, 15–17
Windows Server Backup
backing up and restoring files and
folders, 1566
installing, 1556–1557
overview of, 1555–1556
performing backup with PowerShell,
1561–1562
performing full server backup, 1557–1560
performing full server backup from
command line, 1560
performing full server restore, 1562–1564
performing manual backup of files and
folders, 1566–1567
recovering folder from a backup,
1567–1568
recovering system state of server,
1564–1565
Windows Server Backup (WSB), 1419–1421
Windows Server Gateway (WSG), 1350
Windows Servers. See also servers
ADMT compatibility and, 348, 1262
DCHP failover requirements, 205–206
domain functional levels, 1162, 1206–1207

forest functional levels, 1163, 1208–1209
HVR prerequisites, 1424
IPAM requirements, 177
managing Windows Server 2008 from
Server 2012 R2, 661–664
in-place upgrade from, 1246–1248
promoting Windows Server 2012 R2 to
RODC, 1168–1173
swing migration from, 1255–1257
upgrade capabilities and support,
1244–1245
Windows SharePoint Services (WSS), 402
Windows Software Update Services. See
WSUS (Windows Software Update
Services)
Windows System Image Manager. See WSIM
(Windows System Image Manager)
Windows System Resource Manager, RSAT
tools, 924
Windows System Resource Manager (WSRM),
1020
Windows terminal, 1448
Windows Time Service (W32tm), 307–308
Windows Update, 116
Windows Update Agent (WUA), 1532
Windows-based terminal (WBT), 1448
Windows-on-Windows (WOW32) system, 22
WinRM (Windows Remote Management)
administration of IIS 8.0, 1017
changes in Windows Server 2012, 13
enabling, 920
event subscription and, 1501–1502
issuing PowerShell commands with
WinRS, 922
issuing WMIC commands with WinRS,
921–922
managing remote computer, 661
overview of, 919
using WinRS, 921
winrm qc command, 661
WinRS (Windows Remote Shell)
changes in Windows Server 2012, 13
creating listeners, 124
issuing PowerShell commands, 922
issuing WMIC commands, 921–922
sending commands remotely, 122
testing service with, 131
using, 921
WINS
configuring clients, 236
hostname resolution and, 233
Winsock, 1045
winver.exe, 35
wired networks, accessing with Windows
RT, 946
wireless devices, adding to Windows clients,
963–964
wireless networks, accessing with Windows
RT, 946
WMI (Windows Management
Instrumentation)
BranchCache and, 166
in Hyper-V management OS partition,
1356

managing DCB (Data Center Bridging),
161–163
SMB for, 689
WMIC (Windows Management
Instrumentation Command-line) tool,
921–922
WMSVC (Web Management Services)
configuring, 1019
installing on IIS Server, 1017–1019
overview of, 1017
remote management with, 1017
Work Folders
client configuration, 1322–1323
installing, 1319
managing storage with File and Storage
Services, 565–566
overview of, 1319
Sync Share configuration, 1319–1321
workgroups
in Active Directory, 258
defined, 932
Workplace Join, 374–375, 1323
workstations
DirectAccess requirements, 1112
logon settings, 399
preparing for ADMT migration, 354
security boundaries and, 1186
trust relationships in joining domain, 1226
Work Folders and, 1319
World Wide Port Name (WWPN), 1366
WOW32 (Windows-on-Windows) system, 22
WPAD (Web Proxy Automatic Discovery
Protocol), 242

Write permissions
in list of molecular permissions, 719
NTFS, 667
write-back cache
enabling with PowerShell, 622
overview of, 590–591
WSB (Windows Server Backup), 1419–1421
WSG (Windows Server Gateway), 1350
WSIM (Windows System Image Manager)
adding Windows image to, 89–90
creating answer file in, 91–92
install image, 88
replaces Setup Manager, 81
WSRM (Windows System Resource Manager),
1020
WSS (Windows SharePoint Services), 402
WSUS (Windows Software Update Services)
backing up WSUS database, 1550
complex hierarchies in, 1535–1536
configuring clients, 1547–1550
configuring patch deployment,
1540–1544
deploying patches, 1268
deployment scenarios, 1533–1535
installing WSUS role, 1536–1539
managing updates with Group Policy,
1544–1547, 1551
migrating from WSUS 3.0 to WSUSv6,
1550
patches and, 1422
PowerShell and, 1551
software requirements for, 1532–1533
what's new, 1531–1532

WSUTIL.exe, exporting patches to USB,
1534
WUA (Windows Update Agent), 1532
WWNN (World Wide Node Name), 1366

X

x64, supported upgrade scenarios, 32–33
x86, supported upgrade scenarios, 32–33
xcopy.exe, deploying web sites, 1003
XenServer, testing Windows Server 2012 R2,
34
XML (Extensible Markup Language)
paper specification, 831
XML-based logs, 1491–1492
XPS (XML Paper Specification), 831
XPSDrv printer driver model, 831

Z

zones, DNS
ADI (Active Directory Integrated) zones,
224–226, 299, 1183
background zone loading, 244
configuring DNS servers for RODCs,
1183–1184
database of, 211
dynamic updates and, 238
monitoring, 197–198
for namespace management, 221
reverse lookup zones, 226–228
standard primary zone, 221–222
standard secondary zone, 222–224
stub zones, 226
zone transfer, 223